Organizational Behavior

EIGHTH EDITION

Organizational Behavior

EIGHTH EDITION

Don Hellriegel
Texas A & M University

John W. Slocum, Jr.
Southern Methodist University

Richard W. Woodman
Texas A & M University

SOUTH-WESTERN College Publishing

An International Thomson Publishing Company

■ Production Credits

Acquisitions Editor: John Szilagyi
Developmental Editors: Cinci Stowell and Judith O'Neill
Production Editor: Sandy Gangelhoff
Manufacturing Coordinator: Sue Disselkamp
Marketing Manager: Steve Scoble
Copyediting: Jerrold Moore
Text Design: Roslyn M. Stendahl, Dapper Design
Chapter Opening Art: © 1996 Roslyn M. Stendahl
Composition: Parkwood Composition Service, Inc.
Artwork: Randy Miyake
Cover Art and Design: Roslyn M. Stendahl, Dapper Design

 TEXT IS PRINTED ON 10% POST CONSUMER RECYCLED PAPER

Copyright © 1976, 1979, 1983, 1986, 1989, 1992, 1995
Copyright © 1998
by South-Western College Publishing
Cincinnati, Ohio

Library of Congress Cataloging-in-Publication Data

Hellriegel, Don.
    Organizational behavior / Don Hellriegel, John W. Slocum, Jr.,
  Richard W. Woodman. — 8th ed.
       p. cm.
    Includes bibliographical references and index.
    ISBN 0-538-88024-4 (alk. paper)
    1. Organizational behavior.   I. Slocum, John W.   II. Woodman, Richard W.
III. Title
HD58.7.H44   1998
158.7—dc21   97-13217
                                                              CIP

3456789WST654321098

Printed in the United States of America

International Thomson Publishing
South-Western College Publishing is an ITP Company, The ITP trademark is used under license.

To Jill, Kim, and Lori (DH)
Christopher, Bradley, and Jonathan (JWS)
David and Anna (RWW)

BRIEF CONTENTS

CONTENTS

■ PART II: GROUP AND INTERPERSONAL PROCESSES   227

CHAPTER 10

Leadership: Foundations   298

CHAPTER 11

Leadership: Contemporary Developments   336

CHAPTER **17** ## Organizational Culture 542

CHAPTER **18** ## Organizational Change 572

Preface

This is our eighth edition of *Organizational Behavior.* In each succeeding edition we have tried to represent the best thinking available about each topic covered. To do so again, we carefully analyzed, critiqued, and rewrote, as necessary, each chapter of the seventh edition to reflect the most up-to-date thinking and information available.

The effective design and management of organizations requires the thoughtful application of knowledge concerning the behavior of people at work. Few, if any, of the dramatic challenges facing organizations can be handled effectively without a good understanding of human behavior. Too often in the history of organizations sound plans fail to be implemented, well-designed tasks and processes fail to motivate, innovative technology fails to raise productivity, and workplace cultures fail to support effective behaviors. Many times what poor management, poor designs, and failed strategies have in common is a failure of commitment, caring, and involvement. The human actor is central to organizational success and effectiveness. Organizations fail or succeed, decline or prosper because of people—what people do or fail to do every day on the job. Effective organizational behavior is the bedrock on which productive organizational action rests.

 ## SPECIAL FEATURES OF THIS EDITION

Although this edition is much like the seventh edition in many ways, it is different in several important respects. First, it is shorter, reflecting our continued desire to produce a comprehensive text, yet allow the material to be covered adequately in a single semester. Thus we eliminated chapters on individual problem-solving styles and careers. Additionally, we combined two chapters on group behavior into a single chapter and two chapters on organizational change into a single chapter. However, we expanded the leadership material from one to two chapters, providing a total of eighteen chapters in the book. In each chapter we discarded outdated material and inserted new material on diversity, ethics, global management, leadership, teams, new organizational designs, managing change, managerial core competencies, and information technology.

Among the most significant changes and features of this edition are the following.

- We developed the theme of professional *core competencies* throughout the book. In Chapter 1, which we extensively revised, we introduce this theme, and every chapter contains material dedicated to helping the reader develop various professional competencies. At the end of each chapter is a section entitled "Developing Competencies." It includes questionnaires, exercises, and cases labeled "Self-Insight," "Team Insight," or "Organizational Insight," depending on the focus of the material.

■ Work-force diversity has been a strong theme in our book for several editions. However, we now give it even greater attention. Beginning with a major focus in chapter 1, all chapters contain information and insights designed to help you work and manage more effectively in a culturally diverse workplace.

■ We present the latest thinking about leadership in a new Chapter 11: Contemporary Leadership Developments. Transformational leadership, the seven-habits model, and various substitutes for leadership represent the focus of this new chapter.

■ We continued the popular *Preview Cases* that introduce and frame each chapter.

■ Every chapter contains at least one *Across Cultures* feature in keeping with the continued need for a strong emphasis on the global arena in business school education and the world of work.

■ The other in-chapter features—*Ethics in Practice, Diversity in Practice, Quality in Practice, Technology in Practice,* and *Managing in Practice*—which have been popular in previous editions, focus on crucial ethical, diversity, quality, and technology concerns, as well as concerns of a more general managerial nature. By weaving these issues into a variety of topics within the subject of organizational behavior, we constantly reinforce their importance and relevance.

■ The *Technology in Practice* feature is new to this edition. These selections highlight the impact of technology on jobs and employee behavior.

■ Of the nine *Integrating Cases* at the end of the book, seven are new to this edition. These cases emphasize the major themes developed in the book and integrate the material presented in various chapters.

■ Finally, we added to the usual author and subject indexes an index of the Internet addresses for all companies featured in the book. By visiting these websites, a reader can develop an understanding of how organizations are facing the challenges of this exciting time.

 FRAMEWORK After an introductory chapter, the book is divided into three main parts. Part I (Individual Processes) contains chapters on personality and attitudes, perception and attribution, learning and reinforcement, two chapters on motivation, and a chapter on work stress.

Part II (Group and Interpersonal Processes) consists of chapters on group and team behavior, power and political behavior, two chapters on leadership, and a chapter on conflict and negotiation followed by one on interpersonal communication.

Part III (Organizational Processes) contains chapters on decision making, job design, organization design, organizational culture, and organizational change.

Immediately following the last chapter are an appendix on research methods, the integrating cases, and indexes.

Our approach to introducing students to organizational behavior is to move from the individual to the group to the organizational level. However, the chapters are written to stand alone, which allows material to be covered in any order desired by the instructor.

SUPPLEMENTS

Seven supplements are available for use with the eighth edition of *Organizational Behavior.*

- A new *Instructor's Resource Guide* by Michael McCuddy contains resource materials for lectures; answers to all discussion questions and questions contained in the "Developing Competencies" sections; and instructor notes for questionnaires, exercises, and cases, including the Integrating Cases at the end of the book.
- A new *Test Bank* by David Leuser contains multiple choice, true–false, and essay questions.
- A new *Student Study Guide* by Roger Roderick contains learning objectives, chapter outlines, practice questions, and a programmed study supplement.
- A new edition of *Organizational Behavior: Experiences and Cases* by Dorothy Marcic and Joseph Seltzer contains real-world exercises and cases that parallel the text.
- A new video library is available. A written guide for all videos accompanying the text is included in the *Instructor's Resource Guide.*
- Power Point files prepared by Michael McCuddy are available to supplement the instructor's manual.
- Transparency Masters and four-color acetates of many exhibits in the book are available.

All of these supplements are available from South-Western College Publishing Co., or from your ITP representative.

ACKNOWLEDGEMENTS

We express our grateful appreciation to the following individuals who provided thoughtful reviews and useful suggestions that helped improve this edition of the book.

Gordon Arbogast
Jacksonville University

Amnon V. Ashe
University of District of Columbia, College of Professional Studies

K. Denise Bane
Baruch College

Rafael Bedolla
St. Mary's University

Regis Beighley
Troy State University

Janice M. Beyer
University of Texas

Meg Birdseye
Augusta College

Joan Brett
Southern Methodist University

Filemon Campo-Flores
California State University, Long Beach

Toya Candelari
Texas Woman's University

Stephanie Castro
University of Miami

John A. Chaya
Pennsylvania State University

John Cotton
Marquette University

Michael A. Counte
Saint Louis University

Oya Culpan
West Chester University

Refik Culpan
Penn State University-Harrisburg

Christopher Daniel
Kentucky State University

William E. Farrar
University of Alabama-Birmingham

Bruce Garrison
Houston Baptist University

Janet Henquinet
Metropolitan State University

Michael S. Higgins
Fairleigh Dickinson University

Bill Higley
Lockheed Martin Vought

Raymond Hill
Eastern Michigan University

Manfred Hoffmann
University of Texas at Dallas

Linda Howard
Ottawa University, Phoenix

John N. Hummel
Catholic University of America

Deborah Baker Hulse
University of Texas-Tyler

Sarah Jacobson
North Dakota State University

Jordan Kaplan
Long Island University

Barbara J. Keinath
Metropolitan State University

Bruce Kemelgor
University of Louisville

Donna Klepper
Mary Baldwin College

Joe Labianca
Penn State University

Robert B. Lawson
University of Vermont

Robert Mac Aleese
Spring Hill College

Michael McCuddy
Valpraiso University

Tom McFarland
Jacksonville University

Edward Meyer
SUNY Maritime College

Catherine Michael
St. Edward's University

Ercan Nasif
University of Texas-Pan American

Thomas A. Natiello, Sr.
University of Miami

Linda Neider
University of Miami

Ronald F. Nelson
Indiana University-Purdue University

Judith Oakley
University of Maine

Raj Pillai
University of Miami

Robin Pinkley
Southern Methodist University

Roy Pipitone
Erie Community College

Greg Powell
Southern Utah University

M. Afzalur Rahim
Western Kentucky University

Tina Robbins
Clemson University

Grant T. Savage
Texas Tech University

Valerie B. Scott
Indiana University Southeast

William Martin Sloane
Wilson College

Paul Starkey
Delta State University

Leigh Stelzer
Seton Hall University

Jeff Strese
Southern Methodist University

James Swenson
Moorhead State University

John Taylor
University of Alaska

Edmund L. Toomey
Merrimack College

Richard C. Williams
Troy State University at Dothan

Joan Townley
University of St. Thomas

Warner Woodworth
Brigham Young University

Ebenezer Ugorji
Austin Peay State University

Stuart A. Youngblood
Texas Christian University

In addition, we thank our production editor at West, Sandy Gangelhoff, our copy editor, Jerrold Moore, and South-Western's Cynthia Stowell for their fine, professional assistance at various stages in the production of this book. We extend special thanks to Argie Butler and Patsy Hartmangruber at Texas A&M University, and Billie Boyd at Southern Methodist University for their help with manuscript preparation.

John Slocum acknowledges the insightful comments by Don VandeWalle, who tirelessly read many chapters, Mick McGill, a great colleague and inspirational teacher, whose encouragement from the heart will always be remembered, and his Stonebriar golf buddies, who sacrificed preferred tee times to accommodate his writing schedules.

Don Hellriegel and Dick Woodman express appreciation to their colleagues and friends at Texas A&M University who collectively create a work environment that supports and nurtures their continued learning and professional development.

Don Hellriegel, Texas A&M University

John W. Slocum, Jr., Southern Methodist University

Richard W. Woodman, Texas A&M University

1

Introduction to Organizational Behavior

LEARNING OBJECTIVES

When you have finished studying this chapter, you should be able to:

- Discuss the characteristics and importance of diversity as a key issue for all organizations and employees.
- Describe four additional key issues—quality, technology, global perspective, and ethics—as they relate to organizational behavior.
- State the five core competencies needed by professionals and managers in organizations.
- Outline the portfolio of skills, knowledge, and abilities embedded within each core competency.
- Explain the systems framework for developing the competencies needed in order to use organizational behavior processes and practices.

OUTLINE

PREVIEW CASE

Andrea Cunningham

Andrea Cunningham had just returned to work from her first vacation since starting her public relations agency several years ago. She was preparing to meet with the vice-president she had left in charge. During her European vacation, she had phoned and faxed work to the office between bike rides and excursions with her husband to keep in touch with the business. She also had taken along business books to read, hoping that they would give her some new insights into management.

Located in Silicon Valley, her business was making a profit but had some unresolved internal issues. She had left her previous employer to make more money, take on more responsibility, and be an entrepreneur. Her clients included Hewlett-Packard, Borland International, and Aldus Corporation, among others. Current annual billings were more than $3 million, and she employed twenty people. But Cunningham was dissatisfied. Clients still relied on her personally for most of the advice they had hired her company to provide. She felt that she had failed to delegate and hadn't created the caring and growing organization she had been determined to build. The two top people she had hired to help lead the company had no use for each other, fighting openly despite her efforts to keep the peace. In fact, a year ago she had considered selling the business.

Now she was reviewing the to-do list left with the vice-president. She discovered that many of the items on the list had not been done. Moreover, her secretary told her that the vice-president had led a mini-insurrection against her while she was gone. He had even crumpled up her mission statement and thrown it on the floor, telling the employees that he would be running the show. As she reviewed the to-do list with the vice-president, which he had ignored, something snapped. She said, "I want you to leave. Now. You're fired."

After he left, she tried to figure out what had happened. She had believed that, by dividing people who worked on accounts into teams with each team accountable for its own profit-and-loss record, managing them would be relatively easy. People on each team would earn bonuses based on the team's profits, taking a lot of responsibility themselves and leaving her time to attract new clients. However, team rivalries destroyed company-wide cooperation. People on different teams didn't share ideas because they wanted to protect their own profits. Individuals also balked at taking on responsibility. Andrea had thought that, if she presented them with some goals and gave them a chance to succeed, people would be productive and satisfied. In fact, just the opposite happened. During one six-month period, almost her entire staff had left.[1]

Andrea Cunningham discovered that being a manager isn't easy. She faced ethical and quality control problems along with conflict and motivational challenges. She'd tried many different approaches and had gotten only marginal results. Supervisors didn't follow directives, subordinates didn't accept goals, and employees at all levels quit when they became dissatisfied.

There are no easy or complete answers as to why people and organizations fail to function smoothly. However, your study of organizational behavior should give you a set of competencies for looking at and understanding the behavior of people in organizations. **Organizational behavior** is the study of human behavior, attitudes, and performance in organizations. It is interdisciplinary, drawing concepts from social and clinical psychology, sociology, cultural anthropology, industrial engineering, and organizational psychology.

Why should you study organizational behavior? Most people who do so are or will be employees in organizations and many will eventually become team leaders or managers. Studying organizational behavior should help you attain the competencies needed to be an effective employee, team leader, and/or manager. The knowledge and skills you gain should help you diagnose, understand, and explain what is happening around you in your job.

Although Andrea Cunningham had made organizational changes to remain competitive, she still had some unanswered questions.

- Is my organization designed properly?
- Should I consult with employees about decisions before I make them?
- If I pay people more, will they stay longer and work more effectively?
- How should goals be set for employees?
- How can employees benefit from feedback they receive?

Effective managers try to find answers to these and many other questions. They also try to understand how their behavior affects others in their organization. In this book, we will help you answer such questions and become aware of the importance of behavior (both overt and covert)—including your own—in an organization.

As Figure 1.1 suggests, one way to recognize why people behave as they do at work is to view an organization as an iceberg. What sinks ships isn't always what sailors can see but what they can't see. Using this analogy, let's analyze Andrea Cunningham and her company. Its formal (overt) aspects include

- *goals*, which are to make a profit, be a good community citizen, and let employees make their own decisions;
- *technology*, which comprises the latest computers, fax machines, and electronic equipment to serve clients.
- *structure*, which indicates that the firm is organized around account teams, with each team responsible for its own profit-and-loss record;
- *financial resources*, which are the firm's current assets and liabilities, owner's equity, and the like; and
- *competencies and their corresponding skills*, which are the owner's abilities and those of the employees.

To serve the needs of her clients, Cunningham hired employees with good *surface* competencies. They included research skills, broad-based knowledge of the high-tech industry in which her firm specializes, and an in-depth understanding of how a client's business works. She had tried to discover what hindered employee performance and to remove those obstacles. By looking only at the goals, technology, structure, financial resources, and surface competencies of her employees, she had focused only on the tip of the iceberg.

When Cunningham finally looked below the tip of the iceberg, she found that employee attitudes, communication patterns, team processes, and underlying core competencies—including her own—needed to change. To begin making these changes, Cunningham took several new actions. First, she sent all employees to an off-site meeting and asked her director of human resources to find out what the employees wanted. Interestingly, they didn't complain about money or bonuses; they wanted to help run the company. Second, after receiving this information, she empowered them to design an organization that would allow the firm to satisfy customer demand, reach its financial targets, and maintain employee morale. The employees decided to reorganize into six different types of teams: marketing, professional development, finance, quality, fun, and community relations. Except for finance, every task would be performed by teams of seven to eleven employees. Cunningham now develops goals with each team for the year. Each team then comes up with plans, budgets, and strategies for the year.

Organizational Iceberg

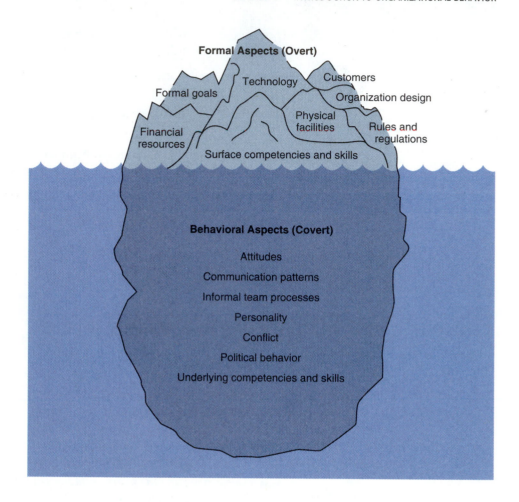

Third, employees learned that it's hard to make decisions, accept trade-offs, and live with their own decisions. Now they are responsible for implementing goals and taking responsibility for meeting them. Teams meet to go over the past month's work and set goals for the next month. Employees adopted the motto, "Don't complain. Fix it." Cunningham also learned that leading the company required an array of competencies.[2] Coaching the teams, helping them stay on track, and removing obstacles became an integral part of her leadership tasks.

An examination of an organization's structure, systems, technologies, goals, and employee surface competencies is only a part of understanding why people behave as they do on the job. These factors set conditions that affect their behavior. Only after Cunningham changed her behavior did the organization's performance improve. As she discovered, what people want from their jobs can be much different from what managers think they want. Thus individuals increasingly need competencies and their corresponding skills to diagnose, assess, interpret, and decide on courses of action that anticipate or respond to changing forces in the external environment, as well as overt and covert issues within the organization.[3] As discussed in the next section, some issues and forces—such as diversity—exist both internally (overtly and covertly) in and externally to the organization.

THE MANY ASPECTS OF DIVERSITY

The media usually focuses on race, gender, and ethnicity when mentioning *diversity*. As suggested in Figure 1.2, however, diversity includes these characteristics and many more.[4] **Diversity** includes all the obvious and more subtle ways in which individuals differ. Even a single aspect of diversity, such as physical abilities and qualities, contains various characteristics that may affect individual or team behaviors. One of the challenges in organizational behavior is to determine whether those effects deny opportunity and thus are wasteful and counterproductive, simply reflect tolerance of differences, or lead to embracing diversity as a value-added organizational resource.[5] A second challenge is to assist in developing individual, team, and organizational competencies—including learning new knowledge, attitudes, skills, and methods of intervention—to value and embrace diversity as a source of creativity and strength.

■ CATEGORIES OF DIVERSITY

Figure 1.2 identifies fourteen of the more common categories of diversity dealt with in organizational behavior. They are subdivided into *primary categories*—generic characteristics that affect a person's self-image and socialization—and *secondary categories*—learned characteristics that a person acquires and modifies throughout life.[6] As suggested by the arrows and dotted lines, these categories aren't independent in their relationship to organizational behavior issues. For example, a woman (gender) with children (parental status) is likely to be directly affected by an organization with *family friendly* or *family unfriendly* policies and attitudes, such as "Your job must always come first to get ahead in this organization."

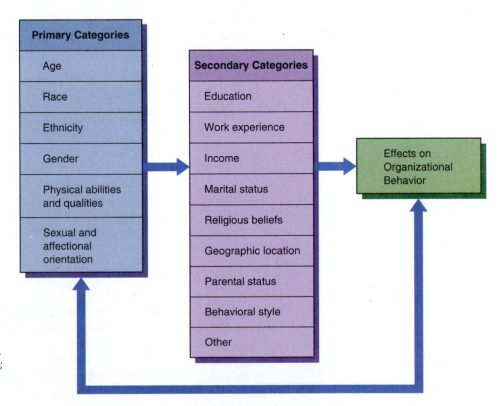

■ FIGURE 1.2

Selected Categories of Diversity

Source: Adapted from Bradford, S. Fourteen dimensions of diversity: Understanding and appreciating differences in the work place. In J. W. Pfeiffer, *1996 Annual: Volume 2 Consulting*. San Diego: Pfeiffer and Associates, 1996, 9–17; Loden, M., and Rosener, J. *Workforce America*. Burr Ridge Ill.: Irwin, 1991.

The following are brief explanations of the primary categories of diversity. Individuals have relatively little influence over these characteristics.

- *Age:* the number of years a person has been alive and the generation in which she or he was born.
- *Race:* the biological groupings within humankind, representing superficial physical differences, such as eye form and skin color. Race accounts for 0.012 percent of the difference in a person's genetic heredity.
- *Ethnicity:* identification with a cultural group that has shared traditions and heritage, including national origin, language, religion, food, customs, and so on. Some people identify strongly with these cultural roots; others do not.
- *Gender:* biological sex as determined by XX (female) or XY (male) chromosomes.
- *Physical abilities and qualities:* a variety of characteristics, including body type, physical size, facial features, specific abilities or disabilities, and visible and invisible physical and mental talents or limitations.
- *Sexual and affectional orientation:* feelings of sexual attraction toward members of the same or opposite gender, such as heterosexual, gay or lesbian, or bisexual.

The following are brief explanations of the secondary categories of diversity. Individuals have relatively more influence over them during their lifetimes by making choices.

- *Education:* the individual's formal and informal learning and training.
- *Work experience:* the employment and volunteer positions the person has held and the array of organizations for which the person has worked.
- *Income:* the economic conditions in which the person grew up and his or her current economic status.
- *Marital status:* the person's situation as a never-married, married, widowed, or divorced individual.
- *Religious beliefs:* fundamental teachings received about deities and values acquired from formal or informal religious practices.
- *Geographic location:* the location(s) in which the person was raised or spent a significant part of her or his life, including types of communities and urban areas versus rural areas.
- *Parental status:* having or not having children and the circumstances in which the children are raised (single parenting, two-adult parenting, and so on).
- *Behavioral style:* tendency of the individual to think, feel, or act in a particular way.[7]

We discuss most of these categories of diversity throughout the book. In addition, many of the chapters contain a Diversity in Practice feature that relates one or more diversity categories to a specific topic in organizational behavior. One such Diversity in Practice feature is the following presentation of how General Electric (GE) Corporation is attempting to embrace the many aspects of diversity through the theme of boundaryless behavior.

DIVERSITY IN PRACTICE

General Electric's Boundaryless Behavior

Recognizing that differences often create barriers to productivity in an organization, GE's CEO Jack Welch, in a recent annual report, called for a company with boundaryless behavior. He stated, "Boundaryless behavior is the soul of today's GE. Simply put, people seem compelled to build layers and walls between themselves and others, and that human tendency tends to be magnified in large, old institutions. . . . These walls cramp people, inhibit creativity, waste time, restrict vision, smother dreams, and above all, slow things down."

To help implement the *boundaryless behavior* concept, GE established a self-assessment program with several key diversity practices:

- top management commitment and involvement in diversity initiatives;
- recruitment goals for diversity;
- support of work-life programs;
- communication of diversity strategy;
- reward and recognition of those who walk the talk; and
- integrate diversity into business strategy.

Dr. Gene Andrews, GE manager of work force diversity, states:

At GE we recognize that we are increasingly relying on teams and that our teams are increasingly diverse. Because of this, it just makes sense for us to put emphasis on ensuring that all of our team members feel and experience a real sense of inclusion and that they are afforded the opportunity to ramp up the learning curve as quickly as possible. We do this through practices such as a buddy system to assist new employees with their transition to GE, a high-impact and business-focused employee orientation, and a mentoring program to help all employees with career and personal development issues. We expect that these practices will also contribute to the bottom line in terms of both individual and team productivity and reduced turnover costs resulting from an anticipated increase in employee retention.[8]

In the remainder of this section, we present a brief overview of the organizational implications for some of the primary diversity categories. As you consider them, you should think about the potential impact of these diversity categories on your career.

■ CHANGING WORK FORCE AND CUSTOMERS

The makeup of the work force and customer base in the United States (and many other countries) will continue to change. The majority of new employees will continue to be women, members of non-Caucasian races, and from ethnically diverse groups (virtually every country in the world is represented in the U.S. population). In addition, an increasing number of business organizations headquartered in many countries have employees, customers, and suppliers in locations around the world. Bank of America's 95,000 employees work in thirty-seven countries and, in the United States, serve some 11 million households in ten western states. The California customer call center staff are fluent in thirteen languages and cover the center twenty-four hours per day. The need for this linguistic capability arises from the fact that 32 million people in the United States speak a language other than English at home, and 8.6 million of them are in California alone. Valerie Crane, senior vice-president and director, corporate diversity development, at Bank of America states, "Those numbers represent a very sizable segment of our actual and potential customer base, as well as our labor force." At another firm, Nicole Bard, manager of Intel's business practices network, comments, "We are global in scope, our values are global in scope. The use of the U.S. paradigm, mostly focused on race and gender, is very constrictive to us. We expect all employees to perform to values. Ours is a more multicultural approach."[9]

Work forces in Asia, Western Europe, Latin America, and North America are growing more complex and diverse. Thus managers and employees need to recognize and embrace differences resulting from this diversity, particularly in terms of what fellow employees want from the job. Let's consider three of the challenges that organizations face with a diverse work force.[10]

First, there are language differences. Unless employees can understand each other, communication is difficult or even impossible. Employees can't train each other or work together if they can't communicate. Translators may be used for hiring, but—for the day-to-day communication that fosters a friendly, informal, and productive work setting—language barriers pose real and often serious problems. Such problems may lead to misunderstandings regarding performance standards, work methods, safety measures, and other essential working conditions.

Second, natural ethnic groupings within an organization may develop. Employees, especially if they don't speak English, may seek out others of the same ethnic group for assistance. Although this may create a strong sense of togetherness within the ethnic group, it may not promote working with others who don't share the same language and cultural heritage. Such tendencies need to be constructively managed.

Third, attitudes and cultural differences are another possible challenge. Most people have developed attitudes and beliefs about others by the time they seek a job. However, some attitudes and beliefs create frustration, anger, and bitterness in those at whom they're aimed. Managers and others who want to foster employee tolerance are opting for major change. Most managers and employees usually accept change only if the potential benefits are clear and worthwhile. In some organizations, women and minorities are bypassed when important, formal decisions are made. Informally, these people often are left out when others go to lunch or a sporting event. These informal get-togethers often give older employees a chance to counsel younger employees about coping with problems.

To create an environment in which everyone can contribute to the organization's goals, attitudes usually must change. What are your attitudes toward diversity? Before reading further, you should complete the Attitudes Toward Diversity Questionnaire in the Developing Competencies section at the end of this chapter.

An example of diversity training is the program started by EDS, a global leader in information services with 95,000 employees in forty-three countries. It offers a diversity awareness workshop as part of an effort to reinforce positive attitudes and behaviors toward diversity. The workshop teaches employees how to work effectively in teams composed of individuals with diverse backgrounds. EDS Customer Services Technologies Division Director, James Coyle, comments, "Our workshop goes beyond race and gender to include religion, age, disabilities, social status and more. And instead of merely teaching white males how to manage women and minorities, we help all employees learn to work with others different from themselves."[11]

■ GENDER

Women now account for nearly half (46 percent) of the work force in the United States. However, the number who have managed to rise to the top of the corporate ladder is small—3 percent to 5 percent—according to a recent study by Catalyst, a New York-based research organization.[12] According to U.S. Labor Department statistics, women will account for 62 percent of the net civilian work force growth through 2005. Consider a few results from a 1995 survey of randomly selected top and middle management female (1880 respondents) and male (230 respondents) subscribers to *Fortune* magazine.[13] These results are fairly typical of those obtained in other such surveys.[14] In this survey, respondents were provided with a list of eighteen attitudes or situations that could potentially erect barriers to women's professional success. The existence of a male-dominated corporate culture was cited by 91 percent of the women and 75 percent of the men as the number one barrier to the advancement of women. Women also felt that the existence of a glass ceiling (88 percent), their exclusion from informal network communication (86 percent), management's attitude that women are less career-oriented than men (84 percent), and the lack of female mentors (78 percent) were among the top five barriers to their advancement.

Men identified the following as primary barriers to women's success: difficulty in balancing work and family life (71 percent), the lack of female mentors (70 percent), few female bosses to serve as role models (67 percent), and exclusion from informal network communication (66 percent). Among men, existence of a glass ceiling ranked only eighth. The **glass ceiling** refers to a barrier so subtle that it is transparent, yet so strong that it prevents women and minorities from moving up in management.[15]

When asked to indicate which initiatives they would like to see their company undertake, female respondents expressed far more interest in almost all of the 23 programs suggested than their male counterparts. The top six initiatives—with the percentage of female and male managers wanting them in their own companies shown in parentheses—were

- leadership development programs for women (43 percent female, 22 percent male);
- regularly surveying women in the company about career satisfaction (40 percent female, 24 percent male);
- mentoring program (39 percent female, 25 percent male);
- career development program focusing on strategies and advice (37 percent female, 24 percent male);
- rotation program to expose women to different areas and operations within the organization (36 percent female, 18 percent male); and
- formal recruitment program to attract senior-level women (33 percent female, 20 percent male).

Deloitte & Touche, a Big Six accounting and consulting services firm, is now recognized as a leading organization in addressing diversity issues, especially those related to women in the work force. Initiatives since 1993 include establishment of a leadership program, with a national partner implementation network; development of programs to enhance working relationships between men and women; enhancement of career opportunities for women through programs or mentoring, networking, and career planning; support for balancing multiple commitments; and continuous communication of information about change, both internally and externally.[16]

Many women—managerial and nonmanagerial—with children hold full-time jobs and still bear primary responsibility for family care. By 2000, approximately 75 percent of working women will be in their child-bearing years. Dupont, Deloitte & Touche, Eli Lilly, Hewlett-Packard, Marriott International, and Motorola are among the firms with family friendly policies and strategies. For example, Dupont offers childcare, flextime (ability to arrive and leave work at varied hours), job-sharing (two individuals, often women, who want to work part-time share a job), telecommuting (opportunity for certain groups of employees to work at home some or most of the time), and flexibility in accommodating employees on family needs.[17]

■ RACE AND ETHNICITY

Each year, one-third of the newcomers to the U.S. work force are minority group members. By 2000, the work force will contain 16.5 million African-Americans, up almost 20 percent from 1988. Hispanics, Asians, and other minorities will comprise 14 percent of the work force, up 4 percent from 1988.[18] Minority group members also face the glass ceiling[19] and **racism,** the notion that a person's race is superior to all others. The three basic forms of racism, which can operate within an organization and the larger society, often are interrelated: (1) *individual racism*—the extent to which a person holds attitudes, values, feelings, and/or engages in behaviors that promote the person's own racial group as superior; (2) *cultural racism*—the arrogant and superiority elevation of the cultural features and achievements of the group's race while actively ignoring or denigrating those of other races; and (3) *institutional racism*—organizational and/or societal rules, regulations, laws, policies, and customs that serve to maintain the dominant status of and control by one racial group. Each form of racism may operate overtly or covertly and intentionally or unintentionally.[20]

Overcoming racism is difficult. Consider the experience of James Wimbush, an African-American who is now a professor of management at Indiana University. Some years ago, Wimbush had just been hired into a managerial position by a company. He recalls how his manager introduced him to other local managers at a West Virginia facility. The manager described Wimbush as a good student, talented, and at the top of his class. Such compliments are always nice to hear, but Wimbush said that his manager didn't say a word about the other managers' credentials, which were equally impressive. Wimbush said that it appeared the manager was trying to explain why the company had hired Wimbush, and brought him to a part of West Virginia where the only African-Americans who wore ties to work were ministers. Wimbush said that white employees quit when they heard of his selection. He wondered whether he should ignore that or respond in some way. In the end, he decided to work hard to earn the respect of fellow managers and employees.[21]

■ AGE

The U.S. and Canadian work forces are aging along with the baby boomers. From 1990 to 2000, the number of people aged 35 to 47 will have increased by 38 percent, whereas the number between 48 and 53 will have increased by 67 percent.[22] In the past, older workers have been less likely than younger workers to relocate or train for new occupations.

The increase in the number of middle-aged employees has collided with organizational efforts to reduce layers of middle management in order to remain competitive. Over time, the skills of many of these employees are valuable only to the firms they work for. Thus older employees who lose jobs often have great difficulty matching previous levels of responsibility and salaries, even when they are able to find new jobs.

The need to manage oneself and career or careers over a lifetime—not just in the early years—is now an imperative rather than an option. Most individuals can no longer count on progressing along a single career path as they age.[23] Moreover, the traditional view that loyalty between the organization and the employee increases with years of service—and thus age—is no longer valid in most U.S. organizations.[24] Consider the case of AT&T, which announced layoffs of 40,000 employees in 1996. Robert E. Allen, who stepped down as chairman of AT&T in 1996, remarked, "Employment at AT&T used to be a lifelong commitment on the employee's part and on our part. But our people now realize that the contract [the implied promise of lifetime job security in exchange for hard work and loyalty] does not exist anymore."[25]

We close this section on diversity with an account of how one organization attempts to embrace diversity as a global imperative. The following Across Cultures feature reflects, for the most part, the views of James E. Preston, chairman and CEO of Avon Products, Inc.

ACROSS CULTURES

Avon's Global Diversity

Let me make it clear at the outset that I do not hold up Avon Products as the model for a diverse work force. It's true that we've made considerable progress over the past decade, not only in the United States but also in the other forty or so countries where we have major operations. From our own experience, and from a close study of similar efforts in other corporations, I would suggest four major principles regarding this important topic of the times.

- First, diversity is a matter of human decency.
- Second, for a commercial enterprise, especially a publicly held company, diversity must be regarded as primarily a business, rather than a social, issue.
- Third, diversity cannot be viewed only on a national basis. We must concern ourselves with what we at Avon call "global differences."
- And fourth—and here's where I sometimes get into trouble—effective diversity is not a matter of set-asides or a numbers-related system, such as affirmative action. They were useful in their time, but I believe that time has largely passed.

Half of the people reporting directly to me are women, including the chief financial officer—not exactly a traditional position for a woman. The head of Avon U.S., our $1.6 billion domestic business and the largest single unit in our

—*Continued*

ACROSS CULTURES—*Continued*

global network, is a woman. Avon is one of only five U.S. corporations with as many as four women on its board of directors—and that number will increase.

African-Americans, Hispanics, and Asians are also coming to prominence. But I have to admit that our percentages of those groups are less impressive because the competition for minority talent is intense. Even, so we don't intend to use this as an excuse.

Globally, Avon is nothing if not multinational. Not too many years ago, our senior management group carried two or at most three passports—American, maybe a Canadian, an occasional Briton. Today, our senior group, called the Global Business Council, carries a total of six passports. Management people around the world are selected on the basis of competencies, not nationality. We look for the best available talent. As a result, our entire European business is now run by a Venezuelan. A Chilean heads our German business. A Chinese-American woman heads our business in Thailand. A Portuguese man is in charge of France.

But diversity at Avon doesn't stop at nationalities. It also includes differences in age, lifestyle, and personal interests. We constantly try for a richness in the decision-making process that we can only get from people with widely diverse backgrounds. Different people—local or global—come at things differently, and that leads to better decisions. To Avon, diversity is making sure we provide an environment where every individual—regardless of ethnicity, religion, lifestyle preferences, dress, whatever—has an opportunity to progress in direct correlation to his or her ability to contribute to the objectives of the company.[26]

ADDITIONAL ORGANIZATIONAL ISSUES

Four additional contemporary organizational issues, which we highlight in this section, are woven into many of the chapters in this book. They are quality, technology, global perspective, and ethics.

■ QUALITY

Quality is the totality of features and characteristics of a product or service that bears on its ability to satisfy given needs. Quality improvement is now an imperative for organizations to remain competitive.[27] A key issue for organizations is how to improve quality. **Total quality management** (TQM) is an organizational philosophy and long-term strategy that makes continuous improvement in quality a responsibility of all employees. It requires dedication to meeting customers' needs and expectations, which includes (1) designing quality into products and services; (2) preventing defects to the greatest extent feasible and correcting those that do appear; and (3) continuously improving the quality of goods and services to the extent economically and competitively feasible.[28]

In 1951, W. Edwards Deming conducted a quality control seminar for Japanese executives. Deming believed that to be more competitive organizations had to begin with quality. He also believed that poor quality is 85 percent a management problem and 15 percent a worker problem. Among his recommendations for improving quality were the following.

■ Establish and maintain zero tolerance for defective materials, workmanship, products, and services.

- Gather statistical facts of quality during the process, not at its end. The earlier an error is caught, the less the cost will be to correct it.
- Rely on a few suppliers that historically have provided quality.
- Depend not on slogans but on training and retraining of employees to use statistical methods in their jobs to improve quality.
- Encourage employees to report any conditions that detract from quality.[29]

Today an increasing number of organizations are committed to productivity and quality improvement. Ford, Chrysler, and General Motors have changed management philosophies and past practices to foster new and creative ways of doing things. Numerous other organizations, including Motorola, Corning, Hewlett-Packard, 3M, FedEx, Xerox, and USAA, have used Deming's concepts or some variation of them to improve quality.

In 1987, Congress established the Malcolm Baldrige Award to recognize organizations that excel in quality achievement and management. Motorola, 3M, FedEx, Xerox, and Corning Telecommunications Products Division are among the firms that have won this prestigious award. The 1997 award criteria (categories) relative weightings out of 1000 total points are leadership (110 points), strategic planning (80 points), customer and market forces (80 points), information and analyses (80 points), human resource development and management (100 points), process management (100 points), and business results (450 points). The business results criterion includes customer satisfaction (130 points), financial and market performance (130 points), supplier and partner results (25 points).[30] Each of the categories contain multiple dimensions for assessment. The award criteria and their interpretation are designed to reflect a *systems approach,* that is, the dynamic linkages among the criteria.

The constant provision of quality services and goods is an ideal that isn't easily attained. How managers and employees respond to quality issues is crucial. Organizations that actually adopt—not just give *lip service* to—TQM generally display the following common characteristics.

- They focus on *satisfying customers,* both internal (other employees, teams, and departments) and external.
- They develop a balanced and integrated *system* for satisfying internal and external customer needs.
- They manage the system to *continuously improve* the satisfaction of internal and external customer needs.
- People are *empowered*—that is, decision-making discretion is moved to individuals and teams where competent decisions about specific situations can be made, often at a lower level than previously in the organization.
- All members in all functions at all levels of the organization use various formal models and techniques to aid decision making and the never-ending process of learning.
- They view all of their human resources as partners and central to their competitiveness, which requires continually investing in developing employee competencies and skills.
- Management, at all levels, provides positive, dynamic leadership to foster an environment having the preceding characteristics.[31]

In much of the book, we discuss the competencies needed for achieving an environment that supports a TQM philosophy and system. The Ritz-Carlton

Hotel Company is a previous winner of the Malcolm Baldrige National Quality Award. The following Quality in Practice account focuses on the customer satisfaction features of its TQM system.

QUALITY IN PRACTICE

Ritz-Carlton Hotel Company

The Ritz-Carlton Hotel Company spent nine years developing a system to deliver premium service and exceed customer expectations. According to its own research, 97 percent of Ritz Carlton customers had their expectations met and reported a "memorable" experience.

The Ritz-Carlton perspective is that, in order to provide complete customer satisfaction, the needs and expectations of the customer must first be fully understood. The hotel gathers information on its customers from a several sources: extensive research by travel industry associations and publications; focus groups with different market segments; surveys of customers who have just used the company's services; and briefings from employees who come in contact with customers daily.

An information system allows Ritz-Carlton employees to enter data regarding customer preferences into a computer. This information then becomes part of the company's online "repeat guest history program." When a repeat customer calls the central reservations number to book a room, the agent can retrieve the individual's preference information directly from the online system. This information is sent to the specific Ritz-Carlton location where the room is reserved. The hotel then outputs the data in a daily guest recognition and preference report, which is circulated to all staff. With this system, hotel staff can anticipate a particular guest's breakfast habits, newspaper choices, and room preferences.

The Ritz-Carlton's employees are well trained to ensure they are able to respond to customers' needs. Its customer management system ensures that the first employee who becomes aware of a customer complaint will be able to resolve the problem quickly and completely. Each employee can reverse a transaction up to $2000 without prior approval—if necessary—to satisfy a customer.[32]

■ TECHNOLOGY

Technology, especially computer-based information technologies, continue to revolutionize how

1. tasks are performed;
2. organizations are structured;
3. customers are served;
4. human resources are led and managed;
5. planning and control systems operate;
6. employees communicate and network with one another and external stakeholders, such as customers, suppliers, competitors, and government agencies;
7. individuals and organizations learn to innovate and adapt; and
8. many other tasks are performed.

Technological change may have positive effects, including higher quality products and services at lower costs. But it also may have negative effects, including erosion of personal privacy, computer-related stress, and health problems (such as eye strain and carpal tunnel syndrome).[33]

James Martin, author of *Cybercorp: The New Business Revolution*, suggests that the next stage in the evolution of business organizations is the creation of **cybercorps,** or organizations that are fully wired with advanced computer-based information technologies, as well as being agile, global, and cybernetic. A cybernetic organization is like a biological organism, but comprises people and electronics instead of cells. According to this view, a cybercorp's senses are constantly on, allowing it to anticipate and react in real time to the external environment. It is an open system that uses computer-based and person-to-person linkages to make it highly agile. A cybercorp is designed to learn and transform itself rapidly. It continually reinvents itself to take advantage of opportunities.[34]

The Internet and intranets are central features of advanced organizations, such as cybercorps. The **Internet** is a worldwide collection of interconnected computer networks. Through an array of computer-based information technologies, the Internet directly links the organization and its employees to customers, suppliers, information sources, the public, and millions of individuals.[35] An **intranet** uses the infrastructure and standards of the Internet and the World Wide Web to provide one or more private networks connecting all the employees or particular sets of employees of an organization, such as all the employees working on a particular project throughout the world.[36] Intranets are protected by passwords to prevent unauthorized outsiders and employees of the organization from accessing certain data and information. Management may give access to *authorized* outsiders—such as customers and suppliers—to one or more of its intranets. For example, several years ago, FedEx put a server on the World Wide Web that gave customers direct access to its package-tracking database. At Ford Motor Company, an intranet with highly restricted access links design centers in Asia, Europe, and the United States.[37]

Throughout this book, we discuss topics that are related to the introduction and use of technology and which, in turn, are affected by it. Our Technology in Practice feature, which appears in several chapters, is another way that we relate the role of technology to organizational behavior. The following Technology in Practice selection presents a brief account of how information technology recently improved service to a special category of Banc One's customers and how it dramatically changed some jobs.

TECHNOLOGY IN PRACTICE

Banc One's Special Intranet

The transaction-processing unit of Banc One Corporation in Columbus, Ohio, handles millions of checks a month for third parties, such as other banks and insurance companies. This task resulted in stacks of paperwork to keep track of checks that have been deposited and accounts that have been debited and credited. Almost all that paperwork has disappeared for about thirty of Banc One's transaction-processing customers. These clients are now using a Banc One intranet through an Internet link.

—Continued

TECHNOLOGY IN PRACTICE—*Continued*

Consider what happens when one of these customers, such as Nationwide Insurance Company, has a question about a check—say, the amount debited from its checking account was incorrect. An employee at the insurance company accesses a World Wide Web browser on a personal computer and keys in a password. That brings the employee into Banc One's intranet setup on the Internet. With a few key strokes, the employee pulls up a computerized image of the check in question to verify the amount. With the same Web browser, the employee can use Banc One's mainframe computers and other databases to see where the mistake was made. A credit to the customer's account in the correct amount can be issued on the spot.

Previously, a Banc One employee would have taken the insurance company's complaint over the phone by filling out a paper form. This action would have triggered a lengthy search through piles of canceled checks in a warehouse to find the one in question. Banc One employees would have had to scan records stored on several computer systems, as well as the paper documents, to locate the error.

"The old world used to be Federal Express and fax and overnight bags—it's a process that took seven to 10 days," says Bill Sheley, a Banc One vice-president who oversees the system, adding that "now it takes less than an hour." Moreover, the new system shaved more than 25 percent off the processing costs of the paper-based system.[38]

■ GLOBAL PERSPECTIVE

A **global perspective** is the mind set and attitudes that view all or most key issues involving stakeholders—customers, employees, suppliers, competitors, shareholders, and governments—as requiring organizational processes and strategies that recognize similarities and differences nation to nation and culture to culture.[39] The competitive strategies that evolve from a global perspective vary widely and aren't central to our discussion of organizational behavior. Rather, we focus on values, perceptions, motivation, leadership, group processes, conflict management, interpersonal communications, and organizational cultures in relation to the concepts and perspectives of different cultures. In addition, virtually all the chapters in this book contain an Across Cultures feature, such as the one presented previously on Avon's global diversity. The effectiveness of a multicultural perspective is measured by success of an organization's competitive strategies in other nations and cultures. In a sense, a global and multicultural perspective is a form of embracing diversity.

Consider these two examples of embracing diversity through a multicultural perspective. Employee networking groups at Silicon Graphics have provided insights into expanding markets globally. Their Asian networking group was pivotal in helping the company gain access to markets in the Pacific Rim. Similarly, their African-American networking group played a significant role in exploring expansion into South Africa. Pitney Bowes is the recipient of important perspectives from employees educated outside the United States. The company's Asian and Japanese employees have raised awareness about cultural issues involved in sending and receiving mail. In the United States, mail is merely a way of getting a message to someone. In Japan, and many other Asian countries, mail reflects the sender. Hence Pitney Bowes has found that quality of printing and other attributes of mailings are much more important in those cultures and subsequently has responded to those cultural norms.[40]

Developments associated with globalization include the following.

- Capital (financial resources), labor (current and potential employees), and ideas are increasingly mobile—especially with the aid of global computer-based information technologies (such as the Internet and intranets).

- Goods and services are increasingly available in many places at the same time. Goods and services, such as personal computers and the Ford Contour, are now often designed with the whole world in mind.

- Easier international travel, deregulation of markets, and privatization of government-owned business, such as Telemex (telephone company) in Mexico.

- Breakup and dispersion of corporate headquarters functions and the creation of centers of excellence around the world reflect an increasingly global perspective. Hewlett-Packard has its corporate headquarters in Palo Alto, California. However, it has world centers in Boston (medical equipment), France (personal computers), Germany (fiber optics research), Singapore (laser printers), and Australia (engineering software development).[41]

■ ETHICS

The ethical issues facing managers and other employees have grown in significance in recent years, fueled by public concern about how business is conducted. Ethical behavior sometimes is difficult to define, especially in a global economy with its myriad beliefs and practices. **Ethics** are the values and rules that distinguish right from wrong.[42] Although ethical behavior in business clearly has a legal component, absolutes aren't always applicable.

Managers and employees alike face situations in which there are no right or wrong answers: The burden is on individuals to make ethical decisions. An **ethical dilemma** occurs when the individual or team must make a decision that involves multiple values. An ethical dilemma doesn't simply involve choosing right over wrong because the opposite of one value may be several other competing values. Some ethical dilemmas arise from competitive and time pressures.[43] Consider the following incident. The minister of a foreign government asks you to pay a special consulting fee of $200,000 to him. In return for the money, the official promises special assistance in obtaining a $100 million contract for your firm that would produce at least a $5 million profit. The contract will be awarded to a foreign competitor if not awarded to your company. Your choice is to pay the fee or not to pay the fee. What would you do? In a survey of *Harvard Business Review* readers, 42 percent said that they would refuse to pay; 22 percent said that they would pay but consider it unethical; 36 percent said that they would pay and consider it ethical in the foreign context.[44]

The first uniform international ethics code, General Principles for Business, was developed recently from a collaboration of business leaders in Europe, Japan, and the United States. This code contains seven general ethical principles and six sets of stakeholder ethical principles that apply to customers, employees, owners and investors, suppliers, competitors, and communities. This code presents global ethical ideals for any organization in every country. Six of the ten ethical responsibilities that relate to employees are

- provide working conditions that respect each employee's health and dignity;
- be honest in communication with employees and open in sharing information, limited only by legal and competitive restraints;
- listen to and, where possible, act on employee suggestions, ideas, requests, and complaints;
- avoid discriminatory practices and guarantee equal treatment and opportunity in areas such as gender, age, race, and religion;
- promote in the business itself the employment of differently abled people in places of work where they can be genuinely useful; and
- be sensitive to serious unemployment problems frequently associated with business decisions and work with governments, employee groups, other agencies, and each other in addressing these dislocations.[45]

Cummins Engine Company, headquartered in Columbus, Indiana, is one organization that strives to adhere to this international ethics code. It designs and manufactures a full line of diesel engines and has more than 24,000 employees worldwide. The following Ethics in Practice piece presents a few of the views of J. A. Henderson, CEO and chairman of Cummins, relative to the global ethical standards that the firm strives to achieve. An Ethics in Practice feature appears in most chapters of this book.

ETHICS IN PRACTICE

Cummins Global Ethics

We manufacture extensively overseas. One of the advantages we have right now is that the expansion of our product line, which enables us to serve many more customers, has coincided with a period when many countries are concerned about quality of life and employment for their people. They want to attract foreign investment, which means lowering trade barriers. It also means that local companies have to compete in world markets. As a result, in many cases, they need to find partners. We are a logical partner, in part because we have a reputation for integrity. We also bring our latest technology to our alliances, and we manufacture and purchase components locally, both of which benefit the local country.

Integrity means that you do what you say you're going to do. You don't do something you wouldn't want to read about in the paper the next day. It means you do what's right, even in the face of difficult circumstances. Here's one example:

Some years ago, when there were real difficulties in South Africa, we were probably that country's leading diesel engine supplier (we weren't manufacturing there, our engines were imported). The South African government decided to put out a bid for a local manufacturer; the engines were to be used not only by commercial people, but also by the police and local defense forces. Because we thought they would be used against the local populace, we declined to participate.

We also took a stand early in the company's history that if the employees thought they needed unions, then they should consider them. We were in the forefront of trying to have a diverse work force long before people thought this was an important thing to do. We want all of our people—our employees, our

—Continued

ETHICS IN PRACTICE—*Continued*

customers, our suppliers, the communities in which we live and work—to be able to trust us, trust what we say, and trust that our actions will be in everybody's best interest, to the extent they can be.[46]

How can you prepare for the challenges and issues of diversity, quality, technology, global perspective, and ethics? A good starting point is to understand the competencies and their coresponding skills that you will need to develop and strengthen to become and remain an effective professional or manager.

CORE COMPETENCIES AND THEIR CORRESPONDING SKILLS

A **competency** comprises the interrelated skills and knowledge bases that enable the individual to bring added value to a general area of job responsibility.[47] A **skill,** which is one element of a competency, refers to a specific set of abilities. Just as organizations need core competencies to compete and achieve their goals, so do employees.[48] In this section we focus on a general model of the core competencies that most professionals and all managers in organizations need to develop and strengthen. For the most part, this section is based on the Evers and Rush base competencies model.[49]

As suggested by the two-way arrows in Figure 1.3, core competencies—and, for that matter, the sets of skills within each competency—are interrelated. For example, to be effective at *mobilizing innovation and change* is difficult without the complementary competency of *managing people and tasks.* Throughout this book, both in the chapter text and in the Developing Competencies section at the end of each chapter, we focus on the development of these core competencies.

■ MOBILIZING INNOVATION AND CHANGE

Mobilizing innovation and change is a core competency that involves the ability to think of ideas about both the present and future and to initiate improvements based on a systematic evaluation of the risks involved in doing so. This competency includes the following interrelated skills.

- **Conceptualization** is the ability to combine information from a number of sources, to integrate information into more general situations and contexts and to apply information to new or broader issues. Individuals with this skill are able to identify key issues and diagnose them by examining the basic questions of *who, what, why, when, where,* and *how.* We focus on this skill throughout the book.

- **Creativity** is the ability to innovate and provide novel solutions to problems and to initiate and adapt to change. Creativity also involves the ability to rethink roles in response to changing demands on the organization and/or one or more of its departments. We focus on this skill in Chapters 17 and 18.

- **Risk taking** is the willingness to take reasonable chances by recognizing and capitalizing on opportunities while also recognizing their potential negative outcomes and monitoring progress toward goals. We focus on this skill in Chapters 14 and 17.

■ FIGURE 1.3

Professional and Managerial Core Competencies Model

Source: Adapted from Evers, F. T., and Rush, J. C. The bases of competence: Skill development during the transition from university to work. *Managing Learning,* 1996, 27, 275–300.

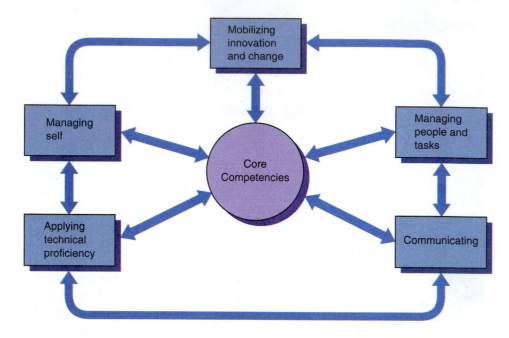

- **Visioning** is the ability to grasp the potential of an organization and/or one or more of its departments and to imagine innovative paths for it to follow. We focus on this skill in several chapters, but especially Chapters 11 and 18.

Mobilizing innovation and change is now viewed as a necessary and vital core competency of organizations as a whole, not just of individual professionals and managers. Bert Roberts, Jr., chairman and CEO of MCI, one of the world's major diversified communications companies, reflects on this imperative:

> We run like mad and then we change directions. It's indicative of the industry we're in. Telecommunications has gone through such radical changes. Many times I've asked, "Can things possibly change in the future more than they've changed in the past?" Fortunately or unfortunately, depending on where you're coming from, the answer always seems to be "Yes." To be successful in this industry, a company not only has to run fast, stay ahead of the pack and make opportunities, but it also has to be able to change directions, because that's what the industry is doing. That's what it's been doing since we started doing business.[50]

■ MANAGING PEOPLE AND TASKS

Managing people and tasks is the core competency associated with many of the traditional management functions but which are now increasingly shared through the empowerment of employees and teams. This competency includes the following interrelated skills.

- **Planning** is the ability to set goals, determine the tasks to be carried out to meet those goals, assigning tasks to others, monitoring progress against the plan, and revising the plan to reflect new information. We focus on this skill in Chapters 7, 16, and 18.
- **Decision making** is the ability to choose effective courses of action on the basis of a thorough assessment of their short- and long-term effects, recognizing their political and ethical implications, and being able to identify the

people and groups who will be affected. We focus on this skill in Chapters 8, 9, and 14.

- **Organizing** is the ability to develop the design of individual jobs, organizational departments, and processes and to integrate them to achieve the organization's goals. We focus on this skill in Chapters 15 and 16.

- **Leading** is the ability to create a sense of direction, guide others in that direction, and delegate tasks in a manner that is effective and motivates others to do their best. Leadership has many aspects, some of which have to do with hiring, evaluating, and rewarding employees. The essence of leading is integrating the needs of individuals with the goals of the organization and its departments. We focus on this skill in Chapters 5, 6, and 8 and devote two full chapters, Chapters 10 and 11, to it.

- **Conflict management** is the ability to identify sources of differences that lead to conflict and take steps to resolve them constructively. Conflict management may involve negotiations with external stakeholders—customers, suppliers, unions, and governments. We focus on this skill in Chapters 8 and 12.

Recall the Preview Case on Andrea Cunningham. She was clearly managing tasks and people, but not with the level of competency needed for the long-term effectiveness of her public relations firm. Fortunately, as suggested in our discussion of how Cunningham looked below the tip of the iceberg (see Figure 1.1), she was able to improve her planning, decision-making, coordinating, leading, and conflict management skills.

■ COMMUNICATING

Communicating is the core competency that involves the capable sending and receiving information and conveying and understanding thoughts, feelings, and attitudes. This competency includes the following interrelated skills.

- **Interpersonal communication** is the ability to interact face-to-face with others (superiors, peers, subordinates, and customers). We focus on this skill in Chapter 13.

- **Listening** is the ability to be attentive when others are speaking and hence to respond effectively to others' comments. We focus on this skill in Chapter 13.

- **Oral communication** is the ability to present information verbally to others, either one-to-one or in groups. We provide the opportunity for you to develop this skill in the Developing Competencies section at the end of each chapter and the Integrating Cases section at the end of the book.

- **Written communication** is the ability to transfer information effectively, either formally (reports, letters) or informally (memos, notes).

The communicating competency may be thought of as the *circulatory system* that nourishes the other competencies. For example, consider how gender, cultural, and ethnic diversity demand new and better communication skills. To overcome language barriers, Pepsi-Cola International developed a system for use by people from many different cultures and countries. The company had found, for example, that the phrase *handle business complexity* might be translated differently in China and France. In China it might mean to produce a product and get it to the loading dock. In France it might mean being concerned with producing, marketing, distributing, and merchandising the product. Because many such words and phrases translate differently, Pepsi-Cola International needed a way to get individuals to behave consistently regardless of country and language. Therefore the company created its own multinational vocabulary to state performance criteria in a consistent, globally acceptable, and easily understood way.[51]

■ ACHIEVING TECHNICAL PROFICIENCY

Achieving technical proficiency is the core competency that involves the ability to apply specific methods, procedures, and techniques in a specialized field. Technical skills are those needed by design engineers, market researchers, tax accountants, computer software developers, and other professionals and specialists. Their skills are concrete and usually are learned both in school and on the job. Managers use technical skills to varying degrees, depending on the problems they face and the tasks they perform. Technical skill requirements change as managers' responsibilities increase. Generally, people are initially promoted into management because of their technical skills. First-line managers need to be technically skilled enough to train new employees and supervise the technical aspects of their work. As managers' responsibilities increase, they may have less need for hands-on, detailed knowledge. But they still have to keep up with changes by learning new skills and applying new information to their tasks. We focus on developing this competency in several chapters in which we present techniques and methods for handling special organizational behavior problems.

Many managers and employees—such as those discussed in the Quality in Practice account of the Ritz-Carlton Hotel Company's system—have had to learn a new management philosophy, new management system, and new set of technical methods and tools with the introduction of total quality management. Four of the many methods and tools in a TQM program that require the development of new technical skills are

- the **run chart,** which turns data into information by plotting a variable over time;
- the **Pareto chart,** which is a bar graph ranking in order of importance the causes, sources, and types of reasons for problems and/or opportunities;
- **Taguchi methods,** which are statistical techniques for conducting experiments to determine the best (lowest cost with highest uniformity) combinations of quality and process variables for making a product; and
- **benchmarking,** which is a continuous process (well-defined series of steps and procedures) of measuring services, practices, or products against organizations recognized as leaders in an industry.[52]

■ MANAGING SELF

Managing self is the core competency that involves being aware of oneself and one's surroundings, motivating oneself and managing one's career, and knowing how to handle and adapt to changing and ambiguous situations. This competency includes the following interrelated skills.

- **Learning** is the ability to gain knowledge from everyday experiences and to keep up to date on developments in one's field. We focus on this skill in Chapters 3 and 4.

■ **Personal time management** is the ability to handle several tasks at once by being able to set priorities and allocate time efficiently in order to meet deadlines. We focus on this skill in Chapters 6 and 7.

■ **Personal attributes** comprise the various personal characteristics that help people deal with day-to-day work situations. Examples include maintaining a high energy level, motivating oneself to function at an optimal level of performance, functioning well in stressful situations, maintaining a positive attitude, being able to work independently, and responding appropriately to constructive criticism. We focus on such personal attributes in Chapters 2, 3, 5, 7, 12, and 13.

■ **Ethical standards** are the beliefs and behaviors that an individual applies in dealing with situations that involve value and moral judgments. We address ethical issues and standards in most of the chapters, but especially Chapters 9, 11, 14, 16, and 17.

Managing self is a key competency for everyone in an organization. It is no longer valid to think that the organization will provide for all of a person's developmental, training, and career needs.[53] The following Managing in Practice feature relates the highlights of how the Ford Motor Company changed its recruitment practices on campuses to emphasize competency based selection of college graduates.

MANAGING IN PRACTICE

Ford's Competency Based Recruitment Program

At the center of the recruitment and selection process are the Ford 2000 Leadership Criteria. These competencies are an agreed-on set of knowledge, experiences, skills, abilities, values, and personal characteristics that the company believes people must possess to be successful and help the business achieve its objectives. Taken together, the competencies identified as essential to each job provide the road map that guides all stages of the recruitment and selection process.

Ford executives are excited about this new opportunity to share more information about the company with candidates as recruiters learn valuable information about the competencies of the candidates.

Ford researched and developed a model of required competencies. The Ford 2000 Leadership Criteria provide the structure on which all the company's human resources systems—not just selection—will be based. At Ford, in addition to having a strong foundation of functional education and experience, an individual should have

■ passion for knowing and meeting customer requirements as well as the business and quality focus to do so in a way that represents value for the company;

■ commitment to working with team members with different perspectives;

■ focus, intensity, persistence, and integrity even under adversity;

■ adaptability in seeking alternative ways of doing business and challenging the status quo;
—Continued

MANAGING IN PRACTICE—*Continued*

■ ability to communicate information clearly and concisely; and

■ ability to solve problems while recognizing the importance of interdependencies.

Consequently, Ford redesigned its selection process to measure a candidate's potential in these areas. In the campus interview and situations inventory, recruiters assess candidates in terms of the four major competency categories of knowledge and experience, skills, personal characteristics, and values.

Ford's recruitment and selection process document includes specific criteria and skills being sought within each of the competency categories.[54]

ORGANIZATIONAL BEHAVIOR FRAMEWORK

One purpose of this book is to present as clearly as possible the basic knowledge about the behavior of people in organizations. Students of physics or accounting learn certain fundamental principles. The law of gravity is the same in Dallas, Paris, and Singapore; a hydrogen atom in New York is the same as a hydrogen atom in Brussels. An account receivable is carried on the books of a company in Calgary the same way it is carried on the books of a company in Atlanta. A cash transaction credit and debit are the same in London as they are in Tokyo. Such uniformity doesn't exist for behavior in the workplace. However, there are some well-established concepts, processes, and models that help (1) explain the behavior of employees and managers in most situations and (2) suggest the competencies and practices that are most likely to achieve effective outcomes.

The framework for understanding the behavior and improving the competencies of employees in organizations consists of four basic components: (1) environmental influences; (2) individual processes; (3) group and interpersonal processes; and (4) organizational processes. Figure 1.4 shows the relationships among these components, as well as the principal aspects of each. These relationships are much too dynamic—in terms of variety and change—to define them as laws or rules. As we preview each component, the dynamics and complexities of organizational behavior will become clear.

■ ENVIRONMENTAL INFLUENCES

Organizations are fundamentally *open systems*, which means that their long-term effectiveness will be determined by their ability to anticipate, manage, and respond to changes in the environment. The external stakeholders and forces that create pressures, demands, and expectations for organizations are numerous—and changing more rapidly than ever. External forces and stakeholders include shareholders, customers, competitors, suppliers, labor force (including current and prospective employees), creditors, government agencies and regulations, the natural environment, the economy, and cultures.

The organizational issues that we have previewed—diversity, quality, technology, global perspective, and ethics—reflect the interplay between environmental forces and the actions of managers and employees. Throughout this book, therefore, we discuss the interplay among various environmental influences and organizational behavior.

■ **FIGURE 1.4**   **Organizational Behavior Framework**

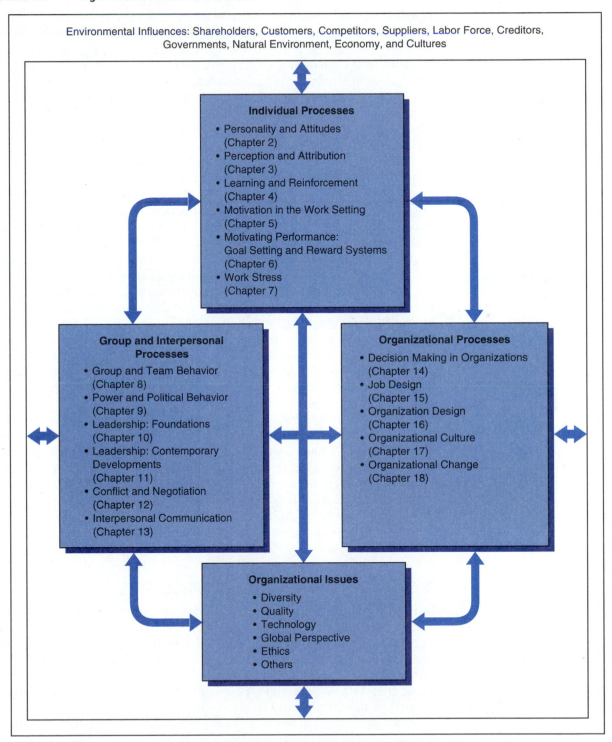

◼ INDIVIDUAL PROCESSES

People make assumptions about those with whom they work, supervise, or spend time in leisure activities. To some extent, these assumptions influence a person's behavior toward others. Effective employees understand what affects their own behavior before attempting to influence the behavior of others. (In Part I, Chapters 2–7, we focus on the behavior of individuals.)

Individual behavior is the foundation of organizational performance. Understanding individual behavior, therefore, is crucial for effective management, as illustrated by the Andrea Cunningham Preview Case. Each person is a physiological system composed of a number of subsystems—digestive, nervous, circulatory, and reproductive—and a psychological system composed of a number of subsystems—attitudes, perceptions, learning capabilities, personality, needs, feelings, and values. In Part I, we concentrate on the individual's psychological system. Both internal and external factors shape a person's behavior on the job. Internal factors include learning ability, motivation, perception, attitudes, personality, and values.

In Chapter 2, we examine how personality and attitudes can affect an individual's behavior at work. In Chapter 3, we discuss perceptions and attributions on the job. Different individuals give their own meaning to situations and so may view the same situation differently. To verify this assertion, compare your score on the Attitudes Toward Diversity Questionnaire with those of others. How similar or dissimilar are they? Think about the reasons for these differences and discuss them with your classmates. In Chapter 4, we identify principles of learning and ways that rewards can be used to communicate decisions and encourage or inhibit employee behaviors. In Chapter 5, we explain how to stimulate, sustain, and stop certain behaviors in organizations. We explore various motivators and the importance of motivation in terms of performance. In Chapter 6, we examine how goal-setting and performance enhancement techniques have been used successfully. In Chapter 7, we focus on work-related stress and how employees at all levels are attempting to cope with it, including the use of organizationally sponsored wellness activities.

Among the external factors that affect a person's behavior are the organization's reward system, organizational politics, group behavior, managerial leadership styles, and the organization's design. We examine these factors in Parts II and III of this book.

◼ GROUP AND INTERPERSONAL PROCESSES

Being inherently social, people generally don't choose to live or work alone. Most of their time is spent interacting with others: People are born into a family group, worship in groups, work in teams, and play in groups. Much of a person's identity is based on the ways that other individuals and groups perceive and treat that person. For these reasons—and because many managers and other professionals spend considerable time with others—skills in interpersonal and team dynamics are vital to all managers and employees.

Many organizational goals can be achieved only with the cooperation of others. The histories of organizations such as the Ritz-Carlton Hotel Company, General Electric, Honeywell, and Boeing clearly illustrate the creative use of teams to improve the quality of life and to satisfy the needs of their employees and customers. The productivity generated by effective team action makes the development of team competencies one of the most essential aspects of professional and managerial development. Furthermore, membership in productive and cohesive teams and groups is essential to maintaining psychological health throughout a person's life.

Being an effective team member requires an understanding of the dynamics within and between teams and other types of groups. Team members must be skillful in eliminating barriers to achieving their goals, solving problems, maintaining productive interaction among team members, and overcoming obstacles to team effectiveness. In Chapter 8, we present methods of increasing team or group effectiveness. Not all behaviors are aimed at improving performance. As Andrea Cunningham discovered when she returned from her vacation, power and political behavior, the topics that we address in Chapter 9, are realities of organizational life. Employees and managers use power to accomplish goals and, in many cases, to strengthen their own positions. A person's success or failure in using or reacting to power is largely determined by understanding power, knowing how and when to use it, and being able to predict its probable effects on others.

Organizations need leaders who can integrate customer, employee, and organizational goals. The ability of organizations to achieve their goals depends on the degree to which leadership abilities and styles enable managers and team leaders to control, influence, and act effectively. In Chapters 10 and 11, we examine how leaders influence others and individuals can develop leadership competencies. Effective leadership involves management of conflict, which may arise over any number of issues. In Chapter 12, we explain why conflict arises and how managers, teams, and employees can effectively resolve conflict, including the process of negotiation. How employees communicate with superiors, peers, subordinates, and others can help make them effective team members or lead to low morale and lack of commitment. For that reason—and because most managers and professionals spend considerable amounts of time dealing with others—we stress interpersonal communication in Chapter 13.

◼ ORGANIZATIONAL PROCESSES

Decision making in organizations isn't particularly orderly or totally within the control of the decision-makers. In Chapter 14, we focus on the factors, both internal and external, that influence individual, team, and organizational decisions. We identify and explore the phases of decision making and some ethical concepts and dilemmas encountered.

To work effectively, all employees must clearly understand their jobs and the organization's design. In Chapter 15, we describe the process of designing jobs, work methods, and relationships among employees at various levels. The technology utilized has a tremendous impact on job design and employee behavior. As we present it in Chapter 16, organization design refers to the features and structure of the organization. An organization chart presents a simplified view of organizational authority, responsibility, and functions. However, organization design is far more complex than can be depicted on such a chart. We identify factors that influence organization design and present some typical organization designs.

Let's return briefly to the Preview Case and diagnose the interaction between design and process in Andrea Cunningham's organization. She had organized her firm by client account (Apple, NeXt, and so on) and had assigned a team of employees to each account. Each team had its own profit goals, on which bonuses were based. Her staff consisted of a vice-president and a secretary. Problems arose when teams didn't share information; they became minicompanies within the firm. Thus Cunningham's organization design fostered self-serving entrepreneurship, not interteam cooperation. Helping other teams solve their client's problems brought no rewards, just more work. Her leadership approach was to hire competent people and let them become entrepreneurs. She also thought that team members would get feedback from profit and loss statements, which would be sufficient motivation. She initially set goals herself without input from others. Her employees felt left out because the decision-making process didn't let them help determine their own goals. They wanted a voice in the decision-making process. Cunningham discovered that she needed to make changes both in design and process for her public relations firm to survive and prosper.

Individuals enter organizations to work, earn money, and pursue career goals. In Chapter 17, we describe how employees learn what is expected of them. Basically, they do so by exposure to the organization's culture. It is the set of shared assumptions and understandings about how things really work—that is, which policies, practices, and norms are important—in the organization. Newcomers have to understand the organization's culture in order to be accepted and become productive. Some organizations use formal introductory programs for new employees; others simply rely on co-workers, and still others use a combination of these methods to teach the newcomer what to do and what not to do on the job.

The management of change involves adapting an organization to the demands of the environment and modifying the actual behaviors of employees. If employees don't learn new behaviors, the organization can't change. Many things must be considered when undertaking organizational change, including the types of pressures being exerted for change, the types of resistance to change that are likely to be encountered, and who should implement change. In Chapter 18, we explore the dynamics of organizational change and discuss several basic strategies for achieving change.

CHAPTER SUMMARY

The themes developed in this chapter have broad implications for everyone who works. Workplace diversity is a reality and increasingly is a key organizational issue. As work-force characteristics change and globalization of the marketplace accelerates, more people from diverse backgrounds have to work together. Few organizations and employees may be exposed to all the possible forms of diversity. We presented a framework of six primary categories of diversity: age, race, ethnicity, gender, physical abilities and qualities, and sexual and affectional orientation. We also identified eight secondary categories, including education, work background, and religious beliefs. We highlighted how several types of diversity—changing work force and customers, gender, race and ethnicity, and age—will affect most employees, managers, teams, departments, and organizations. These types of diversity are important because they often reflect differences in perspectives, life-styles, attitudes, values, and behaviors. How employees embrace and respond to diversity will greatly influence organizational effectiveness.

Next, we previewed four additional issues facing all employees and organizations: individual, group, internal, and organizational processes. As with diversity, these issues are affected by the interplay of environmental influences and internal influences. Diversity and the other organizational issues of quality, technology, global perspective, and ethics are woven into many of the book's chapters. Their direct relationship to organization behavior is reflected in special features that appear in most chapters: Diversity in Practice, Quality in Practice, Technology in Practice, Across Cultures, Ethics in Practice, and Managing in Practice. The five issues that we previewed are requiring organizations and employees to change their traditional practices and behaviors.

To perform effectively, professionals and managers must engage in a lifetime of learning. This learning needs to focus on developing five core competencies and their corresponding skills: mobilizing innovation and change, managing people and tasks, communicating, achieving technical proficiency, and managing self. With the empowerment of teams, team leaders (which may rotate among team members), and individual employees, we noted that the traditional view of managing people and tasks as the exclusive province of those with formal titles of manager or supervisor is no longer valid in many organizations.

The final topic that we previewed in this chapter was organizational behavior from an open systems perspective. This perspective involves the dynamic interplay among environmental influence, individual processes, group and interpersonal processes, and organizational processes. The five organizational issues that we previewed often need to be understood and addressed by considering the interrelationships among these components.

KEY TERMS AND CONCEPTS

Achieving technical proficiency	Global perspective	Pareto chart
Benchmarking	Internet	Personal attributes
Communicating	Interpersonal communication	Personal time management
Competency	Intranet	Planning
Conceptualization	Leading	Quality
Conflict management	Learning	Racism
Creativity	Listening	Risk taking
Cybercorps	Managing people and tasks	Run chart
Decision making	Managing self	Skill
Diversity	Mobilizing innovation and change	Taguchi methods
Ethical dilemma	Open systems	Total quality management
Ethical standards	Oral communication	Visioning
Ethics	Organizational behavior	Written communication
Glass ceiling	Organizing	

DISCUSSION QUESTIONS

1. Identify three categories of diversity that represent significant issues in an organization or group of which you are currently a member. How is this organization and its members addressing these diversity issues?

2. Based on the organization or group identified in Question 1, what do you think needs to happen to create an environment that embraces boundaryless behavior?

3. The most successful organizations will be those that recognize the challenge and opportunity of maintaining a diverse work force. What obstacles stand in the way of maintaining or creating such a work force in an organization or work group of which you are or have been a member, but different than the organization or group identified in Question 1?

4. For the organization identified in Question 3, what quality challenges does it face? Why do they exist?

5. For the most challenging job you now have or have had in the past, list all the technical skills required for performing your tasks.

6. Identify three ethical dilemmas that you have faced. How did you resolve them?

7. One of the core competencies is managing self. What are you currently doing to develop this competency? What do you need to do?

8. One of the core competencies is managing people and tasks. Based on the skills that comprise this competency, evaluate your level of learning and development in relation to it.

9. Develop an outline for life-long learning to develop the core competency of communicating. What are you currently doing to develop this competency? What do you need to do?

■ Developing Competencies

Self-Insight: Attitudes Toward Diversity

Respond to the following statements. Use a scale of 5 to 1 to indicate how strongly you agree with the statements.

SA= Strongly Agree (5)

A= Agree (4)

N= Neutral (3)

D= Disagree (2)

SD= Strongly Disagree (1)

	SA	A	N	D	SD
1. I make a conscious effort to not think stereotypically.	5	4	3	2	1
2. I listen with interest to the ideas of people who don't think like I do.	5	4	3	2	1
3. I respect other people's opinions, even though I may disagree.	5	4	3	2	1
4. If I were at a social event with people who differed ethnically from me, I would make every effort to talk to them.	5	4	3	2	1
5. I have a number of friends who are not my age, race, or gender, or of the same economic status and education.	5	4	3	2	1
6. I recognize the influence that my upbringing has had on my values and beliefs and that my way isn't the only way.	5	4	3	2	1
7. I like to hear both sides of an issue before making a decision.	5	4	3	2	1
8. I don't care how the job gets done, as long as it is done ethically and I see results.	5	4	3	2	1
9. I don't get uptight when I don't understand everything going on around me.	5	4	3	2	1
10. I adapt well to change and new situations.	5	4	3	2	1
11. I enjoy traveling, seeing new places, eating different foods, and experiencing different cultures.	5	4	3	2	1
12. I enjoy people-watching and trying to understand the dynamics of human interactions.	5	4	3	2	1
13. I have learned from my mistakes.	5	4	3	2	1
14. When I am in unfamiliar surroundings, I watch and listen before acting.	5	4	3	2	1
15. When I get lost, I don't try to figure it out for myself but ask for directions.	5	4	3	2	1
16. When I don't understand what someone is telling me, I ask questions.	5	4	3	2	1
17. I really try not to offend or hurt others.	5	4	3	2	1
18. People are generally good, and I accept them as they are.	5	4	3	2	1
19. I watch for people's reactions whenever I'm speaking to them.	5	4	3	2	1
20. I try not to assume anything.	5	4	3	2	1

Scoring

Total your answers. If your score is 80 or above, you probably value diversity and can adapt easily to a multicultural work environment. Continue to look for areas of improvement. If you scored below 50, you probably need to work on understanding the need to value diversity.[55]

Organizational Insight: Executive Dining?

I made the decision to provide one business meeting for our branch managers at a restaurant in my nearby, small hometown instead of at the usual hotel facility in the city. The restaurant overlooked the lake and had a casual atmosphere. A restored farmhouse on the property was available for private parties. I thought that it would be perfect for our party of twelve. I had my secretary make the reservation a month in advance and advised her to make arrangements for the company minivan to provide our transportation for this dinner meeting.

After about ten hours of intensive meetings, we arrived at the restaurant for our 7:30 P.M. reservation. We entered the restaurant, and the manager, whom I knew well, was slumped on a stool behind the bar that was located predominantly in the lobby of the restaurant. I hadn't seen him for months and was taken aback by his sloppy appearance. I walked over to him, and he reached across the bar to shake my hand, while remaining seated. "We're here for our reservation for the Farmhouse." "You must be mistaken," Curtis replied, "your reservation is for tomorrow night." "No," I said, "It's tonight. My secretary said she took care of it. As I left the office today, she said to enjoy our dinner tonight at the Farmhouse." He then got up from the stool and I became even more aware of his sloppy appearance. He retrieved the reservation book and showed me that the reservation was, in fact, for tomorrow night.

I agreed that the reservation was listed for tomorrow night but said, "Curtis, there is obviously a mistake; here I am with my branch managers, *tonight*. What can you do to help me out?" "Smoking or nonsmoking?" he asked. "Well, the privacy is probably more important for us. Is the Farmhouse available?" "No, can't help you out there; I don't have any extra servers to run the food back and forth, but I can pull some tables together here in the restaurant for the twelve of you. It will be in the smoking section. At least it's against the wall, so nobody can be seated behind you." "All right," I said cautiously, "if that's the best you can do!" "There's nothing else I can do," I told my vice-president. "It's 7:30, we're hungry, and this is the only restaurant in town other than Arby's or McDonald's out on the highway."

Curtis had instructed the hostess to pull together three tables in the back room. I made polite conversation with him and asked him how the owner of the restaurant was enjoying his retirement. "He and the Mrs. are enjoying themselves in the Mediterranean, last postcard we received," was Curtis's reply. Shortly, the hostess returned and said that our table was ready. Curtis had already returned to his stool behind the bar.

The hostess and our waitress were busy placing menus and glasses of water in front of us. I asked to see the wine list and was surprised to see only two red wines on the list, this being primarily a steak and prime rib operation. I tried to recall how long it had been since I'd eaten here. Both wines listed were terrible. I knew they retailed in stores for about $4.00. Yet, they were priced at $20.00 a bottle. I told the waitress that I'd been at the Farmhouse some months earlier and that some finer wines had been available. She said she'd get the manager. It took about five long minutes for Curtis to stroll slowly toward our table. I met him part way and explained that I didn't want these managers from every part of the country to have to drink such bad wine. "I know there's a fine collection of wine in the Farmhouse. Couldn't you go and get a few bottles of a good Merlot to go with the steaks I'm sure my associates will be ordering?" He said: "I guess so. I could try and get you some." Then he turned and slowly moved away. I returned to the table and said, loudly enough that the waitress and hostess could hear, "The manager is retrieving wine from their adjacent Farmhouse facility for our pleasure." The hostess and waitress both hurried off after Curtis.

Soon the waitress returned and asked whether we would like a cocktail before she went to get our wine. We all ordered a round of drinks and were served by the bartender. We wouldn't have noticed his shorts and thongs if he'd stayed behind the bar. Serving our drinks to us, he asked, "Okay, who had the martini; what about this gimlet?" His shorts and thongs and hairy legs were very noticeable. He had to serve a second round of drinks before the waitress returned with six bottles of wine cradled in her arms. At this point, the hostess appeared with a "bus tub" full of wine glasses and began placing them in front of us. I asked if there were any red-wine glasses. "Got broken a couple of weeks ago," she replied. "That's why I have to give you white-wine glasses. Sorry." She smiled apologetically.

We ordered our dinner from the waitress and took her suggestion on how to order our steaks cooked. "If you want it medium rare you better order it medium. If you want it rare just plan on sending it back. They're messing up everything in the kitchen tonight."

A party of two were soon seated right next to our table and began smoking. The smoke drifted across out table and our managers, all nonsmokers, began to complain. I asked the waitress if the new arrivals couldn't be moved to a table at the other end of the room since there were plenty of tables available. She said she would ask the seating hostess. The hostess never came. We were all relieved when their dinners came and the smokers put out their cigarettes.

It took fifteen minutes for seven of our salads to arrive. The remaining five of us had ordered the specialty of the house— the Caesar salad. The waitress told us that it would be a little while before they were ready. "We're out of the Caesar dressing at the moment. Cockroaches usually make it up really fast, but they're having to sit out back for a while because they feel so sick." The five of us quickly changed our dressing to blue cheese.

Time passes quickly when you have twelve associates discussing business. However, I was surprised to note that, when our dinners finally began to arrive, we had been there for nearly two hours. It was after 9 P.M. Most of the food was cold, with not a hint that it had ever been warm. Needless to say, eleven dinners were returned to the kitchen. The only dish served hot was the red snapper supreme. The menu described it as stuffed with prosciutto ham and Gruyère cheese and poached in a chardonnay sauce. The youngest manager said that it was hot because "the slice of American cheese and baloney across the top of the fried filet of fish had just come from under the broiler." Within five minutes, the eleven dinners started reappearing at our table as fast as the microwave could turn them out. The only other fish dish was a sautéed sole almondine served over a bed of wild rice. I was surprised that the piece of fried fish was covered with peanuts, complete with their red skins. It was for me. The wild rice had been replaced by noodles; they were "out of the wild rice". The sautéed sole was a memory of days gone by.

We quickly began to discover that none of the baked potatoes were done inside. The waitress retrieved all of them for their turn in the microwave. It was 11 P.M. before I signed the credit card slip for over $500. I left a good tip for the waitress, as she did try hard. I never saw Curtis after he said he would try to get the wine.

As it turned out, we could have had this whole back room to ourselves, as not another customer arrived after the two smokers left. Twelve tables of four sat idle while we were crowded at our table backed against the wall. Many tables also had gone unused in other parts of the restaurant. I guess they weren't doing the business they used to do on a Friday night! I sincerely hoped that the owner had set aside *mucho dinero* for his retirement and wasn't going to rely on income from the current business—or rather the lack of it.[56]

Instructions

Your family and the recently retired owners of Farmhouse Restaurants, Inc., are very good friends. The husband phoned you and offered you the job as assistant manager. He told you, in confidence, that when he returned from his trip in thirty days he would introduce you as the new manager. Obviously, you will have to do as the manager instructs until you are named manager and the present manager is dismissed. You begin work tomorrow.

1. What will you try to accomplish the first week?

2. What will you try to accomplish by the time the owners return?

3. What changes and/or additions will you make when you become the manager?

REFERENCES

1. Adapted from Brokaw, L. Playing for keeps. *INC.*, May 1992, 30–41.

2. Stone, F. M., and Sacks, R. T. *The High Value Manager: Developing Core Competencies Your Organization Demands.* New York: AMACOM, 1995.

3. Handy, C. *Beyond Certainty.* Boston: Harvard Business School Press, 1996.

4. Wheeler, M. L. *Diversity: Business Rationale and Strategies.* New York: The Conference Board, 1996.

5. Cross, E. Y., Katz, J. H., Miller, F. A., and Seashore, E. W. (eds.). *The Promise of Diversity.* Burr Ridge, Ill.: Irwin, 1994.

6. Arredondo, P. *Successful Diversity Management Initiatives.* Thousand Oaks, Calif.: Sage, 1996.

7. Loden, M., and Rosener, J. *Workforce America.* Burr Ridge, Ill.: Irwin, 1991.

8. Adapted from Wheeler, M. L. Diversity: Making the business case. *Business Week,* December 1996 (unpaginated special section); Ashkenas, R., Ulrich, D., Jick, T., and Kerr, S. *The Boundaryless Organization.* San Francisco: Jossey-Bass, 1995.

9. Wheeler, M. L. Diversity: Making the business case.

10. Jackson, S. E., and Ruderman, M. N. *Diversity in Work Teams.* Washington, D.C.: American Psychological Association, 1996.

11. Diversity helps recruitment and customer satisfaction. *Business Week,* December 16, 1996 (unpaginated special section).

12. Ciabattari, J. He said, she said: Women executives and the gender gap. *Parade,* October 20, 1996, 20.

13. Worton, B. Women at work. *Fortune,* March 4, 1996 (unpaginated special section).

14. Swiss, D. J. *Women Breaking Through.* New York: Peterson's/Pacesetter, 1996; Marx Ferree, M., and Yancy Martin, P. (eds.). *Feminist Organizations: Harvest of the New Women's Movement.* Philadelphia: Temple University Press, 1995.

15. Morrison, A. M. *The New Leaders: Guidelines on Leadership Diversity in America.* San Francisco: Jossey-Bass, 1992; Ohlott, P. Ruderman, and McCauley, C. Gender differences in managers' developmental job experiences. *Academy of Management Journal,* 37, 1994, 46–67.

16. Worton, B. Women at work. *Fortune,* March 4, 1996 (unpaginated special section); Briles, J. *Gender Traps.* New York: McGraw-Hill, 1996.

17. Hammonds, K. H. Balancing work and family. *Business Week,* September 16, 1996, 74–80.

18. Kunde, D. Workers cite hesitancy to discuss racial issues. *Dallas Morning News,* November 11, 1992, 1A, 13A; Freedman, J. J. Myths about diversity: What managers should know about change in the U.S. labor force. *California Management Review,* Summer 1996, 54–77.

19. Shakespeare, T. L. Managing is more than skin deep. *Black Enterprise,* October 1995, 62.

20. Gallos, J. V., Ramsey, V. J., and Associates. *Teaching Diversity.* San Francisco: Jossey-Bass, 1996.

21. Sixel, L. M. Black managers travel down difficult road. *Houston Chronicle.* December 18, 1995, 1B, 3B.

22. Green, G. M., and Baker, F. *Work, Health, and Productivity.* New York: Oxford University Press, 1991.

23. Hall, D. T., and Associates. *The Career is Dead—Long Live the Career: A Relational Approach.* San Francisco: Jossey-Bass, 1996; London, M. Redeployment and continuous learning in the 21st century: Hard lessons and positive examples from the downsizing era. *Academy of Management Executive,* November 1996, 67–79.

24. Byron, W. J. Coming to terms with the new corporate contract. *Business Horizons,* January–February 1995, 8–15; Reichheld, F. F. *The Loyalty Effect.* Boston: Harvard Business School Press, 1996.

25. Kramer, S. D., and Rudolph, B. Disconnected. *Time,* January 15, 1996, 44–45.

26. Adapted from Preston, J. E. *Managing Diversity: What It Is and What It Isn't*. St. Louis: Center for the Study of American Business, Washington University, June 1996. Also see: Machan, D. The Makeover, *Forbes*, December 2, 1996, 135–136.

27. Evans, J. R., and Lindsay, W. M. *The Management and Control of Quality*, 2d ed. St. Paul: West, 1993, 9–14.

28. Lindsay, W. M., and Petrick, J. A. *Total Quality and Organization Development*. Delray Beach, Fla.: St. Lucie Press, 1996.

29. Voehl, F. (ed.). *Deming: The Way We Knew Him*. Delray Beach, Fla.: St. Lucie Press, 1995.

30. *Malcolm Baldrige National Quality Award: 1997 Criteria for Performance Excellence*. Gaithersburg, Md.: National Institute of Standards and Technology, United States Department of Commerce, 1996.

31. Amsden, R. T., Ferratt, T. W., and Amsden, D. M. TQM: Core paradigm changes. *Business Horizons*, November–December 1996, 6–14; Miles, R. E., and Snow, C. C. The new network firm: A spherical structure built on a human investment philosophy. *Organizational Dynamics*, Spring 1995, 5–18.

32. Adapted from Band, W. Targeting quality efforts. *Quality Observer*, December 1995, 32–34.

33. Tenner, E. *Why Things Bite Back: Technology and the Revenge of Unintended Consequences*. New York: Knopf, 1996.

34. Martin, J. *Cybercorp: The New Business Revolution*. New York: AMACOM Books, 1996.

35. Cronin, M. J. (ed.). *The Internet Strategy Handbook*. Boston: Harvard Business School Press.

36. Sprout, A. L. The Internet inside your company. *Fortune*, November 27, 1995, 161–168.

37. Cortese, A., and Gross, N. Here comes the intranet. *Business Week*, February 26, 1996, 76–83.

38. Adapted from Ziegler, B. In the net. *Wall Street Journal*, November 18, 1996, R21; Holland, K. Dwyer, P., and Edmondson, G. Technobanding takes off. *Business Week/21st Century Capitalism*, 1995, 52–53.

39. Caves, R. E. *Multinational Enterprise and Economic Analysis*. New York: Cambridge University Press, 1996; Lewis, M., Fitzgerald, C., and Harvey, C. *The Growth of Nations: Culture, Competitiveness, and the Problem of Globalization*. Bristol, England: Bristol Academic Press, 1996.

40. Adapted from Wheeler, M. J. Diversity: Making the business case. *Business Week*, December 9, 1996 (unpaginated special section).

41. Kanter, R. M. *World Class: Thriving Locally in the Global Economy*. New York: Simon & Schuster, 1995.

42. Messick, D. M., and Bazerman, M. H. Ethical leadership and the psychology of decision making. *Sloan Management Review*, Winter 1996, 9–22.

43. Donaldson, T. Values in tension: Ethics away from home. *Harvard Business Review*, September–October 1996, 48–62.

44. Brenner, S. N., and Mollander, E. A. Is the ethics of business changing? *Harvard Business Review*, January–February 1977, 57.

45. Caux Round Table: Principles of Business. *Business Ethics*, January–February 1996 (unpaginated special section).

46. Henderson, J. A. How to build profits with integrity. *Leaders*, October–December 1996, 30–33.

47. Jones, C., and DeFillippi, R. J. Back to the future in film: Combining industry and self knowledge to meet the career challenges of the 21st century. *Academy of Management Executive*, November 1996, 89–103.

48. Marino, K. E. Developing consensus on firm competencies and capabilities. *Academy of Management Executive*, August 1996, 40–51.

49. Evers, F. T., and Rush, J. C. The bases of competence: Skill development during the transition from university to work. *Management Learning*, 1996, 27, 275–300.

50. Roberts, B. C., Jr. Run like mad. *Leaders*, July–September 1996, 104–106.

51. Lei, D., and Slocum, J. W., Jr. Global strategy, competence-building and strategic alliances. *California Management Review*, 1992, 35(1), 81–97.

52. Swanson, R. *The Quality Improvement Handbook: Team Guide to Tools and Techniques*. Delray Beach, Fla.: St. Lucie Press, 1995.

53. Schein, E. H. Career anchors revisited: Implications for career development in the 21st century. *Academy of Management Executive*, November 1996, 80–88.

54. Adapted from Ford 2000: Recruiting and Selection Process. Dearborn, Mich.: Ford Motor Company, September 17, 1996.

55. Adapted from Hill-Storks, H. Diversity Self-Assessment Questionnaire, 1994. Used with permission.

56. Source: Copyright © 1995 by Cis Hawk. The Citizenship Foundation, Houston, Texas. Used with permission.

Individual Processes

PART 1

2

Personality and
Attitudes

LEARNING OBJECTIVES

When you have finished studying this chapter, you should be able to:

- Define personality and describe the basic sources of personality differences.
- Explain the "Big Five" personality factors and identify your own profile in terms of these factors.
- Provide some examples of specific personality traits that have important relationships to work behavior.
- Explain the concept of attitudes and describe their components.
- Describe the general relationship between attitudes and behavior.
- Define job satisfaction and organizational commitment.
- Identify important work outcomes of satisfaction and commitment.

OUTLINE

PREVIEW CASE

Individual Differences in Reactions

Air Designs, Inc., a small manufacturer of airplane cock-pit panel instruments, employs several hundred people at three locations in the southwestern United States. The management of Air Designs has always prided itself on using advanced management techniques and philosophies. Recently, the company has taken steps to create a "high-performance" work culture with emphasis on teamwork, reengineered work processes, and a commitment to the concept of a "boundaryless" organization. Air Design has adopted the credo of "teamwork across boundaries" meaning that no one in the company is free to say "that's not my job"—each individual's responsibilities extend to helping others accomplish their tasks whatever they may be. The expanded notions of teamwork and responsibility have had interesting effects on employee attitudes and behavior. Let's listen in as Anna and David, two team leaders at Air Designs, puzzle over some differences that they have observed in their team members. As we join them, Anna is speaking.

"It happened again today. Amy lost her temper and threatened to quit for probably the fourth time this week. Ever since we reengineered our work, she has been almost impossible to live with."

"I know what you mean," responded David. "Terry has been the same way. The slightest little thing sets him off. It puzzles me. He used to be my best team member, but now doesn't really get along well with anyone."

"Speaking of puzzles," said Anna, "Here's another one. Kate was quite marginal in her performance prior to our latest program, but now has become a real star. Why in the world do these changes seem to be driving behavior in different directions?" "I've had the same positive experience with Reilly and Hanna," responded David. "I don't think you've met them; both have joined my team since our last divisionwide meeting. In any event, my two new people have really responded well to the new culture and their added responsibilities. It seems to fit them."

"Well, one thing about it," said Anna. "The wide range of reactions to our new philosophy and procedures makes me wonder if I know anything at all about people. After all, we're all in the same boat. Why such differences in behavior?"

A s the Preview Case indicates, people often react very differently to organizational changes. Some 2000 years ago, the Greek philosopher Theophrastus asked, "Why is it that while all Greece lies under the same sky and all Greeks are educated alike, it has befallen us to have characters variously constituted?"[1] This question—Why are people different?—is as important for understanding human behavior today as it was in ancient Greece. Managers and employees alike must comprehend and appreciate individual differences in order to understand the behavior of people in complex social settings, which an organization certainly is.[2]

Behavior always involves a complex interaction of the person and the situation. Events in the surrounding environment (including the presence and behavior of others) strongly influence the way people behave at any particular time; yet people always bring something of themselves to the situation. This "something," which represents the unique qualities of the individual, is *personality*.

In Part I of this book we cover individual processes in organizations. We focus first on the individual in order to help you begin to develop an understanding of organizational behavior. The term **individual differences** refers to the fact that people vary in many ways. In this chapter, we discuss the individual differences of personality and attitudes.

CONCEPT OF PERSONALITY

No single definition of personality is accepted universally. However, one key idea is that personality represents personal characteristics that lead to consistent patterns of behavior. Many people quite naturally seek to understand these behavioral patterns in interactions with others. A well-known personality theorist, Salvatore Maddi, proposed the following definition of **personality:**

> Personality is a stable set of characteristics and tendencies that determine those commonalities and differences in the psychological behavior (thoughts, feelings, and actions) of people that have continuity in time and that may not be easily understood as the sole result of the social and biological pressures of the moment.[3]

This definition contains three important ideas. First, the definition doesn't limit the influence of personality only to certain behaviors, certain situations, or certain people. Rather, personality theory is a **general theory of behavior**—an attempt to understand or describe all behavior all the time. In fact, some people argue that attempting to define the concept of personality means trying to explain the very essence of being human.

Second, the phrase "commonalities and differences" suggests an important aspect of human behavior. In certain respects, every person is like

- all other people;
- some other people; and
- no other person.[4]

Theories of personality often describe what people have in common and what sets people apart. To understand the personality of an individual, then, is to understand both what that individual has in common with others and what makes that particular individual unique. Thus each employee in an organization is unique and may or may not respond as others do in a particular situation, as indicated in the Preview Case. This complexity makes managing and working with people extremely challenging.

Finally, Maddi's definition refers to personality as being "stable" and having "continuity in time." Most people intuitively recognize this stability. If your entire personality could change suddenly and dramatically, your family and friends would confront a stranger. Although significant changes normally don't occur suddenly, an individual's personality may change over time. Personality development occurs to a certain extent throughout life, but the greatest changes occur in early childhood.[5]

SOURCES OF PERSONALITY DIFFERENCES

How is an individual's personality determined? This question has no single answer because too many variables contribute to the development of each individual's personality. As Figure 2.1 shows, two primary sources shape personality differences: heredity and environment, or nature and nurture. Examining these categories helps us to understand why individuals are different.

■ HEREDITY

Deeply ingrained in many people's notions of personality is a belief in its genetic basis. Expressions such as "She is just like her father," and "He gets those irritat-

FIGURE 2.1

Sources of Personality Differences

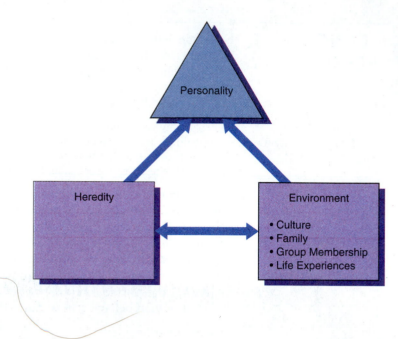

ing qualities from your side of the family, dear," reflect such beliefs. Historically, the **nature–nurture controversy** in personality theory was a sharp disagreement about the extent to which genetic factors influence personality. Those holding the extreme nature position argued that personality is inherited. Those adhering to the extreme nurture position argued that a person's experiences determine personality. Current thinking is more balanced—both heredity (biology) and environment (experiences) are important, although some personality characteristics may be influenced more by one factor than the other. That is, some personality traits seem to have a strong genetic component, whereas other traits seem to be largely learned (based on experiences).

Some personality experts argue that heredity sets limits on the range of development of characteristics and that only within this range do environmental forces determine personality characteristics. Recent research on the personalities of twins who have been raised apart indicates that genetic determinants may play a larger role than many experts had believed. Some studies of twins suggest that as much as 50 to 55 percent of personality traits may be inherited, which has some interesting implications. For example, it explains about 50 percent of the variance in occupational choice.[6] In other words, you probably inherited some traits that will influence your career choices.

ENVIRONMENT

Many behavioral experts still believe that the environment plays a larger role in shaping personality than do inherited characteristics. Environmental components include culture, family, group membership and life experiences.

Culture   **Culture** refers to the distinctive ways that different human populations or societies organize their lives. Anthropologists working in different cultures have clearly demonstrated the important role that culture plays in personality formation.[7] Individuals born into a particular culture are exposed to family and societal values and to their norms of acceptable behavior. Culture also defines how the different roles in that society are to be performed. For example, U.S. culture generally rewards people for being independent and competitive, whereas Japanese culture generally rewards individuals for being cooperative and group oriented.

Culture helps determine broad patterns of behavioral similarity among people, but differences in behavior—which at times can be extreme—usually exist among individuals within a culture. Most cultures aren't homogeneous. For example, the work ethic (hard work is valued; an unwillingness to work is sinful) usually is associated with Western cultures. But this value doesn't influence everyone within those cultures to the same degree. Thus, although culture has an impact on the development of employees' personalities, not all individuals respond to cultural influences equally. Indeed, one of the most serious errors that managers can make is to assume that their subordinates are just like themselves. As indicated in the following Diversity in Practice feature, individuals possess and exhibit many important differences even though they may be raised in the same culture and socialized into the same organization.

DIVERSITY IN PRACTICE

Generational Tension in the Office

As if managers didn't have enough diversity concerns with issues of gender and race, they must also sometimes contend with tensions between different generations of workers. The 78 million Americans born between 1946 and 1964 are popularly known as the Baby Boom generation. The Baby Busters generation comprises the 38 million born from 1965 to 1975. In some respects, we might regard these terms as convenient labels for workers employed, say, fifteen to twenty years, and those in their first few years with an organization. Table 2.1 captures, somewhat tongue-in-cheek, some of the dynamics that exist between these generations in the workplace.

TABLE 2.1   Tension between the "Baby Boom" and the "Baby Bust" Generations

WHAT "BABY BUSTERS" HATE ABOUT "BABY BOOMERS"	THE "BOOMERS" RESPOND
You're blocking our way.	Wait your turn.
Too much political behavior—not enough work.	Can you spell naive?
Too much emphasis on hierarchy and structure.	You have no respect for authority.
You're not current on information technology. You don't know a PC from your left elbow.	You're right. Stop rubbing it in.

Source: Adapted from Ratan, S. Generational tension in the office: Why busters hate boomers. *Fortune*, October 4, 1993, 57–70.

The generation that entered the work force in the 1960s rebelled strongly against authority and a culture it viewed as repressive. Today's twentysomethings (generation X, as some refer to them) face economic and career prospects that seem increasingly bleak. Their concerns center on work and the workplace.

—Continued

DIVERSITY IN PRACTICE—*Continued*

Members of generation X express their concerns about baby boomers in the workplace in terms such as the following. Boomers spend too much time politicking and not enough time working. Boomer managers claim to be seeking younger employees' input when in reality they couldn't care less what Xers think. Worst of all, boomers seem threatened by young, cheap-to-employ hotshots who come in brimming with energy and superior technological savvy. For their part, fortysomethings see Xers as cocky, unwilling to pay their dues, disloyal, and uncommitted to the organization. Paradoxically, the boomers, who came of age challenging all authority, seem upset when a younger generation doesn't defer to *their* authority.

Although the sentiments presented in Table 2.1 have an amusing side, tensions between these generations of employees are all too real. A difficult economic scene for many young job seekers and the clash of workplace values creates a significant managerial challenge. Because organizations always need younger employees' energy and ideas, this challenge in managing diversity involves balancing the attitudes and values of the different generations of workers while at the same time capturing the younger workers' loyalty and enthusiasm.[8]

Family   The primary vehicle for socializing an individual into a particular culture is the person's immediate family. Both parents and siblings play important roles in personality development for most individuals. Members of an extended family—grandparents, aunts, uncles, and cousins—also can influence personality formation. In particular, parents (or a single parent) influence their children's development in three important ways.

- Through their own behaviors, they present situations that bring out certain behaviors in children.
- They serve as role models with which children often strongly identify.
- They selectively reward and punish certain behaviors.[9]

The family's situation also is an important source of personality differences. Situational influences include the family's size, socioeconomic level, race, religion, and geographic location; birth order within the family; parents' educational level; and so on. For example, a person raised in a poor family simply has different experiences and opportunities than does a person raised in a wealthy family. Being an only child is different in some important respects from being raised with several brothers and sisters.

Group Membership   The first group to which most individuals belong is the family. People also participate in various groups during their lives, beginning with their childhood playmates and continuing through teenaged schoolmates, sports teams, and social groups to adult work and social groups. The numerous roles and experiences people have as members of groups represent another important source of personality differences. Although playmates and school groups early in life may have the strongest influences on personality formation, social and group experiences in later life continue to influence and shape personality. Understanding someone's personality requires understanding the groups (both past and present) to which that person belongs.

Life Experiences   Each person's life also is unique in terms of specific events and experiences, which serve as important determinants of personality. For example, the development of self-esteem (a personality dimension that we discuss shortly) depends on a series of experiences that include the opportunity to achieve goals and meet expectations, evidence of the ability to influence others, and a clear sense of being valued by others. Thus a complex series of events and interactions with other people helps shape the adult's level of self-esteem.

PERSONALITY STRUCTURE

The number and variety of specific personality traits or dimensions are bewildering. **Personality trait** typically refers to the basic components of personality. Investigators have identified, named, and examined literally *thousands* of traits over the years. Trait names simply represent the terms that people use to describe each other. However, a list containing hundreds or thousands of terms isn't very useful either in understanding the structure of personality in a scientific sense or in describing individual differences in a practical sense. To be useful these terms need to be organized into a small set of concepts or descriptions. Recent research has done just that, identifying several general factors that describe personality.

Five main factors summarize the structure of an individual's personality.[10] These **"Big Five" personality factors,** as they often are referred to, describe the individual's adjustment, sociability, conscientiousness, agreeableness, and intellectual openness. As shown in Figure 2.2, each factor includes a potentially large number and range of specific traits or dimensions. That is, each factor is both a collection of related traits and a continuum. For example, an individual at one extreme in terms of degree of "agreeableness" might be described as warm and considerate. But with a personality at this factor's other extreme, the person would be considered cold or rude. The Developing Competencies section at the end of this chapter contains a questionnaire that you can use to assess yourself in terms of these five personality factors.

PERSONALITY AND BEHAVIOR

The main reason that we are interested in individual personality in the study of organizational behavior is because of the linkage between personality and behavior. For example, researchers have extensively investigated the relationships between the Big Five personality factors and job performance.[11] Their findings indicate that employees who are responsible, dependable, persistent, and achievement oriented (the *conscientiousness* factor in Figure 2.2), perform better than those who lack these traits.

Although each personality factor represents a collection of related traits, the link between personality and specific behaviors often is most clear when we focus on a single trait rather than one of the five factors. Let's look at several *specific* personality traits that are particularly important for understanding aspects of organizational behavior.[12] Then, throughout the book, we explain additional personality traits as they relate to topics under discussion—for example, in relation to perception (Chapter 3), work stress (Chapter 7), political behavior (Chapter 9), and leadership (Chapter 10).

█ FIGURE 2.2

The "Big Five" Personality Factors

Source: Developed from Hogan, R. T. Personality and personality measurement. In M. D. Dunnette and L. M. Hough (eds.), *Handbook of Industrial and Organizational Psychology*, 2d ed., vol. 2. Palo Alto, Calif.: Consulting Psychologists Press, 1991, 878–879.

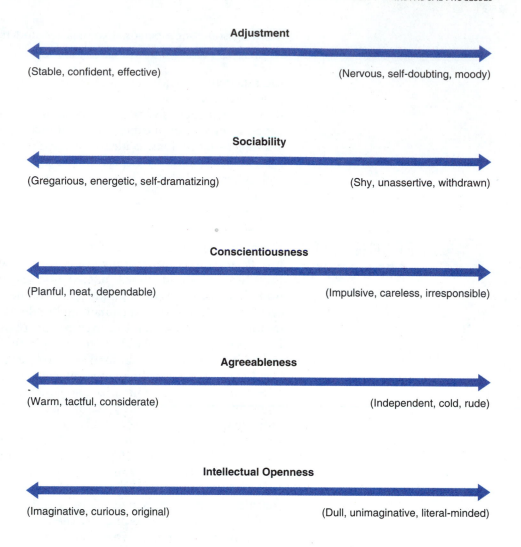

Adjustment

(Stable, confident, effective)   (Nervous, self-doubting, moody)

Sociability

(Gregarious, energetic, self-dramatizing)   (Shy, unassertive, withdrawn)

Conscientiousness

(Planful, neat, dependable)   (Impulsive, careless, irresponsible)

Agreeableness

(Warm, tactful, considerate)   (Independent, cold, rude)

Intellectual Openness

(Imaginative, curious, original)   (Dull, unimaginative, literal-minded)

█ SELF-ESTEEM

Self-esteem is the result of an evaluation that an individual makes of himself or herself. People have opinions of their own behaviors, abilities, appearance, and worth. These general assessments of worthiness are affected by situations, successes or failures, and the opinions of others. Nevertheless, they are stable enough to be widely regarded as a basic personality trait or dimension. In terms of the Big Five personality factors, self-esteem most likely would be part of the *adjustment* factor (see Figure 2.2).

Self-esteem affects behavior in organizations and other social settings in several important ways. Self-esteem is related to initial vocational choice. For example, individuals with high self-esteem take risks in job selection, are attracted to high-status occupations, and are more likely to choose unconventional or nontraditional jobs than are individuals with low self-esteem. A study of college students looking for a job reported that those with high self-esteem (1) received more favorable evaluations from recruiters, (2) were more satisfied with the job search, (3) received more job offers, and (4) were more likely to accept jobs before graduation than were students with low self-esteem.[13]

Self-esteem is also related to numerous social and work behaviors. For example, employees with low self-esteem are more easily influenced than employees with high self-esteem by the opinions of other workers. Employees with low self-esteem set lower goals for themselves than do employees with high self-esteem. Further, employees with high self-esteem place more value on actually attaining those goals than do employees with low self-esteem. Employees with low self-esteem are more susceptible than employees with high self-esteem to adverse job conditions such as stress, conflict, ambiguity, poor supervision, poor working conditions, and the like. In a general sense, self-esteem is positively related to achievement and a willingness to expend effort to accomplish tasks. Clearly, self-esteem is an important individual difference in terms of effective work behavior.[14]

■ LOCUS OF CONTROL

Locus of control refers to the extent to which individuals believe that they can control events affecting them. On the one hand, individuals who have a high **internal locus of control** (internals) believe that their own behavior and actions primarily (but not necessarily totally) affect the events in their lives. On the other hand, individuals who have a high **external locus of control** (externals) believe that chance, fate, or other people primarily determine the events in their lives. Locus of control typically is considered to be a part of the *conscientiousness* factor (see Figure 2.2).

Many differences between internals and externals are significant in explaining some aspects of behavior in organizations and other social settings.[15] Evidence indicates that internals control their own behavior better, are more active politically and socially, and seek information about their situations more actively than do externals. Compared to externals, internals are more likely to try to influence or persuade others and are less likely to be influenced by others. Internals often are more achievement oriented than externals. Compared to internals, externals appear to prefer a more structured, directive style of supervision. A recent study showed that managers with a high internal locus of control adjusted more readily to international transfers than did managers with a high external locus of control.[16]

Recall that we are particularly interested in the relationship between these personality dimensions and specific behaviors. Figure 2.3 shows some of the important relationships between locus of control and job performance.

■ INTROVERSION AND EXTRAVERSION

In everyday usage, the words *introvert* and *extravert* describe a person's congeniality: An introvert is shy and retiring, whereas an extravert is socially gregarious and outgoing. The terms have similar meanings when used to refer to a personality dimension. **Introversion** is a tendency to be directed inward and have a greater sensitivity to abstract ideas and personal feelings. Introverts are quiet, introspective, and emotionally unexpressive. **Extraversion** is an orientation toward other people, events, and objects. Extraverts are sociable, lively, impulsive, and emotionally expressive. Introversion and extraversion are part of the collection of traits that comprise the *sociability* factor (see Figure 2.2).

Although some people exhibit the extremes of introversion and extraversion, most are only moderately introverted or extraverted or relatively balanced between the extremes. Introverts and extraverts appear in all educational, gender,

■ FIGURE 2.3

The Effects of Locus of Control on Performance

Source: Miner, J. B. *Industrial-Organizational Psychology.* New York: McGraw-Hill, 1992, 151. Reprinted with permission of McGraw-Hill.

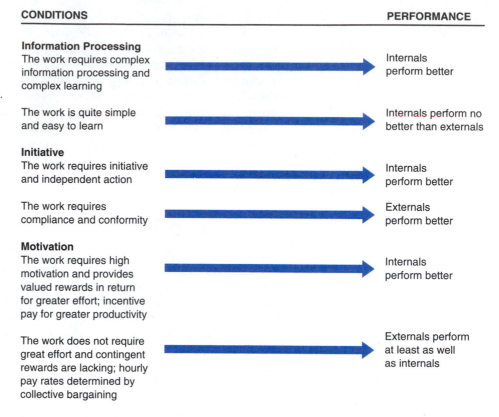

CONDITIONS	PERFORMANCE
Information Processing	
The work requires complex information processing and complex learning	Internals perform better
The work is quite simple and easy to learn	Internals perform no better than externals
Initiative	
The work requires initiative and independent action	Internals perform better
The work requires compliance and conformity	Externals perform better
Motivation	
The work requires high motivation and provides valued rewards in return for greater effort; incentive pay for greater productivity	Internals perform better
The work does not require great effort and contingent rewards are lacking; hourly pay rates determined by collective bargaining	Externals perform at least as well as internals

and occupational groupings. As might be expected, extraverts are well represented in managerial occupations because the manager's decisional role often involves identifying and solving problems with and through other people. Research even suggests that some extraversion may be essential to managerial success. However, either extreme extraversion or extreme introversion can interfere with an individual's effectiveness in an organization.

One of the most striking implications of the introversion–extraversion personality dimension involves task performance in different environments. The evidence suggests that introverts perform better alone and in a quiet environment, whereas extraverts perform better in an environment with greater sensory stimulation, such as a noisy office with many people and a high level of activity.

Recall our discussion of the sources of personality differences among people (nature versus nurture). Interestingly, many experts consider introversion and extraversion to be a personality dimension with a relatively high genetically determined component.[17]

■ DOGMATISM AND AUTHORITARIANISM

Dogmatism refers to the rigidity of a person's beliefs. The highly dogmatic individual perceives the world as a threatening place, often regards legitimate authority as absolute, and accepts or rejects other people on the basis of their agreement or disagreement with accepted authority or doctrine. In short, the high-dogmatic (HD) individual is close-minded, and the low-dogmatic (LD) person is open-minded. As a result, HDs appear to depend more on authority figures in the organization for guidance and direction and are more easily influenced by them than are LDs. Some relationship between the degree of dogmatism and interpersonal and group behavior also seems to exist. For example, HDs typically need more group structure than do LDs to work effectively with others. Hence the performance of HDs on task force and committee assignments may vary somewhat, depending on how the group goes about its work. A high degree of dogmatism is related to a limited search for information in decision-making situations, which sometimes leads to poor managerial performance.

Authoritarianism is closely related to dogmatism but is narrower in scope. The events of World War II spurred the original research on authoritarianism. That research was designed to identify personalities susceptible to fascist or otherwise antidemocratic appeals. Over time, however, the concept broadened. The **authoritarian personality** now describes someone who adheres to conventional values, obeys recognized authority, exhibits a negative view of society, respects power and toughness, and opposes the expression of personal feelings. In organizations, the authoritarian personality probably is subservient to authority figures and may even prefer superiors who have a highly directive, structured leadership style. Both dogmatism and authoritarianism are related to the *intellectual openness* factor (see Figure 2.2).

■ ORGANIZATIONAL IMPLICATIONS

The personality dimensions discussed, and the specific relationships for each, have important implications for organizational behavior. However, managers or work groups should not try to change or otherwise directly control employee personality, which usually is impossible in any event. Even if such control were possible, it would be highly unethical. Rather, the challenge for managers and employees is to understand the crucial role played by personality in explaining some aspects of human behavior in the workplace. Knowledge of important individual differences provides managers, employees, and students of organizational behavior with valuable insights and a framework that they can use to diagnose events and situations. The following Managing in Practice selection describes such a situation—an attempt at Hewlett-Packard to create effective work teams.

MANAGING IN PRACTICE

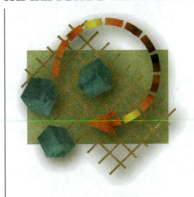

Personality and Teams at Hewlett-Packard

Reed Breland became a team facilitator at Hewlett-Packard's 180-person financial services center in Colorado Springs two years ago. After several months in his new position, Breland noticed that members of one of his teams were having a difficult time working together. "It was a classic case of personality conflict," he says. "They just didn't like each other. But when two people on an eight-person team don't get along, believe me, it's disruptive."

Breland gave the team time to try to work things out. "Of course, I spoke to them about the problems, but I was mainly interested in making sure they understood that the work had to get done, regardless of how they got along," he says. However, after nine months the team was still not working well together. Productivity was inadequate and morale poor. "I knew I had to do something then, because it was beginning to affect their work," explains Breland. He then simply dissolved the team and had its members placed elsewhere rather than trying to

—Continued

MANAGING IN PRACTICE—*Continued*

determine who was right and wrong. Breland says the team members are doing fine in their other assignments. He compares their team dynamics with those of a sports team: "If the chemistry isn't right, it doesn't matter how good or bad the players are. It's not going to work. As a team leader you have to know when it's reached that point. It's more of an art than a science, but that's what makes the job so interesting."[18]

■ THE PERSON AND THE SITUATION

Although understanding differences in personality is important, behavior always involves an interaction of the person and the situation. Sometimes the demands of the situation may be so overwhelming that individual differences are relatively unimportant. For example, if a room is burning, everyone in it will try to flee. However, the fact that everyone behaved the same way says nothing about the personalities of those individuals. In other cases, individual differences may explain more about behavior. At Air Designs (the Preview Case), Terry and Kate faced the same situation, but reacted very differently because of their individual differences.

The relative importance of situational versus personal determinants of behavior continues to be debated, but considerable evidence exists for roles by both. Taking an **interactionist perspective,** that is, considering both the person and the situation, helps in understanding behavior in organizations.[19] For that reason, throughout this book our perspective is consistently interactionist. You will discover that many of the topics covered, such as leadership, political behavior, power differences, stress, and resistance to change, examine both personal and situational causes for the organizational behavior discussed. Both *interact* to determine behavior.

CONCEPT OF ATTITUDES

Attitudes are another type of *individual difference* that affects behavior. **Attitudes** are relatively lasting feelings, beliefs, and behavior tendencies directed toward specific people, groups, ideas, issues, or objects.[20] Attitudes reflect an individual's background and various experiences. As with personality development, significant people in a person's life—parents, friends, and members of social and work groups—strongly influence attitude formation. Also, some evidence points to genetic influences on the attitudes that people develop.[21]

People often think of attitudes as a simple concept, but in reality attitudes and their effects on behavior can be extremely complex. An attitude consists of

- an affective component, or the feelings, sentiments, moods, and emotions about some person, idea, event, or object;

- a cognitive component, or the beliefs, opinions, knowledge, or information held by the individual; and

- a behavioral component, or the predisposition to act on a favorable or unfavorable evaluation of something.[22]

These components don't exist or function separately. An attitude represents the *interplay* of a person's feelings, cognition, and behavioral tendencies with regard to something—another person or group, an event, an idea, and so on. For example, suppose that an individual holds a strong, negative attitude about the use of nuclear power. During a job interview with the representative of a large corporation, he discovers that the company is a major supplier of nuclear power generation equipment. He might feel a sudden intense dislike for the company's interviewer (the affective component). He might form a negative opinion of the interviewer based on beliefs and opinions about the type of people who would work for such a company (the cognitive component). He might be tempted to make an unkind remark to the interviewer or suddenly terminate the interview (the behavioral component). However, the person's actual behavior probably would depend on several factors, including the strength of his attitude toward nuclear power.

ATTITUDES AND BEHAVIOR

To what extent do attitudes predict or cause behavior? For a long time, behavioral scientists believed that individuals' behaviors were consistent with their attitudes. However, they now widely accept the premise that a simple, direct link between attitudes and behavior frequently doesn't exist. In the preceding interviewing example, the person being interviewed might have the negative feelings, opinions, and intentions described and yet choose not to behave negatively toward the interviewer because (1) the individual desperately needs a job; (2) the norms of courteous behavior outweigh the person's desire to express a negative attitude; (3) the individual decides that the interviewer is an inappropriate target for the negative behavior; or (4) the individual acknowledges the possibility of having incomplete information.

Pollsters and others often measure attitudes in attempting to predict subsequent behavior. Anyone doing so should recognize that finding a relationship between attitudes and behavior often is difficult. However, observing three principles can improve predictions of behavior from attitudes.

- General attitudes best predict general behaviors.
- Specific attitudes best predict specific behaviors.
- The less time that elapses between attitude measurement and behavior, the more consistent will be the relationship between attitude and behavior.[23]

For example, attitudes toward women in management in general aren't as good a predictor of whether someone will work well for a female manager as are specific attitudes toward the particular manager. General attitudes toward religion aren't good predictors of specific behavior, such as giving to a certain church-related charity or observing a specific religious holiday. However, these general attitudes may accurately predict general religious behavior, such as the overall level of involvement in church activities. Moreover, attitudes may change over time. Generally, the longer the elapsed time between the measurement of an attitude and a behavior, the less likely it is that the relationship between them will be strong. This third principle is well known to political pollsters (after some earlier embarrassments), and they typically are careful not to predict voting behavior too far ahead of an actual election. (Or they may be careful to add certain qualifiers to published polls, such as: If the election were held today. . . .)

In their model of the attitude–behavior relationship, the **behavioral intentions model,** Ajzen and Fishbein suggested that focusing on a person's specific *intention* to behave in a certain way makes behavior more predictable (and understandable).[24] Figure 2.4 illustrates the model and shows that intentions depend on both attitudes and norms regarding the behavior. **Norms** are rules of behavior, or proper ways of acting, that members of a group or a society have accepted as appropriate. Norms thus impose social pressures to behave or not to behave in certain ways. (We explore more fully the concept of norms in Chapter 8.) If both attitudes and norms are positive with regard to a behavior, an individual's intention to behave in a certain way will be strong. If attitudes and norms conflict, their relative strengths may determine the individual's intention and subsequent behavior.

According to the behavioral intentions model, the individual's beliefs regarding specific behaviors affect both attitudes and norms. In the case of attitudes, beliefs concern the relationship between the behavior and its consequences (outcomes). Beliefs regarding norms reflect an individual's perceptions of how others expect that person to act. The behavioral intentions model helps explain why the relationship between attitudes and behavior sometimes is strong and at other times is weak.

The behavioral intentions model also indicates another possible explanation of behavior: Real or perceived situational or internal obstacles or constraints may prevent a person from behaving in an intended manner.[25] For example, someone might fully intend to perform a task quickly and efficiently but lack the skill to do so. Moreover, the mere perception or belief that he or she lacks the necessary skills might prevent someone from performing the task (having the same effect as the actual lack of skill).

Over the years, behavioral scientists have proposed various models to explain attitude–behavior relationships. However, the simple model shown in Figure 2.4 predicts behavior about as well as more complex explanations do.[26] This model seems particularly useful for predicting certain specific behaviors, such as

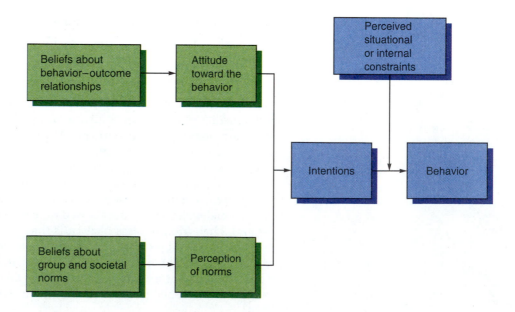

■ **FIGURE 2.4**

Behavioral Intentions Model

Source: Adapted from Ajzen, I., and Fishbein, M. *Understanding Attitudes and Predicting Social Behavior.* Englewood Cliffs, N.J.: Prentice-Hall, 1980, 8.

turnover, in organizations.[27] That is, if a person intends to quit, he or she usually does so. In sum, attitude–behavior relationships are important for understanding some aspects of organizational behavior.

JOB SATISFACTION

In organizational behavior, perhaps the attitude of greatest interest is the general attitude toward work or toward a job, often called **job satisfaction**.[28] Of particular interest to managers are the sources of job satisfaction because they often suggest actions that can be taken to improve employee job satisfaction. Of further interest to managers are the sometimes complex relationship between job satisfaction and job performance. In fact, managers of organizations throughout the world are concerned with workers' attitudes toward work and the satisfactions they get from it. The following Across Cultures piece presents some interesting comparisons of attitudes toward work of Japanese and U.S. workers.

ACROSS CULTURES

A Comparison of Japanese and U.S. Work Attitudes

Investigators gathered data from 8300 employees of 106 factories in the United States and Japan in an effort to identify possible productivity differences in the two countries. Among other things, the investigators suspected that Japanese and U.S. factory workers might have some different attitudes toward work.

Commitment to the company (one of the attitudes measured) seemed to be essentially the same for employees in the two countries. However, responses to questionnaires did reveal important differences in average job satisfaction scores between the two groups of factory workers. Contrary to some people's expectations, U.S. employees reported higher satisfaction than did their Japanese counterparts. Table 2.2 shows the average satisfaction scores obtained, along with some of the questions asked in order to measure job satisfaction.

TABLE 2.2   A Comparison of Job-Satisfaction between U.S. and Japanese Employees

JOB SATISFACTION QUESTION	JAPANESE MEAN	U.S. MEAN
All in all, how satisfied would you say you are with your job? (0 = not at all, 4 = very)	2.12*	2.95
If a good friend of yours told you that he or she was interested in working at a job like yours at this company, what would you say? (0 = would advise against it, 1 = would have second thoughts, 2 = would recommend it)	0.91	1.52

Continued

—*Continued*

ACROSS CULTURES—*Continued*

TABLE 2.2 A Comparison of Job-Satisfaction between U.S. and Japanese Employees—*Continued*

JOB SATISFACTION QUESTION	JAPANESE MEAN	U.S. MEAN
Knowing what you know now, if you had to decide all over again whether to take the job you now have, what would you decide? (0 = would not take job again, 1 = would have some second thoughts, 2 = would take job again)	0.84	1.61
How much does your job measure up to the kind of job you wanted when you first took it? (0 = not what I wanted, 1 = somewhat, 2 = what I wanted)	0.43	1.20

*The differences in average response to each question are statistically significant, which means that the differences between U.S. and Japanese responses are large enough that they do not appear to be chance results.

Source: Adapted from Lincoln, J. R. Employee work attitudes and management practice in the U.S. and Japan: Evidence from a large comparative survey. *California Management Review*, Fall 1989, 91.

Study results also indicated that certain organizational practices had the same positive effects on employee job satisfaction and commitment in both Japanese and U.S. factories. For example, participation in quality circles, company-sponsored recreation opportunities, and training opportunities outside the firm had similar positive effects on work attitudes in both countries.[29]

■ SOURCES OF JOB SATISFACTION

People sometimes regard job satisfaction as a single concept; that is, a person is satisfied or not satisfied with the job. However, it actually is a collection of related job attitudes that can be related to various job aspects. For example, a popular measure of job satisfaction—the job descriptive index (JDI)—measures satisfaction in terms of five specific aspects of a person's job: pay, promotion, supervision, the work itself, and co-workers.[30] Obviously, an employee may be satisfied with some aspects of the job and, at the same time, dissatisfied with others.[31]

The sources of job satisfaction and dissatisfaction vary from person to person. Sources thought to be important for many employees include the challenge of the job, the degree of interest that the work holds for the person, the extent of required physical activity, the characteristics of working conditions, the types of rewards available from the organization (such as the level of pay), the nature of co-workers, and the like. Table 2.3 lists work factors that often are related to levels of employee job satisfaction. An important implication of the relationships suggested is that job satisfaction perhaps should be considered primarily as an outcome of the individual's work experience. Thus high levels of dissatisfaction might indicate to managers that problems exist, say, with the plant's working conditions, the organization's reward system, or the employee's role in the organization.

TABLE 2.3 Effects of Various Work Factors on Job Satisfaction

WORK FACTORS	EFFECTS
Work itself Challenge	Mentally challenging work that the individual can successfully accomplish is satisfying.
Physical demands	Tiring work is dissatisfying.
Personal interest	Personally interesting work is satisfying.
Reward structure	Rewards that are equitable and that provide accurate feedback for performance are satisfying.
Working conditions Physical	Satisfaction depends on the match between working conditions and physical needs.
Goal attainment	Working conditions that promote goal attainment are satisfying.
Self	High self-esteem is conducive to job satisfaction.
Others in the organization	Individuals will be satisfied with supervisors, co-workers, or subordinates who help them attain rewards. Also, individuals will be more satisfied with colleagues who see things the same way they do.
Organization and management	Individuals will be satisfied with organizations that have policies and procedures designed to help them attain rewards. Individuals will be dissatisfied with conflicting roles and/or ambiguous roles imposed by the organization.
Fringe benefits	Benefits do not have a strong influence on job satisfaction for most workers.

Source: Adapted from Landy, F. J. *Psychology of Work Behavior,* 4th ed. Pacific Grove, Calif.: Brooks/Cole, 1989, 470.

■ RELATION TO JOB BEHAVIOR

Of particular interest to managers are the possible relationships between job satisfaction and various job behaviors and other outcomes in the workplace. Common sense suggests that job satisfaction leads directly to effective task performance. (A happy worker is a good worker.) Yet, numerous studies have shown that a simple, direct linkage between job attitudes and job performance often doesn't exist.[32] The difficulty of relating attitudes to behavior is pertinent here. Earlier, we noted that general attitudes best predict general behaviors and that specific attitudes relate most strongly to specific behaviors. These principles explain, at least in part, why the expected relationships often don't exist. Overall job satisfaction, as a collection of numerous attitudes toward various aspects of the job, represents a general attitude. Performance of a specific task, such as preparing a particular monthly report, can't necessarily be predicted on the basis of a general attitude. However, a recent study showed that job satisfaction and the organization's overall performance are linked. That is, organizations with satisfied employees tend to be more effective than organizations with unsatisfied employees.[33]

Although job satisfaction doesn't necessarily lead an individual to perform a specific task well, it is important for several reasons. Satisfaction represents an outcome of work experience, so high levels of dissatisfaction help managers identify organizational problems that need attention. In addition, job dissatisfaction is strongly linked to absenteeism, turnover, and physical and mental health problems.[34] For example, highly dissatisfied employees are likely to be absent from work and are likely to leave a job for other employment. High levels of absenteeism and turnover are costly for organizations. Thus the strong relationship between dissatisfaction and absence and turnover is a compelling reason for concern about employee job satisfaction.

ORGANIZATIONAL COMMITMENT

Another important work attitude that has a bearing on organizational behavior is commitment to the organization. **Organizational commitment** refers to the strength of an employee's involvement in and identification with the organization. Strong organizational commitment, for example, is characterized by

- belief in and acceptance of the organization's goals and values;
- willingness to exert considerable effort on behalf of the organization; and
- desire to maintain membership in the organization.[35]

Organizational commitment goes beyond loyalty to an active contribution in accomplishing organizational goals. Organizational commitment is a broader work attitude than job satisfaction because it applies to the entire organization rather than just to the job. Further, commitment typically is somewhat more stable than satisfaction because day-to-day events are less likely to change it.

■ SOURCES OF COMMITMENT

As with job satisfaction, the sources of organizational commitment may vary from person to person. Employees' initial commitment to an organization is determined largely by their individual characteristics (such as personality and values) and how well their initial job experiences matched their expectations. Later, organizational commitment continues to be influenced by job experiences, with many of the same factors that lead to job satisfaction also contributing to organizational commitment or lack of commitment: pay, relationships with supervisors and co-workers, working conditions, opportunities for advancement, and so on. Over time, organizational commitment tends to become stronger because (1) individuals develop stronger ties to the organization and their co-workers as they spend more time with them; (2) seniority often brings advantages that tend to develop more positive work attitudes; and (3) opportunities in the job market may decrease with age, causing workers to become more strongly attached to their current job.[36]

■ RELATION TO JOB BEHAVIOR

As with job satisfaction, managers are vitally interested in the relationships between organizational commitment and job behavior.[37] To organizations the relationship between organizational commitment and turnover is one of the most important.[38] Simply stated, the stronger an employee's commitment is to the organization, the less likely the person is to quit. Strong commitment also is often correlated with low absenteeism and relatively high productivity. Attendance at work (being on time and taking little time off) is usually higher for employees with strong organizational commitment. Further, committed individuals tend to be more goal directed and waste less time while at work, with a positive impact on typical productivity measures. Effective management can foster increased commitment and loyalty to the organization as the following Quality in Practice feature demonstrates. Merck managers are encouraged to increase commitment by rewarding performance and productivity rather than simply time spent working, and by building relationships based on trust and respect.

QUALITY IN PRACTICE

Building Commitment at Merck

Rose Arnone, a research manager for Merck, works killer hours and travels one-third of the time, including weekends. She used to get mad at a previous boss when she had to report to her desk at 8 A.M. Monday. The supervisor (who has since left Merck) expected employees to work long hours, no matter how little sleep they got as a result. Arnone kept up her performance, but her attitude took a nosedive. She felt, "OK, I'll do the best I can, but you're not getting any more from me." She kept her office door closed much of the time as a symbolic gesture.

In contrast, her next boss made goals very clear and then said, "I trust you to get your job done." The result: "I was completely loyal to her and much more enthusiastic about my work." (She has started keeping her office door open again.)

Senior financial analyst Diane Schweizer didn't expect to get time off when her young child needed tonsil surgery during Merck's year-end rush. To her surprise, Bob Underwood, her boss and controller for Merck's European operations, "just looked at me and said, 'your daughter comes first,'" Schweizer says.

Underwood's attitude and support created intense loyalty from Diane Schweizer. Later, when she was leaving on a long-planned vacation at the shore, Underwood's assistant called to ask for emergency help to prepare data for the head of Merck's European operations. Without hesitating, "I popped into the car and I was there," she says. "You don't think twice when such a boss needs help."[39]

INDIVIDUAL DIFFERENCES AND ETHICAL BEHAVIOR

Ethical behavior in businesses and other organizations has received great attention in recent years. Part of this attention focuses on the influence that individual differences might have on ethical behavior. For example, a study suggested that locus of control and cognitive moral development are important in helping explain whether people will behave ethically or unethically.[40] **Cognitive moral development** refers to an individual's level of moral judgment. People seem to pass through stages of moral reasoning and judgment as they mature. Judgment with regard to right and wrong becomes less dependent on outside influences (such as parents) and less self-centered (It's right because it's right for me.). At higher levels of cognitive moral development, individuals develop a deeper understanding of the principles of justice, ethical behavior, and balancing individual and social rights.

Research has demonstrated that individuals with high internal locus of control exhibit more ethical behavior when making organizational decisions than do individuals with high external locus of control. Further, individuals with higher levels of cognitive moral development are more likely to behave ethically than are others.

■ TYPES OF MANAGEMENT ETHICS

Archie Carroll, a management professor, has suggested that the terms *immoral, amoral,* and *moral* management identify important ethical differences among managers.[41]

Immoral Management   Managerial behaviors devoid of any ethical principles represent **immoral management.** Those practicing immoral management believe in the maximum exploitation of opportunities for corporate or personal gain to the exclusion of other considerations. Any corner will be cut if doing so appears useful. Even legal standards are barriers to be overcome rather than guidelines for appropriate behavior.

The Frigitemp Corporation provides an example of immoral management at the highest levels of the firm. According to testimony provided during federal investigations and criminal trials, corporate officials (including the chairman of the board of directors and the president) admitted making illegal payoffs of millions of dollars. In addition, corporate officers embezzled funds, exaggerated earnings in reports to shareholders, took kickbacks from suppliers, and even provided prostitutes for customers. Frigitemp eventually went bankrupt because of management's misconduct.

Moral Management   The opposite extreme from immoral management is **moral management.** That is, managerial and employee behaviors focus on and follow ethical norms, professional standards of conduct, and compliance with applicable regulations and laws. Moral management doesn't mean lack of interest in profits. However, the moral manager will not pursue profits outside the boundaries of the law and sound ethical principles.

McCulloch Corporation, a manufacturer of chain saws, provides a good example of moral management. Chain saws can be dangerous to use, and studies have consistently shown large numbers of injuries from saws not equipped with chain brakes and other safety features. The Chain Saw Manufacturers Association fought hard against mandatory federal safety standards, preferring to rely on voluntary standards even in the face of evidence that voluntary standards were neither high enough nor working. However, McCulloch consistently supported and practiced higher safety standards; in fact, chain brakes have been standard on McCulloch saws since 1975. McCulloch made numerous attempts to persuade the Chain Saw Manufacturers Association to adopt higher standards when research results indicated that they could greatly reduce injuries. When McCulloch failed to persuade the association to support these higher standards, it withdrew from the association.

Amoral Management   Managerial behaviors that are indifferent to ethical considerations—as though different standards of conduct apply to business than to other aspects of life—characterize **amoral management.** Amoral managers and employees seem to lack awareness of ethical or moral issues and act with no thought for the impact that their actions might have on others.

An example of amoral management was Nestlé's decision to market infant formula in Third World countries. Nestlé received massive amounts of negative publicity for this marketing strategy, and governments in several countries launched investigations. These investigations indicated that Nestlé apparently gave no thought to the possible disastrous health consequences of selling the formula to illiterate and impoverished people in areas where the likelihood was high that it would be mixed with impure, disease-ridden water. The following Ethics in Practice feature, while amusing, presents another example of amoral management.

ETHICS IN PRACTICE

Who's Your Phone Company—I Don't Care

Imagine that you're in Houston and you need assistance calling a relative in Dallas. The local telephone operator asks you to pick a long-distance company. If your answer is, "I don't know," "I don't care," "It doesn't matter," or "Whoever," you may have to pay extra money when the telephone bill arrives. A company in the Fort Worth suburb of Kennedale has registered those phrases as names of Texas long-distance carriers whose rates for operator-assisted calls are about twice those of major phone companies.

"It's not deceptive at all," said Dennis Dees, 38, president of KTNT Communications, Inc., the holding company for the oddly named subsidiaries. Dees also claims the KTNT company name is only coincidentally similar to that of phone giant AT&T. When questioned about the prices they charge and the way his company attracts customers, Dees declared: "There's nothing to be defensive about. I'm charging a fair price compared to the market price for my product. I've come up with a name that's pretty creative and it's successful for us. There's no reason to be embarrassed."

The Texas Public Utility Commission said that it is aware of Dees's companies, which are properly registered with the state. Officials apparently can do nothing but warn consumers to be careful. John Riggins, president of the Better Business Bureau, is of the opinion that Dees's companies do not meet the BBB standard for advertising. "It doesn't give everybody all the information they need to make an informed decision," he says. An editorial in the local paper concluded that what Dees was doing was legal, but "it sure as hell seems wrong." "We're not trying to be anything we're not," countered Dees. "We are 'I Don't Care.' That is our company, and if that's what you want, we're your company."[42]

■ ESTABLISHING ETHICAL ATTITUDES

A story is often told about President Calvin Coolidge, who was famous for being a "man of few words." One Sunday, President Coolidge had attended church without his wife. Later in the day, Mrs. Coolidge inquired as to the subject of the minister's sermon. "Sin," replied Coolidge. "What did he say about it?" his wife persisted. "He was against it," answered Coolidge. This story illustrates part of the problem of dealing with a topic such as ethics or ethical behavior in organizations. To be against unethical behavior isn't enough. Managers and employees need a framework of ethical beliefs and behavior in order to diagnose and address ethical problems in the workplace. In this book, we explore ethical issues involved in various aspects of organizational behavior.

As we discussed earlier, an organization cannot directly manage personality dimensions (such as locus of control) or cognitive individual differences (such as cognitive moral development). Still, managers can take steps such as the following to instill moral management by fostering ethical attitudes in the work force.

- Identify ethical attitudes crucial for the organization's operations. For example, a security firm might stress honesty, whereas a drug manufacturer may identify responsibility as most important to ensure product quality. After identifying important ethical attitudes, training programs can focus on developing such attitudes among employees.

- Select employees with desired attitudes. The organization might develop and use standard interview questions that assess an applicant's ethical values.

- Incorporate ethics in the performance evaluation process. Criteria that individuals are evaluated on will have an important influence on work-related attitudes that they develop. Organizations should make ethical concerns part of the job description and evaluation.

- Establish a work culture that reinforces ethical attitudes. Managers and organizations can take many actions to influence organizational culture. This culture, in turn, has a major influence on ethical behavior in the organization.[43]

(We explore organizational culture, including its relationship to ethical behavior, in detail in Chapter 17.)

Citicorp is one organization that stresses development of ethical attitudes among its employees. Citicorp is a huge, multinational financial services organization. Its concerns about ethical behavior resulted in the development and use of an ethics game, or exercise, entitled "The Work Ethic—An Exercise in Integrity."[44] The game can be played by individuals in a small group or by large groups divided into several teams. Individuals or teams are presented with ethical dilemmas based on actual experiences in the company. Employees can compare their proposed solutions to what Citicorp considers to be the correct, ethical course of action. Managers use the game in training programs, staff meetings, departmental retreats, and to orient new employees. The goals of the game are to help employees recognize ethical dilemmas in decision making, to teach employees how Citicorp responds to misconduct, and to increase understanding of its rules and policies regarding ethical behavior. The ethics game isn't the only ethics training that Citicorp uses, but it is an excellent example of how an organization can foster ethical attitudes among managers and employees.

CHAPTER SUMMARY

Personality is a person's set of relatively stable characteristics and traits that account for consistent patterns of behavior in various situations. Each individual in some ways is like other people and in some ways is unique. An individual's personality is the product both of inherited traits or tendencies and experiences. These experiences occur within the framework of the individual's biological, physical, and social environment—all of which are modified by the culture, family, and other groups to which the person belongs. An individual's personality may be described by a set of factors known as the Big Five. In addition, specific personality dimensions, such as self-esteem, locus of control, and introversion and extraversion, affect behavior. The study of personality and an understanding of interactions between the person and the situation are important for comprehending organizational behavior.

Attitudes are patterns of feelings, beliefs, and behavioral tendencies directed toward specific people, groups, ideas, issues, or objects. Attitudes have affective, cognitive, and behavioral components. The relationship between attitudes and behavior isn't always clear, although important relationships exist. The attitude–behavior relationship may become clearer when an individual's intentions to behave in a certain way are known and the specific attitudes and norms that might be related to the behavior are understood. Job satisfaction—the general collection of attitudes that a worker holds toward the job—is of great interest in understanding organizational behavior. Another work attitude of interest is commitment to the organization. Both satisfaction and commitment are related to important organizational behaviors.

Individual differences, such as locus of control and cognitive moral development, are related to ethical behavior. Organizations can take constructive steps to foster ethical attitudes and behavior among managers and employees.

KEY TERMS AND CONCEPTS

Amoral management	Extraversion	Moral management
Attitudes	General theory of behavior	Nature–nurture controversy
Authoritarian personality	Immoral management	Norms
Behavioral intentions model	Individual differences	Organizational commitment
"Big Five" personality factors	Interactionist perspective	Personality
Cognitive moral development	Internal locus of control	Personality trait
Culture	Introversion	Self-esteem
Dogmatism	Job satisfaction	
External locus of control	Locus of control	

DISCUSSION QUESTIONS

1. Explain the importance of individual differences for understanding behavior in organizations.

2. Discuss the concept of personality. Provide two examples of how personality might affect employee behaviors in the workplace.

3. What are the basic categories of factors that influence personality development?

4. Describe the opposing positions in the nature–nurture controversy over personality formation. What influences on personality formation seem most important to you? Why?

5. Explain the Big Five personality factors. Use these factors to describe your perceptions of the president of the United States.

6. Which of the personality dimensions discussed in this chapter seems most important for managerial behavior? Why?

7. What are attitudes? Describe the basic components of attitudes.

8. How does the behavioral intentions model help explain that attitude–behavior relationships sometimes may appear to be weak and at other times may appear to be strong?

9. What is job satisfaction? Why is it important?

10. What is organizational commitment? Why do organizations seek strong employee commitment?

11. What are the key differences in moral management, immoral management, and amoral management? Give an example of each.

12. Suggest some specific actions that organizations may take to encourage ethical behavior by managers and employees.

■ Developing Competencies

Self-Insight: Assessing the Big Five

The Big Five Locator Questionnaire[45]

Instructions: On each numerical scale that follows, indicate which point is generally more descriptive of you. If the two terms are equally descriptive, mark the midpoint.

1.	Eager	5 4 3 2 1	Calm
2.	Prefer Being with Other People	5 4 3 2 1	Prefer Being Alone
3.	A Dreamer	5 4 3 2 1	No-Nonsense
4.	Courteous	5 4 3 2 1	Abrupt
5.	Neat	5 4 3 2 1	Messy

6.	Cautious	5 4 3 2 1	Confident
7.	Optimistic	5 4 3 2 1	Pessimistic
8.	Theoretical	5 4 3 2 1	Practical
9.	Generous	5 4 3 2 1	Selfish
10.	Decisive	5 4 3 2 1	Open-Ended

11.	Discouraged	5 4 3 2 1	Upbeat
12.	Exhibitionist	5 4 3 2 1	Private

13.	Follow Imagination	5 4 3 2 1	Follow Authority
14.	Warm	5 4 3 2 1	Cold
15.	Stay Focused	5 4 3 2 1	Easily Distracted

16.	Easily Embarrassed	5 4 3 2 1	Don't Give a Darn
17.	Outgoing	5 4 3 2 1	Cool
18.	Seek Novelty	5 4 3 2 1	Seek Routine
19.	Team Player	5 4 3 2 1	Independent
20.	A Preference for Order	5 4 3 2 1	Comfortable with Chaos

21.	Distractible	5 4 3 2 1	Unflappable
22.	Conversational	5 4 3 2 1	Thoughtful
23.	Comfortable with Ambiguity	5 4 3 2 1	Prefer Things Clear-Cut
24.	Trusting	5 4 3 2 1	Skeptical
25.	On Time	5 4 3 2 1	Procrastinate

BIG FIVE LOCATOR SCORE CONVERSION SHEET

Norm Score	Adjustment	Sociability	Openness	Agreeableness	Conscientiousness	Norm Score
80					•	80
79			25			79
78						78
77	22					77
76			24			76
75						75
74						74
73	21		23			73
72		25				72
71				25		71
70	20	24	22			70
69					25	69
68				24		68
67		23	21		24	67
66	19					66
65		22		23	23	65
64			20			64
63					22	63
62	18	21	19	22		62

BIG FIVE LOCATOR SCORE CONVERSION SHEET

Norm Score	Adjustment	Sociability	Openness	Agreeableness	Conscientiousness	Norm Score
61					21	61
60		20				60
59	17		18	21	20	59
58						58
57		19				57
56			17			56
55	16	18		20	19	55
54			16	19		54
53						53
52		17			18	52
51	15					51
50		16	15	18	17	50
49						49
48	14	15			16	48
47			14	17		47
46		14			15	46
45			13			45
44	13			16	14	44
43		13				43
42			12			42
41				15	13	41
40	12	12	11			40
39						39
38				14	12	38
37		11	10			37
36	11					36
35		10		13	11	35
34			9			34
33	10	9			10	33
32				12		32
31			8			31
30		8			9	30
29	9			11		29
28		7	7		8	28
27				10		27
26		6			7	26
25	8		6			25
24				9	6	24
23						23
22			5		22	22
21	7	5				21
20				8		20
Enter Norm Scores Here:	Adj =	S =	O =	A =	C =	

(Norms based on a sample of 161 forms completed in 1993–94.)

Instructions:

1. Find the sum of the circled numbers on the *first* row of each of the five-line groupings (Row 1 + Row 6 + Row 11 + Row 16 + Row 21 = _____). This is your raw score for "adjustment." Circle the number in the ADJUST-MENT: column of the Score Conversion Sheet that corresponds to this raw score.

2. Find the sum of the circled numbers on the *second* row of each of the five-line groupings (Row 2 + Row 7 + Row 12 + Row 17 + Row 22 + = _____). This is your raw score for "sociability." Circle the number in the SOCIA-BILITY: column of the Score Conversion Sheet that corresponds to this raw score.

3. Find the sum of the circled numbers on the *third* row of each of the five-line groupings (Row 3 + Row 8 + Row 13 + Row 18 + Row 23 = _____). This is your raw score for "openness." Circle the number in the OPEN-NESS: column of the Score Conversion Sheet that corresponds to this raw score.

4. Find the sum of the circled numbers on the *fourth* row of each of the five-line groupings (Row 4 + Row 9 + Row 14 + Row 19 + Row 24 = _____). This is your raw score for "agreeableness." circle the number in the AGREEABLENESS: column of the Score Conversion Sheet that corresponds to this raw score.

5. Find the sum of the circled numbers on the *fifth* row of each of the five-line groupings (Row 5 + Row 10 + Row 15 + Row 20 + Row 25 = _____). This is your raw score for "conscientious." Circle the number in the CONSCI-ENTIOUSNESS: column of the Score Conversion Sheet that corresponds to this raw score.

6. Find the number in the far right or far left column that is parallel to your circled raw score. Enter this norm score in the box at the bottom of the appropriate column.

7. Transfer your norm score to the appropriate scale on the Big Five Locator Interpretation Sheet.

BIG FIVE LOCATOR INTERPRETATION SHEET

STRONG ADJUSTMENT: secure, unflappable, rational, unresponsive, guilt free	Resilient	Responsive	Reactive		WEAK ADJUSTMENT: excitable, worrying, reactive, high strung, alert
	35	45	55	65	
LOW SOCIABILITY: private, independent, works alone, reserved, hard to read	Introvert	Ambivert	Extravert		HIGH SOCIABILITY: assertive, sociable, warm, optimistic, talkative
	35	45	55	65	
LOW OPENNESS: practical, conservative, depth of knowledge, efficient, expert	Preserver	Moderate	Explorer		HIGH OPENNESS: broad interests, curious, liberal, impractical, likes novelty
	35	45	55	65	
LOW AGREEABLENESS: skeptical, questioning, tough, aggressive, self-interest	Challenger	Negotiator	Adapter		HIGH AGREEABLENESS: trusting, humble, altruistic, team player, conflict averse, frank
	35	45	55	65	
LOW CONSCIENTIOUSNESS: private, independent, works alone, reserved, hard to read	Flexible	Balanced	Focused		HIGH CONSCIENTIOUSNESS: dependable, organized, disciplined, cautious, stubborn
	35	45	55	65	

Note: The Big Five Locator is intended for use only as a quick assessment for teaching purposes.

Organizational Insight:
Earning Loyalty at A. G. Edwards

Really *earning* employee loyalty—not just backing into it by luck or circumstance—is more than a matter of having the right tools. The right tools (measurements, practices, and poli-cies) are all very important, as the case of A. G. Edwards shows. But the case also shows how important it is to begin with the right philosophy, to *think* in terms of loyalty and value creation before developing strategies and tactics.

A. G. Edwards seeks to employ a different breed of broker than its competitors. Instead of looking for those with a "sales" personality, the firm screens for individuals who share its philosophy: that the broker's role is to act as an agent for the customer. The firm's CEO, Ben Edwards III, puts it this way: "We want someone with character who shares our values and who will fit into our culture. We're looking for a long-term, happy marriage."

The firm's attitude toward growth guides employee selection. The firm has no arbitrary goals or budgets that pressure managers to dip deeper into the talent or character pool than makes them comfortable. Most other firms set hiring goals, then evaluate recruiters on whether the goals have been met. Not surprisingly, recruiters stretch their quality standards, always difficult to measure, in order to meet their volume standards, which are easily measured. A. G. Edwards hires at a relatively steady pace, and has maintained a stable work force of brokers through market ups and downs. Many brokerage firms will hire far more trainees than they can possibly train and assimilate during the boom years, then cut back drastically and hire almost no one in the bust years.

Ben Edwards also avoids the industry practice of using up-front bonuses to lure brokers from the competition. "It would tend to attract the wrong kind of people," he says, "and it would be unfair to our loyal employees. The message would be that the best way to make a lot of money is to jump around from firm to firm."

A. G. Edwards's policy of seldom rotating branch managers provides another link in its high-retention system. When managers come along who are really good at building new branches, the company encourages them and, as new-branch profits are low, pays them on a modified compensation system. The vast majority of branch managers stay where they are, their compensation dependent on how well they build the profits of their own branches. From 90 to 95 percent of promotions come from within the firm, which further reinforces loyalty to the organization. The nine-man executive committee has an average tenure of more than twenty-five years, and all members have a significant financial stake in the firm.

A hallmark of the A. G. Edwards system is treating people fairly. After apologizing for how corny it sounds, Ben Edwards describes the most important element of the firm's management approach as "following the golden rule—treating people the way you would like to be treated." Fairness extends to executive compensation. The firm pays its senior executives less than most of its competitors. Ben Edwards himself has averaged less than $1 million per year over the past several years, which he estimates is probably one-third to one-fifth what his counterparts get at other firms.

The firm works very hard to hire the right kind of trainees, defined as people who will maintain or improve the character and integrity of A. G. Edwards. It works equally hard to earn their loyalty and to help them achieve their income goals. So when defections occur, management tries hard to understand why a successful, productive broker might leave. The firm routinely performs exit interviews to search for the causes of dissatisfaction.

Of course, character and loyalty aren't the only criteria for brokers; trainees must also have the skills to become economically productive. However, the firm has engineered its system so that brokers don't have to sell as much volume as they do at other houses to make a profit for the firm. For one thing, the firm has smaller branches, with eight to ten brokers (compared to an industry average of twenty to thirty). Branch managers act as player–coaches, handling some customers themselves. In addition, space costs are lower per person. Based in St. Louis, the firm is the only major brokerage house to avoid Manhattan overheads by locating its headquarters outside New York City. The firm has historically concentrated on geographic areas that reinforce the loyalty culture, particularly smaller markets and suburban locations. A representative sample of new branch openings include South Hills, Pennsylvania; Lima, Ohio; Tifton, Georgia; Branson, Missouri; Boynton Beach, Florida; and Morgantown, West Virginia.

A. G. Edwards does no national advertising, which not only saves money, but it also reinforces the message that the best source of growth is referrals. The firm also uses a single-tier compensation system, which eases the pressure on brokers who are slow to achieve acceptable sales volumes. Competitors pay reduced commission rates to low-volume producers to weed out the laggards, but that practice encourages new brokers to push products even harder, sometimes in ways that are not in the customer's best interest.

The company passes on some of its efficiencies directly to customers. *Smart Money,* the personal finance magazine of the *Wall Street Journal,* recently ranked brokerage firms on price. To no one's surprise, A. G. Edwards won top honors. The firm also wins the *Smart Money* award for best ongoing broker training. Training receives such high priority that Ben Edwards often leads the seminars himself. But where training at many other firms includes instruction on how to pitch the products that are most profitable to the firm, Edwards concentrates instead on how to serve the customer more effectively.

The firm is unique in the industry in its refusal to manufacture its own investment products, because of the potential for a conflict of interest. Other firms can't resist the fat margins they earn on in-house mutual funds, so some of them pay brokers bigger commissions to push a house fund, even when an outside fund might be a better choice for the customer. Worse yet, when an investment banking department gets stuck with inventory it can't sell (stalled initial public offerings or dubious partnerships) the temptation is to increase commission rates to pressure brokers into unloading the investments on unsuspecting customers. When brokers see their firms placing short-term corporate earnings above the best interests of the customer, they can hardly help concluding that it's all right to put their own interests above the customer's. This kind of thinking is rare at A. G. Edwards, where customer interests receive first priority.

When Ben Edwards writes at the end of an annual report, "We are committed to doing the best job we can for our faithful clients," it's more than lip service. His firm enjoys the lowest level of arbitration awards in the industry—less than half that of the next-best-performing firm, Merrill Lynch. What Edwards does not point out is that the combination of good, dependable income, low-pressure selling environment, and a policy of putting customers first has also produced happier brokers. Broker turnover is less than half the industry average. By engineering a loyalty-based business system that achieves 92 percent broker retention in an industry where 80 to 85 percent is typical, Edwards has made winners of its customers, employees, and investors.[46]

Questions

1. Identify the key ideas and concepts from the chapter that appear in this description of A. G. Edwards.

2. What would you expect job satisfaction and organizational commitment to be like for employees of this firm? Explain your answer.

REFERENCES

1. Quoted in Eysenck, H. J. *Personality, Genetics, and Behavior.* New York: Prager, 1982, 1.

2. George, J. M. The role of personality in organizational life: Issues and evidence. *Journal of Management,* 1992, 18, 185–213; Hartup, W. W., and von Lieshout, C. F. M. Personality development in social context. *Annual Review of Psychology,* 1995, 46, 655–687; Weiss, H. M., and Adler, S. Personality and organizational behavior. In B. M. Staw and L. L. Cummings (eds.), *Research in Organizational Behavior,* vol. 6. Greenwich, Conn.: JAI Press, 1984, 1–50.

3. Maddi, S. R. *Personality Theories: A Comparative Analysis,* 5th ed. Homewood, Ill.: Dorsey, 1989, 10.

4. See, for example, Revelle, W. Personality processes. *Annual Review of Psychology,* 1995, 46, 295–328.

5. Collins, W. A., and Gunnar, M. R. Social and personality development. *Annual Review of Psychology,* 1990, 41, 387–416.

6. Bouchard, T. J. Genes, environment, and personality. *Science,* 1994, 264, 1700–1701; Lykken, D. T., Bouchard, T. J., McGue, M., and Tellegen, A. Heritability of interests. *Journal of Applied Psychology,* 1993, 78, 649–661; Rose, R. J. Genes and human behavior. *Annual Review of Psychology,* 1995, 46, 625–654.

7. Buss, D. M. Evolutionary personality psychology. *Annual Review of Psychology,* 1991, 42, 459–491; Hettma, P. J. (ed.). *Personality and Environment: Assessment of Human Adaptation.* New York: John Wiley & Sons, 1989.

8. Adapted from Ratan, S. Generational tension in the office: Why busters hate boomers. *Fortune,* October 4, 1993, 57–70.

9. Pervin, L. A. *Personality: Theory and Research,* 4th ed. New York: John Wiley & Sons, 1984, 10.

10. Digman, J. M. Personality structure: Emergence of the five-factor model. *Annual Review of Psychology,* 1990, 41, 417–440; Hogan, R. T. Personality and personality measurement. In M. D. Dunnette and L. M. Hough (eds.), *Handbook of Industrial & Organizational Psychology,* 2d ed., vol. 2. Palo Alto, Calif.: Consulting Psychologists Press, 1991, 873–919; Wiggins, J. S., and Pincus, A. L. Personality: Structure and assessment. *Annual Review of Psychology,* 1992, 43, 473–504.

11. Barrick, M. R., and Mount, M. K. Autonomy as a moderator of the relationships between the big five personality dimensions and job performance. *Journal of Applied Psychology,* 1993, 78, 111–118; Barrick, M. R., and Mount, M. K. The big five personality dimensions and job performance: A meta-analysis. *Personnel Psychology,* 1991, 44, 1–26.

12. Descriptions of the following personality dimensions are based on Blass, T. (ed.). *Personality Variables in Social Behavior.* Hillsdale, N.J.: Lawrence Erlbaum Associates, 1977; Engler, B. *Personality Theories,* 3d ed. Boston: Houghton Mifflin, 1991; Jackson, D. N., and Paunonen, S. V. Personality structure and assessment. *Annual Review of Psychology,* 1980, 31, 503–551; Lefcourt, H. M. *Locus of Control: Current Trends in Theory and Research,* 2d ed. Hillsdale, N.J.: Lawrence Erlbaum Associates, 1982; Liebert, R. M., and Spiegler, M. D. *Personality: Strategies and Issues,* 6th ed. Pacific Grove, Calif.: Brooks/Cole, 1990.

13. Ellis, R. A., and Taylor, M. S. Role of self-esteem within the job search process. *Journal of Applied Psychology,* 1983, 68, 632–640.

14. Hollenbeck, J. R., and Brief, A. P. The effects of individual differences and goal origins on goal setting and performance. *Organizational Behavior and Human Decision Processes,* 1987, 40, 392–414; Pierce, J. L., Gardner, D. G., Dunham, R. B., and Cummings, L. L. Moderation by organization-based self-esteem of role condition–employee response relationships. *Academy of Management Journal,* 1993, 36, 271–288; Renn, R. W., and Prien, K. O. Employee responses to performance feedback from the task: A field study of the moderating effects of global self-esteem. *Group & Organization Management,* 1995, 20, 337–354.

15. Lefcourt, H. M. Durability and impact of the locus of control construct. *Psychological Bulletin,* 1992, 112, 411–414.

16. Black, J. S. Locus of control, social support, stress, and adjustment in international transfer. *Asia Pacific Journal of Management,* April 1990, 1–30.

17. Engler, *Personality Theories*, 329–334; Eysenck, *Personality, Genetics, and Behavior*, 161–197.

18. Adapted from Caminti, S. What team leaders need to know. *Fortune*, February 20, 1995, 94, 98.

19. See, for example, Greenberger, D. B., and Strasser, S. The role of situational and dispositional factors in the enhancement of personal control in organizations. In L. L. Cummings and B. M. Staw (eds.), *Research in Organizational Behavior*, vol. 13. Greenwich, Conn.: JAI Press, 1991, 111–145; Mitchell, T. R., and James, L. R. Theory development forum–situational versus dispositional factors: Competing explanations of behavior. *Academy of Management Review*, 1989, 14, 330–407; Woodman, R. W., and Schoenfeldt, L. F. Individual differences in creativity: An interactionist perspective. In J. A. Glover, R. R. Ronning, and C. R. Reynolds (eds.), *Handbook of Creativity*. New York: Plenum, 1989, 77–91.

20. Myers, D. G. *Social Psychology*, 4th ed. New York: McGraw-Hill, 1993, 112; Olson, J. M., and Zanna, M. P. Attitudes and beliefs. In R. M. Baron, W. G. Graziano, and C. Stangor (eds.), *Social Psychology*. Fort Worth, Tex.: Holt, Rinehart, and Winston, 1991, 196.

21. Tesser, A. The importance of heritability in psychological research: The case of attitudes. *Psychological Review*, 1993, 100, 129–142; Weiss, H. M., and Cropanzano, P. Affective events theory: A theoretical discussion of the structure, causes, and consequences of affective experiences at work. In B. M. Staw and L. L. Cummings (eds.), *Research in Organizational Behavior*, vol. 18. Greenwich, Conn.: JAI Press, 1996, 1–74.

22. Breckler, S. J. Empirical validation of affect, behavior, and cognition as distinct components of attitude. *Journal of Personality and Social Psychology*, 1984, 47, 1191–1205; Eagly, A. H., and Chaiken, S. *The Psychology of Attitudes*. San Diego: Harcourt, Brace, Jovanovich, 1992; Olson, J. M., and Zanna, M. P. Attitudes and attitude change. *Annual Review of Psychology*, 1993, 44, 120–122.

23. Penrod, S. *Social Psychology*. Englewood Cliffs, N.J.: Prentice-Hall, 1983, 345–347.

24. Ajzen, I., and Fishbein, M. *Understanding Attitudes and Predicting Social Behavior*. Englewood Cliffs, N.J.: Prentice-Hall, 1980.

25. Ajzen, I. From intentions to actions: A theory of planned behavior. In J. Kuhl and J. Beckmann (eds.), *Action-Control: From Cognition to Behavior*. Heidelberg: Springer, 1985, 11–39.

26. Ajzen, I. The theory of planned behavior. *Organizational Behavior and Human Decision Processes*, 1991, 50, 1–33; Olson and Zanna, Attitudes and attitude change, 131–135.

27. Hulin, C. Adaptation, persistence, and commitment in organizations. In M. D. Dunnette and L. M. Hough (eds.), *Handbook of Industrial & Organizational Psychology*, 2d ed., vol. 2. Palo Alto, Calif.: Consulting Psychologists Press, 1991, 469–471.

28. O'Reilly, C. R. Organizational behavior. *Annual Review of Psychology*, 1991, 42, 427–458.

29. Based on Lincoln, J. R. Employee work attitudes and management practice in the U.S. and Japan: Evidence from a large comparative survey. *California Management Review*, Fall 1989, 89–106.

30. Hanisch, K. A. The job description index revisited. *Journal of Applied Psychology*, 1992, 77, 377–382; Smith, P. C., Kendall, L. M., and Hulin, C. L., *The Measurement of Satisfaction in Work and Retirement.*, Chicago: Rand McNally, 1969.

31. Williams, M. L. Antecedents of employee benefit level satisfaction: A test of a model. *Journal of Management*, 1995, 21, 1097–1128.

32. Iaffaldano, M. T., and Muchinsky, P. M. Job satisfaction and job performance: A meta-analysis. *Psychological Bulletin*, 1985, 97, 251–273.

33. Ostroff, C. The relationship between satisfaction, attitudes, and performance: An organizational level analysis. *Journal of Applied Psychology*, 1992, 77, 963–974.

34. Miner, J. B. *Industrial–Organizational Psychology*. New York: McGraw-Hill, 1992, 119–124; Muchinsky, P. M. *Psychology Applied to Work*, 3d ed. Pacific Grove, Calif.: Brooks/Cole, 1990, 327–337; Saal, F. E., and Knight, P. A. *Industrial/Organizational Psychology: Science and Practice*. Pacific Grove, Calif.: Brooks/Cole, 1988, 312–322.

35. Mowday, R. T., Porter, L. W., and Steers, R. M. *Employee–Organization Linkages: The Psychology of Commitment, Absenteeism, and Turnover*. New York: Academic Press, 1982, 27. See also, Mathieu, J. E., and Zajac, D. M. A review and meta-analysis of the antecedents, correlates, and consequences of organizational commitment. *Psychological Bulletin*, 1990, 108, 171–194.

36. Miner, *Industrial–Organizational Psychology*, 124–128.

37. See, for example, Becker, T. E., Billings, R. S. Eveleth, D. M., and Gilbert, N. L. Foci and bases of employee commitment: Implications for job performance. *Academy of Management Journal*, 1996, 39, 464–482; McCaul, H. S., Hinsz, V. B., and McCaul, K. D. Assessing organizational commitment: An employee's global attitude toward the organization. *Journal of Applied Behavioral Science*, 1995, 31, 80–90; Shore, L. M., Barksdale, K., and Shore, T. H. Managerial perceptions of employee commitment to the organization. *Academy of Management Journal*, 1995, 38, 1593–1615.

38. Cohen, A. Organizational commitment and turnover: A meta-analysis. *Academy of Management Journal*, 1993, 36, 1140–1157; Hulin, Adaptation, persistence, and commitment, 488–491.

39. Adapted from Shellenbarger, S. Enter the new hero: A boss who knows you have a life. *Wall Street Journal*, May 8, 1996, B1.

40. Trevino, L. K., and Youngblood, S. A. Bad apples in bad barrels: A causal analysis of ethical decision making behavior. *Journal of Applied Psychology*, 1990, 75, 378–385.

41. The following examples are from Carroll, A. B. In search of the moral manager. *Business Horizons*, March/April 1987, 2–6.

42. Adapted from Drago, M. Don't care now? You may when telephone bill arrives. *Bryan–College Station Eagle*, July 12, 1996, A1, A5.

43. Goddard, R. W. Are you an ethical manager? *Personnel Journal*, March 1988, 38–47.

44. Trevino, L. K. A cultural perspective on changing and developing organizational ethics. In W. A. Pasmore and R. W. Woodman (eds.), *Research in Organizational Change and Development*, vol. 4. Greenwich, Conn.: JAI Press, 1990, 195–230.

45. Reprinted with permission from Howard, P. J., Medina, P. L., and Howard, J. M. The big five locator: A quick assessment tool for consultants and trainers. In J. W. Pfeiffer (ed.), *The 1996 Annual: Volume 1, Training.* San Diego: Pfeiffer & Company, 1996, 119–122. Copyright © 1996 Pfeiffer, an imprint of Jossey-Bass, Inc., Publishers. All rights reserved.

46. Based on Edwards, B. *1993 Annual Report*, A. G. Edwards, Inc., 5; Reichheld, F. F. *The Loyalty Effect.* Boston: Harvard Business School Press, 1996, 105–108; Siconolfi, M. Rating the brokers. *Smart Money: Personal Finance Magazine of the Wall Street Journal*, December 1993, 100.

3

Perception and Attribution

LEARNING OBJECTIVES

When you have finished studying this chapter, you should be able to:

- Define perception and describe the major elements in the perceptual process.
- Explain perceptual selection and perceptual organization.
- Describe the factors that determine how one person perceives another.
- Discuss the issue of accuracy in person perception.
- Identify five kinds of perceptual errors.
- Explain the process of attribution and describe how attributions influence behavior.
- Identify important attributions that people make in the work setting.

OUTLINE

PREVIEW CASE

The Job Training Opportunity

Frank Biggs and Ernest Garcia are production line team leaders for Air Designs, Inc., a small manufacturer of airplane cockpit panel instruments. Early one Monday morning both received letters delivered by courier to their work stations. The letters, personally signed by the president of Air Designs, notified each that he had been selected to attend a month-long supervisory training program being offered by a nearby college. Other than stating when the training was to begin, the letters provided no additional details concerning why Air Design was using this particular training program nor why Biggs and Garcia had been chosen to receive the training.

Later that same day, Linda Sharpe—manager of production operations—arrived at her office to find both Biggs and Garcia waiting to talk to her. Biggs seemed particularly upset, so Sharpe invited him into the office and asked Garcia to wait.

After she had spent about thirty minutes talking with Biggs, he calmed down and went back to work. Her conversation with Garcia, concerning the same subject, took less than five minutes.

Later Sharpe related this story to friends. "Our invitations to these two team leaders helped me to understand how very different some individuals' perceptions of the same event can be. It turns out that Frank Biggs was worried about his performance. Even though we thought he was doing a reasonably good job, he apparently didn't feel the same way. Then, when the invitation came for the training program, Frank felt very threatened. He perceived the invitation (in our conversation, he described it as an 'order' to take additional training) as confirmation that we were disappointed in his performance.

Ernest Garcia, though, had just dropped by to thank me for the training opportunity. He had perceived the same invitation as a reward for past performance and a vote of confidence from us concerning his future with the firm. Of course, Ernest's interpretation is the one we wanted, and I felt badly that our letter (which I had actually written for the president's signature) could be misperceived in such a negative fashion by Frank Biggs."

The Preview Case illustrates the importance of perceptions in organizational behavior. No two people will necessarily perceive a situation in exactly the same way. People also base their behaviors on what they perceive reality to be, not necessarily what it *is*. In a very real sense, people live in their own perceptual worlds. Recognizing the difference between the perceptual worlds of employees and managers and the reality of the organization is important in understanding organizational behavior. In this chapter, we explore *individual differences* in terms of the important processes of *perception* and *attribution*. First, we describe the perceptual process. Then, we examine the external and internal factors that influence perception, the ways that people organize perceptions, the process of *person perception*, and various errors in the perceptual process. We then turn to the attributions that people make to explain the behaviors of others.

THE PERCEPTUAL PROCESS

Perception is the selection and organization of environmental stimuli to provide meaningful experiences for the perceiver. Perception involves searching for, obtaining, and processing information. It represents the psychological process whereby people take information from the environment and make sense of their worlds.[1]

The key words in the definition of perception are *selection* and *organization*. Different people often perceive a situation differently, both in terms of what they selectively perceive and how they organize and interpret the things perceived. Figure 3.1 summarizes the basic elements in the perceptual process from initial observation to final response.

People receive stimuli from the environment through their five senses: taste, smell, hearing, sight, and touch. Everyone selectively pays attention to some aspects of the environment and selectively ignores other aspects at any particular time. For example, an apartment dweller may listen expectantly for a friend's footsteps in the hall but ignore sounds of the people upstairs. In an office, a secretary may ignore the bell announcing the arrival of the elevator but jump at the sound of the fax machine. A person's selection process involves both external and internal factors, filtering sensory perceptions and determining which will receive the most attention. The individual then organizes the stimuli selected into meaningful patterns.

How people interpret what they perceive also varies considerably. A wave of the hand may be interpreted as a friendly gesture or as a threat, depending on the circumstances and the state of mind of those involved. As indicated in the Preview Case, perceptions are very important. In organizations, managers and employees therefore must recognize that perceptions of events and the behaviors of others may be inaccurate.

A person's interpretation of sensory stimuli will lead to a response, either overt (actions) or covert (motivation, attitudes, and feelings)—or both. Each person selects and organizes sensory stimuli differently and thus has different interpretations and responses. Perceptual differences help explain why people behave differently in the same situation. People often perceive the same things in different ways, and their behavioral responses depend, in part, on these perceptions. The following Across Cultures feature provides another interesting example of perceptual differences.

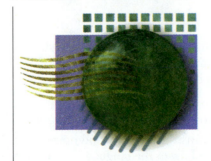

ACROSS CULTURES

British Budweiser Ads Rankle American Indians

Anheuser-Busch is using beer-guzzling American Indians to sell Budweiser in Britain. The television and movie theater ads, which aren't being shown in the United States, have shocked Indian advocacy groups and surprised advertising experts who describe the campaign as insensitive. Budweiser defends the ads, noting that they have become a cult hit in Britain, where consumers are apparently unaware of negative stereotypes about Indians and alcohol.

The controversy points up an increasingly difficult dilemma for global advertising. In ads for foreign markets, should multinational companies be held to the same standards of ethics and taste as they are at home? Does it make a difference whether images that are offensive in one culture are perceived benignly in the market where the ads are shown?

The Budweiser ad, dubbed "Pale Rider," follows a truck driver for a company called Chieftain Cement. The driver enters a dim bar patronized by a crowd of American Indians. The bartender, a silver-haired Indian, is shocked by the man's ghostly pale face, which is covered with cement dust. So the driver dunks his head in a barrel of water, washing the dust away and revealing himself to be an Indian. The camera zooms in as he gulps down a bottle of Budweiser. (Such a shot would

—Continued

ACROSS CULTURES—*Continued*

be prohibited in the United States, where beer can be shown in commercials but not consumed.)

The ad is part of a campaign airing only in Britain that touts Budweiser as "the genuine article" and emphasizes its American roots. Although no one in the ad is misbehaving, American Indian advocates say that it is insensitive and offensive. The reason is the high rate of alcoholism among American Indians, estimated to be five times higher than for the general population.

Suzan Shown Harjo, a Cheyenne and Muskogee who is president of the Indian-rights advocacy group Morning Star Institute in Washington states: "From driving a truck that uses Native American imagery to furthering the impression that Indian people are so closely linked with booze—it's just a continuation of the stereotype."

Anheuser-Busch insists that the main character is perceived positively. "Our British consumers see him as independent and self-confident and very much a genuine person," says Peter Jackson, marketing director for the United Kingdom and Ireland. "In the U.K., there aren't any inappropriate or stereotypical images of Native Americans."[2]

PERCEPTUAL SELECTION

The phone is ringing, your TV is blaring, a dog is barking outside, your PC is making a strange noise, and you smell coffee brewing. Which of these stimuli will you ignore? Which will you pay attention to?

Perceptual selection is the process by which people filter out most stimuli so that they can deal with the most important ones. Perceptual selection depends on several factors, some of which are in the external environment and some of which are internal to the perceiver.[3]

■ EXTERNAL FACTORS

External perception factors are characteristics that influence whether the stimuli will be noticed. The following external factors may be stated as *principles* of perception. In each case we present an example to illustrate the principle.

- *Size.* The larger an external factor, the more likely it is to be perceived. A hiker is far more likely to notice a fully grown fir tree than a seedling.

- *Intensity.* The more intense an external factor (bright lights, loud noises, and the like), the more likely it is to be perceived. Even the language in a memo from a manager to an employee can reflect the intensity principle. A memo that reads, "Please stop by my office at your convenience," wouldn't fill you with the same sense of urgency as a memo that reads, "Report to my office immediately!"

- *Contrast.* External factors that stand out against the background or that aren't what people expect are the most likely to be perceived. In addition, the contrast of objects with others or with their background may influence how they are perceived. Figure 3.2 illustrates this aspect of the contrast principle. Which of the solid center circles is larger? The one on the right appears to be larger, but it isn't: The two circles are the same size. The solid circle on

FIGURE 3.1 Basic Elements in the Perceptual Process

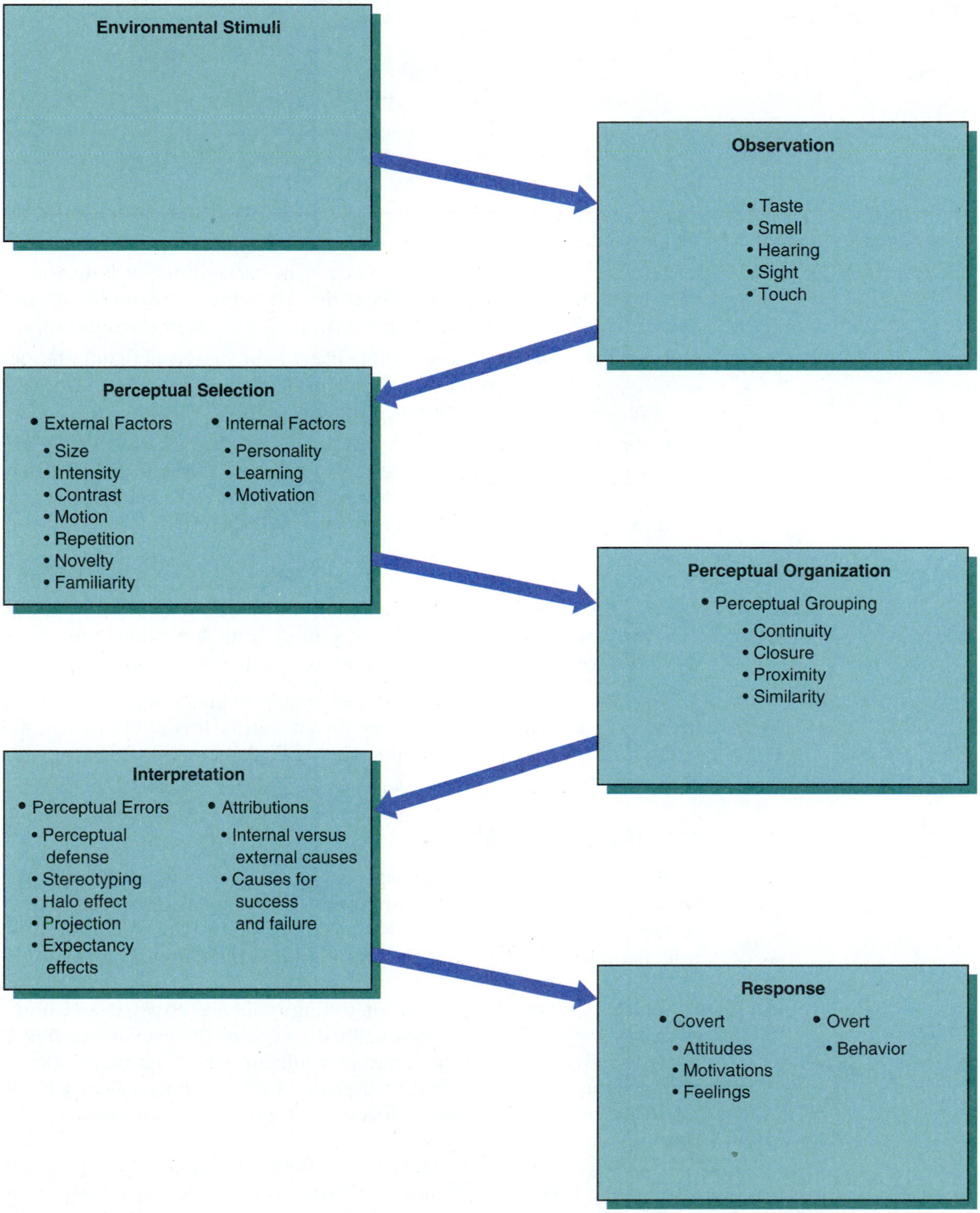

Environmental Stimuli

Observation
- Taste
- Smell
- Hearing
- Sight
- Touch

Perceptual Selection
- External Factors
  - Size
  - Intensity
  - Contrast
  - Motion
  - Repetition
  - Novelty
  - Familiarity
- Internal Factors
  - Personality
  - Learning
  - Motivation

Perceptual Organization
- Perceptual Grouping
  - Continuity
  - Closure
  - Proximity
  - Similarity

Interpretation
- Perceptual Errors
  - Perceptual defense
  - Stereotyping
  - Halo effect
  - Projection
  - Expectancy effects
- Attributions
  - Internal versus external causes
  - Causes for success and failure

Response
- Covert
  - Attitudes
  - Motivations
  - Feelings
- Overt
  - Behavior

■ **FIGURE 3.2**

Contrast Principle of Perception

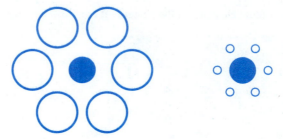

the right appears to be larger because its background, or frame of reference, is composed of much smaller circles. The solid circle on the left appears to be smaller because its background consists of larger surrounding circles.

■ *Motion.* A moving factor is more likely to be perceived than a stationary factor. Soldiers in combat learn this principle very quickly. Video games also demonstrate that motion is quickly detected.

■ *Repetition.* A repeated factor is more likely to be perceived than a single factor. Marketing managers use this principle in trying to get the attention of prospective customers. An advertisement may repeat key ideas, and the ad itself may be presented many times for greater effectiveness.

■ *Novelty and familiarity.* Either a familiar or a novel factor in the environment can attract attention, depending on circumstances. People would quickly notice an elephant walking along a city street. (Both novelty and size increase the probability of perception.) Someone is likely to perceive first the face of a close friend among a group of approaching people.[4]

A combination of these or similar factors may be operating at any time to affect perception. In conjunction with certain internal factors of the person doing the perceiving, they determine whether any particular stimulus is more or less likely to be noticed.

■ INTERNAL FACTORS

Internal perception factors are aspects of the perceiver that influence perceptual selection. Some of the more important internal factors include personality (Chapter 2), learning (Chapter 4), and motivation (Chapter 5). The powerful role that internal factors play in perception manifests itself in many ways.

Personality   Personality has an interesting influence on what and how people perceive. Any of the several personality dimensions that we discussed in Chapter 2, along with numerous other traits, may influence the perceptual process. Under many circumstances, personality appears to affect strongly how an individual perceives other people—the process of *person perception*, which we discuss shortly.[5]

An aspect of the personality called **field dependence/independence** provides insight into the influence of personality on perception. A field-dependent person tends to pay more attention to external environmental cues, whereas a field-independent person relies mostly on bodily sensations. For example, in a test where a subject has to decide whether an object is vertically upright, a field-dependent individual will rely on cues from the environment, such as the corners of rooms, windows, and doors. A field-independent individual will rely mostly on bodily cues, such as the pull of gravity, to make the same judgment. A field-dependent person needs more time to find hidden figures embedded in complex geometric designs than does a field-independent person. A field-dependent person is influenced more by the background or surrounding design than is a field-independent person.

Field dependence/independence has some implications for organizational behavior. For example, compared to a field-dependent employee, a field-independent employee interacts more independently with others. That is, a field-independent employee relies less on cues from others (such as a team leader or supervisor) to identify appropriate interpersonal behavior. In addition, a field-independent employee seems to be more aware of important differences in others' roles, status, and needs.[6]

Learning   Another internal factor affecting perceptual selection is learning, which can lead to the development of perceptual sets. A **perceptual set** is an expectation of a perception based on past experience with the same or similar stimuli. What do you see in Figure 3.3? If you see an attractive, elegantly dressed woman, your perception concurs with the majority of first-time viewers. However, you may agree with a sizable minority and see an ugly, old woman. The woman you see depends on your perceptual set.

In organizations, managers' and employees' past experiences and learning strongly influence their perceptions. For example, studies have indicated that business executives and other decision makers are influenced by their functional backgrounds when making decisions. Thus, under some circumstances, they are likely to frame problems in terms of their own experiences and values. For example, they might perceive their own area of expertise as being the most important to consider when solving certain types of problems. Conversely, studies have also indicated that decision makers can "rise above" their own experiences and limitations, accurately recognizing and effectively solving problems in areas other than their own expertise.[7]

The effects of learning on perception have important implications for organizational behavior. First, managers should avoid overly simplistic assumptions about the abilities of people to process information and make decisions. Internal

■ FIGURE 3.3

Test of Perceptual Set

factors clearly influence and even bias which information managers and employees might pay the most attention to. At the same time, through education and experience, people can overcome perceptual biases. Second, the existence of these biases presents yet another diversity management challenge. That is, employees from different areas of the organization may have trouble working together on task forces and teams because each will tend to see problems and issues from the perspective of their own departments or functions. Thus, in order to be effective, managers and employees must learn how to deal with this type of diversity.

The culture into which a person is born determines many life experiences, and learned cultural differences influence the perceptual process. For example, a study demonstrated differences in perceptions of punctuality among managers in Japan, Mexico, Taiwan, and the United States.[8] On average, U.S. managers would consider a colleague late for an important business meeting after about seven minutes. Managers in the other three countries are somewhat more tolerant of tardiness and would perceive a colleague as late only after about ten or eleven minutes. The following Across Cultures piece examines some other interesting differences in the perception of time in different cultures.

ACROSS CULTURES

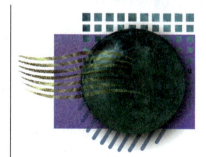

Time Perception

For the traveler or the person attempting to live in another culture, the adjustment to a different perception of time may be quite difficult. An investigation of culture shock among U.S. Peace Corps volunteers revealed that two of the three greatest sources of adjustment difficulties related to perceptions of time: the general pace of life and the punctuality of people.

The general pace at which people live their lives in various cultures has been investigated. One study compared the pace of life in six countries: England, Japan, Indonesia, Italy, Taiwan, and the United States. In each country, researchers collected data from its largest city and one medium-sized city on three measures of the pace or tempo of life.

- *The accuracy of bank clocks.* The researchers checked fifteen clocks in each downtown area and compared the times they showed to a verifiable correct time.

- *The speed at which pedestrians walk.* The researchers timed 100 pedestrians, walking alone, for 100 feet.

- *The length of time needed to purchase a stamp.* The researchers measured the response time to a written request to purchase a commonly used denomination of postage stamp.

Figure 3.4 shows the results of this study. Japanese cities rated the highest on all three measures: They had the most accurate bank clocks, the fastest pedestrians, and the quickest postal clerks. U.S. cities were second in two of the three categories. Indonesian cities had the least accurate clocks and the slowest pedestrians. Italian cities had the slowest postal clerks.

Research thus suggests that a city and a culture have a pace of life that influences people's behaviors. It varies from culture to culture and can be important

—Continued

ACROSS CULTURES—*Continued*

■ FIGURE 3.4

The Pace of Life in Six Countries

Source: Adapted from Levine, R. V. The pace of life. *American Scientist,* September/October, 1990, 453.

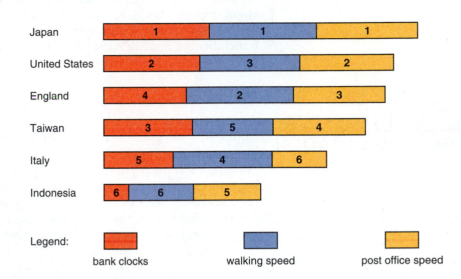

Legend: bank clocks   walking speed   post office speed

Numbers on the chart (1 is the top value) indicate the comparative rankings of cities in each country for each indicator of time sense.

to understanding the perceptions of time in these cultures. Adjusting to a new pace of life is one of the challenges facing employees and managers of multinational corporations when they are transferred from their home country to a foreign assignment.[9]

Motivation   Motivation also plays an important role in determining what a person perceives. A person's most urgent needs and desires at any particular time can influence perception.

For example, imagine that while taking a shower you faintly hear what sounds like the telephone ringing. Do you get out of the shower, dripping wet, to answer it? Or do you conclude that it is only your imagination? Your behavior in this situation may depend on factors other than the loudness of the ringing. If you are expecting an important call, you are likely to leap from the shower. If you aren't expecting a call, you're more likely to attribute the ringing sound to shower noises. Your decision, then, has been influenced by your expectations and motivations.[10]

This example illustrates a significant aspect of perception: Internal factors such as motivation influence the interpretation of sensory information. Similarly, an employee whose firm has just announced the pending layoff of 5000 workers is more sensitive to help-wanted advertisements than is an employee at another firm whose job is not threatened.

In general, people perceive things that promise to help satisfy their needs and that they have found rewarding in the past. They tend to ignore mildly disturbing events (a barking dog) but will perceive dangerous ones (the house being on fire). Summarizing an important aspect of the relationship between motivation and perception is the **Pollyanna principle,** which states that people process pleasant stimuli more efficiently and accurately than they do unpleasant stimuli. For example, an employee who receives both positive and negative feedback during a performance appraisal session may more easily, clearly, and pleasantly remember the positive statements than the negative statements.

PERCEPTUAL ORGANIZATION

Perceptual organization is the process by which people group environmental stimuli into recognizable patterns. In the perceptual process, selection gives way to organization. The stimuli selected for attention now appear as a whole. For example, most people have a mental picture of an object made of wood and having four legs, a seat, a back, and armrests: an image of a chair. Then, when people actually see such an object, they recognize it as a chair. They have organized the incoming information into a meaningful whole.

Much remains to be learned about how the human mind assembles, organizes, and categorizes information.[11] However, certain factors in perceptual organization, such as perceptual grouping, are helpful in understanding perceptual organization. **Perceptual grouping** is the tendency to form individual stimuli into a meaningful pattern by continuity, closure, proximity, and similarity.

Continuity is the tendency to perceive objects as continuous patterns. Continuity is a useful organizing principle, but it may also have negative aspects. For example, the tendency to perceive continuous patterns may result in an inability to perceive uniqueness and detect change. In economic or business forecasting, a common continuity error is to assume that the future will simply reflect current events and trends.

Closure is the tendency to complete an object and perceive it as a constant, overall form. In other words, it is the ability to perceive a whole object, even though only part of the object is evident. Most people somehow perceive the odd-shaped inkblots in Figure 3.5 as a Dalmatian dog walking toward a tree. Someone who had never seen a Dalmatian wouldn't be able to make that closure. People can also organize their perceptions in terms of the closure principle when dealing with ideas and information. For example, a manager facing a complex decision may be able to develop a fairly accurate understanding of the issues even

 FIGURE 3.5

An Example of Closure

Source: Reproduced by permission from Sekuler, R., and Blake, R. *Perception,* 2d ed. New York: McGraw-Hill, 1990, 129.

though some information is lacking. Based on experience and imagination, the manager can fill in the missing pieces needed to make a decision.

The notion of **proximity** suggests that a group of objects may be perceived as related because of their nearness to each other. Employees often perceive other employees working together in a department as a team or unit because of their physical proximity. Suppose that four people on the third floor of a large office building quit their jobs. Even if they did so for completely unrelated reasons, the human resources department may perceive the resignations as a problem on the third floor and examine morale, pay, and working conditions there in an attempt to determine what is wrong.

The concept of **similarity** holds that the more alike objects (or ideas) are, the greater is the tendency to perceive them as a common group. Similarity is very important in most team sports—thus the use of different colors of uniforms by opposing teams. In football, for example, the quarterback must be able to spot an open receiver without a moment's hesitation, which would be extremely difficult (if not impossible) if both teams wore uniforms of the same color. Many organizations, especially those in buildings with open floor plans, color code the partitions and other accessories of each department to define separate functions and responsibilities visually. A company might require visitors to its plant to wear yellow hard hats and employees to wear white hard hats. Employees can then easily identify people who are unfamiliar with everyday safety precautions and routines when they are in work areas.

The ways that individuals organize their perceptions to make sense of their worlds are not something that managers and organizations can safely ignore. The following Managing in Practice account explores the impact that office design, layout, and decor can have on perceptions.

MANAGING IN PRACTICE

Office Design, Layout, and Decor—What Do They Tell You?

Office design—lighting, colors, and arrangement of furnishings and other physical objects—influences the perceptions of customers, suppliers, prospective employees, and visitors. Moreover, the design of their offices may affect employees in various ways. Many managers, though, seem unaware of the relationships between office design and employee perceptions, attitudes, and behaviors.

Office layout—who is located next to whom—influences perceptions of which individuals and functions the organization values most. For example, offices arranged by rank, where the highest level managers occupy the top floors, the most desirable office space, and so on, convey the message that the organization highly values status. By contrast, when Union Carbide moved into new corporate headquarters, all its managers received offices of identical size to emphasize for managers, employees, and visitors alike the importance of equality to the company.

Even the arrangement of furniture influences perceptions of a firm. For example, one study showed that visitors had very different impressions of an organization, depending on whether the chairs in the reception area faced one another or were at right angles to one another. Organizations that placed chairs facing one another were perceived as more "rigid," "tense," and "deliberate" than orga-

—Continued

MANAGING IN PRACTICE—*Continued*

nizations using the right-angle layout for visitor seating. Further, executives visiting the firms where seating was arranged at right angles perceived these organizations as "warmer," "friendlier," and more "comfortable." Significantly, the executive visitors strongly preferred to do business with the "warmer and friendlier" firms.

Finally, office decor influences perceptions. Students perceived that professors who had posters on the wall and plants in their offices were more friendly than professors who didn't display such objects. In organizations, people perceive that items such as flags, corporate logos, and pictures of company officers indicate a highly structured organization in which employees have limited autonomy. People are likely to perceive an organization that displays certificates of achievement, plaques, and trophies as one that values and rewards good performance. Workplace studies consistently show that flowers and plants increase perceptions of warmth and friendliness. Artwork, though, is likely to be tricky. Having art on the walls is generally perceived positively, but the content of some pictures might have the opposite effect. For example, one firm that was having trouble recruiting women discovered that pictures of men on horseback displayed prominently throughout the building gave prospective women employees the impression that the firm was cold, hostile, and generally unfriendly.[12]

PERSON PERCEPTION

Of particular interest in organizational behavior is the process of person or social perception.[13] **Person perception** is the process by which individuals attribute characteristics or traits to other people. It is closely related to the attribution process, which we discuss later in this chapter.[14]

The person perception process is the same as the general process of perception shown in Figure 3.1. That is, the process follows the same sequence of observation, selection, organization, interpretation, and response. However, the object being perceived in the environment is another person. Although perceptions of situations, events, and objects are important, individual differences in perceptions of other people are crucial to understanding behavior in complex social settings. For example, suppose that you meet a new employee. In order to get acquainted and to make him feel at ease, you invite him to lunch. During lunch, he begins to tell you his life history and focuses on his accomplishments. Because he talks only about himself (he asks you no questions about yourself), you may form the impression that he is very self-centered. Later, you may come to see other aspects of his personality, but your perceptions may always be strongly affected by this first impression, which is called the **primacy effect.**

In general, the factors influencing person perception are the same as those that influence perceptual selection. That is, both external and internal factors affect person perception. However, we may usefully categorize factors that influence how a person perceives another as

- characteristics of the person being perceived,
- characteristics of the perceiver, and
- the situation or context within which the perception takes place.

■ THE PERSON PERCEIVED

In perceiving someone else, an individual processes a variety of cues about that person: facial expressions, general appearance, skin color, posture, age, gender, voice quality, personality traits, behaviors, and the like. Some cues may contain important information about the person, but many do not. People seem to have **implicit personality theories** about which physical characteristics, personality traits, and specific behaviors relate to others.[15] Table 3.1 illustrates implicit personality theory in action. People often seem to believe that some voice-quality characteristics indicate that the speaker has certain personality traits. However, you should realize that the relationships contained in Table 3.1 have no real basis. Think about your first contact with someone over the telephone. Later, upon meeting, did that person look and act as you expected?

Implicit personality theories may affect how individuals view, treat, and remember others. At best, the way that people group individual characteristics and personality traits helps them organize their perceptions to understand their worlds better. At worst, implicit personality theories lead to perceptual errors, such as stereotyping (to be discussed shortly).

■ THE PERCEIVER

Listening to an employee describe the personality of a co-worker may tell you as much about the employee's personality as it does about that of the person being described. Does this surprise you? It shouldn't if you recall that factors internal to the perceiver, including personality, learning, and motivation influence perception and that internal factors are particularly important in person perception. A person's own personality traits, values, attitudes, current mood, past experiences, and so on determine, in part, how that person perceives someone else.

Accurately perceiving the personality of an individual raised in another culture often is difficult.[16] For example, Japanese managers in the United States (and U.S. managers in Japan) may face disorienting experiences as they try to learn how to deal with business associates from the other culture.[17] One reason is that the perceiver interprets perceptions of the other person's traits and behavior in light of his or her own cultural experiences, attitudes, and values. Often these factors are inadequate for making accurate judgments about the personality and behavior of people from a different culture.

TABLE 3.1 Personality Judgments on the Basis of Voice Quality

VOICE QUALITY: HIGH IN	MALE VOICE	FEMALE VOICE
Breathiness	Younger, artistic	Feminine, pretty, petite, shallow
Flatness	Similar results for both sexes: masculine, cold, withdrawn	
Nasality	Similar results for both sexes: having many socially undesirable characteristics	
Tenseness	Cantankerous (old, unyielding)	Young, emotional, highstrung, not highly intelligent

Source: Adapted from Hinton, P. R. *The Psychology of Interpersonal Perception.* London: Routledge, 1993, 16.

■ FIGURE 3.6

The Facets of Impression Management

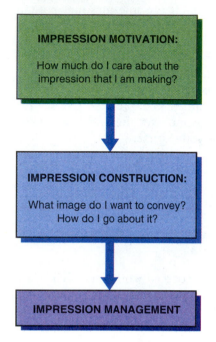

IMPRESSION MOTIVATION:

How much do I care about the impression that I am making?

IMPRESSION CONSTRUCTION:

What image do I want to convey? How do I go about it?

IMPRESSION MANAGEMENT

■ THE SITUATION

The situation or setting also influences how one person perceives another. The situation may be particularly important in understanding first impressions or primacy effects. For example, if you meet someone for the first time and she is with another person that you respect and admire, that may positively influence your assessment of the new acquaintance. But, if she is with someone you dislike intensely, you may form a negative first impression. Of course, these initial perceptions (whether positive or negative) may change over time if you continue to interact with her and get to know her better. Nevertheless, the first impression may continue to color your later perception of the individual.

Thus, in understanding the perceptual process, you have yet another use for the interactionist perspective introduced in Chapter 2. Both person and situation interact to determine how you perceive others.

■ IMPRESSION MANAGEMENT

The use of **impression management** by an individual is an attempt to manipulate or control the impressions that others form about the person.[18]

> We all "put on a show" at times, by using our nonverbal communication to create a deliberate impression. The clothes we choose to wear for an interview or a date, wearing sunglasses even when it's cloudy as it looks "cool," having our hair cut in a certain style, putting on a "telephone voice," feigning interest in a boring lecture given by our instructor, behaving "nicely" when grandparents come to visit; these are all ways of managing impressions.[19]

Impression management has two distinct facets, as Figure 3.6 shows.[20] The first facet, **impression motivation,** concerns the degree to which an individual actively manages the impression he or she makes. Sometimes impression management might be strongly motivated; at other times little or no motivation may exist. For example, someone dressing for a job interview might be acutely conscious of trying to make a favorable impression on an interviewer. But, when meeting old friends, the same person might be far less concerned about the clothing worn.

A second facet in impression management, **impression construction,** refers to an individual's consciously choosing (1) an image to convey, and (2) how to do so. For example, a woman applying for a job as a bank manager might choose to convey stability and conservatism. When interviewing for this position, she probably would wear a conservative business suit. Further, she may rewrite her résumé to emphasize job tenure (to appear stable and dependable) and to omit her skydiving hobby (to not appear reckless).

Impression management provides another example of an individual difference. Some people are preoccupied with impression management; others are less concerned about how they might be perceived. In sum, however, impression management is an important part of understanding person perception. Almost everyone cares about the impression he or she makes on others, at least part of the time.

PERCEPTUAL ERRORS

Because the perceptual process may result in errors in judgment or understanding, we need to consider accuracy of judgment in person perception. We can then examine five of the most common types of perceptual errors: perceptual defense, stereotyping, the halo effect, projection, and expectancy effects.

■ ACCURACY OF JUDGMENT

How accurate are people in their perceptions of others? This question is important in organizational behavior.[21] For example, misjudging the characteristics, abilities, or behaviors of an employee during a performance appraisal review could result in an inaccurate assessment of the employee's current and future value to the firm. Another example of the importance of accurate person perception comes from the employment interview. Many people have long been concerned about errors in judgment and perception that interviewers can easily make when basing employment decisions on information gathered in face-to-face interviews. The following types of interview errors are the most common:

- *Similarity error.* Interviewers are positively predisposed toward job candidates who are similar to them (in terms of background, interests, hobbies, and the like) and negatively biased against job candidates who are unlike them.

- *Contrast error.* Interviewers have a tendency to compare job candidates to other candidates interviewed at the same time, rather than to some absolute standard. For example, an average candidate might be rated too highly if preceded by several mediocre candidates; a candidate might be scored too low if preceded by an outstanding applicant.

- *Overweighting of negative information.* Interviewers tend to overreact to negative information as though looking for an excuse to disqualify a job candidate.

- *Race, sex, and age bias.* Interviewers may be more or less positive about a candidate on the basis of the candidate's race, gender, or age.

- *First-impression error.* The primacy effect previously discussed may play a role in the job interview, as some interviewers are quick to form impressions that are resistant to change.[22]

A good example of first-impression error is presented in the following Managing in Practice selection.

MANAGING IN PRACTICE

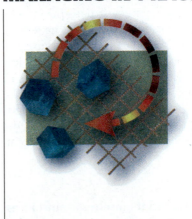

The Fallacy of Instant Insight

John R. Wareham is the founder of Wareham Associates, Inc., an international consulting firm specializing in management selection, evaluation, and development. He was recently interviewed by the editors of *Leaders* magazine. During the interview, Wareham took the position that chief executive officers frequently "get it wrong" when selecting executives and managers for their firms. He argued that some of the selection errors of CEOs stem from making seriously wrong assumptions about people. The interviewer chose to pursue this provocative statement further.

Leaders interviewer: What does the average CEO believe about people that isn't true?

Wareham: For one thing, he believes he can tell how good people are just by

—Continued

MANAGING IN PRACTICE—*Continued*

looking at them. I call this the fallacy of instant insight—the idea that "I'm a pretty good judge of people, and when a person walks into my office, I can sum him up very quickly." In my experience, that's a commonly held belief among many CEOs.

The CEO of a furniture company phoned me recently. He had just employed a person who didn't work out and the CEO asked if I could spend some time with him to analyze where he went wrong. One of the first things that I asked was, "How did you come to hire this individual?"

"I was on the golf course on a Wednesday afternoon," said the CEO, "and so was he. We were paired up for the golf match and we beat everybody. He was an extremely good player, extremely competent. Afterward, we had a few drinks in the clubhouse. He got along with everybody, and I thought to myself: When you find someone like this—an individual who is supercompetent, who gets on with everybody and who, as good fortune would have it, is between jobs—you want to snatch him up immediately instead of asking a whole bunch of questions."

Unfortunately, the CEO had to fire him shortly afterward. The man looked excellent, but he was a hopelessly inept performer. Before acting so quickly, the CEO should have stopped to ask himself a few questions. What was the man doing on a golf course on Wednesday afternoon? It might be OK to be there, but does this reflect a dedicated individual? Perhaps yes, perhaps no. Because he's good at golf, outstanding in fact, does that mean he's equally competent on the job? And just because he gets along well with everybody in the bar, does that mean he'll get on equally well with everybody in the office? When you don't ask the right questions and get the right information, even when you have known an individual for a long time, you can still be completely wrong about him. And you don't really know anyone until that person actually comes to work for you.[23]

There are no easy answers to the general problems of accuracy in person perception. We do know that accuracy in person perception represents another important *individual difference*. That is, some people are quite accurate in judging and assessing others, and some people are extremely inept in doing so. However, people can learn to make more accurate judgments in person perception. Perceptions of others will be more accurate if the perceiver can avoid (1) generalizing from a single trait to many traits; (2) assuming that a single behavior will show itself in all situations; and (3) placing too much reliance on physical appearance. In addition, as person perception is influenced by characteristics of both the perceiver and the situation, accuracy in person perception can be improved when the perceiver understands these potential biases. Unfortunately, the errors that individuals make in person perception (and in other aspects of the perceptual process) are so common that names have been given to some of them.

■ PERCEPTUAL DEFENSE

Perceptual defense is the tendency for people to protect themselves against ideas, objects, or situations that are threatening. A well-known folk song suggests that people hear what they want to hear and disregard the rest. Once established, an individual's way of viewing the world may become highly resistant to change. In the discussion of perceptual selection we noted that people tend to perceive things that are supportive and satisfying and ignore disturbing things. Avoiding unpleasant stimuli often is more than escapism; it may be a sensible defensive device. People can become psychologically deaf or blind to disturbing parts of the environment. Thus employees who really enjoy their work, like most of their colleagues, and are satisfied with their pay, might simply ignore some negative aspect of the work experience (such as an irritating co-worker).

■ STEREOTYPING

Stereotyping is the tendency to assign attributes to someone solely on the basis of a category of people, of which that person is a member.[24] People generally expect someone identified as a doctor, president of a company, or minister to have certain positive attributes, even if they have met some who didn't. A person categorized as a dropout, ex-convict, or alcoholic is automatically perceived negatively. Even identifying an employee by such broad categories as Hispanic, older worker, or female can lead to misperceptions. The perceiver may dwell on certain characteristics expected of everyone in that category and fail to recognize the characteristics that distinguish the person as an individual. For example, disabled workers frequently must overcome stereotypes in order to receive fair consideration for promotion or even to be hired in the first place.[25] The following Diversity in Practice feature identifies some stereotypes common to the work setting.

DIVERSITY IN PRACTICE

Workplace Stereotypes

Managers and employees are often pressured to be aware of major issues involving stereotypes of race and gender. However, other common stereotypes often go unaddressed. The following are several common stereotypes with tips for overcoming them.

- *Techies*—The stereotype: speak in technological tongues, dress poorly, and are shy. To overcome: A well-dressed techie can send a subliminal message that says, I'm not your typical nerd. A more important tactic is to develop good communication skills.

- *MBAs*—The stereotype: are bossy, elitist, and know-it-all. To overcome: Listen and ask questions before issuing orders. Earn respect by involving colleagues in decisions and acknowledging their experience and knowledge.

- *Work–Family Balancers*—The stereotype: are unambitious and can't be counted on in a crisis. To overcome: Make sure projects get done on time. Volunteer for an occasional extra assignment. Rearrange schedules to help out in a crisis.

- *40-plussers*—The stereotype: have less energy and are resistant to change. To overcome: Don't be afraid to deal directly with the age issue. Stress the variety of experiences that you have had and how they relate to the company's needs. Don't try to look younger (inappropriate dress, etc.)—it doesn't work.[26]

■ HALO EFFECT

Evaluation of another person solely on the basis of one attribute, either favorable or unfavorable, is called the **halo effect.** In other words, a halo blinds the perceiver to other attributes that also should be evaluated to obtain a complete, accurate impression of the other person. Managers have to guard against the halo effect in rating employee performance. A manager may single out one trait and use it as the basis for judging all other performance measures. For example, an excellent attendance record may produce judgments of high productivity, quality work, and industriousness, whether they are accurate or not. The CEO who hired the "supercompetent" golfer described in the Managing in Practice feature earlier allowed a halo effect to color his perceptions.

■ PROJECTION

Projection is the tendency for people to see their own traits in other people. That is, they project their own feelings, personality characteristics, attitudes, or motives onto others. This tendency may be especially strong for undesirable traits that perceivers possess but fail to recognize in themselves. For example, employees frightened by rumors of impending organizational changes may not only judge others to be more frightened than they are but may also assess various policy decisions as more threatening than warranted. People whose personality traits include stinginess, obstinacy, and disorderliness tend to rate others higher on these traits than do people who don't have these personality traits.

■ EXPECTANCY EFFECTS

Expectancy effects in the perceptual process are the extent to which prior expectations bias perceptions of events, objects, and people. Sometimes people simply perceive what they anticipate perceiving as indicated in the following dialogue from Shakespeare's *Hamlet.*

> **Polonius**: My lord, the Queen would speak with you, and presently.
> **Hamlet:** Do you see yonder cloud that's almost in the shape of a camel?
> **Polonius**: By th' mass, and 'tis like a camel indeed.
> **Hamlet:** Methinks it is like a weasel.
> **Polonius**: It is back'd like a weasel.
> **Hamlet:** Or like a whale?
> **Polonius**: Very like a whale.
>
> (Act III, scene ii)

Of course, Shakespeare was making a joke about an individual (Polonius) who seemingly would agree with anything to curry favor with the Prince of Denmark (Hamlet). Faced with an ambiguous stimulus (in this case, a cloud), however, many individuals could be led to expect to see a particular object, and this expectation would color their perceptions.

Expectancy effects may also bias perception even in less ambiguous situations. For example, your perception of a committee to which you have been assigned recently may be positive if your supervisor told you that the committee's work is important and that it will be staffed by talented people from several departments. However, your perception may be negative if she told you that the committee exists solely for political reasons and contains some real deadwood from other departments. You might also perceive identical behavior by other members of the committee quite differently under each set of expectations. Earlier we noted that past experiences and learning are important to the perceptual process. As a result, people often approach situations expecting certain things to happen or other people to have certain attributes. These expectations may strongly influence their perceptions of reality.

Another aspect of expectancy effects is the **self-fulfilling prophecy.** Expecting certain things to happen shapes the behavior of the perceiver in such a way that the expected is more likely to happen. For example, a team leader who has been led to believe that a new employee has great potential might do two things: (1) she might assess the employee's performance as being better than it really is (an expectancy effect); and (2) she might behave toward the new employee in such a way (for example, by providing encouragement or additional training) that the new employee's performance is, in fact, very good (a self-fulfilling prophecy).

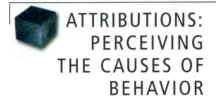

ATTRIBUTIONS: PERCEIVING THE CAUSES OF BEHAVIOR

The **attribution process** refers to the ways in which people come to understand the causes of others' (and their own) behaviors.[27] Attributions play an important role in the process of person perception. Attributions made about the reasons for someone's behavior may affect judgments about that individual's fundamental characteristics or traits (what he or she is really like). Note the attributions made in the following Managing in Practice account.

MANAGING IN PRACTICE

Searching for Causes of Job Applicant Behavior

Christie Johnson decided that she wanted to discuss the job candidates further and attempt to pin down the reasons for their applications. She called the interviewers together to review the files one final time.

"I don't think Richard Thomas would be suitable," said Linda Herrera. "Many of his answers sounded very pat. Our clients would be put off if he's too slick." "It could have been because he was nervous," suggested Kent Smith. "He might be very different on the job." "Well," said Christie, who had Thomas's résumé in front of her, "Don't forget that he's worked for Albanese & Hitt for several years. He must be pretty good with the clients." "So, why is he leaving now?" asked Linda, unconvinced. "Maybe they are trying to get rid of him. He said he wanted a new challenge," answered Christie. "And we would be paying him more than Albanese & Hitt." "It could be, I suppose," said Linda slowly.

"What about the others?" asked Christie. "I was quite impressed with Mary Pat Slavic," said Kent. Now it was Christie's turn to be unconvinced. "I didn't find her very dynamic. Also she's earning the same money as we're offering already. And she would be working longer hours with us." "It could mean that she's really interested," suggested Kent. "Or that she has some other reason. Isn't her company having a rough time? She could be trying to get out while the getting is good," observed Linda. "Possibly," answered Kent, "I've heard the rumors. Still, I don't think that should enter into our decision." "But," Linda persisted, "It could
—*Continued*

MANAGING IN PRACTICE—*Continued*

mean that she's willing to settle for anything to get out and might not stay with us very long. She's not really committed to our position."

"What about David Cohen?" asked Christie. "It is a natural progression from his current job," answered Kent. "And he's been there a few years. It's the right time for him to move on." "But, he didn't seem to have a natural friendliness," interrupted Linda. "He hardly looked at me and sounded rather abrupt."

The others nodded in agreement. . . . And so the discussion went on long past quitting time, as Christie Johnson and her staff explored the characteristics and motivations of the applicants.[28]

The attributions that employees and managers make concerning the causes of behavior are important in understanding organizational behavior. For example, managers who attribute poor performance directly to their subordinates tend to behave more punitively than managers who attribute poor performance to circumstances beyond their subordinates' control. A manager who believes that an employee failed to perform a task correctly because she lacked proper training might be understanding and give the employee better instructions or training. The same manager might be quite angry if he believes that a subordinate made mistakes simply because the subordinate didn't try very hard. The relationship between attributions and behavior will become clearer as we examine the attribution process.

■ THE ATTRIBUTION PROCESS

Basically, people make attributions in an attempt to understand the behavior of other people and to make better sense of their environments. Individuals don't consciously make attributions in all circumstances (although they may do so unconsciously much of the time).[29] However, under certain circumstances, people are likely to make causal attributions consciously. For example, causal attributions are common in the following situations.

- The perceiver has been asked an explicit question about another's behavior. (Why did Anna do that?)

- An unexpected event occurs. (I've never seen him behave that way. I wonder what's going on?)

- The perceiver depends on another person for a desired outcome. (I wonder why my boss made that comment about my expense account?)

- The perceiver experiences feelings of failure or loss of control. (I can't believe I failed my midterm exam!)

Figure 3.7 presents a basic model of the attribution process. People infer "causes" to behaviors they observe in others, and these interpretations often largely determine their reactions to those behaviors. The perceived causes of behavior reflect several antecedents: (1) the amount of information the perceiver has about the people and the situation and how that information is organized by the perceiver; (2) the perceiver's beliefs (implicit personality theories, what other people might do in a similar situation, and so on); and (3) the motivation of the perceiver (for example, the importance to the perceiver of making an accurate

■ FIGURE 3.7

The Attribution Process

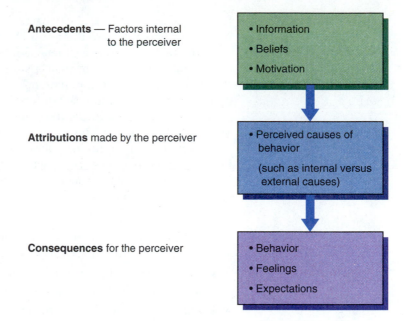

Antecedents — Factors internal to the perceiver
- Information
- Beliefs
- Motivation

Attributions made by the perceiver
- Perceived causes of behavior

  (such as internal versus external causes)

Consequences for the perceiver
- Behavior
- Feelings
- Expectations

assessment). Recall our discussion of internal factors that influence perception—learning, personality, and motivation. These same internal factors influence the attribution process. The perceiver's information and beliefs depend on previous experience and are influenced by the perceiver's personality.

Based on information, beliefs, and motives, the perceiver often distinguishes between internal and external causes of behavior; that is, whether people did something because of a real desire or because of the pressure of circumstances. The assigned cause of the behavior—whether internal or external—helps the perceiver attach meaning to the event and is important for understanding the subsequent consequences for the perceiver. Among the consequences of this attribution process are the subsequent behavior of the perceiver in response to the behavior of others, the impact on feelings or emotions (how the perceiver now feels about events, people, and circumstances), and the effects on the perceiver's expectations of future events or behavior.

■ INTERNAL VERSUS EXTERNAL CAUSES OF BEHAVIOR

Imagine the following scene in a busy department. Hector Gallegos, the office manager, and Jan DiAngelo, a section head for accounts receivable, are arguing loudly in Gallegos's private office. Even though they had closed the door before starting their discussion, their voices have gotten louder until everyone else in the office has stopped working and is staring in discomfort and embarrassment at the closed door. After several minutes, DiAngelo jerks open the door, yells a final, unflattering remark at Gallegos, slams the door, and stomps out of the department.

Anyone observing this scene is likely to wonder about what is going on and make certain attributions about why DiAngelo behaved the way she did. On the one hand, attributions regarding her behavior could focus on internal causes: She gets mad easily because she has a bad temper; she behaves this way because she is immature and doesn't handle pressure well; or she isn't getting her work done, and Gallegos called her on the carpet for it. On the other hand, attributions could focus on external causes: She behaves this way because Gallegos provoked her; or both their behaviors are the result of unreasonable workloads imposed on the department by top management. Some of the individuals who witnessed the events may perceive more than a single cause in such an interaction. Also, as should be clear by now, different individuals in the department are likely to interpret the events they witnessed differently.

A central question in the attribution process concerns how perceivers determine whether the behavior of another person stems from internal causes (such as personality traits, emotions, motives, or ability) or external causes (other people, the situation, or chance). A widely accepted model proposed by Harold Kelley attempts to explain how people determine why others behave as they do.[30] This explanation states that in making attributions, people focus on three major factors:

- *consistency*—the extent to which the person perceived behaves in the same manner on other occasions when faced with the same situation;
- *distinctiveness*—the extent to which the person perceived acts in the same manner in different situations; and
- *consensus*—the extent to which others, faced with the same situation, behave in a manner similar to the person perceived.[31]

As Figure 3.8 suggests, under conditions of high consistency, high distinctiveness, and high consensus, the perceiver will tend to attribute the behavior of the person perceived to external causes. When distinctiveness and consensus are low, the perceiver will tend to attribute the behavior of the person to internal causes. Of course, other combinations of high and low consistency, distinctiveness, and consensus are possible. Some combinations, however, may not provide the perceiver with a clear choice between internal and external causes.

Note that consistency is high under both attribution outcomes in Figure 3.8. When consistency is low, the perceiver may attribute the behavior to either internal or external causes, or both. For example, imagine that a candidate running for the U.S. Senate gives a speech in favor of gun control while campaigning in Washington, D.C., and then speaks in opposition to gun control when addressing the

■ **FIGURE 3.8**　　Kelley's Theory of Causal Attributions

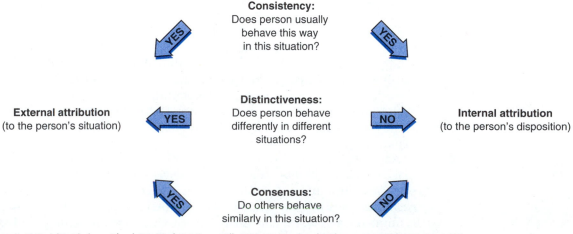

Source: Myers, D. G. *Social Psychology,* 4th ed. New York: McGraw-Hill, 1993, 77. Reprinted with permission from McGraw-Hill.

National Rifle Association. In this case, an observer might make either internal attributions (such as a character flaw "causes" the politician to tell these people what he thinks they want to hear) or external attributions (such as the audience "causes" the politician to change his speech), or both.

In the example of the argument between Gallegos and DiAngelo, an observer would likely attribute causation to DiAngelo if others typically do not have similar arguments with Gallegos (low consensus) and DiAngelo often has similar arguments with others in various work situations (low distinctiveness). But, if other individuals frequently have run-ins with Gallegos (high consensus) and DiAngelo seldom has arguments in other situations with her fellow employees (high distinctiveness), observers may attribute her behavior to external causes (in this case, Gallegos). You may want to reread this paragraph while examining Figure 3.8 to make sure that you understand the differences that lead to either internal or external attributions of behavior.

With regard to internal versus external causes of behavior, observers often make what is known as the **fundamental attribution error.** This type of error is the tendency to underestimate the impact of situational or external causes of behavior and to overestimate the impact of personal or internal causes of behavior when seeking to understand why people behave the way they do.[32] In organizations, employees often tend to assign blame for conflict (Chapter 12), political behavior (Chapter 9), or resistance to change (Chapter 18) to the individuals involved and fail to recognize the effects of the dynamics of the situation. For example, a CEO might attribute a high level of political behavior on the part of his vice-presidents to aspects of their personalities, not recognizing that competition for scarce resources is causing much of the political behavior.

Some cultural differences exist in the fundamental attribution error. For example, in North America, this type of error would be as just described (underestimating external causes and overestimating internal causes). In India, however, evidence indicates that the more common attribution error is to overestimate situational or external causes for the observed behavior.[33] This variance may reflect the way that people view personal responsibility or differences in "average" locus of control beliefs in the two societies.

The fundamental attribution error isn't the only bias that can influence judgments concerning internal versus external causes of behavior. A study of supervisors showed that they were more likely to attribute effective performance to internal causes for high-status employees and less likely to attribute success to internal causes for low-status employees. Similarly, supervisors were more likely to attribute ineffective performance to internal causes for low-status employees and less likely to attribute failure to internal causes for high-status employees.[34]

■ ATTRIBUTIONS OF SUCCESS AND FAILURE

The attributions that employees and managers make regarding success or failure in task performance are very important. Managers may base decisions about rewards and punishments on their perceptions of why subordinates have succeeded or failed at some task. In general, individuals often attribute their own (and others') success or failure to four causal factors: ability, effort, task difficulty, and luck.

■ I succeeded (or failed) because I had the skills to do the job (or because I did not have the skills to do the job). Such statements are ability attributions.

- I succeeded (or failed) because I worked hard (or because I did not work hard). Such statements are effort attributions.
- I succeeded (or failed) because it was easy (or because it was too hard). Such statements are attributions about task difficulty.
- I succeeded (or failed) because I was lucky (or unlucky). Such statements are attributions about luck or the circumstances surrounding the task.[35]

Causal attributions of ability and effort are internal, and causal attributions of task difficulty and luck are external. These attributions about success or failure reflect differences in self-esteem and locus of control—personality dimensions discussed in Chapter 2.[36] For example, individuals with high self-esteem and high internal locus of control are likely to assess their own performance positively and to attribute their good performance to internal causes.

The organizational importance of these success and failure attributions is demonstrated by research in hospitals that examined the feedback provided to nurses by their managers.[37] When the managers perceived that poor performance was the result of lack of effort, their feedback messages to nurses tended to be punitive or negative in tone. Their attributions also affected the specific content of the feedback. When the managers inferred that poor performance reflected lack of ability, their messages to nurses focused on instructions for doing the job better; when they thought that poor performance meant lack of effort, their messages to nurses tended to stress orders to be followed. Thus the managers' attributions about the reasons for performance failures by staff nurses influenced their communications behavior, as suggested by the model of the attribution process shown in Figure 3.7.

Not surprisingly, many people attribute their successes to internal factors (ability or effort) and attribute their failures to external factors (task difficulty or luck). This tendency is known as a **self-serving bias.** The tendency of employees to accept responsibility for good performance but to deny responsibility for poor performance often presents a serious challenge for supervisors during performance appraisals. A self-serving bias may also create other types of problems. For example, it prevents individuals from accurately assessing their own performance and abilities and makes more difficult determining why a manager's course of action has failed. The general tendency to blame others for a person's own failures often is associated with poor performance and inability to establish satisfying interpersonal relationships at work and in other social settings.[38] In general, a version of the self-serving bias seems to operate when people are asked to compare themselves to others in the work setting. That is, managers and employees often view themselves to be more ethical, more effective, better performing, and so on, than the "average" other person.

CHAPTER SUMMARY

Perception is the psychological process whereby people select information from the environment and organize it to make sense of their worlds. Two major components of the perceptual process are selection and organization. People use perceptual selection to filter out less important information in order to focus on more important environmental cues. Both external factors in the environment and factors internal to the perceiver influence perceptual selection. Perceptual organization represents the process by which people assemble, organize, and categorize information from the environment. This process groups environmental stimuli into recognizable patterns (wholes) that allow people to interpret what they perceive.

How people perceive each other is particularly important for understanding organizational behavior. Person perception is a function of the characteristics of the person perceived, the characteristics of the perceiver, and the situation within which the perception takes place. People may go to great lengths to manage the impressions that others form about them. Unfortunately, the perceptual process may result in errors of judgment or understanding, such as in denying the reality of disturbing information or by assigning attributes to someone solely on the basis of some category or group to which the person belongs. Fortunately, through training and experience, individuals can learn to judge or perceive others more accurately.

Attribution deals with the perceived causes of behavior. People infer causes for the behavior of others, and their perceptions of why certain behaviors occur influences their own subsequent behavioral responses and feelings. Whether behavior is internally caused by the nature of the person or is externally caused by circumstances is an important attribution that people make about the behaviors of others. Individuals also make attributions concerning task success and failure, which have important implications for organizational behavior.

KEY TERMS AND CONCEPTS

Attribution process	Impression management	Pollyanna principle
Closure	Impression motivation	Primacy effect
Continuity	Perception	Projection
Expectancy effects	Perceptual defense	Proximity
Field dependence/independence	Perceptual grouping	Self-fulfilling prophecy
Fundamental attribution error	Perceptual organization	Self-serving bias
Halo effect	Perceptual selection	Similarity
Implicit personality theories	Perceptual set	Stereotyping
Impression construction	Person perception	

DISCUSSION QUESTIONS

1. Explain the concepts of perceptual selection and perceptual organization.

2. What are the factors that determine the probability that some stimulus will be perceived?

3. Give an example from your own experience of when people seemed to interpret the same situation differently. Why did they do so?

4. What are the key factors in person perception?

5. Provide two examples of impression management from your own experiences. Did it work in either case? Explain.

6. What are the most common perceptual errors?

7. From your own experience, provide an example of perceptual errors. What was the outcome of the situation?

8. What perceptual errors by managers could create special problems in their evaluation of subordinates' job performance? In their evaluation of job applicants?

9. How can a person determine whether someone else's behavior represents what he or she is truly like or simply reflects the circumstances of the situation?

10. What is the fundamental attribution error? Provide an example—either from your own experience or something you have read—of when an observer apparently made the fundamental attribution error.

11. What attributions did you make following either success or failure at some task?

12. Provide two real examples of the occurrence of a self-serving bias.

■ Developing Competencies

Self-Insight: Measuring Perceptions of Women as Managers

Gender role stereotypes limit the opportunity for women to advance to managerial positions in many firms. Although these stereotypes are slowly changing, the attitudes toward women as managers held by many individuals present a barrier to career opportunities for many women.

Because specific attitudes and stereotypes can be pervasive and powerful influences on behavior, considering their role in the treatment—by both men and other women—of women in managerial positions is important. Attitudes about the managerial abilities of women may affect how a manager or executive judges a woman's performance in a managerial role. In addition, such attitudes may influence the granting or withholding of developmental opportunities. The following questionnaire is designed to help you explore your attitudes toward women as managers.

Instructions

From each set (of three) statements, select the one with which you *most agree* and place an M (for "most agree") in the blank to the right of that statement. For each set, also select the statement with which you *least agree* and place an L (for "least agree") in the blank to the right of that statement. Note that one statement in each set will not be chosen.

1. **A.** Men are more concerned with the cars they drive than with the clothes their wives wear. _____

   B. Any man worth his salt should not be blamed for putting his career above his family. _____

   C. A person's job is the best single indicator of the sort of person he is. _____

2. **A.** Parental authority and responsibility for discipline of the children should be divided equally between the husband and the wife. _____

   B. It is less desirable for women to have jobs that require responsibility than for men. _____

   C. Men should not continue to show courtesies to women, such as holding doors open for them and helping them with their coats. _____

3. **A.** It is acceptable for women to assume leadership roles as often as men. _____

   B. In a demanding situation, a female manager would be no more likely to break down than would a male manager. _____

   C. There are some professions and types of businesses that are more suitable for men than for women. _____

4. **A.** Recognition for a job well done is less important to women than it is to men. _____

   B. A woman should demand money for household and personal expenses as a right rather than a gift. _____

   C. Women are temperamentally fit for leadership positions. _____

5. **A.** Women tend to allow their emotions to influence their managerial behavior more than men. _____

   B. The husband and the wife should be equal partners in planning the family budget. _____

   C. If both husband and wife agree that sexual fidelity is not important, there is no reason why both should not have extramarital affairs. _____

6. **A.** A man's first responsibility is to his wife, not to his mother. _____

   B. A man who is able and willing to work hard has a good chance of succeeding in whatever he wants to do. _____

   C. Only after a man has achieved what he wants from life should he concern himself with the injustices in the world. _____

7. **A.** A wife should make every effort to minimize irritations and inconveniences for the male head of the household. _____

   B. Women can cope with stressful situations as effectively as men can. _____

   C. Women should be encouraged not to become sexually intimate with anyone, even their fiancés, before marriage. _____

8. **A.** The "obey" clause in the marriage service is insulting to women. _____

   B. Divorced men should help to support their children but should not be required to pay alimony if their former wives are capable of working. _____

   C. Women have the capacity to acquire the necessary skills to be successful managers. _____

9. **A.** Women can be aggressive in business situations that demand it. _____

   B. Women have an obligation to be faithful to their husbands. _____

   C. It is childish for a woman to assert herself by retaining her maiden name after marriage. _____

10. **A.** Men should continue to show courtesies to women, such as holding doors open for them or helping them with their coats.

B. In job appointments and promotions, females should be given equal consideration with males. _____

C. It is all right for a wife to have an occasional, casual, extramarital affair. _____

11. A. The satisfaction of her husband's sexual desires is a fundamental obligation of every wife. _____

B. Most women should not want the kind of support that men traditionally have given them. _____

C. Women possess the dominance to be successful leaders. _____

12. A. Most women need and want the kind of protection and support that men traditionally have given them. _____

B. Women are capable of separating their emotions from their ideas. _____

C. A husband has no obligation to inform his wife of his financial plans. _____

Score your responses by using the form and following the instructions given. Your total score indicates your feelings about women managers. The higher your score, the more prone you are to hold negative gender role stereotypes about women in management. Possible total scores range from 10 to 70; a "neutral" score (one that indicates neither positive nor negative attitudes about women as managers) is in the range of 30 to 40.[39]

Instructions

1. Record your response for the indicated items in the spaces provided.

2. On the basis of the information provided, determine the points for each item and enter these points in the space provided to the right. For example, if in item 3, you chose alternative A as the one with which you *most* agree and alternative B as the one with which you *least* agree, you should receive three points for item 3. Note that items 1 and 6 are "buffer items" and are not scored.

3. When you have scored all ten scorable items, add the points and record the total at the bottom of this page in the space provided. That is your total score.

YOUR RESPONSE	ITEM NO.	POINTS PER ITEM RESPONSE*							Points
		1		3		5		7	
	1	Not Scored							
M ____	2	C(M)	A(M)	C(M)	A(M)	B(M)	B(M)		
L ____		B(L)	B(L)	A(L)	C(L)	A(L)	C(L)		
M ____	3	A(M)	A(M)	B(M)	C(M)	B(M)	C(M)		
L ____		C(L)	B(L)	C(L)	B(L)	A(L)	A(L)		
M ____	4	C(M)	C(M)	A(M)	B(M)	A(M)	B(M)		
L ____		B(L)	A(L)	B(L)	A(L)	C(L)	C(L)		
M ____	5	C(M)	C(M)	B(M)	A(M)	B(M)	A(M)		
L ____		A(L)	B(L)	A(L)	B(L)	C(L)	C(L)		
	6	Not Scored							
M ____	7	B(M)	B(M)	C(M)	A(M)	C(M)	A(M)		
L ____		A(L)	C(L)	A(L)	C(L)	B(L)	B(L)		
M ____	8	C(M)	C(M)	A(M)	B(M)	A(M)	B(M)		
L ____		B(L)	A(L)	B(L)	A(L)	C(L)	C(L)		
M ____	9	A(M)	A(M)	C(M)	B(M)	C(M)	B(M)		
L ____		B(L)	C(L)	B(L)	C(L)	A(L)	A(L)		
M ____	10	B(M)	B(M)	C(M)	A(M)	C(M)	A(M)		
L ____		A(L)	C(L)	A(L)	C(L)	B(L)	B(L)		
M ____	11	C(M)	C(M)	B(M)	A(M)	B(M)	A(M)		
L ____		A(L)	B(L)	A(L)	B(L)	C(L)	C(L)		
M ____	12	B(M)	B(M)	C(M)	A(M)	C(M)	A(M)		
L ____		A(L)	C(L)	A(L)	C(L)	B(L)	B(L)		
								Total____	

*M indicates item chosen as "most"; L indicates item chosen as "least."

Organizational Insight: Fudge the Numbers or Leave

It was just after she was yelled at—the sound echoing off the walls of the huge, nearly empty conference room—that Sara recalled the most lasting image from her initial meeting with Kristin Cole seven weeks prior: the crows feet that jetted out of the corners of Kristin's eyes when she became angry. On that day, the two had just sat down for an initial meeting when they were interrupted by a phone call. Kristin's crows feet came out as she masked a flash of intense anger as she talked with the caller. No frown, just a forced smile and those creases cracking like lightning as she hurled a verbal spear to wound the person at the other end of the line.

Now, Sara sensed too late that storm clouds were forming once more, only this time around her. Her new boss was ordering her to do something that caught her by surprise, something that she felt would be terribly wrong. "Do I need to repeat myself, Sara? We have too much at stake here; just make the numbers work!" Sara felt an anxiety attack coming on as she noticed the wrinkle lines deepening around the corners of Kristin's eyes. The meeting had grown into a nightmarish spiral toward panic.

Sara joined MicroPhone—a large telecommunications company with headquarters in Denver—almost two months ago to take over the implementation of a massive customer service training project. The program, lodged in human resources, was rumored to be a favorite of the CEO and was created by Kristin. Industry competition was heating up and the strategies of the company called for being the very best at customer service. That translated into having the most highly trained people in the industry, especially those who would work directly with customers.

Two months ago, Kristin formed a crash team in human resources to develop a new training program that could address those needs. It called for an average of one full week of intense, highly effective training for each of three thousand people, and it had a price tag in the neighborhood of $40 million. Kristin's team—made up of several staffers who already felt overwhelmed with their day-to-day workload—rushed to put the proposal together. It was scheduled to go to the company's board of directors in December.

Kristin needed someone well qualified and dedicated just to manage and implement the project. Sara had eight years of experience, a list of great accomplishments and advanced business degrees in finance and organizational behavior. But perhaps what Kristin failed to see in Sara was the quiet moral compass that she invariably followed, even at risk to her own welfare.

When Sara agreed to come aboard, Kristin expressed her relief and confidence in Sara's ability to make the program work. And those closest to Kristin believed she was hoping this project alone would give her the "star quality" needed to earn a promotion from Jack Davies, a charismatic chief executive who had told her he was pleased with her plans thus far.

But six weeks ago, Sara was asked to look over the plan. "I don't think you'll find any major problems," Kristin said. "Just tidy it up for submission to the guys over at strategic planning. They'll take a look at it before it goes to the board." Sara's first cursory review turned up a few inconsistencies. Kristin's unspoken reaction to Sara's findings seemed odd, as if she were secretly harboring the thought, "You located some mistakes. I hate you for finding them."

When Sara conducted a second and more thorough review, she found some assumptions, built into the formulas of the proposal, that raised red flags. She asked Dan Sotal, the project's team coordinator, about her concerns. The more he tried to explain how the financial projections were derived, the more Sara realized Kristin's proposal was seriously flawed.

But no matter how she tried to work them out, the most that could be squeezed out of the $40 million budget was twenty hours of training a week per person, not forty, as everyone had expected under such a high price tag.

Today was the day Sara was to discuss her review with Kristin, a consultant, and one other human resources staff member. She knew that despite the fact that this proposal was largely developed before she came on board, it would bear her signature. She carefully walked everyone through what she described as significant problems with the program and its potentially devastating consequences. Kristin tapped her pencil on the marble tabletop for a few minutes before she stood up, leaned forward, and interrupted Sara, quietly saying, "Sara, make the numbers work so that is adds up to forty hours and stays within the $40 million figure."

Sara looked up at her and said, "It can't be done unless we either change the number of employees who are to be trained or the cost figure. . . ." Kristin's smile moved into place and the crows feet around the corners of her eyes deepened as she again interrupted: "I don't think you understand what I'm saying: Make the previous numbers work!"

Stunned, Sara belatedly began to realize just what was being asked of her. Kristin adjusted her glasses and continued her cold stare at Sara. The other two people at the meeting sat frozen in their chairs, while Sara wondered what she should do.[40]

Questions

1. Make a list of the possible differences in perceptions between Sara and Kristin.

2. What attributions would you expect Sara to make about Kristin's behavior?

3. What attributions would you expect Kristin to make about Sara's behavior?

4. If you were Sara, what would you do now?

REFERENCES

1. Banks, W. P., and Krajicek, D. Perception. *Annual Review of Psychology*, 1991, 42, 305–331; Bertenthal, B. I. Origins and early development of perception, action, and representation. *Annual Review of Psychology*, 1996, 47, 431–459; Sekuler, R., and Blake, R. *Perception*, 2d ed. New York: McGraw-Hill, 1990.

2. Adapted from Parker-Pope, T. British Budweiser ads rankle American Indians. *Wall Street Journal*, July 16, 1996, B1, B5.

3. Kinchla, R. A. Attention. *Annual Review of Psychology*, 1992, 43, 711–742.

4. Barber, P. *Applied Cognitive Psychology*. London: Methuen, 1988, 35–66.

5. Hogan, R. T. Personality and personality measurement. In M. D. Dunnette and L. M. Hough (eds.), *Handbook of Industrial and Organizational Psychology*, 2d ed., vol. 2. Palo Alto, Calif.: Consulting Psychologists Press, 1991, 886–891.

6. McBurney, D. H., and Collings, V. B. *Introduction to Sensation/Perception*, 2d ed. Englewood Cliffs, N.J.: Prentice-Hall, 1984, 327–345.

7. Dearborn, D., and Simon, H. A. Selective perception: A note on the departmental identifications of executives. *Sociometry*, 1958, 21, 140–144; Walsh, J. P. Selectivity and selective perception: An investigation of managers' belief structure and information processing. *Academy of Management Journal*, 1988, 31, 873–896; Waller, M. J., Huber, G. P., and Glick, W. H. Functional background as a determinant of executive's selective perception. *Academy of Management Journal*, 1995, 38, 943–974.

8. Dorfman, P. W. et al. Perceptions of punctuality: Cultural differences and the impact of time perceptions on job satisfaction and organizational commitment. Paper presented at the Pan Pacific Conference, Beijing, China, June 8–10, 1993.

9. Based on Levine, R. V. The pace of life. *American Scientist*, September/October, 1990, 450–459; Levine, R. V., and Wolff, E. Social Time: The heartbeat of culture. *Psychology Today*, March 1985, 28–35.

10. Example drawn from Sekuler and Blake, 16.

11. Roitblat, H. L., and von Fersen, L. Comparative cognition: Representations and processes in learning and memory. *Annual Review of Psychology*, 1992, 43, 671–710; Squire, L. R., Knowlton, B., and Musen, G. The structure and organization of memory. *Annual Review of Psychology*, 1993, 44, 453–495.

12. Based on Ornstein, S. The hidden influences of office design. *Academy of Management Executive*, 1989, 3, 144–147; Ornstein, S. Impression management through office design. In R. A. Giacalone and T. Rosenfeld (eds.), *Impression Management in the Organization*. Hillsdale, N.J.: Lawrence Erlbaum, 1989, 411–426.

13. See, for example, Ashforth, B. E., and Humphrey, R. H. Labeling processes in the organization: Constructing the individual. In L. L. Cummings and B. M. Staw (eds.), *Research in Organizational Behavior*, 1995, 17, 413–461.

14. Hamilton, D. L., and Sherman, S. J. Perceiving persons and groups. *Psychological Review*, 1996, 103, 336–355; Fiske, S. T. Social cognition and social perception. *Annual Review of Psychology*, 1993, 44, 155–194.

15. Baron, R. M., Graziano, W. G., and Stangor, C. *Social Psychology*. Fort Worth: Holt, Rinehart, and Winston, 1991, 122–123.

16. Bond, M. H., and Smith, P. B. Cross-cultural social and organizational psychology. *Annual Review of Psychology*, 1996, 47, 205–235; Zebrowitz-McArthur, L. Person perception in cross-cultural perspective. In M. H. Bond (ed.), *The Cross-Cultural Challenge to Social Psychology*. Newbury Park, Calif.: Sage, 1988, 245–265.

17. Linowes, R. G. The Japanese manager's traumatic entry into the United States: Understanding the American–Japanese cultural divide. *Academy of Management Executive*, 1993, 7, 21; Thomas, D. C., and Ravlin, E. C. Responses of employees to cultural adaptation by a foreign manager. *Journal of Applied Psychology*, 1995, 80, 133–146.

18. Schlenker, B. R., and Weigold, M. F. Interpersonal processes involving impression regulation and management. *Annual Review of Psychology*, 1992, 43, 133–168; Stevens, C. K., and Kristof, A. L. Making the right impression: A field study of applicant impression management during job interviews. *Journal of Applied Psychology*, 1995, 80, 587–606; Wayne, S. J., and Liden, R. C. Effects of impression management on performance ratings: A longitudinal study. *Academy of Management Journal*, 1995, 38, 232–260.

19. Hinton, P. R. *The Psychology of Interpersonal Perception*. London: Routledge, 1993, 23.

20. Leary, M. R., and Kowalski, R. M. Impression management: A literature review and two-component model. *Psychological Bulletin*, 1990, 107, 34–47.

21. DePaulo, B. M., Kenny, D. A., Hoover, C. W., Webb, W., and Oliver, P. V. Accuracy of person perception: Do people know what kinds of impressions they convey? *Journal of Personality and Social Psychology*, 1987, 52, 303–315; Funder, D. C. On the accuracy of personality judgment: A realistic approach. *Psychological Review*, 1995, 102, 652–670; Kenny, D. A., and DePaulo, B. M. Do people know how others view them? An empirical and theoretical account. *Psychological Bulletin*, 1993, 114, 145–161; Kruglanski, A. W. The psychology of being right: The problem of accuracy in social perception and cognition. *Psychological Bulletin*, 1989, 106, 395–409.

22. Fisher, C. D., Schoenfeldt, L. F., and Shaw, J. B. *Human Resource Management*, 3d ed. Boston: Houghton Mifflin, 1996, 326–327.

23. Adapted from Wareham, J. R. *Leaders*, April, May, June 1996, 182–183.

24. Hilton, J. L., and von Hippel, W. Stereotypes. *Annual Review of Psychology,* 1996, 47, 237–271.

25. Stone, D. L., and Colella, A. A model of factors affecting the treatment of disabled individuals in organizations. *Academy of Management Review,* 1996, 21, 352–401.

26. Adapted from Lancaster, H. You can battle petty stereotypes in the workplace. *Wall Street Journal,* March 5, 1996, B1.

27. Baron, R. A., and Byrne, D. *Social Psychology: Understanding Human Interaction,* 6th ed. Boston: Allyn & Bacon, 1991, 55–83; Harvey, J. H., and Wells, G. (eds.). *Attribution: Basic Issues and Applications.* New York: Academic Press, 1988, 282–311; Myers, D. G. *Social Psychology,* 4th ed. New York: McGraw-Hill, 1993, 74–108.

28. Adapted from Hinton, 138.

29. Azar, B. Influences from the mind's inner layers. *The APA Monitor,* February, 1996, 1, 25.

30. Kelley, H. H. The process of causal attribution. *American Psychologist,* 1973, 28, 107–128.

31. For explanations of Kelley's model see Baron and Byrne, 57–64; Hinton, 143–146.

32. Myers, 78–80.

33. Miller, J. G. Culture and the development of everyday causal explanation. *Journal of Personality and Social Psychology,* 1984, 46, 961–978.

34. Heneman, R. L., Greenberger, D. B., and Anonyus, C. Attributions and exchanges: The effects of interpersonal factors on the diagnosis of employee performance. *Academy of Management Journal,* 1989, 32, 466–476.

35. Babladelis, G. *The Study of Personality.* New York: Holt, Rinehart and Winston, 1984, 76.

36. Levy, P. E. Self-appraisal and attributions: A test of a model. *Journal of Management,* 1993, 19, 51–62.

37. Kim, Y. Y., and Miller, K. I. The effects of attributions and feedback goals on the generation of supervisory feedback message strategies. *Management Communication Quarterly,* 1990, 4, 6–29.

38. Tennen, H., and Affleck, G. Blaming others for threatening events. *Psychological Bulletin,* 1990, 108, 209–232.

39. Adapted from Yost, E. B., and Herbert, T. T. Attitudes toward women as managers. In L. D. Goodstein and J. W. Pfeiffer (eds.), *The 1985 Annual: Developing Human Resources.* San Diego, Calif.: University Associates, 1985, 117–127. Reprinted with permission.

40. Wallace, D. Fudge the numbers or leave. *Business Ethics,* May/June 1996, 58–59. Reprinted with permission from *Business Ethics Magazine,* 52 S. 10th St. #110, Minneapolis, MN 55403. 612/962-4700.

4

Learning and Reinforcement

LEARNING OBJECTIVES

When you have finished studying this chapter, you should be able to:

- Explain the differences among classical, operant, and social-cognitive theory.
- Describe the contingencies of reinforcement.
- List the methods used to increase desired behaviors and reduce undesired behaviors.
- Describe the process and principles of behavioral modification.
- Identify the ethical issues in behavioral modification.

OUTLINE

PREVIEW CASE

Viking Freight

Federal deregulation of the trucking industry created a fiercely competitive market among freight companies. Trucking firms learned that superior employee performance and productivity are the main factors in maintaining their competitive edge. At Viking Freight, one key to developing an effective work force is to compensate employees for superior performance through an incentive pay program that rewards achievement of Viking's goals. Under this plan, employees can earn a maximum of 7.5 percent of their gross pay for a four-week period; supervisors, 11.2 percent; salespeople, 12.5 percent; department managers, 15 percent; and terminal managers, 20 percent when Viking's goals are met.

At each of Viking's forty-seven freight terminals, goals for all employees are based on market conditions and individual performance. Viking's operating ratio, defined as operating expenses divided by revenues before interest and taxes, determines whether incentive payments are made. If the ratio falls below 95 percent for a four-week period, no payouts are made, regardless of performance levels. Performance data are gathered weekly and distributed to employees throughout the company every Monday. Data are presented in easy-to-read bar charts that show performance goals, achievements, and areas needing improvement. Employees at each terminal are encouraged to share ideas about how to improve its performance.[1]

Viking's efficiency is based on specific principles drawn from an area of psychology called learning theory. The **learning theory** approach stresses the assessment of behavior in objective, measurable (countable) terms.[2] Behavior must be publicly observable, which de-emphasizes unobservable, inner, cognitive behavior. In this chapter, we explore the development, maintenance, and change of employee work behaviors, using principles derived from learning theory.

Desirable work behaviors contribute to achieving organizational goals; conversely, undesirable work behaviors hinder achieving these goals. Labeling behavior as *desirable* or *undesirable* is entirely subjective and depends on the value system of the person making the assessment. For example, a team member at Whirlpool's refrigerator assembly line who returns late from a coffee break exhibits undesirable behavior from the manager's viewpoint, desirable behavior from the viewpoint of friends with whom the worker chats during the break, and desirable behavior from the worker's viewpoint because of the satisfaction of social needs.

The work setting and organizational norms are more objective bases for determining whether a behavior is desirable or undesirable. The more a behavior deviates from organizational norms, the more undesirable it is. At Southwest Airlines, undesirable behavior includes anything that results in lost baggage and late departures and arrivals. Norms vary considerably from one organization to another. For example, at Nortel's research and development laboratory, engineers and scientists are encouraged to question top management's directives because professional judgment is crucial to the organization's success in the telecommunications market. A military organization, however, would consider such questioning to be insubordination and justification for severe disciplinary action.

Effective managers do not try to change employees' personalities or basic beliefs. Rather, they focus on identifying observable employee behaviors and the environmental conditions that affect these behaviors. They then attempt to control external events in order to influence employee behavior. As we discussed in Chapters 2 and 3, an individual's personality and attitudes influence behavior. Because uncovering these characteristics in employees often is difficult, focusing on behaviors that others can observe usually is better.

TYPES OF LEARNING

Learning is a relatively permanent change in the frequency of occurrence of a specific individual behavior.[3] In an organization, a manager wants employees to learn and practice productive work behaviors. To a great extent, learning new work behaviors depends on environmental factors. The manager's goal, then, is to provide learning experiences in an environment that will promote employee behaviors desired by the organization. In the work setting, learning can take place in one of three ways: classical conditioning, operant conditioning, and according to social-cognitive theory. Of the three, operant conditioning and social-cognitive theory are most helpful in understanding the behaviors of others.

■ CLASSICAL CONDITIONING

Classical conditioning is the process by which individuals learn to link the information value from a neutral stimulus to a stimulus that would not naturally cause a response. This learned response may not be under an individual's conscious control.[4] Examples of stimuli and responses, or **reflexive behavior,** are shown in Table 4.1. In the classical conditioning process, an unconditioned stimulus (environmental event) brings out a natural response. Then a neutral environmental event, called a conditioned stimulus, is paired with the unconditioned stimulus that brings out the behavior. Eventually, the conditioned stimulus alone brings out the behavior which is called a conditional response.

The name most frequently associated with classical conditioning is Ivan Pavlov, the Russian physiologist whose experiments with dogs led to the early formulations of classical conditioning theory. In Pavlov's famous experiment, the sound of a metronome (the conditioned stimulus) was paired with food (the unconditioned stimulus). The dogs eventually exhibited a salivation response (conditioned response) to the sound of the metronome alone. The classical conditioning process is shown in Figure 4.1.

The process of classical conditioning can help you understand a variety of behaviors that occur in everyday organizational life. At Baylor Hospital's emergency room, special lights in the hallway indicate that a patient who needs treatment has just arrived. Nurses and other hospital staff report that they feel nervous when the lights go on. In contrast, at a recent luncheon in the organization's din-

---

TABLE 4.1 **Examples of Reflexive Behavior**

STIMULUS(S)	RESPONSE(R)
The Individual	
■ is stuck by a pin and	flinches.
■ is shocked by an electric current and	jumps or screams.
■ has something in an eye and	blinks.
■ hits an elbow on the corner of a desk and	flexes arm.

■ **FIGURE 4.1**

Classical Conditioning

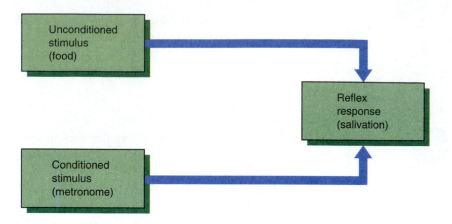

ing room, Linda Seatvet, Manager of Finance at Frito-Lay, was thanked by Farr Fakheri, a friend, for introducing a new work system. Now whenever Seatvet sees the dining room, she feels good.

Organizations spend billions of dollars on advertising campaigns designed to link the information value of a stimulus to customer purchase behavior. In a TV ad Duracell Corporation has successfully created a link between its battery and a pink bunny. The pink bunny is the unconditioned stimulus and the battery is the conditioned stimulus. The positive feelings that buyers have toward the pink bunny are associated with the battery, which Duracell hopes will lead buyers to purchase its batteries. Similarly, McDonald's has linked its jingle, "You deserve a break today," with eating at its restaurants. That is, when people hear the jingle (unconditioned stimulus), they associate it with McDonald's. Associating the upbeat mood created by the jingle with McDonald's is intended to lead customers into its restaurants. Both organizations have successfully used the concepts of classical conditioning to increase sales of their products.

Classical conditioning is probably relatively unused in work settings. The reason is that desired employee behaviors usually don't include responses that can be changed with classical conditioning techniques. There is greater interest in the voluntary behaviors of employees and how they can be changed. We discuss the process of learning voluntary behaviors later in this chapter.

■ OPERANT CONDITIONING

The person most closely linked with this type of learning is B. F. Skinner.[5] He coined the term **operant conditioning** to refer to a process by which individuals learn voluntary behavior. Voluntary behaviors are called operants because they operate, or have some influence, on the environment. Learning occurs from the consequences of behaviors. Many employee work behaviors are operant behaviors. In fact, most behaviors in everyday life (such as talking, walking, reading, or working) are forms of operant behavior. Table 4.2 shows some examples of operant behaviors and their consequences.

Managers are interested in operant behaviors because they can influence, or manage, the results of such behaviors. For example, the frequency of an employee behavior can be increased or decreased by changing the results of that behavior. The crucial aspect of operant conditioning is what happens as a consequence of the behavior. The strength and frequency of apparently conditioned behaviors

TABLE 4.2 Examples of Operant Behaviors and Their Consequences

BEHAVIORS	CONSEQUENCES
The Individual	
■ works and	is paid.
■ is late to work and	is docked pay.
■ enters a restaurant and	eats.
■ enters a football stadium and	watches a football game.
■ enters a grocery store and	buys food.

are determined mainly by consequences. Thus managers must understand the effects of different kinds of consequences on the task behaviors of employees. At Viking, one consequence of a driver's wasting ten minutes at each stop is to have to work an hour and ten minutes more that day to deliver freight.

■ SOCIAL-COGNITIVE THEORY

Albert Bandura and others have extended and expanded Skinner's work by demonstrating that people can learn new behavior by watching others in a social situation and then imitating their behavior.[6] According to the **social-cognitive theory** of learning, people watch others and develop mental pictures of their behaviors and the results. They then try the behaviors; if the results are positive, they repeat the behaviors; if the results are negative, they don't repeat the behaviors. Bandura suggested that observers can often learn faster than those who do not observe the behaviors of others because they don't need to unlearn behaviors and can avoid needless and costly errors.

Social-cognitive theory integrates modeling, symbolism, and self-control. As suggested in Figure 4.2, the three factors that promote social-cognitive learning are vicarious learning, self-control, and self-efficacy.

Vicarious learning occurs when one person (the learner) observes another person's (the model's) behavior and its consequences (rewards or punishments). For the learning to be effective, several conditions must be met.

■ The learner must observe the model when the behavior is being performed.

■ The learner must accurately perceive the model's behavior.

■ The learner must remember the behavior.

■ The learner must have the skills and abilities necessary to perform the behavior.

■ The learner must observe that the model receives rewards for the behavior.

Numerous self-help videos rely on vicarious learning principles. For example, someone wanting to learn how to play golf or improve his or her game can buy videos made by various golf professionals, including Jack Nicklaus and Nancy Lopez. By observing the professional's swing, for example, the learner can form and retain a mental image of that swing. Such mental images can help the learner use the proper stance, approach, and follow-through the next time he or she practices or plays a round of golf.

■ **FIGURE 4.2**   Social-Cognitive Learning Model

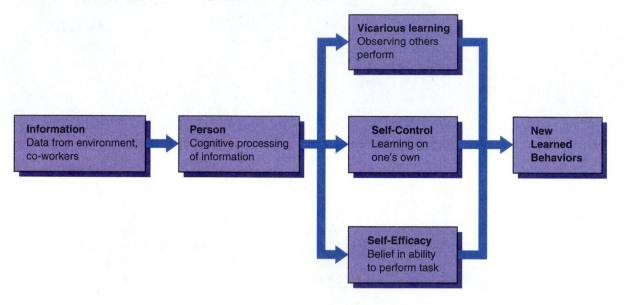

Sears, JC Penney, Wal-Mart, and Home Depot, among other retailers, use vicarious learning to train new salespeople. During formal training sessions, recruits observe the actions of others—both right and wrong behaviors. They also view videos of highly successful salespeople as they give quality customer service and gracefully handle customer inquiries. For such videos to be effective, the learner must observe the model's being rewarded. A reward could simply be having a customer say, thank you, or receiving praise from a manager or fellow employee. By watching experienced salespeople, the recruit is likely to learn appropriate job-related behaviors.

Social-cognitive theory also states that people can learn on their own by exercising **self-control**.[7] Self-control learning occurs when a new behavior is learned even though there is no external pressure to do so. Billie Boyd, an administrative assistant at Southern Methodist University, had a new software package for graphics on her desk for a month. She knew that she had to learn how to use it even though her supervisor hadn't put any pressure on her to do so. She worked Saturdays on her own to learn this new technique. Boyd's goal was to learn to use the software to produce figures for this book. Her approach exhibited self-control.

Most people engage in self-control to learn behaviors on and off the job. Mundane tasks, such as learning how to use e-mail, to more complex tasks, such as preparing to give a subordinate a performance appraisal, can be learned. When an employee learns through self-control, managers don't need to be controlling because the employee takes responsibility for learning and performing the desired behaviors. In fact, if a manager exercises control, it may well be redundant and counterproductive.

At the General Motors Saturn plant, self-control empowers employees to do their jobs better. **Empowerment** means giving employees the authority, skills, and freedom to perform their tasks.[8] The following Managing in Practice feature illustrates how Saturn promoted the use of self-control to empower its employees.

MANAGING IN PRACTICE

Empowerment—The Saturn Way

When General Motors built its new Saturn plant it also redesigned the jobs of employees and managers. This approach entailed permitting the employees to plan their own work; giving them the training, tools, and support they need to do their new jobs; and insisting that managers let employees make more decisions. Working in teams, employees make their own job assignments, plan their work, design their jobs, perform any maintenance necessary on their equipment, select new employees to join their teams, and control their own levels of materials and inventories. Because empowerment without skills and abilities doesn't work, Saturn team members get 320 hours (eight weeks!) of training during their first year and 92 hours annually thereafter. This training not only includes how to fasten bolts and position doors, but it also provides employees with important interpersonal skills.[9]

The third aspect of social-cognitive theory is the concept of self-efficacy. **Self-efficacy** refers to the individual's confidence in their ability to perform a specific task in a particular situation.[10] The greater the perceived ability to perform the task, the higher the employee's self-efficacy will be. Employees with high self-efficacy believe that (1) they have the ability needed, (2) they are capable of the effort required, and (3) no outside events will keep them from performing at a high level. If employees have low self-efficacy, they believe that no matter how hard they try, something will happen to prevent them from reaching the desired level of performance. Self-efficacy influences people's choices of tasks and how long they will spend trying to reach their goals.[11] For example, a novice golfer who has taken only a few lessons might shoot a good round. Under such circumstances, the golfer might attribute the score to "beginner's luck" and not to ability. But, after many lessons and hours of practice, a person with low self-efficacy who still can't break 100 may decide that the demands of the game are too great to justify spending any more time on it. However, a high self-efficacy individual will try even harder to improve his or her game. This effort might include taking more lessons, watching videotapes of the individual's own swing, and practicing even harder and longer.

Self-efficacy affects learning in three ways.

- *Self-efficacy influences the activities and goals individuals choose for themselves.* In a sales contest at Pier 1, salespeople with low self-efficacy didn't set challenging, or "stretch" goals. These people weren't lazy; they simply thought that they would fail to achieve a lofty goal. The high self-efficacy salespeople thought that they were capable of achieving high-performance goals— and did so.

- *Self-efficacy influences the effort that individuals exert on the job.* Individuals with high self-efficacy work hard to learn new tasks and are confident that their efforts will be rewarded. Low self-efficacy individuals lack confidence in their ability to succeed and see their extra effort as futile because they are likely to fail anyway.

- *Self-efficacy affects the persistence with which a person stays with a complex task.* Because high self-efficacy people are confident that they will perform well, they are likely to persist in spite of obstacles or in the face of temporary set-backs. At Frito-Lay, low-performing employees were more likely than high-performing employees to dwell on obstacles hindering their ability to do the task. When people believe that they aren't capable of doing the required work, their motivation to do the task will be low.

What are some sources of self-efficacy that managers can use to help employees learn to believe in themselves? Past experience is the most powerful influence on self-efficacy. At work, the challenge is to create situations in which the employee may respond successfully to the task(s) required. A manager's expectations about a subordinate's behavior also can affect a person's self-efficacy. If a manager holds high expectations for the employee and provides proper training and suggestions, the person's self-efficacy is likely to increase. Small successes boost self-efficacy and lead to more substantial accomplishments later. If a manager holds low expectations for the employee and gives little constructive advice, the employee is likely to form an impression that he or she cannot achieve the goal and, as a result, perform poorly.

Guidelines for using social-cognitive theory to improve behavior in organizations are just starting to emerge.[12] They include the following.

- Identify the behaviors that will lead to improved performance.
- Select the appropriate model for employees to observe.
- Be sure that employees are capable of meeting the technical skill requirements of the required new behaviors.
- Structure a positive learning situation to increase the likelihood that employees will learn the new behaviors and act accordingly.
- Provide positive consequences (praise, raises, or bonuses) to employees who perform in the expected manner.
- Develop organizational practices that maintain these newly learned behaviors.

PepsiCo uses social-cognitive theory to meet the challenges of global competition and maintain its annual growth rate of 17 percent. Chief Executive Officer Wayne Calloway believes that the company needs to train and then assign employees to PepsiCo outlets (Frito-Lay, Pizza Hut, KFC, and Pepsi Cola) around the world. To prepare employees for such assignments and ensure common values, PepsiCo created a Designate Program. This program also helps PepsiCo manage cultural diversity by bringing non-U.S. employees to the United States for a period of time for specialized training in the domestic PepsiCo system, as described in the following Across Cultures piece.

ACROSS CULTURES

PepsiCo's Designate Program

Individuals are selected for this program by their division managers because of significant potential in three areas: (1) their ability to handle business complexities; (2) their ability to lead and manage people; and (3) their belief that they can achieve high sales goals. Furthermore, all non-U.S. employees must agree before starting the program to return to their home countries after completing the program.

—*Continued*

ACROSS CULTURES—*Continued*

What behaviors are stressed? First, employees should listen carefully to what others say, giving recognition to or sharing recognition with others. Teamwork is important. Second, employees should focus on business issues rather than personal issues when giving others feedback on their performance. Although cultural differences are important, sticking to business issues is more important. The goal is to learn business behaviors that transcend cultural beliefs. Through video tapes and working with a trainer, the participants learn how to confront differences openly, stay focused under pressure, act with maturity and good judgment, jointly set goals with others, and judge their own and others' performance in meeting those goals.[13]

In the next section, we return to operant conditioning, or the idea that behavior is influenced by its consequences. It is the most widely used theory of learning and has organizational implications for designing effective reward systems. To understand this theory fully requires a review of its basic elements.

CONTINGENCIES OF REINFORCEMENT

A **contingency of reinforcement** is the relationship between a behavior and the preceding and following environmental events that influence that behavior. A contingency of reinforcement consists of an antecedent, a behavior, and a consequence.[14]

An **antecedent** precedes and is a stimulus to a behavior. The probability that a particular behavior will occur can be increased by presenting or withdrawing a particular antecedent. At Viking, each driver prepares a daily "to do" list. As an antecedent, this list helps the drivers organize their tasks and focus their attention on the specific behaviors required.

A **consequence** is the result of a behavior, which can be either positive or negative in terms of goal or task accomplishment. The manager's response to the employee is contingent on the consequence of the behavior (and sometimes on the behavior itself, regardless of consequence). The consequence for the Viking drivers is completing their tasks on time to help meet the corporation's goals.

Figure 4.3 shows an example of contingent reinforcement. First, the employee and manager jointly set a goal (say, selling $100,000 worth of equipment next month). Next, the employee performs tasks to achieve this goal (such as calling on four new customers a week, having regular lunches with current buyers, and attending a two-day training program on new methods of selling). If the employee reaches the sales goal, the manager praises the employee—an action contingent on achievement of the goal. If the employee fails to reach the goal, the manager doesn't say anything or reprimands the employee.

The contingency of reinforcement concept involves three main types of contingency. First, an event can be presented (applied) or withdrawn (removed), contingent on employee behavior. The event also may be positive or aversive. **Positive events** are desirable, or pleasing, to the employee. **Aversive events** are undesirable, or displeasing, to the employee. Figure 4.4 shows how these events can be combined to produce four types of contingencies of reinforcement. It shows whether a particular type of contingency is likely to increase or decrease

■ FIGURE 4.3   **Example of Contingent Reinforcement**

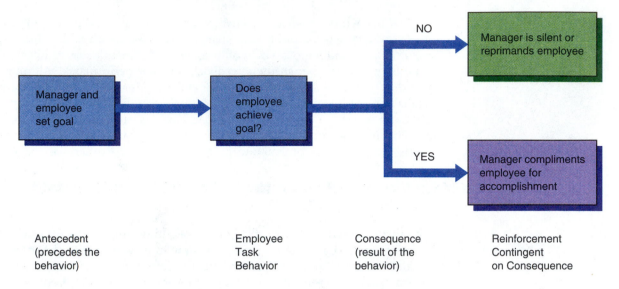

| Antecedent (precedes the behavior) | Employee Task Behavior | Consequence (result of the behavior) | Reinforcement Contingent on Consequence |

the frequency of the behavior. It also is the basis for the following discussion of contingencies of reinforcement. **Reinforcement** is a behavioral contingency that increases the frequency of a particular behavior that it follows. Note that reinforcement, whether positive or negative, always increases the frequency of the employee behavior. Omission and punishment always decrease the frequency of the employee behavior.

■ POSITIVE REINFORCEMENT

Positive reinforcement entails presenting a pleasant consequence after the occurrence of a desired behavior. That is, a manager rewards an employee's behavior that is desirable in terms of achieving the organization's goals.

Reinforcement versus Reward   The terms reinforcement and reward are often confused in everyday usage. A **reward** is an event that a person finds desirable or pleasing. Thus whether a reward acts as a reinforcer is subjective to the individual. A manager who singles out and praises an employee in front of co-workers for finding an error in the group's report believed that the desired behavior was being reinforced. Later, however, the manager learned that the employee was given the silent treatment by co-workers and had stopped looking for errors.

Thus, to qualify as a reinforcer, a reward must increase the frequency of the behavior it follows. Recall that at Viking drivers can earn 7.5 percent more money if they reach their goals and thereby help the organization reach its goals. The extra money can be regarded as a positive reinforcer for a particular individual only if the frequency of desired behavior (in this case, high performance) increases. A reward doesn't act as a reinforcer if the frequency of the behavior decreases or remains unchanged.

Primary and Secondary Reinforcers   A **primary reinforcer** is an event for which the individual already knows the value. Food, shelter, and water are primary reinforcers. However, primary reinforcers don't always reinforce. For example, food may not be a reinforcer to someone who has just completed a five-course meal.

■ FIGURE 4.4

**Types of Contingencies
of Reinforcement**

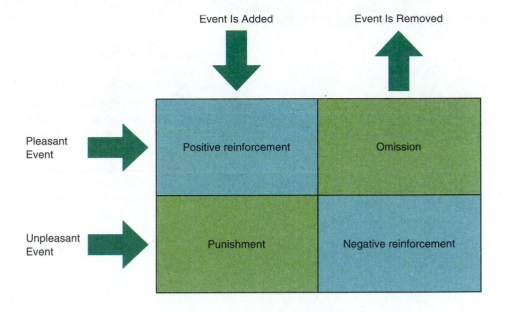

Most behavior in organizations is influenced by secondary reinforcers. A **secondary reinforcer** is an event that once had neutral value but has taken on some value (positive or negative) for an individual because of past experience. Money is an obvious example of a secondary reinforcer. Although it can't directly satisfy a basic human need, money has value because an individual can use it to purchase both necessities and discretionary items. Calvert, a Bethesda Maryland financial firm, groups its secondary reinforcers into three categories: *core benefits*, such as life insurance, sick leave, holiday pay, and a retirement savings plan; *optional benefits*, such as dental and eye-care coverage, and spending accounts for health and dependent care; and *other benefits*, such as tuition reimbursement, car pooling, and career planning.[15]

The following Quality in Practice feature highlights Prudential Insurance Company's use of secondary reinforcers to improve the health of its employees. Prudential designed a wellness program that encourages a healthy lifestyle, focuses on preventive health care, and trains employees in programs that they can use.

QUALITY IN PRACTICE

Prudential Makes Wellness Work

Prudential Insurance Company started a wellness program for its 190 employees at its headquarters in Newark, New Jersey. This program was designed to give employees the tools they needed to maintain a healthy lifestyle. Each person was assigned a fitness category, as defined by the American Heart Association, prior to starting the program. The company provided smoke-free offices, low-cholesterol food in the cafeteria, removed all cigarette and candy machines from the headquarters building, established free aerobics classes, and purchased weight equipment. Employees also were assigned trainers to help them learn the proper way to exercise. A committee of fifteen employees initially examined medical claims,

—Continued

QUALITY IN PRACTICE—*Continued*

health appraisals, and other data to determine employee health levels. As part of the program, the committee meets once a month to update and review these data.

To provide an incentive for participants, employees earn points for watching videos and attending exercise classes, going to HealthFit seminars, and recruiting additional employees for the program. Points may be turned in for prizes quarterly or at the end of the year. The value of the prizes increases with the level of points—from water bottles to tennis balls to beach towels to shorts.

The results of the program have been tremendous. Employees' fitness improved, their average sick days dropped by 20 percent, and medical claims fell by 46 percent in eighteen months. In the annual disability and major medical costs per participant averaged $120.60, compared to $353.88 before the company started the wellness program.[16]

Principles of Positive Reinforcement   Several factors influence the effectiveness of positive reinforcement. These factors can be thought of loosely as principles because they help explain optimum reinforcement conditions.[17]

The **principle of contingent reinforcement** states that the reinforcer must be administered only if the desired behavior is performed. A reinforcer administered when the desired behavior has not been performed is ineffective.

The **principle of immediate reinforcement** states that the reinforcer will be most effective if administered immediately after the desired behavior has occurred. The more time that elapses after the behavior occurs, the less effective the reinforcer will be.

The **principle of reinforcement size** states that the larger the amount of reinforcer delivered after the desired behavior, the more effect the reinforcer will have on the frequency of the desired behavior. The amount, or size, of the reinforcer is relative. A reinforcer that may be significant to one person may be insignificant to another person. Thus the size of the reinforcer must be determined in relation both to the behavior and the individual.

The **principle of reinforcement deprivation** states that the more a person is deprived of the reinforcer, the greater effect it will have on the future occurrence of the desired behavior. However, if an individual recently has had enough of a reinforcer and is satiated, the reinforcer will have less effect.

■ ORGANIZATIONAL REWARDS

What types of rewards do organizations commonly use? Material rewards—salary, bonuses, fringe benefits, and so on—are obvious. However, most organizations offer a wide range of rewards, many of which aren't immediately apparent. They include verbal approval, assignment to desired tasks, improved working conditions, and extra time off. At Toyota's Camry assembly plant in Georgetown, Kentucky, management rewards employees for kaizens. A **kaizen** is a suggestion that results in safety, cost, or quality improvements.[18] The awards are distributed equally among all members of a team. The awards are not cash payments; rather, they are gift certificates redeemable at local retail stores. Toyota learned that an award that could be shared by the employees' families was valued more than extra money in the paycheck. Kaizens instill pride and encourage other employees to scramble for new ideas and products in the hope that they, too, will get awards. In addition, self-administered rewards are important. For example, self-congratulation for accomplishing a particularly difficult assignment can be an important personal reinforcer. Table 4.3 contains an extensive list of organizational rewards. Remember, however, that any of these rewards will act as a reinforcer only if the individual receiving the reward finds it desirable or pleasing.

The Seattle Times Company, publisher of the *Seattle Times* newspaper, recently received the Optima Award from the Society of Personnel Administrators for management of its diversity program. The following Diversity in Practice account highlights the programs that the company undertook to reward diversity initiatives by its managers and employees.

DIVERSITY IN PRACTICE

Seattle Times

Imagine trying to create a diverse workplace without knowing anything about the people you work with. As true in other industries, minority representation in the nation's newsrooms is less than 11 percent, and nearly half the country's daily papers don't employ any minorities at all. However, minorities now make up about 24 percent of the total U.S. population. Although reporters know something of the subjects about which they write, they often perpetuate stereotypes and inadvertently neglect the needs of, and stories of interest to, many readers.

In 1992, the editor of the *Seattle Times* stated that it needed to change how it served the public and how employees related to each other. The company established departmental employment goals and timetables to ensure that its work force reflected the diversity of Seattle. It also established a review cycle and procedures for evaluating departmental accomplishments and instituted programs to achieve a high level of employee awareness of cultural and other differences.

The newspaper holds a two-day mandatory training session, called Exploration into Diversity, for all managers. During the program, the importance of diversity awareness is discussed. After the training session, the company offers two-hour follow-up sessions every other month. Managers do not qualify for promotion unless they have successfully completed this training and are rated by others for encouraging diversity in their departments. This rating is done through an anonymous survey of employees. The manager's pay is linked to the ability to attract and retain a diverse work force.

Editors are encouraged to give reporters space to write stories focusing on diversity issues. Aly Colon, a native of Puerto Rico, wrote an article entitled "Speechless in Seattle," which detailed how people reacted to him as he walked around Seattle. The purpose of the story was to encourage other reporters and the citizens of Seattle to pay more attention to diversity issues. Based on his work and that of others, the paper now helps local teachers deal with current diversity issues in a weekly column, The Times Puts Diversity Talks on Common Ground. The column focuses on the personal or human element of stories.

As a result of these and other initiatives, the paper's daily circulation has increased by 15 percent, and the company has reduced its turnover rate to less than the industry average.[19]

TABLE 4.3 Rewards Used by Organizations

MATERIAL REWARDS	SUPPLEMENTAL BENEFITS	STATUS SYMBOLS
Pay	Company automobiles	Corner offices
Pay raises	Health insurance plans	Offices with windows
Stock options	Pension contributions	Carpeting
Profit sharing	Vacation and sick leave	Drapes
Deferred compensation	Recreation facilities	Paintings
Bonuses/bonus plans	Child care support	Watches
Incentive plans	Club privileges	Rings
Expense accounts	Parental leave	Private restrooms

SOCIAL/INTER-PERSONAL REWARDS	REWARDS FROM THE TASK	SELF-ADMINISTERED REWARDS
Praise	Sense of achievement	Self-congratulation
Developmental feedback	Jobs with more responsibility	Self-recognition
Smiles, pats on the back, and other nonverbal signals	Job autonomy/self-direction	Self-praise
Requests for suggestions	Performing important tasks	Self-development through expanded knowledge/skills
Invitations to coffee or lunch Wall plaques		Greater sense of self-worth

■ NEGATIVE REINFORCEMENT

In **negative reinforcement** (see Figure 4.4), an unpleasant event that precedes the employee behavior is removed when the desired behavior occurs. This procedure increases the likelihood that the desired behavior will occur. Negative reinforcement is sometimes confused with punishment because both use unpleasant events to influence behavior. However, negative reinforcement is used to increase the frequency of a desired behavior, whereas punishment is used to decrease the frequency of an undesired behavior.

Managers frequently use negative reinforcement when an employee hasn't done something that is necessary or desired. For example, air-traffic controllers want the capability to activate a blinking light and a loud buzzer in the cockpits of planes that come too close to each other. The air-traffic controllers wouldn't shut these devices off until the planes moved farther apart. This type of procedure is called **escape learning** because the pilots begin to move their planes away from each other in order to escape the light and buzzer. In escape learning, an unpleasant event occurs until an employee performs a behavior, or escape response, to terminate it.

Avoidance is closely related to escape. In **avoidance learning**, a person prevents an unpleasant event from occurring by completing the proper behavior. For example, after several frustrating encounters with a computer program, you will learn the commands needed to avoid the computer's error messages. Escape and avoidance are both types of negative reinforcement that increase desired behaviors and remove unpleasant events.

■ OMISSION

Omission is the removal of all reinforcing events. Whereas reinforcement increases the frequency of a desirable behavior, omission decreases the frequency and eventually extinguishes an undesirable behavior (see Figure 4.4). Managers use omission to reduce undesirable employee behaviors that prevent achievement of organizational goals. The omission procedure consists of three steps:

1. identifying the behavior to be reduced or eliminated,
2. identifying the reinforcer that maintains the behavior, and
3. stopping the reinforcer.

Omission is a useful technique for reducing and eventually eliminating behaviors that disrupt normal work flow. For example, a group reinforces the disruptive behavior of a member by laughing at the behavior. When the group stops laughing (the reinforcer), the disruptive behavior will diminish and ultimately stop.

Omission can also be regarded as a failure to reinforce a behavior positively. In this regard, the omission of behaviors may be accidental. If managers fail to reinforce desirable behaviors, they may be using omission without recognizing it. As a result, the frequency of desirable behaviors may inadvertently decrease.

Omission may effectively decrease undesirable employee behavior, but it doesn't automatically replace the undesirable behavior with desirable behavior. Often when omission is stopped, the undesirable behavior will return if alternative behaviors haven't been developed. Therefore, when omission is used, it should be combined with other methods of reinforcement to develop the desired behaviors.

■ PUNISHMENT

Punishment (see Figure 4.4) is an unpleasant event that follows a behavior and decreases its frequency. As in positive reinforcement, a punishment may include a specific antecedent that cues the employee that a consequence (punisher) will follow a specific behavior. Whereas a positive contingency of reinforcement encourages the frequency of a desired behavior, a contingency of punishment decreases the frequency of an undesired behavior.

To qualify as a punisher, an event must decrease the undesirable behavior. Just because an event is thought of as unpleasant, it isn't necessarily a punisher. The event must actually reduce or stop the undesired behavior before it can be defined as a punisher.

Organizations typically use several types of unpleasant events to punish individuals. Material consequences for failure to perform adequately include a cut in pay, a disciplinary layoff without pay, a demotion, or a transfer to a dead-end job. The final punishment is the firing of an employee for failure to perform. In general, organizations reserve the use of unpleasant material events for cases of serious behavior problems.

Interpersonal punishers are used extensively. They include a manager's oral reprimand of an employee for unacceptable behavior and nonverbal punishers such as frowns, grunts, and aggressive body language. Certain tasks themselves can be unpleasant. The fatigue that follows hard physical labor can be considered a punisher, as can harsh or dirty working conditions. However, care must be exercised in labeling a punisher. In some fields and to some employees, harsh or dirty working conditions may be considered as just something that goes with the job.

The principles of positive reinforcement discussed earlier have equivalents in punishment. For maximum effectiveness, a punisher should be directly linked to the undesirable behavior (principle of contingent punishment); the punisher should be administered immediately (principle of immediate punishment); and, in general, the greater the size of the punisher, the stronger will be the effect on the undesirable behavior (principle of punishment size).

Negative Effects of Punishment   An argument against the use of punishment is the chance of its negative effects, especially over long or sustained periods of time. Even though punishment may stop an undesirable employee behavior, the potential negative consequences may be greater than the original undesirable behavior. Figure 4.5 illustrates some potential negative effects of punishment.

Punishment may cause undesirable emotional reactions. An employee who has been reprimanded for staying on break too long may react with anger toward the manager and the organization. This reaction may lead to behavior detrimental to the organization. Sabotage, for example, typically is a result of a punishment-oriented management system.

Punishment frequently leads only to short-term suppression of the undesirable behavior, rather than to its elimination. Thus suppression of an undesirable behavior over a long period of time usually requires continued and, perhaps,

■ **FIGURE 4.5**   **Potential Negative Effects of Punishment**

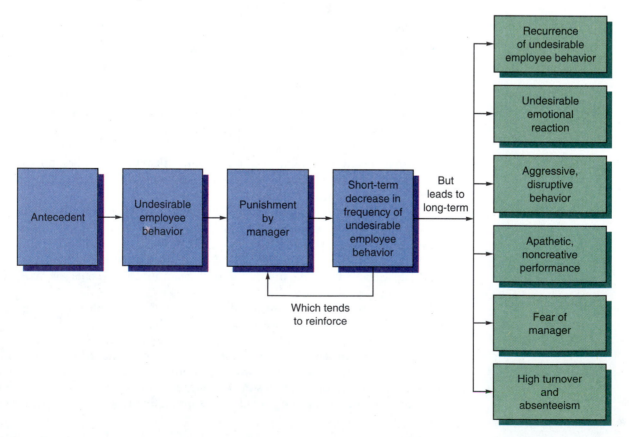

increasingly severe punishment. Another problem is that control of the undesirable behavior becomes contingent on the manager's presence. When the manager isn't around, the undesirable employee behavior is likely to recur.

In addition, the punished individual may try to avoid or escape the situation. From an organizational viewpoint, this reaction may be unacceptable if an employee avoids a particular, essential task. High absenteeism is a form of avoidance that is likely to occur when punishment is used frequently. Quitting is the employee's final form of escape, and organizations that depend on punishment are likely to have high rates of employee turnover. Some turnover is desirable, but excessive turnover is damaging to an organization. Recruitment and training are costly, and competent, high-performing employees are more likely to become frustrated and leave.

Punishment suppresses employee initiative and flexibility. Reacting to punishment, many an employee has said, I'm going to do just what I'm told and nothing more. Such an attitude is undesirable because organizations depend on the personal initiative and creativity that individual employees bring to their jobs.[20] Overusing punishment produces apathetic employees, who are not an asset to an organization. Sustained punishment can also lead to low self-esteem. Low self-esteem, in turn, undermines the employee's self-confidence, which is necessary for performing most jobs (see Chapter 2).

Punishment produces a conditioned fear of management. That is, employees develop a general fear of punishment-oriented managers. Such managers become an environmental cue, indicating to employees the probability that an aversive event will occur. If operations require frequent, normal, and positive interaction between employee and manager, the situation can quickly become intolerable. Responses to fear, such as "hiding" or reluctance to communicate with a manager, may well hinder employee performance.

A manager may rely on punishment because it often produces fast results in the short run. In essence, the manager is reinforced for using punishment because the approach produces an immediate change in an employee's behavior. That may cause the manager to ignore punishment's long-term detrimental effects, which can be cumulative. A few incidents of punishment may not produce negative effects. Its long-term, sustained use by the manager, however, most often results in negative outcomes for the organization.

Effective Use of Punishment   Positive reinforcement is more effective than punishment over the long run. Effectively used, however, punishment does have an appropriate place in management.

The most common form of punishment in organizations is the oral reprimand. It is intended to diminish or stop an undesirable employee behavior. An old rule of thumb is: Praise in public; punish in private. Private punishment establishes a different type of contingency of reinforcement than public punishment. In general, a private reprimand can be constructive and informative. A public reprimand is likely to have negative effects because the person has been embarrassed in front of his or her peers.

Oral reprimands should never be given about behavior in general and especially never about a so-called bad attitude. An effective reprimand pinpoints and specifically describes the undesirable behavior to be avoided in the future. It focuses on the target behavior and avoids threatening the employee's self-image. The effective reprimand punishes specific undesirable behavior, not the person. Behavior is easier to change than the person.

Punishment (by definition) trains a person in what not to do, not in what to do. Therefore a manager must specify an alternative behavior to the employee. When the employee performs the desired alternative behavior, the manager must then reinforce that behavior positively.

Finally, managers should strike an appropriate balance between the use of pleasant and unpleasant events. The absolute number of unpleasant events isn't important, but the ratio of pleasant to unpleasant events is. When a manager uses positive reinforcement frequently, an occasional deserved punishment can be quite effective. However, if a manager never uses positive reinforcement and relies entirely on punishment, the long-run negative effects are likely to counteract any short-term benefits. Positive management procedures should dominate in any well-run organization.

John Huberman, a Canadian psychologist, began promoting the idea of positive discipline in the mid 1960s, but it wasn't until the 1970s when Richard Grote introduced positive discipline at Frito-Lay that the idea became widespread. Grote began searching for a better management technique after a customer discovered a vulgar message written by a disgruntled employee on a corn chip. Grote gave the employee a day off with pay and called it "positive discipline." **Positive discipline** places emphasis on changing employee behaviors by reasoning rather than by imposing increasingly severe punishments.[21] Management's primary duty is to make all employees understand that the needs of the organization require certain standards of behavior and performance. A manager's task is to coach employees, issuing oral and then written reminders only when they fail to maintain behavioral and performance standards. It is the employee's responsibility to exercise self-discipline in achieving those standards. More than 200 companies, including AT&T, General Electric, and Union Carbide, have used positive discipline to change undesirable behaviors of employees. The following Managing in Practice piece describes how New England General Electric used this form of punishment to achieve positive results.

MANAGING IN PRACTICE

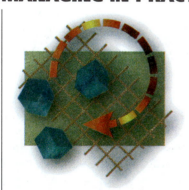

Discipline Without Punishment

New England General Electric uses positive discipline to deal with problem employees. On the face of it, this approach sounds like a contradiction in terms. However, according to Richard Grote, positive discipline places the responsibility for behavioral change with the one person who can best change that behavior— the employee. How does the program work? An employee who comes to work late, does a sloppy job, or mistreats another employee gets an oral reminder about the behavior rather than a written reprimand. If the undesirable behavior persists, the employee is issued a written reminder. If the behavior still persists, the employee is then paid for a day off, called a "decision-making day." The purpose of the day is for the employee to decide whether to conform to the standards.

This procedure accomplishes several things. First, it communicates to the employee that the organization is serious about the matter. Second, it sends a signal to other employees who have been flirting with the idea of challenging the
—Continued

MANAGING IN PRACTICE—*Continued*

standards that the organization doesn't put up with unacceptable behavior. Finally, the suspension provides tangible evidence that the employee's job is at risk.

The New England General Electric method has been very successful. More than 85 percent of the employees going through the positive discipline program have changed their behavior and stayed with the organization. Employees that don't change their behaviors are fired.[22]

■ USING CONTINGENCIES OF REINFORCEMENT

For a positive reinforcer to cause an employee to repeat a desired behavior, it must have value to that employee. If the employee is consistently on time, the manager positively reinforces this behavior by complimenting the employee. But, if the employee has been reprimanded in the past for coming to work late and then reports to work on time, the manager uses negative reinforcement and refrains from saying anything to embarrass the employee. The manager hopes that the employee will learn to avoid unpleasant comments by coming to work on time.

If the employee continues to come to work late, the manager can use either omission or punishment to try to stop this undesirable behavior. The manager who chooses omission doesn't praise the tardy employee but simply ignores the employee. The manager who chooses punishment may reprimand, fine, or suspend—and ultimately fire—the employee if the behavior persists.

The following guidelines are recommended for using contingencies of reinforcement in the work setting.

- Do not reward all employees in the same way.
- Carefully examine the consequences of nonactions as well as actions.
- Let employees know which behaviors will be reinforced.
- Let employees know what they are doing wrong.
- Don't punish employees in front of others.
- Make the response equal to the behavior by not cheating workers out of their just rewards.[23]

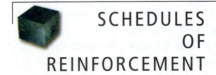

SCHEDULES OF REINFORCEMENT

Schedules of reinforcement determine when reinforcers are applied. Deliberately or not, reinforcement is always delivered according to some schedule.[24]

■ CONTINUOUS AND INTERMITTENT REINFORCEMENT

Continuous reinforcement means that the behavior is reinforced each time it occurs and is the simplest schedule of reinforcement. An example of continuous reinforcement is dropping coins in a soft-drink vending machine. The behavior of inserting coins is reinforced (on a continuous schedule) by the machine delivering a can of soda (most of the time!). Verbal recognition and material rewards generally are not delivered on a continuous schedule in organizations. In organizations such as Mary Kay Cosmetics, Tupperware, and Amway, salespeople are paid a commission for each sale, usually earning commissions of 25 to 50 percent of sales. Merrill Lynch and Company changed the commission rates for its more than 11,000 stockbrokers to help increase the firm's profits. In the past, stockbrokers were paid 30 to 46 percent of the commission income they generated from buying and selling stocks. Under the new plan the minimum commission rate was reduced to 25 percent, and payouts for small trades that generate from $50 to $100 were reduced because small trades aren't as profitable as larger ones. However, most managers who supervise employees other than salespeople seldom have the opportunity to deliver a reinforcer every time their employees demonstrate a desired behavior. Therefore behavior typically is reinforced intermittently.

Intermittent reinforcement refers to a reinforcer being delivered after some, but not every, occurrence of the desired behavior. Intermittent reinforcement can be subdivided into (1) interval and ratio and (2) fixed and variable schedules. In an **interval schedule,** reinforcers are delivered after a certain amount of time has passed. In a **ratio schedule,** reinforcers are delivered after a certain number of behaviors have been performed. These two major schedules can be further subdivided into fixed (not changing) or variable (constantly changing) schedules. Thus there are four primary types of intermittent schedules: fixed interval, variable interval, fixed ratio, and variable ratio.

■ FIXED INTERVAL SCHEDULE

In a **fixed interval schedule,** a constant amount of time must pass before a reinforcer is provided. The first desired behavior to occur after the interval has elapsed is reinforced. For example, in a fixed interval, one-hour schedule, the first desired behavior that occurs after an hour has elapsed is reinforced.

Administering rewards according to this type of schedule tends to produce an uneven pattern of behavior. Prior to the reinforcement, the behavior is frequent and energetic. Immediately following the reinforcement, the behavior becomes less frequent and energetic. Why? Because the individual rather quickly figures out that another reward won't immediately follow the last one until a certain amount of time has passed. A common example of administering rewards on a fixed interval schedule is the payment of employees weekly, biweekly, or monthly. That is, monetary reinforcement comes regularly at the end of a specific period of time. Such time intervals, unfortunately, are generally too long to be an effective form of reinforcement for newly acquired work-related behavior.

■ VARIABLE INTERVAL SCHEDULE

A **variable interval schedule** represents changes in the amount of time between reinforcers. For example, Kevin Mortazavi, Product Manager at AT&T, makes a point of walking through the plant an average of once a day. However, he varies the times. One week, he might walk through the plant twice on Monday, once on Tuesday, not on Wednesday, not on Thursday, and twice on Friday. The following week, Mortazavi changes the days. During these walks, he reinforces any desirable behavior he observes. He must change his schedule or employees will anticipate his tours and adjust their behaviors to get a reward. In the automobile industry, customers have learned to wait, if possible, for the new model year in the fall of each year to buy a car or truck. To push older models off their lots, car dealers give customers large rebates or low finance charges. In this case, the variable interval schedule is known to customers who attempt to wait for the new models to arrive. For automakers and dealers, a variable interval schedule hasn't been able to stimulate sales throughout the year.

■ FIXED RATIO SCHEDULE

In a **fixed ratio schedule,** the desired behavior must occur a specified number of times before it is reinforced. Administering rewards under a fixed ratio schedule tends to produce a high response rate when the reinforcement is close, followed by periods of steady behavior. The employee soon determines that reinforcement is based on the number of responses and performs the responses as quickly as possible in order to receive the reward. The individual piece-rate system used in many manufacturing plants is an example of such a schedule. Production workers are paid on the basis of how many acceptable pieces they produce (number of responses). Other things being equal, the employee's performance should be steady. In reality, other things are never equal, and a piece-rate system may not lead to the desired behavior. The following Ethics in Practice feature highlights what happened at Sears Tire & Auto Centers when the right behaviors were not reinforced.

ETHICS IN PRACTICE

Working at Sears

Sears has tried a variety of selling techniques to boost sales and profitability at its Sears Tire & Auto Centers. A variety of positive reinforcers, such as commissions, quota systems, and other rewards were used to promote repairs and sales. Negative reinforcers, such as threats of being fired if workers didn't meet their quotas for repairs, also were used. Workers believed that meeting a sales quota was more important than high-quality repair and maintenance services to customers.

When Ruth Hernandez drove her car into a Sears Tire & Auto Center in California to have her tires replaced, the mechanic told her that she also needed to have the car's struts replaced, for an additional $419. Hernandez went to another auto center for another opinion and was told that her struts were fine. Enraged, she returned to Sears and confronted the original mechanic, who admitted that he was wrong. She then reported the incident to the California Consumer Affairs Department. After an extensive investigation of her complaint and those of other Sears customers, it found that Sears mechanics were making unneeded repairs in the Tire & Auto Centers. Similar complaints against Sears were found in other states.

Sears pleaded guilty to these charges and agreed to repay customers who had unneeded work done and all court costs, which could exceed $60 million. Sears agreed to stop assigning product quotas in all of its Auto & Tire Centers. Although the fine is costly, the negative effect of the publicity that Sears received in the media is impossible to calculate.

What went wrong at Sears? The company was trying to promote the sale of auto products through the use of positive and negative reinforcers on a fixed ratio
—Continued

ETHICS IN PRACTICE—*Continued*

interval schedule. Employees wanted to avoid being fired at all costs. Sears thought that it was positively reinforcing sales, but it actually was undercutting honest customer service. Mechanics learned that being dishonest with customers and performing repairs that weren't needed were positively reinforced by Sears. The positive reinforcements were bonuses and keeping their jobs.[25]

■ VARIABLE RATIO SCHEDULE

In a **variable ratio schedule,** a certain number of desired behaviors must occur before the reinforcer is delivered, but the number of behaviors varies around some average. Managers frequently use a variable ratio schedule with praise and recognition. Team leaders at Sprint, for example, vary the frequency of reinforcement when they give employees verbal approval for desired behaviors. Gambling casinos, such as Bally's and Harrah's, among others, and state lotteries use this schedule of reinforcement to lure patrons to shoot craps, play poker, feed slot machines, and buy lottery tickets. Patrons win, but not on any regular basis.

■ COMPARISON OF
INTERMITTENT REINFORCEMENT SCHEDULES

Table 4.4 summarizes the four types of intermittent reinforcement schedules. Which is superior? The ratio schedules—fixed or variable—usually lead to better performance than do interval schedules. The reason is that ratio schedules are more closely related to the occurrence of desired behaviors than are interval schedules, which are based on the passage of time.[26]

TABLE 4.4 **Comparison of Schedules of Reinforcement**

SCHEDULE	FORM OF REWARD AND EXAMPLE	INFLUENCE ON PERFORMANCE	EFFECTS ON BEHAVIOR
Fixed interval	Reward on fixed time basis: weekly or monthly paycheck	Leads to average and irregular performance	Fast extinction of behavior
Fixed ratio	Reward tied to specific number of responses: piece-rate pay system	Leads quickly to very high and stable performance	Moderately fast extinction of behavior
Variable interval	Reward given after varying periods of time: unannounced inspections or appraisals and rewards given randomly each month	Leads to moderately high and stable performance	Slow extinction of behavior
Variable ratio	Reward given for some behaviors: sales bonus tied to selling X accounts but X constantly changing around some mean	Leads to very high performance	Very slow extinction of behavior

BEHAVIORAL MODIFICATION

Behavioral modification refers to processes and principles that are based on operant conditioning. Figure 4.6 illustrates the processes of behavioral modification.[27]

■ PINPOINTING RELEVANT BEHAVIORS

Not all employee behaviors are desirable or undesirable from a managerial viewpoint. In fact, many behaviors are neutral; they neither add to nor detract from the achievement of organizational goals. Thus the first and most important step in applying behavioral modification principles is to identify the behaviors that have a significant impact on an employee's overall performance. The manager should then concentrate on them, trying to increase desirable behaviors and

■ **FIGURE 4.6**   Behavioral Modification Procedures and Principles

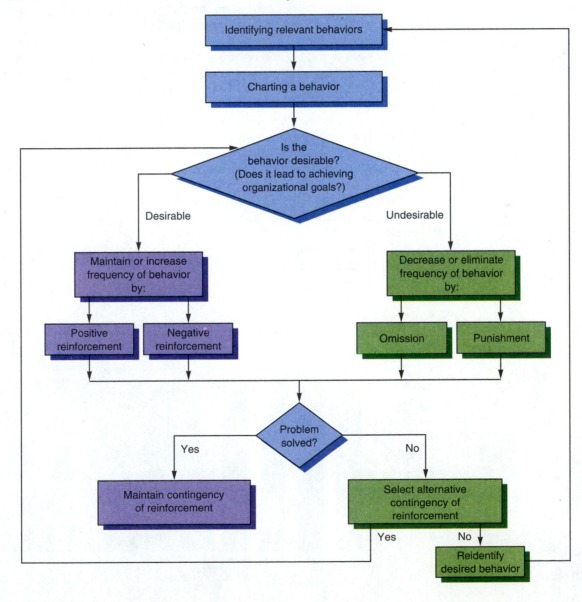

decrease undesirable behaviors. Pinpointing relevant behaviors consists of three activities:

1. observing the behaviors,
2. measuring the behaviors, and
3. describing the situation in which the behaviors occur.

Training is often necessary to enable managers to pinpoint behaviors. Frequently, the untrained manager confuses employee attitudes, feelings, and values with behaviors.

■ CHARTING BEHAVIOR

One of the ways to track employee behaviors is by **charting,** or measuring, them over time. Figure 4.7 shows an example of an employee behavior chart. The horizontal axis reflects time in months. The vertical axis represents employee behavior for past-due projects. Each bar on the chart represents the measurement of the employee's behavior during a one-month period.

An employee behavior chart usually is divided into at least two periods: the baseline period and the intervention period. During the baseline period behavior is measured before any attempt is made to change it. In this case, the baseline period covers the months of June through September. Observations are made by the manager without the employee's knowledge to get an accurate measurement.

During the intervention period, the employee's behavior is measured after one or more contingencies of reinforcement—positive reinforcement, negative reinforcement, omission, or punishment—is used. In this case the intervention period covers the months of October through March. During this time the individual might be shown the chart, providing a type of feedback. Sometimes feedback by itself is enough to cause a change in behavior. However, a reward or penalty frequently accompanies feedback and may have some effect on the behavior.

Charting has two major features. First, observations during the baseline period show the frequency of certain behaviors. Sometimes charting a behavior reveals

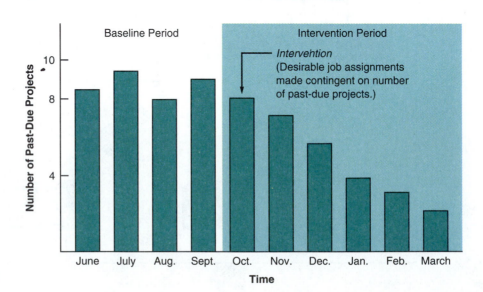

■ FIGURE 4.7

Employee Behavior Chart

that the behavior isn't as much of a problem as originally thought. Second, by charting through the intervention period, the manager can determine whether the intervention strategy is working. Charting then becomes an evaluation method. Sometimes a chart reveals no change in behavior, which means that the intervention wasn't successful.

■ CHOOSING A CONTINGENCY OF REINFORCEMENT

After a behavior has been identified and charted for a baseline period, a contingency of reinforcement aimed at changing the behavior should be selected. The manager must decide which type of reward is most likely to have the desired effect on the employee's behavior. Rewards should be used to increase or maintain desirable behaviors. Obviously, positive reinforcement is the first alternative to consider. The other alternative is to apply negative reinforcement.

If the behavior is undesirable, the manager's goal will be to reduce or eliminate it. Either punishment or omission would be appropriate. A combination of reinforcement contingencies to extinguish undesirable behaviors while reinforcing (increasing) other, desirable behaviors also might be used.

■ PROBLEM SOLVED?

Experience gives the effective manager a valuable tool in choosing contingencies of reinforcement in attempting to modify employee behaviors. The ability to generalize from similar past situations or from similar incidents with the same employee is essential. If the manager is successful in affecting the target behavior, the contingency of reinforcement must be maintained for lasting results.

There is no guarantee that a chosen contingency of reinforcement will be effective. Every manager encounters situations in which the first intervention tactic fails. The manager then should either try a different contingency of reinforcement or reidentify the desired behavior. In either case, the manager must again go through the various steps of the procedure. However, an evaluation of the previous effort can simplify this procedure. The manager may conclude that a different form of positive reinforcement is needed and use it in an attempt to increase the desired behavior. The manager might also try a different contingency of reinforcement—for instance, a change from positive to negative reinforcement. Or the manager might try a combination of contingencies of reinforcement.

Changing behavior may be extremely difficult because people often resist change. An excellent example of the difficulties involved in changing behavior comes from the phenomenon of dieting. Over the past decade, millions of people have tried various weight-loss programs, making the dieting a $35 billion dollar industry.[28] Obesity is on the rise, and more than 33 percent of all adults in the United States are estimated to be overweight, up from 25 percent in 1980. Although the big three—Weight Watchers, Nutri/System, Jenny Craig—have reported losses in sales to Susan Powter Centers and supermarkets, which now stock their shelves with low-calorie cuisine, it is still a huge business. Most diet centers use principles of behavioral modification to change their customers' eating behaviors and, as a result, lose weight. Unfortunately, government studies indicate that most dieters regain two-thirds of the weight lost within a year and that 95 percent of the people who go to a diet center fail to maintain their lower weight. *Consumer Reports* asked more than 19,000 readers who had joined a diet program to rate their satisfaction with it. Based on the responses received, the magazine concluded that people generally were dissatisfied with weight-loss programs. Respondents protested that the programs cost more than they were led to believe and that consultants pressured them to buy their products and to keep coming back.

Using the principles of behavioral modification illustrated in Figure 4.6, a weight-loss center weighs and measures the dieter before the dieter starts the program. The dieter and a counselor jointly establish weight-loss goals. Usually, two or more pounds drop off the first week because early losses are water, not fat. This quick loss gives the dieter positive reinforcement that the diet is working. The dieter normally buys food substitute products from the center, which typically accounts for 85 percent of the center's revenues. At Jenney Craig the typical female dieter wants to lose 30 pounds. At a rate of 1.5 to 2 pounds a week, the food substitute bill would be more than $900. As the dieter loses additional weight, she receives counseling on types of food to eat, attends exercise sessions, and receives motivational reinforcements, including water bottles, T-shirts, and gym bags, among others. The positive reinforcement received from the loss of weight and the counselor encourages the dieter to buy additional food substitutes and enroll in other activities sponsored by the diet center. The diet center's counselor charts progress and celebrates every ounce and inch lost with the dieter.

■ BEHAVIORAL MODIFICATION ISSUES

Three issues are involved in the use of behavioral modification processes and principles: individual differences, group norms, and ethical considerations.[29]

Individual Differences   Behavioral modification often ignores individual differences in needs, values, abilities, and desires. What is reinforcing to one person may not be to another, and effective managers can account for individual differences in two ways. First, they can try to select and hire employees who value the rewards offered by the organization. Proper employee selection can lead to hiring people whose needs most closely match the reinforcers provided by the organization. Although not easy to do, this approach can be an effective way for managers to take individual differences into account.

Second, managers can allow employees to participate in determining their rewards. Thus, if the present contingencies of reinforcement are ineffective, the manager can ask employees to say what they would do to correct the situation. This method allows employees to have a greater voice in designing their work environment and should lead to greater employee involvement. However, if this method is used simply to exploit employees, they will look for ways to get around it.

Group Norms   When employees believe that management is trying to exploit them, group norms emerge to control the degree of cooperation with management. This control typically takes the form of restricting output. When this situation arises, implementation of a program (particularly one that relies on praise and other nonmaterial rewards) is likely to meet with stiff resistance from the work group. Group members feel little need to cooperate with management because this behavior is likely lead to pressure to increase productivity, without a corresponding increase in pay.

The power of group norms can reduce the effectiveness of most reward systems. When employees and managers have a history of distrust, the principles covered in this chapter probably won't help. First, trust must be forged between employee and manager. Once that has been done, these principles have a better chance of working.

Ethical Considerations   Behavioral modification has stirred some controversy in terms of ethics. The criticisms center on a person's freedom and dignity. According to proponents of behavioral modification, the way to manage people effectively is to establish control systems that shape their behaviors. They recognize that behaviors are shaped by their consequences and that managers should administer rewards in ways that promote desirable behaviors from the organization's point of view. They don't worry too much about the individuals' freedom to choose which behaviors to engage in to satisfy their own desires and wants.

Others argue the ethics of someone deciding what is good or beneficial for other people and having enough power to manipulate or impose that decision. They question what manipulation does to a person's sense of self-worth. Promising employees a reward for doing a task they already enjoy doing can lead them to see the reward as the motivation for performing the task, thus undermining their enjoyment of the task. A person may think, If I have to be bribed or forced into doing this, then I must not enjoy doing the task for its own sake. In essence, is it better for an individual to enjoy a task than for managers to manipulate employees into performing it? Furthermore, instead the widespread use of punishment, would not the use of positive reinforcers be more humanitarian?

Managers have some other problems to consider as well. Employees may engage in only those behaviors that can be measured or are being and ignore those that can't be or aren't being measured. For example, managers may reward the quantity of work produced and overlook its quality. Or they may rely on measuring employee tardiness or absenteeism, both of which can easily be measured, rather than evaluate their ideas and other contributions to the work being done, which often are more difficult to measure. Under such conditions, the quality of work may suffer, but employees show up on time for work.

Many managers feel societal pressures to reinforce behaviors that they really don't desire themselves. This emphasis may lead employees to engage in behaviors, such as participating in recycling campaigns or carpools, even though such behaviors may interfere with the employees' effectiveness.

CHAPTER SUMMARY

Classical conditioning began with the work of Pavlov, who studied reflex behaviors. A metronome (conditioning stimulus) was started at the same time food was placed in the dog's mouth (unconditioned stimulus). Soon, the sound of the metronome alone evoked salivation.

Operant conditioning learning focuses on the effects of reinforcement on desirable and undesirable behaviors. Changes in behavior result from the consequences of previous behavior. People tend to repeat a behavior that leads to a pleasant result and not to repeat a behavior that leads to an unpleasant result. In short, when a behavior is reinforced, it is repeated; when it is punished or not reinforced, it is not repeated.

Social-cognitive theory focuses on people learning new behaviors by observing others and then modeling their own behavior on that observed. The three factors emphasized in social-cognitive theory are vicarious learning, self-control, and self-efficacy. Vicarious learning occurs when a person learns from observing others. A person can also learn alone by exercising self-control. Self-efficacy refers to a belief that the person can perform the task. A person's self-efficacy influences how well the person performs in a situation, how long the person persists in doing a task, and how much effort the person will expend on the task.

There are two types of reinforcement: (1) positive reinforcement, which increases a desirable behavior because the person is provided with a pleasurable outcome after the behavior has occurred; and (2) negative reinforcement, which also maintains the desirable behavior by presenting an unpleasant event before the behavior occurs and stopping the event when the behavior occurs. Both positive and negative reinforcement increase the frequency of a desirable behavior. Conversely, omission and punishment reduce the frequency of an undesirable behavior. Omission involves stopping everything that reinforces the behavior. A punisher is an unpleasant event that follows the behavior and reduces the probability that the behavior will be repeated.

There are four schedules of reinforcement. In the fixed interval schedule, the reward is given on a fixed time basis (for example, a weekly or monthly paycheck). In the variable interval schedule, the reward is given around some average time during a specific period of time (for example, the plant manager walking through the plant an average of five times every week). The fixed ratio schedule ties rewards to certain outputs (for example, a piece-rate system). In the variable ratio schedule, the reward is given around some mean, but the number of behaviors varies (as does a payoff from a slot machine).

The process of applying the principles of behavior modification include pinpointing behaviors, charting these behaviors, and choosing a contingency of reinforcement to obtain desirable behaviors and stop undesirable behaviors.

KEY TERMS AND CONCEPTS

Antecedent
Aversive events
Avoidance learning
Behavioral modification
Charting
Classical conditioning
Consequence
Contingency of reinforcement
Continuous reinforcement
Empowerment
Escape learning
Fixed interval schedule
Fixed ratio schedule
Intermittent reinforcement
Interval schedule
Kaizen

Learning
Learning theory
Negative reinforcement
Omission
Operant conditioning
Positive discipline
Positive events
Positive reinforcement
Primary reinforcer
Principle of contingent
    reinforcement
Principle of immediate
    reinforcement
Principle of reinforcement
    deprivation
Principle of reinforcement size

Punishment
Ratio schedule
Reflexive behavior
Reinforcement
Reward
Secondary reinforcer
Self-control
Self-efficacy
Social-cognitive theory
Variable interval schedule
Variable ratio schedule
Vicarious learning

DISCUSSION QUESTIONS

1. What principles of reinforcement did Viking Freight use?

2. Describe the basic differences among classical conditioning, the social-cognitive theory, and the operant conditioning theory. Which type is most important for managers? Why?

3. Which principles of learning are being used by producers of self-help videos?

4. How can a manager raise an employee's level of self-efficacy?

5. When might employees engage in learning through self-control?

6. Visit either a local health club or diet center and schedule an interview with the manager. What types of rewards does it give its members who achieve targeted goals? Does it use punishment?

7. Identify the types of reinforcement used by managers at the Prudential Life Insurance Company to promote wellness.

8. Which are the most effective reinforcement schedules for maintaining desirable behaviors over the long run?

9. Steven Kerr, Vice President for Executive Education at General Electric, wrote an article entitled "On the Folly of Rewarding A While Hoping for B." The essence of the article is that organizations often unintentionally reward behaviors that they don't want to occur. Using this premise, what happened at Sears Tire & Auto Centers? Why did mechanics engage in unethical behaviors?

10. How can a manager use punishment effectively?

11. What ethical considerations should be addressed before introducing a behavioral modification program in the workplace?

Developing Competencies

Self-Insight: What's Your Self-Efficacy?

We have provided you with a chance to gain insights into your self-efficacy to perform activities needed to achieve academic excellence. Please answer the following seven questions in the spaces provided using the following five-point scale. An interpretation of your score follows.

5 = Strongly agree

4 = Agree

3 = Moderate

2 = Disagree

1 = Strongly disagree

1. I am a good student. 5 4 3 2 1

2. It is difficult to maintain a study schedule. 5 4 3 2 1

3. I know the right things to do to improve my academic performance. 5 4 3 2 1

4. I find it difficult to convince my friends who have different viewpoints on studying than mine. 5 4 3 2 1

5. My temperament is not well suited to studying. 5 4 3 2 1

6. I am good at finding out what teachers want. 5 4 3 2 1

7. It is easy for me to get others to see my point of view. 5 4 3 2 1

Add your scores to questions 1, 3, 6, and 7. Enter that score here _____. For questions, 2, 4, and 5, please reverse the scoring key. That is, if you answered question 2 as strongly agree, give yourself 1 point, agree is worth 2 points, etc. Enter your score here for questions 2, 4, and 5 _____. Please enter your combined score here _____. This is your *self-efficacy* score for academic achievement. If you scored between 28 and 35, you believe that you can achieve academic excellence. Scores lower than 18 indicate that you believe no matter how hard you try to achieve academic excellence, something may prevent you from reaching your desired level of performance. Scores between 19 and 27 indicate a moderate degree of self-efficacy. Your self-efficacy may vary with the course you are taking. In courses in your major, you may have greater self-efficacy than in those outside of your major.[30]

Organizational Insight: This Is Going to Cost Me My Job

Background for a role playing exercise is as follows. Ball Corporation is a manufacturer of glass containers, located in Muncie, Indiana. Ball's customers are food packers, such as Heinz or Campbell's. Ball's strengths are its ability to manufacture glass containers that are lighter in weight than tin cans, solve customers' packaging problems, and reduce costs. Most of the company's salespeople sell to existing customers, although each person is expected to bring in new customers.

Salespeople are compensated by salary plus a bonus for achieving their quotas. To earn a bonus, a salesperson must sell at least 90 percent of his or her quota. The bonus amount increases until a salesperson meets the quota at which point the bonus is 20 percent of the person's salary. Salary increases are based on the district manager's performance rating, with one-third of the rating based on quota achievement.

The role play starts with you and another district manager talking at the annual managers' meeting, where each of you has been given your quota for next year. Quotas are set by headquarters, with some input from the district managers. The district managers assign quotas to the salespeople in their districts. Your quota has been increased by 20 percent, whereas the other manager's has been increased by only 12 percent.

As you are packing your briefcase for a meeting, Sandy McGuire stops by, obviously irked. "My quota is wrong," she says. "I exceeded last year's quota by 5 percent and now this year's quota is 20 percent over what I sold last year. How can you do this to me? I need an adjustment." You're running late and don't have much time to talk with McGuire. She is one of your best salespeople and you need her support. You tell her that you're late for the meeting and will get back to her the first thing in the morning.

Just as McGuire leaves, Juan Lopez enters. He is less outspoken than McGuire and is on shaky ground because he didn't make any bonus last year. He follows you down the corridor asking, "How can I make this number? My quota has been increased by 10 percent over last year and I only made 80 percent of last year's quota. This is going to cost me my job." Juan alludes to problems with increased competition, lack of administrative support, stress, and personal problems. You are sympathetic, but emphasized the seriousness of meeting the quota. You tell him to see you first thing tomorrow afternoon to discuss his quota.

The Scene

It's 7:30 the following morning and your meeting with Sandy McGuire is only 30 minutes away. What will you tell her? Think about the problems that may arise because of the upcoming conversation with her.

1. What were your solutions for McGuire and Lopez?
2. How did you come up with these quotas?[31]

REFERENCES

1. Adapted from Stambaugh, T. An incentive pay success story. *Personnel Journal*, April 1992, 48–54; Stambaugh, T. Viking Freight adds "PEP" to its pay for performance plan. *Employee Benefit Plan Review*, June 1993, 58–61.
2. Weiss, H. M. Learning theory and industrial and organizational psychology. In M. D. Dunnette and L. M. Hough (eds.). *Handbook of Industrial & Organizational Psychology*, 2d ed. Palo Alto, Calif.: Consulting Psychologists Press, 1990, 170–221.
3. Kanfer, R. Motivation theory and industrial and organizational psychology. In M. D. Dunnette and L. M. Hough (eds.). *Handbook of Industrial & Organizational Psychology*, 2d ed. Palo Alto, Calif.: Consulting Psychologists Press, 1990, 75–169.
4. Shimp, T. A., Stuart, E. W., and Engle, R. W. A program of classical conditioning experiments testing variations in the conditioned stimulus and context. *Journal of Consumer Research*, 1991, 18, 1–10.
5. Skinner, B. F. *About Behaviorism*. New York: Knopf, 1974; Martinko, M. J. and Fadil, P. Operant technologies: A theoretical foundation for organizational change and development. *Leadership & Organization Development Journal*, 1994, 15(5), 16–21.
6. For excellent overviews, see Wood, R., and Bandura, A. Social cognitive theory of organizational management. *Academy of Management Review*, 1989, 13, 361–384; Bandura, A. *Social-Cognitive Theory*. Englewood Cliffs, N.J.: Prentice-Hall, 1977; Bandura, A. Social-cognitive theory of self-regulation. *Organizational Behavior and Human Decision Processes*, 1991, 50, 248–287.
7. Gist, M. E. Self-efficacy: Implications for organizational behavior and human resource management. *Academy of Management Review*, 1987, 12, 472–485; Cole, B. L., and Hopkins, B. L. Manipulations of the relationship between self-efficacy and performance. *Journal of Organizational Behavior Management*, 1995, 15(1–2), 95–136.
8. Spreitzer, G. M. Psychological empowerment in the workplace: Dimensions, measurement, and validation. *Academy of Management Journal*, 1995, 38, 1442–1465.
9. Adapted from Caudron, S. Create an empowering environment. *Personnel Journal*, September 1995, 28–36.
10. Lindsley, D. H., Brass, D. J. and Thomas, J. B. Efficacy–performance spirals: A multilevel perspective. *Academy of Management Review*, 1995, 20, 645–678; Saks, A. M. Longitudinal field investigation of the moderating and mediating effects of self-efficacy on the relationship between training and newcomer adjustment. *Journal of Applied Psychology*, 1995, 80, 211–226.
11. Latack, J. C., Kinicki, A. J., and Prussia, G. E. An integrative process model of coping with job loss. *Academy of Management Review*, 1995, 20, 311–342; Eden, D., and Zuk, Y. Seasickness as a self-fulfilling prophecy: Raising self-efficacy to boost performance at sea. *Journal of Applied Psychology*, 1995, 80, 628–636.
12. Stone, D. N. Overconfidence in initial self-efficacy judgments: Effects on decision processes and performance. *Organizational Behavior & Human Decision Processes*, 1994, 59, 452–475; Mitchell, T. R., Hopper, H., Daniels, D., George-Falvy, J. and James, L. R. Predicting self-efficacy and performance during skill acquisition. *Journal of Applied Psychology*, 1994, 79, 506–518.
13. Adapted from Fulkerson, J. R., and Schuler, R. S. Managing worldwide diversity at Pepsi-Cola International. In S. E. Jackson and Associates (eds.). *Diversity in the Workplace*. New York: Guilford, 1992, 248–278.
14. Miller, L. *Principles of Everyday Behavior Analysis*. Monterey, Calif.: Brooks/Cole, 1975.

15. Anfuso, D. Creating a culture of caring pays off. *Personnel Journal*, August 1995, 70–77.

16. Adapted from Davis, D., and Cosenza, R. M. *Business Research for Decision Making*, 3rd ed. Belmont, Calif.: Wadsworth, 1993.

17. Latham, G. P., and Huber, V. L. Schedules of reinforcement: Lessons from the past and issues for the future. *Journal of Organizational Behavior Management*, 1992, 12, 125–149.

18. Besser, T. L. Rewards and organizational goal achievement: A case study of Toyota Motor manufacturing in Kentucky. *Journal of Management Studies*, 1995, 32, 383–400.

19. Adapted from Anfuso, D. Diversity keeps newspaper up with the times. *Personnel Journal*, July 1995, 30–40.

20. Ball, G. A., Trevino, L. K., and Sims, H. P., Jr. Just and unjust punishment: Influences on subordinate performance and citizenship. *Academy of Management Journal*, 1994, 37, 299–322; Miles, J. A., and Greenberg, J. Using punishment threats to attenuate social loafing effects among swimmers. *Organizational Behavior & Human Decision Processes*, 1993, 56, 246–266.

21. Grote, D. *Discipline Without Punishment*. New York: AMACOM, 1995.

22. Adapted from Grote, 1995, 164–168.

23. Hamner, W. C., and Hamner, E. Behavior modification on the bottom line. *Organizational Dynamics*, Winter 1976, 2–21; Boettger, R. D., and Greer, C. R. On the wisdom of rewarding A while hoping for B. *Organization Science*, 1994, 569–582.

24. Bandura, A. *Principles of Behavior Modification*. New York: Holt, Rinehart and Winston, 1969.

25. Adapted from Fuschsberg, G. Sears reinstates sales incentives in some centers. *Wall Street Journal*, March 7, 1994, B1, B6; Flynn, J., Del Valle, C., and Mitchell, R. Did Sears take other customers for a ride? *Business Week*, August 3, 1992, 24–25; Patterson, G. A. Sears' Brennan accepts blame for auto flap. *Wall Street Journal*, August 5, 1992, B1–B2.

26. Wright, P. M., Geroge, J. M., Farnsworth, S. R., and Tannenbaum, S. I., Productivity and extra-role behavior: The effects of goals and incentives on spontaneous helping. *Journal of Applied Psychology*, 1993, 78, 374–381.

27. Luthans, F., and Kreitner, R. *Organizational Behavior Modification and Beyond.* Glenview, Ill.: Scott Foresman, 1985; Sutherland, V., Makin, P., Bright, K., and Cox, C. Quality behavior for quality organizations. *Leadership & Organization Development Journal*, 1995, 16(6), 10–16.

28. Vreeland, L. Lean times in fat city. *Working Women*, July 1995, 47–51, 73–75.

29. Stajkovic, A. D., and Luthans, F., Meta-analytic review of the effects of organizational behavior modification on task performance: 1975–1995. *Academy of Management Journal*, 1997, in press.

30. Brown, S., Cron, W. L., and Slocum, J. W., Jr. A longitudinal study of the effects of anticipatory emotions on salesperson volition, behavior, and performance. *Journal of Marketing*, 1997, 61, 39–50. Lee, C., and Bobko, P. Self-efficacy beliefs: Comparison of five measures. *Journal of Applied Psychology*, 1994, 79, 364–370.

31. Adapted from Dalrymple, D. J., and Cron, W. L. *Sales Management: Concepts and Cases.* New York: John Wiley & Sons, 1995, 640–641.

5

Motivation in the Work Setting

LEARNING OBJECTIVES

When you have finished studying this chapter, you should be able to:

- Define motivation and describe the process of motivation.
- Describe and apply four content models of motivation: needs hierarchy model, ERG model, achievement motivation model, and motivator-hygiene model.
- Describe and apply two process models of motivation: expectancy model and equity model.
- State the organizational implications for each of the motivation models.

OUTLINE

PREVIEW CASE

High-Performance Management at UPS

Steve Menkhaus, a UPS delivery driver in Sharonville, Ohio, didn't see himself as a salesperson. However, since UPS began a sales lead incentive program in 1993, more than 62,000 delivery drivers have generated more than 212,000 sales leads. After a driver initiates a lead, a UPS representative follows up, usually in a day, with additional information and a contract offer. Forty-three percent of these new sales leads have turned into new customers, generating an additional $60 million in new company revenue. Menkhaus's efforts in the sales lead incentive program not only added new business for UPS, but they also enabled him to accrue points that he could exchange for merchandise and trips. What Menkhaus did sounds simple, but it represents a dramatic and fundamental change in the way UPS motivated its drivers.

The need to change was fueled by competitors, such as the U.S. Postal Service, Emery, and DLH, all of which expanded their services to attract UPS customers. Offering customized and convenient services, each competitor chipped away at UPS's business as they carved out their own niches. To respond to the competition, UPS cut costs by offering an early retirement program to managers, which many took. This program left UPS with fewer managers and put more demands on front-line employees, such as Menkhaus.

UPS's motivation plan was to involve each employee in soliciting new business. In essence, UPS was entrusting non-management people with determining the best ways to attract and serve customers. Most of the drivers embraced their new autonomy and saw tremendous opportunities to get valued rewards. Before UPS turned its drivers into salespeople, it gave each driver tips on selling.

As of 1997, UPS drivers were allowed to spend up to thirty minutes of unstructured time on the job. (Remember, this is a company that scheduled its drivers to the tenth of an hour, told them how to carry the clipboard (under the right arm) and the package (under the left). As a result, drivers can now spend more time with customers—to listen and to come up with solutions to meet their needs. Thirty minutes a week may not sound like much, but it is a huge financial commitment. At $29 per hour, UPS drivers are the highest paid in the nation. For UPS, thirty minutes per week per driver means a commitment of approximately $36 million a year.

What have been the results? The first six months of 1996 were the best in the company's history. Revenues rose 9.7 percent to more than $11 billion, and profits were up 38.2 percent. In addition, drivers/salespeople all have a vested interest in making this change successful, for their own sakes and for the sake of the company.[1]

Motivation represents the forces acting on or within a person that cause the person to behave in a specific, goal-directed manner. Because the specific work motives of employees affect their productivity, one of management's jobs is to channel employee motivation effectively toward achieving organizational goals. Allan Gomez, chairman and CEO of Thomson, a high-technology French electronics corporation, says that his greatest challenge is to attract, manage, and develop a worldwide work force. With Thomson's RCA and GE brands competing for the high end of the U.S. television market, Gomez must provide motivational systems that will cut costs while maintaining high quality. Permitting employees to participate in incentive programs at the company's Marion, Indiana, plant led to greater productivity. Providing housing and safe working conditions for employees at Thomson's new low-cost TV manufacturing plant in Bangkok, Thailand, accomplished the same thing.[2]

Table 5.1 highlights some of the factors that managers must address when dealing with multicultural work-force motivation. Note the diversity in what employees want. As an effective motivator, a manager must be able to identify and understand these differences and help employees satisfy their wants and needs through the organization.

TABLE 5.1   Diversity in the Work Force: What Do People Want?

Able-Bodied People Want

To develop more ease in dealing with physically disabled people

To give honest feedback and appropriate support without being patronizing or overprotective

Disabled People Want

To have greater acknowledgment of and focus on abilities, rather than on disabilities

To be challenged by colleagues and organizations to be the best

To be included, not isolated

Gay Men and Lesbians Want

To be recognized as whole human beings, not just sexual beings

To have equal employment protection

To have increased awareness among people regarding the impact of heterosexism in the workplace.

Heterosexuals Want

To become more aware of lesbian and gay issues

To have a better understanding of the legal consequences of being gay in America

To increase dialogue about heterosexist issues with lesbians and gay men

Men Want

To have the same freedom to grow/feel that women have

To be perceived as allies, not the enemy

To bridge the gap with women at home and at work

People of Color Want

To be valued as unique individuals, as members of ethnically diverse groups, as people of different races, and as equal contributors

To establish more open, honest, working relationships with people of other races and ethnic groups

To have the active support of white people in fighting racism

White People Want

To have their ethnicity acknowledged

To reduce discomfort, confusion, and dishonesty in dealing with people of color

To build relationships with people of color based on common goals, concerns, and mutual respect for differences

Women Want

To be recognized as equal contributors

To have active support of male colleagues

To have work and family issues actively addressed by organizations

Younger and Older Employees Want

To have more respect for their life experiences

To be taken seriously

To be challenged by their organizations, not patronized

Source: Adapted from Rynes, S. and Rosen, B. A field survey of factors affecting the adoption and perceived success of diversity training. *Personnel Psychology*, 1995, 48, 247–271; Grubb, D. J. Respecting our differences. *Women in Business*, November–December, 1995, 36–39; Graham, E. Demogaphics: Craving closer ties, *Wall Street Journal*, March 4, 1996, B1ff.

Surprisingly, many managers aren't sure which rewards their employees value. According to Don Bohl, Director of Management Studies at the American Management Association, four trends currently affect employee motivation. First, organizations are hiring fewer permanent employees and contracting out (outsourcing) a variety of services. Contract workers—such as engineers, accountants, computer programmers, food preparers, and many others—will be paid fees for completing specific projects. They will have to purchase their own dental, health, and life insurance coverage; will have no paid sick leave, holidays, or vacation; and many will work at home. Second, employees may work for five or six organizations during their careers and should be prepared to work for a foreign corporation. Although many U.S. companies are downsizing and outsourcing work in order to lower their costs, foreign companies are hiring. Understanding how to lead and motivate workers in different cultures will become increasingly important during the remainder of the 1990s and beyond. Third, people should be prepared to work in a team or on their own. Many employees are being asked to work in teams to produce goods and services. Even on the assembly lines at Honda, Saturn, and Nissan, employees work in teams. Thus more and more managers are looking for employees who have developed multiple talents and good interpersonal skills. Fourth, employees must continually upgrade their skills to keep up with the fast-changing technology and workplace requirements. Steve Menkhaus and his fellow drivers at UPS went to school to learn new selling skills.[3]

Experts might not agree about everything that motivates employees—and the effects of working conditions over their careers—but they do agree that an organization must

- attract people to the organization and encourage them to remain with it;
- allow people to perform the tasks for which they were hired; and
- stimulate people to go beyond routine performance and become creative and innovative in their work.

Thus, for an organization to be effective, it must tackle the motivational challenges involved in arousing people's desires to be productive members of the organization.

THE BASIC MOTIVATIONAL PROCESS

A key motivational principle states that performance is based on a person's level of ability and motivation. This principle is often expressed by the formula

$$\text{Performance} = f \, (\text{ability} \times \text{motivation}).$$

According to this principle, no task can be performed successfully unless the person who is to carry it out has the ability to do so. **Ability** is the person's talent for performing goal-related tasks. This talent might include intellectual competencies, such as verbal and spatial skills, and manual competencies, such as physical strength and dexterity.

However, regardless of how intelligent, skilled, or dexterous a person may be, ability alone isn't enough to perform at a high level. The person must also desire to achieve that level of performance. Discussions of motivation generally are concerned with (1) what drives behavior, (2) what direction behavior takes, and (3) how to maintain that behavior.

■ CORE PHASES

The motivational process begins with identifying a person's needs, shown as phase 1 in Figure 5.1. **Needs** are deficiencies that a person experiences at a par-

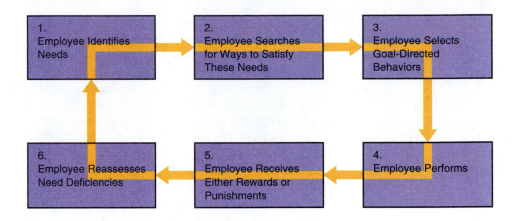

ticular time. These deficiencies may be psychological (such as the need for recognition), physiological (such as the need for water, air, or food), or social (such as the need for friendship). Needs are viewed as energizers. Thus, when needs deficiencies are present, the individual is likely to exert effort (phase 2). Needs deficiencies create tensions within the individual, who finds them uncomfortable and wants to reduce or eliminate them.

Motivation is goal directed (phase 3). A **goal** is a specific result the individual wants to achieve.[4] Accomplishing goals can significantly reduce needs deficiencies. An employee's goals may be viewed as driving forces. For example, some employees have a strong drive for advancement and expectations that working long hours on highly visible projects will lead to promotions, raises and greater influence. Such needs and expectations often create uncomfortable tension within the individuals. Believing that certain specific behaviors can overcome this feeling, these employees act to reduce this tension. Employees striving to advance may seek work on major problems facing the organization to gain visibility and influence with senior managers in helping attain the organization's goals (phase 4). Promotions and raises are two of the ways that organizations attempt to maintain desirable behaviors. They are signals (feedback) to employees that their needs for advancement and recognition and their behaviors are appropriate (phase 5). Once the employees receive either rewards or punishments, they reassess their needs (phase 6).

■ MOTIVATIONAL CHALLENGES

The general model of the motivational process just described is simple and straightforward. In the real world, of course, the process isn't so clear-cut. The first challenge is that motives can only be inferred; they cannot be seen. Linda Seatvet, financial manager for Frito-Lay in Plano, Texas, noticed two employees in her department debugging financial software programs. She knows that both employees are responsible for the same type of work, have similar abilities, and have been with the organization for about five years. One employee is able to spot problems more easily and faster than the other. She knows that both employees have similar abilities and training, so the difference in their output strongly suggests that they have different motivations. Seatvet would have to investigate further to determine what motivates each person.

A second challenge centers on the dynamic nature of needs. At any one time, everyone has many needs, desires, and expectations. These factors change over time and may also conflict with each other. Employees who put in many extra hours at work to fulfill their needs for accomplishment may find that these extra work hours conflict directly with needs for affiliation and their desire to be with their families.

A third challenge involves the considerable differences in people's motivations and in the energy with which people respond to them. Just as organizations differ in the products they manufacture or the services they offer, people differ in terms of what motivates them. Gary Brown knew that he wanted to open a restaurant after visiting his brother one weekend in San Francisco. Working 70 hours a week didn't bother him. Once he developed and perfected his idea, he created his own recipes and opened his first restaurant in Dallas. By mid 1996, his Routh Street Brewery employed more than twenty-five people and Brown was looking for another location to open a second restaurant. He was motivated to be his own boss and operator of an up-scale restaurant in Dallas. In contrast, Mike Doyle, a Salomon Brothers employee, took a one-year job assignment in his firm's Hong Kong office. Doyle joined a group of U.S. managers living in Hong Kong so that he could satisfy his needs to belong and to learn quickly about Chinese business customs. Doyle was advised that Chinese managers are taught to be indirect in conversation, carefully editing remarks to reflect both good manners and the status of their listeners. He also learned that many Chinese managers think that Americans are impatient, noisy, disruptive, and confrontational, often saying things that are better left unsaid.

There is no shortage of models and tactics that can be used to motivate employees.[5] However, we can group the models into two general categories: content and process.

CONTENT MODELS OF MOTIVATION

Content models of motivation focus on the specific factors that energize, direct, and stop a person's behavior. An attractive salary, good working conditions, and friendly co-workers are important to most people. Hunger (the need for food) or a desire for a steady job (the need for job security) are also factors that arouse people and may cause them to set specific goals (earning money to buy food or working in a financially stable industry). Four widely recognized content models of motivation are Maslow's needs hierarchy, Alderfer's ERG model, McClelland's achievement motivation model, and Herzberg's two-factor model.

■ NEEDS HIERARCHY MODEL

The most widely recognized model of motivation is the **needs hierarchy model.** Abraham H. Maslow suggested that people have a complex set of exceptionally strong needs, which can be arranged in a hierarchy.[6] Underlying this hierarchy are the following basic assumptions.

■ Once a need has been satisfied, its motivational role decreases in importance. However, as one need is satisfied, another need gradually emerges to take its place, so people are always striving to satisfy some need.

■ The needs network for most people is very complex, with several needs affecting behavior at any one time. Clearly, when someone faces an emergency, such as desperate thirst, that need dominates until it is gratified.

■ Lower level needs must be satisfied, in general, before higher level needs are activated sufficiently to drive behavior.

■ There are more ways of satisfying higher level than lower level needs.

This model states that a person has five types of needs: physiological, security, affiliation, esteem, and self-actualization. Figure 5.2 shows these five needs categories, arranged in Maslow's hierarchy.

Physiological Needs   The needs for food, water, air, and shelter are all **physiological needs** and are the lowest level in Maslow's hierarchy. People concentrate on satisfying these needs before turning to higher order needs. Managers should understand that, to the extent that employees are motivated by physiological needs, their concerns do not center on the work they are doing. They will accept any job that meets their needs. Managers who focus on physiological needs in trying to motivate subordinates assume that people work primarily for money and are primarily concerned with comfort, avoidance of fatigue, and the like.

Security Needs   The needs for safety, stability, and absence of pain, threat, or illness are all **security needs.** Like physiological needs, unsatisfied security needs cause people to be preoccupied with satisfying them. People who are motivated primarily by security needs value their jobs mainly as a defense against the loss of basic need satisfactions. Managers who feel that security needs are most important focus on them by emphasizing rules, job security, and fringe benefits. Managers who think that subordinates are primarily interested in security neither encourage innovation nor reward risk taking. Their employees, in turn, will strictly follow the rules set for them.

Affiliation Needs   The needs for friendship, love, and a feeling of belonging are all **affiliation needs.** When physiological and security needs have been satisfied, affiliation needs emerge. Managers need to realize that, when affiliation needs are the primary source of motivation, people value their work as an opportunity for finding and establishing warm and friendly interpersonal relationships. Sharon

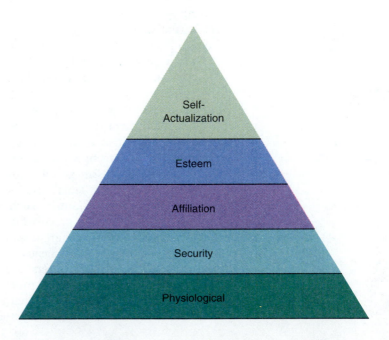

■ **FIGURE 5.2**

Maslow's Needs Hierarchy

Woodson of Colgate-Palmolive Company needed to satisfy her affiliation needs while stationed in China. She and her husband joined a group of U.S. managers and their spouses to help satisfy these needs. Managers and team leaders who believe that employees are striving primarily to satisfy these needs are likely to act supportively. They emphasize employee acceptance by co-workers, extracurricular activities (such as organized sports programs and company celebrations), and team-based norms.

Esteem Needs   Personal feelings of achievement and self-worth and recognition or respect from others meet **esteem needs.** People with esteem needs want others to accept them for what they are and to perceive them as competent and able. Managers who focus on esteem needs try to motivate employees with public rewards and recognition for services. These managers may use lapel pins, articles in the company paper, achievement lists on the bulletin board, and the like to promote their employees' pride in their work. Some people like to be told in private by their manager that they are performing well, and don't like public recognition. In either case, the person's esteem needs are being satisfied. UPS motivated drivers such as Steve Menkhaus by satisfying their esteem needs.

Self-Actualization Needs   Self-fulfillment comes from meeting **self-actualization needs.** People who strive for self-actualization come to accept themselves and others and increase their problem-solving abilities. Managers who emphasize self-actualization may involve employees in designing jobs, make special assignments that capitalize on employees' unique skills, or give employee teams leeway in planning and implementing their work. When Gary Brown opened his first Routh Street Brewery, he achieved fulfillment of his self-actualization needs.

Significance for the Workplace   Maslow's needs hierarchy model also suggests the types of behaviors that will help fulfill various needs. The three lowest needs— physiological, safety, and social—are also known as **deficiency needs.** According to Maslow, unless these needs are satisfied, an individual will fail to develop into a healthy person, both physically and psychologically. In contrast, esteem and self-actualization needs are known as **growth needs.** Satisfaction of these needs helps a person grow and develop as a human being.

   This model provides less complete information about the origin of needs. However, it implies that higher level needs are present in most people, even if they don't recognize or act to meet those needs. These higher level needs will motivate most people if nothing occurs to block their emergence.

   The needs hierarchy is based on U.S. cultural values. In cultures that value uncertainty avoidance, such as Japan and Greece, job security and lifelong employment are stronger motivators than self-actualization. Moreover, in Denmark, Sweden, and Norway, the value and reward of quality of life is more important than productivity. Thus social needs are stronger than self-actualization and self-esteem needs. In countries such as China, Japan, and Korea that value collectivist and community practices over individual achievements, belonging and security are considerably more important than meeting growth needs. Therefore, although the needs that Maslow identified may be universal, the logic or sequence of the hierarchy differs from culture to culture.[7]

   Maslow's work has received much attention from managers, as well as psychologists.[8] Research has found that top managers are better able to satisfy their esteem and self-actualization needs than are lower level managers; part of the reason is that top managers have more challenging jobs and opportunities for self-actualization. Employees who work on teams have been able to satisfy their higher level needs by making decisions that affect their team and company. For example, at Lockheed Martin Vought's Camden, Arkansas, plant, employees are trained to perform multiple tasks, including hiring and training team members—and even firing those who fail to perform adequately. As team members learn new tasks, they start satisfying their higher level needs. Employees who have little or no control over their work (such as assembly-line workers) may not even experience higher level needs in relation to their jobs. Studies have also shown that the fulfillment of needs differs according to the job a person performs, a person's age and background, and the size of the company.

■ ERG MODEL

Clay Alderfer agrees with Maslow that individuals have a hierarchy of needs. However, instead of the five categories of needs suggested by Maslow, Alderfer's **ERG model** holds that the individual has three sets of basic needs: existence, relatedness, and growth.[9] Alderfer describes them in the following way.

- **Existence needs,** or material needs, are satisfied by food, air, water, pay, fringe benefits, and working conditions.
- **Relatedness needs** are met by establishing and maintaining interpersonal relationships with co-workers, superiors, subordinates, friends, and family.
- **Growth needs** are expressed by an individual's attempt to find opportunities for unique personal development by making creative or productive contributions at work.

The arrangement of these categories of needs is similar to Maslow's. Existence needs generally correspond to Maslow's physiological and safety needs; relatedness needs generally correspond to Maslow's affiliation needs; and growth needs generally correspond to Maslow's esteem and self-actualization needs.

The two models differ, however, in their views of how people may satisfy different sets of needs. Maslow states that unfilled needs are motivators and that the next higher level need isn't activated until the preceding lower level need is satisfied. Thus a person progresses up the needs hierarchy as each set of lower level needs is satisfied. In contrast, the ERG model suggests that, in addition to this fulfillment–progression process, a frustration–regression process is at work. That is, if a person is continually frustrated in attempts to satisfy growth needs, relatedness needs will reemerge as a motivating force. The individual will return to satisfying this lower level need instead of attempting to satisfy growth needs, and frustration will lead to regression.

Figure 5.3 illustrates these relationships. The solid line indicates a direct relationship between needs, desires, and needs satisfaction. The dashed lines represent what happens when a set of needs is frustrated. For example, if a person's growth needs are frustrated on the job because of the lack of challenging assignments, the importance of relatedness needs, usually satisfied by their co-workers, increases. The same behavior (performing routine tasks) that had led to the frustration of growth needs now becomes the means for the person to satisfy relatedness needs. Often, when attempts to satisfy relatedness needs have been frustrated, people seek refuge in food and alcohol or drugs to satisfy their existence needs. The frustration–regression idea is based on the assumption that existence,

■ FIGURE 5.3   ERG Needs Model

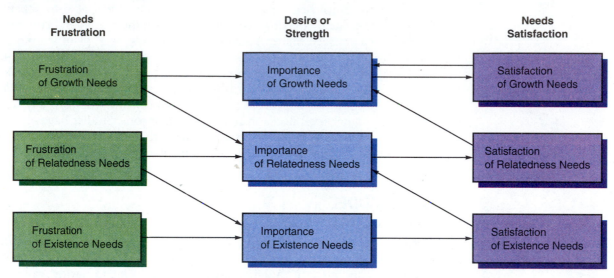

Source: From *Psychology of Work Behavior*, by F. Landy. Copyright © 1989, 1985, 1980, 1976 Brooks/Cole Publishing Company, Pacific Grove, CA 93950, a division of International Thomson Publishing, Inc. By permission of the publisher.

relatedness, and growth needs vary along a continuum of concreteness, with existence being the most concrete and growth being the least concrete. Alderfer further proposes that when lesser concrete needs are not met, more concrete needs fulfillment is sought. (Note that the direction of the dashed lines in Figure 5.3 is downward from needs frustration to needs strength.)

Significance for the Workplace   The ERG model holds that individuals are motivated to engage in behavior to satisfy one of the three sets of needs. Thus Alderfer's ERG model provides an important insight for managers. What should a manager do if a subordinate's growth needs are blocked, perhaps because the job doesn't permit satisfaction of these needs or there are no resources to satisfy them? The answer is that the manager should try to redirect the employee's behavior toward satisfying relatedness or existence needs.[10]

Few research studies have tested the ERG model of motivation. However, several studies do support the three sets of needs presented in the ERG model, rather than the five categories of needs in Maslow's hierarchy. Some managers question the model's universality, finding that it doesn't help them understand what motivates employees in their organizations.

We believe that Maslow's needs hierarchy and Alderfer's ERG models both offer useful ways of thinking about employee motivation. The fact that there is disagreement over the exact number of categories of needs should be noted, but both models agree that satisfying needs is an important part of motivation.

Managers in some global organizations report that the needs models help them understand employee motivation. The following Across Cultures selection indicates how one manager used these models to motivate workers. Note how Bretislav Jackubik manages to satisfy his employees existence, relatedness, and growth needs.

ACROSS CULTURES

Motivating Czech Employees

Bretislav Jackubik is an electrical contractor in Zlechov, Czech Republic. He worked as an electrician for a state-owned company until the collapse of the communist regime. "When that happened, I put my tool bag on my shoulder and went from town to town looking for work," says Jackubik. He found plenty of work, but he didn't like that way of life. Four years ago he started his own electrical wiring and heating systems firm.

In a country where the unemployment rate is among the lowest in all of Europe, hiring and keeping qualified and motivated employees is a challenge. He places ads in the newspaper, goes to the employment office, and lures workers from other firms by offering them high pay or better benefits (existence needs). Each worker is hired at an entry level and monitored for ninety days. During this period, the workers are moved from job to job to determine where they can best perform (growth needs).

To encourage hard work and company loyalty, he bases the pay of all his employees on their performance (existence needs). Supervisors are paid according to how pleased customers are, and other employees are paid according to the speed and quality of their work (growth needs). Jackubik offers workers high salaries and benefits and encourages them to develop disciplined work habits. Drinking on the job, dishonesty, and absence without notice are grounds for immediate dismissal (relatedness needs). To combat workplace theft, Jackubik encourages workers to ask for what they want and sells it to them at his cost (relatedness needs).[11]

Source: "Motivating Czech Employees" by Patricia E. Kriska.

■ ACHIEVEMENT MOTIVATION MODEL

David McClelland proposed a learned needs model of motivation that he believed to be rooted in culture.[12] He argued that everyone has three particularly important needs: for achievement, affiliation, and power. Individuals who possess a strong *power motive* take action that affects the behaviors of others and has a strong emotional appeal. These individuals are concerned with providing status rewards to their followers. Individuals who have a strong *affiliation motive* tend to establish, maintain, and restore close personal relationships with others. Individuals who have a strong *achievement motive* compete against some standard of excellence or unique contribution against which they judge their behaviors and achievements.

McClelland has studied achievement motivation extensively, especially with regard to entrepreneurship. His **achievement motivation model** states that people are motivated according to the strength of their desire either to perform in terms of a standard of excellence or to succeed in competitive situations. According to McClelland, almost all people believe that they have an "achievement motive," but probably only 10 percent of the U.S. population is strongly motivated to achieve. The amount of achievement motivation that people have depends on their childhood, their personal and occupational experiences, and the type of organization for which they work. Table 5.2 shows an application of McClelland's model to presidents of the United States. Presidents' motives can be

TABLE 5.2 Presidents' Needs for Power, Achievement, and Affiliation

	NEEDS		
PRESIDENT	**Power**	**Achievement**	**Affiliation**
Clinton, B.	Moderate	High	High
Bush, G.	Moderate	Moderate	Low
Reagan, R.	High	Moderate	Low
Kennedy, J. F.	High	Low	High
Roosevelt, F. D.	High	Low	Moderate
Lincoln, A.	Moderate	Low	Moderate
Washington, G.	Low	Low	Moderate

Source: Adapted from House, R. J., Spangler, Wm. D., and Woycke, J. Personality and charisma in the U. S. President: A psychological theory of leader effectiveness. *Administrative Science Quarterly*, 1992, 36, 395.

documented by the legislation they have proposed and the policies they have pursued during their tenures.

According to McClelland's model, motives are "stored" in the preconscious mind just below the level of full awareness. They lie between the conscious and the unconscious, in the area of daydreams, where people talk to themselves without quite being aware of it. A basic premise of the model is that the pattern of these daydreams can be tested and that people can be taught to change their motivation by changing these daydreams.

Measuring Achievement Motivation   McClelland measured the strength of a person's achievement motivation with the **Thematic Apperception Test (TAT).** The TAT uses unstructured pictures that may arouse many kinds of reactions in the person being tested. Examples include an ink blot that a person can perceive as many different objects or a picture that can generate a variety of stories. There are no right or wrong answers, and the person isn't given a limited set of alternatives from which to choose. A major goal of the TAT is to obtain the individual's own perception of the world. The TAT is called a projective method because it emphasizes individual perceptions of stimuli, the meaning each individual gives to them, and how each individual organizes them. (The process of perception was discussed in Chapter 3).

One projective test involves looking at the picture shown in Figure 5.4 for ten to fifteen seconds and then writing a short story about it that answers the following questions.

■ What is going on in this picture?
■ What is the woman thinking?
■ What has led up to this situation?

Write your own story about the picture. Then compare it with the following story written by a manager exhibiting strong achievement motivation, whom McClelland would describe as a high achiever.

The individual is an officer in a small entrepreneurial organization who wants to get a contract for her company. She knows that the competition will be tough, because all the big firms are bidding on this contract. She is taking a moment to think how happy she will be if her company is awarded the large contract. It will mean stability for the company and probably a large raise for her. She is satisfied because she has just thought

■ **FIGURE 5.4**

Source: FPG International

of a way to manufacture a critical part that will enable her company to bring in a low bid and complete the job with time to spare.

What motivational profile did you identify? Does it match the executive's?

Characteristics of High Achievers

Self-motivated high achievers have three major characteristics.[13] First, they like to set their own goals. Seldom content to drift aimlessly and let life happen to them, they nearly always are trying to accomplish something. High achievers seek the challenge of making tough decisions. They are selective about the goals to which they commit themselves. Hence they are unlikely to automatically accept goals that other people, including their superiors, attempt to select for them. They exercise self-control over their behaviors, especially the ways they pursue the goals selected. They tend to seek advice or help only from experts who can provide needed knowledge or skills. High achievers prefer to be as fully responsible for attaining their goals as possible. If they win, they want the credit; if they lose, they accept the blame. For example, assume that you are given a choice between rolling dice with one chance in three of winning or working on a problem with one chance in three of solving the problem in the time allotted. Which would you choose? A high achiever would choose to work on the problem, even though rolling the dice is obviously less work and the odds of winning are the same. High achievers prefer to work at a problem rather than leave the outcome to chance or to other people.

Second, high achievers avoid selecting extremely difficult goals. They prefer moderate goals that are neither so easy that attaining them provides no satisfaction nor so difficult that attaining them is more a matter of luck than ability. They gauge what is possible and then select as difficult a goal as they think they can attain. The game of ringtoss illustrates this point. Most carnivals have ringtoss games that require participants to throw rings over a peg from some minimum distance but specify no maximum distance. Imagine the same game but with people allowed to stand at any distance they want from the peg. Some will throw more or less randomly, standing close and then far away. Those with high-achievement motivation will seem to calculate carefully where they should stand to have the greatest chance of winning a prize and still feel challenged. These individuals seem to stand at a distance that isn't so close as to make the task ridiculously easy and isn't so far away as to make it impossible. They set a distance moderately far away from which they can potentially ring a peg. Thus they set personal challenges and enjoy tasks that will stretch their abilities.

Third, high achievers prefer tasks that provide immediate feedback. Because of the goal's importance to them, they like to know how well they're doing. That's one reason why the high achiever often chooses a professional career, a sales career, or entrepreneurial activities. Golf appeals to most high achievers: Golfers can compare their scores to par for the course, to their own previous performance on the course, and to their opponents' score; performance is related to both feedback (score) and goal (par).

Financial Incentives

Money has a complex effect on high achievers. They usually value highly their services and place a high price tag on them. High achievers are usually self-confident. They are aware of their abilities and limitations and thus are confident when they choose to do a particular job. They are unlikely to remain very long in an organization that doesn't pay them well. Whether an incentive plan actually increases their performance is an open question because they normally work at peak efficiency. They value money as a strong symbol of their achievement and adequacy. A financial incentive may create dissatisfaction if they feel that it inadequately reflects their contributions.

When achievement motivation is operating, outstanding performance of a challenging task is likely. However, achievement motivation doesn't operate when high achievers are performing routine or boring tasks or when there is no competition against goals. When Ron Petty was hired to turn around the financial fortunes of Denny's, he used his achievement motivation to solve a thorny problem: Change a company into a model of cultural sensitivity, as described in the following Diversity in Practice piece.

DIVERSITY IN PRACTICE

Petty's Diversity Program

On April 1, 1993, six black Secret Service agents at a Denny's restaurant in Annapolis, Maryland, waited nearly an hour for breakfast. While they were ignored, their white colleagues sitting at a table nearby were served quickly and drank several cups of coffee. When the black agents went public with their treatment, almost overnight Denny's became a national symbol of bigotry.

Within months, Ron Petty was hired. He established challenging goals: 65 percent of Denny's employees would be minority (people of color) and women by the end of 1997. In 1993, there were no nonwhite vice-presidents. Similarly, in 1993, minorities held only 11 percent of the jobs below vice-president; today minorities hold 20 percent of those jobs. Petty worked hard to settle the class action lawsuits filed against Denny's. By 1996, it had paid $54 million to more than 295,000 aggrieved minority customers. Denny's promised to treat all customers equally and train all employees to respect diversity. To accomplish these goals, Petty eliminated three layers of management whose jobs had been to monitor people. He empowered restaurant managers to make decisions; made diversity a performance goal for all managers, and required all employees to attend workshops on racial sensitivity. Employees who refuse to attend such sessions are dismissed. He initiated a management training program to give minorities and women access to executive ranks and a fast-track program to help them become Denny's franchisees. Applicants enroll in this program for as long as three years, during which time they must prove that they can successfully operate a restaurant.

Petty's results have been impressive. Operating income is up 4 percent after rebounding 35 percent in 1994 from its 1993 level. Customer traffic is up by 7 percent, and annual sales now exceed $1 billion.[14]

Significance for the Workplace   Most of the research supporting the achievement motivation model has been conducted by McClelland and his associates at McBer and Company. Based on this research, they recommend the following approach.

■ Arrange tasks so that employees receive periodic feedback on their performance. Feedback will enable employees to modify their behaviors as necessary.

- Provide good role models of achievement. Employees should be encouraged to have heroes to emulate.
- Modify employee self-images. High-achievement individuals accept themselves and seek job challenges and responsibilities.
- Guide employee aspirations. Employees should think about setting realistic goals and the ways that they can attain them.
- Make it known that managers who have been successful are those that are higher in power motivation than in affiliation motivation.

One of the primary problems with the achievement motivation model is also its greatest strength.[15] The TAT method is valuable because it allows the researcher to tap the preconscious motives of people. This method has some advantages over questionnaires, but the interpretation of a story is more of an art than a science. As a result, the method's reliability is open to question. The permanency of the model's three needs has also been questioned. Further research is needed to explore the model's validity.

■ MOTIVATOR-HYGIENE MODEL

The **motivator-hygiene model** is one of the most controversial models of motivation, probably because of two unique features. First, it stresses that some job factors lead to satisfaction, whereas others can prevent dissatisfaction but not be sources of satisfaction. Second, it states that job satisfaction and dissatisfaction do not exist on a single continuum.

Frederick Herzberg and his associates examined the relationship between job satisfaction and productivity in a group of accountants and engineers. Through the use of semistructured interviews, they accumulated data on various factors that these professionals said had an effect on their feelings about their jobs. Two different sets of factors emerged: motivators and hygienes.[16]

Motivator Factors The first set of factors, **motivator factors,** includes the work itself, recognition, advancement, and responsibility. These factors relate to an individual's positive feelings about the job and are related to the content of the job itself. These positive feelings, in turn, are associated with the individual's experiences of achievement, recognition, and responsibility. They reflect lasting rather than temporary achievement in the work setting. In other words, motivators are **intrinsic factors,** which are directly related to the job and are largely internal to the individual. The organization's policies may have only an indirect impact on them. But, by defining exceptional performance, for example, an organization may enable individuals to feel that they have performed their tasks exceptionally well.

Hygiene Factors The second set of factors, **hygiene factors,** includes company policy and administration, technical supervision, salary, fringe benefits, working conditions, and interpersonal relations. These factors are associated with an individual's negative feelings about the job and are related to the environment in which the job is performed. Hygienes are **extrinsic factors,** or factors external to the job. Extrinsic factors serve as rewards for high performance only if the organization recognizes high performance.

Steven Wynn, Chairman of Mirage Resorts, a 3000-room hotel and gaming casino on the Las Vegas strip, uses his knowledge of motivation and hygiene factors to keep staff turnover low and guests coming back. Eighty-nine other casino/hotels in Las Vegas vie for customers. The following Managing in Practice feature describes Mirage Resorts' use of some unique motivational practices with its employees.

MANAGING IN PRACTICE

Mirage Hotels Bets and Wins

When Mirage opened its Treasure Island extravaganza in 1993, it received more than 57,000 applications for its 6500 positions. Why? Mirage Resorts offers several different medical plans, life and disability insurance, paid time off for perfect attendance, and retirement plans (hygienes). In addition, it offers employees classes on everything from how to balance their checkbooks to how to communicate with deaf patrons in sign language. Classes on wallpaper, nutrition, and dieting are very popular. It brings an instructor from the U.S. Immigration and Naturalization Service to help noncitizens get their citizenship. It teaches cocktail servers what the various cocktails are and how to serve them. It also teaches them how to help people if they get too intoxicated and to stop serving them without causing a scene (motivators).

Mirage also provides employees with ample career opportunities. When managers need to hire additional employees, they must first interview internal candidates before going outside to recruit. Employees can move to another more challenging job if they are qualified (motivators). The Mirage recruits from colleges that have hotel-management majors and puts these new recruits through an extensive twenty-six week training program. The program covers everything from food and beverages to identifying customers who cheat the house.[17]

Cultural Influences   One of the important themes of this book is recognizing and addressing cultural diversity in the work force. As U.S. organizations continue to expand overseas and foreign organizations establish manufacturing sites in Canada, Mexico, and the United States, managers must be aware of cultural differences and how these differences can affect the motivation of employees. Herzberg believes that, despite cultural differences, motivators and hygienes affect workers similarly around the world. The data in Table 5.3 support this view. It shows that for U.S. workers about 80 percent of the factors that lead to job satisfaction can be traced to motivators. For workers in the other countries listed, motivators accounted for 60 to 90 percent of the reason for job satisfaction. Hygienes accounted for most of the reasons that workers were dissatisfied with their jobs. In Finland, 80 percent of the workers indicated that hygiene factors contributed mainly to job dissatisfaction, whereas only 10 percent said that hygiene factors contributed to their job satisfaction.

With the passage of the North American Free Trade Agreement (NAFTA), employees in North America will be working closer with others who don't necessarily share similar work motivation. It doesn't take U.S. managers very long to realize that employees in Mexico have different motives toward work. In the United States workers generally favor taking the initiative, having individual

TABLE 5.3 Motivators and Hygienes Across Cultures

MOTIVATORS	SATISFYING JOB EVENTS	DISSATISFYING JOB EVENTS
United States	80%	20%
Japan	82%	40%
Finland	90%	18%
Hungary	78%	30%
Italy	60%	5%
HYGIENES		
United States	20%	75%
Japan	10%	65%
Finland	10%	80%
Hungary	22%	78%
Italy	30%	70%

Source: Adapted from Furnham, A., Kirkcaldy, B. D., and Lynn, R. National attitudes toward competitiveness, money, and work among young people. *Human Relations*, 1994, 47, 119–133; Jacob, R. Secure jobs trump higher pay. *Fortune*, March 20, 1995, 24–26; Herzberg, F. Worker's needs: The same around the world. *Industry Week*, September 21, 1987, 29–32.

responsibility, and taking failure personally. They are competitive, have high goals, and live for the future. In Mexico workers are comfortable operating in groups and the group shares both success and failure. They tend to be cooperative, flexible, and enjoy life as it is, now.[18]

In Mexico, employees' priorities are family, religion, and work. During the year, plant managers host family dinners to celebrate anniversaries of employees who have worked there five, ten, fifteen, and twenty years. Employees may use the company clubhouse for weddings, baptisms, anniversary parties, and other family celebrations. Organizations also host a family day during which employees' families can tour the plant, enjoy entertainment and food, and participate in sports.

The typical workday in Mexico is 8 A.M. to 5:30 P.M. Employees are picked up by the company bus at various locations throughout the city. Employees like to eat their main meal in the middle of the day, the cost of which is heavily subsidized (as much as 70 percent) by the company. Interestingly, managers serve the employees this meal.[19]

The motivator-hygiene model also states that satisfaction and dissatisfaction do not form a single continuum but are on separate and distinct continuums, as indicated in Figure 5.5. Thus a person can be satisfied and dissatisfied at the same time, according to this model.

Significance for the Workplace The research designed to test the motivator-hygiene model hasn't provided clear-cut evidence that either supports or rejects it. One aspect of the model that appeals to managers is the use of common terms to explain how to motivate people. They don't have to translate psychological terms into everyday language. However, because hygiene factors are easy to identify, they have become targets for shareholder complaints when the value of the company's stock drops.

In 1996, AT&T announced that it was laying off 40,000 workers to cut costs and prepare to spin off the company's equipment and computer lines of business. Shortly after this announcement, AT&T's Chairmen Robert Allen's salary of

■ FIGURE 5.5

Motivator-Hygiene Situations

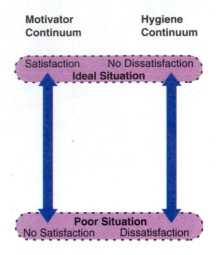

■ FIGURE 5.5

Motivator-Hygiene Situations

$16.2 million and an additional $12.9 million in stock options and other incentive pay plans was reported. Because AT&T's stock performance under Allen's leadership had been about average for all stocks on the New York Stock Exchange, shareholders, employees, and pension fund managers all were critical of his compensation package. Employees in particular were furious over the prospect of being let go while those in top management enriched themselves.[20]

Despite its attractive features, several significant criticisms have been leveled at the motivator-hygiene model.[21] One is that Herzberg used a method-bound procedure; that is, the method he used to measure the factors determined the results. He asked two key questions: "Can you describe, in detail, when you felt exceptionally good about your job?" and "Can you describe, in detail, when you felt exceptionally bad about your job?" In response to such questions, people tend to give socially desirable answers, that is, answers they think the researcher wants to hear or that sound "reasonable." Also, people tend to attribute good job results to their own efforts and to attribute reasons for poor results to others (recall the discussion of the self-serving bias attribution in Chapter 3).

Another serious question about the motivator-hygiene model is whether satisfaction and dissatisfaction really are two separate dimensions, as Figure 5.5 indicates. Research results are mixed. Some researchers have found factors that can contribute to both satisfaction and dissatisfaction, whereas others have found that motivator factors can contribute to dissatisfaction and hygiene factors can contribute to satisfaction. For example, in Hungary, employees reported that, although hygiene factors were related to many dissatisfying features of their jobs, some hygiene factors were also related to satisfying events. These findings, however, haven't disproved the concept that satisfaction and dissatisfaction are two different continuums.

Some evidence, though not strong, links experiences such as increasing job responsibility, challenge, and advancement opportunities to high performance. Unfortunately, researchers have paid little attention to constructing a model that explains why certain job factors affect performance positively or negatively. Similarly, few attempts have been made using content models to explain why certain outcomes are attractive to employees or why they choose one type of behavior over another to obtain a desired outcome.

■ COMPARISONS AMONG CONTENT MODELS

The four content models emphasize the basic motivational concepts of needs, achievement motivation, and hygiene-motivators. Figure 5.6 highlights the relationships among these four models. The needs hierarchy model served as the basis for the ERG model. Therefore there are some important similarities between the two: self-actualization and esteem needs make up growth needs; affiliation needs are similar to relatedness needs; and security and physiological needs are the building blocks of existence needs in the ERG model. A major difference between these two models is that the hierarchy of needs model offers a static needs system based on fulfillment–progression, whereas the ERG model presents a flexible three-needs classification system based on frustration-regression.

The motivator-hygiene model draws on both of the needs models. That is, if hygiene factors are present, security and physiological needs (needs hierarchy) are likely to be met. Similarly, if hygiene factors are present, relatedness and existence needs (ERG model) aren't likely to be frustrated. Motivator factors focus on the job itself and the opportunity for the person to satisfy higher order needs, or growth needs (ERG model).

The achievement motivation model doesn't recognize lower order needs. The need for affiliation can be satisfied if a person meets hygiene factors on the job. If the job itself is challenging and provides an opportunity for a person to make meaningful decisions, it is motivating. These conditions go a long way toward satisfying the need for achievement.

The content models provide an understanding of the particular work-related factors that start the motivational process. These models, however, promote little understanding of why people choose a particular behavior to accomplish task-related goals. This aspect of choice is the major focus of process models of motivation.

PROCESS MODELS OF MOTIVATION

Process models are used to describe and analyze how personal factors (internal to the person) interact and influence each other to produce certain kinds of behavior. An example would be that individuals exert more effort to obtain rewards that satisfy important needs than to obtain rewards that do not. The four best known process models of motivation are expectancy, reinforcement, equity, and goal setting. In this section, we cover the expectancy and equity models of motivation. In Chapter 4, we discussed the reinforcement model, and in Chapter 6 we present the goal-setting model.

■ EXPECTANCY MODEL

The expectancy model differs markedly from the content models just discussed. Instead of focusing on factors in the work environment that contribute to job satisfaction or dissatisfaction, the expectancy model covers the entire work environment.[22] The **expectancy model** states that people are motivated to work when they expect to achieve things they want from their jobs. These things might include satisfaction of safety needs, the excitement of doing a challenging task, or the ability to set and achieve difficult goals. A basic premise of the expectancy model is that employees are rational people. They think about what they have to do to be rewarded and how much the rewards mean to them before they perform

FIGURE 5.6   Matching Content Models

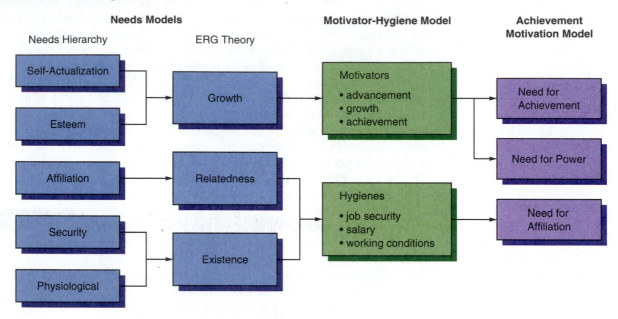

their jobs. Four assumptions about the causes of behavior in organizations provide the basis for this model.

First, a combination of forces in the individual and the environment determines behavior (recall the discussion of the interactionist perspective in Chapter 2). Neither the individual nor the environment alone determines behavior. People join organizations with expectations about their jobs that are based on their needs, motivations, and past experiences. These factors all influence how people respond to an organization. But these factors can and do change over time.

Second, individuals decide their own behaviors in organizations, even though many constraints are placed on individual behavior (for example, through rules, technology, and work-group norms). Most individuals make two kinds of conscious decisions: (1) decisions about coming to work, staying with the same organization, and joining other organizations (membership decisions); and (2) decisions about how much to produce, how hard to work, and the quality of workmanship (job-performance decisions).

Third, different individuals have different needs and goals. Employees want different rewards from their work (for example, job security, promotion, good pay, and challenge). Again, not all employees want the same things from their jobs. As Mike Doyle discovered, Chinese employees have different expectations about their work than do most U.S. workers.

Fourth, individuals decide among alternatives based on their perceptions of whether a specific behavior will lead to a desired outcome. Individuals do what they perceive will lead to desired rewards and avoid doing what they perceive will lead to undesirable outcomes.[23]

In general, the expectancy model holds that individuals have their own needs and ideas about what they desire from their work (rewards). They act on these needs and ideas when making decisions about what organization to join and how hard to work. The model also holds that individuals are not inherently motivated or unmotivated, rather that motivation depends on the situation facing individuals and how it fits their needs.

To understand the expectancy model, we must define its most important variables and explain how they operate. They are first-level and second-level outcomes, expectancy, valence, and instrumentality.

First-Level and Second-Level Outcomes   The results of behaviors associated with doing the job itself are called **first-level outcomes.** They include level of performance, amount of absenteeism, and quality of work. **Second-level outcomes** are the rewards (either positive or negative) that first-level outcomes are likely to produce. They include a pay increase, promotion, acceptance by co-workers, and job security.

Expectancy   The belief that a particular level of effort will be followed by a particular level of performance is called **expectancy.** It can vary from the belief that there is absolutely no relationship between effort and performance to the certainty that a given level of effort will result in a corresponding level of performance. Expectancy has a value ranging from 0, indicating no chance that a first-level outcome will occur after the behavior, to +1, indicating certainty that a particular first-level outcome will follow a behavior. For example, if you believe that you have no chance of getting a good grade on the next exam by studying this chapter, your expectancy value would be 0. Having this expectancy, you shouldn't study this chapter.

Instrumentality   The relationship between first-level outcomes and second-level outcomes is called **instrumentality.** It can have values ranging from −1 to +1. A −1 indicates that attainment of a second-level outcome is inversely related to the achievement of a first-level outcome. For example, Herb Reed wants to be accepted as a member of his work group. His work group has a norm for acceptable levels of performance. If Herb violates this norm, he won't be accepted by his work group. Therefore Herb limits his performance so as not to violate the group's norm. A +1 indicates that the first-level outcome is positively related to the second-level outcome. For example, if you received an A on all your exams, the probability that you would achieve your desired second-level outcome (passing this course) approaches +1. If there were no relationship between your performance on a test and either passing or failing this course, your instrumentality would be 0.

Valence   An individual's preference for a particular second-level outcome is called **valence.** Positive valences include being respected by friends and co-workers, performing meaningful work, having job security, and earning enough money to support oneself and a family. Negative valences are things that you want to avoid, such as being laid off, being passed over for a promotion, or receiving a disciplinary discharge for sexual harassment.

An outcome is positive when it is preferred and negative when it is not preferred or is to be avoided. An outcome has a valence of 0 when the individual is indifferent about receiving it.

Putting It Together   In brief, the expectancy model holds that work motivation is determined by individual beliefs regarding effort–performance relationships and the desirability of various work outcomes associated with different performance levels. Simply put, you can remember the model's important features by the saying:

People exert work effort to achieve performance that leads to valued work-related outcomes.

Expectancy Model in Action These five key variables lead to a general expectancy model of motivation, as shown in Figure 5.7. Motivation is the force that causes individuals to expend effort. Effort alone is not enough, however. Unless an individual believes that effort will lead to some desired performance level (first-level outcome), he or she won't make much of an effort. The effort–performance relationship is based on a perception of the difficulty of achieving a particular behavior (say, working for an A in this course) and the probability of achieving that behavior. On the one hand, you may have a high expectancy that if you attend class, study the book, take good notes, and prepare for exams, you could achieve an A in this class. That expectancy is likely to translate into making the effort required on those activities to get an A. On the other hand, you may believe that even if you attend class, study the book, take good notes, and prepare for exams, your chances of getting an A are only 20 percent. That expectancy is likely to keep you from expending the effort required on these activities to achieve an A.

Performance level is important in obtaining desired second-level outcomes. Figure 5.7 shows four desirable outcomes: passing the course, making the dean's list, gaining admission to graduate school, and gaining further respect from other students and parents. In general, if you feel that a particular level of performance (A, B, C, D, or F) will lead to these desired outcomes, you are more likely to try to perform at that level. If you really desire these four second-level outcomes and you can achieve them only if you get an A in this course, the instrumentality between receiving an A and these four outcomes will be +1. But, if you believe that getting an A in this course means that you will lose some friends and that these friends are more important to you, the instrumentality between an A and this outcome will be negative. That is, the higher the grade, the more your friends will ignore you, and you might choose not to get an A in this course.

Research Findings Researchers are still working on ways to test this model, which has presented some problems.[24] First, the model tries to predict choice or the amount of effort an individual will expend on one or more tasks. However, there is little agreement about what constitutes choice or effort for different individuals. Therefore this important variable is difficult to measure accurately. Second, the expectancy model doesn't specify which second-level outcomes are important to a particular individual in a given situation. Although researchers are expected to address this issue, comparison of the limited results to date is often difficult because each study is unique. Take another look at the second-level outcomes in Figure 5.7. Would you choose them? What others might you choose? Finally, the model contains an implicit assumption that motivation is a conscious choice process. That is, the individual consciously calculates the pain or pleasure that he or she expects to attain or avoid when making a choice. The expectancy model says nothing about unconscious motivation or personality characteristics. In fact, people often do *not* make conscious choices about which outcomes to seek. Can you recall going through this process concerning your grade while taking this course?

Significance for the Workplace Although some research problems remain, the expectancy model has some implications for motivating employees. These implications can be grouped into a series of suggestions for action.[25]

Managers should try to determine the outcomes that each employee values. Two ways of doing so are observing employee reactions to different rewards and asking employees about the types of rewards they want from their jobs. However,

■ FIGURE 5.7   Expectancy Model in Action

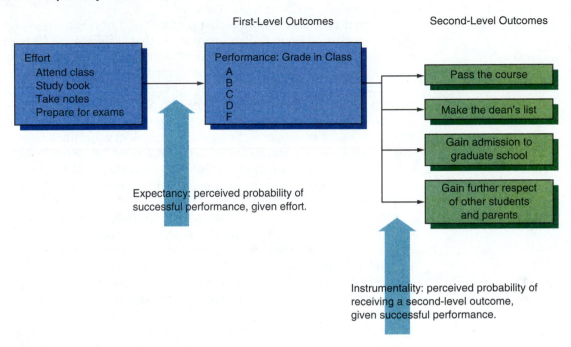

managers must recognize that employees can and do change their minds about desired outcomes over time.

Managers should define good, adequate, and poor performance in terms that are observable and measurable. Employees need to understand what is expected of them and how these expectations affect performance. Baxter Pharmaceutical Company announced a new examination table for doctors. The salespeople wanted to know what behaviors, such as cold-calling on new accounts or trying to sell the new tables to their existing accounts, would lead to more sales. To the extent that Baxter was able to train its salespeople in selling its new product, it was able to link salespeople's efforts with performance.

Managers should be sure that desired levels of performance set for employees can be attained. If employees feel that the level of performance necessary to get a reward is higher than they can reasonably achieve, their motivation to perform will be low. For example, Nordstrom tells its employees: "Respond to Unreasonable Customer Requests." Employees are urged to keep scrapbooks with "heroic" acts, such as hand delivering items purchased by phone to the airport for a customer with a last-minute business trip, changing a customer's flat tire, or paying a customer's parking ticket when in-store gift wrapping has taken longer than expected. It is hardly surprising that Nordstrom pays its employees about twice as much as they could earn at a rival's store. For those who love to sell and can meet its demanding standards, Nordstrom is nirvana.[26]

Managers should directly link the specific performance they desire to the outcomes desired by employees. Recall the discussion in Chapter 4 of how operant conditioning principles can be applied to improve performance. If an employee has achieved the desired level of performance for a promotion, the employee should be promoted as soon as possible. If a high level of motivation is to be created and maintained, it is extremely important for employees to see clearly and quickly the reward process at work. Concrete acts must accompany statements of intent in linking performance to rewards.

Managers should never forget that perceptions, not reality, determine motivation. For example, Robert Allen's conviction that his pay at AT&T wasn't related to AT&T's need to downsize the organization means little if others don't perceive it in the same terms. Too often, managers misunderstand the behavior of employees because they tend to rely on their own perceptions of the situation and forget that employees' perceptions may be different.

Managers should analyze situations for conflicts. Having set up positive expectancies for employees, managers must look at an entire situation to determine whether other factors conflict with the desired behaviors (for example, the informal work group or the organization's formal reward system). Motivation will be high only when employees perceive many rewards and few negative outcomes associated with good performance.

Managers should be sure that changes in outcomes or rewards are large enough to motivate significant efforts. Trivial rewards may result in minimal efforts, if any, to improve performance. Rewards must be large enough to motivate individuals to make the effort required to substantially change performance. Home Depot managers have relied on these practices to create a highly successful retail chain that excels at satisfying the customer. The company has been able to build customer loyalty by doing little extra things for customers and making sure that customers get exactly what they want. The following Quality in Practice selection illustrates some of Home Depot's practices that convert a shopper into a lifetime customer.

QUALITY IN PRACTICE

Working at Home Depot

Once inside the doors of a Home Depot store, you know that you are dealing with a different kind of company. You see a Home Depot employee teaching customers how to install a pedestal sink, rewire an electric outlet, build a fence, or do any number of home improvements. Orange-aproned salespeople are hired not only for their product knowledge, but, as President Art Blank notes, "their ability to raise a customer's enthusiasm about a project. We hire cheerleaders as well as coaches." Contractors asked for special checkout areas near lumber racks and Home Depot obliged. This innovation also speeded up checkout for other customers.

Teaching isn't all focused on the customer. Before a new Home Depot store opens, employees receive nearly four weeks of training. Some of this training is simple, such as having all employees walk repeatedly through the store so that they know where everything is and can tell the customer exactly what aisle to go to for a particular item. Home Depot also holds quarterly Sunday morning meetings in which all 23,000 employees, via a satellite TV hookup in each store, learn about the company's past financial performance and growth plans, and have an opportunity to ask the president any questions they might have. Employees are publicly rewarded for introducing new products, such as a bridal registry for the young homeowner.[27]

■ EQUITY MODEL

Feelings of unfairness were among the most frequent sources of job dissatisfaction reported to Herzberg and his associates. Some researchers have made this desire for fairness, justice, or equity a central focus of their models. Assume that you just received a 7 percent raise. Will this raise lead to higher performance, lower performance, or no change in your performance? Are you satisfied with this increase? Would your satisfaction with this pay increase vary with the consumer price index, with what you expected to get, or with what others in the organization performing the same job and at the same performance level received?

The **equity model** focuses on an individual's feelings of how fairly he or she is treated in comparison with others.[28] The model contains two major assumptions. The first is that individuals evaluate their interpersonal relationships just as they would evaluate the buying or selling of a home, shares of stock, or a car. The model views interpersonal relationships as exchange processes in which individuals make contributions and expect certain results.

The second is that individuals don't operate in a vacuum. They compare their situations to those of others to determine equity of an exchange. In other words, what happens to the individual is important in terms of what happens to the others involved (such as co-workers, relatives, and neighbors).

General Equity Model   The equity model is based on the comparison of two variables: inputs and outcomes. **Inputs** represent what an individual contributes to an exchange; **outcomes** are what an individual receives from the exchange. Some typical inputs and outcomes are shown in Table 5.4. However, The items in the two lists aren't paired and don't represent specific exchanges.

According to equity model, individuals assign weights to various inputs and outcomes according to their perceptions of the situation. Because most situations involve multiple inputs and outcomes, the weighting process isn't precise. However, people generally can distinguish between important and less important inputs and outcomes. After they arrive at a ratio of inputs and outcomes for themselves, they compare it with their perceived ratios of inputs and outcomes of others who are in the same or a similar situation. These relevant others become

TABLE 5.4   Examples of Inputs and Outcomes in Organizations

INPUTS	OUTCOMES
Age	Challenging job assignments
Attendance	Fringe benefits
Interpersonal skills	Job perquisites (parking space
Communication skills	or office location)
Job effort (long hours)	Job security
Level of education	Monotony
Past experience	Promotion
Performance	Recognition
Personal appearance	Responsibility
Seniority	Salary
Social status	Seniority benefits
Technical skills	Status symbols
Training	Working conditions

the objects of comparison for individuals in determining whether they feel equitably treated.

Equity exists whenever the ratio of a person's outcomes to inputs equals the ratio of outcomes to inputs for relevant others. For example, an individual may feel properly paid in terms of what he or she puts into a job compared to what other workers are getting for their inputs. **Inequity** exists when the ratios of outcomes to inputs are unequal. Chet Ciancarelli, an engineer with Computer Language Research, works harder than his co-workers, completes all his tasks on time while others don't, and puts in longer hours than others, but receives the same pay raise as the others. What happens? Ciancarelli believes that his inputs are greater than those of his co-workers and therefore should merit a greater pay raise. Inequity can also occur when people are overpaid. In this case, the overpaid employees might be motivated by guilt or social pressure to work harder to reduce the imbalance between their inputs and outcomes and those of their co-workers.

Consequences of Inequity   Inequity causes tension within an individual and among individuals. Tension is not pleasurable, so a person is motivated to reduce it to a tolerable level. To reduce a perceived inequity and the corresponding level of tension, the person may choose to act in one or more of the following ways. This tension-reduction process is illustrated in Figure 5.8.

- People may either increase or decrease their inputs to what they feel to be an equitable level. For example, underpaid people may reduce the quantity of their production, work shorter hours, be absent more frequently, and so on. Figure 5.9 shows these relationships graphically.

- People may change their outcomes to restore equity. Many union organizers try to attract nonmembers by pledging to improve working conditions, hours, and pay without an increase in employee effort (input).

- People may distort their own inputs and outcomes. As opposed to actually changing inputs or outcomes, people may mentally distort them to achieve a more favorable balance. For example, people who feel inequitably treated may distort how hard they work (This job is a piece of cake.) or attempt to increase the importance of the job to the organization (This is really an important job!).

- People may leave the organization or request a transfer to another department. In doing so, they hope to find a more favorable balance.

- People may shift to a new reference group to reduce the source of the inequity. The star high school athlete who doesn't get a scholarship to a major university might decide that a smaller school has more advantages, thereby justifying a need to look at smaller schools when making a selection.

- People may distort the inputs or outcomes of others. People may come to believe that the comparison group actually works harder than they do and therefore deserves greater rewards.

FIGURE 5.8

Inequity as a Motivational Process

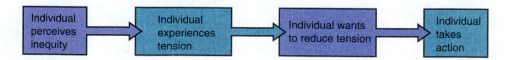

Keeping these six actions in mind, let's take a look at employee theft as a reaction to underpayment. Employee theft is one of the most serious problems facing organizations. The American Management Association estimates that employee theft costs U.S. organizations more than $10 billion a year. After reading both accounts in the following Ethics in Practice feature, decide which you think was associated with greater employee theft.

ETHICS IN PRACTICE

To Steal or Not: That's the Question

The organization reduced its payroll by 15 percent for ten weeks at each of two plants instead of laying people off. Management drafted two accounts concerning the reduction in pay but read only one account at each plant. Before announcing the reduction in pay, overall theft was running about 3 percent annually.

Account A

The reason why I'm sharing this information with you is that I want you to understand what's happening here. As you probably know, we've lost our key contract, which will make things pretty lean around there. Starting Monday, each one of us will take a 15 percent cut in pay. This applies to you, to me, to everyone. Fringe benefits won't be touched. I don't expect this cut to last more than ten weeks. We hope to be stronger than ever after this trying time. I want to thank each and every one of you personally for gutting it out with us.

Account B

It is inevitable in a business like ours that cost-cutting measures are needed. Unfortunately, the time has come for us to take such measures. I know that it won't be easy for anyone, but the president has decided that a 15 percent cut across the board will be instituted starting Monday. All employees, including the president, will share in this effort to save our company. We're pretty sure that the cuts will last only ten weeks. I'll answer a few questions, but then I have to catch a plane for another meeting.

The Outcome

Theft by employees who heard account B increased by more than 250 percent. Why? Employees who heard account B believed that they weren't hearing the entire story. They reduced perceived inequities by acts of theft. To be effective, equity explanations must be perceived to be honest, genuine, and not manipulative.[29]

Procedural Justice   In contrast to equity theory, which emphasizes the *outcome* of the decision, procedural justice theory examines the impact of the *process* used to make a decision. The perceived fairness of rules and procedures is referred to as **procedural justice.**[30] The procedural justice model holds that employees are going to be more motivated to perform at a high level when they perceive as fair the procedures used to make decisions about the distribution of outcomes. Employees are motivated to attain fairness in how decisions are made, as well as in the decisions themselves.

FIGURE 5.9

Performance Levels for Underpaid and Overpaid Employees

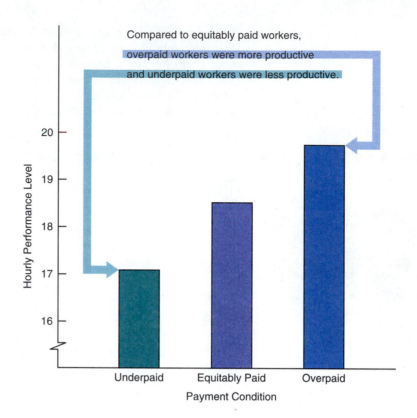

Research has shown that reactions to pay raises, for example, are greatly affected by employees' perceptions about the fairness of the raises. If in the minds of the employees the pay raises were administered fairly, the employees were more satisfied with their increases than if the procedures used to make these increases were judged to be unfair. The perceived fairness of the procedures used to allocate pay raises is a better predictor of satisfaction than the absolute amount of pay received. Similarly, students base their faculty member evaluations on perceptions of fair grading decisions.

In both the pay and evaluation situations, the individual can't directly control the decision but can react to the procedures used to make it. Even when a particular decision has negative outcomes for the individual, fair procedures help ensure that the individual feels that his or her interests are being protected.

Employees' assessments of procedural justice have also been related to their trust in management, intention to leave the organization, evaluation of their supervisor, employee theft, and job satisfaction. Consider some of the relatively small day-to-day issues in an organization that are affected by procedural justice: decisions about who will cover the phones during lunch while others are away from their desks, the choice of the site of the company picnic, or who gets the latest software for a personal computer.

Procedural justice has also been found to affect the attitudes of those workers who survive a layoff. When workers are laid off, survivors (those who remain on the job) are often in a good position to judge the fairness of the layoff in terms of how it was handled. When a layoff is handled fairly, survivors feel more committed to the organization than when they believe that the laid-off workers were unfairly treated.[31]

Organizational Citizenship Behavior

In many organizations, employees perform tasks that are voluntary or not formally required.[32] **Organizational citizenship behavior** is behavior that exceeds formal job duties but is necessary for the organization's survival or important to its image and acceptance. Examples of organizational citizenship behavior include helping co-workers solve problems, making constructive suggestions, volunteering to perform community service work (such as blood drives, United Way campaigns, and charity work). Although not formally required by employers, these behaviors are important in all organizations. Helping co-workers is an especially important form of organizational citizenship behavior when it comes to computers. Every organization has some computer gurus, but often it's the secretary who doesn't go to lunch who can fix the problem easier and without putting down the struggling user. Managers often underestimate the amount of this informal helping that takes place in organizations.

Employees have considerable discretion over whether to engage in organizational citizenship behaviors. Employees who have been treated fairly and are satisfied are more likely to engage in these behaviors than employees who feel unfairly treated. Fairly treated employees engage in citizenship behaviors because they want to give something back to the organization. Most people desire to have fair exchanges with co-workers and others in their organization.

Ray Hertz, President of Hertz and Associates, developed a simple yet innovative method to acknowledge organizational citizenship behaviors at his Dallas advertising firm. At the beginning of the year, Hertz gives each of his ten employees a jar containing twelve marbles. Throughout the year, employees may give marbles to others who have helped them in some way or who have provided an extraordinary service. Employees are recognized throughout the year and are proud of the number of marbles they accumulate, even though they receive no monetary reward from Hertz.

Equity Model Findings

Most of the research on the equity model focuses on pay and other compensation issues.[33] A review of these studies indicates some shortcomings. First, the comparison group is always known. But what happens if the comparison group changes or the situation changes in other respects?

Second, the research focuses mainly on short-term comparisons. Are pay cuts, temporary assignments, longer working hours, and the like such that a person believes that inputs or outcomes are likely to remain the same? That is, do perceptions of inequity or equity increase, decrease, or stabilize over time? In the preceding Ethics in Practice piece, what happens to theft after the ten-week period if salaries aren't restored to their previous levels? Would you expect theft to increase in group A? Answers to these types of questions would help give insight into the dynamic character of equity and inequity.

Third, the equity model doesn't specify the type of action (from among the actions listed) that a person would choose in order to reduce the perceived inequity in a particular situation. That is, is one strategy used primarily when pay is involved, another when theft or absenteeism is involved, and yet another when productivity is involved?

Significance for the Workplace

Despite these questions, managers use the equity model in making a variety of decisions, such as taking disciplinary actions, giving pay raises, allocating office and parking space, and dispensing other perks found in most organizations. The equity model leads to two primary conclusions. First, employees should be treated fairly. When individuals believe that they are not being treated fairly, they will try to correct the situation and reduce tension by means of one or more of the types of actions identified in this section. A sizable inequity increases the probability that individuals will choose more than one type of action to reduce it. For example, individuals may partially withdraw from the organization by being absent more often, arriving at work late, not completing assignments on time, or stealing. The organization may try to reduce the inputs of such employees by assigning them to monotonous jobs, taking away some perquisites, and giving them only small pay increases.

Second, people make decisions concerning equity only after they compare their inputs and outcomes with those of comparable employees.[34] These relevant others may be employees of the same organization or of other organizations. The latter presents a major problem for managers, who cannot control what other organizations pay their employees. For example, the vice-president for human resources at AT&T hired a recent business school graduate for $32,500, the maximum the company could pay for the job. The new employee thought that this salary was very good until she compared it to the $35,250 that fellow graduates were getting at GTE, MCI, and Sprint. She felt that she was being underpaid in comparison with her former classmates, causing an inequity problem for her (and the company).

The idea that fairness in organizations is determined by more than just money has received a great deal of attention from managers. Organizational fairness is influenced by how rules and procedures are used and how much employees are consulted in decisions that affect them.

■ COMPARISONS AMONG PROCESS MODELS

The expectancy and equity models emphasize different aspects of motivation. The expectancy model holds that employees are rational and evaluate how much the reward means to them before they perform their jobs. How well employees will perform depends, in part, on what they believe is expected of them. Once their manager communicates these expectations, then employees assign probabilities that their efforts will lead to desired first-level outcomes (performance, quality, absenteeism, and so on). These outcomes are linked to valued rewards (for example, high pay or job security) they desire from their jobs. It is the manager's job to make the desired rewards attainable by clearly linking rewards and performance. Allowing employees to choose among rewards, such as improved insurance, child-care and elder-care facilities for family members, and additional vacation days, is important because of different employee preferences. **Cafeteria-style benefit plans**—reward systems that permit employees to select their fringe benefits from a menu of alternatives—have become very popular. Because benefits represent 35 percent of payroll costs in many organizations, letting employees choose the ones they prefer and linking them to performance is important to keeping valued employees and controlling costs.[35]

In contrast to the expectancy model, where employees make judgments about the value of rewards, the equity model holds that equity is determined by employees comparing themselves to others in similar situations. According to the equity model, people are motivated to escape inequitable situations and to remain on the job and perform at high levels in equitable situations. Because perceptions of fairness often vary among employees, different employees may react differently in various situations.

Both models emphasize the role of rewards and an individual's decision-making processes. These models suggest that managers concerned about improving employee performance should actively create proper work environments, match employees to jobs, and establish clear performance–reward systems. Motivation for high performance won't exist unless managers recognize such performance when it occurs and reward it quickly.

CHAPTER SUMMARY

A motivational model was presented, indicating that individuals behave in certain ways to satisfy their needs. The reasons that individuals behave in certain ways were the focus of this chapter.

To understand these reasons, we examined two major classes of models of motivation: content and process. Content models focus on the factors within the person that drive, sustain, or stop behavior. They describe the specific needs that motivate people. We examined the content models of motivation developed by Maslow, Alderfer, McClelland, and Herzberg. Process models provide a description and analysis of how behavior is driven, sustained, or stopped. We examined the expectancy and equity process models of motivation.

Maslow assumes that people have five types of needs: physiological, security, affiliation, esteem, and self-actualization. When a need is satisfied, it no longer motivates a person. Alderfer agrees with Maslow that needs motivate people but claims that people have only three types of needs: existence, relatedness, and growth. If a person's growth need can't be satisfied, the person focuses on satisfying relatedness needs. McClelland believes that people have three learned needs (achievement, affiliation, and power) that are rooted in the culture of a society. We focused on the role of the achievement need and indicated the characteristics associated with high achievers. The final content model discussed was Herzberg's. He claimed that two types of factors affect a person's motivation: motivators and hygienes. Motivators, such as job challenge, lead to job satisfaction but not to job dissatisfaction. Hygiene factors, such as working conditions, prevent job dissatisfaction but can't lead to job satisfaction.

The expectancy process model holds that individuals know what they desire from work. They choose activities only after they decide that the activities will satisfy their needs. The primary components of this model are first- and second-level outcomes, expectancy, instrumentality, and valence. An individual must believe that effort expended will lead (expectancy) to some desired level of performance (first-level outcome) and that this level of performance will lead (instrumentality) to desired rewards (second-level outcomes and valences). Otherwise the individual won't be motivated to expend the effort necessary to perform at the desired level.

The equity model focuses on the individual's perception of how fairly he or she is treated in comparison to others in similar situations. To make this judgment, an individual compares his or her inputs (experience, age) and outcomes (salary) to those of relevant others. If equity exists, the person isn't motivated to act. If inequity exists, the person may engage in any one of six behaviors to reduce this inequity. Both procedural justice and organizational citizenship behavior are based on the equity model and have significant implications for employees' perceptions of equity.

KEY TERMS AND CONCEPTS

Ability
Achievement motivation model
Affiliation needs
Cafeteria-style benefit plans
Content models
Deficiency needs
Equity
Equity model
ERG model
Esteem needs
Existence needs
Expectancy
Expectancy model

Extrinsic factors
First-level outcomes
Goal
Growth needs
Hygiene factors
Inequity
Inputs
Instrumentality
Intrinsic factors
Motivation
Motivator-Hygiene model
Motivator factors
Needs

Needs hierarchy model
Organizational citizenship behavior
Outcomes
Physiological needs
Procedural justice
Process models
Relatedness needs
Second-level outcomes
Security needs
Self-actualization needs
Thematic Apperception Test (TAT)
Valence

DISCUSSION QUESTIONS

1. Think about the worst job you have had. What motivational approach was used in that organization? Now think about the best job you have had. What motivation approach was used in that organization?

2. How would the expectancy model explain the behaviors of the employees who stole from their company after it announced that all employees would take a 10 percent pay cut for the next five weeks?

3. Why is job satisfaction not strongly related to job performance?

4. What specific tasks might an organization engage in to raise the level of organizational citizenship behaviors of its employees?

5. How could a manager apply the ERG model to motivate employees on the job?

6. Why might an employee with a low level of motivation be a top performer?

7. What is the value of motivator-hygiene model?

8. If high achievers are better performers, why don't organizations simply hire high achievers?

9. What steps can an organization take to encourage procedural justice by its managers?

10. How can an organization use inequity to motivate employees?

■   ## Developing Competencies

Self-Insight: What Do You Want From Your Job?

We have listed the sixteen most mentioned characteristics that employees want from their jobs in random order.[36] Please rank them in order of both their *importance* to you and then in terms of *satisfaction* for you. Rank these characteristics 1 (most important), 2 (next most important), 3 (next most important), and so on, through 16 (least important). Use the same procedure to rank satisfaction. You may compare your answers to those of managers working in a wide variety of jobs and industries provided at the end of this exercise.

Job Characteristics	Importance Rank	Satisfaction Rank
1. Working independently	_____	_____
2. Chances for promotion	_____	_____
3. Contact with people	_____	_____
4. Flexible Hours	_____	_____
5. Health insurance & other benefits	_____	_____
6. Interesting work	_____	_____
7. Work important to society	_____	_____
8. Job security	_____	_____
9. Opportunity to learn new skills	_____	_____
10. High income	_____	_____
11. Recognition from team members	_____	_____

12. Vacation time   _____   _____

13. Regular hours   _____   _____

14. Working close to
    home   _____   _____

15. Little job stress   _____   _____

16. A job in which I can
    help others   _____   _____

Answers

For *job importance*, the rank order of characteristics is 1-6; 2-14; 3-15; 4-16; 5-1; 6-2; 7-13; 8-3; 9-4; 10-11; 12-5; 13-8; 14-12; 15-10; 16-9.

For *job satisfaction*, the rank order of characteristics is 1-3; 2-14; 3-2; 4-6; 5-13; 6-4; 7-9; 8-7; 9-11; 10-12; 11-15; 12-8; 13-5; 14-1; 15-16; 16-10.

Questions

1. Choose any model of motivation and think about your answers. What situational factors (such as being in school, looking for a new job, desiring more responsibility, desiring to work for a foreign organization, and the like) influenced your ranking of importance?

2. What characteristics gave most of the respondents their greatest job satisfaction? What model of motivation helps you understand these rankings?

Organizational Insight: Working at Nordstrom

Nordstrom has grown from a lone shoe store ninety-five years ago into an eighty-store, $4 billion-a-year national chain in large part by coddling its customers with superior service. Managers tell employees to take care of customers as long as their actions are based on good judgment, are legal, and show care and concern for their fellow employees. They tell employees to think of themselves as independent entrepreneurs and to view their work areas as their own businesses from which they earn a living.

Getting a job at Nordstrom is tough—the competition is fierce. When it recently opened its Dallas store, more than 6000 people applied for 550 jobs. Once a person is hired, an ability to sell and not a pleasing personality is what keeps that person employed. Working for Nordstrom is very competitive. Sales per square foot average $395 compared to $226 at Lord & Taylor, $197 at Macy's, and $159 at JC Penney. Daily sales by employee name and position relative to others are posted in every department. Before the store opens each morning, praise, such as a laudatory customer letter, is broadcast over the intercom, as are blunders (though names are omitted).

The pay structure reflects the competitive spirit at Nordstrom. It is based on an elaborate commission structure that rewards strong sellers and shows up weak ones. A typical salesperson might be credited with $7 to $13 for every $100 in sales. Because sales run hot and cold, people need somewhat predictable paychecks. Nordstrom pays a regular "draw," or base amount, that resembles ordinary hourly wages. The amount a person is able to draw is based on the commission scale for the department and minimum hourly sales targets. For example, a $140-an-hour sales target and a 7 percent commission rate would yield a base draw of $9.80 an hour.

Nordstrom requires salespeople to walk a tightrope. They need to sell but can't oversell, because merchandise bought under pressure often is returned. Accepting returns with a smile builds customer loyalty but can cut the income of the person who made the sale. The original commission is deducted from a future paycheck.

When salespeople miss their sales targets, Nordstrom pays their base draw anyway. But if that happens for two or three weeks, they are fired. Successful sellers take home some of the highest paychecks in the retail industry. The average retail salesperson makes $26,000 a year, compared to $16,000 at other department stores. Last year, six salespeople at Nordstrom sold more than $1 million dollars in merchandise and earned more than $100,000.

Some of Nordstrom's practices have landed them in court. The state of Washington and some West Coast labor unions alleged that Nordstrom didn't pay or underpaid for "off-the-clock" work. Such work included writing thank you notes to customers, making deliveries, attending motivational meetings, and doing favors for customers. The courts ruled in favor of Nordstrom, but now it pays salespeople for such activities.[37]

Discussion Questions

1. What type of person is likely to survive and be effective at Nordstrom?

2. What motivational model best describes the reward system at Nordstrom?

REFERENCES

1. Adapted from Kelly, J. How UPS delivers high performance management. *Global Perspectives*, Fall 1995, 9–11; Bradley, S. One world, one UPS. *Brandweek*, February 5, 1996, 20–21.

2. Adapted from Thomson Corporation's *Annual Report*. Paris 1996; Toor, M. Thomson Bids for Sony Status. *Marketing*, September 5, 1991, 2–3.

3. Bohl, D. L., Luthans, F., Slocum, J. W., Jr., and Hodgetts, R. M. Ideas that will shape the future of management practice. *Organizational Dynamics*, Summer 1996, 7–14.

4. Locke, E. A., and Latham, G. P. *A Model of Goal Setting and Task Performance*. Englewood Cliffs, N.J.: Prentice-Hall, 1990, 6–8.

5. For an excellent overview of motivation models, see Kanfer, R. Motivation model and industrial and organizational psychology. In M. D. Dunnette and L. M. Hough (eds.). *Handbook of Industrial and Organizational Psychology,* vol. 1. Palo Alto, Calif.: Consulting Psychologist Press, 1990, 75–170.

6. Maslow, A. H. *Motivation and Personality.* New York: Harper & Row, 1970.

7. Weiss, J. W. *Organizational Behavior & Change: Managing Diversity, Cross-Cultural Dynamics, and Ethics.* St. Paul, Minn.: West, 1996, 100–104.

8. Woolridge, E. Time to stand Maslow's hierarchy on its head? *People Management,* December 21, 1995, 17–81.

9. Alderfer, C. P. *Existence, Relatedness and Growth: Human Needs in Organizational Settings.* New York: Free Press, 1972.

10. Winer, B. *Human Motivation.* New York: Holt, Rinehart and Winston, 1980; Landy, F. L., and Becker, W. S. Motivation Model Reconsidered. In L. L. Cummings and B. M. Staw (eds.). *Research in Organizational Behavior,* vol. 9. Greenwich, Conn.: JAI Press, 1987, 1–38.

11. Adapted from Kriska, P. *Motivating employees in different cultures.* Unpublished manuscript, Cox School of Business, Southern Methodist University, Dallas, Texas, 1997.

12. McClelland, D. C. *Motivational Trends in Society.* Morristown, N.J.: General Learning Press, 1971.

13. McClelland, D. C., and Burnham, D. Power is the Great Motivator. *Harvard Business Review,* March–April, 1976, 100–111; McClelland, D. C., and Boyatzis, R. E. Leadership Motive Pattern and Long-term Success in Management. *Journal of Applied Psychology,* 1982, 67, 744–751.

14. Adapted from Rice, F. Denny's changes its spots. *Fortune,* May 13, 1996, 133–142; Denny's bias case to yield payments. *New York Times,* December 12, 1995, A11; Mildenberg, D. Grand slam plan. *Dallas Morning News,* January 6, 1996, F1–F2.

15. Winter, D. G. The Power Motive in Women and Men. *Journal of Personality and Social Psychology,* 1988, 54, 510–519.

16. Herzberg, F. I., Mausner, B., and Snyderman, B. B. *The Motivation to Work.* New York: John Wiley & Sons, 1959.

17. Adapted from Anfuso, D. Las Vegas resort bets on training and wins. *Personnel Journal,* September 1995, 78–86; Profits rose 40%, helped by performance at flagship. *Wall Street Journal,* February 9, 1996, B13.

18. Schuler, R. S., Jackson, S. E., Jackofsky, E. F., and Slocum, J. W., Jr. Managing human resources in Mexico: A cultural understanding. *Business Horizons,* May–June 1996, 55–61.

19. Greer, C. R., and Stephens, G. K. Employee relations issues for U.S. companies in Mexico. *California Management Review,* 1996, 38(3), 121–145.

20. Keller, J. J. AT&T's cuts are just the first shot in telecom wars. *Wall Street Journal,* January 4, 1996, A2; Jenkins, H. W., Jr. Business world: 40,000 job cuts. *Wall Street Journal,* March 5, 1996, A15.

21. Boettger, R. D., and Greer, C. R. On the wisdom of rewarding A while hoping for B. *Organization Science,* 1994, 5, 569–582.

22. Vroom, V. H. *Work and Motivation.* New York: John Wiley & Sons, 1964.

23. Tubbs, M. E., Boehme, D. M., and Dahl, J. G. Expectancy, valence, and motivational force functions in goal-setting research: An empirical test. *Journal of Applied Psychology,* 1993, 78, 361–373.

24. Oliver, R. L., Balakrishnan, P. V., and Barry, B. Outcome satisfaction in negotiation: A test of expectancy disconfirmation. *Organizational Behavior & Human Decision Processes,* 1994, 60, 252–276.

25. Snead, K. C., Jr. An application of expectancy model to explain a manager's intention to use a decision support system. *Decision Sciences,* 1994, 25, 499–514.

26. Mehegan, S. Lunch amid the lingerie. *Restaurant Business,* January 20, 1996, 35–37; Halkias, M. Changing the retail landscape. *Dallas Morning News,* March 17, 1996, H1–H3.

27. Adapted from Sellers, P. Can Home Depot fix its sagging stock? *Fortune,* March 4, 1996, 139–144; Sharav, B., and Sirois, C. Retail building supply industry. *Value Line Investment Survey,* January 19, 1996, 883–891.

28. Adams, J. S. Toward an Understanding of Inequity. *Journal of Abnormal and Social Psychology,* 1963, 67, 422–436.

29. Adapted from Greenberg, J. Employee theft as a reaction to underpayment inequity: The hidden costs of pay cuts. *Journal of Applied Psychology,* 1990, 75, 561–568; Wahn, J. Organizational dependence and the likelihood of complying with organizational pressures to behave unethically. *Journal of Business Ethics,* 1993, 12, 245–251.

30. Korsgaard, M. A., and Roberson, L. Procedural justice in performance evaluation: The role of instrumental and non-instrumental voice in performance appraisal decisions. *Journal of Management,* 1995, 21, 657–670; Sapienza, H. J., and Korsgaard, M. A. Procedural justice in entrepreneur–investor relations. *Academy of Management Journal,* 1996, 39, 544–574; Taylor, M. S., Tracy, K. B., Renard, M. K., Harrison, J. K., and Carroll, S. J. Due process in performance appraisal: A quasi-experiment in procedural justice. *Administrative Science Quarterly,* 1995, 40, 95–114.

31. Brockner, J., Wiesenfeld, B. M., and Martin, C. L. Decision frame, procedural justice and survivors' reactions to job layoffs. *Organizational Behavior & Human Decision Processes,* 1995, 63, 59–69.

32. Organ, D. W., and Ryan, K. A meta-analytic review of attitudinal and dispositional predictors of organizational citizenship behavior. *Personnel Psychology,* 1995, 48, 775–803; Robinson, S. L., and Morrison, E. W. Psychological contracts and OCB: The effect of unfilled obligations on civic virtue behavior. *Journal of Organizational Behavior,* 1995, 16, 289–298.

33. Greenberg, J. Looking fair vs. being fair: Managing impressions of organizational justice. In L. L. Cummings and B. M. Staw (eds.). *Research in Organizational Behavior,* vol. 12. Greenwich, Conn.: JAI Press, 1990, 111–158; Ferris, G. R., and Kacmar, K. M. Perceptions of Organizational Politics. *Journal of Management,* 1992, 18, 93–116; Kim,

W. C., and Mauborgne, R. A. Procedural justice, attitudes, and subsidiary top management compliance with multinationals' corporate strategic decisions. *Academy of Management Journal,* 1993, 36, 502–526.

34. Gouveia, M. Equity in model and practice. *Journal of Policy Analysis & Management,* 1995, 14, 481–489.

35. Boes, R. F., and Ransom, G. M. Health care flexible spending arrangements. *Journal of Compensation & Benefits,* 1995, 11, 5–10.

36. Adapted from a survey of employees conducted by Seglin, J. L. The happiest workers in the world. *Inc.,* May 1996, 62–76; Caggiano, C. What Do Workers Want? *Inc.,* November 1992, 101.

37. Adapted from Halkias, M. Eager to please. *Dallas Morning News,* March 17, 1996, A1, A26; Lubove, S. Don't listen to the boss, listen to the customer. *Forbes,* December 4, 1995, 45–47; Solomon, B. Ringing up sales. *Management Review,* February 1995, 38-43.

6

Motivating Performance: Goal Setting and Reward Systems

LEARNING OBJECTIVES

After you have finished studying this chapter, you should be able to:

- Describe the role of customers, suppliers, and others in the goal-setting process.
- State the key factors in goal setting and performance and describe their relationships.
- Explain management by objectives (MBO) as a management philosophy and system.
- Describe four reward systems that help stimulate high performance.

OUTLINE

PREVIEW CASE

Papa John's Pizza

The pizza business in the United States is booming. Annual sales exceed $30 billion and the market is growing at 5 percent a year. The big three—Pizza Hut, Little Caesar's and Dominos'—dominate with more than 65 percent market share. In an industry with more than 60,000 stores nationwide, small pizzerias often find it difficult to compete for customers.

When John Schnatter first opened Papa John's in 1985, he listed the goals he wanted to achieve, including number of stores, sales growth, and return on invested capital. These goals would have to be attained in an industry known for high employee turnover rates—as high as 200 percent. Schnatter's goals for 1995 were to open 232 new restaurants, keep long-term debt at less than $1.5 million, and have stockholders' equity grow to more than $62 million, up $5 million from 1994.

During the past ten years, goal setting has emerged as a key management tool at Papa John's. All employees are encouraged to submit 5 to 10 goals in November and December for the following year. These goals—such as 100 percent on-time safe delivery, answer all telephone calls by the second ring, slash employee turnover by 30 percent, maintain a perfect attendance record, deliver a pizza to a customer in less than thirty minutes—are discussed at meetings with employees at each restaurant. At these meetings store managers grade the previous year's performance, goal by goal, and explain the company's goals (developed from the employees' suggestions) for the next year. What makes a goal good at Papa John's? First, a goal should be attainable by a wide variety of employees, and it must be meaningful and measurable. Drivers who have completed 1000 hours of safe-driving time are given a choice of a VCR or set of new tires for their car. Drivers can also win cellular phones if they maintain their on-time and safe-driving record. Although many things in a restaurant are equally important, all employees must agree on the key goals for the forthcoming year. Second, a goal that is specific and measurable gives people something to relate to because it creates not only a picture of where the company wants to be, but gives all employees something to talk about. Third, a goal set by employees is more likely to bring commitment than is a goal handed down by management.[1]

To survive in today's global competitive market, setting challenging goals that take into account both time and quality is no longer an option. It must happen! AT&T used to take two years to design a new telephone. But, says Jim Jordan, an AT&T manager of sourcing, "We came to the realization that if you get to market sooner with new technology, you can charge a premium until the others follow." AT&T began developing a new cordless phone for the home called the 4200 in early 1988. Rather than trying to save 10 percent in time here and 5 percent there, Jordan's goal was to reduce the development cycle by 50 percent. He says, "It made us change the way we did everything."[2]

The common elements that cut across the achievements noted in the Preview Case are setting goals and developing feedback and reward systems that get individuals and teams to strive to reach those goals. In this chapter, we first outline the role played by customers, suppliers, and other stakeholders of an organization and how they affect goal setting. Second, we present a model of goal setting and performance based on the individual. This model sets the stage for the discussion of management by objectives as a philosophy and system of integrating goal setting into organizational life. In the last section we return to reward systems, which we described in Chapters 4 and 5. Here, we consider the types of reward systems being used by organizations to reinforce desired behaviors of employees.

FUNDAMENTALS OF GOAL SETTING

Goal setting is a process intended to increase efficiency and effectiveness by specifying the desired outcomes toward which individuals, departments, teams, and organizations should work. **Goals** are the future outcomes (results) that individuals and groups desire and strive to achieve.[3] An example of an individual goal is: I am planning to graduate with a 2.5 grade-point average by the end of the spring semester, 1999.

■ REASONS FOR GOAL SETTING

Even though goal setting is no easy task, the process of doing so generally makes the effort worthwhile. The following are among the more important reasons for having goals.

- Goals guide and direct behavior. They increase role clarity by focusing effort and attention in specific directions, thereby reducing uncertainty in day-to-day decision making.
- Goals provide challenges and standards against which individual, departmental, team, or organizational performance can be assessed.
- Goals serve as a source of legitimacy. They justify various activities and the use of resources to pursue them.
- Goals define the basis for the organization's structure. They determine, in part, communication patterns, authority relationships, power relationships, and division of labor.
- Goals serve an organizing function.
- Goals reflect what the goal setters consider important and thus provide a framework for planning and control activities.[4]

■ ROLE OF STAKEHOLDERS

Goals and goal setting are often the object of disagreement and conflict, as we discuss in Chapter 12. Because diverse groups have a stake in organizational decisions, managers are faced with the continuing need to develop, modify, and discard goals. **Stakeholders** are groups having potential or real power to influence the organization's decisions, such as the choice of goals and actions. Stakeholders commonly include customers or clients, employees, suppliers, shareholders, government agencies, unions, public interest groups, and lenders, among others.

Table 6.1 contains several categories of organizational goals of particular interest to five stakeholder groups. Because of the varied concerns of those groups, some of the categories may be incompatible. Creating a unified and logical system of goal setting for an organization is difficult when

- each stakeholder group has substantial power in relation to the organization;
- each stakeholder group pushes to maximize its own interests and perceives the interests of some or all other groups to be incompatible with its own;
- the stakeholders keep changing what they expect (want) from the organization; and/or
- the management team itself is divided into competing groups within the organization.[5]

TABLE 6.1 Goals of Typical Stakeholders

Customers
- Good service
- Competitive prices
- Product quality
- Product variety
- Product satisfaction guaranteed

Employees
- Good compensation and job security
- Opportunity to learn
- Opportunities for fun on the job
- Sense of meaning or purpose in the job
- Opportunities for advancement
- Opportunities for personal development
- Good management of diversity issues

Stockholders
- Growth in dividend payments
- Increase in stock price
- Growth in market share
- Ethical behavior of employees

Bankers
- Financial strength of the organization
- Maintenance of assets that serve as collateral on loans
- Improvements in productivity to keep costs competitive
- Repayment schedule

Suppliers
- Timely debt payment
- Repeat customers
- Prompt service
- Business growth

Taken together, these situations present a worst-case scenario. Thus, if pushed to extremes, some of the goals listed in Table 6.1 will be incompatible and require executives to use keen negotiating skills to balance or resolve the resulting conflicts. Fortunately, managers and employees usually aren't confronted with such diverse and incompatible demands in setting goals.

The most important stakeholders for any organization are its customers or clients. Their goals need to be reflected in the goals of the organization as a whole, as well as in the goals of individual employees and groups within the organization. This perspective was certainly reflected in Papa John's goal-setting process and AT&T's goal of reducing the development cycle time by 50 percent for the 4200 model telephone.

■ QUALITY GOALS IN CUSTOMER SERVICE

What's involved in setting customer service quality goals? Two main issues need to be recognized in answering this question. The first is that customers or clients are the sole judge of service quality. They assess it by comparing the service they receive with the service they desire. Organizations such as Southwest Airlines, Rubbermaid, Coca-Cola, and Procter and Gamble can maintain their strong reputations for quality service only by consistently meeting or exceeding customer service expectations. Second, organizations tend to ignore the first issue when competitors start vying for business.[6]

Customer service goals may be divided into five overall categories. In the following list, each category includes a definition and a sample comment from a dissatisfied customer.

- *Reliability:* The ability to perform the promised service dependably and accurately. Car leasing customer: "Too often they take care of your problems too fast. They fix your car and two days later you have to take it back for the same problem. They could be a little more attentive and fix the problem permanently."

- *Tangibles:* The appearance of physical facilities, equipment, personnel, and communication materials. Hotel customer: "They get you real pumped up with the beautiful ad. When you go in, you expect bells and whistles to go off. Usually, they don't."

- *Responsiveness:* The willingness to help customers and to provide prompt service. Business equipment repair customer: "You put in a service call and wait. No one calls back; there is no communication."

- *Assurance:* The knowledge and courtesy of employees and their ability to convey trust and confidence. Life insurance customer: "I quote pages out of my policy and my agent cannot interpret what it means to me in language that I can understand."

- *Empathy:* The provision of caring, individualized attention to customers or clients. Airline customer: "They'll out-and-out lie to you about how delayed a flight will be so that you won't try to get a flight on another airline."

As demonstrated in the following Quality in Practice feature concerning the Ritz-Carlton Hotel, the setting and achievement of service goals is an evolving process. Because the output of a service organization is intangible, it can't be stored. The customer or client immediately evaluates the quality of a service when it is delivered.

QUALITY IN PRACTICE

Service at the Ritz-Carlton Hotel

The Ritz-Carlton Hotel chain, a winner of the Malcolm Baldrige National Quality Award, is noted for providing exceptional service to its customers. Quality services include twenty-four-hour room service, twice-a-day maid service, complimentary shoeshines, and club rooms with a private lounge and concierge, among others. How does the Ritz achieve this high level of quality? It uses the principles of goal-setting, providing rewards that are valued by employees, and making rewards contingent on performance to direct the behaviors of its employees. The company uses *5 Star Awards* to recognize superior performers who have been nominated by their peers, customers, and managers. Each hotel has five quarterly

—Continued

QUALITY IN PRACTICE—*Continued*

award winners, from which five annual winners are selected. The quarterly winners receive plaques and are recognized at a dinner. The annual winners are treated to a banquet and receive a free trip, including travel and spending money, to any Ritz-Carlton Hotel in the United States. More frequently, managers give *Gold Standard Coupons* to employees who are "caught" meeting the hotel's standards for quality service. The coupons can be exchanged for weekend accommodations at the hotel or merchandise in the hotel's gift shop.

The Ritz is very selective in hiring. In fact, it emphasizes that its employees have been "selected," not hired. As a result, annual employee turnover is 30 percent compared to an industry norm of 90 percent. The careful selection of employees also communicates and clarifies perceptions of service. All employees go through a rigorous and extensive training program that focuses on teaching them the required competencies—empathy, teamwork, low-key demeanor—and instilling in them correct attitudes and behaviors for serving customers.

To make sure that employees know the goals for their departments and the hotel overall, the Ritz utilizes daily line-ups. At these line-ups, department heads inform the employees of special events, potential problems (such as food, language, monetary exchange rates, and transportation) that guests might bring up. Lasting approximately fifteen minutes, the daily line-ups are an important tool in gaining consistent implementation of Ritz's quality service goals.

As a result, Ritz employees achieve exceptional standards of performance. Over 97 percent of the hotel chain's customers are satisfied with the quality of service. However, its goal is to improve quality so that there are, at most, three service defects for every million customer encounters.[7]

GOAL SETTING AND PERFORMANCE

Just as organizations strive to achieve certain goals, individuals also are motivated to strive for and attain goals. In fact, the goal-setting process is one of the most important motivational tools affecting employees in organizations. In this section we consider one of the most widely accepted theories of goal setting and indicate how goal-setting techniques can be applied to motivate individuals and teams.

■ GOAL-SETTING MODEL

Ed Locke and Gary Latham developed a sophisticated model of individual goal setting and performance. Figure 6.1 presents a simplified version of their model.[8] It shows the key variables and the general relationships that can lead to high individual performance, some of which we have discussed in previous chapters. The basic idea behind this model is that a goal serves as a motivator because it causes people to compare their present performance with that required to achieve the goal. To the extent that people believe they will fall short of a goal, they will feel dissatisfied and will work harder to attain the goal so long as they believe that it can be achieved. Having a goal also may improve performance because the goal makes clear the type and level of performance expected. John Schnatter's goals for Papa John's were very clear: Grow the business by 10 percent a year, hire drivers who maintained safe-driving records, and deliver a hot pizza to every customer within thirty minutes. Such goals clearly communicated performance standards

■ FIGURE 6.1   Goal-Setting Model

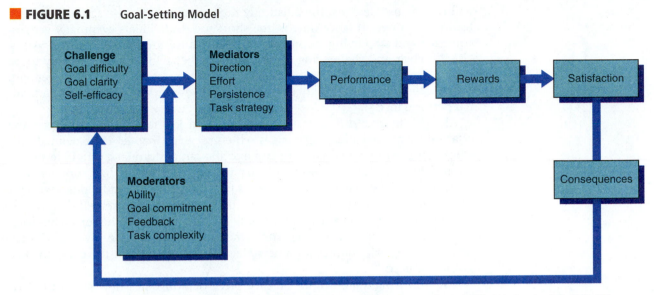

Source: Adapted from Locke, E. A., and Latham, G. P. *A Theory of Goal Setting and Task Performance.* Englewood Cliffs, N.J.: Prentice-Hall, 1990, 253.

to all employees of the company. By reviewing performance against the goals each year, Schnatter also provided information on how well employees were doing in terms of these agreed upon targets. With these general ideas in mind, let's review the basic features of the Locke–Latham goal-setting model.

Challenge   Goal setting is the process of developing, negotiating, and establishing targets that challenge the individual. Employees with unclear goals or no goals are prone to work slowly, perform poorly, exhibit a lack of interest, and accomplish less than employees whose goals are clear and challenging. In addition, employees with clearly defined goals appear to be more energetic and productive. They get things done on time and then move on to other activities (and goals).

Goals may be implicit or explicit, vague or clearly defined, and self-imposed or externally imposed. Whatever their form, goals serve to structure the individual's time and effort. Two key attributes of goals are particularly important.

- **Goal difficulty.** A goal should be challenging. If it is too easy, the individual may delay or approach the goal lackadaisically. If a goal is too difficult, the individual may not accept it and thus not try to meet it.
- **Goal clarity.** A goal must be clear and specific if it is to be useful in directing effort. The individual thus will know what is expected and not have to guess.

Clear and challenging goals lead to higher performance than do vague or general goals. Jeans maker Levi Strauss has offered to reward each of its 37,500 employees worldwide with a one-time bonus equal to about a year's pay if the company achieves its cumulative six-year sales target of $7.6 billion by November 2001.[9] In 1995, sales were slightly over $1 billion. Robert Haas, chairman of Levi Strauss, believes that setting an employee's goal at a specific amount to be sold is better than setting a goal of "trying to increase sales" or "doing your best." Goals that are difficult but not impossible will lead to higher performance than will easy goals. However, unrealistically high goals may not be accepted or may lead to high performance only in the short run. Individuals eventually get discouraged and stop trying, as predicted by expectancy theory (see Chapter 5).

With clear and challenging goals, employee behaviors are more likely to be focused on job-related tasks, high levels of performance, and goal achievement. Table 6.2 provides a summary of the key links between goal setting and individual performance.

Along with goal difficulty and clarity, a third key factor that influences the establishment of challenging goals is self-efficacy. In Chapter 4, we defined self-efficacy as the individual's belief that he or she can perform at a certain level in a given situation. It may be assessed by having individuals rate their confidence in attaining different performance levels. As might be expected, individuals who set high goals perform at a high level when they also have high self-efficacy. A person's self-efficacy is dependent on the task. A golfer with a low handicap has high self-efficacy on the golf course. The same person might have low self-efficacy when meeting sales quotas for a new piece of equipment that the company has just introduced.[10]

The following Managing in Practice piece demonstrates how goal difficulty, goal clarity, and high self-efficacy techniques enabled Steve Forbes to achieve outstanding results at Forbes, Inc., publisher of *Forbes* magazine. In this instance, Forbes outlined several ways to increase revenue of the magazine's advertising pages.

MANAGING IN PRACTICE

Steve Forbes

Forbes designed a goal-setting system to reward employees for increasing the number of advertising pages in the magazine. Employees were first rewarded on the basis of their sales revenue. Employees received 3 percent raises if they increased their paid advertising to $249,999, an additional 6 percent if their increase was from $250,000 to $499,999, and an additional 8 percent if their increase exceeded $500,000. Carlos Gonzalas had a base sales goal of $500,000 but actually sold $1,200,000 worth of advertising last year. He received $7500 for the first $250,000; $15,000 for the second $250,000, and 8 percent, or $16,000, for the remaining $200,000. Thus Gonzalas earned $38,500 in bonuses for his performance.

The second part of the reward system was based on the percentage of the magazine's market share against its competitors, *Fortune* and *Business Week*. An employee would be rewarded at the rate of three-fourths of one-tenth of 1 percent for each 1 percent share of market in total advertising pages. Gonzalas earned another $7500 by achieving a one-third market share against the competitors. His base was $3,000,000, and he had 150 pages of the three-magazine total of 450 pages ($3,000,000 \times 0.00075 \times 33.33 = $7500).

Steve Forbes believed that his goal-setting program targeted two different types of behaviors. First, the sales revenue goal spurred individuals to compete against themselves. Self-efficacy is task specific; that is, people having high self-efficacy for selling can perform very well. The second goal is a benchmark for individuals in terms of competition in the market place.[11]

TABLE 6.2 Impact of Goals on Performance

WHEN GOALS ARE	PERFORMANCE WILL TEND TO BE
Specific and clear	Higher
Vague	Lower
Difficult and challenging	Higher
Set participatively	Higher
Accepted by employees	Higher
Rejected by employees	Lower
Accompanied by positive incentives	Higher

Moderators   Figure 6.1 also shows four of the factors that moderate the strength of the relationship between goals and performance. We start with *ability* because it limits the individual's capacity to respond to a challenge. The relation of goal difficulty to performance is curvilinear, not linear. That is, performance levels off as the limits of a person's ability are approached.

The second factor, **goal commitment,** refers to the individual's determination to reach a goal, regardless of whether the goal was set by that person or someone else. How committed are you to achieving a top grade in this class? Take a minute and complete the questionnaire in Table 6.3. Your commitment to a goal is likely to be stronger if you make a public commitment to achieve it, if you have a high need for achievement, and if you believe that you can control those activities that will assist you in reaching that goal.

The effect of participation on goal commitment is complex. Positive goal commitment is more likely if employees participate in setting their goals, which often leads to a sense of ownership. Not expecting or wanting to be involved in goal setting reduces the importance of employee participation in terms of goal commitment. Even when a manager has to assign goals without employee participation, doing so leads to more focused efforts and better performance than if no goals were set.[12]

TABLE 6.3 Goal Commitment Questionnaire

ITEM	RESPONSE				
	STRONGLY AGREE	AGREE	UNDECIDED	DISAGREE	STRONGLY DISAGREE
1. I am strongly committed to pursuing a top grade.	_____	_____	_____	_____	_____
2. I am willing to expend a great deal of effort beyond what I'd normally do to achieve this top grade.	_____	_____	_____	_____	_____
3. I really care if I achieve a top grade.	_____	_____	_____	_____	_____
4. Much is to be gained by trying to achieve this grade.	_____	_____	_____	_____	_____
5. Revising this goal, depending on how things go this term, isn't likely.					
6. A lot would have to happen for me to abandon this goal.	_____	_____	_____	_____	_____
7. Expecting to reach my goal is realistic for me.	_____	_____	_____	_____	_____

Scoring: Give yourself 5 points for each Strongly Agree response; 4 points for each Agree response; 3 points for each Undecided response; 2 points for each Disagree response; and 1 point for each Strongly Disagree response. The higher your score, the greater your goal commitment to achieve a top grade in this class.

Source: Adapted from Hollenback, J. R., Williams, C. R., and Klein, H. J. An empirical examination of the antecedents of commitment to goals. *Journal of Applied Psychology*, 1989, 74, 18–23.

The expected rewards for achieving goals play an important role in the degree of goal commitment.[13] The greater the extent to which employees believe that positive rewards (merit pay raises, bonuses, promotions, opportunities to perform interesting tasks, and the like) are contingent on achieving goals, the greater their commitment to the goals. These notions are very similar to the ideas contained in the expectancy theory of motivation. Similarly, if employees expect to be punished for not achieving goals, the probability of goal commitment also is higher.[14] However, recall that punishment and the fear of punishment as primary means of guiding behavior may create a number of problems (see Chapter 4).

Employees compare expected rewards against rewards actually received. If the expected and received rewards are in agreement, the reward system is likely to continue to support goal commitment. If employees think that the rewards they receive are much less than the rewards they expected, they may perceive inequity. If perceived or actual inequity exists, employees eventually lessen their goal commitment. Teamwork and peer pressure are other factors that affect a person's commitment to a goal.[15]

Feedback makes goal setting and individual responses to goal achievement (performance) a dynamic process. It provides information to the employee and others about outcomes and the degree of employee goal achievement.[16] Feedback enables the individual to compare the expected rewards against those received. This comparison, in turn, can influence changes in the degree of goal commitment.

Task complexity is the last moderator of the strength of relationship between goals and performance that we consider. On simple tasks (for example, answering telephones at Marriott's reservation center), the effort encouraged by challenging goals leads directly to task performance. In more complex tasks (for example, studying to achieve a high grade), effort doesn't lead directly to effective performance. The individual must also decide where and how to allocate effort. We consider various issues associated with simple and complex jobs in Chapter 15, where we discuss job design.

Mediators   Let's assume that an individual has challenging goals and that the moderating factors support the achievement of these goals. How do the four mediators—direction, effort, persistence and task strategy—affect performance? *Direction* of attention focuses behaviors on activities expected to result in goal achievement and steers the individual away from activities irrelevant to the goals. The *effort* a person exerts depends on the difficulty of the goal. Generally, the greater the challenge, the greater the effort expended, assuming that the person is trying to reach and is committed to the goal. *Persistence* involves a person's willingness to work at the task over an extended period of time until the results are achieved. Most sports require participants to practice long and hard to hone their skills and maintain them at a high level. Finally, *task strategy* is the game plan that the individual has developed through experience and instruction on how to tackle the task.

Performance   Performance is likely to be high when (1) challenging goals are present, (2) the moderators (ability, goal commitment, feedback, and task complexity) are present, and (3) the mediators (direction, effort, persistence, and task strategy) are operating. Emmitt Smith, the star running back for the Dallas Cowboys, uses these three principles each year to improve his performance. Last year, Smith's goals included (1) keep Jesus Christ number 1 in his life, (2) stay healthy, (3) average 125 yards/game, (4) lead the league in rushing and scoring, (5) gain more than 1000 yards rushing in the first eight games, (6) catch 70 passes, (7) have no fumbles, and (8) be named 1st team All Pro.

Three basic types of quantitative outcome measures can be used to assess performance. They are units of production or quality (amount produced or number of errors); dollars (profits, costs, income, or sales); and time (attendance promptness in meeting deadlines).

When such measures are unavailable or inappropriate, qualitative goals and indicators may be used. Many organizations have developed a **code of ethics** to help employees make better ethical decisions. Creating ethics guidelines has several advantages that Boeing, GTE, and Johnson & Johnson, among others, consider important. Some of the advantages for setting ethical goals are

- to help employees identify what their organization recognizes as acceptable business practices;
- to legitimize the consideration of ethics as part of decision making;
- to avoid discussions among employees about what is right and wrong; and
- to avoid ambivalence in decision making caused by an organizational reward system that appears to reward unethical behavior.[17]

Rewards   We discussed rewards at length in Chapters 4 and 5, so we merely summarize them here. When an employee attains a high level of performance, rewards can become important inducements to continue to perform. Rewards can be external (bonuses, paid vacations, and so on) or internal (a sense of achievement, pride in accomplishment, and feelings of success). However, what is viewed as a reward in one culture may not be viewed as a reward in another. For example, doing business in Vietnam requires the exchange of gifts during the first day of a business meeting. Although the gifts may be small and relatively inexpensive, gifts with a company logo are highly valued. The gifts should be wrapped, but white or black paper should not be used because these colors are associated with death. In contrast, exchanging gifts at a business meeting in the United States is generally not expected. Praising an individual in public for achievement in Vietnam will cause the individual to be embarrassed; rewards are not to be given in public. Conversely, public acclaim for achievement in the United States is highly valued.[18]

Satisfaction   Many factors—including challenging work, interesting co-workers, salary, the opportunity to learn, and good working conditions—influence a person's satisfaction with the job (see Chapter 2). However, in the Locke–Latham model, the primary focus is on the employee's degree of satisfaction with goal achievement. Employees who set high, difficult goals may experience less job satisfaction than those employees who set low, easily achievable goals. Difficult goals are less frequently achieved, and satisfaction with performance is associated with success. Thus some compromise on goal difficulty may be necessary in order to maximize both satisfaction and performance. However, some level of satisfaction is associated with simply striving for difficult goals, such as responding to a challenge, making some progress toward reaching the goals, and the belief that benefits may still be derived from the experience regardless of the outcome.

Consequences   Individuals who are both satisfied with and committed to an organization are more likely to stay with the organization and to accept the challenges that it presents than are individuals less satisfied and committed. Turnover and absenteeism rates for satisfied individuals are low. This link brings us full circle to the beginning of the Locke–Latham goal-setting model.

What might happen if things go badly and the individual becomes dissatisfied rather than satisfied? Individual responses fall into at least six possible categories: (1) job avoidance (quitting); (2) work avoidance (absenteeism, arriving late, and leaving early); (3) psychological defenses (alcohol and drug abuse); (4) constructive protest (complaining); (5) defiance (refusing to do what is asked); and (6) aggression (theft or assault). Of course, quitting is the most common outcome of severe dissatisfaction.[19]

Significance for the Workplace   The goal-setting model has important implications for employees, managers, and teams. First, it provides an excellent framework to assist the manager or team in diagnosing the potential problems with low- or average-performing employees. Several diagnostic questions might be: (1) How were the goals set? (2) Are the goals challenging? (3) What is affecting goal commitment? and (4) Does the employee know when he or she has done a good job? Second, it provides concrete advice to the manager on how to create a high-performance work environment. Third, it portrays the system of relationships and interplay among key factors, such as goal difficulty, goal commitment, feedback, and rewards, to achieve high performance.

MANAGEMENT BY OBJECTIVES

Management by objectives (MBO) is a philosophy and system of management that serves as both a planning aid and a way of life in the workplace. This widely used management approach reflects a positive philosophy about people and a participative management style. Management by objectives involves managers and employees in jointly setting goals for work performance and personal development, periodically evaluating the employee's progress toward achieving these goals, and integrating individual, departmental, team, and organizational goals. Hewlett-Packard and Procter & Gamble are among the organizations that use MBO successfully.

Although many people have contributed to the development of MBO, Peter Drucker coined the term *management by objectives* in about 1950.[20] The MBO model contains the four basic components shown in Figure 6.2: goal setting, subordinate participation, implementation, and performance appraisal and feedback. The arrows indicate the strong interrelationship among the components and that an effective MBO process requires all to operate simultaneously.

Goal Setting   Managers and employees define and focus on job goals rather than rules, activities, and procedures. In this discussion, we use the terms *goals, objectives, outputs, quotas, results, ends,* and *performance standards* synonymously. The goal-setting process includes identifying specific areas of job responsibility, developing performance standards in each area, and (possibly) formulating a work plan for achieving the goals. At PageNet, a sales representative for this cellular phone company has a sales goal of selling $3000 worth of equipment a month and five new cellular phone systems every two weeks. To achieve these goals, PageNet management believes that each sales representative should complete thirty-five sales call per week.

What happens when employees don't make their or the organization's goals? When employees are under extreme pressure to meet goals they may resort to cut-

■ **FIGURE 6.2**

Management by Objectives Process

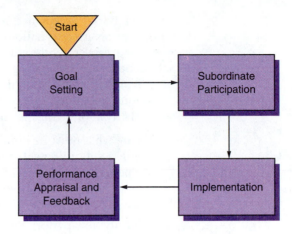

ting corners, overcharging customers, or falsifying research results. Reliance on a numerically based reward system often produces unintended behaviors that harm customers. The following Ethics in Practice selection highlights this problem at Chem-Bio Corporation.

ETHICS IN PRACTICE

Misread Pap Tests

A Wisconsin prosecutor brought charges against Chem-Bio Corporation for reckless homicide. The prosecutor stated that a laboratory technician misread the Pap smears of two women who died of cervical cancer because of the laboratory's goal-setting program.

The prosecutor said that grave errors had been made because the laboratory director paid its technicians on a piecework basis. As a result, the technician read 31,000 slides for Chem-Bio and 16,000 slides for another organization in one year, or more than 22 slides an hour. The American Society of Cytology has recommended that for the sake of quality, technicians read no more than 12,000 slides a year or 6 an hour. The prosecutor also noted that Chem-Bio failed to install random controls to check the quality of the Pap smear analysis, and showed an indifferent attitude toward professional standards and need for continuing education.

A jury decided against the company and awarded the family members of the two women more than $9.8 million. The company also agreed to remove the doctor in charge and not permit him to be responsible for any quality control work in the future. A judge also charged the laboratory with reckless homicide for misreading pap smears and imposed the maximum penalty—$20,000—allowable under Wisconsin law.[21]

Particular job responsibilities usually change less dramatically and less frequently over time than does the specific goal associated with each area of responsibility. At PageNet, the salesperson is responsible for sales volume. However, specific sales volumes can vary greatly because of general economic conditions, changed market acceptance, more or fewer opportunities in a sales territory, and so on. AutoNation, a nationwide franchise operation that specializes in selling preowned cars, recently eliminated daily quotas because they discovered that salespeople were becoming too aggressive with customers. These quotas have been replaced with a monthly goal of selling 800 cars for each franchise.

Various guidelines have been offered to managers and team leaders on how to set goals. The following are some examples.

- State what must be done. A job description may be helpful in setting goals with a subordinate. It should list the tasks to be performed, the outcomes expected, coordination required with other jobs, equipment to be used, any supervisory duties involved, and so on. Factors on which job success depends, can further clarify the job description.

- Specify how performance will be measured. Often time, money, or physical units can be measures. Sometimes, though, success is more subjective and difficult to measure. If so, specifying behaviors or actions that will lead to success can be used an indicators of performance.

- Specify the performance standard. A readily accepted approach is to start goal setting by letting previous performance set the standard. Most employees consider their average previous performance, or that of their team, to be a fair goal. Performance in some jobs, though, can't be measured so precisely. The job may be unique or so new that no previous performance measures are available. If so, goal setting becomes a matter of judgment.

- Set deadlines to reach goals. Some goals lend themselves to daily or weekly accomplishment. Others can be accomplished only monthly, quarterly, or annually.

- Rank goals in order of importance and difficulty. A clear understanding of priorities helps employees focus on what is most important at the time. Also, people work best when they have compelling goals.[22]

Managers at Pacific Bell, Coopers & Lybrand, Pepsi-Cola, American Express, and Digital Equipment, among others, have also used such guidelines to confront diversity issues in their organizations. Work-force diversity is now a fact of organizational life that influences recruitment, retention, motivation, and performance of employees. Although many tools for changing the behaviors of employees exist, setting goals is a key. The following Diversity in Practice feature indicates how Pacific Bell broadened its recruiting practices.

DIVERSITY IN PRACTICE

Beyond Good Faith

Affirmative action programs are supposed to involve a good-faith effort on the part of the organization to seek out, recruit, and encourage minority applicants for jobs. Yet in many organizations, this means placing the words "We are an equal opportunity employer" at the bottom of advertisements, and running those ads in selected "minority publications." Such efforts certainly do not discourage minority applicants, but they do very little to encourage them. Pacific Bell decided to take some actions that went beyond a good-faith program.

—Continued

DIVERSITY IN PRACTICE—*Continued*

It established goals for the number of minority employees by department. To achieve these goals, the company sent recruiters from the human resources and engineering departments to colleges that tended to enroll higher proportions of minority students. Specialists examined standardized test scores to determine possible racial or gender bias. Recruiters contacted minority faculty and staff to identify deserving students. Once they had identified such students, recruiters helped them with basic tools such as résumé writing, preparing for an interview, and job hunting.

To help identify talent further, Pacific Bell's managers developed two programs. First, the company began a summer program for minority students following their junior year that was designed to qualify them for first-level management jobs after graduation. A Bell manager was assigned to coach a student, but, before the coaching started, both coach and student were required to attend a half-day seminar on diversity issues. During the summer, senior managers were introduced to all the students through workshops, recreational events, and other activities. Some 64 percent of the participating students were offered jobs upon graduation from college. Second, the company developed scholarship programs at seventeen California colleges to lessen the financial burdens facing these students.

What were the longer term results of these efforts? A decade ago, the proportion of minority managers at Pacific Bell was 17.5 percent. Today, it is more than 28 percent.[23]

Participation   A moderate- to high-level of participation by subordinates in the goal-setting process is an essential component of MBO. However, before subordinates can participate effectively, they must have some autonomy in their jobs rather than merely doing what they are told. The reason is that management by objectives requires subordinates to plan and control their own tasks. Thus highly routine and programmed jobs should be redesigned before they become part of the MBO process.

Implementation   Implementation of MBO requires translating the outcomes from the goal-setting process into actions that ultimately will lead to the attainment of the desired goals. Action planning, which indicates how goals are to be achieved, often accompanies the implementation phase. During implementation, managers must give greater latitude and choice to employees, perhaps by discontinuing day-to-day oversight of their activities. But managers must be available to coach and counsel employees to help them reach their goals—playing a greater helping or facilitating role and a less judgmental role. Managers should hold periodic meetings during the year with employees to review progress, discuss assistance needed, and make any necessary changes in goals, which should be modified as necessary. This approach allows employees to perceive MBO as a flexible system and encourages them to address major new problems or changes as they occur.

Performance Appraisal and Feedback   Performance appraisal under MBO involves (1) identifying measurement factors or goals against which to evaluate performance; (2) measuring performance against those goals; (3) reviewing performance with the employee; and (4) developing ways to improve future performance. Employees develop a clear understanding of their progress through performance appraisal and feedback. Feedback is a key element of MBO because it identifies the extent to which employees have attained their goals. The knowledge of results is essential to improved job performance and personal development in terms of new skills, attitudes, and motivation. Performance may be recognized and rewarded in many different ways. Ultimately, however, the satisfaction gained from achieving goals becomes one of the most cherished rewards.[24]

Management by objectives encourages self-evaluation of performance. Honest self-evaluation by employees provides insight into their own performance and the possible need to modify their behaviors to achieve their goals. When people are self-motivated and capable of managing many of their own tasks, managers can turn their attention to other issues that must be resolved and other problems that must be solved.

Alamco, a $12 million Clarksburg, West Virginia, oil and gas company, recently won a Wellness Council of America award for using MBO to encourage healthful lifestyles among its ninety-six employees. Yearly cash incentives for six healthful behaviors or conditions were jointly set by all employees: not smoking or chewing tobacco ($100); wearing a seat belt ($25); a cholesterol level below 150 ($100); blood pressure below 135/85 ($50); a waist-to-hip ratio of 0.8 or less for women and 0.95 or less for men ($50); and getting thirty minutes of exercise three times a week ($25). In addition, spouses earn half the incentive amounts. Last year, Alamco distributed $19,000, and the company has saved more than 65 percent on its health insurance premiums. Absenteeism is down and camaraderie is up.[25]

Significance for the Workplace   Critics have attacked MBO, particularly with respect to ways that organizations apply it. These criticisms relate mainly to how managers actually use the process, rather than to how it is supposed to be used. Among the criticisms are the following.

- Too much emphasis is placed on reward–punishment psychology (that is, people are rewarded for accomplishing goals and punished for not doing so).

- An excessive amount of paperwork and red tape develops—the very things that MBO is supposed to reduce.

- The process is controlled and imposed from the top, allowing little opportunity for real employee participation.

- The process turns into a zero-sum (win–lose) game between manager and employee.

- Aspects of jobs that can be objectively rather than subjectively measured receive the most emphasis.

- Too much emphasis on individual goals and performance drives out recognition of the need for collaborative teamwork and group goals. Individuals may satisfy their own goals to the detriment of overall goals.[26]

REWARD SYSTEMS FOR ENHANCING PERFORMANCE

In Chapters 4 and 5 we discussed types of rewards that organizations make available to employees. Also, many employees view fringe benefits, salaries, opportunities to engage in challenging assignments, and the achievement of difficult goals as rewards. In this section, we discuss four popular reward systems that organizations use to motivate employees. These reward systems are gain-sharing, flexible benefit plans, banking time off, and skill-based pay.[27] Their strengths and limitations are summarized in Table 6.4.

■ GAIN-SHARING PLANS

Through **gain-sharing plans,** regular cash bonuses are provided to employees for increasing productivity, reducing costs, or improving quality.[28] According to Tower Perrin, a compensation consulting organization, over 50 percent of all U.S. companies had some type of gain-sharing pay plan for their employees. The average payout for employees was 7.6 percent, up from 5.9 percent just a few years ago. Many organizations, such as Hugh Electronics Corporation, Wal-Mart, and Pizza Hut, are discovering that, when designed correctly, gain-sharing plans can contribute to employee motivation and involvement. Specific formulas tailor made for each organization are used to calculate both performance contributions and gain-sharing awards. Many gain-sharing plans encourage employees to become involved in making decisions that will affect their rewards. Gain-sharing plans are tied to a plant, division, or department's improvement.

In contrast, **profit-sharing plans** give employees a portion of the company's profits.[29] Profit sharing may have a limited impact because employees may feel that they can do little to influence the organization's overall profitability. Moreover, company profits are influenced by many factors, such as competitor's products, state of the economy, and inflation, that are well beyond the employees' control. Profit-sharing plans are very popular in Japan. For example, at Seiko Instruments many managers and workers receive bonuses twice a year that equal four or five months' salary. These bonuses are based on the company's overall performance.[30]

A popular version of gain-sharing is the Scanlon plan, named after Joe Scanlon, a union leader in the 1930s.[31] The Scanlon plan is a system of rewards for improvements in productivity. Working together, employees and managers develop a formula that bases the distribution of rewards on a ratio of total labor costs to total sales volume. If actual labor costs are less than expected, the surplus goes into a bonus pool. The bonus pool is often equally split between the company and employees, with all employees receiving bonuses as a percentage of their salaries.[32]

TABLE 6.4   Reward Systems That Improve Productivity

REWARD SYSTEM	STRENGTHS	LIMITATIONS
Gain-sharing/Scanlon plan	Plans to reward employees who reach specified production levels and control labor costs.	Formula can be complex; trust on part of employees and management is needed.
Flexible benefit plans	Plans are tailored to fit employee needs.	Administrative costs are high for management.
Banking time off	Additional time off is contingent on employee performance.	Managers must give high performers more time off than poor performers.
Skill-based pay	Employee acquires new skills before being paid more.	Training costs to improve employee skills may be high. Employees can "top out." Labor costs increase as employees master more skills.

Although gain-sharing plans sound good, they have had mixed success. Fleet Financial Group recently abandoned its gain-sharing program, but Continental Airlines' adoption of a gain-sharing program was instrumental in revitalizing that company. The following Managing in Practice piece indicates each company's results.

MANAGING IN PRACTICE

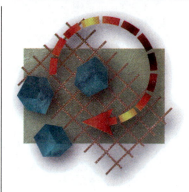

Tying Pay to Performance—A Mixed Bag

As a part of a two-year cost-cutting effort, management at the Fleet Financial Group, Inc., had created a gain-sharing program tied to the company's ratio of expenses to revenue and its stock prices. The more costs were cut and the higher the stock rose, the more employees were supposed to gain. But when Fleet's stock price remained depressed even after cost cutting, workers got the minimum pay-out—averaging $615 per employee. Many employees stated that, considering the blood, sweat, and tears that went into getting the bonus, it turned out to be meaningless. What further enraged employees was that top management received big bonuses that weren't tied to the same measures.

Continental Airlines, Inc., installed gain-sharing programs that have created double-digit productivity gains. Eight times in 1995 Continental Airline employees earned $65 apiece when the airlines ranked in the top half of the Transportation Department's monthly on-time ratings for the industry. When Continental took the number 1 spot in December, the airline paid all employees $100. In 1996, the airline raised the goal: Employees won't get a bonus unless Continental ranks in the top three. The incentive payments may seem small but, because Continental employees make 25 percent less than their industry counterparts, they have been a big morale builder.[33]

■ FLEXIBLE BENEFIT PLANS

Flexible benefit plans allow employees to choose the benefits they want, rather than having management choose for them. According to David Norwood, Vice President at Johnson and Higgins, a global compensation consulting firm, a corporation's benefits plan costs about 37 percent of its total employee cash compensation package.[34] That represents a huge cost, considering that only 5 percent or less is set aside for merit pay increases in most organizations. Under flexible benefit plans, employees decide how they want to receive benefit amounts, tailoring the benefits package to their needs. The idea is that employees can make important and intelligent decisions about their benefits. Some employees take all their benefits in cash; others choose additional life insurance, child or elder care, dental insurance, or retirement plans. Extensive benefits options may be highly attractive to an employee with a spouse and family at home. However, many benefits might be only minimally attractive to a young, single employee. Older employees value retirement plans more than younger employees and are willing to put more money into them. Employees with elderly parents may desire financial assistance in providing care for them. At Traveler's Insurance Company employees can choose benefits of up to $5000 a year for the care of dependent elderly parents.

Thousands of organizations now offer flexible benefits plans.[35] They have become very popular because they offer three distinct advantages. First, they allow employees to make important decisions about their personal finances and to match employees' needs with their benefits plan. Second, such plans help organizations control their costs, especially for health care. Employers can set the maximum amount of benefit dollars they will spend on employees' benefits and avoid automatically absorbing cost increases. Third, such plans highlight the economic value of many benefits to employees. Most employees have little idea of the cost of benefits because the organization is willing to pay for them even though employees might not want some of them or might prefer alternatives.

Moreover, the changing work force is causing employers to consider flexible benefits as a tool to recruit and retain employees. Starbucks Coffee Company believes that its use of flexible benefits plans have cut employee turnover from 150 to 60 percent. Starbucks calculates that hiring an employee costs $550. If so, a competitor with 300 percent turnover would have to hire three people ($3 \times \$550 = \$1650$) per job per year, whereas Starbucks would need to spend only $330 ($0.6 \times \$550$) per year to keep a job filled.

Some limitations are associated with flexible benefits plans. First, because different employees choose different benefits packages, record keeping becomes more complicated. Sophisticated computer systems are essential to keep straight the details of employees' records. Second, accurately predicting the number of employees that might choose each benefit is difficult. That may affect the firm's group rates for life and medical insurance, as the costs of such plans are based on the number of employees covered.

■ BANKING TIME OFF

Time off from work with pay is attractive to some people. Typically, the length of vacations and scheduling them are based on the number of years that employees have worked for an organization. An extension of such a system is basing time off on performance. That is, employees can bank time-off credit contingent on their performance. At Tandem Computers, high-performing employees earn extra vacation time and bank this time for one year. If the employees don't use their vacation time, they can roll the credit over to a savings investment plan. In setting up such programs, organizations should be aware of some potential problems. For example, an employee who wants to use banked time during a busy time for the organization may negatively affect productivity. In addition the organization may incur increased costs because of having to pay overtime or bring in a temporary employee to cover.

A version of banking time off is SelectTime, which is offered by NationsBank, and other organizations. SelectTime offers employees the option of reducing work hours for family reasons. This time can be used for the care of any dependent family member, including a child, spouse, or parent. This time off isn't a vacation. As soon as the need is satisfied, the employee returns to work full time. If the employee's manager agrees, the person's salary and benefits are reduced in proportion to the reduction in hours. NationsBank President Hugh McColl believes that this program permits the bank to utilize its human resources more fully. He says, "The beauty of this concept is that it accommodates people." NationsBank also has lower training costs because the need to recruit new employees has dropped.[36]

■ SKILL-BASED PAY

Paying people according to their value in the labor market makes a great deal of sense. After all, employees who develop multiple skills are valuable assets to the organization. **Skill-based pay** depends on the number and level of job-related skills that an employee has learned.[37] At Toyota, for example, workers not only are expected to operate machines, but also to take responsibility for maintenance and troubleshooting, quality control, and even modifying computer programs. About 40 percent of large U.S. organizations, such as TRW, Honeywell, and Westinghouse, use skill-based pay for at least some production workers in their operations.

Skill-based pay is easiest to describe in terms of a production team in a manufacturing plant. Typically, management can fairly easily identify all the skills needed to perform various tasks and the skills that employees need to learn. Employees' pay is based on their skill levels. The following Across Cultures account illustrates the benefits that General Electric has gained from using skill-based pay.

ACROSS CULTURES

General Electric Appliances

At General Electric's plant in Bayamon, Puerto Rico, there are 172 hourly workers, 15 advisors, and the plant manager. The workers are divided into teams. Each team is responsible for a part of the plant's operation, such as receiving, assembly, or shipping. The advisors assist the teams only when they need help. General Electric agreed to provide the hourly employees with the skills and knowledge needed to perform multiple jobs. It also designed a pay structure to reward employees who learn and use these skills. Hourly workers change jobs every six months so that they learn each job and how it affects the other parts of the plant operations. In return, employees are rewarded with a "triple-scoop" compensation plan that pays for skills, knowledge, and business performance. Workers receive a $0.25 per hour pay increase the first time they go through each of the four six-month rotations. In addition, they can almost double their pay by "declaring a major" and becoming an expert in an area such as maintenance or quality control. Further pay increases can be earned by completing courses in English, business practices, and other subjects. By meeting goals for plant performance and individual attendance, bonuses of more than $200 per quarter also are possible. The Bayamon work force now is 20 percent more productive than the work force in a similar plant.[38]

The most obvious advantage of skill-based pay in a production situation is flexibility. When employees can perform multiple tasks, managers gain tremendous flexibility in work-force utilization. Largely as a result of the Tylenol poisoning tragedy, Johnson & Johnson decided to completely redo its packaging of Tylenol to add greater safety. Because of the firm's skill-based pay system, employees understood the technology involved and were able to introduce quickly the new packaging changes. Johnson & Johnson also found that skill-based pay can increase productivity, while decreasing supervisory costs. Employees are motivated to gain and use new skills because the organization equitably rewards them for doing so.

However, skill-based pay does have some disadvantages. The most obvious one has to do with the high pay rates that the plan tends to produce. By its very nature, the plan encourages individuals to become more valuable to the organization and, as a result, to be paid more. Designed to increase opportunities to learn multiple skills skill-based pay plans require a large investment in training and lost production time as employees learn new skills. Thus the organization sometimes has inexperienced and overpaid employees doing the work, at least in the short run. A worst-case scenario for the organization is that many employees know how to do every job but that all jobs are being done by employees who aren't highly proficient. Finally, employees can be frustrated when no job openings are available in areas for which they have learned new skills. Most skill-based programs require employees to perform skills regularly in order to be paid for them.

CHAPTER SUMMARY

Goal setting is a process intended to increase efficiency and effectiveness by specifying the desired outcomes toward which individuals, departments, teams, and organizations should work. Goal setting doesn't take place in a vacuum. Stakeholders such as customers, shareholders, and employees influence the selection of goals by organizations and their employees. On a day-to-day basis, customers or clients are probably the driving forces in the selection of goals that are most crucial to organizational and employee performance.

A goal-setting model was presented. The model emphasizes the challenges provided for the individual: goal difficulty, goal clarity, and self-efficacy. Four moderating factors—ability, goal commitment, feedback, and task complexity—influence the strength of the relationship between challenging goals and performance. Three mediators—direction, effort, and persistence—act as facilitators of goal attainment. Performance, rewards, satisfaction, and consequences complete the model.

Management by objectives (MBO) is both a philosophy and a management system. It encourages setting general organizational goals and increasingly more specific goals for departments, teams, and individual employees. Its primary emphasis is on manager and employee setting goals jointly, monitoring of performance by the manager, and providing feedback to the employee.

Four reward systems, in particular, are designed to enhance performance: gainsharing, flexible benefits, banking time off, and skill-based pay plans. Each has its own features, advantages, and limitations.

KEY TERMS AND CONCEPTS

Code of ethics	Goal difficulty	Scanlon plan
Flexible benefit plans	Goal setting	Skill-based pay
Gain-sharing plans	Goals	Stakeholders
Goal clarity	Management by objectives (MBO)	
Goal commitment	Profit-sharing plans	

DISCUSSION QUESTIONS

1. Imagine that you are establishing a goal-setting program for a local blood drive campaign. How are various stakeholders likely to influence these goals?

2. Think of an organization for which you currently work or have worked. How does this organization and its employees measure up in terms of the five service quality goals stated in the chapter?

3. List your five most important personal goals. Evaluate the difficulty and clarity of each goal. What are the implications, if any, of this assessment for your future?

4. Think of this course. Evaluate your level of goal commitment. What factors do you think influenced your level of goal commitment? Did your level of commitment influence your performance? Explain.

5. What types of goals should be set for a teller at a branch bank? A supermarket cashier?

6. Why do people sometimes falsify records to achieve goals?

7. Jim Young, Senior Vice President for EDS, has said: "If you don't demand something out of the ordinary, you will not get anything but ordinary results." What implications for goal setting does this statement have for managing others?

8. What are the similarities and differences between gain-sharing and profit-sharing plans? How does each relate to goal-setting techniques?

9. What are some problems that employees might face in an organization that has adopted a skill-based pay program?

10. Can a flexible benefits plan be tied to employee performance? If so, what are the advantages of doing so? The disadvantages?

■ Developing Competencies

Self-Insight: Goal-Setting Questionnaire

Instructions

The following statements refer to a job you currently hold or have held. Read each statement and then select a response from the following scale that best describes your view. You may want to use a separate sheet of paper to record your responses and compare them with the responses of others.

Scale

Almost Never   1   2   3   4   5   Almost Always

_____ 1. I understand exactly what I am supposed to do on my job.

_____ 2. I have specific, clear goals to aim for on my job.

_____ 3. The goals I have on this job are challenging.

_____ 4. I understand how my performance is measured on this job.

_____ 5. I have deadlines for accomplishing my goals on this job.

_____ 6. If I have more than one goal to accomplish, I know which are most important and which are least important.

_____ 7. My goals require my full effort.

_____ 8. My manager tells me the reasons for giving me the goals I have.

_____ 9. My manager is supportive with respect to encouraging me to reach my goals.

_____ 10. My manager lets me participate in the setting of my goals.

_____ 11. My manager lets me have some say in deciding how I will go about implementing my goals.

_____ 12. If I reach my goals, I know that my manager will be pleased.

_____ 13. I get credit and recognition when I attain my goals.

_____ 14. Trying for goals makes my job more fun than it would be without goals.

_____ 15. I feel proud when I get feedback indicating that I have reached my goals.

_____ 16. The other people I work with encourage me to attain my goals.

_____ 17. I sometimes compete with my co-workers to see who can do the best job in reaching our goals.

_____ 18. If I reach my goals, my job security will be improved.

_____ 19. If I reach my goals, my chances for a pay raise are increased.

_____ 20. If I reach my goals, my chances for a promotion are increased.

_____ 21. I usually feel that I have a suitable action plan(s) for reaching my goals.

_____ 22. I get regular feedback indicating how I am performing in relation to my goals.

_____ 23. I feel that my training was good enough so that I am capable of reaching my goals.

_____ 24. Organization policies help rather than hurt goal attainment.

_____ 25. Teams work together in this company to attain goals.

_____ 26. This organization provides sufficient resources (e.g., time, money, equipment) to make goal setting effective.

_____ 27. In performance appraisal sessions, my supervisor stresses problem solving rather than criticism.

_____ 28. Goals in this organization are used more to help you do your job well rather than punish you.

_____ 29. The pressure to achieve goals here fosters honesty as opposed to cheating and dishonesty.

_____ 30. If my manager makes a mistake that affects my ability to attain my goals, he or she admits it.

Scoring and Interpretation

Add the points shown for items 1 through 30. Scores of 120 to 150 may indicate a high-performing, highly satisfying work situation. Your goals are challenging and you are committed to reaching them. When you achieve your goals, you are rewarded for your accomplishments. Scores of 80 to 119 may suggest a highly varied work situation with some motivating and satisfying features and some frustrating and dissatisfying features. Scores of 30 to 79 may suggest a low-performing, dissatisfying work situation.[39]

Organizational Insight: General Stair Corporation

On April 20, Saby Behar worried about the onslaught of competition and the fear of an ugly price war. Behar was the president of General Stair Corporation, a $2.7 million per year maker of prefabricated stairs and railings in Opa-Locka, Florida. Although his company had a leading market share in Southern Florida, he was concerned that competitors would enter the market and start a price war to gain customers.

He and his top management team decided that the best way to stop customer slippage was to guarantee on-time delivery to builders. Late shipments caused builders problems. Remembering that when Domino's pizza first started, it promised the customer a free pizza if it couldn't be delivered within thirty minutes, Behar and his managers guaranteed builders a refund of $50 if stairs weren't delivered on time. However, a problem immediately arose over what constituted "on time." Reports of builders giving crews the wrong lot number and not being able to accept delivery because they weren't far enough along on a house, among others, fueled heated debates within the management team over how to measure on-time delivery.

In order to obtain correct information about deliveries, General Stair decided to overhaul its own communications system. The company hired two field representatives to check houses routinely to see how close the builders were to actually needing stairs. Armed with two-way radios, cellular phones, and portable fax machines, they provided the company with accurate and timely information.

In a meeting involving all thirty-five employees, attention turned to the type of motivational system needed to get employees to make good on the guarantee. Pizza for lunch every Friday, free trips, additional health insurance, and money, among other things, were mentioned. Behar and his management team estimated that, if the company maintained its guarantee and didn't boost on-time from the current rate of 95 percent to 98 percent, it would start losing money. However, if on-time deliveries improved, management decided to put $50 in a fund for each timely delivery to cover employee rewards.

By mid-September, labor costs had been reduced by 30 percent and installers had seen their pay increase by $160 a week. Employees told managers and others how to improve their performance so that they also could get rewards. The field representatives devised a twelve-step check list for quickly indicating how close a house was to needing stairs. Others devised a system for keeping track of screws and tacks, which helped reduce materials costs by 5 percent. Employees started sharing rewards because they realized that, unless everyone was receiving something, the system would break down. The employees also hung a huge board in the factory on which they kept track of the amount of money on hand in the fund, which everyone could see.

To control costs better, the company switched from salary to incentive compensation. To be eligible, employees would have to meet certain criteria: they couldn't be late more than two days a month or absent more than two days a quarter; they couldn't be the cause of a delay; and they had to work accident free.

General Stair's productivity is three times higher than it used to be, and absenteeism is down 20 percent. Despite a downturn in the economy, General Stair's orders are up 20 percent and they have yet to pay $50 to a builder.[40]

Questions

1. What concepts of the Locke–Latham model did Behar use?

2. What role did the reward system play in reinforcing the changes in employee behaviors?

3. What other rewards would you recommend that Behar implement at General Stair to boost productivity?

REFERENCES

1. Adapted from Sullivan, J. Pizza on parade. *Bakery Production & Marketing*, January 25, 1995, 20–24; Sunoo, B. P. Papa John's rolls out hot HR menu. *Personnel Journal*, September 1995, 38–47.

2. Conversation with Jordan, J., Manager, Sourcing, Lucent Technologies, a division of AT&T, State College Pennsylvania, June 16, 1996.

3. Locke, E. A., and Latham, G. P. *A Theory of Goal Setting & Task Performance.* Englewood Cliffs, N.J.: Prentice-Hall, 1990, 7.

4. Locke, E. A., and Kristof, A. L. Volitional choices in the goal achievement process. In *The Psychology of Action: Linking Cognition and Motivation to Behavior*, P. Gollwitzer and J. A. Bargh (eds.). New York: Guilford, 1996, 365–384.

5. Pitts, R. A., and Lei, D. *Strategic Management: Building and Sustaining Competitive Advantage.* St. Paul, Minn.: West, 1996, 21–22, 48–49; Harrison, J. S., and St. John, C. H. Managing and partnering with external stakeholders. *Academy of Management Executive*, 1996, 10, 46–60.

6. Reichfield, F. F. Learning from customer defections. *Harvard Business Review*, March–April, 1996, 56–70; Pine, B. J. II, Peppers, D., and Rogers, M. Do you want to keep your customers forever? *Harvard Business Review*, March–April 1995, 103–119.

7. Adapted from Schulze, H. What makes the Ritz the Ritz? *Across the Board*, May 1994, 58–59; Janjigian, R. Great expectations. *Hospitality Design*, December 1994, 18–24. Also see Milliman, J. F., Zawacki, R. A., Schulz, B., Wigins, S, and Norman, C. A. Customer service drives 360-degree goal setting. *Personnel Journal*, 1995, 74(6), 136–141.

8. Locke and Latham, 252–267.

9. Levi Strauss offers employees bonus if goals are met. *Dallas Morning News*, June 16, 1996, 12H. Also see Lee, C., and Bobko, P. Exploring the meaning and usefulness of measures of subjective goal difficulty. *Journal of Applied Social Psychology*, 1992, 22, 1417–1428.

10. Cole, B. L., and Hopkins, B. L. Manipulations of the relationship between reported self-efficacy and performance. *Journal of Organizational Behavior Management*, 1995, 15, 95–135; Lee, C., and Bobko, P. Self-efficacy beliefs: Comparison of five measures. *Journal of Applied Psychology*, 1994, 79, 364–369; Lindsley, D. H., Brass, D. J., and Thomas, J. B. Efficacy-performance spirals: A multilevel perspective. *Academy of Management Review*, 1995, 20, 645–678.

11. Adapted from Wellington, F. *Managing at Forbes.* Unpublished manuscript, Southern Methodist University, Dallas, Texas, 1995.

12. Wofford, J. C., Goodwin, V. L., and Premack, S. Meta-analysis of the antecedents of personal goal level and of the antecedents and consequences of goal commitment. *Journal of Management*, 1992, 18, 595–615; Wright, P. M., O'Leary-Kelly, A. M., Cortina, J. M., Klein, H. J., and Hollenbeck, J. R. On the meaning and measurement of goal commitment. *Journal of Applied Psychology*, 1994, 79, 795–808.

13. Brett, J. F., Cron, W. L., and Slocum, J. W., Jr. Economic dependency on work: A moderator of the relationship between organizational commitment and performance. *Academy of Management Journal*, 1995, 38, 261–271; Wright, P. M., and Kacmar, K. M. Goal specificity as a determinant of goal commitment and goal change. *Organizational Behavior & Human Decision Processes*, 1994, 59, 242–261.

14. Becker, T. E., Billings, R. S., Eveleth, D. M., and Gilbert, N. L. Foci and bases of employee commitment: Implications for job performance. *Academy of Management Journal*, 1996, 39, 464–482.

15. Brown, S. P., Cron, W. L., and Slocum, J. W., Jr. Effects of goal-directed emotions on salesperson volitions, behavior and performance: A longitudinal study. *Journal of Marketing*, 1997, 60, 39–55.

16. Martin, B. A., and Manning, D. J., Jr. Combined effects of normative information and task difficulty on the goal–commitment–performance relationship. *Journal of Management*, 1995, 21, 65–80; Austin, J. T., and Klein, H. J. Work motivation and goal striving. In *Individual Differences and Behavior in Organizations*, K. Murphy (ed.). San Francisco: Jossey-Bass, 1996, 209–257.

17. Weiss, J. *Organizational Behavior and Change: Managing Diversity, Cross-Cultural Dynamics, and Ethics.* St. Paul, Minn.: West, 1996; Yearta, S. K., Maitlis, S., and Briner, R. B. An exploratory study of goal setting in theory and practice: A motivational technique that works? *Journal of Occupational and Organizational Psychology*, 1995, 68, 237–253.

18. Smith, E. D., Jr., and Pham, C. Doing business in Vietnam: A cultural guide. *Business Horizons*, May–June 1996, 47–51; Von Glinow, M. A., and Clarke, L. Vietnam: Tiger or Kitten? *Academy of Management Executive*, 1995, 9(4), 35–48.

19. Lee, T. W., Mitchell, T. R., Wise, L., and Fireman, S. An unfolding model of voluntary employee turnover. *Academy of Management Journal*, 1996, 39, 5–36.

20. Greenwood, R. G. Management by Objectives: As Developed by Peter Drucker, Assisted by Harold Smidy. *Academy of Management Review*, 1981, 6, 225–230.

21. Adapted from Chem-Bio receives maximum penalty in pap smear case. *Wall Street Journal*, February 23, 1996, B10; A no contest plea by Chem-Bio averts trial over pap smear. *Wall Street Journal*, December 5, 1995, B6; Chem-Bio charged with homicide over pap smears. *Wall Street Journal*, April 13, 1995, B4.

22. Hellriegel, D., and Slocum, J. W., Jr. *Management*, 7th ed. Cincinnati: South-Western, 1996, 246–250.

23. Stoddard, D. B., Jarvenpaa, S. L., and Littlejohn, M. The reality of business reengineering: Pacific Bell's centrex provisioning. *California Management Review*, 1996, 3, 57–76; Roberson, L., and Gutierrez, N. C. Beyond good faith:

Commitment to recruiting management diversity at Pacific Bell. In *Diversity in the Workplace,* S. E. Jackson and Associates (eds.). New York: Guilford, 1992, 65–88.

24. Shalley, C. A. Effects of coaction, expected evaluation, and goal-setting on creativity and productivity. *Academy of Management Journal,* 1995, 38, 483–503.

25. Adapted from Fenn, D. Healthful habits pay off. *Inc.,* April 1996, 111.

26. Latham, G. P. *Increasing Productivity Through Performance Appraisal.* Reading, Mass.: Addison-Wesley, 1992.

27. Lawler, E. E. III. *Strategic Pay: Aligning Organizational Strategies and Pay Systems.* San Francisco: Jossey-Bass, 1990.

28. Zellner, W. Trickle-down in trickling down at work. *Business Week,* March 18, 1996, 34.

29. Welbourne, T. M., and Gomez-Majia, L. R. Gainsharing: A critical review and a future research agenda. *Journal of Management,* 1995, 21, 559–609.

30. Rehfeld, J. E. *Alchemy of a Leader.* New York: John Wiley & Sons, 1994.

31. Schuler, R. S. *Managing Human Resources,* 5th ed. St. Paul, Minn.: West, 1995, 436.

32. Tyler, L. S., and Fisher, B. The Scanlon concept: A philosophy as much as a system. *Personnel Administrator,* July 1983, 33–37.

33. Adapted from Zellner, 34; McCartney, S. Back on course. *The Wall Street Journal,* May 15, 1996, A1.

34. Personal conversation with D. Norwood, Johnson & Higgins, January 9, 1997.

35. Gomez-Majia, L. R., and Balkin, D. B. *Compensation, Organizational Strategy, and Firm Performance.* Cincinnati: South-Western, 1992.

36. Personal conversation with D. Cannon, Executive Vice President, NationsBank, Dallas, Texas, June 24, 1996.

37. French, W. *Human Resources Management,* 3d ed. Boston: Houghton-Mifflin, 1994.

38. McGill, M. E., and Slocum, J. W., Jr. *The Smarter Organization.* New York: John Wiley & Sons, 1994. For another example, see Besser, T. L. Rewards and organizational goal achievement: A case study of Toyota Motor Manufacturing in Kentucky. *Journal of Management Studies,* 1995, 32, 383–399.

39. Adapted from Locke and Latham, 355–358.

40. Adapted from Hyatt, J. Guaranteed growth. *Inc.,* September 1995, 69–78.

LEARNING OBJECTIVES

When you have finished studying this chapter, you should be able to:

- Explain the concepts of stress and stressors.
- Describe the general nature of the body's response to stressors.
- Diagnose the sources of stress in organizations.
- Describe the effects of stress on health.
- Explain the relationship between stress and job performance.
- Describe the nature and causes of job burnout.
- Identify several individual and organizational methods for coping with stress.

OUTLINE

PREVIEW CASE

So Much to Do, So Little Time

Got a minute? Probably not, if you're like most Americans today. Fifty-nine percent of the people in a *Wall Street Journal/NBC News* survey described their lives as busy; for another 19 percent life has become busy to the point of discomfort. Stress is a common complaint. Work consumes a huge portion of the day for many people, although exactly how much is hard to measure. In the age of the virtual office, it has become increasingly difficult for many employees to separate or measure the time they spend at work or leisure.

John Yates of Falls Church, Virginia, knows about overload. On a typical day, the Episcopalian minister and father of five, leaves for work at 6:30 A.M. and gets home at 10 P.M. In his line of work, he sees overextended people everywhere. "The people who attend the PTA meetings are the tiredest folks you've ever seen," says Yates, 50. "They're there because they care, but you know they've been up since before dawn, worked hard all day, raced home, gotten a bite of supper and gone out again. When I talk to people about their schedules, I realize they're completely overloaded and not leaving much in the way of margins in their lives."

Pat Bakkers, 40, a divorced mother of three girls who works as a secretary sighs, "I don't have a morning. I'd love to be able to read the paper and have breakfast with my kids, but the poor things usually end up standing at the counter eating cereal."

If we need proof of stress in modern life, a series of recent studies shows exactly how bad it is. Harvard University economist Juliet Schor used government census and labor data to calculate that the average employee works 163 more hours—an extra month a year—compared to twenty-five years ago. Women, in particular, are more likely to be working year-round today. "The numbers are unprecedented," says Schor. "Recently we've had record levels of overtime in manufacturing and pervasive downsizing, which invariably leads to longer hours for the people who keep their jobs." Record numbers of people—upwards of half—say they'd willingly take less pay for more free time. "The people who trade in comfort for more free time identified more balance and less stress as their motivation," Schor says.

Pagers, e-mail, and fax machines also keep many people connected to other people virtually round the clock. "If technology can make you available twenty-four hours a day, where do we draw the line?" asks Charles Rodgers, a principal of Work/Family Directions in Boston. "The body and mind were not set up to be on call eighteen or nineteen hours a day," says Ruth Klein, a time-management expert in Santa Monica, California.[1]

A great many people experience stress at unacceptable levels. This stress can stem from events in both their personal lives and their work. Although small amounts of stress can have positive effects, excessive stress may seriously and negatively affect a person's health, personal life, and job performance.

In studying organizational behavior, you need to understand the effects of work stress, the relationship between stress and performance, and the sources of stress within an organization. In particular, you should understand the relationships between stress and health. In this chapter, we examine the nature of stress, the sources of stress at work, and the effects of stress. People can handle varying amounts of stress effectively, and we explore some of these individual differences. Finally, we examine ways that employees and organizations can cope with stress.

NATURE OF STRESS

Stress is a consequence of or a general response to an action or situation that places special physical or psychological demands, or both, on a person. In other words, stress involves the interaction of a person and that person's environment.[2] The physical or psychological demands from the environment that cause stress are called **stressors.** Stressors can take various forms, but all stressors have one thing in common: They create stress or the potential for stress when an individual perceives them as representing a demand that may exceed that person's ability to respond.

■ FIGHT-OR-FLIGHT RESPONSE

Numerous changes occur in the human body during a stress reaction. Breathing and heart rates alter so that the body can operate with maximum capacity for physical action. Muscles ready themselves for action. Brain wave activity goes up to allow the brain to function maximally. Hearing and sight become momentarily more acute. These biochemical and bodily changes represent a natural reaction to an environmental stressor: the **fight-or-flight response.**[3] An animal attacked by a predator in the wild basically has two choices: to fight or to flee. The animal's bodily responses to the stressor (the predator) increase its chances of survival. Similarly, our cave-dwelling ancestors benefited from this biological response mechanism. People gathering food away from their caves would have experienced a great deal of stress upon meeting a saber-toothed tiger. In dealing with the tiger, they could have run away or stayed and fought. The biochemical changes in their bodies prepared them for either alternative and contributed to their ability to survive.[4]

The human nervous system still responds the same way to environmental stressors. This response continues to have survival value in a true emergency. However, for most people most of the time, the "tigers" are imaginary rather than real. In work situations, for example, a fight-or-flight response usually isn't appropriate. If an employee receives an unpleasant work assignment from a manager, physically assaulting the manager or storming angrily out of the office obviously is inappropriate. Instead, the employee is expected to accept the assignment calmly and do the best job possible. Remaining calm and performing effectively may be especially difficult when the employee perceives an assignment as threatening and the body is prepared to act accordingly.

Medical science has discovered that the human body has a standard response to demands placed on it—whether psychological or physical. Medical researcher Hans Selye first used the word *stress* to describe the body's biological response mechanisms. Selye considered stress to be the nonspecific response of the human body to any demand made on it.[5] However, the body has only a limited capacity to respond to stressors. The workplace makes a variety of demands on people, and too much stress over too long a time will exhaust their ability to cope with those stressors.

■ THE STRESS EXPERIENCE

Several factors determine whether an individual experiences stress at work or in other situations. Figure 7.1 identifies four of the primary factors: (1) the person's perception of the situation; (2) the person's past experience; (3) the presence or absence of social support; and (4) individual differences with regard to stress reactions.

Perception   In Chapter 3 we defined perception as a key psychological process whereby a person selects and organizes environmental information into a concept of reality. Employee perceptions of a situation can influence how (or whether) they experience stress. For example, let's say that two employees have

■ FIGURE 7.1

The Relationship between Stressors and Stress

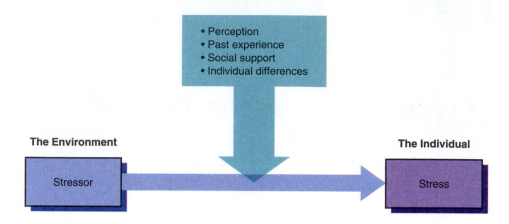

their job duties substantially changed—a situation likely to be stressful for many people. The first employee views the new duties as an opportunity to learn new skills and thinks that the change is a vote of confidence from management in her ability to be flexible and take on new challenges. In contrast, the second employee perceives the same situation to be extremely threatening and concludes that management is unhappy with his performance.

Past Experience   A person may experience a situation as more or less stressful, depending on how familiar that person is with the situation and prior experience with the particular stressors involved. Past practice or training may allow some employees in an organization to deal calmly and competently with stressors that would greatly intimidate less experienced or inadequately trained employees. The relationship between experience and stress is based on reinforcement (see Chapter 4). Positive reinforcement or previous success in a similar situation can reduce the level of stress that a person experiences in the present situation; punishment or past failure under similar conditions can increase stress in the present situation.

Social Support   The presence or absence of other people influences how individuals in the workplace experience stress and respond to stressors.[6] The presence of co-workers may increase an individual's confidence, allowing that person to cope more effectively with stress. For example, working alongside a person who performs confidently and competently in a stressful situation may help an employee behave similarly. Conversely, the presence of fellow workers may irritate some people or make them anxious, reducing their ability to cope with stress.

Individual Differences   Personality characteristics may explain some of the differences in the ways that employees experience and respond to stress. For example, the Big Five personality factor that we labeled *adjustment* in Chapter 2, seems to be particularly important in individual responses to various stressors. Individuals at one extreme of adjustment (described as stable and confident) are more likely to cope well with a wide variety of work stressors; individuals at the other extreme (described as nervous and self-doubting) typically have greater difficulty in coping with the same stressors. Individual differences in motivation, attitudes, and abilities also influence whether employees experience work stress and, if they do, how they respond to it.[7] Simply stated, people are different. What one person considers a major source of stress, another may hardly notice.

The story is told of a Harvard University undergraduate who had to drop out of college because of serious psychological problems brought on by stress from the demands of school. Eventually, this individual enlisted in the U.S. Navy and became a pilot. He was based on an aircraft carrier much of the time. Military pilots usually consider taking off and landing on carriers to be particularly stressful and dangerous. Despite the danger, this particular pilot served with distinction for a number of years and felt psychologically well during the entire time. When he retired from the Navy, he again enrolled in Harvard. As before, he experienced psychological difficulties, which became so severe that he had to be hospitalized.[8] This story dramatically illustrates an individual's reactions to different types of stress. Moreover, situations that cause stress in one individual may not in another. Most people would find flying a plane from an aircraft carrier to be extremely stressful, whereas being a student would be relatively less so. Yet, for this Navy pilot, exactly the opposite was the case. We further discuss relationships between personality and stress later in this chapter.

SOURCES OF STRESS

Individuals commonly experience stress in both their personal and work lives. Understanding these sources of stress and their possible interaction is important. For a manager to consider either source in isolation gives an incomplete picture of the stress that an employee may be experiencing. Note the combined effects of work stress and stress from other aspects of life on the residents of Mexico City, as described in the following Across Cultures feature.

ACROSS CULTURES

Siesta Sunset

Mexicans, particularly residents of Mexico City, are gulping stress medication in record numbers. Mañana-land isn't supposed to be like this—what's going on?

There are signs that Mexico's breakneck pace to urbanize and modernize has brought both opportunities and stress to Mexican workers. During the past few years, Mexican doctors have reported increases in cigarette smoking, drinking, and drug abuse. (However, drug abuse is at relatively low levels compared to that in the United States.) Claudio Garcia Barriga, chief of the outpatient department of a large psychiatric hospital in Mexico City, observed, "In the past five years, there's been a very important increase in the problem of stress, and we continue to see a steady increase in stress crises." Garcia reports that some 15 percent of the hospital's patients show stress symptoms.

Mexico City has 20 million residents, and, traditionally, problems associated with overcrowding were blamed for most stress. Recently however, Mexico's changing economy seemingly is the source of much stress. The North American Free Trade Agreement among Canada, Mexico, and the United States is feeding job insecurity fears among Mexican workers just as it has north of the border. The fears are well founded. As Mexico has opened up to private investment, hundreds of thousands of workers have lost jobs to cost-cutting, downsizing, and closing of businesses in the face of new competition. Time-honored work rules are

—Continued

ACROSS CULTURES—*Continued*

changing as well. For example, many firms no longer tolerate traditional on-the-job siestas. In addition, wage controls and inflation have squeezed average workers' buying power. These economic uncertainties, coupled with the pollution and traffic that are overwhelming Mexico City, have sent stress levels soaring.[9]

■ WORK STRESSORS

According to several nationwide surveys, an average of about 25 percent of all employees suffer from stress-induced problems. Absenteeism surveys show a sharp rise in stress as a cause of unscheduled employee absences. Further, findings such as the following are typical.

- About one in three workers report that they have thought about quitting because of stress.
- One in two workers state that job stress reduces their productivity.
- One in five workers report taking sick leave because of stress.[10]

Work stressors take various forms, and numerous studies have identified specific stressors and their effects. For example, in a worldwide comparative study of work stress, researchers gathered information from 1065 managers in ten countries on five continents: Brazil, the United Kingdom, Egypt, Germany, Japan, Nigeria, Singapore, South Africa, Sweden, and the United States. Fifty-five percent of all respondents mentioned time pressures and deadlines as a stressor, followed closely by work overload, mentioned by almost 52 percent. Other frequently identified stressors included inadequately trained subordinates, long working hours, attending meetings, and conflicts among work and family and other social relationships.[11]

Managers and employees need a framework for thinking about and diagnosing sources of work stress. Figure 7.2 presents such a framework by identifying seven principal sources of work stress. It also shows, as previously discussed, that internal factors influence the ways in which individuals experience these stressors.

Workload   For many people, having too much work to do and not enough time or resources to do it can be stressful. **Role overload** exists when demands exceed the capacity of a manager or employee to meet all of them adequately. Many stressful jobs may perpetually be in a condition of role overload. Surveys commonly identify work overload or "working too hard" as a major source of stress.

Interestingly, the situation of having too little work to do also may create stress.[12] Have you ever had a job with so little to do that the work day seemed never to end? If so, you can understand why many people find an *underload* situation stressful. Managers sometimes are guilty of trying to do their subordinates' work, or *micromanage,* when their jobs aren't challenging enough. Micromanaging might reduce the manager's stress from boredom, but it is likely to increase subordinates' stress as the boss constantly watches them or second-guesses their decisions.

Job Conditions   Poor working conditions represent another important set of job stressors. Temperature extremes, loud noise, too much or too little lighting, radiation, and air pollution are but a few examples of the working conditions that

■ FIGURE 7.2   Sources of Work Stress

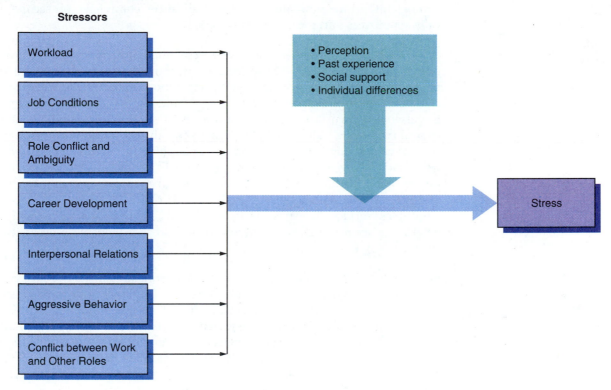

Stressors

- Workload
- Job Conditions
- Role Conflict and Ambiguity
- Career Development
- Interpersonal Relations
- Aggressive Behavior
- Conflict between Work and Other Roles

- Perception
- Past experience
- Social support
- Individual differences

Stress

can cause stress in employees. Job performance deteriorates, sometimes markedly, when these environmental stressors are present. Moreover, their effects are cumulative over time, and they interact with other stressors. Heavy travel demands or long-distance commuting are other aspects of jobs that employees may find stressful. Poor working conditions, excessive travel, and long hours all add up to increased stress and decreased performance.[13]

Role Conflict and Ambiguity   Differing expectations of or demands on a person's role at work produce **role conflict.** (We discuss role conflict in detail in Chapter 12.) **Role ambiguity** describes the situation in which the employee is uncertain about assigned job duties and responsibilities. Role conflict and role ambiguity are particularly significant sources of job-related stress.[14] Many employees suffer from role conflict and ambiguity, but conflicting expectations and uncertainty particularly affect managers. Having responsibility for the behavior of others and a lack of opportunity to participate in important decisions affecting the job are other aspects of employees' roles that may be stressful.

Career Development   Major stressors related to career planning and development involve job security, promotions, transfers, and developmental opportunities. As with too much or too little work, an employee can feel stress by underpromotion (failure to advance as rapidly as desired) or overpromotion (promotion to a job that exceeds the individual's capabilities).

The current wave of reorganization and downsizing may seriously threaten careers. When jobs, departments, work teams, or entire organizations are restructured, employees often have numerous career-related concerns: Can I perform competently in the new situation? Can I advance? Is my new job secure? Typically, employees find these concerns stressful.

Interpersonal Relations   Groups have a tremendous impact on the behavior of people in organizations. (We explore these dynamics in Chapter 8.) Good working relationships and interactions with peers, subordinates, and superiors are crucial aspects of organizational life, helping people achieve personal and organizational goals; when lacking, they are sources of stress. For example, a study of clerical employees indicated that intrusions by others—interruptions from noisy co-workers, ringing telephones, and other people walking into and around their work stations—were principal sources of stress.[15] A high level of political behavior, or "office politics," also may create stress for managers and employees (see Chapter 9). The nature of relationships with co-workers may influence how employees react to other stressors. In other words, interpersonal relationships can be either a source of stress or the social support that helps employees react to stressors.

Aggressive Behavior   A frightening category of work stressors is overly aggressive behavior in the workplace, often taking the form of violence or sexual harassment. Aggressive behavior that causes actual physical or psychological harm to an employee is classified as **workplace violence.** An American Management Association survey found that almost 25 percent of responding organizations reported that an employee had been physically attacked or killed in the workplace. Homicide is second only to transportation accidents as the most common cause of workplace fatalities. Although homicide is the most extreme example of workplace violence, several million employees a year are subjected to violence of one form or another, ranging from actual physical assaults to threats or other forms of unwanted harassment. Individuals subject to violence or the threat of violence in the workplace are more likely to experience negative stress reactions, have lower productivity, and have higher absenteeism. Lost productivity and legal expenses related to workplace violence cost employers more than $4 billion annually, according to recent estimates.[16] The current level of violence in organizations is a major source of work stress that needs to be understood and dealt with.

A second form of overly aggressive behavior in the workplace is sexual harassment. **Sexual harassment** is defined as unwanted contact or communication of a sexual nature.[17] In a *New York Times/CBS News* poll, fully 30 percent of female employees reported that they had been the object of unwanted sexual advances, propositions, or discussions at work. As with workplace violence, this problem seems to be growing. Management clearly has a strong responsibility to do everything in its power to prevent sexual harassment from occurring. When it does occur, it needs to be dealt with firmly. Some practical suggestions for managers who have to deal with this disruptive issue include the following.

- Don't think of yourself as a judge. Your job is to gather the facts.
- Take the complaint seriously.
- Contact your human resource department before taking any action.
- Document all conversations pertaining to the situation.
- Collect the facts confidentially.
- Don't try to solve the problem by transferring to a different department the person making the complaint or the person accused.

■ Follow up any action you take by making sure that the harassment has stopped, that there have been no reprisals, and that the complaining employee is getting along well with colleagues.[18]

Organizations need to have policies that clearly identify what constitutes sexual harassment, procedures for dealing with it, and penalties for engaging in this unacceptable behavior. Having policies in place, however, isn't sufficient if managers don't back them up with serious and prompt action, as described in the following Ethics in Practice account.

ETHICS IN PRACTICE

Sexual Harassment Charges at Mitsubishi

The Equal Employment Opportunity Commission (EEOC) has sued Mitsubishi Motor Manufacturing of America, Inc., for alleged widespread sexual harassment of female employees. According to the lawsuit, women at the company's automobile assembly plant in Normal, Illinois, have been subjected to physical abuse of a sexual nature for the past several years. Harassment reportedly included name calling with sexual overtones, unwanted physical touching and grabbing, and exposing the workers to sexually offensive drawings. In addition to the EEOC suit, more than two dozen female employees have sued Mitsubishi in a private lawsuit.

According to the EEOC, most of the harassment has occurred in the plant's production and maintenance areas and involves line workers, their supervisors, and some lower level managers. The EEOC is particularly concerned because it claims that Mitsubishi had knowledge of the alleged behavior and did nothing to eliminate it. Gary Schultz, vice president and general counsel of Mitsubishi, denies that assertion. He maintains that the company does not tolerate discrimination or harassment in the workplace and provides swift punishment for anyone violating company policies. Schultz claims that the EEOC lawsuit is "politically motivated."

The EEOC class-action suit could be huge. With as many as 500 female workers potentially involved, each eligible for as much as $300,000 in damages, the total cost to Mitsubishi if found guilty could be as high as $150 million. Paul Igasaki, the EEOC's vice-chairman, stated, "This case is going to show that sexual harassment in the workplace is bad for the bottom line."[19]

Conflict between Work and Other Roles   A person has many roles in life, only one of which is typically associated with work (although some individuals may hold more than one job at a time). These roles may present conflicting demands that become sources of stress. Furthermore, work typically meets only some of a person's goals and needs. Other goals and needs may conflict with career goals, presenting an additional source of stress. For example, employees' personal needs to spend time with their families may conflict with the extra hours they must work to advance their careers. Current demographic trends, such as the increasingly large number of dual-career couples, have brought work and family role conflicts into sharp focus.[20] Such conflicts are obvious in the following Diversity in Practice feature.

DIVERSITY IN PRACTICE

The Complex Dance of the Dual-Career Couple

It is an hour before dawn and the outline of the mountain behind Rick and Barbara Mauntel's Phoenix home hasn't yet emerged from the darkness. However, Rick Mauntel has already showered, dressed for work, read the paper, and had coffee. At 6 A.M. he awakens four-year-old Jeffrey and two-year-old Jillian. As Barbara Mauntel gets ready for work, her husband dresses the kids and makes them breakfast, then drops them at day care before heading for his job as a project manager at Motorola. Barbara Mauntel's turn comes at 6 P.M. She will leave her job as a Motorola payroll manager to take care of the children, feeding and bathing them before reading to them and tucking them into bed. Later, the couple will "fight for the computer" in their home office as both try to get some more work done before going to bed.

The Mauntels are involved in the complex dance of the dual-career couple, with their lives interwoven with work and family. Each carries a mobile phone and pager, with agreed on private emergency signals. Recently, when a day-care center called because Jeffrey was ill and needed to be picked up at midday, Rick Mauntel rearranged his schedule to go. Fitting their schedules together requires a great deal of give-and-take. Neither makes work commitments such as after-hours meetings, travel plans, or day-care plans for the kids without checking with the other. Importantly, neither could reach their long-term financial goals, including a secure retirement and college education for the kids, without the help of the other.

Traditional gender roles with their tidy division of labor just don't fit the Mauntels. Both feel guilty a lot, worrying that they spend too much time away from both their jobs and their children. Their careers have waxed and waned with family demands. Barbara Mauntel coasted briefly in a job as a tax-department analyst at Motorola after Jeffrey was born so that she could manage all the child care. But "I paid a big price for that" with a slowdown in career growth, she says. Now, with her husband's help, her career is starting to take off again while his seems to be on a plateau despite his team's string of impressive inventions. At the same age, some of his friends are vice-presidents, including some who admitted to not having children for career reasons. But, Rick Mauntel states, "I don't think about it. . . . I'm not saying I'm not ambitious. But there's more to life than just the job."[21]

■ LIFE STRESSORS

The distinction between work and nonwork stressors isn't always clear. For example, as the preceding Diversity in Practice feature indicates, one source of stress lies in conflicts between work and family. As Figure 7.3 illustrates, both work and family stressors may contribute to work–family conflict because stress in one area can reduce a person's ability to cope with stress in the other. This

■ FIGURE 7.3 **Stressors and Work–Family Conflict**

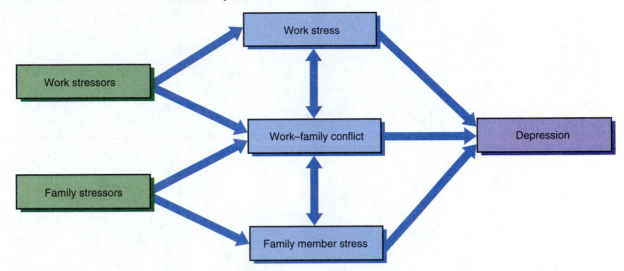

Source: Adapted from Frone, M. R., Russell, M., and Cooper, M. L. Antecedents and outcomes of work–family conflict: Testing a model of the work–family interface. *Journal of Applied Psychology,* 1992, 77,

conflict represents a further source of stress, which in turn leads to problems such as depression.

Much of the stress felt by managers and employees may stem from stressors in their personal lives, or **life stressors.** As in the work setting, people must cope with a great variety of life stressors. In addition, different individuals deal with life stressors differently. Events that cause stress for one person may not do so for another person. However, life stressors that affect almost everyone are those caused by major changes: divorce, marriage, death of a family member, and the like. As mentioned previously, the human body has a limited capacity to respond to stressors. Too much change too quickly can exhaust the body's ability to respond, with negative consequences for physical and mental health.

Table 7.1 contains some stressful events that college students typically face. These events are rated on a 100-point scale, with 1 indicating the least stressful event and 100 the most stressful. Events labeled "high levels of stress" might be assigned 71 to 100 points, depending on the specific circumstances of the student being evaluated. "Moderate levels of stress" might be scored from 31 to 70 points, and "low levels of stress" assigned scores from 1 to 30 points. During the course of a year, if a student faces events that total 150 points or more, the student has a 50–50 chance of getting sick as a result of excessive stress.[22]

Recall that stress is the body's general response to any demand made on it. Note that the list of stressful events in Table 7.1 contains both unpleasant events, such as failing a course, and pleasant events, such as finding a new love interest. This dual nature of life stressors demonstrates that they involve both negative and positive experiences. For example, vacations and holidays actually may be quite stressful for some people but very relaxing and refreshing for others. In addition, viewing unpleasant life events as having only negative effects is incorrect. People often can both cope with and grow from experiencing unpleasant events. They also can enjoy the positive effects and stimulation of pleasurable events, such as significant accomplishments, vacations, gaining a new family member, and so on.

TABLE 7.1 Stressful Events for College Students

Events Having High Levels of Stress
- Death of parent
- Death of spouse
- Divorce
- Flunking out
- Unwed pregnancy

Events having Moderate Levels of Stress
- Academic probation
- Change of major
- Death of close friend
- Failing important course
- Finding a new love interest
- Loss of financial aid
- Major injury or illness
- Parents' divorce
- Serious arguments with romantic partner

Events Having Relatively Low Levels of Stress
- Change in eating habits
- Change in sleeping habits
- Change in social activities
- Conflict with instructor
- Lower grades than expected
- Outstanding achievement

Source: Adapted from Baron, R. A., and Byrne, D. *Social Psychology: Understanding Human Interaction*, 6th ed. Boston: Allyn & Bacon, 1991, 573.

EFFECTS OF STRESS

Work stress also may have both positive and negative effects. However, our concern with work stress tends to focus on its negative effects. This focus seems well founded, for the American Institute of Stress estimates the cost to the U.S. economy from stress-related medical problems and lost productivity at $300 billion per year.[23] Other estimates are more conservative, but they invariably run into billions of dollars. These costs include lost productivity, mistakes, and medical treatment.

The effects of work stress occur in three main areas: physiological, emotional, and behavioral. Examples of the effects of excessive stress in these three areas are as follows.

- **Physiological effects of stress** include increased blood pressure, increased heart rate, sweating, hot and cold spells, breathing difficulties, muscular tension, and increased gastrointestinal disorders.

- **Emotional effects of stress** include anger, anxiety, depression, lowered self-esteem, poorer intellectual functioning (including an inability to concentrate and make decisions), nervousness, irritability, resentment of supervision, and job dissatisfaction.

- **Behavioral effects of stress** include decreased performance, absenteeism, higher accident rates, higher turnover rates, higher alcohol and other drug abuses, impulsive behavior, and difficulties in communication.

These effects of work stress have important implications for organizational behavior. We examine some of them in terms of health and performance, including the phenomenon of job burnout.

HEALTH AND STRESS

Stress and coronary heart disease are strongly linked. Other major health problems commonly associated with stress include back pain, headaches, stomach and intestinal problems, upper respiratory infections, and various mental problems. Medical researchers recently have discovered possible links between stress and cancer. Although determining the precise role that stress plays in individual cases is difficult, many illnesses appear to be stress-related.[24]

Stress-related illnesses place a considerable burden on people and organizations. The costs to individuals often are more obvious than the costs to organizations. However, identifying at least some of the organizational costs associated with stress-related disease is possible.[25] First, costs to employers include not only increased premiums for health insurance but also lost work days from serious illnesses (such as heart disease) and less-serious illnesses (such as stress-related headaches). Estimates are that each employee who suffers from a stress-related illness loses an average of sixteen days of work a year. Second, over three-fourths of all industrial accidents are caused by a worker's inability to cope with emotional problems worsened by stress. Third, legal problems for employers are growing. The number of stress-related workers' compensation claims is increasing at a tremendous rate. In a recent development, courts are recognizing **post-traumatic stress disorder** as an illness or injury that may justify a damage claim against an employer. We normally think of post-traumatic stress disorder as a psychological disorder brought on, for example, by horrible experiences suffered in combat during wartime. However, employees have successfully claimed suffering from this stress disorder as a result of sexual harassment, violence, and other unpleasant circumstances in the workplace. Damages in the millions of dollars have been reported from court cases.[26]

PERFORMANCE AND STRESS

The positive and negative aspects of stress are most apparent in the relationship between stress and performance. Figure 7.4 depicts the general performance–stress relationship. At low levels of stress, employees may not be sufficiently alert, challenged, or involved to perform at their best. As the curve indicates, increasing a low amount of stress may improve performance—but only up to a point. An optimal level of stress probably exists for most tasks. Beyond that point, performance begins to deteriorate.[27] At excessive levels of stress, employees are too agitated, aroused, or threatened to perform at their best. The following Managing in Practice selection provides an example of the relationship between performance and stress.

MANAGING IN PRACTICE

"Just Enough but Not Too Much"

Kathy Taylor was puzzled. During the past several months, she had presented three major reports to the executive committee of the board of directors. The first had been a catastrophe. She had been so nervous that she could actually remember little that had gone on. Taylor did know, however, that she had somehow gotten through her formal presentation—which seemed to go okay—before disaster struck. It came in the form of a series of questions, each more confusing than the last. The board members eventually took pity on her and stopped the questioning. They thanked her for her efforts and turned their attention to other matters. Later, Elizabeth Rainey—her boss and the firm's president—helped Taylor analyze her performance. They determined that, with one or two exceptions, Taylor actually knew the answers to the questions asked. What seemed to happen, they decided, was that she had been far too agitated to think clearly. Indeed, Taylor had been so upset that she even had trouble focusing on what was being asked. Several times she had had to ask that questions be repeated. Rainey's advice was preparation and practice. "You have to make stress work for you—but you can't be so stressed out that you can't think straight."

Taylor didn't fully understand the implications of Rainey's last comment, but she carefully prepared for her next presentation. Like a highly trained athlete before the big game, she was actually looking forward to the presentation. Although "keyed up" when the time came, Taylor made a superb presentation, full of energy and enthusiasm, and fielded the board members' questions with confidence. The board members were effusive in their praise (and probably a little relieved because the first presentation had gone so badly).

Now Taylor had just come from her third presentation to the board. Even though well prepared, today she had been "flat." She hadn't been nervous. In fact, she had been working on another project right up until the time she went into the boardroom. Although her presentation certainly went better than the first one, she knew without being told that it hadn't measured up to the peak performance of last time. "What's going on?" she wondered. With Rainey's help, she again attempted to diagnose her performance. After some discussion, they finally decided that, whereas Taylor had felt too much stress during her first presentation, this time she had, ironically, probably not felt enough.

Managers often want to know the optimum stress points for both themselves and their subordinates. This information, however, is difficult to obtain. For example, an employee may be absent from work frequently because of boredom (too little stress) or because of overwork (excessive stress). Also, the curve in Figure 7.4 changes with the situation; that is, the curve varies for different people and different tasks. Too little stress for one employee may be just right for another on a particular task. Similarly, the optimum amount of stress for a specific individual for one task may be too much or too little for that person's effective performance of other tasks.

As a practical matter, managers should be more concerned about the excessive stress side of the curve than with how to add to employee stress. Motivating indi-

■ **FIGURE 7.4**

Typical Relationship between Performance and Stress

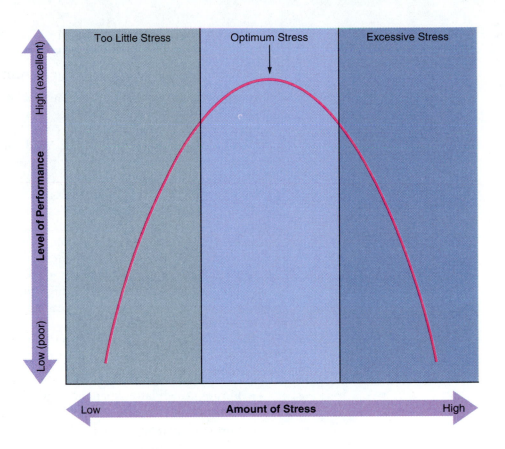

viduals to perform better is always important, but attempting to do so by increasing the level of stress is shortsighted.

The downsizing of many organizations yields good examples of the effects of excessive stress on performance. A survey of 531 large companies indicated that 85 percent expected their restructuring to raise profits. However, only 46 percent actually had increased earnings after restructuring. An examination of Jostens Learning Corporation, the largest U.S. maker of educational software, revealed some reasons for these disappointing results. Although layoffs may lower direct labor costs, these lower costs are often more than offset by declines in productivity because of increased stress and lowered morale among the survivors.[28]

Studies of the performance–stress relationship in organizations often show a strong negative correlation between the amount of stress in a work team or department and its overall performance.[29] That is, the greater the stress that employees are experiencing, the lower will be their productivity. This negative relationship indicates that these work settings are operating on the right-hand side (excessive stress) of the curve in Figure 7.4. Managers and employees in these situations need to find ways to reduce the number and magnitude of stressors.

■ JOB BURNOUT

Job burnout refers to the adverse effects of working conditions where stressors seem unavoidable and sources of job satisfaction and relief from stress seem unavailable. The burnout phenomenon typically contains three components:

- a state of emotional exhaustion;
- depersonalization of individuals; and
- feelings of low personal accomplishment.[30]

Depersonalization refers to the treatment of people as objects. For example, a nurse might refer to the "broken knee" in room 107, rather than use the patient's name.

Most job-burnout research has focused on the human services sector of the economy—sometimes called the "helping professions." Burnout is thought to be most prevalent in occupations characterized by continuous direct contact with people in need of aid. The professionals who may be most vulnerable to job burnout include social workers, nurses, physicians, police officers, air traffic controllers, teachers, and lawyers. Burnout also may affect managers, shopowners, professionals, and others who constantly face stressors with little relief or who must deal extensively with other people as part of their jobs. Figure 7.5 suggests that the highest probability of burnout occurs among those professionals who have both a high frequency and a high intensity of interpersonal contact. This level of interpersonal contact may lead to emotional exhaustion, a key component of job burnout.

Individuals who experience job burnout seem to have some common characteristics. Three characteristics in particular are associated with a high probability of burnout.

- Burnout candidates experience a great deal of stress as a result of job-related stressors.
- Burnout candidates tend to be idealistic and self-motivating achievers.
- Burnout candidates often seek unattainable goals.[31]

Job burnout thus represents a combination of certain individual characteristics and job situations. Individuals who suffer from burnout often have unrealistic expectations concerning their work and their ability to accomplish desired goals because of the nature of the situation in which they find themselves. Unrelieved stressful working conditions, coupled with an individual's unrealistic expectations or ambitions, may lead to physical, mental, and emotional exhaustion. In burnout, the individual can no longer cope with job demands, and the willingness to even try drops dramatically.

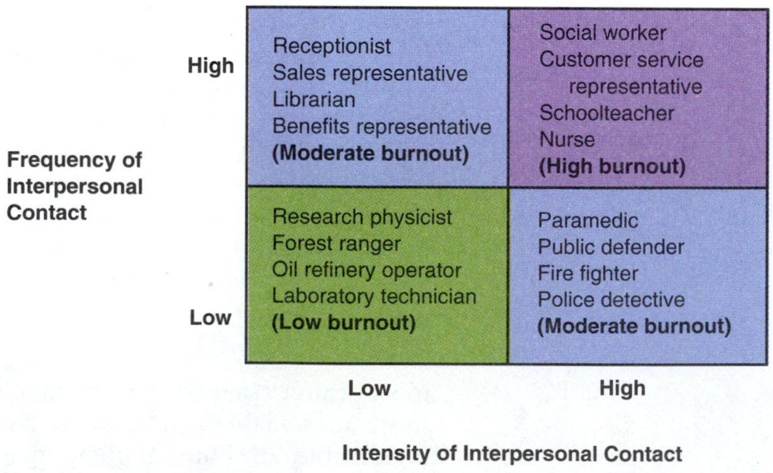

■ **FIGURE 7.5**

Predicted Level of Job Burnout Based on Frequency and Intensity of Interpersonal Contact

Source: Cordes, C. L., and Dougherty, T. W. A review and integration of research on job burnout. *Academy of Management Review,* 1993, 18, 643. Reprinted with permission.

	Low Intensity of Interpersonal Contact	**High** Intensity of Interpersonal Contact
High Frequency of Interpersonal Contact	Receptionist Sales representative Librarian Benefits representative **(Moderate burnout)**	Social worker Customer service representative Schoolteacher Nurse **(High burnout)**
Low Frequency of Interpersonal Contact	Research physicist Forest ranger Oil refinery operator Laboratory technician **(Low burnout)**	Paramedic Public defender Fire fighter Police detective **(Moderate burnout)**

Intensity of Interpersonal Contact

Evidence suggests that women, on average, are somewhat more likely to face burnout than are men. For example, surveys have indicated that 11 percent more women than men report that high stress has affected their health. A Northwestern Life Insurance study found that the job burnout rate was 36 percent for women versus 28 percent for men. Note also that the "high burnout" cell in Figure 7.5 contains occupations that have traditionally attracted more women than men. Women comprise much of the "new collar" group of employees described in the following Diversity in Practice feature.

DIVERSITY IN PRACTICE

The "New-Collar" Workers

Bev Demille is having a bad night. The fifty-one-year-old telemarketer is on her fourteenth phone call of the shift, but so far she has sold just one magazine renewal. "Come on computer, move it," she says, waiting for the next beep in her headset and the next name to flash on her screen. Around her, co-workers tethered to their desks by telephone cords gesture as they speak and signal supervisors to listen to the confirmation of a sale. A supervisor half DeMille's age reprimands her: "You're low, girl—one in 14."

DeMille glares at her video screen. "I don't know where he gets off saying that," she says. But she knows that pressure goes with the job. Working for nine other employers in her ten years in telemarketing, she has seen co-workers take tranquilizers to relieve stress. She has seen people fired for missing sales targets. When confronted once on a previous job for leaving her desk to go to the ladies' room without permission, she retorted: "My bladder couldn't see you."

Many of the estimated 3 to 4 million telephone sales representatives in the United States feel this type of stress. A telemarketer often talks to hundreds of indifferent or hostile customers during a shift. Supervisors constantly monitor them, expecting them to stick closely to a prepared script and remain cheerful no matter how rudely they are treated. It is little wonder, then, that telemarketers feel unappreciated and tend to burn out quickly. About 70 percent of telemarketers are women.

Sometimes called *new-collar* workers, telemarketers, other similar sales people, and data processors comprise about 40 percent of the work force born after 1945. These new-collar workers, working primarily with computers and telephones, in a sense perform blue-collar work in a white-collar world. In terms of stress, lack of variety in their work, limited opportunity for advancement, and heavy performance pressure, the new-collar worker has been described as similar to "turn-of-the-century factory workers except that they are educated and use high technology."[32]

PERSONALITY AND STRESS The problems caused by stress depend substantially on the type of person involved. Personality influences (1) how individuals are likely to perceive situations and stressors and (2) how they will react to these environmental stressors.

Many personality dimensions or traits are related to stress, including self-esteem and locus of control (personality traits discussed in Chapter 2). A personality trait may affect the likelihood that someone will perceive a situation or an event as a stressor. For example, an individual with low self-esteem is more likely to experience stress in demanding work situations than is a person with high self-esteem. The reason may be that individuals high in self-esteem typically have more confidence in their ability to meet job demands. Employees with high internal locus of control may take more effective action, more quickly, in coping with a sudden emergency (a stressor) than might employees with high external locus of control. Individuals high in internal locus of control are likely to believe that they can moderate the stressful situation.

Before reading further, please respond to the statements in Table 7.2. This self-assessment exercise is related to the discussion that follows.

■ TYPE A AND B PERSONALITIES

People with a **Type A personality** are involved in a never-ending struggle to achieve more and more in less and less time. Characteristics of this personality type include

- a chronic sense of urgency about time;[33]
- an extremely competitive, almost hostile orientation;
- an aversion to idleness; and
- an impatience with barriers to task accomplishment.

Two medical researchers first identified the Type A personality when they noticed a recurrent personality pattern in their patients who suffered from premature heart disease.[34] In addition to the characteristics mentioned, extreme Type A individuals often speak rapidly, are preoccupied with themselves, and are dissatisfied with life.

The questionnaire in Table 7.2 measures four sets of behaviors and tendencies associated with the Type A personality: (1) time urgency, (2) competitiveness and hostility, (3) polyphasic behavior (trying to do too many things at once), and (4) a lack of advance planning. Medical researchers have discovered that these behaviors and tendencies often relate to life and work stress. They tend to cause stress or to make stressful situations worse than they otherwise might be.

Evidence links Type A behavior with a vulnerability to heart attacks. For years, the conventional wisdom among medical researchers was that Type A individuals were two to three times more likely to develop heart disease than were Type B individuals. The **Type B personality** is considered to be the opposite of the Type A personality. Type B individuals tend to be more easy-going and relaxed, less concerned about time pressures, and less likely to overreact to situations in hostile or aggressive ways. Recent research, however, suggests that the Type A personality description is too broad to predict coronary heart disease accurately. Rather, research indicates that only certain aspects of the Type A personality—particularly anger, hostility, and aggression—are strongly related to stress reactions and heart disease.[35]

■ THE HARDY PERSONALITY

A great deal of interest has emerged in identifying aspects of the personality that might buffer or protect individuals from, in particular, the negative health consequences of stress. A collection of personality traits that seem to counter the

TABLE 7.2 A Self-Assessment of Type A Personality

Choose from the following responses to answer the questions below:

A. Almost always true   C. Seldom true
B. Usually true   D. Never true

Answer each question according to what is generally true for you:

_____ 1. I do not like to wait for other people to complete their work before I can proceed with my own.

_____ 2. I hate to wait in most lines.

_____ 3. People tell me that I tend to get irritated too easily.

_____ 4. Whenever possible, I try to make activities competitive.

_____ 5. I have a tendency to rush into work that needs to be done before knowing the procedure I will use to complete the job.

_____ 6. Even when I go on vacation, I usually take some work along.

_____ 7. Even when I make a mistake, it is usually due to the fact that I have rushed into the job before completely planning it through.

_____ 8. I feel guilty for taking time off from work.

_____ 9. People tell me I have a bad temper when it comes to competitive situations.

_____ 10. I tend to lose my temper when I am under a lot of pressure at work.

_____ 11. Whenever possible, I will attempt to complete two or more tasks at once.

_____ 12. I tend to race against the clock.

_____ 13. I have no patience for lateness.

_____ 14. I catch myself rushing when there is no need.

Score your responses according to the following key:

- *An intense sense of time urgency* is a tendency to race against the clock, even when there is little reason to. The person feels a need to hurry for hurry's sake alone, and this tendency has appropriately been called "hurry sickness." Time urgency is measured by items 1, 2, 8, 12, 13, and 14. Every A or B answer to these six questions scores one point.

  Your Score = [   ]

- *Inappropriate aggression and hostility* reveals itself in a person who is excessively competitive and who cannot do anything for fun. This inappropriately aggressive behavior easily evolves into frequent displays of hostility, usually at the slightest provocation or frustration. Competitiveness and hostility is measured by items 3, 4, 9, and 10. Every A or B answer scores one point.

  Your Score = [   ]

- *Polyphasic behavior* refers to the tendency to undertake two or more tasks simultaneously at inappropriate times. It usually results in wasted time due to an inability to complete the tasks. This behavior is measured by items 6 and 11. Every A or B answer scores one point.

  Your Score = [   ]

- *Goal directedness without proper planning* refers to the tendency of an individual to rush into work without really knowing how to accomplish the desired result. This usually results in incomplete work or work with many errors, which in turn leads to wasted time, energy, and money. Lack of planning is measured by items 5 and 7. Every A or B response scores one point.

  Your Score = [   ]

  TOTAL SCORE = _____

If your score is 5 or greater, you may possess some basic components of the Type A personality.

Source: Reproduced with permission of the Robert J. Brady Co., Bowie, Maryland, 20715, from its copyrighted work *The Stress Mess Solution: The Causes and Cures of Stress on the Job*, by G. S. Everly, and D. A. Girdano, 1980, 55.

effects of stress is known as the hardy personality. As a personality type, **hardiness** is defined as "a cluster of characteristics that includes feeling a sense of commitment, responding to each difficulty as representing a challenge and an opportunity, and perceiving that one has control over one's own life."[36] Hardiness includes

- a sense of positive involvement with others in social situations;
- a tendency to attribute one's own behavior to internal causes (recall the discussion of attribution in Chapter 3); and
- a tendency to perceive or welcome major changes in life with interest, curiosity, and optimism.[37] (Recall the earlier discussion in this chapter of change as a major life stressor).

A high degree of hardiness reduces the negative effects of stressful events.[38] Hardiness seems to reduce stress by altering the way that people perceive stressors. The concept of the hardy personality provides a useful insight into the role of individual differences in reactions to environmental stressors. An individual having a high level of hardiness perceives few events as stressful; an individual having a low level of hardiness perceives many events as stressful. A person with a high level of hardiness isn't overwhelmed by challenging or difficult situations. Rather, faced with a stressor, the high-hardiness individual copes or responds constructively by trying to find a solution—to control or influence events. This behavioral response typically reduces stress reactions, lowers blood pressure, and reduces the probability of illness.

STRESS MANAGEMENT

Organizational and individual programs to help managers and employees cope with stress have become increasingly popular as the tremendous toll taken by stress has become more widely known. Methods are available to individuals and organizations for managing stress and reducing its harmful effects. **Stress management** refers to any program that reduces stress by helping people understand the stress response, recognize stressors, and use coping techniques to minimize the negative impact of stress.[39]

■ INDIVIDUAL METHODS

Stress management by individuals includes activities and behaviors designed to (1) eliminate or control the sources of stress and (2) make the individual more resistant to or better able to cope with stress. The first step in individual stress management involves recognizing the stressors that are affecting the person's life. Next, the individual needs to decide what to do about them. Figure 7.6 shows how personal goals and values, coupled with practical stress management skills, can help individuals cope with stressors and reduce negative stress reactions.

Practical suggestions for individual stress management include the following.

- Plan ahead and practice good time management.
- Get plenty of exercise, eat a balanced diet, get adequate rest, and generally take care of yourself.
- Develop a sound philosophy of life and maintain a positive attitude.
- Concentrate on balancing your work and personal life. Always take the time to have fun.
- Learn a relaxation technique.

■ FIGURE 7.6   Individual Strategy for Stress Management

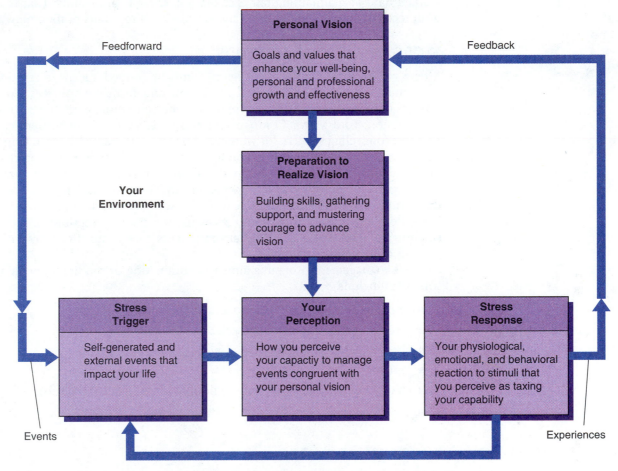

Source: Kindler, H. S., and Ginsburg, M. Stress Training for Life. New York: Nichols Publishing Company. Reprinted with permission.

Among the advantages of relaxation techniques are that individuals can use them during the workday to cope with job demands. For example, a common approach to learning a "relaxation response" when stressed is to (1) choose a comfortable position, (2) close your eyes, (3) relax your muscles, (4) become aware of your breathing, (5) maintain a passive attitude when thoughts surface, and (6) continue for a set period of time (for example, twenty minutes).[40]

An in-depth study of six successful top executives revealed that they used similar methods of coping with stress.[41] First, they worked hard at balancing work and family concerns. Work was central to their lives, but it wasn't their sole focus. These executives also made effective use of leisure time to reduce stress. In addition, they were skilled time managers and goal setters. Important components of their effective use of time were identifying crucial goals and constructively planning their attainment. Finally, these executives cited the essential role of social support in coping with stress. They didn't operate as loners; rather they received emotional support and important information from a diverse network of family, friends, co-workers, and industry colleagues. Additionally, these executives worked hard at maintaining fair exchanges in these relationships. That is, they both received support from others and gave support to others in their networks.

◼ ORGANIZATIONAL METHODS

After a major layoff, Phillips Petroleum Company formed a team to respond to problems created by stress among its current and former employees. Further, Phillips paid for outside help to supplement the counseling available within the organization. Ford Motor Company currently offers stress management classes and free counseling services for workers who feel overloaded. Chevron Corporation conducts workshops to help employees deal with stress.[42] A large percentage of organizations have in place or are developing stress management programs.

As Figure 7.7 shows, stress management by organizations is designed to reduce the harmful effects of stress in three ways: (1) identify and then modify or eliminate work stressors, (2) help employees modify their perceptions and understandings of work stress, and (3) help employees cope more effectively with the consequences of stress.[43]

Stress management programs aimed at eliminating or modifying work stressors often include

■ improvements in the physical work environment;

■ job redesign to eliminate stressors;

■ changes in workloads and deadlines;

■ structural reorganization;

■ changes in work schedules, more flexible hours, and sabbaticals;

◼ FIGURE 7.7   Targets of Organizational Stress Management Programs

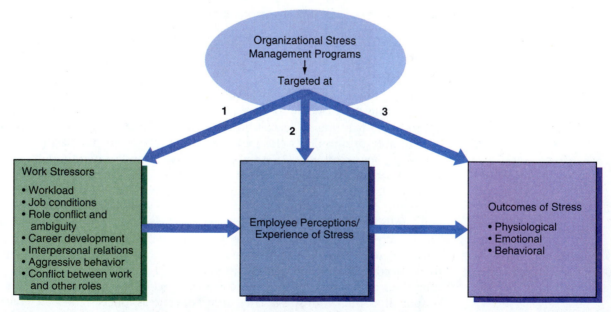

Source: Adapted from Ivancevich, J. M., Matteson, M. T., Freedman, S. M., and Phillips, J. S. Worksite stress management interventions. *American Psychologist,* 1990, 45, 253.

- management by objectives or other goal-setting programs;
- greater levels of employee participation, particularly in planning changes that affect them; and
- workshops dealing with role clarity and role analysis.

Programs that promote role clarity and role analysis can be particularly useful in removing or reducing role ambiguity and role conflict—two major sources of stress. When diagnosing stressors in the workplace, managers should be particularly aware of the large amount of research showing that uncertainty and perceived lack of control heighten stress. For example, Figure 7.8 shows the relationships commonly observed between work stressors and an individual's control over his or her work. Note that the greatest stress occurs when jobs are high in stressors and low in controllability. Thus involvement of employees in organizational change efforts, work redesign that reduces uncertainty and increases control over the pace of work, and improved clarity and understanding of roles all should help reduce employee stress.

Programs of stress management targeted at perceptions and experiences of stress and outcomes of stress include

- team building;
- behavior modification;
- career counseling and other employee assistance programs;
- workshops on time management;
- workshops on job burnout to help employees understand its nature and symptoms;
- training in relaxation techniques; and
- physical fitness or "wellness" programs.

Dividing stress management programs into these categories doesn't mean that they are necessarily unrelated in practice. In addition, programs that appear in the preceding lists might overlap in terms of their impact on the three target areas shown in Figure 7.7. For example, a workshop dealing with role problems might clarify roles and thus reduce the magnitude of this potential stressor. At the same time, through greater knowledge and insight into roles and role problems,

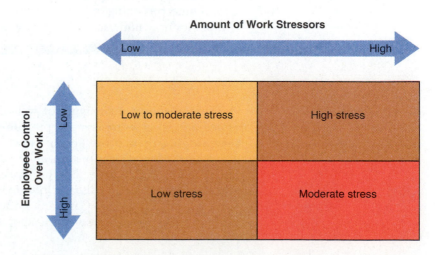

■ FIGURE 7.8

Impacts of Employee Control and Amount of Work Stressors

Source: Adapted from Fox, M. L., Dwyer, D. J., and Ganster, D. C. Effects of stressful job demands and control on physiological and attitudinal outcomes in a hospital setting. *Academy of Management Journal*, 1993, 36, 291.

employees might be able to cope more effectively with this source of stress. Similarly, career counseling might reduce career concerns as a source of stress while improving the ability of employees to cope with career problems.

Currently, wellness programs are extremely popular. In general, **wellness programs** are activities that organizations sponsor to promote good health habits or to identify and correct health problems.[44] Estimates indicate that more than 50,000 U.S. firms provide some type of company-sponsored health promotion program. The following Quality in Practice account describes part of the wellness program at Tenneco.

QUALITY IN PRACTICE

Tenneco's Wellness Program

Deep in the Louisiana bayous, a team of leathery pipeline workers—of all people—celebrate the rigors of healthy living. A few years ago the fourteen men who operate a 22-acre natural gas platform in the gulf of Mexico near the Cajun town of Cocodrie shared a sedentary, gluttonous existence. At work they gorged on deep-fried crawfish or spicy, sausage-laced gumbos, topped off by slabs of cheesecake. Chefs risked getting fired for holding the Tabasco or serving anything too healthy, like an overdose of vegetables. Gerald Thurston, a Tenneco manager who supervises the platform, stated: "The attitude was, the more you eat, the more you earn."

Workers regularly added five pounds a year. Their age could be judged by the size of their bellies, like counting the rings on trees. Prior to the start of the wellness program, ten of the fourteen platform workers had dangerously high cholesterol. Fearing a medical time bomb, Tenneco began urging employees to get healthy. Today it brings in nurses by helicopter about twice a year to conduct tests and dispense advice. In addition, each employee has frequent appointments with physicians. Employees fill their plates with baked chicken and salad prepared by Tenneco's hand-picked caterer, and pump iron in a well-equipped fitness area. The five fattest employees have lost an average of twenty-six pounds each. Although half the workers are forty-five or older, not one has suffered from heart problems.

By turning a group of coronary candidates into a relatively fit, diet-conscious crew, Tenneco is doing more than saving lives. It and a growing number of other companies now understand that it pays to keep workers healthy.[45]

There are three main types of wellness programs.[46] The first are programs aimed at raising awareness and providing information. These programs may or may not directly improve health; rather they are designed to inform employees about the consequences of unhealthy behavior. For example, Sara Lee provides female employees with a series of workshops on prenatal care, nutrition, and strategies for preventing disease. Johnson & Johnson has lunch-hour seminars on stress-coping techniques. Companies often use these programs to generate interest in more active exercise and life-style change programs.

A second type of wellness program involves employees in ongoing efforts to modify their life-styles. Such efforts might involve physical fitness programs (such as jogging or walking), smoking cessation programs, weight control programs, and the like. For example, L. L. Bean has a running club for employees and programs that offer lessons in ballroom dancing and cross-country skiing. Bonne Bell encourages employees to ride bicycles to work and has arranged for its employees to purchase bikes at cost. The company also provides an extensive series of exercise programs for employees and has built tennis and volleyball courts, a running track, and shower and locker facilities. Employees may use all of these facilities at no cost and even get an extra thirty minutes for lunch if they want to exercise. The firm sells running suits and shoes at discount prices and currently offers a $250 bonus for employees who exercise at least four days a week.

A third variety of wellness program has as its goal the creation of an environment that will help employees maintain the healthy life-style developed in the other programs. For example, AT&T employees formed support groups to help each other maintain their healthy life-style changes as a result of AT&T's Total Life Concept wellness program. The exercise facilities provided free of charge to employees by Bonne Bell are another example. At Safeway, employees built their own fitness center on company property. The firm now provides a full-time fitness director to oversee the exercise programs and activities.

Wellness programs can provide substantial benefits to both individuals and organizations. Safeway estimates that its wellness program has almost completely eliminated workplace accidents and reduced tardiness and absenteeism by more than 60 percent. AT&T has obtained dramatic health benefits in terms of reduced blood pressure and cholesterol levels from its Total Life Concept program. Many other companies report similar positive health consequences.

At Johnson & Johnson locations that used the wellness program, hospital costs during the first five years increased by only one-third as much as they did at company locations that didn't use the program. Johnson & Johnson's wellness program also reduced absenteeism by 18 percent. In addition to showing a substantial improvement in employee morale, an evaluation of Honeywell's wellness program indicated that the cost of its health-care services is increasing an average of only 4 percent a year, compared to nationwide increases that average about 14 percent.[47] Each year, the Health Project (a nonprofit group composed of business executives, labor leaders, professors, and government officials) awards the C. Everett Koop National Health Award to companies having the most successful wellness programs. The most recent winners of this award are shown in Table 7.3.

CHAPTER SUMMARY

Stress is a consequence of or a response to a situation that places either physical or psychological demands (stressors) on a person. The body's general biological response to stressors prepares the individual to fight or flee—behaviors generally inappropriate in the workplace. Many factors determine how employees experience work stress, including their perception of the situation, past experiences, the presence or absence of other employees, and a variety of individual differences.

Stressors at work stem from many sources, including (1) workload, (2) job conditions, (3) role conflict and ambiguity, (4) career development, (5) interpersonal relations, (6) aggressive behavior, including violence and sexual harassment, and (7) conflict between work and other roles. In addition, significant

TABLE 7.3 Winning Health Care Programs

COMPANY	WINNING WELLNESS PROGRAM
Aetna	Aetna boasts five state-of-the-art health clubs with 7,600 enrollees. Exercise machines cost $282 less per year than is needed to insure couch potatoes.
L.L. Bean	L.L. Bean pays up to $200 to employees whose families quit smoking or take prenatal classes. Its annual health insurance premiums are $2,000 per employee, half the national average.
Champion	Champion's 18,000 mill workers pay no deductible on preventive exams and immunizations. This creates big savings from early detection of cancer and diabetes.
Coors	Coors pays bonuses for healthy habits. Employees can use the award of $500 per family to buy extra holidays or pay for financial planning.
Dow	Dow's Backs in Action program encourages exercise and dieting. On-the-job strains and sprains have decreased by 90%.
DuPont	DuPont budgets $20 million per year on tests and checkups for employees. Free treatment includes frequent mammographies and flu shots.
First Chicago	First Chicago pays for 800 births each year in its female work force. Educational programs have reduced C-sections and underweight babies.
Johnson & Johnson	J&J employees receive free checkups six times annually for their infants. Prevention saves $13 million a year.
Quaker	Quaker grants $500 bonuses for exercise, not smoking, and using seat belts.
Steelcase	Steelcase tests 4,000 employees for health problems and safety awareness. Estimated savings from promoting healthy lifestyles are $20 million over 10 years.
Tenneco	Among other things, Tenneco promotes healthy eating habits for 1,500 pipeline workers. Health costs are shrinking along with waistlines.
Union Pacific	UP motivates employees to focus on healthy lifestyles. A $1.2 million per year investment in wellness programs generates 3-to-1 return.

Source: Adapted from Tully, S. America's healthiest companies. *Fortune*, June 12, 1995, 99.

changes or other events in an individual's personal life may also be sources of stress.

Stress affects people physiologically, emotionally, and behaviorally. Researchers have linked stress to several serious health problems, particularly coronary heart disease. An inverted U-shaped relationship exists between stress and performance. An optimal level of stress probably exists for any particular task, and less or more stress than that level may lead to reduced performance. Job burnout is a major result of unrelieved job-related stress.

Several personality dimensions are related to stress. Individuals having a Type A personality are prone to stress and have an increased chance of heart disease. Some specific dimensions of the Type A personality, such as hostility, are particularly important in terms of stress-related illness. In contrast, the collection of personality traits known as hardiness seems to reduce the effects of stress.

Stress is a crucial issue for both individuals and organizations. Fortunately, various techniques and programs can help people manage stress in the workplace. These programs may focus on identifying and removing workplace stressors and helping employees cope with stress. Wellness programs are particularly promising in this latter regard.

KEY TERMS AND CONCEPTS

Behavioral effects of stress	Physiological effects of stress	Stress management
Depersonalization	Post-traumatic stress disorder	Stressors
Emotional effects of stress	Role ambiguity	Type A personality
Fight-or-flight response	Role conflict	Type B personality
Hardiness	Role overload	Wellness programs
Job burnout	Sexual harassment	Workplace violence
Life stressors	Stress	

DISCUSSION QUESTIONS

1. Based on your own experience, briefly describe a work situation that you found stressful. Use Figures 7.1 and 7.2 to identify the factors causing the stress and explain their impact.

2. Explain the role of individual differences (such as age, gender, past experience, and personality) in experiencing stress.

3. Describe some of the stressors in a job that you have held. Which were the most difficult ones to deal with? Why?

4. Give an example of a time when the fight-or-flight response seemed particularly inappropriate for your own behavior.

5. Identify the possible health consequences of excessive stress.

6. What is the general relationship between performance and stress?

7. Discuss the conditions and circumstances leading to job burnout.

8. Compare and contrast the hardy personality with the Type A personality.

9. Design a stress management program for an organization. Justify the various components of your suggested program.

10. What can be done to avoid sexual harassment at work?

◼ Developing Competencies

Self-Insight: Strategies for Coping with Stress

On a separate sheet of paper, develop responses to the following questions. Be prepared to share your responses with other members of your group or class.[48]

Successful Experience

1. Describe a situation in which you coped well with stress. (How did you perceive and/or assess the situation? What did you think was happening?)

2. What perceptions, thoughts, feelings, behaviors, and resources helped you to succeed in this situation?

3. How have you integrated these perceptions, thoughts, feelings, behaviors, and resources into your typical style of dealing with stress?

4. What other perceptions, thoughts, feelings, behaviors, and resources could you use in order to cope even better with stress?

Unsuccessful Experience

1. Describe a situation in which you did not cope well with stress. (How did you perceive and/or assess the situation? What did you think was happening?)

2. What perceptions, thoughts, feelings, and behaviors prevented you from dealing with this situation effectively?

3. As a result of this experience, what did you learn about coping with stress? What would (or did) you do differently the next time?

Comparison

Review your responses to the "successful experience" and the "unsuccessful experience." Describe the differences in how you perceived and handled the two situations.

Organizational Insight:
Stress Management at Metropolitan Hospital

This stress management program was carried out over a two-year period at Metropolitan Hospital. The initial impetus for the project was widespread complaints from middle managers about feeling stress, overworked, and subject to unexpected changes in policies and procedures. Top administrators sought help in dealing with these problems from external organization development (OD) consultants with skills and experience in stress management.

The initial stage of the project consisted of diagnosing the causes and consequences of experienced stress at the hospital. Understanding the sources of stress was seen as a necessary prelude to developing an appropriate plan for managing stress. The consultants developed a questionnaire to collect data from the forty-five middle managers responsible for almost every phase of operation of the hospital. The design of the questionnaire was guided by a conceptual model of stress similar to that shown in Figure 7.2. The questionnaire included items about various organizational stressors, including ongoing, recurrent stressors as well as those associated with recent changes. It also included questions about the manager's use of stress management techniques, such as exercise, nutritional awareness, and the creation of support systems. The questionnaire ended with items about possible immediate stress effects (for example, irritability, sleep difficulty, and changes in eating and drinking patterns) and longer-term impacts (such as reduced general health, job dissatisfaction, and poor work performance).

. Analysis of the diagnostic data showed that many of the organizational change events and ongoing working conditions were significantly related to managers' levels of perceived stress. Among the most stressful organizational change events were major and frequent changes in instructions, policies, and procedures; numerous unexpected crises and deadlines; and sudden increases in the activity level or pace of work. The ongoing working conditions contributing most to stress included work overload, feedback only when performance is unsatisfactory, lack of confidence in management, and role conflict and ambiguity. The managers reported little if any use of stress management techniques to help them to cope with these stressors. Only 20 percent engaged in regular physical exercise, and surprisingly, 60 percent had marginally or poorly balanced diets. Among the most commonly reported health problems were tension headaches, diarrhea or constipation, common colds, and backaches.

Based on the diagnostic data, senior management with the help of the consultants implemented several organizational improvements. In order to reduce work overload and role ambiguity, each managerial position was analyzed in terms of work distribution, job requirements, and performance standards. This resulted in more balanced workloads across the jobs and in clearer job descriptions. Hospital administrators also began working with department managers to define job expectations and to provide ongoing performance feedback. The managers were given training in time management, how to better organize their workload, and in how to more effectively delegate work to subordinates.

The "fire-fighting" climate at the hospital had caused many managers to focus on their own departments while neglecting important lateral relations with other units. Monthly cross-departmental meetings were implemented to improve lateral relations among department heads and supervisors. Efforts were also made to provide an organizational culture supporting the building of peer-support groups.

In order to reduce uncertainty about organizational changes, senior managers spent more time informing and educating managers about forthcoming changes. Top management also held information meetings with first-line supervisors on a quarterly basis in order to clear up misunderstandings, misinterpretations, and rumors.

While the above changes were aimed at reducing organizational stressors, additional measures were taken to help managers to identify and cope with stress more effectively. The hospital instituted yearly physical examinations to detect stress-related problems. It also trained managers to identify stress symptoms and problems both in themselves and subordinates. The hospital developed an exercise club and various sports activities and offered weekly yoga classes. It also created a training program combining nutritional awareness with techniques for coping with tension headaches and backaches. Fresh fruit was made available as an alternative to doughnuts in all meetings and training sessions.

Initial reactions to the stress management program were positive, and the hospital is assessing the longer-term effects. Measures of stressors and experienced stress will be taken every twelve to eighteen months to monitor the program so that changes can be made if necessary.[49]

Questions

1. Identify the primary ideas and concepts from the chapter that appear, in one form or another, in this case.

2. Using Figure 7.2, diagnose the work stressors at Metropolitan Hospital.

3. Using Figure 7.7, analyze Metropolitan's stress management program.

REFERENCES

1. Adapted from Graham, E., and Crossen, C. The overloaded American: Too many things to do, too little time to do them. *Wall Street Journal*, March 8, 1996, R1, R4; Sharp, D. So many lists, so little time. *USA Weekend*, March 15–17,

1996, 4–6.

2. Edwards, J. R. An examination of competing versions of the person environment fit approach to stress. *Academy of Management Journal*, 1996, 39, 292–339; Kahn, R. L., and Byosiere, P. Stress in organizations. In M. D. Dunnette and L. M. Hough (eds.), *Handbook of Industrial and Organizational Psychology*, vol. 3, 2d ed. Palo Alto, Calif.: Consulting Psychologists Press, 1992, 571–650.

3. Contrada, R., Baum, A. S., Glass, D., and Friend, R. The social psychology of health. In R. M. Baron, W. G. Graziano, and C. Stangor (eds.), *Social Psychology*. Fort Worth: Holt, Rinehart and Winston, 1991, 620–624.

4. This example is based on Matteson, M. T., and Ivancevich, J. M. *Controlling Work Stress: Effective Human Resource and Management Strategies*. San Francisco: Jossey-Bass, 1987, 12–14.

5. Selye, H. History and present status of the stress concept. In L. Goldberger and S. Breznitz (eds.), *Handbook of Stress*. New York: Free Press, 1982, 7–17; Selye, H. *The Stress of Life*, rev. ed. New York: McGraw-Hill, 1976, 1.

6. See, for example, Cummins, R. C. Job stress and the buffering effect of supervisory support. *Group & Organization Studies*, 1990, 15, 92–104; Manning, M. R., Jackson, C. N., and Fusilier, M. R. Occupational stress, social support, and the costs of health care. *Academy of Management Journal*, 1996, 39, 738–750.

7. Burke, M. J., Brief, A. P., and George, J. M. The role of negative affectivity in understanding relations between self-reports of stressors and strains: A comment on the applied psychology literature. *Journal of Applied Psychology*, 1993, 78, 402–412; Lazarus, R. S. From psychological stress to the emotions: A history of changing outlooks. *Annual Review of Psychology*, 1993, 44, 1–21; Schaubroeck, J., Ganster, D. C., and Fox, M. L. Dispositional affect and work-related stress. *Journal of Applied Psychology*, 1992, 77, 322–335.

8. This story is attributed to Henry Murray, as described by Pervin, L. A. Persons, situations, interactions: The history of a controversy and a discussion of theoretical models. *Academy of Management Review*, 1989, 14, 350–360.

9. Adapted from Ellison, K. Siesta sunset: Stress invades mañana-land. *Houston Chronicle*, July 28, 1992, 7A.

10. O'Boyle, T. F. Fear and stress in the office take toll. *Wall Street Journal*, November 6, 1990, B1, B3; Shellenbarger, S. Was that 24-hour flu that kept you home really just the blahs? *Wall Street Journal*, July 24, 1996, B1; Stewart, T. A. Do you push your people too hard? *Fortune*, October 22, 1990, 121–128.

11. Cooper, C. L., and Arbose, J. Executive stress goes global. *International Management*, May 1984, 42–48; see also, Peterson, M. F. et al., Role conflict, ambiguity, and overload: A 21-nation study. *Academy of Management Journal*, 1995, 38, 429–452.

12. Melamed, S., Ben-Avi, I., Luz, J., and Green, M. S. Objective and subjective work monotony: Effects on job satisfaction, psychological distress, and absenteeism in blue-collar workers. *Journal of Applied Psychology*, 1995, 80, 29–42.

13. Nykodym, N., and George, K. Stress busting on the job. *Personnel*, July 1989, 56–59; Shostak, A. B. *Blue-Collar Stress*. Reading, Mass.: Addison-Wesley, 1980, 19–28; van de Vliert, E. and van Yperen, N. W. Why cross-national differences in role overload? Don't overlook ambient temperature. *Academy of Management Journal*, 1996, 39, 986–1004.

14. See, for example, Leigh, J. H., Lucas, G. H., and Woodman, R. W. Effects of perceived organizational factors on role stress-job attitude relationships. *Journal of Management*, 1988, 14, 41–58; Miner, J. B. *Industrial-Organizational Psychology*. New York: McGraw-Hill, 1992, 158–159; Peterson et al., Role conflict, ambiguity, and overload.

15. Sutton, R. I., and Rafaeli, A. Characteristics of work stations as potential occupational stressors. *Academy of Management Journal*, 1987, 30, 260–276.

16. Statistics in this section are drawn from O'Leary-Kelly, A. M., Griffin, R. W., and Glew, D. J. Organization-motivated aggression: A research framework. *Academy of Management Journal*, 1996, 21, 225–253. See also Allen, R. E., and Lucero, M. A. Beyond resentment: Exploring organizationally targeted insider murder. *Journal of Management Inquiry*, 1996, 5, 86–103.

17. Hollway, W., and Jefferson, T. PC or not PC: Sexual harassment and the question of ambivalence. *Human Relations*, 1996, 49, 373–394; Lengnick-Hall, M. L. Sexual harassment research: A methodological critique. *Personnel Psychology*, 1995, 48, 841–865; Serepca, B. Sexual harassment. *Internal Auditor*, October 1995, 60–63.

18. Investigating harassment charges. *The Manager's Intelligence Report*. Chicago: Lawrence Ragan Communications, 1996, 3.

19. Adapted from Sharpe, R. EEOC sues Mitsubishi unit for harassment. *Wall Street Journal*, April 10, 1996, B1, B8.

20. Dolby, V. J. Organizational stress as threat to reputation: Effects on anxiety at work and at home. *Academy of Management Journal*, 1995, 38, 1105–1123; Frone, M. R., Russell, M., and Cooper, M. L. Antecedents and outcomes of work–family conflict: Testing a model of the work–family interface. *Journal of Applied Psychology*, 1992, 77, 65–78.

21. Adapted from Shellenbarger, S. Couple orchestrates complex dance needed in two-career home. *Wall Street Journal*, February 28, 1996, B1.

22. Baron, R. A., and Byrne, D. *Social Psychology: Understanding Human Interaction*, 6th ed. Boston: Allyn & Bacon, 1991, 571–573; the type of rating scale shown in Table 7.1 is based on the work of Holmes, T. H., and Rahe, R. H. The social readjustment rating scale. *Journal of Psychosomatic Medicine*, 1967, 11, 213–218.

23. Sharp, 4.

24. Ader, R., and Cohen, N. Psychoneuroimmunology: Conditioning and stress. *Annual Review of Psychology*, 1993, 44, 53–85; Cohen, S. Psychological stress, immunity, and upper respiratory infections. *Current Directions in Psychological Science*, 1996, 5, 86–90; Cohen, S., and Williamson, G. M. Stress and infectious disease in humans. *Psychological Bulletin*, 1991, 109, 5–24.

25. Allen, D. S. Less stress, less litigation. *Personnel*, January 1990, 32–35; Hollis, D., and Goodson, J. Stress: The legal and organizational implications. *Employee Responsibilities and Rights Journal*, 1989, 2, 255–262.

26. McMorris, F. A. Can post-traumatic stress arise from office battles? *Wall Street Journal*, February 5, 1996, B1, B10.

27. Xie, J. L., and Johns, G. Job scope and stress: Can job scope be too high? *Academy of Management Journal*, 1995, 38, 1288–1309.

28. Cascio, W. F. Downsizing: What do we know? What have we learned? *Academy of Management Executive*, 1993, 7, 95–104; Lublin, J. A. Walking wounded: Survivors of lay-offs battle angst, anger, hurting productivity. *Wall Street Journal*, December 6, 1993, A1.

29. See, for example, Greer, C. R., and Castro, M. A. D. The relationship between perceived unit effectiveness and occupational stress: The case of purchasing agents. *Journal of Applied Behavioral Science*, 1986, 22, 159–175; Motowidlo, S. J., Packard, J. S., and Manning, M. R. Occupational stress: Its causes and consequences for job performance. *Journal of Applied Psychology*, 1986, 71, 618–629; Sullivan, S. E., and Bhagat, R. S. Organizational stress, job satisfaction, and job performance: Where do we go from here? *Journal of Management*, 1992, 18, 353–374.

30. Cordes, C. L., and Dougherty, T. W. A review and integration of research on job burnout. *Academy of Management Review*, 1993, 18, 621–656; Lee, R. T., and Ashforth, B. E. A meta-analytic examination of the correlates of the three dimensions of job burnout. *Journal of Applied Psychology*, 1996, 81, 123–133; Lee, R. T., and Ashforth, B. E. On the meaning of Maslach's three dimensions of burnout. *Journal of Applied Psychology*, 1990, 75, 743–747.

31. Niehouse, O. I. Controlling burnout: A leadership guide for managers. *Business Horizons*, July–August 1984, 81–82; See also, Levinson, H. When executives burn out. *Harvard Business Review*, July–August 1996, 152–163.

32. Milbank, D. "New-collar" work: Telephone sales reps do unrewarding jobs that few can abide. *Wall Street Journal*, September 9, 1993; Offerman, L. R., and Armitage, M. A. Stress and the woman manager: Sources, health outcomes, and interventions. In E. A. Fagenson (ed.), *Women in Management*, vol. 4. Newbury Park, Calif.: Sage, 1993, 131–161.

33. Conte, J. M., Landy, F. J., and Mathieu, J. E. Time urgency: conceptual and construct development. *Journal of Applied Psychology*, 1995, 80, 178–185; Landy, F. J., Rastegary, H., Thayer, J., and Colvin, C. Time urgency. *Journal of Applied Psychology*, 1991, 76, 644–657.

34. Friedman, M., and Rosenman, R. *Type A Behavior and Your Heart*. New York: Knopf, 1974.

35. Friedman, H. S., and Booth-Kewley, S. Personality, Type A behavior and coronary heart disease: The role of emotional expression. *Journal of Personality and Social Psychology*, 1987, 53, 783–792; Ganster, D. C., Schaubroeck, J., Sime, W. E., and Mayes, B. T. The nomological validity of the Type A personality among employed adults. *Journal of Applied Psychology*, 1991, 76, 143–168; Lee, C., Jamieson, L. F., and Earley, P. C. Beliefs and fears and Type A behavior: Implications for academic performance and psychiatric health disorder symptoms. *Journal of Organizational Behavior*, 1996, 17, 151–168; Lyness, S. A. Predictors of differences between Type A and B individuals in heart rate and blood pressure reactivity. *Psychological Bulletin*, 1993, 114, 266–295.

36. Baron and Byrne, 606.

37. Contrada, Baum, Glass, and Friend, 626-627.

38. Baron and Byrne, 574–575; Contrada, R. J. Type A behavior, personality hardiness, and cardiovascular responses to stress. *Journal of Personality and Social Psychology*, 1989, 57, 895–903; Roth, D. L., Wiebe, D. J. Fillingham, R. B., and Shay, K. A. Life events, fitness, hardiness, and health: A simultaneous analysis of proposed stress-resistance effects. *Journal of Personality and Social Psychology*, 1989, 57, 136–142.

39. Byrum-Robinson, B. Stress-management training for the nineties. In J. W. Pfeiffer (ed.), *The 1993 Annual: Developing Human Resources*. San Diego: Pfeiffer & Company, 1993, 264.

40. Byrum-Robinson, 277.

41. Nelson, D. L., Quick, J. C., and Quick, J. D. Corporate warfare: Preventing combat stress and battle fatigue. *Organizational Dynamics*, Summer 1989, 65–79; see also, Delbecq, A. L., and Friedlander, F. Strategies for personal and family renewal: How a high survivor group of executives cope with stress and avoid burnout. *Journal of Management Inquiry*, 1995, 4, 262–269.

42. Trost, C. Workplace stress. *Wall Street Journal*, December 1, 1992, A1.

43. Ivancevich, J. M., Matteson, M. T., Freedman, S. M., and Phillips, J. S. Worksite stress management interventions. *American Psychologist*, 1990, 45, 252–261.

44. Gebhardt, D. L., and Crump, C. E. Employee fitness and wellness programs in the workplace. *American Psychologist*, 1990, 45, 262–272.

45. Adapted from Jeffrey, N. A. Wellness plans try to target the not-so-well. *Wall Street Journal*, June 20, 1996, B1, B2; Tully, S. America's healthiest companies. *Fortune*, June 12, 1995, 98–106.

46. Gebhardt and Crump.

47. Company examples in this section are drawn from Jeffrey; Roberts, M., and Harris, T. J. Wellness at work. *Psychology Today*, May 1989, 54–58.

48. Gregory, A. M. Coping strategies: Managing stress successfully. Reproduced from *The 1992 Annual: Developing Human Resources*, J. W. Pfeiffer (ed.). Copyright 1992 by Pfeiffer & Company, San Diego, California. Used with permission.

49. Cummings, T. G., and Worley, C. G. *Organization Development and Change*, 5th ed. Copyright © 1993. By permission of South-Western College Publishing, a division of International Thomson Publishing Inc., Cincinnati, Ohio 45227.

Group and
Interpersonal Processes

PART 2

8

Group and Team Behavior

LEARNING OBJECTIVES

When you have finished studying this chapter, you should be able to:

- Identify the tensions that can arise between individuals and teams or groups.
- Describe the most common types of teams and groups in organizations.
- Discuss the increasing impact of groupware tools on teams and groups.
- Explain the five-stage model of team development.
- Describe six of the key influences on team and group outcomes.
- Explain the six-phase model of self-managing team decision making.
- Apply the nominal group technique and electronic brainstorming to stimulate team creativity.

OUTLINE

Preview Case: Macy's New Team System

Individual–Team Relations

Individualism and Collectivism

Individual and Team Goals

Managing in Practice: Individual and Team Pay

Varieties of Teams and Groups

Types of Task Groups

Types of Teams

Quality in Practice: Honeywell's Self-Managed Teams

Coalitions

Stages of Team Development

Influences on Teams and Groups

Context

Technology in Practice: Surfacing Options

Goals

Diversity in Practice: Standard Motor Products Reduces Barriers

Size

Member Roles and Diversity

Ethics in Practice: Texas Instrument's Ethics of Diversity

Norms

Cohesiveness

Leadership

Team Decision Making

Self-Managing Team Model

Assessment of Model

Across Cultures: General Motors Work Teams in Mexico

Stimulating Team Creativity

Nominal Group Technique

Brainstorming

Technology in Practice: Electronic Brainstorming at North American Life and Casualty

Developing Competencies

Team Insight: Assessing Team Diversity

Organizational Insight: Great Majestic Company

229

PREVIEW CASE

Macy's New Team System

Macy's Herald Square flagship store in New York City presents major logistics challenges. The retailer recently made dramatic improvements in what had been one of its greatest problem areas: the flow of merchandise from the receiving dock to the selling floor.

Roy G. Seher, vice-president of operations for the ninety-one store Macy's East Division comments, "We implemented a new program that brought what had been a merchandising function—the processing, handling and replenishment of goods—into operations, setting up functional teams with specialized job responsibilities. The changes, which encompassed everything from markdowns to stock replenishment, involved a major job restructuring for the stock associates. Job teams were created along functional lines. The associates were allowed to pick their team based on seniority."

Under the new system, the receiving and delivery team unloads the trailers and segregates and delivers the merchandise by delivery zone. The processing team organizes all the soft goods to floor presentation standards and tags them for security purposes. The receiving and delivery team and the processing team work overnight. Seher notes, "Previously, the merchandise was brought to the floor from the receiving platform and dumped into the freight well. The stock associates would get to it when they could. If the workload was too great or if the sales manager had to set other priorities for the day, the merchandise would just pile up on the receiving dock, eventually backing up in the distribution center."

The first team to appear in the morning after the merchandise has been processed and delivered is the placement team. It distributes fashion merchandise to the proper locations for further handling by the fill-in team. This team comes in about midmorning. It is the largest team with sixty-four associates. It is responsible for filling the holes created by sales from merchandise displays during the day. Smaller subteams maintain stock reserves and fitting rooms. The recovery team, whose shift starts in the afternoon, fills and straightens displays, ensuring that the merchandise on tables is folded properly. The team also helps maintain the fitting rooms.

An administrative team handles all damaged goods, merchandise returns to vendors, markdowns, and price changes. This team is also responsible for hanger and security tag pickup at the cash registers and wrapping areas.

Macy's previous system required an average of five to seven days to process goods and get them onto the selling floor (the turn time was even longer at peak receipt times, averaging seven to ten days). Since the new team system was implemented, the time as been slashed to twenty-four hours or less. Seher states, "We have reduced our receiving and stocking budget by about 22 percent, with significant savings coming from the increased productivity of our employees."[1]

Macy's isn't alone in using teams and other types of groups to accomplish organizational goals. There is no simple formula for creating and maintaining effective formal teams (those specifically created by management) or informal groups (those that form from the day-to-day interactions of individuals.[2] To date, the introduction and use of the team system at Macy's has been effective and accepted by employees and managers alike. According to Roy Seher, "The stock associates like the structure of the teams. They like knowing their agenda. One of our initial objectives was to free up our managers for other key functions, such as improved customer service. Judging by the feedback we have received, I do think we achieved that objective."[3]

In this chapter, we present ways to analyze formal and informal groups and—based on the analysis—ways to increase their performance and effectiveness. We emphasize (1) the relations between individuals and groups, (2) the principal variables that influence team and group effectiveness, (3) how effective teams make decisions, and (4) how to encourage team creativity. Many of the topics discussed in this book—such as leadership, interpersonal communication, and conflict management—contribute to the competencies needed for effective management of and participation in teams and groups.

A **group** comprises people with shared goals who often communicate with one another over a period of time and are few enough so that each individual may communicate with all the others, person-to-person.[4] In other words, a group is a small number of individuals who communicate person-to-person to achieve one or more common goals. In this chapter, we focus on small groups and don't consider large groups such as political parties, ethnic groups, or occupational groups.

INDIVIDUAL–TEAM RELATIONS

In some countries, including the United States and Canada, many people strongly believe in the importance and uniqueness of the individual. In these countries, educational, government, and business institutions frequently state that they exist to serve individual goals and needs. Individualism and collectivism are two cultural values that influence how teams and groups are likely to be accepted and operate.

■ INDIVIDUALISM AND COLLECTIVISM

Individualism means being distinct and separate from the group, emphasizing personal goals, and showing little concern and emotional attachment to groups, especially in the work setting. Employees in cultures that espouse individualism are expected to act on the basis of their personal goals and self-interests. This cultural belief can, and often does, cause uneasiness over the influence that teams and groups have in organizations.

Collectivism means being an integral part of the group, subordinating personal goals to group goals, showing deep concern for the welfare of the group, and feeling intense emotional ties to the group.[5] The cultural belief in collectivism in countries such as China and Japan seems to have an effect opposite to that of individualism: The use of teams is a natural extension of cultural values. Uneasiness revolves around the potential influence and assertiveness of the individual in teams. Thus we might characterize the basic difference between individualism and collectivism in certain cultures as the uneasiness between "fitting into the group" versus "standing out from the group."[6]

Even in societies that value individualism, the use of teams and groups is increasing, as demonstrated by Macy's experience. The company encourages many associates and managers to contribute to various functional teams through (1) intensive training in team participation and decision making; (2) empowerment of functional and administrative teams to implement improvements and take corrective action (which serves to increase participation); and (3) assessment, recognition, and reward of individuals for their contributions to team decision making and goal achievement. Even with Macy's new team system, though, employees spend most of their time performing tasks individually.

■ INDIVIDUAL AND TEAM GOALS

Work team and individual goals need not conflict and, in fact, usually are compatible.[7] However, the potential exists for a work team or group and its individual members to have incompatible goals, as suggested by the following observations. Goal conflicts

- do exist, and all employees need to take them into account;
- mobilize powerful forces that have significant effects on individuals and their behaviors;
- may produce both good and bad results; and can be managed to increase their benefits.[8]

As discussed in the following Managing in Practice feature, the relative emphasis given to individual and team-based pay is a clear example of the potential for conflicting goals. It reflects the underlying tension caused by individualism versus collectivism.

MANAGING IN PRACTICE

Individual and Team Pay

According to a study by the Hays Group (a management consulting firm), a problem for information system (IS) teams and others is how to isolate the performance of a particular team member. Both outstanding and mediocre individual performance may be hidden in team settings.

The impact on IS organizations is of particular concern because of the project-team orientation of most of their systems and applications work. Steve Ross, vice-president of the Hays Group, stated, "The longer a team is together, the more troubling the pay issues become [because] people begin asking the proverbial question of 'what's in it for me?' People created teams without changing the human resources infrastructure—specifically the pay system."

Xerox has been experimenting with team-based pay for three years. "But I think we've only broken the code in the last year," said Bob Monastero, director of human resources for global IS at Xerox. The Xerox formula is that half an IS worker's merit pay increase is determined by managers and the other half is determined by teammates. Interestingly, the range of bonuses determined by teammates is much greater than those given by managers. "Those closer to the work know better than the manager who's pulling the weight," Monastero said.

At Monsanto in St. Louis, where almost all IS work is team-based, management recently implemented a new IS compensation plan. Now, IS employees' merit pay is divided into thirds: a third determined by project-team performance, a third by individual performance, and a third by the company's overall financial performance. Merit compensation previously was based largely on business unit performance and subjective criteria.[9]

The free-rider concept is another example of conflicting team and individual goals. The term **free rider** refers to a team member who obtains benefits from membership but doesn't bear a proportional share of the responsibility for generating those benefits.[10] Students sometimes experience the free-rider problem when a faculty member assigns a team project for which all the members receive the same (team) grade. Let's say that seven students were on a team that received an A but that two members contributed little or nothing to the project. The non-contributing members obtained the benefit of the team grade but didn't bear a proportional share of the work that earned the team grade. Free riders are likely to be highly individualistic people who believe that they can minimize their contribution to a team effort so long as they themselves aren't held accountable.

Most team and group members dislike free riders. First, free riders violate an equity standard: Team members don't want others to receive the same rewards for less effort. Second, free riders violate a standard of social responsibility: All should do their fair share. Third, free riders violate a standard of reciprocity or exchange. A team will perform poorly if too many of its members are free riders who fail to contribute significantly to the task.[11]

VARIETIES OF TEAMS AND GROUPS

Most individuals belong to various teams and groups, which can be classified in several ways. For example, a person concerned with obtaining membership in a group or gaining acceptance as a group member might classify groups as open or closed to new members. A person evaluating groups in an organization according to their primary goals might classify them as friendship groups and task groups. A **friendship group** evolves informally to meet its members' personal security, esteem, and belonging needs. A **task group** is created by management to accomplish certain organizational goals. However, a single group or team in an organization may serve both friendship and task purposes. The receiving and delivery team, processing team, placement team, fill-in team, recovery team, and administrative team at Macy's are examples of task groups. The primary focus of this chapter is on task groups.

■ TYPES OF TASK GROUPS

Task groups may be classified by the relationships between groups or team members. The three basic types of task groups are counteracting, coacting, and interacting.[12]

A **counteracting group** exists when members interact to resolve some type of conflict, usually through negotiation and compromise. A labor–management negotiating group is one example of a counteracting group. Management and union representatives usually believe that at least some of their goals conflict.

A **coacting group** exists when group members perform their jobs relatively independently in the short run. The terms *relatively* and *in the short run* indicate that, without interdependence over time, there would be no task group. For example, college students enrolled in the same course may participate relatively independently of each other in class discussions but act interdependently with others in undertaking a team project. Another example of a coacting group is a bowling team, with the team score being the sum of the team members' scores. Coacting groups are likely to be effective when individual efforts don't require much cooperation and coordination. For example, a regional sales manager may need to bring sales representatives together quarterly to review common problems and issues. However, the day-to-day activities of each sales representative don't involve communication and coordination with the other sales representatives. In addition, total regional sales and profits are primarily the sum of each sales representative's performance.

An **interacting group** exists when a group can't accomplish its goal(s) until all its members have completed their shares of the project. Recall the Managing in Practice feature on individual and team pay. The development and application of information systems requires a team orientation.

Common forms of interacting groups include teams, committees, task forces, boards, advisory councils, work crews, review panels, and the like. An increasing portion of the work force is being called on to work in a team environment, as at Macy's, Xerox, and Monsanto. The types of issues and decisions that a team or group addresses may vary widely. Table 8.1 provides a brief questionnaire for assessing the degree of autonomy and responsibility that resides with a team or group versus higher management. As you review Table 8.1, relate it to your own experience—such as the autonomy and responsibilities of a class project team relative to your instructor (higher management). In general, the greater the number of marks in the team/group column in Table 8.1, the greater is the autonomy and empowerment of the team or group.

■ TYPES OF TEAMS

In an organization, a **team** is a small number of employees with complementary skills and knowledge (competencies) who are committed to common performance goals and interacting relationships for which they hold themselves mutually accountable.[13] The heart of any team is a shared commitment by the members to their collective performance. Team goals could be as basic as responding to all customers within twenty-four hours to reducing defects by 20 percent over the next six months. The key is that these goals can't be achieved without the cooperation and interaction of team members. A team must be formed with or develop the right mix of complementary skills and knowledge among the members to achieve its goals. Also, the members need to be able to influence how they will work together to accomplish the team's goals.[14] Of the many types of teams, let's consider four of the most common: functional teams, problem-solving teams, cross-functional teams, and self-managed teams.

TABLE 8.1 Questionnaire for Assessing Team or Group Empowerment

Instructions: Check the appropriate column for each of the 12 types of issues or decisions.
For the most part in my team/group, the autonomy and responsibility for handling the following issues or decisions resides with:

ISSUE OR DECISION	TEAM/GROUP	HIGHER MANAGEMENT
1. Primary influence on its qualitative goals	_____	_____
2. Primary influence on its quantitative goals	_____	_____
3. Propose and/or formulate budget	_____	_____
4. Monitor activities against budget	_____	_____
5. Rotate tasks and assignments among members	_____	_____
6. Decide on team leadership	_____	_____
7. Assess performance and progress toward goals	_____	_____
8. Call and conduct meetings	_____	_____
9. Implement solutions within scope of team responsibilities	_____	_____
10. Inspect quality of team's outputs	_____	_____
11. Evaluate and dismiss team members	_____	_____
12. Other (add other types of issues or decisions relevant to the team)	_____	_____

Functional teams usually represent individuals who work together daily on a cluster of ongoing and interdependent tasks. Macy's new team structure included the following functional teams: receiving and delivery, placement, fill-in, recovery, and administrative. Recall that the administrative team handles all damaged goods, merchandise returns to vendors, markdowns and price changes, and hanger and security tag pickup at the cash register and wrapping areas. Functional teams often exist within functional departments—marketing, production, finance, auditing, human resources, and the like. Within the human resources department, one or more functional teams could operate within the recruiting, compensation, benefits, safety, training and development, affirmative action, industrial relations, and similar functions.

Problem-solving teams focus on specific issues in their areas of responsibility, develop potential solutions, and often are empowered to take action within defined limits.[15] Such temporary teams frequently address quality or cost problems. The members usually are employees of a specific department and meet at least once or twice a week for an hour or two. The teams may have the authority to implement their own solutions if those solutions don't require major changes in procedures that might adversely affect other departments, teams, or external stakeholders (customers, suppliers, regulatory agencies, and the like) or require substantial new resources. Problem-solving teams do not fundamentally reorganize work or change the role of managers. In effect, managers delegate certain problems and decision-making responsibilities to a team. This approach contrasts with delegating specific tasks and authority to individuals.[16] Wabash National, a truck-trailer factory located in Lafayette, Indiana, recently began to use various types of teams. One problem-solving team saved the company hundreds of thousands of dollars by finding a way to eliminate many time-consuming welds on a coupler for a Wabash trailer that doubles as a railroad car.[17]

Cross-functional teams bring together the knowledge and skills of people from various work areas to identify and solve mutual problems. Cross-functional teams draw members from several departments or functions, deal with problems that cut across departmental and functional lines, and disband after the problems are solved. They are often most effective in situations that require adaptability, speed, and a focus on responding to customer needs.[18] Cross-functional teams may design and introduce quality improvement programs and new technology, meet with customers and suppliers to improve inputs or outputs, and link separate functions (such as marketing, finance, manufacturing, and human resources) to increase product or service innovations. The development of Boeing's 777 jetliner made extensive use of cross-functional teams. Previously, design engineers worked independently of the production and operations people who actually built the planes. The traditional approach was for the designers to say, Here are the plans, go build it. For production of the Boeing 777, hundreds of integrated "design–build" teams were formed. Their members were drawn from diverse functional areas. Each design–build team focused on a specific plane component—tail section, wings, electrical systems, and so on. These teams were then coordinated by integration teams that included higher levels of management.[19]

Self-managed teams normally consist of employees who must work together and cooperate daily to produce an entire good (or major identifiable component) or service. These teams perform a variety of managerial tasks, such as (1) scheduling work and vacations, (2) rotating tasks and assignments among members, (3) ordering materials, (4) deciding on team leadership (which can rotate among team members), (5) setting key team goals, (6) budgeting, (7) hiring replacements for departing team members, and (8) sometimes even evaluating one another's performance.[20] Each member often learns all the jobs that have to be performed by the team. The impact of self-managed teams may be enormous. They have raised productivity 30 percent or more and have substantially raised quality in organizations that have used them. They fundamentally change how work is organized and empower the team to make many decisions (see Table 8.1).[21] The introduction of self-managed teams typically eliminates one or more managerial levels, thereby creating a flatter organization. We discuss additional aspects of self-managed teams throughout this chapter, including a model of decision making for self-managed teams. The following Quality in Practice account outlines the features and importance of self-managed teams at a Honeywell plant in Ontario, Canada.

QUALITY IN PRACTICE

Honeywell's Self-Managed Teams

Ten employees at the Honeywell Ltd. plant in Scarborough, Ontario, recently shut down the production line. The issue was a tiny nick in the control knob of a baseboard heater, and these employees formed the team that assembled it. After plant engineers traced the problem to one of the plastic molds, a meeting with team members resulted in decisions on how to sort the good knobs from the bad and then work resumed.

A few years ago these employees wouldn't have dared call an engineer, much less stop the assembly line. But the half-hour shutdown saved the company several thousand dollars in rework costs. The employees say the self-managed team concept deserves the credit. "When you manage your own team, you learn all the jobs, not just one," says team member Karen Orr, a twelve-year veteran at the plant. She added, "You become more aware of what's going on and you notice immediately if anything's wrong."

Employees who once followed the routine of assembling a small piece of a product now do several jobs on teams that make, test, and pack entire assemblies. They've also taken over many managerial tasks that allow them much more control over their daily routine: changing work assignments, ordering materials, maintaining equipment, and training new staff.

At this Honeywell facility, thirty-five teams draw members from various parts of the plant. They include engineers, skilled tradespeople, maintenance workers, electricians, materials planners, purchasing staff, and others. The old style of supervisor is obsolete—now they're "coaches" or "facilitators." Teams are automatically entitled to take an hour every two weeks to meet with any other group of employees, a facilitator, an engineer, or the plant manager. It isn't a privilege, but a right.

Team members look for ways to improve quality, slash costs, save time, and improve the product. One result of teams at this Honeywell plant was the elimination of most quality control inspectors. Now, teams are trained to inspect their own work, and they're asking questions seldom raised by employees in the past. Karen Orr further states, "The team may have a question for engineering or sales or about job rotation. It depends on what's happening on your line."[22]

■ COALITIONS

A **coalition** is a group of individuals (or organizations) who band together to pursue a specific goal. An informal group that operates to control and reduce the influence of higher management is one type of coalition. A coalition has four key features: (1) it is deliberately created by the members, (2) it operates independently of the formal organization, (3) it is formed to achieve a specific and mutual goal, and (4) it requires united action by the members.[23] A coalition could even be ten students banding together to try to reverse a decision to deny tenure to their favorite faculty member.

■ STAGES OF TEAM DEVELOPMENT

Effective teams and groups don't just happen. In fact, one author suggests that there is no solid evidence that teams, especially cross-functional teams, have delivered on their promise. She states, "The danger is that, as teams fail to realize their potential, the team form will be discarded as just another organizational fad."[24] This chapter and the book as a whole provides insights and guidance for avoiding or correcting team failures.

To provide a sense of the potential for failure, let's consider a basic five-stage developmental sequence that teams or other types of groups may go through: forming, storming, norming, performing, and adjourning.[25] The types of work-related and socially related behaviors that may be observed in teams and groups differ from stage to stage. Figure 8.1 shows the five stages on the horizontal axis and the level of team maturity on the vertical axis. Figure 8.1 also indicates that a team or other type of group can fail and disband during a stage or when moving from one stage to another. Pinpointing the developmental stage of a team at any specific time is difficult. Nevertheless, managers and team members need to understand these developmental stages because each can influence a team's effectiveness. We present behaviors that might occur in each stage. As we do so, you need to realize that teams and groups may not evolve in the straightforward manner shown.[26] For example, the competencies in team processes that members bring to the team could speed up or change its evolution.

Forming   In the forming stage, members focus on defining or understanding goals and developing procedures for performing their tasks. Team development in this stage involves getting acquainted and understanding leadership and other member roles. In terms of social behaviors it should also deal with members' feelings and the tendency of most members to depend too much on one or two other members. Otherwise, individual members might (1) keep feelings to themselves until they know the situation, (2) act more secure than they actually feel, (3) experience confusion and uncertainty about what is expected of them, (4) be nice and polite, or at least certainly not hostile, and (5) try to size up the personal benefits relative to the personal costs of being involved with the team or group.[27]

Storming   During the storming stage, conflicts emerge over work behaviors, relative priorities of goals, who is to be responsible for what, and the task-related guidance and direction of the leader. Social behaviors are a mixture of expressions of hostility and strong feelings. Competition over the leadership role and conflict over goals may dominate this stage. Some members may withdraw or try to isolate themselves from the emotional tension generated. The key is to man-

■ **FIGURE 8.1**

Stages of Team Development

Source: Adapted from Tuckman, B. W., and Jensen, M. A. C. Stages of small-group development revisited. *Groups and Organization Studies,* 1977, 2, 419–442; Kormanski, C. Team interventions: Moving the team forward. In J. W. Pfeiffer (ed.), *The 1996 Annual: Volume 2 Consulting.* San Diego: Pfeiffer and Company, 1996, 19–26.

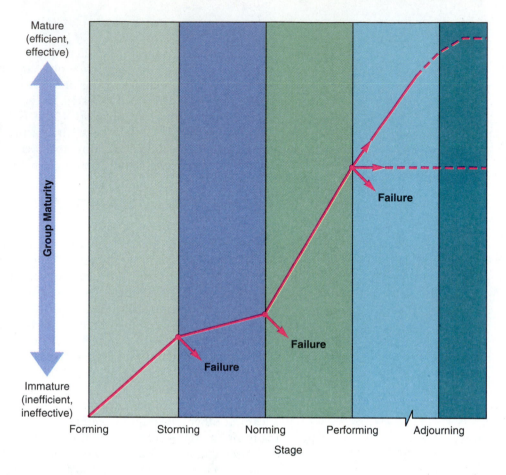

age conflict during this stage, not to suppress it or withdraw from it. The team can't effectively evolve into the third stage if its members go to either extreme. Suppressing conflict will likely create bitterness and resentment, which will last long after team members attempt to express their differences and emotions. Withdrawal may cause the team to fail.

This stage may be shortened or mostly avoided if the members use a team-building process from the beginning. This process involves the development of decision-making, interpersonal, and technical competencies when they are lacking. Team-building facilitators can help members work through the inevitable conflicts that will surface during this and the other stages.[28] When Honeywell created self-managed teams, even though the members had extensive training in how to work in teams, conflicts and shouting on the facility floor occurred when the teams first started making their own decisions.[29]

Norming   Work behaviors in the norming stage evolve into a sharing of information, acceptance of different options, and positive attempts to make decisions that may require compromise. During this stage, the team helps to set the rules by which it will operate. Social behaviors focus on empathy, concern, and positive expressions of feelings that lead to a sense of cohesion. Cooperation and a sense of shared responsibility develop among team members.

Performing   During the performing stage, the team shows how effectively and efficiently it can achieve results. The roles of individual members are accepted and understood. The members have learned when they should work independently and when they should help each other. The two dashed lines in Figure 8.1 suggest that teams may differ after the performing stage. Some teams continue to learn and develop from their experiences, becoming more efficient and effective. Other teams—especially those that developed norms not fully supportive of efficiency and effectiveness—may perform only at the level needed for their survival. Excessive self-oriented behaviors, development of norms that inhibit task effectiveness and efficiency, poor leadership, or other factors may hurt effectiveness.[30]

Adjourning   The termination of work behaviors and disengagement from social behaviors occurs in the adjourning stage. Some teams, such as a problem-solving team or a cross-functional team created to investigate and report on a specific issue within six months, have well-defined points of adjournment. Other teams, such as the functional teams at Macy's, may go on indefinitely. Macy's functional teams adjourn when top management decides to revise the team system. In terms of relations-oriented behaviors, some degree of adjourning occurs when team members resign or are reassigned.

The developmental stages of teams or groups—regardless of the framework used to describe and explain them—are not easy to traverse.[31] Failure can occur at any point in the sequence, as indicated in Figure 8.1. Several primary factors influence team or group behaviors and effectiveness. These influences help explain variations in outcomes between teams and within a specific team over time.

INFLUENCES ON TEAMS AND GROUPS

The factors that influence team and group outcomes, as you might expect, are interrelated. Figure 8.2 identifies seven of these factors. They should be analyzed both separately and in relation to each other. This approach is necessary to gain an understanding of team dynamics and outcomes and to develop the competencies needed to be effective team members and leaders.

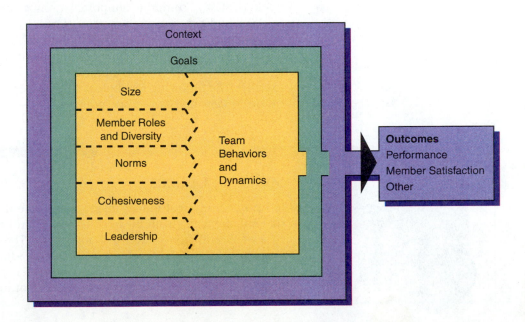

■ **FIGURE 8.2**

Some Influences on Team or Group Outcomes

■ CONTEXT

The **context** (external environment) can directly affect each of the six other factors shown in Figure 8.2 that influence team or group behaviors and outcomes. The context includes the conditions that apply to a team. The team's context might include technology, physical working conditions, management practices, formal organizational rules, influences of higher management, and organizational rewards and punishments. We focus here on one of the contextual influences that fundamentally shapes the ways individuals and teams work and interact, namely, the growing array of information technologies.

Information Technology   The term **information technology** refers to the means of assembling and electronically storing, transmitting, processing, and retrieving words, numbers, images, and sounds, as well as to the electronic means for controlling machines of all kinds—from everyday appliances to automated factories.[32] Information technology isn't just computers and computer software. It also includes communications aids (including telephone, video, and radio) and office equipment (such as word processors, copiers, and fax machines). If a company's management wants to introduce a technological change, such as automatically controlled machines, it might well turn the matter over to a problem-solving team. The team's investigation and findings will influence how this technology is introduced into the organization.

Groupware   Computer-based information technologies are beginning to have a significant impact on how team and group members network with each other. These technologies are part of a concept known as **groupware,** an approach to using specialized computer aids, communications tools, and designated physical facilities. Groupware helps teams work faster, share information, make decisions, and achieve their goals. Common groupware tools are the telephone, the computer (with software), real-time video capabilities, and the conference room. As is typical of rapidly developing technologies and approaches, these tools may initially be known by a variety of names. A few of the other names for groupware include computer-mediated communications, computer-supported cooperative work (CSCW), computer-supported groups, group decision support systems (GDSS), and group support systems (GSS).

Groupware tools revolve around four combinations of time and place.[33] Face-to-face networking involves the same time/same place combination. Obviously, it is the most common mix of time and place in terms of team members working together. The following Technology in Practice piece reveals one interesting application of *same time/same place* groupware.

TECHNOLOGY IN PRACTICE

Surfacing Options

Jeff Jury, an internal management consultant at Westinghouse, remembers getting an urgent call from the head of a $150 million per year manufacturing division of Westinghouse Electric Corporation. The division had reached a critical juncture. The top management team was deadlocked in its attempts to formulate a new strategic business plan. Jury called a meeting of the division's top managers. He took his laptop computer out of his briefcase, along with a dozen

—Continued

TECHNOLOGY IN PRACTICE—*Continued*

small electronic voting keypads. Within minutes, Jury had distributed one of the devices to every executive in the room. The keypads were linked by thin wires to the laptop, which was running a voting software application called Option-Finder.

Jury began probing the team's attitudes by asking questions about the division's fundamental strategy. Participants answered the questions by pressing the keypads in front of them. Questions included: "Are you trying to be a low-priced competitor?" "Do you differentiate on value?" and "Serve the entire market or just a niche?" Jury showed the executives the results, displayed in full-color graphs on an overhead projector. The team was stunned to find that "answers were scattered across the board, with absolutely no agreement or consensus," says Jury. "Yet if I'd asked them this question vocally, we probably wouldn't have gotten any challenge."

Through Option-Finder, team members can see not only which issues "won" but by how much—and whether the team is splintered. They can even calculate subgroups of agreement and disagreement according to preset characteristics of the attendees. Because the process is totally anonymous, people feel freer to express (vote) their own minds.[34]

The *same time/different place* combination comes into play when team members can't get together face-to-face because they work in different locations and travel time and costs are substantial. The conference call is the simplest form of groupware for meetings held at the same time in different locations. Also, participants can exchange personal computer (PC), fax, and graphic images and messages simultaneously with a conference call. Videoconferencing, a new groupware tool, is a dramatic application; its cost has fallen by a factor of 10 in recent years. With digital technology, the quality of images is improving rapidly. The New York City law firm of Parnon & Pratt LLP has several small law offices around the country. The firm pays for continuous video links among these offices. The cost is several thousand dollars a month. However, the link enables high-level talent at multiple locations to be available continuously to collaborate on difficult cases.[35]

On the surface, the *different time/same place* combination may be difficult to imagine. However, consider these examples. A team in a manufacturing plant could include members from different work shifts. A bedside workstation in a hospital may be served by a team of health care providers round the clock. The groupware tools most often used in this situation include voice mail and computers (including electronic mail, or e-mail). Shift workers may then need to meet face-to-face only infrequently, such as once a month.

The *different time/different place* combination is the most extreme and difficult configuration for team members. Groupware tools focus on storing and forwarding information about issues, making suggestions, and the like. Once again, e-mail and voice mail are commonly used groupware tools. Team members check into the system, see what has been entered since their last check, record comments, and leave the system. The main advantage of this use of groupware tools is flexibility, as gathering team members at the same time and place regularly may be difficult. Limitations of this method include stretching "meetings" out over time, not getting immediate feedback, and not being able to receive visual (including nonverbal) communication cues.

Because of the revolution in groupware tools, the work of teams and groups clearly is no longer limited to being in the same place at the same time.

■ GOALS

We discussed many aspects of goals in Chapter 6. Throughout the book, we return repeatedly to the concept that goals influence individual, team, and organizational outcomes. Obviously, individual and organizational goals are likely to influence team or group goals and behaviors in pursuit of these goals. **Team goals** are the outcomes desired for the team or group as a whole, not just the individual goals of the individual members.[36]

Both compatible and conflicting goals often exist within a team. Moreover, teams typically have both relations-oriented and task-oriented goals. Effective teams spend two-thirds or more of their time on task-oriented issues and roughly one-third or less of their time on relations-oriented issues. The pursuit of only one or the other type of goal over the long run can hurt performance, increase conflicts, and cause the team or group to disband. The influence of goals on group dynamics and outcomes becomes even more complex when the possible compatibilities and conflicts among member goals, broader team goals, and even broader organizational goals are considered.

One mechanism for dealing with these issues is **superordinate goals,** which two or more individuals, teams, or groups might pursue but can't be achieved without their interaction and cooperation.[37] Such goals do not replace or eliminate individual or team goals and may be qualitative or quantitative. An example of a qualitative goal is: We need to pull together for the good of the team. An example of a quantitative goal is: We need to work together if we are to reach the team goal of launching a new line within nine months. Superordinate goals are likely to have a more powerful effect on the willingness of individuals or teams to cooperate if they are accompanied by superordinate rewards. Superordinate rewards are the benefits received by members of the interacting and cooperating individuals or teams that are determined by the results of their joint efforts. The following Diversity in Practice selection provides an example of how self-managed teams, superordinate goals, and superordinate rewards can work together to achieve positive outcomes.

DIVERSITY IN PRACTICE

Standard Motor Products Reduces Barriers

For years, language barriers among production employees at Standard Motor Products (SMP)—an auto supply company in Edwardsville, Kansas—blocked communication between African-American and white production employees (who are actually in the minority) and the company's Latino and Asian employees. The introduction of English language classes, partially supported by SMP, didn't help because few production workers attended them. In the face of increasing foreign competition, SMP implemented self-managed teams to make operations more cost-efficient. Team members take responsibility, on a rotating basis, for various tasks. At some point, each member heads the team. Thus plant employees

—Continued

DIVERSITY IN PRACTICE—*Continued*

can no longer rely on a bilingual supervisor or claim language ignorance when something doesn't get done. Many employees, some of whom had been with the company for more than a decade, had to learn English for the first time.

Downtime at SMP has dropped by about 60 percent, according to Ernest Lewis, chairman of Local 710 of the United Auto Workers, which represents some 300 employees at the plant. "Work teams have allowed the communication lines to open. In the past, employees who didn't speak English would not participate or mingle with those who did," he says. "Now, productivity is up, along with camaraderie. There is more dialogue between individuals from diverse groups so they are learning more about each other," adds Lewis.

Generally, they're also earning more. The company implemented an employee gainsharing program. Quarterly cash awards are based on the amount of money the company saves on productivity, quality, returned products, and safety costs resulting from team efforts. Other factors such as attendance and customer satisfaction also affect how much an employee receives. In the first year, gainsharing awards averaged $2000 for each production employee.[38]

■ SIZE

The effective size of a team or group can range from two members to a normal upper limit of about sixteen members. Groupware tools such as e-mail and the Internet are enabling larger teams to work on some tasks. Twelve members probably is the largest size that allows each member to interact easily with every other member face-to-face.[39] Table 8.2 shows six dimensions of teams in terms of leader behaviors, member behaviors, and team process. The likely effects of team size on each dimension are highlighted. Note that members of teams of seven or less interact differently than do members of teams or groups of thirteen to sixteen. A sixteen-member board of directors will operate differently from a seven-member board. Large boards of directors often form committees of five to seven members to consider specific matters in greater depth than can the entire board.

As with all influences on teams, the effects identified in Table 8.2 need to be qualified.[40] For example, adequate time and sufficient member commitment to the team's goals and tasks might lead to better results from a team of eight or more members than from a hurried and less committed team of the same size. If a team's primary task is to tap the knowledge of the members and arrive at decisions based primarily on expertise rather than judgment, a larger team won't necessarily reflect the effects identified in Table 8.2.

■ MEMBER ROLES AND DIVERSITY

Similarities and differences among members and their roles influence team behavior, dynamics, and outcomes. Obviously, managers can't alter the basic personalities or attributes of team members (see Chapters 1 and 2). Therefore attempts to influence the behavioral roles in a team or group is more useful.[41] These roles may be formally classified as task-oriented, relations-oriented, and self-oriented. Each member has the potential for performing all of these roles over time.

TABLE 8.2 Typical Effects of Size on Teams

Dimension	TEAM SIZE		
	2–7 Members	8–12 Members	13–16 Members
1. Demands on leader	Low	Moderate	High
2. Direction by leader	Low	Low to moderate	Moderate to high
3. Member tolerance of direction by leader	Low to moderate	Moderate	High
4. Member inhibition	Low	Low to moderate	High
5. Formalization of rules and procedures	Low	Low to moderate	Moderate to high
6. Time required for reaching judgment decisions	Low to Moderate	Moderate	Moderate to high

Task-Oriented Role   The **task-oriented role** of a member involves facilitating and coordinating work-related decision making. This role may include

- *initiating* new ideas or different ways of considering team problems or goals and suggesting solutions to difficulties, including modification of team procedures;
- *seeking information* to clarify suggestions and obtain pertinent facts;
- *giving information* that is relevant to the team's problem or issue;
- *coordinating* and clarifying relationships among ideas and suggestions, pulling ideas and suggestions together, and coordinating members' activities; and
- *evaluating* the team's effectiveness, including questioning the logic, facts, or practicality of other members' suggestions.

Relations-Oriented Role   The **relations-oriented role** of a member involves building team-centered feelings and social interactions. This role may include

- *encouraging* members through praise and acceptance of their ideas, as well as indicating warmth and solidarity;
- *harmonizing* and mediating intrateam conflicts and tensions;
- *encouraging* participation of others by saying: Let's hear from Sue or Why not limit the length of contributions so all can react to the problem? or Rahul, do you agree?
- *expressing* standards for the team to achieve or apply in evaluating the quality of team processes, raising questions about team goals, and assessing team movement in light of these goals; and
- *following* by going along passively or constructively and serving as a friendly member.

Self-Oriented Role   The **self-oriented role** focuses only on a member's own (individual) needs, possibly at the expense of the team or group. This role may include

- *blocking progress* by being negative, stubborn, and unreasoningly resistant—for example, the person may repeatedly try to bring back an issue that the team had considered carefully and rejected;

- *seeking recognition* by calling attention to oneself, including boasting, reporting on personal achievements, and, in various ways, avoiding being placed in an inferior position;

- *dominating* by asserting authority, manipulating the team or certain individuals, using flattery or proclaiming superiority to gain attention, and interrupting the contributions of others; and

- *avoiding* involvement by maintaining distance from others, remaining insulated from interaction.

Effective problem-solving teams and groups often are composed of members who play both task-oriented and relations-oriented roles. Again, each individual may demonstrate various behaviors over time. A particularly adept individual who reveals behaviors valued by the team probably has relatively high *status*—the relative rank of an individual in a group or team. A team dominated by individuals who are performing mainly self-oriented behaviors is likely to be ineffective.

Table 8.3 provides a questionnaire for evaluating some of your task-oriented, relations-oriented, and self-oriented behaviors as a team member. The questionnaire asks you to assess your tendency to engage in each role, on a scale of 1 to 5 (or almost never to almost always). Member composition and roles greatly influence team or group behaviors. Either too much or too little of certain member behaviors can adversely affect team performance and member satisfaction.[42] Scores of 20–25 on task oriented behaviors, 16–20 on relations-oriented behaviors, and 3–6 on self-oriented behaviors by each member probably would indicate an effectively functioning team.

TABLE 8.3   Assessing Your Behaviors as a Team Member

	ALMOST NEVER	RARELY	SOMETIMES	OFTEN	ALMOST ALWAYS
Task-oriented behaviors: In this team, I . . .					
1. initiate ideas or actions.	1	2	3	4	5
2. facilitate the introduction of facts and information.	1	2	3	4	5
3. summarize and pull together various ideas.	1	2	3	4	5
4. keep the team working on the task.	1	2	3	4	5
5. ask whether the team is near a decision (determine consensus).	1	2	3	4	5
Relation-oriented behaviors: In this team, I . . .					
6. support and encourage others.	1	2	3	4	5
7. harmonize (keep the peace).	1	2	3	4	5
8. try to find common ground.	1	2	3	4	5
9. encourage participation.	1	2	3	4	5
Self-oriented behaviors: In this team, I . . .					
10. express hostility.	1	2	3	4	5
11. avoid involvement.	1	2	3	4	5
12. dominate the team.	1	2	3	4	5

Team Diversity   The growing diversity of the work force adds complexity—beyond individual differences in personality and behavioral roles in teams—to understanding team behavior and processes.[43] As discussed in previous chapters, the composition of the work force is undergoing continued change in terms of age, gender, race, cultural values, physical well-being, life-style preferences, ethnicity, educational background, religious preference, occupational background, and the like. Team effectiveness will be hampered if members hold false stereotypes about each other in terms of such differences.[44] As illustrated in the following Diversity in Practice feature, some organizations base diversity initiatives on ethical principles and implement them through team and group processes.

ETHICS IN PRACTICE

Texas Instrument's Ethics of Diversity

Texas Instruments (TI) states its ethical commitment to employees as: "We will expect the highest levels of performance and integrity from our people. We will create an environment where people are valued as individuals and treated with respect and dignity, fairness and equality. We will strive to create opportunities for them to develop and reach their full potential and to achieve their professional and personal goals." This vision aims to create an environment that recognizes understands, values, and utilizes the unique skills and abilities of all employees.

In addition to participating in awareness training, TI employees have formed various groups to help TI, and themselves, move toward full acceptance of diversity. To date, TI employees have formed some twenty different diversity groups for women, African-Americans, Hispanics, Asians, and others. The groups focus on issues facing them in the workplace and community.

One example is TI's African-American Employees Initiative. Initially, it was formed as a quality improvement team to focus on professional development, employee advancement, community action, and networking for TI's African-American employees. The group has five primary goals:

1. develop leadership skills, with special emphasis on diverse role modeling;
2. continue to develop the next generation of potential leaders for TI;
3. create a positive impact on perceptions and awareness of African-Americans' abilities;
4. establish a mentoring program for new employees; and
5. position TI to compete better in an increasingly diverse environment.

The company also has integrated diversity into its successful use of self-managed teams. Not only have self-managed teams made headway toward flattening the management hierarchy at TI, they have helped enrich cultural diversity at all levels.[45]

Although attitudes are changing in some organizations, diversity too often is viewed more negatively than positively. This negative reaction may be due, in large part, to six underlying attitudes involving stereotypical false assumptions.

1. Otherness is a deficiency.
2. Diversity poses a threat to the organization's effective functioning.
3. Expressed discomfort with the dominant group's values is perceived as oversensitivity by the minority groups.
4. Members of all groups want to become and should be more like the dominant group.
5. Equal treatment means the same treatment.
6. Managing diversity simply requires changing the people, not the organizational culture.[46]

The goal of achieving diversity creates unique challenges in making it work for rather than against the long-term interests of individuals, teams, and organizations. Once a we–they distinction is perceived, people tend to discriminate against others who are different. Moreover, they tend to perceive these others as inferior, adversaries, and competitive.[47]

The attitude expressed throughout this book about diversity is that of **positive multiculturalism.** This condition allows an individual to acquire new skills, perspectives, and attitudes that improve that person's chances of relating effectively to others within the same or other teams and groups—regardless of their backgrounds and characteristics. Positive multiculturalism is additive; that is, individuals can maintain their self-defining attributes, while adding competencies and positive attitudes to help them form and maintain work relationships with others. Thus a person can become bilingual by learning English but retain a native language, as at SMP.[48] Positive multiculturalism at TI is expressed this way:

> Texas Instruments recognizes that a diverse empowered work force is a means for achieving a sustained competitive business advantage. Because of this belief, TI has taken great strides in recent years on its journey toward not only embracing diversity, but weaving it through the very fabric of the corporation.[49]

■ NORMS

Norms are the rules and patterns of behavior that are accepted and expected by members of a team or group.[50] They help define the behaviors that members believe to be necessary to help them reach their goals. Over time, every team or group establishes norms and enforces them on its members. Such norms may further or inhibit achievement of organizational goals.

Norms Versus Organizational Rules   Norms differ from organizational rules. Managers may write and distribute formal organizational rules to employees in the form of manuals and memorandums. At times, employees refuse to accept such rules and ignore them. In contrast, norms are informal, often unwritten expectations that are enforced by team or group members. If a member consistently and excessively violates the team's or group's norms, the other members sanction the individual in some way. Sanctions may range from physical abuse to threats to ostracism to positive inducements (rewards) for compliance. Those who consistently adhere to the team's or group's norms typically receive praise, recognition, and acceptance from the other members.

Members may be only vaguely aware of some of the norms that operate in their team or group. They should be made aware of these norms for at least two reasons. First, awareness increases the potential for individual and group freedom and maturity. Second, norms can positively or negatively influence the effectiveness of individuals, teams, and organization.[51] For example, group norms of minimizing and correcting defects are likely to reinforce an organization's formal quality standards.

Relation to Goals   Teams often adopt norms to help them attain their goals.[52] Moreover, some organizational development efforts are aimed at helping members evaluate whether their team's norms are consistent with, neutral with respect to, or conflict with organizational goals. (See Chapter 18 for a discussion of organizational development.) For example, a team may claim that one of its goals is to become more efficient to help it meet organizational goals. However, the team members' behaviors might reveal norms inconsistent with this stated goal; that is, the norms might actually inhibit production and making changes.

Even if team members are aware of such norms, they may rationalize them as being necessary in order to achieve their own goals. Members may claim that producing more than the norm will "burn them out" or reduce product or service quality, resulting in lower long-term effectiveness. If a team's goals include minimizing managerial influence and increasing the opportunity for social interaction, its members could perceive norms restricting employee output as desirable.

Enforcing Norms   Teams and groups don't establish norms for every conceivable situation. They generally form and enforce norms with respect to behaviors that they believe to be particularly important. Members are most likely to enforce norms under one or more of the following conditions.[53]

- The norms aid in group survival and provide benefits. For instance, a team might develop a norm not to discuss individual salaries with other members in the organization to avoid calling attention to pay inequities in the team.
- The norms simplify or make predictable the behaviors expected of members. When colleagues go out for lunch together, there can be some awkwardness about how to split the bill at the end of the meal. A group may develop a norm that results in some highly predictable way of behaving: Split the bill evenly, take turns picking up the tab, or individually pay for what each ordered.
- The norms help avoid embarrassing interpersonal situations. There might be norms about not discussing romantic involvements (so that differences in moral values don't become too obvious) or about not getting together socially in members' homes (so that differences in taste or income don't become too obvious).

Norms express the central values and goals of the team or group and clarify what is distinctive about its identity. Employees of an advertising agency may wear unconventional but stylish clothing. Other professionals may view their doing so as deviant behavior. However, the advertising agency personnel may say, We think of ourselves, personally and professionally, as trendsetters, and being fashionably dressed conveys that to our clients and the public.

Conforming to Norms   The pressures to adhere to norms may result in conformity.[54] The two basic types of conformity are compliance and personal acceptance. **Compliance conformity** occurs when a person's behavior reflects the team's or group's desired behavior because of real or imagined pressure. In fact, some individuals may conform for a variety of reasons, even though they don't personally agree with the norms. They may think that the appearance of a united front is necessary for success in accomplishing group goals. On a more personal level, someone may comply in order to be liked and accepted by others. Meeting this need may apply especially to members of lower status in relation to those of higher status, such as a subordinate and a superior. Finally, someone may comply because the costs of conformity are much less than the costs of nonconformity, which could threaten the personal relationships in the group or team.

The second type of conformity is based on positive personal support of the norms. In **personal acceptance conformity**, the individual's behavior and attitudes are consistent with the team's or group's norms and goals. This type of conformity is much stronger than compliance conformity because the person truly believes in the goals and norms. At its Camry assembly plant in Georgetown, Kentucky, Toyota makes explicit use of teams to develop norms and peer pressure in support of organizational goals. Management makes extensive use of *community of fate* as a superordinate goal at all levels—that is, we're all in this together—as a means of achieving personal acceptance conformity.[55]

All of the preceding helps explain why some members of highly conforming teams and groups may easily change their behavior (compliance type of conformity), whereas others may oppose changes and find them highly stressful (personal acceptance type of conformity). Without norms and reasonable conformity to them, teams would be chaotic, and few tasks could be accomplished. Conversely, excessive and blind conformity may threaten expressions of individualism and a team's ability to change and learn.

■ COHESIVENESS

Cohesiveness reflects the strength of the members' desire to remain in the team or group and their commitment to it. It is influenced by the degree of compatibility between group goals and individual members' goals. Members who have a strong desire to remain in the group and personally accept its goals form highly cohesive teams or groups.

This relationship between cohesiveness and conformity isn't a simple one. Low cohesiveness usually is associated with low conformity. However, high cohesiveness doesn't exist only in the presence of high conformity. High performing teams may have high member commitment and a desire to stick together while simultaneously respecting and encouraging individual differences in behavior and thought. This situation is more likely to develop when cohesion is based on a common commitment to performance goals. In confronting complex problems, members of a cohesive team are likely to encourage and support nonconformity.[56] A **hot group** is one such example. Such a group performs extremely well and is dedicated; it usually is small, and its members are turned on by an exciting and challenging goal. Hot groups completely engage their members, capturing their attention to the exclusion of almost everything else. Whether it is called a team, a committee, or even a task force, the characteristics of a hot group are the same: vital, absorbing, full of debate and laughter, and very hard working.[57] They may arise from the need for dealing with major challenges and changes, innovation, complex projects, or crises. For example, development of the Boeing 777 spawned some hot groups.

Relation to Groupthink   When decision-making teams are both conforming and cohesive, a phenomenon called groupthink can emerge. **Groupthink** is an agreement-at-any-cost mentality that results in ineffective team decision making

■ FIGURE 8.3   The Groupthink Process

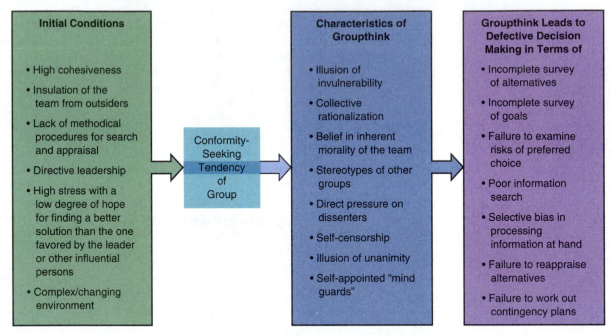

and poor decisions. Irving L. Janis, who coined the term, focused his research on high-level government policy teams faced with difficult problems in a complex and dynamic environment. Team decision making is common in all types of organizations, so the possibility of groupthink exists in both private-sector and public-sector organizations. Figure 8.3 outlines the initial conditions that are likely to lead to groupthink, its characteristics, and the types of defective decision making that result from it.

The characteristics of groupthink include the following.

■ An *illusion of invulnerability* is shared by most or all team members, which creates excessive optimism and encourages taking extreme risks. Statements such as No one can stop us now or The other group has a bunch of jerks often are made by members suffering from an illusion of invulnerability.

■ *Collective rationalization* discounts warnings that might lead the members to reconsider their assumptions before committing themselves to major policy decisions. Statements such as "We are confident that only a small segment of auto buyers are willing to buy Japanese-made autos" were made by U.S. auto executives in the early 1970s.

■ An *unquestioned belief* in the team's inherent morality leads members to ignore the ethical or moral consequences of their decisions.

■ *Stereotypical views* of rivals and enemies (other groups) picture them as too evil to warrant genuine attempts to negotiate or too weak or stupid to counter whatever attempts are made to defeat their purpose.

■ *Direct pressure* is exerted on any member who expresses strong arguments against any of the team's illusions, stereotypes, or commitments, making clear that such dissent is contrary to what is expected of all loyal members. The leader might say, What's the matter? Aren't you a team member anymore?

- *Self-censorship* of deviations from any apparent team consensus reflects the inclination of members to minimize the importance of their doubts and not present counter-arguments. A member might think, If everyone feels that way, my feelings must be wrong.

- A *shared illusion of unanimity* results, in part, from self-censorship and is reinforced by the false assumption that silence implies consent.

- The emergence of *self-appointed "mind-guard"* members serves to protect the team from adverse information that might shatter the shared complacency about the effectiveness and morality of their decision.[58]

In a recent study of twenty-three top management teams, the chief executive officers (CEOs) of six expressed concern about groupthink in their teams. The CEOs of a large financial retailing company and a global financial services firm commented:

> We're all too much on the same wavelength. We were all part of a management buyout four years ago. We've been through some tough battles together, and now we share a lot of common views. But in this industry you have to be fresh and experimental. If we all agree on everything, how new or exciting can our ideas be?
>
> There's a lack of genuine debate. Sometimes there's a half-hearted "devil's advocate" gesture, but they really don't confront each other or me on the big issues. We're too comfortable, too self-congratulatory. It's gotten obvious to me in the past few months. I have to find a way to shake things up.[59]

Groupthink isn't inevitable, and several steps can be taken to avoid it. For example, a leader should try to remain neutral and encourage dialogue and new ideas. Small subgroups or outside consultants can be used to introduce new viewpoints. People holding diverse views can be encouraged to present them.

Impact on Outcomes   Cohesiveness is important because it can affect both team performance and productivity. **Productivity** is the relationship between the inputs consumed (labor hours, raw materials, money, machines, and the like) and the outputs created (quantity and quality of goods and services). Cohesiveness and productivity can be interrelated, particularly for teams having high performance goals. If the team is successful in reaching those goals, the positive feedback of its successes may heighten member commitment and satisfaction. For example, a winning basketball team is more likely to be cohesive than one with a poor record, everything else being equal. Also, a cohesive basketball team may be more likely to win games. Conversely, low cohesiveness may interfere with a team's ability to achieve its goals. The reason is that members aren't as likely to communicate and cooperate to the extent necessary to reach the team's goals. High team cohesiveness actually may be associated with low efficiency if team goals conflict with organizational goals. Team members might think that the boss holds them accountable rather than that they hold themselves accountable to achieve results. Therefore the relationships among cohesiveness, productivity, and performance can't be anticipated or understood unless the team's goals and norms are also known.

■ LEADERSHIP

Studies of teams and small groups in organizations emphasize the importance of emergent, or informal, leadership in accomplishing goals. An **informal leader** is an individual whose influence in the group grows over time and usually reflects a unique ability to help the group reach its goals.

Multiple Leaders   Team or group leadership is often thought of in terms of one person. Recall that self-managed teams usually are very flexible in terms of having different leaders over time and for different tasks. Moreover, because a group often has both relations-oriented and task-oriented goals, it may have two or more leaders. The reason is that achieving these two types of goals may require different skills and leadership styles, creating a total set of demands that one person may have difficulty satisfying.[60] Informal leaders of work teams aren't likely to emerge unless the formal leader ignores task-related responsibilities or lacks the necessary skills to carry them out.[61] In contrast, relations-oriented leaders of task groups are likely to emerge informally.

Effective Team Leaders   Leaders greatly influence virtually all aspects of team or group composition and behaviors (such as size, members and roles, norms, goals, and context). A leader often assumes a key role in the relations between the team and external groups or higher management and often influences the selection of new members. Even when the team participates in the selection process, the team leader may screen potential members, thereby limiting the number and range of candidates.

Based on the seven key influences on team and group behaviors and dynamics reviewed so far (see Figure 8.2), the creation and maintenance of effective teams clearly is no easy leadership task. We discuss leadership and the qualities and characteristics of effective leaders in detail in Chapters 10 and 11.

TEAM DECISION MAKING

In an organization, the many different types of goals, problems, and tasks confronted require varying degrees of interdependency among individuals, teams, and external groups. Dealing with them requires both individual and team decision making. Organizations can incur excessive costs if either individual or team decision-making approaches are used improperly. The unnecessary use of team decision making is wasteful because the participants' time could have been used more effectively on other tasks; it creates boredom, resulting in a feeling that time is being squandered, and reduces motivation. Conversely, the improper use of individual decision making can result in poor coordination, less creativity, and more errors.[62] In brief, team decision making is likely to be superior to individual decision making when (1) the greater diversity of information, experience, and approaches to be found in a team are important to the tasks at hand; (2) acceptance of the decisions arrived at is crucial for effective implementation by team members; (3) participation is important for reinforcing the democratic values of representation versus authoritarianism and demonstrating respect for individual members through team processes; and (4) the team members rely on each other in performing their jobs.

■ SELF-MANAGING TEAM MODEL

What does the process of effective team decision making involve when a team has been fully empowered? Figure 8.4 shows one possible model for effective self-managing team decision making.[63] Its use may improve decision making in all types of teams—from a class project team to the cross-functional teams at Macy's to the self-managed teams at Honeywell, Standard Motor Products, and Texas Instruments. The model is based on the assumption that the team has achieved

■ FIGURE 8.4   *Self-Managing Team Model*

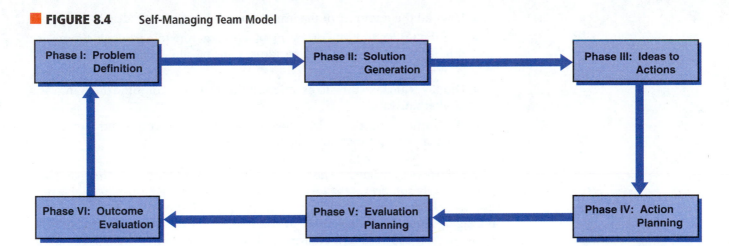

the performing stage of development (see Figure 8.1). In general, self-managed teams are empowered to engage regularly in all phases of decision making, as depicted in the model.

Phase I: Problem Definition   Team members may assume that they know what the problem is in a situation, but they may be wrong. They could be looking at only a symptom or a part of the problem. In phase I, a self-managing team should fully explore, clarify, and define the problem. Even when it has correctly identified the problem, the team may need to collect more detailed information and define it more sharply. Thus a key part of problem definition is the generation and collection of information. Problem definition also requires that the team identify or recognize the goals that it is trying to achieve by solving the problem. When team members are clear about goals—which in itself may be a major problem area—they can determine better whether the problem really exists and, if it does, the relative priority that should be assigned to solving it. If members can respond *yes* to questions such as the following, the team dynamics involved in phase I probably were effective.

- Was everyone who might have relevant data present or represented at the team meeting?
- Were those most directly involved in defining the problem encouraged by the leader and other team members to give information?
- Did the team take the information relating to the problem and consider how it all fits together?
- Was everyone asked whether he or she agrees with the final problem statement as written?

Phase II: Solution Generation   Teams may tend to be more solution-oriented than problem-oriented. They may choose the first or one of the first solutions suggested. Phase II prolongs the idea-generating process and discourages premature conclusions. An eventual solution can be much better if the self-managing team considers many ideas and several alternative solutions. The more ideas generated and creativity encouraged, the more likely the team is to come up with good potential solutions. The team dynamics involved in phase II probably were effective if members can respond *yes* to questions such as the following.

- Have all the resources of the team been used to generate ideas?

- Did the leader and other team members take time to encourage those who might be slower at expressing ideas, pausing and asking for more ideas when necessary?

- Did the team take time to examine all the ideas and combine them into sets of alternatives?

- Was criticism tactfully discouraged and evaluative comments postponed (such as asking for another alternative instead of criticism)?

Phase III: Ideas to Actions   The team's evaluation of ideas and alternatives leading to a likely solution is the focus of phase III. Even though one alternative may not work alone, it could provide a useful part of the solution. Thus a self-managing team should take time to combine the best parts of alternative solutions. It then can carefully evaluate each possibility. Rather than weeding out poor alternatives (and making those who suggested them feel defensive), the team should select the best ones and concentrate on them until everyone can agree on a solution or recognize the need to move on. A *yes* to questions such as the following suggests that team dynamics were on target in phase III.

- Did the team examine the alternatives in terms of human, financial, and other costs associated with each and in terms of new problems that might arise?

- Was the team able to evaluate ideas critically without attacking individuals who proposed or supported those ideas?

- Is the chosen solution related to the problem statement and goals developed earlier?

- Was final consensus reached on a trial solution? If not, was the extent of agreement among team members clearly established?

Phase IV: Action Planning   This phase involves deciding on the actions needed to make the plan work smoothly. A self-managing team should anticipate implementation problems, make plans to involve those whose support will be needed, and assign and accept responsibilities for taking action. Only if the team determines who is to do what and when can the agreed-on solution get a fair test. Key questions requiring a *yes* response in phase IV include the following.

- Did the team identify the various forces that might help or hinder the actions being planned?

- Were all team members involved in the discussion, particularly in giving information needed to define actions and ensure that essential steps weren't left out?

- Were all the needed resources (material as well as human, including people not present) for taking each of the actions clearly identified?

- Did each person who accepted responsibility for a task make a clear commitment to carry out that responsibility?

Phase V: Evaluation Planning   Sometimes teams stop at phase IV, losing the chance to learn from experience. Even if a solution is a tremendous success, a team benefits from knowing what made the solution work so that it can be applied, when appropriate, to the solution of other problems. If a solution is a total disaster, team members may feel like hiding the fact that they had anything to do with it. However, a self-managing team that knows what went wrong can avoid making the same mistakes in the future. In real life, solutions generally work moderately well; most are neither great successes nor great failures. By keeping track of what is happening, a team can make minor improvements or adjustments that will help significantly in other team problem-solving efforts. Diagnosis should not be based on guesswork but on hard, accurate information about the effect of actions. Evaluation planning offers the greatest potential for team learning in decision making. To take advantage of this opportunity, a team must determine the type of information needed, who will obtain it, and when it must be collected. Questions requiring a *yes* response for effective team dynamics in phase V include the following.

- Has the team reviewed the desired outcomes and developed measures to indicate the degree of success achieved in attaining the outcomes?
- Were any differences among team members regarding definitions and measures of success openly discussed, explored, and resolved?
- Were contingency plans outlined for critical steps so that the overall plan could continue with modification but without major interruption?
- Was a timetable developed for step-by-step interim evaluation (monitoring of effects as actions were taken)?

Phase VI: Outcome Evaluation   When enough information has been collected to evaluate how well the solution worked, a self-managing team should make a comprehensive evaluation of the outcome. The outcome demonstrates whether the problem was solved. If the problem or some part of it remains, the team can recycle it by looking at the information, perhaps even redefining the problem, and coming up with new ideas or trying a previously rejected alternative. This phase also involves a review and evaluation of how well the team members worked together. As we suggested in the discussion of team development stages, mature teams and groups can openly and constructively evaluate outcomes. A response of *yes* to each of the following questions indicates effective team dynamics during phase VI.

- Was the team able to compare, in detail, the outcomes with the goals set earlier?
- Were all team members involved in influencing both what the team did and how the team operated?
- Did the team determine whether any new problems were created and, if so, then make plans to deal with them?
- Did the team learn to solve problems in accordance with this model (Figure 8.4)?

■ ASSESSMENT OF MODEL

Team decision making rarely proceeds so neatly or systematically as suggested in the descriptions of these six phases.[64] Self-managed and other types of empowered teams may jump around or skip phases because of the nature of the problem being solved or the team's makeup. However, this self-managing team decision-making model, if followed as closely as possible, should improve the decision making of most teams. It stresses the need for competence and a norm of full participation by members during the process. Teams and other types of groups—even if operating properly—probably are more effective in phase III (ideas to actions) through phase V (evaluation planning) than in phases I, II, and VI. Phase I (problem definition) and phase II (solution generation) benefit from processes different from the usual face-to-face interactions of individuals.

In addition to those suggested here, various other processes and procedures have been developed for improving the effectiveness of decision-making teams. For example, in the last section of this chapter, we consider two aids especially designed to improve team effectiveness in phases I and II. First, however, we present an Across Cultures feature to demonstrate the commonalities that may exist in the use of teams in different cultures. This feature is based on the views of Lee Crawford, who has been the managing director of General Motors' Delphi Packard Electric Division in Mexico since 1986. He is based in Ciudad Juarez and has overall responsibility for twenty-two manufacturing operations in Mexico that employ 20,000 workers.

ACROSS CULTURES

General Motors Work Teams in Mexico

You have to blend your management style to the situation you are in. In Ohio, I was very participatory. When I came here, I had to become sort of a benevolent dictator for a period of time. I think we as a company have evolved now through understanding and education and training of the Mexican managers. Now, I am more participatory again. But I can be very flexible. I can be a benevolent dictator or totally participatory. I would say that my style overall is more participatory. I have seen the Mexican managers mature. As they have matured, they have gained confidence in their management style, and we have been able to phase in more participatory management.

The plants that are actually the farthest along in terms of teams, self-managed teams, are in the interior. Our Meoqui plant is our shining star. It is 100 percent work teams. I think that teams work well in the interior because a more family atmosphere exists there. We saw what was happening on the border. We saw what was happening at that point in time, the high turnover and high growth in Juarez. We just thought it would be better to go to the interior. We made the plants smaller than the original plants on the border. That was by design. For example, Casas Grandes is one community where we have a small plant. People there know each other. A lot of families work in the plants. When we went to the interior, we intended to stay out of industrial parks and instead to go into neighborhoods. Another example is our Los Mochis plant. In Los Mochis, most of the people walk to work. Most of them are brothers and sisters. There is a lot more esprit de corps there than on the border.

We are doing the same thing in the interior that we are doing in some plants in the States. There we have plants that have no supervisors. People want to be involved. They want to be committed. We can take work teams from here and take them to Mississippi. We have actually done this. Everybody had told us that Mexican workers require a benevolent dictator; that you can't use work teams. We proved them wrong.[65]

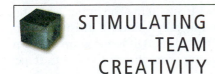

STIMULATING TEAM CREATIVITY

Let's now turn to two approaches for stimulating team and group creativity. These approaches can assist team members with problem definition (phase I), solution generation (phase II), and the initial part of the ideas to action phase (phase III) in the self-managing decision-making model (see Figure 8.4).

■ NOMINAL GROUP TECHNIQUE

The **nominal group technique** (NGT) is a structured process designed to stimulate creative team decision making where agreement is lacking or the members have incomplete knowledge of the nature of the problem. This technique has a special purpose: to make individual judgments the essential inputs in arriving at a team decision. That is, members must pool their judgments in order to solve the problem and determine a satisfactory course of action.

The NGT is most beneficial for (1) identifying the crucial variables in a specific situation; (2) identifying key elements of a plan designed to implement a particular solution to some problem; or (3) establishing priorities with regard to the problem to be addressed and goals to be attained. The NGT isn't particularly well suited for routine team meetings that focus primarily on task coordination or information exchange. Nor is it usually appropriate for the negotiating that takes place in counteracting groups (such as a union and management committee, if the parties have conflicting goals). The NGT consists of four distinct stages: generating ideas, recording ideas, clarifying ideas, and voting on ideas.[66] Various suggestions have been made for modifying or tailoring these stages to specific situations.[67]

Generating Ideas   The first stage in the process is to have the members generate ideas. Each participant separately writes down ideas in response to a statement of the problem, a stimulus question, or some other central focus of the team. A question could be something as simple as: What problems do you think we should consider over the next year? Followed by, take five minutes to write some of your own ideas on the piece of paper in front of you. The generation of ideas or solutions privately by team members avoids the direct pressures of status differences or competition among members to be heard. Yet it retains some of the peer and creative tension in the individual generated by the presence of others. This stage and the subsequent stages provide time for thinking and reflection to avoid premature choices among ideas.[68]

Recording Ideas   The second stage is to record one idea (generated in the first stage) from each group member in turn on a flip chart or other device visible to all team members. A variation is to have members submit their ideas anonymously on index cards. The process continues until the team members are satisfied that the list reflects all the ideas individually generated. This round-robin approach emphasizes equal participation by the members and avoids losing ideas that individuals consider significant. Listing the ideas for everyone to see depersonalizes the ideas and reduces the potential for unnecessary conflict. Team members often are impressed and pleased with the list of ideas presented, which provides momentum and enthusiasm for continuing the process.

Clarifying Ideas   The team then discusses in turn each idea on the list during the third stage. The purpose of this discussion is to clarify the meaning of each idea and allow team members to agree or disagree with any item. The intent is to present the logic behind the ideas and minimize misunderstanding. It isn't to win arguments concerning the relative merits of the ideas. Differences of opinion aren't resolved at this stage, but rather by the voting procedure in the fourth stage.

Voting on Ideas   Using the list developed, which may contain at least twelve and perhaps as many as thirty ideas, the team may proceed in one of several ways. Perhaps the most common is a voting procedure that has the team members individually select a specific number (say, five) of the ideas that they believe are the most important. Each person writes these five ideas on individual index cards. The team leader then asks the members to rank their items from most to least important. The index cards are collected and the votes tabulated to produce a priority list. An alternative to this single vote is to feed back the results of a first vote, allow time for discussion of the results, and then vote again. Feedback and discussion are likely to result in a final decision that most closely reflects the members' actual preferences.

Regardless of format, the voting procedure determines the outcome of the meeting: a team decision that incorporates the individual judgments of the participants. The procedure is designed to document the collective decision and provide a sense of accomplishment and closure.

Assessment of the Nominal Group Technique   The advantages of the NGT over traditional team discussion include greater emphasis and attention to idea generation, increased attention to each idea, and greater likelihood of balanced participation by each member. Nominal groups may not be superior when the task of problem identification is performed by people who are both aware of existing problems and willing to communicate them. The approach may be most effective when certain blockages or problems exist in a team, such as domination by a few team members.

◼ BRAINSTORMING

Traditional Brainstorming   Usually done with five to twelve people, **brainstorming** is a process in which individuals state as many ideas as possible during a twenty to sixty minute period. Guidelines for brainstorming include (1) the wilder the ideas the better, (2) don't be critical of any ideas, and (3) hitchhike on or combine previously stated ideas. The group setting for brainstorming was supposed to generate many more and better ideas than if the same number of individuals worked alone.[69] However, research indicates that brainstorming isn't nearly as effective as once thought. In fact, the nominal group technique has proven to be much more effective than traditional brainstorming as an aid for generating ideas.[70]

To brainstorm effectively is to think of an idea, express it, and get on with thinking of and expressing more new ideas. In face-to-face brainstorming, however, people may be prevented from doing so because someone else is talking. As a result, team members may get bogged down waiting for other people to finish talking. Team members also may be anxious about how others will view them if they express their ideas. This problem may be particularly acute when ideas can be interpreted as critical of current practice or when superiors or others who may affect team members' futures are present. Withholding ideas for these reasons defeats the purpose of brainstorming.[71] Electronic brainstorming is a type of groupware that can reduce such problems.

Electronic Brainstorming   In **electronic Brainstorming,** computer technology is used to enter and automatically disseminate ideas in real time to all team members, each of whom may be stimulated to generate other ideas. For example, GroupSystems has a software tool called Electronic Brainstorming. For this approach to work, each member must have a computer terminal that is connected to all other members' terminals. The software allows individuals to enter their ideas as they think of them. Every time an individual enters an idea, a random set of the team's ideas is presented on each person's screen. The individual can continue to see new random sets of ideas at will by pressing the appropriate key.[72]

Preliminary research on electronic brainstorming is encouraging. Electronic brainstorming tends to produce significantly more fresh ideas than traditional brainstorming.[73] It also removes the main barrier of traditional brainstorming: members seeing and hearing which ideas are whose; that is, it permits anonymity and thus lets team members contribute more freely to idea generation. They need not fear "sounding like a fool" to other employees and managers when spontaneously generating ideas. These advantages appear to be greater for teams of seven or more people.[74] The following Technology in Practice account reveals how the elements of brainstorming, the nominal group technique, and the ideas to action phase of team decision making may be integrated by means of several groupware tools.

TECHNOLOGY IN PRACTICE

Brainstorming at North American Life and Casualty

Jim Westland, regional vice-president of North American Life and Casualty (NALC), decided that fresh ideas were needed about ways to cut costs and improve efficiency at the northeast regional office. He decided to gather his senior management team and selected lower level employees at a one-day, electronic brainstorming session at a local university's computer-supported decision center. The team consisted of seven senior managers, two clerical staff, and one sales representative. The day began with an electronic brainstorming session. The question was: How can we cut costs at NALC? The process started tentatively, with people typing in an idea and hitting a function key to enter it. People saw a random selection of their own and other people's ideas on their screens to help them think of other ideas. Suddenly everyone was typing and entering ideas. In twenty minutes, the team produced more than eighty-five cost-cutting ideas.

The team used the Idea Organizer software tool to put the ideas into categories for easier evaluation. Each person scanned the ideas and created categories, which appeared on a large screen at the front of the room. There were some common, well-defined categories, and most participants agreed about how the ideas fit into them. The outcome of the process was a list of forty-nine ideas divided into seven categories. Each person rated each idea in the first category on feasibility and benefits (using a 10-point scale). Then the software collected the ratings and displayed them for the team on the large screen.

The participants decided that two ideas were outstanding and should be implemented immediately. They rated ideas in the rest of the categories (with a
—*Continued*

TECHNOLOGY IN PRACTICE—*Continued*

break for lunch) and selected six more good ideas. Then they fleshed out these eight ideas and assigned responsibilities for implementing them, using the Topic Commentator tool.[75]

CHAPTER SUMMARY

Teams and groups have far-reaching effects on organizations and life in general. The cultural belief in individualism can cause an uneasiness over their possible impacts on people's lives. One potential source of tension between group and individual interests is that of the free rider.

Teams and groups are classified in numerous ways. In organizations, a basic classification is by the group's primary purpose, including friendship groups and task groups. Task groups may be classified further as counteracting, coacting, or interacting. The four types of interacting teams discussed were functional teams, problem-solving teams, cross-functional teams, and self-managed teams.

Several models for understanding the developmental sequence of teams and groups are available. The five-stage developmental model focuses on forming, storming, norming, performing, and adjourning. The issues and challenges a team faces change with each stage.

Team dynamics and outcomes are affected by the interplay of context, goals, size, member roles, norms, cohesiveness, and leadership. One type of changing contextual influence on how teams work, interact, and network with other teams is that of information technology, especially the rapid developments in group-ware tools. Teams no longer are limited to face-to-face meetings (same time/same place) in carrying out their tasks and goals. Member behavioral roles may be task-oriented, relations-oriented, or self-oriented. Norms differ from rules in important ways and can positively or negatively affect performance. The pressures to adhere to norms may result in either compliance conformity or personal acceptance conformity. Another factor affecting teams or groups is cohesiveness, which is related to conformity, groupthink, and productivity. Team leaders may be selected formally or emerge informally.

Three approaches to improving team decision making and creativity are the self-managing team decision-making model, the nominal group technique, and brainstorming. They can help both team members and leaders become more effective. Key factors involved in the use of team decision making include when to use team decision making versus individual decision making; the relationship between team processes and the team's relative autonomy and empowerment; and suggestions for improving team processes and creativity to increase performance outcomes and member satisfaction.

KEY TERMS AND CONCEPTS

Brainstorming	Cohesiveness	Context
Coacting group	Collectivism	Counteracting group
Coalition	Compliance conformity	Cross-functional teams

Electronic brainstorming	Informal leader	Relations-oriented role
Free rider	Information technology	Self-managed teams
Friendship group	Interacting group	Self-oriented role
Functional teams	Nominal group technique	Superordinate goals
Group	Norms	Task group
Groupthink	Personal acceptance conformity	Task-oriented role
Groupware	Positive multiculturalism	Team
Hot group	Problem-solving teams	Team goals
Individualism	Productivity	

DISCUSSION QUESTIONS

1. Think about a team of which you have been a member. Were there any free riders on the team? Why was free riding present or not present?

2. For the same team, was there any evidence that the team evolved according to the five-stage developmental sequence presented in Figure 8.1?

3. What were the effects of the size of that team in terms of the dimensions shown in Table 8.2? Were these effects consistent with those predicted in Table 8.2?

4. Was it a self-managed team? Use Table 8.1 to explain your answer.

5. For another team or group of which you have been a member, describe its environment (context) in terms of technology, organizational rules, influence of higher level management, and organizational rewards and punishments. In what ways did the context appear to affect the team's or group's dynamics and outcomes?

6. What were the formal and informal goals of this team or group? Were the informal goals consistent and supportive of the formal goals? Explain.

7. How would you describe this team or group as a whole in terms of task-oriented behaviors, relations-oriented behaviors, and self-oriented behaviors? Which of the behaviors seemed to contribute the most to its performance? The least?

8. State three possible norms of positive multiculturism of a team or group of which you have been a member. Did you or other members conform to these norms on the basis of compliance or personal acceptance? Explain.

9. The self-managing decision-making model depicted in Figure 8.4 presents a phased sequence that empowered teams can follow. How may the factors identified in Figure 8.2 work for or against the use of this model?

10. What are the similarities and differences between the nominal group technique (NGT) and electronic brainstorming?

■ Developing Competencies

Team Insight: Assessing Team Diversity

Instructions

Think of a work-related team or group and organization of which you have been or are a member. Some of the following statements focus on the overall work environment (context) and others on your specific work team or group. The statements are worded as if you were still an employee of this organization, which may or may not be the case. Use a scale of 10 to 1 to indicate how strongly you agree with the statements (10 is strongly agree and 1 strongly disagree).

> SA = Strongly Agree (10)
>
> A = Agree (7)
>
> N = Neutral (5)

> D = Disagree (3)
>
> SD = Strongly disagree (1)

	SA	A	N	D	SD
1. If someone who is not included in the mainstream tries to get information or makes a request, others stall or avoid helping them out in subtle ways.	10	7	5	3	1
2. It seems that the real reason people are denied promotions or raises is that they are seen as not fitting in.	10	7	5	3	1
3. Some people have to prove themselves more and work a lot harder					

to get into that next position because of their gender, race, or ethnic background.   10   7   5   3   1

4. When people from different backgrounds work together in groups, some people feel slighted because their ideas are not acknowledged.   10   7   5   3   1

5. People are reluctant to get involved in a project that requires them to balance ideas from different gender, racial, and cultural points of view.   10   7   5   3   1

6. Individuals with different backgrounds have a difficult time getting their ideas across.   10   7   5   3   1

7. Individuals in our group have a difficult time really listening with an open mind to the ideas presented by those who are different.   10   7   5   3   1

8. When people who are culturally different or of different genders work together in our group, there is always some amount of miscommunication.   10   7   5   3   1

9. Women and people of color are interpreted differently than white males, even when they say the same thing.   10   7   5   3   1

10. When fellow employees are confronted for giving a person a hard time because of his or her uniqueness, they usually deny the problem.   10   7   5   3   1

Scoring

Total the points of your responses. If your score is 60 or higher, there probably is no *positive multiculturalism* in this work team or group and organization. There probably is a need for an intensive effort to create a work environment that values diversity. Scores of 59 to 41 suggest some problems and a lack of consistency in addressing diversity issues but a greater readiness for change by team or group members. Scores of 40 to 10 suggest a somewhat to very positive embracing of diversity and multiculturalism.[76]

Organizational Insight: Great Majestic Company

Susan Hoffman, manager of the Great Majestic Lodge, was sitting at her desk and debating what she would say and what action she would take at a meeting with her bellmen, which was scheduled to begin in two hours. She has just weathered a stormy encounter with Bob Tomblin, the general manager of the Great Majestic Company's recreational and lodging facilities in the area.

Tomblin was visibly upset by an action taken by the bellmen at Great Majestic Lodge three weeks ago. At the end of the explosive meeting, Tomblin roared, "Sue, I don't care if you fire the whole bunch! I want you to do something about this right now!"

Background

The Great Majestic Lodge was located in a popular park in the western United States. It was rather remote, yet offered all the modern conveniences of a fine large-city hotel. Because of its size and accommodations, the lodge was a favorite spot for large, organized tours. Most of the tours stayed one night and none stayed more than two days. They were good moneymakers for the lodge because they always met their schedules, paid their bills promptly, and usually were gone early on checkout day.

Most of the employees hired by the Great Majestic Company were college students. This situation was ideal because the opening and closing dates of the lodge corresponded to most universities' summer vacations. The employees lived and ate at the company facilities and were paid about $400 a month.

The Lodge Bellmen

The bellmen at the Great Majestic Lodge were directly responsible to Hoffman. They were college students who, before being chosen for a bellman position, had worked for the company at least three summers. A total of seven were chosen on the basis of their past performance, loyalty, efficiency, and ability to work with the public. However, Tomblin chose the bellmen.

Employees considered the position of bellman to be prestigious and important. In the eyes of the public, the bellmen represented every aspect of the Great Majestic Lodge. They were the first ones to greet the guests upon arrival, the people the guests called when anything was needed or went wrong, and the last ones to see the guests off upon their departure. Clad in their special cowboy apparel complete with personalized name tags and company insignia, the bellmen functioned as an effective public relations team for the lodge, as well as providing prompt and professional service for each guest.

The bellmen all lived together in the back area of the most secluded employees' dorm at the lodge. They shared this facility with other lodge employees who had been with the company for two years or more. The older student employees were especially close-knit, and all were looking forward to the time they would have the opportunity to be chosen as bellmen. The first-year employees usually occupied a dorm to themselves, adjacent to the senior dorm. For the most part, a warm team spirit existed among all the staff at the lodge. Traditionally, the bellmen had a comfortable relationship with Tomblin, so this latest incident was of great concern to Hoffman. She realized that Tomblin was dead serious about firing them. It was midsummer, and finding qualified replacements would be difficult. The bellmen this year had been especially productive. They received $2.50 per hour plus tips, which they pooled and divided equally at the end of each week; daily tips averaged

$35 per person. Hoffman was particularly concerned about the situation because it involved employees for whom she was directly responsible.

Organized Tours

The bellmen had the responsibility of placing the tour luggage in the guests' rooms as soon as the bus arrived. The front desk provided them with a list of guests' names and the assigned cottage numbers. Speed was particularly important because the guests wanted to freshen up and wanted their bags to be delivered promptly. On the morning of departure, the guests left their packed bags in their rooms while they went to breakfast. The bellmen picked up the bags, counted them, and then loaded them on the bus.

As payment for the service rendered by the bellmen, tour directors paid the standard gratuity of $1.00 per bag. It was considered a tip, but it was included in the tour expenses by each company. For large tours, the tip could be as high as $125, although the average was $75.

Jones Transportation Agency

The Jones Transportation Agency had a reputation throughout the area of being fair and equitable with its tips. However, one of its tour directors, Don Sirkin, didn't live up to the company's reputation. On a visit to the Great Majestic Lodge, Sirkin had not given a tip. The bellmen knew that their service to Sirkin's group had been very good. They were upset about the situation but assumed that Sirkin had forgotten the tip in the rush before his tour departed. The tour was large and the tip would have amounted to $110. Sirkin's tour also stayed at several other nearby resorts. Several of the Great Majestic Lodge bellmen knew the bellmen at the other lodges and, in discussing the situation, discovered that Sirkin had neglected the tip at each of the other lodges. Sirkin apparently had pocketed almost $1000 on his group's four-day tour through the region.

The Letter

Upon hearing of Sirkin's actions, the Majestic Lodge bellmen decided that some action had to be taken. They immediately ruled out telling Hoffman. On previous occasions when there had been a problem, Hoffman had done very little to alleviate the situation.

Roger Sikes, a first-year bellman and a business undergraduate, suggested that they write a letter directly to the president of Jones Transportation Agency. He felt that the agency would appreciate knowing that one of its tour directors had misused company funds. After some discussion, the other bellmen present agreed. Sikes prepared a detailed letter, which told the Jones president the details of the Sirkin incident. The bellmen didn't expect to recover the money from the tour, but they felt that this was the appropriate action to take.

Five of the bellmen signed the letter as soon as it was completed. Two more opposed, but after more discussion and con-siderable peer pressure, agreed to sign the letter. They mailed it with the expectation of a speedy reply and justice for the offending Don Sirkin.

Reaction to the Letter

Three weeks after the bellmen's letter had been mailed to the Jones Transportation Agency, Tomblin was thumbing through his morning mail. He noticed a letter from his good friend Grant Cole, the president of the Jones Transportation Agency. Tomblin opened this letter first. Cole had written that there was a problem at the Great Majestic Lodge and he thought that Tomblin should be made aware of it. He enclosed the letter from the bellmen and suggested that, if the bellmen had any problems with any Jones tour directors in the future, it might be wise for them to speak to Tomblin before taking any action. Cole informed Tomblin that Jones was investigating the Sirkin incident.

Tomblin was enraged. The bellmen had totally ignored their supervisor and had written a letter without first consulting the lodge manager or any of the other managers of the Great Majestic Company. This action not only was a breach of company policy, but also a personal humiliation for Tomblin. Tomblin, yelling with outrage, leaped to his feet and charged through the lobby to Hoffman's office. He spotted bellman George Fletcher and ordered him to get out of his sight. The bewildered Fletcher quickly obeyed. Hoffman's meeting with Tomblin was unpleasant. She had never seen Tomblin so upset at the actions of employees. Tomblin was a proud person, and, because his pride has been hurt, he wanted revenge. He showed Hoffman the bellmen's letter and the reply from Cole. Tomblin made it clear that he expected some quick action. Hoffman knew that the action had to meet Tomblin's approval. Her position as lodge manager suddenly was precarious.

Several employees had been in the lobby when Tomblin roared through. Hoffman knew that gossip would spread quickly throughout the lodge. The bellmen were well liked by the other employees, and she knew that they would be concerned about the bellmen's fate. Hoffman called the still shaken George Fletcher into her office and told him to summon the off-duty bellmen for a meeting. After Fletcher left, she attempted to think of alternatives that would satisfy Tomblin and also maintain the quality of service expected by guests.[77]

Questions

1. What social influences and norms appear to have played a part in the behaviors of the bellmen?

2. What contextual influence and goals are relevant in this situation to (1) the bellmen, (2) Hoffman, and (3) Tomblin?

3. What should Hoffman do? Why?

REFERENCES

1. Adapted from: New system keeps the goods flowing, *Chain Store Age,* September 1996, 42–48; Munk, N. Shopping at Macy's, *Forbes,* February 12, 1996, 37–38.

2. Lawler, E. J. (ed.). *Advances in Group Processes,* vol. 13. Greenwich, Conn.: JAI Press, 1996; Markovsky, B., Lovaglia, M. J., and Simon, R. (eds.). *Advances in Group Processes,* vol. 14. Greenwich, Conn.: JAI Press, 1997.

3. New system keeps the goods flowing, 42–48.

4. Homans, G. C. *The Human Group.* New York: Harcourt, Brace and World, 1959, 2. Also see Miller, J. Living systems: The group. *Behavioral Science,* 1971, 16, 302–398.

5. Erez, M. Toward a model of cross-cultural industrial and organizational Psychology. In H. C. Triandis, M. D. Dunnette, and L. M. Hough (eds.), *Handbook of Industrial and Organizational Psychology,* vol. 4, 2d ed. Palo Alto: Calif.: Consulting Psychologists Press, 1994, 559–607.

6. Hofstede, G., Neuijen, B., Ohayv, D. D., and Sanders, G. Measuring organizational cultures: A qualitative and quantitative study across twenty cases. *Administrative Science Quarterly,* 1990, 35, 286–316.

7. Wadner, J. A. III. Studies of individualism and collectivism: Effects on cooperation in groups. *Academy of Management Journal,* 1995, 38, 152–172.

8. Zander, A. *Making Groups Effective,* 2d ed. San Francisco: Jossey-Bass, 1994.

9. Adapted from King, J. Pay inequities sap team spirit. *Computerworld,* November 4, 1996, 1; Johnson, S. T. High performance work teams: One firm's approach to team incentive pay. *Compensation & Benefits Review,* September/October 1996, 47–50.

10. George, J. M. Extrinsic and intrinsic origins of perceived social loafing in organizations. *Academy of Management Journal,* 1992, 35, 191–202

11. Kidwell, R. E., Jr., and Bennett, N. Employee propensity to withhold effort: A conceptual model to intersect three avenues of research. *Academy of Management Review,* 1993, 18, 429–456.

12. Fiedler, F. E., and Garcia, J. E. *New Approaches to Effective Leadership.* New York: John Wiley & Sons, 1987, 3–4.

13. Hammer, M. *Beyond Reengineering.* New York: HarperBusiness, 1996.

14. Katzenbach, J. R., and Smith, D. K. *The Wisdom of Teams: Creating the High Performance Organization.* Boston: Harvard Business School Press, 1993.

15. Albers Mohrman, S., Cohen, S. G., and Mohrman, A. M., Jr. *Designing Team-Based Organizations.* San Francisco: Jossey-Bass, 1995.

16. Nelson, R. B. *Empowering Employees Through Delegation.* Burr Ridge, Ill.: Richard D. Irwin, 1994.

17. Rose, R. L. A productivity push at Wabash National puts firm on a roll. *Wall Street Journal,* September 7, 1995, A1, A6.

18. Parker, G. M. *Cross-Functional Teams.* San Francisco: Jossey-Bass, 1994.

19. Lubove, S. Destroying the old hierarchies. *Forbes,* June 3, 1996, 62–71.

20. Mankin, D., Cohen, S. G., and Bikson, T. K. *Teams and Technology.* Boston: Harvard Business School Press, 1996.

21. Randolph, W. A. Navigating the journey to empowerment. *Organizational Dynamics,* Spring 1995, 19–32.

22. Adapted from Southerst, J. Now everyone can be a boss. *Canadian Business,* May 1994, 48–50; Williams, R. Self directed work teams: A competitive advantage. *Quality Digest,* November 1995, 50–52; Caudron, S. How pay launched performance. *Personnel Journal,* September 1996, 70–76.

23. Stevenson, W. B., Pearce, J. L., and Porter, L. W. The concept of "coalition" in organization theory and research. *Academy of Management Review,* 1985, 10, 256–268.

24. Donnellon, A. *Team Talk.* Boston: Harvard Business School Press, 1996, 1–4.

25. Tuckman, B. W. Development sequence in small groups. *Psychological Bulletin,* 1965, 62, 384–399; Tuckman, B. W., and Jensen, M. A. C. Stages of small group development revisited. *Group & Organization Studies,* 1977, 2, 419–427; Obert, S. L. Developmental patterns of organizational task groups: A preliminary study. *Human Relations,* 1983, 36, 37–52.

26. Gersick, C. J. Time and transition in work teams: Toward a new model of group development. *Academy of Management Journal,* 1988, 31, 9–41.

27. McCaffrey, D. P., Faerman, S. R., and Hart, D. W. The appeal and difficulties of participative systems. *Organization Science,* 1995, 6, 603–627.

28. Lawler, E. E. III. *From the Ground Up.* San Francisco: Jossey-Bass, 1996.

29. Southerst, J. Now everyone can be a boss, 48.

30. Hirokawa, R. Y., and Keyton, J. Perceived facilitators and inhibitors of effectiveness in organizational work teams. *Management Communication Quarterly,* 1995, 8, 424–446.

31. Gersick, C. J. G. Revolutionary change theories: A multi-level exploration of the punctuated equilibrium paradigm. *Academy of Management Review,* 1991, 16, 10–36; Montebello, A. R. *Work Teams That Work.* Minneapolis: Best Sellers, 1995.

32. Gerstein, M. S. *The Technology Connection.* Reading, Mass.: Addison-Wesley, 1987, 5; Johansen, R. *Groupware: Computer Support for Business Teams.* New York: Free Press, 1988.

33. Zack, M. H., and McKenney, J. L. Social context and interaction in ongoing computer-supported management groups. *Organization Science,* 1995, 6, 394–422.

34. Adapted from La Plante, A. Brainstorming. *Forbes ASAP,* October 25, 1993, 45–61; Hart, P., Svenning, L., and Ruchinskas, J. From face-to-face meeting to video teleconferencing: Potential shifts in meeting genre. *Management Communication Quarterly,* 1995, 4, 395–423; Walter, K. Employee ideas make money. *HR Magazine,* April 1996, 36–39.

35. Strom, D. You oughta be in pixes. *Forbes ASAP,* December 4, 1995, 48–49.

36. Herman, S. M. *A Force of Ones.* San Francisco: Jossey-Bass, 1994.

37. Sherif, M. Superordinate goals in the reduction of intergroup conflict. *American Journal of Sociology,* 1958, 68, 349–358.

38. Adapted from Hayes, C. The new spin on corporate work teams. *Black Enterprise,* June 1995, 229–234.

39. Berelson, B., and Steiner, G. A. *Human Behavior: An Inventory of Scientific Findings.* New York: Harcourt, Brace and World, 1964, 356–360.

40. Stoneman, K. G., and Dickinson, A. M. Individual performances as a function of group contingencies and group size. *Journal of Organizational Behavior Management,* 1989, 10, 131–150; Benedict Bunker, B. and Alban, B. T. *Large Group Interventions.* San Francisco: Jossey-Bass, 1996.

41. Wageman, R. Interdependence and group effectiveness. *Administrative Science Quarterly,* 1995, 40, 145–180.

42. Bales, R. F. *Personality and Interpersonal Behavior.* New York: Holt, Rinehart and Winston, 1970; Lustig, M. W. Bales' interpersonal rating forms: Reliability and dimensionality. *Small Group Behavior,* 1987, 18, 99–107.

43. Murphy, K. R. (ed.) *Individual Differences and Behavior in Organizations.* San Francisco: Jossey-Bass, 1996.

44. Milken, F. J., and Martins L. L. Searching for common trends: Understanding the multiple effects of diversity in organizational groups. *Academy of Management Review,* 1996, 21, 402–433.

45. Adapted from Paton, S. M. Diversity at Texas Instruments. *Quality Digest,* October 1995, 26–33; Griggs, L. B., and Louw, L. (ed.). *Valuing Diversity.* Englewood Cliffs, N.J.: Prentice-Hall, 1996; Laabs, J. J. Eyeing future HR Concerns. *Personnel Journal,* January 1996, 28–37.

46. Laden, J., and Rosener, J. B. *Workforce America: Managing Employee Diversity as a Vital Resource.* Homewood, Ill.: Business One–Irwin, 1991, 27–30; Ibarra, H. Race, opportunity, and diversity of social circles in managerial networks. *Academy of Management Journal,* 1995, 38, 673–703.

47. Barry, B., and Bateman, T. S. A social trap analysis of the management of diversity. *Academy of Management Review,* 1996, 21, 757–740.

48. Triandis, H. C., Kurowski, L. L., and Gelfand, M. J. Workplace diversity. In H. C. Traindis, M. D. Dunnette, and L. M. Hough (eds.), *Handbook of Industrial and Organizational Psychology,* vol. 4, 2d ed. Palo Alto, Calif.: Consulting Psychologists Press, 1994, 796–827.

49. Paton, S. M. Diversity at Texas Instruments, 26.

50. Bettenhausen, K. L., and Murnighan, J. K. The development of an intragroup norm and the effects of interpersonal and structural changes. *Administrative Science Quarterly,* 1991, 36, 20–35.

51. Nemetz, P. L., and Christensen, S. L. The challenge of cultural diversity: Harnessing a diversity of views to understand multiculturalism. *Academy of Management Review,* 1996, 21, 434–362.

52. Roethlisberger, F. J., and Dickson, W. J. *Management and the Worker: Technical versus Social Organization in an Industrial Plant.* Cambridge, Mass.: Harvard University Press, 1939.

53. Feldman, D. C. The development and enforcement of group norms. *Academy of Management Review,* 1984, 9, 47–53. Also see Spich, R. S., and Keleman, R. S. Explicit norm structuring process: A strategy for increasing task-group effectiveness. *Group and Organization Studies,* 1985, 10, 37–59.

54. Hackman, J. R. Group influences on individuals. In M. D. Dunnette and L. M. Hough (eds.), *Handbook of Industrial and Organizational Psychology,* vol. 3, 2d ed. Palo Alto: Calif.: Consulting Psychologists Press, 1992, 199–267.

55. Besser, T. L. *Team Toyota.* Ithaca, N.Y.: State University of New York Press, 1996.

56. Cosier, R. A., and Schwenk, C. R. Agreement and thinking alike: Ingredients for poor decisions. *Academy of Management Executive,* February 1990, 69–74.

57. Leavitt, H. J. Hot groups. *Harvard Business Review,* July–August 1995, 109–116; Leavitt, H. J. The old days, hot groups, and managers' lib. *Administrative Science Quarterly,* 1996, 41, 288–300.

58. Janis, L. L. Groupthink, 2d ed. Boston: Houghton Mifflin, 1982; Whyte, G. Groupthink reconsidered. *Academy of Management Review,* 1989, 14, 40–56; Sims, R. R. Linking groupthink to unethical behavior in organizations. *Journal of Business Ethics,* September 1992, 651–652.

59. Hambrick, D. C. Fragmentation and the other problems CEOs have with their top management teams. *California Management Review,* Spring 1995, 110–127.

60. Randolph, W. A. Navigating the journey to empowerment. *Organizational Dynamics,* Spring 1995, 19–32.

61. Rothstein, L. R. The empowerment effort that came undone. *Harvard Business Review,* January–February 1995, 20–31.

62. McLagan, P., and Nel, C. *The Age of Participation.* San Francisco: Berrett-Kohler, 1996.

63. Morris, W. C., and Sashkin, M. *Organization Behavior in Action: Skill Building Experiences.* St. Paul: West, 1976; Ford, R. C., and Fattler, M. D. Empowerment: A matter of degree. *Academy of Management Executive,* August 1995, 21–31; Hartman, J. J., and Nelson, B. H. Group decision making in the negative domain. *Group & Organization Management,* 21, 1996, 146–162.

64. Priem, R. L., Harrison, D. A., and Kanoff Muir, N. Structured conflict and consensus outcomes in group decision making. *Journal of Management,* 1995, 21, 691–710; Mulvey, P. W., Veiga, J. F., and Elsass, P. M. When teammates raise a white flag. *Academy of Management Executive,* February 1996, 40–49.

65. Adapted from Gowan, M., Ibarreche, S., and Lackey, C. Doing the right things in Mexico. *Academy of Management Executive,* February 1996, 74–81.

66. Major portions of this discussion for the nominal group technique were excerpted from: Woodman, R. W. Use of the nominal group technique for idea generation and deci-

sion making. *Texas Business Executive*, Spring 1981, 50–53; Delbecq, A. L., Van de Ven, A. H., and Gustafson, D. H. *Group Techniques for Program Planning: A Guide to Nominal and Delphi Processes*. Glenview, Ill.: Scott, Foresman, 1975.

67. Foster, J. *How to Get Ideas*. San Francisco: Berrett-Kohler, 1996.

68. Kao, J. *Jamming: the Art and Discipline of Business Creativity*. New York: HarperBusiness, 1996.

69. Osborn, A. F. Applied Imagination, rev. ed. New York: Scribner, 1957; Beaubien, E. E. Doing groupthink, *Successful Meetings*, July 1996, 45–50.

70. Diehl, M., and Strobe, W. Productivity loss in brainstorming groups: Toward the solution of the riddle. *Journal of Personality and Social Psychology*, 1987, 53, 497–509.

71. Mullen, B., Johnson, C., and Salas, E. Productivity loss in brainstorming groups: A meta-analytical integration. *Basic and Applied Social Psychology*, 12, 1991, 3–23.

72. Gallupe, R. B., Cooper, W. H., Grise, M. L., and Bastianutti, L. M. Blocking electronic brainstorms. *Journal of Applied Psychology*, 1994, 79, 77–86.

73. Olaniran, B. A. Group performance in computer-mediated and face-to-face communication media. *Management Communication Quarterly*, 1994, 7, 256–281; Aiken, M., Vanjani, M., and Paolillo, J. A Comparison of two electronic idea generation techniques. *Information Management*, 30, 1996, 91–99.

74. Gallupe, R. B., Dennis, A. R., Cooper, W. H., Valacich, J. S., Bastianutti, L. M., and Nunamaker, J. F., Jr. Electronic brainstorming and group size. *Academy of Management Journal*, 1992, 35, 350–359.

75. Adapted from Gallupe, R. B., and Cooper, W. H. Brainstorming electronically. *Sloan Management Review*, Fall 1993, 27–36.

76. Adapted from Larkey, L. K. The development and validation of the workforce diversity questionnaire. *Management Communication Quarterly*, 1996, 9, 296–337. Reprinted by permission of Sage Publications, Inc.

77. Prepared by and adapted with permission from Barnes, F. C., professor, University of North Carolina at Charlotte (presented at Southern Case Research Association).

9

Power and Political Behavior

LEARNING OBJECTIVES

When you have finished studying this chapter, you should be able to:

- Explain the concepts of organizational power and organizational politics.
- Identify five interpersonal sources of power.
- Describe the major categories of structural sources of power.
- Discuss effective and ineffective uses of power.
- Diagnose personal and situational factors that contribute to political behavior.
- Describe some personality dimensions that are related to political behavior.

OUTLINE

PREVIEW CASE

Graziano's Last Stand

The Board of Directors of Apple Computer faced a full agenda as they gathered in Austin, Texas, for a meeting. Joseph Graziano, the Chief Financial Officer of Apple, had his own agenda—nothing less than the survival of the company. Graziano intended to lay out for the directors his objections to CEO Michael Spindler's 1996 business plan. Graziano had serious concerns that underlying financial and marketing problems at Apple were being masked by year-to-year earnings gains. In addition, Graziano was convinced that Apple should merge with a larger company. Finally, at the heart of his suggestions for Apple was a recommendation that the CEO be removed from his job.

The response to Graziano's presentation? "As soon as he walked out of the room we all looked at each other and turned thumbs down," said one Apple director. The director remembers some board members actually trembling with anger at Graziano. Graziano resigned the next day. While he knew he hadn't swayed the board, he was surprised to learn just how bad an impression he had left with his powerful audience.

Different pictures have emerged of what has been called "Graziano's Last Stand." The Austin episode has been characterized by some board members as a palace coup against Spindler, or alternatively by others as a quiet presentation of Graziano's views about the deteriorating finances at Apple, after which the board deliberated and chose to back the CEO.

Events since his departure suggest that Graziano was on target concerning Apple's troubles. Within four months of the meeting, Spindler was ousted due to financial setbacks caused by inventory and marketing miscalculations at the computer maker. As 1996 wore on, losses widened beyond the most dismal predictions of many industry observers.

So, why did Apple's board shoot the messenger if he was essentially right about pending problems? "There wasn't any news that Joe brought that day that we hadn't heard before," says one Apple director. He remembers Graziano as providing no real financial data to support his assertions. "The presentation as I remember it was more that we should have sold the company to IBM." IBM had previously turned down such a proposal from Apple, but Graziano apparently blamed Spindler for somehow blocking Apple's sale and botching its financial plans. Although Graziano claims to have told the board that his remarks were not intended as a coup and that he "didn't want to replace Spindler as CEO," many board members apparently viewed the presentation differently. Said one, "Graziano's personal attacks on Spindler were tantamount to a coup." You live by the sword, you die by the sword.[1]

I n this chapter, we focus on power and political behavior in organizations. People often are uncomfortable discussing the concepts of power and organizational politics. Both terms carry emotional, often negative, implications. We argue that this should not be the case; these labels are simply descriptive terms that apply to certain aspects of the behavior of people in organizations. Managers and employees need to be aware of power and political behavior in order to understand organizational behavior fully.[2]

Certainly, political behavior can be unproductive for an organization, and people can use power in unfair or harmful ways. Managers and employees must try to avoid such outcomes, but they cannot change reality by refusing to accept the existence of power differences or political behavior. In this chapter, we discuss the nature of power, the sources of power in organizations, and the effective and ineffective uses of power. We also explore political behavior in organizations and some relationships between personality and political behavior.

POWER

Power is the capacity to influence the behavior of others.[3] The term power may be applied to individuals, groups, teams, organizations, and countries. For example, a certain group or team within an organization might be labeled as powerful, which suggests that it has the ability to influence the behavior of individuals in other groups or departments. This influence may affect resource allocations, space assignments, goals, hiring decisions, or many other outcomes and behaviors in an organization.

People continually attempt to influence the behavior of others in the normal course of everyday living. For example, people quite naturally attempt to reinforce the pleasing or satisfying behaviors of family members and friends. Likewise—and often without conscious awareness—people fail to reinforce or even attempt to punish undesirable behaviors. The behavior of people at work is no different.

Power is a social term; that is, an individual has power in relation to other people, a group or team has power in relation to other groups, and so on. The concept of power characterizes interactions among people—more than one person must be involved for the concept to apply. Further, power is never absolute or unchanging. It is a dynamic relationship that changes as situations and individuals change. For example, a manager may strongly influence the behavior of one subordinate but, at the same time, only marginally influence another. Managers may be powerful with respect to their own subordinates, yet be unable to influence the behavior of employees in other departments. In addition, relationships change with time. Last month's successful influence attempt may fail tomorrow, even though the same people are involved in both situations. The following Managing in Practice account illustrates the dynamic, changing nature of CEO power in corporate America.

MANAGING IN PRACTICE

The King Is Dead

American industry is going through a reversal of a decades-old trend that saw corporate power accrue to top managers and executives. If the Chief Executive Officer (CEO) ever was King, those days are gone. The King is dead. Gigantic institutions that hold large amounts of stock (such as retirement funds like TIAA), activist shareholders, boards of directors, and even lower level managers increasingly are wielding power formerly exercised almost exclusively by CEOs.

Chief executive officers report major changes in who has power in their organizations and how that power is used. According to a survey of top executives of the largest U.S. corporations, formerly powerful headquarters staffs have been reduced in size, and their power has shrunk. Louis Pepper, CEO of Washington Mutual Savings Bank in Seattle, states: "The headquarters staff, at one point, were running the entire show. That power has been diminished to allow more of management to become involved." Moreover, the corporate hierarchy has been flattened and layers of management reduced. One result has been to push decision making lower in the organization. Consequently, the majority of CEOs surveyed report that middle management's power has increased.

In comparing the balance of power between organizations and their customers, these CEOs say that customer power is growing. In response, Square D, an electrical equipment manufacturer, reorganized to give employees who deal with customers greater autonomy and power, says Jerry Stead, CEO. In addition, CEOs must listen more to their boards of directors, which increasingly contain

—*Continued*

MANAGING IN PRACTICE—*Continued*

more outside representatives. The majority of these CEOs report that their boards are more powerful than they were a few years ago.

The CEOs agree that consensus building characterizes their management style. Compared to the traditional, more autocratic or "imperial" CEO, 74 percent of these CEOs describe themselves as more participatory, more consensus-oriented, and more reliant on communication skills than on "command and control" skills. Harry Todd, CEO of Rohr Industries, says, "No more one-man band. We're all group-oriented." This theme was echoed by Vincent Sarni of PPG Industries, who describes the new style of successful CEOs as team-oriented and participatory. In this view, CEOs should set a strategic direction, get employees to agree, give them resources and authority, and leave them alone.

Indeed, these powerful corporate heads agree that personality and leadership skills are the most important sources of power in today's organization. The exercise of control has become less important than the exercise of leadership. Reuben Mark, CEO of Colgate-Palmolive, sums up the new power-sharing philosophy: "The more [power] you have, the less you should use. You consolidate and build power by empowering others."[4]

The terms *power* and *authority*, although closely related, do not mean exactly the same thing. **Authority** is power legitimated by (1) being formally granted by the organization and (2) being accepted by employees as being right and proper.[5] The most obvious organizational example is the superior–subordinate relationship. An organization has a formal authority structure with individuals, groups, teams, departments, and divisions being charged with responsibility for certain activities and functions. When individuals join an organization, they generally recognize the authority structure as legitimate; that is, employees accept the manager's right to set policy and give direction. So long as directives are reasonable and related to the job, employees generally obey them. Authority is narrower in scope than power and applies to fewer behaviors in an organization.

In addition to exercising authority, an individual or group may be able to influence the behavior of other people in an organization for many other reasons. In general, power sources in an organization may be categorized as (1) interpersonal and (2) structural, as shown in Figure 9.1.

 **INTERPERSONAL SOURCES OF POWER**

Many studies of power in organizations have focused on interpersonal relationships between manager and subordinates or leader and followers. French and Raven identified five interpersonal sources of power: reward power, coercive power, legitimate power, expert power, and referent power.[6]

■ REWARD POWER

Reward power is an individual's ability to influence others' behavior by rewarding their desirable behavior. For example, to the extent that subordinates value rewards that the manager can give—praise, promotions, money, time off, and so

■ FIGURE 9.1 **Sources of Power in Organizations**

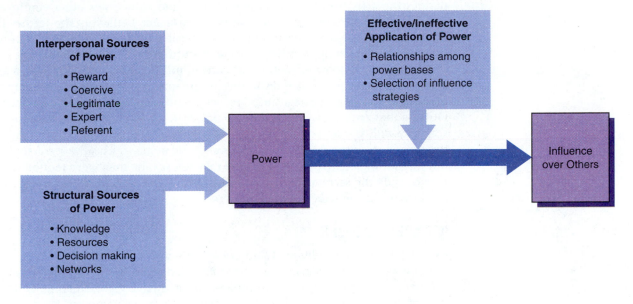

on—they may comply with requests and directives. A manager who controls the allocation of merit pay raises in a department has reward power over the employees in that department. In sum, employees may comply with some influence attempts by managers because they expect to be rewarded for their compliance.

■ COERCIVE POWER

Coercive power is an individual's ability to influence others' behavior by means of punishment for undesirable behavior. For example, subordinates may comply because they expect to be punished for failure to respond favorably to managerial directives. Punishment may take the form of reprimands, undesirable work assignments, closer supervision, tighter enforcement of work rules, suspension without pay, and the like. The ultimate punishment, from the organization's perspective, is to fire the employee.

Recall, however, that punishment can have undesirable side effects (see Chapter 4). For example, the employee who receives an official reprimand for shoddy work may find ways (other than the obvious one the organization wants) to avoid the punishment, such as by refusing to perform the task, falsifying performance reports, or being absent frequently.

■ LEGITIMATE POWER

Legitimate power most often refers to a manager's ability to influence subordinates' behavior because of the manager's position in the organizational hierarchy. Subordinates may respond to such influence because they acknowledge the manager's legitimate right to prescribe certain behaviors. Sometimes nonmanagerial employees possess legitimate power. For example, a safety inspector at Lockheed Martin Vought's plant in Camden, Arkansas, has the legitimate power to shut down production if there is a safety violation, even if the plant manager objects.

Legitimate power is an important organizational concept. Typically, a manager is empowered to make decisions within a specific area of responsibility, such as quality control, marketing, or accounting. This area of responsibility, in effect, defines the activities for which the manager (and sometimes other employees) can expect to exercise legitimate power to influence behavior. The farther that managers get from their specific area of responsibility, the weaker their legitimate power becomes. Employees have a **zone of indifference** with respect to the exercise of managerial power.[7] Within the zone of indifference, employees will accept certain directives without questioning the manager's power, and the manager may have considerable legitimate power to influence subordinates' behavior. Outside that zone, however, legitimate power disappears rapidly. For example, a secretary will type letters, answer the phone, open the mail, and do similar tasks for a manager without question. However, if the manager asks the secretary to go out for a drink after work, the secretary may refuse. The manager's request clearly falls outside the secretary's zone of indifference. The manager has no legitimate right to expect the secretary to comply.

■ EXPERT POWER

Expert power is an individual's ability to influence others' behavior because of recognized skills, talents, or specialized knowledge. To the extent that managers can demonstrate competence in implementing, analyzing, evaluating, and controlling the tasks of subordinates, they will acquire expert power. Expert power often is relatively narrow in scope. For example, a team member at Overhead Door Company might carefully follow the advice of her team leader about how to program a numerically controlled lathe, yet ignore advice from the team leader regarding which of three company health plans she should choose. In this instance, the team member is recognizing expertise in one area while resisting influence in another. A lack of expert power often plagues new managers and employees. Even though a young accountant might possess a great deal of knowledge about accounting theory and procedures, that expertise must be demonstrated and applied over time to be recognized and accepted. Similarly, employees or managers from underrepresented groups may have difficulty getting their expertise recognized by others, as illustrated by the following incident.

> The head of a large division of a multinational corporation was running a meeting devoted to performance assessment. Each senior manager stood up, reviewed the individuals in his group, and evaluated them for promotion. Although there were women in every group, not one of them made the cut. One after another, each manager declared, in effect, that every woman in his group didn't have the self-confidence needed to be promoted. The division head began to doubt his ears. How could it be that all the talented women in the division suffered from a lack of self-confidence?[8]

An analysis of this situation led to the conclusion that the firm, in fact, had many promotable women. The managers conducting the performance appraisal sessions had failed to recognize the knowledge and potential of their female subordinates. The reason, in part, was differences often found in men's and women's interpersonal styles, communication styles, approaches to problem solving, and the like.

■ REFERENT POWER

Referent power is an individual's ability to influence others' behavior as a result of being liked or admired. For example, subordinates' identification with a manager often forms the basis for referent power. This identification may include the desire of the subordinates to emulate the manager. (See Chapter 11 for an explanation of how this source of power is related to charismatic leadership.) A young manager may copy the leadership style of an older, admired, and more experienced manager. The older manager thus has some ability—some referent power—to influence the behavior of the younger manager. Referent power usually is associated with individuals who possess admired personality characteristics, charisma, or a good reputation. Thus it often is associated with political leaders, movie stars, sports figures, or other well-known individuals (hence their use in advertising to influence buying behavior). However, managers and employees also may have considerable referent power because of the strength of their personalities. Anita Roddick, CEO of the Body Shop, and Herb Kelleher, CEO of Southwest Airlines, use their referent power to motivate employees to achieve their organization's goals.

■ KEY RELATIONSHIPS

Managers and employees alike possess varying amounts of interpersonal sources of power. As implied by Figure 9.1, these sources don't operate independently. A study conducted in two paper mills provides an example of how power sources are related.[9] One of the mills dropped an incentive pay plan based on performance in favor of a pay plan based strictly on seniority. Compared to the second plant, which retained the incentive system, subordinates' perceptions of the use of various sources of power by supervisors in the first plant changed noticeably. Discontinuing the incentive plan lowered the perceived reward power of supervisors, as might be expected, but other results were more complex. Perceptions of supervisors' use of punishment increased (attributable perhaps to less control over rewards). The perceived use of referent and legitimate power decreased, but expert power appeared to be unaffected. These findings suggest that the interpersonal sources of power that influence behavior are complex and interrelated.

The ways in which managers and employees use one type of power can either enhance or limit the effectiveness of power from another source. For example, managers who administer rewards to subordinates also tend to be well liked and seem to have greater referent power than managers who don't give out rewards. However, the use of coercive power can reduce referent power. The threatened or actual use of punishment appears to reduce liking or admiration, leading to a reduction in referent power. Further, employees often view managers who possess knowledge valuable to them as having greater legitimate power in addition to having expert power.

These five sources of interpersonal power may be divided into two broad categories: organizational and personal. Reward power, coercive power, and legitimate power have organizational bases; that is, top managers can give to or take away from lower level managers or others the right to administer rewards and punishments. The organization can change employees' legitimate power by changing their positions in the authority hierarchy or by changing job descriptions, rules, and procedures. Referent power and expert power, however, depend much more on personal characteristics—personalities, leadership styles, and knowledge brought to the job. In the long run, the organization may influence expert power by, for example, making additional training available. But the individuals determine how they use that training, that is, the extent to which they apply the new knowledge. Recall that, in the Managing in Practice description of CEO power, CEOs reported that personal sources of power (expert and referent power) were more important than organizational sources (legitimate, reward, and coercive power).

STRUCTURAL SOURCES OF POWER

Much of the attention directed at power in organizations tends to focus on the power of managers over subordinates. An additional perspective is that the characteristics of the situation affect or determine power. Situational characteristics include the design of the organization, the type of departmental structure, the *opportunity* to influence, access to powerful individuals and critical resources, the nature of the position an individual holds, and so on.[10] For example, the power associated with a particular position or job is affected by its visibility to upper management and its importance or relevance with respect to the organization's goals or priorities. Table 9.1 contains some examples of position characteristics that determine relative power within an organization. Note that, whereas the legitimate power previously discussed applies primarily to managerial positions, the characteristics described in Table 9.1 are relevant for both managerial and nonmanagerial positions.

Structural and situational sources of power reflect the division of labor and membership in different departments, teams, and groups. These work assignments, locations, and roles naturally result in unequal access to information, resources, decision making, and other people. Any of an almost infinite variety of specific situational factors could become a source of power in an organization. Important structural sources of power include knowledge, resources, decision making, and networks.

■ KNOWLEDGE AS POWER

Organizations are information processors that must use knowledge to produce goods and services. The concept of **knowledge as power** means that individuals, teams, groups, or departments that possess knowledge crucial to attaining the organization's goals have power. People and groups in a position to control information about current operations, develop information about alternatives, or acquire knowledge about future events and plans have enormous power to influence the behavior of others. Thus certain staff and support activities—a data processing center, for example—sometimes seem to have influence disproportionate to their relationship to the organization's goals and main activities.

TABLE 9.1   Position Characteristics Associated with Power

CHARACTERISTIC	DEFINITION	EXAMPLE
Centrality	Relationship among positions in a communication network	More-central positions will have greater power.
Criticality	Relationships among tasks performed in a work-flow process	Positions responsible for the most critical tasks will have more power.
Flexibility	Amount of discretion in decision making, work assignments, and so on	More-autonomous positions will have more power.
Visibility	Degree to which task performance is seen by higher management in the organization	More-visible positions will have more power.
Relevance	Relationship between tasks and high-priority organizational goals	Positions most closely related to important goals will have more power.

Source: Adapted from Whetten, D. A., and Cameron, K.S. *Developing Managerial Skills.* Glenview, Ill.: Scott, Foresman, 1984, 259.

The increased use of personal computers and computerized workstations is having a dramatic impact on access to and use of information—and thus on power relationships—in many organizations. Information is rapidly becoming more widely available to many employees. Greater access to information tends to flatten the hierarchy and make hoarding information by individuals and departments more difficult. Further, computer networks provide workers with information that previously was available only to management. Information sharing has important implications for the quality of decision making and other aspects of performance. The extensive use of computer networks is spreading and presenting management with both opportunities and challenges.

Some experts now claim that intellectual capital is corporate America's most valuable asset. **Intellectual capital** represents the knowledge, know-how, and skill that exists in the organization. This intellectual capital can provide an organization with a competitive edge in the marketplace. However, perhaps because knowledge is power, at some firms sharing of information doesn't come easily. A study at Price Waterhouse found that some junior employees wouldn't share information on the computer network because of the firm's intensely competitive culture. Esther Dyson, an industry consultant, observes that computer networks can "create a flatter, more democratic organization. But that really only happens if the organization is ready for it."[11]

RESOURCES AS POWER

Organizations need a variety of resources, including human resources, money, equipment, materials, supplies, and customers, to survive. The importance of specific resources to a firm's success and the difficulty of obtaining them vary. The concept of **resources as power** suggests that departments, groups, or individuals who can provide essential or difficult-to-obtain resources acquire power in the organization. Which resources are the most important depends on the situation, the organization's goals, the economic climate, and the goods or services being produced. The old saying that "he who has the gold makes the rules" sums up the idea that resources are power.

At Weirton Steel, employees own 77 percent of the voting stock in the company. Employees and management had a bitter battle for control of the board of directors, stemming from disagreements over strategies (such as issuing new stock) the firm should pursue. Although some employees were angry that they didn't wield as much power as they wanted, the employees undoubtedly had more power over corporate strategy as a result of their ownership interests than they would have had otherwise.[12]

DECISION MAKING AS POWER

Decisions in organizations often are made sequentially, with many individuals or groups participating (see the discussion in Chapter 14). The decision-making process creates additional power differences among individuals or groups. The concept of **decision making as power** means that individuals or groups acquire power to the extent that they can affect the decision-making process. They might influence the goals being developed, premises being used in making a decision, alternatives being considered, outcomes being projected, and so on. For example, Southern California Edison uses a technique known as *scenario planning* to develop strategic plans for the future of the electric utility.[13] Scenario planners might look ahead ten years and develop a dozen possible versions of the future—another Middle East oil crisis, heightened environmental concerns, an economic boom in southern California, a major recession, and so on. Each scenario has implications for needed capacity, investment funds, human resources, and the like. The individuals and departments involved in scenario planning at Edison wield considerable influence, regardless of whether they make the final decisions about resource allocations.

The ability to influence the decision-making process is a subtle and often overlooked source of power. Decision-making power doesn't necessarily reside with the final decision-maker in an organization. A powerful machine politician in New York City once reportedly said, "I don't care who does the electing, as long as I have the power to do the nominating."

Although decision making is an important aspect of power in every organization, cultural differences make for some interesting differences in the relationship, as the following Across Cultures piece indicates.

ACROSS CULTURES

Power in Chinese and British Organizations

Relationships between power and decision making were examined in several Chinese and British companies. Data were collected about making decisions in eighteen areas, such as assigning employees to training, selecting supervisors, and assigning specific tasks to be performed. Organizations studied represented both manufacturing and service industries. Patterns of decision making revealed both organizational and cultural differences.

In the Chinese organizations, decision-making power was more decentralized in manufacturing firms than in service organizations. The reverse was true in British firms, with power being more decentralized in the service organizations than in the manufacturing firms. Organizational and cultural differences were more pronounced for medium- and long-range decisions than for short-term decisions. In China, the service sector of the economy is relatively new, which may account for its greater centralization of power compared to manufacturing firms. However, the central government has attempted to decentralize power in manufacturing firms as part of its economic reforms. In the United Kingdom, by contrast, the service sector of the economy is well developed and prosperous and is characterized by decentralized decision-making procedures.

In the British firms, managers and trade union representatives had larger differences in perceptions of which individuals had decision-making power than did their counterparts in the Chinese firms. Chinese management and trade unions seemed to have more common objectives, and they more readily agreed about who held power and who didn't. In part because of the strong influence of the Communist party, management and unions cooperate more in Chinese organizations than is typical of British organizations.

Decision-making power was more centralized at the middle and top levels of Chinese firms than it was in British organizations. This condition, too, may reflect important cultural differences between China and the United Kingdom. In general, Chinese society relies more on strong central authority than does British society. Thus the study demonstrated that decision-making power is affected by various factors, including the type of decision-making task, the type of industry, and the prevailing culture.[14]

■ NETWORKS AS POWER

The existence of structural and situational power depends not only on access to information, resources, and decision making, but also on the ability to get cooperation in carrying out tasks. Managers and departments that have connecting links with other individuals and departments in the organization will be more powerful than those who don't. Certainly, traditional superior–subordinate vertical relationships are important aspects of power, but these linkages don't begin to tell the whole story. Horizontal linkages provided by both internal and external networks help explain a lot of power differences. The concept of **networks as power** implies that various affiliations, channels of information, and coalitions, both inside and outside the organization, represent sources of power.

For example, the following Managing in Practice feature shows just how important social networks can be in terms of influence. The quoted statement is from the treasurer and controller of a *Fortune 500* consumer products firm who wished to remain anonymous.

MANAGING IN PRACTICE

Using Networks to Build Support

I just felt like the time was right to establish an offshore trading division of the company. At that time, I had been with the firm for eighteen years. Even though I was convinced that the time was perfect for such a venture, I puzzled for some time about how to proceed. My power base just didn't seem strong enough to get the permission I needed. I finally decided that I needed an alliance with key stakeholders to gain internal support for such a project.

It was important for me to convince my company's president of the viability of this idea. I have expertise in this area and my reputation as a winner is well known. I decided that if I could parlay these two assets into gaining the support of others, then the total package would sell to the two top people.

I personally visited all of the division vice-presidents overseas, ostensibly to seek support for the project. In my discussions with them, I stressed the innovative aspects of the project. I implied that the trading company would be established and hinted strongly that their support would make them part of a successful project.

Soon after I returned, I gave a formal presentation to the president, emphasizing the benefits of the project. I also stressed the strong support given to the project by the vice-presidents of all the subsidiaries. I was given the go-ahead to establish the offshore trading company. I don't really believe that I could have received this permission without the support of my "network."[15]

Power is provided by the following connecting links, each of which relates to factors already discussed.

■ *Information links.* To be effective, managers and employees must be "in the know" in both the formal and informal sense. (Knowledge is power.)

- *Supply links.* Outside links provide managers with the opportunity to bring materials, money, or other resources into their departments or teams. (Resources are power.)

- *Support links.* A manager's job must allow for decision-making discretion—the exercise of judgment. Managers must know that they can make decisions and take on innovative, risk-taking ventures without each decision or action having to go through a stifling, multilayered approval process. Managers and other professionals need the backing of important people in the organization, whose support becomes another resource they bring to their own work and group. (Participation in decision making is power and an important indicator of support links.)[16]

Understanding internal networks is the key to understanding how the organization gets work done. To identify and determine how they operate, managers and employees can undertake a **network analysis,** whereby they attempt to diagram important relationship networks within the organization. For example, the *advice network* reveals employees that others depend on to solve problems and provide technical information. The *trust network* shows which employees share delicate political information with each other. The *communication network* (see Chapter 13) indicates who talks to whom on a regular basis.[17] By understanding these and other networks, managers can diagnose the informal organization and understand more about how work actually gets done (or fails to get done) in the organization, as well as identify power differences among individuals and groups.

■ LOWER LEVEL EMPLOYEE POWER

Although people commonly think of power as something that managers have, lower level employees also may wield considerable power. Some sources of interpersonal power—expert power, in particular—may allow subordinates to influence their managers. For example, the secretary who can set up and use a *Windows 95* spreadsheet has the power to influence a manager's decisions if the manager is unable to use the spreadsheet and must rely on the secretary's expertise.

Although lower level employees may have some interpersonal power, their ability to influence others' behavior more likely stems from structural or situational sources. Figure 9.2 suggests that their power is a result of their positions in the organization. Refer back to Table 9.1 for a description of important position characteristics related to power. In addition to these characteristics, lower level employees may be able to control access to information or resources and important aspects of the decision-making process. Networks or affiliations with powerful individuals or groups may be yet another source of their power. Further, the expertise of employees and the amount of effort expended also influence the extent of their power. As Figure 9.2 illustrates, whether expertise and effort increase employees' power depends, in part, on their superior's expertise and effort. If an employee's manager has little knowledge about a certain task and the employee has considerable knowledge, the relative power of the employee increases. Employees also can acquire power by expending effort in areas where management puts little effort. For example, language skills can increase the relative power of bilingual employees, as demonstrated in the following Diversity in Practice feature.

■ FIGURE 9.2

Model of Lower Level Employee Power

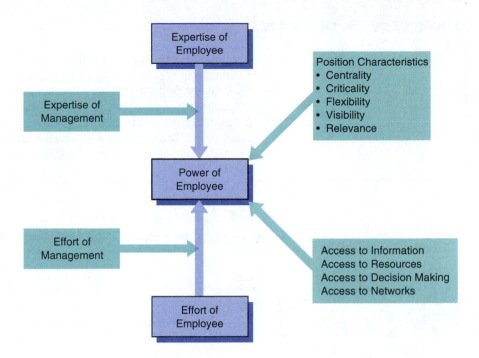

DIVERSITY IN PRACTICE

Bilingual Employees Acquire Power

At the first hint of Spanish, Southwestern Bell directory-assistance operators in San Antonio, a heavily Hispanic city, push a button to route callers to a bilingual operator such as Maggie Morales. Morales and other workers state that this new system, while effective, has made their jobs a lot tougher. Sifting through differences in language and culture means that she can't always meet the company's goal for getting off the phone in 21.5 seconds or less. "In Spanish, it can take a while to figure out that 'eternity general' isn't a hospital, but the attorney general's office," she says.

Maggie Morales doesn't mind the extra work. But like many of her colleagues, she wants the company to pay her more for her language skills. "The more computer languages you know, the more you make," says fellow operator Lillian Stevens, who taught herself Spanish. "Why shouldn't that be the same for languages?"

That question is being asked by bilingual employees in many organizations. As U.S. companies expand overseas and reach out to more non-English–speaking customers at home, demand for workers with language skills is rising fast. These workers' pay expectations are rising fast as well.

But the debate is complex. Many other workers find it unfair to pay someone extra for a skill that may come as naturally as talking. Employers who want to reward workers for their second languages are finding that it isn't easy to figure out how to do so in a way that will be perceived as equitable.

Still, workers at companies from AT&T to the U.S. Postal Service are pressing their demands with greater insistence. Early in 1996, about 2500 bilingual U.S.

—Continued

DIVERSITY IN PRACTICE—*Continued*

Customs Service inspectors threatened to slow down international travel in Florida, New York, and California by refusing to speak a foreign language unless the Treasury Department paid them more.

The bilingual issue has moved to center stage because of business and social trends. Corporate recruitment of bilingual workers has increased dramatically in recent years. Companies are more aggressively marketing to the estimated 20 million U.S. residents for whom English is a second language. Accompanying the marketing shift is a big change in the way foreign languages are perceived. As recently as the early 1980s, Southwestern Bell operators in Texas could be reprimanded for speaking Spanish on the job. Today, the company advertises extensively for bilingual workers.[18]

THE EFFECTIVE USE OF POWER

When managers, employees, or teams face a situation in which they want to influence the behavior of others, they must choose a strategy. **Influence strategies** are the methods by which individuals or groups attempt to exert power or influence others' behavior. Table 9.2 lists various influence strategies that managers and employees use in the workplace.

Researchers and others are interested in identifying effective influence strategies and understanding the situations in which each might be used. Research indicates that the influence strategies of rational persuasion, inspirational appeal, and consultation often are the most effective in a variety of circumstances. Overall, the least effective strategies seem to be pressure, coalition, and legitimating.[19] However, it is a mistake to assume that certain strategies always will work and that others won't. Differences in effectiveness occur when attempts to influence are downward rather than upward or lateral in the hierarchy and when they are used in combination rather than independently. In general, a manager or employee must take into account the power sources available, the direction of attempts to influence, and the goals being sought when selecting an influence strategy.[20]

Having the *capacity* to influence (power) the behavior of others and effectively using this capacity aren't the same thing. Managers who believe that they can effectively influence the behavior of others by acquiring enough power to simply order other people around generally are unsuccessful. In addition, the evidence indicates that the ineffective use of power has many negative implications, both for the individual and the organization. For example, one study examined the consequences of overreliance on assertiveness and persistence as an influence strategy (the "pressure" strategy in Table 9.2). Managers who were very assertive and persistent with others—characterized by a refusal to take no for an answer, reliance on repeated reminders, frequent use of face-to-face confrontations, and the like—suffered negative consequences. Compared to other managers studied, these aggressive managers (1) received the lowest performance evaluations, (2) earned less money, and (3) experienced the highest levels of job tension and stress.[21]

In addition to selecting the correct strategy, effective influence in organizations often depends on an exchange process somewhat related to the "exchange" influence strategy in Table 9.2. The **exchange process** in power relationships is based

TABLE 9.2 Influence Strategies

INFLUENCE STRATEGY	DEFINITION
Rational persuasion	Use logical arguments and factual evidence.
Inspirational appeal	Appeal to values, ideals, or aspirations to arouse enthusiasm.
Consultation	Seek participation in planning a strategy, activity, or change.
Ingratiation	Attempt to create a favorable mood before making request.
Exchange	Offer an exchange of favors, share of benefits, or promise to reciprocate at later time.
Personal appeal	Appeal to feelings of loyalty or friendship.
Coalition	Seek aid or support of others for some initiative or activity.
Legitimating	Seek to establish legitimacy of a request by claiming authority or by verifying consistency with policies, practices, or traditions.
Pressure	Use demands, threats, or persistent reminders.

Source: Adapted from Yukl, G., Guinan, P. J., and Sottolano, D. Influence tactics used for different objectives with subordinates, peers, and superiors. *Group & Organization Management,* 1995, 20, 275.

on the "law of reciprocity"—the almost universal belief that people should be paid back for what they do.[22] Imagine a situation in which an employee is asked by her manager to work through the weekend on an important project. The employee does so but receives no recognition, no extra time off, no extra pay—not even a "thank you." The employee later discovers that her manager took sole credit for the project, which was quite successful. This employee, and most observers, would agree that the manager violated an important aspect of a good working relationship: giving recognition or other rewards when due.

The expectation of reciprocal actions, or exchange, occurs repeatedly in organizations. In part, because people expect to be "paid back," influence becomes possible in many situations. The exchange process is particularly important in relationships such as networks of peers or colleagues, where formal authority to compel compliance is absent. Power in the exchange process stems from the ability to offer something that others need. The metaphor of currencies provides a useful way to understand how the exchange process influences behavior. Table 9.3 provides some interesting examples of the many types of currencies traded in organizations. Note the similarities between these currencies and the sources of power previously discussed.

The effective use of power is a difficult challenge for managers, employees, and organizations. The goal is to influence the behavior of others in ways that are consistent with both the needs of the organization and its employees. If the use of power isn't carefully managed, powerful individuals may exploit those with less power in the organization and substitute their self-interests for the legitimate interests of the organization. Effective managers and employees often possess five characteristics.[23]

First, they understand both the interpersonal and the structural sources of power and the most effective methods of using them to influence people. For example, professionals (e.g., research and development scientists, engineers, lawyers, or professors) tend to be more readily influenced by expertise than by other interpersonal sources of power. Effective managers and employees often recognize the structural and situational problems that exist in a power relation-

TABLE 9.3 Organizational Currencies Traded in the Exchange Process

CURRENCY	EXAMPLE
Resources	Lending or giving money, budget increases, personnel, space
Assistance	Helping with existing projects or undertaking unwanted tasks
Cooperation	Giving task support, providing quicker response time, approving a project, or aiding implementation
Information	Providing organizational or technical knowledge
Advancement	Giving a task or assignment that can aid in promotion
Recognition	Acknowledging effort, accomplishment, or abilities
Network/contracts	Providing opportunities for linking with others
Personal support	Giving personal and emotional backing

Source: Adapted from Cohen, A. R., and Bradford, D. L. Influence without authority: The use of alliances, reciprocity, and exchanges to accomplish work. *Organizational Dynamics*, Winter 1989, 11.

ship and modify their own behavior to fit the actual situation. As a result, they tend to develop and use a wide variety of power sources and influence strategies. Some ineffective managers rely too much on one or a few power bases or influence strategies.

Second, they understand the nature of the exchange process underlying many successful attempts to influence others. They recognize that, over time, unless reciprocal exchanges are roughly equivalent and fair, hard feelings will result and their ability to influence others will decline.

Third, they understand what is and what is not legitimate behavior in acquiring and using power. The misuse or lack of understanding of a source of power can destroy its effectiveness. For example, individuals erode expert power if they attempt to demonstrate expertise in areas in which they lack the required knowledge. Individuals may lose referent power by behaving in ways that are inconsistent with characteristics or traits that are attractive to others.

Fourth, they tend to seek positions that allow the development and use of power. In other words, they choose jobs that immerse them in the crucial issues and concerns of an organization. These jobs provide opportunities for and, indeed, demand influencing the behavior of others. Successful performance in these positions, in turn, allows the individual to acquire power.

Finally, they temper their use of power with maturity and self-control. They recognize that their actions influence the behaviors and lives of others. Although they are not necessarily reluctant or afraid to use their power—recognizing that influencing the behavior of employees is a legitimate and necessary part of the manager's role—they nevertheless exercise power carefully. They do so in principled and fair ways that are consistent with organizational needs and goals.

POLITICAL BEHAVIOR

Political behavior of individuals and groups consists of their attempts to influence the behavior of others and the course of events in the organization in order to protect their self-interests, meet their own needs, and advance their own goals. Described in this way, almost all behavior may be regarded as political. Labeling behavior as political, however, usually implies a judgment that individuals or groups are gaining something at the expense of other employees, groups, or the organization. However, you need to develop a balanced understanding of political behavior and its consequences. People often are self-centered and biased when labeling actions as political behavior. Employees may justify their own behavior as defending legitimate rights or interests, yet call similar behavior by others "playing politics." In any event, the following Quality in Practice piece dramatically illustrates outcomes typically perceived as negative that might stem from unchecked political behavior by powerful actors.

QUALITY IN PRACTICE

The Politics of Innovation

In 1873, Christopher Sholes invented the typewriter. Well over a century later, this same typewriter keyboard is still the principle tool that most of us use to communicate with our computers. What is unknown to most people, however, is that the particular configuration of keys (referred to as the QWERTY keyboard) was purposely engineered to *slow down* typists in order to accommodate the limitations of the typewriter introduced in 1873. The original typewriters, which relied on gravity to return struck keys to their resting positions, could jam if keys were struck in quick succession. Thus the keyboard was designed to prevent typists from striking keys too rapidly, particularly keys located next to each other. This mechanical problem with modern typewriters no longer exists, nor is it a problem with PC keyboards.

Surprisingly, a keyboard with a significantly improved configuration of keys has been in existence since 1932. The Dvorak simplified keyboard (DSK) has repeatedly been shown to be faster and more accurate than the standard keyboard in use, yet this innovation has never been adopted. Why?

The story of the DSK keyboard pits a solitary inventor against large organizations with a stake in maintaining the status quo. For some thirty years, Dr. August Dvorak fought to have his keyboard adopted as the standard. Dvorak and his associates conducted time and motion studies, participated in international typing contests, and even arranged for trial tests to be conducted by the federal government. Studies and tests showed the DSK keyboard to result in productivity improvements in the range of 35 to 100 percent with approximately 50 percent fewer mistakes. From 1934 to 1941, DSK-trained typists won the World Typewriting Championships. Dvorak failed to gain a government contract for his typewriters despite government tests that showed an average 74 percent gain in productivity. Both the U.S. Navy and the General Services Administration rejected converting to the DSK keyboard based on the costs of replacing obsolete equipment and retraining typists. The U.S. Navy assigned a security classification to test results of the DSK, thereby assuring that few people would be aware of them.

Dvorak also faced active resistance from typewriter manufacturers. Manufacturers sponsored most of the typing contests and routinely attempted to prevent DSK typists from competing. Results of typing contests typically failed to list the machines that typists used in instances when DSK typists won. There were even documented instances of sabotage of Dvorak's machines.

Adoption of the DSK was defeated by political resistance on the part of typewriter manufacturers who had little incentive to use the improved keyboard. The increased productivity from the new keyboard could reduce sales of typewriters, as an office would need less machines if each typist could produce more. Further, manufacturers would have been required to pay royalties on the DSK, which was a patented invention.

—Continued

QUALITY IN PRACTICE—*Continued*

Today, of course, the QWERTY keyboard is still with us in PC use. Cynthia Crossen, a *Wall Street Journal* reporter, states, "Take a good look at your computer keyboard, and behold one of the worst-designed, least-friendly tools in the workplace today." Crossen points out that the computer keyboard contains a number of keys, such as print scrn, scroll lock, and pause, that were developed during the earliest days of personal computers (primarily for the early DOS operating system) and have little or no use in cutting-edge software. Even the function keys across the top of the keyboard are unneeded for programs using a "mouse." Although some companies, such as Apple, have experimented with different keyboard layouts, in general computer makers have little desire to redesign them. In addition to believing that people need to have a layout that matches their typing training, computer makers cite the tremendous cost of making a change since most current software is written for the standard keyboard. Sound familiar?[24]

■ ORGANIZATIONAL POLITICS

Organizational politics involves actions by individuals or groups to acquire, develop, and use power and other resources in order to obtain preferred outcomes when there is uncertainty or disagreement about choices.[25] When people share power but differ about what must be done, many decisions and actions quite naturally will be the result of a political process.

Employees often are concerned about office politics.[26] Typically, they also believe that an ideal work setting would be free from political behavior. Negative attitudes about political behavior and organizational politics can block understanding of this crucial aspect of organizational behavior. People tend to assume that political behavior doesn't yield the best organizational decisions or outcomes—that somehow, by pushing for their own positions, individuals or groups produce inferior actions or decisions. Although this result can occur, political behavior isn't always detrimental to an organization. For example, a study involving managers in thirty organizations indicated that these managers were able to identify beneficial, as well as harmful, effects of political behavior. Beneficial effects included career advancement, recognition and status for individuals looking after their legitimate interests, and achievement of organizational goals—getting the job done—as a result of the normal political process in the organization. Harmful effects included demotions and loss of jobs for "losers" in the political process, a misuse of resources, and creation of an ineffective organizational culture.[27] The effect on culture may be among the most undesirable consequences of continual political behavior. Organizational politics may arouse anxieties that cause employees to withdraw emotionally from the organization. This withdrawal, in turn, makes creating an organizational culture characterized by high performance and high commitment very difficult (see Chapter 17).

Political behavior, then, can meet appropriate and legitimate individual and organizational needs, or it can result in negative outcomes. In any event, managers and employees must understand political behavior because it will occur. Eliminating political behavior isn't possible—it can only be managed.

■ FORCES CREATING POLITICAL BEHAVIOR

The probability of political behavior increases in proportion to disagreements over goals, unclear goals, different ideas about the organization and its problems, different information about the situation, the need to allocate scarce resources, and so on. If these forces didn't exist, perhaps political behavior wouldn't occur. Unfortunately, outcomes are never certain, resources are never infinite, and people must make difficult choices among competing goals and methods to attain them. Thus political behavior will occur as employees and groups attempt to obtain their preferred outcomes. Managers shouldn't try to prevent the inevitable, but rather should try to ensure that these activities not have negative consequences for the organization and its employees.

One perspective on political behavior suggests that managers and employees are likely to act politically when (1) decision-making procedures and performance measures are highly uncertain and complex and (2) competition among individuals and groups for scarce resources is strong. Conversely, in more stable and less complex environments where decision processes are clear and competitive behavior is less, excessive political behavior is unlikely.[28] Figure 9.3 illustrates these ideas.

Whereas certain individual differences may contribute to political behavior, such behavior probably is more strongly influenced by aspects of the situation. Organizations make engaging in political behavior easier when they provide few rules or policies. Ambiguous circumstances allow individuals to define situations in ways that satisfy their own needs. Further, when employees want more of a resource (such as computer time or office space) than is available, political behavior is likely to occur.[29]

In addition to the dimensions shown in Figure 9.3, political behavior will be higher in organizations that reward such behavior. A reward system may focus solely on individual accomplishment and minimize group and team contributions. When that is the case, individuals may be tempted to behave politically to ensure that they receive some of the rewards. If their political actions result in rewards, employees may be even more likely to engage in such actions in the

■ **FIGURE 9.3**

Probability of Political Behavior in Organizations

Source: Adapted from Beeman, D. R., and Sharkey, T. W. The use and abuse of corporate politics. *Business Horizons,* March–April 1987, 27.

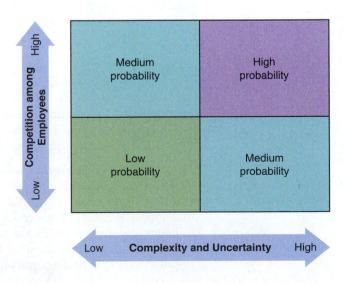

future. Similarly, individuals who had avoided political behavior, may start behaving politically when they observe such behavior being rewarded. In sum, the organizational reward system can be a major factor in the occurrence of political behavior.[30]

Decisions in some areas can be made less political by increasing the resources available (thus reducing conflict over scarce resources) or by making the decisions seem less important than they really are. However, strategies to reduce the political behavior associated with organizational decisions may have some unintended consequences that translate into real costs for the firm. Table 9.4 shows several examples of strategies used to avoid organizational politics and the potential costs associated with each strategy.

The performance appraisal process provides a good example of forces in the workplace that may create political behavior. Performance for many employees isn't easily measured, and the process results in the allocation of scarce resources based on complex criteria. The following Ethics in Practice account describes political behavior in the performance appraisal process.

ETHICS IN PRACTICE

The Politics of Employee Appraisal

There is really no getting around the fact that whenever I evaluate one of my people, I stop and think about the impact—the ramifications of my decisions on my relationship with the guy and his future here. I'd be stupid not to. Call it being politically minded, or using managerial discretion, or fine-tuning the guy's ratings, but in the end, I've got to live with him, and I'm not going to rate a guy without thinking about the fallout. There are a lot of games played in the rating process, and whether we (managers) admit it or not, we are all guilty of playing them at our discretion.

That statement comes from one of sixty executives that participated in in-depth interviews concerning their performance appraisal processes. These sixty executives—from seven large corporations—had performance appraisal experience in a total of 197 different companies. An analysis of these interviews resulted in the following conclusions.

- Political considerations were nearly always part of the performance evaluation process.

- Politics played a role in the performance appraisal process because (1) executives took into consideration the daily interpersonal dynamics between them and their subordinates; (2) the formal appraisal process results in a permanent written document; and (3) the formal appraisal can have considerable impact on the subordinate's career and advancement.

In addition, these executives believed there was usually a justifiable reason for generating appraisal ratings that were less than accurate. Overall, they felt it was within their managerial discretion to do so. Thus the findings suggest that the formal appraisal process is indeed a political process and that few ratings are determined without some political consideration.

Perhaps the most interesting finding from the study (because it debunks a popular belief) is that accuracy is not the primary concern of these executives

—Continued

ETHICS IN PRACTICE—*Continued*

when appraising subordinates. Their main concern is how best to use the appraisal process to motivate and reward subordinates. Hence managerial discretion and effectiveness, not accuracy, are the real goals. Managers made it clear that they would not allow excessively accurate ratings to cause problems for themselves and that they attempted to use the appraisal process to their own advantage.[31]

Many organizations ignore the existence of politics in the appraisal process or may assume that use of the proper performance appraisal instruments will minimize it. However, research indicates that, as indicated in the preceding Ethics in Practice account, political behavior may be a fact of life in many appraisal processes. In particular, because of the ambiguous nature of managerial work, appraisals of managers are susceptible to political manipulation. What is the risk, ethical or otherwise, of using performance appraisal as a political tool? Among other things, overly political performance appraisals can

- undermine organizational goals and performance;
- compromise the link between performance and rewards (see Chapters 5 and 6);
- encourage politics in the rest of the organization; and
- expose an organization to litigation if managers are terminated.[32]

Some experts who have studied politics in the appraisal process suggest that organizations adopt the following guidelines to help cope with the problem.

- Articulate goals and standards as clearly and specifically as possible.
- Link specific actions and performance results to rewards.
- Conduct structured, professional reviews, providing specific examples of observed performance and explanations for ratings given.

TABLE 9.4   Strategies for Avoiding the Use of Political Behavior in Decision Making and Their Possible Costs

STRATEGY	COSTS
Slack or excess resources, including additional administrative positions	Inventory, excess capacity, extra personnel and salary
Strong-culture—similarity in beliefs, values, and goals produced through recruitment, socialization, use of rewards and punishments	Fewer points of view, less diverse information represented in decision making, potentially lower quality decisions
Make decisions appear less important	Decision avoided; critical analysis not done; important information not uncovered
Reduce system complexity and uncertainty	Creation of rigid rules and procedures; reduction of capacity for change

Source: Adapted from Pfeffer, J. *Power in Organizations.* Marshfield, Mass.: Pitman, 1981, 93; and Pfeffer, J. *Managing with Power: Politics and Influence in Organizations.* Boston: Harvard Business School Press, 1993.

- Offer performance feedback on an ongoing basis, rather than once a year.
- Acknowledge that appraisal politics exists and make this topic a focus of ongoing discussions throughout the organization.[33]

PERSONALITY AND POLITICAL BEHAVIOR

So far, we have stressed the situational and structural determinants of political behavior. Just as power has both personal and situational sources, some individuals appear more likely to engage in political behavior than others. Several personality traits are related to a willingness to use power and political behavior. We discuss four of them: the need for power, Machiavellianism, locus of control, and risk-seeking propensity.

■ NEED FOR POWER

The **need for power** is a motive, or basic desire, to influence and lead others and to control the current environment. As a result, individuals with a high need for power are likely to engage in political behavior in organizations. Successful managers often have high needs for power.[34] The desire to have an impact, to control events, and to influence others often is associated with effective managerial behaviors, equitable treatment of subordinates, and hence higher morale.

However, some aspects of strong power needs may not be particularly useful for effective management. The need for power may take two different forms: personal power and institutional power. On the one hand, managers who emphasize personal power strive to dominate others; they want loyalty to themselves, rather than to the organization. When this type of manager leaves the organization, the work group may fall apart. On the other hand, managers who emphasize institutional power demonstrate a more socially acceptable need for power. They create a good climate or culture for effective work, and their subordinates develop an understanding of and loyalty to the organization. Interestingly, some research indicates that female managers often demonstrate greater needs for institutional power and lesser needs for personal power than their male counterparts.[35]

■ MACHIAVELLIANISM

Niccolo Machiavelli was a sixteenth-century Italian philosopher and statesman whose best-known writings include a set of suggestions for obtaining and holding governmental power. Over the centuries, Machiavelli has come to be associated with the use of deceit and opportunism in interpersonal relations. Thus **Machiavellians** are people who view and manipulate others for their own purposes.

As a personal style of behavior toward others, **Machiavellianism** is characterized by (1) the use of guile and deceit in interpersonal relationships, (2) a cynical view of the nature of other people, and (3) a lack of concern with conventional morality.[36] A person who scores high on a test to measure Machiavellianism probably agrees with the following statements.

- The best way to handle people is to tell them what they want to hear.
- Anyone who completely trusts anyone else is asking for trouble.
- Never tell anyone the real reason you did something unless it is useful to do so.

■ It is wise to flatter important people.

Machiavellians are likely to be effective manipulators of other people. They often are able to influence others, particularly in face-to-face contacts, and tend to initiate and control social interactions. As a result, Machiavellianism can be associated with a tendency to engage in political behavior. For example, a study that examined the relationship between a propensity to engage in political behavior in organizations and a variety of individual differences reported that Machiavellianism was the strongest correlate of political behavior among the variables investigated.[37] The study concluded that Machiavellianism may be a good predictor of political behavior in many organizational situations.

■ LOCUS OF CONTROL

Recall that **locus of control** refers to the extent to which individuals believe that they can control events that affect them (see Chapter 2). Individuals with a high internal locus of control believe that events result primarily from their own behavior. Those with a high external locus of control believe that powerful others, fate, or chance primarily determine events that affect their lives. Internals tend to exhibit more political behaviors than externals and are more likely to attempt to influence other people. Further, they are more likely to assume that their efforts will be successful. The study of relationships among political behavior and individual differences referred to in the preceding section also supported the notion that the propensity to engage in political behavior is stronger for individuals who have a high internal locus of control than for those who have a high external locus of control.

■ RISK-SEEKING PROPENSITY

Individuals differ (sometimes markedly) in their willingness to take risks, or in their **risk-seeking propensity.** Some people are risk avoiders, and others can be described as risk seekers.[38] Negative outcomes (such as demotions, low performance ratings, and loss of influence) are possible for individuals and groups who engage in political behavior in organizations. Engaging in political activity isn't risk free; to advocate a position and to seek support for it is to risk being perceived as opposing some other position. In many situations, risk seekers are more willing to engage in political behavior, whereas risk avoiders tend to avoid such behavior because of its possible consequences.

CHAPTER SUMMARY

Power is the capacity to influence the behavior of others. Sources of power stem from interpersonal and structural factors in an organization. Interpersonal power sources can be categorized as reward power, coercive power, legitimate power, expert power, and referent power. Structural power differences stem from unequal access to information, resources, decision making, and networks with others. Lower level employees, despite their location in the organizational hierarchy, may have considerable power to influence events and behavior. Individuals who can effectively influence others' behavior usually understand clearly the sources of power—and the appropriate and fair uses of power. Such individuals also usually understand the important role that the exchange process plays in the ability to influence the behavior of others.

Organizational politics involves the use of power and other resources by individuals or groups to obtain their own preferred outcomes. Political behavior is inevitable, owing to naturally occurring disagreements and uncertainty about choices and actions. Political behavior can have both positive and negative consequences; it may or may not result in optimal decisions, and some real costs are associated with avoiding political behavior. Political behavior is more likely to occur when resources are scarce or rules and procedures are unclear. The performance appraisal process often invites political behavior, sometimes with negative consequences.

Certain personality traits predispose some people to political behavior. Specifically, the probability that individuals will engage in political influence attempts increases if they have (1) a high need for power, (2) a Machiavellian interpersonal style, (3) a high internal locus of control, and (4) a preference for risk taking.

KEY TERMS AND CONCEPTS

Authority
Coercive power
Decision making as power
Exchange process
Expert power
Influence strategies
Intellectual capital
Knowledge as power

Legitimate power
Locus of control
Machiavellianism
Machiavellians
Need for power
Network analysis
Networks as power
Organizational politics

Political behavior
Power
Referent power
Resources as power
Reward power
Risk-seeking propensity
Zone of indifference

DISCUSSION QUESTIONS

1. Compare and contrast interpersonal and structural sources of power in organizations.

2. What bases of power did Joseph Graziano, formerly of Apple Computer, attempt to use? (See the Preview Case.) In your opinion, why did his attempt to influence Apple's board of directors fail?

3. Were you ever in a situation in which you had the power to influence the behavior of others? If so, explain the source or sources of your power.

4. Were you ever in a situation in which someone else had the power to influence your behavior? If so, explain the source or sources of their power.

5. Make some suggestions for the effective use of power.

6. What is the nature of the exchange process in power relationships? Provide some examples of currencies that were commonly exchanged in an organization with which you are familiar.

7. Based on your own experiences, give examples of both effective and ineffective uses of power. Explain why each outcome occurred.

8. Define political behavior. What are some of the factors that can contribute to organizational politics?

9. Based on your own experience, describe a situation in which political behavior seemed to be excessive. Why did it occur?

10. Why is the performance appraisal process prone to political abuse? How can the probability of political behavior be minimized in this process?

■ Developing Competencies

Team Insight: How Much Power Do You Have in Your Group?

Instructions

Think of a group of which you are a member. It could be a work group or team, a committee, a group project at your school, or the like. Use the scale shown to respond to the following statements.

1 = Strongly Disagree

2 = Disagree

3 = Slightly Disagree

4 = Neither Agree nor Disagree

5 = Slightly Agree

6 = Agree

7 = Stongly Agree

_____ 1. I am one of the more vocal members of the group.

_____ 2. People in the group listen to what I have to say.

_____ 3. I often volunteer to lead the group.

_____ 4. I am able to influence group decisions.

_____ 5. I often find myself on "center stage" in group activities or discussions.

_____ 6. Members of the group seek me out for advice.

_____ 7. I take the initiative in the group for my ideas and contributions.

_____ 8. I receive recognition in the group for my ideas and contributions.

_____ 9. I would rather lead the group than be a participant.

_____ 10. My opinion is held in high regard by group members.

_____ 11. I volunteer my thoughts and ideas without hesitation.

_____ 12. My ideas often are implemented.

_____ 13. I ask questions in meetings just to have something to say.

_____ 14. Group members often ask for my opinions and input.

_____ 15. I often play the role of scribe, secretary, or note taker during meetings.

_____ 16. Group members usually consult me about important matters before they make a decision.

_____ 17. I clown around with other group members.

_____ 18. I have noticed that group members often look at me, even when not talking directly to me.

_____ 19. I jump right into whatever conflict the group members are dealing with.

_____ 20. I am very influential in the group.

Scoring

Visibility		Influence	
Item	Your Score	Item	Your Score
1. _____		2. _____	
3. _____		4. _____	
5. _____		6. _____	
7. _____		8. _____	
9. _____		10. _____	
11. _____		12. _____	
13. _____		14. _____	
15. _____		16. _____	
17. _____		18. _____	
19. _____		20. _____	
Total _____		Total _____	

Use the scores calculated and mark your position on the visibility/influence matrix shown in Figure 9.4. The combinations of visibility and influence shown are described as follows.

1. *High visibility/high influence.* Group members in quadrant I exhibit behaviors that bring high visibility and allow them to exert influence on others. In organizations, these people may be upwardly mobile or on the "fast track."

2. *High visibility/low influence.* Group members in quadrant II are highly visible but have little real influence. This condition could reflect their personal characteristics but also could indicate that formal power resides elsewhere in the organization. Often these people may hold staff, rather than line, positions that give them visibility but that lack "clout" to get things done.

3. *Low visibility/low influence.* Group members in quadrant III, for whatever reason, are neither seen nor heard. Individuals in this category may have difficulty advancing in the organization.

4. *Low visibility/high influence.* Group members in quadrant IV are "behind the scenes" influencers. These individuals often are opinion leaders and "sages" who wield influence but are content to stay out of the limelight.[39]

■ FIGURE 9.4

Visibility/Influence Matrix

Source: Adapted from Reddy, W. B., and Williams, G. The visibility/credibility inventory: Measuring power and influence. In J. W. Pfeiffer (ed.), *The 1988 Annual: Developing Human Resources.* San Diego: University Associates, 124.

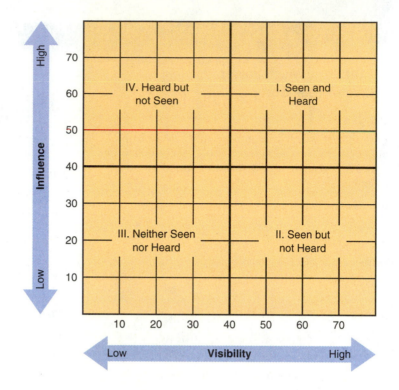

Organizational Insight:
The NASA Moonlander Monitor

As a young engineer, Chuck House played a key role at Hewlett-Packard (H-P) in developing new applications for oscilloscope technology. The company's technology eventually was used in NASA's moon missions, although this happy ending was not without its political battles.

The story began when the Federal Aviation Administration (FAA) advertised for an improved airport control tower monitor. Hewlett-Packard developed such a monitor but lost out when the FAA selected another firm's design. However, House was convinced that the H-P design represented a significant technological breakthrough. The model that his team developed was smaller, faster, more energy efficient, and brighter than conventional monitors. Unfortunately, the model didn't seem to have a niche in the marketplace.

House set out to convince H-P of the merits of his team's monitor, even though the firm had lost the FAA contract. He proved to be a master political gamesman who violated a number of organizational rules and procedures. First, he collected his own market research data in direct violation of organizational policies, circumventing the marketing department. During an unauthorized trip, he visited forty computer manufacturers to demonstrate the prototype. Not only did this arouse the ire of the marketing department, but it violated a security rule against showing prototypes to potential customers. However, based on marketing information gathered during the trip, House was able to convince senior management at H-P to continue development of the monitor, at least temporarily.

The next obstacle to continuation of the project came during an annual review of progress by senior management. The marketing department conducted a telephone survey and concluded that the total projected demand for the product was thirty-two monitors. House argued that the marketing data were flawed and that marketing was resistant to the project because of his invasion of their "turf." Further, the marketing department failed to understand the appropriate strategy for marketing the new monitor and had called only on current oscilloscope customers. House's position was that new products required new customers. In addition, because the product was difficult to describe, only in-person demonstrations could sell it. Despite this reasoning, management accepted the marketing department's projection of potential demand rather than House's projection. (House again had obtained data through organizationally illegitimate means.) As if the political resistance from marketing weren't enough, the project also lacked the support of the chief corporate engineer, who favored an alternative technology.

Not surprisingly, the senior management annual review concluded that there was insufficient market demand and a lack of technological support from others in the organization for this product. The project was to be canceled. David Packard, one of the two founders of H-P, even said: "When I come back next year, I don't want to see that project in the lab!"

At this point, House's political skills were put to their greatest test. House chose to interpret Packard's statement to mean that the project should be out of the lab in one year and in production, rather than that the project should be scrapped. With covert support from his boss, House and his group hid the development cost of the new monitor under other items in the budget. They then raced to complete the project within a year's time (easily only one-half of the normal time such development might be expected to take). The marketing department mounted continual opposition to the project, but House countered by convincing interested potential customers to intervene personally with senior management and express interest in the monitor.

Fortunately for House and the project, he and his team made the deadline. When Packard returned for the next annual review, the monitor was in the marketplace. Packard was said to be both angered and amused by this obvious reinterpretation of his order. However, perhaps because he himself was something of a maverick, Packard now chose to support the monitor. Rather than being punished, House and his development team were given the green light to continue to seek additional applications. The eventual uses for this oscilloscope monitor included the NASA moon mission, the medical monitor used in the first artificial heart transplant, and a large-screen oscilloscope that was part of a television special effects system that won an Emmy award. These important innovations could easily have fallen victim to opposing political forces in Hewlett-Packard.[40]

Questions

1. List and explain the sources of power that House used.

2. Identify and explain the factors that increased political behavior in Hewlett-Packard during this time. Although he wasn't the only one to behave politically, what factors do you think were particularly critical for increasing House's political behavior?

3. Did House use power effectively or ineffectively? Defend your answer.

4. Suggest some strategies that House might have utilized to reduce the political resistance to this innovation.

REFERENCES

1. Adapted from Harris, R. Graziano's last stand. *CFO*, May 1996, 26–36.

2. Hollander, E. P. Power. In N. Nicholson (ed.), *Blackwell Encyclopedic Dictionary of Organizational Behavior*. Oxford: Blackwell, 1995, 437–440; Wilson, P. A. The effects of politics and power on the organizational commitment of Federal executives. *Journal of Management*, 1995, 21, 101–118.

3. Finkelstein, S. Power in top management teams: Dimensions, measurement, and validation. *Academy of Management Journal*, 1992, 35, 505–538; Hollander, E. P., and Offerman, L. R. Power and leadership in organizations. *American Psychologist*, 1990, 45, 179-189; Keys, B., and Case, T. How to become an influential manager. *Academy of Management Executive*, 1990, 4(4), 38–51; Pfeffer, J. *Managing with Power: Politics and Influence in Organizations*. Boston: Harvard Business School Press, 1993.

4. Adapted from Stewart, T. A. The king is dead. *Fortune*, January 11, 1993, 34–40. See also, Bourget, L. The changing face of power. In J. W. Pfeiffer (ed.), *The 1996 Annual: Volume 2, Consulting*. San Diego: Pfeiffer & Company, 1996, 199–206; Zajac, E. J., and Westphal, J. D. Director reputation, CEO-based power, and the dynamics of board interlocks. *Administrative Science Quarterly*, 1996, 41, 507–529.

5. Biggart, N. W., and Hamilton, G. G. The power of obedience. *Administrative Science Quarterly*, 1984, 29, 540–549; Hamilton, G. G., and Biggart, N. W. Why people obey: Theoretical observations on power and obedience in complex organizations. *Sociological Perspectives*, 1985, 28, 3–28; Pfeffer, J. *Power in Organizations*. Marshfield, Mass.: Pitman, 1981, 4–6.

6. French, J. R. P., and Raven, B. The bases of social power. In D. Cartwright (ed.), *Studies in Social Power*. Ann Arbor: University of Michigan Institute for Social Research, 1959, 150–167. Also see Hinkin, T. R., and Schriesheim, C. A. Development and application of new scales to measure the French and Raven (1959) bases of social power. *Journal of Applied Psychology*, 1989, 74, 561–567; Podsakoff, P. M., and Schrieshiem, C. A. Field studies of French and Raven's bases of power: Critique, reanalysis, and suggestions for future research. *Psychological Bulletin*, 1985, 97, 387–411; Yukl, G., and Falbe, C. M. Importance of different power sources in downward and lateral relations. *Journal of Applied Psychology*, 1991, 76, 416–423.

7. See, for example, the classic work by Barnard, C. I. *The Functions of the Executive*. Cambridge, Mass.: Harvard University Press, 1938. For additional perspectives on this issue, see Zelditch, M., and Walker, H. A. Legitimacy and the stability of authority. In S. B. Bacharach and E. J. Lawler (eds.), *Advances in Group Processes*, vol. 1. Greenwich, Conn.: JAI Press, 1984, 1–25.

8. Tannen, D. The power of talk: Who gets heard and why. *Harvard Business Review*, September–October, 1995, 138.

9. Greene, C. N., and Podsakoff, P. M. Effects of withdrawal of a performance-contingent reward on supervisory influence and power. *Academy of Management Journal*, 1981, 24, 527–542.

10. Atwater, L. E. The relationship between supervisory power and organizational characteristics. *Group & Organization Management*, 1995, 20, 460–485; Brass, D. J., and Burkhardt, M. E. Potential power and power use: An investigation of structure and behavior. *Academy of Management Journal*, 1993, 36, 441–470; Krackhardt, D. Assessing the political landscape: Structure, cognition, and power in organizations. *Administrative Science Quarterly*, 1990, 35, 342–369; Pfeffer, J. *Power in Organizations*, 101–122.

11. Wilke, J. R. Computer links erode hierarchical nature of workplace culture. *Wall Street Journal*, December 9, 1993, A1, A7.

12. Baker, S., and Alexander, K. L. The owners vs. the boss at Weirton Steel. *Business Week*, November 15, 1993, 38.

13. Henkoff, R. How to plan for 1995. *Fortune*, December 31, 1990, 70–81.

14. Adapted from Wang, Z., and Heller, F. A. Patterns of power distribution in managerial decision making in Chinese and British industrial organizations. *International Journal of Human Resource Management*, 1993, 4(1), 113–128.

15. Adapted from Cummings, T. G., and Worley, C. G. *Organization Development and Change*, 5th ed. St. Paul: West, 1993, 156.

16. Kanter, R. M. Power failure in management circuits. *Harvard Business Review*, July–August 1979, 66. Also see Ibarra, H., and Andrews, S. B. Power, social influence, and sense making: Effects of network centrality and proximity on employee perceptions. *Administrative Science Quarterly*, 1993, 38, 277–303.

17. Krackhardt, D., and Hanson, J. R. Informal networks: The company behind the chart. *Harvard Business Review*, July–August, 1993, 104–111.

18. Adapted from Fritsch, P. Bilingual employees are seeking more pay and many now get it. *Wall Street Journal*, November 13, 1996, A1, A6.

19. Falbe, C. M., and Yukl, G. Consequences of managers using single influence tactics and combinations of tactics. *Academy of Management Journal*, 1992, 35, 638–652; Yukl, G., Falbe, C. M., and Youn, J. Y. Patterns of influence behavior for managers. *Group & Organization Management*, 1993, 18, 5–28; Yukl, G., Guinan, P. J., and Sottolano, D. Influence tactics used for different objectives with subordinates, peers, and superiors. *Group & Organization Management*, 1995, 20, 272–296; Yukl, G., and Tracey, J. B. Consequences of influence tactics used with subordinates, peers, and the boss. *Journal of Applied Psychology*, 1992, 77, 525–535. See also, Morand, D. A. Dominance, deference, and egalitarianism in organizational interaction: A sociolinguistic analysis of power and politeness. *Organization Science*, 1996, 7, 544–556.

20. Maslyn, J. M., Farmer, S. M., and Fedor, D. B. Failed upward influence attempts. *Group & Organization Management*, 1996, 21, 461–480; Thacker, R. A. and Wayne, S. J. An examination of upward influence tactics and assessments of promotability. *Journal of Management*, 1995, 21, 739–756; Yukl, G., Kim, H., and Falbe, C. M. Antecedents of influence outcomes. *Journal of Applied Psychology*, 1996, 81, 309–317.

21. Schmidt, S. M., and Kipnis, D. The perils of persistence. *Psychology Today*, November 1987, 32–34. Also see Judge, T. A., and Bretz, R. D. Political influence behavior and career success. *Journal of Management*, 1994, 20, 43–65.

22. Cohen, A. R., and Bradford, D. L. Influence without authority: The use of alliances, reciprocity, and exchange to accomplish work. *Organizational Dynamics*, Winter 1989, 5–17.

23. These characteristics of managerial effectiveness are based, in part, on Kotter, J. P. Power, dependence, and effective management. *Harvard Business Review*, April 1977, 125–136; Kotter, J. P. *Power and Influence*. New York: Free Press, 1985.

24. Adapted from Crosson, C. Print scrn, numlock and other mysteries of the keyboard. *Wall Street Journal*, October 22, 1996, B1, B8; Frost, P. J., and Ergi, C. P. The political process of innovation. In L. L. Cummings and B. M. Staw (eds.), *Research in Organizational Behavior*, vol. 13. Greenwich, Conn.: JAI Press, 1991, 230, 251–252.

25. Ferris, G. R., Frink, D. D., Bhawak, D. P. S., Zhou, J., and Gilmore, D. C. Reactions of diverse groups to politics in the workplace. *Journal of Management*, 1996, 22, 23–44; Pfeffer, J. *Power in Organizations*, 7.

26. Ferris, G. R., and Kacmar, K. M. Perceptions of organizational politics. *Journal of Management*, 1992, 18, 93–116; Gilmore, D. C., Ferris, G. R., Dulebohn, J. H., and Harrell-Cook, G. Organizational politics and employee attendance. *Group & Organization Management*, 1996, 21, 481–494; Parker, C. P., Dipboye, R. L, and Jackson, S. L. Perceptions of organizational politics: An investigation of antecedents and consequences. *Journal of Management*, 1995, 21, 891–912.

27. Madison, D. L., Allen, R. W., Porter, L. W., Renwick, P. A., and Mayes, B. T. Organizational politics: An exploration of managers' perceptions. *Human Relations*, 1980, 33, 79–100.

28. Beemon, D. R., and Sharkey, T. W. The use and abuse of corporate politics. *Business Horizons*, March–April 1987, 26–30.

29. Galbraith, C. S., and Merrill, G. B. The politics of forecasting: Managing the truth. *California Management Review*, Winter 1996, 29–43.

30. Kacmar, K. M., and Ferris, G. R. Politics at work: Sharpening the focus of political behavior in organizations. *Business Horizons*, July–August, 1993, 70–74.

31. Excerpted with permission from Longenecker, C. O., Sims, H. P., and Gioia, D. A. Behind the mask: The politics of employee appraisal. *Academy of Management Executive*, 1987, 1, 183–193.

32. Gioia, D. A., and Longenecker, C. O. Delving into the dark side: The politics of executive appraisal. *Organizational Dynamics*, Winter 1994, 54.

33. Longenecker, Sims, and Gioia, Behind the mask, 56.

34. McClelland, D. C. *Human Motivation*. Glenview, Ill.: Scott, Foresman, 1985; McClelland, D. C., and Boyatzis, R. E. Leadership motive pattern and long-term success in management. *Journal of Applied Psychology*, 1982, 67, 737–743; Sankowsky, D. Understanding the abuse of power. *Organizational Dynamics*, Spring 1995, 57–71.

35. Ragins, B. R., and Sundstrom, E. Gender and power in organizations: A longitudinal perspective. *Psychological Bulletin*, 1989, 105, 70.

36. Christie, R., and Geis, F. L. *Studies in Machiavellianism*. New York: Academic Press, 1970; Wilson, D. S., Near, D., and Miller, R. R. Machiavellianism: A synthesis of the evolutionary and psychological literatures. *Psychological Bulletin*, 1996, 119, 285–299.

37. Woodman, R. W., Wayne, S. J., and Rubinstein, D. Personality correlates of a propensity to engage in political behavior in organizations. *Proceedings of the Southwest Academy of Management,* 1985, 131–135. Also see Nelson, G., and Gilbertson, D. Organizational Machiavellianism: The ruthlessness of opportunism. *Proceedings of the Southwest Academy of Management,* 1991, 119–122.

38. Sitkin, S. B., and Pablo, A. L. Reconceptualizing the determinants of risk behavior. *Academy of Management Review,* 1992, 17, 9–38.

39. Adapted from Reddy, W. B., and Williams, G. The visibility/credibility inventory: Measuring power and influence. In J. W. Pfeiffer (ed.), *The 1988 Annual: Developing Human Resources.* San Diego: University Associates, 1988, 115–124.

40. Adapted from Frost, P. J., and Egri, C. P. The political process of innovation. In L. L. Cummings and B. M. Staw (eds.), *Research in Organizational Behavior,* vol. 13. Greenwich, Conn.: JAI Press, 1991, 246–248.

10

Leadership: Foundations

LEARNING OBJECTIVES

When you have finished studying this chapter, you should be able to:

- Identify the differences between leaders and managers.
- List the competencies and sources of power that leaders can use to influence others.
- Describe the traits model of leadership.
- Define two key behavioral leadership dimensions.
- Describe Fiedler's contingency model.
- Explain the leadership and contingency variables in Hersey and Blanchard's situational model and House's path-goal model.
- Discuss the situational variables in the Vroom-Jago model.

OUTLINE

PREVIEW CASE

Stirring It Up at Campbell Soup

In the late 1980s, Campbell soup was beset by falling earnings, weak marketing, and a lack of leadership. Since David Johnson took over as CEO in 1990, earnings have increased at the annual rate of nearly 18 percent, new products have been introduced, and sales have increased dramatically. Such feats are difficult to achieve when a leader has to motivate more than 44,000 employees scattered throughout the world.

Johnson's leadership style is informal, and he is accessible to all employees. He regularly eats with employees, talking with them about new products they would like Campbell to make and problems they encounter at work. When an employee comes up with a new idea, he holds that person accountable for developing the product and joins in celebrating his or her success. When British employees recommended that Campbell introduce low-fat cream soups, the new soup became a big seller in England. Dressed in a red cape as "Souperman, Top Spoon," he praised the employees for their suggestion at one of their plant's pep rallies. He suggested that Campbell transplant the recipe to the United States. The approach worked, and now Campbell is a leader in that segment of the U.S. market. Similarly, an employee noticed that, when people eat soup, many put saltines, croutons, or pieces of bread in it. A suggestion was made to market Pepperidge Farm Goldfish, a Campbell Soup product, with its soup lines. As a result, Goldfish sales jumped 22 percent in one year.

Although cheerleading and communication are important, so is measurement. Johnson believes that measurement creates discipline and that numbers always tell the story. He doesn't accept excuses when numbers point to weaknesses. Managers who miss their numbers the first time are rarely fired, but are counseled not to miss them twice. Johnson focuses employees' attention on a single number—increasing net earnings faster than competitors. Scoreboards comparing Campbell's net-profit increases with other food companies—Nestlé and Heinz among others—are prominently posted throughout the company. People are rewarded for thinking like owners of their own small business. Salary increases are based on the entire company hitting its net earning numbers. He requires that his top 300 executives own up to three times their annual salaries in Campbell stock. Members of the board of directors are paid in stock, not cash. He bans directors from repricing their stock options when the market slumps.

To reach the shared vision of Campbell Soup as a global food leader, the management team is focusing on Asia. Campbell's strategy is to customize its brands to local tastes. Its cream of pumpkin soup has become Australia's top-selling canned soup, and in Hong Kong it sells watercress-and-duck-gizzard soup. Johnson wants managers who have extensive international experience, who can make decisions, and who can motivate local employees to excel.[1]

David Johnson is an effective leader. If we examine how he steered the rebirth of Campbell Soup, two important behaviors stand out. First, he developed an agenda for himself and the company that included a new vision of what the company could and should be. It was a vision of a competitive and profitable firm that produced high-quality, innovative products. Second, he gained cooperation from employees by motivating them to buy into this vision. He worked hard to delegate decision making to teams of employees who could make decisions, such as the British employees who created the new soup. These employees gained a sense of belonging, recognition, and self-esteem, along with a feeling of control over their lives and the ability to live up to their own ideals. These feelings elicited a powerful motivational response from all team members. Johnson maintained these feelings by regularly providing support (financial and marketing) for all employees. As a result, employees' work became intrinsically motivating.

Leadership is the process whereby one person influences others to achieve a goal.[2] A **leader** is someone who does the right things to inspire others to help accomplish that person's vision. David Johnson exercised leadership because he was able to guide, steer, and influence employees in developing new product lines for this 127-year-old company.

Not all employees or managers exercise leadership. An employee may be good at his or her job but not be a leader; a good manager may not be an effective leader. The origin of the word *manage* is a word meaning "hand." Basically, managing is about "handling" things, about maintaining order, and about organization and control. A **manager** directs the work of others and is responsible for results. An effective manager brings a degree of order and consistency to the work setting and his or her employees. The origin of the word *lead* means to "go in advance, to guide." They're pioneers, venturing into unexplored territory and guiding their followers to new and unfamiliar destinations. Therefore leadership, in contrast to management, is about coping with change. Let's explore these differences more closely.[3]

Managers handle complexity through *planning* and *budgeting*. They set goals, determine how to achieve those goals, and then allocate resources to achieve those goals. By contrast, leaders start with a *direction* or *vision* of what the future might look like and then develop innovative strategies to achieve that vision. According to Norman Brinker, chairman and CEO of Brinker International, vision is the art of seeing beyond the present to seeing the possible. In uncertain times, employees look to leaders for vision. Like yeast, vision is a leavening agent, and it stimulates the organization to grow and change. In its earliest days, Brinker's vision of leadership in the restaurant industry kept the company on course. This vision helped Brinker's International beat the competition and enabled employees to take risks and be innovative entrepreneurs. Now, Brinker International has some of the nation's fastest growing restaurants in its chain, including On The Border, Macaroni Grill, Chili's, and Cozymel's.

Effective managers achieve their goals by *organizing* and *staffing*. They create an organizational structure and design jobs to accomplish the plan's requirements, staffing the jobs with qualified employees, communicating goals to those employees, and devising systems to monitor employees' progress in achieving those goals. Leaders try to *recruit* and *keep* employees who share their vision. This approach involves creating teams of people who not only understand and share the leader's vision but also are given the opportunity to decide how best to achieve it.

Finally, managers ensure that employees reach goals by *controlling* their behaviors. That is, they monitor results in great detail by means of reports and meetings, and they note failure to reach the goals. Effective leadership requires *motivating* and *inspiring* teams of employees, as David Johnson has done at Campbell Soup. It taps their needs, values, and emotions.[4] Johnson was able to motivate employees to overcome obstacles, such as the lack of product development, that the company faced when he became CEO by empowering employees to make decisions. By empowering employees, he viewed his role to be motivational, not controlling.

Some managers are leaders, but others aren't, as Figure 10.1 shows. The roles of manager and leader often require different behaviors, but the roles can over-

■ **FIGURE 10.1**

Behaviors of Leaders and Managers

Managers Who Also Are Leaders

Leaders' Behaviors
• Vision and direction
• Align employees
• Inspire and motivate

Managers' Behaviors
• Plan and budget
• Organize and staff
• Control

lap. Return to the Preview Case and evaluate David Johnson's behaviors. How did his behaviors help Campbell Soup achieve its vision?

KEYS TO EFFECTIVE LEADERSHIP

Leadership always has been, and probably always will be, important to organizations. The need for effective managerial leadership and the difficulty of providing it have increased rapidly because of the accelerating complexity of organizational life. Hundreds of firms and dozens of industries have been restructured to remain competitive. The banking industry provides a good example. Since federal deregulation, a local bank's competition is not just the other bank down the street. It is also Sears, Merrill Lynch, American Express, foreign banks, and General Electric. The airline, insurance, automobile, health care, and other industries face new competitive pressures every day. Effective leadership is required to cope with such changes.

■ LEADER-SUBORDINATE RELATIONSHIPS

Leaders become an integral part of an organization, group, or team only after proving their value to subordinates. Their rewards are both economic and psychological rewards. The top people in many organizations are paid up to eighty-five times as much as their lowest-paid employees. (Notwithstanding the possibility that some people may not be worth that much more than others, someone thinks so.) However, people seek leadership roles even when there are no economic rewards. The captain of a collegiate basketball team, a union steward, and the chairperson of a civic or church committee don't hold paid positions, but they usually exercise leadership. Leadership rewards people with power over others; with this power, people believe that they can influence to some extent the well-being of others and can control their own futures.

Leaders receive their authority from subordinates because the subordinates have accepted them as leaders. To maintain a leadership position, a person must enable others to gain satisfactions that are otherwise beyond their reach. In return, they satisfy the leader's need for power and prominence and give the leader the support necessary to reach organizational goals.

■ COMPETENCIES OF LEADERS

The leadership practices of David Johnson and Norman Brinker obviously have been successful. Both share several common competencies, as shown in Figure 10.2, with many other successful leaders.[5]

Creating a Vision   Leaders have the ability to pull employees toward them by creating a new vision. Many people want to be part of an organization that has a vision larger than reality. When a leader can share such a vision with others and get them committed to it, the vision "grabs" them. Both David Johnson and Norman Brinker are visionary leaders. Employees become so caught up in pursuing a vision that they absorb and commit themselves to the goals and values of such leaders. Moreover, the visions that leaders convey often instill confidence in others, leading them to believe that they can succeed.

Meaning through Communication   Successful leaders have the ability to communicate effectively with employees. Such leaders can present a compelling vision of the future, generating enthusiasm and commitment in others. The old method of telling people what to do just doesn't work in many cases anymore. In Johnson's case, he used pep rallies at Campbell's plants to build enthusiasm and commitment.

Empowerment   The sharing of influence and control with employees is **empowerment.** The leader allows employees to share in developing goals and strategies and the satisfactions derived from reaching those goals. Campbell Soup employees are urged to talk directly to customers and involve them in new product development and introduction, such as selecting a price range for the soup, judging its taste and aroma, and the like. Effective leaders are sensitive to the needs of employees. They tap the motivations and capabilities in others to pursue shared goals. The behaviors associated with empowerment include taking delight in employees' development, realizing that visions are achieved by teams and not by single employees, and helping employees reach their personal goals.[6] Responsi-

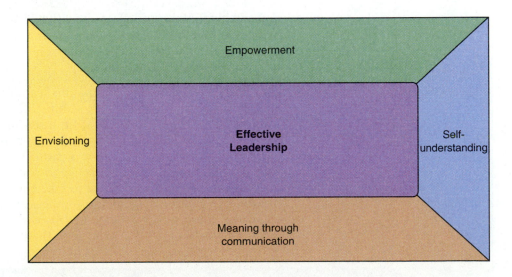

■ FIGURE 10.2

Leaders' Competencies

ble employees will not make decisions that are inconsistent with their goals and those of the organization, especially goals that they helped shape.

Self-Understanding   Effective leaders have the skill to recognize their own strengths and weaknesses. They tend to hire employees who can offset their weaknesses. They are eager to receive feedback on their performance. Effective leaders continually take an inventory of themselves, asking themselves questions such as: What am I really good at? What are my strengths? What do I lack? and What do I need to work on?

These leadership competencies can be learned. In many organizations, such as Texas Instruments, General Foods, and Johnson & Johnson, potential leaders get the types of job experience early in their careers that help them develop these competencies. The following Across Cultures account describes how Gillette grooms global talent.

ACROSS CULTURES

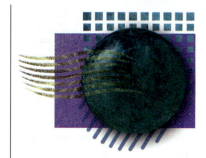

Grooming Global Leaders

When King Camp Gillette founded the Gillette Company in 1903, he laid the foundation for the company that not only would be renowned the world over, but also would be guided by two principles: quality and market dominance. Although best known for its shaving products, it also manufactures Papermate and Waterman Pens, Oral-B Toothbrushes, coffee grinders, hair dryers, and dental hygiene products sold under the Braun label. Over 70 percent of Gillette's more than $6 billion in annual revenues are derived outside the United States.

In an effort to achieve world-class leadership, Gillette recruits people who

- hold university degrees,
- have good social skills,
- are mobile and globally career-oriented,
- are fluent in English and at least one other language, and
- are young—under thirty—who are enthusiastic and aggressive.

What happens after they are hired? The management trainee is paired with a Gillette senior manager in one of its businesses in a foreign country. The trainee will spend as long as eighteen months learning about marketing, finance, and manufacturing and how to work within Gillette's organization in that country. Trainees typically work in two or three areas during their training assignments. In addition to their daily assignments, trainees participate in monthly seminars on topics such as business practices in a particular country, finance for nonfinancial managers, and presentation skills. Upon completion of their training program, graduates can either return home to take entry-level positions or go to another country. Subsequent assignments in other countries are made for those moving up in the company. Eventually, the most successful graduates return to their home countries as general managers. These general managers have spent ten years or more in various countries honing their leadership competencies.[7]

■ SOURCES AND USES OF POWER

To influence others, a person must appeal to one or more of their needs. If a robber is pointing a gun at a bank teller and is ready to fire it, chances are that the teller will do what the robber asks. History proves, however, that in many situations people refuse to obey an order even when faced with death. Thus effective leadership depends as much on acceptance of direction by the follower as on the leader giving it.

Power and influence are central to a leader's job. In Chapter 9, we described the sources of a manager's power as legitimate, reward, coercive, referent, and expert. It's useful to think of a leader's power in the same way, so let's briefly review those sources of power.[8]

Legitimate Power   Employees may do something because the leader has the right to request them to do it and they have an obligation to comply. This **legitimate power** comes from the leader's position in the organization. Employees at The Body Shop usually follow the directions of CEO Anita Roddick because she has legitimate power. Speeders usually pull over when they see red or blue lights flashing from a police car because they believe that police have legitimate authority to issue citations to speeders.

Reward Power   Employees may do something to get rewards that the leader controls (such as promotions, pay raises, and better assignments). Thus **reward power** comes from the leader's ability to provide something desired by team members in return for their desired behaviors. Roddick's goal for The Body Shop is to become a major competitor in the cosmetics industry, enabling it to give employees salary increases, honor its commitment not to test drugs on animals, and use its profits to help finance projects such as Greenpeace, Amnesty International, or rain-forest survival.[9]

Coercive Power   Employees may do something to avoid punishments that the leader controls (such as demotions, reprimands, no pay raises, and termination). **Coercive power** is the potential to influence others through the use of sanctions or punishment. Unfortunately, coercive power doesn't necessarily encourage desired behavior. In Chapter 4, we described how employees whom managers have reprimanded for poor workmanship may suddenly slow production, stop working altogether, be absent more often, and take other negative actions.

Referent Power   Employees may do something because they admire the leader, want to be like the leader, and want to receive the leader's approval. **Referent power** usually is associated with individuals who possess admired personal characteristics, such as charisma, integrity, and courage. Michael Dell, CEO of Dell Computer, has referent power because of his instinctive feel for technology and marketing, which has propelled his company into a world-class mail-order computer retailer.

Expert Power   Employees may do something because they believe that the leader has special knowledge and knows what is needed to accomplish a task. **Expert power** has a narrow scope: Employees are influenced by a leader only within that leader's area of expertise. The expert power of Janet Reno, U.S. Attorney General and a member of President Clinton's cabinet, is confined to the Justice Department, whereas Roddick's expert power is confined to the cosmetics industry and social programs.

Figure 10.3 classifies these sources of power as personal and organizational. Legitimate, reward, and coercive powers are organizational, and the organization's policies and culture prescribe them. Part of the leader's job is to use them wisely to motivate members of the organization. A team probably won't achieve exceptional levels of performance if its leader relies solely on formal organizational power. Thus reliance on referent and expert power—personal power—can lead to higher job satisfaction and less absenteeism or turnover. However, an effective leader uses multiple sources of power and is flexible in their use, depending on the situation.[10]

The bases of power are changing within organizations because of changing technology, the rapidly increasing ability of employees to use information to make decisions, and the flattening of the management hierarchy. Leaders must now empower employees to get results. One leader who has done so is Ralph Stayer, CEO of Johnsonville Foods, a specialty foods and sausage maker in Sheboygan, Wisconsin. Said Stayer, "Flattening pyramids doesn't work if you don't transfer the power, too. Before, I didn't have power because I had people wandering around not giving a damn. Real power is getting people committed. It comes from giving it to others who are in a better position to do things than you are. The only control a leader can possibly have comes when people are controlling themselves."[11]

TRADITIONAL LEADERSHIP MODELS

Many people believe that they have the intuitive ability to identify outstanding leaders. Often they believe that people with pleasing personalities will be highly successful leaders and recommend as leaders those who have personal charm.

FIGURE 10.3   Sources of a Leader's Power and Effectiveness

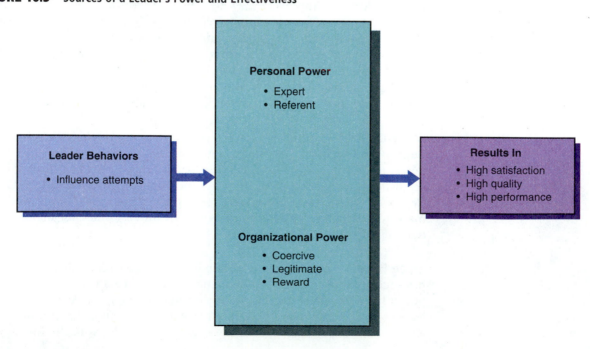

Leader Behaviors
- Influence attempts

Personal Power
- Expert
- Referent

Organizational Power
- Coercive
- Legitimate
- Reward

Results In
- High satisfaction
- High quality
- High performance

However, most people do *not* have the intuitive ability to select individuals who become good leaders. In fact, there are better ways to assess leadership effectiveness and potential. In the remainder of this chapter, we present and examine three general approaches to assessing leadership: the traits, behavioral, and contingency models.

■ TRAITS MODEL

The **traits model** is based on observed characteristics of many leaders—both successful and unsuccessful. The resulting lists of traits—drive, originality, high energy, extraversion, introversion, and the like—are then compared to those of potential leaders to assess their likelihood of success or failure. There is support for the notion that effective leaders have interests and abilities and, perhaps, even personality traits that are different from those of less effective leaders. Most researchers, however, believe that the traits approach is inadequate for successfully predicting leadership performance for at least three reasons.[12]

First, although more than 100 personality traits of successful leaders have been identified, no consistent patterns have been found. (In fact, the list of personality traits never ends.) The trait stereotypes of successful leaders of salespeople include optimism, enthusiasm, and dominance. Successful production leaders are usually progressive, introverted, cooperative, and genuinely respectful of employees. These descriptions also are simply stereotypes. Many successful leaders of salespeople and production employees do not have all, or even some, of these characteristics. There also is often disagreement over which traits are the most important for an effective leader. However, two leaders with significantly different traits have been successful in the same situation.[13]

Despite these difficulties, the evidence does suggest that four traits are shared by most (but not all) successful leaders. These traits are more likely to be found in middle-level and top leaders than in team leaders or first-line supervisors.

- *Intelligence.* Leaders tend to have somewhat higher intelligence than their subordinates.
- *Maturity and breadth.* Leaders tend to be emotionally mature and have a broad range of interests.
- *Inner motivation and achievement drive.* Leaders want to accomplish things; when they achieve one goal, they seek another. They do not depend primarily on employees for their motivation to achieve goals.
- *Employee-centered.* Leaders are able to work effectively with employees in a variety of situations. They respect others and realize that to accomplish tasks they must be considerate of others' needs and values.

The second criticism of the traits model is that it relates physical characteristics such as height, weight, appearance, physique, energy, and health to effective leadership. Most of these factors are related to situational demands that can significantly affect a leader's effectiveness. For example, military or law enforcement people must be a particular minimum height and weight in order to perform certain tasks well. Although these characteristics may help an individual to rise to a leadership position in such organizations, neither height nor weight correlates highly with effective leadership. In educational and business organizations height and weight play no role in performance and thus are not requirements for a leadership position.

The final criticism of the traits model is that leadership itself is complex. A relationship between personality and a person's interest in particular types of jobs could well exist, which a study relating personality and effectiveness might not identify. For example, one study found that high earners (a measure of success) in small firms were more ambitious, were more open-minded, and described themselves as more considerate than low earners.

◼ BEHAVIORAL MODELS

Behavioral models focus on what leaders actually *do* and how they do it. These models suggest that effective leaders assist individuals and teams in achieving their goals in two ways: (1) by having task-centered relations with members that focus attention on the quality and quantity of work accomplished; and (2) by being considerate and supportive of members' attempts to achieve personal goals (such as work satisfaction, promotions, and recognition), settling disputes, keeping people happy, providing encouragement, and giving positive reinforcement.

Ohio State University Leadership Studies   The greatest number of studies of leader behavior have come from the Ohio State University leadership studies program, which began in the late 1940s under the direction of Ralph Stogdill.[14] That research was aimed at identifying those leader behaviors that are important for attaining team and organizational goals. These efforts resulted in the identification of two dimensions of leader behavior: consideration and initiating structure.

Consideration is the extent to which leaders are likely to have job relationships characterized by mutual trust, two-way communication, and respect for employees' ideas consideration for their feelings. Leaders with this style emphasize the satisfaction of employee needs. They typically find time to listen, are willing to make changes, look out for the personal welfare of employees, and are friendly and approachable. A high degree of consideration indicates psychological closeness between leader and subordinates; a low degree shows greater psychological distance and a more impersonal leader.

Initiating structure is the extent to which leaders are likely to define and structure their roles and those of employees in order to accomplish the organization's goals. Leaders with this style emphasize direction of group activities through planning, communicating information, scheduling, assigning tasks, emphasizing deadlines, and giving directions. They maintain definite standards of performance and ask subordinates to follow standard rules. In short, leaders with a high degree of initiating structure concern themselves with accomplishing tasks by giving directions and expecting them to be followed.

Studies also suggest that a leader who emphasizes initiating structure generally improves productivity, at least in the short run. However, leaders who rank high on initiating structure and low on consideration generally have large numbers of grievances, absenteeism, and high turnover rates among employees. We might rank David Johnson of Campbell Soup as high on both consideration and initiating structure, and Anita Roddick as high on consideration and moderate on initiating structure.

The Ohio State University researchers made an assumption that leader behavior is related not only to indirect measures of performance, such as absenteeism, grievances, and turnover, but also to direct measures of performance, such as the number of units produced. Later studies by others have failed to show a significant relationship between leadership behavior and group performance. This failure indicates that individual productivity is influenced by other factors, including

(1) the employee's social status within the group; (2) the technology used; (3) employee expectations of a certain style of leadership; and (4) employee psychological rewards from working with a particular type of leader.

When Is Consideration Effective?   The most positive effects of leader consideration on productivity and job satisfaction occur when (1) the task is routine and denies employees any job satisfaction; (2) employees are predisposed toward participative leadership; (3) team members must learn something new; (4) employees feel that their involvement in the decision-making process is legitimate and affects their job performance; and (5) few status differences exist between leader and subordinate.

When Is Initiating Structure Effective?   The most positive effects of leader initiating structure on productivity and job satisfaction occur when (1) a high degree of pressure for output is imposed by someone other than the leader; (2) the task satisfies employees; (3) employees depend on the leader for information and direction on how to complete the task; (4) employees are psychologically predisposed toward being told what to do and how to do it; and (5) more than twelve employees report to the leader.[15]

The following Managing in Practice account highlights the leadership style of two different but effective leaders. After reading these descriptions, who would you rather work for?

MANAGING IN PRACTICE

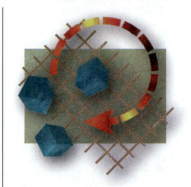

A Tale of Two Leaders

Linda Wachner, CEO of Warnco, is the only female CEO of a Fortune 500 industrial company. Employees describe her as a person who's so impatient to achieve results that she will do almost anything, including humiliating employees in front of others. Employees carry notebooks to meetings with the words DO IT NOW! inscribed on the front cover. She regularly arrives at work early and often holds meetings until 1:00 A.M. Over one Thanksgiving, she called a manager thirty-one times to ask him questions. She also asked a newly hired vice-president, "Have you fired anyone yet?" He replied, "No." "Well," she said, "you'd better start firing people so they'll understand that you are serious." She tells people, "If you don't like it, leave. It's not a prison."

Anita Roddick is instantly recognized as the CEO of the Body Shop when she drives her diesel-powered Volkswagen Golf to her Littlehampton headquarters in the rolling pastures of Sussex, England. Roddick and her husband are actively exploring ways to take the company private and turn it over to a nonprofit foundation that could use profits to finance good works rather than to pay shareholders dividends. She rails about administrative systems that are killing the entrepreneurial spirit of the Body Shop. She realizes, however, that hiring professional managers, installing tighter inventory controls, and streamlining management processes are needed to keep the company alive. To pursue these projects, she has delegated the day-to-day running of the company to a team of employees. Rather than trying to operate its own stores, The Body Shop now franchises stores and permits franchisees to make decisions regarding hiring, advertising, and merchandising.[16]

Limitations of the Behavioral Model   The major limitation of the Ohio State University research was the limited attention it gave to the effects of the situation on leadership style. It paid attention to relationships between leader and members of an organization but gave little attention to the situation in which the relationships occurred. For example, compare the situations facing Anita Roddick at Body Shop and David Johnson at Campbell Soup. Can these different situations account for the success of their different styles of leadership? The importance of the situation is considered by the contingency, or situational, models of leadership.

CONTINGENCY MODELS

Research into the leadership process before the mid 1960s showed no consistent relationship between leadership style and measures of performance, group processes, and job satisfaction. Although many researchers concluded that the situation in which a leader functions plays a significant role in determining the leader's effectiveness, they did little to identify the key situational variables.

Contingency leadership theorists, in contrast, aimed their research at discovering the variables that permit certain leadership characteristics and behaviors to be effective in a given situation. For example, contingency theorists would suggest that a team leader at Chaparral Steel in charge of buying a new $2.3 million steel mill and the director of marketing at Baxter International creating an advertising strategy for a new drug sold to physicians are facing substantially different situations. Because of the situation, they may choose different leadership styles to reach their goals. According to contingency models, both leaders could be effective if they did so.

Four variables frequently cited as having an influence on a leader's behavior are (1) a leader's personal characteristics; (2) employees' personal characteristics; (3) the group's characteristics; and (4) the structure of the group, department, or organization. These contingency variables, shown in Figure 10.4, don't act independently but interact to influence a leader's style of behavior. Thus the leadership process is complex, and simple prescriptions (such as "democratic leaders have more satisfied employees than autocratic leaders") just aren't valid.

In this section, we present and discuss four specific contingency models of leadership: Fiedler's contingency model, Hersey and Blanchard's situational leadership model, House's path-goal model, and the Vroom-Jago model. Each of these models focuses primarily on one of the four contingency variables.

■ FIEDLER'S CONTINGENCY MODEL

Fred Fiedler and his associates developed the first contingency model of the leadership process.[17] **Fiedler's contingency model** specifies that a performance is contingent upon both the leader's motivational system and the degree to which the leader controls and influences the situation. The model's three contingency variables—group atmosphere, task structure, and the leader's position power—are shown in Figure 10.5. In combination, the three contingency variables create eight situations, as shown in Figure 10.6.

Group Atmosphere   A leader's acceptance by the team is called **group atmosphere.** A leader who is accepted by and inspires loyalty in employees needs few signs of rank to get them to commit themselves to a task. When leader and employees get

■ **FIGURE 10.4**   **Contingency Variables That Affect Leader Behavior**

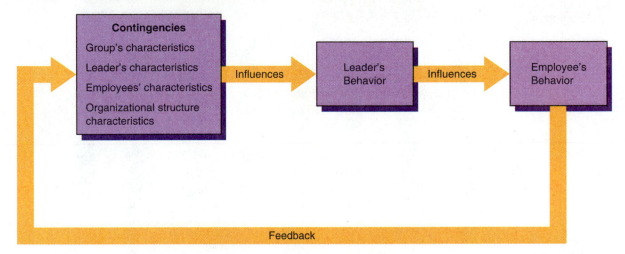

along well together, there is less friction. In groups that reject the leader, the leader's basic problem is to keep from having employees go around him or her or sabotaging the task.

Task Structure   The extent to which a task performed by employees is routine or nonroutine is the degree of **task structure** that exists. A routine task is likely to have clearly defined goals, to consist of only a few steps or procedures, to be verifiable, and to have a correct solution. At the other extreme is the task that is completely nonroutine. In this situation, the leader may no more know how to perform the task than the employees do. Such a task is likely to have unclear or changing goals and multiple paths to accomplishment; the task cannot be done by the "numbers."

Eckhard Pfeiffer is the CEO of Compaq Computer. He describes his role as unstructured and himself as an orchestra leader. Pfeiffer spends sixty-five to seventy hours a week running the fifth largest computer company in the world. He rarely shoots from the hip, and his meticulous nature helps Compaq avoid mistakes. His thoroughness when contemplating a business decision has driven sub-

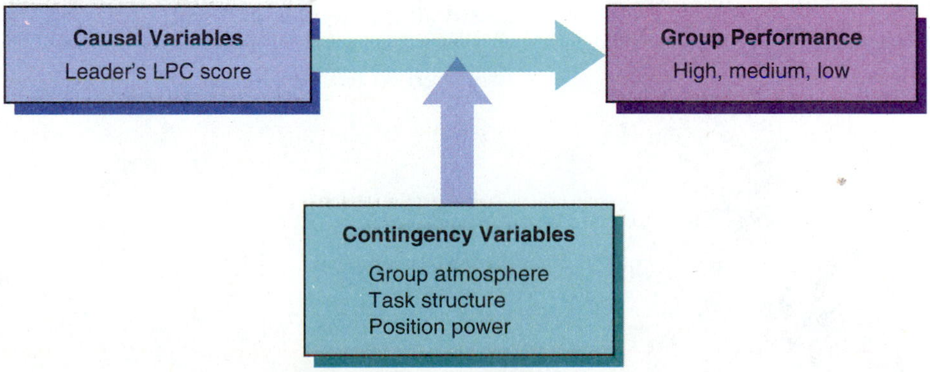

■ **FIGURE 10.5**

Variables in Fiedler's Contingency Model

Source: Yukl, G. A. *Leadership in Organizations,* 196. Copyright © 1989 by Prentice-Hall, Inc., Englewood Cliffs, N.J. Adapted with permission.

Causal Variables	**Group Performance**
Leader's LPC score	High, medium, low

Contingency Variables

Group atmosphere
Task structure
Position power

■ **FIGURE 10.6**   Continuum of the Three Basic Leadership Variables

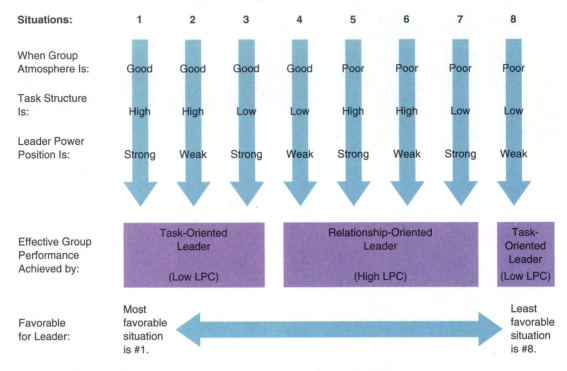

ordinates wild. When speaking, his words are so carefully considered that they seem rehearsed. He uses speeches primarily to get employees to dream the impossible. He evaluates Compaq mainly on how well it has done this year compared to last year and how it stacks up against other industry leaders—IBM, Fujitsu, Hewlett-Packard, and NEC.[18]

Position Power   The extent to which a leader has reward, coercive, and legitimate power is known as **position power.** In most business organizations, leaders such as Eckhard Pfeiffer have high position power. He has the authority to hire, discipline, and fire employees. In most voluntary organizations, committees, and social organizations, leaders tend to have low position power.

Leadership Style   Fiedler developed the **least preferred co-worker (LPC)** scale to measure leadership style. Scores are obtained by asking employees first to think about all the people with whom they have worked and then to identify the individual with whom they have worked least well. The person then rates this least preferred co-worker on a set of eighteen scales, five of which are as follows:

Pleasant									Unpleasant
	8	7	6	5	4	3	2	1	
Friendly									Unfriendly
	8	7	6	5	4	3	2	1	
Accepting									Rejecting
	8	7	6	5	4	3	2	1	

Relaxed   Tense

          8   7   6   5   4   3   2   1

Close   Distant

          8   7   6   5   4   3   2   1

Low-LPC leaders describe their least preferred co-worker in negative terms. Low-LPC leaders are primarily motivated by the task and gain satisfaction from accomplishing the task. If tasks are being accomplished satisfactorily, low-LPC leaders will try to form and maintain relationships with their subordinates. Thus low-LPC leaders focus on improving relationships with their subordinates *after* they are assured that the assigned tasks are being completed. *High-LPC* leaders give a more positive description of their least preferred co-worker and are sensitive to others. They are primarily motivated by establishing and maintaining close interpersonal relationships. If high-LPC leaders have established good relationships with their subordinates, *then* they will focus on task accomplishment.

How Well Does It Work?   Fiedler's answer to how well it works is: "It all depends." What it all depends on are situational factors—leader-member relations, task structure, and leader power. Fiedler suggests that whether low-LPC or high-LPC leaders are more effective depends on the degree to which the situation allows the leader to influence others.

Let's return to Figure 10.6, which represents Fiedler's contingency model. It is based on the average results of the studies conducted by Fiedler and his associates. Task-oriented (low-LPC) leaders performed more effectively than high-LPC leaders in the most favorable situations (1, 2, and 3) and in the least favorable situation (8). Task-oriented leaders are motivated basically by task accomplishments. In the most favorable situation—when their group supports them, their power position is high, and the task is structured (situation 1)—leaders will strive to develop pleasant work relations in directing group members. They realize that conditions are very good and that successful task performance is likely. As a result, they can turn their attention to improving their relations with team members and often adopt a "hands off" style. Employees value such treatment, and satisfaction and performance remains high. In many respects, this situation reflects Anita Roddick's approach at the Body Shop. In the least favorable situation (8)—when the task is unstructured, leaders lack group support, and their position power is low—leaders will devote their energies to achieving organizational goals by telling employees what to do.

Figure 10.6 also shows situations in which relationship-oriented leaders (high-LPC) will probably perform more effectively than low-LPC leaders. Relationship-oriented leaders get the best performance under conditions that are moderately favorable (situations 4 through 7). Situations 4 and 5 describe cases in which (1) the group has a structured task but dislikes the leader, who must demonstrate concern for the emotions of employees; or (2) the group likes the leader but has an unstructured task, and the leader must depend on the willingness and creativity of group members to accomplish the group's goals. As a result, high-LPC leaders may shift their attention to task performance. Ygnacio Dominquez, a business development manager at IBM, is a high-LPC leader who provides guidance to his team members when they start a new task. Once they have learned how to proceed and their task becomes more structured, he delegates decision-making authority to them and supports them in their decisions.

Limitations of Fiedler's Model   Fiedler's contingency model has several limitations.[19] In particular, critics have questioned the use of the least preferred co-worker, arguing that better measures of leader behaviors are needed. The LPC has been called a one-dimensional concept; that is, it implies that, if individuals are highly motivated to accomplish tasks, they aren't unconcerned about their relations employees and vice versa. Fiedler's assumptions that a person's LPC score is constant over time, is unlikely to change, and is a trait of a leader have been questioned. In addition, Fiedler's model doesn't consider that leaders can influence both the task structure and group atmosphere because of their knowledge of the situation. Thus, because the leader can change the task, it isn't a contingency variable in the model. The nature of a task can be determined, at least in part, by the leader's style. That is, a leader can take a messy, ill-defined problem and structure it before presenting it to the team.

Implications for Leaders   Despite these limitations, Fiedler's contingency model has three important implications for leaders. First, both relationship-motivated and task-motivated leaders perform well in certain situations but not in others. Outstanding people at one level who are promoted may fail at the higher level because their leadership style doesn't match the demands of the situation.[20]

Second, leaders' effectiveness depends on the situation. Therefore an organization can affect a leader's effectiveness with a group by changing the reward system or by modifying the situation itself.

Third, leaders themselves can do something about their situations. Table 10.1 presents some of Fiedler's suggestions for changing particular contingency variables. He believes that leaders can be taught how to become better leaders. **Leader match** is a self-teaching process utilizing a programmed learning text that teaches the individual how to match his or her LPC level to the situation. This match could be achieved by changing the situation to mesh with the leader's style or by the leader moving to a new position in the organization.

The Semco Manufacturing Company in Brazil is prospering at a time when many other manufacturers in the country are going bankrupt. Most attribute Semco's good fortunes to its leader, Ricardo Semler. The following Across Cultures piece illustrates how leaders and the situation can match to increase organizational effectiveness. After reading this account, you should be able to identify the applicable contingency variables, how Ricardo Semler's style of leadership fit the situation, and how he was able to implement change.

TABLE 10.1   **Leadership Actions to Change Contingency Variables**

Modifying Group Atmosphere

1. Spend more—or less—informal time with your employees (lunch, leisure activities, etc.).
2. Request particular people to work in your team.
3. Volunteer to direct difficult or troublesome employees.
4. Suggest or effect transfers of particular employees into or out of your department.
5. Raise morale by obtaining positive outcomes for team members (e.g., special bonuses, time off, attractive jobs).

Continued

> **TABLE 10.1**   Leadership Actions to Change Contingency Variables—*Continued*
>
> ---
>
> *Modifying Task Structure*
>
> If you want to work with less structured tasks, you can
>
> **1.** ask your leader, whenever possible, to give you the new or unusual problems and let you figure out how to get them done; and
>
> **2.** bring the problems and tasks to your team members and invite them to work with you on the planning and decision-making phases of the tasks.
>
> If you want to work with more highly structured tasks, you can
>
> **1.** ask your leader to give you, whenever possible, the tasks that are more structured or to give you more detailed instructions; and
>
> **2.** break the job down into subtasks that can be more highly structured.
>
> ---
>
> *Modifying Position Power*
>
> To raise your position power, you can
>
> **1.** show others "who's boss" by exercising fully the powers that the organization provides; and
>
> **2.** make sure that information to others gets channeled through you.
>
> To lower your position power, you can
>
> **1.** call on team members to participate in planning and decision making functions; and
>
> **2.** delegate decision making to others.
>
> Source: Developed from Fiedler, F. E., and Garcia, J. E. *New Approaches to Effective Leadership.* New York: John Wiley & Sons, 1987, 49–93.

ACROSS CULTURES

Ricardo Semler

When Ricardo Semler took over the family business in 1979, Semco operated like many other Brazilian companies. Leaders used fear as a governing principle. Armed guards patrolled the factory floor, timed employees' trips to the rest rooms, and frisked employees for contraband when they left the building. Employees who broke equipment had their paychecks docked to replace it. Revenues from the manufacture of industrial pumps, mixers, and other products averaged $10,800 per employee.

Semler decided to replace fear with freedom. He reduced the organization's hierarchy from eight levels to three. The new levels were designed as concentric circles. One tiny circle contains six employees who develop business strategies and coordinate the activities of the company as a whole. The second circle contains the heads of the divisions. The third circle contains all other employees.

Employees are called associates. Associates make most day-to-day decisions, dress as they want, choose their own supervisors, and have no time clocks. All associates attend classes to learn how to read and understand financial statements. A union leader teaches the course. Every month, each associate gets a balance sheet, a profit-and-loss analysis, and a cash flow statement for his or her division. Almost a third of the associates set their own salaries.

Associates also evaluate their supervisors. These evaluations are posted for everyone to see. If a manager's evaluation is consistently low, that manager steps down. Senior managers in the tiny circle are also graded by their subordinates.

—Continued

After all these changes, what are the results? In 1996, on sales of more than $35 million, more than $434,000 was set aside for profit sharing. Employees decide who gets what amount because they know the numbers and who is contributing to profits. Sales per employee exceeded $139,000, more than four times Semco's competitors. Semco gets 1000 job applications for every job opening.[21]

■ HERSEY AND BLANCHARD'S SITUATIONAL MODEL

Hersey and Blanchard's situational model is based on the amount of relationship (supportive) and task (directive) behavior that a leader provides in a situation. In turn, the amount of either relationship or task behavior is based on the readiness of the follower.[22]

Task behavior is the extent to which a leader spells out to followers what to do, where to do it, and how to do it. Leaders who use task behavior structure, control, and closely supervise the behaviors of their followers. **Relationship behavior** is the extent to which a leader listens, provides support and encouragement, and involves followers in the decision-making process. **Follower readiness** is subordinates' ability and willingness to perform the task. Followers have various degrees of readiness, as shown in Figure 10.7. In R1, the followers are either unable or unwilling to perform the task, whereas in R4, they are able, willing, and confident that they can achieve the task. In R2, followers are unable but are willing to perform a task and are confident that they can do so. In R3, followers are able to do the task but are either unwilling to do so or aren't confident that they can. According to the situational leadership model, as the readiness level of individuals increases from R1 to R4, a leader should change his or her style to increase subordinates' commitment, competence, and performance.

Style of Leader and Readiness of Followers   Figure 10.7 also shows the linkages between task and relationship leader behaviors and follower readiness. The appropriate style of leadership is shown by the curve running through the four leadership quadrants, S1-S4.

A **telling style** provides clear and specific instruction. Because followers are either unable or unwilling to perform the task, specific direction and close supervision are needed. That is, the leader tells subordinates what to do and how to perform various tasks.

A **selling style** is most effective when followers are willing but still unable to carry out their tasks. The selling style provides both task and relationship leader behaviors. This style encourages two-way communication between the leader and followers and helps subordinates build confidence in their ability to perform the tasks.

A **participating style** works best when the followers are able but not fully confident of their ability to perform their tasks. This moderate level of follower readiness requires the leader to maintain two-way communication and to encourage and support followers in the use of the skills they have developed.

When followers are able and willing to perform their tasks and confident that they can do so, a delegating style of leader behavior is most appropriate. A **delegating style** provides little task or relationship behaviors because subordi-

■ FIGURE 10.7

Hersey and Blanchard's Situational Leadership Model

Source: Hersey, P., and Blanchard, K. H. *Management of Organizational Behavior: Utilizing Human Resources,* 5th ed. Englewood Cliffs, N.J.: Prentice-Hall, 1988. Used by permission form Ronald Campbell, President, Leadership Studies, Escondido, California, June 1994.

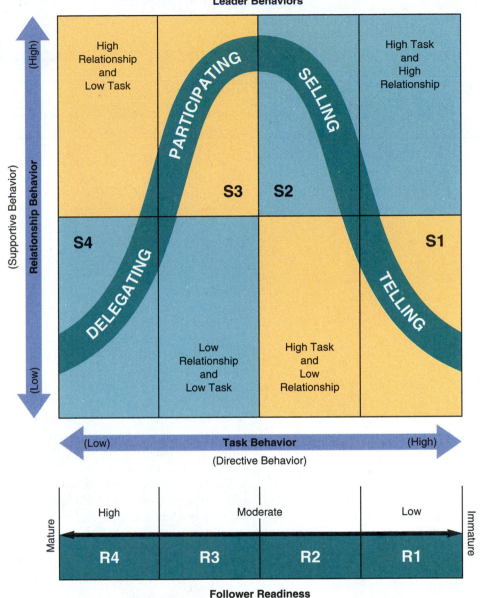

nates are empowered to make decisions. They decide how and when to do things.

To help you understand the dynamics of the situational leadership model, let's review the leadership behaviors of William Agee. In 1980, William Agee and Mary Cunningham were playing leading roles at Bendix Corporation. He was the CEO and she was his young, smart, and charming executive assistant with an MBA from Harvard Business School. In two years, she rose to executive vice-president but was forced to leave the company when she became Mrs. Agee. After a takeover attempt by Martin Marietta Corporation, Agee lost his job. In 1988, he became CEO of Morrison Knudsen Corporation, a giant construction and rail-equipment company headquartered in Boise, Idaho. The following Ethics in Practice feature highlights his leadership style and the problems it presented to the employees and shareholders of Morrison Knudsen.

ETHICS IN PRACTICE

William Agee

Upon arriving in Boise, Idaho, the Agees were lightning rods in the town and its largest employer. Mary was brilliant, charming, and gracious. In this small city where everyone knew everyone else, the lavish parties and the Agees' Hollywood friends astounded the locals. William and Mary Agee enjoyed the full support of the board of directors because of their charisma, performance records, and vision of huge contracts that would turn the company around. William Agee immediately secured some small contracts, started selling off businesses, and quickly improved the firm's financial picture. He sought little input from others and simply announced decisions.

Initially, these decisions paid off. The company's stock rose from $15 to $29 in three years. By 1991, its financial fortunes started slipping. Managers questioned Mary Agee's use of company operations for her personal benefit (e.g., making life-size unicorns for an Agee birthday party and rushing orders for her social causes through the print shop while company business had to wait or be done outside). Agee defended his wife's actions by stating that organizations should encourage employees to participate in community activities and causes. When the company's chief financial officer politely tried to tell him that his personal life-style, use of the corporate jet, and $2.2 million dollar salary was excessive, Agee promptly reassigned him. When Agee informed employees not to leak information to the press about internal morale problems, he had security employees wire-tap employees' phones. When bad news eventually got out, he identified who was leaking it to the press and fired them. Quickly, morale dropped to an all-time low.

As financial and employee troubles mounted, Agee became more remote and quickly moved the company headquarters to his seaside estate in Pebble Beach, California, and ran the company by phone, fax, and weekly briefings from executives. When he tried to sell off the company's start-up locomotive and maintenance operation, he was more concerned about how the sale would affect his salary than whether the sale was good for the company. As the board of directors became more concerned about the company's financial plight, he replaced senior managers with inexperienced people who wouldn't question his decisions. Without experienced personnel, Knudsen lost huge transportation contracts. The board of directors fired him in 1995, but by 1996, Knudsen's stock price had plummeted to a low of $1.24 a share after a proposed reorganization plan failed.[23]

Implications for Leaders   Hersey and Blanchard's situational leadership model is relatively simple to understand, and its recommendations are straightforward. The readiness level of followers must be checked constantly in order for the leader to determine what combination of task and relationship behaviors would be most appropriate in the situation. An inexperienced employee (low readiness) may perform at as high a level as an experienced employee if given direction and close supervision. If the style is appropriate, it should also help followers increase their levels of readiness. Thus, as a leader develops a team and helps its members learn to manage themselves, the leadership style used should be changed to fit the changing situation.

The model has some limitations.[24] First, if each individual has a unique readiness level, how does a leader address those different readiness levels in a team situation? Does the leader assume the average level and choose a leadership style accordingly? Second, the model relies only on one contingency factor—follower readiness. In most situations, time and work pressures also influence a leader's choice of behavior. A leader needs to take these and other factors into account when choosing a leadership style. Third, an assumption of the model is that a leader can adapt his or her leadership style to fit the situation. How adaptable are William Agee's leader behaviors? Fourth, although the model is used in thousands of organizations to help people improve their diagnostic abilities, it isn't strongly supported by scientific research. That is, some studies have supported the model while others haven't been able to confirm the model's basic premises.

■ HOUSE'S PATH-GOAL MODEL

Puzzled by the contradictory research findings on leadership, Robert J. House developed a model based on the expectancy theory of motivation (see Chapter 5). **House's path-goal model** suggests that, in order to be effective, a leader must select a style that will enhance employees' satisfaction with their jobs and increase their performance levels. House believes that a leader can do so—and motivate employees—by clarifying the nature of the task, reducing roadblocks to successful task completion, and increasing the opportunities for them to obtain job satisfactions. Employees are satisfied with their jobs to the extent that performance leads to rewards they value highly.[25] Figure 10.8 illustrates House's general model.

Leader Styles The model identifies four distinct styles of leader behavior:

- **Supportive leadership,** which refers to considering the needs of employees, displaying concern for their welfare, and creating a friendly climate in the work group. This behavior is similar to the consideration style identified by the Ohio State University researchers.

- **Directive leadership,** which involves letting members know what they are expected to do, giving them specific guidance, asking them to follow rules and regulations, scheduling and coordinating their work, and setting stan-

■ **FIGURE 10.8**   House's Path-Goal Model

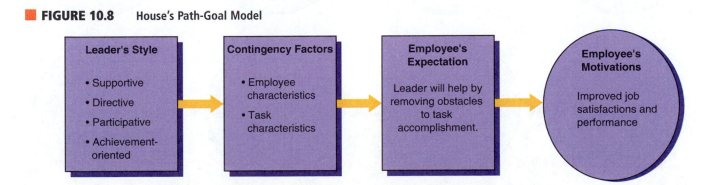

dards of performance for them. This behavior is similar to the initiating structure style identified by the Ohio State University researchers.

- **Participative leadership,** which refers to consulting with others and evaluating their opinions and suggestions when making decisions.
- **Achievement-oriented leadership,** which entails setting challenging goals, seeking improvements in performance, emphasizing excellence in performance, and showing confidence that members will achieve high standards of performance.

Contingency Variables   House's path-goal model has two key contingency variables: *employees needs* and *task characteristics.* The needs (e.g., safety, esteem, belongingness, etc.) of employees determine how they will react to a leader's behavior. Employees with strong needs for acceptance and affiliation may find their needs satisfied by a supportive leader. Employees with strong needs for autonomy, responsibility, and self-actualization are more likely to be motivated by participative and achievement-oriented leaders than by supportive leaders.

Recall that tasks may be either routine or nonroutine and that their characteristics vary. A routine task (1) doesn't call for the use of a variety of skills, (2) represents bits and pieces of a job rather than the whole job, (3) requires few decisions regarding scheduling and methods to be used, and (4) provides little information about how well it has been performed. A nonroutine task has the opposite characteristics. Figure 10.9 illustrates the application of supportive and directive leadership styles to routine and nonroutine tasks.

Effects of Different Styles   When employees have a task that is tedious, boring, or routine, a leader can make performing the task more pleasant by considering and

■ **FIGURE 10.9**   Applying House's Path-Goal Model

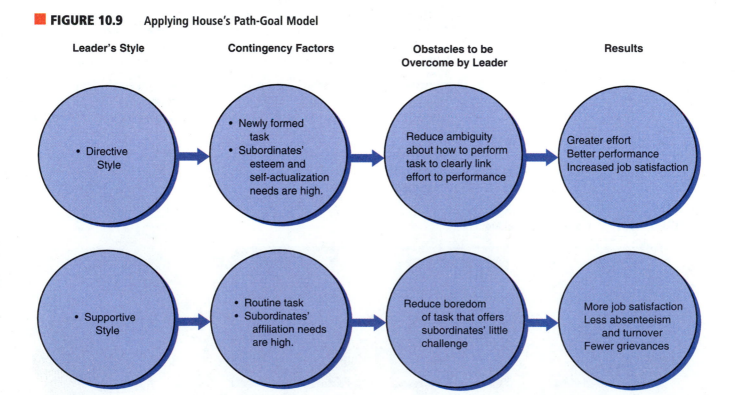

supporting the employees' needs. For example, employees taking parking tolls at airports all day long derive little self-esteem or self-actualization from performing this highly structured and routine task. They probably would perceive a directive leadership style as excessive and unnecessary. A leader with a supportive style, however, could increase employee satisfaction with the work by asking the employee about his or her interests and preferred working hours.

A more directive leadership style is appropriate for highly unstructured, complex, and nonroutine tasks. Directive leaders can help employees cope with task uncertainty and clarify the paths to high job satisfaction and performance. Employees wouldn't perceive this style to be excessive when they are given guidance and direction about how to improve the manufacturing process. Rather, directive leadership helps employees gain a sense of job satisfaction when they properly complete their tasks and gain a reward.

Participative leaders share information, power, and influence with managers and employees. When the task is clear and employees' egos aren't involved in the work, participative leaders will likely contribute to satisfaction and performance only for highly independent employees. For ambiguous, ego-involving tasks, participative leaders will have positive effects on performance and job satisfaction regardless of an employee's needs for self-esteem or achievement.

Achievement-oriented leaders set challenging goals, expect employees to perform at the highest level, and show a high degree of confidence that employees will assume responsibility for accomplishing complex tasks. This type of leader can motivate employees to strive for high standards and build confidence in meeting challenging goals, especially among employees who are working on unstructured tasks. The Preview Case illustrates how an achievement-oriented team leader such as David Johnson can get great results from employees.

Implications for Leaders   Research findings show that employees who perform highly routine or tedious tasks report higher job satisfaction when their leader uses a supportive (as opposed to directive) leadership style.[26] However, employees who perform unstructured tasks are more productive and satisfied when their leader uses a more directive style.

Achievement-oriented leaders have little effect on followers' performance and job satisfaction when they are performing routine and repetitive tasks. Unless employees have some discretion over the what, when, and how of performing a task, the achievement-oriented leader can have little impact on employees' performance and job satisfaction. Participative leaders have the greatest effect on performance if employees are performing an unstructured task. When they participate in decision making about a task, goals, plans, and procedures, employees learn more and feel that they have a better chance of successfully completing the necessary task. If employees have a highly structured task and a clear understanding of the job, however, participative leaders have little effect on performance.

Let's see how this model works by looking at the leadership of Bernard Walsh, president of Johnson & Johnson's (J&J's) Vistakon company. He changed Vistakon into one of J&J's most aggressive and successful companies. Walsh was lured by the challenge of taking a company with barely $20 million in sales and low profits and turning it into a successful and highly profitable organization. Headquarters' managers promised to leave him alone as he attempted to develop this company. In the following Quality in Practice feature note that Walsh varied his leadership style to fit the situation (each style is identified in parentheses).

QUALITY IN PRACTICE

Bernard Walsh

In 1983, a J&J employee got word of a new Danish technology to produce disposable contact lenses cheaply. Johnson & Johnson bought the rights and, under Bernard Walsh's leadership, began developing the packaging and manufacturing processes. Within a few years, J&J's Vistakon company had assembled a management team and built a high-volume plant in Jacksonville, Florida, to manufacture Acuvue, J&J's disposable lens. Walsh hired employees because of their ability to make decisions without close supervision and their attention to quality (achievement-oriented leadership). Choosing the right employees was crucial because Acuvue lenses cost the consumer about $150 a year more to wear than conventional extended-wear lenses. Today, sales of its contact lenses bring in more than $250 million annually.

One reason for Acuvue's success is Walsh's leadership. His company was so small that he and his employees could make decisions (participative leadership) quickly on issues ranging from work-force diversity to manufacturing processes to marketing. When the customers' initial reaction to the new lenses weren't what Walsh expected because competitors challenged the lenses' safety, Vistakon FedExed some 17,000 lenses to eye-care professionals. The speedy reaction to this complaint built goodwill in the marketplace and indicated to eye-care professionals how much service they could expect from J&J (achievement-oriented leadership). Walsh urged Vistakon employees to think about new products, and they responded with Surevue lenses. Unlike Acuevue lenses, Surevue lens users can't sleep with them in place, but users get twice the wear from them.[27]

■ VROOM-JAGO LEADERSHIP MODEL

Victor Vroom and Arthur Jago developed a leadership model that focuses on the role played by leaders in making decisions.[28] The **Vroom-Jago leadership model** indicates that various degrees of participative decision making are appropriate in different situations. These researchers assume that the leader can choose a leadership style along a continuum, ranging from highly autocratic to high participative, as shown in Table 10.2.

Vroom and Jago use the shorthand notation AI to refer to instances in which the leader makes the decision alone without further information collection. The notation AII is similar but permits the leader to request certain specific information from others. (The letter A stands for *autocratic,* and the roman numerals refer to degrees of autocratic processes.) The notation CI refers to *consultation* on a one-to-one basis with another party. The notation CII refers to consultation in a group setting. The notation GII refers to group decision making, with consensus as the goal.

Decision Effectiveness   **Decision effectiveness** depends on decision quality, acceptance, and timeliness. *Decision quality* is the extent to which a method of handling a situation produces a quality decision. *Decision acceptance* is the degree to which employee commitment is generated by a process. Employees are more likely to implement a decision that is consistent with their values and preferences

TABLE 10.2   Decision Styles for Leading a Group

Leading a Group

AI   You solve the problem or make the decision yourself, using information available to you at that time.

AII   You obtain any necessary information from employees, then decide on the solution to the problem yourself. The role played by your employees in making the decision is clearly one of providing specific information that you request, rather than generating or evaluating solutions.

CI   You share the problem with relevant team members individually, getting their ideas and suggestions without bringing them together as a group. Then you make the decision. This decision may or may not reflect their influence.

CII   You share the problem with your employees in a group meeting. In this meeting, you obtain their ideas and suggestions. Then you make the decision, which may or may not reflect their influence.

GII   You share the problem with your subordinates as a group. Together you generate and evaluate alternatives and attempt to reach a consensus on a solution. Your role is much like that of chairperson, coordinating the discussion, keeping it focused on the problem, and making sure that the critical issue are discussed. You do not try to influence the group to adopt "your" solution, and you are willing to accept and implement any solution that has the support of the entire group.

Source: Vroom, V. H., and Yetton, P. W. *Leadership and Decision Making*. Pittsburgh: University of Pittsburgh Press, 1973, 13.

than one that they view as harmful to them (such as a layoff, demotion, or cut in pay). *Decision time penalty* is the negative result of decisions not being made in a timely manner. Leaders make most decisions when time is of the essence. For example, air traffic controllers, emergency rescue squad leaders, and nuclear energy plant supervisors may have limited time to get inputs from others before having to make a decision. The time penalty is zero when there are no severe time pressures on the leader to make a decision. Decision effectiveness may be expressed as

$$\text{Decision effectiveness} = \text{Decision quality} + \text{Decision acceptance} - \text{Decision time penalty.}$$

Decision effectiveness criteria apply only when a leader has ample time to make a decision and team member decision-making development isn't important. If time isn't available or decision-making development is important, another criterion, **overall effectiveness,** is needed. It is influenced by decision effectiveness, by time, and by the need for employees' decision-making development. Overall effectiveness may be expressed as

$$\text{Overall effectiveness} = \text{Decision effectiveness} - \text{Cost} + \text{Development.}$$

Negative effects on what Vroom and Jago call "human capital" occur because participative and consultative leadership processes use time and energy, which can be translated into costs even if there are no severe time constraints. Many managers spend almost 70 percent of their time in meetings. Time always has a value, although its precise cost varies with the reasons for the meetings. For example, while Chuck Walker, a marketing manager for El Chico Mexican restaurants, is in a meeting, which other marketing decisions are being delayed? What's the cost to El Chico for these delays? Some of the benefits from employees participating in meetings include being members of a team, strengthening their commitment to the organization's goals, and contributing to the development of their leadership skills (mainly self-understanding and communication). Thus the cost of holding a meeting must be compared to the cost of not holding a meeting. One cost therefore is the value of time lost through the use of participative decision making.

If participation has negative effects on human capital, it can also have some positive effects, as illustrated by Bernard Walsh at Vistakon. Participative leader behaviors help develop the technical and managerial talents of employees, help build teamwork, and help build loyalty and commitment to organizational goals. Walsh used these positive outcomes to build Vistakon into one of J&J's most profitable companies.

Decision Tree   The Vroom-Jago model considers the trade-offs among four criteria by which a leader's decision-making behavior can be evaluated: decision quality, employee commitment, time, and employee development. Figure 10.10 shows the decision tree representing the Vroom-Jago model. Note the eight problem attributes, or situational variables, that can be used to describe differences among decision-making situations.

At the end of each branch of the decision tree, the letters and Roman numerals correspond to those used to identify leadership styles in Table 10.2. That is, AI represents a leadership style in which you solve the problem yourself, using the information available to you at that time, and so on, for the various leadership styles. Leader style and problem attributes are combined through a series of complex equations that are beyond the scope of this book. The decision tree, however, represents the solution of those equations.

Starbucks Coffee Company has a relatively short history. It began in Washington state in 1971 when three young entrepreneurs began to sell coffee at Pike Place Market in Seattle. The original Starbucks store was named after the first mate in Moby Dick. Today, it is the largest specialty retail coffee roaster in North America with more 800 company-owned stores serving more than 1.5 million customers a week. It opens a store each working day. The person in charge of each store's design team is Brooke McCurdy. The following Diversity in Practice selection highlights some of the challenges facing her. Following this account, we will walk you through the decision tree solution.

DIVERSITY IN PRACTICE

Brooke McCurdy

When she joined Starbucks in 1990, Brooke McCurdy found that the employees working there had a passion for and believed in the product. She now heads a seventy-person team that includes five regional project managers, ten project captains and thirty job captains who spend most of their time at construction sites. In addition, McCurdy oversees the design and development group, which develops new store designs, and the remodel team, which remodels existing stores.

As much as possible, Starbucks tries to stay away from cookie-cutter designs. Each restaurant is designed to fit into the neighborhood. McCurdy likens the stores to sisters: They share certain family characteristics, but maintain their own unique personality.

Her team consists of diverse professionals who have lived all over the world. Each person brings a unique perspective to the job and draws heavily on his or her understanding of the mythology surrounding the coffee bean and coffee

—Continued

DIVERSITY IN PRACTICE—*Continued*

making process. (To continue this mythology, Starbucks financially assists people in the coffee-producing countries where they do business.) Getting the team to reach consensus on a store's design is no easy task because each team member has unique perspectives. The regional project managers want the new stores in their areas, whereas the job captains want locations where building codes are favorable for Starbucks and construction crews can easily work the site.[29]

If you were Brooke McCurdy and using the decision tree in Figure 10.10, what leadership style should you choose when making a decision about which store to build? Start with State the Problem on the left-hand side of the tree. The first box to the right is QR (quality requirement). You must make a decision about whether the importance of quality requirements is high or low. After you make that decision, go to the next box, CR (commitment required). Once again you must make a decision about the importance of having staff members committed to the final design of a new store. After you have made that decision, you face another decision and then another. As you make each decision, follow the proper line to the next box. Eventually, at the far right-hand side of the tree, you will arrive at the best style of leadership to use, based on your previous eight decisions. We used this method to determine the style of leadership that we would recommend Brooke McCurdy use.

Analysis		Answers
QR	*Quality requirement:* How important is the technical quality of the decision?	Highly important
CR	*Commitment Requirement:* How important is employee commitment to the decision?	Highly important
LI	*Leader's information:* Does Brooke have sufficient information to make a high-quality decision?	Probably not
ST	*Problem structured?* Is the problem well structured?	No
CP	*Commitment probability:* If Brooke were to make the decision herself, would her team members likely be committed to her decision?	Probably not
GC	*Goal congruence:* Do team members share the organizational goals to be attained in solving this problem?	Yes
CO	*Subordinate conflict:* Is conflict likely among team members over preferred solutions?	Yes
SI	*Subordinate information:* Do team members have sufficient information to make a high-quality decision?	Yes

■ **FIGURE 10.10**   Vroom-Jago Decision Tree

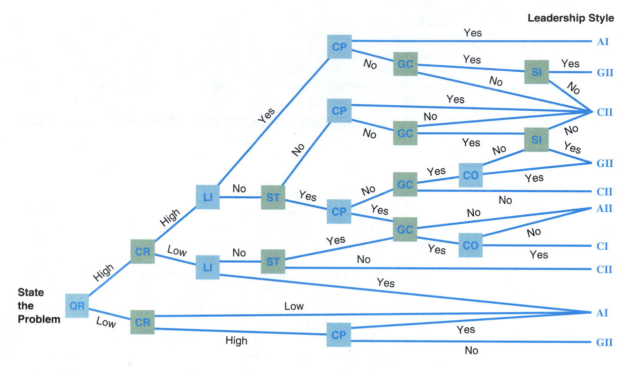

Problem Attributes

QR	Quality requirement:	How important is the technical quality of this decision?
CR	Commitment requirement:	How important is subordinate commitment to the decision?
LI	Leader's information:	Do you have sufficient information to make a high-quality decision?
ST	Problem structure:	Is the problem well structured?
CP	Commitment probability:	If you were to make the decision by yourself, is it reasonably certain that your subordinate(s) would be committed to the decision?
GC	Goal congruence:	Do subordinates share the organizational goals to be attained in solving this problem?
CO	Subordinate conflict:	Is conflict among subordinates over preferred solutions likely?
SI	Subordinate information:	Do subordinates have sufficient information to make a high-quality decision?

Source: Reprinted from Vroom, V. H., and Jago, A. G. *The New Leadership.* Englewood Cliffs, N.J.: Prentice-Hall, 1988, 184.

Factors Not Considered by Brooke McCurdy

TC   *Time constraints:* Are time constraints important?

MD   *Motivation development:* Does McCurdy want to develop her employees' skill levels?

Answer

We recommend the GII style of leadership. Which did you choose?

The GII style of leadership seems most appropriate when someone is leading a diverse group of team members who have the ability to make decisions. McCurdy also recognized that, unless she was able to gain the commitment of these professionals, the location decision would be delayed.

Implications for Leaders   The Vroom-Jago model represents a significant break-through in thinking about leadership.[30] Moreover, it is consistent with earlier work on group and team behaviors (see Chapter 8). If leaders can diagnose situations correctly, choosing the best leadership style for those situations becomes easier. These choices, in turn, will enable them to make high-quality, timely decisions. If the situation requires delegation, the leader must learn how to establish the desired goals and limitations—and then let employees determine how best to achieve the goals within those limitations. If the situation calls for the leader alone to make the decision, the leader should be aware of potential positive and negative consequences of not asking others for their input.

However, the model does have some drawbacks. First, most subordinates have a strong desire to participate in decisions affecting their jobs regardless of the model's recommendations for a more autocratic decision. If subordinates are kept in the dark, they are likely to become frustrated and not be committed to the decision. Second, certain competencies of the leader play a key role in determining the relative effectiveness of the model. For example, in situations involving conflict, only leaders skilled in conflict resolution should use the kind of participative decision-making strategy suggested by the model. A leader who hasn't developed these competencies would obtain better results with a more autocratic style, even though this style is opposite from what the model predicts. Third, the model is based on the premise that decisions involve a single process. Often, decisions go through several cycles and are part of a solution to a bigger problem. In McCurdy's case, a design decision made for a store in Dallas might affect a subsequent decision for another store in Austin, Texas.

■ COMPARING THE FOUR CONTINGENCY MODELS

Choosing the most appropriate leadership style can be difficult. A strongly stated preference for democratic, participative decision making in organizations prevails in the business community today. Evidence from Anita Roddick, David Johnson, and Ricardo Semler, among others, shows that this leadership style can result in productive, healthy organizations. However, participative management is not appropriate for all situations, as contingency theorists note. Table 10.3 shows the differences in leader behaviors, situational variables, and outcomes for the four contingency models that we have discussed.

Leadership Differences   Fiedler's model is based on the LPC style of a leader (high or low LPC) and the degree to which the situation is favorable for the leader. The leadership style of a leader is considered to be relatively rigid, and the model suggests that the leader choose a situation that matches his or her leadership style. Hersey and Blanchard use the same two leadership dimensions that Fiedler identified: task and relationship behaviors. They went one step further by considering each as either high or low and then combining them into four specific leadership styles: directive, supportive, participating, and delegating. House's path-goal model states that leaders should try to improve the job satisfaction and performance of employees by removing roadblocks that stand in their way. The leader can choose a supportive, participative, directive, or achievement-oriented leadership style. Vroom and Jago believe that leaders can choose from among a variety of leadership styles, ranging from highly autocratic to highly consultative. The leader's role in choosing a style is to (1) improve the quality and acceptance of the decision; (2) increase the probability that employees will accept and implement the decision on a timely basis; and (3) develop effective leadership competencies in employees. Thus each of the four contingency models identifies different styles of leadership and views the leader's ability to choose among styles differently.

Contingency Variables   All four models emphasize somewhat different contingency variables. Fiedler's model suggests that the way the variables (group atmosphere, task structure, and leader position power) are arranged in a situation determines whether and to what extent the situation is favorable or unfavorable to the leader. As the combination of the three contingency variables changes, so do the leadership requirements. A leader who is effective in one situation may not be effective in another. He believes that changing the situation is easier than changing the leader's style.

Hersey and Blanchard's contingency variable is the readiness of the employee. An employee having a low level of readiness is unable or unwilling to take responsibility or do something independently. An employee having a high readiness level is both willing to take responsibility and knows what to do, can work independently, and always meets deadlines. As the readiness level of subordinates change, the leader's style should change to match their readiness level. A directive style is most appropriate for employees having a low-readiness level, whereas a delegating style is most appropriate for employees having a high-readiness level.

TABLE 10.3 Comparing the Four Contingency Leadership Models

MODEL	LEADER BEHAVIORS	CONTINGENCY VARIABLES	LEADER EFFECTIVENESS CRITERIA
Fiedler's	Task-oriented: Low LPC Relationship-oriented: High LPC	Group atmosphere Task structure Leader position power	Performance
Hersey and Blanchard's	Task and Relationship	Readiness level of team members	Performance and job satisfaction
House's Path-Goal	Supportive Directive characteristics Participative Achievement- oriented	Employee satisfaction Task character- istics	Employee job Job performance
Vroom-Jago	Continuum of autocratic to group consensus	Eight problem attributes	Employee development Time Decision effectiveness Overall effectiveness

House's model uses the contingency variables of task characteristics and the employees' needs. Employees who believe that rewards are based on their own efforts generally feel more satisfied with a participative style of leadership. If the task is unstructured, a directive style of leadership will lead to higher job satisfaction and performance than a participative style because it eases the "unknown" for the employee.

The Vroom-Jago model identifies eight different contingencies for the leader to consider in deciding whether a more autocratic or a more participative style would be effective in a particular situation. Subordinate participation in the decisions that a leader encounters increases quality, generates commitment, and develops employee leadership competencies—but increases the time required for the leader to make a decision and the need for the leader to develop subordinates' competencies.

Leadership Effectiveness   All four models use somewhat different criteria for evaluating leadership effectiveness. Fiedler emphasizes performance; Hersey and Blanchard and House use both employee job satisfaction and performance; and Vroom and Jago emphasize decision effectiveness and overall effectiveness. If a decision must be made with a group, the Vroom-Jago model may best assist leaders in choosing the most appropriate leadership style. If improving individual performance is most important, perhaps Fiedler's, Hersey and Blanchard's, or House's model may be more useful.

CHAPTER SUMMARY

Leadership is the process of creating a vision for others and having the power to translate the vision into reality. The ways in which leaders attempt to influence others depend in part of the power available to them and in part on their competencies. Leaders draw on five sources of power to influence the actions of others: legitimate, reward, coercive, referent, and expert. Vision, empowerment, meaning through communication, and self-understanding are the competencies that help leaders become more effective.

The traditional leadership models include traits and behavioral. The traits model emphasizes the personal qualities of leaders and attributes success to certain abilities, skills, and personality characteristics. However, this model fails to explain why certain people succeed and others fail as leaders. The behavioral model emphasizes leaders' actions instead of their personal traits. We focused on two leader behaviors—initiating structure and consideration—and how they affect employee performance and job satisfaction. The behavioral models tended to ignore the situation in which the leader was operating. This omission was the focal point of the contingency approach.

The contingency approach emphasizes the importance of various situations, or contingencies. The four contingency models are those of Fiedler, Hersey and Blanchard, House, and Vroom and Jago. Fiedler focuses on the effective diagnosis of the situation in which the leader will operate. He emphasizes understanding the nature of the situation and then matching the correct leadership style to that situation. According to this model, three contingency variables need to be diagnosed: group atmosphere. task structure, and the leader's position power. Fiedler believes that all leaders have a least-preferred-co-worker trait that is stable and determines the situations in which their particular leadership style will be effective.

Hersey and Blanchard state that leaders should choose a style that matches the readiness level of their subordinates. If subordinates are not ready to perform the task, a directive leadership style will be more effective than a relationship style. As the readiness level of the subordinate increases, the leader's style should become more participative and less directive.

House suggests that leadership behavior—supportive, directive, participative, achievement-oriented—is contingent on the personal needs—esteem, belongingness, safety—of the subordinates and the nature of the task. The leader's purpose is to reduce the obstacles that keep employees from reaching their goals. For a routine task and subordinates who have belongingness needs, a considerate leader is more likely to have satisfied and productive subordinates than a leader who is less considerate. Vroom and Jago base their model on an analysis of how a leader's style affects decision effectiveness and overall effectiveness of his or her subordinates. The Vroom-Jago model proposes five leadership styles, ranging from autocratic to group decision making, that leaders can use. Its set of rules can help a leader determine the leadership style to avoid in a given situation because decision effectiveness and overall effectiveness might be low.

KEY TERMS AND CONCEPTS

Achievement-oriented leadership
Coercive power
Consideration
Decision effectiveness
Delegating style
Directive leadership
Empowerment
Expert power
Fiedler's contingency model
Follower readiness
Group atmosphere
Hersey and Blanchard's situational model

House's path-goal model
Initiating structure
Leader
Leader match
Leadership
Least-preferred co-worker (LPC)
Legitimate power
Manager
Overall effectiveness
Participating style
Participative leadership
Position power
Referent power

Relationship behavior
Reward power
Selling style
Supportive leadership
Task behavior
Task structure
Telling style
Traits model
Vroom-Jago leadership model

DISCUSSION QUESTIONS

1. What competencies must a person gain to become a successful leader?

2. Are leaders born or made? Explain.

3. When Norman Brinker, CEO of Brinker International, speaks on leadership, he says, "I don't send for people. For the most part, I go to other people's offices to see them instead of having them come see me." What kind of leadership style does this suggest? Under what conditions might it be most effective?

4. Make a list of the conditions under which you failed to exercise effective leadership. Make another list of the con-

ditions under which you exercised successful leadership. What are the differences in the lists? How did you build trust and respect? How did you recognize others? What lessons did you learn about leadership from these experiences?

5. How do you involve others?

6. What conclusions can be drawn from the Ohio State University leadership studies?

7. Suppose that a leader's style doesn't match the situation. What does Fiedler recommend?

8. When someone asked Robert Hernandez, regional manager for Boston Market, what it took to be an effective restaurant store manager, his response was "Great team members who are self-disciplined to serving the customer." Using Hersey and Blanchard's model, what style of leadership produces these results? What assumptions is Hernandez making about his team members?

9. Assume that you have been assigned to do a team project with five other classmates. How might House's path-goal model help you choose an appropriate leadership style?

10. Sue Allen, field manager for Trammell Crow real estate, discovered that she could improve the performance of her team by making decisions autocratically rather than consultatively. According to the Vroom-Jago model, under what conditions would her autocratic leadership style be effective? What are some drawbacks to this style that she might want to consider?

11. What are some conditions under which leaders don't seem to make a difference in team members' performances?

■ Developing Competencies

Self-Insight: What's Your Leadership Style?

The following questions analyze your leadership style according to the Ohio State model. Read each item carefully. Think about how you usually behave when you are the leader. Then, using the following key, circle the letter that most closely describes your style. Circle only one choice per question.[31]

A = Always   O = Often   ? = Sometimes
S = Seldom   N = Never

1. I take time to explain how a job should be carried out.   A O ? S N

2. I explain the part that co-workers are to play in the group.   A O ? S N

3. I make clear the rules and procedures for others to follow in detail.   A O ? S N

4. I organize my own work activities.   A O ? S N

5. I let people know how well they are doing.   A O ? S N

6. I let people know what is expected of them.   A O ? S N

7. I encourage the use of uniform procedures for others to follow in detail.   A O ? S N

8. I make my attitude clear to others.   A O ? S N

9. I assign others to particular tasks.   A O ? S N

10. I make sure that others understand their part in the group.   A O ? S N

11. I schedule the work that I want others to do.   A O ? S N

12. I ask that others follow standard rules and regulations.   A O ? S N

13. I make working on the job more pleasant.   A O ? S N

14. I go out of my way to be helpful to others.   A O ? S N

15. I respect others' feelings and opinions.   A O ? S N

16. I am thoughtful and considerate of others.   A O ? S N

17. I maintain a friendly atmosphere in the group.   A O ? S N

18. I do little things to make it more pleasant for others to be a member of my group.   A O ? S N

19. I treat others as equals.   A O ? S N

20. I give others advance notice of change and explain how it will affect them.   A O ? S N

21. I look out for others' personal welfare.   A O ? S N

22. I am approachable and friendly toward others.   A O ? S N

Scoring Form

The following boxes are numbered to correspond to the questionnaire items. In each box, circle the number next to the letter of the response alternative you picked. Add up the numbers you circled in each of the columns.

Interpretation

The questions scored in Column 1 reflect an initiating structure or task leadership style. A score of greater than 47 would indicate that you describe your leadership style as high on initiating or task structure. You plan, direct, organize, and control the work of others. The questions scored in Column 2 reflect a considerate or relationship style. A total score of greater than 40 indicates that you are a considerate leader. A considerate leader is one who is concerned with the comfort, well-being, and personal welfare of his or her subordinates. In general, managers rated high on initiating structure and moderate on consideration tended to be in charge of higher-producing teams than those whose leadership styles are the reverse.

Column 1   Column 2

1	2	13	14
A = 5	A = 5	A = 5	A = 5
O = 4	O = 4	O = 4	O = 4
? = 3	? = 3	? = 3	? = 3
S = 2	S = 2	S = 2	S = 2
N = 1	N = 1	N = 1	N = 1

3	4	15	16
A = 5	A = 5	A = 5	A = 5
O = 4	O = 4	O = 4	O = 4
? = 3	? = 3	? = 3	? = 3
S = 2	S = 2	S = 2	S = 2
N = 1	N = 1	N = 1	N = 1

5	6	17	18
A = 5	A = 5	A = 5	A = 5
O = 4	O = 4	O = 4	O = 4
? = 3	? = 3	? = 3	? = 3
S = 2	S = 2	S = 2	S = 2
N = 1	N = 1	N = 1	N = 1

7	8	19	20
A = 5	A = 5	A = 5	A = 5
O = 4	O = 4	O = 4	O = 4
? = 3	? = 3	? = 3	? = 3
S = 2	S = 2	S = 2	S = 2
N = 1	N = 1	N = 1	N = 1

9	10	21	22
A = 5	A = 5	A = 5	A = 5
P = 4	P = 4	O = 4	O = 4
? = 3	? = 3	? = 3	? = 3
S = 2	S = 2	S = 2	S = 2
N = 1	N = 1	N = 1	N = 1

11	12
A = 5	A = 5
O = 4	O = 4
? = 3	? = 3
S = 2	S = 2

Total Column 1 = _____   Total Column 2 = _____

Organizational Insight

Herb Kelleher Is No Ordinary Leader at Southwest Airlines

Herbert D. Kelleher is wearing a mischievous grin and clutching a Merit Ultima. Kelleher the jokemeister, who relishes the chance to tell another of his wild stories, explains how he stole four boxes of the American Airlines' logo lighters when he visited Bob Crandall, the chairman of Fort Worth-based American, who had just quit smoking. Laughter, tall tales, and an unabashed fondness for cigarettes and whiskey are as much a part of Kelleher's fun-loving persona as his stature as one of the airline industry's greatest revolutionists. His unconventional methods have helped him build and promote America's most successful low-fare airline, a carrier that has grown from a Texas puddle jumper into the nation's fifth-largest carrier when measured by number of U.S. passengers flown.

Over the years, Kelleher has shown up in public dressed as Elvis, Cpl. Clinger of M*A*S*H*, a hippie, and a biker. He accepted a challenge from a South Carolina aviation firm to an arm-wrestling match after it claimed rights to a company slogan, "Just Plane Smart." (Kelleher lost, saying he had suffered a wrist fracture diving in front of a bus to save a small child.) Last year, he lost a game of H-O-R-S-E at Hobby Airport to Houston Rockets Coach Rudy Thomjanovich. The antics have made Kelleher a winner, endearing him to employees and passengers for nearly two decades.

Kelleher grew up in southern New Jersey, one of four children and nine years younger than his next older brother. His father was general manager of Campbell Soup Company's plant in Camden, and Kelleher credits his parents for providing a strong example of how to treat people right. "They'd just talk to me all the time about the ethical way to treat people, how important they were as individuals. It's a way of living." A star basketball player and student body president in high school and college, Kelleher majored in English and contemplated becoming a journalist. Instead, he got a law degree from New York University in 1956, clerked for the New Jersey Supreme Court and went into private law practice.

In the early 1960s, Kelleher moved his family to San Antonio, believing that in Texas he'd have a better chance of finding an entrepreneurial opportunity. He got one in 1967 when a client, a Mr. King, came to him for help in starting a new intrastate airline. At the time, King ran a business that flew eight-seat Beech prop planes and catered mostly to businessmen flying from San Antonio to such places as Eagle Pass and Kerrville. King's idea was to expand by flying a far more lucrative market, the triangle of Dallas, Houston, and San Antonio. Kelleher liked the idea and became a minor investor. The company was incorporated as Air Southwest on March 15, 1967. But during the era when airline routes and prices were regulated by the government, the carrier was grounded by legal challenges brought by rival carriers Braniff International, Trans Texas Airways, and Continental Airlines. They argued that the markets Southwest wanted to serve were "thoroughly mature" and Southwest would simply take a piece of their business. After three and a half years of legal battles, during which Kelleher was forced to work for no pay and to pay some legal costs himself, the airline was cleared to take off in December 1970, when the U.S. Supreme Court refused to hear the rival carriers' appeal. Renamed Southwest Airlines, its inaugural flight was in June 1971.

Although Kelleher was a director and general counsel of the Dallas-based airline, he at first remained at his law firm in San Antonio. He didn't take over as chairman until 1978, when the company's first chairman, Lamar Muse, resigned after a dispute with the board. In 1981, Kelleher took over permanently as chief executive and president, moving to a townhouse in Dallas. His wife of forty years still lives in San Antonio, and Kelleher has commuted back and forth ever since. ("I'm one of the nomads," he jokes.)

Kelleher and Southwest have succeeded by breaking nearly every operating rule other airlines follow. The basic strategy—rolling easily off Kelleher's tongue—is to offer short-haul, high-frequency, low-fare, point-to-point service. As part of its no-frills approach, passengers don't get assigned seats—it's first come, first served—nor do they get meals. (A billboard near Dallas Love Field shows a bag of peanuts and the caption: "Still nuts after all these years.")

Southwest doesn't force passengers to fly to central "hub" airports to connect to their final destinations like other major airlines. Instead, it keeps costs low by flying directly between pairs of U.S. cities that merit frequent service. If loads on a route get full, instead of reducing demand by raising prices as other carriers typically do, Southwest adds more flights. With its average flight only 400 miles and costing $60, Southwest considers its biggest competition to be the automobile. But other airlines see Southwest as a formidable competitor. The low-fare carrier has come to dominate most of the forty-seven U.S. cities it serves. Even in Houston, home to Continental, Southwest has 135 flights a day and claims nearly as big a share of passengers whose flights originate in Houston—33.6 percent compared with Continental's 34.9 percent. In 1996, while many other airlines were digging their way out of five years of record losses, Southwest notched record profits for the fifth straight year. It also countered a direct threat from United Airlines' new low-fare shuttle on the West Coast and helped bury Continental's discount operation in the East called Continental Lite.

Having a winning strategy makes the rest simple. "Once you establish clearly who you are and you have that fundamental in place, then everything flows from that easily and you gain speed because you don't have a big debate about everything you do," Kelleher says. "We have agreed what we're going to do and how we're going to do it; then it's just a question of where and when—not what." Admitting that he has been criticized in the past for being a workaholic, Kelleher says that his critics miss the point: he doesn't consider what he does to be work. "I used to tell them if your vocation is your avocation as well—it's what you enjoy—it's not stress. It's not work. It's fun."

Kelleher finds it impossible not to schmooze with employees at every opportunity. "I like people," he explains, "and enjoy being with them, particularly the type of person Southwest has."

Albert Craus, a Southwest marketing manager in Houston, recalls walking through Hobby's terminal with Kelleher last year when Kelleher greeted by name more than a dozen employees manning ticket counters. Employees are astounded by his ability to remember their names. "He's got to have a photographic memory," said Gary Kelly, the company's chief financial officer. "He's amazing."

Wall Street analysts in large part attribute Southwest's success to Kelleher's leadership skills, which have helped him build the best management-labor relations in the industry despite having the highest percentage of unionized workers—84 percent. Beloved by employees, he'll go out with a couple of mechanics and have a few drinks until 5 A.M., listen to what needs to be changed and go out the next day and fix it. Analysts note that Southwest is the only major airline that has never had a layoff. That says a lot for a person and for a company that has been around for twenty-five years, especially in an industry as competitive as this one.

Kelleher's leadership skills are applied to passengers, as well as employees. Southwest prides itself on paying close attention to the needs of customers, a word the company capitalizes whenever it is used—in ads, brochures and its annual report. Frequent fliers are mailed birthday cards every year, and some have reported that it was the only card they received. Airport employees are known to give out goodies as prizes to customers with the largest hole in his or her sock, or the person brave enough to sing a company jingle over the airplane's PA system.

Kelleher believes that his workers should have fun, even as they focus intently on serving the customer. At many corporations, employees don't really focus on the customer. They're focusing on procedures and rules and internal things, rather than pleasing their customers. His simple idea is: "If you like the people of Southwest Airlines, you're going to fly it more often."

Company executives now tell anyone who will listen that Kelleher has built a strong management team that can step in whenever necessary. Kelleher won't mention the names of any possible heirs apparent, fearing that if they are talked about publicly, people will become very competitive, stooping to office politics and backstabbing. He absolutely refuses to do that.[32]

Questions

1. What leadership competencies does Herb Kelleher use to influence others at Southwest Airlines?

2. Choose a contingency model of leadership and analyze Kelleher's leadership style.

3. Is Kelleher an effective leader? Explain.

REFERENCES

1. Adapted from Grant. L. Stirring it up at Campbell. *Fortune*, May 13, 1996, 80–86; Redman, R. Campbell stirs up marketing consolidation. *Supermarket News*, February 19, 1996, 34–35.

2. Yulk, G., and VanFleet, D. D. Theory and research on leadership in organizations. In M. D. Dunnette and L. M. Hough (eds.), *Handbook of Industrial and Organizational Psychology*, vol. 3. Palo Alto, Calif.: Consulting Psychologists Press, 1992, 147–198.

3. Kouzes, J. M., and Posner, B. Z. *The Leadership Challenge*. San Francisco: Jossey-Bass 1995; Spreitzer, G. M. Social structural characteristics of psychological empowerment. *Academy of Management Journal*, 1996, 39, 483–502; Hooijberg, R. A multidimensional approach toward leadership: An extension of the concept of behavioral complexity. *Human Relations*, 1996, 49, 917–946.

4. Fiedler, F. E., and House, R. J. Leadership theory and research: A report of progress. In C. L. Cooper and I. T. Robertson (eds.), *Key Reviews in Managerial Psychology*. Chichester, U.K.: John Wiley & Sons, 1994, 97–116.

5. Bennis, W., and Townsend, R. *Reinventing Leadership*. New York: William Morrow, 1995; Farkas, C. M., and Wetlaufer, S. The ways chief executive officers lead. *Harvard Business Review*, May-June 1996, 110–122.

6. Sayles, L. R. *The Working Leader*. New York: Free Press, 1993; Brinker, N., and Phillips, D. T. *On the Brink*. Arlington, Tex.: Summit, 1996.

7. Adapted from Labbs, J. L. How Gillette grooms global talent. *Personnel Journal*, August 1993, 65–75; Mallory, M., and Whitelaw, K. The power brands. *U.S. News & World Report*, May 13, 1996, 58–60; Zeien, A. M. An iconoclast in a cutthroat world. *Chief Executive*, March 1996, 34–39; Farkas, C. M., and De Backer, P. *Maximum Leadership*. New York: Holt, 1996.

8. French, J. R. P., and Raven, B. H. The bases of social power. In D. Cartwright and A. Zander (eds.), *Group Dynamics: Research and Theory*, 2d ed. New York: Harper & Row, 1960, 607-623; Yukl, G., Kim, H., and Falbe, C. M. Antecedents of influence outcomes. *Journal of Applied Psychology*, 1996, 81, 309–317.

9. Roddick, A. *Body and Soul*. New York: Crown Trade Paperbacks, 1991; Reilly, P. M. Retailing: Shoppers buy up a bounty of natural beauty products. *Wall Street Journal*, June 8, 1994, B1ff.

10. Bass, B. M. *Bass and Stogdill's Handbook of Leadership*, 3d ed. New York: Free Press, 1990; Suchman, M. C. Managing legitimacy: Strategic and institutional approaches. *Academy of Management Review*, 1995, 20, 571–610.

11. Belasco, J. A., and Stayer, R. C. *Flight of the Buffalo*. New York: Warner Books, 1993, 16–23.

12. Campbell, R. J., Sessa, V. I., and Taylor, J. *Choosing Top Leaders: Learning to Do Better*. Greensboro, N.C.: Center for Creative Leadership, 1995.

13. Bass, 43–96.

14. Schriesheim, C. A., and Kerr, S. Theories and measures of leadership: A critical appraisal. In J. G. Hunt and L. L Larson (eds.), *Leadership: The Cutting Edge*. Carbondale, Ill.: Southern Illinois University Press, 1977, 9–45.

15. For a discussion of factors that affect leader behavior, see Podsakoff, P. M., MacKenzie, S. B., Ahearne, M., and Bommer, W. H. Searching for a needle in a haystack: Trying to identify the illusive moderators of leadership behaviors. *Journal of Management*, 1995, 21 (Special Issue: Yearly Review), 423–471.

16. Adapted from Dumaine, H. America's toughest bosses. *Fortune*, October 18, 1993, 39–50; Chief Linda Wachner got about $9.8 million for year. *Wall Street Journal*, April 11, 1996, B10; Wallace, C. P. Can the Body Shop shape up? *Fortune*, April 15, 1996, 119–120; Davidson, A, Anita Roddick. *Management Today*, March 1996, 42–46.

17. Fiedler, F. E. *A Theory of Leadership*. New York: McGraw-Hill, 1967; Fiedler, F. E. Research on leadership selection and training: One view of the future. *Administrative Science Quarterly*, 1996, 41, 241–250.

18. Kirpatrick, D. At Compaq. *Fortune*, April 1996, 121–128.

19. Fiedler, F. E. *Leadership Experience and Leadership Performance*. Alexandria, Va.: U.S. Army Research Institute, 1994.

20. Fiedler, F. E., and Chemers, M. M. *Improving Leadership Effectiveness: The Leader Match Concept*, 2d ed. New York: John Wiley & Sons, 1982; Fiedler, F. E. Cognitive resources and leadership performance. *Applied Psychology—An International Review*, 1995, 44, 5–28.

21. Adapted from Semler, R. Why my former employees still work for me. *Harvard Business Review*, January-February 1994, 64–72; Perrault, M. World's most unusual workplace? *Denver Business Journal*, August 27, 1993, 2Cff; Personal communication with D. Bitterman, vice president, Alex Brown and Company, Dallas, Texas, August 1996.

22. Hersey, P., and Blanchard, K. H. *Management of Organizational Behavior: Utilizing Human Resources*. Englewood Cliffs, N.J.: Prentice-Hall, 1993; Blanchard, K. H., and Hersey, P. Great ideas revisited. *Training & Development Journal*, January 1996, 42–48.

23. Adapted from Lublin, J. S. Management: Irate shareholders target ineffective board members. *Wall Street Journal*, November 6, 1995, B1ff; MK rail corp. plans a quarterly charge, layoffs to cut costs. *Wall Street Journal*, January 9, 1996, C18; Richards, B. Morrison Knudsen's stock skids 50% as reorganization plan details emerge. *Wall Street Journal*, February 27, 1996, C1. Also see Messick, D. M., and Bazerman, M. H. Ethical leadership and the psychology of decision making. *Sloan Management Review*, 1996, 37(2), 9–23.

24. Yulk, G. A., and VanFleet, D. D., Theory and research in organizations. In M. D. Dunnette and L. M. Hough (eds.), *Handbook of Industrial and Organizational Psychology*, vol. 3.

Palo Alto, Calif.: Consulting Psychologist Press, 1992, 147–198; Blanchard, K. H., Zigarmi, D., and Nelson, R. B. Situational leadership after 25 years: A retrospective. *Journal of Leadership Studies,* 1993, 1, 21–36.

25. House, R. J., and Mitchell, T. R. Path-goal theory of leadership. *Journal of Contemporary Business,* 1974, 3, 81–97.

26. Wofford, J. C., and Liska, L. Z. Path-Goal theories of leadership: A meta-analysis. *Journal of Management,* 1993, 19, 857–876; Podsakoff, P. M., Mac Kenzie, S. B., Ahearne, M., and Bommer, W. H. Searching for a needle in the haystack: Trying to identify the illusive moderators of leadership behaviors. *Journal of Management,* 1995, 21, 422–470.

27. Adapted from Weber, J. How J&J's foresight made contact lenses pay. *Business Week,* May 4, 1992, 132; Gonzales, A. Daily disposable contacts hit market. *The Business Journal* (Phoenix), August 26, 1994, B26–28; Markey, K. A. et al. Medical supplies industry. *The Value Line Investment Survey,* March 15, 1966, 195–235.

28. Vroom, V. H., and Jago, A. G. *The New Leadership.* Englewood Cliffs, N.J.: Prentice-Hall, 1988.

29. Adapted from McCurdy, B. Starbucks rides the caffeine wave. *Chain Store Age,* April 1996, 80–82.

30. Field, R. H. G., and House, R. J. A test of the Vroom-Yetton model using manager and subordinate reports. *Journal of Applied Psychology,* 1990, 75, 362–366; Pasewark, W. E., and Strawser, J. R. Subordinate participation in audit budgeting decisions. *Decision Sciences,* 1994, 25, 281–299.

31. Schriesheim, C. *Leadership Instrument.* Used by permission, University of Miami, Miami, Florida, 1997.

32. Adapted from Boisseau, C. Southwest's pilot. *Houston Chronicle,* March 10, 1996, 1Dff; Strope, L. Kelleher: Southwest will stay on top. *Dallas Business Journal,* April 21, 1995, 1–6; Sunoo, B. P. How fun flies at Southwest airlines. *Personnel Journal,* June 1996, 62–72; Farkas, C. M., and DeBacker, P. *Maximum Leadership.* New York: Holt, 1996, 86–88.

11

Leadership: Contemporary Developments

LEARNING OBJECTIVES

When you have finished studying this chapter, you should be able to:

- Describe how leaders' attributions affect their leadership behaviors.
- Identify the behaviors of charismatic, transactional, and transformational leaders.
- Explain the seven habits of highly effective people.
- Describe conditions under which leadership may be irrelevant.

OUTLINE

PREVIEW CASE

Orit Gadiesh

Bain and Company is one of the old-line firms in the consulting business. When Orit Gadiesh took over as CEO in 1993, the company had rebounded from several years of poor financial performance and had successfully downsized to help achieve its goals. Largely because of Gadiesh's leadership, Bain has since grown from 900 to more than 1400 employees and revenues are increasing by 25 percent a year. She accomplished these feats by achieving a "pride turnaround" at Bain.

There is an "Orit mystique" at Bain. The daughter of an Israeli army commander, she served two years in the Israeli army, enrolled at Harvard Business School knowing little English, and graduated in the top 5 percent of her class. Bain hired Gadiesh in 1977 because of her high energy level and thoughtful and original answers to questions. She's succeeded at Bain because she's able to get people excited about their work. Employees describe her as driven, intense, painfully direct, empathetic, and a lot of fun.

She doesn't think of herself as the leader but as part of the company's leadership team. She involves people in decisions, trusts them, and believes that if employees trust her the company will prosper. She firmly believes in and promotes Bain's core values. Employees succeed at Bain because they are a team and love to compete as a team. Bain has its own band that plays the Bain theme song at company outings and recruiting dinners. Gadiesh joins in such events, which gives her a chance to congratulate people for jobs well done. During such occasions she maintains personal contact with many people and listens to their concerns. Although other consulting firms typically downplay the emotional aspect of the business, Gadiesh has been able to restore in Bain's employees a shared passion for their work at Bain.[1]

T he four contingency theories of leadership that you studied in Chapter 10 don't answer all our questions about leadership. All four theories attempt to describe which leadership style is the most effective in a particular situation. But none consistently answers the full range of questions about what makes an effective leader. For example, what impact do leaders' perceptions of their employees have on their choices of leadership style? What role does a leader's charisma play? Have effective leaders developed habits that they can apply in a variety of situations to help others improve their performance? Is leadership always necessary? In this chapter, we focus on four contemporary developments in leadership that attempt to answer these questions.

THE ATTRIBUTION MODEL

In Chapter 3, we discussed attribution theory in relation to perception. Recall that attribution theory is an attempt to understand what causes behavior. In other words, when someone behaves in a certain way, why does he or she do so? The **attribution model** suggests that a leader's judgment about employees is influenced by the leader's interpretation of the causes of the employees' performance.[2] The leader's attributions, as much as the employees' behaviors, determine how the leader responds to their performance. A leader obtains information about employees and their behaviors through daily observations of their work. Based on this information, the leader interprets the reasons for the employees' behaviors and takes actions to deal with them when necessary. Orit Gadiesh's attributions about employees' behaviors included their desire to compete, have fun, and display their emotions at work.

■ LEADERS' ATTRIBUTIONS

As part of diagnosing the situation, leaders must determine whether personal or situational factors cause behavior. As explained in Chapter 3, a leader's attributions reflect an ability to process information about three dimensions of behavior: *distinctiveness* (Did the behavior occur during performance of this task only?), *consensus* (Is this level of performance usual for other employees?), and *consistency* (Is this level of performance usual for this employee?). The answers to these three questions identify for the leader either external (situational) or internal (personal) causes for employee performance.

This distinction is crucial to good leader–employee relations.[3] An employee whose successes or failures are attributed to personal skills is likely to have different interpersonal relations with the leader than an employee whose successes or failures are attributed to factors over which the employee has little, if any, control. Leaders should attempt to change an employee's behavior only after attributing poor performance to an internal cause. For example, if Peggy Field, an assistant vice-president at Sprint, believes that a subordinate's poor performance is caused by the situation, she is more likely to provide additional resources, redesign the job, or otherwise change the situation in some way. But, if she believes that his poor performance is attributable to personal reasons, she will more likely try to motivate him to improve his behavior, offer him training to improve his skills, or reprimand him. Figure 11.1 illustrates the attribution model of leadership.

■ EMPLOYEES' ATTRIBUTIONS

Employees also attribute certain causes to their leader's behavior. Employees tend to believe that their leader affects their performance, whether true or not, and develop either positive or negative attitudes about their leader. Because employ-

■ FIGURE 11.1   Attributional Leadership Model

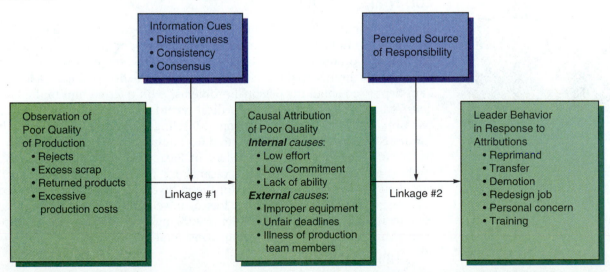

Source: Adapted from Mitchell, R., and Wood, R. E. An empirical test of an attribution model of leaders' responses to poor performance. In Richard C. Huseman (ed.), *Academy of Management Proceedings.* Starkville, Miss.: Academy of Management, 1979, 94.

ees want to believe that their leader can influence their performance, their past performance often influences their rating of the leader's effectiveness. When employees succeed at a task, they tend to rate their leader as successful. When they don't succeed, employees perceive their leader as ineffective and attribute their failure to the leader's actions, rather than to their own. (Recall our discussion of the self-serving bias in Chapter 3.) In sports, it is often the manager, not the players, who gets fired; in organizations, it's the CEO. The firing of the leader symbolizes top management's or the board of directors' conviction that steps must be taken to improve effectiveness.[4]

■ IMPLICATIONS FOR LEADERS

Leaders often tend to make internal attributions about poor employee performance, often leading to the punitive actions. Such actions usually are resented by employees who often do not feel responsible for the problem. Once the leader attributes performance problems to employees, the leader is less likely to give them support, coaching, and resources. Moreover, when employees make mistakes or have difficulty performing tasks, the leader is likely to blame them rather than recognizing situational causes or the leader's own contribution to the problem. Therefore leaders must learn to be careful, fair, and systematic about evaluating employee performance. They need to aware of the many options available for dealing with different causes of performance problems and the importance of selecting an appropriate one.

The following Ethics in Practice account describes an ethical problem facing a manager. After reading the case, please answer the questions. We have provided you with responses from a sample of managers working in 260 different companies.

ETHICS IN PRACTICE

You Make the Decision

Baxter Corporation has an Employee Assistance Program (EAP) that offers counseling for alcohol and substance abuse and mental and psychiatric problems. In 1992, Bob Gordon, a 20-year sales staff veteran and frequent winner of annual performance awards, told his boss Paula Hill, "I have been drinking a lot because I am depressed about my personal problems." Hill referred him to the EAP. Hill doesn't have access to Gordon's medical records and doesn't know whether he ever obtained or is currently receiving counseling for depression. However, he has continued to perform well since he told her about his drinking problem. In 1997, Paula Hill was promoted to president of Baxter Corporation. She received an application from Gordon to fill a vacancy for the high-stress position of vice-president for sales and marketing for the midwest region. The position requires supervising thirty-five salespeople, lots of travel, and making decisions on the spot to fix customer service problems. Judging by Gordon's past sales performance, his application merits serious consideration.

1. Hill should (pick one):
   A. Ask Gordon if he is still "depressed"; his response is relevant to whether he qualifies for the job.

—Continued

ETHICS IN PRACTICE—*Continued*

    B. Not discuss the issue with Gordon, but his complaint about being depressed should be considered.

    C. Ignore Gordon's depression. His performance is high.

    D. Exclude the depression incident because it occurred more than five years ago.

2. In making her decision Hill (pick one):

    A. Is confronting ethical as well as business issues.

    B. Can resolve the issue by conforming to the human resources practices stated in the company's manual.

3. Hill's policy with respect to known employee health complaints should be to (pick one):

    A. Exclude health issues in making any promotions.

    B. Consider them when they are related to performance.

    C. Consider them if they are related to performance but exclude them if they occurred more than three years ago.[5]

Which answers did you pick? The managers who participated chose the following: 1A, 37%; 1B, 1%; 1C, 33%; 1D, 29%; 2A, 72%; 2B, 28%; 3A, 5%; 3B, 75%; 3C, 20%.

The managers' reactions to the Baxter case indicate that most perceived Gordon's problems to stem from external rather than internal sources and would promote him. Did you make the same attribution?

VISIONARY LEADERS

Leadership is inherently future-oriented. It involves helping people move from where they are (here) to some new place (there). However, different leaders define or perceive *here* and *there* differently. For some, the journey between here and there is relatively routine, like driving on a familiar road. Others see the need to chart a new course through unexplored territory. Such leaders perceive fundamental differences between the way things are and the way things can or should be. They recognize the shortcomings of the present situation and offer a vision of how to overcome them. Thus **visionary leaders** see beyond the current realities, define new goals, and generate ideas about how to achieve those goals.

History is replete with examples of individuals who have had extraordinary success in generating deep changes in the beliefs, values, and actions of their followers.[6] These individuals (Abraham Lincoln, Franklin D. Roosevelt, John F. Kennedy, Martin Luther King, Gandhi, Mother Teresa, Martin Luther, and Joan of Arc, to name but a few) transformed entire societies through their words, actions, and visions. In today's organizations, such people include Yotaro Kobayashi of Fuji Xerox, Jean Kvasnica of Hewlett-Packard, Ray Lane of Oracle, and many others. Individuals who set great changes in motion are often described as visionary leaders. Their behaviors may be classified as charismatic, transactional, and transformational. We can best describe the differences between these types of leaders in the workplace and their behaviors by examining their sources of power (recall our discussion of sources of power in Chapter 9).

■ CHARISMATIC LEADERS

Charismatic leaders concern themselves with developing a vision of what could be, discovering or creating opportunities, and increasing employees' desire to control their own behaviors.[7] Charismatic leaders rely on the power they obtain through followers' identification with them. Followers identify with and are inspired by charismatic leaders in the hope (and with the leaders' promises) that they will succeed or even become as powerful as the leader. Charismatic leaders also have the ability to distill complex ideas into simple messages, communicating with symbols, metaphors, and stories. Charismatic leaders relish risk and emotionally put themselves on the line, working on hearts as well as minds. Are you likely to be a charismatic leader? To get an idea, before reading any further, complete the questionnaire in Table 11.1.

TABLE 11.1   Is Charismatic Leadership Your Preference?

To determine whether you would prefer to be a charismatic—rather than another type of—leader, please think how you would likely lead in the following situations. Circle the answer that best describes your preferred leader behaviors.

1. I would worry most about
   a. my current situation.
   b. my future situation.
2. I would be at ease thinking in
   a. generalities.
   b. specifics.
3. I would tend to focus on
   a. missed opportunities.
   b. opportunities that I could take advantage of.
4. I would prefer to
   a. promote traditions that have made my team great.
   b. create new team traditions.
5. I would prefer to communicate an idea via
   a. a written report.
   b. a one-page chart.
6. I tend to ask,
   a. How can we do this better?
   b. Why are we doing this?
7. I believe that
   a. there's always a way to minimize risk.
   b. some risks are too high.
8. When I disagree with others, I typically
   a. coax them nicely to change their views.
   b. bluntly tell them, You're wrong.
9. I tend to sway people by using
   a. emotion.
   b. logic.

Continued

TABLE 11.1   Is Charismatic Leadership Your Preference?—Continued

10. I think this questionnaire is

   a. ridiculous.

   b. fascinating.

To determine your charismatic leadership score, please use the following key and give yourself one point for each of these answers: (1) b; (2) a; (3) a; (4) b; (5) b; (6) b; (7) a; (8) b; (9) a; (10) b. Enter your total score: _____. If your total is less than four points, you do not prefer to be a charismatic leader. If your total is seven or more points, you have a strong charismatic leadership preference.

Source: Adapted from Sellers, P. What exactly is charisma? *Fortune,* January 15, 1996, 74.

Orit Gadiesh at Bain, Larry Bossidy at Allied Signal, Herb Kelleher at Southwest Airlines, Oprah Winfrey at Harpo Entertainment, and Charlotte Beers at Ogilvy & Mather are all charismatic leaders. When Arthur Martinez, former vice-president at Saks Fifth Avenue, became CEO of Sears in 1992, he knew he had problems. He used the metaphor about the Titanic to rally people behind his vision of what Sears could be. He told the company's employees that Sears was going to do what no other retailer in history had done: refloat a sinking ship. He told them that it would be risky and that they would be called on to make courageous decisions. Once they accomplished this feat, they would be filled with a great sense of team pride and accomplishment.[8]

Lars Kolind, president of Oticon Holding A/S, a maker of hearing aids, is a charismatic leader. Working from a three-tier loft space in Copenhagen, Kolind and his partners built a company that has captured a large share of the hearing aid market. It has become the world's leading producer of digital hearing aids, and operating profits have risen to nearly ten times their 1990 level. The following Across Cultures feature highlights some of the charismatic behaviors that Kolind displayed.

ACROSS CULTURES

Lars Kolind

At first glance, Oticon's headquarters seem almost deserted. There are plenty of workstations, but few employees are sitting at them. Rather, employees use mobile phones to communicate with each other and are constantly moving their offices to form new self-managed teams. When they join the organization, employees are given caddies, a file that can hold as many as thirty hanging folders, a few binders, and space perhaps for a family photo. Teams are formed, disbanded, and formed again as the work requires. Employees are always on the move, their office nothing more than where they park their caddies for the duration of the project. Project leaders (anyone with a compelling idea) attract resources and people in order to develop their ideas and deliver results. Members of Kolind's top management team provide advice and support but make few day-to-day decisions. The company has 100 or so projects at any one time, and most employees work on several projects at once.   —*Continued*

Kolind believes that Oticon isn't about making hearing aids but is about creating an atmosphere in which people have the freedom to do what they want and can do best. Kolind believes that employees should be encouraged to think the unthinkable. Every morning, Kolind and his employees meet in the company's second floor "paper room" to sort through the incoming mail. They may keep a few magazines but run everything else through an electronic scanner and throw the originals into a shredder.[9]

William Agee provides a good example of a charismatic leader whose use of power was misdirected. As we related in Chapter 10, Agee was consumed by a need to win. He and his wife found Boise, Idaho, the headquarters of Morrison-Knudsen, too small for their lifestyle. He had the company purchase a multimillion dollar residence for them on California's Pebble Beach. Thus executives had to fly to California to meet with him. His need for dominance and control eventually bankrupted the company and forced the board of directors to fire him.

■ TRANSACTIONAL LEADERS

Transactional leaders use power derived from rewards and punishments to influence their followers.[10] Unlike charismatic leaders, transactional leaders create visions that don't capture the emotional spirit of their followers. Their visions focus on the exchange of rewards and punishers for achieving results. Leaders help followers identify what must be done to accomplish the desired results. In helping followers identify what must be done, the leaders take into consideration the followers' needs.

This type of leadership is based on some sort of contractual exchange (often implicit) between leader and follower.[11] A factory work crew supervisor expects subordinates to follow directions, and the supervisor's subordinates expect to follow such directions. Each party has these expectations because of a contract between them specifying that, if the employees do the work required, they will receive a certain amount of money. However, exchanges need not involve material things. In fact, most exchanges are based on intangible social or nonmaterial rewards or feelings. Designing and maintaining exchanges in organizations so that people can work together effectively is crucial.[12] Robert Crandall, CEO of AMR Corporation (parent of American Airlines) is an example of a transactional leader. His negotiations with American's pilots and flight attendants saved the company significant labor costs and gave it a competitive advantage over its competitors, notably Delta and United Airlines. As a result, American has been able to expand its flights into new markets and not lay off personnel.

Richard Rosenberg, CEO of BankAmerica, used his transactional leader behaviors to change radically how that organization does business. In the following Quality in Practice piece, we highlight some of his behaviors.

QUALITY IN PRACTICE

Richard Rosenberg

BankAmerica, with more than 96,000 employees and $216 billion in assets, is the second largest bank holding company in the United States. It processes more than 20 million checks a day, operates more than 5500 ATMs, and handles more than 15 million customer account inquiries every month. Rosenberg and his staff have installed a set of rules, systems, and procedures that essentially control the behavior of employees within well-defined jobs to achieve consistent high-quality results. Through these practices the bank's management clearly defines the tasks and its expectations of employees. These practices also provide employees with the authority needed to do their jobs effectively. Rosenberg spends more than 40 percent of his time selecting, motivating, and training employees to maintain the bank's competitive advantage. He describes his job as that of making people feel good about what they are doing.

BankAmerica has 107 different incentive plans to motivate employees. Rosenberg believes that these incentives are fair, but they are designed to make sure that employees don't get too comfortable. If employees fail to reach their financial goals, it may be "damaging to their health." He also tries hard to send handwritten notes to employees who have made outstanding contributions to the bank and tells the public relations department to feature them in the bank's newsletter. As a result of such practices, since 1990 the bank has been among the most successful in the United States.[13]

■ TRANSFORMATIONAL LEADERS

Transformational leaders rely on their referent and personal sources of power to arouse intense feelings and motivate their employees.[14] Unlike charismatic or transactional leaders, transformational leaders' influence derives from their followers' personal acceptance of certain values. Values provide guidance in making decisions and behaving, so the followers, who share the leader's values, aren't dependent on the leader's orders.

Frances Hesselbein, former president of the Girl Scouts, strove to define and make explicit certain important values—trust, empathy, openness, and honesty—that she and her subordinates held in common. Faced with falling membership, she challenged the organization's policies, practices, and procedures, but never its values, purpose, or mission.[15] Such values guide action, enabling the transformational leader to rely on the followers' judgment. Transformational leaders are described by others as servants or stewards rather than bosses. One task of a transformational leader, then, is to turn subordinates into self-directed leaders.[16]

What methods do transformational leaders use that have such a profound effect on their followers and generate this type of relationship? Transformational leaders exhibit three behaviors: vision, framing, and impression management. These behaviors and followers' reactions are illustrated in Figure 11.2. The self-insight questionnaire at the end of this chapter allows you to diagnose your preference for transformational leader behaviors, which you might want to do before reading further.

■ FIGURE 11.2

Transformational Leadership Model

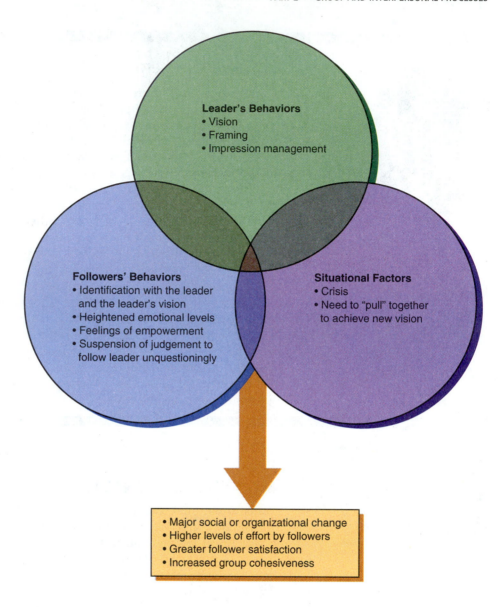

Leader's Behaviors
- Vision
- Framing
- Impression management

Followers' Behaviors
- Identification with the leader
  and the leader's vision
- Heightened emotional levels
- Feelings of empowerment
- Suspension of judgement to
  follow leader unquestioningly

Situational Factors
- Crisis
- Need to "pull" together
  to achieve new vision

- Major social or organizational change
- Higher levels of effort by followers
- Greater follower satisfaction
- Increased group cohesiveness

Vision   Perhaps the most important behavior of transformational leaders is their
ability to create a vision that emotionally binds people together.[17] People may
become exhausted, frustrated, disenchanted, and tempted to give up. Visionary
leaders encourage others' "hearts" to carry on. Such encouragement can come in
simple gestures or actions. At Mobil Oil, Continuous Improvement Advisor Steve
Butt occasionally puts on a clown's suit and gives out balloons to employees
when certain quality milestones are reached. Such acts always get a good laugh
from people, and Butt enjoys playing the role.

At the beginning of this chapter we noted the importance of a leader's having
a vision. A dramatic example of a vision is Martin Luther King's "I Have a Dream"
speech, in which he said:

> It is a dream rooted in the American dream that one day this nation will rise up and
> live out the true meaning of its creed—we hold these truths to be self-evident, that all
> men are created equal.

In this speech, King provided the world with an emotional message that inspired and motivated many people to change their attitudes and behaviors toward civil rights issues in the United States. Norman Brinker, president of Brinkers International (operators of Chili's, On the Border, Cozymel's, and Macaroni Grill), uses emotional appeals when leading his company. After a near fatal polo accident, he returned one year later to a joyous headquarters welcoming party and told his employees that he loved them. It was an emotional moment for everybody; all cried. Brinker said that he was determined to make it back to a company that had a real sense of direction and compassion. At Brinker, he has created a vision that employees can believe in and gives them a sense of direction.[18] Both leaders had more than just a vision: They also had a road map for attaining it. What is important is that followers "buy into" the vision and that the leader has a plan to energize their actions to achieve it.

Framing   Mary Kay Ash, founder and president of Mary Kay Cosmetics, began her company in 1963 to help women earn as much money as men. She wanted her salespeople to be paid on the basis of their contributions and not because they were women or men. She framed her vision by giving women a purpose for working for her new organization.

Transformational leaders are willing to take risks and nontraditional career paths to reach their goals. In short, they challenge the status quo by **framing** their vision of the future. That is they may champion a new product through its development, get a groundbreaking piece of legislation enacted into law, initiate a campaign to get teenagers to join an environmental cleanup, or whatever. Joan Lappin vividly remembers her introduction into the men's-club world of Wall Street. As an analyst with Equity Research Corporation, she had been invited to lunch at the New York Stock Exchange's lunch club. The security guard wouldn't let her in because the club rules prohibited women. Undaunted by this rule, and after several years of training, she founded her own firm, Gramacy, which specializes in investing in stocks that she believes are grossly underpriced. Since forming her organization in 1986, her firm now is recognized as one of the best investment firms on Wall Street. Now she gets a kick out of declining luncheon invitations to the NYSE's club (now open to women).[19]

Impression Management   Transformational leaders use tactics designed to enhance their attractiveness and appeal to others, referred to as **impression management** (see Chapter 3). When Mary Kay Ash arrives at her company's annual meeting to present awards to her beauty consultants, her entrance befits a queen. She is lowered on a throne from above into billowing clouds below. She descends from her throne in a long flowing pink ball gown, adorned with jewels. The more than 8000 beauty consultants are captivated by her presence, setting the mood for the event. She leads them in songs, crowns top performers, and personally asks each winner to repeat the "Mary Kay oath." Obviously, she has the ability to inspire others through her words, vision, and actions.

Transformational leaders lead by example. Their actions are designed to express and reinforce organizational values and beliefs. Often they do so in mundane ways, in contrast to Mary Kay's extravaganzas. Ken Wilkinson is the general manager for information systems at Greyhound Lines. On a tour of the Austin, Texas, bus terminal with local terminal management, he sees a passenger wandering around the terminal looking for something. He excuses himself from the group, approaches the person, and asks, "Is there something I can help you find?"

Such actions do more than could dozens of memoranda on the importance of customer service.

Steve Jobs of Apple Computer, Wayne Huizenga of Blockbuster Video, Anita Roddick of The Body Shop, Ben Cohen of Ben & Jerry's Ice Cream, and Herb Kelleher of Southwest Airlines are among the transformational leaders that you might have read about. Through their leadership, these people have been able to motivate employees and change their organizations in unique ways.

Transformational leaders may be found anywhere in an organization.[20] Emily Morgan personifies what a transformational leader can do in a large organization. Currently, Morgan's title is vice-president for customer fulfillment Asia at Levi Strauss & Company. The following Diversity in Practice selection illustrates her application of the three behaviors of transformational leaders.

DIVERSITY IN PRACTICE

Emily Morgan

When Tom Kasten (CEO of Levi Strauss) recruited Emily Morgan, he told her that she would either be an ambassador or an assassin. Ambassadors are people who can help others understand what the organization is doing; assassins try to kill new ideas. Kasten gave her one order: Help transform the company into one that emphasizes participation, diversity, accountability, and teamwork. Kasten considers her his ultimate ambassador because when she leads others she paints a vision, explaining its impact on them and getting people excited (vision). She decided that there would be no private offices, turning all of them into cubicles. One day an employee was on the phone singing "Happy Birthday" to his young daughter. When he hung up, everyone clapped. He'd forgotten he wasn't in his private office!

Morgan's job requires her to oversee a web of Asia-based textile mills, button factories, sewing centers, and other contractors that make Levi's products in eight different countries. She constantly throws out ideas and watches others shape and turn them into reality. She believes that people can learn to deal with task ambiguity but that they need a clear vision of goals (framing). Her staff works with suppliers to lower their costs, improve quality, and increase on-time performance. She has the ability to communicate with a wide variety of people and generate commitment.

Morgan describes herself as a catalyst, not a controller. Her motivational approach is to identify, articulate, and help others internalize Levi Strauss's values and beliefs. She spends time with her subordinates, helping them derive values and beliefs that support the organization's (impression). Through this process, subordinates develop greater self-confidence in their work and in turn empower lower level employees. Her task is to make leaders of her followers. She lets others who are going to do the work fill in the blanks between concepts and what's needed to implement them.[21]

Transformational leaders consider themselves as change agents, are courageous risk takers, believe in the abilities of their followers, and can dream and share this dream with others. Transformational leaders build confidence among their followers by helping them increase their self-efficacy and giving them freedom to take the initiative. Seeing themselves as teachers and stewards, they empower their followers to become partners in their endeavors.

Implications for Leaders   Transformational leadership may be most appropriate when an organization is new or when its survival is threatened. The problems faced by such organizations call for leaders with vision, confidence, and determination. These leaders will have to influence others to assert themselves, to join enthusiastically in team efforts, and arouse positive feelings about what they are attempting to do.[22]

Transformational leadership isn't a cure-all for organizations. Because transformational leaders' effects can be more emotional than rational, they have certain limitations. First, followers of such leaders may be so zealous that they are blind to conditions surrounding the leader, a bit like the children who followed the Pied Piper of Hamelin. For example, Steve Jobs at Apple Computer achieved unwavering loyalty and commitment from his employees during the late 1970s and early 1980s. He created a vision for them that personal computers would dramatically change the way people lived. However, once the need for this vision was fulfilled, Jobs became a liability to Apple. He was unable to listen to what experts in the PC industry were saying about Apple, became uncomfortable when employees challenged his views, and began to hold an unjustifiable belief in his "rightness" about issues. Because of these problems, he was replaced by a less charismatic leader, John Sculley, who has since been replaced himself as Apple's profits and market share dwindled.

At worst, transformational leaders emotionally manipulate followers and create visions for their own self-aggrandizement. They can even wreak havoc on the rest of the world. A tragic example of the negative aspects of transformational leadership was David Koresh, the Branch Davidian cult leader who died along with his followers in a fiery farmhouse near Waco, Texas, in 1993. A similar tragedy occurred when 912 followers of the Jim Jones cult drank a flavored drink containing cyanide in Jonestown, Guyana, killing all members. Jones said that they all must commit mass suicide for the glory of socialism.

Second, such leaders may lack communications and impression management skills. Organizations that become dependent on transformational leaders run the risk that they will surround themselves with "yes people" and thus fail to receive information that might be important but challenging to their visions.

Finally, some transformational leaders are known for their autocratic management style. Ross Perot, for example, was used to running his own organization at Electronic Data Systems (EDS). When EDS merged with General Motors and Perot was made a GM board member, he became one of GM's most outspoken critics. He insisted that any changes in EDS's procedures be cleared through him. His style and outspokenness were revealed again during his 1993 TV campaign against NAFTA, including his TV face-off with Vice President Al Gore.

These limitations must be considered, but organizations such as Wal-Mart and Home Depot have found that transformational leadership and its philosophy can become an important part of their operating style. That is, organizations in the 1990s must understand, appreciate, and support those employees who are willing to make unpopular decisions, who know when to reject traditional ways of doing something, and who can accept reasonable risks. A "right to fail" must be nurtured and embedded in the organization's culture.

THE SEVEN HABITS OF HIGHLY EFFECTIVE PEOPLE

Stephen Covey, author of *The 7 Habits of Highly Effective People*, has proposed another, widely acclaimed view of leadership.[23] It provides an integrated approach to personal and interpersonal effectiveness. He defines **habits** as the intersection of knowledge, skill, and desire. Covey's **seven habits** are arranged along a maturity continuum from dependence (you take care of me) to independence (I am responsible and self-reliant) to interdependence (we can do it). A *dependent* person expects things that happen to them to be taken care of, much like an infant who is dependent on others. Being dependent keeps people from assuming responsibility for their own actions and enables them to blame others when things go wrong. In contrast, an *independent* person has worked out a sense of security and self-worth, discovering in the process what it takes to be productive and satisfied. Finally, an *interdependent* person realizes that goals can't be achieved without the help of others. Such a person seeks to establish ways to work cooperatively with others. By so doing, the individual can sharpen abilities and enjoy the emotional richness that comes from close interpersonal relationships and teamwork. Figure 11.3 illustrates this cycle, showing each habit at the appropriate place on the maturity continuum. Each habit also builds on the previous ones.[24]

■ INDEPENDENCE

The first three habits deal with self-mastery. They move the individual from dependence to independence.

Habit 1: Be Proactive   More than simply taking the initiative, this habit means that people are responsible for their own lives. Highly proactive people recognize that responsibility means the ability to choose and to exercise integrity. People base choices on their values and don't blame circumstances for their outcomes. Recall in the Preview Case that, when Gadiesh accepted the CEO position at Bain, she took on the dual responsibility to help the company grow and to return pride to it.

■ **FIGURE 11.3**   **The Seven Habits Cycle**

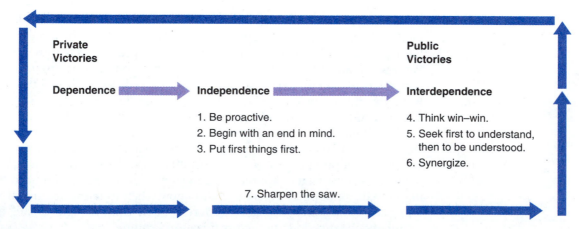

Source: Adapted from Covey, S. R. *The 7 Habits of Highly Effective People.* New York: Simon & Schuster, 1989.

Habit 2: Begin with an End in Mind   This habit entails creating a mental image of what a person wants to create. A home builder begins with a blueprint. Song writers put on paper sounds that exist in their minds. The authors of this text work from written outlines. Beginning with an end in mind also entails clearly thinking about specific goals and plans and establishing guiding values and principles. At Oticon, Kolind began with an end in mind (vision) for his company to become the largest hearing aid company in the world in terms of sales. From this mental image, he created an organization to achieve his vision.

Habit 3: Put First Things First   Rather than focusing on things to do, this habit requires people to gain control of time and events by relating them to their goals and by managing themselves. Important things serve a mission and urgent things have pressing deadlines. Putting first things first involves accomplishing results by focusing on managing relationships and not just activities. At Bain, a client's call takes precedence over any other activity that Gadiesh may be engaged in.

■ INTERDEPENDENCE

Moving from independence (self-mastery and self-discipline) to interdependence (productive relationships with others) involves open communication, effective team building, and caring for others. Creating effective relationships are what Covey calls "public victories."

Habit 4: Think Win–Win   Win–win means understanding that people must cooperate in order for the organization to succeed. When people understand that, they can dedicate themselves to cooperating with people in ways that ensure their mutual success and allow everyone to come out a winner. The win–win habit means that decisions are mutually satisfying to everyone, leading to commitment. When Gadiesh took over the reins at Bain, she noticed that employees had lost their collective pride. Her charismatic leadership style helped employees to realize that they would rather succeed or fail together than succeed alone.

Habit 5: Seek First to Understand, Then to Be Understood   Most people don't listen with the intent to understand; they listen with the intent to reply. They are either speaking or preparing to speak, filtering everything they hear through their own perceptions. Listening with the intent to understand requires people to be nonjudgmental and develop empathy for the other person's situation. When both parties fully understand the other's point of view, they can have a meaningful conversation. Gadiesh tries to focus completely on the person she's talking with and not on what needs to get done. As a result, she stays attuned both to her clients and to her employees.

Habit 6: Synergize   When two or more people work together to understand something, they create synergy. **Synergy** occurs when people create new alternatives and solutions. The greatest chance for achieving synergy is when people don't see things the same way; that is, differences present opportunities. Relationships don't break down because of differences but because people fail to grasp the value of their differences and how to take advantage of them. Synergy is created by people who have learned to think win–win, and listen to understand the other person. In other words, this habit builds directly upon the two that precede it. One of the messages of Martin Luther King's "I Have A Dream" speech was that of synergy. He challenged people to confront their differences and to learn from them. Stereotyping keeps people from appreciating their differences because they limit listening for understanding.

Habit 7: Sharpen the Saw   The seventh habit integrates the previous six. Actually, it is a process of renewal that encompasses the physical, the mental, the spiritual, and the social aspects of a person's life. Covey recommends that people continually renew themselves in order to maintain high levels of performance. The following Managing in Practice feature illustrates how Ofelia Gonzales used the seven habits model to create effective teamwork in organizations.

MANAGING IN PRACTICE

Ofelia Gonzales

Ofelia Gonzales, a team leader for the physical therapy department at Presbyterian Hospital in Dallas, Texas, attended a seven habits seminar as part of the hospital's leadership development program. This hospital is the flagship for a large not-for-profit health-care system.

The emergence of managed care and cost controls were factors that made Presbyterian Hospital look at its business processes to find ways to increase efficiency. One way was to form self-managed teams. From benchmarking other hospitals that had gone to self-managed teams, Presbyterian learned that it had to spend time training employees in group dynamics before forming these teams. In an attempt to provide members of these teams with leadership tools, the hospital sponsored the seven habits course.

The focus was on learning how to use each habit on a daily basis to manage teams. Gonzales focused on habit 4, "Think win–win." This habit provided team leaders with a set of guidelines for building an effective team environment. The following five guidelines gave Gonzales and her team a common language and philosophy, enabling them to create a win–win attitude. They then applied these guidelines effectively to their operations. First, she carefully explained the objectives of her team so that all team members had the same ends (patient satisfaction and effective patient planning) in mind. Second, team members had to agree on specific roles (nursing, physical therapy, occupational therapy, and others) that each member was responsible for performing and deadlines for their accomplishment. Third, team members had to list the human, financial, and technical resources they needed. This strategy garnered commitment and support from key administrators, lessening resistance and creating trust. Fourth, team members had to develop methods to measure the team's progress and accomplishments. Because teams would now be accountable for a patient's care, their members would have to be cross-trained to provide different types of therapy for a patient. Finally, each team would be responsible for determining its own rewards (financial and nonfinancial) and methods of recognition for outstanding performance.

Gonzales felt that, by establishing a win–win agreement before her team became operational, she could resolve differences and remove barriers before they could hinder her team's performance. The time and effort spent on creating a win–win agreement with other departments paid off for these leaders as implementation began. The results were favorable patient responses and lower costs.[25]

■ IMPLICATIONS FOR LEADERS

The 7 Habits of Highly Effective People and *Principle-Centered Leadership* have become two of the best-selling books of all time. They have been on the *New York Times* best-seller list for more than 220 weeks, have sold more than 5 million copies, and have been translated into more than forty languages. Covey's management training center trains more than 300,000 people a year. These statistics are impressive, but little systematic research has been done to evaluate Covey's views. The research that has been reported is anecdotal.[26]

DOES LEADERSHIP MATTER?

The underlying thrust of all the models presented in Chapter 10 and this chapter is that leaders *can* and *do* make a difference. Although the various models make contradictory recommendations about leadership style (that is, use a consideration or an initiating structure, use an autocratic or a consultative approach, and so on), all are based on the assumption that leaders make a difference in organizations.[27] Several researchers have attacked this assumption, concluding that the varying nature of a situation or type of followers cast doubt on the relative importance of leaders in organizations. These researchers suggest that leaders sometimes have little impact on the attitudes and behaviors of their followers. Sometimes, no matter what a leader does, employees are satisfied or dissatisfied with their jobs, attain or fail to reach their goals, and perform well or poorly without a leader exerting much influence. The evidence surrounding these arguments isn't conclusive, but we believe that it warrants your attention. These arguments can be classified as (1) leader irrelevance and (2) substitutes for leadership.

■ LEADER IRRELEVANCE

Jeffrey Pfeffer has argued that leadership is irrelevant for many organizational outcomes.[28] He stresses a situation-based approach to understanding leadership, emphasizing that situations are more important determinants of organizational effectiveness than leaders' behaviors. His argument stresses three point.

First, *factors outside the leader's immediate control* affect profits and other success factors more than anything a leader might do. Consider the recent situation facing Lockheed Martin. Lockheed Martin, the largest defense contractor in the United States, was formed in 1995 by the merger of Martin Marietta, Lockheed Corporation, and Loral Vought. Much of Lockheed Martin revenues comes from U.S. defense contracts. When the federal government announced that it was cutting defense contracts, Norman Augustine, CEO, found that he had to slash millions of dollars from its budget to keep the company operating. In addition, he had to sell off operations that weren't part of the company's core businesses in order to reduce debt.

Second, *only rarely do leaders unilaterally control the resources needed* to influence others. The leader's power to reward or punish people is constrained by organizational policies, politics, and/or the power of stakeholders outside of the company. As Augustine discovered, shareholders and creditors exerted pressures on Lockheed Martin to divest noncore businesses so that it could raise $1.8 billion in cash to improve its financial position.[29]

Third, the *selection process* through which all leaders pass filters people in such a way that those in leadership positions tend to act similarly. Therefore the impact of a leader on the organization is reduced. For example, in the 1996 presidential election campaign it was virtually impossible for some leaders—extremists whether right or left—to be elected. People who eventually win elections are more alike than different.[30] Therefore selection processes generally reduce the impact of any change in high-level leadership. In some organizations, such as JC Penney, Allstate Insurance, Brooklyn Union, The Associates, and Alcoa, leaders tend to be long-time employees who have paid their dues while climbing the corporate ladder. They have followed proven career paths that their predecessors used. For example, in the 1980s, many CEOs rose through the ranks of marketing. In the 1990s, the trend is for engineers and technical people to rise to positions of leadership.

■ SUBSTITUTES

A **leadership substitute** is something that acts in place of a formal leader and makes leadership unnecessary.[31] According to the substitutes model, the success of a particular leader depends on the characteristics of the followers, team, situation, and organization. Each can act as a substitute for a particular leader behavior. Consider the case of Robert Kennedy, an ophthalmologist at the University of Texas, Southwestern Medical Center. The tasks that his staff perform are intrinsically challenging for them. Hence the substitutes model suggests that leader consideration (see Chapter 10) would have little impact on his followers because the tasks that they are performing give them considerable job satisfaction. Therefore it is unnecessary for Kennedy to engage in considerate behaviors to influence his followers. The model also suggests that Kennedy direct his considerate behavior toward followers performing routine tasks that provide little job challenge and satisfaction. In essence, substitutes can free up a leader's time to concentrate on other activities that need attention.

A recent review of the research on leadership substitutes provides some support for this model.[32] Leader substitutes, such as employee maturity, group norms and cohesiveness, team performance, task structure, and professional recognition, affect subordinates' behaviors. That is, actions by leaders influence the substitutes through employee selection, task design, work group assignments, and the design of reward systems. Part of being an effective leader is knowing when to use substitutes to influence others. For example, a charismatic leader who is in charge of a highly effective team needs to provide less active leadership than a transactional leader in the same situation. Leader substitutes are important but do not eliminate the role of the leader.

CHAPTER SUMMARY

Leadership is a process of creating a vision for others and having the ability to translate that vision into reality and sustain it. Four contemporary developments in leadership were presented. The attribution leadership model suggests that a leader's judgment about subordinates is influenced by the leader's interpretation of the causes of the employees' behaviors. These causes may either be external or internal. Effective leaders correctly identify the cause and then act accordingly.

The visionary leadership models focus on the ability of the leader to create new ideals by means of charismatic, transactional, or transformational skills. Charismatic leaders concern themselves with developing a vision that followers can identify with, have the ability to distill complex messages into simple ones, and are empathetic toward others. Transactional leaders help followers identify tasks to be done and the exchanges of rewards and punishments needed to obtain compliance. Transformational leaders rely on their referent power to arouse intense feelings in followers. Through a leader's vision, framing, and impression behaviors, followers come to internalize the leader's values.

The seven habits of highly effective people provide an integrated approach to personal and interpersonal effectiveness. The seven habits are arranged along a continuum from dependence to independence to interdependence. When leaders master the first three habits—be proactive, begin with an end in mind, and put first things first—they create the necessary conditions for moving from dependence to interdependence. The next three habits are win–win; seek first to understand, then to be understood; and synergize. The final habit, sharpen the saw, involves a continual renewal of the person through physical, mental, spiritual, and social actions.

The question, Does leadership matter?, focuses attention on situations in which leaders are constrained and their behaviors have little impact on their followers. The issues of leader irrelevance and leader substitutes relate to the characteristics of situations that make it difficult for the leader to effectively influence others.

KEY TERMS AND CONCEPTS

Attribution model	Impression management	Transactional leaders
Charismatic leaders	Leadership substitute	Transformational leaders
Framing	Seven habits	Visionary leaders
Habits	Synergy	

DISCUSSION QUESTIONS

1. What factors could affect a leader's attribution of a subordinate's performance?

2. Why do some followers attribute their failures to leaders?

3. Are transformational leaders really different from transactional leaders? If so, in what ways?

4. What sources of power do charismatic leaders rely on to influence follower behaviors?

5. How do transformational leaders lead?

6. According to Jonathan Wheeler, President of the C. T. Film Division of Rexene Chemical Company, "At Rexene, our philosophy is that some of the best ideas come from employees in the plant rather than managers sitting in their offices." Using the seven habits model, what habits underlie Wheeler's statement?

7. Norman Brinker, CEO of Brinker International says, "I'm not afraid to fail. I'm not afraid to make mistakes. For me, when you take all the risks out, it just isn't as much fun." What does this statement say about Brinker's leadership style?

8. What is the "dark side" of transformational leadership?

9. List some conditions under which leaders don't seem to make a difference.

10. Consider all the men who have been president of the United States since you were born. How many of them would be classified as transformational? How would you rate their performances as president?

11. Briefly describe the relationship between the seven habits model and the transformational leader behaviors.

■ Developing Competencies

Self-Insight: Are You a Transformational Leader?

Instructions:

The following statements refer to the possible ways in which you might prefer to behave toward others when you are in a leadership role. Please read each statement carefully and decide to what extent it applies to your preferred or actual behaviors. Then put a check on the appropriate number.[33]

To a Very Great Extent	5
To a Considerable Extent	4
To a Moderate Extent	3
To a Slight Extent	2
To Little or No Extent	1

Your preference is to . . .

1. pay close attention to what others say when they are talking.   5 4 3 2 1
2. communicate clearly.   5 4 3 2 1
3. be trustworthy.   5 4 3 2 1
4. care about other people.   5 4 3 2 1
5. not put excessive energy into avoiding failure.   5 4 3 2 1
6. make the work of others more meaningful.   5 4 3 2 1
7. seem to focus on the key issues in a situation.   5 4 3 2 1
8. get across your meaning effectively, often in unusual ways.   5 4 3 2 1
9. be relied on to follow through on commitments.   5 4 3 2 1
10. have a great deal of self-respect.   5 4 3 2 1
11. enjoy taking carefully calculated risks.   5 4 3 2 1
12. help others feel more competent in what they do.   5 4 3 2 1
13. have a clear set of priorities.   5 4 3 2 1
14. keep in touch with how others feel.   5 4 3 2 1
15. rarely change once you have taken a clear position.   5 4 3 2 1
16. focus on strengths, of yourself and of others.   5 4 3 2 1
17. seem most alive when deeply involved in some project.   5 4 3 2 1
18. show others that they are all part of the same group.   5 4 3 2 1
19. get others to focus on the issues you see as important.   5 4 3 2 1
20. communicate feelings as well as ideas.   5 4 3 2 1
21. let others know where you stand.   5 4 3 2 1
22. know just how you "fit" into a group.   5 4 3 2 1
23. learn from mistakes, do not treat errors as disasters, but as learning.   5 4 3 2 1
24. be fun to be around.   5 4 3 2 1

Interpretation

The questionnaire measures each of the six basic leader behavior patterns, as well as a set of emotional responses, usually associated with transformational leaders. Your score can range from four to twenty. Each question is stated as a measure of the extent to which you prefer or actually engage in a behavior. The higher your score, the more you prefer or actually demonstrate transformational leader behaviors.

Index 1: Management of Attention (1, 7, 13, 19).
Your score _____.

You pay especially close attention to people with whom you are communicating. You prefer to "focus in" on the key issues under discussion and help others to see clearly these key points. You have clear ideas about the relative importance or priorities of different issues under discussion.

Index 2: Management of Meaning (2, 8, 14, 20).
Your score _____.

This set of items centers on your communication skills, specifically your ability to get the meaning of a message across, even if this means devising some quite innovative approach.

Index 3: Management of Trust (3, 9, 15, 21). Your score _____.

The key factor is your perceived trustworthiness as shown by your willingness to follow through on promises, avoidance of "flip-flop" shifts in position, and preference to take clear positions.

Index 4: Management of Self (4, 10, 16, 22). Your score _____.

This index concerns your general attitudes toward yourself and others; that is, your overall concern for others and their feelings, as well as for "taking care of" feelings about yourself in a positive sense (e.g., self-regard).

Index 5: Management of Risk (5, 11, 17, 23). Your score _____.

Effective transformational leaders are deeply involved in what they do. They do not spend excessive amounts of time or energy on plans to "protect" themselves against failure (a "CYA" approach). These leaders are willing to take risks, not on a hit-or-miss basis, but after careful estimation of the odds of success or failure.

Index 6: Management of Feelings (6, 12, 18, 24).
Your score _____.

Transformational leaders seem to consistently generate a set of feelings in others. Others feel that their work becomes more meaningful and that they are the "masters" of their own behavior; that is, they feel competent. They feel a sense of community, a "we-ness" with their colleagues and co-workers.

Organizational Insight: Malden Mills

On December 11, 1995, at about 8 p.m., a large portion of the Malden Mills complex in Lawrence, Massachusetts, was seriously damaged by fire. Several employees were injured, some critically burned. The cause of the fire has been blamed on a faulty boiler. The fire put 1400 of the company's 3200 employees out of work. Many thought that Aaron Feuerstein, the company's president, would take the insurance money and retire to Florida. But, in the following week, Feuerstein did something that astonished his employees and earned him a trip to the White House to meet President Clinton. He announced that he would keep all his workers on the payroll for a month while he started rebuilding the ninety-year old business. In January, Feuerstein announced that he would pay them a second month. In February, he said that he would pay them for a third month. By March, most of the employees had returned to full-time work and by midsummer, 85 percent were back at work. Those who hadn't returned were offered help in making other arrangements. Feuerstein estimates that this approach cost him millions of dollars.

Immediately after the fire, Feuerstein gathered all his employees in the gym at Catholic Central High School and told them of his decision to keep paying their wages. It was a highly charged, emotional meeting. People wept, hugged each other, and employees lifted the seventy-year-old Feuerstein onto their shoulders and carried him around the gym while others sang songs.

Founded in 1906, the company originally made bathing suits and uniforms for the U.S. Army. Since 1945, the company has focused on fabrics for clothing and sleepware. The company faced intense foreign competition from low-cost mills and mills operating in the Sun Belt states where labor costs were lower than in Massachusetts. The result of such competition forced the company into bankruptcy in 1981. In 1982, employees in its research and development laboratory patented Polartec, a 100 percent polyester thermal fabric, whose sales are expected to bring in more than $400 million this year. Coats, hats, gloves, and other apparel made from Polartec keep skiers and hikers warm.

Feuerstein says that the fundamental difference between his leadership philosophy and that of most other American CEOs is that he considers employees assets and not expenses. He believes that his job goes beyond just making money for shareholders, even though the only shareholders of Malden Mills are members of his immediate family. He has arranged for several heart by-pass operations for employees and provides free soft drinks when the temperature is more than 90° on the manufacturing lines.

He feels a responsibility to the employees and community. Feuerstein found it unconscionable to put 3000 people on the street and deliver a death blow to the town. How can you tell long-time employees who just spent $1000 on Christmas gifts that they have just collected their last paycheck and would have to go on unemployment? His answer: He couldn't. Feuerstein believes in the American Dream that those who work hard should make a good living and be able to retire comfortably. He could get rid of permanent employees who earn $15 an hour and replace them with temporary employees for $7 an hour, but that would violate the spirit of trust that he has established with his workers and the community.

Ten days after the fire, employees had set up temporary facilities in a parking lot to continue manufacturing the synthetic fabrics. Using new equipment, people were willing to work long hours to make sure that orders would be filled. Employees called L. L. Bean, a major customer, and assured them that Malden Mills would deliver their goods on time.[34]

Questions

1. What leader attributions did Feuerstein make about his employees?

2. Choose among the three types of visionary leaders and analyze Feuerstein's leader behaviors. Indicate specific actions to support your choices.

3. Are Feuerstein's leader behaviors applicable to CEOs of other organizations? Why haven't others tried it? Is there a dark side to use of this leadership style? If so, what is it?

Source: "Are You a Transformational Leader?" by Marshall Sashkin.

REFERENCES

1. Adapted from Sellers, P. What exactly is charisma? *Fortune*, January 15, 1996, 68–75; Conger, J., and Rothard, N. Orit Gadiesh: Pride at Bain & Co. (A). Boston: Harvard Business School Case number 9-494-031 (rev. January 5, 1995).

2. Gooding, R. Z., and Kinicki, A. J. Interpreting event causes: The complementary role of categorization and attribution process. *Journal of Management Studies*, 1995, 32, 1–23; Ashkanasy, N. M., and Gallois, C. Leader attributions and evaluations: Effects of locus of control, supervisory control, and task control. *Organizational Behavior & Human Decision Processes*, 1994, 59, 24–51.

3. Schein, E. H. *Organizational culture and leadership.* San Francisco: Jossey-Bass, 1993.

4. Bennis, W., and Townsend, R. *Reinventing Leadership.* New York: Morrow, 1995.

5. Adapted from Bernheim, R. E. The corporate ethics test. *Business and Society Review,* Spring 1992, 77–89.

6. Burns, J. McG. *Leadership.* New York: Harper & Row, 1978.

7. Conger, J. A., and Kanungo, R. N. Charismatic leadership in organizations: Perceived behavioral attributes and their measurement. *Journal of Organizational Behavior,* 1994, 15, 439–452; Howell, J. M. Two faces of charisma: Socialized and personalized leadership in organizations. In J. A. Conger and R. N. Kanungo (eds.), *Charismatic Leadership: The Elusive Factor in Organizational Effectiveness.* San Francisco: Jossey-Bass, 1988, 213–236; Sankowsky, D. The charismatic leader as narcissist: Understanding the abuse of power. *Organizational Dynamics,* Spring 1995, 57–72; Kirkpatrick, S. A., and Locke, E. A. Direct and indirect effects of three core charismatic leadership components on performance. *Journal of Applied Psychology,* 1996, 81, 36–51.

8. Byrne, J. A. Strategic warfare. *Business Week,* August 26, 1996, 46–51; personal communication, Richard Haayen, Retired CEO, Allstate Insurance Company, September, 1996.

9. Adapted from Labarre, P. This organization is disorganization. *Fast Company,* June/July 1996, 77–81.

10. Sashkin, M., Rosenbach, Wm. E., and Sashkin, M. G. Development of the power need and its expression in management and leadership with a focus on leader–follower relations. Paper presented at 12th Scientific Meeting of the A. K. Rice Institute, Washington, D.C., May, 1995; Cawthon, D. L. Leadership: The great man theory revisited. *Business Horizons,* May–June 1996, 1–5.

11. Bycio, P., Hackett, R. D., and Allen, J. S. Further assessments of Bass's (1985) conceptualization of transactional and transformational leadership. *Journal of Applied Psychology,* 1995, 80, 468–479.

12. Sashkin, M., Rosenbach, W. E., and Sashkin, M. G. One more time: What's the difference between leaders and managers. Unpublished manuscript, George Washington University, September 1996; Bass, B. M. Is there universality in the full range model of leadership? *International Journal of Public Administration* (Special issue on transformational leadership), 1996, 19, 731–762.

13. Adapted from Farkas, C. M., and DeBacker, P. *Maximum Leadership: The World's Leading CEOs Share Their Five Strategies for Success.* New York: Holt, 1996, 142–145.

14. Podsakoff, P. M., MacKenzie, S. B., and Bommer, Wm. H. Transformational leader behaviors and substitutes for leadership as determinants of employee satisfaction, commitment, trust, and organizational citizenship behaviors. *Journal of Management,* 1996, 22, 259–299.

15. Sherman, S. Tomorrow's best leaders are learning their stuff. Fortune, November 25, 1995, 98; Hesselbein, F. The "How to be" leader. In F. Hesselbein, M. Goldsmith, and R. Beckhard (eds.), *The Leader of the Future.* San Francisco: Jossey-Bass Publishers, 1996, 121–125.

16. Atwater, L. E., and Wright, W. J. Power and transformational and transactional leadership in public and private organizations. *International Journal of Public Administration* (Special issue on transformational leadership), 1996, 19, 963–990.

17. Larwood, L., Falbe, C. M., Kriger, M. P., and Missing, P. Structure and meaning of organizational vision. *Academy of Management Journal,* 1995, 38, 740–769.

18. Brinker, N., and Phillips, D. T. *On The Brink.* Arlington, Tex.: Summit Group, 1996.

19. Marcial, G. G. Very fancy returns. *Business Week,* June 8, 1992, 83.

20. Ashkenas, R., Ulrich, D., Jick, T. and Kerr, S. *The Boundaryless Organization: Breaking the Chains of Organizational Structure.* San Francisco: Jossey-Bass, 1996, 326–332.

21. Adapted from Sheff, D. Levi's changes everything. *Fast Company,* June/July 1996, 66–74.

22. Shamir, B., House, R. J. and Arthur, M. B. The motivational effects of charismatic leadership: A self-concept based theory. *Organization Science,* 1993, 4, 577–594; Lewis, K. M. Leadership, emotion and gender: The consequences of a leader's emotional display in the workplace. Paper presented at the Academy of Management meeting, Cincinnati, August 1996.

23. Covey, S. R. *The 7 Habits of Highly Effective People.* New York: Simon and Shuster, 1989; Covey, S. R. Principle-Centered Leadership. New York: Summit, 1991. Also see Covey, S. R., Merrill, A. R., and Merrill, R. R. *First Things First.* New York: Simon & Schuster, 1994.

24. Smith, T. K. What's so effective about Stephen Covey? *Fortune,* December 12, 1994, 116–126.

25. Used with permission from Strese, J., Organizational Development Officer, Southern Methodist University, Dallas, Texas, October 1996.

26. Whitferd, D. Therapist to the new economy. *Inc.,* September 1996, 76–83.

27. McGill, M. E., and Slocum, J. W. What We Need Is a Little Leadership. Unpublished manuscript, Southern Methodist University, Dallas, 1997.

28. Pfeffer, J. Why do smart organizations occasionally do dumb things? *Organizational Dynamics,* Summer 1996, 33–44; Pfeffer, J. The ambiguity of leadership. *Academy of Management Review,* 1977, 2, 104–112.

29. Zunitch, V. M. Lockheed Martin now concentrates on slashing debt. *Wall Street Journal,* April 26, 1996, A7.

30. Barone, M. Great men need not apply: We are living in a time of lesser dangers and lesser leaders. *U.S. News & World Report,* February 19, 1996, 40–41.

31. Kerr, S., and Jermier, J. M. Substitutes for leadership: Their meaning and measurement. *Organizational Behavior and Human Performance,* 1978, 22, 374–403.

32. Podsakoff, P. M., MacKenzie, S. B., and Bommer, W. H. Meta-analysis of the relationships between Kerr and Jermier's substitutes for leadership and employee job attitudes, role perceptions, and performance. *Journal of Applied Psychology,* 1996, 81, 380–399.

33. Sashkin, M. *Visionary Leadership*. Washington, D.C.: George Washington University, 1997. Used with permission.

34. Adapted from Ryan, M. They call their boss a hero. *Parade*, September 8, 1996, 4–5; Lee, M. Corporate focus: Malden looks spiffy in New England textile gloom. *Wall Street Journal*, November 10, 1995, B4; 1randall@ecst.csuchico.edu, and mullen@world.std.com.

12

Conflict and Negotiation

LEARNING OBJECTIVES

When you have finished studying this chapter, you should be able to:

- Define four basic forms of conflict.
- Explain the negative, positive, and balanced views of conflict.
- Compare the primary levels of conflict within organizations.
- Use five interpersonal conflict handling styles.
- Discuss the basic types of negotiations.
- Describe various negotiation strategies.

OUTLINE

PREVIEW CASE

Charlie Olcott

Charlie Olcott had the career most of us only dream of. By the time he was thirty-nine years old, he'd worked his way up the corporate ladder to become president of Burger King USA, a division of Minneapolis-based Pillsbury Corporation. "I thought I had it all figured out," he says. "I ran a $5 billion company with 250,000 employees and five thousand stores. But I hope I'm never again as smart as I was in my thirties."

"I was taught growing up that each rung of the ladder would give me more satisfaction, but I found the view from the top held no more real satisfaction than the other rungs. I was supposed to feel better about having a big bank account, but I was still searching for fulfillment. The needs in my life just weren't being met by having a corporate jet, a seven-figure salary, or controlling a boardroom. Still, you don't suddenly leave something you've worked your whole life to achieve. Sometimes, you need a little push."

Pillsbury management began what Olcott calls a desperate attempt to defend the company from a hostile takeover by Grand Metropolitan PLC. "A professional difference of opinion on the accuracy of the numbers used in the defensive strategy forced a showdown with Pillsbury's new chairman," Olcott says. "The chairman told me, 'Defend my numbers or you're off the team.'" Olcott refused, walked out, and called his wife to tell her

he had been fired. "This was a career vaporizing move, and I knew it. You don't get to that position at thirty-nine by being a rabble rouser—the most radical thing I'd done in corporate life was not shave on vacation."

His wife was supportive, though, and the family of five had enough savings to live on while Olcott began searching for something more satisfying. After nearly a year of searching, Olcott became a partner in a four-person small business consulting practice in Miami, where he'd continued to live after he left Burger King. Still, after two years, the business wasn't making much money and the family's savings were depleted. "If I'd focused on the loss of title and money, I could have been extremely unhappy," he says. "Instead, we found that this was the happiest time we'd ever had as a family. I was largely never home when I was with Burger King, but now I had time with my three sons."

It wasn't long before he was introduced to Tim Joukowsky and his Boston-based social venture capital firm, HFG Expansion Fund. Olcott liked what he saw and became a general partner as well as chairman and CEO of two of the fund's four portfolio companies. He's making a lot less money than before and he doesn't control the resources he used to, but Olcott couldn't be happier. "The particulars of your circumstance are less important than your attitude," he says. "I've been rich and poor, and I would like to be rich again. But it doesn't matter because I realize that you win in the end."[1]

The need to manage conflict is an everyday event in organizations. **Conflict** is the process in which one party perceives that its interests are being opposed or negatively affected by another party.[2] This definition implies some interdependence and interaction, along with the perception of incompatible concerns, among the people involved. It is sufficiently broad to cover a variety of conflict issues and events. As Charlie Olcott demonstrated, a person's attitudes, values, and style play an important role in determining whether conflict leads to beneficial or destructive outcomes.

In this chapter we consider conflict and negotiation from several viewpoints. First, we present the basic forms of conflict and examine three views of it. Second, we identify four levels of conflict often present in organizations. Third, we discuss five interpersonal styles in conflict management and the conditions under which each style may be appropriate. Fourth, we address the essentials of negotiation, basic negotiation strategies, and some of the complexities involved in negotiating when the parties are from different cultures. We conclude with some highlights of third-party mediation in the negotiation process.

CONFLICT MANAGEMENT

The ability to understand and correctly diagnose conflict is essential to managing it. **Conflict management** consists of diagnostic processes, interpersonal styles, negotiating strategies, and other interventions that are designed to avoid unnecessary conflict and reduce or resolve excessive conflict.[3] Charlie Olcott resolved his work–family conflicts by deciding that time with his family was more important than the relentless pursuit of bigger titles and more money.

■ FORMS OF CONFLICT

As highlighted in Table 12.1, conflict takes four basic forms. Regardless of form, though, the essence of conflict is incompatibility.

Goal conflict refers to incompatible preferred or expected outcomes. Goal conflict includes inconsistencies between the individual's or group's values and norms (such as standards of behavior) and the demands or goals assigned by higher levels in the organization.[4] Recall Charlie Olcott's comment in the Preview Case: "A professional difference of opinion on the accuracy of the numbers used in the defensive strategy forced a showdown with Pillsbury's new chairman. The chairman told me, 'Defend my numbers or you're off the team.'" Olcott's personal goal was honesty in reporting the numbers accurately, whereas Olcott's perception of the demands from Pillsbury's chairman was to distort the numbers to ward off the hostile takeover effort by Grand Metropolitan PLC.

A more common type of goal conflict occurs when an individual or group is assigned or selects incompatible goals. A student may set goals of earning $200 a week and achieving a 3.50 grade point average (on a 4.0-point system) while being enrolled full-time during the coming semester. A month into the semester, the student may realize that there aren't enough hours in the week to achieve both goals. **Goal incompatibility** refers to the extent to which an individual's or group's goals are at odds with the capacity to achieve the goals. Thus, even without the goal of earning $200 per week, the student could face inner conflict because of the difficulty in achieving a 3.50 grade point average.

Cognitive conflict refers to incompatible ideas and thoughts within an individual or between individuals. In the Preview Case, Charlie Olcott appeared to be reflecting on one of his cognitive conflicts when he stated, "I thought I had it all figured out. I ran a $5 billion company with 250,000 employees and five thousand stores. But I hope I'm never again as smart as I was in my thirties."

Affective conflict refers to incompatible feelings and emotions within an individual or between individuals. Charlie Olcott's reflection on inner affective conflict is implied when he comments, "I was supposed to feel better about having a big bank account, but I was still searching for fulfillment. The needs in my life weren't being met by having a corporate jet, a seven-figure salary, or controlling

TABLE 12.1 Basic Forms of Conflict

FORM	CORE MEANING
Goal conflict	Incompatible preferences
Cognitive conflict	Incompatible thoughts
Affective conflict	Incompatible feelings
Procedural conflict	Incompatible views on process

a boardroom." The more obvious forms of affective conflict occur between individuals, such as the anger by the chairman of Pillsbury when he told Olcott: "Defend my numbers or you're off the team."

Procedural conflict refers to people differing over the process to use for resolving a matter. Union–management negotiations often involve procedural conflicts before negotiations actually begin. The parties may have procedural conflicts over who will be involved in the negotiations, where they will take place, and when sessions will be held (and how long they will last). Different interpretations about how a grievance system is to operate provide another example of procedural conflict.

■ VIEWS OF CONFLICT

The presence of the four basic forms of conflict need not necessarily harm an organization or keep its members from being effective. In fact, of the three views of conflict—positive, negative, and balanced—only one is concerned with its harmful aspects.

Positive View   Conflict in organizations can be a positive force. The creation and/or resolution of conflict may lead to constructive problem solving. The need to resolve conflict can lead people to search for ways of changing how they do things. The conflict resolution process can be a stimulus for positive change within an organization. This process may not only lead to innovation and change, but it may also make change more acceptable.[5] A recent study of managers demonstrated this view. The positive effects they noted generally fell into three main categories: beneficial effects on productivity ("Our work productivity went up" and "We produced quality products on time"), relationship outcomes ("Sensitivity to others was increased" and "Better communication methods were developed"), and constructive organizational change ("We adopted more effective controls" and "Better job descriptions and expectations were drawn up").[6]

The intentional introduction of conflict into the decision-making process may even be beneficial. In team decision making, a problem may arise when a cohesive team's desire for agreement interferes with its ability to consider alternative solutions. A team may encounter groupthink (see Chapter 8), which it can reduce by introducing conflict in the form of one or more dissenting opinions. Finally, people may come to quite different conclusions about what is fair and ethical in specific situations. A positive view of conflict encourages people to work out their differences, participate in developing an ethical and fair organization, and deal directly with injustices.[7]

Negative View   Conflict also may have serious negative effects, diverting efforts from goal attainment, and depleting resources, especially time and money. Conflict also may negatively affect the psychological well-being of employees and cause stress (see chapter 7). If severe, conflicting thoughts, ideas, and beliefs may lead to resentment, tension, and anxiety. These feelings appear to result from the threat that conflict poses to important personal goals and beliefs. Over an extended period of time, conflict may make the creation and maintenance of supportive and trusting relationships difficult. In one study, the vast majority of women participants revealed personal images of conflict that were negative. They viewed conflict as a battle that proceeds at great personal cost, creates negative results, and may even be hopeless. Words that they associated with conflict were *pain, loss, danger,* and even *death.* Their other principal image of conflict was as a process in which they had little or no input. Many of the women saw themselves, at worst, as victims in conflict and, at best, as bystanders ("I'm in the middle" and "A losing proposition—the good old boys support each other strongly").[8]

Severe conflict and competition when cooperation is required typically hurts performance. Pressure for results tends to emphasize immediate and measurable goals—such as reducing sales costs—at the expense of longer range and more important goals—such as product quality. When high product quality is a primary organizational goal, conflict based on competition between co-workers is often ill-advised.[9] Deep and lasting conflicts that aren't addressed may even trigger violence between employees and others.[10]

Balanced View   Our perspective is that conflict may sometimes be desirable and at other times destructive. Although some conflicts can be avoided and reduced, others have to be resolved and properly managed. The balanced view is sensitive to the consequences of conflict, ranging from negative outcomes (loss of skilled employees, sabotage, low quality of work, stress, and even violence) to positive outcomes (creative alternatives, increased motivation and commitment, high quality of work, and personal satisfaction).

The balanced view acknowledges that conflict arises in organizations whenever interests collide. Sometimes, employees will think differently, want to act differently, and pursue different goals. When these differences divide interdependent people, they must be constructively managed.[11] The following Quality in Practice feature describes the cognitive, affective, and even procedural conflicts that Motorola recently triggered by issuing new requirements for dealers who handle its cellular phones. Motorola issued new rules that required Signature retailers to carry its full cellular phone line. Some conflict probably was inevitable, but Motorola's action triggered more and deeper forms of conflict than the company had anticipated.

QUALITY IN PRACTICE

Motorola's Dilemma with Retailers

Headquartered in Schaumburg, Illinois, Motorola is a worldwide leader in wireless communications. The firm manufactures cellular telephones, pagers, two-way radios, semiconductors, and other electronic items.

When Motorola executives asked Robert Qureshi to meet in a side room at a Dallas cellular telephone conference, he thought they wanted his opinion on a new distribution policy. Instead, they told him that at least three-quarters of the cellular phones he carries in his fifty stores must be made by Motorola. If he didn't meet that quota, Motorola wouldn't supply him with its new products, including StarTac, the sleek model that's wowing customers. "I thought they were crazy," said Qureshi, president of Cellular Concepts, a cellular phone retailer. "This is going to drive Motorola's market share into the toilet."

Qureshi was not the only one concerned. Other retailers bristled at what they called Motorola's strong-arm tactics as it tried to boost its slumping market share. They say the strategy is backfiring, tempting vendors to turn to competitors, further eroding Motorola's position as the world's number 1 cell phone maker.

—Continued

QUALITY IN PRACTICE—*Continued*

Motorola said that it doesn't plan to change the policy because it makes good business sense. "We want a say in how our products are displayed and promoted," said Jim Caile, vice-president of marketing for Motorola's General Systems division. Motorola said that it wants retailers to carry a full line of its products, not just pick their favorites. It asked retailers whether they want to be Signature retailers. Signature retailers must promise that 75 percent or more of their phones will be Motorola's or they don't get the company's StarTac, the world's smallest cell phone. "There is supposed to be a choice in whether or not they (retailers) want to be a Signature retailer," Caile said.

Retailers and carriers contend that there was no real choice. Increasing the array of Motorola phones would mean pushing rivals' models off the shelf. At the same time, not having StarTac could mean turning customers away. No other major cell phone company is trying to tie up its retailers through Motorola's approach.

Carriers and retailers are in conflict with Motorola over the policy. "I want to have a good relationship with all my vendors, but I refuse to distribute under Motorola's current terms," said Cynthia White, chief operating officer of Bell Atlantic Nynex Mobile, the nation's number 3 cellular phone provider.[12]

LEVELS OF CONFLICT

Five primary levels of conflict may be present in organizations: intrapersonal (within an individual), interpersonal (between individuals), intragroup (within a group), intergroup (between groups), and interorganizational (between organizations), which we discuss only briefly in this chapter. These levels of conflict are often cumulative and interrelated, as Figure 12.1 suggests. For example, an employee struggling with whether to stay on a certain career path may act aggressively toward fellow workers, thus triggering interpersonal conflicts.

■ INTRAPERSONAL CONFLICT

Intrapersonal conflict occurs within an individual and usually involves some form of goal, cognitive, or affective conflict. It is triggered when a person's behavior will result in outcomes that are mutually exclusive.[13] Inner tensions and frustrations commonly result. For example, a graduating senior may have to decide between jobs that offer different challenges, pay, security, and locations. Trying to make such a decision may create one (or more) of three basic types of intrapersonal goal conflict.

- **Approach–approach conflict** means that an individual must choose among two or more alternatives, each of which is expected to have a positive outcome (such as a choice between two jobs that appear to be equally attractive).

- **Avoidance–avoidance conflict** means that an individual must choose among two or more alternatives, each of which is expected to have a negative outcome (such as relatively low pay or extensive out-of-town traveling).

FIGURE 12.1

Levels of Conflict in Organizations

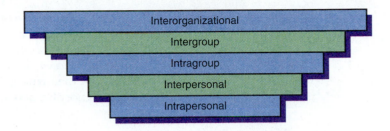

- **Approach–avoidance conflict** means that an individual must decide whether to do something that is expected to have both positive and negative outcomes (such as accepting an offer of a good job in a bad location).

Day-to-day decisions frequently involve the resolution of intrapersonal goal conflict. However, its intensity generally increases under one or more of the following conditions: (1) several realistic alternative courses of action are available for handling the conflict; (2) the positive and negative consequences of the alternative courses of action are roughly equal; or (3) the source of conflict is important to the individual.

Cognitive Dissonance   Intrapersonal conflict may also be a consequence of **cognitive dissonance,** which occurs when individuals recognize inconsistencies in their own thoughts and/or behaviors.[14] Substantial inconsistencies are usually stressful and uncomfortable, but sufficient discomfort usually motivates a person to reduce the dissonance and achieve balance. Balance is often achieved by (1) changing thoughts and/or behaviors or (2) obtaining more information about the issue that is causing the dissonance. Both goal conflict and cognitive conflict accompany many important personal decisions. The greater the goal conflict before the decision, the greater the cognitive dissonance is likely to be after the decision. Individuals experience dissonance because they know that the alternative accepted has negative (avoidance) outcomes and that the alternative rejected has positive (approach) outcomes. The more difficulty individuals have in arriving at the original decision, the greater is their need to justify the decision afterward. Some cognitive dissonance is inevitable.

Neurotic Tendencies   **Neurotic tendencies** are irrational personality mechanisms that an individual uses—often unconsciously—which create inner conflict. In turn, inner conflict often results in behaviors that lead to conflict with other people.[15] Although the psychological sources of neurotic tendencies are beyond the scope of this book, we briefly describe several ways that those with strong neurotic tendencies may think and act in the workplace.[16] Neurotic managers make excessive use of tight organizational controls (budgets, rules and regulations, and monitoring systems) because they distrust people. They are often fearful of uncertainty and risk, not just distrustful of others. Neurotic managers are often driven to plan and standardize every detail of their departments' operations by emphasizing rules and procedures. Still others are excessively bold and impulsive in their actions. They rely on hunches and impressions rather than available facts and advice. Such managers usually don't use participation and consultation in their decision making unless required to do so by some higher authority.

Individuals with strong neurotic tendencies struggle unsuccessfully with intrapersonal conflict, unable to resolve their own problems. Their excessive distrust and need to control triggers conflict with others, especially subordinates who come to feel micromanaged and distrusted. A common reaction to leaders with neurotic tendencies is either open or covert (hidden) aggression and hostility. Subordinates often try to even the score and protect themselves from further abuse. These actions give the manager an even stronger sense of employee worthlessness. The manager's hostility and attempts to control and punish become ever more vigorous.[17]

Workplace Violence   Severe unresolved intrapersonal conflicts within employees, customers, or others may trigger violent interpersonal conflict. Much violence in the workplace has its source in severe intrapersonal conflicts.[18] Research suggests that 50 percent of employees who were victimized didn't report the incident to police. Forty percent of those who didn't report the incident said that it was either too minor or too personal to report. However, in the United States, twenty employees are the victims of work-related homicide each week and four additional employees die each week of self-inflicted injuries that occur at work. About 17,000 assaults of employees occur each week while the employees are working or on duty. Moreover, an estimated 6 million employees are threatened each year with some form of aggression or violent act.[19] What's behind these grim statistics? They emphasize the potential dire consequences of not adequately diagnosing and managing the forms, levels, and sources of intense conflicts in the workplace.

■ INTERPERSONAL CONFLICT

Interpersonal conflict refers to two or more individuals who perceive that their attitudes, behaviors, or preferred goals are in opposition. As with intrapersonal conflicts, many interpersonal conflicts are based on some type of role conflict or role ambiguity.

Role Conflict   A **role** is the cluster of tasks and behaviors that others expect a person to perform in doing a job. Figure 12.2 presents a role episode model, which involves role senders and a focal person. Role senders are individuals who have expectations of how the focal person should behave. A role episode begins before a message is sent because role senders have expectations, perceptions, and evaluations of the focal person's behaviors. These attributions, in turn, influence the actual role messages that the senders transmit. The focal person's perceptions of these messages and pressures may then lead to role conflict. **Role conflict** refers

■ FIGURE 12.2

Role Episode Model

Source: Based on Kahn, R. L., et al. *Organizational Stress: Studies in Role Conflict and Ambiguity.* New York: John Wiley & Sons, 1964, 26.

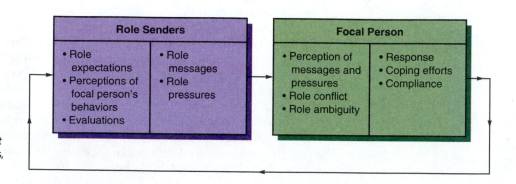

to a focal person perceiving incompatible messages and pressures from the role senders. The focal person responds with coping behaviors that serve as inputs to the role senders' attribution process. A **role set** is the group of role senders that directly affect the focal person. A role set might include the employee's manager, other team members, close friends, immediate family members, and important clients or customers served.

Four types of role conflict may occur as a result of incompatible messages and pressures from the role set.

- **Intrasender role conflict** may occur when different messages and pressures from a single member of the role set are incompatible.

- **Intersender role conflict** may occur when the messages and pressures from one role sender oppose messages and pressures from one or more other senders.

- **Interrole conflict** may occur when role pressures associated with membership in one group are incompatible with pressures stemming from membership in other groups.

- **Person–role conflict** may occur when the role requirements are incompatible with the focal person's own attitudes, values, or views of acceptable behavior.[20] Intrapersonal conflict typically accompanies this type of role conflict.

Officials of public agencies often are subjected to extreme role pressures and conflicts. One such agency is the U.S. Food and Drug Administration (FDA). The FDA is responsible for regulating the introduction and purity of a variety of drug and food products. Many of the role conflicts created for the agency's leadership evolve from goal conflicts (such as the incompatible pressures of fully protecting the public versus giving early public access to new drugs that haven't been exhaustively tested), cognitive conflict (such as incompatible views of the need for greater versus less regulatory control), and procedural conflict (such as incompatible views on how the safety of a particular drug or food should be determined). The following Technology in Practice account focuses on the pressures and intersender role conflicts experienced by Dr. David Kessler, the commissioner of the FDA. Many of these role pressures and conflicts have been brought about by new technology and scientific information. The desire for firms, and sometimes the public, to be freer from restrictions in bringing technological advances to the market more quickly often conflicts with the FDA's goal of public safety.

TECHNOLOGY IN PRACTICE

David Kessler at the FDA

Consider the headlines from three major newspapers on the same day: "Doctor's Cancer Cure Attacked by the FDA," "America's Editorial Writers Join the Call for FDA Reform" (from an ad), and "RU-486's FDA Approval Based on Facts Not Myths" (about the abortion pill). "Welcome to the world of controversial FDA decisions," says Dr. David Kessler. To his critics, Kessler is the far too powerful commissioner of the federal Food and Drug Administration. Kessler had his way

—Continued

TECHNOLOGY IN PRACTICE—*Continued*

in extending its regulatory authority over tobacco by limiting children's access and exposure to cigarettes.

Consumer groups praise him for overhauling the agency. He has speeded up the drug-approval process from an average of thirty months in 1990 to sixteen months today (six months for breakthrough drugs), insisted that food companies tell the truth about what is "fresh" and what is "lite," built a criminal investigation unit, and brought the nation more explicit food labels. But the "pounding," as he calls it, continues to rise with Kessler's profile. Opponents want to curb his power—or even eliminate it.

Kessler speaks forcefully about the pressures on him and his determination to resist them. "I'm opposed to reducing all review periods to six months. We've gone about as far as we can go safely. I think twelve months for standard drugs [the agency's goal] and six months for breakthrough drugs is acceptable. If we push any further, there is a risk we could start compromising on those standards. Two things could happen. One, we have enormously well-trained officers. They could, as the deadline approaches, either simply say "no" more often because they still have unanswered questions—so there may be an increase in the number of rejections, which I don't think is necessarily in the public interest—or they can start taking shortcuts. I don't think a well-trained medical review officer would do that."

The response to Kessler's proposal to further regulate access to tobacco products was intense. He commented, "The pounding is intense. The pounding is more intense than anything I've experienced. But we get paid to resist that pressure. I'm not saying it's easy. I'm just saying that if you were a public health official, if you were in this job, what would you do? We are standing firm. We are moving forward. We will finish this."[21]

Role Ambiguity   **Role ambiguity** is the uncertainty or lack or clarity surrounding expectations about a single role.[22] Like role conflict, severe role ambiguity causes stress and triggers subsequent coping behaviors. These coping behaviors often include (1) aggressive action (theft, violence, verbal abuse) and hostile communication, (2) withdrawal, or (3) approaching the role sender or senders to attempt joint problem solving. Research findings aren't clear-cut on the relationships among role conflict, role ambiguity, and their effects. These effects include stress reactions, aggression, hostility, and withdrawal behaviors (turnover and absenteeism).[23] Stress is a common reaction to severe role conflict and role ambiguity (see Chapter 7). However, effective managers and professionals possess the ability to cope with the many ambiguities inherent in their roles.[24]

■ INTRAGROUP CONFLICT

Intragroup conflict involves clashes among some or all of the group's members, which often affect the group's processes and effectiveness. Family-run businesses can be especially prone to severe intragroup and other types of conflicts.[25] These conflicts are most evident when an owner–founder approaches retirement, retires, or dies.

Only three in ten family-run businesses make it to the second generation, and one in ten survives into the third generation. The most formidable obstacles to succession are the relationships among the family members who own the business and bear responsibility for keeping it alive for another generation. What determines whether a family business soars or nose-dives? It depends, in large part, on the respect family members give each other in the workplace, their willingness to take on work roles different from those they have at home, and their ability to manage conflict. Randall Carlock, a consultant on family business and founder of the Audio King electronic stores chain, comments, "Families don't express their needs and wants clearly and don't deal with conflict very well. When that moves into their place of business, that spells real trouble. Take the way most parents negotiate with their kids in the business. They basically tell them what they're going to do, or they threaten them, or they tell them, 'You're lucky to have this job.' That's not how you handle an employee, and that's not how you develop a future leader."[26]

■ INTERGROUP CONFLICT

Intergroup conflict refers to opposition and clashes between groups or teams. It often occurs in union–management relations, such as in the recent dispute between American Airlines and the pilots union. Such conflicts may be highly intense, drawn out, and costly to those involved. Under extreme conditions of competition and conflict, the parties develop attitudes toward each other that are characterized by distrust, rigidity, a focus only on self-interest, failure to listen, and the like. We briefly consider four categories of intergroup conflicts within organizations.

Vertical Conflict   Clashes between employees at different levels in an organization are called **vertical conflict.** It often occurs when superiors attempt to control subordinates too tightly and the subordinates resist.[27] Subordinates may resist because they believe that the controls infringe too much on their freedom to do their jobs. Vertical conflicts also may arise because of inadequate communication, goal conflict, or a lack of agreement concerning information and values (cognitive conflict).

Horizontal Conflict   Clashes between groups of employees at the same hierarchical level in an organization are called **horizontal conflict.** It occurs when each department or team strives only for its own goals, disregarding the goals of other departments and teams, especially if those goals are incompatible. Contrasting attitudes of employees in different departments and teams may also lead to conflict.

Consider the intergroup, vertical and horizontal conflicts that were created at Lanteck, a manufacturer of packaging machinery in Louisville, Kentucky, as a result of a poorly designed bonus pay system. The firm is privately owned and has about 300 employees. At one time, each of the company's five manufacturing divisions received a bonus, the amount of which was determined by how much profit it made. An individual worker's share of the bonus could amount to as much as 10 percent of regular pay. However, the divisions were so interdependent that sorting out who was entitled to what amount of bonus was extremely difficult. "That led to so much secrecy, politicking, and sucking noise that you wouldn't believe it," says CEO Jim Lancaster. For example, the division that built standard machines and the one that added custom design features to those machines depended on each other for parts, engineering expertise, and other assistance. Inevitably, when the groups clashed, each tried to assign costs to the other and claim credit for revenues. At the end of each month, the divisions would rush to fill orders from other parts of the company. This behavior created profits for the division filling the order but generated unnecessary and costly inventory in the receiving division. The company's chairman, Pat Lancaster, states, "I was spending 95 percent of my time on conflict resolution instead of on how to serve our customers." Lantech abandoned individual and division performance incentive pay. It now relies on a profit-sharing system in which all employees get bonuses based on salary and overall firm profits. This system is working fine.[28]

Line–Staff Conflict   Clashes over authority relationships often involve **line–staff conflict.** Most organizations have staff departments (human resources, legal, accounting) to assist the line departments. Line managers normally are responsible for some process that creates part or all of the firm's goods or services. Staff personnel often serve an advisory or control function that requires specialized technical knowledge.[29] They also may specify the methods and partially control the resources used by line managers. For example, in many manufacturing organizations, staff engineers specify how each product is to be made and what materials are to be used. At the same time, line managers are held responsible for results (downtime, rework, labor costs per unit). Thus line managers may feel that staff personnel are encroaching on their areas of legitimate authority and actually directing production tasks. Line managers often think that staff personnel reduce their authority over workers while their responsibility for the results remains unchanged. That is they perceive that their authority is less than their actual responsibility because of staff involvement.

Diversity-Based Conflict   As discussed in previous chapters, serious intergroup conflicts may arise from work-force diversity. The toughest diversity-based conflicts in organizations appear to relate to issues of race, gender, ethnicity, and religion.[30] They may encompass all five levels of conflict—intrapersonal, interpersonal, intragroup, intergroup, and interorganizational. Interorganizational conflicts come into play, for example, in disputes between an organization and the U.S. Equal Employment Opportunity Commission (EEOC), which pursues discrimination charges by individuals or groups.

The following Diversity in Practice piece presents highlights of the pressures and conflicts experienced by some organizations in attempting to manage and control relationships between women and men in the workplace.

DIVERSITY IN PRACTICE

Women and Men in the Workplace

"Outside of work, we face an incredibly permissive society," notes Louis DiLorenzo, a senior partner at Bond, Schoeneck & King, in Syracuse, New York, which represents companies in sexual harassment cases. "Yet we're told, at work, make sure no one talks about race or sex."

Sheila Wellington heads Catalyst, a New York firm that researches the advancement of women in the workplace. She says, "If men and women can't be comfortable together as colleagues, it has an impact on every aspect of the business.

—Continued

DIVERSITY IN PRACTICE—*Continued*

If men are worried about interacting with women and women with men, it can't be a healthy organization where people focus on the tasks at hand."

Consider the conflicting pressures on Wal-Mart with 650,000 employees and annual sales of $100 billion. Punitive damages are allowed in sexual harassment cases, so companies with the deepest pockets, such as Wal-Mart, are hit hardest. In one recent case, for example, a jury awarded $50 million to Peggy Kimzey, a freight clerk at a Wal-Mart store in Warsaw, Missouri. The jury agreed that Kimzey's supervisor had made crude comments about her body and that Wal-Mart management failed to stop him. The award was later reduced to $5 million. This amount doesn't include the legal costs for the company or the diversion of executive time and energy. Wal-Mart is appealing the decision.

For years, Wal-Mart had a policy that barred dating between two people from the same office or store. Also banned was any dating that involved employees married to others. Offenders faced dismissal if caught. In brief, Wal-Mart tried to ban office romances. It faced at least two lawsuits from employees who were fired for dating colleagues. New York State also sued Wal-Mart on behalf of two employees who charged that the company's no-fraternization policy violated state labor laws.

Wal-Mart has changed its policy. Now Wal-Marters can date if they are on the same level, but a supervisor still can't date a subordinate.[31]

CONFLICT HANDLING STYLES

Individuals handle interpersonal conflict in various ways.[32] Figure 12.3 provides a basic model for understanding and comparing five interpersonal conflict handling styles. They are identified by their locations on two dimensions: *concern for self* and *concern for others*. The desire to satisfy your own concerns depends on the extent to which you are *assertive* or *unassertive* in pursuing personal goals. Your desire to satisfy the concerns of others depends on the extent to which you are *cooperative* or *uncooperative*. The five interpersonal conflict handling styles thus represent different combinations of assertiveness and cooperativeness. Although you may have a natural tendency toward one or two of the styles, you may use all of them as the context and people involved change.[33] For example, the style you use in working through a conflict with a good friend may be quite different from that you utilize with a stranger after a minor auto accident.

■ AVOIDING STYLE

The **avoiding style** refers to unassertive and uncooperative behaviors. A person uses this style to stay away from conflict, ignore disagreements, or remain neutral. This approach reflects an aversion to tension and frustration and may involve a decision to let a conflict work itself out. Because ignoring important issues often frustrates others, the consistent use of this interpersonal conflict handling style usually results in unfavorable evaluations by others.[34] The avoiding style is illustrated by the following statements.

- If there are rules that apply, I cite those. If there aren't, I leave the other person free to make his or her own decision.

■ FIGURE 12.3

Interpersonal Conflict-Handling Styles

Source: Adapted with permission from
Thomas, K. W. Conflict and conflict
management. In M. D. Dunnette (ed.),
*Handbook of Industrial and Organizational
Psychology.* Chicago: Rand McNally, 1976, 900.

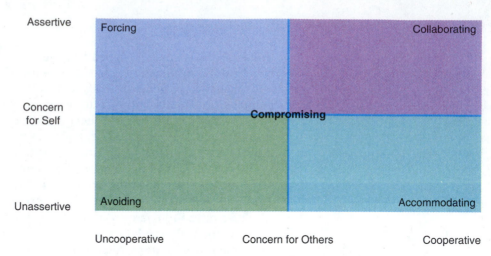

I usually don't take positions that will create controversy.

I shy away from topics that are sources of disputes with my friends.

That's okay. It wasn't important anyway. Let's leave well enough alone.

When unresolved conflicts affect goal accomplishment, the avoiding style will lead to negative results for the organization. This style may be desirable under some situations, as when (1) the issue is minor or only of passing importance and thus not worth the individual's time or energy to confront the conflict; (2) there isn't enough information available to the individual to deal effectively with the conflict at that time; (3) the individual's power is so low relative to the other person's that there's little chance of causing change (such as disagreement with a new strategy approved by top management); and (4) other individuals can more effectively resolve the conflict.

■ FORCING STYLE

The **forcing style** refers to assertive and uncooperative behaviors and reflects a win–lose approach to interpersonal conflict. Those who use this style try to achieve their own goals without concern for others. The forcing style includes aspects of coercive power and dominance.[35] The forcing person feels that one side must win and that one side must lose. This style sometimes helps a person achieve individual goals, but like avoidance, forcing tends to result in unfavorable evaluations by others. The forcing style is suggested by the following statements.

I like to put it plainly: Like it or not, what I say goes, and maybe when others have had the experience I have, they will remember this and think better of it.

I convince the other person of the logic and benefits of my position.

I insist that my position be accepted during a disagreement.

I usually hold on to my solution to a problem after the controversy starts.

Forcing-prone individuals assume that conflict involves win–lose situations. When dealing with conflict between subordinates or departments, forcing-style managers may threaten or actually use demotion, dismissal, negative performance evaluations, or other punishments to gain compliance. When conflict occurs between peers, an employee using the forcing style might try to get his or her own way by appealing to the manager. This approach represents an attempt to use the manager to force the decision on the opposing individual. Recall from the Preview Case that Charlie Olcott said, "The chairman told me, Defend my numbers or you're off the team."

Overreliance on forcing by a manager lessens employees' work motivation because their interests haven't been considered. Relevant information and other possible alternatives usually are ignored. In some situations the forcing style may be necessary, such as when (1) emergencies require quick action, (2) unpopular courses of action must be taken for long-term organizational effectiveness and survival (such as cost-cutting and dismissal of employees for unsatisfactory performance), and (3) the person needs to take action for self-protection and to stop others from taking advantage of him or her.

As discussed elsewhere, **whistle-blowing** refers to the disclosure by current or former organizational members of illegal, immoral, or illegitimate organizational practices in an attempt to change the practice. All too often top management believes that whistle-blowers are creating negative rather than positive conflict. As a result, role senders, especially from within the organization, commonly use the forcing style of conflict handling on whistle-blowers.[36] The following Ethics in Practice selection contains some examples of the coercive pressures, including threat of, or actual, dismissal experienced by two whistle-blowers in their efforts to be ethical.

ETHICS IN PRACTICE

Whistle-Blowers As Objects of the Forcing Style

"Think back to when you were a kid," stated Ohio State University business professor Marcia Micelli, who has studied whistle-blowers for twenty-two years. "Nobody likes someone who tattles."

Consider the experience of George Galatis, an engineer at Northeast Utilities, which operates five nuclear plants in New England. After repeated, unsuccessful efforts over two years to have safety concerns and violations addressed, he went directly to the U.S. Nuclear Regulatory Commission (NRC). Galatis told his manager and a vice-president that he was going to the NRC. He experienced what he calls "subtle forms of harassment, retaliation, and intimidation." His performance evaluation was downgraded, and his personnel file was forwarded to Northeast's lawyers. His manager "offered" to move him out of the nuclear group. He would walk into a meeting, and the room suddenly would go silent.

A senior vice-president issued a memo warning employees that "experienced antinuclear activists" had "the intention of shutting the station down and eliminating 2500 jobs." The memo stirred up some of Galatis's colleagues. "You're taking food out of my girl's mouth," one of them told him. "If I had it to do over again," says Galatis, "I wouldn't." He believes that his nuclear career is over. Though still employed by Northeast, he feels that whistle-blowers are routinely shut out by the industry.

Consider the experience of Robert Manley. He had been president of Valencia National Bank (Valencia, California) since he helped found it in 1987. He was fired in 1995, ostensibly for poor performance. But in pending suits in state and federal courts, he claims that the firing stemmed from the controversy he created

—*Continued*

QUALITY IN PRACTICE—*Continued*

by exposing bad loans to bank directors. The bank later conceded that two directors defaulted on loans totaling $300,000. It maintains that Manley's firing was unrelated.

Manley was out of work for two months, and his next job was temporary. His current position, as first vice-president of correspondent banking for Community Bank in Pasadena, pays considerably less than he made at Valencia. A long commute has forced him to withdraw from many community activities in his hometown of Santa Clarita, California.[37]

■ ACCOMMODATING STYLE

The **accommodating style** refers to cooperative and unassertive behaviors. Accommodation may represent an unselfish act, a long-term strategy to encourage cooperation by others, or a submission to the wishes of others. Accommodators usually are favorably evaluated by others, but they also are perceived as weak and submissive. An accommodating style is suggested by the following statements.

- Conflict is best managed through the suspension of my personal goals to maintain good relationships with those whom I value.
- If it makes other people happy, I am all for it.
- I like to smooth over disagreements by making them appear less important.
- I ease conflict by suggesting that our differences are trivial and then show good will by blending my ideas into those of the other person.

When using the accommodating style, an individual may act as though the conflict will go away in time and appeal for cooperation. The person will try to reduce tensions and stress by reassurance and support. This style shows concern about the emotional aspects of conflict but little interest in working on its substantive issues. The accommodating style simply results in the individual covering up or glossing over personal feelings. It is generally ineffective if used as a dominant style.[38] The accommodating style may be effective in the short run when (1) the individual is in a potentially explosive emotional conflict situation, and smoothing is used to defuse it; (2) keeping harmony and avoiding disruption are especially important in the short run; and (3) the conflicts are based primarily on the personalities of the individuals and cannot be easily resolved.

■ COLLABORATING STYLE

The **collaborating style** refers to strong cooperative and assertive behaviors. It is the win–win approach to interpersonal conflict handling. The collaborating style represents a desire to maximize joint results. An individual who uses this style tends to (1) see conflict as natural, helpful, and even leading to a more creative solution if handled properly; (2) exhibit trust in and candor with others; and (3) recognize that when conflict is resolved to the satisfaction of all, commitment to the solution is likely. An individual who uses the collaborating style is often seen as dynamic and evaluated favorably by others. Charlie Olcott's comments in the Preview Case, when taken as a whole, suggest that he primarily uses the collaborating style. Statements consistent with this style include the following:

- I first try to overcome any distrust that might exist between us. Then I try to get at the feelings that we both have about the topics. I stress that nothing we decide is cast in stone and suggest that we find a position we can both give a trial run.
- I tell the other person my ideas, actively seek out the other person's ideas, and search for a mutually beneficial solution.
- I like to suggest new solutions and build on a variety of viewpoints that may have been expressed.
- I try to dig into an issue to find a solution good for all of us.

With this style, conflict is recognized openly and evaluated by all concerned. Sharing, examining, and assessing the reasons for the conflict should lead to development of an alternative that effectively resolves it and is fully acceptable to everyone involved.[39] Collaboration is most practical when there is (1) sufficient required interdependence to make expending the extra time and energy needed with collaboration to work through individual differences worthwhile; (2) sufficient parity in power among individuals so that they feel free to interact candidly, regardless of their formal superior–subordinate status; (3) the potential for mutual benefits, especially over the long run, for resolving the dispute through a win–win process; and (4) sufficient organizational support for taking the time and energy to resolve disputes through collaboration. The norms, rewards, and punishments of the organization—especially those set by top management—provide the framework for encouraging or discouraging collaboration.[40]

■ COMPROMISING STYLE

The **compromising style** refers to behaviors at an intermediate level of cooperation and assertiveness. This style is based on give and take, typically involves a series of concessions, and is commonly used and widely accepted as a means of resolving conflict. The compromising style is illustrated by the following statements.

- I want to know how and what others feel. When the timing is right, I explain how I feel and try to show them where they are wrong. Of course, it's often necessary to settle on some middle ground.
- After failing in getting my way, I usually find it necessary to seek a fair combination of gains and losses for both of us.
- I give in to others if they are willing to meet me halfway.
- As the old saying goes, half a loaf is better than nothing. Let's split the difference.

An individual who compromises with others tends to be evaluated favorably. Various explanations are suggested for the favorable evaluation of the compromising style, including: (1) it is seen primarily as a cooperative "holding back;" (2) it reflects a pragmatic way for dealing with conflicts; and (3) it helps maintain good relations in the future.

In one study, individuals with a preference for the compromising style felt that it did provide a solution ("not coming up with a solution is weak") but that it required strength to accept the other person's ideas as important. These two ideas suggest that insisting on your own viewpoint can be self-indulgent because it fails to recognize the ideas of others. Most thought that the initially positive reactions to a compromise are soon replaced by doubts about the fairness of the outcome, the equality of each person's concessions, and the other person's motives and honesty.[41] The compromising style usually is most effective as a backup to the collaborating style.

The compromising style shouldn't be used early in the conflict resolution process. First, the people involved are likely to compromise on the stated issues rather than on the real issues. The first issues raised in a conflict often aren't the real ones, so premature compromise will prevent full diagnosis or exploration of the real issues. For example, students telling professors that their courses are tough and challenging may simply be trying to negotiate an easier grading system. Second, accepting an initial position presented is easier than searching for alternatives that are more acceptable to everyone involved. Third, compromise is inappropriate to all or part of the situation when it isn't the best decision available. Further discussion may reveal a better way of resolving the conflict.

Compared to the collaborating style, the compromising style doesn't maximize joint satisfaction. Compromise achieves moderate, but only partial, satisfaction for each person. This style is likely to be appropriate when (1) agreement enables each person to be better off, or at least not worse off than if no agreement were reached; (2) achieving a total win–win agreement simply isn't possible; and (3) conflicting goals or opposing interests block agreement on one person's proposal.

■ EFFECTIVENESS OF THE VARIOUS STYLES

Studies conducted on the use of different interpersonal conflict handling styles indicate that collaboration tends to be characteristic of (1) more successful rather than less successful individuals and (2) high-performing rather than medium- and low-performing organizations. People tend to perceive collaboration in terms of the constructive use of conflict. The use of collaboration seems to result in positive feelings in others, as well as favorable self-evaluations of performance and abilities.

In contrast to collaboration, forcing and avoiding often have negative effects. Forcing and avoiding tend to be associated with a less constructive use of conflict, negative feelings from others, and unfavorable evaluations of performance and abilities. The effects of accommodation and compromise appear to be mixed. The use of accommodation sometimes results in positive feelings from others. But these individuals do not form favorable evaluations of the performance and abilities of those using the accommodating style. The use of the compromising style generally is followed by positive feelings from others.[42]

NEGOTIATION IN CONFLICT MANAGEMENT

Negotiation is a process in which two or more individuals or groups, having both common and conflicting goals, state and discuss proposals for specific terms of a possible agreement. Negotiation normally includes a combination of compromise, collaboration, and possibly some forcing on vital issues.[43]

■ BASIC TYPES OF NEGOTIATIONS

The four basic types of negotiations are distributive, integrative, attitudinal structuring, and intraorganizational.[44]

Distributive Negotiations   Traditional win–lose, fixed-amount situations—where one party's gain is another party's loss—characterize **distributive negotiations.**

They often occur over economic issues. The interaction patterns may include guarded communications, limited expressions of trust, use of threats, and distorted statements and demands. In short, the parties are engaged in intense, emotion laden conflict. The forcing and compromise conflict handling styles are dominant in distributive negotiations.

During 1996, Andersen Worldwide, top management of the world's largest accounting firm, decided against splitting into two separate organizations despite severe conflicts between the accounting and consulting operations. Management debated for more than a year whether to sell or spin off its consulting arm, which is the faster growing part of Andersen's business. Those favoring a breakup weren't able to get the two-thirds vote needed among Andersen's approximately 2800 partners.

Some analysts think that the continued turmoil could eventually hurt the firm's business. "Fortune 500 companies want stability," said Byron Reimus, an industry analyst who consults with numerous Andersen partners. "Why would clients want to do business with a company where they're bad-mouthing each other? They can't even talk about how they should talk to be organized for the future. They can't seem to resolve anything." To complicate matters, the accounting unit set up its own consulting practice, which now competes directly with Andersen Consulting. The accounting unit now takes in about $1 billion a year in revenue from business, tax, and other financial consulting services.[45]

Integrative Negotiations   Joint problem solving to achieve results benefiting both parties is called **integrative negotiations.** The parties identify mutual problems, identify and assess alternatives, openly express preferences, and jointly reach a mutually acceptable solution. Rarely perceived as equally acceptable, the choice is simply advantageous to both sides. Those involved are strongly motivated to solve problems, exhibit flexibility and trust, and explore new ideas. The collaborative and compromise conflict handling styles are dominant in integrative negotiations.

For years, the labor relationships and negotiations between the major luxury hotels in San Francisco and Culinary Local 2, with more than 8000 members, were characterized by distrust, hostile confrontation, and distributive negotiations. The opening of new nonunion hotels and other common competitive threats to their mutual survival set the stage for a major shift to integrative negotiations and practices. The transition wasn't easy or quick, as the following Managing in Practice feature discloses.

MANAGING IN PRACTICE

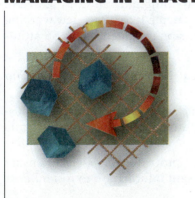

Union–Management Negotiations

Several of the hotels openly discussed their financial condition and profitability with the union leadership as the initial step. They presented in graphic detail the anticipated decline in hotel food and beverage operations if current trends continued. They revealed the real, and abysmal, economics of hotels in the 1990s. The hotels' controllers made these presentations and were told to be totally candid by top management. This was an unprecedented move in the hotel industry in San Francisco.

Both sides then agreed to create formal joint-negotiation and fact-finding teams to take the results of the study phase and turn them into real proposals and
—*Continued*

MANAGING IN PRACTICE—*Continued*

contractual programs. The first joint team was asked to arrive at a common factual understanding of the state of the health and welfare trust fund and the unique situation that its surplus of tens of millions of dollars presented. The second joint fact-finding team was asked to develop proposals for the training programs that the study phase had identified as absolutely necessary if cross-classification work (such as waiters doing the job of bartenders) and improved quality were to be achieved. A third team was formed to develop a new grievance system. Still other teams were formed to develop a new sick-leave system and to develop pilot projects using cross-classification work and other work redesign concepts. The focus was on these joint fact-finding teams during the first few months of the formal negotiations. Using this strategy, management and labor were able to develop *joint proposals* in all areas that the study phase had identified as urgent problems. Instead of unilateral proposals that were dead on arrival, these were joint proposals that both sides understood and took ownership of from the very beginning. As a result, all of them were eventually incorporated into the new labor contract.

The most important changes in the new labor contract are the establishment of joint problem-solving and employee-involvement teams within each hotel and a permanent Joint Steering Committee representing both the hotel multi-employer group and the union. These employee involvement teams and Joint Steering Committee, in effect, created *living contracts* under which management, union, and workers are committed to continue working together for change throughout the terms of the agreements.[46]

Attitudinal Structuring   Throughout any negotiations, the parties exhibit certain interpersonal approaches (such as hostility or friendliness and competitiveness or cooperativeness) that influences their interactions. **Attitudinal structuring** is the process by which the parties seek to establish desired attitudes and relationships.

As indicated in the preceding Managing in Practice feature, hostile and competitive attitudes had prevailed between the major San Francisco hotels and the members of Culinary Local 2. One element in their attitudinal restructuring was the use of La Vonne Ritter as a third-party mediator. She spent several days with union and hotel leadership developing a training program for the twelve problem-solving teams and creating a mission statement for their new working relationships. The following elements of the mission statement focus on attitudinal structuring.

- It shall be the mission of the San Francisco Hotels Multi-employer Group and the unions to create a new partnership in labor relations.
- We are committed to jointly creating world class models in the hotel industry demonstrating that union–employer partnerships can achieve a truly successful competitive edge.
- Acknowledging that joint ownership of the process is necessary to ensure success of the parties, we will share all relevant information to foster better communication.

- To accomplish this mission, we commit ourselves to openness, human dignity, courtesy, mutual respect, and an ever increasing level of trust.[47]

Intraorganizational Negotiations   Groups often negotiate through representatives. However, these representatives first may have to obtain the agreement of their respective groups before they can agree with each other. In **intraorganizational negotiations,** each set of negotiators tries to build consensus for agreement and resolve intragroup conflict before dealing with the other group's negotiators. For example, the members of the hotel multiemployer group had to spend a considerable amount of time negotiating over the new concepts, attitudes, and practices that were necessary to change from distributive to integrative negotiations.

■ INTEGRATIVE PROCESS[48]

In the best-seller, *Getting to Yes*, R. Fisher and W. Ury outline four key concepts for integrative (win–win) negotiations. These concepts comprise the foundation of an integrative negotiation strategy, which they call "principled negotiation," or "negotiation on the merits."[49]

- *Separate the people from the problem.* The first concept in reaching a mutually agreeable solution is to disentangle the substantive issues of the negotiation from the interpersonal relationship issues between the parties and deal with each set of issues separately. Negotiators should perceive themselves as working side by side, attacking the substantive issues or problems instead of attacking each other.

- *Focus on interests, not positions.* People's egos tend to become identified with their negotiating positions. Furthermore, focusing only on stated positions often obscures what the participants really need or want. Rather than focusing only on the positions taken by each negotiator, a much more effective strategy is to focus on the underlying human needs and interests that had caused them to adopt those positions.

- *Invent options for mutual gain.* Designing optimal solutions under pressure in the presence of an adversary tends to narrow people's thinking. Searching for the one right solution inhibits creativity, particularly when the stakes are high. These blinders can be offset by establishing a forum in which a variety of possibilities are generated before decisions are made about which action to take.

- *Insist on using objective criteria.* The parties should discuss the conditions of the negotiation in terms of some fair standard such as market value, expert opinion, custom, or law. This approach steers the focus away from what the parties are willing or unwilling to do. By using objective criteria, neither party has to give in to the other, and both parties may defer to a fair solution.

■ DISTRIBUTIVE PROCESS

Some individuals and groups still believe in extreme distributive (win–lose) negotiations, and, as a negotiator, you have to be prepared to counter them. Awareness and understanding probably are the most important means for dealing with win–lose negotiation ploys by the other party. Four of these more common win–lose strategies are as follows.[50]

- *I want it all.* By making an extreme offer and then granting concessions grudgingly, if at all, the other party hopes to wear down your resolve. You will know that you have met such a negotiator when you encounter the following tactics: (1) the other party's first offer is extreme; (2) minor concessions are made grudgingly; (3) you are pressured to make significant concessions, and (4) the other party refuses to reciprocate.

- *Time warp.* Time can be used as a very powerful weapon by the win–lose negotiator. When any of the following techniques are used, you should refuse to be forced into an unfavorable position: (1) the offer is valid only for a limited time; (2) you are pressured to accept arbitrary deadlines; (3) the other party stalls or delays the progress of the negotiation; and (4) the other party increases pressure on you to settle quickly.

- *Good cop, bad cop.* Negotiators using this strategy hope to sway you to their side by alternating sympathetic with threatening behavior. You should be on your guard when you are confronted with the following tactics: (1) the other party becomes irrational or abusive; (2) the other party walks out of a negotiation; and (3) irrational behavior is followed by reasonable, sympathetic behavior.

- *Ultimatums.* This strategy is designed to try to force you to submit to the will of the other party. You should be wary when the other party tries any of the following: (1) you are presented with a take-it-or-leave-it offer; (2) the other party overtly tries to force you to accept its demands; (3) the other party is unwilling to make concessions; and (4) you are expected to make all the concessions.

■ MATRIX OF OUTCOMES

Negotiators increasingly realize the importance of cooperatively creating value by means of the integrative negotiation process. However, they must also acknowledge the fact that both sides may eventually seek gain through the distributive process. The **negotiator's dilemma** means that the tactics of self-gain tend to repel moves to create greater mutual gain. An optimal solution normally results when both parties openly discuss the problem, respect each other's substantive and relationship needs, and creatively seek to satisfy each other's interests. However, such behavior doesn't always occur.[51]

Win–win negotiators are vulnerable to the tactics of win–lose negotiators. As a result, negotiators often develop an uneasiness about the use of integrative strategies because they expect the other party to use distributive strategies. This mutual suspicion often causes negotiators to leave joint gains on the table. Moreover, after being stung in several encounters with experienced win–lose strategists, the pull toward self-gain tactics becomes insidious. Win–win strategists soon "learn" to become win–lose strategists. Finally, if both negotiators use distributive strategies, the probability of achieving great mutual benefits is virtually eliminated. The negotiations will likely result in both parties receiving only mediocre benefits.

Graphically, the integrative and distributive negotiating strategies may be placed on vertical and horizontal axes, representing the two negotiating parties. Then, a matrix of possible outcomes emerging from the negotiation process can be developed to illustrate the negotiator's dilemma, as shown in Figure 12.4, for parties A and B.

■ **FIGURE 12.4**

Matrix of Negotiated Outcomes

Source: Adapted from Anderson, T. Step into my parlor: A survey of strategies and techniques for effective negotiation. *Business Horizons,* May–June 1992, p. 75.

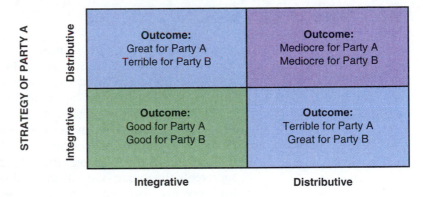

■ NEGOTIATING ACROSS CULTURES

The numerous issues and complexities relevant to domestic negotiations are compounded when negotiators are from different cultures.[52] Table 12.2 provides a thumbnail sketch of the complexities and sensitivities involved in such negotiations. It presents the traditional cultural assumptions that underlie the Japanese, U.S. and Canadian, and Latin American approaches toward negotiations in terms of five dimensions: emotions, power, decision making, social interaction, and persuasion. Recently, however, leading organizations in the United States and other countries have begun to move away from these traditional assumptions.

The traditional assumptions and generalizations shown may not always apply to negotiations and conflict resolution between the parties when long-term and insider relationships have been established. This situation applies particularly to negotiations by the Japanese with those whom they view as insiders. Almost by definition, Japanese businesspeople consider Westerners to be outsiders. Thus Westerners often incorrectly assume that the Japanese never use direct or confrontational approaches to conflict resolution and negotiations. In fact, they often are very direct in resolving differences of opinion with *insiders*. They explicitly state the principal differences among group members and state demands, rejections, and counteroffers directly.[53]

The following Across Cultures account highlights some of the unique aspects of negotiations and union–management relations in Mexico.

ACROSS CULTURES

Business Negotiations in Mexico

Personal relationships are an important part of business negotiations in Mexico. Hospitality is a first priority in doing business, and negotiations are initiated with social graces. Trust and respect must be secured for successful negotiations. Executives in Mexico express strong objections to U.S. negotiators' tendency to "get to the point." They find this urgency to produce results distasteful and ill-mannered.

Mexican negotiators initially tend to be cautious, perhaps even suspicious. Their wanting not to appear ill-informed and not to be taken advantage of may

—*Continued*

ACROSS CULTURES—*Continued*

slow the opening phases of negotiations. Therefore the opening conversation should be indirect, cautious, and exploratory. Direct questions or statements should be postponed until later. Consequently, although talk will be plentiful, little time will be spent on substantive negotiations.

Mexican negotiators prefer to start with a general proposal and then define the issues. The ultimate conclusions will be arrived at with minimal consideration of details. Mexican negotiators prefer agreements that are bound by a strong oral understanding. They believe that the written agreement is secondary and only represents the strong bond of the oral obligation. At times, however, the seemingly positive oral statements during negotiations are simply used to save face. A negative decision may come later by mail.

Equality in union–management relations in Mexico is valued by employees, management, and the union. This norm is sometimes difficult for U.S. managers to understand because they are accustomed to union and management being adversaries. Under Mexican labor law, union and management roles often are complementary and equal. They both strive to maintain a "foundation of employment," one accountable for workers and the other for managing the business. However, day-to-day relations often fall short of this ideal. Direct management communications to the work force are welcomed by unions as a way to cement relations, and management solicitation of grievances is encouraged. The union cooperates in disciplining workers, and management's role is to discipline supervisors. Few significant problems arise so long as wages don't fall below the legal minimum, supervisors act reasonably, and recreational or other social activities are available. Mexican employees view peaceful relations between the union and management as normal and desirable. The recognition of an individual's place through symbolic formalities or a bit of flattery is the bedrock of human relations and negotiations in Mexico. For example, a union president was deeply insulted when a U.S. plant manager failed to introduce him to visitors from the home office. The plant manager regarded him as just another employee. However, the union leader's place was that of commander of the entire labor force and, under labor law, he and the employer had equal status.[54]

■ MEDIATION

Mediation is a process by which a third party helps two or more other parties resolve one or more issues. Most of the actual negotiations occur directly between the involved parties. But, when the parties appear likely to become locked into win–lose conflict, a mediator, acting as a neutral party, may be able to help them resolve their differences.[55]

Competencies and Functions   Mediators need special competencies. They must (1) be able to diagnose the conflict, (2) be skilled at breaking deadlocks and facilitating discussions at the right time, (3) show mutual acceptance, and (4) have the ability to provide emotional support and reassurance. In brief, a mediator's style must instill confidence in and acceptance by the parties in conflict.[56]

Key functions of the mediator's role include the following.

- *Ensure mutual motivation.* Each party should have incentives for resolving the conflict.

- *Achieve a balance in situational power.* If the situational power of the parties isn't equal, establishing trust and maintaining open lines of communication may be difficult.

- *Coordinate confrontation efforts.* One party's positive moves must be coordinated with the other party's readiness to do likewise. A failure to coordinate positive initiatives and readiness to respond can undermine future efforts to work out differences.

- *Promote openness in dialogue.* The mediator can help establish norms of openness, provide reassurance and support, and decrease the risks associated with openness.

- *Maintain an optimum level of tension.* If the threat and tension are too low, the incentive for change or finding a solution is minimal. However, if the threat and tension are too high, the parties may be unable to process information and see creative alternatives. They may begin to polarize and take rigid positions.[57]

TABLE 12.2 Traditional Negotiating Assumptions About Three Cultural Groupings

	TRADITIONAL NEGOTIATING ASSUMPTIONS		
DIMENSION	**Japanese**	**U.S. and Canadian**	**Latin American**
Emotions	Emotions valued but must be hidden.	Emotions not highly valued. Transactions with others mostly unemotional.	Emotional sensitivity valued. Highly emotional and even passionate interactions.
Power	Subtle power plays. Conciliation sought.	Power games played all the times. Litigation, not so much conciliation, pursued. Strength highly valued.	Great power plays. To be stronger than the others particularly valued.
Decision making	Team decision making.	Team inputs for decision makers.	Decisions made by individuals in charge.
Social interaction	Face-saving crucial. Decisions often made on the basis of saving someone from embarrassment.	Decisions made on a cost/benefit basis. Face-saving not openly important.	Face-saving for oneself critical to preserve honor and dignity.
Persuasion	Not argumentative. Quiet when right. Respectful and patient. Modesty and self-restraint highly valued.	Argumentative when right or wrong. Impersonal when arguing. Practical when presenting arguments.	Passionate and emotional when arguing. Enjoys a warm interaction and a lively debate.

Source: Adapted from Casse, P., and Doel, S. Managing *Intercultural Negotiations: Guidelines for Trainers and Negotiators.* Washington, D.C.: SEITAR International, 1985, p. 10.

Intergroup Dialogue Technique   A mediator usually tries to assist negotiations without setting down a specific set of procedures for the parties to follow. Occasionally, however, a structured approach is useful to ensure that the negotiators concentrate on the real issues and direct their efforts toward resolving them. One example of such an approach is the **intergroup dialogue technique,** which refers to the following process.[58]

- Each group meets in a separate room and develops two lists. On one list, the members indicate how they perceive themselves as a group, particularly in their relationship with the other group. On the second list, they indicate how they view the other group.

- The two groups come together and share perceptions. The mediator helps them clarify their views and come to a better understanding of themselves and the other group.

- The groups return to their separate rooms to look at the issues further, diagnose the current problem, and determine what each group contributes to the conflict.

- The groups meet again to share their new insights. The mediator urges them to identify common issues and plan the next stages for seeking solutions.

Like most methods of negotiation and conflict management, the intergroup dialogue technique doesn't guarantee successful conflict resolution. Instead, it provides a process for the parties in conflict to explore and work through their differences. A competent mediator uses the technique to move the parties toward a resolution.

CHAPTER SUMMARY

Conflict is a part of organizational life. Four basic forms of conflict are goal conflict, cognitive conflict, affective conflict, and procedural conflict. Conflict need not have destructive outcomes for individuals or an organization. Through effective conflict management, its negative effects may be minimized and its positive effects maximized, yielding a balanced view of conflict. Effective conflict management requires an understanding of the different ways in which conflict develops and can be resolved.

Conflict occurs at five different levels within organizations: intrapersonal, interpersonal, intragroup, intergroup, and interorganizational. We discussed the main features of each level, with the exception of interorganizational conflict. The model presented for understanding and comparing interpersonal conflict handling styles identifies them as avoiding, forcing, accommodating, collaborating, and compromising. An individual may have a natural preference for one or two of these styles but is likely to use all of them over time when dealing with various interpersonal conflict situations.

Negotiation is an important process in conflict management. The four basic types of negotiations are distributive, integrative, attitudinal structuring, and intraorganizational. The two basic approaches to negotiating tactics and behaviors are the win–win and win–lose processes. Negotiations involving parties from different cultures is even more complex than negotiations involving only domestic parties. Mediation can be helpful when the negotiating parties anticipate or experience difficulties in reaching agreement.

KEY TERMS AND CONCEPTS

Accommodating style
Affective conflict
Approach–approach conflict
Approach–avoidance conflict
Attitudinal structuring
Avoidance–avoidance conflict
Avoiding style
Cognitive conflict
Cognitive dissonance
Collaborating style
Compromising style
Conflict
Conflict management
Distributive negotiations

Forcing style
Goal conflict
Goal incompatibility
Horizontal conflict
Integrative negotiations
Intergroup conflict
Intergroup dialogue technique
Interpersonal conflict
Interrole conflict
Intersender role conflict
Intragroup conflict
Intraorganizational negotiations
Intrapersonal conflict
Intrasender role conflict

Line–staff conflict
Mediation
Negotiator's dilemma
Negotiation
Neurotic tendencies
Person–role conflict
Procedural conflict
Role
Role ambiguity
Role conflict
Role set
Vertical conflict
Whistle-blowing

DISCUSSION QUESTIONS

1. Reread the Quality in Practice feature on Motorola. What types of conflict were triggered by Motorola's policy? Should Motorola have handled this situation differently? Explain.

2. Would you have any difficulties in negotiating in Mexico or Latin America? Explain why or why not and identify the competencies you possess or may need to develop to overcome any difficulties.

3. Have you been involved in negotiations where the other party used or tried to use win–lose tactics? If yes, describe the situation. What did you do in response to these tactics? How did you feel? What was the outcome?

4. Have you experienced diversity-based conflict? If yes, explain what happened and why.

5. What is your personal view of conflict—positive, negative, or balanced? Cite two incidents from personal experience to illustrate your view.

6. How might goal conflict, cognitive conflict, and affective conflict all come into play in a conflict situation? Illustrate your answer by referring to a personal experience.

7. Give personal examples of your experience with approach–approach conflict, avoidance–avoidance conflict, and approach–avoidance conflict.

8. Give an example of intrasender role conflict, intersender role conflict, and person–role conflict that you have experienced.

9. In which of your roles do you experience the most role ambiguity? Explain.

10. What difficulties might an individual encounter in trying to apply win–win tactics in negotiations?

◼ Developing Competencies

Self-Insight: Conflict Handling Styles[59]

Instructions

Each numbered item contains two statements that describe how people deal with conflict. Distribute 5 points between each pair of statements. The statement that more accurately reflects your likely response should receive the highest number of points. For example, if response (a) strongly describes your behavior, then record

  _5_   a.
  _0_   b.

However, if (a) and (b) are both characteristic, but (b) is slightly more characteristic of your behavior than (a), then record

  _2_   a.
  _3_   b.

1._____   a. I am most comfortable letting others take responsibility for solving a problem.

_____ b. Rather than negotiate differences, I stress those points for which agreement is obvious.

2. _____ a. I pride myself in finding compromise solutions.

_____ b. I examine all the issues involved in any disagreement.

3. _____ a. I usually persist in pursuing my side of an issue.

_____ b. I prefer to soothe others' feelings and preserve relationships.

4. _____ a. I pride myself in finding compromise solutions.

_____ b. I usually sacrifice my wishes for the wishes of a peer.

5. _____ a. I consistently seek a peer's help in finding solutions.

_____ b. I do whatever is necessary to avoid tension.

6. _____ a. As a rule, I avoid dealing with conflict.

_____ b. I defend my position and push my view.

7. _____ a. I postpone dealing with conflict until I have had some time to think it over.

_____ b. I am willing to give up some points if others give up some too.

8. _____ a. I use my influence to have my views accepted.

_____ b. I attempt to get all concerns and issues immediately out in the open.

9. _____ a. I feel that most differences are not worth worrying about.

_____ b. I make a strong effort to get my way on issues I care about.

10. _____ a. Occasionally I use my authority or technical knowledge to get my way.

_____ b. I prefer compromise solutions to problems.

11. _____ a. I believe that a team can reach a better solution than any one person can working independently.

_____ b. I often defer to the wishes of others.

12. _____ a. I usually avoid taking positions that would create controversy.

_____ b. I'm willing to give a little if a peer will give a little, too.

13. _____ a. I generally propose the middle ground as a solution.

_____ b. I consistently press to "sell" my viewpoint.

14. _____ a. I prefer to hear everyone's side of an issue before making judgments.

_____ b. I demonstrate the logic and benefits of my position.

15. _____ a. I would rather give in than argue about trivialities.

_____ b. I avoid being "put on the spot."

16. _____ a. I refuse to hurt a peer's feelings.

_____ b. I will defend my rights as a team member.

17. _____ a. I am usually firm in pursuing my point of view.

_____ b. I'll walk away from disagreements before someone gets hurt.

18. _____ a. If it makes peers happy, I will agree with them.

_____ b. I believe that give-and-take is the best way to resolve any disagreement.

19. _____ a. I prefer to have everyone involved in a conflict generate alternatives together.

_____ b. When the team is discussing a serious problem, I usually keep quiet.

20. _____ a. I would rather openly resolve conflict than conceal differences.

_____ b. I seek ways to balance gains and losses for equitable solutions.

21. _____ a. In problem solving, I am usually considerate of peers' viewpoints.

_____ b. I prefer a direct and objective discussion of any disagreement.

22. _____ a. I seek solutions that meet some of everyone's needs.

_____ b. I will argue as long as necessary to get my position heard.

23. _____ a. I like to assess the problem and identify a mutually agreeable solution.

_____ b. When people challenge my position, I simply ignore them.

24. _____ a. If peers feel strongly about a position, I defer to it even if I don't agree.

_____ b. I am willing to settle for a compromise solution.

25. _____ a. I am very persuasive when I have to be to win in a conflict situation.

_____ b. I believe in the saying, "Kill your enemies with kindness."

26. _____ a. I will bargain with peers in an effort to manage disagreement.

_____ b. I listen attentively before expressing my views.

27. _____ a. I avoid taking controversial positions.

_____ b. I'm willing to give up my position for the benefit of the group.

28. _____ a. I enjoy competitive situations and "play" hard to win.

_____ b. Whenever possible, I seek out knowledgeable peers to help resolve disagreements.

29. _____ a. I will surrender some of my demands, but I have to get something in return.

_____ b. I don't like to air differences and usually keep my concerns to myself.

30. _____ a. I generally avoid hurting a peer's feelings.

_____ b. When a peer and I disagree, I prefer to bring the issue out into the open so we can discuss it.

Scoring

Record your responses (number of points) in the space next to each statement number below and then sum the points in each column.

Column 1	Column 2	Column 3	Column 4	Column 5
3 (a) ___	2 (a) ___	1 (a) ___	1 (b) ___	2 (b) ___
6 (b) ___	4 (a) ___	5 (b) ___	3 (b) ___	5 (a) ___
8 (a) ___	7 (b) ___	6 (a) ___	4 (b) ___	8 (b) ___
9 (b) ___	10 (b) ___	7 (a) ___	11 (b) ___	11 (a) ___
10 (a) ___	12 (b) ___	9 (a) ___	15 (a) ___	14 (a) ___
13 (b) ___	13 (a) ___	12 (a) ___	16 (a) ___	19 (a) ___
14 (b) ___	18 (b) ___	15 (b) ___	18 (a) ___	20 (a) ___
16 (b) ___	20 (b) ___	17 (b) ___	21 (a) ___	21 (b) ___
17 (a) ___	22 (a) ___	19 (b) ___	24 (a) ___	23 (a) ___
22 (b) ___	24 (b) ___	23 (b) ___	25 (b) ___	26 (b) ___
25 (a) ___	26 (a) ___	27 (a) ___	27 (b) ___	28 (b) ___
28 (a) ___	29 (a) ___	29 (b) ___	30 (a) ___	30 (b) ___
Total ___	Total ___	Total ___	Total ___	Total ___

Next, carry over the totals from the column totals and then plot your total scores on the following chart to show the profile of your conflict handling styles. A total score of 36 to 45 for each style, such as the forcing style in column 1, may indicate a strong preference and use of that style. A total score of 0 to 18 for each style, such as the compromising style in column 2, may indicate little preference and use of that style. A total score of 19 to 35 for each style may indicate a moderate preference and use of that style.

	Total	0	10	20	30	40	50	60
Column 1 (Forcing)	_____		•	•	•	•	•	•
Column 2 (Compromising)	_____		•	•	•	•	•	•
Column 3 (Avoiding)	_____		•	•	•	•	•	•
Column 4 (Accommodating)	_____		•	•	•	•	•	•

		0	10	20	30	40	50	60
Column 5 (Collaborating)	_____		•	•	•	•	•	•

Interpretation

When used appropriately, each of these styles can be an effective approach to conflict handling. Any one style or a mixture of the five can be used during the course of a dispute. Are you satisfied with this profile? Why or why not? Is this profile truly representative of your natural and primary conflict handling styles?

Organizational Insight: The Reluctant Loan Officer

Betty Hampton graduated from State College with a bachelor's degree in English. For three years she had worked for a local bank during the day and attended classes at night. At the bank Hampton had held various jobs, such as teller, loan clerk, secretary, new accounts clerk, and loan processor. Although her major area was English, she had taken enough courses to have a second, unofficial major in business administration. Upon graduation, Hampton had difficulty finding a challenging job. Finally, in desperation, she accepted a secretarial position with Third National Bank of Brookfield, her hometown. She was easily able to master the routine secretarial work and handle some other areas of responsibility, such as new accounts, loan documentation, statement analysis, and computer output.

Ralph Wheelen, the senior commercial loan officer, soon noticed Hampton's work. He remarked to others that, as she seemed to be doing such a good job processing loan applications, she might make a good loan officer. Top management was somewhat reluctant to have a female loan officer because they felt that it was "well known" that women are easily swayed by their emotions. Some feared that customers might take advantage of her. Carlos Louis, the bank president, feared that a young, attractive woman might not project the stable and conservative image that he felt necessary in a good loan officer. At that time, only three women in the bank had supervisory responsibilities. Two women were in operations—one supervising the bookkeeping department and the other overseeing tellers. There also was one female branch manager, Susan Spriggs (with whom Carlos Louis quite openly had more than a simple business relationship). Louis believed these women to be appropriately placed because they primarily supervised other women and had nothing to do with what he considered to be the key profit area in the bank—commercial loans. Nevertheless, on the basis of Wheelen's recommendation and Equal Employment Opportunity considerations, Louis gave Hampton the chance to move up to the position of loan officer.

Hampton realized that the bank was using her as a test case and that the president was concerned that she project the proper image. Consequently, she dressed in long-sleeved blouses with high-neck collars. She wore mainly dark colors and attempted to maintain a serious appearance and demeanor at all times, both on the job and in the community.

Of eight banks in the city, only Third National had a female loan officer.

The first few months on the job were challenging ones for Hampton. She enjoyed her job and seemed to be progressing well. She was having no real problems getting commercial customers to accept her as a loan officer or in visiting local business-people to encourage them to do business with Third National.

One morning Hampton joined eleven other loan officers and branch managers in the conference room for the weekly business development meeting. The meeting was conducted, as usual, by the senior vice-president, Bill Weber. After discussing the week's officer call reports, Weber asked the group how the bank could increase its holdings of mortgage loans. John Sullivan, a loan officer of many years, suggested that someone talk with Amos McLaren, a successful realtor in the community. "If someone could just talk Amos into mentioning Third National to his customers," suggested Sullivan, "we could really pick up business!"

"That's an excellent idea," responded Weber, "but we have to be careful how we approach him." Turning to Hampton, Weber said, "Betty, I think you ought to take Amos out tomorrow night and do whatever is necessary to get his business."

Betty was astounded at the implications of Weber's statement. Who does he think I am? she wondered to herself as she looked at the eleven other people in the conference room. Susan, the branch manager and the only other female in the room, was looking at the floor and nervously adjusting her watch. No one else seemed to be reacting except for Joe Bibbins, a young but experienced loan officer, who seemed to have a slight smirk on his face. Hampton had heard the rumors circulating around the bank of various people sleeping together, but she never realized how far things seemed to have gone!

After a moment's hesitation, Betty Hampton looked the senior vice-president in the eye and said, "You have other women on the staff you've hired for that purpose. Let them do it."[60]

Questions

1. What types of conflicts exist in this case?
2. What are the basic causes of these conflicts?
3. Did Betty say the right thing? What is the basis for your response?

REFERENCES

1. Adapted from Kaeter, M. From hell to happiness. *Business Ethics,* July/August 1993, 22–26. This article was reprinted with permission from *Business Ethics Magazine,* 52 S. 10th St., Suite 110, Minneapolis, MN 55403-2001.
2. Walls, J. A., Jr. Conflict and its management. *Journal of Management,* 1995, 21, 515–558.
3. Kottler, J. *Beyond Blame: A New Way of Resolving Conflicts in Relationships.* San Francisco: Jossey-Bass, 1994.
4. Kolb, D. M., and Bartunek, J. M. (eds.). *Hidden Conflict in Organizations: Uncovering Behind-the-Scenes Disputes.* Thousand Oaks, Calif.: Sage, 1992; Genest, M. A. *Conflict and Cooperation.* San Diego: Harcourt Brace Jovanovich, 1996.
5. Amason, A. C. Distinguishing the effects of functional and dysfunctional conflict on strategic decision making: Resolving a paradox of top management teams. *Academy of Management Journal,* 1996, 39, 123–148.
6. Baron, R. A. Positive effects of conflict: A cognitive perspective. *Employee Responsibilities and Rights Journal,* 1991, 4, 25–35; Mescon Group. *Managing Conflict in Teams.* Cincinnati: South-Western, 1996.
7. Amason, A. C., Hochwarter, W. A., Thompson, K. R., and Harrison, A. W. Conflict: An important dimension in successful management teams. *Organizational Dynamics,* Autumn 1995, 20–35.
8. Burrell, N. A., Buzzanell, P. M., and McMillan, J. J. Feminine tensions in conflict situations as revealed by metaphoric analyses. *Management Communication Quarterly,* 1992, 6, 115–149.
9. Kohn, A. *No Contest: The Case Against Competition.* Boston: Houghton Mifflin, 1986.
10. Labig, C. E. *Preventing Violence in the Workplace.* New York: AMACOM, 1995.
11. Costantino, C. A., and Merchant, C. S. *Designing Conflict Management Systems.* San Francisco: Jossey-Bass, 1996.
12. Adapted from Motorola may have blundered by strong-arming some retailers. *Houston Chronicle,* September 8, 1996, 10E; Alleven, M. Motorola Inc's new Signature retail program has upset dealers. *Wireless Week,* September 16, 1996, 1; Motorola aims to maintain prestige of top-of-the-line cellular phone units; will create new category of 'signature' dealers. *Chicago Tribune,* May 13, 1996, 1, 3+.
13. Locke, E. A., Smith, K. G., Erez, M., Chah, D., and Schaeffer, A. The effects of intra-individual goal conflict on performance. *Journal of Management,* 1994, 20, 67–91.
14. Festinger, L. *A Theory of Cognitive Dissonance.* Evanston, Ill.: Row, Peterson, 1967.
15. Czander, W. H. *The Psychodynamics of Work and Organizations: Theory and Applications.* New York: Guilford, 1993.
16. Kets de Vries, M. F. R., and Miller D. *The Neurotic Organization.* San Francisco: Jossey-Bass, 1984.
17. Kets de Vries and Miller, 73–94; Zaleznik, A. *Learning Leadership: Cases and Commentaries on Abuse of Power in Organizations.* Chicago: Bonus Books, 1993.
18. VandenBos, G. R., and Bulatao, E. Q. (eds.). *Violence on the Job: Identifying Risks and Developing Solutions.* Washington, D.C.: American Psychological Association, 1996.

19. Myers, D. W. The mythical world of workplace violence—Or is it? *Business Horizons,* July–August 1996, 31–36; O'Leary-Kelly, A. M., Griffin, R. W., and Glew, D. J. Organization-motivated aggression: A research framework. *Academy of Management Review,* 1996, 21, 225–253.

20. Kahn, R. L., Wolfe, D. M., Quinn, R. P., Snoek, J. D., and Rosenthal, R. A. *Occupational Stress: Studies in Role Conflict and Ambiguity.* New York: John Wiley & Sons, 1964.

21. Adapted from Sexton, J., and Biddle, W. The pounding is intense. *USA Weekend,* August 16–18, 1996, 4–6.

22. Ilgen, D. R., and Hollenbeck, J. R. The structure of work: Job design and roles. In M. D. Dunnette and L. M. Hough (eds.), *Handbook of Industrial and Organizational Psychology,* vol. 2, 2d ed. Palo Alto, Calif.: Consulting Psychologists Press, 1991, 165–207.

23. Peterson, M. F. and Associates. Role conflict, ambiguity and overload: A 21-nation study. *Academy of Management Journal,* 1995, 38, 429–452.

24. Hesselbein, F., Goldsmith, M., and Beckhard, R. (eds.). *The Leader of the Future.* San Francisco: Jossey-Bass, 1996.

25. Kabanoff, B. Equity, equality, power, and conflict. *Academy of Management Review,* 1991, 16, 416–441; Alvesson, M. *Communication Power and Organization.* New York: Walter D. deGruyter, 1996.

26. Kahn, A. Taking on a family business can call for greater expertise. Bryan–College Station Eagle, March 20, 1994, C6; Lenzner, R., and Upbin, B. Brother vs. brother vs. mother vs. cousin. *Forbes,* June 17, 1996, 44–46.

27. Pondy, L. R. Organizational conflict: Concept and models. *Administrative Science Quarterly,* 1967, 12, 296–320.

28. Adapted from Nulty, P. Incentive pay can be crippling. *Fortune,* November 13, 1995, 235–236; Nelson, E. Gas company's gain-sharing plan turns employees into cost-cutting vigilantes. *Wall Street Journal,* September 29, 1995, B1.

29. March, S., and Simon, H. *Organizations,* 2d ed. Cambridge, Mass.: Blackwell, 1993.

30. Harriman, A. *Women/Men/Management,* 2d ed. Westport, Conn.: Praeger, 1996; Stockdale, M. S. *Sexual Harassment in the Workplace.* Thousand Oaks, Calif.: Sage, 1996.

31. Adapted from Alger, A., and Flanagan, W. G. Sexual politics. *Forbes,* May 6, 1996, 106–110; Crock, S. Sexual harassment at McKinsey. *Business Week,* December 6, 1996, 44–46.

32. Thomas, K. W. The conflict handling modes: Toward more precise theory. *Management Communication Quarterly,* 1988, 1, 430–436. For a more complex model of conflict-handling styles, see Nicotera, A. M. Beyond two dimensions: A grounded theory model of conflict-handling behavior. *Management Communication Quarterly,* 1993, 6, 282–306.

33. King, W. C., and Miles, E. W. What we know—and don't know—about measuring conflict: An examination of the ROCI-OO and the OCCI conflict instruments. *Management Communication Quarterly,* 1990, 4, 222–243.

34. Sorenson, P. S., Hawkins, K., and Sorenson, R. L. Gender, psychological type and conflict style preference. *Management Communication Quarterly,* 1995, 9, 115–126.

35. Weider-Hatfield, D., and Hatfield, J. D. Superiors' conflict management strategies and subordinate outcomes. *Management Communication Quarterly,* 1996, 10, 189–208.

36. Near, J. P., and Micelli, M. P. Effective whistle-blowing. *Academy of Management Review,* 1995, 20, 679–708.

37. Adapted from Pooley, E. Nuclear warriors. *Time,* March 4, 1996, 46–54; Lancaster, H. Workers who blow the whistle on bosses often pay a high price. *Wall Street Journal,* July 8, 1995, B1; Weber, C. E. *Stories of Virtue in Business.* Lanham, Md.: University Press of America, 1995.

38. Martocchio, J. J., and Judge, T. A. When we don't see eye to eye: Discrepancies between supervisors and subordinates in absence disciplinary decisions. *Journal of Management,* 1995, 21, 251–278.

39. Blanchard, K., and O'Connor, M. *Managing by Values.* San Francisco: Berrett-Kohler, 1997.

40. Blake, R. R., and Mouton, J. S. *Solving Costly Organizational Conflicts.* San Francisco: Jossey-Bass, 1984.

41. Kabanoff, B. Why is compromise so favorably viewed? In F. Hoy (ed.), *Academy of Management Best Paper Proceedings.* Mississippi State, Miss.: Academy of Management, 1987, 280–284.

42. Rahim, M. A. *Managing Conflict in Organizations,* 2d ed., New York: Praeger, 1992.

43. Lewicki, R. J., *Essentials of Negotiation.* Burr Ridge, Ill.: Irwin, 1996; Mintzberg, H., Dougherty, D., and Jorgensen, J. Some surprising things about collaboration: Knowing how people connect makes it work better. *Organizational Dynamics,* Summer 1996, 60–71.

44. Walton, R. E., and McKersie, R. B. *A Behavioral Theory of Labor Negotiations.* New York: McGraw-Hill, 1965.

45. Adapted from MacDonald, E. Andersen Worldwide rules out breakup. *Wall Street Journal,* December 23, 1996, A2; Berton, L. Andersen flap could presage formal split. *Wall Street Journal,* July 29, 1996, B1, B7.

46. Adapted from Korshak, S. R. Negotiating trust in the San Francisco hotel industry. *California Management Review,* Fall 1995, 117–137; *Labor Management Committees Contained in HERE Contract* with *San Francisco Hotels.* BNA Daily Report No. 178, September 16, 1994.

47. Korshak, S. R., 136.

48. This section was adapted from Anderson, T. Step into my parlor: A survey of strategies and techniques for effective negotiations. *Business Horizons,* May–June 1992, 71–76.

49. Fisher, R., and Ury, W. *Getting to Yes: Negotiating Agreement Without Giving In.* New York: Penguin Books, 1981; Fisher, R. *Getting Ready to Negotiate: The Getting to Yes Workbook.* New York: Viking Penguin, 1995; Benedict Bunker, B., Rubin, J. Z., and Associates. *Conflict, Cooperation, and Justice.* San Francisco: Jossey-Bass, 1995.

50. Economy, P. *Business Negotiating Basics.* Burr Ridge, Ill.: Irwin, 1994; Mayer, R. *Power Plays: How to Negotiate, Persuade, and Finesse Your Way to Success in Any Situation.* New York: Times Books, 1996.

51. Friedman, R. A. *Front Stage Backstage: The Dynamic Structure of Labor Negotiations.* Cambridge, Mass.: MIT Press, 1994.

52. Zartman, I. W. (ed.). *International Multilateral Negotiation: Approaches to the Management of Complexity.* San Francisco: Jossey-Bass, 1994; Ghauri, P. N., and Usunier, J. C. *International Business Negotiations.* New York: Elsevier Science, 1996.

53. Black, J. S., and Mendenhall, M. Resolving conflicts with the Japanese: Mission impossible. *Sloan Management Review,* Spring 1993, 49–59;

54. Adapted from de Forest, M. E. Thinking of a plant in Mexico. *Academy of Management Executive,* February 1994, 33–40; Hellweg, S. A., Samovar, L. A., and Skow, L. Cultural variations in negotiation styles. In L. A. Samovar and R. E. Proter (eds.), *Intercultural Communications: A Reader,* 2d. ed. Belmont, Calif.: Wadsworth, 1994, 286–292; Kras, E. *Management in Two Cultures: Bridging the Gap Between U.S. and Mexican Managers,* rev. ed. Yarmouth, Me.: Intercultural Press, 1995.

55. Slaikeu, K. L., *When Push Comes to Shove: A Practical Guide to Mediating Disputes.* San Francisco: Jossey-Bass, 1995; Weiss, D. S. *Beyond the Walls of Conflict: Mutual Gains Negotiating in Unions & Management.* Burr Ridge, Ill.: Irwin, 1996.

56. Susskind, L. E., and Field, P. T. *Dealing with an Angry Public: The Mutual Gains Approach to Resolving Disputes.* New York: Free Press, 1996.

57. Moore, C. W. *The Mediation Process: Practical Strategies for Resolving Conflict.* San Francisco: Jossey-Bass, 1996; Pinkley, R. L., and Northcraft, G. B. Cognitive interpretations of conflict: Implication for dispute processes and outcomes. *Academy of Management Journal,* 1994, 37, 193–205.

58. Blake, R. R., Shepard, H. A., and Mouton, J. S. *Managing Intergroup Conflict in Industry.* Houston: Gulf, 1964. Also see: Bush, R. A., and Folger, J. P. *The Promise of Mediation: Responding to Conflict Through Empowerment and Recognition.* San Francisco: Jossey-Bass, 1994.

59. Adapted from Baskerville, D. M. How do you manage conflict. *Black Enterprise,* May 1993, 63–66; Holton, B., and Holton, C. *The Manager's Short Course: A Complete Course in Leadership Skills for the First-Time Manager.* New York: John Wiley & Sons, 1992; Thomas, K. W., and Kilmann, R. H. *The Thomas–Kilmann Conflict Mode Instrument.* Tuxedo, N.Y.: Xicom, 1974; Rahim, M. A. A measure of styles of handling interpersonal conflict. *Academy of Management Journal,* 1983, 26, 368–376.

60. Adapted with permission from J. D. Hunger, Iowa State University. Copyright © 1979 by J. D. Hunger. Distributed by the Intercollegiate Case Clearing House, Soldiers Field, Boston, MA 02163. All rights reserved to the contributors.

13

Interpersonal Communication

LEARNING OBJECTIVES

When you have finished studying this chapter, you should be able to:

- Describe the essentials of interpersonal communication.
- Identify the interpersonal and cultural hurdles to dialogue.
- Evaluate the effects of communication networks.
- Describe how groupware supports networking.
- Explain the skills and abilities that foster dialogue.
- Know how to give feedback, engage in selfdisclosure, and actively listen.
- State how nonverbal cues may support dialogue between individuals.

OUTLINE

PREVIEW CASE

New Employee Encounters

When people enter organizations, they typically encounter situations or events about which they experience a great deal of uncertainty. This uncertainty may take the form of questions such as: What should I do now? What does this mean? Now what? What am I going to do? Think back to the situation you faced in your new work setting which was characterized by the most uncertainty. Did the interpersonal communications you encountered help to reduce these uncertainties or were they more like those shared by an older college student, who we call Joe, in the following account?

"Before taking an inventory, a meeting was called in the store's back room. I walked in and joined the group of about twenty. No one said a thing to me. I finally had to ask who my team leader was; she wasn't there. I knew no one. I said to a lady next to me that I was new and what was I to do. She told me in a very matter of fact way. After the meeting we went out into the store. Again, I was not instructed as to what to do. I asked a young man and he pointed to an area and said start there. I had only received four hours of verbal training, and this line of work was completely different from my previous eighteen years as a bookkeeper.

"I had been told in training someone would be working with me. What a joke! I was totally on my own. I made mistakes and was chewed out by a young lady. I tried to explain I was new and no one assisted me; she didn't care. No one was friendly; I felt like running. I wondered how a business could operate like this and [thought that] their turnover must be huge. My second day was just as bad. I was ready to quit. I told my team leader on the phone what had happened. She said not to worry. I would catch on.

"After a month I was called back in, along with two others, for detailed training. It seems once you prove to the company that you are willing to work, the company will help you develop the necessary skills. I am still working, but I wonder how many good employees the company has lost because of this practice. I needed the money so I stuck it out."[1]

J oe's encounters as a new employee suggest a pattern of difficult and strained interpersonal communication. Three basic patterns of interpersonal communication were available to Joe, the team leader, and his co-workers: assertive, nonassertive, and aggressive.[2] **Assertive communication** means confidently expressing what you think, feel, and believe (values)—and standing up for your rights while respecting the rights of others. By actions and words, you convey meaning and expectations without humiliating or degrading the other person. Assertive communication is based on respect for yourself and respect for other people's needs and rights. Unfortunately, there did not seem to be much, if any, assertive communications in the encounters reported by Joe.

Nonassertive communication is a reluctance or inability to express consistently what you think, feel, and believe (values), as well as allowing others to violate your rights without challenge. It reflects a lack of respect for your own preferences. With this approach, others can easily disregard your thoughts, feelings, and beliefs. A variation of this approach is *passive–aggressive communication*, which involves some degree of resentment and subtle hostility—pouting, stewing, and fretting. It may involve a sense of being a victim, even if such a feeling isn't valid. In the Preview Case, Joe appeared to exhibit the passive–aggressive communication approach in several of his comments, such as: "I had been told in training someone would work with me. What a joke! I was totally on my own. . . . I needed the money, so I stuck it out." The team leader also demonstrated nonassertive communication: "I told my team leader on the phone what had happened. She said not to worry, I would catch on." A co-worker appeared to exhibit a degree of nonassertive communication in this encounter: "I [Joe] said to a lady next to me that I was new and what was I to do. She told me in a very matter of fact way."

Aggressive communication means expressing yourself in ways that intimidate, demean, or degrade another person and pursuing what you want in ways that violate the rights of that person. This approach carries messages such as: I (we) don't really care about you. This is what I think. You're dumb for not knowing. and Do as I say or you're out of here. Recall this encounter by Joe: "I made mistakes and was chewed out by a young lady. I tried to explain I was new and no one assisted me; she didn't care." Joe also reflected what he experienced as an aggressive communication environment in these words: "No one said a word to me. . . . No one was friendly. . . . I am still working but I wonder how many good employees the company lost because of this practice."

We identified *communicating* as a core competency in Chapter 1. Effective interpersonal communication is the focus of this chapter. We discuss the process, types, and patterns of verbal, nonverbal, and other forms of interpersonal communication used by employees on the job. We present ways to foster effective dialogue in organizations. Finally, we examine the nature and importance of nonverbal communication.

Interpersonal communication is the transmission and reception of thoughts, facts, beliefs, attitudes, and feelings—through one or more information media— that produce a response. Through active listening, the messages intended by the sender are likely to be accurately understood and interpreted by the receiver.[3] In the Preview Case, the team leader wasn't listening to Joe nor were several of his co-workers. Of course, these encounters were made even worse when Joe, as a new employee, was unwilling to engage in assertive communication.

ESSENTIALS OF INTERPERSONAL COMMUNICATION

What needs to happen for accurate interpersonal communication to take place? The thoughts, facts, beliefs, attitudes, or feelings that the sender intended to transmit must be the same as those understood and interpreted by the receiver. Management at American Airlines and labor representatives of pilots of the Allied Pilots Association disagreed with each other while negotiating a new labor contract. But so long as their opposing viewpoints are being transmitted, received, and understood with the intended meaning, accurate interpersonal communication is taking place. Interpersonal communication obviously requires two or more people. Figure 13.1 presents the essentials of interpersonal communication involving only two people.

■ SENDER AND RECEIVER

Exchanges between people is an element of interpersonal communication. Thus labeling one person as the sender and the other as the receiver is arbitrary. These roles shift back and forth, depending on where the individuals are in the process. When the receiver responds to the sender, the original receiver becomes the sender and the initiating sender becomes the receiver.

Consider the comment of a supervisor of security services about dealing with a vice-president of operations:

> I wanted an assistant so that I could have some help in managing my department and would not have to handle the petty problems of my employees. I [sender] tried to convince my general manager [receiver] that I was overworked since my staff had almost

■ **FIGURE 13.1** Elements of Interpersonal Communication

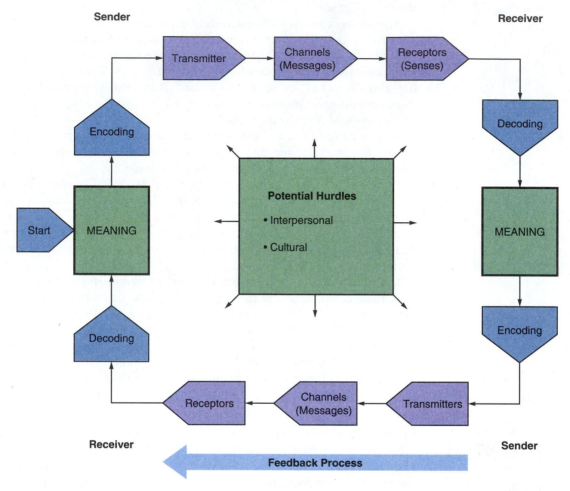

doubled and I was having a lot of people problems. I failed because I was just trying to make it easier on myself and wanted an assistant to do the job that I was supposed to be doing. I was also asking to increase the payroll of the company with no plans to increase revenue or profits. After my general manager [sender] turned me [receiver] down, I pouted for a few weeks and later learned that he thought I was immature. I then decided to forget about past disappointments and only worry about the future.[4]

The supervisor's statement suggests that the goals of the sender and receiver substantially influence the communication process. For example, the sender may have certain goals for communicating, such as adding to or changing the thoughts, beliefs, attitudes, and/or behaviors of the receiver or changing the relationship with the receiver. These intentions may be presented openly (the supervisor wanted a new assistant) or developed deceptively.[5] If the receiver doesn't agree with them, the probability of distortion and misunderstanding can be quite high (the general manager concluded that the supervisor was immature). The fewer the differences in goals, attitudes, and beliefs, the greater is the probability that accurate communication will occur. This quote also suggests that the sender used a passive–aggressive communication approach with his general manager.

■ TRANSMITTERS AND RECEPTORS

Transmitters (used by the sender) and **receptors** (used by the receiver) are the means (media) available for sending and receiving messages. They usually involve one or more of the senses: seeing, hearing, touching, smelling, and tasting. Transmission can take place both verbally and nonverbally. Once transmission begins, the communication process moves beyond the direct control of the sender. A message that has been transmitted cannot be brought back. How many times have you thought to yourself: I wish I hadn't said that?

Various types of communication media are available for transmitting and receiving messages. They vary in terms of **media richness,** which are the medias' capacities for carrying multiple cues and providing rapid feedback. The richness of each medium involves a blend of four factors: (1) the rapidity and use of feedback to correct and/or confirm intended meanings; (2) the customizing of messages to the personal circumstances of the receiver; (3) the ability to convey multiple cues simultaneously; and (4) language variety.[6] Figure 13.2 relates nine different media to these four factors. The factors are labeled *feedback* (slow to rapid), *personalization* (low to high), *cues* (single to multiple), and *language* (standard to varied). A medium may vary somewhat in richness along these continua, depending on its use by the sender and receiver.[7] Electronic mail (e-mail) may be associated with slower or quicker feedback than shown in Figure 13.2. The speed depends on the accessibility of e-mail messages and the receiver's tendency to reply immediately or later. Messages that require a long time to digest or that can't overcome biases are low in richness.

Data simply are the output of communication. The various forms of data include words spoken face-to-face, telephone calls, letters, memos, and computer printouts. They become information when they reinforce or change the receivers' understanding of their thoughts, feelings, attitudes, or beliefs. The use of *groupware* (various information technologies) may help such information exchange but can't always substitute for face-to-face dialogue.[8] Why? As suggested in Figure 13.2, face-to-face dialogue is considered to be the richest medium. It provides immediate feedback so that receivers can check the accuracy of their understanding and correct if they need to. It also allows the sender and receiver simultaneously to observe body language, tone of voice, and facial expression. These observations communicate more than just the spoken words. Finally, it enables the sender and receiver to identify quickly and use language that is natural and personal. Because of these characteristics, solving important and tough problems—especially those involving uncertainty and ambiguity—almost always requires face-to-face dialogue.[9]

■ MESSAGES AND CHANNELS

Messages include the transmitted data and the coded (verbal and nonverbal) symbols that give particular meanings to that data. The sender hopes that messages are interpreted as meant. To understand the difference between the original meaning and the received message, think about an occasion when you tried to convey inner thoughts and feelings of happiness, rage, or fear to another person. Did you find it difficult or impossible to transmit your true "inner meaning"? The greater the difference between the interpreted meaning and the original message, the poorer will be the interpersonal communication. Words and nonverbal symbols have no meaning by themselves. Their meaning is created by the sender, the receiver, and the situation or context.[10] In our discussion of potential interper-

■ FIGURE 13.2   Examples of Media Richness for Sending and Receiving Messages

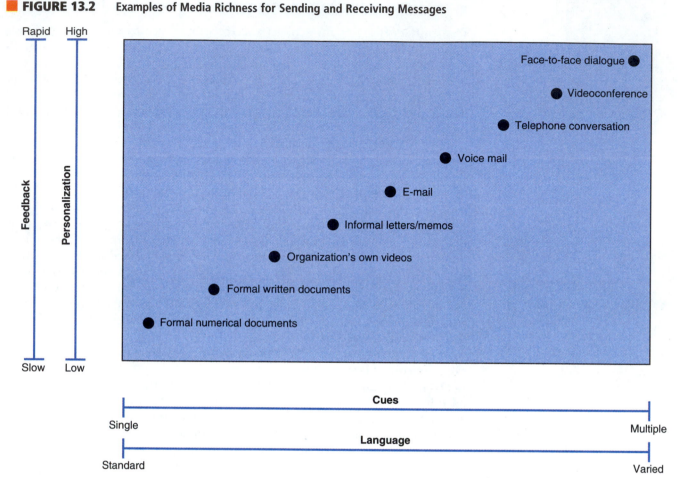

Source: Adapted from Daft, R. L., and Lengel, R. H. Organizational information requirements, media richness, and structural design. *Management Science*, 1986, 32, 554–571.

sonal and cultural hurdles, we explain why messages aren't always interpreted as they were meant to be. **Channels** are the means by which messages travel from sender to receiver. For example, a conversation may be carried by the air during face-to-face conversation or by a telephone line during long-distance conversation.

■ MEANING, ENCODING, DECODING, AND FEEDBACK

The sender's message is transmitted through channels to the receiver's five senses. As Figure 13.1 suggests, the received messages are changed from their symbolic form (such as spoken words) to a form that has meaning. **Meaning** represents a person's thoughts, feelings, beliefs (values), and attitudes.

Encoding is the personal translation of meaning into messages that can be sent. Vocabulary and knowledge play an important role in the sender's ability to encode. Unfortunately, some professionals have difficulty communicating with people in general. They often encode meaning in a form that only other professionals in the same field can understand. Lawyers often encode (write) contracts that directly affect consumers on the assumption that only other lawyers will decode them. Consumer groups have pressed to have such contracts written in language that most everyone can understand. As a result, many banks, credit card firms, and other organizations have simplified the language in their contracts.

Decoding is the personal translation of received messages into interpreted meanings. Through a shared language, people can decode many messages so that the meanings received are reasonably close to the meanings transmitted. Decoding messages accurately is often a major challenge in communicating across cultures. The following comments made by Japanese and Japanese-Americans who have worked closely with North Americans illustrate the gaps that may occur between sent messages and interpreted meanings.

■ Sometimes Americans don't understand that we are smiling and laughing not because we like what they are doing but because they are making us nervous.

■ Americans ought to watch us more carefully as we are not as verbal as they are. We don't like to say no for instance, but when we suck air in through our teeth and grab the back of our necks, we mean no.

■ Americans just don't understand the process of establishing relationships with the Japanese; the investment of time and expense seems like too much for them. They just aren't comfortable with the expectations, and they are not used to creating lasting, permanent business relationships. They think once the deal is done, it's over. They need to learn how to nurture relations: pay attention, follow up, make return visits—not only when something goes wrong.[11]

Interpersonal communication accuracy should be evaluated in relation to the ideal state. It occurs when the sender's intended meaning and the receiver's interpretation of it are the same. The transmission of factual information of a nonthreatening nature approximates the ideal state. For example, the sharing of the time, place, and procedures for high school or college commencement generally results in easy and accurate interpersonal communication. The communication between a manager and a subordinate during a performance feedback session is another matter.

The receiver's response to the message is **feedback.** It lets the sender know whether the message was received as intended. Interpersonal communication becomes a dynamic, two-way process, through feedback, rather than just an event. Reread the Preview Case. It provides several examples of the lack of constructive feedback.

■ INTERPERSONAL HURDLES

Numerous interpersonal communication hurdles exist, many of which we discussed in previous chapters. Let's review the more important hurdles that stem from individual differences in personality and perceptions.

■ Individual personality traits that serve as hurdles include low adjustment (nervous, self-doubting, moody), low sociability (shy, unassertive, withdrawn), low conscientiousness (impulsive, careless, irresponsible), low agreeableness (independent, cold, rude), and low intellectual openness (dull, unimaginative, literal-minded). Introverts are more likely to be quiet and emotionally unexpressive. Dogmatics are rigid and closed-minded and accept or reject other people on the basis of their agreement or disagreement with accepted authority or their own beliefs. (See Chapter 2.)

- Individuals with a low level of cognitive moral development, which is associated with extreme self-centeredness (It's right because it's right for me.), are likely to present hurdles to interpersonal communication. (See Chapter 2.)

- Individual perceptual errors include perceptual defense (protecting oneself against ideas, objects, or situations that are threatening), stereotyping (assigning attributes to someone solely on the basis of a category in which the person has been placed), halo effect (evaluating another person based solely on one impression, either favorable or unfavorable), projection (tendency for people to see their own traits in others) and high expectancy effect (prior expectations serving to bias how events, objects, and people are actually perceived). Individuals who make the fundamental attribution error (underestimating the impact of situational or external causes of behavior and overestimating the impact of personal causes of behavior when seeking to understand why people behave the way they do) are less likely to communicate effectively. This error too readily results in communicating blame or credit to individuals for outcomes. A related attribution error is the self-serving bias (communicating personal responsibility for good performance but denying responsibility for poor performance). (See Chapter 3.)

In addition to these underlying interpersonal communication hurdles, there also are some direct hurdles. Most of them are caused, at least in part, by one or more of the underlying hurdles.

Communication Approach   We identified several basic interpersonal communication approaches—assertive, nonassertive, passive–aggressive, and aggressive—early in the chapter. With the exception of the assertive approach, they are characterized by transmission and reception processes that create potential hurdles to effective communication between two or more individuals. For example, the aggressive approach creates communication hurdles by criticizing, belittling, reprimanding, threatening, failing to be open to options, stressing conformity, focusing on weaknesses, and the like.[12]

Noise   Any interference with the intended message in the channel represents **noise.** A radio playing loud music while someone is trying to talk to someone else is an example of noise. Noise sometimes can be overcome by repeating the message or increasing the intensity (for example, the volume) of the message.

Semantics   The special meanings assigned to words is called **semantics.** However, the same words may mean different things to different people.[13] Consider this comment by Jing, a manager, to Phil: How about the report for production planning? Don't they want it soon! She could have intended one of several meanings in her comment to Phil.

Directing: You should get the report to me now. That's an order.

Suggesting: I suggest that we consider getting the report out now.

Requesting: Can you do the report for me now? Let me know if you can't.

Informing: A report is needed soon by production planning.

Questioning: Does production planning want the report soon?[14]

Consider the semantics for basic words such as *sale, airport,* and *train* in the following organizations. At Digital Equipment Corporation, a sale to the indirect marketing organization happens when a distributor or reseller orders a computer.

To direct marketing (sells to the ultimate customer), a sale occurs only when the end customer takes delivery. Even within direct marketing, there are differences of opinion: Salespeople record a sale when the order is placed, manufacturing and logistics when the product is delivered, and finance when it is paid for. At American Airlines, some managers argue that an airport is any location to which American has scheduled service; others count an airport as any facility granted that status by the international standards body. At Union Pacific Railroad, there's little consensus on what a train is. Is it a locomotive, all cars actually moved from an origin to a destination, or a scheduling sheet?[15]

Language Routines   A person's verbal and nonverbal communication patterns that have become habits are **language routines.**[16] They can be observed by the ways that employees greet one another each morning. In many instances, language routines are quite useful because they reduce the amount of thinking time needed to produce common messages. They also provide predictability in terms of being able to anticipate what was going to be said and how it was going to be said. The unique culture of Ford Motor Company and its identity is reinforced through language routines, including slogans such as "Quality is Job 1."

Conversely, language routines sometimes cause discomfort, offend, and alienate when they put down or discriminate against others. Many demeaning stereotypes of individuals and groups are perpetuated through language routines.[17] The following Diversity in Practice feature provides examples of the stereotypic biases and several language routines used to communicate some of those stereotypes. This feature is based on specific incidents reported by Dr. Alan Weis, an organizational consultant.

DIVERSITY IN PRACTICE

Communicating Biases

The anecdotes and accounts presented are from some of the best run and most successful organizations in the United States. In a group of all white men, one participant responsible for interviewing candidates in research and technical areas reported that "if I see ten candidates, only one is likely to be a minority, and that person will never be the best of the group." I asked, "Do you mean because he or she is a minority, that person will not be the best?" He replied, "Absolutely." To my greater astonishment, not one of the other fourteen people in the room saw fit to contradict or qualify that statement.

In a group of women, a woman silenced the room during her revelation that she was four months pregnant and afraid to tell anyone in her work unit. "I wake up every morning praying that I don't 'show' for a little while longer," she explained. Although the company has a competitive family leave program, all the women acknowledged that there was intense pressure from superiors to return to work as soon as possible, despite the provisions in the leave policy. (And it was a "career-ender" for a man to use the family leave policy.) A group of minorities and women stated flatly that "we have to be twice as good as the white males to obtain equivalent positions." When I asked if they felt that this was an arrogant attitude and whether it was difficult to arise every morning feeling you have to be twice as good just to be treated equally, a woman responded—to applause from
—*Continued*

DIVERSITY IN PRACTICE—*Continued*

the group—"That's the way it is, so why be bitter about it? Let's just get on with work, whatever the rules may be."

African-American men repeatedly cited instances during interviews of white males approaching them when talking in an all-black group and asking, "Hey, what are you guys up to?" Although stated jokingly, the respondents pointed out that there was never an analogous situation when a group of white males were clustered in discussion. "It's as if we were engaged in some drug deal going down right in the hallway," stated one interviewee. Asian-Americans frequently cited "labeling" which included two career-stopping elements: "Asians are excellent in technical areas, but are unable to serve as leaders because they cannot muster the assertiveness necessary to confront tough situations." Consequently, Asian-Americans were relegated to technical areas with career paths that excluded management positions.[18]

Lying and Distortion   The extreme form of deception in which the sender states what is believed to be false in order to seriously mislead one or more receivers is **lying.** The intention to deceive implies a belief that the receiver will accept the lie as a fact. In contrast, **honesty** means that the sender abides by consistent and rational ethical principles to respect the truth. Everyday social flattery in conversations usually isn't completely honest, but it is normally considered acceptable and rarely regarded as dishonest (lying).[19] **Distortion** represents a wide range of messages that a sender may use between the extremes of lying and complete honesty. Of course, the use of vague, ambiguous, or indirect language doesn't necessarily indicate the sender's intent to mislead.[20] This form of language may be viewed as acceptable political behavior (see Chapter 9). Not wanting to look incompetent or take on a manager in a departmental meeting, a subordinate may remain quiet instead of expressing an opinion or asking a question.[21]

Personal distortion in interpersonal communications may occur through **impression management,** or the process by which a sender consciously attempts to influence the perceptions that the receivers form (see Chapter 3). Three impression management strategies are commonly used:

- *ingratiation*, which involves using flattery, supporting others' opinions, doing favors, laughing excessively at others' jokes, and so on;

- *self-promotion*, which involves describing one's personal attributes to others in a highly positive and exaggerated way; and

- *facesaving*, which involves using various tactics, such as (1) apologizing in a way to convince others that the bad outcome isn't a fair indication of what the sender is really like as a person; (2) making excuses to others by admitting that one's behavior in some way caused a negative outcome, but strongly suggesting that the sender isn't really as much to blame as it seems (because the outcome wasn't intentional or there were extenuating circumstances); or (3) presenting justifications to others by appearing to accept responsibility for an outcome, but denying that the outcome actually led to problems.[22]

Impression management strategies can range from relatively harmless and minor forms of distortion (being courteous to another even if you don't like the individual) to messages that use extreme ingratiation and self-promotion to obtain a better raise or promotion relative to others. The personal ethics and self-awareness of the sender and the political nature of the individual's organization (see Chapter 9) combine to influence the degree to which distortion tactics are used.[23] In brief, the greater the frequency of distortion tactics and the more they approach the lying end of the distortion continuum, the more they will serve as a hurdle to interpersonal communication.

■ CULTURAL HURDLES

Culture refers to the distinctive ways that different populations, societies or smaller groups organize their lives or activities. **Intercultural communication** occurs whenever a message sent by a member of one culture is received and understood by a member of another culture.[24] The effects of cultural differences on hurdles to interpersonal communications can be wide ranging. They depend on the degree of difference (or similarity) between people in terms of language, religious beliefs, economic beliefs, social values, physical characteristics, use of nonverbal cues, and the like. The greater the differences, the greater are the hurdles to achieving intercultural communication.

Cultural Context   The conditions that surround and influence the life of an individual, group, or organization is its **cultural context.** Differences in cultural context may represent a hurdle to intercultural communication. Nations' cultures vary on a continuum from low context to high context.[25] Figure 13.3 shows the approximate placement of various countries along this continuum. In a **high-context culture,** interpersonal communication is characterized by (1) the establishment of social trust before engaging in work-related discussions, (2) the value placed on personal relationships and goodwill, and (3) the importance of the surrounding circumstances during an interaction. People rely on paraphrasing, tone of voice, gesture, posture, social status, history, and social setting to interpret spoken words. High-context communication requires time. Factors such as trust, relationships between friends and family members, personal needs and difficulties, weather, and holidays must be considered. For example, Japanese executives—when meeting foreign executives for the first time—do not immediately "get down to business." There is a period of building trust and getting to know each other that foreign executives often are impatient with but must conform to.

In contrast, a **low-context culture** is characterized by (1) directly and immediately addressing the tasks, issues, or problems at hand; (2) the high value placed on personal expertise and performance; and (3) the importance of clear, precise, and speedy interactions. The *One-Minute Manager,* a management best seller in North America, promotes a managerial approach based on low-context communication. The book describes how a manager can motivate employees with one-minute statements focusing on positive or corrective feedback and goal setting.[26] In a heterogeneous country, such as the United States, multiple subcultures have their own unique characteristics. In contrast, the cultural context of a homogeneous country, such as Japan, reflects the more uniform characteristics of its people.

Let's now consider three of the challenges in cross-cultural nonverbal communication—body language, personal space around an individual, and ethno-

■ FIGURE 13.3   Examples of Cultures on the Cultural Context Continuum

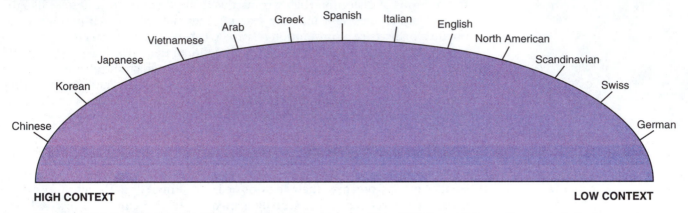

HIGH CONTEXT   **LOW CONTEXT**

Source: Based on Hall, E. *Understanding Cultural Differences.* Yarmouth, Me.: Intercultural Press, 1989; Munter, M. Cross-culture communication for managers, *Business Horizons,* May–June 1993, 67–78.

centrism.[27] While considering them, we give some tips for nonverbal communication across cultures.

Body Language   Ideas of appropriate posture, gestures, eye contact, facial expression, touching, voice pitch and volume, and speaking rate differ from one culture to another. As a simple but potentially disastrous example, nodding the head up and down in Bulgaria means "no," not "yes." In cross-cultural communication, you must avoid using any gestures considered rude or insulting. For instance, in Buddhist cultures, the head is considered sacred, so you must never touch anyone's head. In Muslim cultures, the left hand is considered unclean, so never touch, pass, or receive with the left hand. Pointing with the index finger is rude in cultures ranging from the Sudan to Venezuela to Sri Lanka. The American circular "A-OK" gesture carries a vulgar meaning in Brazil, Paraguay, Singapore, and Russia. Crossing your ankle over your knee is rude in Indonesia, Thailand, and Syria. Pointing your index finger toward yourself insults the other person in Germany, the Netherlands, and Switzerland. Avoid placing an open hand over a closed fist in France, saying "tsk tsk" in Kenya, and whistling in India.

Prepare yourself to recognize gestures that have meaning only in the other culture. Chinese stick out their tongues to show surprise and scratch their ears and cheeks to show happiness. Japanese suck in air, hissing through their teeth to indicate embarrassment or "no." Greeks puff air after they receive a compliment. Hondurans touch a finger to the face below the eyes to indicate caution or disbelief. Finally, resist applying your own culture's nonverbal meanings to other cultures. Vietnamese may look at the ground with their heads down to show respect, not to be "shifty." Russians may exhibit less facial expression and Scandinavians fewer gestures than Americans are accustomed to, but that doesn't mean that they aren't enthusiastic.

Personal Space   A second aspect of nonverbal communication has to do with norms regarding space. North Americans generally feel comfortable in the following zones of space: 0–18 inches for intimacy only (comforting or greeting); 18 inches to 4 feet for personal space (conversing with friends); 4–12 feet for social space (conversing with strangers); and more than 12 feet for public space (standing in lobbies or reception areas). Different cultures define the acceptable extents of these zones differently. Venezuelans tend to prefer much closer personal and social space and might consider it rude if you back away. The British may prefer more distant personal and social space and might consider it rude if you move too close. Closely related to this is the concept of touch. Anglos usually avoid touching each other very much. In studies of touching behaviors, researchers observed people seated in outdoor cafes in each of four countries and counted the number of touches during one hour of conversation. The results were: San Juan, Puerto Rico, 180 touches per hour; Paris, 110 per hour; Gainesville, Florida, 1 per hour; and London, 0 per hour.

Ethnocentrism   The greatest barrier to intercultural communication occurs when a person believes: Only my culture makes sense, espouses the "right" values, and represents the "right" and logical way to behave. This type of thinking is called **ethnocentrism.** When two ethnocentric people from different cultures interact, there is little chance that they will achieve understanding. Common ethnocentric reactions to strongly differing views are anger, shock, or even amusement.[28]

Consider the intercultural communication blunders in the following Across Cultures account. It presents several incidents related to business communications with Arabs, who represent *high-context* cultural orientations. Also, ethnocentrism is reflected in all three of the blunders.

ACROSS CULTURES

Business Communication with Arabs

Richard Larson, an American businessman, wanted to sell a large quantity of automobile parts to his Arab client, Mohammed Al-Salaami. Larson faxed and phoned his client several times, but Al-Salaami postponed his decision. Eager to close the sale, Larson set a twenty-four-hour deadline for al-Salaami to decide. Deeply offended by the deadline, he took his business elsewhere. Why did Larson lose this deal? Because he didn't understand al-Salaami's cultural background and inclinations. Al-Salaami delayed a decision in order to establish trust and to investigate Larson's references—a common practice of Arab businessmen, who strive to create personal friendships with their business acquaintances.

Franz Kerr, a German executive, was transferred to Syria to manage a manufacturing plant. During his first week on the job, Kerr noticed that his employees socialized and drank tea every morning for between ten and twenty minutes—leading many to arrive well after the 8 A.M. starting time. Accustomed to punctual employees, Kerr posted a notice on the bulletin board informing the employees that their wages would be docked if they didn't begin promptly on time. Soon thereafter, Kerr began to notice that the employees weren't working as hard as they used to. In fact, they seemed to resent his presence in the plant. Kerr's mistake was not to recognize that he needed to accommodate the Arab employees' desire to socialize each morning. Kerr didn't realize that Arabs commonly socialize at the beginning of each shift. By compelling them to eliminate their morning ritual, Kerr lost their respect. Kerr should have joined the employees as they enjoyed a cup of tea during their morning gathering.

Pierre LeBlanc, a French negotiator, was invited home for dinner by Ahmet Faud, a Saudi businessman. Eager to display his appreciation for Arab culture,

—*Continued*

ACROSS CULTURES—*Continued*

LeBlanc arrived in an Arab shirt that he had purchased at the market. He was carrying a US$100 bottle of perfume and a bouquet of flowers for Faud's wife. For a while things seemed to go well. Faud and his family were very cordial that evening, and LeBlanc departed with the conviction that he was close to sealing the deal. LeBlanc was shocked the next morning when he received a call from Faud's assistant, informing him that the deal had been canceled. LeBlanc shouldn't have offered the bottle of perfume or flowers to Faud's wife. Family privacy is very important to Arabs, and the gift made Faud very uncomfortable. A more appropriate gift would have been chocolates for the entire family.[29]

INTERPERSONAL NETWORKS

An **interpersonal communication network** is the pattern of communication flows over time between individuals.[30] It focuses on communication *relationships* among them over time, rather than on the individuals themselves. Networks involve the ongoing flow of oral, written, and nonverbal signals (data) between two people or between one person and all other network members simultaneously. The concept doesn't focus on whether a specific signal sent was received as intended by the sender. However, communication networks can influence the likelihood of a match between messages as sent and as actually received and interpreted.

■ TYPES OF NETWORKS

The essentials of interpersonal communication shown in Figure 13.1 are based on the involvement of only two people. Obviously, communication often takes place among many individuals and larger groups. Claudia Gonzales, a telecommunications manager for Abaco Grupo Financiero in Mexico, normally has ongoing links with many people both inside and outside her organization. Her communication network extends laterally, vertically, and externally. *Vertical networks* typically include her immediate superior and subordinates and the superior's superiors and the subordinates' subordinates. *Lateral networks* include people in the same department at the same level (peers) and people in different departments at the same level. *External networks* include customers, suppliers, regulatory agencies, pressure groups, professional peers, and friends. Thus an employee's communication network can be quite involved. It usually is based on a combination of formally prescribed and informally developed relationships.[31]

Size limits the possible communication networks within a group. In principle, as the size of a group increases arithmetically, the number of possible communication interrelationships increases exponentially. Accordingly, communication networks are much more varied and complex in a twelve-person team than in a five-person team. Although every group member (theoretically) may be able to communicate with all the others, the direction and number of communication channels often are somewhat limited. In committee meetings, for example, varying levels of formality influence who may speak, what may be discussed, and in what order. The relative status or ranking of group members also may differ. Members having higher status probably will dominate a communication network more than those with lower status. Even when an open network is encouraged, group members may actually use a limited network arrangement.

To provide a sense of the potential and powerful effects of communication networks, let's consider a single group—which could be a work team or informal social group—of five members. This example reduces the complicating effects of multiple groups and different group sizes. A five-person group has about sixty possible communication networks but only five basic networks—the *star* (sometimes called the *wheel*), the *Y*, the *chain*, the *circle*, and the *all-channel* network— as shown in Figure 13.4. Each line between each pair of names represents two-way communication. The degree of restriction on members in communicating with each other differentiates the networks. At one extreme, the star network is the most restricted: All communication between members must flow through Jane. At the other extreme, the all-channel network is the least restricted and most open: Each member communicates with all other members directly.

◼ EFFECTS OF NETWORKS

Communication networks can affect the selection of group leaders, the ease and speed of group learning, the effectiveness and efficiency of the group, and member satisfaction with the group's progress.[32] Table 13.1 provides a brief comparison of the five basic communication networks in terms of four assessment criteria. The first criterion, *degree of centralization*, is the extent to which some group members have access to more communication possibilities than other members.

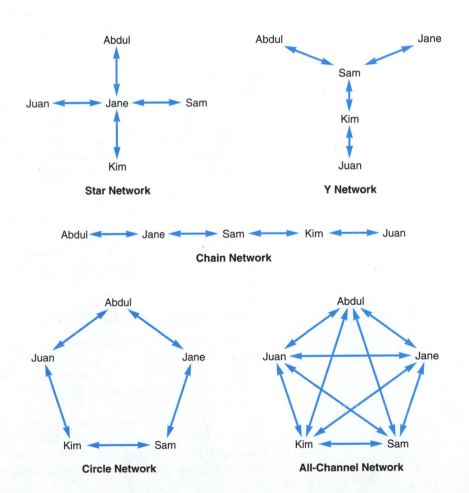

◼ **FIGURE 13.4**

Five Alternative Communication Networks for a Five-Person Group

TABLE 13.1　Effects of Five Communication Networks

FACTOR	TYPES OF COMMUNICATION NETWORKS				
	Star	Y	Chain	Circle	All-Channel
Degree of centralization	Very high	High	Moderate	Low	Very low
Leadership predictability	Very high	High	Moderate	Low	Very low
Average group satisfaction	Low	Low	Moderate	Moderate	High
Range in individual member satisfaction	High	High	Moderate	Low	Very low

The star network is the most centralized because all communication flows from and to only one member. The all-channel network is the least centralized because any member can communicate with all other members. The second criterion, *leadership predictability*, indicates the ability to anticipate which group member is likely to emerge as the leader. In Figure 13.4, the following individuals are likely to emerge as leaders: Jane in the star network, Sam in the Y network, and possibly Sam in the chain network. In each of these three networks, the anticipated leaders have more information and greater control over its dissemination than the other members.

The third and fourth assessment criteria in Table 13.1, *average group satisfaction* and *range in individual member satisfaction*, reflect the levels and range of satisfaction of group members. Several interesting relationships exist between these two criteria. In the star network, the average member satisfaction in the group is likely to be the lowest compared to the other networks. However, the range in individual member satisfaction is likely to be the highest relative to the other networks. Jane might find the star network highly satisfying, because she is the center of attention and has considerable influence over the group. In contrast, the other members are highly dependent on Jane and may well play a small role in the decision process. Accordingly, the average satisfaction of the group as a whole is likely to be relatively low. The all-channel network creates the potential for greater participation by all members in terms of their interests and abilities to contribute to the group. Average group satisfaction may be relatively high, and the range of satisfaction scores for individuals probably will be smaller than for the other networks.

■ IMPORTANCE OF NETWORKS

Knowing the types of communication networks used is especially important in understanding power and control relationships among employees in organizations.[33] Powerful individuals may limit access to information by others as one way of maintaining or increasing their power (see Chapter 9).

Problems may range from simple to complex. Simple problems, such as scheduling overtime work, make few demands on group members. Simple networks (such as superior to subordinate) often are effective for solving simple problems. However, complex problems (such as deciding whether to build a new plant) generate many decision-making demands on group members. All-channel or open networks (as in a self-managed team) often are more effective for solving complex problems.

Another factor is the degree to which members must work together to accomplish the team's tasks. With problems requiring little member interdependence, communication may be handled effectively through one of the more centralized networks. Think about various sports and the types of communication networks needed in them. In swimming, track, and golf, the coach usually is the central person in task coordination and communication. Team members can perform most of their tasks with minimal interactions with other team members. With a high degree of member interdependence—as in basketball, ice hockey, and soccer—the all-channel network is much more effective than a simple, centralized network. A complex communication network is required—both between coach and players and among players—as they perform their tasks.

Networks also are important for day-to-day communication in organizations. First, no single network is likely to prove effective in all situations for a team with a variety of tasks and goals. The apparently efficient, low-cost, and simple method of a superior instructing subordinates is likely to be ineffective if used exclusively. Dissatisfaction may become so great that members will leave the team or lose their motivation to contribute. Second, teams that face complex problems requiring high member interdependence may deal with them ineffectively because of inadequate sharing of information, consideration of alternatives, and the like. Third, a team must consider trade-offs or opportunity costs. A team committed to the exclusive use of the all-channel network may deal inefficiently with simple problems and tasks that require little member interdependence. In such cases, members also may become bored and dissatisfied with team meetings. They often simply come to feel that their time is being wasted. Another trade-off with the all-channel network is higher labor costs. That is, team members must spend more time on a problem and its solution in meetings with the all-channel network than with a star network. Hence a team should use the type of network that is most appropriate to its goals and tasks.[34]

Informal networks in many organizations often create barriers for minorities and women as they seek opportunities and representation in white male–dominated roles and departments, especially in upper level managerial networks. These informal managerial networks may value similarities among members in terms of gender, race, educational level, and the like.[35] Xerox is one of a few organizations that support the establishment of *caucus groups* as a way to manage, value, and nurture diversity. The caucus groups encourage networking to (1) link caucus members and upper management, (2) assist with personal and professional development, (3) provide support within the caucus, and (4) serve as role models to majority employees in managing diversity.[36]

■ GROUPWARE-BASED NETWORKING

An increasing range of groupware aids (information technologies) is available to support and extend interpersonal communication networks. Groupware aids (see Chapters 1 and 8) increasingly are being substituted for direct face-to-face communication. In this section, we highlight a few of the groupware aids that make it easier for people at work to communicate with one another.

Electronic mail (e-mail) is a computer-based system that enables individuals to exchange and store messages with their computers. In sophisticated e-mail systems, the user gets a digest of all the incoming mail, with headings noting the name of the sender, the time and date an item was sent, and what it is about. The user can then choose which full messages to call up. In addition to transmitting messages between employees down the hall or overseas, e-mail technology even permits computer-to-computer exchanges of purchase orders, invoices, electronic payment of bills, and so on.[37] Thus e-mail reduces barriers of time and distance in the creation of communication networks. It also minimizes "phone tag," in which individuals trade numerous phone calls before catching up with each other. According to *Fortune* magazine, 200 million e-mail messages are sent each day and the number is continuing to increase.[38]

Voice mail is a computer-based message system that people access by telephone. They may use it as they would an answering machine to receive recorded messages or as they would memorandums to send recorded messages to others. Although more expensive to operate than an e-mail system, voice mail is a richer information medium than e-mail. Voice mail is an excellent medium for sending short, simple, and noncontroversial messages.[39]

Telecommuting is the practice of working at home while being linked to the office or plant with groupware. It also includes those who work out of a customer's office or communicate with the office or plant via a laptop computer or mobile phone. Telecommuting often incorporates computer-based software, e-mail, voice mail, fax machines, and related technologies. Telecommuting jobs usually involve some combination of

- tasks that can be performed and transmitted with the use of groupware aids;
- regular telephone use;
- routine information handling;
- tasks that can be performed independently of others and, if necessary, be coordinated with others via groupware aids; and/or
- project-oriented jobs with well-defined targets and schedules.

Telecommuting jobs include salesperson, real estate agent, computer systems analyst, data entry clerk, consultant, author, security broker, and copy editor. Millions of employees have already formed telecommuting arrangements with their employers, and the number is growing. Among the more well-known companies with successful telecommuting programs for some employees are IBM, Xerox, American Express, Du Pont, Pacific Bell, J.C. Penney, and Apple Computer.[40] However, telecommuting isn't for everyone. Some telecommuters experience a sense of isolation, stagnation, or compulsive overwork. Julie Rohrer, who works full time from her home as a transcriber for a hospital in Madison, Wisconsin, says: "Every day is the same. You put in your eight hours and there isn't anybody to talk to, and you miss what's going on in the outside world. You feel you're in your house constantly."[41] Rohrer clearly misses face-to-face interactions on the job.

The potential advantages of groupware aids are fairly obvious. They allow people to communicate with one another more easily, quickly, and less expensively. However, some problems need to be guarded against. First, these aids haven't been effective for relationship building or complex team problem solving where face-to-face dialogue is needed. Brad Silverberg, a senior vice-president of Microsoft, comments, "E-mail doesn't have the nuances of real-time conversation. Senior level managers lose track of the impact their mail may have on people."[42] Second, groupware aids can break down the boundaries between work time and nonwork time. These boundaries are especially useful for many employees in managing work stress (see Chapter 7). If not managed carefully, these technologies can evolve into a continuous invasion of privacy by enabling managers and other workers to contact the employee easily at any time. Third, groupware aids may erode the delegation of authority by creating too much and too frequent communications between superiors and subordinates. That is, superiors may start to oversupervise the work of subordinates because giving and getting constant feedback is too easy. Fourth, groupware aids open the possibility of wasting time on increased volumes of meaningless data (junk) with the consequence of unnecessary work overload. Fifth, groupware aids, for most individuals, lack confidentiality. For example, most e-mail messages can easily be read by others who have computers and access to the same intranet or to the Internet.

Mr. Lynch, an executive at Auto Desk, a software maker, comments: "I get eighty e-mails a day, and sixty of them are because I'm copied from multiple levels. I can put filters on my mailbox. But, I tell my people the best filter is to show self-restraint."[43] These problems are not inevitable, and awareness is the first step in avoiding them.[44]

The following Technology in Practice selection tells how 3M is using several groupware aids—including video conferencing.

TECHNOLOGY IN PRACTICE

3M's Video Conferencing

3M currently has seventy-seven video conferencing suites around the world. The company has created a culture of video conferencing that is woven into the fabric of the corporation.

Memo Izzi is the manager of the silver halide lab at 3M's St. Paul, Minnesota, headquarters. This particular chemical compound is crucial to photography and other uses. Although Izzi is based in St. Paul, he works closely with 3M's other photographic labs around the world via video conferencing. Izzi says, "The real impetus for us to use video conferencing was the outbreak of the Gulf War in 1991. I was literally getting on a plane, heading for Europe, when my assistant had me paged and told me that the corporation had decided no employees should travel to Europe. It was a critical time in the dry halide development project and some of my key engineers were in Europe."

Izzi soon had a video conferencing linkup with 3M's photographic lab in Harlow, England. Shortly thereafter, the labs in Ferrania, Italy, Neuss, Germany, and Rochester, New York, joined in. At first the scientists were uncomfortable looking at each other—and at themselves—on television. "After all, most of our work is done in the dark," he explains. "But today we couldn't work without it."

Now when Izzi needs specific knowledge to help him out on a project, he consults 3M's corporate technical directory. This is an in-house online compendium that includes most of the staff's specialties, a cross-reference to all the company's patents, and a listing of every current research and development project worldwide. Once Izzi finds a person with the needed knowledge, he starts a dialogue by e-mail, then proceeds directly to face-to-face communication through video conferencing, no matter where the expert is located.

Izzi brings his team to the meeting via the corporation's web of Picture Tel video conferencing systems. Izzi comments, "This way I get lots of team members

—Continued

TECHNOLOGY IN PRACTICE—*Continued*

involved with the expert. Not just the one guy who would have traveled to the meeting in the past. We get a kind of teamwork that just couldn't have happened before. And we get knowledge that might come from across the country or from around the world."[45]

FOSTERING DIALOGUE

The skills and behaviors that directly foster dialogue between individuals are the focus of the remainder of this chapter. The lack of these skills and behaviors hinder or prevent dialogue. **Dialogue** is a process through which people have learned to suspend their defensive exchanges to enable a free flow of inquiry into their own and others' assumptions and beliefs. As a result, dialogue can build mutual trust and common ground.[46] A necessary condition for dialogue is assertive communication. Recall that, in the Preview Case, there was no evidence of assertive communication. True dialogue requires that interacting individuals demonstrate multiple skills and behaviors. Figure 13.5 illustrates the idea that dialogue is characterized by a specific network of skills and behaviors. They include communication openness, constructive feedback, appropriate self-disclosure, active listening, and supportive nonverbal cues.

■ COMMUNICATION OPENNESS

Communication openness may be viewed as a continuum ranging from closed, guarded, and defensive to open, candid, and nondefensive.[47] Figure 13.6 shows

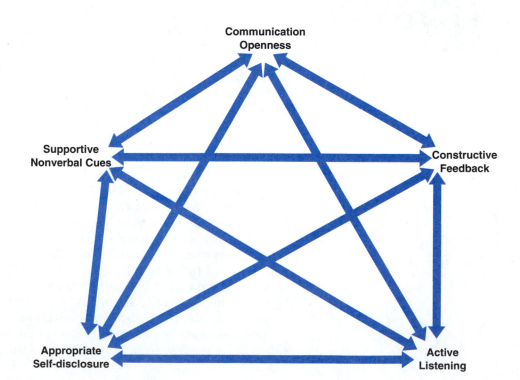

■ **FIGURE 13.5**

Network of Skills and Behaviors That Foster Dialogue

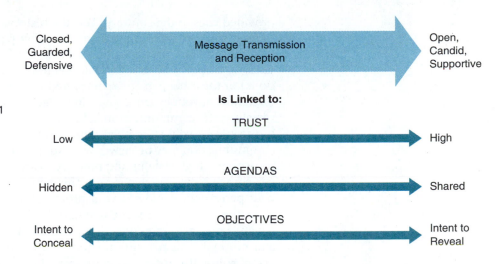

that, at the extreme left side of the continuum, every message (regardless of the medium of transmission) is weighed, analyzed, and scrutinized. Communication occurs on a direct level and a meta-communication level. **Meta-communication** is the (hidden) assumptions, inferences, and interpretations of the parties that form the basis of open messages. In closed communications, senders and receivers consciously and purposely hide their real agendas and "messages" and game playing is rampant. Meta-communications focus on inferences such as: (1) what I think you think about what I said; (2) what I think you really mean; (3) what I really mean but hope you don't realize what I mean; (4) what you're saying but what I think you really mean; and (5) what I think you're trying to tell me but aren't directly telling me because . . . (you're afraid of hurting my feelings, you think being totally open could hurt your chances of promotion, and so on). At the extreme right side of the continuum, the communications are totally open, candid, and supportive. The words and nonverbal cues sent convey an authentic message that the sender chose without a hidden agenda. The purpose of communication is to reveal intent, not conceal it. The individuals express what they mean and mean what they convey. Breakdowns in communication at this end of the continuum are due primarily to honest errors (such as the different meanings that people assign to words—for example, *soon* or *immediately*). Communication openness usually is a matter of degree rather than an absolute. The nature of language, linguistics, and different interpersonal relationships (co-worker to co-worker, subordinate to superior, friend to friend, or spouse to spouse) create the situational forces that allow for degrees of shading, coloring, amplification, and deflection in the use of words and nonverbal cues as symbols of meaning.

Contextual Factors   The degree of openness must be considered in relation to the context associated with such openness. (We addressed contextual factors at length in Chapter 9 in terms of power and political behavior, Chapter 12 in terms of conflict and negotiation, and Chapter 17 in terms of organizational culture.) We note just three of these factors here briefly. First, the history of the relationship is perhaps the most significant factor affecting trust and risk taking in interpersonal communication. Has the other person violated your or others' trust in the past? Has the other person provided cues (verbal and/or nonverbal) soliciting or reinforcing your attempts to be open and candid? Or has the other person provided cues to the contrary? Has the history of the relationship created a level of such comfort that both you and the other person can focus on direct communication, rather than meta-communication?[48] Second, if the communication is likely to be partly adversarial (such as union and management in wage negotiations) or the other person is committed to damaging or weakening your position or gaining at your expense, engaging in guarded communication is rational. Conversely, if the communication is likely to be friendly and the other person is trying to please you, strengthen your position, or enhance your esteem, guarded communication may be viewed as irrational. Third, when you communicate with someone of higher status and power, you are communicating with someone who has some control over your fate. This person may be responsible for appraising your performance, judging your promotability, and determining the amount of your merit pay increase. The tendency is to project a favorable image, to encode negative messages in euphemisms and qualifiers, which may be understandable and rational. This perception is especially valid if past encounters reinforce the use of some distortion over completely honest disclosures.[49] Consider the comment by a top manager of a Fortune 500 company:

> Listen, I've attended enough seminars and read enough self-help books to know that relationships ought to be based on honesty, mutual support, and open communications. But I've also managed long enough in this company and other companies to know that complete honesty can hurt both parties and the organization. The principle isn't always worth the cost of hurt feelings and ruined relationships.[50]

An individual or organization that fosters communication openness faces the potential of a few individuals—either within or outside the organization—exploiting such openness. As suggested in the following Ethics in Practice piece, individuals need to recognize how openness of communication in one context may be used by others to gain access to private information about them. Consider the experience of John Kaufman.

ETHICS IN PRACTICE

Individual Privacy Versus Openness

John Kaufman was well aware that his postings and ruminations were considered public on Usenet, a global bulletin board made up of more than 15,000 separate discussion groups on every topic imaginable. He was surprised by the ease with which someone who had taken such an overwhelming interest in his life was able to track down everything he'd ever said online.

The story Kaufman relates started innocently enough: He had posted a note on a local computer bulletin board about a program he wanted to sell. A woman e-mailed that she was interested. They agreed on a price. A few days later, she stopped by his apartment to pick it up. Everything seemed normal, he said, until the next day. "She sent me e-mail saying she'd conducted a search of Usenet, looking at the posts I'd made, and she was very interested in me and the things I'd done," Kaufman said.

A San Francisco-based writer, Kaufman's words have appeared in numerous national magazines. They also appear in many areas of the Internet, where he takes part in many of the free-floating conversations on Usenet.   *—Continued*

ETHICS IN PRACTICE—*Continued*

It was those words that came back to haunt him when his admirer began sending him daily e-mail messages. They often commented on things he'd posted in newsgroups on topics ranging from Latin American politics to the weather in the Shetland Islands. Finally, she sent a message that shook him—a three-page letter that basically was a dossier of his entire life. "When this thing flashed on the screen, my mouth dropped open," he said. "Here was a total stranger who knew my cat's name."

Lori Fena, director of an online rights organization comments, "I think this is a situation where there has been a great step forward in technology, but how we absorb it into society and use it responsibly hasn't quite been defined yet. The rules have changed, but people's actions haven't changed." "Before," she said of posting, "it was a public act in a private room. These new search engines are going back into those private rooms, listening to the recordings and making everything said there available to everyone else."[51]

■ CONSTRUCTIVE FEEDBACK

In giving feedback, people share their thoughts and feelings about others with them. Feedback may involve personal feelings or abstract thoughts, as when someone reacts to others' ideas or proposals. The emotional impact of feedback varies according to how personally it is focused. When you attempt to achieve dialogue, feedback should be supportive (reinforcing ongoing behavior) or corrective (indicating that a change in behavior is appropriate). The following are principles of constructive feedback that can foster dialogue.

- Constructive feedback is based on a foundation of trust between sender and receiver. What happens if the organization is characterized by extreme personal competitiveness? There is an emphasis on the use of power to punish and control, rigid superior–subordinate relationships, and a lack of trust for constructive feedback.

- Constructive feedback is specific rather than general. It uses clear and recent examples. Saying, You are a dominating person, is not as useful as saying, Just now when we were deciding the issue, you did not listen to what others said. I felt I had to accept your argument or face attack from you.

- Constructive feedback is given at a time when the receiver appears to be ready to accept it. When a person is angry, upset, or defensive, that probably isn't the time to bring up other, new issues.

- Constructive feedback is checked with the receiver to determine whether it seems valid. The sender can ask the receiver to rephrase and restate the feedback to test whether it matches what the sender intended.

- Constructive feedback covers behaviors that the receiver may be capable of doing something about.

- Constructive feedback doesn't include more than the receiver can handle at any particular time. For example, the receiver may become threatened and defensive if the feedback includes everything the receiver does that annoys the sender.[52]

Constructively sharing how you feel helps others examine their behaviors. However, people who are given and accept accurate feedback don't necessarily change their behaviors. Individual change usually isn't that easy. Consider this description of how one manager, who was eventually fired, communicated and provided destructive feedback:

> He is a great strategic thinker, . . . but he lashes out at people, he can't build trusting relationships. He is very smart, but he achieves superiority through demeaning others. He is abusive, he hits people with intellectual lightning. He instinctively goes after people. Many people have tried to work on this flaw because he has such extraordinary skills, but it seems hopeless.[53]

■ APPROPRIATE SELF-DISCLOSURE

Self-disclosure is any information that individuals communicate (verbally or nonverbally) about themselves to others. People often unconsciously disclose much about themselves by what they say and how they present themselves to others.[54] The ability to express yourself to others usually is basic to personal growth and development. The relationship between self-disclosure and effectiveness in an organization appears to be curvilinear. Nondisclosing individuals may repress their real feelings because to reveal them is threatening. Conversely, total-disclosure individuals, who expose a great deal about themselves to anyone they meet, actually may be unable to communicate with others because they are too preoccupied with themselves. The presence of appropriate self-disclosure, say, between superior and subordinate or team members and customers, can facilitate dialogue and sharing of work-related problems. The ties among personality and self-disclosure have been expressed as follows:

> Healthy personality is manifested by a model of what we call authenticity, or more simply, honesty. Less healthy personalities, people who function less than fully, who suffer recurrent breakdowns or chronic impasses, may usually be found to be liars. They say things they do not mean. Their disclosures have been chosen more for cosmetic value than for truth. The consequences of a lifetime of lying about oneself to others, of saying and doing things for their sound and appearance, is that ultimately the person loses contact with his or her real self. The authentic being manifested by healthier personalities takes the form of unself-conscious disclosure of self in words, decisions, and actions.[55]

A person's level in the organization often complicates self-disclosure. Individuals are likely to dampen self-disclosure to those with higher formal power because of their ability to give raises and promotions or demotions and dismissals. Even when a subordinate is able and willing to engage in "appropriate" forms of self-disclosure at work, a perception of the superior's trustworthiness in not using the revealed information to punish, intimidate, or ridicule is likely to influence the amount and form of self-disclosure.

■ ACTIVE LISTENING

Active listening is necessary to encourage maximum levels of feedback and openness. **Listening** is a process that integrates physical, emotional, and intellectual inputs in a search for meaning and understanding.[56] Listening is effective when the receiver understands the sender's message as intended.

As much as 40 percent of an eight-hour work day of many employees is devoted to listening. However, tests of listening comprehension suggest that people often listen at only 25 percent efficiency.[57] Listening skills influence the quality of peer, manager–subordinate, and employee–customer relationships. Employees who dislike a manager may find it extremely difficult to listen attentively to the manager's comments during performance review sessions. The following guidelines are suggested for increasing listening skills to foster dialogue.

- Active listening involves having a reason or purpose for listening. Good listeners tend to search for value and meaning in what is being said, even if they are not predisposed to be interested in the particular issue or topic. Poor listeners tend to rationalize any or all inattention on the basis of a lack of initial interest.

- Active listening involves suspending judgment, at least initially. Good listening requires concentrating on the sender's whole message, rather than forming evaluations on the basis of the first few ideas presented.

- Active listening involves resisting distractions, such as noises, sights, and other people, and focusing on the sender.

- Active listening involves pausing before responding to the sender.

- Active listening involves rephrasing in your own words the content and feeling of what the sender seems to be saying, especially when the message is emotional or unclear.

- Active listening seeks out the sender's important themes in terms of the overall content and feeling of the message.

- Active listening involves using the time differential between the rate of thought (400 or 500 words per minute) and the rate of speech (100 to 150 words per minute) to reflect on content and search for meaning.[58]

Most of these active listening skills are interrelated. That is, you can't practice one without improving the others. Unfortunately, like the guidelines for improving feedback, the guidelines for improving active listening are much easier to understand than to develop and practice. The more you practice active listening skills, the more likely you will be able to enter into effective dialogue. The following Quality in Practice account relates how several top executives at Pillsbury introduced a system that encourages listening to lower level employees, who are viewed as key *internal customers* by top management.

QUALITY IN PRACTICE

Pillsbury's Special Listening System

Pillsbury and a few other companies are encouraging employees to telephone a third party anonymously. Every word of every call is transcribed. Every transcript reaches the hands of Pillsbury Chief Executive Paul Walsh and other managers, as appropriate. Lou de Ocejo, the vice president for human resources comments: "The No. 1 objective was for the senior management of this company to have employees get in our face."

The InTouch phone number and the Pillsbury identification code were printed on stickers, wallet cards and ultimately refrigerators magnets. "We wanted people to call whenever a thought hit them," says Karen Gustafson, director of employee communications.

—Continued

QUALITY IN PRACTICE—*Continued*

When de Ocejo and the top managers began reading the transcripts, they were stunned to see how much genuinely useful knowledge had been bottled up by fear of ridicule or recrimination. One caller pointed out that the time clock was running five minutes fast at the Pillsbury bakery in Eden Prairie, Minnesota. Another employee suggested a new topping for a Pillsbury frozen pizza. Callers identified retail locations where a certain product wasn't on the shelf. A ground swell against lags in expense reimbursement caused the company to overhaul the way people accounted for travel and entertainment costs. Existing communication channels—a whistle-blower hot line for reporting fraud, for instance, and the usual suggestion-box programs—did nothing to turn dissent into constructive feedback. The InTouch phone system allows anyone with a corporate pass code to call at any time on any subject from any telephone. Pillsbury employees sound off to a recording machine. The transcripts do not even identify the gender of the caller.

Understandably, some middle managers resent responding to top management regarding messages from nameless messengers, but others are positive. A plant manager in Tennessee being second-guessed by higher management for shutting down in a snowstorm became a hero at headquarters after dozens of appreciative employees phoned. Pillsbury's top management recognizes that an anonymous phone call is inferior to an open face-to-face discussion. But, some employees, because of fear or distrust, are reluctant to be as open in their communication as desired by higher management. This program gives those employees an alternative and helps convince others throughout the organization of the need to encourage feedback and to actively listen to it.[59]

NONVERBAL COMMUNICATION

Nonverbal communication includes nonlanguage human responses (such as body motions and personal physical attributes) and environmental effects (such as a large or small office). Nonverbal cues may contain many hidden messages and can influence the process and outcome of face-to-face communication. Even a person who is silent or inactive in the presence of others may be sending a message, which may or may not be the intended message (including boredom, fear, anger, or depression).[60]

■ TYPES OF NONVERBAL CUES

The basic types of nonverbal cues are presented in Table 13.2, along with the numerous ways people can and do communicate without saying or writing a word. Nonverbal communication is important to verbal communication in that neither is adequate by itself for effective dialogue. Verbal and nonverbal cues can be related by

- *repeating,* as when verbal directions to some location are accompanied by pointing;
- *contradicting,* as in the case of the person who says, What, me nervous? while fidgeting and perspiring anxiously before taking a test—a good example of

how the nonverbal message might be more believable when verbal and nonverbal signals disagree;

- *substituting* nonverbal for verbal cues, as when an employee returns to the office with a stressful expression that says, I've had a horrible meeting with my manager, without a word being spoken; and

- *complementing* the verbal cue through nonverbal "underlining," as when a person pounds the table, places a hand on the shoulder of a co-worker, uses a tone of voice indicating the great importance attached to the message, or presents a gift as a way of reinforcing an expression of gratitude or respect.[61]

Nonverbal cues have been linked to a wide variety of concepts and issues. We briefly consider two: (1) status, in terms of the relative ranking of individuals and groups; and (2) gender differences.

■ NONVERBAL CUES AND STATUS

The following are only three of the many relationships between nonverbal cues and organizational status.

- Employees of higher status typically have better offices than employees of lower status. For example, executive offices at EDS are more spacious, located on the top floors of the building, and have finer carpets and furniture than those of first-line managers. Most senior offices at EDS are at the corners, so they have windows on two sides.

- The offices of higher status employees are better "protected" than those of lower status employees. Here, *protected* means how much more difficult it would be for you to arrange to visit the governor of your state than for the governor to arrange to visit you. Top executive areas are typically least accessible and are often sealed off from others by several doors and assistants. Even lower level managers and many staff personnel are protected by having an office with a door and a secretary who answers the telephone.

- The higher the employee's status, the easier that employee finds it to invade the territory of lower status employees. A superior typically feels free to walk

TABLE 13.2	**Basic Types of Nonverbal Cues**
TYPE OF CUE	**EXPLANATION AND EXAMPLES**
Body motion	Gestures, facial expressions, eye behavior, touching, and any other movement of the limbs and body
Personal physical characteristics	Body shape, physique, posture, body or breath odors, height, weight, hair color, and skin color
Paralanguage	Voice qualities, volume, speech rate, pitch, nonfluencies (saying "ah," "um," or "uh"), laughing, yawning, and so on
Use of space	Ways people use and perceive space, including seating arrangements, conversational distance, and the "territorial" tendency of humans to stake out a personal space
Physical environment	Building and room design, furniture and other objects, interior decorating, cleanliness, lighting, and noise
Time	Being late or early, keeping others waiting, cultural differences in time perception, and the relationship between time and status

right in on subordinates, whereas subordinates are more careful to ask permission or make an appointment before visiting a superior.[62]

Carried to excess, these and other nonverbal status cues are likely to create barriers to dialogue, especially from the perspective of the employees with lower formal status. However, effective managers often use supportive nonverbal cues when meeting with subordinates, such as (1) lightly touching subordinates on the arm when they arrive and shaking hands, (2) smiling appropriately, (3) nodding to affirm what was said, (4) slightly pulling their chairs closer to subordinates and maintaining an open posture, and (5) engaging in eye contact to further demonstrate listening and interest.[63]

■ NONVERBAL CUES AND GENDER DIFFERENCES

Physical differences between women and men contribute to differences in their nonverbal behaviors. However, they are minor compared to the differences based on cultural influences. In addition to communicating gender, body language may communicate status and power. Many signs of dominance and submission are exchanged through nonverbal communication. Some nonverbal behaviors are associated with the subordinate position of either gender. But many of these same behaviors have been associated with women, regardless of status. In this section, we describe three nonverbal patterns and note how they may differ by gender.[64] These patterns reflect generalities and certainly do not apply to all men and women. Moreover, we know that in some segments of the U.S. and Canadian societies, these patterns have changed or are changing.

Use of Space   Women's bodily behavior more often is restrained and restricted than men's. In fact, their femininity is gauged by how little space they occupy. Masculinity is judged by men's expansiveness and the strength of their gestures. Men control greater territory and personal space, a property associated with dominance and status. Studies have found that people tend to approach women more closely than men, seat themselves closer to women, and cut across women's paths in hallways, and so on.

Eye Contact   Gender may influence eye contact. In personal interactions, women tend to look more at the other person than men do—and they maintain more woman-to-woman eye contact. Some research suggests that women are more skilled than men in accurately decoding nonverbal cues.[65] People tend to maintain more eye contact with those from whom they want approval. Women are stared at and reciprocate by not looking back more than men. Men routinely stare at women in public. Our language even has specific words, ogling and leering, for this practice.

Touching   Touching may be another gesture of dominance. Cuddling in response to touch may be a corresponding gesture of submission. Just as a manager can put a hand on a worker, a master on a servant, and a teacher on a student, so men frequently put their hands on women.

Another side to touching is much better understood: Touching symbolizes friendship and intimacy. The power aspect of touching doesn't rule out its intimacy aspect. A particular touch may have both components and more, but it is the pattern of touching between individuals that tells us the most about their relationship. When touching is reciprocal—that is, when both people have equal touching privileges—we have information about the intimacy of the relationship. Much touching indicates closeness, whereas little touching indicates distance. The freedom of one person to touch the other but not vice versa provides information about status and power. The person with greater touching privileges probably has higher status or more power. Consider the experience of one information systems (IS) manager. He found himself the subject of a sexual harassment complaint. The IS manager, who wants to remain anonymous, says that he was training a female software engineer. While she sat at her workstation, he stood behind her and briefly put his hand on her shoulder. He says, "When I was called down to human resources and told about my inappropriate behavior I was stunned. Now, I keep my distance—literally. I stand three feet away with my hands in my pockets."[66] Nonverbal communication can, indeed, have powerful consequences.

Changing Patterns   Many women have been reversing these nonverbal interaction patterns. Women now feel freer to stop smiling when they are unhappy, stop lowering their eyes, stop getting out of men's way on the street, and stop letting themselves be interrupted. They can stare people in the eye, address someone by first name if that person addresses them by their first name, and touch when they feel that it is appropriate. Men need to become more aware of what they are signifying nonverbally. Men can restrain their invasions of personal space by avoiding staring, touching (if not by mutual consent), and interrupting.[67]

CHAPTER SUMMARY

Individuals increase their own sense of well-being and become more productive when they engage in effective interpersonal communication. The essential elements in the communication process—senders, receivers, transmitters, receptors, messages, channels, noise, meaning, encoding, decoding, and feedback—are interrelated. Individuals may approach communication differently by being assertive, nonassertive, or aggressive.

Face-to-face interpersonal communication has the highest degree of information richness. An information-rich medium is especially important for performing complex tasks and resolving social and emotional issues that involve considerable uncertainty and ambiguity. Important issues usually contain significant amounts of uncertainty, ambiguity, and people-related (especially social and emotional) problems.

There are many potential hurdles to effective interpersonal communication. We briefly reviewed the underlying interpersonal hurdles discussed in previous chapters. Direct hurdles include the nonassertive and aggressive communication approaches, noise, semantics, demeaning language, and lying and distortion. The hurdles stemming from cultural differences always is present. They may be especially high when the interaction takes place between individuals from high-context and low-context cultures.

Through their many communication networks, individuals may repeat the interpersonal communication process dozens of times each day. These networks operate both vertically and laterally. They can range from closed and centralized to open and decentralized and may hinder or support organizational diversity. Groupware-based networking by means of e-mail, voice mail, teleconferencing, and telecommuting is now quite common. The skills and behaviors that foster dialogue include communication openness, constructive feedback, active listening, appropriate self-disclosure, and supportive nonverbal cues. Nonverbal cues play a powerful role in fostering dialogue, either supporting or contradicting what is being said. For example, formal organizational status often is tied to nonverbal cues, and status and gender differences in the use of nonverbal cues exist. If not used appropriately, nonverbal cues will hinder dialogue.

KEY TERMS AND CONCEPTS

Aggressive communication	High-context culture	Media richness
Assertive communication	Honesty	Messages
Channels	Impression management	Meta-communication
Cultural context	Intercultural communication	Noise
Data	Interpersonal communication	Nonassertive communication
Decoding	Interpersonal communication	Nonverbal communication
Dialogue	network	Receptors
Distortion	Language routines	Self-disclosure
Electronic mail (E-mail)	Listening	Semantics
Encoding	Low-context culture	Telecommuting
Ethnocentrism	Lying	Transmitters
Feedback	Meaning	Voice mail

DISCUSSION QUESTIONS

1. Give an example of your use of assertive or aggressive communication. What was the result?

2. Give two examples of how interpersonal classroom communication is likely to vary in a high-context culture and in a low-context culture.

3. Describe your communication network. Would you like to make any changes in it? Why or why not?

4. What types of problems are less likely to be communicated effectively by e-mail than in face-to-face discussion? What are three ethical concerns with e-mail?

5. Think of an organization or team of which you are a member. How would you assess it in terms of the continuum of communication openness? (See Figure 13.6.)

6. What types of issues limit appropriate self-disclosure between you and an important person in your work life?

7. How are constructive feedback skills and active listening similar and different?

8. Describe the common nonverbal cues used by someone you have worked for or by someone you know well. Are they usually consistent or inconsistent with that person's verbal expressions? Explain.

9. If your job immerses you in a foreign culture, what communication practices must you be sensitive to?

10. If you are supervised by a person of a different gender, what nonverbal problems might you encounter?

■ Developing Competencies

Self-Insight: Individual Communication Practices[68]

Instructions

This survey is designed to assess your interpersonal communication practices. For each item on the survey, you are requested to indicate which of the alternative reactions would be more characteristic of the way you would handle the situation described. Some alternatives may be equally characteristic of you or equally uncharacteristic. Although this is a possibility, please choose the alternative that is relatively more characteristic of you. For each item, you will have five points that you may distribute in any of the following combinations, where 5 = most characteristic and 0 = least characteristic. The following are example responses.

	A	B
1.	5	0
2.	4	1
3.	3	2
4.	2	3
5.	1	4
6.	0	5

Thus, there are six possible combinations for responding to the pair of alternatives presented to you with each survey item. Be sure the numbers you assign to each pair sum to 5. To the extent possible, please relate each situation in the survey to your own personal experience. In this survey, we alternate the words he/she and him/her to include both the feminine and masculine genders with balanced frequency.

1. If a friend of mine had a personality conflict with a mutual acquaintance of ours with whom it was important for her to get along, I would:

    _____ A. Tell my friend that I felt she was partially responsible for any problems with this other person and try to let her know how the person was being affected by her.

    _____ B. Not get involved because I would not be able to continue to get along with both of them once I had entered into the conflict.

2. If one of my friends and I had a heated argument in the past and I realized that he was ill at ease around me from that time on, I would:

    _____ A. Avoid making things worse by discussing his behavior and just let the whole thing drop.

    _____ B. Bring up his behavior and ask him how he felt the argument had affected our relationship.

3. If a friend began to avoid me and act in an aloof and withdrawn manner, I would:

    _____ A. Tell her about her behavior and suggest she tell me what was on her mind.

    _____ B. Follow her lead and keep our contacts brief and aloof since that seems to be what she wants.

4. If two of my friends and I were talking and one of my friends slipped and brought up a personal problem of mine that involved the other friend, and of which he was not yet aware, I would:

    _____ A. Change the subject and signal my friend to do the same.

    _____ B. Fill in my uninformed friend on what the other friend was talking about and suggest that we go into it later.

5. If a friend were to tell me that, in her opinion, I was doing things that made me less effective than I might be in social situations, I would:

    _____ A. Ask her to spell out or describe what she has observed and suggest changes I might make.

    _____ B. Resent the criticism and let her know why I behave the way I do.

6. If one of my friends aspired to an office in our student organization for which I felt he was unqualified and if he had been tentatively assigned to that position by the president of the student society, I would:

    _____ A. Not mention my misgivings to either my friend or the president and let them handle it in their own way.

    _____ B. Tell my friend and the president of my misgivings and then leave the final decision up to them.

7. If I felt that one of my friends was being unfair to me and her other friends, but none of them had mentioned anything about it, I would:

    _____ A. Ask several of those people how they perceived the situation to see if they felt she was being unfair.

    _____ B. Not ask the others how they perceived our friend but wait for them to bring it up to me.

8. If I were preoccupied with some personal matters and a friend told me that I had become irritated with him and others and that I was jumping on him for unimportant things, I would:

    _____ A. Tell him I was preoccupied and would probably be on edge a while and would prefer not to be bothered.

    _____ B. Listen to his complaints but not try to explain my actions to him.

9. If I had heard some friends discussing an ugly rumor about a friend of mine that I knew could hurt her and she asked me what I knew about it, if anything, I would:

    _____ A. Say I didn't know anything about it and tell her no one would believe a rumor like that anyway.

    _____ B. Tell her exactly what I had heard, when I had heard it, and from whom I had heard it.

10. If a friend pointed out the fact that I had a personality conflict with another friend with whom it was important for me to get along, I would:

    _____ A. Consider his comments out of line and tell him I didn't want to discuss the matter any further.

    _____ B. Talk about it openly with him to find out how my behavior was being affected by this.

11. If my relationship with a friend has been damaged by repeated arguments on an issue of importance to us both, I would:

    _____ A. Be cautious in my conversations with her so the issue would not come up again to worsen our relationship.

    _____ B. Point to the problems the controversy was causing in our relationship and suggest that we discuss it until we get it resolved.

12. If in a personal discussion with a friend about his problems and behavior, he suddenly suggested we discuss my problems and behavior as well as his own, I would:

    _____ A. Try to keep the discussion away from me by suggesting that other, closer friends often talked to me about such matters.

    _____ B. Welcome the opportunity to hear what he felt about me and encourage his comments.

13. If a friend of mine began to tell me about her hostile feelings about another friend who she felt was being unkind to others (and I wholeheartedly agreed), I would:

    _____ A. Listen and also express my own feelings to her so she would know where I stood.

    _____ B. Listen but not express my own negative views and opinions because she might repeat what I said to her in confidence.

14. If I thought an ugly rumor was being spread about me and suspected that one of my friends had quite likely heard it, I would:

    _____ A. Avoid mentioning the issue and leave it to him to tell me about it if he wanted to.

    _____ B. Risk putting him on the spot by asking him directly what he knew about the whole thing.

15. If I had observed a friend in social situations and thought that she was doing a number of things that hurt her relationships, I would:

    _____ A. Risk being seen as a busybody and tell her what I had observed and my reactions to it.

    _____ B. Keep my opinions to myself, rather than be seen as interfering in things that are none of my business.

16. If two friends and I were talking and one of them inadvertently mentioned a personal problem that involved me but of which I knew nothing, I would:

    _____ A. Press them for information about the problem and their opinions about it.

    _____ B. Leave it up to my friends to tell me or not tell me, letting them change the subject if they wished.

17. If a friend seemed to be preoccupied and began to jump on me for seemingly unimportant things and to become irritated with me and others without real cause, I would:

    _____ A. Treat him with kid gloves for a while on the assumption that he was having some temporary personal problems that were none of my business.

    _____ B. Try to talk to him about it and point out to him how his behavior was affecting people.

18. If I had begun to dislike certain habits of a friend to the point that it was interfering with my enjoying her company, I would:

    _____ A. Say nothing to her directly but let her know my feelings by ignoring her whenever her annoying habits were obvious.

    _____ B. Get my feelings out in the open and clear the air so that we could continue our friendship comfortably and enjoyably.

19. In discussing social behavior with one of my more sensitive friends, I would:

    _____ A. Avoid mentioning his flaws and weaknesses so as not to hurt his feelings.

    _____ B. Focus on his flaws and weaknesses so he could improve his interpersonal skills.

20. If I knew I might be assigned to an important position in our group and my friends' attitudes toward me had become rather negative, I would:

    _____ A. Discuss my shortcomings with my friends so I could see where to improve.

    _____ B. Try to figure out my own shortcomings by myself so I could improve.

Scoring Key

In the Personal Communication Practices Survey, there are ten items that deal with your receptivity to feedback and ten that are concerned with your willingness to self-disclose. Transfer your scores from each item to this scoring key. Add the scores in each column. Now, transfer these scores to Figure 13.7 by drawing a vertical line through the feedback score and a horizontal line through the self-disclosure line.

Receptivity to Feedback		Willingness to Self-Disclose	
2. B	_____	1. A	_____
3. A	_____	4. B	_____
5. A	_____	6. B	_____
7. A	_____	9. B	_____
8. B	_____	11. B	_____
10. B	_____	13. A	_____
12. B	_____	15. A	_____

14. B	_____	17. B	_____
16. A	_____	18. B	_____
20. A	_____	19. B	_____
Total:	_____	Total:	_____

As Figure 13.7 suggests, higher scores in receptivity to feedback and willingness to self-disclose indicate a greater willingness to engage in personal openness in interpersonal communications. Of course, you need to be mindful of the situational factors that may influence your natural personal preference to be relatively more open or closed in interpersonal communication.

Organizational Insight: The Irate Customer[69]

SystemBase was a leading vendor of high-performance relational database software. Established in 1989, SystemBase shipped its first product in 1992.

Since the initial product shipments, SystemBase has served more than one thousand customers in various industries. Recently, however, SystemBase has experienced difficulties satisfying its clients due to staff cuts. Its New York City office, which predominantly serves the financial district, typifies SystemBase's present customer satisfaction problems.

Most of the New York City staff, led by its district sales manager, Tom, were aggressive in pursuit of their goals. Competition between sales representatives was keen. Tom's philosophy, often reiterated during sales training sessions, was "Stress is good. If you don't feel stress, then you must be leaving money on the table."

Based on SystemBase New York's encouraging 1993–1994 sales growth, an even higher sales growth rate in 1995 was planned. Consequently, additional sales representatives and technicians were hired at the New York City location during late 1995 and early 1996.

Downsizing

Projected revenues, corporationwide and at the New York City office, were not achieved for 1996. SystemBase executives believed that sales projections were not achieved because of poor internal practices and an unanticipated downturn in the software market. Their conclusion was that the company had been overstaffed. Consequently, a decision was made to furlough fifty employees and impose a hiring freeze. The aim of a new focus on "working smarter and faster" was to build a solid foundation for satisfying customers and achieving desired growth and profitability. The New York City office was hit particularly hard by the layoff. It lost three technicians and a secretary. Consequently, on the technical side only the district technical manager, Anne, supported by two technicians remained. However, the salesforce of Tom and six sales representatives was left intact.

With at least two less technical support personnel than required, Anne often found it necessary to help with presenta-

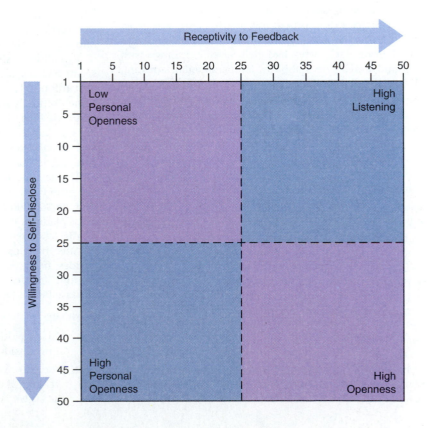

■ FIGURE 13.7

Personal Openness in Interpersonal Communications

tions and demonstrations. Despite the need for the sales and technical teams to work together, management of the teams was not centralized at the local office level. Tom and Anne reported to different home office corporate managers. However, Tom, as the leader of the revenue-bearing sales team, had the greater power in the New York City office.

Office Tensions

The reduction in technical support staff, a downturn in the software market, and no relief from high sales quotas raised tensions in the New York City office. Sales representatives, struggling to make their quotas, felt squeezed by the demands made on them. They, in turn, pressured the understaffed technical team for sales support. The technical team, responsible for supporting both new sales and existing accounts, felt pulled in many directions. The result was frustration for all.

Infonet's Order

Pressure to meet quarterly quotas peaked near the end of the third quarter of 1996. Jack, the district's most productive sales representative, expected to receive a $60,000 order from Infonet. This firm wanted to upgrade its software to run on a more powerful computer system. Infonet, a U.S. subsidiary of the French company RTR, had already invested $250,000 in SystemBase software. In 1996, this represented a moderately sized SystemBase customer. RTR had also made a significant investment in SystemBase technology and Jack was hoping that it would recommend SystemBase as its corporationwide standard for workstation-based database systems.

Infonet's director of information systems, Pierre, was based in New York City. He was a French national, raised and educated in Europe. Jack, who had had several dealings with Pierre, found him to be stubborn, temperamental, arrogant, and elitist. He typified many European businessmen by valuing and demanding attention from contractors and expecting the work to be properly performed the first time. Sloppy, untimely support sent him into a tirade. Reporting to Pierre was Lance, a database administrator. The local SystemBase technician assigned to support Infonet was Rick.

The Incident

Two weeks prior to the end of the third quarter of 1996, Lance called Rick concerning an ongoing "case" that he had opened at SystemBase's Technical Support Center, which was based at corporate headquarters in California. SystemBase Technical Support provided hotline telephone support to help solve customer problems. Customers were required to work through Technical Support to resolve moderate and major technical issues requiring significant effort. However, clients such as Infonet could also call on local technician support staff like Rick for help in solving minor problems that didn't require too much time.

While Lance was speaking with Rick, Pierre called Jack to complain about the same problems. Pierre warned Jack that someone better come to the Infonet office and fix the problem. Meanwhile, Rick listened to Lance's description of the problem and then asked Lance to run a few tests and send him the output. Rick found the requested output on the fax machine the following morning. Upon reviewing the information, Rick determined that he was unable to identify the problem conclusively. However, he knew that Infonet's database software, which was an old version, contained some "bugs" and that the software should be updated before they continued. He hoped that installation of the new software would solve the problem.

Lance had the latest version of the software available but hesitated to install it without guidance. Rick and Lance discussed the installation procedure over the phone. As a result, Rick believed that Lance was now comfortable in proceeding with the upgrade with the help of the Technical Support hotline in California. However, Lance preferred to be informed officially of the recommended course of action by SystemBase and asked Rick to apprise Pierre of the situation. Rick agreed, relieved that he wouldn't have to help with the upgrade. He was already overloaded, and other sales representatives were lining up to see him.

Rick reported the incident to Anne. They agreed that it would be futile for Rick to visit Lance until he had upgraded the Infonet system. In accordance with Lance's request, they drafted a letter to Pierre and sent it via fax. The letter said that Lance and Rick had agreed that the software upgrade to the latest version should be made before Rick continued to give technical support. Additionally, the letter stated that SystemBase was confident that the upgrade would correct the situation and that Lance was comfortable proceeding with the upgrade because of the help from SystemBase Technical Support in California.

Rick didn't visit Infonet that afternoon. Jack, committed to seeing another client, was unaware that there were no plans to visit Infonet. Later that evening, a fax from Pierre arrived at Anne's office. It was a copy of the letter faxed earlier by Anne and Rick. Pierre had scribbled "not true" over the section stating that Lance was comfortable proceeding with the upgrade and had added a note demanding "proof" that the latest version did not have any bugs.

The next morning Jack was in his office when he received a call from Pierre. Pierre was extremely upset and shouted at Jack that the $60,000 deal would not go through in the third quarter as planned. Pierre then placed a call to Tom and demanded that Jack be fired.

After hanging up, Tom began to examine the options. Besides firing Jack, Tom could take Jack off the Infonet account, rigorously defend jack, or arrange to have Jack appease Pierre. He wondered what he should do.

Questions

1. How should Tom respond to Pierre? What issues should Tom consider before replying?

2. Does downsizing appear to have played a role in this incident? If the answer is "yes," what in the case supports the answer and what should be done about it?

3. What vendor–customer miscommunication transpired during the incident? What can SystemBase do to improve such communication in the future?

4. Did cultural differences contribute to the problems between SystemBase and Infonet? Explain.

REFERENCES

1. Adapted from Teboul, J. C. B. Facing and coping with uncertainty during organizational encounter. *Management Communication Quarterly*, 1994, 8, 190–224.

2. Based on Carr-Ruffino, N. *The Promotable Woman: Advancing Through Leadership Shells*, 2d ed. Belmont, Calif.: Wadsworth, 1993, 164–208; Lange, A., and Jakubowski, P. *Responsible Assertive Behavior*. Champaign, Ill.: Research Press, 1983.

3. Axley, S. R. *Communication at Work: Management and the Communication Intensive Organization*. Westport, Conn.: Quorum Books, 1996.

4. Adapted from Keys, J. B., and Case, T. L. How to become an influential manager. *Academy of Management Executive*, November 1990, 38–51.

5. Robinson, W. P. *Deceit, Delusion, and Detection*. Thousand Oaks, Calif.: Sage, 1996.

6. Russ, G. S., Daft, R. L., and Lengel, R. H. Media selection and managerial characteristics in organizational communications. *Management Communication Quarterly*, 1990, 4, 151–175.

7. Mankin, D., Cohen, S. G., and Bikson, T. K. *Teams and Technology*. Boston: Harvard Business School Press, 1996.

8. Hart, P. Svenning, L., and Ruchinskas, J. From face-to-face meeting to video teleconferencing: Potential shifts in meeting genre. *Management Communication Quarterly*, 1995, 8, 395–423.

9. Kikoski, J. F. and Kikoski, C. K. *Reflexive Communication in the Culturally Diverse Workplace*. Westport, Conn.: Quorum Books, 1996.

10. Stohl, C. *Organizational Communication: Connectedness in Action*. Thousand Oaks, Calif.: Sage, 1995.

11. Barnum, C. F. Mirror on the wall: Who's the wisest one of all? *International Executive*, July–August 1989, 39–41; Gudykunst, W. B., Ting-Toomey, S. and Nishida, T. *Communication in Personal Relationships Across Cultures*. Thousand Oaks, Calif.: Sage, 1996.

12. Mortensen, C.D. *Miscommunication*. Thousand Oaks, Calif.: Sage, 1997.

13. Musgrave, J. and Anmis, M. *Relationship Dynamics: Theory and Analysis*. New York: Free Press, 1996.

14. Sullivan, J., Kameda, N., and Nobu, T. Bypassing in managerial communications. *Business Horizons*, January–February 1991, 73.

15. Davenport, T. H. Saving IT's soul: Human-centered information management. *Harvard Business Review*, March–April 1994, 119–131.

16. Daily, B., and Finch, M. Benefiting from nonsexist language in the workplace. *Business Horizons*, March–April 1993, 30–34.

17. Tannen, D. The power of talk: Who gets heard and why. *Harvard Business Review*, September–October 1995, 138–148.

18. Adapted from Weiss, A. A hidden bias. Reprinted with permission from *Managing Diversity Newsletter*, JALMC, P.O. Box 819, Jamestown, NY 14702-0819; Phone: (716) 665-3654.

19. Murphy, K. R. *Honesty in the Workplace*. Pacific Grove, Calif.: Brooks/Cole, 1993.

20. Cupach, W. R. and Spitzberg, B. H. (eds.). *The Dark Side of Interpersonal Communication*. Hillsdale, N.J.: Lawrence Erlbaum Associates, 1994.

21. Bing, S. Are you a master of (in)sincerity? *Fortune*, November 13, 1995, 63–64.

22. Gardner, W. L. III. Lessons in organizational dramaturgy: The art of impression management. *Organizational Dynamics*, Summer 1992, 33–46.

23. Bird, F. B. *The Muted Conscience: Moral Silence and the Practice of Ethics in Business*. Westport, Conn.: Quorum Books, 1996.

24. Varner, I., and Beamer, L. *Intercultural Business Communication in the Global Workplace*. Burr Ridge, Ill.: Irwin, 1995.

25. Hall, E. *Understanding Cultural Differences*. Yarmouth, Me.: Intercultural Press, 1989; Wiseman, R. L. (ed.) *Intercultural Communication Theory*. Thousand Oaks, Calif.: Sage, 1995.

26. Halverson, C. B. Cultural-context inventory: The effects of culture on behavior and work style. In J. W. Pfeiffer (ed.), *The 1993 Annual: Developing Human Resources*. San Diego: Pfeiffer & Company, 1993, 131–145; Blanchard, K., and Johnson, S. *The One-Minute Manager*, New York: Berkeley, 1987.

27. Adapted from Munter, M. Cross-cultural communication for management. *Business Horizons*, May–June, 1993, 76–77; Shanahan, D. From language learner to multicultural manager. *European Management Journal*, 14, 1996, 315–320.

28. Mowlana, H. *Global Communication in Transition*. Thousand Oaks, Calif.: Sage, 1996.

29. Adapted from Elashmawi, F. Communicating effectively with your Arab partner. *Trade & Culture*, January 1996, 55–56; Elashmawi, F., and Harris, P. R. *Multicultural Management: New Skills for Global Success*. Houston: Gulf, 1994; Anderson, J. W. A comparison of Arab and American conceptions of persuasion. *Howard Journal of Communication*, 1989, 2, 81–114.

30. Krackhardt, D., and Hanson, J. R. Informal networks: The company behind the chart. *Harvard Business Review*, July–August 1993, 104–111; Marschan, R. New structural forms in multinational corporations at the expense of

communication networks? *International Journal of Technology Management*, 1996, 11, 192–206.

31. Yeung, I. Y. M., and Tung, R. L. Achieving business success in Confucian societies: The importance of Guanxi (connections). *Organizational Dynamics*, Autumn 1996, 54–65.

32. Toshio, Y., Gilmore, M. R., and Cook, K. S. Network connections and the distribution of power in exchange networks. *American Journal of Sociology*, 1988, 93, 833–851; Powell, W. W., Koput, K. W., and Smith-Doer, L. Interorganizational collaboration and the locus of innovation: Networks of learning in biotechnology. *Administrative Science Quarterly*, 1996, 41, 116–145.

33. Simon, H. A. *Administrative Behavior: A Study of Decision-Making Processes in Administrative Organization*, 4th ed. New York: Free Press, 1997.

34. Donnellon, A. *Team Talk: The Power of Language in Team Dynamics.* Boston: Harvard Business School Press, 1996.

35. Ibarra, H. Personal networks of women and minorities in management: A conceptual framework. *Academy of Management Review*, 1993, 18, 56–87; Ibarra, H. Race, opportunity, and diversity of social circles in managerial networks. *Academy of Management Journal*, 1995, 38, 673–703

36. Sessa, V. I. Managing diversity at the Xerox Corporation: Balanced workforce goals and caucus groups. In S. E. Jackson and Associates (eds.), *Diversity in the Workplace: Human Resource Initiatives.* New York: Guilford, 1992, 37–64; Lesly, E. Sticking it out at Xerox by sticking together. *Business Week*, November 29, 1993, 77.

37. Mankin, D., Cohen, S. G., and Bikson, T. K. *Teams and Technology: Fulfilling the Promise of the New Organization.* Boston: Harvard Business School Press, 1996.

38. Behar, R. Who's reading your e-mail? *Fortune*, February 3, 1997, 57–70; Federico, R. F., and Bowley, J. M. The great e-mail debate. *HR Magazine*, January 1996, 67–72.

39. Reinsch, N. L., Jr., and Beswick, R. W. Voice mail versus conventional channels: A cost minimization analysis of individuals' preferences. *Academy of Management Journal*, 1990, 33, 801–816; Clapper, D. L., and Massey, A. P. Electronic focus groups: A framework for exploration. *Information & Management*, 1996, 30, 43–50.

40. Berner, J. *The Joy of Working from Home: Making a Life While Making a Living*, San Francisco: Berrett-Kolhler, 1994.

41. Shellenbarger, J. Some thrive, but many wilt working at home. *Wall Street Journal*, December 14, 1993, B1, B10; Shellenbarger, S. I'm still here! Home workers worry they're invisible. *Wall Street Journal*, December 16, 1993, B1, B2.

42. Markels, A. Managers aren't always able to get the right message across with e-mail. *Wall Street Journal*, August 8, 1996, B1.

43. Merkels, B1.

44. Fulk, J., Schmitz, J., and Ryu, D. Cognitive elements in the social construction of communication technology. *Management Communication Quarterly*, 1995, 8, 259–288.

45. Adapted from Young, J. 3M: Whole earth corp. *Forbes ASAP*, December 4, 1995, 56–57; Young, J. Downlinks in the out-

back, *Forbes ASAP*, December 4, 1995, 68–69; Hasenyager, B. W. *Managing the Information Ecology: Information Technology Management.* Westport, Conn.: Quorum Books, 1996; 3M test drives AT&T Uniworld VPN. Network-World, July 8, 1996, 17.

46. Isaacs, U. N. Taking flight: Dialogue, collective thinking, and organizational learning. *Organizational Dynamics*, Autumn 1993, 24–39; Pye, A. Strategy through dialogue and doing: A game of "Mornington Crescent?" *Management Learning*, 1995, 26, 445–462.

47. This section draws heavily from Sussman, L. Managers: On the defensive. *Business Horizons*, January–February 1991, 81–87; Sejersted, F. Managers and consultants as manipulators: Reflections on the suspension of ethics. *Business Ethics Quarterly*, 1996, 6, 67–86.

48. Preston, D., Smith, A. Buchanan, D., and Jordon, S. Symbols of the culture and communication processes of a general hospital. *Management Learning*, 1996, 27, 343–357.

49. Denton, D. K. Open communication. *Business Horizons*, September–October 1993, 64–69.

50. Sussman, L., Managers: On the defensive. *Business Horizons*, January-February 1991, 82.

51. Adapted from Weise, E. Internet's search tools and perceived privacy. *Bryan-College Station Eagle*, March 4, 1996, B5; Behar, R. Who's reading your e-mail? *Fortune*, February 3, 1997, 57–70.

52. Karp, K. The lost art of feedback. In J. W. Pfeiffer (ed.), *The 1987 Annual: Developing Human Resources.* San Diego: University Associates, 1987, 237–245; Waldroop, J. and Butler, T. The executive as coach. *Harvard Business Review*, November–December 1996, 11-1-130.

53. Van Velsor, E., and Brittain Leslie, J. Why executives derail: Perspectives across time and culture. *Academy of Management Executive*, November 1995, 62–70.

54. Derlega, V. J., Metts, S., Petronio, S., and Margulis, S. T. *Self-Disclosure.* Newbury Park, Calif.: Sage, 1993.

55. Jourard, S. M. *Disclosing Man to Himself.* New York: Van Nostrand Reinhold, 1968, 46–47.

56. Nichols, M. P. *The Lost Art of Listening.* New York: Guilford, 1995.

57. Hamlin, S. *How to Talk So People Listen.* New York: Harper & Row, 1988; Weisberg, J. Hit or misunderstandings. *Folio: The Magazine for Magazine Management.* May 15, 1996, 57–61.

58. Brownell, J. *Building Active Listening Skills.* Englewood Cliffs, N.J.: Prentice-Hall, 1986; Horowitz, A. S. Hey! Listen Up. *Computerworld*, July 1, 1996, 63–65.

59. Petzinger, T., Jr. Two executives cook up way to make Pillsbury listen. *Wall Street Journal*, October 27, 1996, B1; A more worldly view. *Minneapolis Star-Tribune-*, March 18, 1996, DI.

60. Wiseman, J. M., and Harrison, R. P. (eds.), *Nonverbal Interaction.* Newbury Park, Calif.: Sage, 1983.

61. Harper, R. G., Wiens, A. N., and Matarzzo, J. D. *Nonverbal Communication: The State of the Art.* New York: John Wiley & Sons, 1978; Bruhn, M. Business gifts: A form of non-

verbal and symbolic communication. *European Management Journal*, 1996, 14, 61–68.

62. Strati, A. Aesthetic understanding of organizational life. *Academy of Management Review*, 1992, 17, 568–581; Rafaeli, A., and Pratt, M. G. Tailored meanings: On the meaning and impact of organizational dress. *Academy of Management Review*, 1993, 18, 32–55.

63. Heintzman, M., Leathers, D. G., Parrot, R. L., Cairns, A. B. III. Nonverbal rapport-building behaviors/effects on perceptions of a supervisor. *Management Communication Quarterly*, 1993, 7, 181–208.

64. Zorn, T. E., and Violanti, M. T. Communication abilities and individual achievement in organizations. *Management Communication Quarterly*, 1996, 10, 139–167; Tear, J. They just don't understand gender dynamics. *Wall Street Journal*, November 20, 1995, A14.

65. Briles, J. *Gendertraps*. New York: McGraw-Hill, 1997.

66. DiDio, L. This one's for the guys. *Computerworld*, January 6, 1997, 66.

67. Arliss, L. P. *Gender Communication*. Englewood Cliffs, N.J.: Prentice-Hall, 1991.

68. Source: Douglas Roberts, formerly Manager of Training, LTV Missiles and Electronics Group, Grand Prairie, Texas. Used with permission.

69. Source: This case was prepared by Bridget Piraino and James W. Lawson of Saint Peter's College, Jersey City, New Jersey. Presented and accepted by the refereed Society for Case Research. All rights reserved to the authors and the SCR. Copyright © 1993 by Bridget Piraino and James W. Lawson. Original updated and edited for *Organizational Behavior*, 8th ed. Used with permission.

Organizational Processes

CHAPTERS

PART

3

LEARNING OBJECTIVES

After you have finished studying this chapter, you should be able to:

- Explain the key issues in ethical decision making.
- Describe three models of decision making in organizations.
- Outline the primary phases of managerial decision making.
- Identify the common human biases in decision making.
- Describe two methods for stimulating creativity.

OUTLINE

PREVIEW CASE

Decisions!?!

The passengers of an America West flight from Dallas were intrigued when they learned their plane was returning to the airport to pick up some celebrity travelers—the entire California Angels baseball team. But their excitement turned to fury when they were kicked off the plane to make room for the Angels, whose chartered flight had been grounded because of mechanical problems. "They can't commandeer a plane like this," complained passenger Jeri Chapman. "We're paying passengers. What are we, trash?" "I don't think it's a public relations disaster," an airline spokesman said.

R.J. Reynolds' Chairman Charles Harper was asked about the dangers of exposing children to secondhand smoke. Harper said that kids could leave a smoky room if they didn't like it. What about newborns? "At some point, they will learn to crawl," he said.

The administrators at Southwest Elementary School in Lexington, North Carolina, applied a get-tough attitude toward sexual harassment. They accused six-year-old Johnathan Prevette of sexual harassment after he kissed a classmate on the cheek. Johnathan was promptly suspended from school. When the school board was exposed to international ridicule, it reduced the charge to "unwarranted and unwelcome touching" and returned Johnathan to class.

Journalist Joe Klein initially lied when asked if he was the author of the best-selling book, *Primary Colors*. But the truth leaked out as the novel was readied for a paperback edition. Although controversy sells books, Klein and his publisher denied that the leak was a matter of convenient timing. "It's not easy telling the truth," Klein explained.

The American Society of Composers, Authors and Publishers (ASCAP) sent a letter to summer camps warning them to pay up if they wanted to sing copyrighted songs such as *Edelweiss* and *This Land Is Your Land*. As a result, several cash-strapped camps stopped singing the songs. After television talk shows and newspapers reported the story, ASCAP took out full-page ads saying that it "never sought, nor was it ever its intention to license Girl Scouts singing around the campfire." The credibility of that denial wilted under the light of ASCAP's admission that it would reimburse money to sixteen Girl Scout councils that had already paid fees ranging from $77 to $257.[1]

What do these five incidents have in common? First, all were blunders that resulted in negative consequences. Second, all were the result of flawed decision-making processes. Can organizations and individuals eliminate all bad decisions? No. Can they reduce the likelihood of bad decisions, especially blunders? Yes.

In several previous chapters, we presented recommendations for assessing and improving decision making in organizations. In this chapter, we expand on those earlier discussions. We start with five core issues related to ethics and decision making.[2] Then, we review the features of three major decision-making models. Next, we describe several features of those models in outlining the phases of managerial decision making. Finally, we present approaches for stimulating creativity in decision making. By mastering the learning objectives of this chapter and the related discussions of decision making in other chapters, you should be able to reduce the possibility of making blunders like those presented in the Preview Case.

KEY ETHICAL ISSUES

Decision making in organizations reflects underlying ethical principles and rules. Because of its importance, we have emphasized this point by discussing one or more ethical issues relevant to the content of each chapter. **Ethics** deals with right or wrong in the decisions and actions of individuals and the organizations of which they are a part. Ethical issues in organizations are more common and complex than generally recognized. In fact, ethical issues influence the decisions that employees make daily.[3] Some ethical issues involve factors that blur the distinction between "right" and "wrong." As a result, many employees experience ethical dilemmas.[4] Table 14.1 shows twenty ethical issues facing U.S. industries, ranked according to their importance. This table is based on a survey of managers in 711 of the largest U.S. corporations. The managers who responded identified the five most important ethical issues as drug and alcohol abuse, employee theft, conflicts of interest, quality control, and discrimination.[5]

Ethical decision making is extremely complex because no simple rules exist for making decisions that have important ethical content. As with our earlier presentations of ethical issues, our intent here is to help you to learn how to apply ethics to reasoning and decision making. Evaluation of alternatives can be improved by an examination of five key aspects of ethical decision making: ethical intensity, decision principles and rules, affected individuals, benefits and costs, and determination of rights.[6]

■ ETHICAL INTENSITY

The ethical issues identified in Table 14.1 aren't equally important to decision makers. Thus **ethical intensity** is the degree of importance given to an issue-related moral imperative and varies from issue to issue.[7] Ethical intensity is determined by the combined impact, as interpreted by the decision maker, of six factors.

- **Magnitude of consequences** is the total of the harm or benefits accruing to individuals affected by an action. A decision that causes a thousand people to suffer a particular injury has greater consequences than a decision that causes ten people to suffer the same injury. A decision that causes the death of a human being is of greater consequence than a decision that causes a minor personal injury.

- **Probability of effect** is the joint result of the likelihood that a decision will be implemented and that the decision will cause the harm or benefit pre-

TABLE 14.1 Twenty Ethical Issues Facing U.S. Industries: In Rank Order of Importance

RANK	ISSUE	RANK	ISSUE
1.	Drug and alcohol abuse	11.	Misuse of other's information
2.	Employee theft	12.	Methods of gathering competitor's information
3.	Conflicts of interest	13.	Inaccuracy of books and records
4.	Quality control	14.	Receiving excessive gifts and entertainment
5.	Discrimination	15.	False or misleading advertising
6.	Misuse of proprietary information	16.	Giving excessive gifts and entertainment
7.	Abuse of expense accounts	17.	Kickbacks
8.	Plant closings and layoffs	18.	Insider trading
9.	Misuse of company assets	19.	Relations with local communities
10.	Environmental pollution	20.	Antitrust issues

Source: Ethics Resource Center and Behavior Research Center. *Ethics Policies and Programs in American Business: Report of a Landmark Survey of U.S. Corporations.* Washington, D.C.: Ethics Resource Center, 1990, 17. Used with permission.

dicted. The production of an automobile that would be dangerous to occupants during routine driving has greater probability of harm than the production of a car that endangers occupants only when curves are taken at high speed. The sale of a gun to a known armed robber has a greater probability of harm than the sale of a gun to a law-abiding citizen.

■ **Social consensus** is the degree of public agreement that a proposed decision is evil or good. The evil involved in actively discriminating against minority job candidates has greater public agreement than the evil involved in not actively seeking out minority job candidates. The evil involved in bribing a customs official in Canada has greater public agreement than the evil involved in bribing a customs official in a country where such behavior is generally accepted as a way of doing business, such as the Philippines (illegal under U.S. law). Managers and employees will have difficulty deciding what is and isn't ethical if they aren't guided by a high degree of social consensus, which reduces the likelihood of ambiguity.

■ **Temporal immediacy** is the length of time between the making of a decision and the beginning of consequences of that decision. A shorter length of time implies greater immediacy. Releasing a drug that will cause 1 percent of the people who take it to have acute nervous reactions within one month has greater temporal immediacy than releasing a drug that will cause 1 percent of those who take it to develop nervous disorders after thirty years. The reduction in the retirement benefits of current retirees has greater temporal immediacy than the reduction in the future retirement benefits of employees who are currently between twenty and thirty years of age.

■ **Proximity** is the feeling of nearness (social, cultural, psychological, or physical) that the decision maker has for victims or beneficiaries of the decision. Layoffs in a person's department have greater ethical proximity (physical and psychological) than do layoffs in a remote plant. For North Americans, the sale of dangerous pesticides in Canadian, U.S., and Mexican markets has greater ethical proximity (social, cultural, and physical) than does the sale of such pesticides in Australia.

■ **Concentration of effect** is the inverse function of the number of people affected by a decision. A change in a warranty policy denying coverage to 10 people with claims of $10,000 each has a more concentrated effect than a change denying coverage to 10,000 people with claims of $10 each. Cheating an individual or small group of individuals out of $1000 has a more concentrated effect than cheating an organization, such as General Motors or the Internal Revenue Service, out of the same sum.

All six factors of ethical intensity potentially are characteristics of the issue itself. As a result, they are likely to have combined effects. Moreover, ethical intensity will increase with increases in one or more of its factors and decrease with decreases in one or more of its factors, assuming that all other conditions remain constant. However, individuals may rate ethical intensity differently, simply because they place different values on the various principles of ethical decision making.

Ethical intensity often comes into play in coping with diversity issues such as racism. The following Diversity in Practice feature illustrates ethical intensity factors related to the intense controversy surrounding the diversity training and related initiatives at R. R. Donnelley & Sons Company. This large commercial printing firm is headquartered in Chicago.

DIVERSITY IN PRACTICE

Controversy Over Donnelley's Initiatives

Since 1993, when this commercial printer settled a class-action racial discrimination lawsuit involving one of its facilities, R. R. Donnelley & Company has spent millions on diversity training and related initiatives. Yet some of these activities are implicated in two lawsuits alleging widespread racial discrimination and harassment at the company, which has 38,000 employees.

About 550 employees have joined one suit since its filing in U.S. District Court in Chicago in November 1996. Several employees allege discrimination and harassment related to their participation in the company's diversity training. The other suit, filed in the same court in December 1996, alleges harassment related to work by Ward Campbell, a former sales associate at Donnelley, in preparing a "diversity plan" that management didn't like.

Thomas Kochman, author of *Black and White Styles in Conflict*, says, "For African-Americans, sincerity is measured by what you do—it's the numbers that count." Yet at Donnelley, which started its diversity initiative in 1993, black employment fell from 8 percent in 1992 to 6.6 percent in 1997.

There are so few black managers and employees that some are asked to attend multiple diversity training programs to ensure the presence of diverse groups. That has drawn resentment from black employees, many of whom already view the stressful sessions as a poor substitute for significant improvements in employment practices. "Diversity training was just window dressing," says Roslyn Houston, a former manager who was asked to attend two training programs.

Former sales associate Ward Campbell, who is black, alleges in his lawsuit that, after management asked him to help develop a "diversity plan," he determined that "Donnelley maintained minimal minority-group representation in upper management." During and after his work on the plan, his complaint alleges, his immediate managers made "racially offensive and abusive remarks" about him. Upon completion of the plan, according to the complaint, Campbell's managers "were displeased with [his] expressed views and findings" and sought ways to induce him to resign voluntarily. A representative of Donnelley says, "Ward Campbell was fired for cause. It had nothing to do with his race or involvement in the diversity initiative."[8]

■ DECISION PRINCIPLES AND RULES

No agreed-upon principles and rules exist for resolving ethical issues.[9] In addition, individuals and groups differ over what influences both ethical and unethical behaviors and decisions. Table 14.2 presents the results of a survey of consumers and chief executives on the factors that they believe strongly influence ethical and unethical behaviors and decisions in organizations.[10] These findings, and those of other studies, clearly show some areas of general agreement, as well as some significant differences, between the two groups. For example, 88 percent of the executives viewed *company values or culture* as a strong influence on ethical and unethical behaviors and decisions but only 45 percent of the consumers did so. Thus a large majority of the executives but less than half of the consumers surveyed believe that a company's values and culture encourage individual managers and employees to make ethical or unethical decisions (see Chapter 17).

TABLE 14.2 Factors Rated as Strong Influences on Determining Ethical and Unethical Decisions and Behaviors

FACTORS	CONSUMERS	CEOs
▪ An individual's moral code	59%	82%
▪ Behavior of an employee's immediate supervisor	59	84
▪ Example set by CEO or company president	57	92
▪ Fear of getting caught or losing one's job	57	50
▪ Company's economic situation	46	26
▪ Customer opinions	46	41
▪ What others would think	46	56
▪ Company code of ethics	45	62
▪ Company values or culture	45	88
▪ Level of ethical behavior of coworkers	40	72

Source: Adapted from Laczniak, G. R., Berkowitz, M. W., Brooker, R. G., and Hale, J. P. The ethics of business: Improving or deteriorating? Reprinted from *Business Horizons*, January–February, 1995, 40. Copyright © 1995 by the Foundation for the School of Business at Indiana University. Used with permission.

Various principles and rules have been advanced by people in business, philosophy, religion, and politics to provide an *ethical* justification for a person's decisions and behaviors.[11] They range from those that justify self-serving decisions to those that require careful consideration of others' rights and costs. The following ethical principles attempt to justify self-serving decisions and behaviors.

▪ **Hedonist principle:** Do whatever you find to be in your own self-interest.

▪ **Might-equals-right-principle:** You are strong enough to take advantage without respect to ordinary social conventions and widespread practices or customs.

▪ **Conventionalist principle:** Bluff and take advantage of all legal opportunities and widespread practices or custom.

▪ **Intuition principle:** Go with your "gut feeling," or what you understand to be right in a situation.

▪ **Organization ethics principle:** Ask whether actions are consistent with organizational goals and do what is good for the organization.

Recall the incidents presented in the Preview Case. Those initially based on one or more of these underlying self-serving principles were: (1) removing passengers on an America West flight to accommodate the California Angels baseball team (might-equals-right principle); (2) the comment on children's exposure to secondhand smoke by R.J. Reynolds' chairman (hedonist principle and organization ethics principle); (3) school suspension of six-year old Johnathan Prevette for sexual harassment (intuition principle); (4) Joe Klein first lying about not being the author of *Primary Colors* and then the publisher leaking the truth that he was the author just prior to release of the paperback edition (hedonist principle, conventionalist principle, and organization ethics principle); and (5) the American Society of Composers, Authors and Publishers initially threatening lawsuits unless royalties were paid for singing popular songs at children's camps (hedonist principle and organization ethics principle).

The following are ethical principles that tend to justify decisions and actions on the basis of attempting to balance multiple interests.

- **Means–end principle:** Ask whether some overall good justifies any moral transgression.
- **Utilitarian principle:** Determine whether the harm inherent in the action is outweighed by the good in it.
- **Professional ethics principle:** Do only that which can be explained before a group of your peers.

These principles likely provide the foundation for discretionary decision making in most of the organizations that are viewed as progressive. They provide the justification for decisions in situations that create ethical dilemmas—for example, justifying employee layoffs but recognizing certain responsibilities for the well-being of those employees.

The following are ethical principles that emphasize the need to consider decisions and behaviors from the perspective of those affected and the public as a whole.

- **Disclosure principle:** Ask how a wide audience would likely respond to disclosure of the thinking and details of the decision.
- **Distributive justice principle:** An individual's treatment should not be based on arbitrarily defined characteristics.
- **Categorical imperative principle:** Act in a way that you believe would be right and just for any other person in a similar situation.
- **Golden rule principle:** Place yourself in the position of someone affected by the decision and try to determine how that person would feel.

These principles are often *imposed* on certain categories of decisions and behaviors through the enforcement of laws, regulations, and court rulings. In effect, governments impose ethical principles and rules that organizations are expected to comply with in certain situations. For example, Title VII of the 1964 U.S. Civil Rights Act forbids organizations from considering personal characteristics such as race, gender, religion, or national origin in decisions to recruit, hire, promote, or fire employees. This law is based on the ethical principle of distributive justice. This principle requires that the treatment of individuals differently shouldn't be based on arbitrarily defined characteristics such as age, race, or gender.[12] It states that (1) employees who are similar in relevant respects should be treated similarly and (2) employees who differ in relevant respects should be treated differently in proportion to the differences between them. On this basis, the U.S. Equal Pay Act of 1963 asserts that paying women and men different wages is illegal when their jobs in the same organization require equal skill, effort, responsibility, and working conditions.

The culture of a country influences, in part, the behaviors and decisions that are viewed as ethical or unethical.[13] Figure 14.1 presents the generally accepted views of ethical and unethical behaviors and decisions in Russia and the United States. Some business activities are recognized as ethical by businesspeople in both countries (cell I), whereas other activities are considered to be unethical in both (cell II). Other behaviors, however, may be viewed as ethical by Russians but unethical to Americans (cell III), as well as the opposite situation (cell IV). For example, many Russians would consider as unethical the extreme salary differentials between the employees and top management in the United States. The fact that some U.S. executives have compensation packages that pay them some 200 times the compensation of the average worker conflicts with the Russian values

FIGURE 14.1

Sample of Russian and U.S. Views of Business Ethics

Source: Adapted from Puffer, S. M., and McCarthy, D. J. Finding the common ground in the Russian and American business ethics. Copyright © 1995, by The Regents of the University of California. Reprinted from the *California Management Review*, Winter 1995, 35. By permission of The Regents.

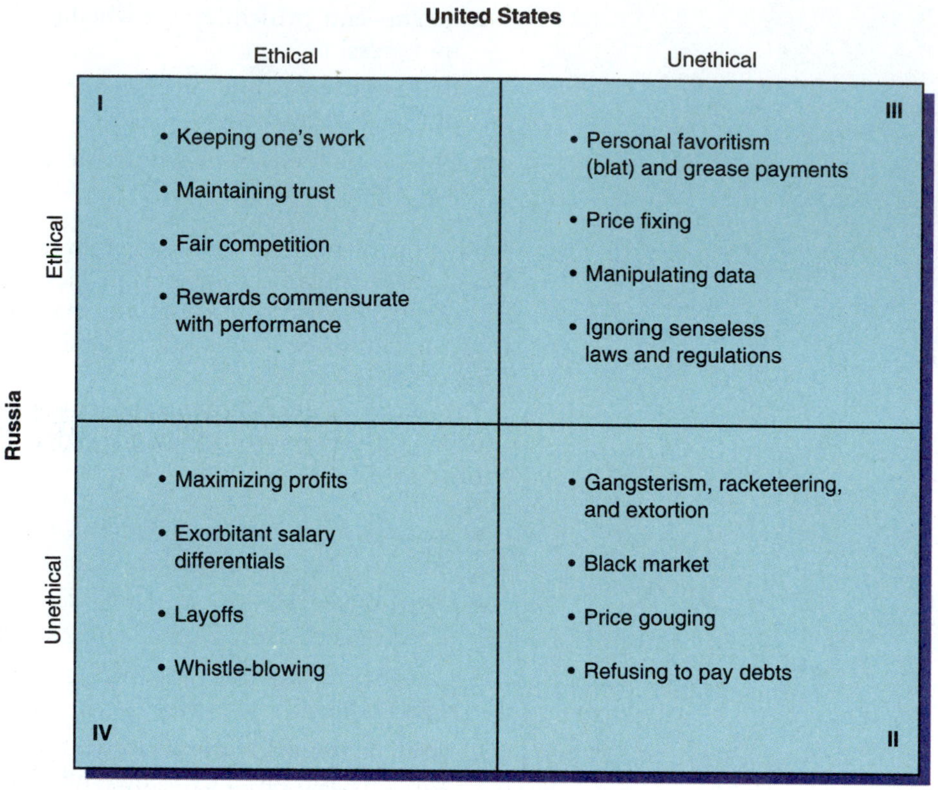

United States

	Ethical	Unethical
Ethical (Russia)	**I** • Keeping one's work • Maintaining trust • Fair competition • Rewards commensurate with performance	**III** • Personal favoritism (blat) and grease payments • Price fixing • Manipulating data • Ignoring senseless laws and regulations
Unethical (Russia)	**IV** • Maximizing profits • Exorbitant salary differentials • Layoffs • Whistle-blowing	**II** • Gangsterism, racketeering, and extortion • Black market • Price gouging • Refusing to pay debts

of fairness and equality.[14] In essence, this practice violates the Russian interpretation of the distributive justice principle.

As suggested previously in Table 14.2, no one factor influences the degree to which decisions and behaviors by managers and employees are likely to be ethical or unethical. However, the following actions have been suggested for integrating ethical decision making into the day-to-day life of an organization.

- Secure a commitment to ethical behaviors and decisions by top management and use their commitment as a model for other managers and employees.
- Develop a clear code of ethics and follow it.
- Establish a whistle-blowing and/or ethical concerns procedure and follow it.
- Involve employees in the identification of ethical problems to achieve a shared understanding and resolution of them.
- Include ethical decision making in the performance appraisal process.
- Publicize the organizational priorities and efforts related to ethical issues.[15]

AFFECTED INDIVIDUALS

The highest form of ethical decision making requires an assessment of who will receive benefits or incur costs as a result of a particular decision. For significant decisions, this assessment may include a variety of stakeholders—shareholders, customers, lenders, suppliers, employees, and government agencies, among others. The more specific a decision maker can be about who may benefit and who may lose from a particular decision, the more likely it is that ethical decisions will be made.

The ethical interpretation of the effects of decisions on identifiable individuals can change over time. Consider **employment at will,** a doctrine that holds that parties to an employment agreement have equal bargaining power and that therefore the right to fire is absolute and creates little cost to either party. The employer presumably can easily find another employee, and the employee presumably can easily find another job.[16]

Based on the distributive justice principle, the categorical imperative principle, and the golden rule principle, the employment-at-will doctrine increasingly has been challenged successfully in wrongful termination cases in the courts. Before 1980, companies in the United States were free to fire most nonunion employees "at will." That is, they could be fired for any reason and without explanation. Employees rarely went to court to challenge a termination. The vast majority who did had their suits dismissed. The courts have increasingly ruled in favor of exceptions to at-will employment, especially if questionable termination procedures were followed.[17]

▪ BENEFITS AND COSTS

Judging the benefits and costs of a proposed decision requires determination of the interests and values of those affected. When individuals value something, they want that situation to continue or to occur in the future. **Values** are the relatively permanent and deeply held desires of individuals. A sample of business managers were asked to rank a set of eighteen values they considered most important in their lives. The top five were self-respect, family security, freedom, accomplishment, and happiness. The bottom five were pleasure, beauty, salvation, social recognition, and equality.[18] Managers need to guard against assuming that others attach the same importance to the managers' values or even hold all the same values. Conflicting values between stakeholders can lead to different interpretations of ethical responsibilities. Greenpeace and other environmental groups, which have as one of their top values a world in which quality of life is paramount (both for human beings and other species), often consider the managers of some organizations as both irresponsible and unethical in not showing more concern about air and water pollution, land use, protection of endangered species, and the like.

One common approach to the assessment of benefits and costs is utilitarianism. **Utilitarianism** emphasizes the provision of the greatest good for the greatest number in judging the ethics of decision making. An individual who is guided by utilitarianism considers the potential effect of alternative actions on those who will be affected and then selects the alternative benefiting the greatest number of people. The individual accepts the fact that this alternative may harm others. However, so long as potentially positive results outweigh potentially negative results, the individual considers the decision to be both good and ethical.[19]

Some critics suggest that utilitarianism has been carried to extremes in North America. They suggest that there is too much short-run maximizing for personal advantage and too much discounting of the long-run costs of disregarding ethics. Those costs include rapidly widening gaps in income between rich and poor, creation of a permanent underclass with its hopelessness, and harm done to the environment. These critics believe that too many people and institutions are acquiring wealth for the purpose of personal consumption and power and that the end of acquiring wealth justifies any means of doing so. As a result, these critics suggest that trust of leaders and institutions, both public and private, has declined.[20] According to one study, total compensation of chief executive officers at thirty large U.S. corporations has increased to 212 times that of the average U.S. worker as of 1996, up from a factor of 44 in 1965. Another study claims that the average CEO of a large corporation made 187 times the wage of the average factory worker, up from a factor of 41 in 1960.[21]

■ DETERMINATION OF RIGHTS

The notion of rights also is complex and has changed over time. One aspect of rights focuses on who is entitled to benefits or to participation in the decision to change the allocation of benefits and costs.[22] Union–management negotiations frequently involve conflicts and dilemmas over management's rights to hire, promote, fire, and reassign union employees. For example, a major issue in the 1997 negotiations between American Airlines and the pilots was the *right* of the firm to outsource (that is, use some flight crews from nonunionized firms.) Slavery, racism, gender and age discrimination, and invasion of privacy often have been attacked by appeals to values based on concepts of fundamental rights.

Responsibilities and rights issues in the workplace are numerous and vary greatly. A few examples include unfair and reverse discrimination, sexual harassment, employee rights to continued employment, employer rights to terminate employment "at will," employee and corporate free speech, due process, and the right to test for substance abuse and acquired immune deficiency syndrome (AIDS). According to some experts, the attention to workplace rights and the establishment of trust with employees is the most crucial internal issue facing organizations today.[23]

Privacy rights have become ethical dilemmas in terms of (1) distribution and use of employee data from computer-based human resource information systems; (2) increasing use of paper-and-pencil honesty tests as a result of polygraph testing being declared illegal in most situations; (3) procedures and bases for substance abuse and AIDS testing; and (4) genetic testing. The ethical dilemmas in each of these areas revolve around balancing the rights of the individual, the needs and rights of the employer, and the interests of the community at large.[24]

The following Ethics in Practice account presents a scenario related to a determination of rights and other ethical issues. You are asked to answer the question: Would you consult the psychologist? Then, illustrative narrative responses reflecting the ethical reasoning by individuals for the decisions made are given. Finally, the responses to that question obtained from eighty-eight marketing and sales managers in a single organization (forty-eight males and forty females) are summarized.

ETHICS IN PRACTICE

Consult the Psychologist?

You sell corporate financial products, such as pension plans and group health insurance. You are currently negotiating with Paul Scott, treasurer, of a Fortune 500 firm, for a sale that could amount to millions of dollars. You feel that you are in a strong position to make the sale, but two competitors are also negotiating with Scott, and it could go either way. You have become friendly with Scott, and over lunch one day he confided in you that he has recently been treated for manic depressive illness. You happen to have a staff psychologist who does employee counseling for your firm. The thought has occurred to you that such a

—Continued

ETHICS IN PRACTICE—*Continued*

trained professional might be able to coach you on how to act with and relate to a personality such as Scott's, so as to persuade him to choose your product.

Would you consult the psychologist? Select one of the following responses: *would consult, would not consult,* or *unsure.* Write down one or two sentences that serve as basis for your decision. *Please do not read further until you have completed these tasks.*

Illustrative responses from the female marketing and sales managers included the following.

- How cruel and degrading it would be to even consider doing such a thing!
- Absolutely not—I would never play with a person's mental health.
- I certainly would not do it, nor ever countenance anyone working for me doing it.
- It would be totally unethical to use information you acquired in confidence for your own selfish gain.

Illustrative responses from the male marketing and sales managers included the following.

- Yes, I would seek such advice. I use many behavioral techniques in dealing with customers, and as long as I don't lie to them or cheat them, there is no ethical issue involved.
- Yes, as long as I believe in my product, seeking professional advice as to how to sell it better is not unethical; indeed, the customer will benefit from my helping him to make the right choice.
- Yes, when I train salespeople part of it is how to learn to deal with different customer types—and that is all this situation comes down to.
- Yes. Actually, I would be acting in his best interests by doing this.

The overall responses were as follows:

	Would consult	Would not consult	Unsure
Males	84%	12%	4%
Females	32%	62%	6%

The responses to this scenario and the other scenarios that were a part of the study revealed that the ethical explanations and justifications for the decisions by females and males differed considerably.[25]

DECISION-MAKING MODELS

In this section we present briefly the primary features of three decision-making models: the rational, bounded rationality, and political models. Our goal is to demonstrate the different ways in which decision making is perceived and interpreted. These models are useful for identifying the complexity and variety of decision-making situations in an organization.

■ RATIONAL MODEL

The **rational model** emphasizes decision making that involves intentionally choosing among alternatives to maximize benefits to the organization. The rational perspective requires comprehensive problem definition, an exhaustive consideration of alternatives, and thorough data collection and analysis. Evaluation criteria are developed early in the process, and information exchange presumably is unbiased and accurate. Individual preferences and organizational choices are a function of the best alternative for the entire organization.[26] Thus the rational model of decision making is based on the explicit assumptions that (1) complete information concerning alternatives is available, (2) these alternatives can be ranked according to objective criteria, and (3) the alternative selected will provide the maximum gain possible for the organization (or decision makers). An implicit assumption is that ethical dilemmas do not exist in the decision-making process and that the *means–end principle* and *utilitarian principle* will dominate the consideration of ethical issues.

Xerox developed a companywide six-step process for making virtually all decisions of any importance, a portion of which is presented in Table 14.3. Column 1 identifies the six steps of the process. Column 2 presents the key question to be answered in each step. Column 3 indicates what's needed to proceed to the next step. Through this process, Xerox attempts to obtain rational decision making companywide. Managers and employees receive extensive training about various decision-making tools to help them work through these steps.[27] In terms of the individual, the rational model puts a premium on logical thinking.[28]

Computer-based technologies can help people use the rational model in making decisions. The following Technology in Practice selection provides some examples of how such technology aids in making human resource decisions more rational at McCormick & Company, the 8000 employee spice company.

TABLE 14.3 Portion of Xerox's Rational Decision-Making Process

STEP	QUESTION TO BE ANSWERED	WHAT'S NEEDED TO GO TO THE NEXT STEP
1. Identify and select problem	What do we want to change?	Identification of the gap; "desired state" described in observable terms
2. Analyze problem	What's preventing us from reaching the "desired state"?	Key cause(s) documented and ranked
3. Generate potential solutions	How *could* we make the change?	Solution list
4. Select and plan the solution	What's the *best* way to do it?	Plan for making and monitoring the change; measurement criteria to evaluate solution effectiveness
5. Implement the solution	Are we following the plan?	Solution in place
6. Evaluate the solution	How well did it work?	Verification that the problem is solved, or agreement to address continuing problems

Source: Adapted from Garvin, D. A Building a learning organization. *Harvard Business Review,* July–August 1993, 78–91; Brown, J. S., and Walton, E. Reenacting the corporation: Organizational change and restructuring of Xerox. *Planning Review,* September/October 1993, 5–8.

TECHNOLOGY IN PRACTICE

HR Technology at McCormick & Company

Michael Traskey remembers the dark ages of human resources (HR). Back then, every time the director of organizational development at McCormick & Company wanted to fill a management position internally, he had to wait for days as faxes and voice-mail messages went back and forth to HR offices in California, Canada, and the United Kingdom. Personnel managers in the field pored over files and employees' qualifications before forwarding lists to Traskey, who then went through them to find the right candidate. In the end, it was a highly inexact science. "We couldn't always locate the best candidate as quickly as we would have liked," Traskey recalls. "It was slow and frustrating."

Today, managers at the company can tap a central database of everyone in the 8000 employee organization, including their education, training, language skills, and preferences. "We wanted to automate the internal résumé process and have a system do the searches for us," Traskey explains. "If we needed a person with manufacturing experience, an MBA, and a willingness to relocate to Morocco, we didn't want to have to spend weeks trying to find the individual." McCormick's sophisticated computer system can provide a list of qualified candidates in minutes rather than days. Perhaps more important, managers virtually anywhere in McCormick's far-flung empire can now do the search. That relieves the company's central HR staff of the burden of doing every search while also giving managers away from the corporate center greater control over their operations' future.

McCormick's Traskey opted to use an IBM mainframe linked to hundreds of PCs connected over local- and wide-area networks. The company installed elaborate succession planning and internal résumé software. Data flows instantly between offices across town and around the world. And Traskey, from his desk at the firm's headquarters in Sparks, Maryland, can gather information simply by tapping a few keys on his PC.

At McCormick and other firms, an HR professional sitting at a workstation can do sophisticated spreadsheet modeling or management succession planning. Software has automated record keeping by allowing employees to update appropriate portions of their own files at terminals or kiosks; yet it also protects everyone's privacy and corporate confidentiality. New programs track hiring, firing, and promotion patterns and provide details about how managers deal with women and minorities; offer sophisticated modeling for downsizing or reengineering efforts; and even handle changes in business rules and government requirements. All of these developments are consistent with the rational model of decision making.[29]

■ BOUNDED RATIONALITY MODEL

The **bounded rationality model** emphasizes the limitations of rationality and reveals the day-to-day decision-making processes actually used by individuals. It partially explains why different individuals make different decisions when they have exactly the same information. As suggested in Figure 14.2, the bounded rationality model reflects the individual's tendencies to (1) select less than the

■ FIGURE 14.2

Bounded Rationality Model

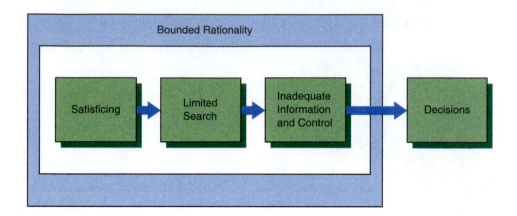

best goal or alternative solution (that is, to *satisfice*), (2) engage in a limited search for alternative solutions, and (3) have inadequate information and control of external and internal environmental forces influencing the outcomes of decisions.[30] This model also recognizes the reality that complete information—concerning available alternatives or the outcome of some course of action—may be impossible for an individual to obtain, regardless of how much time and resources are used.

Satisficing　　The practice of selecting an acceptable goal or solution is called **satisficing.** In this case, *acceptable* might mean easier to identify and achieve, less controversial, or otherwise safer than the best available alternative. For example, profit goals often are quantified, such as a 12 percent rate of return on investment or a 6 percent increase in profits over the previous year. These goals may not be the maximum attainable. They may, in fact, represent little more than top management's view of reasonable goals, that is, challenging but not too difficult to achieve.[31]

In an interview almost thirty-five years after introducing the bounded rationality model, Herbert Simon described satisficing in these words for a management audience:

> Satisficing is intended to be used in contrast to the classical economist's idea that in making decisions in business or anywhere in real life, you somehow pick, or somebody gives you, a set of alternatives from which you select the best one—maximize. The satisficing idea is that first of all, you don't have the alternatives, you've got to go out and scratch for them—and that you might have shaky ways of evaluating them when you do find them. So you look for alternatives until you get one from which, in terms of your experience and in terms of what you have reason to expect, you will get a reasonable result.
>
> But satisficing doesn't necessarily mean that managers have to be satisfied with what alternative pops up first in their minds or in their computers and let it go at that. The level of satisficing can be raised—by personal determination, setting higher individual or organizational standards, and by use of an increasing range of sophisticated management science and computer-based decision-making and problem-solving techniques.
>
> As time goes on, you obtain more information about what's feasible and what you can aim at. Not only do you get more information, but in many, if not most, companies there are procedures for setting targets, including procedures for trying to raise individuals' aspiration levels [goals]. This is a major responsibility of top management.[32]

Limited Search   Individuals usually make a limited search for possible goals or solutions to a problem, considering alternatives only until they find one that seems adequate. For example, in choosing the best job, college graduates can't evaluate every available job in a particular field. They might hit retirement age before obtaining all the information needed for a decision. Even the rational decision-making model recognizes that identifying and assessing alternatives cost time, energy, and money. In the bounded rationality model, individuals stop searching for alternatives as soon as they discover an acceptable goal or solution.

Inadequate Information and Control   Individuals frequently have inadequate information about problems and face environmental forces that they can't control. These conditions often influence the results of their decisions in unanticipated ways.

The individuals who made the decision to remove the passengers on the American West flight to accommodate the California Angels baseball team, as described in the Preview Case, used the bounded rationality model. They appeared to engage in a limited search for alternatives. They had inadequate information regarding the consequences of their decision—outraged customers and a public relations blunder. They falsely assumed that the consequences of their action wouldn't be serious. They assumed that giving priority to professional baseball players at the direct cost (delayed departure and wasted time) to customers who had already boarded their scheduled flight was acceptable. In fact, their action violated American West's contractual obligation and its customers' trust. Consistent with learning from experience with the bounded rationality model, American West isn't likely to make the same mistake again.

Rules are a natural part of the bounded rationality model. They provide quick and easy ways to reach a decision without a detailed analysis and search. They can be explicitly stated and easily applied. A general type of rule used by organizations—as well as by individuals—is the **dictionary rule.** This rule ranks items the same way a dictionary does: one criterion (analogous to one letter) at a time. The dictionary rule gives great importance to the first criterion. It is valid in decision making only if this first criterion is known to be of overriding importance.[33] Perhaps a dictionary rule was incorrectly used by individuals at American West. Such a rule might read: Always give priority and preference to our most influential and frequent customers.

In sum, the bounded rationality model provides insights into the limitations of decision making in organizations. It implicitly recognizes the potential for ethical dilemmas in decision-making situations but provides no guidance for resolving them. Also, it provides no specific guidance for navigating between two extremes: "paralysis by analysis" on the one hand and "extinction by instinct" on the other.[34]

■ POLITICAL MODEL

The **political model** emphasizes decision making that reflects the desires of individuals to satisfy their own interests. Preferences are established early, usually on the basis of personal self-interest goals, and seldom change as new information is acquired. Problem definitions, data searches and collection, information exchange, and evaluation criteria are merely methods used to tilt (bias) the outcome in someone's favor.

Decisions reflect the distribution of power in the organization and the effectiveness of the tactics used by the various participants in the process. Although the model doesn't allow for ethical dilemmas, it often draws on the following self-serving ethical principles discussed previously: (1) *hedonistic principle*—do whatever you find to be in your own self-interest; (2) *might-equals-right principle*—you are strong enough to take advantage without respect to ordinary social conventions and widespread practices or customs; and (3) *conventionalist principle*—bluff and take advantage of all legal opportunities and widespread practices or customs.

Deception is a common tactic of the political model. For example, to make top management look better to various stakeholders, some firms distort future revenue flows and expenses. These doctored figures are even presented in documents such as venture capital business plans, real estate prospectuses, and corporate earnings forecast announcements.[35]

The following Across Cultures feature reviews aspects of the political model as it operates in French organizations. The French culture values relatively high power distance, which indicates that relationships between superiors and subordinates are unequal, with both sides occupying different levels of status and privilege as a normal state.

ACROSS CULTURES

Political Model in French Organizations

The political model in French organizations is based on a number of underlying assumptions and expected behaviors. Four of them are as follows.

- Power, once attained, should not be shared except with the inside group of senior managers. Some are born to lead and others to follow; it is difficult for people to change. Secretaries are there to follow orders. Middle managers need to consult with their bosses as well as many others in the company before making a decision.

- If individuals have been recognized as being of senior management material, it does not matter if they are put in a job where they have no experience. Being of superior mettle, they should be able to learn how to do their jobs as they go along.

- It is harmful to reveal information unnecessarily, because then the decision-making process cannot be controlled. When, where, and how to communicate information is a delicate question that often only the upper echelons can decide.

- The upper echelons of the company are the older members of an elite circle of society, having frequented the best educational circles. They must maintain dignity and are a reference to be cited and an example to be followed. Their surroundings should reflect their importance. The senior manager's role is to control decisions, down to the smallest detail.

Some U.S. managers working in France chafe under the iron hand of a French boss. For example, one American, complaining of a lack of autonomy in his job, said, "The decision-making process is so hierarchical. In the U.S., I was completely responsible for my decisions. Here everything is so boxed I can just do a

—Continued

ACROSS CULTURES—*Continued*

few things. I'm required to carry out my defined responsibility and then pass the project on. No one is individually responsible. Your project could die in the next person's hands." He went on to condemn what he saw as "the blind following of power," which he declared led to "poor decisions." Thus, although he had exactly the same job as he had held in the United States, this disgruntled manager has much less responsibility at French headquarters. Forced to share projects with others, he is powerless to influence their outcome and is left without the satisfying feeling of accomplishment he had back home.[36]

PHASES OF MANAGERIAL DECISION MAKING

Managerial decision making begins with a recognition of problems and concludes with an assessment of the results of actions taken to solve those problems. Figure 14.3 illustrates the phases of managerial decision making.[37] Although these phases appear to proceed in logical order, managerial decision making actually may be quite disorderly and complex as it unfolds. There seemingly is no beginning or end. Managers usually deal with the unexpected crises and petty problems that require much more time than they're worth. The manager may well go from a budget meeting involving millions of dollars to a discussion of what to do about a broken decorative water fountain. Thus managerial work is hectic and fragmented and requires the ability to shift continually from person to person, from subject to subject, and from problem to problem.[38]

■ PROBLEM RECOGNITION

Managerial decision making rarely begins with a clean slate. Previous decisions and experiences and new information may determine whether a manager even recognizes a problem. Moreover, the characteristic of individual managers play an important role in problem recognition.[39]

With **structured problems,** the problem recognition phase is straightforward. For example, a marketing manager promises the delivery of an order within thirty days. After forty-five days, the customer calls and angrily complains: The order hasn't arrived. I need it pronto. What are you going to do? The marketing manager is suddenly and forcefully made aware of a problem and the need to resolve it immediately.

With **unstructured problems,** the problem recognition phase, itself, often is a problem. The "problem" of problem recognition can result from unclear or inadequate information about developments and trends in the environment. For example, Walt Disney, Hilton Hotels, and other organizations have marketing research departments to collect information about their customers to determine whether changing customer tastes and preferences are likely to create new problems. A challenge for successful organizations is to avoid the error of perceptual defense (see Chapter 3). In other words, people have a tendency to deny and protect themselves against threatening ideas or situations, especially when current success is at stake.[40] Mark Newton heads the department at Cincinnati Gas & Electric and is charged with helping the utility move into the future. He comments, "I look at denial as an unconscious coping mechanism to block out and not deal with major change that may have some pain associated with it."[41]

FIGURE 14.3

Phases of Managerial Decision Making

Source: Adapted from McCall, M. W., Jr., and Kaplan, R. E. Whatever It Takes: The Realities of Managerial Decision Making, 2d ed. Englewood Cliffs, N.J.: Prentice-Hall, 1990.

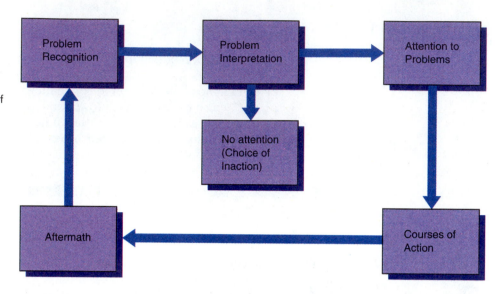

Let's return to the marketing manager who was called by an irate customer. This manager also has had a 200 percent turnover in sales representatives. When asked about this level of turnover, he replies: That's the way it's always been, even before I became the marketing manager. I guess it's just part of the cost of doing business and the nomadic nature of sales reps. This response shows no awareness that a problem of high turnover might exist. Six months later, a new marketing manager is appointed. When reviewing the personnel files, she is astounded to find: a major turnover problem, which must be corrected if we are ever to establish long-term and trusting relationships with our customers and eventually increase our sales to them.

Recognition of a problem usually triggers activities that may either lead to a quick solution or be part of a long, drawn-out process. The amount of time required to solve it depends on the nature and complexity of the problem. For example, the new marketing manager may be confronted by a subordinate with an easily solved problem: We're fifteen days late in the delivery of the South-Western Publishing Company order. Should we ship it by our regular freight line, by air express, or what? The marketing manager may immediately respond: Send it air express. However, the 200 percent annual turnover in sales personnel represents a major problem. She may need several months to (1) determine the reasons for the turnover, (2) implement a program to reduce turnover, and (3) assess the results of the program.

A variety of conditions can increase the likelihood of incorrect problem recognition and formulation. The following are seven such conditions.

- *Someone gives you a problem.* When you are asked to help solve a problem that someone else has defined, you are likely to take that problem as a "given" and work within the constraints of the problem statement. The more authority or power that the other person wields, the more likely you are to accept, without question, the statement of the problem.

- *A quick solution is desired.* If a decision is needed quickly, the amount of time spent in formulating or reformulating a problem is likely to be cut short. Recall the incident in the Preview Case regarding administrators who promptly suspended six-year-old Johnathan Prevette for sexual harassment after he kissed a classmate on the cheek. Their quick solution resulted in international ridicule.

■ *A low-quality solution is acceptable.* People attach a lower priority to some problems than to others. They are likely to spend less time formulating and solving a problem requiring only a low-quality solution than if a high-quality solution were essential. Recall from the Preview Case the comment by R.J. Reynolds' Chairman Charles Harper about exposing newborns to a smoky room. He clearly expressed a low-quality solution in his comment, "At some point, they will learn to crawl."

■ *The problem seems familiar.* A seemingly familiar problem is likely to get a ready-made solution rather than a tailor-made solution. Familiarity can lead to a quick solution or a fix. Recall from the Preview Case the American Society of Composers, Authors and Publishers requiring children's camps to pay fees if the youngsters sang certain copyrighted songs around their camp-fires. Initially, the warning and requirement to pay fees was based on the assumption that this practice violated copyrights as would the use of such material by commercial enterprises, such as radio stations, without payment of the required royalties.

■ *Emotions are high.* Stressful or emotional situations often lead to an abbreviated search for a satisfactory statement of the problem.

■ *Prior experience in handling challenging problem definitions is lacking.* For most people, questioning a problem statement requires training and practice. The habit of questioning is hard to get into (and easy to fall out of). Those unaccustomed to challenging or reformulating a problem statement are unlikely to do so.

■ *The problem is complex.* When a situation involves many variables and the variables are hard to identify and measure, the problem is more difficult to formulate and solve.[42]

■ PROBLEM INTERPRETATION

The second phase in the decision-making process requires an interpretation of the problem. A high turnover rate for sales representatives might be the result of looking for applicants in the wrong places, poor selection procedures and training, lack of supervision, a poor compensation system, an unacceptable level of work stress, or some combination of these inadequacies. **Problem interpretation** refers to the process of giving meaning and definition to concerns and issues that have been recognized.[43] Problem recognition doesn't mean that the problem will get attention. According to Figure 14.3, one option for managers simply is not to give a recognized problem any attention—the choice of inaction. This choice may be a consequence of (1) demands on the manager to deal with too many high-priority problems, (2) a belief that the problem will go away with time, or (3) the judgment that an attempt to do something about the problem will fail or only worsen the situation.

Preconceptions, the filtering out of new information, and defensiveness contribute to ineffective problem interpretation. Some of the key influences on problem interpretation include perceptions and attributions, organizational culture, and organization design. A common thread in these influences is the way information is processed and used to interpret problems. There is no simple one-to-one relationship between the availability of "objective" information and how it is processed in the problem interpretation phase. Various biases can affect decision making, including risk propensity, problem framing, availability bias, confirmation bias, selective perception bias, and law of small numbers bias.

Risk Propensity   **Risk propensity** is the general tendency of an individual or group to make or avoid decisions in which the anticipated outcomes are unknown (see Chapter 9). A risk-averse individual or group is likely to focus on potentially negative outcomes. The probability of loss is overestimated relative to the probability of gain. Therefore the decision maker requires a high probability of gain to tolerate exposure to failure. Conversely, a risk-seeking decision maker is likely to focus on potentially positive outcomes. Probability of gain is overestimated relative to the probability of loss. Thus risk seekers may be willing to tolerate exposure to failure with a low probability of gain.[44] Many decisions can be understood in terms of a desire to avoid the unpleasant consequences of a decision that turns out poorly. Making a choice can be personally threatening because a poor outcome can undermine the decision maker's sense of competence, cause significant problems for the organization, and even get the decision maker fired. In general, most people have a low-risk propensity. People buy countless varieties of insurance to avoid the risk of large but improbable losses. They invest in savings accounts, CDs, and money market funds in order to avoid the risk of extreme price changes for individual stocks and bonds. Generally, they prefer courses of action that are likely to produce satisfactory outcomes to risky courses of action that are likely to have the same or higher expected outcomes.[45]

Problem Framing   The tendency to perceive issues in positive or negative terms is called **problem framing.** Individuals in favorable circumstances tend to be risk averse because they may feel that they have more to lose. In contrast, those in unfavorable situations may feel that they have little to lose and therefore may be risk seeking. Stressing the potential losses implied by a decision heightens the importance of risk. In contrast, stressing potential gains lessens the perception that serious risks are involved. Specifically, positively framed situations foster risk taking by drawing managerial attention to opportunities rather than risks.[46] An example of positive versus negative framing is that of the certainty of winning $3000 or the 80 percent probability of winning $4000. Most people prefer the certain gain to the uncertain chance of larger gain. Which would you choose? Although risk aversion commonly is assumed to hold for most decisions, many exceptions have been documented. People prefer to take risks when making a choice between a certain loss and a risky loss. For example, what happens when individuals are asked to choose between the certainty of losing $3000 and the 80 percent probability of losing $4000? In this case, most people prefer the risky alternative.[47] Which would you choose?

Availability Bias   The tendency to recall specific instances of an event and therefore to overestimate how often it occurs (and vice versa) is called the **availability bias.** Individuals who have been in a serious automobile accident often overestimate the frequency of such accidents. This type of bias may be expressed as what's out of sight often is out of mind. In other words, evident limited alternatives may carry more weight in judgments concerning the likelihood of an event than they should.[48] Bridge players provide a telling example. Experienced bidders take into account unusual events or ways to win hands by relying on various decision rules. Less experienced players believe that they can make hands they often cannot, precisely because they fail to consider uncommon occurrences.

Confirmation Bias   The tendency to seek support for an initial view of a situation rather than to look for disconfirming evidence is called the **confirmation bias.** Unfortunately, the more complex and uncertain a situation, the more easily one-sided support can be found. Realistic confidence requires seeking negative, as well as positive, evidence. People tend to overstate the strength of evidence (how well a candidate did in an interview) relative to the credibility of that type of evidence (the limited insight gained from any single interview). Whenever source credibility is low and the strength of the evidence is highly suggestive, overconfidence is likely to occur (see Chapter 3).[49] Thus people may predict too readily that the interviewed candidate will win or lose, based on the fallible, limited evidence obtainable from a short interview.

Selective Perception Bias   The tendency to see what people expect to see is called the **selective perception bias.** People seek information consistent with their own views and often downplay information that conflicts with their perceptions (see Chapter 3).[50] An example might be parents who are unwilling to acknowledge that the reasons their child received a falling grade are poor performance and lack of effort, rather than poor instruction or instructor bias.

Law of Small Numbers Bias   The tendency to consider small samples to be representative of a larger population (a few cases "prove the rule"), even when they aren't, is called the **law of small numbers bias.**[51] Some Arab-Americans were the targets of hostile comments and actions by some non-Arabs after the invasion of Kuwait by Iraq. Apparently, these individuals incorrectly attributed the unsavory characteristics of Saddam Hussein's government (sample of 1) to Arabs and Arab-Americans in general.

Another potential bias is occupational specialization, which may lead to a form of tunnel vision. Specialization fosters the channeling of information and problems to particular experts and departments, which can both aid and hinder problem recognition and interpretation. When the marketing manager and her staff have been assigned goals to ensure customer satisfaction—such as 98 percent of all orders are to reach customers on the promised date of delivery—and to take corrective action when the goals are not achieved, specialization probably aids problem recognition and interpretation. Generally, however, unless there are cross-functional teams in the organization, specialization may well lead to ineffective efforts and conflicts between specialties and departments. Employees have been known to conceal and distort information as a means of advancing their individual and departmental goals. Someone also may fail to recognize the importance of new information if it doesn't clearly fall within that person's specialty or area of responsibility. Unfortunately, this tendency is most likely in a complex and uncertain environment, the very environment in which effective problem recognition and interpretation are crucial. The likelihood of managers and employees learning to recognize and interpret problems effectively is also strongly influenced by the organization's culture (see Chapter 17).[52]

■ ATTENTION TO PROBLEMS

After problems have been recognized and interpreted, judgments need to be made about which problems are to receive attention, how much of it they are to receive, and in what order they are to receive it. Managers must be aware of the relative priorities they place, sometimes unconsciously, on the problems they deal with. The problems receiving the highest priority are likely to meet the following criteria.

- Attention to the problem is supported by strong external pressure (the executive vice-president insists on a report being completed within two weeks).

- Attention to the problem is supported by the necessary resources to take action (authorization given to approve overtime pay and hire temporary workers to complete the report within two weeks).

- Attention to the problem represents an irresistible opportunity (the report deals with assessing a proposed expansion in production capacity that could lead to a larger and more profitable firm, a promotion from production supervisor to production manager, or the potential of larger bonuses).

The number and variety of recognized problems needing attention almost always exceeds the manager's capacity for addressing and solving all of them within the desired time frame. In addition, pressures from the external environment can change the most carefully planned priorities for attending to recognized problems.[53]

■ COURSES OF ACTION

The development and evaluation of courses of action (alternatives) and the implementation of the selected alternative can range from a quick-action process to a convoluted-action process. A *quick-action process* is appropriate when (1) the nature of the problem is well structured (two subordinates fail to show up for work, creating a problem in meeting a deadline for the next day); (2) a single manager (or at most, two managers) is clearly recognized as having the authority and responsibility to resolve the problem (the manager authorizes overtime for some employees to meet the deadline); and (3) the search for information about the problem and alternatives is quite limited (the manager might call the customer to determine the actual urgency of delivery to determine whether to schedule overtime, bring in help from a temporary employment service, or check with other managers to find out whether their departments are less busy and could loan some workers). This quick-action process may well take place within a matter of minutes or take as long as several days.

At the other extreme, the *convoluted-action process* is drawn-out and mazelike. This process is often applied to problems and issues that have the following characteristics.

- The problem is unstructured.
- A long period of time is required to develop, evaluate, and implement alternatives.
- Many vested interests and power relationships are involved.
- Many people are involved in an extensive search for solutions.

Recent issues that involved a convoluted-action process include (1) Donnelley's efforts to deal with diversity issues (see previous Diversity in Practice); (2) the introduction and use of computer-based information to aid human resource decisions at McCormick & Company (see previous Technology in Practice), (3) Microsoft's development, market testing, and introduction of Windows 95 and subsequent updating to Windows 97; and (4) attempts to negotiate a new contract over more than a two-year period between American Airlines and its

pilots. In either the convoluted-action or quick-action processes, trade-offs, negotiations, conflict, and political processes usually are involved. Managers continuously face a variety of problems, many of which can be addressed by the quick-
action process; far fewer require initiating the convoluted-action process.
However, quick action may lead to poor decisions, when a deliberate approach
would have been more appropriate.[54]

■ AFTERMATH

The **aftermath** phase refers to evaluation of the results from the actions taken.
With structured problems, evaluation usually is rather simple. The benefits and
costs associated with alternative actions can easily be calculated. Recall the example of the manager who scheduled overtime to meet a deadline when two workers failed to show up. If the overtime hours resulted in meeting the deadline,
there is clear feedback that the decision led to the intended result.

The selection of a course of action and its implementation to deal with an
unstructured problem may involve many individuals, teams, and subjective judgments, as in the American Airlines–pilots negotiations. The assessment of the
course of action taken may require months or even years before the outcomes are
known and their consequences can be determined. Whether the pilots' fear of
losing jobs to outsourcing by American Airlines will be borne out won't be fully
known for several years after a new contract is approved. Also, the potential for
the contract to reduce American Airlines' competitiveness with other carriers
won't be known for several years. Unstructured problems thus require implementing a course of action in the face of risk and uncertainty.

Even the best managers and employees make mistakes. The challenge is to recognize and learn from these mistakes. Most managers and employees guard their
reputations as capable people and may go to extremes not to acknowledge their
mistakes. Moreover, individuals and teams tend to overestimate the effectiveness
of their judgment decisions.[55] Sometimes the negative aftermath of a decision
will result in an escalating commitment. **Escalating commitment** is a process of
continuing or increasing the allocation of resources to a course of action, even
though a substantial amount of feedback indicates that the action is wrong.[56]
Consider the following reflections on the Vietnam War and the anticipation of
the escalating commitment process.

> At an early state of the U.S. involvement in the Vietnam War, George Ball, then Under-
> secretary of State, wrote the following statement in a memo to Lyndon Johnson: "The
> decision you face now is crucial. Once large numbers of U.S. troops are committed to
> direct combat, they will begin to take heavy casualties in a war they are ill-equipped to
> fight in a noncooperative if not downright hostile countryside. Once we suffer large
> casualties, we will have started a well-nigh irreversible process. Our involvement will be
> so great that we cannot—without national humiliation—stop short of achieving our
> complete objectives. Of the two possibilities I think humiliation would be more likely
> than the achievement of our objectives—even after we have paid terrible costs." (Memo
> dated July 1, 1965, from Pentagon papers, 1971).[57]

One of the explanations for escalating commitment is that individuals feel
responsible for negative consequences, which motivates them to justify previous
decisions. In addition, individuals may become committed to a course of action
simply because they believe that consistency in action is a desirable form of
behavior. Our discussion of perception and attributions in Chapter 3 gives additional insights into the possible reasons for escalating commitment.

The following comment by a manager is instructive of the need to learn from the aftermath of a course of action, including those that turned out to be mistakes.

> Everybody knows you make mistakes, so why not admit it. I make it a point to admit the blunders. Once I admit it, I feel better about it. It doesn't bother me. It's really a painful thing to keep trying not to admit some things. You have to carry that around as a burden until you get it off your chest.[58]

STIMULATING CREATIVITY

Organizational creativity is the production of novel and useful ideas by an individual or team in an organization. Innovation builds on novel and useful ideas. Accordingly, **organizational innovation** is the implementation of creative and useful ideas through unplanned or planned organizational change.[59]

Creativity helps employees uncover problems, identify opportunities, and undertake novel courses of action to solve problems. We presented two approaches for stimulating creativity in organizations in Chapter 8, namely, the nominal group technique and electronic brainstorming. Moreover, we have repeatedly addressed issues and discussed processes for reducing barriers to creative and innovative thought and action. Some of these barriers include perceptual blocks, cultural blocks, and emotional blocks. *Perceptual blocks* include such factors as the failure to use all of the senses in observing, failure to investigate the obvious, difficulty in seeing remote relationships, and failure to distinguish between facets of cause-and-effect relationships. *Cultural blocks* include a desire to conform to established norms, overemphasis on competition or conflict avoidance and smoothing, the drive to be practical and narrowly economical above all things, and a belief that indulging in fantasy or other forms of open-ended exploration is a waste of time. Finally, *emotional blocks* include fear of making a mistake, fear and distrust of others, grabbing the first idea that comes along, and the like.[60]

For many organizations, fostering creativity and innovation are essential to their ability to offer high-quality products and services. The following Quality in Practice selection reviews some of the ways that Hallmark Cards, Inc., headquartered in Kansas City, Missouri, attempts to nourish creativity in its artists and writers.

QUALITY IN PRACTICE

Creativity at Hallmark

Keeping its artists and writers creative is a top priority at Hallmark, the nation's largest greeting card seller with more than $3.5 billion in sales annually. Hallmark traditionally captures about 42 percent of the market.

Staffers can desert Hallmark's midtown Kansas City headquarters for a downtown loft, where teams of writers and artists get away from phones to exchange ideas. They may spend days in retreat at a farm in nearby Kearney, Missouri, taking part in fun exercises like building birdhouses. Some go farther afield, sent by the company on trips overseas to soak up atmosphere and culture. Not all the methods are high-budget. For the creators of the irreverent Shoebox line, there are free movie passes and daily screenings of the hippest television shows.

—Continued

QUALITY IN PRACTICE—*Continued*

About 5500 of Hallmark's 19,000 full-time employees work at the company's huge corporate headquarters. Tucked away in thousands of cubicles, they seem to have their own methods of working. "Right now I'm trying to think like a cat," said Barbara Loots, a writer in the traditional cards section who's also a well-known local poet. A few cubicles away, Linda Staton describes herself as a poetry pack rat, saving poems she likes and trying to distill their essence for a card with broad appeal. She reads children's books in search of a writing tip that can pep up a card. Her best work comes when she's daydreaming. "I stare out that window for an inordinate amount of time," she said. "Some of my best ideas have turned up in my head at the end of the day when all defenses are down."

Nurturing the creative spirit reaches its wackiest heights at the Shoebox Cards division, where a team of seven writers and four editors usually starts its day by watching a tape of the previous night's David Letterman show. They flip through magazines, even work out in the middle of the workday. Sounds like fun, but there are deadlines. The group is expected to turn out seventy cards a week. To do that, they'll generate an average of 150 pieces of writing a day. At the end of the day, the staff's efforts are sifted at a raucous conference led by Chief Editor Steve Finken. With a practiced ear for the staff's reaction, Finken reads each card aloud and swiftly separates them into two piles. The reject pile is much larger than the save pile.

There's the same pressure as in any other business. Each card's success is rated through surveys and information gathered by electronic cash registers, and staff members know exactly how well their work is doing.[61]

We conclude this section with a description of two methods for stimulating creativity with virtually any individual, team, or group: the lateral thinking and devil's advocate methods.

■ LATERAL THINKING METHOD

The **lateral thinking method** is a deliberate process for generating new ideas by changing the individual's or team's typical logical pattern for processing and storing information. In contrast, the **vertical thinking method** is the logical step-by-step process of developing ideas by proceeding on a continuous path from one bit of information to the next. Table 14.4 presents the major differences between lateral thinking and vertical thinking. Edward de Bono, the British physician and psychologist who developed the lateral thinking method, stated that the two processes are complementary, not antagonistic.

Lateral thinking is useful for generating ideas and approaches, and vertical thinking is useful for developing them. Lateral thinking enhances the effectiveness of vertical thinking by offering it more to select from. Vertical thinking multiplies the effectiveness of lateral thinking by making good use of the ideas generated. An individual might use vertical thinking most of the time, but when that person needs to use lateral thinking, excellence in vertical thinking won't suffice.[62]

The lateral thinking method includes some special techniques for (1) developing an awareness of current ideas and practices, (2) generating alternative ways of looking at a problem, and (3) assisting in the development of new ideas. Here,

TABLE 14.4 Characteristics of Lateral Versus Vertical Thinking

LATERAL THiNKING	VERTICAL THINKING
1. Tries to find new ways for looking at things; is concerned with change and movement.	1. Tries to find absolutes for judging relationships; is concerned with stability.
2. Avoids looking for what is "right" or "wrong." Tries to find what is different.	2. Seeks a "yes" or "no" justification for each step. Tries to find what is "right."
3. Analyzes ideas to determine how they might be used to generate new ideas.	3. Analyzes ideas to determine why they do not work and need to be rejected.
4. Attempts to introduce discontinuity by making "illogical" (free association) jumps from one step to another.	4. Seeks continuity by logically proceeding from one step to another.
5. Welcomes chance intrusions of information to use in generating new ideas; considers the irrelevant.	5. Selectively chooses what to consider for generating ideas; rejects information not considered to be relevant.
6. Progresses by avoiding the obvious.	6. Progresses using established patterns; considers the obvious.

Source: Based on de Bono, E. *Lateral Thinking: Creativity Step by Step.* New York: Harper & Row, 1970; de Bono, E., *Six Thinking Hats.* Boston: Little, Brown, 1985.

we consider four lateral thinking techniques for assisting in the development of new ideas: reversal, cross-fertilization, analogy, and random-word stimulation.[63]

Reversal The process of examining a problem and turning it completely around, inside out, or upside down is called the **reversal technique.** Engineers at Conoco asked, "What's good about toxic waste?" By so doing, they discovered a substance in waste that they now are turning into both a synthetic lubricant and—they hope—a promising new market. Ronald Barbaro, president of Prudential Insurance, considered the idea, "You die before you die," and came up with "living benefit" life insurance. It pays death benefits to people suffering from terminal illnesses before they die. Prudential has sold more than a million such policies.[64]

Cross-Fertilization The process of asking experts from other fields to view the problem and suggest methods for solving it from their own areas is called the **cross-fertilization technique.** For the technique to be effective, these outsiders should be from fields entirely removed from the problem. An attempt can then be made to apply these methods to the problem. As suggested in the previous Quality in Practice selection, Hallmark Cards has its own variation of cross-fertilization. In addition, Hallmark brings in some thirty speakers a year to stimulate novel thinking. Writers and artists also are sent on what seem like vacations to soak up new atmospheres and obtain inspiration. Artist and manager Marita Wesely-Clough, after two weeks in Mexico, found "stimulus galore." It led her to suggest new products such as a line of cards whose colors mimic the shades of adobe walls.

Analogies The process of developing a statement about similarities between objects, persons, or situations is called the **analogy technique.** Some examples of analogies are: This organization operates like a beehive or This organization operates like a fine Swiss watch. The method involves translating the problem into an analogy, refining and developing the analogy, and then retranslating to the problem to judge the suitability of the analogy. If an analogy is too similar to the problem, little will be gained. Concrete and specific analogies should be selected over more abstract ones. Analogies should describe a specific, well-known issue or process in the organization. For an organization that is ignoring increased environmental change, an analogy might be: We are like a flock of ostriches with our heads buried in the sand.

Random-Word Stimulation   The process of selecting a word from a dictionary or specially prepared word list and then seeking links between the word and a problem is called the **random-word stimulation technique.** One option is to select a word by using a table of random numbers to choose a page in a dictionary and then a position on a page. For most problems, however, a less-than-random procedure probably is adequate. One important point about using this method is: Try to stay with a word once it has been selected. A premature judgment about a word's relevance could result in many useful ideas being overlooked.

We presented only a few of the techniques and ideas for stimulating lateral thinking. Organizations such as Hallmark, Unilever, General Electric, Shell, Motorola, Microsoft, and 3M have formally introduced this approach through their development programs.[65]

■ DEVIL'S ADVOCATE METHOD

The process by which a person or team develops a systematic critique of a recommended course of action is called the **devil's advocate method.** It involves pointing out weaknesses in the assumptions underlying the proposal, internal inconsistencies in it, and problems that could lead to failure if it were followed. The devil's advocate acts like a good trial lawyer by presenting arguments against the majority position as convincingly as possible.[66] Figure 14.4 illustrates the basic decision-making process when this method is utilized.

People assigned to the devil's advocate role should be rotated to avoid any one person or task force being identified as a critic on all issues. The devil's advocate role may be advantageous for a person and the organization. Steve Huse, chairperson and CEO of Huse Food Group, indicates that the devil's advocate role is an opportunity for employees to demonstrate their presentation and debating skills. How well someone understands and researches issues is apparent when that person presents a critique. The organization avoids costly mistakes by hearing viewpoints that identify potential pitfalls. In addition, the use of the devil's advocate approach may increase the probability of creative solutions to problems and reduce the probability of groupthink.[67] Recall that groupthink in decision making is caused by excessive consensus and similarity of views in groups—a sure

■ **FIGURE 14.4**   **Decision Making with a Devil's Advocate**

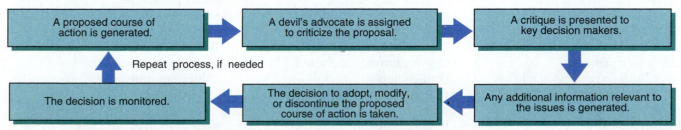

Source: Adapted from Cosier, R. A., and Schrivenk, C. R. Agreement and thinking alike: Ingredients for poor decisions. *Academy of Management,* February 1991, 71.

way to kill organizational creativity (see Chapter 8). The devil's advocacy method is effective in helping to bring to the surface and challenge assumptions on which a proposed course of action is based—an essential element in stimulating creativity. Of course, the devil's advocate method shouldn't be overused. It is best applied to especially important and complex issues.

CHAPTER SUMMARY

Individuals experience ethical dilemmas when making some decisions. Five basic issues, which can be stated as questions, should be considered in ethical decision making: What is the ethical intensity? What are the principles and rules? Who is affected? What are the benefits and costs? Who has rights?

Approaches commonly used to understand decision making in organizations are the rational, bounded rationality, and political models. Each captures some aspects of the decision-making situations and processes experienced by managers and employees. All three models are needed to understand the complexity and range of decision-making processes.

Managerial decision making often is an unending flow and cross-current of processes. The phases of managerial decision making include problem recognition, problem interpretation, attention to problems, courses of action, and aftermath. Although we discussed these phases separately, they don't unfold in a neat and orderly sequence.

Creativity often is needed in the most difficult situations. These situations arise when there is ambiguity or disagreement over both the goals to be sought and the best course of action to pursue. Organizational creativity and innovation are crucial to the discovery and implementation of novel and useful ideas. Two approaches for stimulating organizational creativity are the lateral thinking method and the devil's advocate method.

KEY TERMS AND CONCEPTS

Aftermath
Analogy technique
Availability bias
Bounded rationality model
Categorical imperative principle
Concentration of effect
Confirmation bias
Conventionalist principle
Cross-fertilization technique
Devil's advocate method
Dictionary rule
Disclosure principle
Distributive justice principle
Employment at will
Escalating commitment
Ethical intensity
Ethics

Golden rule principle
Hedonist principle
Intuition principle
Lateral thinking method
Law of small numbers bias
Magnitude of consequences
Managerial decision making
Means–end principle
Might-equals-right principle
Organization ethics principle
Organizational creativity
Organizational innovation
Political model
Probability of effect
Problem framing
Problem interpretation
Professional ethics principle

Proximity
Random-word stimulation
    technique
Rational model
Reversal technique
Risk propensity
Satisficing
Social consensus
Selective perception bias
Structured problems
Temporal immediacy
Unstructured problems
Utilitarian principle
Utilitarianism
Values
Vertical thinking method

DISCUSSION QUESTIONS

1. Think of an issue that created an ethical dilemma for you. How would you evaluate this dilemma in terms of each of the six components of ethical intensity?

2. Of the six ethical intensity components, which two are likely to be most important in the majority of situations? Explain.

3. What are the similarities and differences between the distributive justice principle and utilitarianism?

4. Arrange the ethical principles presented in this chapter in rank order from your most preferred to least preferred principle. What does this ranking tell you about how you are likely to interpret situations involving ethical dilemmas?

5. What are three potential ethical dilemmas that managers may experience when conducting performance appraisals?

6. At which managerial level—first-line, middle, and top—is a manager most likely to use each of the decision-making models (rational model, bounded rationality model, and political model)?

7. How is the decision-making process for professionals likely to differ from that of nonprofessional employees?

8. What are the most common difficulties you have in recognizing problems?

9. How might creativity help you in achieving effective problem identification and interpretation?

10. What are two differences between the lateral thinking method and the devil's advocate method?

■ Developing Competencies

Self-Insight: Individual Ethics Profile

The Individual Ethics Profile (IEP) is designed to help individuals identify the ethical preferences that guide their actions. The results can be useful for individuals who want to understand better the determinants of their own actions and gain new and broader ethics perspectives.

Instructions

Twelve pairs of statements or phrases follow. Read each pair and check the one that you most agree with. You may, of course, agree with neither statement. In that case, you should check the statement that you least disagree with.

You must select one statement in each pair; your IEP cannot be scored unless you do so.

_____ 1. The greatest good for the greatest number.

_____ 2. The individual's right to private property.

_____ 3. Adhering to rules designed to maximize benefits to all.

_____ 4. Individuals' rights to complete liberty in action, as long as others' rights are similarly respected.

_____ 5. The right of an individual to speak freely without fear of being fired.

_____ 6. Engaging in technically illegal behavior in order to attain substantial benefits for all.

_____ 7. Individuals' rights to personal privacy.

_____ 8. The obligation to gather personal information to ensure that individuals are treated equitably.

_____ 9. Helping those in danger when doing so would unduly endanger oneself.

_____ 10. The right of employees to know about any danger in the job setting.

_____ 11. Minimizing inequities among employees in the job setting.

_____ 12. Maintaining significant inequities among employees when the ultimate result is to benefit all.

_____ 13. Organizations must not require employees to take actions that would restrict the freedom of others or cause others harm.

_____ 14. Organizations must tell employees the full truth about work hazards.

_____ 15. What is good is what helps the organization attain ends that benefit everyone.

_____ 16. What is good is equitable treatment for all employees of the organization.

_____ 17. Organizations must stay out of employees' private lives.

_____ 18. Employees should act to achieve organizational goals that result in benefits to all.

_____ 19. Questionable means are acceptable if they achieve good ends.

_____ 20. Individuals must follow their consciences, even if doing so hurts the organization.

_____ 21. Safety of individual employees above all else.

_____ 22. Obligation to aid those in great need.

_____ 23. Employees should follow rules that preserve the individual's freedom of action while reducing inequities.

_____ 24. Employees must do their best to follow rules designed to enhance organizational goal attainment.

Instructions

Circle the numbers of the statements that you checked, indicating a preference for those statements over their paired alternatives. When you have circled the numbers of all your choices, add the *number of circles* in each of the three columns. The total for any column can range from 0 to 8.

1	2	4
3	5	8
6	7	9
12	10	11
15	14	13
18	17	16
19	20	22
24	21	23

Total number circled   _____   _____   _____

Divide the totals for each of the columns by 8. Enter the results on the following chart.

1.00 _____	1.00 _____	1.00 _____
.90 _____	.90 _____	.90 _____
.80 _____	.80 _____	.80 _____
.70 _____	.70 _____	.70 _____
.60 _____	.60 _____	.60 _____
.50 _____	.50 _____	.50 _____
.40 _____	.40 _____	.40 _____
.30 _____	.30 _____	.30 _____
.20 _____	.20 _____	.20 _____
.10 _____	.10 _____	.10 _____
Utilitarian	Moral rights	Justice

Interpretation

The IEP measures a person's preferences in terms of three primary sets of ethical concepts. The first set is called *utilitarian* because it is based on the premise that actions must be judged good or bad in terms of their effects, especially the effect of producing the greatest good for the greatest number. Although this value set is consistent with the common organizational aims of efficiency and effectiveness, it may be limited in that affected parties who are not heard from can easily be ignored. The utilitarian concept is consistent with what many believe to be a dangerous premise, that is, that the ends can justify the means.

The second ethical concept is called *moral rights*. It is based on the idea that individuals' personal rights must not be violated. Such rights include the right to life and safety, the right to know information that directly affects them and their choice of actions, the right to privacy, the right to act in line with their beliefs or conscience without fear of reprisal, the right to speak freely (including the right to speak about illegal or unethical actions by their employer, without fear of reprisal), and the right to private property. Clearly in some cases the moral rights concept may conflict with the utilitarian concept.

The third ethical concept is called *justice*. It is based on the belief that benefits and burdens should be allocated fairly, that is, based on equity and impartiality. In other words, each person has a right to the greatest possible freedom consistent with similar freedom for all others. Further, justice demands that social and economic inequities be dealt with so that those who are the most disadvantaged receive the greatest benefits. The concept of affirmative action is one illustration of this value in action. At the same time, the justice concept set calls for all persons to be treated equitably and not arbitrarily. Thus one employee should not be paid more than another who has the same skills and is doing the same job because of gender or race.[68]

Team Insight: Olson Medical Systems

Olson Medical Systems (OMS) offers computer-based financial systems to hospitals and nursing homes throughout the United States. Founded ten years ago by T. G. Olson, a former health care administrator, OMS employs more than forty analysts and programmers.

Once a month, the executive team of OMS meets to discuss plans, problems, and opportunities of the company. T. G. Olson calls and chairs the meetings. The other members include Frank Telsor (marketing), Karen Smith (operations), Terry Heath (systems development), Damien O'Brien (finance/accounting), and Ali Hassan (systems analyst). At a recent meeting, "maintenance contracts" appeared on the agenda, producing the following discussion.

Olson: Okay. Our last item is "maintenance contracts." Damien, this was your item.

O'Brien: Yes. I've been looking into the software maintenance contracts we have with some of our clients and I don't think we are getting a good return on investment. Based on my calculations, we would be better off selling enhanced versions of our Medicalc package every two years than offering maintenance contracts . . . unless, of course, we increase the price of the maintenance agreement.

Olson: How much would we have to increase the price?

O'Brien: Right now, we are breaking even.

Olson: So, what are you proposing?

O'Brien: I think we should increase the annual fee for Medicalc by at least two hundred dollars.

Telsor: If we do that, we're going to lose some business . . . maybe not the people who are with us already but some potential clients.

Olson: How many Medicalc users have maintenance contracts with us?

Telsor: I don't know.

O'Brien: I think it's about 80 percent.

Olson: What is the standard price, on a percentage basis, for maintenance packages?

Telsor: It varies slightly with the price of the software, but it is related to the frequency of changes.

Heath: Maybe we shouldn't be making so many changes. Last year, we made those changes to Schedule B and then Health and Social Services changed their minds. We could have been spending our time converting to the new IBM system.

Smith: It didn't help that we lost Stan Freedson. He knew Medicalc inside and out.

Olson: Yeah. Stan was good. Why don't we try to market the Medicalc maintenance agreement better? Does Health Data Systems or TMS make the kinds of changes we do and as frequently as we do? Let's let our clients know that our system is the most up-to-date in the market.

Telsor: Sometimes I think they'd rather buy the enhanced version every two years.

O'Brien: There are two hospitals in the Southwest that purchased the maintenance agreement, went off it for a year, and then renewed. Why, I wonder?

Telsor: One of them had a change of financial directors.

Olson: Ali, we haven't heard from you yet. Any thoughts on how to keep the cost of maintenance down?

Hassam: Not really. This sounds like a marketing problem to me . . . how to sell the service contracts.

Smith: I think we need more data. Maybe we should table this item until we know more about our clients' need and so forth.

O'Brien: What, specifically, do we need to know?

Olson: We need to know the projected changes in the schedules for the next couple of years and what it will cost to keep current.

Smith: Excuse me, I have to leave. I have a meeting with Joe Bergmann at eleven.

O'Brien: Why don't we just raise the price $75 for new clients and see what happens? TMS raised theirs $150 last year.

Olson: What do you think, Frank?

Telsor: Well, we can try it. We may lose some potential clients.

Olson: Okay, let's try it.[69]

Questions

1. What problem statements were offered (explicitly or implicitly) during this meeting?

2. How are these statements related to each other (that is, which statements are the means of solving others)?

3. What different purposes do problem statements serve (such as to keep people involved in the process, to avoid blame, and so on)? For what purposes were the statements offered in this case, in your opinion?

4. What other problem perspectives can you think of that might be useful to this team?

5. Which model of decision making (rational, bounded rationality, or political) best describes the decision-making process in this case? Explain and justify your answer.

REFERENCES

1. Adapted from G. Hassell, Memorable PR missteps of '96. *Houston Chronicle*, January 15, 1997, C1.

2. Freeman, E. E. (ed.). *Business Ethics: The State of the Art.* New York: Oxford University Press, 1991.

3. Donaldson, T., and Dunfee, T. W. Toward a unified conception of business ethics: Integrative social contracts theory. *Academy of Management Review*, 1994, 19, 252–284.

4. Frederick, R. E., and Petry, E. S., Jr. (eds.). *Emerging Global Business Ethics.* Westport, Conn.: Quorum Books, 1994.

5. Ethics Resource Center and Behavior Research Center. *Ethics Policies and Programs in American Business: Report of a Landmark Survey of U.S. Corporations.* Washington, D.C.: Ethics Resource Center, 1990.

6. Freeman, R. E., and Gilbert, D. R., Jr. *Corporate Strategy and the Search for Ethics.* Englewood Cliffs, N.J.: Prentice-Hall, 1988; Verbeke, W., Ouwerkerk, C., and Peelen, E. Exploring the contextual and individual factors on ethical decision making of salespeople. *Journal of Business Ethics*, 1996, 15, 1175–1187.

7. This section is based primarily on James, T. M. Ethical decision making by individuals in organizations: An issue-contingent model. *Academy of Management Review*, 1991, 16, 366–395. Also see Petrick, J. A., and Quinn, J. F. *Management Ethics and Organization Integrity.* Thousand Oaks, Calif.: Sage, 1997.

8. Adapted from Markels, A. A diversity program can prove divisive. *Wall Street Journal*, January 30, 1997; B1; Santosus,

M. Personnel matters. *CIO*, May 1, 1995, 44–52; Melcher, R. A. The press of new business! *Business Week*, January 15, 1996, 64–65.

9. Quinn, D. P., and Jones, T. M. An agent morality view of business policy. *Academy of Management Review*, 1995, 20, 22–42; Hartman, E. M. *Organizational Ethics and the Good Life*. New York: Oxford University Press, 1996.

10. Laczniak, G. R., Berkowitz, M. W., Brooker, R. G., and Hale, J. P. The ethics of business: Improving or deteriorating. *Business Horizons*, January–February, 1995, 39–47.

11. Adapted from Lewis, P. V. Ethical decision-making guidelines: Executive/student perceptions. In L. H. Peters and K. A. Vaverek (eds.), *Proceedings of the Annual Meeting of the Southwest Division of the Academy of Management*, 1988, 44–48; Chenko, L. B., Tanner, J. F., Jr., and Weeks, W. A. Ethics in salesperson decision making: A synthesis of research approaches and an extension of the scenario method. *Journal of Personal Selling & Sales Management*, Winter 1996, 35–52.

12. Greenberg, J. *The Quest for Justice on the Job*. Thousand Oaks, Calif.: Sage, 1995.

13. Husted, B. W., Brinker Dozier, J., McMahon, J. T., and Kattan, M. W. The impact of cross-cultural carriers of business ethics on attitudes about questionable practices and forms of moral reasoning. *Journal of International Business Studies*, 1996, 27, 391–411; Johnson, P. C., and Wolfe, D. M. Toward global integrity ethics: Challenges for the field of OD. *Organization Development Journal*, Winter 1996, 70–96.

14. Puffer, S. M., and McCarthy, D. J. Finding the common ground in Russian and American business ethics. *California Management Review*, Winter 1995, 29–46; Puffer, S. M., and Associates. *Business and Management in Russia*. Chiltenham, U.K.: Edward Elger, 1996.

15. France, M., Elstrom, P., and Maremont, M. Ethics for hire. *Business Week*, July 16, 1996, 26–28; Messeck, D. M., and Bazerman, M. H. Ethical leadership and the psychology of decision making. *Sloan Management Review*. Winter 1996, 9–22; Raiborn, C., and Payne, D. TQM: Just what the ethicist ordered. *Journal of Business Ethics*, 1996, 15, 963–972.

16. Sheppard, B. H., Lewicki, R. J., and Minton, J. W. *Organizational Justice: The Search for Fairness in the Workplace*. New York: Lexington Books, 1992.

17. Krueger, A. B. The evolution of unjust-dismissal legislation in the United States. *Industrial Labor Relations Review*, 1991, 44, 644–660.

18. Wartzman, R. Nature or nurture? Study blames ethical lapses on corporate goals. *Wall Street Journal*, October 9, 1987, 21.

19. Badaracco, J. L., Jr., and Webb, A. Business ethics: A view from the trenches. *California Management Review*, Winter 1995, 8–28.

20. Fukuyama, F. *Trust: The Social Virtues and the Creation of Prosperity*. New York: Free Press, 1996.

21. Boisseau, C. Workers foot bill for boosts in bosses pay. *Houston Chronicle*, June 19, 1996, A1, A21.

22. Eide, A., and Hagtvet, B. *Human Rights in Perspective: A Global Assessment*. Cambridge, Mass.: Blackwell, 1992; Thomas, D. A., and Ely, R. J. Making differences matter: A new paradigm for managing diversity. *Harvard Business Review*, September–October 1996, 79–90.

23. Robinson, S. L. Trust and breach of the psychological contract. *Administrative Science Quarterly*, 1996, 41, 574–599; Handy, C. Trust and the virtual corporation. *Harvard Business Review*, May–June 1995, 40–50.

24. Weiss, J. W. *Business Ethics: A Managerial, Stakeholder Approach*. Belmont, Calif.: Wadsworth, 1994.

25. Adapted from Dawson, L. M. Women and men, morality and ethics. *Business Horizons*, July–August 1995, 61–68; Dawson, L. M. Will feminization change the ethics of the sales profession? *Journal of Personal Selling and Sales Management*, Winter 1992, 21–32.

26. Hogart, R. M., and Reder, M. W. (eds.). *Rational Choice: The Contrasts Between Economics and Psychology*. Chicago: University of Chicago Press, 1986; Priem, R. L., Rasheed, A. M., and Kotulic, A. G. Rationality in strategic decision processes, environmental dynamism and firm performance. *Journal of Management*, 1995, 21, 913–929.

27. Garvin, D. A. Building a learning organization. *Harvard Business Review*, July–August 1993, 78–91.

28. Vos Savant, M. *The Power of Logical Thinking*. New York: St. Martin's Press, 1996.

29. Adapted from Greengard, S. The next generation. *Personnel Journal*, March 1994; Port, O. Computers that think are almost here. *Business Week*, July 17, 1995, 68–73; Goodman, P. S., and Darr, E. D. Exchanging best practices through computer-aided systems. *Academy of Management Executive*, May 1996, 7–19.

30. March, J., and Simon, H. *Organizations*, 2d ed. Cambridge, Mass.: Blackwell, 1993; Gigerenzer, G., and Goldstein, D. G. Reasoning the fast and frugal way: Models of bounded rationality. *Psychological Bulletin*, 1996, 103, 650–659.

31. March, J. G. *A Primer on Decision Making: How Decisions Happen*. New York: Free Press, 1994.

32. Roach, J. M. Simon says: Decision making is a "satisficing" experience. *Management Review*, January 1979, 8–9. Also see Simon, H. A. Bounded rationality and organizational learning. *Organization Science*, 1991, 2, 125–134.

33. Schoemaker, P. J. H., and Russo, J. E. A pyramid of decision approaches. *California Management Review*, Fall 1993, 9–31.

34. Langley, A. Between "paralysis by analysis" and "extinction by instinct." *Sloan Management Review*, Spring 1995, 63–76; Pfeffer, J. *Managing with Power: Politics and Influence in Organizations*. Boston: Harvard Business School, 1994.

35. Galbraith, C. S., and Merrill, G. B. The politics of forecasting: Managing the truth. *California Management Review*, Winter 1996, 29–43.

36. Adapted from Gouttefarde, C. American values in the French workplace. *Business Horizons*, March–April 1996, 60–69. Copyright © 1996 by the Foundation for the School of Business at Indiana University. Used with permission.

37. The perspective of this discussion was developed from McCall, M. W., Jr., and Kaplan, R. E. *Whatever It Takes: The Realities of Managerial Decision Making.* 2d ed. Englewood Cliffs, N.J.: Prentice-Hall, 1990.

38. Warglien, M., and Masuch, M. (eds.). *The Logic of Organizational Disorder.* New York: Walter De Gruyter, 1996.

39. Fairhurst, G. T., and Sarr, R. A. *The Art of Framing: Managing the Language of Leadership.* San Francisco: Jossey-Bass, 1996.

40. Daudelin, M. W. Learning from experience through reflection. *Organizational Dynamics,* Winter 1996, 36–48.

41. Kiechel, W. III. Facing up to denial. *Fortune,* October 18, 1993, 163.

42. Adapted from Volkema, R. J. Factors which promote "solving the wrong problem." Unpublished statement. Fairfax, Va.: Institute for Advanced Study in the Integrative Sciences, George Mason University, 1988.

43. Janis, I. L., and Mann, L. *Decision Making: A Psychological Analysis of Conflict, Choice, and Commitment.* New York: Free Press, 1977, 81.

44. Shapira, Z. *Risk Taking: A Managerial Perspective.* New York: Russell Sage Foundation, 1996; March, J. G. Learning to be risk averse. *Psychological Review,* 1996, 103, 309–319.

45. Bernstein, P. L. *Against the Gods: The Remarkable Story of Risk.* Somerset, N.J.: John Wiley & Sons, 1997.

46. Bernstein, P. L. The new religion of risk management. *Harvard Business Review,* March–April 1996, 47–51; Wang, X. Framing effects: Dynamics and task domains. *Organizational Behavior & Human Decision Processes,* 1996, 68, 145–157.

47. Kahneman, D., and Tversky, A. Prospect theory: An analysis of decision under risk. *Econometricka,* 1987, 47, 263–291.

48. Schwenk, C. R. Strategic decision making. *Journal of Management,* 1995, 21, 471–493.

49. Larson, E. W., and King, J. B. The systematic distortion of information. *Organizational Dynamics,* Winter 1996, 49–60.

50. Starbuck, W. H., and Mezias, J. M. Opening Pandora's box: Studying the accuracy of managers' perceptions. *Journal of Organizational Behavior,* 1996, 17, 99–117.

51. Kahneman, D. Judgment and decision making: A personal view. *Psychological Science,* 1991, 2, 142–145.

52. Price Waterhouse (firm). Change Integration Team. *The Paradox Principles.* Chicago: Irwin Professional Publishing, 1996.

53. Pablo, A. L., Sitkin, S. B., and Jemison, D. B. Acquisition decision-making processes: The central role of risk. *Journal of Management,* 1996, 22, 723–746.

54. Bazerman, M. H. *Judgment in Managerial Decision Making,* 3d ed. New York: John Wiley & Sons, 1993.

55. Weick, K. E. *Sensemaking in Organizations.* Thousand Oaks, Calif.: Sage, 1995.

56. Brockner, J. The escalation of commitment to a failing course of action: Toward theoretical progress. *Academy of Management Review,* 1992, 17, 39–61.

57. Staw, B. M. The escalation of commitment: A review and analysis. *Academy of Management Review,* 1981, 6, 577–587.

58. McCall, M. W., and Kaplan, R. E. *Consequences, Issues and Observations:* Greensboro, N.C.: Center for Creative Leadership, February 1985, 7.

59. Woodman, R. W., Sawyer, J. E., and Griffin, R. W. Toward a theory of organizational creativity. *Academy of Management Review,* 1993, 18, 293–321; Amabile, T. M., Conti, R., Coon, H., Lazenby, J., and Herron, M. Assessing the work environment for creativity. *Academy of Management Journal,* 1996, 39, 1154–1184.

60. Ford, C. M. A theory of individual creative action in multiple social domains. *Academy of Management Review,* 1996, 21, 1112–1142; Goswami, A. Creativity and the quantum: A unified theory of creativity. *Creativity Research Journal,* 1996, 9, 47–61.

61. Adapted from Hallmark goes the extra mile to keep employees creative. *Bryan–College Station Eagle,* June 5, 1996, A10; Flynn, G. Hallmark cares. *Personnel Journal,* March 1996, 50–58; Dutton, G. Enhancing creativity. *Management Review,* November 1996, 44–46.

62. de Bono, E. *Serious Creativity: Using the Power of Lateral Thinking to Create New Ideas.* New York: HarperCollins, 1992.

63. This discussion is based on Van Gundy, A. B. Techniques of Structured Problem Solving. New York: Van Nostrand, 1981, 234–244; Peterson, T. O., and Lunsford, D. A. Parallel thinking: A technique for group interaction and problem solving. *Journal of Management Education* (in press); Krohe, J., Jr. Managing creativity. *Across the Board,* September 1996, 16–21.

64. Farnham, A. How to nurture creative sparks. *Fortune,* January 10, 1994, 94–100.

65. Foster, J. *How to Get Ideas.* San Francisco: Berrett–Koehler, 1996.

66. Schwenk, C. R. Devil's advocacy and the board: A modest proposal. *Business Horizons,* July–August 1990, 22–27.

67. Cosier, R. A., and Schwenk, C. R. Agreement and thinking alike: Ingredients for poor decisions. *Academy of Management Executive,* February 1990, 69–74; Bennis, W., and Biederman, P. W. *Organizing Genius: The Secrets of Creative Collaboration.* Reading, Mass.: Addison-Wesley, 1997.

68. Adapted from Sashkin, M., and Morris, W. C. *Experiencing Management.* Reading, Mass.: Addison-Wesley, 1987, 60–62. Reprinted by permission of Addison-Wesley Longman Inc.

69. Volkema, R. J. Problem Formulation at Olson Medical Systems. Used with permission. This case was developed under a grant from the National Institute for Dispute Resolution, 1988.

15

Job Design

After you have finished this chapter, you should be able to:

- Explain and compare five common approaches to job design.
- Discuss the relationship between job design and reengineering.
- Outline the effects of poorly designed jobs.
- State the potential impact of technology on job design.
- Describe the job characteristics enrichment model and explain how it increases empowerment and work motivation.
- Explain the sociotechnical systems model and state how it increases empowerment and work motivation.

OUTLINE

PREVIEW CASE

Pillars of Job Design at the Fed

Management of the Federal Reserve Bank of Dallas (Eleventh District of the Federal Reserve System, or the Fed) developed a statement of *Strategic Direction, 1996 through 1998.* This statement discusses the Bank's mission, core values, pillars, and key initiatives. The two pillars—*customer driven quality* and *people*—serve as the foundation for its job design expectations and practices.

The Dallas Fed's statement says in part: The first major pillar of our organization is *Customer Driven Quality.* We will apply the following management precepts across all functions of the Bank and at all Eleventh District Offices.

- *Continuous Improvement.* We will focus our energies on making constant, long-term improvement in all areas of the Bank.

- *Teamwork.* Eleventh District Offices and departments will join forces to satisfy our customers' changing business requirements. We will take a team approach to management which values individual accomplishment but recognizes the far-reaching benefits of teamwork. Management will work rigorously to capture the synergies associated with collective problem solving and consensus decision making. Teamwork will provide all employees with an opportunity to contribute to the District's success.

- *Customer Service Excellence.* In the years ahead, the District will face new and complex demands that will stress our relationships with the Federal Reserve System, account holders, the public, and Bank staff. To meet these challenges, we will respond with creativity, industry, and perseverance.

- *Communication.* Satisfying our customers requires that we share information with openness, candor, and clarity. We will nurture communication in the context of a learning environment where the exchange of ideas, suggestions for change, and the expression of all viewpoints are accommodated.

- *Leadership.* For the organization to be fully effective, all employees must take ownership in the Eleventh District mission, vision, and core values. Management will achieve this commitment by fully involving all employees in the execution of our mission, allowing them to openly present their ideas and take initiative in their work. Employees who demonstrate leadership will be recognized for their contributions to the Bank's goals and objectives.

The second pillar of our organization is people. We believe that highly competent and highly motivated employees are paramount to the long-term success of the Bank. Toward this end, the Eleventh District will sustain a well-trained workforce, harness the talents and knowledge of our employees, and demonstrate fundamental respect for and appreciation of individuals. Employee training and development will keep pace with the increasing sophistication of technology and the rapid rate of change in the market. As a continually learning organization, we will place a high priority on knowledge, skills, and competency.

To bolster job satisfaction and to tap our employees' talents and ideas, employees will be encouraged to deploy the wealth of knowledge, life experience, and common sense that they bring to the job. The Bank will promote employee involvement by empowering employees to make decisions, providing the necessary technology and resources, lending supportive leadership, and rewarding excellent performance. Employee retention, recruitment of high-potential candidates, and management development will take on heightened importance as our responsibilities grow in complexity. Recognizing the dignity of the individual, management will provide the opportunity for personal growth, pride, and professionalism.[1]

T he Preview Case illustrates the underlying values, management principles, and strategic imperatives in the design or redesign of jobs. At the Federal Reserve Bank of Dallas (which we refer to as the Dallas Fed from here on), individual jobs are perceived to be interwoven with a broader pattern of tasks, responsibilities, and goals: continuous improvement (total quality management), teamwork, customer service excellence, communication openness, a learning environment, shared leadership and commitment, employee involvement and empowerment, among others. Hence job design there isn't viewed as defining tasks and responsibilities that are undertaken in isolation. Unfortunately, this approach to job design isn't typical of that taken by many organizations.

This chapter contains five sections. First, we introduce job design by (1) defining it, (2) explaining its relationship to reengineering, and (3) presenting a framework for comparing job design approaches. Second, we summarize five common job design approaches, two of which we discuss in greater detail in the last two sections of the chapter. Third, we outline the potential impact of technological factors on job design. Fourth, we describe the job characteristics enrichment model and extensions of it. Finally, we consider the sociotechnical systems model, the most complex and significant job design approach presented in this chapter. Job design at the Dallas Fed draws on both the sociotechnical systems model and the job characteristics enrichment model.

INTRODUCTION TO JOB DESIGN

We have emphasized the importance of effectively designed jobs in several previous chapters. For example, we discussed the need to design jobs to give individuals challenging goals and a sense of meaning at work in Chapter 5. In Chapter 8 we presented many ideas relevant to job design with regard to the use of teams. Problem-solving teams, special-purpose teams, and self-managed teams change and enlarge the tasks performed by employees. In this chapter, we further develop and extend these and other job design concepts and issues introduced earlier.

The specification of goals and tasks to be accomplished by employees, including expected interpersonal and task relationships, comprises **job design.** It occurs every time individuals are assigned work, given instructions, or empowered to perform tasks and pursue goals. Consciously or unconsciously, managers, team members, or others may change the job-related tasks of employees. Because both the tasks and the best means for performing them change, managers and teams need to know how to design and redesign jobs formally to make them as motivating, meaningful, and productive as possible. Thus the needs and goals of both the employee and the organization should be considered in the design of jobs.[2] The Dallas Fed's job design approach strives to give employees and the organization as a whole the tools needed to provide high-quality and efficient services to the organization's customers.

The ideal is to use employees' competencies to create and deliver quality products and services. Although this ideal isn't always attainable, substantial improvements in job design usually are possible and can also benefit the customer. For example, improving the design of U.S. production workers' jobs in automobile plants has improved the quality of cars. These efforts directly benefited the workers, improved the automakers' market positions, and provided customers with better cars.

■ RELATION TO REENGINEERING

Job design is one of the cornerstones of organizational reengineering efforts. **Reengineering** involves radically new ways of thinking about organizations, including breaking away from the outdated rules and assumptions that underlie task relationships and how tasks have been performed in the past. The purpose of reengineering is to eliminate—or prevent—the erection of barriers that separate employees and customers. Organization design, which we cover in Chapter

16, should be based on collections and flows among tasks that create value. The term used to describe such flows is *processes*. Processes are value-adding and value-creating flows of activities and tasks. Some examples are product development, customer acquisition, customer service, and order fulfillment.[3] The primary role of job design in reengineering has been stated as follows:

> The reason we are slow to deliver results is not that our people are performing their individual tasks slowly and inefficiently. We are slow because some of our people are performing tasks that need not be done at all to achieve the desired result and because we encounter agonizing delays in getting the work from the person who does one task to the person who does the next one. . . . We do not provide unsatisfactory service because our employees are hostile to customers, but because no employee has the information and the perspective needed to explain to customers the status of the process whose results they await.[4]

The reengineering process is more comprehensive than four of the five job design approaches discussed in this chapter. The three "R's" of reengineering—rethink, redesign, and retool—represent separate but related phases.

- *Rethink:* This phase requires examining the organization's current goals and underlying assumptions to determine how well they reflect a commitment to customer satisfaction. Another element in this phase is to examine crucial success factors, or those areas that set the organization apart from its competition. Do they contribute to the goal of customer satisfaction?

- *Redesign:* This phase requires an analysis of the way an organization produces the goods or services it sells–how jobs are structured, who accomplishes what tasks, and what results are obtained. Then, a determination must be made as to which elements should be redesigned to increase job satisfaction and customer focus.

- *Retool:* This phase requires a thorough evaluation of the current use of advanced technologies, especially groupware aids, to identify opportunities for change to improve the quality of services, products, and customer satisfaction.[5]

Reengineering initiatives often are accompanied by the use of advanced computer-based systems to streamline the flow of processes and assist in the introduction of new services. The following Technology in Practice feature on the U.S. Postal Service is one such example.

TECHNOLOGY IN PRACTICE

U.S. Postal Service Pursues High Tech

Postmaster General Marvin Runyon, a former auto industry executive, understands that in the digital age the U.S. Postal Service (USPS) must look to private industry to help it provide new and improved services. That's why the USPS has Pitney Bowes and other companies vying to develop a new digital postmark for metered mail. Printed from a standard office printer, the new postmark will contain a bar code that contains far more data than the Universal Product Code found on products in the supermarket and elsewhere.

The new postmarks would help the USPS cut down on postage theft and schedule its workers and vehicles more efficiently. The postmarks could also allow the
—Continued

TECHNOLOGY IN PRACTICE—*Continued*

USPS to link data about the sender and the recipient in a database. Out of concern for individual privacy, the USPS probably wouldn't sell personal data but instead aggregate it into neighborhood blocks, as the Census Bureau does with the data it collects. "If we get the privacy issue right and continue the tradition of trust, that information could be valuable," states Robert Reisner, the Postal Service's vice-president of strategic planning. Reisner adds that selling such data might make a lot of sense for the USPS because of its dominant role as a delivery service for direct mail, whose volume is rising faster than the volume of first-class mail.

The Postal Service also wants to turn the same encryption techniques used in the proposed postmarks into a business of certifying digital signatures. Today the average person who sends documents electronically has no way of guaranteeing that the document will arrive unaltered and that it will be received by the right person. And the recipient can't be sure that it is from the person named on it as the sender. The Postal Service proposes to serve as the agency that will certify that you are who you say you are and that documents are not altered en route. Implementation of this process is expected sometime in the year 2000.[6]

■ COMPARATIVE FRAMEWORK

Five of the most common approaches to job design, contrasted in terms of impact and complexity, are shown in Figure 15.1. *Impact* refers to the extent to which a job design approach is likely to be linked to factors beyond the immediate job, such as reward systems, performance appraisal methods, leadership practices of managers, organization structure, physical working conditions, and team composition and norms—as well as its likely effects on changes in productivity and quality. *Complexity* refers to the extent to which a job design approach is likely to require (1) changes in many factors, (2) the involvement of individuals with diverse competencies at various organizational levels; and (3) a high level of decision-making competency for successful implementation. In relation to Figure 15.1, the job design philosophy and practices at the Dallas Fed are characterized as high impact and high complexity.

The five approaches shown in Figure 15.1 and summarized in the next section don't by any means represent all the important job design approaches actually used. For example, there is renewed interest in the **human factors approach** to job design. It focuses on minimizing the physical demands (costs) and biological risks of work and sometimes is referred to as *ergonomics*. The goal of this approach is to ensure that job demands don't exceed people's physical capabilities to perform them. It involves the design of aids (ranging from hand tools to computer software to instruments) used to perform jobs.[7]

COMMON JOB DESIGN APPROACHES

In this section we provide an overview of the five common job design approaches shown in Figure 15.1: job rotation, job engineering, job enlargement, job enrichment, and sociotechnical systems. We expand on the job enrichment and sociotechnical systems approaches in later sections of this chapter.

■ FIGURE 15.1

Comparison of Five Job Design
Approaches

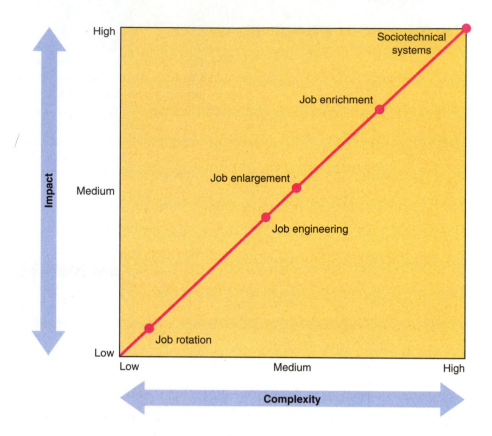

■ JOB ROTATION

Moving employees from job to job to give them opportunities to perform a variety of tasks is called **job rotation.** It is low in both impact and complexity because its primary purpose is to move employees among current jobs. Most often, job rotation focuses on adding variety to reduce employee boredom. Maids International, a housecleaning service franchise, uses job rotation with its four-person housecleaning teams by, for example, having a maid clean the kitchen in one house and the bedroom in another.[8] However, if all the tasks are similar and routine, job rotation may not have the desired effect. For example, rotating automobile assembly-line workers from bolting bumpers on cars to bolting on tire rims isn't likely to reduce their boredom. Job rotation may be of benefit if it is part of a larger redesign effort and/or it is used as a training technique to improve the skills and flexibility of employees.

■ JOB ENGINEERING

Late in the nineteenth century, Frederick W. Taylor established the foundation for modern industrial engineering. It is concerned with product design, process design, tool design, plant layout, work measurement, and operator methods. **Job engineering** focuses on the tasks to be performed, methods to be used, work flows among employees, layout of the workplace, performance standards, and interdependencies between people and machines. Analysts often examine these job design factors by means of time-and-motion studies, determining the time required to do each task and the movements needed to perform it efficiently.

Specialization of labor and efficiency are two of the cornerstones of job engineering. High levels of specialization are intended to (1) allow employees to learn a task rapidly, (2) permit short work cycles so that performance can be almost automatic and involve little or no mental effort, (3) make hiring easier because low-skilled people can be easily trained and paid relatively low wages, and (4) reduce the need for supervision, owing to simplified jobs and standardization.

Many managers and industrial engineers now recognize that traditional job engineering also can create boring jobs. Yet it remains an important job design approach because its immediate cost savings can be measured easily. In addition, this approach is concerned with appropriate levels of automation, that is, looking for ways to replace workers with machines to perform the most physically demanding and repetitive tasks.[9] The following questions define the intent of the job engineering approach.

- *Job specialization:* Is the job highly specialized in terms of purpose and/or activity?

- *Task simplification:* Are the tasks simple and uncomplicated?

- *Job simplification:* Does the job require relatively little skill and training time?

- *Repetition:* Does the job require performing the same activity or activities repeatedly?

- *Automation:* Are many of the activities of this job automated or assisted by automation?[10]

The job engineering approach continues to be widely and often successfully used, especially when it is combined with a concern for the social context in which the jobs are performed. The following Managing in Practice selection provides one such example.

MANAGING IN PRACTICE

Making Godfather's Pizza

As special projects manager and regional director at Minit Mart, Kelly Slavens has overseen the rollout of labor-scheduling software. Time studies, she contends, form the foundation of good labor scheduling.

"If you want software to produce good schedules, you've got to give it good information," Slavens says. "That means analyzing how long it takes employees to complete various tasks associated with their jobs. And you don't just look at one employee. You look at dozens and try to come up with mean task times. And, if you think you can perform a task more efficiently, you just try it yourself."

Godfather's Pizza counter sections are among Minit Mart's fast-food options. According to Slavens, "Under Godfather's, we have four jobs: pizza prep, food cashier, drive-through clerk, and a 'pivot person' who brings the food to the drive-through clerk and answers the phone." She adds that each of the Godfather's jobs have from nine to twelve tasks associated with them. "With so many tasks, you can see how important good time studies are," Slavens points out. "I literally go into the stores with a stop watch and time people as they perform their jobs," she

—Continued

MANAGING IN PRACTICE—*Continued*

explains. "It was a little weird for the employees at first, but now they are so used to me they joke about it."

"I visit the stores at random because I don't want to time the most productive or the least productive person. I watched morning, noon and night shifts in three stores. I observed thirty-five to forty people doing pizza prep alone. For the Godfather's counter section, I ended up with fifty pages of tasks referring to the four job titles—complete with the times it takes to perform them. Then I did some condensing to make it easier for the software to juggle those tasks. I grouped some together and came up with very sound data to feed into the program."

"After you feed that kind of information into the software program, it compares task times to point of sale data," Slavens says. "The software tracks how many pizzas are sold in fifteen-minute blocks. The same is true for the other registers in the stores. Once the system knows how much time the tasks take that support those sales, it can schedule amazingly well."[11]

■ JOB ENLARGEMENT

The expansion in the number of different tasks performed by an employee is called **job enlargement.** For example, one automobile assembly-line worker's job was enlarged from installing just one taillight to installing both taillights and the trunk. An auto mechanic switched from only changing oil to changing oil, greasing, and changing transmission fluid. Job enlargement attempts to add somewhat similar tasks to the job so that it will have more variety and be more interesting. As Figure 15.1 suggests, job enlargement is viewed as an extension of job engineering. However, it is more responsive to the higher level needs of employees by providing more variety in their jobs. At Minit Mart a form of job enlargement, along with job rotation, would be to have employees develop the skills to perform all four pizza-making jobs: pizza prep, food cashier, drive-through clerk and the pivot person.

Although the job enlargement approach often has positive effects, employees may resist it. Some employees view job enlargement as just adding more routine, repetitive tasks to their already boring job. Other employees may view it as eliminating their ability to perform their jobs almost automatically. These employees may value the opportunity to daydream about a big date that night or a vacation next month. Others may simply prefer to spend their time socializing with co-workers. If an enlarged job requires greater attention and concentration than the original job, some employees may find it interesting or challenging but others may view the added demands negatively. Management shouldn't underestimate the importance of individual differences in attempting to anticipate or understand the reactions of employees to redesigned jobs.

■ JOB ENRICHMENT

The empowerment of employees to assume more responsibility and accountability for planning, organizing, controlling, and evaluating their own work is called **job enrichment.**[12] The job enrichment approach originated in the 1940s at International Business Machines (IBM). In the 1950s, the number of companies interested in job enrichment grew slowly. However, successful and widely publicized experiments at AT&T, Texas Instruments (TI), and Imperial Chemicals eventually led to an increasing awareness of job enrichment and interest in this approach in the 1960s.[13] The techniques used for enriching jobs often are specific to the job being redesigned. We discuss enrichment techniques when we present the job characteristics enrichment model later in this chapter.

■ SOCIOTECHNICAL SYSTEMS

The **sociotechnical systems model** is based on the premise that every organization is made up of people with various competencies (the *social system*) who use tools, machines, and techniques (the *technical system*) to produce goods or services valued by customers. Thus the social and technical systems need to be designed with respect to one another—and to the demands of stakeholders in the external environment. To a large extent, this method of job design determines how effective an organization will be. All organizations are sociotechnical systems, but all don't necessarily reflect the principles underlying this approach.

The fundamental goal of sociotechnical systems analysis is to find the best possible match among the technology available, the people involved, and the organization's needs.[14] A crucial aspect of this approach is recognition of task interdependence, which becomes the basis for forming teams. After teams have been formed, the specific tasks to be performed by team members are considered, along with the relationships among all these tasks. This approach has been applied most successfully—as has the job enrichment approach—to industrial organizations.

The sociotechnical systems approach emphasizes the diagnosis of demands by external stakeholders (customers, suppliers, shareholders, regulatory agencies, creditors, and others) and the internal adaptations needed to respond to those demands. From a job design perspective, passage of the Americans with Disabilities Act (ADA) in 1990 created one such demand for many U.S.-based organizations. The following Diversity in Practice account reviews the accommodations that Benteler Automotive Corporation made on behalf of Brian Capshaw so that he could continue to work.

DIVERSITY IN PRACTICE

The Brian Capshaw Story

On his way to work at the Benteler Automotive Corporation (located near South Bend, Indiana), Brian Capshaw was in a severe accident that paralyzed him from the waist down.

Although he's in a wheelchair, Capshaw, 35, isn't confined. He coaches a kids' basketball team. He drives himself around in a hand-controlled van. And he still travels the familiar route to Benteler, where he works as an accountant.

Under the Americans with Disabilities Act, employers may be required to adapt their workplace to get disabled employees back on the job. Generally, however, "all the employer has to do is make 'reasonable' accommodations," says Pete Carroll, senior vice-president at CNA, the insurance company that provides group long-term disability coverage for Benteler. "It doesn't have to be anything

DIVERSITY IN PRACTICE—*Continued*

extraordinary." In fact, CNA estimates that the average cost of accommodating a disabled employee is less than $500.

Capshaw's injury was extraordinary and so were Benteler's efforts on his behalf. While he was still in rehabilitation, the company installed a wheelchair ramp, three electronic doors, and an eye-activated water fountain and redesigned a bathroom. The cost came to $30,000, all of it paid by CNA. By late summer 1995, Capshaw had returned to his job. His manager drove him to and from work every day until he was able to drive himself.

Benteler's and CNA's willingness to go the extra mile was the humane thing to do, but it made good business sense as well. In Capshaw's case, going back to work was a realistic possibility. This enabled Benteler to keep a valuable, productive employee rather than spend money to recruit and train a replacement. CNA was able to keep its costs down, too. If Capshaw had not returned to work, he would have been eligible for long-term-disability payments until he turned sixty-five—money that CNA would have had to pay.

Benteler Automotive Corporation and its insurer, CNA, obviously more than met the standard of reasonable accommodation. The ADA says that reasonable accommodation may include (1) modifying existing employment facilities to make them readily accessible to individuals with disabilities; and (2) making modifications such as job restructuring, part-time or modified work schedules, reassignment to vacant positions, acquiring, adjusting, or modifying equipment or devices, adjusting or modifying examinations, developing new training materials or policies, providing qualified readers or interpreters, and other similar accommodations.[15]

TECHNOLOGY AND JOB DESIGN

Recall that the use of techniques, tools, and machines to transform objects (material, information, and people) is called **technology**. Hence the technical system of an organization comprises the tools, techniques, methods, procedures, and machines used by employees to acquire inputs, transform inputs into outputs, and provide goods or services to clients and customers.[16] Our technology–job design discussion relates the concepts of work-flow uncertainty, task uncertainty, and task interdependence to job design. We also present some examples of how various information technologies are being used to implement these concepts. In terms of other approaches for relating technology to job design, recall the various ways that the work of individuals and teams is being changed by new information technologies, especially with groupware (see Chapters 8, 13, and 14).

■ WORK-FLOW AND TASK UNCERTAINTY

Work-flow uncertainty is the degree of knowledge that an employee has about when inputs will be received and require processing. When there is little work-flow uncertainty, an employee may have little discretion (autonomy) to decide which, when, or where tasks will be performed. For the most part, the production workers at an automobile assembly plant experience a low degree of work-flow uncertainty. In fact, the application of the job engineering approach in automobile assembly plants is intended to minimize work-flow uncertainty. In contrast,

task uncertainty is the degree of knowledge that an employee has about how to perform the job and when it needs to be done. When there is little task uncertainty, an employee has a lot of knowledge about how to produce the desired results.[17] Through extensive training and the standardization of jobs, management typically attempts to minimize task uncertainty in the automobile assembly plant. However, production employees in a plant experience somewhat more task uncertainty if they work as teams to study problems and refine procedures. At such a plant, teams often are asked to participate in proposing continuous improvements, which is one of the elements in total quality management.

With high task uncertainty, few (if any) prespecified ways exist for dealing with the job's tasks. This condition means that experience, judgment, intuition, and problem-solving ability usually are required of the employee. A number of employees at the Dallas Fed (Preview Case) face moderate to high levels of task uncertainty.

The main combinations of work-flow uncertainty and task uncertainty are shown in Figure 15.2. Each of the four cells contains examples of jobs that fall primarily into each category. Be careful not to stereotype particular jobs by thinking of them only in terms of a single position on the grid. Redesign often modifies jobs and changes their levels of task and work-flow uncertainty. Managerial jobs—including some top-management jobs—could range from the extreme upper right corner in cell 3 to closer to the center of the grid. Also, some jobs don't fit neatly into a single cell. For example, an auditor's job at an accounting firm might generally be plotted somewhere in the middle of the grid.

Job enrichment programs generally increase task uncertainty and/or work-flow uncertainty. However, the assembly-line job shown in cell 1 of Figure 15.2 could be enriched but still be generally classified as a cell-1 type of job. Figure 15.2 also suggests how jobs could become too enriched. Some people who occupy cell-3 types of jobs could experience stress from too much work-flow and task uncertainty.

■ TASK INTERDEPENDENCE

Task interdependence is the degree to which decision making and cooperation between two or more employees is necessary for them to perform their jobs. The construction of the structural steel framework of a high-rise building involves a

■ **FIGURE 15.2**

Technology Framework and Job Design

Source: Adapted from Slocum, J. W., Jr., and Sims, H. P., Jr. Typology for integrating technology, organization and job design. *Human Relations*, 1980, 33, 196; Susman, G. I. *Autonomy at Work—A Sociotechnical Analysis of Participative Management.* New York: Praeger, 1980, 132.

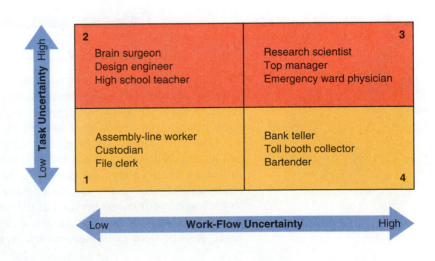

high degree of task interdependence among the crane operator, ground crew, and assembly crew in moving and joining the steel girders.

The three basic types of interdependent task relations are pooled, sequential, and reciprocal.[18] **Pooled interdependence** refers to the ability of an employee (or team) to act independently of others in completing a task or tasks. The William Raveis Real Estate firm is primarily a residential brokerage firm based in Shelton, Connecticut. It has forty offices and 1200 sales associates, each of whom acts as an independent contractor. Each agent maintains a database of potential property buyers and sellers. Until a property is listed in the local multiple listing service (MLS), the sales associates control access to their data. The sales associates purchase the laptop computers and printers they use in their work—and even pay for part of the software required. The software is capable of producing the company's actual contract forms on the laptop so that the agents can negotiate deals and print out a final agreement in one meeting with buyer and seller. The laptops have "pen capabilities" so that agents can take and record notes during property "walk throughs."[19] Clearly, most of the time the jobs of the 1200 associates of the William Raveis Real Estate firm fit the concept of pooled interdependence.

Sequential interdependence refers to the need for an employee (or team) to complete certain tasks before other employees (or teams) can perform their tasks. In other words, the outputs from some employees (teams) become the inputs for other employees (teams). The sequence of interdependencies can be a long chain in some mass-production technologies. The automobile assembly line is an example of sequential interdependence.

Reciprocal interdependence refers to outputs from an individual (or team) becoming the inputs for others and vice versa. Reciprocal interdependencies are common in everyday life. Examples include (1) a family, (2) a basketball team, (3) a surgical team, (4) a decision-making team, and (5) a class project assigned to a small team of students. Reciprocal interdependence usually requires a high degree of collaboration, communication, and team decision making. The following Managing Quality piece about the Metz Baking Company demonstrates how groupware has affected the reciprocal interdependencies involved in producing, delivering, and maintaining shelves full of quality baked goods at grocery stores. Metz is headquartered in Sioux City, Iowa, and does business in sixteen states.

QUALITY IN PRACTICE

Metz Baking Company

Prior to the introduction of groupware aids, the company's 1400 sales representatives manually estimated demand for baked goods on their daily routes. A route includes approximately thirty grocery stores, delis, and restaurants. "They'd make their best guess of what they needed for their entire route over the next week; we'd bake that amount of product, roughly divided by day; and they'd attempt to sell it on a daily basis," recalls Larry Hames, vice-president of MIS for Metz. These estimates weren't always on the mark. "If you ended up short by the end of your route, one of your accounts would have to do without. Or you might end up dumping all your excess product at the last stop," Hames says.

The fact that shoppers often buy baked goods on impulse also meant that these weekly sales estimates—which were translated into nightly bake sched-
—Continued

QUALITY IN PRACTICE—*Continued*

ules—frequently were wrong. A sales rep would deliver too much product at the beginning of the week and run out by the weekend, according to Ken Franklin, senior vice-president of sales. "We have stringent seventy-two-hour stale requirements. Our product has to be on the shelf the day the consumer is in the store, or we run the risk of not being able to sell it at all."

Metz invested more than $7.5 million in its sales automation efforts, which included 1400 palmtop computers. Now, all product data, price changes, and new-customer data are downloaded each evening from remote minicomputers into each sales rep's palmtop. At night, the palmtops are kept in a "docking station" at each of 250 Metz distribution centers scattered across sixteen states. Just after dawn Metz sales reps pick up their hand-held units and verify that the type and number of bakery products they ordered have been correctly recorded and loaded onto their trucks.

The sales representative is then ready to drive the route. At each store, the sales rep takes all stale Metz products off the shelves, enters the data into the palmtop and then fills the shelves with freshly baked goods. The palmtop automatically generates an invoice that takes into account how much stale product from the previous day wasn't sold and how much fresh product was delivered. The sales rep then enters the estimate of the next day's order. "This is the beauty of the new system," says Hames. Previously, a driver might jot down notes during the day of how product seemed to be moving at individual stores. "But more likely, they'd wait until the end of the day, look at the amount of stale product in the truck and estimate how much fresh product the entire route might need the next day," adds Hames. "Now our drivers can track demand on a daily basis by account. No more ballpark figures."[20]

Task uncertainty, work-flow uncertainty, and/or task interdependence must be considered in job design. An increase in pooled interdependence decreases the amount of required coordination among jobs. Less coordination means less sequential and/or work-flow uncertainty for employees. New information technologies often change task interdependence and reduce work-flow uncertainty. The introduction of groupware (laptop computers) for use by the 1200 sales associates at the William Raveis Real Estate firm increased the use of pooled interdependence and reduced some task uncertainty for the organization. The introduction of groupware (palmtop computers) for use by the 1400 sales representatives at the Metz Baking Company enhanced the reciprocal interdependencies of the sales and baking functions. These aids also appeared to reduce both task and work-flow uncertainty for the sales representatives.

JOB CHARACTERISTICS ENRICHMENT MODEL

The job characteristics enrichment model is one of the best known approaches to job enrichment.[21] However, before reading further, please complete the questionnaire in Table 15.1.

■ BASIC FRAMEWORK

The **job characteristics enrichment model** focuses on increasing the amounts of skill variety, task identity, task significance, autonomy, and feedback in a job. The

TABLE 15.1   Job Characteristics Inventory

Directions

The following list contains statements that could be used to describe a job. Please indicate the extent to which you agree or disagree with each statement as a description of a job you currently hold or have held, by writing the appropriate number next to the statement. Try to be as objective as you can in answering.

1	2	3	4	5
Strongly disagree	Disagree	Uncertain	Agree	Strongly agree

This job . . .

_____ 1.   provides much variety.

_____ 2.   permits me to be left on my own to do my work

_____ 3.   is arranged so that I often have the opportunity to see jobs or projects through to completion.

_____ 4.   provides feedback on how well I am doing as I am working.

_____ 5.   is relatively significant in my organization.

_____ 6.   gives me considerable opportunity for independence and freedom in how I do the work.

_____ 7.   provides different responsibilities.

_____ 8.   enables me to find out how well I am doing.

_____ 9.   is important in the broader scheme of things.

_____ 10.   provides an opportunity for independent thought and action.

_____ 11.   provides me with considerable variety of work.

_____ 12.   is arranged so that I have the opportunity to complete the work I start.

_____ 13.   provides me with the feeling that I know whether I am performing well or poorly.

_____ 14.   is arranged so that I have the chance to do a job from the beginning to the end (i.e., a chance to do the whole job).

_____ 15.   is one where a lot of other people can be affected by how well the work gets done.

Scoring

For each of the five scales, compute a score by summing the answers to the designated questions.

	SCORE
	_____
Skill variety: Sum the points for items 1, 7, and 11.	_____
Task identity: Sum the points for items 3, 12, and 14.	_____
Task significance: Sum the points for items 5, 9, and 15	_____
Autonomy: Sum the points for items 2, 6, and 10.	_____
Job feedback: Sum the points for items 4, 8, and 13.	_____
Total Score	_____

Summary Interpretation

A total score of 60–75 suggests that the core job characteristics contribute to an overall positive psychological state for you and, in turn, leads to desirable personal and work outcomes. A total score of 15–30 suggests the opposite. We present additional interpretative comments later in this section of the chapter.

Source: Adapted from Sims, H. P., Jr., Szilagyi, A. D., and Keller, R. T. The measurement of job characteristics. *Academy of Management Journal,* 1976, 19, 195–212.

model suggests that the levels of these job characteristics affect three critical psychological states: (1) experienced meaningfulness of the tasks performed; (2) experienced personal responsibility for task outcomes; and (3) knowledge of the results of task performance. If all three psychological states are positive, a reinforcing cycle of strong work motivation based on self-generated rewards is activated. A job without meaningfulness, responsibility, and feedback is incomplete and presumably doesn't strongly motivate an employee. Because of our previous coverage of motivation (see Chapters 5 and 6), we focus here on the job characteristics and individual differences components of the model. Figure 15.3 shows an outline of the elements of the job characteristics enrichment model and their relationships.

■ JOB CHARACTERISTICS

Five job characteristics are key to job enrichment efforts in this model. They are defined as follows.

- **Skill variety**—the degree to which a job requires a variety of personal competencies to carry out the work.
- **Task identity**—the degree to which a job requires completion of a whole and identifiable piece of work, that is, doing a task from beginning to end with a visible outcome.
- **Task significance**—the degree to which the employee perceives the job as having a substantial impact on the lives of other people, whether those people are within or outside the organization.

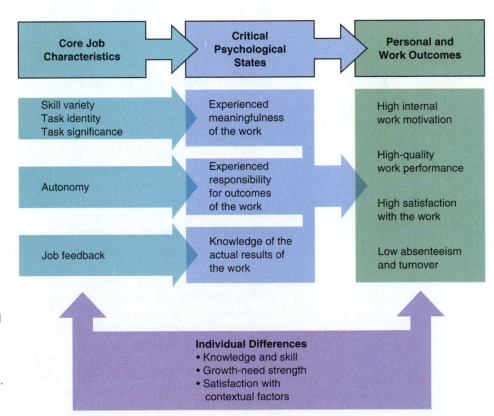

■ FIGURE 15.3

Job Characteristics Enrichment Model

Source: Hackman, J. R., and Oldham, G. R. Work Redesign. Copyright © 1980. Addison-Wesley Publishing Co., Inc., Reading, Massachusetts (adapted from Fig. 4.6 on p. 90). Reprinted by permission of Addison-Wesley Longman Inc.

■ **Autonomy**—the degree to which the job provides empowerment and discretion to the employee in scheduling tasks and in determining procedures to be used in carrying out the tasks.

■ **Job feedback**—the degree to which carrying out the job-related tasks provides the individual with direct and clear information about the effectiveness of his or her performance.[22]

Skill variety, task identity, and task significance may be especially powerful in influencing the experienced meaningfulness of work. Autonomy usually fosters increased feelings and attitudes of personal responsibility and empowerment for work outcomes. Job feedback directly gives the employee the knowledge of results from performing the job. This type of feedback comes from the work itself, not from a superior's performance appraisal. Refer back to Table 15.1 and your scores on each of the job characteristics. A score of 12–15 for a job characteristic is likely to contribute positively to one or more critical psychological states. A score of 3–6 for a job characteristic, in contrast, is likely to contribute negatively to one or more critical psychological states.

The job of surgeon can be used to further illustrate these points. This job seems to rate high on all core job characteristics. It provides a constant opportunity for using highly varied skills, abilities, and talents in diagnosing and treating illnesses. Task identity is high because the surgeon normally diagnoses a problem, performs an operation, and monitors the patient's recovery. Task significance also is high because the surgeon's work can mean life or death to the patient. Autonomy is high because the surgeon often is the final authority on the procedures and techniques used. However, the growing prevalence and threat of malpractice suits may have lowered the surgeon's sense of autonomy recently. Finally, the surgeon receives direct feedback from the job, knowing in many cases almost immediately whether an operation is successful.

■ INDIVIDUAL DIFFERENCES

The individual differences (see Figure 15.3) included in this model influence how employees respond to enriched jobs. They include competencies, strength of growth needs, and satisfaction with contextual factors.[23] These individual differences have an impact on the relationship between job characteristics and personal or work outcomes in several important ways. Managers therefore should consider them when designing or redesigning jobs.

Competencies   Employees with the competencies needed to perform an enriched job effectively are likely to have positive feelings about the tasks they perform. Employees who aren't competent to perform an enriched job effectively may experience frustration, stress, and job dissatisfaction. These feelings and attitudes may be especially intense for employees who desire to do a good job but realize that they are performing poorly and lack certain skills and knowledge. Accordingly, diagnosing the competencies of employees whose jobs are to be enriched is important. A training and development program may be needed along with an enrichment program to help such employees attain the competencies they need now and will need in the future.

To help its employees develop needed competencies, Motorola based a program on the idea of lifelong learning. The company has increased the training of all employees—from factory floor to executive suite. The goal is a disciplined, yet free-thinking work force. This initiative (1) trains employees in the use of advanced techniques and procedures so that they can perform more effectively and (2) helps employees develop competencies that the company needs to remain competitive in terms of rapidly changing technologies and markets. Motorola's program also ties education to business goals and thus doesn't involve learning for its own sake. For example, management might set a goal to reduce product development cycle time and then create a formal course on how to do so. Employees are coached in specific tasks until they get them right, whether it's operating a tool or persuading customers.[24]

Growth-Need Strength   The degree to which an individual desires the opportunity for self-direction, learning, and personal accomplishment at work is called **growth-need strength.** This concept is essentially the same as Alderfer's growth needs and Maslow's esteem needs and self-actualization needs concepts (see Chapter 5). Individuals with high growth needs tend to respond favorably to job enrichment programs. They derive greater satisfaction from work and are more highly motivated than people who have low growth needs. High growth-need individuals are absent less and produce better quality work when their jobs are enriched. In contrast, one study suggested that the level of growth-need strength doesn't moderate the relationships between job characteristics and personal or work outcomes.[25] It reported that the sense of satisfaction with work and internal work motivation didn't appear to change after job enrichment. In general, research hasn't shown job enrichment to be negatively related to satisfaction or performance for individuals with low growth needs. Employee responses to enriched jobs usually range from indifferent to highly positive.[26]

Satisfaction with Contextual Factors   The degree to which employees are satisfied with contextual factors at work often influence their willingness or ability to respond positively to enriched jobs. *Contextual factors* include organizational policies and administration, technical supervision, salary and benefit programs, interpersonal relations, and work conditions (lighting, heat, safety hazards, and the like). Employees who are extremely dissatisfied with their superiors, salary levels, and safety measures are less likely to respond favorably to enriched jobs than are employees who are satisfied with these conditions. Other contextual factors (such as employee satisfaction with the organization's culture, power and political processes, and team norms) also can affect employee responses to their jobs.[27]

One controversial contextual factor is the growing use of electronic monitoring of work through the use of computers, video cameras, and telephones to "listen in" or "observe" employees as they perform their tasks. More than ten million employees are electronically monitored each day. Such monitoring often occurs without employees being aware exactly when it is taking place. Information technologies are being used to monitor attendance, tardiness, work speed (such as recording the number of computer keystrokes an employee performs per minute or hour), break length and frequency, types of messages being transmitted on computer networks, nature and quality of conversations with customers or others, among other activities. Such intrusiveness raises serious ethical concerns, which focus on the excessive invasion of privacy of employees while at work and a widespread concern that "Big Brother is watching."[28]

Another contextual factor is the extent to which policies and rules prescribe appropriate behaviors on the job. The following Ethics in Practice feature describes the ethics policy adopted by General Motors Corporation in 1996, which changes the *context* of working relationships between GM employees and vendors.

ETHICS IN PRACTICE

GM's New Ethics Policy

Read the following scenario:

> A distinguished investment banking firm has successfully concluded a major acquisition for GM and invites, at the firm's expense, all the GM employees who worked with it to a dinner in New York at which each will be given a nice mantle clock, appropriately inscribed, as a memento of the successful venture.

Assume that you are a senior executive at GM. What would be your response to this invitation? Why?

The response in GM's new ethics policy document to this scenario states:

> The dinner and clock should be politely declined. While "thank you" gestures are a nice custom socially, they can create wrong appearances if they are lavish or extravagant. Firms that provide high value services should be rewarded by being considered for future work. There is no need or expectation that they "thank" individual GM employees with gifts, entertainment, or other gratuities. Consistent with business custom and management approval, items of no or nominal commercial value commemorating significant accomplishments or expressing appreciation for past GM support, such as a Lucite block, certificate or baseball cap, may be accepted from suppliers on an infrequent basis.

GM's new ethics policy is a twelve-page document that includes instructional scenarios involving fictional characters. It does provide some flexibility for GM employees outside the United States. GM employees in certain countries may accept meals, gifts or outings to comply with local business practices and to avoid being put at a competitive disadvantage.

The policy also permits GM employees to continue providing gifts and meals to *their* customers, but only within limits. The most expensive restaurant in town is no longer appropriate for treating GM car dealers. Transporting them by limousine from dinner to the theater is also prohibited. The new policy requires GM employees to avoid violating the customer's gift policy.

GM's policy has changed the way business is conducted in Detroit, where the concentration of automakers and suppliers has created a culture in which personal relationships often influence business deals. "We can't give them anything!" says a Detroit-based supplier. He didn't know what to do with all the baseball tickets he had planned to offer his GM customers during the summer of 1997.

The revised policy is among the toughest in corporate America. It puts an end to the stadium box seats, steak dinners and weekend golf outings that employees have long enjoyed at the expense of GM's suppliers and vendors. Taking gifts, except for the most nominal trinkets, is now forbidden. Throughout corporate America, "a lot of companies are seriously rethinking their gift and entertainment policies," says W. Michael Hoffman, executive director of the Center for Business Ethics at Bentley College in Waltham, Massachusetts.[29]

■ JOB DIAGNOSIS

A variety of methods may be used to diagnose jobs, determine whether job design problems exist, and estimate the potential for job enrichment success. We limit the discussion to two of these methods: structural clues and survey.

Structural Clues Method   The process of checking for contextual factors often associated with deficiencies in job design is called the **structural clues method**.[30] The analysis of five specific structural factors usually reveals potential job design problems and possible employee acceptance of job enrichment.

- *Inspectors or checkers.* Autonomy usually is much lower when inspectors or checkers, rather than the employee or team, examines work. Feedback is less direct because it doesn't come from the job itself.

- *Troubleshooters.* The existence of troubleshooters usually means that the exciting and challenging parts of a job have been taken away from the employees. Thus they have less sense of responsibility for work outcomes. Task identity, autonomy, and feedback usually are poor.

- *Communications and customer relations departments.* These departments usually cut the link between employees who do the job and customers or clients. These departments often dilute direct feedback and task identity for those creating the products or services.

- *Labor pools.* On the surface, pools of word processors, computer programmers, and other employees are appealing because they seem to increase efficiency and the ability to meet workload fluctuations. However, such pools often destroy feelings of ownership and task identity.

- *Narrow span of control.* A manager with only a few subordinates (say, five to seven) is more likely to become involved in the details of their day-to-day tasks than a manager with a wider span of control. Centralization of decision making and overcontrol may result from too narrow a span of control and seriously reduce autonomy and a sense of empowerment.

Survey Method   Several types of questionnaires, one of which is the **job diagnostic survey** (JDS), make diagnosing jobs relatively easy and systematic.[31] The questionnaire in Table 15.1 measures the job characteristics in Figure 15.3. You can develop your own job profile by using the totals on the scales in Table 15.1, each of which has a score of 3–15. You can calculate an overall measure of job enrichment, called the **motivating potential score** (MPS), as follows:

$$MPS = \frac{\text{Skill variety} + \text{Task identity} + \text{Task significance}}{3} \times \text{Autonomy} \times \text{Feedback}.$$

The MPS formula sums the scores for skill variety, task identity, and task significance and divides the total by 3. Thus the combination of these three job characteristics has the same weight as autonomy and job feedback. The reason is that the job characteristics enrichment model (see Figure 15.3) requires that both *experienced responsibility* and *knowledge of results* be present for high internal job motivation. This outcome can be achieved only if reasonable degrees of autonomy and job feedback are present. The minimum MPS score, using Table 15.1, is 1. The maximum possible MPS score is 3375, a clearly positive MPS score starts at 1728, and a purely neutral MPS score is 729 (based on an average score of 9 per scale). What is your MPS score? Use the results from your completed questionnaire to calculate it.

■ IMPLEMENTATION APPROACHES

Any one of five approaches, or a combination of them, may be used to implement a job enrichment program. All need not be used in every job enrichment effort, nor are they mutually exclusive. The two main approaches are vertical loading and the formation of natural work teams. The other three—establishment of customer relationships, employee ownership of the product, and employee receipt of direct feedback—often are used within one of the two principal approaches.

Vertical Loading   The delegation to employees of responsibilities and tasks that were formerly reserved for management or staff specialists is called **vertical loading.** The elements of vertical loading include the empowerment of employees to

- set schedules, determine work methods, and decide when and how to check on the quality of the work produced;
- make their own decisions about when to start and stop work, when to take breaks, and how to assign priorities; and
- seek solutions to problems on their own, consulting with others only as necessary, rather than calling immediately for the manager when problems arise.

Many employees schedule their own work after vertical loading, although a manager may set deadlines or goals. Within these guidelines, employees are allowed some freedom in setting their own schedules and pace. **Flextime** allows employees, within certain limits, to vary their arrival and departure times to suit their individual needs and desires and helps in self-scheduling of work. With the new information technology capabilities (such as computer-based networks), an increasing number of jobs can be performed, at least part of the time, at the employee's residence, in hotels while traveling, and at customer locations.[32]

Natural Teams   The formation of natural teams combines individual jobs into a formally recognized unit (such as a section, team, or department). The criteria for the grouping are logical and meaningful to the employee and include the following.

- *Geographic:* Salespeople might be given a particular section of the city, state, or country as their territory.
- *Types of business:* Insurance claims adjusters might be assigned to teams that serve specific types of businesses, such as utilities, manufacturers, or retailers.
- *Organizational:* Word-processing operators might be given work that originates in a particular department.
- *Alphabetic or numeric:* File clerks could be made responsible for materials in specified alphabetical groups (A to D, E to H, and so on); library-shelf readers might check books in a certain range of the library's cataloging system.
- *Customer groups:* Employees of a public utility might be assigned to particular residential or commercial accounts.

Customer Relationships   One of the most important concepts of job enrichment is putting employees in touch with the users of their output. The establishment of customer relationships often is a logical outcome if natural teams are formed. Employees too often end up working directly for their superiors rather than for customers or clients. Consider the approach used by Home Depot, a large retailer primarily for residential fixer-uppers. It encourages employees to build long-term relationships with customers. Workers are trained in home repair techniques and can spend as much time as necessary to help customers. There are no high-pressure sales tactics, and employees are on straight salary. In order to satisfy customers consistently, the leadership of Home Depot believes that employees must be committed. Every salesperson's bright-orange apron reads, "Hi. I'm _____, a Home Depot stockholder. Let me help you." Instead of receiving discounts on merchandise, employees get shares in the company's stock. Salespeople are trained not to let customers overspend. "I love it when shoppers tell me they were prepared to spend $150 and our people have showed them how to do the job for four or five bucks," says Bernard Marcus, the chief executive of Home Depot. He further states: "Every customer has to be treated like your mother, your father, your sister, or your brother."[33]

Ownership of Product   Employees who assemble entire television sets or washing machines or type entire reports identify more with the finished products than do employees who perform only part of the same job. Allowing employees to build entire products or complete entire task cycles is likely to generate a sense of pride and achievement. The assignment of as much responsibility as possible for a certain geographic area also may create the feeling of ownership.

At Aetna Life and Casualty Company, changes in the way insurance policies are issued have improved customer service and given employees a sense of ownership in providing this service. Not long ago, Aetna had twenty-two business centers, with a staff of 3000. About fifteen days were required to get a basic policy out of the office, in part, because 60 different employees had to handle the application. Now, the entire operation is handled by 700 employees in four centers—and customers get their policies within five days. How? A single Aetna representative sitting at a PC tied to a network can now perform all the necessary processing steps. This representative may access an actuarial database, for example, to begin processing an application immediately. When all the relevant information has been gathered, the policy is passed along the network to company headquarters in Hartford, Connecticut. It is printed and mailed within a day from Hartford. Computer-based technology also gave Aetna's salesforce more autonomy. Work teams of about 17 people have replaced the old hierarchy of managers and agents.[34]

Direct Feedback   The job-enrichment approach stresses feedback to the employee directly from performance of the task.[35] Reports or computer output may go directly to employees, instead of just to their supervisors. A common technique is to let people check their own work so that they can catch most of their own errors before others do. This technique also increases employee autonomy. Direct communication with customers or clients also may improve the timeliness and accuracy of feedback, thereby eliminating distortions and delays.

■ TECHNOLOGY AND JOB CHARACTERISTICS

We now merge the concepts of technology and job design—and the technology framework (see Figure 15.2)—with that of the job characteristics enrichment model (see Figure 15.3). To change one or more of the five job characteristics usually means making changes in one or more of the three technological dimensions. To avoid excessive complexity, we consider only a basic job redesign situation where management decides to use a combination of vertical loading and the formation of natural work teams.

Vertical loading increases the amount of task and work-flow uncertainty that employees must handle in redesigned jobs. Some of the changes caused by vertical loading tend to increase pooled interdependence and decrease sequential and reciprocal interdependence. For example, there is usually less need to obtain a quality control specialist's approval before proceeding with other tasks, which lessens sequential interdependence. The formation of natural work teams has the most direct impact on reducing task interdependence among departments or teams, with each team becoming self-managed. All the criteria for forming natural work teams tend to increase pooled interdependence and decrease sequential and reciprocal interdependence among departments, teams, and higher levels of the organization.

Figure 15.4 shows the technological changes that are likely to accompany a job redesign program involving vertical loading and the formation of natural work teams. These changes, in turn, can be expected to lead to changes in job characteristics. In brief, technological dimensions and job characteristics are closely and intricately linked.[36]

■ SOCIAL INFORMATION PROCESSING

The job characteristics enrichment model is based on the assumption that employees can respond reasonably, accurately, and objectively about the characteristics of their jobs. Their perceptions of job characteristics may be influenced by social information, which refers to comments, observations, and similar cues provided by people whose view of the job an employee values. Social information may be provided by people directly associated with the job, such as co-workers, managers, and customers, and by people not employed by the organization, such as family members and friends. Some aspects of a job aren't likely to be influenced by cues from others (a hot work environment will be hot despite what anyone tells an employee). However, most of an employee's perceptions of job characteristics are subject to the influence of others with whom the employee has contact.[37]

Based on this perspective, the **social information processing model** states that the individual's social context provides

- cues as to which dimensions might be used to characterize the work environment;

- information concerning how the individual should weigh the various dimensions—whether autonomy is more or less important than skill variety or whether pay is more or less important than social usefulness or worth;

■ **FIGURE 15.4**   Sample Job Characteristic and Technological Links

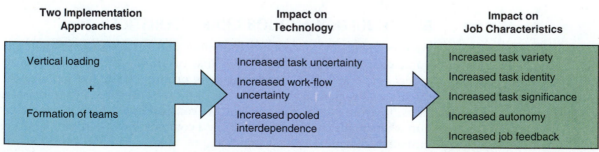

Two Implementation Approaches	Impact on Technology	Impact on Job Characteristics
Vertical loading + Formation of teams	Increased task uncertainty Increased work-flow uncertainty Increased pooled interdependence	Increased task variety Increased task identity Increased task significance Increased autonomy Increased job feedback

- cues concerning how others have come to evaluate the work environment on each of the selected dimensions; and
- direct positive or negative evaluation of the work setting, leaving the individual to construct a rationale to make sense of the generally shared affective reactions.[38]

The potential impact of the social information processing model can be illustrated with a simple example. Two employees performing the same tasks with the same job characteristics under different managers might respond differently to the objective characteristics of their jobs on the JDS. The differences in perceived social information cues might account for some of the variation in the employees' responses. For example, one manager may praise subordinates a great deal, whereas the other manager may criticize subordinates repeatedly. The social information processing model suggests that receiving praise or criticism affects how employees respond to the JDS. An integrated perspective is more accurate than one or the other points of view. The integrative perspective suggests that (1) job characteristics and social information (cues) combine to affect employees' reactions to their jobs and (2) introducing changes in the work environment can produce those reactions. However, the intricate and varied ways that social information in the workplace can affect the perceptions of job characteristics is beyond the scope of this discussion.[39] To reduce possible distortions caused by social information influences, the employees' managers, and possibly a trained job analyst, should also rate the characteristics of jobs being considered for redesign.

SOCIOTECHNICAL SYSTEMS MODEL

One particular model, the **sociotechnical systems model,** has always recognized the importance of technology in job design. It also emphasizes grouping jobs by team when the reciprocal and/or sequential interdependence among jobs can't be reduced.[40] The use of pooled interdependence therefore tends to occur among teams rather than among individual jobs. Use of the model involves vertical job loading to a cluster of jobs within a team as a whole, rather than to each individual job. Many of the concepts and diagnostic tools of this model are being used by the advocates of reengineering. After accounting for the demands of the external environment, management can use the sociotechnical systems model to design work that integrates people and technology and to optimize the relationships between the technological and social systems. When applied to manufacturing, the needed changes in technology sometimes are too difficult and costly to make in an existing plant. Thus the sociotechnical systems model more frequently works best in designing jobs for an entirely new plant. Numerous organizations in Western Europe and North America, including General Foods, GM, Weyerhauser, TRW, Rushton Mining, Volvo, and the Tennessee Valley Authority, have implemented sociotechnical systems projects. Although successes have been reported, so have failures.[41]

Figure 15.5 presents the sociotechnical systems model. It has four main parts: environmental forces, social system, technological system, and moderators. We don't review the environmental forces (such as customers, suppliers, and regulatory agencies) in this model because we have described them elsewhere in the book.

■ SOCIAL SYSTEM

The social system includes those aspects of the organization's "human side" that can influence how individuals and teams perform tasks and their attitudes

■ FIGURE 15.5   Sociotechnical Systems Model

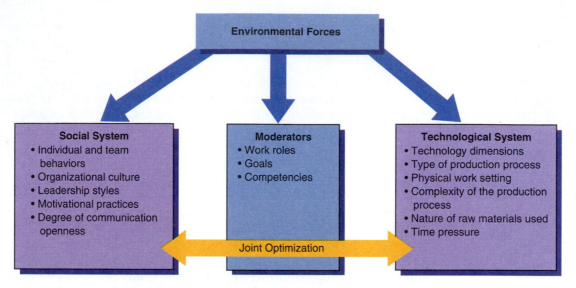

toward work and the organization. The social system factors shown in Figure 15.5 are discussed in other chapters. (Chapters 8, 10, and 17, in particular, present the main elements and processes of the work-related social system). For example, if employees characterize their organization as one marked by distrust, back-stabbing, and infighting, the creation of self-managed work teams is likely to be counterproductive until some degree of trust and cooperation can be established.

■ TECHNOLOGICAL SYSTEM

Task uncertainty, work-flow uncertainty, and task interdependence need to be diagnosed. These three technological dimensions are likely to vary with the type of production process being used or planned. For example, the type of production process in a factory (assembly line or small unit) is an important technological characteristic. Thus different production processes require different approaches to job design. In a process-technology operation, such as an EXXON oil refinery, most work is automated. Relatively few workers spend much of their time monitoring dials and performing maintenance tasks. By contrast, small-unit technologies—plumbing, television repair, sales, and investment brokering—involve relatively large amounts of labor to achieve the required outputs.

Another technological characteristic is the physical work setting (amount of light, temperature, noise, pollution, geographical isolation, and orderliness). For example, if the workplace is too hot or noisy, employees may have difficulty performing tasks that require intense thought and concentration.

Complexity of the production process also is an important technological characteristic. A person might easily learn how to build an entire toaster, but one person probably could not learn how to build a major system of a complex jet aircraft. The more complex the production process, the greater are the degrees of task and work-flow uncertainty and the requirements for reciprocal task interdependence.

Other important technological characteristics are the nature of raw materials used in production and the time pressure inherent in the production process. For example, newspapers are published on a rigid time schedule. Bottlenecks must be dealt with quickly, and employees must speed up their pace if production falls behind schedule by even a few minutes.

■ MODERATORS

Work roles act as moderators in the sociotechnical systems model, establishing a set of expected employee behaviors. They define the relationships between the people who perform tasks and the technological requirements of those tasks, binding the sociotechnical systems to each other. Goals and values also moderate the relationship between the social and technical systems. Recall that in the Preview Case the two pillars that represent superordinate goals for the Dallas Fed are *customer driven quality* and their own *people*. The Dallas Fed's strategic statement asserts: "We believe that highly competent and highly motivated employees are paramount to the long-term success of the Bank."

A final moderator includes employee competencies. The sociotechnical systems model is most effective in an organization with a highly competent and educated work force. The Dallas Fed's statement goes on to say: "Employee training and development will keep pace with the increasing sophistication of technology and the rapid rate of change in the market. As a continually learning organization, we will place a high priority on knowledge, skills, and competency."

■ CORE PRINCIPLES

The degree to which an organization operates according to the sociotechnical systems model can be assessed in terms of six core principles, all of which are reflected in the Preview Case.

- *Innovativeness*—Organizational leaders and members maintain a futuristic versus historical orientation, including a propensity for risk taking and provision of rewards for innovation.
- *Human resource development*—The talents, knowledge, skills, and abilities of organizational members are developed and tapped through job design, supervisory roles, organizational structure, and the work-flow process.
- *Environmental agility*—The organization maintains awareness of the environment and responds appropriately to it by recognizing customer importance, proactivity versus reactivity, and structural, technical, and product or service flexibility.
- *Cooperation*—Individuals, teams, and departments work together to accomplish common goals through openness, mutual support, shared values, and common rewards.
- *Commitment and energy*—Employees are dedicated to accomplishing organizational goals and are prepared to expend energy in doing so.
- *Joint optimization*—The organization uses both its social and technical resources effectively, including the design of technology to support teamwork and flexibility.[42]

The following Across Cultures account reveals some of the contrasting ways that Volvo's Uddevalla automobile plant in Sweden and the New United Motor Manufacturing, Inc. (NUMMI) automobile plant in Fremont, California, utilized design features of the sociotechnical systems model. (NUMMI is a joint venture of GM and Toyota.) The Uddevalla plant suffered from inadequate diagnosis of changing environmental forces and a lack of adequate attention to several crucial technological issues. Because Volvo was operating at low production levels, this relatively new plant had to be shut down. Its operation appeared to become "out-of-balance" because of an overemphasis on democratizing and humanizing the plant versus focusing on performance and productivity. The contrasts with the NUMMI plant dramatize the core idea of the sociotechnical systems model, namely, the need to balance and integrate environmental forces, the technological system, the social system, and various moderators in the design of jobs, teams, and plants.

ACROSS CULTURES

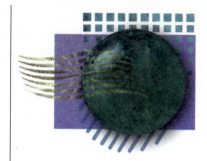

Volvo's Uddevalla Versus NUMMI

The Uddevalla plant in Sweden evolved at a time when Volvo was experiencing production capacity bottlenecks in a relatively protected market. There were no efficient Japanese competitors for its niche at that time. In the mid 1980s, Volvo was selling everything it could make, and lack of production capacity was a key problem. The major constraint in breaking the capacity bottleneck was the tight Swedish labor market. The design of the Uddevalla plant was labor-market driven, not product-market driven. As one of the key managers involved in the plant design expressed it, "The problem we had was how could we make the plant attractive for Swedish workers to want to work in it."

In the newly designed plant, each of eight production teams took full responsibility for assembling the vehicle from the subsystems up—a work cycle of about two hours. The plant abolished the assembly line, and the eight teams worked in parallel. Because the work cycle was so much more flexible, Uddevalla teams paid much less attention than NUMMI teams to detailed, movement-by-movement standardization. Instead, the teams focused on the more general balance of tasks within the whole assembly cycle. The Uddevalla teams decided job rotation schedules, selected their own employees, and decided on their own overtime schedules. At NUMMI, union representatives and managers jointly selected team leaders based on objective tests. At Uddevalla, teams selected their own leaders and often rotated the role. Both plants put great emphasis on worker training. NUMMI invested more time and effort than Uddevalla did in training employees in the principles and techniques of job engineering and its production system.

As a place to work, Uddevalla probably was more desirable than NUMMI. Uddevalla offered a much less regimented environment, more task variety, more autonomy, and more team self-management. However, NUMMI's production system delivered the greatest efficiency and quality. One Volvo executive stated that Uddevalla wouldn't have been built in today's circumstances. The context that produced Uddevalla had changed: The labor bottleneck had disappeared and efficient Japanese competitors was hurting Volvo in its export markets.

Uddevalla employees had specific information on their work cycle performance. But this cycle was two hours long. They had no way to track task performance in more detail. This problem was compounded by the organizational culture that encouraged the employees to think that they should have considerable latitude in how they performed each cycle. Some proponents of the Uddevalla design principles argue that it offered a way around the line-balancing problems

—*Continued*

ACROSS CULTURES—*Continued*

that limit the efficiency of traditional sequential assembly lines. NUMMI resolved those problems through a combination of modest doses of employee flexibility (far less extensive than Uddevalla's) and aggressive efforts to reduce setup times. The standardization of detailed work methods helped reduce setup times. Moreover, as the variety of models produced in a plant increases, employees have more difficulty recalling the correct procedure for each job. Shorter cycle times and well-defined methods help ensure quality at NUMMI. As a result, its assembly line could handle a relatively broad range of product types with minimal disruption.

No detailed documentation describing how to perform each task and specifying how long it should take was available to Volvo employees. One of the Uddevalla employees commented, "You don't really need all that detail because you can feel it when the task isn't going right; you can feel the sticking points yourself." The employees at Uddevalla had no mechanisms for identifying, testing, or disseminating the improvements that individual workers might make to eliminate problems. Sustaining continuous improvements in the production of goods as standardized as automobiles without clear and detailed methods and standards is extremely difficult.[43]

NUMMI's sociotechnical systems may be the more appropriate type for relatively repetitive, labor-intensive activities such as auto assembly. In the long run, however, NUMMI's sociotechnical systems could be undermined by progressive automation of assembly tasks, changing employee expectations, and a continuing shift toward volatile markets, lower volumes, and greater product variety. If Uddevalla had survived, it probably would have had to evolve in dramatically new ways to be competitive. Whether Uddevalla could have done so quickly enough and whether it could have retained its distinctive sociotechnical systems is unclear.

■ IMPLEMENTATION ISSUES

The factors to be diagnosed in designing jobs under the sociotechnical systems model are complex. The basic issue is the management philosophy and values that define the organization's culture. Managers interested in improving both the social system and organizational effectiveness may find either the job enrichment or sociotechnical systems models to be appropriate. Managers interested only in production and efficiency may concentrate on the job engineering, job enlargement, or job rotation approaches.

Technology is a primary variable in job design. Some jobs cannot be enriched without redesigning an entire operation. When changing a job is impossible, other techniques (such as flextime) may soften the effects of a boring job. Moreover, new information technologies, especially those involving robotics in manufacturing, are being used increasingly to eliminate routine jobs and thus the need to redesign them. Perhaps the best approach is to understand fully the various job design approaches and to use the approach or combination of approaches that best fits the organization and employees.[44]

For example, **telecommuting** involves employees performing their jobs at virtually any location, including home, while remaining connected to other employees and their employer on a real-time basis through various communication technologies. For example, Xerox now has more than 3000 sales and marketing representatives with no personal office space. District offices serve as hubs that sales employees can use to meet or grab an unassigned workstation when necessary.[45]

CHAPTER SUMMARY

Ideally, the process of job design takes into account the goals of employees, the organization, and external stakeholders. Job design is interwoven with the underlying values, management principles, and strategic imperatives of the organization. The most common job design approaches are job rotation, job engineering, job enlargement, job enrichment, and the sociotechnical systems model. These approaches vary significantly in terms of their relative impact on the organization and complexity of implementation. Job engineering includes traditional industrial engineering techniques that simplify a job in order to make it more efficient. Job enlargement and job rotation seek to make boring jobs more interesting by adding variety.

Job enrichment makes jobs more meaningful and challenging. The job characteristics enrichment model focuses on modifying five job characteristics: task variety, task identity, task significance, autonomy, and job feedback. Usually, technological factors that affect these job characteristics must be changed. Three important technological factors are task uncertainty, work-flow uncertainty, and task interdependence (pooled, sequential, and reciprocal). The job enrichment approach is often implemented through vertical loading, formation of natural work teams, establishment of client relationships, employee ownership of the product, and employee receipt of direct feedback. Properly designed jobs are likely to result in more satisfied and higher performing employees. Individual differences are important in redesigning jobs because some people may not want enriched jobs or may not want to work in teams. Also, some organizational or technological situations may not permit job enrichment.

The sociotechnical systems model attempts to integrate the organization's technical and social systems after careful assessment of the environmental forces acting on the organization. Three moderators—work roles, goals, and competencies—influence optimization of the social and technical systems. Relative to the other approaches to job design, it is the most complex and offers the greatest potential impact on the organization as a whole. The six core principles of this model address are innovativeness, human resource development, environmental agility, cooperation, commitment and energy, and joint optimization.

Job design decisions, like other decisions, contain many contingencies that must be diagnosed, understood, and balanced. Perhaps the best way to address these contingencies is by having a thorough knowledge of the various job design approaches that can be applied.

KEY TERMS AND CONCEPTS

Autonomy

Flextime

Growth-need strength

Human factor approach

Job characteristics enrichment
    model

Job design

Job diagnostic survey

Job engineering

Job enlargement

Job enrichment

Job feedback

Job rotation

Motivating potential score

Pooled interdependence

Reciprocal interdependence

Reengineering

Sequential interdependence

Skill variety

Social information processing
    model

Sociotechnical systems model

Structural clues method

Task identity

Task interdependence

Task significance

Task uncertainty

Technology

Telecommuting

Vertical loading

Work-flow uncertainty

DISCUSSION QUESTIONS

1. Assume that you are the dean of the college in which you are majoring. Respond to the statement attributed to a faculty member: There is no need to be interested in how the jobs are designed in our college. We are better off letting people do their own thing.

2. How are job design and reengineering interrelated?

3. How does job rotation differ from job enlargement?

4. From the perspective of employees, is job engineering good or bad? Explain.

5. Think about your role as a student as though it were a job. Analyze your "job" in terms of task uncertainty, work-flow uncertainty, and task interdependence. Can this analysis vary by specific course and instructor? Explain.

6. Why does technology often need to be changed as a first step in changing job characteristics?

7. Electronic monitoring of employees is ethical and necessary from the perspective of organizations. Do you agree or disagree with this statement? Explain.

8. How would you compare each of the job characteristics in your instructor's job with those in your "job" as a student? Discuss their similarities and differences.

9. What clues might you look for in determining whether the manager's job of a local sports store needs to be redesigned?

10. Why might some managers and employees welcome the sociotechnical systems approach to job design and others oppose it?

■ Developing Competencies

Team Insight: Job of Service Representative

Introduction

The purpose of this exercise is to pinpoint the kind of job design changes that are involved when a job is "enriched." The example used in the exercise is based on an actual job enrichment case.[46]

Process

1. Everyone reads the "Background" sheet.

2. Keeping in mind the five goals stated in the *Situation* part of this exercise, everyone fills out the "Corrective Action Rating Form," using the right-hand column to rank *only* those corrective actions judged to be most helpful.

3. The class forms teams of five or six people. Team members discuss their top five corrective actions, explaining why they selected or rejected certain actions. Teams attempt to arrive at a consensus on five actions. Then, each team attempts to rank order its top five actions.

4. Each team reports its results to the entire class. The results are discussed and the job design principles on which corrective actions should be based are reviewed.

Discussion Questions

1. Which corrective actions were most often listed among the top four?

2. Identify actions that relate to increased autonomy for workers, meaningful task completion, and co-worker task interactions.

3. Which of the corrective actions are least likely to have a positive effect? Why?

Situation

The job of *service representative* is to answer, either by letter or phone, complaints from shareholders. Complaints range from alleged mismanagement of the organization to lost dividend checks.

You are faced with the current situation. Five groups of service representatives (reps) were divided along natural supervisory lines, with a total of sixty reps answering shareholder complaint letters and another group of nine reps handling calls from shareholders. The organization needed highly literate and intelligent employees (approximately 70 percent were college graduates). The problems raised, questions asked, and information sought by the shareholders could be complex. After letters are written, they are typed by clerk-typists.

The turnover rate was high, and employee morale was low. Although management regarded the job as complex and challenging, as it required many weeks of training, exit interviews indicated that the reps didn't share this view. The quality of the shareholder service index was relatively poor. This index contains items such as speed of response, accuracy of details, and correctness of the response to a stockholder's letter.

In studying this case, you have five goals:

1. improve the shareholder service index;

2. maintain or improve productivity;

3. reduce turnover;

4. reduce costs; and

5. increase the reps' job satisfaction.

Corrective Actions Rating Form

The following list identifies some corrective actions that might improve the performance of the service reps. Read through the list and decide whether each proposed corrective action would be helpful. Check the appropriate line next to each corrective action. You may rank the top five corrective actions as an individual and/or team. We have provided blank spaces to insert "other" possible corrective actions that you think might also be helpful.

Corrective Action	Helpful	Not Helpful	Rank
1. Setting firm quotas of letters to be answered each day.	_____	_____	_____
2. Allowing service representatives to sign their own names to letters from the first day on the job after training.	_____	_____	_____
3. Rotating the service representatives through the telephone unit to units handling different customers and then back to their own units.	_____	_____	_____
4. Developing better verifying measures for catching errors.	_____	_____	_____
5. Letting the service representatives type the letters themselves, as well as compose them, or take on other clerical functions such as reviewing the files or obtaining detailed information.	_____	_____	_____
6. Developing a better set of form letters on the basis of analysis of types of complaints.	_____	_____	_____
7. Having the work of the more experienced service representatives reviewed less frequently, at their desks.	_____	_____	_____
8. Encouraging the verifiers and supervisors to be more alert in catching errors.	_____	_____	_____
9. Encouraging service representatives to answer letters in a more personalized way, avoiding the form-letter approach.	_____	_____	_____
10. Increasing the number of supervisors and/or verifiers.	_____	_____	_____
11. Telling service representatives that they will be fully accountable for the quality of their work.	_____	_____	_____
12. Calling the group together and impressing on them the need for increased production and fewer errors.	_____	_____	_____
13. Encouraging the service representatives to check with the supervisor about questions.	_____	_____	_____
14. Encouraging the service representatives to discuss questions with each other before involving the supervisor.	_____	_____	_____

15. Other?   _____ _____ _____ _____
16. Other?   _____ _____ _____ _____
17. Other?   _____ _____ _____ _____
18. Other?   _____ _____ _____ _____

Organization Insight: McGuire Industry

In spite of its modern $60 million facility for overhauling engines, McGuire Industry, a Department of Defense industrial facility, is having trouble meeting its production goals. The morale of the civilian employees is low—absenteeism and tardiness are major problems.

The plant is located in the southwestern United States, and approximately 70 percent of the 2000 employees are Hispanic; however, only a few of them are supervisors. The engine facility is directed by a colonel who has had extensive management experience in military units but has never directed an industrial organization.

The engine facility was designed to utilize the latest technology in engine overhaul. Engines enter at one end of the quarter-mile-long plant, where they are disassembled and placed on conveyor lines for delivery to the areas that specialize in repairing, replacing, and cleaning various components, such as turbine wheels and fuel controls. Highly specialized

teams consist of ten to fifteen workers and a supervisor. The pace of incoming components determines their work load. After a team has cleaned and repaired an item, it is sent to a testing group and then on to the next team for combination with other parts into a subassembly. When the subassemblies finally arrive at the other end of the building, the engine is assembled and sent to the testing department for an operational run-up. Any problems are corrected by troubleshooting teams. Finally, the engines are packed for shipment to the organization that uses them.

The engine facility controls its employees tightly. They punch time clocks and take breaks only when a buzzer sounds. Management limits the employees' mobility and even tightly controls the rest rooms; production employees may only use shop rest rooms. Supervisors and white-collar employees, however, have their own separate rest rooms.

Discussion Questions

1. Are the sociotechnical systems balanced at the engine facility?
2. How could these jobs be enriched?
3. How could goal setting be used to improve the jobs?
4. How would you improve performance and morale?

REFERENCES

1. Adapted from *Federal Reserve Bank of Dallas: Strategic Direction, 1996–1998.* Dallas: Federal Reserve Bank of Dallas, 1996.
2. Mohrman, S. A., Cohen, S. G., and Mohrman, A. M., Jr. *Designing Team-Based Organizations: New Forms for Knowledge Work.* San Francisco: Jossey-Bass, 1995.
3. Johann, B. *Designing Cross-Functional Business Processes.* San Francisco: Jossey-Bass, 1995.
4. Hammer, M. *Beyond Reengineering: How Process-Centered Organization Is Changing Our Work and Our Lives.* New York: Harper Business, 1996, 4–5.
5. Omachonu, V. K., and Ross, J. E. *Principles of Total Quality,* Delray Beach, Fla.: St. Lucie Press, 1994, 297–308; Hammer, M., and Stanton, S. A. *The Reengineering Revolution: A Handbook.* New York: Harper Business, 1995.
6. Adapted from Darlin, D. Data-mining the mail. *Forbes,* February 24, 1997, 112; Darlin, D. Innovate or die. *Forbes,* February 24, 1997, 108–112; Avery, S. New postal regs may spur technology, alter market. *Purchasing,* September 19, 1996, 54–68; U.S. Post Office testing electronic postmarks. *Marketing News,* October 21, 1996, 16.
7. McCann, K. B., and Sulzer-Azaroff, B. Cumulative trauma disorders: Behavioral injury prevention at work. *Journal of Applied Behavioral Science,* 1996, 32, 277–291; Bencivenga, D. The economics of ergonomics: Finding the right fit. *HR Magazine,* August 1996, 68–75; La Bar, G. Ergonomics: Are automakers on the right track? *Occupational Hazards,* October 1996, 96–104.
8. Denton, D. K. I hate this job. *Business Horizons,* January–February 1994, 46–52.
9. Swanson, R. A. *Analysis for Improving Performance: Tools for Diagnosing Organizations & Documenting Workplace Expertise.* San Francisco: Berrett-Koehler, 1994.
10. Campion, M. A., and Thayer, P. W. Job design: Approaches, outcomes, and trade-offs. *Organizational Dynamics.* Winter 1987, 66–79.
11. Adapted from How long does a task take? *Chain Store Age,* October 1996, 12C; Intelligent scheduling. *Chain Store Age,* October 1996, 9C–11C.
12. Roberts, H. V., and Sergesketter, B. F. *Quality Is Personal: A Foundation for Total Management.* New York: Free Press, 1994.
13. Herzberg, F., Mausner, B., and Synderman, B. *The Motivation to Work.* New York: John Wiley & Sons, 1959.
14. Becker, F., and Steele, F. *Workplace by Design: Mapping the High-Performance Workscape.* San Francisco: Jossey-Bass, 1995.
15. Adapted from Roha, R. R. The long road to recovery. *Kiplinger's Personal Finance Magazine,* March 1997, 163; Wilhelm, P. G. Productive employment of the handicapped: Compliance strategies for the Americans with Disabilities Act. *SAM Advanced Management Journal,* Summer 1993, 9–15.
16. Schonberger, R. J. *World Class Manufacturing: The Next Decade.* New York: Free Press, 1996.

17. Slocum, J. W., Jr., and Sims, H. P., Jr. A typology for integrating technology, organization, and job design. *Human Relations*, 1980, 33, 193–212; Doerr, K. H., Mitchell, T. R., Klastorin, T. D., and Brown, K. A. Impact of material flow policies and goals on job outcomes. *Journal of Applied Psychology*, 1996, 81, 142–152.

18. Thompson, J. D. *Organizations in Action*, New York: McGraw-Hill, 1967; Adler, P. S., and Borys, B. Two types of bureaucracy: Enabling and coercive. *Administrative Science Quarterly*, 1996, 41, 61–89.

19. La Plante, A. It's wired Willy Loman! *Forbes ASAP*, April 11, 1994, 46–55.

20. Adapted from La Plante, 46–55.

21. Hackman, J. R., and Oldham, G. R. *Work Redesign*. Reading, Mass.: Addison-Wesley, 1980.

22. Hackman and Oldham, 77–80.

23. Hackman Oldham, 82–88.

24. Kelly, K. Motorola: Training for the millennium. *Business Week*, March 28, 1994, 158–162; Baker, S., and Armstrong, L. The new factory worker. *Business Week*, September 30, 1996, 59–68.

25. Tiegs, R. B., Tetrick, L. E., and Fried, Y. Growth need strength and context satisfactions as moderators of the relations of the job characteristics model. *Journal of Management*, 1992, 18, 575–593.

26. Campion, M. A., and McClelland, C. L. Interdisciplinary examination of the costs and benefits of enlarged jobs: A job design quasi-experiment. *Journal of Applied Psychology*, 1991, 76, 186–198; Thorlakson, A. J. H., and Murray, R. P. An empirical study of empowerment in the workplace. *Group & Organization Management*, 1996, 21, 67–83.

27. Henderson, H. *Building a Win–Win World: Life Beyond Global Economic Warfare*. San Francisco: Berrett-Koehler, 1996.

28. Stanton, J. M., and Barnes-Farrell, J. L. Effects of electronic performance monitoring on personal control, task satisfaction, and task performance. *Journal of Applied Psychology*, 1996, 81, 738–745; Smolowe, J. My boss, big brother. *Time*, January 22, 1996, 56.

29. Adapted from Stern, G., and Lublin, J. S. New GM rules curb wining and dining. *Wall Street Journal*, June 5, 1996, B1, B4; *Policies on Gifts, Entertainment and Other Gratuities*. Detroit: General Motors Corporation, 1996.

30. Whitsett, D. A. Where are your enriched jobs? *Harvard Business Review*, January–February 1975, 74–80.

31. Ilgen, D. R., and Hollenbeck, J. R. The structure of work: Job design and roles. In M. D. Dunnette and L. M. Hough (eds.), *Handbook of Industrial and Organizational Psychology*, vol. 2, 2d ed. Palo Alto, Calif.: Consulting Psychologists Press, 1991, 165–207.

32. Niles, J. *Making Telecommuting Happen: A Guide for Telemanagers and Telecommuters*. Florence, Ky.: Van Nostrand Reinhold, 1996.

33. Sellers, P. Companies that serve you best. *Fortune*, May 31, 1993, 74–88; Lieber, R. B. Storytelling: A new way to get closer to your customer. *Fortune*, February 3, 1997, 102–110.

34. Gleckman, H. The technology payoff: A sweeping reorganization of work itself is boosting productivity. *Business Week*, June 14, 1993, 57–68.

35. Minnick, A. and Pischke-Winn, K. Work redesign. *Nursing Management*, October 1996, 61–65; Renn, R. W., and Prein, K. O. Employee responses to performance feedback from the task. *Group & Organization Management*, 1995, 20, 337–354.

36. Sviokla, J. J. Knowledge workers and radically new technology. *Sloan Management Review*, Summer 1996, 25–40; Baker, S., and Armstrong, L. The new factory worker. *Business Week*, September 30, 1996, 59–68.

37. Thomas, J. G., and Griffin, R. W. The power of social information in the workplace. *Organizational Dynamics*, Winter 1989, 63–75; Brown, S. P., and Leigh, T. W. A new look at psychological climate and its relationship to job involvement, effort, and performance. *Journal of Applied Psychology*, 1996, 81, 358–368.

38. Hinz, V. P., Tindale, R. S., and Volbrath, D. A. The emerging conceptualization of groups as information processors. *Psychological Bulletin*, 1997, 121, 43–64; Griffin, R. W., Bateman, T. S., Wayne, S. J., and Head, T. C. Objective and social factors as determinants of task perceptions and responses: An integrated perspective and empirical investigation. *Academy of Management Journal*, 1987, 30, 501–523.

39. Baldwin, M. W. Relational schemas and processing of social information. *Psychological Bulletin*, 1992, 112, 461–484; Hemmer, T. On the interrelation between production technology, job design, and incentives. *Journal of Accounting & Economics*, 1995, 19(23), 209–245.

40. Cherns, A. Principles of sociotechnical design revisited. *Human Relations*, 1987, 40, 153–162; Trist, E., and Murray, H. (eds.). *The Social Engagement of Social Science: A Anthology, Vol. II: The Socio-Technical Perspective*. Philadelphia: University of Pennsylvania Press, 1993.

41. Wall, T. D., Kemp, N. J., Jackson, P. R., and Cleff, C. W. Outcomes of autonomous workgroups: A long-term field experiment. *Academy of Management Journal*, 1986, 29, 280–304; Jordan, A. T. Critical incident story creation and culture formation in a self-directed work team. *Journal of Organizational change Management*, 1996, 9(5), 27–35.

42. Pasmore, W. A. *Creating Strategic Change: Designing the Flexible, High-Performing Organization*. New York: John Wiley & Sons, 1994.

43. Adapted from Adler, P. S., and Cole, R. E. Designed for learning: A tale of two auto plants. *Sloan Management Review*, Spring 1993, 85–93; Adler, P. S. (ed.). *Technology and the Future of Work*. New York: Oxford University Press, 1992; Adler, P. S. Time and motion regained. *Harvard Business Review*, January–February 1993, 97–108.

44. Davis, J. H., Schoorman, F. D., and Donaldson, L. Toward a stewardship theory of management. *Academy of Management Review*, 1997, 22, 20–47; Pfeffer, J. *Competitive Advan-

tage through People: Unleashing the Power of the Workforce. Boston: Harvard Business School Press, 1996.

45. Corbett, M. L. Telecommuting: The new workplace trend. *Black Enterprise,* June 1996, 256–260; La Plante, A. Telecommuting: Round two—Voluntary no more. *Forbes ASAP,* October 9, 1995, 133–138.

46. Adapted from Huse, E. *Organization Development and Change.* St. Paul: West, 1980; Sashkin, M., and Morris, W. C. *Organizational Behavior: Concepts and Experiences.* Reston, Va.: Reston Publishing, 1984, 257–259.

16

Organization Design

When you have finished studying this chapter, you should be able to:

- Explain the influence of environmental forces, strategic choices, and technological factors on the design of organizations.
- Indicate the relationship between reengineering and organization design.
- State the differences between mechanistic and organic systems.
- Describe functional, place, product, horizontal, and matrix designs and when they are most effective.
- Discuss multidivisional, multinational, and network designs and conditions favoring their effectiveness.

OUTLINE

PREVIEW CASE

Corning, Inc.

Corning, Inc., produces more than 5000 different products. These products include television tubes, fiber optical cables, eyeglass lens, cookware, laboratory diagnostic equipment, and ceramics. Although these products are dissimilar in appearance and use, they are related in two important ways. First, all are made of glass. Second, most represent special applications based on Corning's superb distinctive competencies in glass chemistry, manufacturing, and specialty materials. This emphasis on high-quality product development and innovative applications has enabled Corning to earn high profits and avoid competition from flat glass manufacturers, such as Anchor Hocking, Pittsburgh Plate Glass, and Libby Owens Glass.

To manage its diverse products, Corning had used a form of organization design consisting of seven divisions (television, consumer, lighting, electronic, science, medical, and technical products) in the United States. Each division was responsible for only one product. This responsibility included manufacturing, distribution, personnel selection, sales and marketing, and purchasing raw materials. Corning believed that the television tube business, for example, was quite unlike the cookware business in terms of investment required, technologies, product features, and type of customer.

Internationally, Corning was organized along geographic rather than product lines. Each plant was responsible for producing and distributing all of Corning's products within a geographic area. For example, Corning's Sovirel plant was responsible for manufacturing all of Corning's products in France; its Jobling plant oversaw all products in the United Kingdom.

This type of organization design had worked efficiently for years. Recently, however, Corning adopted a new organization design to respond to customer demands for applications of glass technology that were housed in different divisions and to new technological opportunities. Manufacturing engineering and research and development (R&D) are now coordinated from the company's headquarters in Corning, New York. By coordinating its efforts in these two areas, Corning gains skills in new technologies, saves development costs, and achieves coordination across product lines that wouldn't be possible in its divisional structure. Technologies used in ceramics are now being applied in catalytic converters. Diagnostic technologies, such as chemicals and enzymes, have found applications beyond medical and industrial applications. These advances require the sharing of information and manufacturing expertise across product lines. Globally, it also has created twenty-three business alliances with host-country firms in order to respond more quickly to changes in these markets. In Mexico it has joined with Vitro to manufacture glass containers, and with Siemens of Germany to manufacture fiber optics for telecommunications.[1]

Organization design is the process of diagnosing and selecting the structure and formal system of communication, division of labor, coordination, control, authority, and responsibility necessary to achieve the organization's goals.[2] The Preview Case demonstrated how Corning for years used its design. Increased competitive pressures and changing technologies triggered a reevaluation of Corning's organization design.

Organization design decisions often involve the diagnosis of multiple factors, including the organization's culture, power and political behaviors, and job design. Organization design represents the outcomes of a decision-making process that encompasses environmental forces, technological factors, and strategic choices. Specifically, organization design should

- ease the flow of information and decision making in meeting the demands of customers, suppliers, and regulatory agencies;
- clearly define the authority and responsibility for jobs, teams, departments, and divisions; and
- create the desired levels of integration (coordination) among jobs, teams, departments, and divisions.

One cornerstone of organization design is the design of individual jobs (see Chapter 15). A second cornerstone is the formation and use of teams—such as problem-solving teams, special-purpose teams, and self-managed teams (see Chapter 8). The third cornerstone includes both organizational power and political behavior and organizational culture (see Chapters 9 and 17). **Organizational culture** is a set of shared philosophies, values, assumptions, and norms that influence organizational decisions and actions. The organization's culture is likely to influence organization design decisions about the delegation of authority or the use of teams. Power and political behavior usually come into play when major changes in organization design are being considered. Corning changed from a design that concentrated power and influence in product divisions to one that concentrated power and influence in research and development and manufacturing engineering at headquarters. Top managers at Corning had to deal with the potential loss of power and related political behavior in each division before they could implement these changes.

In this chapter, we frequently refer to departments and divisions as we discuss organization design. The term *department* typically is used to identify a specialized function within an organization, such as human resources, production, accounting, and purchasing. In contrast, the term *division* typically is used to identify a broader, often autonomous part of an organization that performs many, if not all, of the functions of the parent organization with respect to a product or large geographic area.

In this chapter, we first note how environmental forces, strategic choices, and technological factors can influence the design of an organization.[3] We present a broad framework to suggest how particular patterns of these influences tend to fit different organization designs and briefly discuss how reengineering and organization design are related. Then, we introduce and compare mechanistic and organic systems and show how each type reflects a basic strategic choice by top managers. Next, we describe the functional, place, and product bases of design. Then, we explain how to use the horizontal and matrix designs to improve integration across units. Next, we present multinational design options as ways to respond to multiple demands, primarily owing to diversity in the customers, cultures, and geographic markets served. Finally, we describe the newest approach to organization design—the network organization—a method intended to overcome the limitations of the others in the face of complex, diverse, and changing environments, technologies, and strategic choices.

KEY FACTORS IN ORGANIZATION DESIGN

Organization design decisions (such as greater decentralization and empowerment of employees) may solve one set of problems but create others. Because every organization design has some drawbacks, the key is to select an organization design that minimizes them. Table 16.1 identifies several variables for each of the three primary factors—environmental forces, strategic choices, and technological capabilities—that affect organization design decisions.

■ ENVIRONMENTAL FORCES

The environmental forces that managers and employees need to assess are (1) the characteristics of the present and possible future environments and (2) how these demands affect the organization's ability to process information, cope with

TABLE 16.1 Factors In Organization Design Decisions

FACTORS	INDICATORS
Environmental forces	Degree of complexity Degree of dynamism
Strategic choices	Low cost Differentiation Focused
Technological capabilities	Work-flow uncertainty Task uncertainty Task interdependence

changes in markets and technologies, and achieve desired levels of differentiation (division of labor) and integration (coordination). Hypercompetition in some industries, including consumer electronics, airlines, personal computers, is requiring managers to adopt new ways of thinking about their environment. As government regulation increases and markets become global, the quest for productivity, quality, and speed has spawned a remarkable number of new organization designs. Many organizations have been frustrated by their inability to redesign themselves to stay ahead of their rivals.

Environmental Characteristics   The environment includes those external stakeholders and forces that directly affect the organization's survival. Major stakeholders include customers, suppliers, regulatory agencies, shareholders, and creditors. After identifying the relevant stakeholders and forces in the environment, management should assess their characteristics and relative importance to the organization. Environmental characteristics basically vary in terms of complexity and dynamism.

Complexity refers to whether characteristics are few and similar (homogeneous) or many and different (heterogeneous). Carmike Cinemas, for example, operates in a homogeneous environment. It owns movie theaters located exclusively in cities and towns with populations under 200,000.[4] It serves its customers through standardized low-cost theater complexes requiring few screens and unsophisticated projection technology. A single manager can run the entire theater. Operating in small towns allows Carmike to use a highly personal form of marketing in which the theater manager knows patrons and promotes attendance through personal contacts, such as sponsoring Little League teams. By being the dominant theater in the market, its main competition is often the local high school football and basketball teams. It is also able to negotiate better rental terms from landlords than if it were in competition for sites. In contrast, Tinsletown, a firm that builds large theaters that show as many as twenty movies simultaneously in major metropolitan areas, faces a much more competitive environment. Each theater has a manager and three assistant managers, ten ticket takers, five concession stations, seating for 5200 patrons, and movies showing eighteen hours a day. The theaters often face typical urban problems such as crime and lack of parking space. Intense competition from other movie theaters, including SONY and AMC, and other forms of entertainment—opera, symphony, legitimate theater, and professional sports teams, among others—add to the complexity of operating in this environment.

Rating an environment as homogeneous or heterogeneous depends on the number of factors involved. As suggested by the Preview Case, the formation of seven product divisions in the United States and separate global divisions that manufactured Corning products proved too complex and did not provide customer satisfaction. Customers were demanding products that called for specific technologies housed in various product divisions. Corning needed a design to integrate these technologies or lose customers to competitors that offered such coordination.

Dynamism relates to whether environmental characteristics remain basically the same (are stable) or change (are unstable). Corning identified a changing environment and decided to make its organization design more responsive to those changes. Dynamism also relates to the need for speed in responding to customers' and other stakeholders' demands. Organizations increasingly must be able to respond quickly and flexibly, a need specifically addressed by Corning in choosing alliance partners for joint ventures.

Types of Environments   Figure 16.1 illustrates the basic classification of task environments. The four "pure" types of task environments are homogeneous–stable, heterogeneous–stable, homogeneous–unstable, and heterogeneous–unstable. You can use this grid to determine the environment for any organization.

The simplest organization design can be effective in a *homogeneous–stable environment* (box 1).[5] The environment holds few surprises, and the manager's role is to ensure that employees consistently follow established routines and proce-

■ **FIGURE 16.1**   **Basic Types of Task Environments**

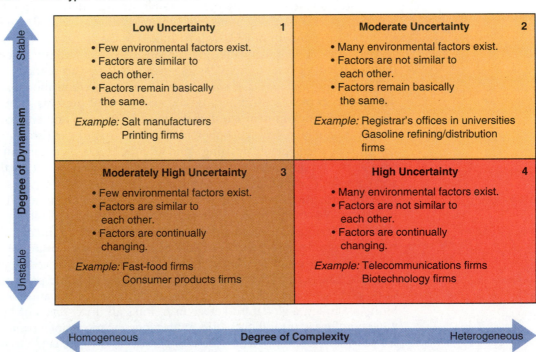

	Low Uncertainty 1	**Moderate Uncertainty** 2
Stable	• Few environmental factors exist. • Factors are similar to each other. • Factors remain basically the same. *Example:* Salt manufacturers Printing firms	• Many environmental factors exist. • Factors are not similar to each other. • Factors remain basically the same. *Example:* Registrar's offices in universities Gasoline refining/distribution firms
Unstable	**Moderately High Uncertainty** 3 • Few environmental factors exist. • Factors are similar to each other. • Factors are continually changing. *Example:* Fast-food firms Consumer products firms	**High Uncertainty** 4 • Many environmental factors exist. • Factors are not similar to each other. • Factors are continually changing. *Example:* Telecommunications firms Biotechnology firms

Degree of Dynamism (vertical axis)

Homogeneous ← **Degree of Complexity** → Heterogeneous

Source: Adapted from Rasheed, A., and Prescott, J. E. Dimensions of organizational task environments: Revisited. Paper presented at 1987 Academy of Management meeting, New Orleans, 1987; Duncan, R. What is the right organization structure? Decision tree analysis provides the answer. *Organizational Dynamics,* Winter 1979, 60–64.

dures. Managers and employees need relatively fewer competencies and less formal training and job experience to operate successfully in this environment than in the others. Organizations that primarily operate in this environment include basic lawn care firms, local delivery service firms, car wash firms, mail service firms, and self-service storage firms. Of course, these firms do face uncertainties created by competitors' actions, customers' changing preferences, and potential substitutes for their products and services.

The *heterogeneous–stable environment* (box 2) poses some risks for managers and employees, but the environment and the alternatives are fairly well understood. The environment is relatively stable, but employees may need considerable training and experience to understand it and make it work. For example, at Southwest Airlines, ground crew members must learn multiple tasks to turn planes around in fifteen minutes. This requires extensive training in maintenance, fuel loading, baggage handling, and other ground functions.

The *homogeneous–unstable environment* (box 3) requires managers, employees, and organization designs to be flexible. Frequent changes can be handled with reasonable levels of skill and motivation. Computer-based information systems often help keep track of the changes. Procter & Gamble, Kraft Foods, Unilever, and Colgate-Palmolive, among other consumer product firms, frequently create new products to attract and retain customers. Procter & Gamble, for example, has aggressively redesigned its organization to sell different products.[6] Its Foods division accounts for 12 percent of corporate sales and its Beauty division 80 percent, but its newly formed Drug division contributes only 8 percent. John Pepper, P&G's CEO, believes that, with the growth of managed care, gross margins for pharmaceuticals will be higher than for food and beauty products. Therefore P&G plans to spend more than $1.2 billion dollars on pharmaceutical research and development and has charged that division with developing medicines that attack bacterial infections, bone diseases, and cardiovascular ailments. According to Pepper, the growth of P&G will be linked to the success of the new products created and sold in its drug division. New plants and distribution centers around the world will be built to help P&G aggressively enter this market.

The *heterogeneous–unstable environment* (box 4) represents the most difficult situation for an organization because the environment presents numerous uncertainties. This environment requires the most managerial and employee sophistication, insight, and problem-solving abilities. Managers can't solve the problems confronting them merely by using standard procedures. New computer networks, such as the World Wide Web, have created organizations to satisfy the changing and complex demands of customers.[7] Once found only at "techie" organizations such as Sun Microsystems or Digital Equipment, intranets are driving entire industries. Netscape Communications, America Online, and other providers create webs for organizations that allow employees to call up internal data, such as customer profiles and product inventory. Previously such information was hidden in databases and was accessible only to technicians. A FedEx customer, for example, can track packages by logging onto FedEx's home page on the World Wide Web, which is linked to the company's internal databases. The intranet at Morgan Stanley, a global brokerage firm, links all thirty-seven of its offices and 9600 employees around the world. With money markets open somewhere in the world twenty-four hours a day, the Web permits money managers to move money from New York to Tokyo to London continually. Moreover, brokers can continually update customers' portfolios, based on the latest financial information.[8]

Each type of task environment requires different approaches to designing and managing an organization. As we go through this chapter, we relate different organization designs to the general type of environments in which they are most likely to be effective.

■ STRATEGIC CHOICES

Many of top management's strategic choices affect organization design decisions. **Strategic choice** enables the organization to capitalize on its unique competitive advantages in order to be successful.[9] Organizations have attempted to build competitive advantage in various ways. However, three underlying strategies appear to be essential to building a competitive advantage: low cost, differentiation, and focused.[10] These strategies are shown in Figure 16.2. Let's examine how each affects the design of an organization.

Low Cost   **Low-cost strategies** are based on an organization's ability to provide a product or service at a lower cost than its rivals. Management's intent is to attain a significant cost advantage over other competitors that can be passed on to consumers in order to gain a large market share. Such a strategy aims at selling a standardized product that appeals to an "average" customer in a broad market. Because the environment is homogeneous and stable, few product modifications are needed to satisfy customers. Organizations that have successfully used a low-cost strategy include Carmike Cinemas in movie theaters, Whirlpool in washers and dryers, Black & Decker in power tools, BIC in ballpoint pens, Wal-Mart in discount stores, PetSmart in pet stores, and Procter-Silex in coffee makers. The risks involved in following this strategy are (1) getting "locked in" to a technology and organization design that is expensive to change, (2) the ability of competitors to copy the strategy (for example, Target copying Wal-Mart), or, most important, (3) management not paying attention to shifts in the environment, such as customer demand for different types of products and/or services. In the early 1970s, for example, one of every two watches sold in the United States was a Timex. However, Timex didn't change its mechanical watch when the new electronic watch entered the market, and today Timex's market share is only about 5 percent.

Differentiation   **Differentiation strategies** are based on providing customers with something that is unique and makes the organization's product or service distinctive from its competition. The key managerial assumption behind this

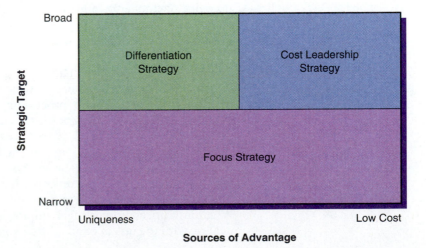

■ **FIGURE 16.2**

Strategies Model

Source: Adapted with the permission of The Free Press, a division of Simon & Schuster, from *Competitive Strategy: Techniques for Analyzing Industries and Competitors* (p. 39) by Michael E. Porter. Copyright © 1980 by The Free Press.

strategy is that customers are willing to pay a higher price for a product that is distinctive in some way. Superior value is created because the product is of higher quality, is technically superior, or has special appeal. Toyota's strategy with Lexus is based on exceptional manufacturing quality, the use of genuine wood paneling, advanced sound systems, high engine performance, and comparatively high fuel economy for luxury cars. These organizations typically operate in a heterogeneous–unstable environment and are organized by product. Corning Glass (as noted in the Preview Case), American Express in credit cards, Nordstrom in department stores, Krups in coffee and espresso makers, and 3M in coatings and adhesives are some organizations that have successfully used this strategy. The biggest disadvantage these organizations face is maintaining a price premium as the product becomes more familiar to customers. Organizations may also overdo product differentiation, which places a burden on their financial and human resources.

Focused   **Focused strategies** are designed to help an organization target a specific niche within an industry. Unlike both the low-cost and the differentiation strategies, which are designed to target industrywide markets, focused strategies aim at a specific niche. These niches could be a particular buyer group, a regional market, or customers that have special tastes, preferences, or requirements. The basic idea is to specialize in ways that other organizations can't match effectively. Operating in either heterogeneous–stable or homogeneous–unstable environments, these organizations are successful in changing and/or complex environments. Cooper Tire and Rubber, Southwest Airlines, Nucor, and Chaparral Steel are some of the organizations that have adopted this strategy. Southwest Airlines is among the most profitable airlines in the industry. It has achieved its success by focusing on short-haul routes, flying into airports located close to cities, not serving meals, not transferring baggage, and offering no reserved seating. The greatest disadvantage that the focused strategy organization faces is the risk that the underlying market niche may gradually shift toward the characteristics of a broader market. Distinctive customer tastes may "blur" over time, thus reducing the defensibility of the niche.

■ TECHNOLOGICAL FACTORS

In Chapter 15, we noted how the technological factors of work-flow uncertainty, task uncertainty, and task interdependence affected job design. These same technological factors also influence organization design in terms of the creation of teams and departments, the delegation of authority and responsibility, and the need for formal integrating mechanisms.

Work-Flow and Task Uncertainty   In terms of organization design, *work-flow uncertainty* involves the extent to which managers and employees know when inputs will be received for processing. When work-flow uncertainty is low, a department has little discretion to decide which, when, or where tasks will be performed. At the General Motors assembly plant in Arlington, Texas, trucks move along the assembly line at predetermined speeds. Departments know exactly when their work will arrive. *Task uncertainty* involves the degree of knowledge that managers and employees have about making a product. When task uncertainty is low, employees generally know how to make the desired product. When task uncertainty is high, employees have few (if any) prespecified ways of dealing with the task at hand. The personnel at the Ceiba-Geigy, Merck, and Gentech laboratories who are attempting to find cures for cancer and AIDS face high task uncertainty. In the case of high task uncertainty, key members of the department usually have to apply experience, judgment, and intuition—and jointly define and solve problems—in order to achieve the desired outcome.

Parallel to the discussion of job design and technology in Chapter 15 (see, especially, Figure 15.3), we first consider the effects of work-flow uncertainty and task uncertainty on organization design and then discuss the effects of task interdependence on organization design. Figure 16.3 shows possible linkages between work-flow uncertainty and task uncertainty. Both can range from low to high, again yielding four combinations.

An organization's department may fit into more than one of these cells. Through organization redesign, a department's task uncertainty and work-flow uncertainty may be changed. The office of the president and the strategic planning department generally are characterized by high task uncertainty and high work-flow uncertainty. However, some of the specific tasks that they perform could be classified anywhere on the matrix. Some departments don't fit neatly into a single cell. For example, the auditing department of Arthur Andersen might fit somewhere in the middle of Figure 16.3. One of the implications of the framework for managers is to recognize similarities in technological characteristics and create functional departments, such as those shown.

Task Interdependence   *Task interdependence* may be pooled, sequential, or reciprocal. In terms of organization design, we can characterize them in the following manner.[11]

- *Pooled interdependence* occurs when departments or teams are relatively autonomous and make an identifiable contribution to the organization. For example, the many sales and services offices of State Farm Insurance don't engage in day-to-day decision making, coordination, and communication with each other. The local offices are interdependent with regional offices that coordinate and set policies for the local offices. The performance of each local office is readily identifiable.

- *Sequential interdependence* occurs when one department or team must complete certain tasks before one or more other departments or teams can per-

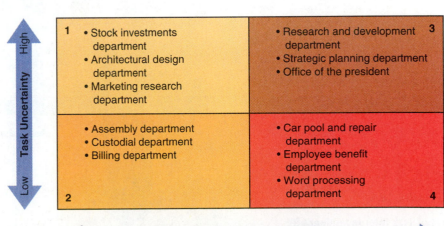

■ FIGURE 16.3

Technology and Organization Design Framework

Source: Adapted from Slocum, J. W., Jr., and Sims, H. P., Jr. Typology for integrating technology, organization, and job design. *Human Relations,* 1980, 33, 196; Susman, G. I. *Autonomy at Work: A Sociotechnical Analysis of Participative Management.* New York: Praeger, 1980, 132.

form their tasks. For example, at Whirlpool's washing machine factory, the fabrication department provides its outputs to the assembly department, which, in turn, provides its outputs to the painting and finishing department, and so on.

■ *Reciprocal interdependence* occurs when the outputs from one department or team become the inputs for another department or team and vice versa. One of Corning Glass's problems pointed out in the Preview Case was that customers were demanding products that required the integration of technologies from various product lines to satisfy their needs. Until the establishment of centralized manufacturing engineering and R&D departments, each product line operated in pooled interdependence.

Figure 16.4 shows that reciprocal interdependence is the most complex type and that pooled interdependence is the simplest type. As Corning Glass found out, greater interdependence among its seven product divisions required more integration. Placing reciprocally interdependent departments or teams under a common superior often improves integration and minimizes information processing costs. For example, at Brooklyn Union, the marketing research, advertising, and sales departments report to the vice-president of marketing. Employees in these departments must communicate and coordinate more with each other than, for example, with employees in the maintenance department.

In previous chapters, we discussed how new information technologies are changing many jobs. These information technologies also affect the design of

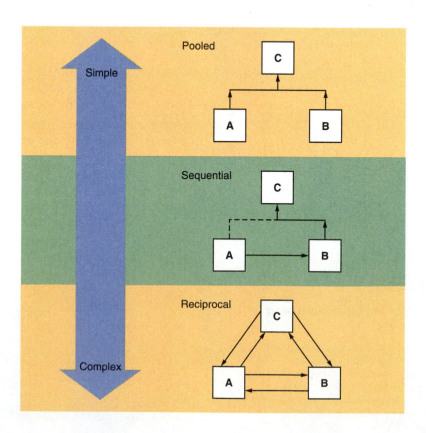

■ **FIGURE 16.4**

Types of Task Interdependence in Organization Design

organizations and the flows of information through them. The following Technology in Practice feature reveals how US West is using information technology in its organization to enhance productivity.

TECHNOLOGY IN PRACTICE

US West

Margaret Tumey, a top financial executive at US West, was looking for a way to show employees how fast-changing technologies would affect the telephone services that their organization offered. She asked Sherman Woo, the company's director of information tools and technologies, to help her. Little did she realize that her request would result in the Global Village, an intranet that now connects 15,000 employees at US West and has changed the way the company operates.

Woo believed that the best way to interest employees in new technology was to have them experience it for themselves. He created a basic intranet in a conference room by linking a number of computers to communication lines and a videoscreen. He gave browser software to any computer users who wanted it, and connected their machines to his web. In exchange, Woo requested that the new users show at least two other employees how the web worked. Almost everyone who saw it wanted to be connected too.

Today employees in fourteen states work together on the intranet. Some meet in online chat rooms to exchange documents and discuss ongoing projects. Salespeople use the web to keep in touch with managers in Denver, US West's headquarters. The intranet also functions as an electronic suggestion box. Employees in different departments create their own home pages and keep their own documents current.

Customers also have benefited from US West's internal web. The company lets service representatives use the intranet to fill orders for features (such as call waiting) immediately while the customer is on the phone. The service rep simply enters the order on the web browser, which sends it to the phone switching network. Within a few minutes, the customer's call waiting is activated. Under the old system, that process took days.[12]

■ COMPARATIVE FRAMEWORK

Figure 16.5 illustrates seven approaches to common organization design. These approaches, and the conditions under which they are most likely to be effective, are contrasted in terms of the key factors in organization design. Environmental forces comprise a single continuum on the vertical axis, ranging from simple, stable environment to a complex, dynamic environment. Technological factors comprise a single continuum on the horizontal axis, ranging from simple to complex. At one end of the continuum is a cluster of choices that reflect uniformity in customers, technologies, and geographic markets, represented by firms such as Avis Rent-a-Car, Allstate Insurance Company, and Motel 6. At the other end are organization design choices that reflect diversity in customers, technologies, and

■ **FIGURE 16.5**

Options of Organizational Designs

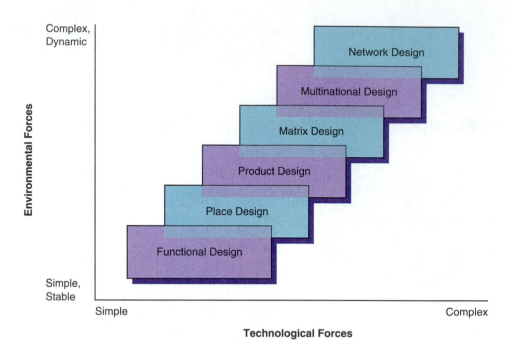

geographic markets, represented by firms such as Corning Glass, Ford Motor Company, and IBM.

The comparative framework broadly portrays how the design of an organization may differ and change as a result of various patterns of environmental forces and technological factors. The simplest environment (lower left) implies that some version of the functional organization design is likely to be appropriate. The most complex environment (upper right) implies that some form of the network organization design is likely to be appropriate. In general, designs become more complex as an organization moves from a functional design to a network design.

■ RELATION TO REENGINEERING

In our discussion of the relationship of reengineering to job design (see Chapter 15), we defined *reengineering* as radically new ways of thinking about organizing and breaking away from outdated assumptions, rules, and procedures.[13] The need to diagnose and address environmental forces, technological factors, and strategic choices in organization design is consistent with the reengineering approach. Therefore managers need to ask two fundamental questions when involved in reengineering in order to determine the appropriate organization design: Why do we do what we do? and Why do we do it the way we do?

We don't suggest that "starting all over" or "starting from scratch" in changing the organization's design is always necessary or feasible. At Corning Glass and other organizations, slight changes may be more feasible and effective. However, a central tenet in reengineering is to make fundamental changes in business processes, which in turn affects organization design. The following Quality in Practice feature reveals how Ford Motor Company reengineered its accounts payable process after comparing it to Mazda's. Ford discovered that its process was slow, confusing, expensive, and error prone—and needed to be overhauled.

QUALITY IN PRACTICE

Ford Reengineers Its Accounts Payable Process

Under the old system, Ford's purchasing department would send a purchase order to a supplier, with a copy going to the accounts payable department. When the goods arrived at Ford, a clerk at the receiving dock completed a form describing the goods and then sent it to the accounts payable department. Meanwhile, the supplier sent accounts payable an invoice. The system was ponderous. Many of the department's 500 clerks spent most of their time straightening out discrepancies in purchase order, receiving, and invoice documents. Sometimes a resolution required weeks of time and enormous amounts of work to trace and correct documents.

Ford's reengineered accounts payable process is radically different. Accounts payable clerks no longer match the purchase order and receiving document because the new process eliminated the invoice entirely. Now, when a buyer in the purchasing department issues a purchase order to a vendor, the buyer simultaneously enters the order into an online database. Suppliers, as before, send goods to the receiving dock. When they arrive, someone in receiving uses a computer terminal to determine whether the received shipment corresponds to the purchase order in the database. Only two possibilities exist: It does, or it doesn't. If it does, the employee at the dock accepts the goods and pushes a button on the terminal keyboard to tell the database that the goods have arrived. The receipt of the goods is now recorded in the database. The computer will automatically issue and send a check to the supplier at the appropriate time. If the goods don't correspond to the purchase order in the database, the employee on the dock refuses the shipment and sends it back to the supplier.

The basic concept of the change at Ford is simple. Payment authorization, which used to be performed by accounts payable personnel, is now accomplished by receiving dock personnel. The new process allowed Ford to reduce the number of people involved in supplier payment from 500 to 125.[14]

MECHANISTIC AND ORGANIC SYSTEMS

A **mechanistic system** is characterized by reliance on formal rules and regulations, centralization of decision making, narrowly defined job responsibilities, and a rigid hierarchy of authority. In contrast, **an organic system** is characterized by low to moderate use of formal rules and regulations, decentralized and shared decision making, broadly defined job responsibilities, and a flexible authority structure with fewer levels in the hierarchy.[15]

Top management typically makes decisions that determine the extent to which an organization will operate as a mechanistic system or an organic system. At Corning Glass, product divisions had operated relatively autonomously until top management decided to coordinate manufacturing engineering and R&D at headquarters. Although mechanistic and organic systems are organization design choices, environmental forces (such as a dynamic, complex environment versus a stable, simple environment), strategic choices (low cost, differentiation, focused), and technology (work-flow uncertainty and task uncertainty) also influence whether the design is mechanistic or organic.

A mechanistic system is essentially a bureaucracy. Max Weber, a German sociologist and economist in the early 1900s, defined a bureaucracy as an organization having the following characteristics.[16]

- The organization operates according to a body of rules or laws that are intended to tightly control the behavior of employees.
- All employees must carefully follow extensive impersonal rules and procedures in making decisions.
- Each employee's job involves a specified area of expertise, with strictly defined obligations, authority, and powers to compel obedience.
- The organization follows the principle of hierarchy; that is, each lower position is under the tight control and direction of a higher one.
- Candidates for jobs are selected on the basis of "technical" qualifications. They are appointed, not elected.
- The organization has a career ladder. Promotion is by seniority or achievement and depends on the judgment of superiors.

The word **bureaucracy** often brings to mind rigidity, incompetence, red tape, inefficiency, and ridiculous rules. In principle, though, the basic characteristics of a mechanistic system may make a bureaucratic organization design feasible in some situations. Any discussion of a mechanistic system must distinguish between the way it should ideally function and the way some large-scale organizations actually operate.

The degrees to which an organization emphasizes a mechanistic or an organic system can vary substantially, as suggested in Figure 16.6. Radio Shack, McDonald's, and Target are organizations that have a relatively mechanistic system in terms of the selected dimensions. Such organizations are identified as "B" in Figure 16.6. Ben & Jerry's Ice Cream Company, Bain and Company, and The Body Shop are organizations that place more emphasis on the dimensions that represent an organic system. Such organizations are identified as "A" in Figure 16.6. The organic system emphasizes employee competence, rather than the employee's formal position in the hierarchy, as a basis for rewards, including promotion. This system has a flexible hierarchy and empowers employees to deal with uncertainties in the environment.

■ HIERARCHY OF AUTHORITY

Hierarchy of authority represents the extent to which decision-making processes are prescribed and where formal power resides. In a mechanistic system, higher level departments set or approve goals and detailed budgets for lower level departments and issue orders to them. A mechanistic system has as many levels in its hierarchy as necessary to achieve tight control. An organic system has few levels in its hierarchy, which makes coordination and communication easier and fosters innovation.

The hierarchy of authority is closely related to centralization. **Centralization** means that all major, and oftentimes many minor, decisions are made only at the top levels of the organization. Centralization is common in mechanistic systems, whereas decentralization and shared decision making between and across levels are common in an organic system. At McDonald's and Radio Shack, top executives make nearly all decisions affecting store operations. Rules and regulations are sent from headquarters to each store, and reports from the store are sent up the hierarchy.

■ DIVISION OF LABOR

Division of labor refers to the various ways of dividing up tasks and labor to achieve goals. Adam Smith, the father of capitalism, recognized the importance of this concept in his book *An Inquiry into the Nature and Cause of the Wealth of Nations,* first published in 1776.[17] Smith suggested that, in general, the greater the division of labor in organizations, the greater would be the efficiency of the organizations and the amount of wealth created.

The mechanistic system typically follows Smith's views. However, a continued increase in the division of labor may eventually become counterproductive. Employees who perform only very routine and simple jobs that require few skills may become bored and frustrated. The results may be low quality and productivity, high turnover, and high absenteeism. In addition, the managerial costs (volume of reports, more managers, and more controls to administer) of integrating highly specialized functions usually are high. In contrast, the organic system tends to reduce these costs by delegating decision making to lower levels in the organization. Delegation also encourages employees and teams to take on responsibility for achieving their tasks and linking them to those of others in the organization. The organic system takes advantage of the benefits from the division of labor, but it is sensitive to the negative results of carrying the division of labor too far.

■ RULES AND PROCEDURES

Rules are formal statements specifying acceptable and unacceptable behaviors and decisions by employees. One of the paradoxes of rules that attempt to reduce individual autonomy is that someone must still decide which rules apply to specific situations. Rules are an integral part of both mechanistic and organic systems. In a mechanistic system, the tendency is to create detailed uniform rules to cover tasks and decisions whenever possible. In an organic system, the tendency is to create rules only when necessary (such as safety rules to protect life and property). Managers and employees alike tend to question the need for new rules, as well as existing rules. In a mechanistic system, the tendency is to accept the need for extensive rules and to formulate new rules in response to new situations.

Procedures refer to a preset sequence of steps that managers and employees must follow in performing tasks and dealing with problems. Procedures often comprise rules that are to be used in a particular sequence. For example, in order to obtain reimbursement for travel expenses in most organizations, employees must follow specific procedures. Procedures have many of the same positive and negative features that characterize rules, and they often proliferate in a mechanistic system.

Managers in organic systems usually know that rules and procedures can make the organization too rigid and thus dampen employee motivation, stymie innovation, and inhibit creativity. In a mechanistic system, rules and procedures tend to be developed at the top and issued through memorandums. Such memos may convey the expectation of strict compliance and the adverse consequences of not complying. In an organic system, employee input is likely to be sought on changes in current rules and procedures or on proposed rules and procedures when they are absolutely necessary. In an organic system employees at all levels are expected to question, evaluate, and make suggestions about such proposals, with an emphasis on collaboration and interdependence.

■ IMPERSONALITY

Impersonality is the extent to which organizations treat their employees, customers, and others according to objective, detached, and rigid characteristics. Managers in a highly mechanistic system are likely to emphasize matter-of-fact indicators (college degrees, certificates earned, test scores, training programs completed, length of service, and the like) when making hiring, salary, and promotion decisions. Although these factors may be considered by managers in an organic system, the emphasis is likely to be on the actual achievements and professional judgments of individuals rather than on rigid quantitative indicators. Merck is a leading pharmaceutical company and operates as an organic system. A college graduate applying for a job at Merck goes through an extensive interview process. This process may involve several managers, many (if not all) of the employees with whom the applicant would work, and even a casual and informal "interview" by a team of employees. The person responsible for filling the open position solicits opinions and reactions from these employees before making a decision. In some instances, the manager may even call a meeting of the employees and other managers who participated in the interview process to discuss a candidate.

■ CHAIN OF COMMAND

Early writers on organization design stressed two basic ideas about the chain of command.[18] First, in a scalar **chain of command,** authority and responsibility are arranged hierarchically. They flow in a clear, unbroken vertical line from the highest executive to the lowest employee. Clarity of direction is at the core of the chain. Second, these writers emphasized **unity of command,** which holds that no subordinate should receive orders from more than one superior. Although some organizations don't rigidly follow unity of command in their designs, overlapping lines of authority and responsibility can make both managing and production tasks more difficult than they should be. Without unity of command, who may direct whom to do what may become cloudy and confusing. Of course, the issues of chain of command and span of control don't just apply to mechanistic design. They must be addressed in all organization designs.

■ SPAN OF CONTROL

Span of control refers to the number of employees reporting directly to one manager. When the span of control is broad, relatively few levels exist between the top and bottom of the organization. Conversely, when the span of control is narrow, more levels are required for the same number of employees. Although there is no "correct" number of subordinates that a manager can supervise effectively, the competencies of both the manager and employees, the similarity of tasks being supervised, and the extent of rules and operating standards all influence a manager's span of control. A manager at Carmike Cinemas faces a relatively homogeneous environment and asks employees to perform simple and repetitive operations, such as taking tickets, operating the concession stands, and performing housekeeping duties. At higher organizational levels, however, a regional manager might effectively supervise fifteen or fewer theater managers who are geographically spread over a wide area.

In both mechanistic and organic systems, well-defined rules and procedures may have to be developed and applied through a relatively impersonal process in certain instances. For example, laws, court rulings, and regulatory agency decisions may even mandate impersonality, extensive rules, and rigid procedures.

Organizations have used some of these aspects of design to support employees who voice concern about ethical practices in their organizations. **Whistle-blowing** is employee disclosure of illegal, immoral, or illegitimate practices on the part of the organization.[19] Many organizations have adopted mechanistic systems to protect whistle-blowers from retaliation (transfer to lower level or make-work positions or even being fired) because of their ethical concerns. The following Ethics in Practice selection highlights whistle-blowing at Darling International.

ETHICS IN PRACTICE

Whistle-Blowing at Darling International

Dallas-based Darling International's top managers recently pleaded guilty to five felonies and agreed to pay a $4 million fine to settle federal criminal charges that one of its meat processing plants had continuously polluted a Minnesota stream since 1993. Employees at the company's Blue Earth plant complained to state regulators that animal carcasses, untreated wastes, blood, and solvents were dumped into a stream near the plant. Hazardous chemicals were used to wash company trucks over a drain pipe that also led directly into a stream, the employees claimed. When Minnesota state regulators used dye to follow water through the plant's drainage system, they found pipes carrying wastes that bypassed the plant's water treatment system and dumped directly into the stream. Dennis

—Continued

ETHICS IN PRACTICE—*Continued*

Longmire, Darling's chief executive officer, assured the Environmental Protection Agency that violations will not reoccur.

The federal judge ordered the company to protect the whistle-blowers by adopting four practices. First, whistle-blowers' names are to remain confidential. If their identity were made known, they probably would be subject to social retaliation by other employees. Although the plant's general manager and two other managers were fired, no production workers can be fired. Second, an ethics department is to be established at corporate headquarters where wrongdoings can be reported and investigated. The head of this department must report directly to the president. The department is to be responsible for responding to questions about illegal procedures or practice. Third, training programs are to be held to inform all employees about ethical guidelines and the various rules and regulations designed to protect employees. Fourth, clearly stated rules and procedures are to be established and enforced, leading to compliance with all relevant EPA regulations.[20]

Now that we have examined the various factors that affect managers' choice of an organization design, let's consider some of the design choices available. As we discuss these choices, we refer to the factors that influence a particular choice of design.

FUNCTIONAL DESIGN

Functional design involves the creation of positions and units on the basis of specialized activities. Functional grouping of employees is the most widely used and accepted form of departmentalization. Although the functions vary widely, depending on the organization (for example, Presbyterian Hospitals do not have production departments nor does Chemical Bank), grouping tasks and employees by function can be both efficient and economical.

■ KEY CHARACTERISTICS

Departments of a typical manufacturing firm with a single product line often are grouped by function—engineering, human resources, manufacturing, shipping, purchasing, sales, and finance. Tasks also are usually divided functionally by the process used—receiving, stamping, plating, assembly, painting, and inspection (sequential interdependence). Figure 16.7 shows how the Callaway Golf Corporation uses both managerial functions and processes in its design. This firm is the largest golf club manufacturer in the United States.[21] A common theme of functional design proponents was the desirability of standardizing and routinizing repetitive tasks whenever possible. Management could then concentrate on exceptions to eliminate any gaps or overlaps.

■ CONDITIONS FOR USE

A functional design has both advantages and disadvantages. On the positive side, it permits clear identification and assignment of responsibilities, and employees

■ **FIGURE 16.7**   Callaway Golf's Design by Function and Process

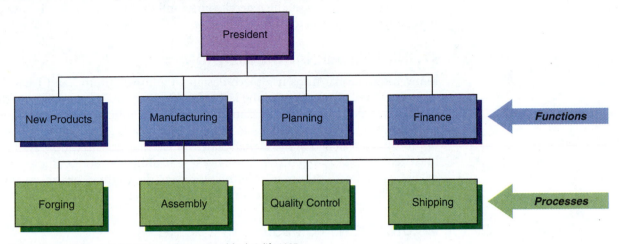

Source: Adapted from *Callaway Golf 1996 Annual Report*. Carlsbad, Calif., 1997.

easily understand it. People doing similar tasks and facing similar problems work together, thus increasing the opportunities for interaction and mutual support. A disadvantage is that a functional design fosters a limited point of view that focuses on a narrow set of tasks. Employees may lose sight of the organization as a whole. Horizontal integration across functional departments often becomes difficult as the organization increases the number of geographic areas served and the range of goods or services provided. With the exception of marketing, most employees in a functionally designed organization have no direct contact with customers and may lose touch with the need to meet or exceed customer expectations.

A functional design may be effective when an organization has a narrow product line, competes in a homogeneous environment, pursues a low-cost or focused business strategy, and doesn't have to respond to the pressures of serving different types of customers. The addition of specialized staff departments to a functional design may enable an organization to deal effectively with some degree of environmental complexity and dynamism. Staff departments may provide line departments with expert advice, such as dealing with certain technologies. As shown in Figure 16.5, functional design is the most elementary type of organization design and often represents a base from which other types of designs evolve.

PLACE DESIGN

Place design involves establishing an organization's primary units geographically while retaining significant aspects of functional design. All functional groups for one geographic area are in one location.

■ KEY CHARACTERISTICS

Many of the tasks required to serve a geographic territory are placed under one manager, rather than grouping functions under different managers or all tasks in one central office. Large companies such as American Airlines, FedEx, and Allstate Insurance Company use place design in the form of regional and district offices.

Similarly, many government agencies such as the Internal Revenue Service (IRS), the Federal Reserve Board, the federal courts, and the U.S. Postal Service use place design in providing their services.

◼ LINK TO INTERNATIONALIZATION

Many international firms use place design to address cultural and legal differences in various countries and the lack of uniformity among customers in different geographic markets.[22] For example, Kendall Healthcare Products Company established a German subsidiary to manufacture locally and market a broad line of products developed in the United States for German consumption. In this case localized manufacturing makes sense because health-care product standards vary considerably from country to country. Moreover, the German health-care system has long been a major consumer of Kendall's products.[23]

◼ CONDITIONS FOR USE

Place design has several potential advantages. Each department or division is in direct contact with customers in its locale and can adapt more readily to their demands. For Hoechst Celanese Chemical Corporation, it means locating plants near raw materials or suppliers. Potential gains may include lower costs for materials, freight rates, and (perhaps) labor costs. For marketing, locating near customers might mean lower costs or better service. Salespeople can spend more time selling and less time traveling. Being closer to the customer may help them pinpoint the marketing tactic most likely to succeed in that particular region.

Organizing by place clearly increases control and coordination problems. If regional units have different personnel, purchasing, and distribution procedures, management may have difficulty achieving integration. Further, regional and district managers may want to control their own internal activities to satisfy local customers. Employees may begin to emphasize their own geographically based unit's goals and needs more than those of the organization as a whole. To help ensure uniformity and coordination, organizations such as the IRS, Southland (7-Eleven stores), Steak and Ale, Jiffy Lube, and Hilton Hotels make extensive use of rules that apply in all locations.

PRODUCT DESIGN

Product design involves the establishment of self-contained units, each capable of developing, producing, and marketing its own goods or services. The Preview Case related how Corning used this type of organization design and emphasized pooled interdependence among its seven divisions. Figure 16.8 shows part of the product organizational structure of Vencor, Inc., a health-care provider.[24]

Vencor, Inc., was founded in 1985 to develop a niche (focused-business strategy) in the health-care industry for critically ill patients requiring quality respiratory care services over an extended period of time. In 1995, it acquired a competitor and is now an integrated long-term health-care network. In addition to its 36 acute care hospitals, Vencor operates 311 skilled nursing centers, 55 institutional pharmacies, and 23 retirement centers. The advantage of this product design for Vencor is that it can move patients from hospitals to nursing centers as the patient's medical condition dictates. Its pharmacies supply medications for all its patients. Vencor has developed its own intraweb, which enables its personnel at each facility to have complete access to all of its patients' medical histories.

■ **FIGURE 16.8**

Vencor, Inc.

Source: Vencor, Inc., 1996 Annual Report to Shareholders. Louisville, Ky., 1996.

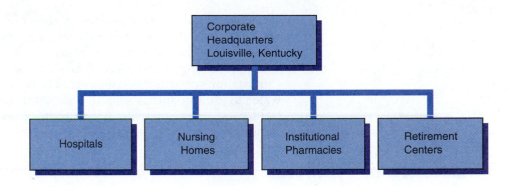

The intraweb lessens the administrative overhead associated with delivery of patient care by reducing the number of employees needed to maintain patient records.

■ TYPICAL EVOLUTION

Organizations that produce multiple goods or services, such as Procter & Gamble, Heinz, PepsiCo, and American Brands, utilize some form of product design. It reduces the complexity that managers and others would face in a purely functional organization design. Under a purely functional design, a single vice-president of marketing at such a firm wouldn't be able to manage the diversity of products, customers, and geographic markets served. When the diversity of goods or services and types of customers reach a certain point, the creation of multiple marketing vice-president positions (one vice-president for each product line), to handle the resulting complexity can be more effective. This is the organization design used by PepsiCo, which owns Frito-Lay, Taco Bell, Pepsi, Hot-n-Now, and Chevy's. Moreover, a product design is an attractive alternative to a functional design when the environmental and technological factors for each product line are different. Hot-n-Now, Chevy's, and Taco Bell are fast-food restaurants and face a different environment (competitors, customers, and suppliers) than does Frito-Lay. Organizations with a product design usually began with a functional design and then added some place design features as they began to serve new geographic markets. Eventually, serving multiple customers creates management problems that can't be effectively dealt with in a functional design or place design alone. The addition of new product lines, diverse customers, and technological advances also may increase complexity and uncertainty. When changing to a product design, however, companies usually don't discard functional or place designs altogether. Instead, the product design may incorporate features of functional and place designs into the organization of each product division.[25]

■ MULTIDIVISIONAL DESIGN

A variation of the product design is the multidivisional design, sometimes referred to as the M-Form.[26] **Multidivisional design** organizes tasks by division on the basis of the product or geographic markets in which their goods or services are sold. Divisional managers are primarily responsible for day-to-day operating decisions within their units. Freed from day-to-day operating responsibilities, top corporate-level managers concentrate on strategic issues, such as allocating resources to the various divisions, assessing new businesses to acquire and divisions to sell off, and communicating with shareholders and others. These top managers often are supported by elaborate accounting and control systems and specialized staff. Top management delegates to product divisions the authority to develop their own strategic plans.

The following Managing in Practice account describes Johnson & Johnson Corporation's multidivisional design. The company manufactures and markets a wide range of products, including anesthetics, Band-Aids, baby powder, and contact lenses. This account also reveals some of J&J's efforts to overcome the limitations of this type of design.

MANAGING IN PRACTICE

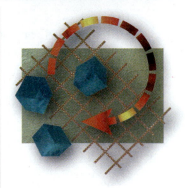

Johnson & Johnson's Multidivisional Design

At Johnson & Johnson (J&J), the presidents of its 166 multidivisional companies aren't just encouraged to act independently—they're expected to. They travel at will and decide who will work for them, what products to produce, and which customers to sell to. They prepare budgets and marketing plans, and many oversee their own R&D operations. Although they are accountable ultimately to executives at corporate headquarters, some of the presidents see headquarters executives as rarely as four times a year. The J&J approach "provides a sense of ownership and responsibility for a business that you simply cannot get any other way," says CEO Ralph S. Larsen.

However, this multidivisional design caused problems with some large customers. Dozens of J&J representatives called on the same customers (for example, Wal-Mart and Kmart). But big retailers increasingly want to simplify their dealings with manufacturers by reducing the number of contacts with a supplier. Another concern for a multidivisional company is overhead expenses. Overhead at J&J was 41 percent of sales, compared with 30 percent for its more integrated rival, Merck & Company, and 28 percent for Bristol-Myers Squibb Company. At J&J, divisions perform their own purchasing, billing, and distribution functions. Duplication of these functions is part of the reason that J&J's overhead is high.

The J&J organization design isn't static. Since taking over as CEO, Larsen has pushed the J&J companies to achieve more integration among common functions, such as payroll processing, computer services, purchasing, distribution, accounts payable, and employee fringe benefits. This push is intended to share more services efficiently among divisions to cut down on duplication of efforts and improve relations with J&J's largest customers. To keep large retailers happy, J&J established "customer-support centers." The centers' employees work on-site with major retailers to ease distribution and ordering problems. Giant customers, such as Kmart, still get sales calls from dozens of different J&J units. But the goods from most of J&J's divisions are now delivered to retailers' warehouses in single large shipments. "We're very excited about it," says James A. Glime, manager of business development at Kmart. "This makes sense, and it certainly supports our business."

Larsen also launched an effort to unite customer service and credit functions. Code-named Pathfinder, it replaced four separate departments that used to do credit reviews, sometimes on the same customers. "If a customer has a question about a delivery, they don't have to call the baby company, then our consumer-products organization, and so on," says Larsen. "They make one phone call to one person who specializes in them, and no matter where the problem is, that person takes care of it."[27]

CONDITIONS FOR USE

A multidivisional design eases problems of integration by focusing expertise and knowledge on specific goods or services. For example, the sales efforts of a single marketing department at a firm such as Johnson & Johnson would likely be ineffective in marketing products ranging from anesthetics to contact lenses to baby powder. Each product line is best handled by a department or division thoroughly familiar with it and its set of customers. Such a design clearly meets the needs of a company such as J&J, which provides diverse products to diverse customers (ranging from family-run pharmacies to global retailers to hospitals to government agencies) in geographic locations throughout the world.

One disadvantage of the multidivisional design is that a firm must have a large number of managerial personnel to oversee all the product lines.[28] Another disadvantage is the higher cost that results from the duplication of various functions. Johnson & Johnson addressed it by combining some processes and introducing horizontal mechanisms to link its independent units in dealing with common issues.

Adoption of a multidivisional design often reduces the environmental complexity facing any one team, department, or division. Employees in a product-based unit can focus on one product line, rather than be overextended across multiple product lines. As with a functional design, an organization with a multidivisional design can deal with complex environments by adding horizontal mechanisms, such as linking roles, task forces, integrating roles, and cross-functional teams. Johnson & Johnson did so with its payroll, computer services, purchasing, distribution, accounts payable, and benefits functions.

INTEGRATION OF UNITS

Another essential part of organization design is to determine the desired horizontal integration among individuals, teams, departments, and divisions. **Horizontal integration** refers to the processes and mechanisms for linking teams and departments that are related to each other laterally, such as between marketing and manufacturing departments. Many of the dynamics between teams and groups (see Chapter 8) apply to horizontal relations. Horizontal integration processes and mechanisms include team goals and rewards, plans, linking roles, cross-functional teams, integrating roles and teams, and various groupware aids. Horizontal integration is affected primarily by three variables: (1) the degree of differentiation between departments; (2) the degree of required integration between departments; and (3) the degree of uncertainty (including task, work-flow, and environmental) confronting each department. As Figure 16.9 shows, each variable has a range from low to high. The diagnosis of these variables and their impact on operations is a necessary step in designing an effective organization.

HORIZONTAL DESIGN

Differentiation   **Differentiation** is the degree to which departments differ in structure (low to high), members' orientation to a time horizon (short to long), managers' orientation to other people (permissive to authoritarian), and members' views of the task environment (certain to uncertain).[29] Production departments often have a high degree of formal structure with many rules and procedures, tight supervisory control, frequent and specific reviews of individual and departmental performance, and structured relationships among co-workers

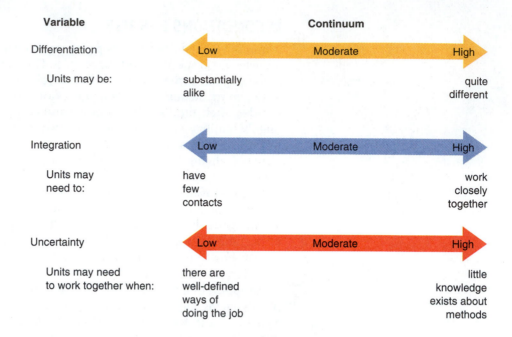

■ FIGURE 16.9

Variables That Affect Horizontal Relations between Units

(mechanistic system). Research departments and planning departments often are just the opposite with their personnel needing open and close working relationships (organic system). Production workers have short time horizons (minutes, hours, and days) and think about immediate problems. Research and planning employees think in terms of months and even years into the future. In general, the greater the differences between departments, the greater management's challenge is to get them to work together (such as marketing with production).

Integration   **Integration** is the degree of collaboration and mutual understanding required among departments to achieve their goals. Integration is greatest between departments that are reciprocally interdependent and least when they are in a pooled interdependent relationship.

Management must be careful not to establish too much or too little horizontal integration. Too little integration probably will lead to lower quality decisions and the misuse of resources because each unit will "do its own thing." The costs associated with too much integration are likely to far exceed any possible benefits. With excessive horizontal integration, departments often get in the way of each other, rather than help each other perform their tasks and achieve their goals.

In Chapter 8, we discussed several approaches for fostering effective dynamics and outcomes between horizontal and interdependent teams and groups. Achieving horizontal integration between products also is important. Recall that Corning Glass has seven product divisions. It achieved horizontal integration between them with the adoption of common manufacturing engineering and R&D facilities located at corporate headquarters. Uncertainty is a key to determining how complex and varied such horizontal mechanisms need be.

Uncertainty   **Uncertainty** is the gap between what is known and what needs to be known to make effective decisions and perform tasks effectively. Factors that should be evaluated in determining the degree of uncertainty that a department faces include

- the completeness of information and guidelines available to help employees perform their tasks;
- the frequency with which departments can be expected to face problems that they have to solve jointly; and
- the probability that departments can be reasonably certain of the results of their independent and mutual efforts.

Conditions for Use   The combinations of the three variables—differentiation, required integration, and level of uncertainty—have several significant implications for horizontal organization design. The simplest situation involves low uncertainty, low differentiation, and low integration between departments. Such departments produce standardized goods or services and are practically independent of each other.

An increase in the degree of differentiation, integration, and uncertainty is costly. It requires an increase in the expenditure of resources, the number of formal horizontal mechanisms (such as cross-functional teams), and the use of behavioral processes (reward systems, leadership and communication styles) to obtain integration.[30] For example, extensive collaboration among manufacturing, marketing, planning, design, and engineering at General Motors and its Oldsmobile Division was required to create the new Aurora automobile.

The most difficult interdepartmental situation involves high differentiation, high required integration, and high uncertainty. Organizations must expend considerable resources and use a variety of horizontal mechanisms and behavioral processes to manage interdepartmental relations under such conditions.

▮ MATRIX DESIGN

Matrix design is based on multiple support systems and authority relationships whereby some employees report to two superiors rather than one.[31] As Figure 16.10 illustrates, matrix design usually involves a combination of functional and product designs through the use of dual authority, information, and reporting

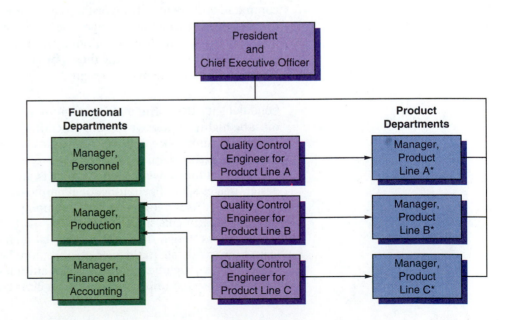

▮ FIGURE 16.10

Partial Illustration of Basic Matrix Design

*These product managers also have full responsibility for the marketing activities associated with their own product lines.

relationships and systems. Every matrix contains three unique sets of role relationships: (1) the top manager, who heads up and balances the dual chains of command; (2) the managers of functional and product departments, who share subordinates; and (3) the managers (or specialists) who report to both a functional manager and a product manager. In an organization that has major operations throughout the world, matrix managers could be designated for each of the firm's main geographic areas, such as Europe, South America, North America, the Pacific Rim, and the Middle East.

Boeing, Lockheed Martin, and other aerospace companies were the first to use the matrix design. Today, organizations in many industries (including chemical, banking, insurance, packaged goods, electronics, and computer) and fields (including hospitals, government agencies, and professional organizations) use various adaptations of the matrix design.

Typical Evolution   The matrix design typically evolves in stages.[32] The first stage may be the use of a temporary task force. Let's say that a task force composed of representatives from different departments or divisions of an organization is created to study a problem and make recommendations. Task force members retain their usual departmental affiliations (an engineer continues to report to the head of engineering and a market analyst to the head of marketing). But these temporary members also are accountable to the task force's leader.

The second stage usually involves the creation of a permanent team or committee to address a specified need or problem. Again, representatives from the various functional and product departments comprise the team or committee, each representing the view of his or her department.

The third stage may occur when a project manager is appointed and held accountable for integrating the team's activities and inputs for its final output. Project managers often must negotiate or "buy" the human resources necessary to carry out the tasks from the managers of functional departments. With the appointment of project managers, an organization is well on the way to a matrix design and faces all the difficulties and benefits of multiple-authority relationships. These new relationships replace the simple, straightforward, single chain of command and are the distinguishing characteristic of the matrix design. Whereas the traditional hierarchical design rests on formal reward or position power, the matrix design demands negotiations by peers with a high tolerance of ambiguous power relationships. Managing these power relationships is one of the most challenging aspects of the matrix design.

Conditions for Use   The matrix design may be appropriate when (1) employees must be highly responsive to both functional or product line (or place) concerns; (2) organizations face complex, dynamic environments coupled with unproved technologies that require employees to process lots of data and information; and (3) organizations have multiple products and limited resources.[33] This type of design makes specialized, functional employees' knowledge available to all projects. Also, it uses people flexibly, as employees are assigned to functional and product departments simultaneously.

The matrix design demands substantial managerial support while employees learn how to operate in the new organization. Learning may require two or three years because significant changes in attitudes and behaviors are required. Employees used to unity of command, a clear authority structure, and top-down orders may be uncomfortable with the dual-authority structure required under a matrix design. Special training programs often are needed to implement the new design. In order to work properly, a matrix design must maintain a continuing tension between multiple orientations (such as functional specialty and product line). This tension, in turn, requires effective interpersonal skills in communication, conflict resolution, and negotiation.

MULTINATIONAL DESIGN

A **multinational design** attempts to maintain coordination across products, functions, and geographic areas.[34] Meeting the need for extensive three-way cooperation is especially difficult because operating divisions are separated by distance and time. A further complication is that managers often are separated by culture and language. A "perfect" balance, if such were possible, between these perspectives would require a very complex matrix design. Hence most multinational designs focus on the relative emphasis that should be given to place and product organization design.

■ BASIC OPTIONS

Figure 16.11 suggests the various combinations that might be selected. It also shows the likely effects of choosing a design based primarily on place or product line. At Campbell Soup, strong delegation of authority by place gives country or

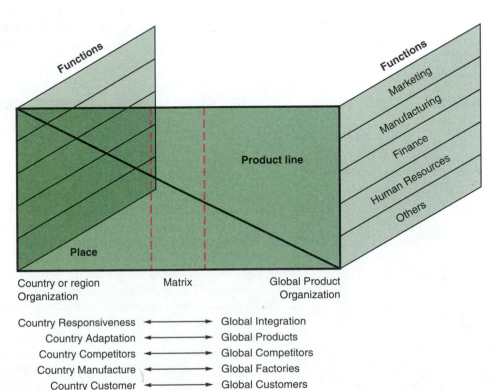

■ FIGURE 16.11

Basic Options in Multinational Design

Source: Adapted from Galbraith, J. R., and Kazanijian, R. K. *Strategy Implementation: Structure Systems and Process,* 2d ed. St. Paul: West, 1986, 159.

Country Responsiveness	⟷	Global Integration
Country Adaptation	⟷	Global Products
Country Competitors	⟷	Global Competitors
Country Manufacture	⟷	Global Factories
Country Customer	⟷	Global Customers

regional managers the ability to respond and adapt to local food preferences. In contrast, product-line managers with worldwide authority may focus on achieving global efficiencies (integration) in production and universal (standard) products.

■ CONDITIONS FOR USE

The forces generating more global integration in many industries include (1) the growing presence and importance of global competitors and customers, (2) the global rise in market demand for products, (3) new information technologies, and (4) efficient factories that can manufacture goods for customers throughout the world.[35] Worldwide product divisions in firms dealing with such forces are likely to dominate decisions, overpowering the interests of geographically based divisions. Pressures from national governments and local markets also may be strong, often requiring multinational corporations to market full product lines in all the principal countries they serve. Marketing opportunities, however, may not be open to companies unless they negotiate terms with the host government. Therefore a worldwide product-line division may not be as effective at opening new markets as a geographically organized division because local managers can respond more effectively to local governments' concerns. A division operating under a place design often can establish relations with host governments, invest in distribution channels, develop brand recognition, and build competencies that no single product-line division could afford. Thus valid reasons still exist for country or regional (Europe, North America, Latin America, the Pacific Rim, and the Middle East) organization.

The following Across Cultures feature relates the shift at Black & Decker from a multinational product design that emphasized regional operations to one that emphasizes global operations. It reveals some of the tensions inherent in multinational design when top management tries to balance place, function, and product-line considerations.

ACROSS CULTURES

Black & Decker's Worldwide Design

Black & Decker (B&D), manufacturer of power tools for home and professional use, has manufacturing plants in ten countries and sells its products in more than ninety. Design centers, manufacturing plants, and marketing programs focus on making and selling products worldwide. But it wasn't always that way.

Earnings had begun to slip in the early 1980s, and a worldwide recession caused a significant downturn in the power tools segment of B&D's business. However, B&D's problems were partly a result of its own organization design. The corporation operated twenty-five manufacturing plants in thirteen countries on six continents. It had three operating groups and a headquarters group, in Maryland. In addition, individual B&D companies, such as B&D of West Germany, operated autonomously in each of more than fifty countries where B&D sold its products. The company's philosophy had been to let the company in each country adapt products to fit the unique characteristics of its market. The Italian firm produced power tools for Italians, the U.K. firm made tools for Britons, and so on.

—Continued

ACROSS CULTURES—*Continued*

As a result, these companies didn't communicate well with each other. Successful products in one country often took years to introduce in others. The highly successful Dustbuster, introduced in the United States in the late 1970s, wasn't introduced in Australia until 1983. When efforts were made to introduce B&D home products into European markets, the European managers refused to comply. They felt that home appliances and products were uniquely American and wouldn't sell well outside the United States.

Because of the tailor-made specifications for different markets, design centers weren't being used efficiently. At one point, eight design centers around the world were producing 260 different motors, even though market research had revealed that the firm needed fewer than ten. Plant utilization was quite low, employment levels were high, and output per employee was unacceptably low.

As B&D moved into the mid 1980s, management realized that something had to be done. One area in which the Japanese had not made significant inroads was housewares and small appliances. So B&D acquired the small-appliances division of General Electric in 1984 to give itself more shelf space in housewares and also a large enough line of products to provide economies of scale in manufacturing.

To gain some efficiencies from being a global corporation, starting in 1987, B&D tried to match staffing requirements with sales and limited the number of motors it was going to market around the world. Standardizing motors allowed B&D to develop a global product strategy, letting B&D change features for local market tastes but retaining a product's essential design. Currently, B&D organizes its businesses around product lines. These product lines (such as vacuum cleaners) have common distribution channels, technologies, customers, competitors, and geographic markets. Product-line managers are responsible for all functions, including manufacturing, advertising, and sales, for their product lines.[36]

NETWORK DESIGN

All the organization designs discussed so far have limitations that often hinder organizations in coping with turbulent environments and technologies. The network design is intended to overcome those limitations and facilitate the management of highly diverse and complex organizations involving multiple departments and many people. A primary concern in all the other organization designs was how to allocate authority and resources among positions, teams, departments, and divisions. The **network design** focuses on sharing authority, responsibility, and resources among people and departments that must cooperate and communicate frequently to achieve common goals.[37] Various designs (functional, product, or place) must be available in a network organization as the tasks to be performed and the goals to be achieved change.

The following Managing in Practice account presents the features of the network design recently adopted by Eastman Chemical Company. This company is a large division ($3.5 billion in annual sales) of the Eastman Kodak Company.

MANAGING IN PRACTICE

■ **FIGURE 16.12**

Eastman Chemical's Network (Pizza) Design

Source: Office of Public Affairs, Eastman Chemical Company, 1994.

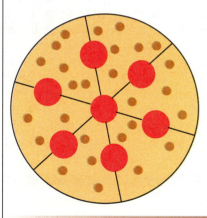

Eastman Chemical's Network Design

Figure 16.12 shows a schematic representation of Eastman Chemical's new network design. "Our organization chart is now called the pizza chart because it looks like a pizza with a lot of pepperoni sitting on it," says Ernest W. Davenport, Jr., who as president is the "pepperoni" at the center of the pie. "We did it in circular form to show that everyone is equal in the organization. No one dominates the other. The space inside the circles is more important than the lines."

The large "pepperoni" typically represent the major cross-functional teams responsible for managing a key product line, a geographic area, a function, or a "core competence" in a specific technology or area such as innovation. The space around them is where collaborative interaction is supposed to occur. The small pepperoni typically represent support teams (such as human resources) or special project teams that will be discontinued after their goals are accomplished.

Self-managed teams replaced several of the senior vice-presidents who had been responsible for key functions. Instead of having a head of manufacturing, for example, the company uses a team consisting of all its plant managers. "It was the most dramatic change in the company's seventy-year history," maintains Davenport. "It makes people take off their organization hats and put on their team hats. It gives people a much broader perspective and brings decision-making down at least another level."

In creating the new organization, the senior managers agreed that the primary role of the functions was to support Eastman's businesses in chemicals, plastics, fibers, and polymers. "A function does not and should not have a mission of its own," insists Davenport. But over the years, the functional departments had grown strong and powerful, often at the expense of the company overall as they fought to protect their own turf and build their own empires. The company's managers now work on at least one cross-functional team, and most work on two or more. Tom O. Nethery, a group vice-president, leads an industrial-business group. He also serves on three teams that deal with such diverse issues as human resources, cellulose technology, and product-support services.[38]

■ KEY CHARACTERISTICS

The network design is sometimes called a spiderweb or cluster organization (as at Eastman Chemical). It resembles a mosaic of mutually interdependent departments and managerial processes. This mosaic can't be woven from typical organization charts that show vertical authority and reporting relationships. A network organization exists only when most of the following factors operate in support of one another.

- *Distinctive competence.* The organization maintains superiority through innovation and adaptation by combining resources in novel ways.
- *Responsibility.* People who must collaborate to perform their tasks share responsibility. The organization's design includes extensive use of cross-functional, special-purpose, and self-managed teams. At Eastman Chemical, each large "pepperoni" (see Figure 16.12) typically represents a key cross-functional team responsible for managing a product line, a geographic area,

a function, or a core competence in a specific technology (or an area such as innovation).

- *Goal setting.* Common goals linked to satisfying the needs of one or more important external stakeholders (such as customers or clients, suppliers, shareholders, lenders, and governments) are formulated.

- *Communication.* The primary focus is on lateral rather than vertical communication. The information necessary to make decisions is widely shared and distributed, and open communication is the norm.

- *Information technology.* Many information technologies (including groupware) assist employees in networking internally (with others in the organization who may even be separated geographically by great distances) or externally (with customers, suppliers, regulatory agencies, and others). Typical information technologies and related groupware include e-mail, special PC software decision aids, voice mail, mobile phones, fax, telecommuting, teleconferencing, local and wide-area computer networks, and the like.

- *Organizational culture.* The culture has a bias toward the organic system and as few organization levels as possible. Recall the comment of Eastman Chemical's Ernest Davenport: "We did it (organization chart) in circular form to show that everyone is equal in the organization. No one dominates the other. The space inside the circles is more important than the lines."

- *Balanced view.* Individuals, teams, departments, and divisions do not view themselves as isolated islands having only their unique goals and ways of doing things. They view themselves in relation to others with common goals and rewards. Forms of cooperation and trust evolve over time, based on a history of past performance. The basic assumption of trust is that each person or department depends on resources controlled by others and that mutual gains are obtained by pooling resources and finding win-win solutions for all.

■ ROLE OF INFORMATION TECHNOLOGIES

The principal developments in information technologies over the past ten years have both pushed and enabled organizations to move toward the network design.[39] Four of the information technology advances that have enabled organizations to utilize internal and external networking are open systems, distributed computing, real time, and global networking.

Open Systems   Portable software and compatible technology now exist. These capabilities extend to the external network of suppliers, consumers, regulatory agencies, and even competitors. The shift is away from departments or divisions with their own unique computing capability to a network of linked business processes. In addition, organizations can be in closer touch with their customers, suppliers, and others, enabling people to act not only in their own self-interests, but with a shared vision and commitment.

Distributed Computing   The shift is from centralized computing where all access was limited to a few people or departments to network computing whereby information is available to the primary user. Centralized and limited access computing systems are typical of a mechanistic system. In contrast, planning, information processing, and the application of knowledge to business problems are being distributed throughout organic organizations by empowered individuals and teams.

Real Time   The new information technologies now capture information online and update information banks in real time. These capabilities provide an instantaneous, accurate picture of many processes, such as sales, production, and cash flow. At Frito-Lay, a real-time network allows the company's manufacturing plants to continuously adjust to changing market conditions. Just-in-time receipt of raw materials from suppliers and delivery of products to customers minimizes the need for warehousing and allows Frito-Lay to shift from mass production to custom online production. Customer orders can arrive electronically and be processed instantly. Corresponding invoices can be sent electronically and databases automatically updated.[40]

Global Networking   Information networks are the backbone of network organization design.[41] Global networking permits both real-time communication and access of electronically stored information at will from anywhere in the world. For global organizations such as Intel, Texas Instruments, Samsung, and NEC, the network organization design redefines time and space for both employees and suppliers, customers, and competitors. In an open network design, any individual, team, or department can quickly communicate and share information with any other individual, team, or department. Work can be performed at a variety of locations, including employees' homes, with the office becoming part of a network rather than a place.

■ EXTERNAL NETWORKING

The network design is particularly effective in creating alliances of flexible partnerships.[42] Partners in an alliance could be customers, suppliers, and firms that would be defined as competitors under different circumstances. Corning, Inc., uses its twenty-three joint ventures with foreign partners such as Siemens (Germany), Samsung (South Korea), Asahi Chemical (Japan), and CIBA-GEIGY (Switzerland), to compete in a growing number of related high-technology markets. The flexibility with which Corning approaches its partnerships—letting the form be determined by the goals and letting the ventures evolve over time—is one reason for its success. But even more important is the time and effort expended by Corning executives to create the conditions for long-lasting, mutually beneficial relationships.

The network design is intended to create successful external relationships by having "six I's" in place: importance, investment, interdependence, integration, information, and institutionalization. Because the relationships are important, they get adequate resources, management attention, and sponsorship. Agreement to provide long-term investment tends to help equalize benefits and costs over time. The participants are interdependent, which helps maintain a balance of power. The participants are integrated in order to maintain essential points of contact and communication. Each partner is informed about the plans and directions of the other. Finally, when the networking design is institutionalized, it is bolstered by a framework of supporting mechanisms from legal requirements to social ties to shared values. These mechanisms solidify trust.

The following Across Cultures selection reports on the new network design adopted at Procter & Gamble (P&G) to make it more responsive to global customers. It has required fundamental changes in P&G's organizational culture, and complete implementation is likely to take several more years. A large number of managers who couldn't change from the old mechanistic system have already left for other jobs, retired early, or are seeking to leave.

ACROSS CULTURES

Procter & Gamble's New Network Design

Procter & Gamble (P&G) has redesigned the way it develops, manufacturers, distributes, prices, markets, and sells products in order to deliver better value at every point in the supply chain. The new design has eliminated three management levels to make the company a more responsive global marketer. Products will be tailored more swiftly to the wishes of consumers everywhere.

Achieving lower costs required fundamental changes in P&G's overmanaged organization. Under Edwin Artze's leadership, eleven teams collectively examined every part of the company. They were given four mandates: change the work, do more with less, eliminate rework, and reduce costs that can't be passed on to the consumer. Stephen David, a vice-president in charge of one of the teams, stated, "The first thing we learned is that if you don't make the commitment to take some of your best people and pull them off line, you will not get the results." His project, originally scheduled for six to nine months with part-time participants, had to be converted to a full-time, year-long effort.

David's team, guided by consultants from Booz Allen, spent six months benchmarking the costs of the sales organization. The team analyzed forty-one work processes that the company calls its customer management system. It found that P&G had the highest overhead in the industry and marketed thirty-four product categories, each with seventeen basic pricing brackets and endless variations. The quarterly sales promotion plan for health and beauty products alone ran to more than 500 pages and was sent to every salesperson. Five P&G trucks used to pull up to a retailer's dock on any day, representing five separate contacts for order verification and delivery times. Richard E. Fredericksen, an executive at American Stores, a Salt Lake City–based multiregional food and drug retailer stated, "There were so many levels and so many parts; to get a purchase order correct was almost an act of God."

One goal of the overhaul is to make the distribution chain linking supplier, wholesaler, retailer, and consumer more like a continuous loop. Networking replaces the old piecemeal ordering system with continuous product replenishment (CPR). When a box of detergent is scanned at the checkout counter, the information is transferred directly to the manufacturer's computer. The computer is programmed to replenish the product automatically. This paperless exchange minimizes mistakes and bill-backs, reduces inventory, decreases out-of-stock situations, and improves cash flow.

The company now requires that suppliers to the feminine products, diaper, hair care, and laundry detergent categories bid for global business. Artze also wants P&G to get improved products to market faster. Formerly, forty-four months were required to make a diaper change worldwide. In contrast, Kimberly Clark required only twenty months to bring its Huggies Pull-Ups diapers to market. Although P&G has long sought to make world products, the company has been slow to coordinate R&D, purchasing (suppliers), and marketing strategy. The company has modified its global management matrix. In that matrix, an executive might have had operating responsibilities for both the U.S. diaper business and a global diaper strategy. The company now stresses regional management over country management. In South America a regional network focused on customers has replaced a country-by-country design. Executives say that this network can handle twice the business with the same staff, facilitated by a computer-based global information network.[43]

CHAPTER SUMMARY

Organization design is an intricate decision-making process. It is heavily influenced by the combination of environmental forces, technological factors, and strategic choices. The environment(s) confronting an organization, its teams, departments, and divisions can vary greatly. This variability must be assessed in terms of degrees of complexity, dynamism, diversity, and uncertainty.

Strategic choices—low cost, focused, or differentiation—have a direct impact on organization design. Organizations pursuing a low-cost strategy usually seek designs that emphasize functional lines and operate in homogeneous–stable environments. Focused strategies are intended to help an organization target a specific niche within an industry. The basic idea behind a focused strategy is to specialize in products or services that other firms find hard to copy. Differentiation strategies are based on providing customers with something that is different or unique. The key assumption is that the environment is constantly changing and that these firms offer customers superior value for their dollar.

If top management supports tight, centralized control of day-to-day decisions, a mechanistic system is more likely to be used than an organic system. Different departments or divisions within the same organization may vary along the mechanistic to organic continuum. A production department may operate as a mechanistic system, whereas the research and development department may operate as an organic system. The adoption of total quality values often requires a shift to a more organic system.

Technological considerations are important in organization design. The potential impact of three technological variables—work-flow uncertainty, task uncertainty, and task interdependence (pooled, sequential, and reciprocal)—on organization design can be considerable.

Four of the more traditional designs are functional, product, place, and matrix. The conditions under which each may be appropriate were described. An organization or its departments facing a somewhat simple, stable environment and simple technology generally can utilize a functional design effectively. Its top managers may integrate the functional areas as needed with some horizontal mechanisms, such as committees and cross-functional teams. Multidivisional design—a form of product design—is an option for firms providing a range of goods or services to geographically dispersed markets. The need for linking units also affects organization design. Horizontal and matrix designs support linking. The amount of horizontal integration needed is strongly influenced by three variables: differentiation, integration, and uncertainty. Diagnosis of these variables is an essential aspect of horizontal organization design. Horizontal mechanisms include group goals and rewards, task forces, formal planning activities, linking roles, cross-functional teams, and the like.

Multinational design attempts to maintain three-way organization perspectives and capabilities among products, functions, and geographic areas. Numerous options are available in multinational design. Network organization design represents a fundamental breakthrough in overcoming the disadvantages inherent in the other types of design. The network design emphasizes horizontal mechanisms and processes needed to manage complex sequential and reciprocal interdependencies among individuals, teams, departments, and divisions. This design also draws on the revolution in information technologies (including groupware) that enable formation of convenient and low-cost networks and change as needs and goals change. This design generally requires a management philosophy and organizational culture that supports an organic system.

KEY TERMS AND CONCEPTS

Bureaucracy

Centralization

Chain of command

Complexity

Differentiation

Differentiation strategies

Division of labor

Dynamism

Focused strategies

Functional design

Hierarchy of authority

Horizontal integration

Impersonality

Integration

Low-cost strategies

Matrix design

Mechanistic system

Multidivisional design

Multinational design

Network design

Organic system

Organization design

Organizational culture

Place design

Procedures

Product design

Rules

Span of control

Strategic choice

Uncertainty

Unity of command

Whistle-blowing

DISCUSSION QUESTIONS

1. What are the basic environmental forces that shape the organization design of your college or university?

2. What is the basic strategy of a business organization with which you are familiar? What impact does this choice of strategy have on the design of this organization?

3. How does technology affect an organization's design?

4. Which organization design is used by your college or university? How do the environment, strategy, and technology influence its organization design?

5. Visit a local bank or department store. How is it organized?

6. Describe the mechanistic or organic characteristics of an organization of which you are a member. Are any changes needed? Explain.

7. What are some limitations of a functional design?

8. ARAMARK Corporation, a global provider of managed services, is organized by product line, including campus din- ing, business dining, uniform rentals, corrections (feeding prisoners), and sports and recreation (managing concessions at various sports arenas). The sports and recreation division, for example, recently served more than 60,000 meals each day for seventeen days at the Olympic Village in Atlanta, Georgia. What are some likely organization design problems that Joe Neubauer, ARAMARK'S chief executive officer, faces?

9. What difficulties are associated with the matrix design? Why did this type of design start in the aerospace industry?

10. What forces work for and against the establishment of a network design?

11. How does information technology affect the design of a global organization?

Developing Competencies

Self-Insight: Inventory of Effective Design[44]

Instructions: Listed are statements describing an effective organization design. Please indicate the extent to which you agree or disagree with each statement as a description of an organization you currently work for or have worked for in the past. Write the appropriate number next to the statement.

1. Strongly disagree

2. Disagree

3. Somewhat disagree

4. Uncertain

5. Somewhat agree

6. Agree

7. Strongly agree

_____ 1. Employees who try to change things are usually recognized and supported.

_____ 2. The organization makes it easy to get the skills needed to progress.

_____ 3. Employees almost always know how their work turns out, whether it is good or bad.

_____ 4. Employees have flexibility over the pace of their work.

_____ 5. Managers facilitate discussion at meetings to encourage participation by subordinates.

_____ 6. Few policies, rules, and regulations restrict innovation in this organization.

_____ 7. Boundaries between teams, departments, and divisions rarely interfere with solving joint problems.

_____ 8. There are few hierarchical levels in this organization.

_____ 9. Everyone knows how their work will affect the work of the next person or team and the quality of the final product or service.

_____ 10. The organization is well informed about technological developments relevant to its processes, goods, or services.

_____ 11. The organization is constantly trying to determine what the customer wants and how to meet customer needs better.

_____ 12. The organization can adapt to most changes because its policies, organization design, and employees are flexible.

_____ 13. Different parts of the organization work together; when conflict arises, it often leads to constructive outcomes.

_____ 14. Everyone can state the values of the organization and how they are used to make decisions.

_____ 15. A great deal of information is shared openly, as appropriate.

Scoring and Interpretation

Sum the points given to statements 1–15. A score of 75–105 suggests an effective organization design. A score of 70–89 suggests a mediocre design that probably varies greatly in terms of how specific aspects of the organization work for or against the design's effectiveness. A score of 50–69 suggests a great deal of ambiguity about the organization and how it operates. A score of 15–49 suggests that the design is contributing to serious problems.

Organizational Insight: Asea-Brown-Boveri

Asea-Brown-Boveri (ABB) is one of Europe's leading producers of power generation equipment, factory automation systems, robotics and machine tools, high-speed trains, and environmental monitoring systems. The company is becoming well known for its wide range of high-quality products and for its organizational structure. In 1997, the company's revenues exceeded $25 billion, and it has close to 200,000 employees worldwide. ABB spends nearly 8 percent of sales on R&D ($2.5 billion) per year. It is a technological leader in the development of factory automation systems. Recently it extended its market share gains in power transmission and distribution systems.

Originally, ABB was two separate companies, Asea (a Swedish engineering group) and Brown-Boveri (a Swiss manufacturer of electric motors). The current ABB came into being in 1987 with a merger of the companies. Despite the long history and growth that both companies enjoyed on their own, the new ABB is a model for managing operations around the world. During the past six years, ABB has restructured its European operations to achieve economies of scale for its products. It has also undertaken an aggressive acquisition strategy to build market share abroad. In 1989, ABB purchased Westinghouse Electric's power transmission and distribution business. In the same year, it purchased Combustion Engineering, an innovative U.S. firm with specialized technologies in the turbine and the power automation field. In 1991, it acquired the robotics business from Cincinnati Milacron, one of the largest U.S. producers of machine tools and integrated factory systems. Through these acquisitions, ABB has numerous factories, R&D centers, and other facilities around the world, so it now manages a global empire of companies. The company continues to expand and look for new business and market opportunities.

The organizational tasks and pressures facing ABB managers are enormous. On the one hand, they need to ensure that each ABB business remains responsive to the individual markets it serves. On the other hand, ABB must develop and produce products at a cost low enough to compete against other global electrical equipment giants. In other words, ABB needs to balance low-cost production with fast response to local markets. This daunting task represents a major organizational challenge.

To accommodate these two goals (low cost and fast response), ABB is organized as a global matrix, or grid, organization. The idea behind a matrix is to develop core technologies and low-cost production without sacrificing the firm's ability to respond to local markets. The essence of ABB's matrix is that each person reports to two bosses simultaneously: a country manager and a product manager. Each country manager runs local operations with a unique set of strategies for dealing with local markets, customers, competitors, legal regulations, and other issues. Each product manager deals on a worldwide basis with the technical specifications and costs of product design and manufacture. Both types of managers must work together to design leading-edge products that fit local market conditions. In practice, the matrix system is often "tilted" toward the product or country manager, depending on the strategy needed for a particular product at the time.

Chief Executive Officer Percy Barnevik believes that the global matrix gives ABB a competitive advantage. It allows ABB to coordinate its operations against General Electric, Westinghouse, Toshiba Hitachi, and Mitsubishi. These companies compete directly with ABB in many markets. Also, the matrix encourages a diversity of perspectives, ideas, and cultures. This diversity is vital to the stimulation of new product and market ideas. By using the matrix organization design carefully, ABB is trying to become a truly global firm with both technological leadership and a strong local presence. The company has been described as neither Swiss, nor Swedish, nor even European; the primary language spoken is English.[45]

Questions

1. How would you characterize the environment that ABB operates in? How has it affected its strategy?

2. What are some potential limitations to ABB's choice of organizational design?

REFERENCES

1. Adapted from Seligram, P. M. Electrical equipment industry. *Value Line*, October 25, 1996, 1001–1020; Diverse consortium plans glass factory across border. *New York Times*, August 7, 1996, C4; *Annual Report*. Corning, New York: Corning Glass, 1997.

2. Bulter, R. Organizational design. In N. Nicholson (ed.). *Encyclopedic Dictionary of Organizational Behavior*. Cambridge, Mass.: Blackwell, 1996, 384–390.

3. Hamel, G., and Prahalad, C. K. *Competing for the Future*. Boston: Harvard Business School, 1994.

4. Porter, M. E. What is strategy? *Harvard Business Review*, November-December 1996, 61–78.

5. Duncan, R. B. Characteristics of organizational environments and perceived environmental uncertainty. *Administrative Science Quarterly*, 1972, 17, 314; Amburgey, T. L., and Rao, H. Organizational ecology: Past, present and future directions. *Academy of Management Journal*, 1996, 39, 1265–1286.

6. Henkoff, R. P&G new and improved. *Fortune*, October 14, 1996, 151–160.

7. Gates, B. *The Road Ahead*. New York: Penguin USA, 1996.

8. Cronin, M. J. *The Internet Strategy Handbook*. Boston: Harvard Business School Press, 1996.

9. Pitts, R. A., and Lei, D. *Strategic Management: Building and Sustaining Competitive Advantage*. St. Paul: West, 1996.

10. Porter, M. E. *Competitive Strategy*. New York: Free Press, 1980.

11. Fry, L. W., and Slocum, J. W., Jr. Technology, structure and workgroup effectiveness: A test of a contingency model. *Academy of Management Journal*, 1984, 17, 221–246; Miller, C. C., Glick, W. H., Wang, Y. D., and Huber, G. P. Understanding technology–structure relationships: Theory development and meta-analytic theory testing. *Academy of Management Journal*, 1991, 34, 370–399.

12. Sprout, A. L. The Internet inside your company. *Fortune*, November 27, 1995, 164.

13. Hammer, M. *Beyond Reengineering*. New York: Harper Business, 1996.

14. Adapted from Hammer, M., and Champy, J. *Reengineering the Corporation: A Manifesto for Business Revolution*. New York: Harper Business, 1993; Sherman, S. How to bolster the bottom line: Investments in information technology; Profiles of five companies. *Fortune*, Autumn 1993 (Special 1994 information technology guide), 14–18.

15. Burns, T., and Stalker, G. M. *The Management of Innovation*. London: Social Science Paperbacks, 1961, 96–125.

16. Adapted from Weber, M. *The Theory of Social and Economic Organization* (trans., T. Parsons). New York: Oxford University Press, 1947, 329, 334; Adler, P. S., and Borys, B. Two types of bureaucracy: Enabling and coercive. *Administrative Science Quarterly*, 1996, 41, 61–89.

17. Smith, A. *An Inquiry into the Nature and Causes of the Wealth of Nations* (1776). New York: Modern Library, reprint, 1937, 48.

18. Hellriegel, D., and Slocum, J. W., Jr. *Management*. Cincinnati: South-Western, 1996, 49–51.

19. Near, J. P., and Miceli, M. P. Whistle-blowing: Myth and Reality. *Journal of Management*, 1996, 507–526.

20. Pasztor, D. Darling will cough up $4 million. *Dallas Observer*, January 2–8, 1997, 5.

21. *Callaway 1997 Annual Report*. Carlsbad, Calif.: Callaway Golf, 1997.

22. Lomi, A., and Larsen, E. R. Interacting locally and evolving globally: A computational approach to the dynamics of organizational populations. *Academy of Management Journal*, 1996, 39, 1287–1321.

23. Morrison, A. J., Ricks, D. A., and Roth, K. Globalization versus regionalization: Which way for the multinational? *Organizational Dynamics*, Winter 1991, 17–29.

24. *Vencor 1996 Annual Report to Shareholders*. Louisville, Ky.: Vencor, 1996.

25. Tallman, S., and Li, J. Effects of international diversity and product diversity on the performance of multinational firms. *Academy of Management Journal*, 1996, 39, 179–190.

26. Ashkenas, R., Ulrich, D., Jick, T., and Kerr, S. *The Boundaryless Organization*. San Francisco: Jossey-Bass, 1995.

27. Adapted from Ettore, B. James Burke: The fine art of leadership. *Management Review*, 1996, 85(10), 13–17; Rudnitsky, H. One hundred sixty companies for the price of one. *Forbes*, February 26, 1996, 54–60; Weber, J. A big company that works. *Business Week*, May 4, 1992, 124–132; Tully, S. A dickens of a tale. *Fortune*, May 31, 1993, 167–169.

28. Robins, J. A., and Wiersema, M. F. A resource-based approach to the multibusiness firm: Empirical analysis of portfolio relationships and corporate financial performance. *Strategic Management Journal*, 1995, 16, 277–300.

29. Allmendinger, J., and Hackman, J. R. Organizations in changing environments: The case of East German symphony orchestras. *Administrative Science Quarterly*, 1996, 41, 337–369.

30. Lawrence, P. R. Organization and environment perspective: The Harvard research program. In A. H. Van de Ven and W. F. Joyce (eds.), *Perspectives on Organization Design and Behavior.* New York: John Wiley & Sons, 1981, 311–337.

31. Ford, R. C., and Randolph, W. A. Cross-functional structures: A review and integration of matrix organization and project organization. *Journal of Management*, 1992, 18, 267–294.

32. Galbraith, J. R. *Competing with Flexible Lateral Organizations.* Reading, Mass.: Addison-Wesley, 1994.

33. Joyce, W. F., McGee, V. E., and Slocum, J. W., Jr. Designing lateral organizations: An analysis of the benefits, costs and enablers of nonhierarchical organizational forms. *Decision Sciences* (in press).

34. Young, S. T., and Nie, W. *Managing Global Operations.* Westport, Conn.: Greenwood, 1996.

35. Joyce, W. F. *Megachange: Reforming the Corporation.* Homewood, Ill.: Irwin, 1997.

36. Adapted from Brady, J. Lessons learned from the brink of disaster. *Washington Business Journal*, May 17, 1996, 63ff; Cosco, J. Black & Deckering Black & Decker. *Journal of Business Strategy*, January–February 1994, 59–62;

37. Miles, R. E., and Snow, C. C. *Fit, Failure and the Hall of Fame.* New York: Free Press, 1994; Miles, R. E., and Snow, C. C. The new network firm: A spherical structure built on a human investment philosophy. *Organizational Dynamics*, Spring 1995, 5–18.

38. Adapted from Birchard, B. Closing the strategy gap. *CFO, The Magazine for Senior Financial Executives*, October 1996, 26–34; Taylor, S. Eastman Chemical strives for better than world class. *Industrial Engineering*, 1993, 25(11), 28–32; Byrne, J. A. The horizontal organization: It's about managing across not up and down. *Business Week*, December 20, 1993, 76–81.

39. Lucas, H. C., Jr. *The T-Form Organization.* San Francisco: Jossey-Bass, 1995.

40. Conversation with Ralph Sorrentino, Manager, Management Information Systems, Frito-Lay, Plano, Texas, January, 1997.

41. Pfeffer, J. When it comes to "best practices"—Why do smart organizations occasionally do dumb things? *Organizational Dynamics*, Summer 1996, 33–44.

42. Slocum, J. W., Jr., and Lei, D. Designing global strategic alliances: Integrating cultural and economic factors. In G. P. Huber and W. M. Glick (eds.), *Organizational Change for Improving Performance.* New York: Oxford University Press, 1993, 295–322.

43. Adapted from Kaplan, A. P&G plan to reward "efficiency." *U.S. Distribution Journal*, October 15, 1995, 10–11; Saporito, B. Behind the tumult at P&G. *Fortune*, March 7, 1994, 74–81; Laing, J. R. New and improved: Procter & Gamble fights to keep its place on the top shelf. *Barrons*, November 29, 1993, 8–11; Arzt, E. L. Customers want performance, price, and value: Procter & Gamble's revamped logistics system within a total quality management context. *Transportation & Distribution*, July 1993, 32–34.

44. Adapted from Pasmore, W. A. *Designing Effective Organizations: The Sociotechnical Systems Perspective.* New York: John Wiley & Sons, 1988, 157–186.

45. Adapted from Holman, R. L. ABB's net income surges. *Wall Street Journal*, October 23, 1996, A16; Guyon, J. ABB fused units with one set of values; managers get global strategies to work locally. *Wall Street Journal*, October 2, 1996, A12; Bredin, P., Fletcher, P., Gee, J., and McClenahen, J. S. Europe's best practices. *Industry Week*, October 2, 1995, 66–70; Smart, T. and Edmondson, G. Slow boil for ABB in the U.S. *Business Week*, September 12, 1994, 72–74.

17

Organizational Culture

LEARNING OBJECTIVES

When you have finished studying this chapter, you should be able to:

- Define the concept of organizational culture.
- Explain how organizational cultures are developed, maintained, and changed.
- Identify the potential relationships between organizational culture and performance.
- Discuss the implications of organizational culture for ethical behavior in organizations.
- Explain the importance of effectively managing cultural diversity.
- Describe the process of organizational socialization and explain its relationship to organizational culture.

OUTLINE

PREVIEW CASE

"The Firm"

Members of McKinsey & Co. have long called their organization "The Firm"—doing so before release of the popular book and movie of the same title. McKinsey & Co. has been called the "most well-known, most secretive, most high-priced, most prestigious, most consistently successful, most envied, most trusted, and the most disliked management consulting firm on earth." The culture of McKinsey—unique and eccentric—seems to set it apart from other consulting firms. This organizational culture often mystifies outsiders, including McKinsey's clients.

Marvin Bower is McKinsey's founding father. (Mac McKinsey, Bower's partner in starting the firm, and whose name the firm still bears, died in 1937 at a relatively young age.) Bower has been likened to Sam Walton of Wal-Mart and Tom Watson of IBM in terms of his impact on the organization's culture. Bower laid down principles that have been emphasized so consistently over the years that they now define the culture.

First, McKinsey consultants are supposed to put the client's interests ahead of consulting revenues. They should keep their mouths shut about the client's activities. They should always tell the truth and not be afraid to disagree with a client's opinion. They should agree only to perform work that is truly needed and that McKinsey has the expertise to do. Bower prefers "professional" to "business" language as part of the culture. Thus McKinsey is "The Firm," never the "company"; jobs are "engagements"; and The Firm doesn't have a business—it has a "practice."

A defining moment in the McKinsey culture came in 1960 when Bower sold his shares back to the firm for book value, rather than selling to outsiders at a huge multiple of earnings. This incident set an example for partners that they still follow.

One view of why the McKinsey culture seems to function so well is that the firm only recruits consultants that fit with the prevailing culture. A former employee says, "Basically they hire the same people over and over. At other consulting firms there is a lot more diversity." Of the 465 partners, 21 are women and only 2 are African-American. Only 3 of 151 firm directors (a higher rank than partner) are women. The vast majority of people who run McKinsey were educated at one of only seven universities.[1]

The effectiveness and success of an organization are not determined solely by the abilities and motivations of employees and managers. Nor is effectiveness measured solely by how well groups and teams work together, although both individual and group processes are crucial for organizational success. According to R. H. Kilmann:

> The organization itself has an invisible quality—a certain style, a character, a way of doing things—that may be more powerful than the dictates of any one person or any formal system. To understand the soul of the organization requires that we travel below the charts, rule books, machines, and buildings into the underground world of corporate cultures.[2]

In this chapter, we examine the concept of organizational culture and how such cultures are formed, maintained, and changed. We also explore some possible relationships between organizational culture and performance; the relationship between organizational culture and ethical behavior; the challenge of managing a culturally diverse work force; and, finally, how organizations socialize individuals to their particular cultures. We begin with a brief overview of several types of organizational cultures.

TYPES OF ORGANIZATIONAL CULTURE

The labels of baseball team, club, academy, and fortress have been used to describe some common types of organizational cultures in the business world.[3] Each has distinctive characteristics.

Organizations with a **baseball team culture** attract entrepreneurs, innovators, and risk takers and pay employees for what they produce. Top performers often receive large salaries or other financial rewards and considerable autonomy. However, risks are high and long-term security is virtually nonexistent. High performers tend to see themselves as free agents, much like professional athletes. Job hopping is common, with employees readily leaving one firm for greater rewards or freedom at another. Baseball team cultures are common in advertising agencies, biotechnology firms, consulting firms, investment banks, law firms, and computer software developers, such as Microsoft and Lotus.

Age and experience are valued in the **club culture.** Organizations with a club culture reward seniority and provide stable, secure employment. The club culture also rewards loyalty, commitment, and "fitting in." Managers typically work at various jobs in different functions during a slow, steady progression up the corporate hierarchy; quick upward mobility is unusual. Employees often start young and may spend thirty-five to forty years with the same firm. At United Parcel Service (UPS), the CEO and his entire top management team began their UPS careers as clerks, delivery drivers, or management trainees. Darryl Hartley-Leonard rose from being a desk clerk to become the CEO of Hyatt Hotels. At Nynex, CEO Ivan Seidenberg started as a splicer's assistant earning $89.50 per week.[4] Other club cultures include Delta Airlines, most commercial banks, many utilities (such as the Bell companies), government agencies, and the U.S. military.

Organizations with an **academy culture** tend to hire recruits early—often directly from college—as do organizations with club cultures. However, academy cultures emphasize training employees to become expert in a particular function. For example, someone hired as a marketing representative would be unlikely to serve a stint in manufacturing. The academy culture stresses continuity of service, functional expertise, and institutional wisdom. Although there is some opportunity for "fast trackers," the academy culture is more likely to appeal to the steady climber who enjoys mastering the job. Academy cultures exist at Coca-Cola, IBM, Procter & Gamble and many other consumer product firms, the big three U.S. automakers, pharmaceutical companies, and many electronics and office products companies.

The **fortress culture** is preoccupied with survival. Organizations with a fortress culture promise little in the way of job security and have difficulty rewarding employees for good performance. Typically, they downsize or restructure periodically, dismissing many employees in the process. A fortress culture might appeal to individuals who relish the challenge of turning a company around. It wouldn't appeal to those who desire a sense of belonging, opportunities for professional growth, or secure future income. Some organizations with a fortress culture that have fallen on hard times previously had baseball team, club, or academy cultures. Others are firms in industries characterized by periodic boom and bust cycles. Currently, the ranks of fortress companies include some forest products firms, oil and gas companies, publishers, large retailers, and textile firms.

Most organizations probably can't be categorized neatly as having a baseball team, club, academy, or fortress culture. Some may be a blend of these cultures;

others may be in transition between cultures or even have different cultures at different times. Bank of America began as a baseball team culture, matured into a club culture, and then returned to its original culture. Apple Computer also started with a baseball team culture but matured into an academy culture.

These brief descriptions of various cultures are offered as a way of introducing the concept of organizational culture and making some important distinctions among organizations. However, other labels or categories of cultures are commonly used.[5] Labels are interesting, colorful, and help convey some understanding of organizational culture, but oversimplyfying the concept of culture through the use of labels should be avoided. Two organizations might be in essentially the same industry, be located in the same geographic area, have similar forms of organizational structure, and yet, somehow, be very different places to work. What makes organizations different? How do they get that way? The concept of organizational culture provides a useful way to answer such questions.

DYNAMICS OF ORGANIZATIONAL CULTURE

Organizational culture represents a complex pattern of beliefs, expectations, ideas, values, attitudes, and behaviors shared by the members of an organization.[6] More specifically, organizational culture includes

- *routine behaviors* when people interact, such as organizational rituals and ceremonies and the language commonly used;
- the *norms* that are shared by work groups throughout the organization, such as "a fair day's work for a fair day's pay";
- the *dominant values* held by an organization, such as "product quality" or "price leadership";
- the *philosophy* that guides an organization's policies toward its employees and customers;
- the *rules of the game* for getting along in the organization or the "ropes" that a newcomer must learn in order to become an accepted member; and
- the *feeling* or *climate* conveyed in an organization by the physical layout and the way in which members of the organization interact with customers or other outsiders.[7]

None of these components individually represents the culture of the organization. Taken together, however, they reflect and give meaning to the concept of organizational culture.

Organizational culture exists on several levels, as indicated by Figure 17.1, which differ in terms of visibility and resistance to change. The least visible or deepest level is that of basic, **shared assumptions,** which represent beliefs about reality and human nature that are taken for granted. For example, a basic assumption that guides some organizations in the development of reward systems, rules, and procedures is that employees are naturally lazy and must be tightly controlled in order to enhance their performance.

The next level of culture is that of **cultural values,** which represent collective beliefs, assumptions, and feelings about what things are good, normal, rational, valuable, and so on. Cultural values might be very different in different companies; in some, employees may care deeply about money but, in others, about

Levels of Organizational Culture

Source: Adapted from Cummings, T. G., and Worley, C. G. *Organization Development and Change,* 5th ed. St. Paul: West, 1993, 527.

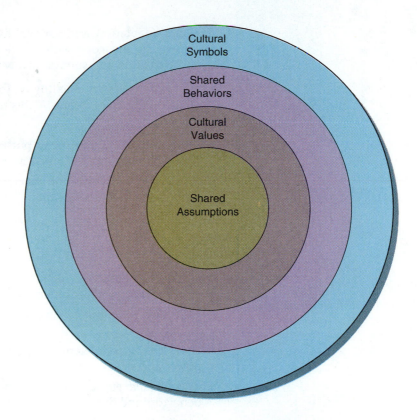

technological innovation or employee well-being. These values tend to persist over time even when organizational membership changes.

The next level is that of **shared behaviors,** including norms (see Chapter 8), which are more visible and somewhat easier to change than values. The reason, at least in part, is that people may be unaware of the values that bind them together.

The most superficial level of organizational culture consists of symbols. **Cultural symbols** are words (jargon or slang), gestures, and pictures or other physical objects that carry a particular meaning within a culture. Some expressions used at McDonald's provide an example of corporate jargon. McDonald's employees take training classes at Hamburger University; loyal employees are said to have "ketchup in their veins." Important cultural symbols sometimes take the form of **cultural heroes,** or people (alive or dead, real or imaginary) who possess characteristics highly valued by the culture and thus serve as role models.[8] For example, at the University of Virginia, which was founded by Thomas Jefferson, administrators reportedly still ask, "What would Mr. Jefferson do?" when faced with a challenging decision.

■ DEVELOPING ORGANIZATIONAL CULTURE

How does an organizational culture develop? Edgar Schein suggests that organizational culture forms in response to two major challenges that confront every organization: (1) external adaptation and survival; and (2) internal integration.[9]

External adaptation and survival has to do with how the organization will find a niche in and cope with its constantly changing external environment. External adaptation and survival involves addressing the following issues.

- *Mission and strategy:* Identifying the primary mission of the organization; selecting strategies to pursue this mission.
- *Goals:* Setting specific goals.
- *Means:* Determining how to pursue the goals; means include selecting an organizational structure and reward system.
- *Measurement:* Establishing criteria to measure how well individuals and teams are accomplishing their goals.

Internal integration has to do with the establishment and maintenance of effective working relationships among the members of an organization. Internal integration involves addressing the following issues.

- *Language and concepts:* Identifying methods of communication; developing a shared meaning for important concepts.
- *Group and team boundaries:* Establishing criteria for membership in groups and teams.
- *Power and status:* Determining rules for acquiring, maintaining, and losing power and status.
- *Rewards and punishments:* Developing systems for encouraging desirable behaviors and discouraging undesirable behaviors.

An organizational culture emerges when members share knowledge and assumptions as they discover or develop ways of coping with external adaptation and internal integration issues. Figure 17.2 shows a common pattern in the emergence of organizational cultures. In new companies, such as Dell Computers or Intel, the founder or a few key individuals may largely determine the organization's culture. Later in the life of the organization, its culture will reflect a complex mixture of the assumptions, values, and ideas of the founder or other early top managers and the subsequent learning and experiences of organizational members.

The national culture, customs, and societal norms of the country within which the firm operates also shape organizational culture. In other words, the culture of the larger society influences the culture of organizations operating within it.[10]

The dominant values of a national culture may be reflected in the constraints imposed on organizations by their environments. For example, the form of government may have a dramatic impact on how an organization does business in a country. In addition, the members of the organization have been raised in a particular society and thus bring the dominant values of the society into the firm. For example, individuals learn values, such as freedom of speech or respect for individual privacy, from their societies. The presence or absence of these and other values within the larger society has implications for organizational behavior. Finally, increased global operations have forced an awareness that differences in national culture may seriously affect organizational effectiveness. Multinational corporations have discovered that organizational structures and cultures that might be effective in one part of the world may be ineffective in another.[11] The following Across Cultures account illustrates the impact of a society's culture on the organizational culture of firms operating in that society.

■ **FIGURE 17.2**

One Common Pattern in the Emergence of Corporate Cultures

Source: Reprinted with the permission of The Free Press, an imprint of Simon and Schuster, from *Corporate Culture and Performance* by John P. Kotter and James L. Heskett. Copyright © 1992 by Kotter Associates, Inc., and James L. Heskett.

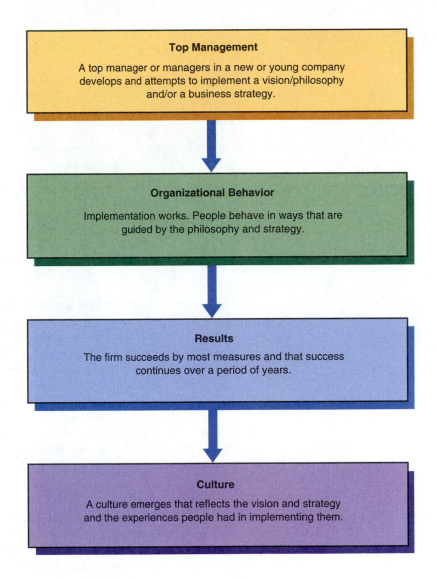

Top Management

A top manager or managers in a new or young company develops and attempts to implement a vision/philosophy and/or a business strategy.

Organizational Behavior

Implementation works. People behave in ways that are guided by the philosophy and strategy.

Results

The firm succeeds by most measures and that success continues over a period of years.

Culture

A culture emerges that reflects the vision and strategy and the experiences people had in implementing them.

ACROSS CULTURES

National Cultural Values and Organizations

Geert Hofstede, a Dutch social scientist, has developed a framework of several cultural dimensions that can be used to compare national cultural values. A particularly important cultural dimension is power distance.

Power distance refers to the extent to which a society encourages unequal distributions of power among people. In low power distance societies, more interaction takes place among people from different social classes, and individuals can move up in social status more easily. Examples of low power distance societies include Austria, Sweden, and the United States. In high power distance societies, the distance between individuals of high and low status typically is considerable, and advancement into the upper classes often is difficult. Examples of high power distance countries are India, Mexico, and the Philippines. Table 17.1

—Continued

ACROSS CULTURES—*Continued*

TABLE 17.1 Some Effects of Power Distance	
HIGH POWER DISTANCE CULTURE	**LOW POWER DISTANCE CULTURE**
• High centralization and focus on order	• Less centralization
• Well-defined, stable hierarchies with many levels	• Flat organizations: fewer levels in hierarchy
• Large numbers of supervisory personnel	• Use of exchange relations
• Paternal managers	• Democratic managers
• Large wage differentials	• Smaller wage differentials

Source: Adapted from Schuler, R. S., Jackson, S. E., Jackofsky, E., and Slocum, J. W. *Managing human resources in Mexico: A cultural understanding. Business Horizons,* May–June 1996, 56.

shows some differences between organizations in low and high power distance cultures.

These organizational characteristics can lead to important differences in organizational culture. For example, managers and employees are highly interdependent in low power distance societies and may prefer a more democratic style of management. In high power distance societies, a more autocratic style of managing people may be expected and even preferred by employees.

One implication for global corporations is that an organizational culture that fits one society might not be readily transferable to other societies. For example, a recent study used the power distance dimension to compare Mexican and U.S. organizations. Some observations from this study follow.

Hierarchy

Mexican organizations reflect the hierarchical structures of church and government. Most organizations have a bureaucratic structure with power vested at the top. Employees below the upper levels have little authority. In Mexico, workers are rewarded for being loyal and following directions from the person in charge. The United States is currently characterized by an extremely wide variance with regard to types of hierarchical relations, although on average, U.S. organizations tend to be much flatter and somewhat less bureaucratic than Mexican organizations (see Chapter 16).

Formality

Mexicans tend to prefer a more distant relationship between workers and managers than is typically found in a society that ranks low on power distance, such as the United States. Despite this need for distance and formality, Mexican employees value working conditions in which supervisors are understanding. They admire bosses that treat them in a warm but dignified manner.

Rules and Regulations

In Mexican organizations, formal rules and regulations aren't adhered to unless someone in authority is present. Managers are more likely to be obeyed than a rule because of who they are. Without a strong emotional bond between people,

—*Continued*

ACROSS CULTURES—*Continued*

rules tend to be ignored. Conversely, U.S. managers believe that rules establish a system of justice that emphasizes fairness and thus should be applied impersonally.[12]

■ MAINTAINING ORGANIZATIONAL CULTURE

The ways in which an organization functions and is managed may have both intended and unintended effects on maintaining or changing organizational culture. Figure 17.3 illustrates one basic method of maintaining an organization's culture: The organization hires individuals who seem to fit the organizational culture; the organization then maintains its culture by removing employees who consistently or markedly deviate from accepted behaviors and activities.

Specific methods for maintaining organizational culture, however, are a great deal more complicated than just hiring the right people and firing those who don't work out. The most powerful reinforcers of the organization's culture are (1) what managers and teams pay attention to, measure, and control; (2) the ways that managers (particularly top managers) react to critical incidents and organizational crises; (3) managerial and team role modeling, teaching, and coaching; (4) criteria for allocating rewards and status; (5) criteria for recruitment, selection, promotion, and removal from the organization; and (6) organizational rites, ceremonies, and stories.[13]

What Managers and Teams Pay Attention To   One of the more powerful methods of maintaining organizational culture involves the processes and behaviors that managers and teams pay attention to, that is, the events that get noticed and commented on. Dealing with events systematically sends strong signals to employees about what is important and expected of them. For example, a large toy manufacturer installed a management by objectives (MBO) performance appraisal system (see Chapter 6). After a few years, top management discovered that the MBO process was working well in one part of the company but not in

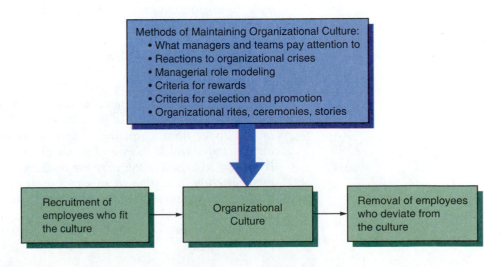

■ FIGURE 17.3

Methods of Maintaining Organizational Culture

another. An investigation revealed that MBO was working well where senior management was enthusiastic and committed. These managers perceived real benefits from the program and conveyed these beliefs to others. Where MBO was failing, senior management viewed MBO as just another bureaucratic exercise. Subordinates quickly learned to complete the paperwork but ignore the purpose of the MBO system. The firm's top management concluded that MBO would work only when employees believe that managers care about the results and pay attention to them.[14]

Reactions to Incidents and Crises   When an organization faces a crisis, the handling of that crisis by managers and employees reveals a great deal about the culture. The manner in which the crisis is dealt with can either reinforce the existing culture or bring out new values and norms that change the culture in some way. For example, an organization facing a dramatic reduction in demand for its product might react by laying off or firing employees. Or it might reduce employee hours or rates of pay with no work-force reduction. The alternative chosen indicates the value placed on human resources and can reinforce and maintain the current culture or indicate a major change in the culture. Such a situation occurred at Hewlett-Packard early in its history. The company responded to declining demand for its products by reducing hours. It went to a schedule of working nine days every two weeks—a 10 percent reduction in time with a corresponding cut in pay—rather than fire or lay off employees. Hewlett-Packard thus sent a clear message to its employees about their value to the company. This response became deeply ingrained in the company's folklore and now reinforces this aspect of its culture.

Role Modeling, Teaching, and Coaching   Aspects of the organization's culture are communicated to employees by the way managers fulfill their roles. In addition, managers and teams may specifically incorporate important cultural messages into training programs and day-to-day coaching on the job. For example, training films shown to new employees might emphasize customer service. Also, managers might demonstrate good customer or client service practices in their interactions with customers. The repeated emphasis on good customer relations in both training and day-to-day behavior would help create and maintain a customer-oriented culture throughout the organization. Arthur Andersen, the large public accounting firm, sends all newly hired accountants to an extensive training program, not only to learn accounting procedures used by the firm, but also to become steeped in the organization's culture.

Allocation of Rewards and Status   Employees also learn about their organization's culture through its reward system. The rewards and punishments attached to various behaviors convey to employees the priorities and values of both individual managers and the organization. Similarly, the organization's status system maintains certain aspects of its culture. The distribution of *perks* (a corner office on an upper floor, carpeting, a private secretary, or a private parking space) demonstrates which roles and behaviors are most valued by the organization. However, an organization may use rewards and status symbols ineffectively and inconsistently. If it does, it misses a great opportunity to influence its culture because an organization's reward practices and its culture appear to be strongly linked in the minds of its members. In fact, some authorities believe that the most effective method for influencing organizational culture may be through the reward system.

Recruitment, Selection, Promotion, and Removal   As Figure 17.3 suggests, one of the fundamental ways that organizations maintain a culture is through the recruitment process. In addition, the criteria used to determine who is assigned to specific jobs or positions, who gets raises and promotions and why, who is removed from the organization by firing or early retirement, and so on reinforce and demonstrate basic aspects of a culture. These criteria become known throughout the organization and can maintain or change an existing culture.

Organizational Rites, Ceremonies, and Stories   **Organizational rites and ceremonies** are organized, planned activities or rituals that have important cultural meaning.[15] Certain managerial or employee activities can become organizational rituals that are interpreted as part of the organizational culture. Rites and ceremonies that sustain organizational culture include rites of passage, degradation, enhancement, and integration. Table 17.2 contains examples of each of these four types of rites and identifies some of their desirable consequences.

A ceremony used at Mary Kay Cosmetics Company provides a good example of rites of enhancement. During elaborate awards ceremonies, gold and diamond pins, fur stoles, and the use of pink Cadillacs are presented to saleswomen who achieve their sales quotas. The ceremonies are held in a setting reminiscent of a Miss America pageant with all the participants dressed in glamorous evening clothes. The setting is typically an auditorium with a stage in front of a large, cheering audience.[16] The ceremonies clearly are intended to increase the identity and status of high-performing employees and emphasize the rewards for excellence.

Many of the underlying beliefs and values of an organization's culture are expressed as legends and stories that become part of its folklore. These stories and legends transmit the existing culture from older to new employees and emphasize important aspects of that culture. Some stories may persist for a long time. For example, a Fortune 500 manufacturer had a factory with a history of hostile labor–management relations, low productivity, and poor quality. The company hired a consultant who started out by talking with the employees in the plant. They eagerly told him about the plant manager, a 300-pound gorilla named Sam with a disposition that made King Kong look like Bonzo the chimp. Employees

TABLE 17.2   Organizational Rites and Ceremonies

TYPE	EXAMPLE	POSSIBLE CONSEQUENCES
Rites of passage	Basic training, U.S. Army	Facilitate transition into new roles; minimize differences in way roles are carried out
Rites of degradation	Firing a manager	Reduce power and identity; reaffirm proper behavior
Rites of enhancement	Mary Kay Cosmetics Company ceremonies	Enhance power and identity; emphasize value of proper behavior
Rites of integration	Office party	Encourage common feelings that bind members together

Source: Adapted from Trice, H. M., and Beyer, J. M. *The Cultures of Work Organizations.* Englewood Cliffs, N.J.: Prentice-Hall, 1993, 111.

told a number of outrageous stories about Sam's behavior. The stunned consultant made an appointment to see the plant manager. When the consultant walked into the manager's office, he saw a slim, pleasant-looking man behind the desk who introduced himself as Paul. "Where's Sam?" asked the consultant. Paul, looking puzzled, replied, "Sam has been dead for nine years."[17]

■ CHANGING ORGANIZATIONAL CULTURE

The same basic methods used to maintain an organization's culture may be used to change it. Culture might be changed by (1) changing what managers and teams pay attention to, (2) changing how crises are handled, (3) changing criteria for recruiting new members, (4) changing criteria for promotion within the organization, (5) changing criteria for allocating rewards, and (6) changing organizational rites and ceremonies. For example, an organizational culture that tends to punish risk taking and innovation and reward risk avoidance might be deliberately altered through changes in the reward system. Employees could be encouraged to set riskier and more innovative goals for themselves in coaching and goal-setting sessions. In performance appraisal sessions and through merit raises, individuals could be rewarded for attempting more challenging tasks, even if they failed sometimes, than for attaining safe goals that required no innovative behavior.

Changing organizational culture can be tricky, and at least two concerns suggest caution. One is articulated by well-known management expert Peter Drucker who has questioned whether the deeply held, core values of organizational culture are amenable to change.[18] In his view, focusing managerial efforts on changing ineffective behaviors and procedures is more meaningful than attempting to change organizational culture. Drucker further argues that changing behavior will work only if it can be based on the existing culture.

A second concern that suggests caution in cultural change involves the difficulties in accurately assessing organizational culture. Most large, complex organizations actually have more than one culture. General Electric, for example, has distinctly different cultures in different parts of its multidivisional, worldwide operations. Sometimes these multiple cultures are called **subcultures.** Schein even goes so far as to argue that *every* organization has at least three cultures—an operating culture (the "line" employees), an engineering culture (the "technical" people), and an executive culture (top management)—stemming from the very different world views typically held by individuals in these three groups.[19] Faced with a variety of subcultures, management may have difficulty (1) in accurately assessing them and (2) in effecting needed changes.

Despite these concerns, we believe that changing organizational cultures is both feasible and, in the case of failing organizations, sometimes essential. Successfully changing organizational culture requires

- understanding the old culture first because a new culture can't be developed unless managers and employees understand from where they're starting;
- providing support for employees and teams who have ideas for a better culture and are willing to act on those ideas;
- finding the most effective subculture in the organization and using it as an example from which employees can learn;
- not attacking culture head-on but finding ways to help employees and teams do their jobs more effectively;

- treating the vision of a new culture as a guiding principle for change, not as a miracle worker;

- recognizing that significant organizationwide cultural change takes five to ten years; and,

- living the new culture because actions speak louder than words.[20]

We cover planned organizational change extensively in Chapter 18. Many of the specific techniques and methods for changing organizational behaviors presented in that chapter also may be used to change organizational culture. Indeed, any comprehensive program of organizational change, in some sense, is an attempt to change the culture of the organization.[21]

We can't overemphasize how difficult changing organizational cultures may be. In fact, the incompatibility of organizational cultures and their resistance to change has been one of the most significant barriers to successful corporate mergers.[22] For a merger to be effective, at least one (and sometimes both) of the merging organizations may need to change its culture.

PERFORMANCE AND ORGANIZATIONAL CULTURE

An underlying assumption of cultural change is that an organization's culture and its performance or effectiveness are directly related. Thus the rationale for attempting cultural change is to create a more effective organization.

The common theme of several popular books about management and organizations is that strong, well-developed cultures are an important characteristic of organizations that have outstanding performance records.[23] The term **strong culture** implies that most managers and employees share a set of consistent values and methods of doing business.[24] Strong cultures can be found in many organizations, including Wal-Mart, Procter & Gamble, Mary Kay, Hewlett-Packard, and Pier 1.

Strong cultures may be associated with strong performance for three reasons. First, a strong culture often provides for a good fit between strategy and culture. This fit is considered essential for successfully implementing corporate strategy. Second, a strong culture may lead to the alignment of goals among employees. That is, the majority of organizational participants share the same goals and have some basic agreement as to how to pursue them. Finally, a strong culture leads to employee commitment and motivation. In this view, culture is crucial for developing the dedication to excellent performance that characterizes successful organizations.

Organizational culture and performance clearly are related, although the evidence regarding the exact nature of this relationship is mixed. For example, strong cultures may not always be superior to weak cultures. Some studies indicate that the *type* of culture may, in fact, be somewhat more important than its strength. A comparison of the cultures of 334 institutions of higher education revealed no differences in organizational effectiveness between those with strong cultures and those with weak cultures.[25] However, the type of culture possessed by these institutions was related to their effectiveness. Colleges and universities that possessed a type of culture that matched their market niche and strategy were more effective than institutions whose cultures lacked such a match.

Another cautionary note comes from studies showing that the relationship between many cultural attributes (featured in the popular press as being important for performance) and high performance hasn't been consistent over time. Based on what we know about culture–performance relationships, a contingency approach seems to be a good one for managers and organizations to take. Further investigations of this issue are unlikely to discover one "best" organizational culture (either in terms of strength or type).

A four-year study of a large number of organizations resulted in the following conclusions about the relationships between culture and performance.

- Organizational culture can have a significant impact on a firm's long-term economic performance.

- Organizational culture will probably be an even more important factor in determining the success or failure of firms in the next decade.

- Organizational cultures that inhibit strong long-term financial performance are not rare; they develop easily, even in firms that are full of reasonable and intelligent people.

- Although tough to change, organizational cultures can be made more performance enhancing.[26]

High degrees of participative management and an emphasis on teamwork often are cited as characteristics of successful, effective organizational cultures. In **participative management,** managers share decision-making, goal-setting, and problem-solving activities with employees. Of course, high levels of participation don't fit all settings and tasks. Further, changing an organization from a more traditional management approach to greater collaboration with employees may be extremely difficult. A type of organizational culture designed to foster high performance with high levels of employee involvement is called a **high performance–high commitment work culture.** As with participative management, cultures that foster high involvement and commitment on the part of employees often exist in organizations that have a record of high performance. We examine high performance–high commitment work cultures or systems in greater detail in Chapter 18.

Another type of organizational culture often associated with organizational effectiveness is a **total quality culture,** which values customers, continuous improvement, and teamwork. Employees in such a culture believe that customers are the key to the organization's future. Employees expect their jobs to change as they constantly strive to improve and seek better ways of doing things. Moreover, employees in such a culture almost instinctively act as a team. Gillette provides an example of an organization with a focus on customers, continuous improvement, and teamwork, as the following Quality in Practice account demonstrates.

QUALITY IN PRACTICE

Gillette's Total Quality Culture

Gillette dominates the "wet shaving" market and has for several generations. For example, in 1923 Gillette was the market share leader and remained so in 1996. In today's rapidly changing economy this observation, by itself, indicates something rather remarkable about the Gillette organization.

Gillette has about two-thirds of the U.S. market, and its share of the world market is even higher. In Latin America, for example, Gillette's market share is over 80 percent. In some parts of the world, the word Gillette *means* razor blade. Global sales continue to expand with joint ventures in China, Russia, and India.

QUALITY IN PRACTICE—*Continued*

Over the years, Gillette faced numerous competitive challenges, yet has always responded with improved products.

This type of success doesn't just happen. It is the result of a relentless quest for improvements in shaving technology and high levels of commitment and teamwork from employees. The CEO of Gillette shaves half of his face with his product and half with a competitor's to compare the closeness of the shaves. Each day, about 200 employees come to work unshaven (including women with unshaven legs) in order to test their own and competitors' shaving products. Gillette maintains laboratories dedicated to shaving and whisker research. Gillette can tell you how long it takes a whisker lifted by a passing blade to snap back to the skin (one-eighth of a second), the ideal beard length for shaving (about 24 hours, just after the hairs have cleared skin level), and how much hair the average man scrapes off of his face during his lifetime (about 27 feet).

This continuous improvement and ongoing desire to satisfy the customer is expressed by Donald Chaulk, vice-president in charge of Gillette's shaving technology lab: "We test the blade edge, the blade guard, the angle of the blades, the balance of the razor. . . . What happens to the chemistry of the skin? What happens to the hair when you pull it? What happens to the follicle? We own the face. We know more about shaving than anybody. I don't think obsession is too strong a word."[27]

We can summarize the effects of organizational culture on employee behavior and performance with four key ideas. First, knowing the culture of an organization allows employees to understand the firm's history and current approach. This knowledge provides guidance about expected behaviors for the future. Second, organizational culture can foster commitment to corporate philosophy and values. This commitment generates shared feelings of working toward common goals. Third, organizational culture, through its norms, serves as a control mechanism to channel behaviors toward desired and away from undesired behaviors. Finally, certain types of organizational cultures may be related directly to greater effectiveness and productivity than others.

ETHICAL BEHAVIOR AND ORGANIZATIONAL CULTURE

Ethical problems in organizations continue to concern managers and employees greatly. As an example of this concern, KPMG Peat Marwick, the Big Six accounting firm, recently formed a new unit designed to help its clients create a "moral organization."[28] In its promotional literature, the firm maintains that the process of auditing ethics can promote good business practices and benefit the corporate culture.

Researchers are only now beginning to explore the potential impact that organizational culture can have on ethical behavior. The ethics component of organizational culture is a complex interplay of formal and informal systems that may support either ethical or unethical organizational behavior. The formal systems include leadership, structure, policies, reward systems, orientation and training programs, and decision-making processes. Informal systems include norms, heroes, rituals, language, myths, sagas, and stories.

Organizational culture appears to affect ethical behavior in several ways.[29] For example, a culture emphasizing ethical norms provides support for ethical behavior. In addition, top management plays a key role in fostering ethical behavior. Moreover, all authority figures—managers and other professionals—in the organization can encourage or discourage ethical behavior. The presence or absence of ethical behavior in managerial actions both influences and reflects the prevailing culture. The organizational culture may promote taking responsibility for the consequences of actions, thereby increasing the probability that individuals will behave ethically. Alternatively, the culture may diffuse responsibility for the consequences of unethical behavior, thereby making such behavior more likely. In sum, ethical business practices stem from ethical organizational cultures. The following Ethics in Practice feature demonstrates the potential effect of these dynamics.

ETHICS IN PRACTICE

Bath Iron Works Enforces Ethics

A U.S. Navy consultant attending a meeting at Bath Iron Works Corporation in Bath, Maine, left a document containing proprietary information about a competitor in a conference room there. In rapid succession, three top managers, including Bath's vice-president of contracts and the vice-president of finance, saw the document. None took any further action to return the material—in direct violation of the company's ethical compliance program. But Bath's president, upon learning of this event, alerted the Navy to his colleagues' transgression. In addition to his desire to foster an ethical culture at the company, the president had the practical concern that repercussions could cost the firm its lucrative government contracts if the truth was discovered independently.

Although coming clean eventually cost three executives their jobs, the privately held shipbuilder emerged from the incident almost unscathed. The Navy didn't suspend or bar the firm from bidding on government contracts, but Bath had to sign an agreement to do certain things to enhance its ethics program. Certainly firing three executives provided a powerful example for employees about the consequences of unethical behavior. In addition, Bath created a day-long ethics seminar for senior executives and the board of directors. Further, Bath now provides enhanced ethics training for all new employees.[30]

An important concept linking organizational culture to ethical behavior is **principled organizational dissent,** by which individuals in an organization protest, on ethical grounds, some practice or policy.[31] Some cultures permit and even encourage principled organizational dissent; other cultures punish such behavior.

An employee might use various strategies in attempting to change unethical behavior, including

■ secretly or publicly blowing the whistle within the organization;

- secretly or publicly blowing the whistle outside the organization;

- secretly or publicly threatening an offender or a responsible manager with blowing the whistle; or

- quietly or publicly refusing to implement an unethical order or policy.[32]

As a form of principled organizational dissent, **whistle-blowing** refers to the disclosure by current or former employees of illegal, immoral, or illegitimate organizational practices to people or organizations that may be able to change the practice.[33] As discussed in Chapter 16, the whistle-blower lacks the power to change the undesirable practice directly and so appeals to others either inside or outside the organization.

An example of publicly blowing the whistle inside an organization occurred when John Young, the chief of the National Aeronautic and Space Administration's (NASA's) astronaut office, wrote a twelve-page internal memorandum following the Challenger explosion that killed seven astronauts. He sent the memo, which detailed a large number of safety problems that endangered space shuttle crews, to ninety-seven key individuals in NASA. This communication was instrumental in broadening NASA's safety investigations and implementing safety improvements.

An example of secretly blowing the whistle outside an organization occurred when an employee of Commonwealth Electric Company anonymously sent a letter to the U.S. Justice Department that identified instances of bid rigging among the largest U.S. electrical contractors. These contractors paid more than $20 million in fines as a result of investigations into illegal bidding practices.

These types of whistle-blowing activities aren't without risk. The individual engaging in principled organizational dissent risks dismissal, demotion, isolation, ostracism, and even threats to self and family. Often millions or even billions of dollars are at stake. Moreover, the whistle-blower could be wrong about individual or organizational actions. Thus misguided attempts to stop apparently unethical behavior might unnecessarily harm employees or organizations.

Much remains to be learned about creating organizational cultures that encourage ethical behavior. The following suggestions are a beginning.

- Be realistic in setting values and goals regarding employment relationships. Do not promise what the organization cannot deliver.

- Encourage input from throughout the organization regarding appropriate values and practices for implementing the culture. Choose values that represent the views of both employees and managers.

- Do not automatically opt for a "strong" culture. Explore methods of providing for diversity and dissent, such as grievance or complaint mechanisms or other internal review procedures.

- Provide training programs for managers and teams on adopting and implementing the organization's values. These programs should stress the underlying ethical and legal principles and present the practical aspects of carrying out procedural guidelines.[34]

An effective organizational culture should encourage ethical behavior and discourage unethical behavior. Admittedly, ethical behavior may "cost" the organization and individuals. A global firm that refuses to pay a bribe to secure business in a particular country may lose sales. An individual may lose financially by not accepting a kickback. Similarly, an organization or individual might seem to gain from unethical actions. An organization may flout U.S. law by quietly paying bribes to officials in order to gain entry to a new market. A purchasing agent for a large corporation might take kickbacks for purchasing all needed office supplies from a particular supplier. However, such gains are often short term. The Sears experience provides a clear example of short-term gain but long-term loss for an organization. Sears spent $60 million in settling lawsuits and giving customers refunds after being accused of selling unnecessary auto parts and repair services in more than forty states.[35]

In the long run, an organization can't successfully operate if its prevailing culture and values aren't congruent with those of society. That is just as true as the observation that, in the long run, an organization cannot survive unless it provides goods and services that society wants and needs. An organizational culture that promotes ethical behavior is not only more compatible with prevailing cultural values but also makes good business sense.

MANAGING CULTURAL DIVERSITY

In Chapter 1, we emphasized that organizations are becoming increasingly diverse in terms of gender, race, ethnicity, and nationality. More than half the U.S. work force consists of women, minorities, and recent immigrants. The growing diversity of employees in many organizations can bring substantial benefits, such as more successful marketing strategies for different types of customers, improved decision making, and perhaps greater creativity and innovation. At DuPont, a group of African-American workers recently opened up promising new markets for the firm by focusing on black farmers. A multicultural team gained the company about $45 million in new business by changing the way DuPont designs and markets decorating materials (such as countertops) in order to appeal more to overseas customers.[36]

There are costs and concerns as well, including communication difficulties, intraorganizational conflict, and turnover. Effectively managing cultural diversity promises to continue to be a significant challenge for organizations.[37] To succeed, organizations have to work hard at acculturation. **Acculturation** refers to methods by which cultural differences between a dominant culture and minority or subcultures are resolved and managed.[38] Both the benefits and the challenges stemming from a multicultural work force are described in the following Diversity in Practice piece.

DIVERSITY IN PRACTICE

Diversity at Marriott International

The staff of the Marriott Marquis in New York's Times Square is a model of diversity. The hotel's 1700 employees represent every race, hail from seventy countries, and speak forty-seven languages. At a hotel with a multicultural guest register, such diversity can be a competitive advantage. "We have a diverse clientele, and we need a diverse work force to serve them," says Human Resources Director Ray Falcone. But managing people from such a wide range of backgrounds presents a constant management challenge.

Prickly racial, ethnic, and gender concerns are an undercurrent in virtually every interaction at the Marriott. Some workers are quick to charge discrimina-

—Continued

DIVERSITY IN PRACTICE—*Continued*

tion when conflicts with managers arise. Just maintaining a basic level of civility can be a daily struggle. In required diversity training classes, managers are taught that the best way to cope with diversity-related conflict is to focus narrowly on performance and never to define problems in terms of gender, culture, or race. Marriott managers are instructed to bend over backward to be fair about issues large and small. To ensure that days off are spread equitably, for example, Rooms Director Susan Gonzalez agonizes over each week's schedule for the housekeeping department's nearly 400 workers. Her records tracking holiday requests go back four years, and she uses the data to show that choice days are doled out evenly.

Managers in the Marriott organization believe that in the years ahead managing multiethnic and multiracial employees is likely to become an increasingly important skill throughout the business world. More and more people from diverse backgrounds are expected to enter more industries and rise higher on corporate ladders. In addition to needing that skill on its own staff, Marriott clearly hopes that members of this diverse work force will stay in its hotels during their business travels.[39]

The Prudential Insurance Company provides another example of managing cultural diversity.[40] Prudential became alarmed because many African-American employees were leaving the company. Surveys showed that the complaints of African-Americans actually were shared by female, Asian, and other minority employees as well. Among other problems uncovered, Prudential management was viewed as insensitive to diversity issues. Prudential embarked on a massive diversity training effort that by now has included 12,000 managers. During their diversity training, managers must develop personal goals and plans that identify actions and behaviors to improve organizational diversity. Top management then holds them financially accountable for accomplishing the goals. Even the most senior-level executives in the organization are required to submit plans for addressing diversity concerns. Prudential also established diversity councils throughout the firm to monitor the effectiveness of the effort. Prudential believes that its diversity effort has gone beyond a mere program and has become institutionalized. The company believes that the core values of the culture now promote respect for diversity.

There are no easy answers to the challenges of managing a culturally diverse work force. However, research has revealed some common characteristics of employee values, managerial philosophy, and organizational culture that are present in organizations having effective diversity management programs. These characteristics have been distilled into the following helpful guidelines.

- Managers and employees must understand that a diverse work force will embody different perspectives and approaches to work and must truly value variety of opinion and insight.

- The leadership of the organization must recognize both the learning opportunities and the challenges that the expression of different perspectives presents for an organization.

- The organizational culture must create an expectation of high standards of performance from everyone.
- The organizational culture must stimulate personal development.
- The organizational culture must encourage openness.
- The organizational culture must make workers feel valued.
- The organization must have a well-articulated and widely understood mission.
- The organization must have a relatively egalitarian, nonbureaucratic structure.[41]

Table 17.3 contains a questionnaire that you can use to examine your awareness of diversity issues.

ORGANIZATIONAL SOCIALIZATION

Organizational socialization is the systematic process by which an organization brings new employees into its culture. The general meaning of the term *socialization* is the process by which older members of a society transmit to younger members the social skills and knowledge needed to function effectively in that society. Organizational socialization has a similar meaning: the transmission of culture from senior to new employees, providing the social knowledge and skills needed to perform organizational roles and tasks successfully.[42]

Socialization provides the means by which individuals learn the ropes upon joining an organization. It includes learning work group, departmental, and organizational values, rules, procedures, and norms; developing social and working relationships; and developing the competencies needed to perform the new job. Interestingly, the stages that an employee goes through during socialization resemble, in many respects, the stages in group development discussed in Chapter 8.

TABLE 17.3   Diversity Questionnaire

Answer the following questions true (T) or false (F).

1. I know about the rules and customs of several different cultures. _____

2. I know that I hold stereotypes about other groups. _____

3. I feel comfortable with people of different backgrounds from my own. _____

4. I associate with people who are different from me. _____

5. I find working on a multicultural team satisfying. _____

6. I find change stimulating and exciting. _____

7. I enjoy learning about other cultures. _____

8. When dealing with someone whose English is limited, I show patience and understanding. _____

9. I find that spending time building relationships with others is useful because more gets done. _____

The more true responses you have, the more adaptable and open you are to diversity. If you have five or more true responses, you probably are someone who finds value in cross-cultural experiences.

    If you have less than five true responses, you may be resistant to interacting with people who are different from you. If that is the case, you may find that your interactions with others are sometimes blocked.

Source: Adapted from Gardenswartz, L., and Rowe, A. What's your diversity quotient? *Managing Diversity Newsletter*, Jamestown, New York (undated).

■ SOCIALIZATION PROCESS

Figure 17.4 presents an example of an organizational socialization process. It isn't intended to depict the socialization process of every organization. However, many firms with strong cultures—such as Arthur Andersen, Disney, Procter & Gamble, Southwest Airlines, and Wal-Mart—frequently follow these steps for socializing new employees.

Step One. Entry-level candidates are selected carefully. Trained recruiters use standardized procedures and seek specific traits that tie to success in the business.

■ FIGURE 17.4 An Example of an Organizational Socialization Process

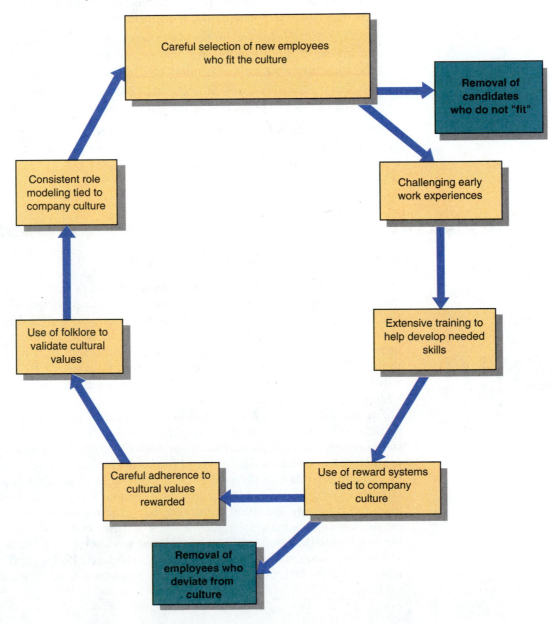

Step Two.   Humility-inducing experiences in the first months on the job cause employees to question their prior behaviors, beliefs, and values. Such experiences might include giving a new employee more work to do than can reasonably be done. The self-questioning promotes openness toward accepting the organization's norms and values.

Step Three.   In-the-trenches training leads to mastery of one of the core disciplines of the business. Promotion is tied to a proven track record.

Step Four.   Careful attention is given to measuring operational results and rewarding individual performance. Reward systems are comprehensive and consistent and focus on those aspects of the organization that are tied to success and corporate culture.

Step Five.   Adherence to the organization's values is emphasized. Identification with common values allows employees to justify personal sacrifices caused by their membership in the organization.

Step Six.   Reinforcing folklore provides legends and interpretations of important events in the organization's history that validate its culture and goals. Folklore reinforces a code of conduct for "how we do things around here."

Step Seven.   Consistent role models and consistent traits are associated with those recognized as being on the fast track to promotion and success.[43]

Southwest Airlines has developed a strong culture based on customer service. The following Managing in Practice account describes the main characteristics of its strong culture and socialization process.

MANAGING IN PRACTICE

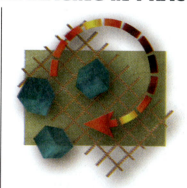

Herb Kelleher and Southwest Airlines

Herb Kelleher of Southwest Airlines attributes the firm's success to a simple corporate philosophy: "We dignify the customer." This sounds strange coming from the CEO of an airline that has no first-class seating, no assigned seats, and no transfers of bags to other airlines—and serves no food on flights other than peanuts, potato chips, and cookies. However, Southwest must be doing something right. At a time when airlines as a group are consistently losing money, Southwest's revenues are increasing 15 percent annually and the company is adding 200 new employees a month.

For starters, Southwest charges about one-third as much as competitors for its tickets. But cheap fares aren't all that is going on here. Southwest takes its customer-oriented culture seriously. For example, the job of one executive vice-president is to oversee every aspect of the business that touches the public and to make that contact as pleasant as possible. The word *customer* is always capitalized in company ads and publications. Frequent fliers receive birthday cards from the company. The 1000 customers that write the company during a typical week receive a personal response—not a form letter—within one month. When five medical students who commuted weekly to their out-of-state medical school complained that their regularly scheduled flight got them to class fifteen minutes late, Southwest moved the departure time forward by fifteen minutes.

—Continued

MANAGING IN PRACTICE—*Continued*

For Kelleher, treating the customer right begins with treating employees right. "If you don't treat your own people well, they won't treat other people well," he has said. Kelleher believes that work should be fun, and this belief permeates the organizational culture. For example, every Friday at noon, employees in the Dallas office gather in the parking lot for a cookout. Employees throughout the organization typically wear costumes on Halloween, Valentine's Day, and other special occasions and "fun uniforms" on Fridays. Upper level managers reinforce an egalitarian culture by working as baggage handlers, ticket agents, and flight attendants once each quarter.

As do many firms with a strong culture and socialization process, Southwest places a great deal of emphasis on its hiring practices. Kelleher believes so strongly that work should be fun and too much seriousness is ineffective, that a sense of humor is actually one of the criteria for hiring new employees. Kelleher looks for people with a certain attitude and approach to life that is humorous, broad-minded, and tolerant of individual differences. In keeping with its customer orientation, Southwest uses frequent fliers to help select new flight attendants.[44]

■ SOCIALIZATION OUTCOMES

All organizations and groups socialize new members in some way, but the process can vary greatly in terms of how explicit, comprehensive, and lengthy it is. Generally, rapid socialization is advantageous. For the individual, it quickly reduces the uncertainty and anxiety surrounding a new job. For the organization, it helps the new employee become productive quickly. Organizations with strong cultures may be particularly skillful at socializing individuals. If the culture is effective, the socialization process will contribute to organizational success. However, if the culture needs changing, a strong socialization process reduces the prospects for making the needed changes.

Some additional dilemmas are created by strong socialization processes. For example, business schools are concerned with issues surrounding the socialization of their students. How strong should their socialization be? Does the business school want students to think alike, at least in terms of a certain level of logic and intelligent analysis? To have the same appropriate values and sense of professionalism? In some sense, the answer to these questions has to be "yes." Yet, oversocialization runs the risk of creating rigid, narrow-minded corporate men and women. The ideal goal of business school socialization, then, may be to develop independent thinkers committed to what they believe to be right, while at the same time educating students to be collaborative team players who have good interpersonal skills and are able to relate well to others. These goals pose a challenge for the socialization process, which, in order to be effective, must balance these demands. Although this example is of the business school, to a certain extent the same need for balance exists for all organizations.

The socialization process may affect employee and organizational success in a variety of ways.[45] Table 17.4 lists some possible socialization outcomes. We don't claim that these outcomes are determined solely by an organization's socialization process. For example, job satisfaction is a function of many things, including the

TABLE 17.4   Possible Outcomes of Socialization Process

SUCCESSFUL SOCIALIZATION IS REFLECTED IN	UNSUCCESSFUL SOCIALIZATION IS REFLECTED IN
• Job Satisfaction	• Job dissatisfaction
• Role Clarity	• Role ambiguity and conflict
• High work motivation	• Low work motivation
• Understanding of culture, perceived control	• Misunderstanding, tension, perceived lack of control
• High job involvement	• Low job involvement
• Commitment to organization	• Lack of commitment to organization
• Tenure	• Absenteeism, turnover
• High performance	• Low performance
• Internalized values	• Rejection of values

nature of the task, the individual's personality and needs, the nature of supervision, opportunities to succeed and be rewarded, and so on (see Chapter 2). Rather, the point here is that successful socialization may contribute to job satisfaction, whereas unsuccessful socialization may contribute to job dissatisfaction.

CHAPTER SUMMARY

Organizational culture is the pattern of beliefs and expectations shared by members of an organization. Culture includes norms, common values, company philosophy, the "rules of the game" for getting along and getting things done, and ways of interacting with outsiders, such as customers. Some aspects of organizational culture are indicated by cultural symbols, heroes, rites, and ceremonies.

Organizational culture develops as a response to the challenges of external adaptation and survival and of internal integration. The formation of an organization's culture also is influenced by the culture of the larger society within which the firm must function.

The primary methods for both maintaining and changing organizational culture include (1) what managers and teams pay attention to, measure, and control; (2) the ways managers and employees react to crises; (3) role modeling, teaching, and coaching; (4) criteria for allocating rewards; (5) criteria for recruitment to, selection and promotion within, and removal from the organization; and (6) organizational rites, ceremonies, and stories.

Organizational culture can affect employee behaviors and commitment to the organization. Culture may be related to effective organizational performance, although no "best" organizational culture exists. Organizational culture also can have a strong effect on ethical behavior by managers and employees alike. Finally, managing cultural diversity is expected to be one of the principal managerial challenges for many years to come.

Socialization is the process by which new members are brought into an organization's culture. At firms having a strong culture, the socialization process is well developed and the focus of careful attention. All organizations socialize new members, but depending on how it is done, the outcomes could be either positive or negative in terms of job performance, satisfaction, and commitment to the organization.

KEY TERMS AND CONCEPTS

Academy culture
Acculturation
Baseball team culture
Club culture
Cultural heroes
Cultural symbols
Cultural values
External adaptation and survival

Fortress Culture
High performance-high
    commitment work culture
Internal integration
Organizational culture
Organizational rites and ceremonies
Organizational socialization
Participative management

Principled organizational dissent
Shared assumptions
Shared behaviors
Strong culture
Subcultures
Total quality culture
Whistle-blowing

DISCUSSION QUESTIONS

1. Provide three examples of how culture is expressed in your college or university.

2. Describe how that culture affects your behavior.

3. How did your college or university develop its culture?

4. What are the primary methods used to maintain that organizational culture? How easy or difficult would this culture be to change? Explain your answer.

5. What role do reward systems play in maintaining or changing an organization's culture?

6. How do organizational culture and performance seem to be related in an organization where you have worked?

7. How might an organization use culture to increase the probability of ethical behavior and decrease the probability of unethical behavior by its members?

8. Why is managing cultural diversity difficult? How can organizations and managers deal with this challenge?

9. Identify and discuss the key issues in organizational socialization.

10. Describe the socialization process used by an organization with which you are familiar. What were the results of this socialization process?

■ Developing Competencies

Self-Insight: Assessing Ethical Culture

Instructions

Think of a job you currently hold or used to have. Indicate whether you agree or disagree with the following statements about that organization. Use the scale shown and write the number of your response in the space next to each question.

Completely	Mostly	Somewhat	Somewhat	Mostly	Completely
False	False	False	True	True	True
1	2	3	4	5	6

_____ 1. In this organization, employees are expected to follow their own personal and moral beliefs.

_____ 2. Employees are expected to do anything to further the organization's interest.

_____ 3. In this organization, employees look out for each other's welfare.

_____ 4. It is very important to follow the rules and procedures of this organization strictly.

_____ 5. In this organization, the major consideration is whether a decision violates any law or ethical code.

_____ 6. In this organization, employees protect their own interests above other considerations.

_____ 7. An important consideration is what is best for everyone in the organization.

_____ 8. The most efficient way is always the right way in this organization.

_____ 9. In this organization, employees are always expected to do what is right for the customer and the public.

Scoring

Add the responses to questions 1, 3, 5, 7, and 9:   _____

Reverse the scores on questions 2, 4, 6 and 8

$(1 = 6, 2 = 5, 3 = 4, 4 = 3, 5 = 2, 6 = 1)$ and

add these responses: _____

Total: _____

Scores can range from 9 to 54. Scores of 36 and higher indicate an organizational culture that tends to support or encourage ethical behavior. Scores of 28 to 35 indicate a culture that may be somewhat ambivalent with regard to ethical issues. Scores of 27 or below indicate a culture that tends to increase the probability that individuals will behave unethically.[46]

Organizational Insight:
Cultural Change at Texaco

Corporate culture manifests itself in many ways, such as the kinds of people it employs, company values, and reaction to crises. A company's actions often display culture clearer than policies tacked on office walls or well-rehearsed statements made by spokespersons. Corporations change cultures when faced with calamities or a change in leadership. Currently, Texaco is experiencing both—an embarrassing racial discrimination situation and a new CEO.

Founded in 1902, Texaco is one of the world's largest oil-producing companies and the fourteenth largest company in the United States. In 1995, Texaco's net income was $607 million. Texaco employs more than 19,000 people, of whom 7 percent are black.

The Lawsuit and the Tapes

In 1994, six of its African-American employees filed a racial discrimination suit against Texaco. In June 1996, the U.S. Equal Employment Opportunity Commission (EEOC) found that Texaco had failed to promote blacks because of race and that Texaco's evaluation system did not meet federal guidelines. In addition, the EEOC found that, from 1992 to 1994, blacks "were selected at rates significantly below that of their nonblack counterparts" because of race. Rather than trying to find a solution immediately, Texaco asked the EEOC to reconsider its findings.

Richard Lundwall, a former human resource official for Texaco, recorded conversations at various 1994 meetings attended by several Texaco executives: Robert Ulrich (who later retired, in March 1995), then Texaco treasurer and head of the finance department; Peter Meade (later suspended), assistant general manager in the fuel and marine marketing department; and David Keough (later suspended), chief financial officer for a Texaco subsidiary in Bermuda. The entire work force at this subsidiary, except Keough, was black.

Lundwall stated that he made the tapes to help him keep an accurate record of meetings for which he served as secretary. The tapes revealed several racist statements by the executives. In addition, the group later suggested destroying and altering documents to keep records from the plaintiffs. (Ulrich's department was directly targeted in the lawsuit.) Lundwall also made negative comments about blacks and Jews on the tapes. According to a Texaco spokesperson, Lundwall was terminated because departments were consolidated, eliminating his job. Shortly thereafter, he told the plaintiff's attorneys that he had useful information for them—the tapes, which proved to be the "smoking gun."

Texaco's Stated Values

Texaco's mission is "to be one of the most admired, profitable, and competitive companies in the world." The company's principles include: commitment to quality, teamwork, leadership, technological excellence, and customer service. Texaco stresses corporate responsibility, respect for the individual, high ethical standards, open communication, and fully competitive shareholder return. Texaco's 1995 Annual Report states that the company is committed to diversity, an "inclusive process, grounded in our core value of respect for the individual and in our long-standing policies of equal opportunity for all employees." Peter Bijur, the new Texaco CEO, said that it is "utterly reprehensible to deny another person his or her self-respect and dignity because of race, color, religion, or sex." Despite the stated values and principles supportive of diversity, documents and testimony during the trial revealed a long history of discrimination and racist attitudes that were tolerated at Texaco. Internal surveys (which an in-house attorney told Texaco to hide) indicated that only 37 percent of employees believed that promotions were consistent and fair. Furthermore, only 38 percent felt like they could speak out against unfairness without retribution.

Texaco's Challenge: Changing Organizational Culture to Appreciate Cultural Diversity

An effective change in corporate culture must come from the top. First, a company's culture and values must be clearly articulated. Texaco's stated values already include cultural diversity and sensitivity. Now Texaco must work to implement those ideals. Bijur responded to the tapes quickly and decisively. He suspended the two current employees recorded on the tapes and suspended the benefits of the two retired employees (including Lundwall). Bijur said that other penalties may be imposed if warranted by additional investigation. (Bijur's actions are markedly different from Mitsubishi's executives, who initially defended management against allegations of discrimination at Mitsubishi; see Chapter 7.) Rather than align Texaco with those caught on tape, Bijur distanced himself and the company from that type of behavior.

Second, Bijur must earn the trust of Texaco employees, its shareholders, and its customers. Quickly settling the case (for $176 million) is evidence that Bijur recognizes that racial strife may hurt Texaco's profits. In the week after the tapes surfaced, Texaco's stock dropped five points, which cost shareholders an estimated $1 billion! In addition, various civil rights leaders threatened boycotts. The $176 million settlement includes payment of some $115 million to current and former non-supervisory black Texaco employees, $26 million for salary increases for African-American employees over the next five years, and $35 million to fund a diversity program managed by an outside task force.

Third, real diversity learning must occur at Texaco. In 1995, Texaco had begun a two-day seminar for managers and supervisors designed to "eliminate subtle ethnic, cultural, and gender barriers." Bijur stated that this program will be redesigned and expanded to include all employees. The diversity training is a beginning, but formal training programs alone won't eradicate long-held prejudices and stereotypes. Learning to accept diversity must occur daily in a variety of ways. Building diversity into the structure of teams or work groups is one method of achieving this objective.

Fourth, defining an organization's culture may begin at the top, but that culture won't take hold if a vast majority of the company's employees don't believe in it and try to make it work. One of the easiest ways to ensure a diverse work force is to hire and promote people of different racial, gender, and ethnic backgrounds. In addition, Texaco must deal effectively with existing employees who espouse racist sentiments and exhibit racist behaviors. Dyrus Mehri, an attorney for the plaintiffs, said, "This incident wouldn't have happened if a corporate culture of disrespect for minorities hadn't existed."

Finally, Texaco must honor the various promises made in the settlement, such as increasing the amount of business it does with minority-owned companies and expanding the number of women and minority-owned gasoline stations and other franchises. Texaco hired a black-owned advertising agency, UniWorld Group, to produce ads targeted at minorities on the same day the suit was settled.

Only long-term commitments will convince Texaco's employees, shareholders, and customers that the company won't tolerate racism and discrimination. Texaco, like many other companies, faces the challenge of modifying its organizational culture to include diversity. Companies that fail to curb racism and gender discrimination will face increased litigation, lost customers, and stock devaluation. By restructuring their organizational cultures, human resource departments, and job assignments, companies can ensure that diversity isn't just another legal requirement, but a fundamental part of their cultures.[47]

Questions

1. List the major issues and ideas from this chapter that are reflected in this case.

2. Using the suggestions for effective diversity management presented in this chapter, assess the culture at Texaco.

3. Are the remedies that Texaco is implementing likely to change its culture? Why or why not?

REFERENCES

1. Adapted from Hue, J. How McKinsey does it. *Fortune*, November 1, 1993, 56–81.

2. Kilmann, R. H. Corporate culture. *Psychology Today*, April 1985, 63.

3. The description of these cultural types is based on Thompson, G. Fitting the company culture. In T. Lee (ed.), *Managing Your Career*. New York: Dow Jones & Company, 1990, 16.

4. Lancaster, H. It's harder, but you can still rise up from the mail room. *Wall Street Journal*, June 18, 1996, B1.

5. See, for example, Klein, A. S., Masi, R. J., and Weidner, C. K. Organization culture, distribution and amount of control, and perceptions of quality. *Group & Organization Management*, 1995, 20, 122–148; Wilkof, M. V., Brown, D. W., and Selsky, J. W. When the stories are different: The influence of corporate culture mismatches on interorganizational relations. *Journal of Applied Behavior Science*, 1995, 31, 373–388.

6. Hatch, M. J. The dynamics of organizational culture. *Academy of Management Review*, 1993, 18, 657–693; Schein, E. H. Culture: The missing concept in organization studies. *Administrative Science Quarterly*, 1996, 41, 229–240; Trice, H. M., and Beyer, J. M. *The Cultures of Work Organizations*. Englewood Cliffs, N.J.: Prentice-Hall, 1992.

7. Schein, E. H. *Organizational Culture and Leadership*. San Francisco: Jossey-Bass, 1985, 6.

8. Hofstede, G., Neuijen, B., Ohayv, D. D., and Sanders, G. Measuring organizational cultures: A qualitative and quantitative study across twenty cases. *Administrative Science Quarterly*, 1990, 35, 286–316.

9. Schein, E. H. How culture forms, develops, and changes. In R. H. Kilmann, M. I. Saxton, and R. Serpa (eds.), *Gaining Control of the Corporate Culture*. San Francisco: Jossey-Bass, 1985, 17–43; Schein, E. H. *Organizational Culture and Leadership*, 49–84; Schein, E. H. Organizational culture. *American Psychologist*, 1990, 45, 109–119.

10. Kane, K. An inside view of management in a People's Republic of China global enterprise. *Journal of Management Inquiry*, 1995, 4, 381–387; Fedor, K. J., and Werther, W. B. Creating culturally responsive international alliances. *Organizational Dynamics*, Autumn 1996, 39–53; Triandis, H. C. Cross-cultural industrial and organizational psychology. In H. C. Triandis, M. D. Dunnette, and L. M. Hough (eds.), *Handbook of Industrial and Organizational Psychology*, vol. 4, 2d ed. Palo Alto, Calif.: Consulting Psychologists Press, 1994, 103–172.

11. Greer, C. R., and Stephens, G. K. Employee relations issues for U.S. companies in Mexico. *California Management Review*, Spring 1996, 121–145; Hofstede, G. Cultural constraints in management theory. *Academy of Management Executive*, 1993, 7(1), 81–94; Solomon, C. M. Transplanting corporate cultures globally. *Personnel Journal*, October 1993, 78–88.

12. Jackofsky, E. F., Slocum, J. W., Jr., and McQuaid, S. J. Cultural values and the CEO: Alluring companions? *Academy of Management Executive*, 1988, 2, 39–49; Schuler, R. S., Jackson, S. E., Jackofsky, E., and Slocum, J. W. Managing human resources in Mexico: A cultural understanding. *Business*

Horizons, May–June, 1996, 55–61; Stephens, G. K., and Greer, C. R. Doing business in Mexico: Understanding cultural differences. *Organizational Dynamics,* Summer 1995, 39–55.

13. The description of these methods is based on Schein, *Organizational Culture and Leadership,* 223–243; Schein, Organizational culture, 109–119.

14. O'Reilly, C. R. Corporations, culture, and commitment: Motivation and social control in organizations. *California Management Review,* Summer 1989, 9–25.

15. Trice, H. M., and Beyer, J. M. Using six organizational rites to change culture. In R. H. Kilmann, M. I. Saxton, and R. Serpa (eds.), *Gaining Control of the Corporate Culture.* San Francisco: Jossey-Bass, 1985, 372.

16. Farnham, A. Mary Kay's lessons in leadership. *Fortune,* September 20, 1993, 68–77.

17. Dumaine, Creating a new company culture, 127–131.

18. Drucker, P. F. Don't change corporate culture—Use it! *Wall Street Journal,* March 28, 1991, A14.

19. Schein, E. H. Three cultures of management: The key to organizational learning. *Sloan Management Review,* Fall 1996, 9–20.

20. Dumaine, B. Creating a new company culture. *Fortune,* January 15, 1990, 128.

21. Schneider, B., Brief, A. P., and Guzzo, R. A. Creating a climate and culture for sustainable organizational change. *Organizational Dynamics,* spring 1996, 7–19.

22. Cartwright, S., and Cooper, C. L. The role of culture capability in successful organizational marriage. *Academy of Management Executive,* 1993, 7(2), 57–70; Kneale, D., Roberts, J. L., and Cauley, L. Why the mega-merger collapsed: Strong wills and a big culture gap. *Wall Street Journal,* February 25, 1994, A1, A16.

23. Deal, T. E., and Kennedy, A. A. *Corporate Cultures: The Rites and Rituals of Corporate Life.* Reading, Mass.: Addison-Wesley, 1982; Peters, T. J., and Austin, N. *A Passion for Excellence.* New York: Random House, 1985; Peters, T. J., and Waterman, R. H. *In Search of Excellence.* New York: Harper & Row, 1982. See also, Jacob, R. Corporate reputations. *Fortune,* March 6, 1995, 54–64.

24. Kotter, J. P., and Heskett, J. L. *Corporate Culture and Performance.* New York: Free Press, 1992, 15.

25. Cameron, K. S., and Freeman, S. J. Cultural congruence, strength, and type: Relationships to effectiveness. In R. W. Woodman and W. A. Pasmore (eds.), *Research in Organizational Change and Development,* vol. 5. Greenwich, Conn.: JAI Press, 1991, 23–58.

26. Kotter, and Heskett, *Corporate Culture and Performance,* 11–12.

27. Adapted from Dean, J. W., and Evans, J. R. *Total Quality: Management, Organization, and Strategy.* St. Paul: West, 1994, 150–152. See also, Carton, B. To make Gillette bristle, ask about the razor's edge. *Wall Street Journal,* July 30, 1996, A1, A9; Lowenstein, R. Blades, batteries, and fifth of Gillette. *Wall Street Journal,* September 19, 1996, C1.

28. Petzinger, T. This auditing team wants you to create a moral organization. *Wall Street Journal,* January 19, 1996, B1.

29. Near, J. P., and Dworkin, T. M. Corporate responses to legislative protection for whistle blowers: Survey results. In S. Wartick and D. Collins (eds.), *1994 Proceedings of the International Association for Business and Society,* 398–400; Sinclair, A. Approaches to organizational culture and ethics. *Journal of Business Ethics,* 1993, 12, 63–73; Stark, A. What's the matter with business ethics? *Harvard Business Review,* May–June 1993, 38–48; Trevino, L. K., and Victor, B. Peer reporting of unethical behavior: A social context perspective. *Academy of Management Journal,* 1992, 35, 38–64; Wimbush, J. C., and Shepard, J. M. Toward an understanding of ethical climate: Its relationship to ethical behavior and supervisory influence. *Journal of Business Ethics,* 1994, 12, 101–111.

30. Adapted from Gross, D. School for scandal. *CFO,* July 1995, 71–75.

31. Graham, J. W. Principled organizational dissent: A theoretical essay. In B. M. Staw and L. L. Cummings (eds.), *Research in Organizational Behavior,* vol. 8. Greenwich, Conn.: JAI Press, 1986, 2.

32. Intervention strategies and the following examples are based on Nielsen, R. P. Changing unethical organizational behavior. *Academy of Management Executive,* 1989, 3, 123–130.

33. Near, J. P., and Miceli, M. P. Effective Whistle Blowing. *Academy of Management Review,* 1995, 20, 679–708.

34. Drake, B. H., and Drake, E. Ethical and legal aspects of managing corporate cultures. *California Management Review,* Winter 1988, 120–121.

35. Fuchsberg, G. Sears reinstates sales incentives in some centers. *Wall Street Journal,* March 7, 1994, B1, B6; Paine, L. S. Managing for organizational integrity. *Harvard Business Review,* March–April, 1994, 106–117.

36. Labich, K. Making diversity pay. *Fortune,* September 9, 1996, 177–180.

37. Friedman, J. J., and DiTomaso, N. Myths about diversity: What managers need to know about changes in the U.S. labor force. *California Management Review,* Summer 1996, 54–77; Nemetz, P. Z., and Christensen, S. L. The challenge of cultural diversity: Harnessing a diversity of views to understand multiculturalism. *Academy of Management Review,* 1996, 21, 434–462; Watson, W. E., Kumar, K., and Michaelsen, L. K. Cultural diversity's impact on interaction process and performance: Comparing homogeneous and diverse task groups. *Academy of Management Journal,* 1993, 36, 590–602.

38. Cox, T. The multicultural organization. *Academy of Management Executive,* 1991, 5(2), 35.

39. Adapted from Markels, A. How one hotel manages staff's diversity. *Wall Street Journal,* November 20, 1996, B1, B11.

40. Caudron, S. Training can damage diversity efforts. *Personnel Journal,* April 1993, 54.

41. Thomas, D. A., and Ely, R. J. Making differences matter: A new paradigm for managing diversity. *Harvard Business Review,* September–October, 1996, 79–90.

42. Adkins, C. L. Previous work experience and organizational socialization: A longitudinal examination. *Academy of*

Management Journal, 1995, 38, 839–862; Harrison, J. R., and Carroll, G. R. Keeping the faith: A model of cultural transmission in formal organizations. *Administrative Science Quarterly,* 1991, 36, 552–582; Major, D. A., Kozlowski, S. W. J., Chao, G. T., and Gardner, P. D. A longitudinal investigation of newcomer expectations, early socialization outcomes, and the moderating effects of role development factors. *Journal of Applied Psychology,* 1995, 80, 418–431; Morrison, E. W. Longitudinal study of the effects of information seeking on newcomer socialization. *Journal of Applied Psychology,* 1993, 78, 173–183.

43. Pascale, R. The paradox of "corporate culture": Reconciling ourselves to socialization. *California Management Review,* Winter 1985, 29–33. See also, O'Reilly, C. A., and Chatman, J. A. Culture as social control: Corporations, cults, and commitment. In B. M. Staw and L. L. Cummings (eds.), *Research in Organizational Behavior,* vol. 18. Greenwich, Conn: JAI Press, 1996, 157–200.

44. Adapted from Quick, J. C. Crafting an organizational culture: Herb's hand at Southwest Airlines. *Organizational Dynamics,* Autumn 1992, 45–56; Teitelbaum, R. S. Southwest Airlines: Where service flies right. *Fortune,* August 24, 1992, 115–116; Trice and Beyer, *The Cultures of Work Organizations,* 3.

45. Abelson, M. A. Turnover cultures. In G. Ferris (ed.), *Research in Personnel and Human Resources Management,* vol. 11. Greenwich, Conn.: JAI Press, 1993, 339–376; Allen, N. J., and Meyer, J. P. Organizational socialization tactics: A longitudinal analysis of links to newcomer's commitment and role orientation. *Academy of Management Journal,* 1990, 33, 847–858; Ashforth, B. E., and Saks, A. M. Socialization Tactics: Longitudinal effects on newcomer adjustment. *Academy of Management Journal,* 1996, 39, 149–178; O'Reilly, C. R., Chatman, J., and Caldwell, D. F. People and organizational culture: A profile comparison approach to assessing person–organization fit. *Academy of Management Journal,* 1991, 34, 487–516.

46. Adapted from Cullen, J. B., Victor, B., and Stephens, C. An ethical weather report: Assessing the organization's ethical climate. *Organizational Dynamics,* Autumn 1989, 56.

47. Adapted with permission from White, R. Cultural Change at Texaco, November 1996. Case written under the supervision of John W. Slocum, Southern Methodist University.

18

Organizational Change

LEARNING OBJECTIVES

When you have finished studying this chapter, you should be able to:

- Understand why coping with change is one of the major challenges that organizations must meet.
- Identify characteristics of effective change programs.
- Explain the importance of an accurate diagnosis of organizational functioning and problems.
- Describe sources of individual and organizational resistance to change.
- Provide suggestions for overcoming resistance to change.
- Identify some of the major features of OD approaches to change.
- Give examples of behavioral, cultural, task, technology, strategy, and design change approaches.

OUTLINE

PREVIEW CASE

A Grim Fairy Tale

Once upon a time, an American automobile company and a Japanese automobile company decided to have a boat race on the Mississippi River. Teams from both companies practiced long and hard to reach their peak rowing performance. On the big day, the teams were as ready as they could possibly be.

The Japanese team won by a mile. After the race, the American team became discouraged by the loss and their morale sagged. Corporate management decided that the reason for the crushing defeat had to be found. A task force of executives was created to diagnose the problem and to recommend appropriate corrective action.

After much study, the task force concluded that the problem seemed to center on the fact that the Japanese team had eight people rowing and one person steering. The American team, in contrast, had one person rowing and eight people steering. Not wanting to rush to judgment, the task force recommended that a consulting firm be employed to further study the problem. After some time and the accumulation of considerable consulting fees, the consulting firm also concluded that "too many people were steering and not enough rowing."

To prevent further losses to the Japanese team, the Americans decided that the management structure of the rowing enterprise needed to be redesigned. The new management team consisted of four steering managers, three area steering managers, and one staff steering manager. In addition, a new incentive system was developed for the lone rower in order to provide motivation for that person to work harder.

A new race was agreed upon and this time the Japanese team won by two miles. The American company then decided to downsize. The rower was laid off for poor performance. The company sold off the boat and paddles, canceled capital investments planned for a new boat, granted a large performance award to the consulting firm, and distributed the money budgeted for next year's race as bonuses for senior executives.[1]

The Preview Case contains a tongue-in-cheek parable that appeared on an organization's computer bulletin board. Like much satire, it contains a kernel of wisdom and truth. The world that organizations face is changing, and "business as usual" for many firms is a sure prescription for disaster. We can easily imagine the story in the Preview Case being composed by a disgruntled employee irritated by his or her company's unimaginative approach to needed organizational change.

Managing organizational change presents complex challenges.[2] Planned changes may not work, or they may have consequences different from those intended. In many sectors of the economy, organizations must have the capacity to adapt quickly and effectively in order to survive. Often the speed and complexity of change severely test the capabilities of managers and employees to do so. However, when organizations fail to change, the costs of that failure may be quite high. Hence managers and employees must understand the nature of the changes needed and the likely effects of alternative approaches to bring about that change.

To a certain extent, all organizations exist in a changing environment and are themselves constantly changing. Increasingly, organizations that emphasize bureaucratic or mechanistic systems are ineffective. Organizations with rigid hierarchies, high degrees of functional specialization, narrow and limited job descriptions, inflexible rules and procedures, and impersonal management can't respond adequately to demands for change. Organizations need designs that are flexible and adaptive. They also need systems that both require and allow greater commitment and use of talent on the part of employees and managers.

In this chapter, we examine the pressures on organizations that create the need for change, identify characteristics of effective change programs, and emphasize the importance of accurate organizational diagnosis. We explore the difficult issue of resistance to change at both the individual and organizational level and examine ways to cope with the inevitable resistance. We briefly examine the field of organization development as a major approach to managing organizational change. In addition, we identify some specific approaches and techniques for making organizational and behavioral changes. Finally, we explore some ethical issues associated with programs of organizational change.

THE CHALLENGE OF CHANGE

Organizational change can be difficult and costly. Despite the challenges, many organizations successfully make needed changes. Adaptive, flexible organizations have a competitive advantage over rigid, static ones.[3] Thus managing change has become a central focus of effective organizations worldwide. This focus is creating its own vocabulary. For example, Table 18.1 presents some of the current concepts made popular by the increasing emphasis on effective organizational change. These ideas have appeared in various forms throughout the book. In many respects, then, managing change effectively means understanding and using many of the important principles and concepts of organizational behavior that we have explored in this book.

■ PRESSURES FOR CHANGE

Both advanced industrialized societies and developing countries are changing in important ways that have significant impacts on organizations.[4] Many organizations have had to undergo radical, and sometimes complete, reorientation with regard to the way they do business. The resulting changes may be comparable in scale to the Industrial Revolution of the nineteenth century. George Bennett, chairman of Symmetrix, a consulting firm, asks the provocative question: "If 2% of the population can grow all the food we eat, what if another 2% can manufacture all the refrigerators and other things we need?" From the bewildering variety of **pressures for change** that organizations face, we selected three significant ones to examine: (1) the globalization of markets, (2) the spread of information technology and computer networks, and (3) changes in the nature of the work force employed by organizations. We examine these three categories because they parallel major themes first introduced in Chapter 1 and repeatedly stressed throughout this book.

Globalization   Organizations face global competition on an unprecedented scale. Increasingly, the main players in the world's economy are international or multinational corporations.[5] The emergence of these global organizations creates pressures on domestic corporations to redesign and, in turn, internationalize their operations. Global markets now exist for most products, but in order to compete effectively in them, firms often must transform their cultures, structures, and operations.

The primary forces at work in **globalization** include

- the economic recoveries of Germany and Japan after their defeat in World War II;
- the emergence of "newly industrialized" countries, such as Korea, Taiwan, Singapore, and Spain;
- the dramatic shift from planned economies to market economies occurring in Eastern Europe, Russia and other republics of the former Soviet Union, and, to a lesser extent, China; and

TABLE 18.1   The Language of Organizational Change

CONCEPT	EXPLANATION
The learning organization	The notion that learning is central to success and effectiveness. Management must learn to see the "big picture" and understand subtle relationships among parts of the system.
Reengineering	A fundamental rethinking and redesign of systems and processes. Work should be organized around outcomes not tasks or functions.
Core competencies	The notion that companies need to identify and organize around what they do best. Strategy should be based on these core competencies rather than products or markets.
Organizational architecture	The idea that managers need to think broadly about the organization in terms of how work, people, and designs fit together.
Time-based competition	The notion that time is money. Time is manageable and can be a source of competitive advantage affecting productivity, quality, and innovation.

Source: Adapted from Byrne, J. A. Management's new gurus. *Business Week*, August 31, 1992, 45.

■ the emergence of new "power blocks" of international traders, such as the economic unification of Europe (which eventually will involve currency, some government operations, and lowered tariff barriers) and the "yen block" (Japan and its Pacific Rim trading partners).[6]

These powerful forces for globalization mean that domestic organizations must recognize that the rest of the world does in fact exist. Although successful globalization strategies aren't easy to implement, many organizations have effectively moved outside their domestic markets. For example, Ford, Merck & Company, IBM, and Hewlett-Packard have strong, profitable operations in Europe. McDonald's, Walt Disney, DuPont, and Amway have successful Asian operations. Amway sells more than $500 million worth of housewares door to door in Japan each year. At Aluminum Company of America (Alcoa), international operations contributed only 33 percent of its revenue and 46 percent of its operating profit in 1987. By the end of 1995 Alcoa's growing global operations provided 44 percent of the company's revenue and 59 percent of its profits.[7]

Moreover, the globalization of markets and other pressures for change affect managers and organizations around the world, as the following Across Cultures feature indicates.

ACROSS CULTURES

12,000 World Managers View Change

The *Harvard Business Review* collected data (by survey questionnaire) on a variety of organizational issues from almost 12,000 managers throughout the world. Twenty-five business publications in twenty-five countries on six continents assisted the journal in this effort. Each publication reproduced the survey questionnaire in its own language.

The questionnaire examined a number of issues, but one strong theme particularly stood out in the survey results. Change is occurring everywhere—regardless of country, culture, or organization—with managers reporting a rapidly changing business environment. Figure 18.1 contains data from six countries, showing the

—Continued

ACROSS CULTURES—*Continued*

◼ FIGURE 18.1

Percentage of Respondents Reporting Major Redesign of Their Organizations

Source: Adapted from Kanter, R. M. Transcending business boundaries: 12,000 world managers view change. *Harvard Business Review,* May–June, 1991, 154.

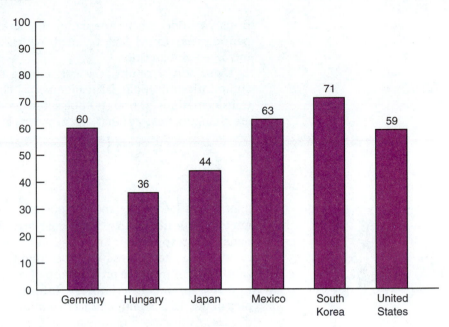

percentage of the respondents' organizations that underwent a major redesign during a recent two-year period. For example, during that period, an incredible 71 percent of South Korean firms were restructured. Among the six countries shown in Figure 18.1, Hungary had the smallest amount of organizational redesign, at 36 percent. However, even that is a significant amount of reorganization for any two-year period.

Figure 18.2 summarizes results from the same six countries with regard to international expansion. Almost half the German and Japanese respondents'

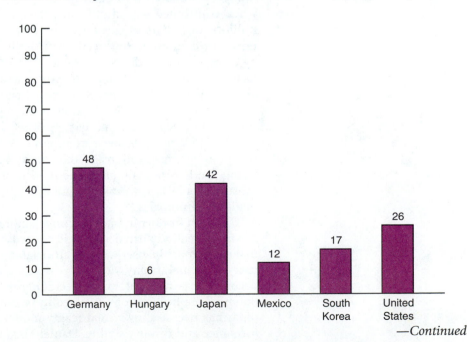

◼ FIGURE 18.2

Percentage of Respondents Reporting International Expansion by Their Organizations

Source: Adapted from Kanter, R. M. Transcending business boundaries: 12,000 world managers view change. *Harvard Business Review,* May–June, 1991, 154.

—Continued

ACROSS CULTURES—*Continued*

firms expanded their international operations during the two-year reporting period. The United States trailed, with 26 percent of the managers reporting increased globalization.

These survey results reveal that increasingly global markets, instantaneous communication, political realignments, changing demographics, technological transformations in both products and production, and new corporate alliances are changing the ways that organizations are designed and conduct business.[8]

Information Technology and Computers   Coping with international competition requires a flexibility that traditional organizations often do not possess. Fortunately, the revolution in information technology permits many organizations to develop the needed flexibility. A second major category of change facing organizations stems from the proliferation of computer networks and the use of sophisticated information technology. **Information technology** (IT) comprises complex networks of computers, telecommunications systems, and remote-controlled devices. As discussed mainly in Chapters 1 and 8 and elsewhere throughout this book, information technology is having a profound impact on organizational operations, interpersonal relationships, power relationships, the development of markets, and the implementation of strategies.[9]

For example, information technology might affect a J.C. Penney store manager who sees an attractive sweater at Neiman-Marcus. She buys the sweater, photographs it, and faxes the photograph to Penney buyers around the world. Soon, a buyer in Bangkok locates a factory that can produce the sweater. Within two weeks, thousands of replicas are on their way to Penney stores. Information technology permits an IBM engineer to ask colleagues around the world for help when confronted with a difficult problem. General Electric spent hundreds of millions of dollars to create its own private global phone network. Employees now can communicate directly with each other from anywhere in the world by using just seven digits. Information technology allows CRSS, the giant architectural firm, to exchange drawings with 3M, one of its largest clients, almost instantly. In an event of great historic (and perhaps symbolic) significance, the London Stock Exchange replaced its trading floor with a computer–telecommunications network.[10]

Table 18.2 presents some examples of information technologies that will be common in organizations of the future. Some, such as electronic data interchange and voice mail, are being used in many organizations already. In time, most (if not all) organizations will utilize these and even more advanced information technologies.

The latest frontier in information technology is a computer application known as virtual reality. **Virtual reality** is created by a display and control technology that surrounds the user with an artificial environment that mimics real life. The user of virtual reality doesn't passively view a computer screen but rather becomes a participant in a three-dimensional setting. Boeing is investigating potential applications of virtual reality to the design and testing of aircraft. Caterpillar has been testing virtual reality models of its earthmovers to improve performance and driver visibility. Daniel Ling, leader of a research team on virtual

TABLE 18.2   Information Technology of the Future

INDIVIDUAL WORK SUPPORT	GROUP WORK SUPPORT	ADVANCED ORGANIZATIONAL AUTOMATION	ENHANCED COMMUNICATION
High bandwidth portable compute	Groupware	Electronic data interchange (EDI)r	Language speech translator
Knowbot*	Cyberspace†	Virtual reality sales	E-mail and voice mail
Advanced forms of multimedia	Virtual reality for teams	Automated customer response systems	Videophone and deskphone videoconferencing
Virtual reality			Videoconferencing Telepresence‡

*A *knowbot* resides inside an individual's PC and is programmed to organize data and work for the user.
†The next step beyond virtual reality; incorporates the user's thoughts into computer processible form.
‡The transmission of holographic images from one office to another.

Source: Adapted from Thach, L., and Woodman, R. W. Organizational change and information technology: Managing on the edge of cyberspace. *Organizational Dynamics,* Summer 1994, 34.

reality at IBM, stated, "Virtual reality will eventually change the way people use computers. The applications are countless."[11]

Changing Nature of the Work Force   In addition to coping with the challenges presented by globalization and rapid changes in information technology, organizations must attract employees from a changing labor market. For this reason, we have explored the challenges of managing cultural diversity throughout this book.

As discussed in Chapter 1, the labor market continues to grow more diverse in terms of gender and ethnicity. Thus equal opportunity pressures on hiring practices and promotion decisions will persist for some time to come. Other trends add to the challenge for organizations. For example, the dual-career family rapidly is becoming the norm, rather than the exception, in many advanced societies. Further, the number of temporary workers continues to grow as a percentage of all workers, almost doubling in the United States in just five years. The **contingency work force** includes part-time employees, free-lancers, subcontractors, and independent professionals hired by companies to cope with unexpected or temporary challenges. By some accounts, almost 25 percent of U.S. workers now fall into these categories.[12] Experts expect this percentage to continue to grow as companies find efficiencies by operating with a small core of permanent employees surrounded by a changing cast of temporary help. Temporary-employment agencies, such as Manpower and Kelly Services, grew by 240 percent in just ten years and now employ some 1.6 million people. Manpower, the largest of these firms has more employees than General Motors or IBM—a truly incredible statistic. Among the challenges facing organizations are those of motivating and rewarding part-time employees whose morale and loyalties may be quite different from those of permanent employees.

Increasingly, the work force is better educated, less unionized, and characterized by changing values and aspirations. Although changing values and aspirations won't lessen the motivation to work, they will continue to affect the rewards that people seek from work and the balance they seek between work and other aspects of their lives. The **quality of work life** represents the degree to which people are able to satisfy important personal needs through their work and is an important goal for many, if not most, working women and men. More than ever before, employees desire pleasant working conditions, more participation in decisions that affect their jobs, and support facilities, such as day-care centers for their children. These and other employee expectations put additional pressures on organizations and affect their ability to compete effectively in the labor market.

■ CHARACTERISTICS OF EFFECTIVE CHANGE PROGRAMS

Distinguishing between change that inevitably happens to all organizations and change that is planned by members of an organization is important. Our focus is primarily on intentional, goal-oriented organizational change. **Planned organizational change** represents a purposeful attempt by managers and employees to improve the functioning of groups, teams, departments, divisions, or an entire organization in some important way.[13]

Effective planned change efforts are often characterized by some common antecedents. For example, Cummings and Worley believe that effective change programs involve

- motivating change by creating a readiness for it among employees and attempting to overcome resistance to change;
- creating a shared vision of the desired future state of the organization; and
- developing political support for the needed changes.[14]

Similarly, Porras and Robertson have identified conditions that are related to effective change programs, including the following.

- The organization's members must be the key source of energy for the change, not some external party.
- Key members of the organization must recognize the need for change and be attracted by the potentially positive outcomes from the change program.
- A willingness to change norms and procedures, in order to become more effective, must exist.[15]

Note the similarities in the preceding lists. Change needs to come from inside the organization, and people must be aware of the need for change, believe in the potential value of the changes, and be willing to change their behaviors in order to make the team or organization more effective. Absent these beliefs and behaviors, effective organizational change is problematic.

In addition, effective change must be organizationwide and rely on a contingency perspective that is open to trying different things at different times.

Organizationwide Change   Meeting the challenge posed by organizational change often means not doing things piecemeal. To be successful, change usually must be organizationwide.[16] Figure 18.3 shows a systems model that provides a useful way to think about organizationwide change.

The **systems model of change** describes the organization as six interacting variables that could serve as the focus of planned change: people, culture, task, technology, design, and strategy. The **people variable** applies to the individuals working for the organization, including their individual differences—personali-

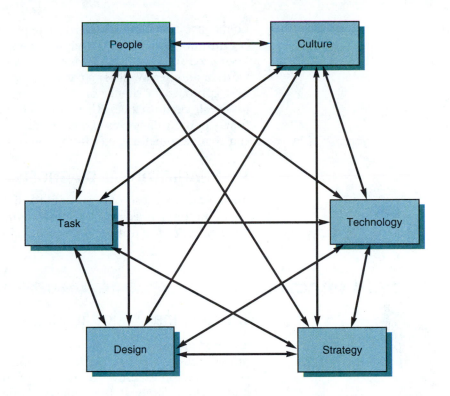

ties, attitudes, perceptions, attributions, needs, and motives (see Chapters 2, 3, and 5). The **culture variable** reflects the shared beliefs, values, expectations, and norms of organizational members (see Chapter 17). The **task variable** involves the nature of the work itself—whether the job is simple or complex, novel or repetitive, standardized or unique. The **technology variable** encompasses the problem-solving methods and techniques used and the application of knowledge to various organizational processes. It includes such things as the use of information technology, robots and other automation, manufacturing processes, tools, and techniques (see Chapter 15). The **design variable** is the formal organizational structure and its systems of communication, control, authority, and responsibility (see Chapter 16). Finally, the **strategy variable** comprises the organization's planning process. It typically consists of activities undertaken to identify organizational goals and prepare specific plans to acquire, allocate, and use resources in order to accomplish those goals.

As Figure 18.3 indicates, these six variables are highly interdependent. A change in any one variable usually results in a change in one or more of the others. For example, a change in the organization's strategic plan might dictate a change in organization design to an adaptive or network form. This change, in turn, could result in the reassignment of people. At the same time, the redesign may also lead to a change in the technology used, which would affect the attitudes and behaviors of the employees involved, and so on. All of these changes would occur within a particular organizational culture, which might either support or resist them. Moreover, change itself may either modify or reinforce the existing culture. An advantage of a systems approach to organizational change is that it helps managers and employees think through such interrelationships. The systems approach reminds them that they can't change part of the organization without, in some sense, changing the whole.

Contingency Perspective   Disagreement exists about the best ways to achieve organizational change. Many different approaches to organizational change have been used successfully, but what works in one organization may not necessarily work in another. We favor a contingency perspective, which recognizes no single best approach to change and holds that no approach is likely to be effective under all circumstances. The contingency perspective leads directly to the need for an accurate diagnosis of organizational functioning and problems. Before you can change something effectively, you must understand it.

■ ORGANIZATIONAL DIAGNOSIS

An accurate diagnosis of organizational problems is absolutely essential as a starting point for planned organizational change.[17] In a humorous way, the following Quality in Practice feature suggests the importance of organizational diagnosis.

QUALITY IN PRACTICE

The Chairman's Rice Pudding

A senior manager was given the responsibility of examining all operations and procedures at corporate headquarters. She formed a task force to help with this review. The top executives of the organization had their own private kitchen and dining room. Although this perk wasn't high on its list of priorities, the task force eventually got around to taking a look at the kitchen's operation.

The task force discovered that two rice puddings were made every day at 12:15 P.M. and thrown away at 2:45 P.M. Mysteriously, the rice puddings were not listed on the dining room's menu. When the chef was questioned about this practice, he admitted that, to the best of his knowledge, no one had ever eaten one of these puddings. Nor did he know why they were being made. The practice was in place when he joined the organization, and he had simply continued it. (Amazingly, he had been the chef for eight years.)

Intrigued, the task force decided to investigate the origin of this odd ritual and discovered the following. Seventeen years before, the then-chairman of the organization had strolled through the kitchen one day. In a conversation with the chef at the time, he had mentioned how much he liked rice pudding. The chef then instructed his kitchen staff to prepare two rice puddings each day but not to include them on the menu. When the chairman came to lunch, his waiter could then offer him a rice pudding. The second rice pudding was made in case anyone else in the chairman's lunch party also should request one.

The chairman, who apparently had a rice pudding occasionally, retired four years later. Thirteen years after his retirement, the kitchen staff was still making rice puddings. By now, however, none of them knew why they were doing so, nor did any of the patrons of the dining room know that the pudding was available.[18]

All organizations have "rice puddings"—patterns of behavior and procedures that, at one time and place, made perfect sense but no longer do. Diagnosing needed change, in part, means uncovering the organization's "rice puddings." Four basic steps should be undertaken in **organizational diagnosis:**

- recognize and interpret the problem and assess the need for change;
- determine the organization's readiness and capability for change;
- identify managerial and work-force resources and motivations for change; and
- determine a change strategy and goals.[19]

Information needed to diagnose organizational problems may be gathered by questionnaires, interviews, or observation, and from the firm's records. Typically, some combination of these data gathering methods is used. An advantage of the information collecting process is that it increases awareness of the need for change. Even when widespread agreement exists concerning the need for change, people may have different ideas about the approach to be used and when, where, and how it should be implemented. Thus some systematic attempt should be made to determine the focus and goals of a change effort.

Any planned change program requires a careful assessment of individual and organizational capacity for change. Two important aspects of individual readiness for change are the degree of employee satisfaction with the status quo and the perceived personal risk involved in changing it. Figure 18.4 shows the possible combinations of these concerns. When employees are dissatisfied with the current situation and perceive little personal risk from change, their readiness for change probably would be high. In contrast, when employees are satisfied with the status quo and perceive high personal risk in change, their readiness for change probably would be low.

With regard to individual readiness for change, another important variable is employee expectations regarding the change effort.[20] Expectations play a crucial role in behavior. If people expect that nothing of significance will change, regardless of the amount of time and effort they might devote to making it happen, this belief can become a self-fulfilling prophecy. And when employee expectations for improvement are unrealistically high, unfulfilled expectations can make matters worse. Ideally, expectations regarding change should be positive yet realistic.

In addition, the organization's capacity for change must be accurately assessed. Approaches that require a massive commitment of personal energy and organizational resources probably will fail if the organization has few resources and its members do not have the time or opportunity to implement the needed changes. Under such circumstances, the organization may benefit most from starting with

■ **FIGURE 18.4**

Employee Readiness for Change

Source: Adapted from Zeira, Y., and Avedisian, J. Organizational planned change: Assessing the chances for success. *Organizational Dynamics*, Spring 1989, 37.

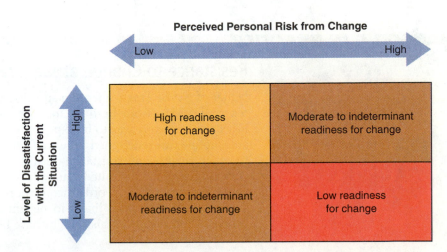

a modest effort. Then, as the organization develops the necessary resources and employee commitment, it can increase the depth and breadth of the change.

When managers and employees conduct an organizational diagnosis, they should recognize two additional important factors. First, organizational behavior is the product of many interacting forces. Therefore what is observed or diagnosed—employee behaviors, problems, and the current state of the organization—has multiple causes. Trying to isolate single causes for complex problems can lead to simplistic and ineffective change strategies. Second, much of the information gathered about an organization during a diagnosis will represent symptoms rather than causes of problems. Obviously, focusing change strategies on symptoms won't solve underlying problems. For example, in one organization, an awards program that recognized perfect attendance failed to reduce absenteeism because it didn't deal with the causes of the problem. Careful diagnosis revealed that employees were absent from work because of pressures created by excessive workloads and an inefficient, frustrating set of procedures for doing their jobs. The awards offered weren't sufficient to change employee behaviors and, more important, didn't address the real problems of work overload and job design.

Potential resistance to change represents another important aspect of readiness and motivation for change. Both individual and organizational resistance to change must be diagnosed.

RESISTANCE TO CHANGE

Inevitably, change will be resisted, at least to some extent, by both individuals and organizations. **Resistance to change** often is baffling because it can take so many forms. Overt resistance may be manifested in strikes, reduced productivity, shoddy work, and even sabotage. Covert resistance may be expressed by increased tardiness and absenteeism, requests for transfers, resignations, loss of motivation, lower morale, and higher accident or error rates. One of the more damaging forms of resistance is lack of participation in and commitment to proposed changes by employees, even when they have opportunities to participate.[21] The following Managing in Practice account indicates some of the difficulties in developing commitment to needed changes.

MANAGING IN PRACTICE

Resistance to Change at Jaguar

Jaguar of North America faced a surprising source of resistance during its recent reorganization—from both its top management and North American dealers. Resistance certainly was to be expected from the company's rank-and-file. As the automobile was redesigned, so were factories and jobs—changes that were likely to cause anxiety and resistance on the part of employees. However, since sales were slumping in the United States, the dealers might have been expected to welcome enthusiastically Ford's acquisition of the company and its proposed changes. Key managers, likely to benefit a great deal from Ford's infusion of expertise and resources, also might have been expected to be enthusiastic. Such was far from the case.

—*Continued*

MANAGING IN PRACTICE—*Continued*

Ford bought the English carmaker in 1990 and spent a couple of years helping Jaguar reengineer its manufacturing operations to produce a more reliable car in less time. "That was the easy part," says vice-president of customer care Dale Gambill. The hard part began in July 1991, when Jaguar responded to falling sales and profits with a total reorganization, splitting North American operations into three parts and shedding one-third of the staff. Managerial survivors lost titles, fancy offices, company cars, and other perks they'd come to cherish. They also had to work harder, usually with different people, than before.

Enter Gambill, intent on polishing Jaguar's customer service image, which had been badly tarnished. Gambill thought the main problem was that dealers had lost enthusiasm for selling the cars. That was true. But when Gambill stood before a gathering of Jaguar managers to tell them to think harder about pleasing dealers and customers, he got a shock. "As soon as I started in on customer care, these people said, 'Hey, let's forget the customer for a minute here. You aren't taking care of us,'" Gambill says. "I hadn't realized how much pent-up frustration there was. These people spent two days venting. They said we had no clear vision for the future. They said we had too many competing sets of values among the departments. They said we never learned anything from our mistakes and were just constantly going around putting out fires. Then they told *me* we had to start getting more customer-focused. I went there thinking I was going to do all the talking. I barely got a word in edgewise."

Gambill and Jaguar President Mike Dale reacted with a change strategy that had worked in other difficult situations: Put the loudest dissenters in charge of solutions, then get out of their way. Over the past three years, employee involvement groups, called "egg groups" in a whimsical adaptation of the acronym EIG, have corrected so many of Jaguar's shortcomings that even dealers are pleasantly surprised. "I was suspicious and instinctively resisted the notion that Jaguar was finally getting serious about customers," says Martin Bennett, a plain-spoken Brit who owns Thoroughbred Motorcars in Nashville. "But they've really changed. They've convinced me." Customers appear to agree: By 1995, Jaguar ranked in the top ten of J.D. Power's customer satisfaction survey, up from twenty-fourth four years earlier.[22]

As Figure 18.5 shows, resistance to change stems from a variety of sources. Some are traceable to individuals, but others involve the nature and structure of organizations. Managers and employees need to understand the reasons for and sources of resistance to change.[23]

■ INDIVIDUAL RESISTANCE TO CHANGE

Figure 18.5 shows six important sources of individual resistance to change. They aren't the only reasons why individuals may resist change at work, but they are common and may be deep seated.

Perceptions Recall the perceptual error called *perceptual defense* (see Chapter 3). It's the notion that people tend to perceive selectively those things that fit most comfortably into their current view of the world. Once individuals establish an

■ FIGURE 18.5

Sources of Resistance to Change

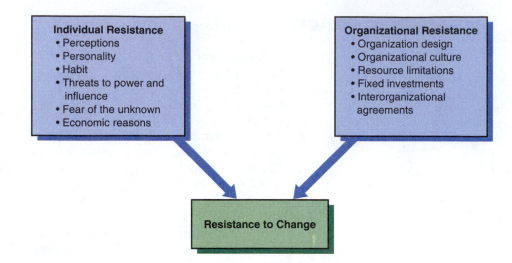

understanding of reality, they resist changing it. Among other things, people may resist the possible impact of change on their lives by (1) reading or listening only to what they agree with, (2) conveniently forgetting any knowledge that could lead to other viewpoints, and (3) misunderstanding communication that, if correctly perceived, wouldn't fit their existing attitudes and values. For example, managers enrolled in management training programs are exposed to different managerial philosophies and techniques. In the classroom, they may effectively discuss and answer questions about these philosophies, yet carefully segregate in their minds the approaches that they believe wouldn't work from those that they already practice.

Personality   Some aspects of their personalities (such as dogmatism and dependency) may predispose some individuals to resist change (see Chapter 2). *Dogmatism* is the rigidity of a person's beliefs. The highly dogmatic individual is close-minded and more likely to resist change than a less dogmatic person. Another example is dependency.[24] If carried to extremes, dependency on others can lead to resistance to change. People who are highly dependent on others often lack self-esteem. They may resist change until those they depend on endorse the change and incorporate it into their behavior. Employees who are highly dependent on their supervisors for performance feedback probably will not accept any new techniques or methods unless the supervisors personally endorse them and indicate to the employees how these changes will improve performance and benefit them.

A cautionary note: Don't overemphasize the role played by personality in resistance to change. Recall the *fundamental attribution error* (see Chapter 3). People tend to "blame" resistance to change in the workplace on individual personalities. Although personality may be a factor, it seldom is the most important dynamic in the situation.

Habit   Unless a situation changes dramatically, individuals may continue to respond to stimuli in their usual ways. A habit may be a source of satisfaction for individuals because it allows them to adjust to and cope with the world. A habit also provides comfort and security. Whether a habit becomes a primary source of resistance to change depends, to a certain extent, on whether individuals perceive advantages from changing it. For example, if an organization suddenly announced that all employees would immediately receive a 20 percent pay raise, few would object because the raise probably would permit significant beneficial changes in life-style. However, if the organization announced that all employees could receive a 20 percent pay raise only if they switched from working from 9:00 A.M. to 5:00 P.M. to working during the evenings and nights, many would object. Employees would have to change many habits—when they sleep, eat, interact with their families, and so on.

Threats to Power and Influence   Some people in organizations may view change as a threat to their power or influence. The control of something needed by other people, such as information or resources, is a source of power in organizations (see Chapter 9). Once a power position has been established, individuals or groups often resist changes that they perceive as reducing their power and influence. For example, programs to improve the quality of work life (QWL programs) in organizations tend to focus on nonmanagerial employees and often are perceived as increasing their power. As a result, managers and supervisors may resist such programs. Novel ideas or a new use for resources also can disrupt the power relationships among individuals and departments in an organization and therefore often are resisted.

Fear of the Unknown   Confronting the unknown makes most people anxious. Each major change in a work situation carries with it an element of uncertainty. People starting a new job may be concerned about their ability to perform adequately. Women starting a second career after raising a family may be anxious about how they will fit in with other workers after a long absence from the workplace. An employee may wonder what might happen if he or she relocates to company headquarters in another state: Would my family like it? Will I be able to find friends? What will top managers think of me if I refuse to relocate? Uncertainty in such situations arises not just from the prospective change itself, but also from the potential consequences of the change. To avoid both the fear of the unknown and having to make more demanding types of decisions, some employees may refuse promotions that require relocating or that require major changes in job duties and responsibilities.

Economic Reasons   Money weighs heavily in people's thinking, and they certainly can be expected to resist changes that might lower their incomes. In a very real sense, employees have invested in the status quo in their jobs. That is, they have learned how to perform their work well, how to get good performance evaluations, and how to interact with others. Changes in established work routines or job duties may threaten their economic security. Employees may fear that, after changes are made, they won't be able to perform as well and thus won't be as valuable to the organization, their supervisors, or their co-workers.

■ ORGANIZATIONAL RESISTANCE TO CHANGE

To a certain extent, the nature of organizations is to resist change. Organizations often are most efficient when doing routine tasks and tend to perform more poorly, at least initially, when doing something for the first time. To ensure operational efficiency and effectiveness, organizations may create strong defenses against change. Moreover, change often opposes vested interests and violates certain territorial rights or decision-making prerogatives that groups, teams, and departments have established and accepted over time. Figure 18.5 shows several of the more significant sources of organizational resistance to change.

Organization Design   Organizations need stability and continuity in order to function effectively. Indeed, the term *organization* implies that individual, group, and team activities have a certain structure. Individuals have assigned roles, established procedures for getting the job done, consistent ways of getting needed information, and the like. However, this legitimate need for structure also may lead to resistance to change. Organizations may have narrowly defined jobs; clearly spelled-out lines of authority, responsibility, and accountability; and limited flows of information from the top to the bottom. The use of a rigid design and an emphasis on the hierarchy of authority usually causes employees to use only specific channels of communication and to focus narrowly on their own duties and responsibilities. Typically, the more mechanistic the organization, the more numerous are the levels of the organization through which an idea must travel (see Chapter 16). This organizational design, then, increases the probability that any new idea will be screened out because it threatens the status quo. More adaptive and flexible organizations are designed to reduce the resistance to change created by rigid organizational structures.

Organizational Culture   Organizational culture plays a key role in change. Cultures are not easy to modify and may become a principle source of resistance to needed change (see Chapter 17). One aspect of an effective organizational culture is whether it has the flexibility to take advantage of opportunities to change. An ineffective organizational culture (in terms of organizational change) is one that rigidly socializes employees into the old culture even in the face of evidence that it no longer works.

IBM and General Motors dominated their industries by creating organizations with cultures that were excellent at producing very large products—mainframe computers and large, powerful cars. When the demand for their products dropped off dramatically, both IBM and GM were forced to undertake drastic cultural changes in order to remain profitable. Among other things, the sheer size of these organizations has made it difficult for them to change their cultures quickly.

Resource Limitations   Some organizations want to maintain the status quo, but others would change if they had the resources to do so. Change requires capital, time, and skilled people. At any particular time, an organization's managers and employees may have identified changes that could or should be made, but they may have to defer or abandon some of the desired changes because of resource limitations. Continental Lite, formerly a division of Continental Airlines, quickly learned that it didn't have the resources (planes, ground crews, and terminals) to compete effectively against Southwest Airlines for the budget-conscious traveler. Without these resources, Continental was unable to change quickly and had to abandon its attempt to compete with Southwest.

Fixed Investments   Resource limitations aren't confined to organizations with insufficient assets. Wealthy organizations may be unable to change because of fixed capital investments in assets that they can't easily alter (equipment, buildings, and land). The plight of the central business districts in many cities illustrates this resistance to change. Most large cities developed before the automobile and can't begin to accommodate today's traffic volumes and parking demands.

The fixed investments in buildings, streets, transit systems, and utilities are enormous and usually prevent rapid and substantial change. Therefore many older central areas are unable to meet the competition of suburban shopping centers.

Fixed investments aren't always limited to physical assets; they also may be expressed in terms of people. For example, consider employees who no longer are making a significant contribution to an organization but have enough seniority to maintain their jobs. Unless they can be motivated to perform better or retrained for other positions, their salaries and fringe benefits represent, from the organization's perspective, fixed investments that can't easily be changed.

Interorganizational Agreements   Agreements between organizations usually impose obligations on people that can restrain their behaviors. Labor negotiations and contracts provide some examples. Ways of doing things that once were considered the prerogatives of management (the right to hire and fire, assign tasks, promote and demote, and so on) may become subject to negotiation and fixed in the negotiated contract. Other types of contracts also constrain organizations. For example, proponents of change may face delay because of arrangements with competitors, commitments to suppliers and other contractors, and pledges to public officials in return for licenses, permits, or financing.

■ OVERCOMING RESISTANCE TO CHANGE

Realistically, resistance to change will never cease completely. Managers and employees, however, can learn to identify and minimize resistance and thus become more effective change agents.

People often have difficulty with clearly understanding situations that involve change. Part of the reason is that even analyzing a change problem may be quite complex when a large number of variables must be considered. Kurt Lewin, a pioneering social psychologist, developed a way of looking at change that has proved to be highly useful to action-oriented managers and employees.[25] Lewin viewed change not as an event but as a dynamic balance of forces working in opposite directions. His approach, called **force field analysis,** suggests that any situation can be considered to be in a state of equilibrium resulting from a balance of forces constantly pushing against each other. Certain forces in the situation—various types of resistance to change—tend to maintain the status quo. At the same time, various pressures for change are acting opposite to these forces and are pushing for change. The combined effect of these two sets of forces results in the situation shown in Figure 18.6. It illustrates the forces that are likely to have an impact on a potential change in group performance.

To initiate change, someone must act to modify the current equilibrium of forces by

- increasing the strength of pressure for change;
- reducing the strength of the resisting forces or removing them completely; or
- changing the direction of a force, that is, changing a resistance into a pressure for change.

Using force field analysis to understand the processes of change has two primary benefits. First, managers and employees are required to analyze the current situation. By becoming skillful at diagnosing the forces pressing for and resisting change, individuals should be able to understand better the relevant aspects of any change situation. Second, a force field analysis highlights the factors that can

■ FIGURE 18.6

Force Field Analysis

Source: Adapted from Zand, D. E. Force field analysis. In N. Nicholson (ed.), *Blackwell Encyclopedic Dictionary of Organizational Behavior.* Oxford, England: Blackwell, 1995, 181.

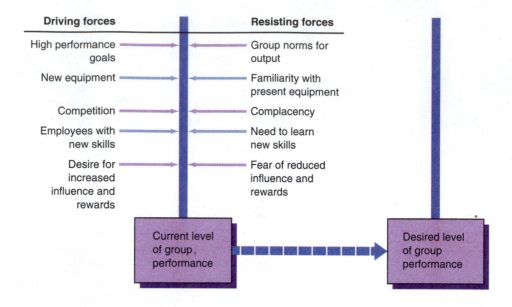

be changed and those that cannot. People often waste a great deal of time considering actions related to forces over which they have little, if any, control. When individuals focus on the forces over which they do have some control, they increase the likelihood of selecting effective options to change the situation.

Of course, careful analysis of a situation doesn't guarantee successful change. For example, people in control have a natural tendency to increase the pressure for change in any situation in order to produce the change they desire. Increasing such pressure may result in short-run changes, but it may have a high cost: Strong pressure on individuals and groups may create conflicts that disrupt the organization. Often the most effective way to make needed changes is to identify existing resistance to change and focus efforts on removing resistance or reducing it as much as possible.

An important part of Lewin's approach to changing behaviors consists of carefully managing and guiding change through a three-step process.

- *Unfreezing.* This step usually involves reducing those forces maintaining the organization's behavior at its present level. Unfreezing is sometimes accomplished by introducing information to show discrepancies between behaviors desired by employees and behaviors they currently exhibit.

- *Moving.* This step shifts the behavior of the organization or department to a new level. It involves developing new behaviors, values, and attitudes through changes in organizational structures and processes.

- *Refreezing.* This step stabilizes the organization at a new state of equilibrium. It is frequently accomplished through the use of supporting mechanisms that reinforce the new organizational state, such as organizational culture, norms, policies, and structures.[26]

Successful methods for dealing with resistance to change often include the following components.

- *Empathy and support.* Understanding how employees are experiencing change is useful. It helps identify those who are troubled by the change and understand the nature of their concerns. When employees feel that those managing change are open to their concerns, they are more willing to provide information. This openness, in turn, helps establish collaborative problem solving, which may overcome barriers to change.

- *Communication.* People are more likely to resist change when they are uncertain about its consequences. Effective communication can reduce gossip and unfounded fears. Adequate information helps employees prepare for change.

- *Participation and involvement.* Perhaps the single most effective strategy for overcoming resistance to change is to involve employees directly in planning and implementing change. Involvement in planning change increases the probability that employee interests will be accounted for and thus lowers resistance to change. Involved employees are more committed to implementing the planned changes and more likely to ensure that they work.[27]

ORGANIZATION DEVELOPMENT

Organization development (OD) is a planned, systematic process of organizational change based on behavioral science research and theory.[28] The goal of OD is to create adaptive organizations capable of repeatedly transforming and reinventing themselves, as needed, to remain effective.[29] As a field of behavioral science, OD draws heavily from psychology, sociology, and anthropology. Organization development relies on information from personality theory, learning theory, and motivation theory (see Chapters 2, 4, 5, and 6) and on research in group dynamics, power, leadership, and organization design (see Chapters 8, 9, 10, 11, and 16). It is based on many well-established principles regarding the behaviors of individuals and groups in organizations. In short, OD rests on many of the facets of organizational behavior presented in this book.

Organization development isn't a single technique but a collection of techniques that have a certain philosophy and body of knowledge in common. The basic tenets that set OD approaches apart from other organizational change approaches include the following.

- OD seeks to create self-directed change to which people are committed. The problems and issues to be solved are those identified by the organization's members who are directly concerned with and affected by them.

- OD is an organizationwide change effort. Making lasting changes that create a more effective organization requires an understanding of the entire organization. Changing part of the organization isn't possible without changing the entire organization in some sense.

- OD typically places equal emphasis on solving immediate problems and the long-term development of an adaptive organization. The most effective change program isn't one that just solves present problems but one that also prepares individuals to solve future problems.

- OD places more emphasis than do other approaches on a collaborative process of data collection, diagnosis, and action for arriving at solutions to problems.

- OD has a dual emphasis on organizational effectiveness and human fulfillment through the work experience.[30]

A recent survey of 110 of the Fortune 500 industrial corporations revealed that all but 3 of these organizations had viable OD change activities underway. Some

82 percent of these organizations considered their OD change programs to be effective.[31]

A primary change process used in most OD programs is action research. **Action research** is a data-based, problem-solving process of organizational change that closely follows the scientific method.[32] It represents a powerful approach to organizational change and consists of three essential steps:

- gathering information about problems, concerns, and needed changes from the members of an organization;

- organizing this information in some meaningful way and sharing it with those involved in the change effort; and

- planning and carrying out specific actions to correct identified problems.

An organizational change program may go through repeated cycles of data gathering, information sharing, and action planning and implementation. The action research sequence often concludes with a follow-up evaluation of the implemented actions.

The strength of the action research approach to change lies in (1) its careful diagnosis of the current situation in the organization and (2) its involvement of employees in the change process. In other words, effective group or organizational change can occur only if those involved understand the current situation, including what tasks are done well and what tasks need to be improved. Moreover, employee involvement can spur change for at least two reasons. First, people are more likely to implement and support a change that they have helped create. Second, once managers and employees have identified the need for change and have widely shared this information, the need becomes difficult for people to ignore. The pressure for change thus comes from within the group, department, or organization, rather than from outside. Such internal pressure is a particularly powerful force for change.[33]

CHANGE MANAGEMENT

The major objective of planned organizational change is to alter the behavior of individuals within the organization. In the final analysis, organizations survive, grow, prosper, decline, or fail because of employee behaviors—the things that employees do or fail to do.

An example of the importance of changing employee behaviors occurred when the new CEO of an international bank announced a companywide change program. The bank's traditional hierarchical organization seemed ill-suited to respond to serious challenges stemming from deregulation in the United States and increased global competition. The only solution was a fundamental change in how the company operated. The CEO held a retreat with fifteen top executives of the bank. They carefully examined the organization's culture and purpose and drew up a new mission statement. Following the retreat, the bank recruited a new vice-president for human resources from another organization well known for its excellent management. In a quick succession of moves, the bank adopted a new organization design, performance appraisal system and compensation plan, and training programs. The CEO implemented quarterly attitude surveys to track the progress of the change program. All these steps would seem to represent a textbook example of successful organizational change. Unfortunately, there was one principal problem: The employees didn't buy into the change program, and two years after the CEO started it, virtually no changes in organizational behavior had occurred.[34] What went wrong?

The CEO and his top management team correctly identified the need for change. But they incorrectly assumed that they alone knew how best to proceed. They believed that simply adopting a new mission statement, new programs, and a new organization design would achieve the change they desired. However, unless employee behaviors actually change, new programs and structures probably will have little, if any, impact on organizational effectiveness—as the bank's management learned to its chagrin.

Behavior should be a primary target of planned organizational change. Change programs must have an effect on employee roles, responsibilities, and working relationships. At some fundamental level, all organizational change depends on changes in behavior. Using Figure 18.3 as an organizing framework, let's explore specific approaches to change that focus on people, culture, task, technology, design, and strategy.

■ CHANGING BEHAVIOR

Change programs focused on behavior (the people variable) tend to rely on active involvement and participation by many employees. Successfully changing behaviors can improve individual and group processes in decision making, problem identification, problem solving, communication, working relationships, and the like.

Four approaches to organizational change that initially focus on people are survey feedback, team building, process consultation, and quality of work life (QWL) programs.

Survey Feedback   **Survey feedback** consists of (1) collecting information (usually by questionnaire) from members of an organization or work group, (2) organizing the information into an understandable and useful form, and (3) feeding it back to the employees who provided it.[35] Some or all of the employees then use this information as a basis for planning actions to deal with specific issues and problems. Survey feedback typically follows the action research process. The primary objective of survey feedback is to improve the relationships among the members of groups or teams or between departments through the discussion of common problems, rather than to introduce a specific change, such as a new computer system. Survey feedback also is frequently used as a diagnostic tool to identify team, department, and organizational problems. Because of its value in organizational diagnosis, survey feedback often is utilized as part of large-scale, long-term change programs in combination with other approaches and techniques.

Team Building   **Team building** is a process by which members of a work group or team diagnose how they work together and plan changes to improve their effectiveness. Many different work groups comprise an organization, and much of its success depends on how effectively those groups and the people in them can work together.[36]

Effective team building often involves use of the action research process. Team building begins when members recognize a problem in group functioning for which this approach seems appropriate. An effective team can recognize barriers to its own effectiveness and design and take actions to remove them. During team building, members of the work group contribute information concerning their perceptions of issues, problems, and working relationships. They may gather information informally during group meetings or prior to meetings, using interviews or questionnaires. They then analyze the information and diagnose work problems. Using problem diagnosis as the starting point, members of the team plan specific actions and assign individuals to implement them. At some later stage, team members evaluate their plans and progress to determine whether their actions solved the problems identified. As team effectiveness grows, the potential impact on organizational performance increases. Another good way to define team building is that it consists of the activities designed to move the team up the performance curve shown in Figure 18.7.

About 20 percent of U.S. corporations are operating with self-managed teams, considered by many to be the best example of high-performance teams. These teams comprise perhaps 7 to 9 percent of all employees. Estimates are that some 40 to 50 percent of all employees will work in such teams in just a few years. At Chrysler Corporation, high-performance teams saved the firm's oldest plant in New Castle, Indiana, from almost certain closure. Chrysler's teams assign tasks, talk to customers, order repairs, and schedule their own work hours. Absenteeism and grievances have plummeted, defects per million parts made have dropped from 300 to 20, and production costs have shrunk. At Ford Motor Company, a group known as "Team Mustang" saved the Mustang model from extinction by developing a new version of the popular car in 25 percent less time and using 30 percent less money than required to introduce any other comparable new car in the automaker's history.[37]

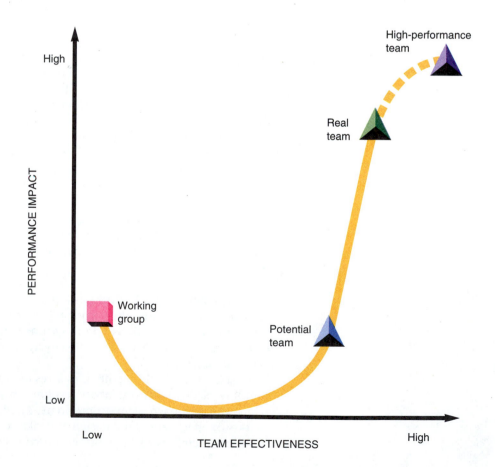

■ **FIGURE 18.7**

The Team Performance Curve

Source: Adapted from Katzenbach, J. R., and Smith, D. K. *The Wisdom of Teams*. Boston: Harvard Business School Press, 1993, 84.

Process Consultation   **Process consultation** is guidance provided by a consultant to help members of an organization perceive, understand, and act on process events that occur in the work environment.[38] Process events are the ways in which employees do their work, including the behavior of people at meetings; formal and informal encounters among employees at work; and, in general, any of the behaviors involved in performing a task.

Process consultation involves the use of a skilled third party, or facilitator, who may be an outsider to the organization (say, an external behavioral science consultant) or a member of the organization (say, a human resource professional or a manager skilled in process activities). Process consultation is typically used to address communication issues, leadership problems, decision-making processes, role problems, and conflict resolution. Process consultation is seldom the sole component of an organizational change program; rather, it usually is used in combination with other approaches.

Quality of Work Life Programs   **Quality of work life (QWL)** programs are activities undertaken by an organization to improve conditions that affect an employee's experience with an organization. Many QWL programs focus on security, safety and health, participation in decisions, opportunities to use and develop talents and skills, meaningful work, control over work time or place, protection from arbitrary or unfair treatment, and opportunities to satisfy social needs.[39] Such programs became popular in response to demands from employees for better working conditions. In addition, QWL programs have been undertaken to increase productivity and quality of output through greater involvement and participation by employees in decisions that affect their jobs.

Organizations increasingly are attempting to improve employee quality of work life through the use of alternative work schedules. **Alternative work schedules** might include flextime (giving employees some control over their own work schedules), part-time employment, job sharing (where two individuals share the same job, each working part of the day or week), or work at home. A survey of companies affiliated with the Conference Board found that 92 percent used flextime, 69 percent allowed compressed work schedules, 95 percent utilized part-time employees, 67 percent allowed some job sharing, and 76 percent had some employees who were allowed to do at least part of their jobs at home (called telecommuting).

Aetna Life and Casualty Company is using nearly all these alternative work schedule options with good results. Making alternative work schedules available allowed Aetna to retain some highly valued employees who otherwise would have quit. One Aetna manager said, "We're not doing flexible work scheduling to be nice, but because it makes business sense." Xerox shares that conclusion. After Xerox adopted flexible work schedules (employees have total freedom to set their own work hours), absenteeism fell by one-third, teamwork increased, and morale improved. Xerox feels that, in particular, productivity among dual-career couples with child-care problems has risen and that these employees also now report less job stress.[40]

◼ CHANGING CULTURE

Earlier, we explored changing organizational culture and pointed out just how difficult such changes can be (see Chapter 17). To begin with, there are problems just in assessing the culture accurately before any plans for changes can be developed. In addition, some aspects of culture (such as the deepest core values shared by employees) may be almost impossible to change. Despite these challenges, some organizations have successfully changed their cultures. How did they do it?

A detailed examination of cultural change, conducted by Trice and Beyer, suggests that the odds for success can be increased by giving attention to seven main issues.[41] First, *capitalize on dramatic opportunities.* The organization needs to take advantage of the moment when obvious problems or challenges that are not being met "open the door" to needed change. When Ford acquired Jaguar, obvious quality problems with the Jaguar automobile made justifying needed changes easier.

Second, *combine caution with optimism.* Managers and employees need to be optimistic with regard to the advantages of cultural change; otherwise they will be unwilling to make the attempt. Yet, because cultural change can have negative impacts, the organization needs to proceed with caution. Expectations for improvement must be positive, yet realistic.

Third, *understand resistance to cultural change.* Resistance to change needs to be diagnosed. Identifying and reducing sources of resistance is valuable in cultural change as well as in other change programs.

Fourth, *change many elements but maintain some continuity.* "Don't throw the baby out with the bathwater" is a common saying that sums up the importance of recognizing what is of value and retaining it. Hewlett-Packard successfully changed its culture as it grew and prospered, yet managed to retain a core of cultural ideas and beliefs that have served it well.

Fifth, *recognize the importance of implementation.* One survey indicated that over 90 percent of planned changes in strategy and culture were never fully implemented. A large percentage of failed change programs are failures of implementation rather than failures of ideas. Management needs to recognize that having a vision and a plan, although important, are only part of the battle. Planned changes must be carried through.

Sixth, *modify socialization tactics.* Socialization is the primary way that people learn about a culture. Thus changing socialization processes can be an effective approach to cultural change.

Finally, *find and cultivate innovative leadership.* Cultural change must begin at the top of the organization, and good leadership is crucial. When Lockheed got into serious trouble with its L-1011 jet airliner, an ineffective culture at its primary manufacturing facility was identified as a major part of the problem. The turnaround at Lockheed began with the appointment of Dale Daniels as vice-president of manufacturing at the L-1011 plant. Daniels brought a change in managerial philosophy that effectively changed the culture of the firm.

High Performance–High Commitment Work Systems   The goal of many cultural change efforts is to produce a "high-involvement" type of work culture. One example of this type of culture is known as a **high performance–high commitment (HP–HC) work system.**[42] These systems blend technology and teamwork to create a sense of ownership among employees while utilizing the most sophisticated work practices and technologies.

High performance–high commitment work systems have the following characteristics.

- *Delegation.* People who have the most relevant and timely information or the most appropriate skills for a task are given responsibility for decisions and actions.

■ *Teamwork across boundaries.* All employees in the organization are focused on the product and serving the customer for the product, rather than their function or department.

■ *Empowerment.* Everyone is expected to accept and exercise the responsibility necessary to do their jobs and help others accomplish theirs. Providing opportunities to be responsible empowers people—the opposite of limiting roles and contributions. No one feels free to say, It's not my job.

■ *Integration of people and technology.* People are in charge of the technology, instead of the technology being in charge of the people.

■ A *shared sense of purpose.* People in the work culture share a vision of the organization's purpose and the methods for accomplishing this purpose.[43]

An assumption underlying the HP–HC work system is that superior technology, efficient task design, matching organizational design and processes, good planning, and the like are necessary, but not sufficient, for high performance. Individuals and teams must be committed to make the technology, task design, structure, and strategy work. The HP–HC work system is designed to manage human, technological, and financial resources efficiently and to engage the talents and capacities of employees more fully.

Learning Organizations   A second popular goal of cultural change programs is to create an organization capable of adapting to changes in the external business environment through continual renewal of processes and practices.[44] The **learning organization** has a culture based on the notion that learning is central to success and effectiveness (see Table 18.1). This notion is similar to our earlier description of the goals of organization development (OD): creating adaptive organizations capable of repeatedly transforming and reinventing themselves as needed to remain effective. What does having an organization with this type of culture actually mean?

At Techtronics Corporation, a high-tech electronics firm, an important cultural value is a desire to learn from customers in order to meet their needs better. When a customer calls with a problem, the phone does not ring in some office devoted solely to public relations, but rather it rings on the shop floor. The manufacturing employees who actually worked on the product are the ones who take the call and respond to customer questions, suggestions, or concerns. Motorola is another firm committed to providing employees with continuous learning. At Motorola, new products are developed by cross-functional teams drawn from those responsible for designing, manufacturing, and marketing the product. In some respects, this approach initially takes more time. However, Motorola believes that it pays off in the long run as team members learn from each other and as they learn how to develop the *systems* needed to introduce successful products.[45]

■ CHANGING TASK AND TECHNOLOGY

Approaches to change focusing on the task emphasize modifying the work of individuals, groups, and teams. Approaches focusing on technology concentrate on the technological processes and tools used to perform the work. We examine task and technology together because several change approaches—such as job design, sociotechnical systems, quality circles, reengineering, and total quality management—often affect these areas simultaneously. As discussed earlier, the challenges of technological change increasingly are having an impact on organizations. Some of the concerns about technology are expressed in the following Technology in Practice selection.

TECHNOLOGY IN PRACTICE

The Technology Challenge

Hugh McColl is scared, and he doesn't like it one bit. This, after all, is the usually fearless chairman and chief executive of NationsBank Corporation, an ex-Marine who keeps a hand grenade in his office and who once told a takeover target to respond promptly, "or I will launch my missiles." This is the man who braved the scorn of his peers by predicting the wave of consolidation now sweeping the banking industry—and followed up by building his own bank into one of the country's powerhouses.

So what fills him with trepidation? In a word, technology. McColl believes that technological change threatens to remake the banking industry. But how swiftly, and in what form, these changes will come is still anyone's guess. And that's what is bugging McColl. He is convinced that if he makes the wrong bet, or the right bet at the wrong time, the company he nursed from a regional bank to a player on the national stage will fade into obscurity. "This thing," he says, referring to technology, "is like a tidal wave. If you fail in the game, you're going to be dead."

Across the country, thousands of chief executives in industries ranging from banking to publishing to retailing to manufacturing are similarly scared. Once, mastering technology meant learning to use a personal computer and figuring out how to tweak productivity gains. Suddenly, the march of technological change means rethinking corporate strategies. Products and delivery systems face drastic changes. Competitors emerge from unexpected places. And the internet is the wild card. Here are two examples—one successful and one not—of companies that faced rapid technological change.

Philips Electronics NV attempted to introduce a combination compact disk and interactive game player that attached to a TV set. It was a game player, a teaching tool, and a music system rolled into one. It even had a port that could provide access to the internet. But, five years after its introduction, the product has almost disappeared in the United States, rendered obsolete by rapid advances in personal computers and a new generation of lightning fast game machines. Some estimates are that Philips lost more than $1 billion dollars by investing its hopes too heavily in a technology that few customers easily understood. The product was so complicated that it required a thirty-minute demonstration, something few retailers or customers liked. Critics complained that the item was overpriced and that sufficient software wasn't available. Most important, rapidly changing technology quickly brought superior products to market.

A more positive outcome in the technology wars comes from Fidelity Investments. Fidelity manages more than $400 billion in assets, a portfolio that tripled in size between 1990 and 1996. Investment management firms send a huge volume of mail to their customers—prospectuses, promotional materials, personal statements, and the like. When its mailing facilities in Dallas and Boston proved to be inadequate, Fidelity built a new, state-of-the-art printing and mailing facility in Covington, Kentucky. Drawing on tracking and storage techniques used by

—Continued

TECHNOLOGY IN PRACTICE—*Continued*

manufacturers, including extensive use of robotics to store and retrieve spare parts, the nation's largest mutual fund company has reinvented the inglorious task of sorting, stuffing and stamping mail. With cutting-edge technology, Fidelity has changed processing mail from a back-room function to a core business designed to satisfy and retain customers. When a customer calls to ask for material, it will be in the mail within one day.[46]

Job Design   As a change approach, **job design** represents a deliberate, planned restructuring of the way work is performed in order to increase employee motivation, involvement, and efficiency—and ultimately to improve performance. Recall that job design encompasses a group of specific organizational change techniques, including job engineering, job rotation, job enlargement, job enrichment, and the redesign of core task characteristics (see Chapter 15).

Each technique is an effective approach to organizational change under certain conditions. However, managers sometimes use specific job design approaches inappropriately. For example, job enrichment programs may fail if managers wrongly assume that all employees want enriched work and do not allow for differences in employee needs and values. Job design techniques perhaps are most successful in the context of a comprehensive organizational change program that examines the complex fit among the tasks to be performed, the types of technology used, the design and culture of the organization or team, and the nature and characteristics of the people doing the work.

Sociotechnical Systems   The **sociotechnical systems** (STS) approach simultaneously focuses on changing both the technical and social aspects of the organization to optimize their relationship and thus increase organizational effectiveness.[47] The STS approach regards the organization as more than just a technical system for making products and providing services. Ultimately, the organization is a collection of human beings—a social system. Changes made in the technical system affect the social fabric of the organization. Thus managing organizational change effectively means dealing with both the social and technical aspects of that change.

Sociotechnical approaches to organizational change usually incorporate a major redesign of the way work is done (the task variable), in addition to emphasizing technological and social issues (the technology and people variables). We described the sociotechnical systems approach to job design in detail in Chapter 15.

We have discussed self-managed teams throughout this book. From the perspective of organizational change, the idea of autonomous, or self-managed, work groups is a major contribution of sociotechnical systems theory. **Autonomous groups** are self-managed teams that plan their work, control its pace and quality, and make many of the decisions traditionally reserved to management.[48] The STS approach involves redesigning work groups to give them as much control as possible over virtually all the resources and competencies needed to manufacture a specific product or deliver a specific service to a customer. The role of management in STS is to ensure that teams have sufficient resources to accomplish their tasks.

Quality Circles   **Quality circles** are work groups, generally containing less than a dozen volunteers from the same work area, who meet regularly to monitor and solve job-related quality or production problems.[49] Quality circles also may be utilized to improve working conditions, increase the level of employee involvement and commitment, and encourage employee self-development. In these instances, they frequently are an important component of QWL programs. Adapted initially from Japanese quality control practices, their use spread rapidly in the United States.

Quality circles typically have a narrower focus than many of the other change techniques described. They also differ from other approaches in that management retains more control over the activities of the employees than is possible, or desirable, in most of the other approaches. Although quality circles may make a contribution relatively quickly, sustaining an initial success over a period of time requires considerable energy and creating new challenges to maintain employee interest. Quality circles may not fit well into an organization's culture and are not likely to move the organization toward a highly participative culture if other changes are not made at the same time. Quality circles appear to cope successfully with only a limited range of problems; accurate diagnosis is essential to ensure that the problems facing the organization can be best addressed by this approach.

Reengineering   Reengineering is another term that has appeared frequently throughout this book. It also represents a major change approach currently popular with organizations. **Reengineering,** sometimes called process redesign, is a fundamental rethinking and radical redesign of business processes to reduce costs and improve quality, service, and speed.[50] Reengineering represents a more radical approach to change than do most of the other methods discussed. During reengineering, the most fundamental ideas and assumptions of the organization are challenged. Recall that reengineering begins with no assumptions and asks fundamental questions such as: Why does the organization do what it does? and Why does it do it the way that it does?

At GE, chairman Jack Welch compared his company to a 100-year-old attic that collected a lot of useless junk over the years. Welch views reengineering as the process of cleaning all the junk out of the attic, and GE calls its reengineering activities "workout."[51]

When an organization reengineers its business processes, the following changes typically occur.

- Work groups change from functional departments to process teams.
- Individual jobs change from simple to multidimensional tasks.
- People's roles change from being controlled to being empowered to make decisions.
- Performance appraisal changes from measuring activities (attending meetings or arriving at work on time) to measuring results (customer satisfaction, costs, and performance).
- Managers change from supervisors to coaches.
- Organization designs change from tall to flat hierarchies.[52]

Reengineering shares many of the objectives of other change approaches. Despite these similarities, reengineering programs (if they truly are reengineering) represent a dramatic and revolutionary, rather than an evolutionary or gradually transformational, approach to organizational change.

Total Quality Management   **Total quality management** (TQM) focuses on meeting or exceeding customer expectations. Quality ultimately is defined by the customer. When an organization achieves "total quality," all activities and processes are designed and carried out to meet all customer requirements while reducing both the time and cost required to provide them.[53]

Total quality management is partly technical. Just-in-time (JIT) inventory systems, for example, frequently are utilized by TQM organizations.[54] It also is partly cultural—the shared values must emphasize quality, and employees must be empowered to carry out needed changes. The concept of **continuous improvement** is central to TQM. One-time programs or "quick-fix" solutions for productivity or quality problems are unacceptable.

A focus on quality and continuous improvement is crucial to competing effectively in the global economy. The U.S. government created the Malcolm Baldrige National Quality Award to honor organizations that attain "world-class" quality in their products, services, and operations. One winner of the award, Motorola, provides a good example of the payoff from emphasizing quality. The company is the market leader in cellular phones, pagers, two-way radios, and some types of microprocessors. It is beating Japanese rivals by manufacturing consumer electronics with better quality at lower prices. Part of its strategy is a TQM program that earned the company a Baldrige award and, more important, has reduced its defect rate in manufacturing by an astounding 99 percent. This reduction in defects, in turn, generated savings currently running at about $900 million a year.[55]

■ CHANGING ORGANIZATION DESIGN

Organizationwide change programs frequently are aimed at changing organization design. Approaches to change that focus on the design variable involve redefining positions or roles and relationships among positions and redesigning department, division, and/or organization structure. Unfortunately, implementing design or structural change has sometimes been used as an excuse for organizations simply to downsize their work forces without recognizing why more adaptive organization designs are needed. Some of the negative consequences of poorly thought out organizational changes are presented in the following Managing in Practice piece.

MANAGING IN PRACTICE

Dumbsizing

Corporate America loves to talk about the nimbleness and efficiency gained by restructuring. Pressured by low-cost foreign competitors that threaten to snare their customers and by Wall Street's demands for quick returns, executives have taken to cutting costs by reducing the number of employees with fervor. Despite warnings about downsizing becoming dumbsizing, many companies continue to make flawed decisions—hasty across-the- board cuts—that come back to haunt them, on the bottom line, in negative public relations, in strained relationships with customers and suppliers, and in demoralized employees.   —*Continued*

MANAGING IN PRACTICE—*Continued*

At AT&T, CEO Robert Allen has long been one of America's most admired executives. He has guided the world's most powerful telecommunications company through wrenching changes, transforming a staid monopoly into a competitive powerhouse. Now, however, in the twilight of his career, Allen came under attack when he announced the pending layoff of an additional 50,000 employees, layoffs that presumably would not be necessary if previous reorganizations had been successful. To critics Allen now appears to be an uncaring and unaccountable chief whose numerous restructurings wiped out $15 billion in earnings during the last decade.

Eastman Kodak Company expected to save thousands of dollars a year when it laid off Maryellen Ford in a companywide downsizing. But within weeks, Kodak was paying more for the same work. Ford, a computer-aided designer, was snapped up by a local contractor that gets much of its work from Kodak. Ford says, "I took the project I was working on at Kodak and finished it here." But instead of paying her $15 an hour, Kodak now pays the contractor $65 an hour.

Cutbacks that result in poor customer service can also lead to problems. Nynex Corporation was recently ordered by New York's Public Service Commission to rebate $50 million to customers because its reduced staff fell behind in responding to problems. Nynex has hired back hundreds of employees including managers already receiving pensions. Even greater than the rehiring expense is the blight on Nynex's reputation for customer service. "Their past reputation for customer service is their key competitive advantage," says Joe Kraemer, a management consultant at A. T. Kearney. "They've put all that at risk, just to gain a few cents per share in a given quarter. It's just plain dumb."

Even reengineering guru Michael Hammer has been humbled by the negative results of some restructuring and downsizing stemming from reengineering. He states that he and other leaders in the reengineering movement sometimes forgot about people. "I wasn't smart enough about that," he says, "I was reflecting my engineering background and was insufficiently appreciative of the human dimension. I've learned that's critical."[56]

As organizations grow increasingly complex and face the challenge of managing constant change, they often need new ways of organizing their activities. They particularly need more flexibility and adaptive capabilities than the traditional mechanistic system, with its rigid hierarchy and standardized procedures, allows. Here, we explore three forms of organizational design that characterize flexible, adaptive organizations: collateral organization, matrix organization, and network organization.

Collateral Organization   A **collateral organization** is a parallel, coexisting organization that can be used to supplement an existing formal organization.[57] The collateral, or parallel, organization utilizes groups of people outside normal communication and authority channels to identify and solve difficult problems that the formal organization may be unwilling or unable to solve. A collateral organization has norms—ways of working together, making decisions, and solving problems—that are different from those of the rest of the organization. However, the collateral organization requires no new people, is carefully linked to the formal organization, and coexists with it. Collateral organizations have the following characteristics.

- All communication channels are open and connected. Managers and employees freely communicate without being restricted to the formal channels of the organizational hierarchy.

- Relevant information about problems and issues is exchanged rapidly and completely. The outputs of the collateral structure are ideas, solutions to problems, and innovation.

- The norms in use encourage critical questioning and careful analysis of goals, assumptions, methods, alternatives, and evaluation criteria.

- Managers can approach and enlist others in the organization to help solve a problem; they are not restricted to using their subordinates in the formal organizational hierarchy.

- Mechanisms are developed to link the collateral and formal organization.[58]

Matrix Organization   Many organizations have turned to a matrix design to address the limitations of mechanistic or bureaucratic structures. Recall that a **matrix organization** represents a balance between organizing resources by product or function (see Chapter 16).

A mutually beneficial relationship often exists between the matrix form of organization and the capacity to change. For example, many features of OD programs, such as an emphasis on collaborative behavior and the effective use of teams, also are important for implementing a matrix structure with its decentralized decision making and extensive use of temporary task forces and teams. In general, the matrix form helps create a culture receptive to organizational improvement efforts.

Changing an organization to a matrix form is never easy. Often, managers need a change strategy focusing on people to facilitate the transition. For example, team building has helped organizations introduce matrix designs successfully. One senior executive put it this way: "The challenge is not so much to build a matrix structure as it is to create a matrix in the minds of our managers."[59]

Network Organization   The **network organization,** as described in Chapter 16, is a complex mosaic of lateral communication, decision-making, and control processes. Although a network organization might have an organization chart showing the typical hierarchical authority and communication relationships, such a chart cannot begin to describe the reality of this complex organizational form. Figure 18.8 shows three basic types of network organizations.

The components business of General Motors represents an internal network. Corporate headquarters serves a "brokerage function" that coordinates the activities of eight components producing divisions. The separate divisions sell some of their products on the open market. In contrast, the Bavarian Motor Works (BMW) is a stable network. Every part of the BMW automobile is a candidate for outsourcing and some 55 to 75 percent of the total cost of the car is in outside parts. Even more decentralized is Lewis Galoob Toys, which operates as a dynamic network. It has only about 100 permanent employees, who run the core business. Most of its products are invented, designed, and engineered outside the firm. Galoob also contracts for manufacturing and packaging with other organi-

■ FIGURE 18.8   Examples of Network Designs

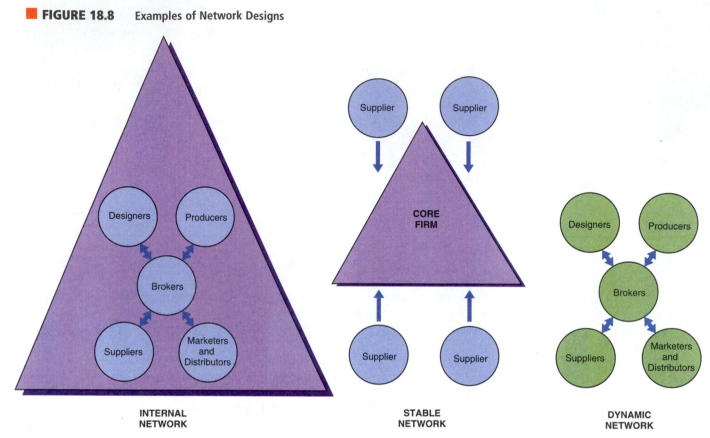

Source: Snow, C. C., Miles, R. E., and Coleman, H. J. Managing 21st century network organizations. *Organizational Dynamics,* Winter 1992, 12. Reprinted by permission of publisher, from Organizational Dynamics, Winter/1992 © 1992. American Management Association, New York. All rights reserved.

zations. Thus it operates as a "broker," coordinating the activities of independent specialty firms.[60]

The dynamic network design shown in Figure 18.8 is also called a virtual organization. A **virtual organization** is defined as a temporary network of independent companies linked by information technology to share skills, costs, and access to customers.[61] Galoob Toys clearly fits the definition of a virtual organization. AeroTech Service Group, a spin-off from McDonnell Douglas, is another example. AeroTech operates virtual factories where several thousand individuals, including outside suppliers, designers, and customers are linked to factory operations through sophisticated information technology networks. Virtual organizations obviously demand new competencies of managers and employees. Managers are challenged to build relationships, negotiate win–win deals, be able to find competent venture partners, and provide employees with the appropriate balance of freedom and control. Employees, in turn, must possess or gain greater skills and knowledge in order to function effectively in this work environment.

Network organizations share some features with both matrix and collateral organizations, yet place more emphasis on sophisticated information technologies to coordinate activities and perform work. Managers in a network organization function much like switchboard operators in terms of coordination and control. They can pull together temporary teams of employees to bring expertise to bear on projects and concerns as needed. The collaborative behaviors and attitudes characterizing the network organization are similar to those typical of the high performance–high commitment work system described earlier. Many adaptive organizations use some version of network design, especially global organizations that need the flexibility to function effectively in the international arena.

■ CHANGING STRATEGY

Issues of strategic change need to be addressed in comprehensive organizational change programs. At its most basic level, a strategy is a *plan*—an intended course of action to attain organizational goals. **Strategic change** is planned organizational change designed to alter the organization's intended courses of action to attain its goals. Strategic change may include assessment and redefinition of the goals themselves.

BankAmerica Corporation made one of the most dramatic turnarounds in U.S. banking history after sustaining almost $2 billion in losses, in large part by adopting a new strategic vision when the old one no longer worked. BankAmerica reassessed its entire business structure and approach to banking. The firm developed new strategic objectives that included concentrating on providing banking services to the western United States, and reducing its banking services in other regions of the country. Had BankAmerica attempted minor, piecemeal changes, rather than a comprehensive organizationwide change in strategy, culture, and design, the firm probably would not have survived as an independent organization.[62]

A good example of a strategic change program is provided by the process of **open systems planning.** Open systems planning is designed to help an organization systematically assess its environment and develop a strategic response to it. It consists of the following steps.

- Assess the external environment in terms of its expectations and demands on the organization's behavior.
- Assess the organization's current response to these environmental demands.
- Identify the organization's core mission.
- Create a realistic scenario of future environmental demands and organizational responses.
- Create an ideal scenario of future environmental demands and organizational responses.
- Compare the present with the ideal future and prepare an action plan for reducing the discrepancy.[63]

ETHICAL ISSUES IN ORGANIZATIONAL CHANGE

Serious ethical issues may arise in any organizational change program, no matter how carefully thought out and well-managed it might be. Certainly one of the most wrenching changes that organizations can undergo is the layoff of employees. This situation is fraught with potential ethical dilemmas, as illustrated in the following Ethics in Practice feature.

ETHICS IN PRACTICE

Layoff Ethics

Tom Derkas sat at his desk in his crowded office. The surface of every desk and table was piled high with files, catalogs, and promotional calendars waiting to be sold. He knew that his business was failing, but was reluctant to pronounce it dead.

It had been two years since he founded Ad World, an advertising specialties company. Like any other entrepreneur, Derkas went into the venture thinking only of the upside: creating a good working environment, developing a positive relationship with customers, and establishing a business that would generate a decent income. At first all went smoothly. But unexpected problems came up, revenues did not grow fast enough to cover costs, and credit from the banks began to dry up. Despite its best efforts, Ad World would have to be shut down or, at a minimum, operate with a skeleton crew while Derkas tried to build up the business. The worst thing about reaching that conclusion, thought Derkas, was the realization that it meant he would have to utter the word "layoff."

If Derkas followed conventional wisdom, he would (1) try to keep employees in the dark as long as possible about what is going to happen and (2) force employees to leave their place of employment, physically, within an hour after being laid off. In contrast, a growing number of managers and owners are ignoring traditional ways of letting employees go, for both ethical and financial reasons.

Gunn Denhart, owner of the children's mail-order clothing company Hanna Anderson, gave the employees in her distribution center eighteen months notice that the plant would be moving from the company's headquarters in Portland, Oregon, to Kentucky. The firm didn't have an immediate defection of key personnel, and by the time the transition took effect, employees had found new jobs, retired, or transferred to the new location.

Nelson Carlo, owner of Abbott Products in Chicago, employs some 300 people in a small plant that manufactures products for the defense industry. Carlo thinks that the idea that employees can be fooled about pending layoffs is absurd. "Employees know when new orders are not coming in," he says. Because of the cyclical nature of the defense business, Abbott Products has a lot of experience with laying off and rehiring the same people. Its goal is to communicate openly at all times and to treat its employees with great dignity and respect. Carlo's experience is that "the loyal ones will stay loyal—the transient ones will leave anyway on the basis of the slightest rumor." And although the former employee may be out of sight, what he or she is saying about the employer is still alive and well in the industry and around town.[64]

Managers and employees need to be aware of potential ethical issues in four main areas: change approach selection, change target selection, managerial responsibilities, and manipulation.[65]

When choosing the change approach or combination of approaches deemed best for the situation, managers and employees should recognize the ethical issues involved in selecting the criteria to be used. Does the manager or change agent have a vested interest in using a particular technique so that other alternatives might not receive a fair hearing? Do individuals involved in the organizational diagnosis have biases that might predetermine the problems identified and thus influence the change approach chosen?

Selection of the change target raises ethical concerns about participation in the change program. What is to be the target of change? Which individuals, teams, or departments of the organization will the change effort focus on? Which members of the organization participate in diagnosing, planning, and implementing the change and to what degree? Who will make this determination? Issues of power and political behavior raise serious ethical concerns when managers attempt to make inappropriate changes or choices concerning what is to be changed that overstep the boundaries of their legitimate roles. To what extent can managers make choices about changing the behaviors of employees, and where should the line be drawn in this regard?

A major ethical concern in the area of managerial responsibility involves whose goals and values are to guide the change effort. The reason is that organizational change is never value neutral. The value systems of managers and employees always underlie assumptions about what the organization should be doing. Ethical concerns arise if managers involved in the change process fail to recognize the potential problems associated with incompatible goals and values held by the organization's members. Whose vision guides the change? Whose values influence the adoption of goals and methods chosen to accomplish them?

Finally, the possibility of manipulation also raises the question of power in the change process. Making changes in organizations without some employees feeling manipulated in some way is difficult. Often the organization needs to make changes that do, in fact, result in some individuals or groups being worse off after the change than they were before. Ethical issues concern the degree of openness surrounding planned changes. To what extent should the organization disclose all aspects of the change in advance? To what degree do employees have the right to participate in, or at least be aware of, changes that affect them, even indirectly?

These questions are not easily addressed. Hence managers and employees need some basis for recognizing the potential ethical concerns involved in organizational change so that fair and informed choices can be made. As a starting point, organizations need to be sensitive to the probability that ethical problems will emerge during planned change programs.

CHAPTER SUMMARY

A rapidly changing environment places many demands on managers and employees, including the need to plan for and manage organizational change effectively. Pressures for change stem from globalization, increasingly heavy use of computers and information technology, and the changing nature of the work force.

Planned organizational change attempts to alter the design and processes of an organization to make it more effective and efficient. For planned change programs to be effective, employees must be aware of the need for change, believe in the potential value of the changes, and be willing to change their behaviors. Typically, change is also more effective when it is organizationwide. The systems model of change—focusing on the variables of people, culture, task, technology, design, and strategy—provides a useful way to conceptualize organizationwide change. An accurate, valid diagnosis of current organizational functioning, activities, and problems is an essential foundation for effective organizational change. The readiness for change, availability of resources for change, and possible resistance to change are among the factors that should be diagnosed.

Individuals may resist change because of their perceptions or personalities. In addition, habitual behaviors, fear of the unknown, economic insecurities, and threats to established power and influence may generate further resistance to change. Organizational resistance to change may be caused by organizational structure and culture, resource limitations, fixed investments not easily altered, and interorganizational agreements. Force field analysis can help managers and employees diagnose and overcome resistance to change. Such resistance can be reduced through good communications and high levels of employee involvement in the change process.

Organization development (OD) is a field of applied behavioral science that focuses on understanding and managing organizational change. Successful change programs often utilize an action research sequence of information gathering, feedback, and action planning.

Managers and employees must understand the likely effects of various change approaches and carefully match change programs to the problems they are intended to solve. When the initial focus of the change effort is on people, managers might choose to use survey feedback, team building, process consultation, or quality of work life programs. Comprehensive change often means that the culture of the organization must be considered. Although cultural change is difficult, the probability of success can be increased by careful attention to some key issues. Creating a high performance–high commitment work system or a learning organization often are goals of cultural change efforts. When the initial focus is on task or technology, managers typically utilize job design, sociotechnical systems, quality circles, reengineering, or total quality management. The last two may involve significant changes in organizational culture. Approaches to change that focus on organization design might include creating more adaptive organizational structures, such as collateral, matrix, or network designs. Strategic change often is the focus of organizationwide change efforts. Open systems planning is one method of achieving strategic change. No approach to organizational change is likely to be successful unless it addresses several, if not all, of the people, culture, task, technology, design, and strategy variables. Comprehensive organizational change programs, regardless of their initial focus, often make simultaneous changes in several aspects of the organization. In practice, the approaches presented in this chapter are commonly used in combination to manage organizational change.

Managers and employees need to be aware of and knowledgeable about potential ethical issues that can arise during organizational change. Ethical issues may emerge during selection of the change approach, selection of the change targets, managerial responsibilities for the goals selected, and potential manipulation of employees.

KEY TERMS AND CONCEPTS

Action research	Design variable	Job design
Alternative work schedules	Force field analysis	Learning organization
Autonomous groups	Globalization	Matrix organization
Collateral organization	High performance–high	Network organization
Contingency work force	commitment (HP–HC) work	Open systems planning
Continuous improvement	system	Organization development
Culture variable	Information technology	Organizational diagnosis

People variable
Planned organizational change
Pressures for change
Process consultation
Quality circles
Quality of work life
Quality of work life (QWL)
    programs

Reengineering
Resistance to change
Sociotechnical systems
Strategic change
Strategy variable
Systems model of change
Survey feedback
Task variable

Team building
Technology variable
Total quality management
Virtual organization
Virtual reality

DISCUSSION QUESTIONS

1. What are some of the pressures for change at your college or university? Explain. (You might consider funding, student life, curriculum development, or similar types of pressures.)

2. Use Figure 18.5 to analyze and identify the primary types of resistance to change that exist at your college or university. Which seem the most important. Why?

3. Based on your own work experience, use force field analysis to analyze a situation that needed changing. Start by describing the setting. What were the main pressures and types of resistance to change operating?

4. Use the three-step process of unfreezing, moving, and refreezing to describe some major behavioral change from your own experience.

5. Based on your own work experience, analyze a change situation in terms of the readiness for change on the part of the individuals involved.

6. What are six primary systems variables that affect an organization's ability to change? Describe them and give an example to show how they are interrelated.

7. What does the process of action research involve? Suggest a situation in which it might be used effectively.

8. Describe an ideal "adaptive organization" and then describe an organization with which you are familiar. Compare the two descriptions and suggest how the real organization could become more like your ideal of an adaptive, flexible organization.

9. Can employees always have a high level of participation in organizational change programs? Why or why not?

10. Based on your own experience, describe an organization, group, or team that needed to change. Which of the change approaches presented would you have used? Why?

■ Developing Competencies

Self-Insight: Measuring Support for Change

Instructions

This questionnaire is designed to help you understand the inherent level of support or opposition to change within an organization. Please respond to each item according to how true it is in terms of an organization for which you are currently working or used to work. Circle the appropriate number on the scale that follows the item.

Usually Not True	Somewhat Not True	Somewhat Untrue	Neutral	Somewhat True	Usually True	True
1	2	3	4	5	6	7

Values and Visions

1. Do people throughout the organization share values or visions?

| 1 | 2 | 3 | 4 | 5 | 6 | 7 |

History of Change

2. Does the organization have a good track record in implementing change smoothly?

| 1 | 2 | 3 | 4 | 5 | 6 | 7 |

Cooperation and Trust

3. Is there a lot of cooperation and trust throughout the organization (as opposed to animosity)?

| 1 | 2 | 3 | 4 | 5 | 6 | 7 |

Culture

4. Does the organization's culture support risk taking (as opposed to being highly bureaucratic and rule bound)?

| 1 | 2 | 3 | 4 | 5 | 6 | 7 |

Resilience

5. Are people able to handle change (as opposed to being worn out from recent, unsettling changes)?

| 1 | 2 | 3 | 4 | 5 | 6 | 7 |

Punishments and Rewards

6. Does the organization reward people who take part in change efforts (as opposed to subtly punishing those who take the time off other work to get involved)?

| 1 | 2 | 3 | 4 | 5 | 6 | 7 |

Respect and Status

7. Will people be able to maintain respect and status when the change is implemented (as opposed to losing these as a result of the change)?

| 1 | 2 | 3 | 4 | 5 | 6 | 7 |

Status Quo

8. Will the change be mild (and not cause a major disruption of the status quo)?

| 1 | 2 | 3 | 4 | 5 | 6 | 7 |

Interpretation

Even though 1, 2, and 3 should be considered low scores; 4 and 5, mid-range scores; and 6 and 7, high scores—these are just numbers. One person's "5" is another person's "3." The value lies in understanding the meanings that people attach to their scores.

Generally, low to mid-range scores should be cause for concern. Lower scores indicate fertile soil for the growth of resistance.

Values and Visions

Low scores may indicate that values may be in conflict and that individuals and groups may not perceive any common ground. This situation is serious and almost guarantees that any major change will be resisted unless people learn how to build a shared set of values. In contrast, low scores may indicate a communication problem. In some organizations, values and visions remain secret, with people not knowing where the organization is headed. Although this communication problem needs to be solved, it may not indicate deeper potential resistance.

History of Change

Low scores indicate a strong likelihood that a change will be resisted with great force. Those who want the change will need to demonstrate repeatedly that they are serious this time. People are likely to be very skeptical, so persistence will be crucial.

Cooperation and Trust

Low scores should be taken seriously. Building support for any major change without some degree of trust is difficult, if not impossible. The opposite of trust is fear, so a low score indicates not just the absence of trust but the presence of fear.

Culture

Mid-range to low scores indicate that people may have difficulty carrying out changes even though they support the changes. They are saying that the systems and procedures in the organization hinder change. The change agents must be willing to examine these deeper systemic issues.

Resilience

Low scores probably indicate that people are burned out. Even though they may see the need for change, they may have little strength to give to the effort. Two important questions should be asked:

- Is this change really necessary at this time?
- If it is, how can the organizations support people so that the change causes minimal disruption?

Punishments and Rewards

Low scores indicate strong potential resistance. Who in their right minds would support something that they knew would harm them? If the respondents' perceptions are accurate, the change agents must find a way to move forward with the change *and find ways to make it rewarding for others.* If the low scores indicate a misperception, the change agents must let people know why they are misinformed. This message will likely need to be communicated repeatedly (especially if trust is low as well).

Respect and Status

Low scores indicate that change agents must find ways to make this a win–win situation.

Status Quo

Low scores indicate that people regard the potential change as very disruptive and stressful. The more involved people are in the change process, the less resistance they are likely to experience. Most often, people resist change when they feel out of control.[66]

Organizational Insight: Planned Change at the Piedmont Corporation

The Piedmont Corporation produces and markets a variety of computer products for the global market. In order to compete in this industry, firms need to introduce new products rapidly to meet changing customer demand. This requires close coordination among different functional departments, including research and development, marketing, production, and sales. For major new products, Piedmont creates special task forces responsible for coordinating the different contributions needed to develop, produce, and sell the product. Each task force is headed by a product manager and includes representatives from the different functional departments.

Stan Ledford headed the Omega task force, which was in the early stages of developing a plan for introducing the new Omega word processor. The task force was just starting its activities and had held four half-day meetings since its inception about a month earlier. Stan felt frustrated by the progress of these meetings and attributed these feelings to members' inability to work well together. They frequently interrupted each other and strayed from the agenda that Stan gave out at the start of each meeting. They also had forceful yet divergent opinions on how the Omega should be rolled out, and they had difficulty making even minor decisions. In talking these problems over with a close friend and fellow product manager, Stan was advised that members of his division's human resources department might be able to help. He was quickly put in touch with Sue Srebla, an internal consultant for Piedmont who specialized in organization development. Sue suggested that the two of them meet and explore Stan's problems and determine whether Sue (or someone else) might help to resolve them.

At the meeting, Stan shared his ideas about the task force's problems. Sue listened attentively, periodically asking questions to clarify what Stan was saying. She then talked about her experience helping groups to solve such problems and tentatively outlined a team-building strategy for Stan's consideration. The strategy would be aimed at helping team members to examine their meetings and task interactions and to devise ways of improving them. Sue would facilitate this process by interviewing team members about their perceptions of the problems and feeding the data back to members at a special meeting. Sue would help members analyze the interview data and devise appropriate solutions. Sue suggested that Stan should take an active leadership role in the team building and that team members should be involved in deciding whether to proceed with the team building and whether to use Sue as their consultant. Stan agreed to put this issue on the agenda for the team's next meeting and asked Sue to attend to answer questions and to establish relations with members.

At the team's next meeting, Stan explained his frustration with the group's progress and his desire to do something constructive about it. He described his meeting with Sue and outlined the team-building proposal as well as Sue's expertise in this area. Members were encouraged to ask questions and to share their reactions. This led to a spirited discussion about the need for good task interactions among group members. It also led to sharing their expectations about Sue's role in the team building as well as her expectations of members' roles. All members agreed to try the team building, and they set a date for the interviews and the subsequent feedback and problem-solving meeting.

Over the next week, Sue conducted a one-hour interview with each member of the Omega task force. Although she asked several questions, they were aimed at three major areas: things the team did well, things that impeded task performance, and suggestions for improvement. Sue summarized the interview data under those three headings and placed them on large sheets of newsprint that could be affixed to the walls of the meeting room. Only general themes appeared on the newsprint in order to preserve the anonymity of members' responses. Members could choose to be as open as they wanted at the feedback meeting. On the evening before the meeting, Sue shared the summarized data with Stan so that he would be prepared to lead the meeting and to help the group address important issues.

The feedback session started with members setting expectations for the meeting and agreeing to share perceptions openly with a spirit of constructive problem solving. Sue briefly reviewed the major themes on the newsprint and encouraged members to elaborate on their responses and to share opinions about the underlying causes of the problems. Several strengths of the team were identified, including member's expertise, willingness to work hard, and fierce loyalty to the product. Among the impediments to team performance were members' lack of input into the agenda for meetings, Stan's laissez-faire leadership style, and one or two members' domination of the meetings.

Members engaged in an open discussion of the feedback and ended the meeting with concrete suggestions for improvement. These included setting clearer parameters for group decision making, allowing members to gain greater involvement in setting the agenda, and paying more attention to members' interactions and to how the group is functioning. Sue provided conceptual input about the role of group norms in determining members' behaviors, and the group decided to list norms that it would like to operate under. Members also agreed to set aside some time at the end of each meeting to review how well their behaviors matched those norms. This would enable the group to detect ongoing problems and to solve them. At the end of the feedback session, the group thanked Sue for the help and asked whether she would be willing to provide further assistance if new problems emerged that the group could not handle. Sue assented to this request and ended this cycle of consulting with the Omega task force.

Over the next few months, Stan and his team implemented most of the suggestions from the feedback session. Although they had some problems taking time to assess their norms at each meeting, members gradually saw the benefits of doing this and made it a regular part of meetings. Periodically, the team encountered new problems that were difficult to deal with, such as bringing new members on board, and asked Sue for help. Her inputs helped team members solve their own problems, and with time, the team called on her less and less. Although far from perfect, the Omega team was judged by Piedmont executives to be one of its most effective new-product task forces.[67]

Questions

1. Using the force field analysis techniques discussed in the chapter, analyze this case. Be specific about the pressures for change and the resistance to change that seem to be operating in this situation. Identify the types of pressure and resistance that are likely to be the strongest.

2. Use the systems model of change to identify key variables that might be changed in order to increase the overall effectiveness of Piedmont Corporation.

3. Describe the readiness for change that seems to be exhibited by individuals in this case.

4. Would you describe the change approach in use as action research? Why or why not?

REFERENCES

1. Adapted from a story posted on a computer bulletin board and reprinted on the Internet. Author unknown.

2. Greenwood, R., and Hinings, C. R. Understanding radical organizational change. *Academy of Management Review,* 1996, 21, 1022–1054; Kanter, R. M., Stein, B. A., and Jick, T. D. *The Challenge of Organizational Change.* New York: Free Press, 1992; Van de Ven, A. H., and Poole, M. S. Explaining development and change in organizations. *Academy of Management Review,* 1995, 20, 510–540; Woodman, R. W., and Pasmore, W. A. (eds.), *Research in Organizational Change and Development,* vol. 9. Greenwich, Conn.: JAI Press, 1996.

3. Hammer, M., and Champy, J. *Reengineering the Corporation.* New York: Harper Business, 1993; *High Performance Work Practices and Firm Performance.* Washington, D. C.: U.S. Department of Labor, 1993; Neal, J. A., and Tromley, C. L. From incremental change to retrofit: Creating high-performance work systems. *Academy of Management Executive,* February 1995, 42–53; Rao, R. M. The struggle to create an organization for the 21st century. *Fortune,* April 3, 1995, 90–99.

4. Offermann, L. R., and Gowing, M. K. Organizations of the future. *American Psychologist,* 1990, 45, 95–108; Stewart, T. A. Welcome to the revolution. *Fortune,* December 13, 1993, 66–80.

5. Griffin, R. W., and Pustay, M. W. *International Business: A Managerial Perspective.* Reading, Mass.: Addison-Wesley, 1996; Overholt, W. H. *The Rise of China: How Economic Reform in Creating a New Superpower.* New York: W. W. Norton, 1993; Woronoff, J. *Asia's Miracle Economies,* 2d ed. Armonk, N.Y.: M. E. Sharpe, 1992.

6. Peters, T. Prometheus barely unbound. *Academy of Management Executive,* November 1990, 70–84.

7. Norton, E. Global makeover. *Wall Street Journal Reports: World Business,* September 26, 1996, R14; Wysocki, B. Going global in the new world. *Wall Street Journal Reports: World Business,* September 21, 1990, 3.

8. Adapted from Kanter, R. M. Transcending business boundaries: 12,000 world managers view change. *Harvard Business Review,* May–June 1991, 151–164.

9. Gleckman, H. The technology payoff. *Business Week,* June 14, 1993, 56–68; Hardy, Q. Wireless wagers. *Wall Street Journal Reports: Telecommunications,* September 16, 1996, R18, R21; Thach, L., and Woodman, R. W. Organizational change and information technology: Managing on the edge of cyberspace. *Organizational Dynamics,* Summer 1994, 30–46.

10. These examples are drawn from Peters, Prometheus barely unbound, 72–73.

11. Bylinsky, G. The marvels of "virtual reality." *Fortune,* June 3, 1991, 138–142.

12. Aley, J. The temp biz boom: Why it's good. *Fortune,* October 16, 1995, 53, 55; Fierman, J. The contingency work force. *Fortune,* January 24, 1994, 30–36.

13. Cummings, T. G., and Worley, C. G. *Organization Development and Change,* 5th ed. St. Paul: West, 1993, 52–71. See also, Woodman, R. W. Change methods. In N. Nicholson (ed.), *Blackwell Encyclopedic Dictionary of Organizational Behavior.* Oxford, England: Blackwell, 1995, 59–60.

14. Cummings and Worley, *Organization Development and Change,* 145.

15. Porras, J. I., and Robertson, P. J. Organizational development: Theory, practice, and research. In M. D. Dunnette and L. M. Hough (eds.), *Handbook of Industrial and Organizational Psychology,* 2d ed., vol. 3. Palo Alto, Calif.: Consulting Psychologists press, 1992, 719–822.

16. Macy, B. A., and Izumi, H. Organizational change, design, and work innovation: A meta-analysis of 131 North American field studies—1961–1991. In R. W. Woodman and W. A. Pasmore (eds.), *Research in Organizational Change and Development,* vol. 7. Greenwich, Conn.: JAI Press, 1993, 235–313; Robertson, P. J., Roberts, D. R., and Porras, J. I. An evaluation of a model of planned organizational change: Evidence from a meta-analysis. In R. W. Woodman and W. A. Pasmore (eds.), *Research in Organizational Change and Development,* vol. 7. Greenwich, Conn.: JAI Press, 1993, 1–39; Robertson, P. J., Roberts, D. R., and Porras, J. I. Dynamics of planned organizational change: Assessing empirical support for a theoretical model. *Academy of Management Journal,* 1993, 36, 619–634.

17. Burke, W. W. *Organization Development: A Process of Learning and Changing,* 2d ed. Reading, Mass.: Addison-Wesley, 1994, 96–124; Cummings and Worley, *Organizational Development and Change,* 84–109; Woodman, R. W. Issues and concerns in organizational diagnosis. In C. N. Jackson and M. R. Manning (eds.), *Organization Development Annual Volume III: Diagnosing Client Organizations.* Alexandria, Va.: American Society for Training and Development, 1990, 5–10.

18. Adapted from Carnall, C. A. *Managing Change in Organizations.* London: Prentice-Hall, 1990, 68–69.

19. Beckhard, R. Strategies for large system change. *Sloan Management Review,* 1975, 16, 43–55; Beckhard, R., and Harris, R. T. *Organizational Transitions: Managing Complex Change.* Reading, Mass.: Addison-Wesley, 1987, 29–44.

20. Eden, D. Creating expectation effects in OD: Applying self-fulfilling prophecy. In W. A. Pasmore and R. W. Woodman (eds.), *Research in Organizational Change and Development,* vol. 2. Greenwich, Conn.: JAI Press, 1988, 235–267; Woodman, R. W., Organizational change and development: New arenas for inquiry and action. *Journal of Management,* 1989, 15, 209–210; Woodman, R. W., and Tolchinsky, P. D. Expectation effects: Implications for organization development interventions. In D. D. Warrick (ed.), *Contemporary Organization Development: Current Thinking and Applications.* Glenview, Ill.: Scott, Foresman, 1985, 477–487.

21. Neumann, J. E. Why people don't participate in organizational change. In R. W. Woodman and W. A. Pasmore (eds.), *Research in Organizational Change and Development,* vol. 3. Greenwich, Conn.: JAI Press, 1989, 181–212; Pasmore, W. A., and Fagans, M. A. Participation, individual development, and organizational change: A review and synthesis. *Journal of Management,* 1992, 18, 375–397.

22. Adapted from Fisher, A. B. Making change stick. *Fortune,* April 17, 1995, 124.

23. Dirks, K. T., Cummings, L. L., and Pierce, J. L. Psychological ownership in organizations: Conditions under which individuals promote and resist change. In R. W. Woodman and W. A. Pasmore (eds.), *Research in Organizational Change and Development,* vol. 9. Greenwich, Conn.: JAI Press, 1996, 1–23; Hollander, E. P. Resistance to change. In N. Nicholson (ed.), *Blackwell Encyclopedic Dictionary of Organizational Behavior.* Oxford, England: Blackwell, 1995, 483–484; Strebel, P. Why do employees resist change? *Harvard Business Review,* May–June 1996, 86–92.

24. Bornstein, R. F. The dependent personality: Developmental, social and clinical perspectives. *Psychological Bulletin,* 1992, 112, 3–23.

25. Lewin, K. *Field Theory in Social Science.* New York: Harper & Row, 1951; Lewin, K. Frontiers in group dynamics. *Human Relations,* 1947, 1, 5–41. See also, Zand, D. E. Force field analysis. In N. Nicholson (ed.), *Blackwell Encyclopedic Dictionary of Organizational Behavior.* Oxford, England: Blackwell, 1995, 180–181.

26. Cummings and Worley, *Organization Development and Change,* 53.

27. Cummings and Worley, *Organization Development and Change,* 148–149. See also, Larkin, T. J., and Larkin, S. Reaching and changing frontline employees. *Harvard Business Review,* May–June 1996, 95–104.

28. Porras and Robertson, Organizational development: Theory, practice, and research; Woodman and Pasmore, *Research in Organizational Change and Development,* vol. 9

29. Woodman, R. W. Observations on the field of organizational change and development from the lunatic fringe. *Organization Development Journal,* 1993, 11, 71–74.

30. Beer, M. *Organization Change and Development: A Systems View.* Santa Monica, Calif.: Goodyear, 1980, 10; Woodman, R. W. Organization development. In N. Nicholson (ed.), *Blackwell Encyclopedic Dictionary of Organizational Behavior.* Oxford, England: Blackwell, 1995, 359–361.

31. McMahan, G. C., and Woodman, R. W. The current practice of organization development within the firm: A survey of large industrial corporations. *Group & Organization Management,* 1992, 17, 117–134. See also, Church, A. H. and Burke, W. W. Practitioner attitudes about the field of organization development. In W. A. Pasmore and R. W. Woodman (eds.), *Research in Organizational Change and Development,* vol. 8. Greenwich, Conn.: JAI Press, 1995, 1–46.

32. For a description of action research, see French, W. L., and Bell, C. H. *Organization Development: Behavioral Science Interventions for Organization Improvement*, 4th ed. Englewood Cliffs, N.J.: Prentice-Hall, 1990, 98–111. See also, Agunis, H. Action research and scientific method: Presumed discrepancies and actual similarities. *Journal of Applied Behavioral Science*, 1993, 29, 416–431.

33. See, for example, the classic statement by Cartwright, D. Achieving change in people: Some applications of group dynamics theory. *Human Relations*, 1951, 4, 381–392.

34. Beer, M., Eisenstat, R. A., and Spector, B. Why change programs don't produce change. *Harvard Business Review*, November–December 1990, 158. See also, Kotter, J. P. Leading change: Why transformation efforts fail. *Harvard Business Review*, March–April, 1995, 59–67.

35. For descriptions of survey feedback and its effects, see Cummings and Worley, *Organization Development and Change*, 136–142; French and Bell, *Organization Development: Behavioral Science Interventions for Organization Improvement*, 169–172.

36. Guzzo, R. A., and Dickson, M. W. Teams in organizations: Recent research on performance and effectiveness. *Annual Review of Psychology*, 1996, 47, 307–338; Hirschhorn, L. *Managing in the New Team Environment*. Reading, Mass.: Addison-Wesley, 1991; Katzenbach, J. R., and Smith, D. K. *The Wisdom of Teams: Creating the High-Performance Organization*. Boston: Harvard Business School Press, 1993.

37. Lublin, J. S. Trying to increase worker productivity, more employers alter management style. *Wall Street Journal*, February 13, 1992, B3; White, J. B., and Suris, O. How a "skunk works" kept the mustang alive—on a tight budget. *Wall Street Journal*, September 21, 1993, A1, A12.

38. Schein, E. H. *Process Consultation, Vol. I: Its Role in Organization Development*, 2d ed. Reading, Mass.: Addison-Wesley, 1988, 11.

39. Pasmore, W. A. A comprehensive approach to planning an OD/QWL strategy. In D. D. Warwick (ed.), *Contemporary Organization Development: Current Thinking and Applications*. Glenview, Ill.: Scott, Foresman, 1985, 205.

40. Hymowitz, C. As Aetna adds flextime, bosses learn to cope. *Wall Street Journal*, June 18, 1990, B1, B5; Shellenbarger, S. More companies experiment with workers' schedules. *Wall Street Journal*, January 13, 1994, B1; Trost, C. To cut costs and keep the best people, more concerns offer flexible work plans. *Wall Street Journal*, February 18, 1992, B1.

41. Trice, H. M., and Beyer, J. M. *The Cultures of Work Organizations*. Englewood Cliffs, N.J.: Prentice-Hall, 1993, 393–428.

42. Woodman, R. W. Organizational change and development: New arenas for inquiry and action. *Journal of Management*, 1989, 15, 218–219.

43. Sherwood, J. J. Creating work cultures with competitive advantage. *Organizational Dynamics*, Winter 1988, 5–26.

44. Burgoyne, J. Learning organization. In N. Nicholson (ed.), *Blackwell Encyclopedic Dictionary of Organizational Behavior*.

Oxford, England: Blackwell, 1995, 292–293; Wishart, N. A., Elam, J. J., and Robey, D. Redrawing the portrait of a learning organization: Inside Knight-Ridder, Inc. *Academy of Management Executive*, February 1996, 7–20.

45. Barrett, F. J. Creating appreciative learning cultures. *Organizational Dynamics*, Autumn 1995, 36–49.

46. Deogun, N. A tough bank boss takes on computers, with real trepidation. *Wall Street Journal*, July 25, 1996, A1, A18; Hirsch, J. S. A high-tech system for sending the mail unfolds at Fidelity. *Wall Street Journal*, March 20, 1996, A1, A11; Trachtenberg, J. A. How Philips flubbed its U.S. introduction of electronic product. *Wall Street Journal*, June 28, 1996, A1, A6.

47. Pasmore, W. A. *Designing Effective Organizations: The Sociotechnical Systems Perspective*. New York: John Wiley & Sons, 1988; Vansina, L. S., and Taillieu, T. Business process reengineering or socio-technical design in new clothes? In R. W. Woodman and W. A. Pasmore (eds.), *Research in Organizational Change and Development*, Vol. 9. Greenwich, Conn.: JAI Press, 1996, 81–100.

48. Manz, C. Beyond self-managing work teams: Toward self-leading teams in the workplace. In W. A. Pasmore and R. W. Woodman (eds.), *Research in Organizational Change and Development*, vol. 4. Greenwich, Conn.: JAI Press, 1990, 273–299.

49. Bruning, N. S., and Liverpool, P. R. Membership in quality circles and participation in decision making. *Journal of Applied Behavioral Science*, 1993, 29, 76–95; Steel, R. P., and Jennings, K. R. Quality improvement technologies for the 90s: New directions for research and theory. In W. A. Pasmore and R. W. Woodman (eds.), *Research in Organizational Change and Development*, vol. 6. Greenwich, Conn.: JAI Press, 1992, 1–36.

50. Hammer and Champy, *Reengineering the Corporation*; Stoddard, D. B., Jarvenpaa, S. L., and Littlejohn, M. The reality of business reengineering. *California Management Review*, spring 1996, 57–76.

51. Dean, J. W., and Evans, J. R. *Total Quality: Management, Organization, and Strategy*. St. Paul: West, 1994, 159. See also, Ashkenas, R. N., and Jick, T. D. From dialogue to action in GE work-out. In W. A. Pasmore and R. W. Woodman (eds.), *Research in Organizational Change and Development*, vol. 6. Greenwich, Conn.: JAI Press, 1992, 267–287.

52. Hammer and Champy, *Reengineering the Corporation*, 65–82.

53. Hackman, J. R., and Wageman, R. Total quality management: Empirical, conceptual, and practical issues. *Administrative Science Quarterly*, 1995, 40, 309–342; Lawler, E. E. Total quality management and employee involvement. *Academy of Management Executive*, February 1994, 68–76; Reed, R., Lemak, D. J., and Montgomery, J. C. Beyond process: TQM content and firm performance. *Academy of Management Review*, 1996, 21, 173–202.

54. Flynn, B. B., Sakahibara, S., and Schroeder, R. G. Relationship between JIT and TQM: Practices and performance. *Academy of Management Journal*, 1995, 38, 1325–1360.

55. Hill, G. C., and Yamada, K. Motorola illustrates how an aged giant can remain vibrant. *Wall Street Journal*, December 9, 1992, A1.

56. Keller, J. J. AT&T's Robert Allen gets sharp criticism over layoffs, losses. *Wall Street Journal*, February 22, 1996, A1, A6; Markels, A., and Murray, M. Call it dumbsizing: Why some companies regret cost-cutting. *Wall Street Journal*, March 14, 1996, A1, A6; Stewart, T. A. Watch what we did, not what we said. *Fortune*, April 15, 1996, 140–141; White, J. B. Re-engineering gurus take steps to remodel their stalling vehicles. *Wall Street Journal*, November 26, 1996, A1, A13.

57. Bushe, G. R., and Shani, A. B. *Parallel Learning Structures: Increasing Innovation in Bureaucracies.* Reading, Mass.: Addison-Wesley, 1991; Woodman, R. W. Collateral organization. In N. Nicholson (ed.), *Blackwell Encyclopedic Dictionary of Organizational Behavior.* Oxford, England: Blackwell, 1995, 70–71.

58. Bushe, G. R., and Shani, A. B. Parallel learning structure interventions in bureaucratic organizations. In W. A. Pasmore and R. W. Woodman (eds.), *Research in Organizational Change and Development*, vol. 4. Greenwich, Conn.: JAI Press, 1990, 167–194; Zand, D. E. Collateral organization: A new change strategy. *Journal of Applied Behavioral Science*, 1974, 10, 63–89.

59. Bartlett, C. A., and Ghoshal, S. Matrix management: Not a structure, a frame of mind. *Harvard Business Review*, July–August 1990, 145.

60. Snow, C. C., Miles, R. E., and Coleman, H. J. Managing 21st century network organizations. *Organizational Dynamics*, Winter 1992, 5–20. See also, Miles, R. E., and Snow, C. C. The new network firm: A spherical structure built on a human investment philosophy. *Organizational Dynamics*, Spring 1995, 5–18.

61. Handy, C. Trust and the virtual organization. *Harvard Business Review*, May–June 1995, 40–50; Upton, D. M., and McAfee, A. The real virtual factory. *Harvard Business Review*, July–August 1996, 123–133.

62. Clausen, A. W. Strategic issues in managing change: The turnaround at BankAmerica Corporation. *California Management Review*, Winter 1990, 98–105.

63. Cummings and Worley, *Organization Development and Change*, 505–506.

64. Adapted from Spears, D. Layoff ethics. *Business Ethics*, January/February, 1996, 62–65.

65. Boccialetti, G. Organization development ethics and effectiveness. In W. Sikes, A. B. Drexler, and J. Gants (eds.), *The Emerging Practice of Organization Development.* Alexandria, Va.: NTL Institute for Applied Behavioral Sciences, 1989, 83–92; Connor, P. E., and Lake, L. K. *Managing Organizational Change.* New York: Praeger, 1988, 171–175.

66. Adapted from Maurer, R. Working with resistance to change: The support for change questionnaire. In J. W. Pfeiffer (ed.), *The 1996 Annual: Volume 2 Consulting.* San Diego: Pfeiffer & Company, 1996, 161–174.

67. From *Organization Development and Change*, 5th ed., by T. G. Cummings and C. G. Worley. Copyright © 1993. By permission of South-Western College Publishing, a division of International Thomson Publishing Inc., Cincinnati, Ohio 45227.

Tools and Techniques for Studying Organizational Behavior

In this appendix we introduce you to the tools and techniques used to assess problems in organizational behavior. We suggest ways to think about issues and apply sound research methods to solve them. We also use examples to illustrate how several organizations used research to answer specific questions that puzzled their managers.

THE SCIENTIFIC APPROACH

Good management involves the ability to understand job-related problems and to make valid predictions about employee behavior. The key is understanding the **scientific approach,** a method for systematically collecting and analyzing information in an unbiased manner. Figure A.1 illustrates the three basic steps of the scientific approach: observation, measurement, and prediction. These steps are so basic that, without even realizing it, most people use them every day.

Organizations are now using the scientific approach to understand how family issues affect productivity.[1] *Business Week* recently surveyed some 8000 employees of more than 100 organizations to assess whether their employers' business practices were "family-friendly." Based on its survey, *Business Week* identified the top ten family-friendly organizations: DuPont, Eddie Bauer, Eli Lilly, First Tennessee Bank, Hewlett-Packard, Marriott International, MBNA America Bank, Merrill Lynch, Motorola, and UNUM Life Insurance.

First Tennessee Bank is one of the organizations that used the scientific approach to improve performance. The bank began by observing the behaviors of employees who weren't performing as expected. Then it measured the impact of a family-friendly organization philosophy on those employees. Finally, it predicted that instituting such a philosophy would improve overall bank operations and profitability.

Let's review what the bank did. First, it got rid of a lot of work rules and let employees set schedules because they know best what work needs to be done and when. The bank then sent all 1000 employees through a $3\frac{1}{2}$-day training program, during which child care, flexible hours, on-site day care or vouchers, job-sharing, and other issues were discussed. It used questionnaires and interviews to measure a variety of employees' attitudes toward their work.

■ FIGURE A.1

The Scientific Approach

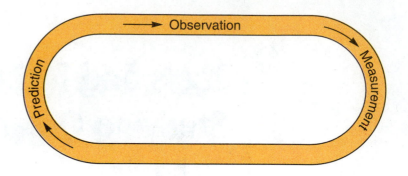

What were the results? Freed from attendance guidelines, employees adjusted their schedules to match their work and personal lives. When one team member worked overtime, her team let her four-year-old daughter wait in the office until they had finished. Another group chose to work fewer hours in the middle of the month to balance the overtime they put in at the end of the month to post customer account statements and mail them. As employees gained more control over their work lives and managers changed the way they did business (for example, no more 7:30 a.m. breakfast meetings), the bank's profitability improved. Moreover, the bank retained employees twice as long as before, cut turnaround time on monthly statements in half, and kept 7 percent more retail customers. Higher employee retention rates contributed to a 55 percent increase in profits over two years.

Another of the family-friendly organizations noted by *Business Week*, Marriott, used the scientific approach to solve a managerial problem. Of its 134,417 employees, more than half are women, a large percentage work part-time, they speak and read more than sixty-five languages, and one-third have children younger than twelve years of age. Most Marriott employees live in major metropolitan areas, where the company has intense labor competition for the $7.40 an hour employee. Marriott managers had some anecdotal information that employees were having difficulty satisfying both their work and home demands. According to Donna Klein, Director of Work and Family Life, many Marriott employees quit at the beginning of summer because they didn't have anyone to take care of their children.

To assess the size of the problem, Marriott undertook a nationwide, large-sample survey (using questionnaires, interviews, and observation) to document its employees' problems. Klein's team collected data from more than 1600 employees in five metropolitan areas: Atlanta, Boston, Chicago, Los Angeles, and Washington, D.C. The results indicated that family issues strongly affected Marriott's work force. The company also obtained data that hadn't been collected before: average number of children (2.2); percentage of employees who have dependents under age twelve (35 percent); and the percentage who have children under age five (15 percent). The survey also discovered the amount of work time employees missed because of child-care problems and the types of child care needed. The company found that, on average, employees with children younger than twelve were absent four days a year and were late five days a year because of child-care problems. Each year, nearly 33 percent of the employees took two days off because they couldn't find a replacement when their day-care arrangements broke down. Moreover, 20 percent of all Marriott employees had left a previous employer because of work–family conflicts. The survey also indicated that male and female employees reported an equal number of problems, that elder-care issues were growing in importance, and that problems with child-care arrangements limited an employee's ability to work certain schedules and overtime. Marriott managers predicted that, unless the organization took some action to remedy these problems, turnover, absenteeism, and tardiness would continue at their present levels or even increase.

In response to the needs identified, Marriott made the following programs available nationwide to its employees. As a result, retention levels rose, training costs fell, and stress and pressure on employees at work declined.

- The Child Care Choices referral program provides employees with professional help in locating affordable child care.
- The Child Care Discount program gives employees a 10 percent discount or waives registration fees for employees.
- The Family Care Spending Account enables employees to use a payroll deduction plan to pay for child care, tax free.
- The Elder Care Program provides information and seminars about services available to older employees and their relatives.

The scientific approach also requires a systematic test of assumptions. Such testing may reveal that a problem doesn't exist or is less or more serious than initially assumed. The scientific approach guards against preconceptions or personal bias by requiring as complete an assessment of the problem or issue as resources permit.

PREPARATION OF RESEARCH DESIGNS

A **research design** is a plan, structure, and strategy of investigation intended to obtain answers to one or more questions.[2] The plan is the researcher's overall program for the research. It includes a list of everything the researcher will do during the project from its beginning through analysis of the data to submission of the final report. The plan should identify the types of data to be collected, the target population and sample(s) to be drawn, research instruments, methods of analysis, tentative completion dates, and the like. The structure is an outline of the specific variables to be measured. Diagrams may be used to show how the variables—and their assumed relationships—are to be examined. The strategy presents the methods to be used to validate the data, to achieve research objectives, and to resolve problems encountered during the research.

■ PURPOSES OF RESEARCH DESIGNS

A research design has two major purposes: to provide answers to questions and to provide control for nonrelevant effects that could influence the results of the study.[3] Investigators devise research designs to obtain answers to questions as objectively, accurately, and economically as possible. The design determines the observations to be made and how they are to be obtained and analyzed. A nonrelevant effect is anything the investigator has little control over but that could affect study results. In the First Tennessee Bank and Marriott Corporation examples, nonrelevant effects might include national health-care reform proposals that could reduce employees' family-related problems.

■ FUNDAMENTALS OF RESEARCH DESIGNS

Rarely does a research design satisfy all the criteria associated with the scientific approach, but investigators should try to satisfy as many as possible in choosing a design. The ultimate findings of a poorly conceived research design may be invalid or have limited applicability. The ultimate product of a well-conceived design is more likely to be valid and receive serious attention.

■ HYPOTHESIS

The design of a research project typically involves stating a hypothesis so that inferences of a causal relationship between an independent (causal) variable and a dependent (effect) variable can legitimately be drawn or discarded. A **hypothesis** is a statement about the relationship between two or more variables. It asserts that a particular characteristic or occurrence of one of the factors (the independent variable) determines the characteristic or occurrence of another factor (the dependent variable). A manager might state the following hypotheses with regard to drug testing.

- Employees who use illegal drugs are more likely to steal from the organization and be absent more than employees who do not use illegal drugs.
- Spending $12,000 a year testing for the presence of illegal drugs will be less costly than not testing for these drugs.
- Customers will use the services of organizations that have drug-free—and particularly zero tolerance—policies for their employees more often than the services of organizations that do not have such policies.

After researchers state a hypothesis, they collect facts and analyze them (usually statistically) to determine whether the facts support or fail to support the hypothesis. A cause-and-effect relationship often isn't easy to establish. With all this in mind, let's examine the basic parts of an experimental design.

■ EXPERIMENTAL DESIGN

Some types of research designs provide more valid grounds for drawing causal inferences than others. The concept of causality in relation to experimental designs is complex,[4] and a thorough analysis is beyond the scope of this appendix. Here, we limit the discussion to points that are essential to understanding adequate research design requirements. We use the example of physical fitness and wellness programs in organizations to introduce these points.

During the past fifteen years, organizations have become much more aware of the importance of physical fitness and wellness in the workplace (see Chapter 7). The estimated costs of medical treatment for workers and lost productivity combined are more than $175 billion per year.[5] According to a RAND Corporation study, couch potatoes cost an employer about $1900 annually in lost productivity, higher payments for health insurance, lost time owing to disability, and sick leave. The tremendous growth of workplace health programs has resulted partially from the belief that an organization should take some of the responsibility for the welfare of its most valuable asset, its employees. Organizations sponsoring fitness and wellness programs include Fortune 500 companies, municipal public safety agencies (such as fire and police departments), insurance providers, federal and state agencies, manufacturing companies, and universities.

Many organizations have adopted one of three levels of fitness and wellness programs to control costs, maintain a healthier work force, and reduce stress (see Chapter 7). Level I programs are aimed at making individuals aware of specific consequences of unhealthy habits. Such programs include newspaper articles, health fairs, screening sessions, posters, flyers, and classes. Level II programs involve jogging, help for employees to stop smoking, and various aerobic exercises and strength training that last some eight to twelve weeks. Level III programs help individuals maintain healthy life-styles and behaviors. Level III programs foster ongoing participation in a healthy life-style by providing on-site fitness centers (including equipment, space, and locker facilities) making healthy food (such as low-fat, low-cholesterol items) available in lounges and cafeterias, and removing unhealthy temptations (for example, candy and cigarettes) from the workplace.

Johnson & Johnson wanted to test the hypothesis that employees who participated in Level III fitness and wellness programs would have lower health insurance and treatment costs than employees who participated in Level I or II programs.[6] The company believed that the Level III approach, with its constant reinforcing messages, would change the health-related behaviors of employees more permanently than would Level I or II programs. The company also believed that participation in Level III programs would change the work environment, providing additional positive reinforcement for changes in employee behaviors. More than 11,000 employees were divided into two groups. All agreed to participate in either a Level I and II or a Level III program for thirty months. Initial analysis of the groups indicated that medical costs and other factors, such as age, gender, and marital status, prior to the experiment were about the same. After thirty months, the company concluded that employees participating in Level III programs had fewer admissions to hospitals, visited doctors less, were absent from work less, and performed better than employees who had participated in Level I and II programs.

Two groups—experimental and control—are always used in an experiment. Members of the **experimental group**—in the Johnson & Johnson case, employees who participated in Level III fitness programs—are exposed to the treatment, or the independent variable. Members of the **control group**—employees in the Johnson & Johnson Level I and II fitness programs—aren't exposed to the treatment.

Random selection ensures that an experimenter's preconceptions or biases don't influence the choice of participants or assignment to either the control group or the experimental group. In the Johnson & Johnson case, employees were randomly chosen to participate, with each person having an equal chance of being selected. Then members of the control and experimental groups were randomly selected from the participants.

One way to obtain a random selection is to assign each person a number and then consult a table of random numbers. Another way is to flip a coin for each person; heads are participants (or members of the experimental group); tails are nonparticipants (or members of the control group).

Another way of selecting participants is by matching people who are alike in all aspects relevant to the experiment. For example, in the Johnson & Johnson case, employees could have been matched by length of employment, job level, prior medical costs, marital status, age, educational level, and so on. Participants who fit the same profile are then divided into experimental and control groups (probably by random selection).

The use of a control group permits investigators to rule out other causes for the experimental results. In the Johnson & Johnson case, other factors affecting improvements in job performance that had to be controlled for included the following significant possibilities.

■ *Natural maturing or development.* Day-to-day experiences and activities that had nothing to do with the training received during the experiment could have affected participants' performance. Moreover, employees could have reduced their medical expenses and time off for illness during the experimental period (thirty months) by doing things on their own that weren't part of their fitness program level. However, if the maturing process were assumed to be the same for members of both the experimental and control groups—and if it were assumed further that the effect of the fitness program wasn't caused by any extraordinary circumstances—the effects of maturation could be ruled out when comparing the results achieved by the two groups.

■ *Influence of the measurement process itself.* If the employees felt like guinea pigs being studied, they might respond differently than if they didn't feel that way. Also, if they felt that they were being tested and had to make a good impression, their responses and thus the measurements obtained could distort the experimental results. Complex variations in experimental designs can be used to account for the effects of the measuring process.[7]

■ *Contemporaneous events other than the exposure of the employees to the program.* Events that occurred during training for the experiment that the researcher couldn't control might have affected employee performance and the outcome. For example, while employees were participating in the fitness programs, a feature story in the *Wall Street Journal* indicated that the Surgeon General of the United States believed that everyone should exercise regularly and vigorously. The article also said that, before beginning a regular exercise program, people should be screened medically. The story indicated that people who exercised regularly had lower medical expenses and were more productive than those who didn't. If Johnson & Johnson employees participating in the experiment had read the story, they might have started exercising regardless of what their fitness program called for. Like maturational effects, however, if such an event had affected members of the experimental and control groups the same way, it wouldn't have affected the comparisons between the two groups.

TYPES OF RESEARCH DESIGN

Many different types of research design exist, and numerous textbooks have been written on the subject.[8] There is growing recognition that managers and others need a basic knowledge of certain research methods in order to understand the contributions and limitations of research in organizational behavior. An understanding of these methods should rein in the tendency to rush into cause-and-effect analyses and solutions to problems.

Managers should familiarize themselves with several research designs so that they can select the best design for the problem at hand. They should select the design that will do the most complete job, which depends on

■ the types of information the design provides;

■ the validity of the data, that is, how confident the investigator can be about inferences based on the findings; and

■ the amounts of time, money, and other resources required and available to perform the research.

Instead of properly evaluating these and other considerations, managers often approve a research design, become comfortable with it, and then apply it inappropriately to situations. Unfortunately, prior habits, experiences, and biases often determine the choice of a research design. Instead of becoming solely interested in, say, laboratory experiments or field surveys, managers should understand and appreciate the usefulness and limitations of various types of research design.

The four most common types of research design are the case study, the field survey, the laboratory experiment, and the field experiment. They may be interrelated in many ways; Figure A.2 suggests one logical sequence of research.

■ CASE STUDY

In a **case study** a researcher seeks detailed information about an individual or a group through records, interviews, questionnaires, and observations.[9] The case study is particularly useful for stimulating insights into problems in relatively new areas where there is little experience to guide the researcher.

Three distinctive features of the case study make it an important tool for stimulating new insights. First, the researcher can adopt an attitude of alert receptivity, of seeking rather than testing. The factors being studied guide the investigator, who isn't limited to testing existing hypotheses. Second, the case study is intense. The researcher attempts to obtain sufficient information to characterize and explain the unique aspects of the case being studied and other cases having factors in common with it. Third, the case study tests the researcher's ability to assemble many diverse bits of information and base a unified interpretation on them.

If the investigator is comfortable with these three key features, the case study can be an effective way to analyze organizational behavior. It is highly adaptable to many problems that arise in organizations, such as in obtaining the reactions of a newcomer to an established work group. A newcomer to a group tends to be sensitive to social customs and practices that members probably take for granted. For example, let's say that a six-person work group loses one member because of retirement and that a newcomer to the plant fills this vacancy. The social practices of the group (for example, taking lunch breaks together, kidding each other while working, and playing on the same softball team) and its production standard (no more than 100 axles per day) must be communicated to this newcomer. In an

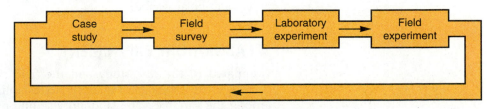

■ FIGURE A.2

One Type of Relationship Among Research Designs

Note: A logical sequence of research might follow the above diagram.

analysis of the newcomer's reactions, the depth of understanding that can be attained through the case study is its major advantage.

The investigator must also consider the limitations of the case study. The method's main disadvantage is that generalizing the results of one case study to other cases usually isn't practical or logical. That is, only rarely can two cases be compared meaningfully in terms of their essential characteristics (for example, growth potential, number of employees, location, number of products made, levels of hierarchy, and the technology used to manufacture goods). Therefore case studies rarely can be repeated exactly or their findings applied validly to other settings. A further disadvantage is that a case study usually doesn't lend itself to a systematic investigation of cause-and-effect relationships. Although a case study extending over time can help identify changes that have occurred, the range of variations observed may be too limited for practical cause-and-effect analysis. Case studies therefore may not allow the researcher to accept or reject a hypothesis. However, they frequently provide many clues and insights for further investigation.

■ FIELD SURVEY

In a **field survey** data are collected through interviews or a questionnaire from a sample of people selected to represent the group being studied. Using a sample avoids an expensive and time-consuming census (contacting every person in the group being studied).[10]

The intent of a field survey is to gather information—to discover how people feel and think—and not to change or influence the respondents. You may be familiar with the ABC–Lou Harris Poll. This field survey asks people to express their opinions about topics such as the economy, presidential decisions, and proposed legislation in Congress. Each person in the sample is asked the same series of questions. A field survey generally requires a large sample for valid conclusions to be drawn from the responses. Of those initially selected, many fail to respond: Typically, only about 20 to 30 percent of the people who receive a questionnaire fill it out and return it. Researchers tabulate the responses, analyze them, draw conclusions, and state the results.

The field survey isn't the best research design for obtaining some types of data; its use is limited to data about things of which the respondents are consciously aware. If people's unconscious motivations are important, an in-depth personal interview would be more productive and valid. Problems with inferring cause-and-effect relationships also arise in the field study. Consider an analysis of the relationships between job satisfaction, leadership styles, and performance. Does job satisfaction lead to higher performance, causing leaders to change their personal styles? Or is leadership related to job satisfaction, causing high performance? Because of the large number of unmeasured variables usually involved in a field survey, such questions concerning causal relationships among the variables can't be answered.

■ LABORATORY EXPERIMENT

Compared to the case study and the field survey, the laboratory experiment increases the investigator's ability to establish cause-and-effect relationships among the variables. The laboratory setting permits the investigator to control the conditions under which the experiment is carried out.

The essence of the **laboratory experiment** is to manipulate one or more independent variables and observe the effect on one or more dependent variables. For example, an autocratic leader *tells* one group of three blindfolded subjects to build a tower as high as possible with Tinker Toys. A democratic leader *asks* another group of blindfolded subjects to perform the same task. The dependent variable is the height of the tower; the independent variable is leadership style.

Laboratory experiments are most useful when the conditions required to test a hypothesis aren't practical or readily obtainable in natural situations and when the situations can be replicated under laboratory conditions. For example, Chili's restaurants has built a challenge course to demonstrate how teamwork can improve managerial effectiveness. The challenge course comprises fifteen events performed close to the ground, such as having members of a group exchange places while standing on a horizontal telephone pole suspended six inches off the ground, and eight events performed high off the ground, such as climbing and then rappelling down a sixty-foot tower. By manipulating the types of challenges facing the group, Wade Bibbee, the course's director, can observe the changes in team effectiveness, cooperation, and commitment and draw some conclusions about ways to increase teamwork in a restaurant.[11]

Using the laboratory research design has several disadvantages. For practical reasons, college students are the most common source of subjects in studies of organizational behavior. However, arguing that they represent managers actually involved in making decisions is difficult. Many students are young, are transient, haven't yet occupied positions of responsibility, and don't depend on successful completion of a task under laboratory conditions for their livelihoods. To what populations and treatment variables, then, can the laboratory results of experiments involving students be generalized? Most such results aren't valid when broadly interpreted because the experiments usually are limited in scope—to narrowly defined behaviors.

In addition, simulating many of the properties of organizational structure and process in the laboratory can be extremely difficult. For example, many behavioral problems in organizations can't be isolated to permit their simulation and examination under laboratory conditions. Conversely, much of the work undertaken in the laboratory deals with matters that can't be reproduced in or applied to real-life situations. For example, a firm couldn't readily redesign its organizational hierarchy to fit an ideal model. Even if it could find and hire "perfect" personnel, the changeover likely would result in serious morale and productivity problems. Investigators thus tend to focus narrowly on problems that can be addressed in the laboratory. These experiments should be derived from studies of real-life situations, and results should be continually checked against them.

■ FIELD EXPERIMENT

A **field experiment** is an attempt to apply the laboratory method to ongoing real-life situations.[12] A field experiment permits the manipulation of one or more independent variables. The researcher can study the changes in the dependent variables and infer the direction of causality with some degree of confidence.

The subjects in a field experiment ordinarily know that they are being observed, so the researcher must use procedures that minimize the possibility of subjects changing their behavior simply because they are being observed. Compared to the laboratory experiment, the field experiment provides the investigator with fewer controls.

Let's consider how the Prudential Insurance Company used a field experiment to determine the success of its general fitness program.[13] The company developed a general fitness program and for five years studied its effects on 190 white-collar workers who held sedentary jobs. The program was designed to provide participants with a healthy work environment. The company provided smoke-free offices, an on-site fitness center with an instructor, and low-cholesterol food in the cafeteria and removed candy and cigarette machines from the premises, among other things. The study included employees who worked for the company at least a year before and a year after their participation. Doctors measured the participants' level of cardiorespiratory fitness (aerobic capacity) with a treadmill exercise test prior to the field experiment. Each individual was placed in one of five fitness categories (low to high), as defined by the American Heart Association in relation to that person's age, gender, and aerobic activity. The results of the study showed that the percentage of individuals in the experimental group who were in the low and fair fitness categories declined from 57 to 33 percent. These individuals moved into the average, good, and high fitness categories. The proportion of the participants in the high and good categories increased from 16 to 39 percent. Participants in the control group all remained in their original categories, with neither improvement nor regression.

One striking result in the experimental group was that average sick days dropped 20 percent from the year before the program began. When these days were converted to dollars, the experimental group had achieved a 32 percent reduction in costs for the program's first year. Similarly, their major medical costs dropped by 46 percent during a period when national health care costs increased by 13.9 percent. Moreover, during the five years of the study, the medical costs for the control group rose by 29 percent. The savings in annual disability and major medical costs per participant in the experimental group were $353.88, compared to the fitness program's cost of $120.60 per participant.

■ COMPARISON OF RESEARCH DESIGNS

Each of the four types of research design has both strong and weak points. By selecting one, the researcher must often forgo some of the advantages of the others but, at the same time, can avoid their disadvantages.

■ REALISM

A primary advantage of doing research in a natural setting, such as a field experiment within an organization, is the ability to increase the level of realism. The researcher can be confident that the participants are generally behaving under natural and ongoing conditions. This approach offers an advantage over the laboratory setting, which typically involves artificial conditions. However, the investigator in the field loses the ability to manipulate the independent variable or variables as freely as in the laboratory.

■ SCOPE

Case studies and field surveys usually are broad in scope and contain many variables of interest to the investigator. Laboratory experiments, by their nature, are the most limited in scope, and field experiments often are simply extensions of laboratory experiments.

■ PRECISION

Laboratory research usually is more precise than field research. In the laboratory, the use of multiple measures of the same variable or variables under controlled conditions allows the researcher to obtain more accurate information about the variables than do other methods. The use of videotape, for example, permits the investigator to record an entire experiment and then study it later, examining behavior, expressions, gestures, and the like.

■ CONTROL

Investigators try to control an experiment so that the events being observed will be related to hypothesized causes, not to some unknown, unrelated events. The laboratory experiment allows researchers to reproduce a situation repeatedly so that they don't have to rely on a single observation for their conclusions. By replicating a study, predictions about cause-and-effect relationships can be refined from "sometimes" to, say, "ninety-five times in one hundred." The laboratory experiment also avoids many factors present in the field over which the investigator has little control (personnel changes or employees forgetting to fill out questionnaires, for example). However, the results obtained from ideal circumstances may not fit the real situation.

■ COST

Research designs differ in terms of relative costs and resources required. Designs vary in initial setup costs, that is, in the time and resources needed to plan and initiate them. They also vary in the cost per additional sample. For example, a laboratory experiment has relatively low setup costs, requires relatively few other resources, and costs relatively little for additional subjects—and the resources required can be found in most colleges. Because of high costs, field experiments and surveys tend to be carried out by large research organizations rather than by a researcher and a few assistants. These designs require a large number of subjects and computer facilities to analyze the data.

DATA COLLECTION METHODS

Managers observe events and gather data all day, every day. Some data they reject, some they store away, and some they act on. The problem with this ordinary method of data gathering, as opposed to scientific data gathering, is that day-to-day observations of behavior frequently are unreliable or biased by personal attitudes or values. Also, the sample of behaviors observed often is limited and doesn't truly represent typical behavior, making it a poor basis for generalizations. Hence erroneous conclusions frequently are drawn from observations of human behavior.

The quality of research depends not only on the adequacy of the research design but also on the adequacy of the data-collection methods used. The investigator can collect data in various ways: by interviews, questionnaires, observation, nonreactive measures, or qualitative methods.[14] The rules for using these data-collection methods to make statements about the relevant subject matter may be built into the data-collecting technique, or they may be developed during the investigator's study. The First Tennessee Bank used interviews, observations, and questionnaires to study the relationship of employee productivity to family needs.

■ INTERVIEWS

The **interview** is one of the oldest and most often used methods for obtaining information. It relies on the willingness of people to communicate. Asking someone a direct question can save considerable time and money if that person is willing to talk and responds honestly.

An interview's quality depends heavily on the mutual trust and goodwill established between interviewer and respondent. A trained interviewer builds these relationships early in the interview so that the greatest number of responses will be useful. One way to build trust is to assure the respondent that all answers will be confidential. In addition, an interviewer must be a good listener in order to draw information from the respondent.

However, the interview method has several major shortcomings. First, people may be unwilling to provide certain types of information readily to an interviewer, face-to-face. Employees, for example, may be unwilling to express negative attitudes about a superior when the interviewer is from the organization's human resources department. Getting employees to talk openly—even to a skilled outsider—and answer questions about their jobs, other individuals, and the organization is a difficult task. Thus the importance of establishing trust cannot be overstated. The second shortcoming of this method is that interviews take time, which costs money. Third, to achieve reliability, interviewers must be well-trained, present questions in a way that ensures validity, and eliminate personal biases. Their questions must be tested in advance of the actual interviews for hidden biases. Fourth, the questions asked by the interviewer limit the answers that respondents may freely give.

■ QUESTIONNAIRES

Questionnaires are sets of written items to which the subject is asked to respond. They probably are the most frequently used data-gathering device. Questionnaires are used to measure the respondent's attitudes, opinions, or demographic characteristics and usually cover a wide variety of variables. Numerous types of questionnaires are used to measure variables such as job satisfaction, needs fulfillment, company satisfaction, job stress, leadership style, values, vocational interest, and the like.

Developing a questionnaire requires some art as well as some science.[15] Factors such as the research budget, the purpose of the study, and the nature of the population to be sampled must be addressed before a sound decision can be made about the use of a questionnaire. After carefully thinking through the reasons for using a questionnaire and deciding to use this method, an investigator must construct the specific questionnaire to fit the intended purpose. To illustrate how the structure of questionnaire items can vary, let's consider the measurement of job satisfaction. At one end of the continuum, an investigator could measure satisfaction by asking, Are you satisfied with your job? A person would respond by checking either (a) yes or (b) no, the only two alternatives provided for a highly structured question. A somewhat less structured question is one that asks the person to indicate agreement with the statement, I find my job quite satisfying, with the response categories of (a) strongly agree, (b) agree, (c) neither agree nor disagree, (d) disagree, and (e) strongly disagree. An example of a totally unstructured question is one that asks, What do you like or dislike about your job? for which the response is open-ended.

Using questionnaires to collect data has both advantages and disadvantages. Among the advantages of questionnaires are the following:

- They provide a relatively inexpensive way to collect data.
- They can be administered by relatively unskilled people.
- They can be mailed to people individually or given to people in groups.
- They provide the same stimulus to everyone surveyed.
- They often can be answered anonymously, which may lead to more open and truthful responses than might be obtained, for example, during an interview.

Questionnaires may have one or more of the following disadvantages.

- Missing data may be a problem if people do not answer all the questions.
- A low response rate (less than 20 percent) may invalidate the results.
- This method cannot be used with individuals who have severe reading problems. When employees cannot read English, translations are needed. Unfortunately, translations aren't always precise.
- The respondent has no flexibility in answering, which limits the amount of information that can be obtained.

Suppose that you wanted to study the ethical considerations of software piracy. Software piracy—the illegal duplication of commercially available computer software in order to avoid fees—is costing U.S.-based companies $15.2 billion annually. Annual piracy losses also exceed $6 billion in Europe and $4.3 billion in Asia. It has been estimated that software piracy produces between two and ten illegal copies for every legitimate copy sold. In fact, software piracy threatens the survival of a number of firms in this industry.[16]

The questionnaire in Table A.1 has been used to measure the extent to which someone would likely engage in software piracy. Before designing this questionnaire, the researchers actually observed software piracy behaviors. They also asked others whether they considered these questions relevant to studying software piracy. This questionnaire uses a 5-point Likert scale to indicate the extent to which an individual's ethical position would lead that person to engage in software piracy. Complete the questionnaire yourself to measure your ethical position on software piracy.

To score your responses, add the points that you assigned to each question. The (R) after questions 9, 10, 11, and 14 means to reverse the score for that question before adding the scores. That is, if you answered question 9 as "Completely disagree" and gave yourself 1 point, when you reverse the score of that question, you would give yourself 5 points. Designers of questionnaires often use this technique so that respondents simply do not "blindly" respond similarly to all questions. Otherwise, many respondents might use only one end of the 5-point scale to describe their attitudes.

■ OBSERVATION

Managers observe the actions of others and, based on these observations, infer others' motivations, feelings, and intentions. A principal advantage of the **observation** method is that the observer actually can see the behavior of individuals

TABLE A.1   Ethical Position Questionnaire

Instructions

Below is a series of statements designed to allow you to indicate the extent to which you agree with each statement. In answering, use the following response scale and write the number corresponding to your level of agreement with each statement in the space provided beside that statement.

Completely disagree	Moderately disagree	Neither agree nor disagree	Moderately agree	Completely agree
1	2	3	4	5

1. _____ A person should make certain that his or her actions never intentionally harm another, even to a small degree.

2. _____ Risks to another should never be tolerated, irrespective of how small the risks might be.

3. _____ The existence of potential harm to others is always wrong, irrespective of the benefits to be gained.

4. _____ One person should never psychologically or physically harm another person.

5. _____ One person should not perform an action that might in any way threaten the dignity and welfare of another individual.

6. _____ If an action could harm an innocent other, then it should not be taken.

7. _____ The dignity and welfare of people should be the most important concern in any society.

8. _____ There are ethical business principles that are so important that they should be a part of any code of ethics.

9. _____ What is ethical varies from one situation to another. (R)

10. _____ Moral standards should be seen as being individualistic; what one person considers to be moral may be judged to be immoral by another person. (R)

11. _____ Different types of moralities cannot be compared as to "rightness." (R)

12. _____ Rightly codifying an ethical option that prevents certain types of actions is needed in businesses.

13. _____ No rule concerning ethical acts can be formulated.

14. _____ Whether an act is judged to be unethical depends upon the circumstances surrounding the action. (R)

Scoring Key

56–70 High ethical position. Piracy of software always is illegal and unethical.

45–55 Strong ethical position. Piracy of software violates the inventor's rights and should not be done.

30–44 Moderate ethical position. Piracy of software depends on the situation.

<29   Rip them off.

Source: Adapted from Barnett, T., Bass, K., and Brown, G. Religiosity, ethical ideology and intentions to report a peer's wrongdoing. *Journal of Business Ethics,* 1996, 15, 1161–1174; and Glass, R. S., and Wood, W. A. Situational determinants of software piracy. *Journal of Business Ethics,* 1996, 15, 1189–1198.

rather than relying on verbal or written descriptions of it, which may be inaccurate or biased. One problem with the observation method is inherent in observers. They must absorb the information noted and then draw inferences from what they have observed. Often, however, these inferences are incorrect. Suppose, for example, that a person intensely dislikes college football because of its violence, corruption in recruiting of athletes, and emphasis on winning. These previously formed personal opinions may well invalidate any observations and inferences that person might make during and after watching a game.

■ NONREACTIVE MEASURES

A manager who wants to know something about someone might turn to nonreactive sources of information instead of asking or observing that person directly. **Nonreactive measures** don't require the cooperation of the person. Company records provide investigators with valuable data on absenteeism, turnover, grievances, performance ratings, and demographics. In some cases, these sources may yield more accurate data than that obtained by directly questioning the employee. Nonreactive measures have the advantage of being inconspicuous because they are generated without the person's knowledge of their use. For example, radio dial settings can be used to determine the listener appeal of different radio stations. A Dallas automobile dealer estimates the popularity of different radio stations by having mechanics record the radio dial position on all cars brought in for service. The dealer then uses this information to select radio stations to carry his advertising. The wear on library books, particularly on the corners where the pages are turned, offers another example of a nonreactive measure that librarians can use to learn the popularity of a book.

■ QUALITATIVE METHODS

Investigators also use qualitative methods to describe and clarify the meaning of naturally occurring events in organizations. These methods are open-ended and interpretative because qualitative data are rarely quantifiable. Hence the researcher's interpretation and description are highly significant.

   Qualitative methods rely on the experience and intuition of the investigator to describe the organizational processes and structures being studied. The type of data collected requires the qualitative researcher to become involved in the situation or problem being studied. For example, a qualitative method used for years by anthropologists is ethnography. As applied to organizational behavior, ethnography requires the investigator to study the organization for long periods of time as a participant observer. That is, the investigator takes part in the situation being studied in order to understand what it is like for those involved in it. One researcher studying a big-city police department accompanied police officers as they performed their duties. This person informally interviewed police officers, read important police documents, used nonreactive methods (e.g., police records) to gather other data, and, as a result, provided vivid descriptions of what police work was really like.[17]

■ CRITERIA FOR DATA COLLECTION

Any data-collection method used to measure attitudes or behaviors must meet three important requirements: reliability, validity, and practicality.[18]

Reliability   The accuracy of measurement and the consistency of results determine **reliability,** which is one of the most important characteristics of any good data-collection method. A bathroom scale would be worthless if you stepped on it three times in sixty seconds and got a different reading each time. Similarly, a questionnaire would be useless if the scores obtained on successive administrations were inconsistent. Different scores obtained for the same individual at different times reflects low reliability, unless something happened (experimental change) between each measurement to warrant the change. Control normally is the only prerequisite for reliability. So long as the directions for a data-collection method are clear, the environment is comfortable, and ample time is given for the subject to respond, the method should give reliable results. Furthermore, all data-collection methods, except those utilizing nonreactive sources, are affected to some degree by random changes in the subject (e.g., fatigue, distraction, or emotional strain). These conditions also can affect the researcher's reliability, especially in making observations. Finally, changes in the setting, such as unexpected noises or sudden changes in weather, also can affect data reliability.

Validity   Even a reliable data-collection method isn't necessarily valid. **Validity** is the degree to which a method actually measures what it claims to measure. Validity is an evaluation, not a fact, and usually is expressed in broad terms, such as high, moderate, or low, instead of precise quantities. A method can reliably measure the wrong variables. For example, a low score on a math test denies a job to a potential machine repairer. The test may have reliably measured the applicant's abstract math ability. However, it may not be a valid measure of the applicant's actual skill at repairing machines.

The validity of many psychological tests used by organizations in employee selection is being questioned. The U.S. Equal Employment Opportunity Commission insists that the use of tests that cannot be validated be discontinued. Tests that are not valid are worse than useless: They are misleading and dangerous. At times, such tests have been used—either consciously or unwittingly—to discriminate against members of minority groups. Those who challenge the use of vocabulary tests in the hiring process question not their reliability but their validity.

Practicality   Don't underestimate the importance of **practicality,** the final requirement of a good data-collection method. Questionnaires, interviews, and other methods should be acceptable to both management and the employees who are asked to participate in a study. Unions and various civil rights groups have raised questions about what management has the right to know. In the case of testing for drugs, the question of who has the right to know the results of the tests is crucial. Most organizations maintain confidentiality by recording positive test results only on the doctor's records.

Many organizations now test job applicants for the presence of illegal drugs in the following way.[19] First, the applicant is notified of the screening test and procedures on the physical examination form. It identifies the types of tests, such as hair analysis or urinalysis, that will be used. Second, the applicant isn't permitted to change a test date after appearing at the doctor's office and realizes that drug testing is part of the physical examination. Third, in the event of positive test results, another portion of the same sample is retested in order to ensure validity. Samples are kept in the doctor's office for 180 days in case of a lawsuit. Fourth, all records are confidential. Only the applicant and the doctor know the test results.

Where employees are unionized, the union typically must approve the data-collection method. The use of a planning committee composed of representatives from each management level and the unions can help gain widespread acceptance of the method to be used. The method chosen also should ensure accessibility to both participants and investigators to save time and money and to minimize disruption of normal operations.

ETHICS IN RESEARCH

Investigators who obtain data from the general public, students, or employees must recognize the ethical and legal obligations they have to their subjects. Generally, managers and researchers face three types of ethical issues:

- misrepresentation and misuse of data;
- manipulation of the participant; and
- value and goal conflict.

■ MISREPRESENTATION AND MISUSE OF DATA

Misrepresentation and misuse of data are widespread problems. The issue for the investigator is to decide between fully disclosing all the information obtained or sharing just some of it. For example, a manager may easily gather data about a department's performance under the guise of asking about a competitor's. People might talk freely and give the manager essential information about the department. What happens, however, if a higher level manager asks for that information? The dilemma for the manager is whether to reveal data gathered confidentially, breaking the trust of the employees, or to refuse to furnish the data, incurring the wrath of the boss.

Many organizations use electronic surveillance to measure performance. **Electronic surveillance** refers to the collection of detailed, minute-by-minute information on employee performance through electronic devices for management's use.[20] New technology allows employers to monitor many aspects of their employees' jobs, especially those who work on telephones, computer terminals, and use voice mail. Often electronic surveillance techniques are sold to employees as ways to help them improve their performance and gain valuable rewards, such as prizes (including T-shirts, gym bags, and coffee mugs) or bonuses. An estimated 30 million workers currently are being monitored electronically, often without their knowledge. Employers eavesdrop on an estimated 400 million telephone conversations every year or more than 750 calls every minute. Those monitored include employees who work at computer terminals in data-processing service bureaus and those who provide insurance, airline ticketing, telemarketing, and telephone services. However, many managers in these organizations collect such data to discipline employees who talk too long on the phone with customers, make personal calls, and the like.

In laboratory experiments, investigators sometimes present false statements or attribute true statements to false sources. The code of ethics of the American Psychological Association states: "Only when a problem is significant and can be investigated in no other way is the psychologist justified in giving misinformation to research subjects." Many researchers feel an ethical obligation to inform the subjects of any false information presented as soon as possible after terminating the research.

Several years ago the U.S. Department of Health, Education, and Welfare issued an extensive report recommending research requirements to protect human subjects. One recommendation was that a committee conduct objective and independent reviews of research projects and activities involving the use of human subjects when federal funds are involved. Most universities, for example, have an independent review committee composed of various directors of research from the colleges within the university. Each member uses professional judgment to determine whether proposed research will place the participants at risk. If a majority of the review committee members believe that the procedure employed will not put the subjects at risk, the committee will approve the proposal. After this approval, each subject must sign an agreement of informed consent. The basic elements of informed consent include

- a fair explanation of the procedures to be followed, including those that are experimental;
- a description of the study;
- an offer to answer any inquiries concerning the procedures;
- an announcement that the subject is free to withdraw consent and to discontinue participation in the activity at any time; and
- upon completion of the research, an offer to make available an abstract of the report to all participants.

■ MANIPULATION

Manipulation involves tampering with a person's exercise of free will. Basically, manipulation occurs when the investigator requires subjects to do something opposed to their personal values. Many college students participating in laboratory experiments are asked to lie to others about the results of the experiment. Such practices are inappropriate unless the experimenter, immediately after the experiment, tells all subjects the reasons for such manipulation.

■ VALUE AND GOAL CONFLICTS

The third major issue is that of value and goal conflict. The American Civil Liberties Union and other organizations protest the use of employee alcohol and drug testing unless the organization can show probable cause. Some experts estimate that one fourth of the U.S. work force may be substance abusers, which cost businesses more than $160 billion in 1996.[21] Although no single symptom is indicative of substance abuse, behavioral changes (including increased absenteeism, disappearance from the work area, failure to complete tasks, accidents, and changes in work quality) may suggest substance abuse. General Motors and Pennzoil, among others, have set up sting operations to uncover substance abusers in their organizations. Such operations are extremely controversial because they entail surveillance, search, and detection to identify employees involved in the sale and abuse of illegal drugs. Drug testing, commonly through urinalysis, is used by many U.S. corporations to detect substance abuse. Urinalysis can detect the beer and alcohol consumed during the previous 6–12 hours, marijuana up to 12 weeks, and barbiturates from 2–12 days. Organizations must be careful not to violate federal, state, and local laws, especially a constitutionally protected right to privacy. Some courts have decided that random drug testing violates this right.

CHAPTER SUMMARY   All research designs have both strengths and weaknesses. Too much has been written about the reasons that one strategy is weak or one strategy is better than others. *No one strategy is best in every case.* Far more important is determining how each type of research design differs from and complements the others. Rather than search for the ideal, effective investigators select the research design that is best for their purposes and circumstances at the time, use all the strengths of that design, and limit or offset its weaknesses whenever possible.

Data collection may involve the use of interviews, questionnaires, observation, nonreactive measures, and qualitative methods. Each has advantages and disadvantages and may be appropriate in some cases but not in others. Data-collection methods used to measure attitudes or behaviors must meet three conditions: They must be reliable, valid, and practical. Investigators have certain ethical obligations when collecting data from people, analyzing it, and reporting it. They should not misrepresent or misuse the data, not manipulate the participants, and resolve any value and goal conflicts involved in the research.

KEY TERMS AND CONCEPTS

Case study	Hypothesis	Qualitative methods
Control group	Interview	Questionnaires
Electronic surveillance	Laboratory experiment	Reliability
Experimental group	Nonreactive measures	Research design
Field experiment	Observation	Scientific approach
Field survey	Practicality	Validity

REFERENCES

1. Hammonds, K. H. Balancing work and family: Big returns for companies willing to give family strategies a chance. *Business Week*, September 16, 1996, 34ff; Yang, C., Palmer, T., Browder, S., and Cuneo, A. Low-wage lessons. *Business Week*, November 11, 1996, 46ff.

2. Creswell, J. W. *Research Design*. Thousand Oaks, Calif.: Sage, 1996.

3. Slife, B. D., and Williams, R. N. *What's Behind the Research?* Thousand Oaks, Calif.: Sage, 1995.

4. Hedrick, T. E., Bickman, L., and Rog, D. J. *Applied Research Design*. Thousand Oaks, Calif.: Sage, 1993.

5. Wendel, S. The healthy workplace: Promoting wellness for a profitable company. *Inc.*, August 1996, 71–78.

6. Bly, J. L., Jones, R. C., and Richardson, J. E. Impact of worksite health promotion on health care costs and utilization: Evaluation of Johnson and Johnson's live for life program. *JAMA*, 1986, 256(23), 3235–3240.

7. Sackett, P. R., and Larson, J. R., Jr. Research strategies and tactics in industrial and organizational psychology. In *Handbook of Industrial & Organizational Psychology*, 2d ed., vol. 1. M. D. Dunnette and L. M. Hough (eds.). Palo Alto, Calif.: Consulting Psychologists Press, 1990, 419–490.

8. Harrison, M. J. *Diagnosing Organizations*. Thousand Oaks, Calif.: Sage, 1994.

9. Stake, R. E. *The Art of Case Study Research*. Thousand Oaks, Calif.: Sage, 1995.

10. Weisberg, H. F., Krosnick, J. A., and Bowen, B. D. *An Introduction to Survey Research*. Thousand Oaks, Calif.: Sage, 1996.

11. Personal communications with W. Bibbee, Director, Challenge Course, Brinker International, Dallas, November 1996.

12. Cook, T. D., Campbell, D. T., and Peracchio, L. Quasi experimentation. In *Handbook of Industrial & Organizational Psychology*, 2d ed., vol. 1. M. D. Dunnette and L. M. Hough (eds.). Palo Alto, Calif.: Consulting Psychologists Press, 1990, 491–576.

13. Browne, D. W., Russell, M. L., Morgan, S. A., Optenberg, S., and Clark, A. Reduced disability and health care costs in an industrial fitness program. *Journal of Occupational Medicine*, 1984, 26, 809–816.

14. Sapsford, R., and Jupp, V. *Data Collection and Analysis*. Thousand Oaks, Calif.: Sage, 1996.

15. Fink, A. *How to Ask Survey Questions*. Thousand Oaks, Calif.: Sage, 1995.

16. Results of a survey conducted by Business Software Alliance. HTTP://www.mbo.com/STAT.HTM#BSA.

17. Jermier, J., Slocum, J. W., Fry, L. W., and Gaines, J. Organizational subcultures in a soft bureaucracy: Resistance behind the myth and facade of an official culture. *Organization Science*, 1991, 2, 170–194.

18. Wright, D. *Understanding Statistics*. Thousand Oaks, Calif.: Sage, 1996.

19. Drug testing in the workplace. HTTP://www.aclu.org/library/pbp5.html

20. *Employee Monitoring in the Workplace*. San Diego: University of San Diego, Center for Public Interest Law, 1996.

21. Workplace Rights. HTTP://www.aclu.org/news/no90196a.html

Turner's Dilemma

Nancy Turner, a recent graduate from a four-year degree program in interior design, was new to the East Coast. She was looking for a change of scenery and for career opportunities not available in the small town in the Midwest where she grew up. She had joined a former college roommate, now living in Massachusetts, to start her new life. The pace of life in the Northeast was decidedly different from that at home. But Turner kept an open mind and enjoyed the challenge of assimilating into a new culture. After briefly getting to know the area with her girlfriend, Turner started her job search in earnest.

She was pleasantly surprised, and felt fortunate, to receive a job offer within a week of sending out résumés. She hadn't expected such a quick response, especially since she was new to the area. She had feared that graduating from a relatively unknown state university in the Midwest would be a strike against her in this part of the country.

A friendly sounding young woman, Tracy Benton, phoned one morning, identifying herself as an associate of Interior Specialties. She explained that they were interested in Turner's résumé and the samples of work that she had submitted. Turner readily accepted the offer to schedule an interview. During the conversation, she learned that the reason for the immediate opening was that an employee had quit the week before. She chalked this opportunity up to "being in the right place at the right time."

Four days later, Turner went to her interview. She thought it went well, but she wasn't very experienced in these matters and thus wasn't quite sure what to make of the process. Joyce Hutchens, owner, head designer, and a professional member of the American Society of Interior Designers (ASID), seemed pleasant enough. She was middle-aged and a little dramatic looking, Turner thought. She had never seen hair or a manicure quite like those Hutchens was sporting. Tracy Benton, the junior designer who had called Turner, seemed to be just a couple of years older than Turner. That was the entire company, just the two women and the open position.

Most of the questions and discussion during the interview centered on Turner's portfolio and her classroom work. During a tour of the store, Hutchens caught Turner off guard with a casual remark. She explained that, owing to the custom nature of the work done at Interior Specialties, clients sometimes became impatient with delays or were overly anxious about imperfections. "Do you think you can handle people yelling and making a scene?" she asked Turner lightheartedly. Although Turner disliked confrontation, she guessed that this would be an insignificant part of the job and felt that she could cross that bridge when she came to it.

Turner was both pleased and relieved when the phone call came just two days later informing her that she had been hired. Turner began work the following week, and the job went smoothly at first. She was given mostly "gofer" type jobs, which

weren't very challenging. Hutchens was often out of the store checking on clients, suppliers, or subcontractors. When Benton and Turner had the store to themselves, Benton would fill Turner in on the history of Interior Specialties and Hutchens's way of operating. Benton's stories included accounts of high employee turnover, a battle with a client that had resulted in arbitration, and mistakes on jobs that took too long to fix. Turner found these stories fascinating but a little disturbing. It was incredulous that a woman with Hutchens's experience could get herself into such predicaments.

As the days passed, it became clear to Turner that Hutchens's personality was demanding and erratic. In one day she could have a fight with a subcontractor, woo a client, flirt with another subcontractor, and demand that Benton collect money from a delinquent client *now*. This range of emotions was unsettling to Turner, and she often felt as though she were walking on eggs. She marveled at how Hutchens could turn her charm off and on at will. Although Turner witnessed these mood swings and exhibitions, she was rarely the brunt of them. Nevertheless, she began to notice that a nervous knot would form in her stomach during her drive to work each day. The knot lasted until Hutchens finally walked in the door, settling the question: What's Joyce's mood today?

Gradually, as Turner became more experienced, she dealt directly with subcontractors, suppliers, and clients. Consequently, she found herself increasingly caught up in unpleasant confrontations not of her making. A "good cop/bad cop" routine would result. Hutchens lashed out at subcontractors, berating them for delaying jobs. Turner made follow-up calls and visits, pleading with them to make life easier for everyone, begging, "*Please* rush this job, Hutchens is making our lives miserable!" However, Turner was unable to smooth over some situations. One subcontractor became so irate with Hutchens that he came to the store and became threatening enough to cause Hutchens to call the police. They never told me about this in my design classes, Turner would often think to herself.

Although run-ins with clients weren't infrequent, jobs didn't start off poorly. The beginning of a new job was always exciting and fun for both the client and the women of Interior Specialties. Turner and Benton both enjoyed searching for just the right fabric, wall covering, or tile for a client. Sketching floor plans and going over the choices with clients also was enjoyable. This time was the "honeymoon" period when the new client made initial selections, contracts were drawn up, and deposits were made. With most clients though, the honeymoon ended all too soon and tension took its place.

Although jobs often involved tens of thousands of dollars, cash flow was a persistent problem. Benton and Turner were paid weekly, and most weeks Hutchens warned the two women that there was no money for payroll. Then the burden fell to Benton and Turner to call delinquent clients and ask for payment. This task was complicated by the fact that most delinquent clients were withholding payment pending satisfactory completion of some aspect of the job. Despite threats and theatrics, Hutchens never missed a payroll.

Cash deposits and payments by clients were common. This method suited Hutchens as she preferred to avoid "paper trails." She tried to support herself in a lifestyle comparable to that of her wealthy clients, as keeping up appearances was important. Cash deposits often went to pay for Hutchens's designer clothes, jewelry, or furnishings for her 100-year-old home. The combination of Hutchens's lifestyle and her erratic bookkeeping methods resulted in a situation of almost perpetual financial crisis.

The financial problems, in turn, created client problems. Interior Specialties did mostly customized work with suppliers who required deposits and partial payments up front before even starting on a client's custom wall covering, carpet, or window treatment. Because of the typical eight- to ten-week delivery time for custom goods, clients were often in for a long wait once contracts were signed, even under the best of conditions. Turner noticed that this usually was the point at which the honeymoon faded and the battles began. Clients were always eager to receive what they had contracted for, and once they had finally decided on a purchase, they often became impatient with delays. Hutchens's lack of attention to finances kept her from paying deposits and balances due to suppliers in a timely manner. This carelessness added two, three, four, or more weeks to the already standard eight- to ten-week delivery time.

Clients would often become testy, but Hutchens usually sweet-talked them into a more compliant mood. She was a master of manipulation, and Turner was always astounded by Hutchens's attitude when faced by an irate client. It never seemed to faze her, and she seemed to be able to say whatever the client needed to hear. However, this approach only worked for a couple of months. Eventually the clients began to figure out that Hutchens wasn't taking their concerns seriously. When this realization sank in, they would begin to call on Benton and Turner in search of an advocate. When Hutchens was out of the office, Turner or Benton was left to smooth clients' ruffled feathers.

Turner had been at Interior Specialties for over a year when the Martins came to Hutchens to have her design and furnish the entire interior of their new home in a retirement community. The Martins were a friendly couple and doted on Turner and Benton, treating them like young nieces. During the job, Benton quit and a woman closer to Hutchens's age, Fran Reed, was hired as the office administrator. This made Turner the employee with seniority. Clients now looked to her more than ever to intercede on their behalf with Hutchens.

The Martin job started well, but, as Turner knew to expect by now, the calm wouldn't last. For a while, Hutchens's usual tactics kept the Martins at bay. It also helped that they had ordered so many items that enough things came in to keep them generally satisfied. However, a dining table with a special finish had become a real source of contention. The Martins frequently inquired about it when they came to the store each week or so to check on the progress of their orders.

Turner and Reed knew that the table hadn't been started because Hutchens hadn't sent the deposit. Hutchens, too, was aware that the Martins were worried about their table, but according to her, enough money was never available. Before long, Turner and Reed dreaded the Martins' regular visits. They were running out of plausible excuses for the table's delay, and Hutchens wasn't much help at this point. Whiny clients got on her nerves. The more they complained, the less interest she showed in the job.

After putting off the Martins for several weeks, things finally came to a head. When the Martins arrived on a Friday afternoon, Hutchens was gone but both Turner and Reed were there. After Turner told them yet again that there was no new information on their table, Mrs. Martin became very angry. Assuming that the fault for the delay lay with the furniture company, Mrs. Martin insisted that Turner call them "right now and get to the bottom of this!"

Turner felt trapped. Mrs. Martin was standing on the other side of her desk. Turner knew why the table hadn't been shipped. She also knew that she couldn't make a scene with customer service at the furniture company because the fault wasn't theirs. Yet, there stood Mrs. Martin demanding satisfaction *now!* Turner finally had come to a bridge that she didn't know how to cross. Reluctantly, she dialed the number of the furniture company and asked to speak to customer service. Her mind was racing; how was she going to get out of this? Then, pretending that she needed information from the invoice located in another office, she put the phone on hold and excused herself. Once in the relative privacy of the other office, she asked the only question she could think of: "If we sent the deposit *today*, how quickly could the table be shipped?" The answer, as Turner knew it would be, was that delivery would be weeks away.

Steadying herself, Turner returned to face Mrs. Martin. "They are still having trouble with their wood supplier, and the best they can promise is a three-week delivery." The Martins were still upset, and so was Turner. She resented being put in such an impossible situation. She encouraged the Martins to take the issue up with Hutchens. Turner hoped that if they put enough pressure on Hutchens she would finally pay the deposit.

Later, when Hutchens returned, Turner told her about the scene. Apparently Hutchens sensed that the Martins had been pushed to the edge. She managed to find the money for the deposit on the table and sent it to the supplier.

Questions

1. What factors should an employee in Turner's position consider when faced with such a situation?

2. Did Turner handle the Martins' concerns in an ethical manner? Explain.

3. How could Turner have approached Hutchens about feeling uncomfortable with the delay of paying deposits to wholesalers?

4. Should Turner's loyalty be to Hutchens when faced with such a situation? Explain.

5. How might Turner have handled the situation differently?

Source: This case was prepared by Kelly Edmondson and Ron Stepehens of Central Missouri State University, Warrensburg, Missouri. It has been presented to and accepted by the refereed

Society for Case Research. All rights reserved to the authors and the SCR. Copyright ©1994 by Kelly Edmondson and Ron Stephens. This case was edited for *Organizational Behavior*, 8th edition, and used with permission.

ABP Auto Repair Shop

Founded in the late 1940s, ABP, Inc., had grown from a three-person collision repair facility in San Diego, California, to a corporation employing more than 100 people in 1997. The firm had gained considerable local market share, and owner Gene Garrett wanted ABP to continue to grow and eventually to expand substantially. By late 1993, however, Mike Barclay, ABP's chief operating officer, believed that solutions to various operational problems were needed before expansion beyond the one suburban facility under construction could be considered. The problems that Barclay alluded to were a growing market, a six-week backlog of work, consistently decreasing profit margins, and, most important, declining employee morale. For Garrett, the solution was simple: "Let's build another facility!" Unfortunately, expansion wasn't going to alleviate the situation because the number of facilities weren't the problem.

In the collision repair industry, success stems from efficient operations, which means fast through-put, high employee morale, and high customer service ratings (CSI)—all resulting in good profits. As of 1993, all of these indicators were heading in the wrong direction for APB. The main problem, which ABP's management didn't understand, was that through-put was the key to operational efficiency and exerted substantial influence over the other factors. The inability to increase productivity, while maintaining quality, was the cause of the declining profitability, employee morale, and CSI scores.

Costs, revenue, and profits are calculated for four main areas: labor, parts, materials, and sublet, representing 48, 40, 10, and 2 percent of total sales, respectively. Parts, materials, and sublet profits hinge on APB's ability to negotiate with, and exert influence over, vendors in making volume purchases. Well-run repair facilities should achieve profits of 28 percent on parts, 10 percent on materials, and 20 percent on sublet. These profits are relatively easy to attain because they depend on a company's ability to negotiate and utilize its buying power. Labor, with an optimal profit of 60 percent, is a different matter.

In order to obtain volume business, auto repair companies need to get their names on the Direct Repair Program (DRP) lists. These lists are utilized by insurance companies to select preferred facilities to which they can refer clients who have had accidents. In addition, preferred facilities can negotiate agreements with local rental companies, corporate fleet accounts, and dealerships to handle all their collision repairs. This method of generating business results in exponential sales increases. However, repair shops are required to discount their labor rates in order to get on these lists. For example, ABP posted a "door" labor rate of $30 per hour. However, under

most of the DRP contracts they were charging actual rates of $24 to $28 per "insurance hour." Thus to receive such jobs, ABP had to take a cut in labor profits.

Another restriction involved the "insurance hours" that ABP could work. They are the number of hours allowed by insurance companies for each type of repair. For example, the shop will only receive sixteen repair hours on a job that normally requires twenty labor hours to complete. Thus companies are forced to take a cut in hours in addition to a cut in labor rates if they want the insurance company business.

In 1996, ABP was making profits of 32 percent on parts, 10 percent on materials, 20 percent on sublet, and a low 40 percent on labor. The high parts' profit reflected parts' sales of $172,000 per month on gross income of $430,000. ABP was able to command large discounts from its vendors because of its buying power and excellent credit rating. The parts' profits were offset by unrealized labor profits of $19,814 per month. Thus ABP's gross margin was 33.4 percent versus the optimal 41.4 percent, which produced a net income of only 5.4 percent per month after overhead expenses. Most of ABP's successful competitors were earning profits of 11 to 14 percent per month.

Because of these low profits, ABP couldn't provide regular raises and employee health and retirement benefits. As a result, turnover had risen from 15 to 28 percent. This situation led to a decline in employee morale, which in turn lowered the quality of the work done and, inevitably, CSI ratings. Lower CSI ratings meant possible removal from DRP lists and lost business.

Mike Barclay convinced Gene Garrett to seek the help of Kodiak consulting group. After reviewing various auto repair operations, the consultants reported that ABP was 63 percent efficient, compared to the 150–160 percent average efficiency of the other repair shops studied. In other words, ABP's employees were turning a 0.63 insurance hour for every hour worked, whereas efficient competitors were turning 1.5 insurance hour—and with higher relative quality. The consultants also noticed that ABP was carrying forty-three employees, of which thirty-three were engaged in actual repair work. Each production employee was producing $13,030 in monthly sales, compared to a benchmark of $20,000 per month. This finding indicated either overstaffing, underproduction, or both.

In response to this part of the consultant's report, Garrett and Barclay agreed to make the following operational changes.

- Cut costs and hold to an overhead budget rate of 25 percent.
- Change the production employee pay plan from hourly to a flat rate. Under this plan, employees are to be paid 40

percent of the revenue generated by the insurance hours they work. Thus employees who aren't as productive as others would be paid less.

- Initiate a bonus and penalty pool to reflect the quality of work done. CSI ratings for each repair were to be calculated. If employees received favorable ratings, they received points that were applied to a bonus pool.
- Introduce profit-sharing, hoping that it would encourage employees to take a vested interest in the company's performance.
- Switch the nonrepair employees to performance-pay structures, including the receptionist, whose pay is to be based on a portion of the CSI score for the entire shop.

Garrett and Barclay didn't stop there. The consultants had studied each job and interviewed all the employees, discussing their individual responsibilities and where they fit in the overall process. No single focus emerged from these discussions because each employee was worried about his or her own tasks. The consultants had found that duplication of tasks was common and that little cooperation existed between departments (such as paint and metal-working). In addition, the consultants felt that there were too many managers, who often assigned competing tasks to the same employees. This situation further explained the low through-put and resulting low employee pay and morale. As a result, the consultants believed that the organization needed a solution that would increase production, reduce the number of managers and employees, and cut costs.

The consultants recommended implementation of self-directed work teams (SDWT). SDWTs represent a group of trained employees responsible for carrying out a specific process with minimal leadership. Such teams can be highly beneficial for certain companies, but aren't workable for all organizations. The consultants believed that SDWTs could be successful at ABP because top management was committed to creating a corporate culture and work environment that supports involvement, teamwork, and cooperation. In addition, the collision repair process involves multifaceted, interactive tasks demanding a wide range of employee skills. Garrett and Barclay agreed and believed that such teams could develop clear goals, from which each member could benefit.

Garrett and Barclay discussed self-directed teams with key employees, and found that they were willing to support the implementation 100 percent. The consultants explained that such teams could not be created overnight and that changing the existing culture at ABP would be a challenge. The entire process from training and team selection to actual self-directed teams was projected to take as long as nine months.

The first step—interviewing all employees to see how their tasks were related—had already been completed. The second step was to meet with the employees to see if they were willing to support the required drastic changes and help implement them. Once they realized that they would be empowered to make many decisions that were currently being made for them, most employees readily agreed. The fact that their income was

expected to increase also was an incentive. The only part of the proposal that they were reluctant to accept was downsizing. However, Garrett told them that employees not working on a team at the main location in San Diego would be able to work at the new suburban location in Santee, which was slated to open soon. Garrett had already committed to implementing SDWTs in the new location. Thus he agreed to carry these employees on the payroll until the new facility opened; they would take part in the SDWT training and conversion downtown and then act as a seed team at the suburban location. Additionally, employees not willing to make the conversion to SDWTs would receive placement assistance to help them find jobs at other collision repair facilities. There would no longer be a place for them at ABP.

After management and employees had learned how a team-based organization should operate, meetings were held to determine how the shift to a team structure would be made. Background was provided through books on teams, seminars, and visits to other companies who had already adopted SDWTs. Once the decision was made about how the switch would be made, Garrett appointed Greg Kneff as general manager. Kneff would be responsible for coordinating production and providing direction for the teams.

How many teams to create was the next decision. The production goals indicated that three teams would be appropriate—two for the day shift and one for the night shift. The night team would be sent from the main facility to the new facility as the seed team. The plan was to bring this team back to the main repair shop later as the night team.

To facilitate team formation, elections were held for team leaders, who were then evaluated in terms of their desire and ability to lead a team. Team leaders, along with Kneff and one of the consultants, interviewed the employees to determine their interpersonal and technical competencies and determine which team they could work best in. Three teams were formed, each consisting of one salesperson, five body technicians, two assistant painters, one painter and a detailer. In addition, overhead staff was trimmed from eight to five people. Thus the downtown facility was expected to operate with an initial staff of twenty-five, which would increase to thirty-four after the addition of the night shift. It was currently operating with forty-three employees. Garrett was expected to trim nine employees from the payroll as a result of the conversion.

Once the teams were formed, specialists were brought in to train the teams further in team building and team dynamics, including shared leadership, coaching, goal-setting, problem-solving, decision making, and communication. In addition, Kneff held sessions on quality control, inter- and intra-departmental responsibility, repair and allocation of jobs. This approach allowed the employees to have input in setting goals and standards of production, which solidified the employee buy-in of SDWTs.

Upon completion of team training and goal setting, the first team meetings were held. Compensation, skill training, hiring and firing standards, individual responsibility and productivity goals were discussed during these sessions. Kneff, along with a consultant, took part in each meeting to assist the team leader with direction and to document the various goals agreed on by the teams. The teams also decided that Kneff should sit in on all future lunch-hour team meetings to be held once a week. The purpose of his presence was to act as a resource and ensure equality between members. In addition, no member of management, including Kneff, would intervene unless a particular problem threatened the future of the group or appeared to be unmanageable.

With the norms and goals of the groups forming, the firm embarked on the final stages of conversion. Management slowly backed away from managing the groups, and the teams began to operate as businesses within a business. They hired and fired their own employees, enforced training requirements, and tracked their efficiency and cost effectiveness. Additionally, the two teams at the main facility customized their uniforms and selected different colors (red and gold) to identify their respective teams. They also began to challenge each other on productivity, cost reduction, and quality. Management provided prizes for the winners, as long as the competition didn't conflict with the corporate goals.

In November 1997, the night team was added to the main repair shop, and the conversion was completed. The results were phenomenal. The facility's efficiency increased to 87 percent, producing sales of $500,000 to $550,000 per month. In addition, gross profit jumped to 40.6 percent, with labor profits increasing from 40 to 55 percent. These increases, coupled with a 3 percent decline in overhead, resulted in net income of

15 percent. Thus the switch to SDWTs increased efficiency, reduced costs, and added $693,360 to ABP's annual profits.

Other benefits of the team structure included the following.

■ More flexible methods and procedures were introduced. The teams were empowered to make the decisions on how they would operate.

■ Turnover fell to 7 percent. Employees knew that they could not be so empowered anywhere else. They were, in essence, running their own businesses.

■ The number of supervisors dropped, as the teams assumed many of the duties previously performed by managers and other staff.

Questions

1. What were the principles of self-managed teams in ABP's change effort?

2. What changes did ABP make in its structure to increase its effectiveness?

3. What changes in reward systems were made? Why were they effective?

Source: This case was prepared by Joe Dougherty under the supervision of Professor John W. Slocum, Cox School of Business, Southern Methodist University, Dallas, Texas, 1997. It was edited for *Organizational Behavior*, 8th edition, and used with permission.

Bob Knowlton

Bob Knowlton was sitting alone in the conference room of the laboratory. The rest of the group had gone. One of the secretaries had stopped and talked for a while about her husband's coming induction in the Army, and had finally left. Knowlton, alone in the laboratory, slid a little farther down in his chair, looking with satisfaction at the results of the first test run of the new photon unit.

He liked to stay after the others had gone. His appointment as project head was still new enough to give him a deep sense of pleasure. His eyes were on the graphs before him, but in his mind he could hear Dr. Jerrold, the head of the laboratory, saying again, "There's one thing about this place that you can bank on. The sky is the limit for a person who can produce." Knowlton felt again the tingle of happiness and embarrassment. Well, dammit, he said to himself, he had produced. He had come to Simmons Laboratories two years ago. During a routine testing of some rejected Clanson components he had stumbled on the idea of the photon correlator, and the rest just happened. Jerrold had been enthusiastic; a separate project had been set up for further research and development of the device, and he had gotten the job of running it. The whole sequence of events still seemed a little miraculous to Knowlton.

He had shrugged off his reverie and bent determinedly over the sheets when he heard someone come into the room behind him. He looked up expectantly. Jerrold often stayed late himself, and now and then dropped in for a chat. This always made his day's end especially pleasant. But it wasn't Jerrold. The man who had come in was a stranger. He was tall, thin, and rather dark. He wore steel-rimmed glasses and had on a very wide leather belt with a large brass buckle. The stranger smiled and introduced himself. "I'm Simon Fester. Are you Bob Knowlton?" Bob said "yes," and they shook hands. "Doctor Jerrold said I might find you in. We were talking about your work, and I'm very much interested in what you're doing." Knowlton waved him to a chair. Fester didn't seem to belong in any of the standard categories of visitors: customers, visiting fireman, shareholder. Bob pointed to the sheets on the table. "These are the preliminary results of a test we're running. We've got a new gadget by the tail and we're trying to understand it. It's not finished, but I can show you the section that we're testing." He stood up, but Fester was deeply engrossed in the graphs. After a moment he looked up with an odd grin. "These look like plots of a Jennings surface. I've been playing around with some autocorrelation functions of surfaces—you know that stuff." Knowlton, who had no idea what Fester was referring to, grinned back and nodded, and immediately felt uncomfortable. "Let me show you the monster," he said, and led the way to the workroom.

After Fester left, Knowlton slowly put the graphs away, feeling vaguely annoyed. Then, as if he had made a decision, he quickly locked up and took the long way out so that he would pass Jerrold's office. But the office was locked. Knowlton wondered whether Jerrold and Fester had left together.

The next morning Knowlton dropped into Jerrold's office, mentioned that he had talked with Fester, and asked who he was.

"Sit down for a minute," Jerrold said. "I want to talk to you about him. What do you think of him?" Knowlton replied truthfully that he thought Fester was very bright and probably very competent. Jerrold looked pleased.

"We're taking him on," he said. "He has a very good background at a number of laboratories, and he seems to have ideas about the problems we're tackling here." Knowlton nodded in agreement, instantly wishing that Fester not be placed with him.

"I don't know yet where he will finally land," Jerrold continued, "but he seems interested in what you're doing. I thought he might spend a little time with you by way of getting started." Knowlton nodded thoughtfully. "If his interest in your work continues, you can add him to your group."

"Well, he seemed to have some good ideas even without knowing exactly what we are doing," Knowlton answered. "I hope he stays; I'd be glad to have him."

Knowlton walked back to the lab with mixed feelings. He told himself that Fester would be good for the group. He was no dunce; he'd produce. Knowlton thought again of Jerrold's promise when he had promoted him: "The person who produces gets ahead in this outfit." The words now seemed to him to carry the overtones of a threat.

The next day, Fester didn't appear until midafternoon. He explained that he had had a long lunch with Jerrold, discussing his place in the lab. "Yes," said Knowlton, "I talked with him this morning about it, and we both thought that you might work with my group for a while."

Fester smiled in the same knowing way that he had smiled when he mentioned the Jennings surfaces. "I'd like to," he said.

Knowlton introduced Fester to the other members of the lab. Fester and John Link, the mathematician of the group, hit it off well together. They spent the rest of the afternoon discussing a method of analysis of patterns that Link had been worrying over for the last month.

It was 6:30 when Knowlton finally left the lab that night. He had waited almost eagerly for the end of the day to come—when all the lab personnel would all be gone and he could sit in the quiet room, relax, and think it over. Think what over? he asked himself. He didn't know. Shortly after 5:00 they had all gone except Fester, and what followed was almost a duel. Knowlton was annoyed that he was being cheated out of his quiet period, and finally resentful, determined that Fester would leave first.

Fester was sitting at the conference table reading, and Knowlton was sitting at his desk in the little glass-enclosed office that he used during the day when he needed to be undisturbed. Fester had gotten last year's progress reports out and was studying them carefully. Time dragged. Knowlton doodled on a pad, the tension growing inside him. What the hell did Fester think he was going to find in the reports?

Knowlton finally gave up, and they left the lab together. Fester took several of the reports with him to study that evening. Knowlton asked him if he thought the reports gave a clear picture of the lab's activities.

"They're excellent," Fester answered with obvious sincerity. "They're not only good reports; what they report is damn good too!" Knowlton was surprised at the relief he felt, and grew almost jovial as he said goodnight.

Driving home, Knowlton felt more optimistic about Fester's presence in the lab. He had never fully understood the analysis that Link was attempting. If there was anything wrong with Link's approach Fester would probably spot it.

And if I'm any judge, he thought, he won't be especially diplomatic about it.

He described Fester to his wife, Lucy, who was amused by the broad leather belt and the brass buckle.

"It's the kind of belt the Pilgrims must have worn," she laughed.

"I'm not worried about how he holds his pants up," Knowlton laughed with her. "I'm afraid that he's the kind that just has to make like a genius twice each day. And that can be pretty rough on the group."

Knowlton had been asleep for several hours when he was jarred awake by the telephone. He realized it had rung several times. He swung off the bed, muttering about damn fools and telephones. It was Fester. Without any excuses, apparently oblivious of the time, he plunged into an excited recital of how Link's patterning problem could be solved.

Knowlton covered the mouthpiece to answer his wife's stage whisper, "Who is it?"

"It's the genius."

Fester, completely ignoring the fact that it was 2:00 in the morning, proceeded excitedly to explain a completely new approach to certain of the photon lab problems that he had stumbled onto while analyzing some past experiments. Knowlton managed to put some enthusiasm in his own voice and stood there, still half-dazed and very uncomfortable, listening to Fester talk endlessly, it seemed, about what he had discovered. He said that he not only had a new approach but also an analysis that showed how inherently weak the previous experiment. He finally concluded by saying that further experimentation along that earlier line certainly would have been inconclusive.

The following morning Knowlton spent the entire morning with Fester and Link, the usual morning group meeting having been called off so that Fester's work of the previous night could be gone over intensively. Fester was very anxious that this be done, and Knowlton wasn't too unhappy to call the meeting off for reasons of his own.

For the next several days Fester sat in the back office that had been turned over to him and did nothing but read the progress reports of the work that had been done in the last six months. Knowlton caught himself feeling apprehensive about the reaction that Fester might have to some of his work. He was a little surprised at his own feelings. He had always been proud—although he had put on a convincingly modest face—of the way his team had broken new ground in the study of photon measuring devices. Now he wasn't sure. It seemed to him that Fester might easily show that the line of research they had been following was unsound or even unimaginative.

The next morning, as was customary, the members of Knowlton's group, including the secretaries, sat around the table in the conference room for a group meeting. He had always prided himself on the fact that the team as a whole guided and evaluated its work. He was fond of repeating that it was not a waste of time to include secretaries in such meetings. He would point out that, often what started out as a boring recital of fundamental assumptions to a naive listener, uncovered new ways of regarding these assumptions that wouldn't have occurred to the lab member who had long ago accepted them as a necessary basis for the research he was doing. These group meetings also served another purpose. He admitted to himself that he would have felt far less secure if he had had to direct the work completely on his own. Team meetings, as a principle of leadership, justified the exploration of blind alleys because of the general educative effect of the team. Fester and Link were there, as were Lucy Martin and Martha Ybarra. Link sat next to Fester, the two of them continuing their conversation concerning Link's mathematical study from yesterday. The other group members, Bob Davenport, George Thurlow, and Arthur Oliver, sat there waiting quietly.

Knowlton, for reasons that he didn't quite understand, brought up a problem that all of them had previously spent a great deal of time discussing. The team had come to an implicit conclusion that a solution was impossible and that there was no feasible way of treating it experimentally. Davenport remarked that there was hardly any use of going over it again. He was satisfied that there was no way of approaching the problem with the equipment and the physical capacities of the lab.

This statement had the effect of a shot of adrenaline on Fester. He said he would like to know in detail what the problem was, and walking to the blackboard, began setting down "the factors" as various members of the group began both discussing the problem and simultaneously listing the reasons why it had been abandoned. Very early in the description of the problem it became evident that Fester was going to disagree about the impossibility of solving it. The group realized this and finally the descriptive materials and their recounting of the reasoning that had led to its abandonment dwindled away. Fester began his analysis, which as it proceeded might have well been prepared the previous night although Knowlton knew that to be impossible. He couldn't help being impressed with the organized and logical way that Fester was presenting ideas that must have occurred to him only a few minutes before.

However, Fester said some things that left Knowlton with a mixture of annoyance, irritation and, at the same time, a rather smug feeling of superiority in at least one area. Fester was of the opinion that the way that the problem had been analyzed was typical of what happened when such thinking was attempted by a team, and with an air of sophistication that made it difficult for a listener to dissent, he proceeded to make general comments on the American emphasis on team ideas, satirically describing the ways in which they led to a "high level of mediocrity."

Knowlton observed that Link stared studiously at the floor and was conscious of George Thurlow's and Bob Davenport's glances at him at several points of Fester's little speech. Inwardly, Knowlton couldn't help feeling that this was one point at least in which Fester was off on the wrong foot. The whole lab, following Dr. Jerrold's lead, talked, if not actually practiced, the theory of small research teams as the basic organization for effective research. Fester insisted that the problem could be solved and that he would like to study it for a while himself.

Knowlton ended the session by remarking that the meetings would continue and that the very fact that a supposedly insoluble experimental problem was now going to get another look was yet another indication of the value of such meetings. Fester immediately remarked that he was not at all averse to meetings for the purpose of informing the group of the progress of its members. He went on to say that the point he wanted to make was that creative advances were seldom accomplished in such meetings, that they were made by the individual "living with" the problem closely and continuously, forming a sort of personal relationship with it. Knowlton responded by saying that he was glad Fester had raised these points and that he was sure the team would profit by reexamining the basis on which they had been operating. Knowlton agreed that individual effort was probably the basis for making major advances but that he considered the group meetings useful primarily because of the effect they had on keeping the team together and on helping the weaker members of the team keep up with the advances of the ones who were able to move more easily and quickly when analyzing problems.

As days went by and the meetings continued, Fester came to enjoy them because of the direction the meetings soon took. Typically, Fester would hold forth on some subject, and it became clear that he was, without question, more brilliant and better prepared on the topics germane to the problems being studied. He probably was more capable of going ahead on his own than anyone there, and Knowlton grew increasingly disturbed as he realized that his leadership of the team had been, in fact, taken over. In Knowlton's occasional meetings with Dr. Jerrold, whenever Fester was mentioned, he would comment only on Fester's ability and obvious capacity for work, somehow never quite feeling that he could mention his own discomforts. He felt that they revealed a weakness on his own part. Moreover, Dr. Jerrold was greatly impressed with Fester's work and with the contacts he had with Fester outside the Photon Laboratory.

Knowlton began to feel that the intellectual advantages that Fester had brought to the team might not quite compensate for evidences of a breakdown in the cooperative spirit that had been evident in the group before Fester's coming. More and more of the morning meetings were skipped. Fester's opinion concerning the abilities of others of the team, with the exception of Link's, was obviously low. At times during morning meetings or in smaller discussions he had been rude, refusing at certain times to pursue an argument when he claimed that it was based on the other person's ignorance of the facts involved. His impatience with the others also led him to make remarks of this kind to Dr. Jerrold. This Knowlton inferred from a conversation he had had with Jerrold. The head of the lab had asked whether Davenport and Oliver were going to be retained, but he hadn't mentioned Link. This conversation led Knowlton to believe that Fester had had private conversations with Jerrold.

Knowlton had little difficulty making a convincing case regarding whether Fester's brilliance actually was sufficient recompense for the beginning of his team's breaking up. He spoke privately with Davenport and Oliver. Both clearly were uncomfortable with Fester's presence. Knowlton didn't press the discussion beyond hearing them in one way or another say that they sometimes felt awkward around Fester. They said that sometimes they had difficulty understanding the arguments he advanced. In fact, they often felt too embarrassed to ask Fester to state the grounds on which he based such arguments. Knowlton didn't talk to Link in this manner.

About six months after Fester's coming to the Photon lab, meetings were scheduled at which the sponsors of much of the ongoing research were coming to get some idea of its progress. At special meetings, project heads customarily presented the research being conducted by their groups. The other members of the laboratory groups were invited to other, more general meetings later in the day and open to all. The special meetings usually were restricted to project heads, the head of the laboratory, and the sponsors. As the time for his special meeting approached, Knowlton felt that he must avoid the presentation at all costs. He felt that he couldn't present the ideas that Fester had advanced—and on which some work had been done—in sufficient detail and answer questions about them. However, he didn't feel that he could ignore these newer lines of work and present only the work that had been started or completed before Fester's arrival (which he felt perfectly competent to do). It seemed clear that keeping Fester from attending the meeting wouldn't be easy in spite of the fact that he wasn't on the administrative level that had been invited. Knowlton also felt that it wouldn't be beyond Fester, in his blunt and undiplomatic way, if he was present at the meeting, comment on Knowlton's presentation and reveal the inadequacy that he felt.

Knowlton found an opportunity to speak to Jerrold and raised the question. He remarked to Jerrold that, of course, with the interest in the work and Fester's contributions he probably would like to come to these meetings. Knowlton said that he was concerned about the feelings of the others in the group if Fester were invited. Jerrold brushed this concern aside by saying that he felt the group would understand Fester's rather different position. He thought that, by all means, Fester should be invited. Knowlton then immediately said that he had thought so too and further that Fester should make the presentation because much of it was work that he had done. As Knowlton put it, this would be a nice way to recognize Fester's contributions and to reward him because he was eager to be recognized as a productive member of the lab. Jerrold agreed, and so the matter was decided.

Fester's presentation was very successful and in some ways dominated the meeting. He held the interest and attention of those attending, and following his presentation the questions persisted for a long period. Later that evening at the banquet, to which the entire laboratory was invited, a circle of people formed about Fester during the cocktail period before the dinner. Jerrold was part of the circle and discussion concerning the application of the theory Fester was proposing. Although this attention disturbed Knowlton, he reacted and behaved characteristically. He joined the circle, praised Fester to Jerrold and the others, and remarked how able and brilliant some of his work was.

Knowlton, without consulting anyone, began to consider the possibility of a job elsewhere. After a few weeks he found that a new laboratory of considerable size was being organized in a nearby city. His training and experience would enable him to get a project-head job equivalent to the one he had at the lab, with slightly more money.

He immediately accepted it and notified Jerrold by letter, which he mailed on a Friday night to Jerrold's home. The letter was brief, and Jerrold was stunned. The letter merely said that Knowlton had found a better position; that there were personal reasons why he didn't want to appear at the lab any more; that he would be glad to come back later (he would be only forty miles away), to assist if there was any problems with the past work; that he felt sure that Fester could, however, supply any leadership that was required for the group; and that his decision to leave so suddenly was based on some personal problems (he hinted at family health problems involving his mother and father, which was fictitious). Dr. Jerrold took it at face value but still felt that Knowlton's behavior was very strange and quite unaccountable. Jerrold had always felt that his relationship with Knowlton had been warm; that Knowlton was satisfied and, as a matter of fact, quite happy and productive.

Jerrold was considerably disturbed because he had already decided to place Fester in charge of another project that was going to be set up soon. He had been wondering how to explain this decision to Knowlton in view of the obvious help, assistance, and value Knowlton had been getting from Fester and the high regard in which Knowlton held him. In fact, Jerrold had considered letting Knowlton add to his staff another person with Fester' background and training, which apparently had proved so valuable.

Jerrold did not make any attempt to contact Knowlton. In a way he felt aggrieved about the whole thing. Fester, too, was surprised at the suddenness of Knowlton's departure and when Jerrold, in talking to him, asked him whether he preferred to stay with the photon group rather than to head the Air Force project that was being organized, he chose the Air Force project and moved into that job the following week. The photon lab was hard hit. The leadership of the photon group was given to Link, with the understanding that it would be temporary until someone else could be brought in to take over.

Questions

1. What attributions did Bob Knowlton make?

2. What team norms seemed to be operating in Knowlton's team.

3. What leadership style did Knowlton *need* from Dr. Jerrold after Fester arrived? Explain.

4. What leadership style did Knowlton seem to get from Dr. Jerrold *before* and *after* Fester arrived?

5. What leadership style did Knowlton use with his subordinates?

6. What leadership style did Knowlton use with Fester? Was it effective? Explain.

7. What would you have done with Fester if you were Knowlton?

8. What would you have done to influence Dr. Jerrold if you were Knowlton?

Source: This case was developed by Dr. Alex Bavelas. Edited for *Organizational Behavior*, 8th edition, and used with permission.

Conscience or the Competitive Edge

The plane touched down at Bombay airport precisely on time. Olivia Jones made her way through the usual immigration bureaucracy without incident and was finally ushered into a waiting limousine, complete with uniformed chauffeur and soft black leather seats. Her already considerable excitement at being in India for the first time was mounting. As they cruised the dark city streets, she asked her chauffeur why so few cars had their headlights on at night. The driver responded that most drivers believe that headlights used too much petrol! Finally, she arrived at her hotel, a black marble monolith, grandiose and decadent in its splendor, towering above the bay.

The goal of her four-day trip was to sample and select swatches of woven cotton from the mills in and around Bombay, to be used in the following season's youthwear collection of shirts, trousers, and underwear. She was treated with the utmost deference by her hosts, who were invariably Indian factory owners or British agents for Indian mills. For three days she was ferried from one air-conditioned office to another, sipping iced tea or chilled lemonade, poring over leather-bound swatch catalogues, which featured every type of strip and design possible. On the fourth day, Jones made a request which she knew would cause some anxiety on the part of her hosts: "I want to see a factory," she declared.

After much consultation and several attempts at dissuasion, she was once again ushered into a limousine and driven through a part of the city she hadn't previously seen. Gradually the hotel and western-style shops dissolved into the background and Jones entered downtown Bombay. All around was a sprawling shantytown, constructed from sheets of corrugated iron and panels of cardboard boxes. Dust rose in choking spirals from the dirt roads. An almost overpowering stench rose from open drains. The car crawled along the unsealed roads behind carts hauled by man and beast alike, laden to overflowing with straw or city refuse—the treasure of ghetto. More than once the limousine had to halt and wait while a lumbering white bull crossed the road.

Finally, in the very heart of the ghetto, the car came to a stop. "Are you sure you want to do this?" asked her host. Determined not to be fainthearted, Jones got out of the car.

White-skinned, blue-eyed, and blond, clad in a city suit and stiletto-heeled shoes, and carrying a briefcase, Jones was indeed conspicuous. It was hardly surprising that the inhabitants of the area found her an interesting and amusing subject, as she teetered along the dusty street and stepped gingerly over the open sewers.

Her host led her down an alley, between the shacks and open doors and inky black interiors. Some shelters, Jones was told, were restaurants, where at lunchtime people would gather on the rush mat floors and eat rice together. In the doorway of one shack a table served as a counter, laden with ancient cans of baked beans, sardines, and rusted tins of a fluorescent green substance that might have been peas. The eyes of the young man behind the counter were smiling and proud as he beckoned her forward to view his wares.

As Jones turned another corner, she saw an old man in the middle of the street, clad in a waist cloth, sitting in a large tin bucket. He had a tin can in his hand with which he poured water from the bucket over his head and shoulders. Beside him played two little girls in brilliant white nylon dresses, bedecked with ribbons and lace. They posed for her with smiling faces, delighted at having their photograph taken in their best frocks. The men and women moved around her with great dignity and grace, Jones thought.

Finally, her host led her up a precarious wooden ladder to a floor above the street. At the top Jones was warned not to stand up straight as the ceiling was just 5 feet high. There, in a room not 20 feet by 40 feet, twenty men were sitting at treadle sewing machines, bent over yards of white cloth. Between them on the floor were rush mats, some occupied by sleeping workers awaiting their next shift. Jones learned that these men were on a twenty-four-hour rotation, twelve hours on and twelve hours off, every day for six months of the year. During the remaining six months they returned to their families in the countryside to work the land, planting and building with the money they had earned in the city. The shirts they were working on were for an order she had placed four weeks earlier in London, an order of which she had been particularly proud because of the low price she negotiated. For Jones this sight was the most humbling experience of her life. When she questioned her host about these living and working conditions, she was told that they were typical for her industry—and for most of the Third World, as well.

Eventually, she left the heat, dust, and din of the little shirt factory and returned to the protected, air-conditioned world of the limousine.

What I've experienced today and the role I've played in creating this living hell will stay with me forever, she thought. Later in the day, she asked herself whether what she had seen was an inevitable consequence of pricing policies that enabled the British customer to purchase shirts at £12.99 instead of £13.99 and at the same time allowed the company to make its mandatory 56 percent profit margin? Were her negotiating skills—the result of many years of training—an indirect cause of the terrible conditions she had seen?

When Jones returned to the United Kingdom, she considered her position and the options open to her as a buyer for a large, publicly traded, retail chain operating in a highly competitive environment. Her dilemma was twofold: Can an ambitious person afford to exercise a social conscience in his or her career? And can career-minded individuals truly make a difference without jeopardizing their futures?

Questions

1. What should Jones do?

2. What would you do if you were in the same situation?

Source: This case was prepared by Kate Button, journalist, and Dr. Christopher K. Bart, McMaster University, Hamilton, Ontario, Canada. Copyright © 1993 by the *Case Research Journal* and Kate Button and Christopher K. Bart. This case appeared in the *Case Research Journal*, Winter 1994, 68–72. It was edited for *Organizational Behavior*, 8th edition, and used with permission.

NORDSTROM, INC.

Nordstrom, Inc., based in Seattle, Washington, is a fashion specialty retailer that operates sixty-one full-time stores in fourteen states. In 1996, sales were more than $4 billion. The company has been named by *Hispanic* magazine as one of the best workplaces for Hispanics. Nordstrom demonstrates its concern with diversity in its catalogs, not just in terms of age, but also in terms of race and disabilities. Since 1989, Nordstrom has had a Supplier Diversity Program that purchases goods and service from women- and minority-owned businesses. In 1994, Nordstrom introduced The Nordstrom Partnership, a set of guidelines for its foreign and domestic partners. The guidelines focus on five areas: legal requirements, health and safety standards, employment practices, environmental standards, and documentation and inspection. For example, the guidelines prohibit the use of child or forced labor to produce goods for Nordstrom. Labor Secretary Reich praised Nordstrom for its efforts to prevent abusive working conditions by its partners.

Throughout the industry, Nordstrom is well known for its superb customer service. The level of customer service and amount of sales per square foot represent the most valuable measures of success in a retail environment. Nordstrom is consistently a leader in the retail industry in both categories. The Nordstrom corporate philosophy places the responsibility for achieving this superiority in the hands of the people who deal with Nordstrom customers daily—the sales force. Because the company's prosperity depends on the efficacy of its sales associates, their motivation is crucial. Nordstrom explicitly defines its job expectations for employees and corresponding rewards in the form of promotion, salary increases, liberal merchandise discounts, and other benefits.

Nordstrom has identified three performance categories in which they expect sales associates to excel: customer service, team play, and productivity. An equilateral triangle, with each side of the triangle representing one of the categories, illustrates the importance of meeting stated expectations in order to achieve desired results (see Figure 1). That is,

Customer service + Team play + Productivity = Results.

Each new Nordstrom sales associate must attend an orientation session before beginning his or her first assignment with the company. At that time, employees receive a list of qualities, known as the Expectation List, representative of each performance category. Demonstration of product knowledge and always putting the customer first indicates exemplary customer service; the notion of a customer being "our" customer rather than "my" customer illustrates teamwork; and prompt and satisfactory completion of assignments and projects demonstrates an employee's productivity. (Figure 1 contains the complete Expectation List.)

Through actively practicing the attributes on the list, associates display their commitment to the values that Nordstrom promotes. Department managers evaluate the overall performance of sales associates in terms of the qualities identified in the Expectation List. An employee's success in meeting the teamwork, customer service, and productivity goals manifests itself in the "ranking of the schedule." Sales associates receive a new work schedule bimonthly. Each new schedule lists all the employees in the department in the order in which they have succeeded in accomplishing those goals. The schedules are posted for everyone to see and are frequently used as the main source of information for assessing employee performance. A common question that Nordstrom managers ask their sales associates is: "Where are you on the schedule?" In other words, "How well are you performing within the framework of our expectations?"

Employees' ranks on the schedule indicate their status/power positions in the department's hierarchy. Sales associates ranked among the top 25 percent of employees in their departments gain additional responsibilities and serve in a managerial capacity in the department manager's absence.

■ FIGURE 1

Customer Service

Results

Productivity

Team Player

PRODUCTIVITY	CUSTOMER SERVICE	TEAM PLAY
Stock Work	Greeting	Save Sales
Areas of Responsibility	Aisle Smiles	Communication
Initiative	Listening	Honest
Safety	Product Knowledge	Ethical
Ownership	Follow-through	On-Time
Assignments/Projects	Multiple Selling	Gossip-Free
Organized	Gift Boxes	Pride
Time Management	Phone	Respect
Attention to Detail	Thank-you Notes	Flexibility
No Wasted Motion	Customer Name	Positive
Merchandising	Employee Service	Focus on Solutions
Accuracy	Good Judgement	"Our" Customer
Open to Learning	Professionalism-Appearance	Enthusiasm
Proactive	Professionalism-Communications	Supportive
Creativity	Peripheral Vision	Fun
Sales Per Hour	Sense of Urgency	Leadership
Make Draw	Holds	Golden Rule
Achieve Sales Goals	"No Problem" Returns	
	See Through Customer's Eyes	
	Under Promise, Over Deliver	
	Accountabilty	

These top-ranked employees typically receive the first shot at filling vacated managerial positions.

Sales associates determine the level of compensation they want to receive, which is based on their productivity. Through a program called Write Your Own Paycheck, employees state the amount of commission they want to earn during a particular pay period. Once the associate settles on a dollar figure, the productivity level needed to attain it can be calculated. Thus the sales associates can determine in advance the effort required to reach a desired financial outcome.

Nordstrom sets an annual sales goal within each department, which is known as the Pacesetter mark. All employees have a fair chance of meeting the goal and attaining Pacesetter status—an elite group of top salespeople. Associates receive a calendar page to chart their progress in meeting this goal. Bulletin boards in each stockroom serve as a constant reminder of everybody's status. The Customer Service All-Star Award has a less tangible goal than a sales figure; progress toward achieving it is measured by the volume of favorable customer service letters and other feedback.

The recognition associated with reaching either of these achievement levels is significant. Pacesetters and All-Stars receive a 33 percent house discount (as opposed to the standard 20 percent), an awards dinner-dance in their honor sponsored by the Nordstrom family, recognition in the local papers and the Nordstrom newsletter, special business cards reflecting the award, and mounted photographs in the stores. The required level of performance to achieve these rewards is known to everyone in the organization and is calculated in a straightforward manner. Sales associates know the requirements for becoming a Pacesetter or All-Star and can adjust their efforts accordingly.

However, Nordstrom has encountered some difficulties in following these practices. The most prevalent discrepancy lies in the area of productivity, measured in sales per hour (SPH). The SPH defines each associate's sales performance by dividing total sales by the number of hours worked. The logical step for an employee wanting to appear to maximize productivity in order to receive a reward is to reduce the number of hours worked without reducing sales volume. The problem of employees "clocking out" but continuing to work on the sales floor has arisen. The employees most likely to clock out but continuing to work often have been those nearest the top of the ranking schedule, leaving employees working fairly on the clock at a great disadvantage.

Despite the controversy over SPH, it does provide a tangible measurement of a sales associate's productivity. Customer service and teamwork present an entirely different type of problem because their less concretely defined expectations are more difficult to measure performance against. The department manager's best judgment, in the end, represents the only appraisal of performance in these categories.

Chad Reynolds's Dilemma

Park Plaza Hotel was a chain of twelve full-service upscale suburban hotels located in large cities throughout the Midwest and Southeast. Each hotel offered complete food and beverage service, including restaurants, bars, and banquet facilities catering to the needs of the traveling public, conventions, and the local community. Each hotel in the chain was operated as a free-standing unit but received support through functional departments headed by vice-presidents at the corporate level. The smallest hotel in the chain had 300 rooms, and the largest had 500 rooms. Figure 1 shows organization charts of key corporate positions and a typical hotel.

Hotel management has traditionally experienced high levels of turnover. Rapid growth in the industry created many new job opportunities, and burnout caused by the demanding nature of the work and long hours opened others. To meet the need for developing managerial talent, most hotel companies operate management trainee and/or internship programs. Employees who successfully complete these programs are then placed on well-defined career paths. They are given special assignments or projects and supervisory assignments in all functional areas of hotel operations, including rooms, food and beverage, accounting, personnel, and maintenance.

Chad Reynolds had been recruited directly out of college. After completing Park Plaza's management trainee program, he was initially assigned to the Atlanta hotel. After rotating through various departmental assignments and accepting several promotions and two transfers, Reynolds felt ready to prove himself as an executive assistant manager. This position would be the final step in preparation for becoming the general manager in one of the chain's hotels.

When the executive assistant manager's position became open in Atlanta, Reynolds accepted it immediately. It would be like old home week. The promotion and transfer to Atlanta would give him a chance to work with several people who had helped him establish his career. In addition, the corporate personnel director assured Reynolds that he would be considered for the general manager's position at the new Orlando hotel when he had successfully completed this assignment. With his ultimate objective of being a general manager in sight, all the

Questions

1. What motivational principles does Nordstrom use to reward its employees?
2. What attributions might managers make about sales associates who don't achieve their sales targets?
3. What are some of the potential barriers that sales associates would face if they wanted to form effective teams?

Source: This case was prepared by Susan Summers under the direction of Professor John W. Slocum, Cox School of Business, Southern Methodist University, Dallas, Texas, 1997. Edited for *Organizational Behavior*, 8th edition, and used with permission.

long hours and six- to seven-day work weeks finally seemed to have been worth the effort.

Reynolds's "homecoming" was better than he had expected. He quickly renewed many acquaintances and rekindled friendships he had previously made in the hotel and community. However, the excitement of settling into his new position was quickly dampened by the following conversation he had with Nancy Benson, the hotel's controller.

Benson: Chad, do you have time for a cup of coffee and a few questions?

Reynolds: Sure, let's go down to the coffee shop.

Benson: No, I've got the coffee pot on in my office, and I want to talk to you in private anyway.

Reynolds: By your tone of voice, this sounds serious.

Benson: Chad, you and I have known each other for almost six years, and I need to talk to someone I can trust. I'm not sure, but I think we may have a problem in our food and beverage department.

Reynolds: I'm all ears.

Benson: For the past six months, our food and beverage costs have been anywhere from 1 to 2 percent over budget.

Reynolds: That sounds a little off, but not too bad.

Benson: Not too bad? This could be serious, and it's my responsibility to spot potential problems! On our combined annual food and beverage budgets of $2.7 million, this could amount to over $50,000 a year.

Reynolds: Okay, I get your point. Have you talked with Mike Schwerzek (food and beverage director) about your concerns?

Benson: Yes, on several occasions. He assures me that all control procedures are being adhered to, and the only problem is that the catering sales staff is cutting too many special deals with banquet customers, forcing up the costs.

Reynolds: I'm sure you've checked into this. Does his reasoning make any sense?

FIGURE 1

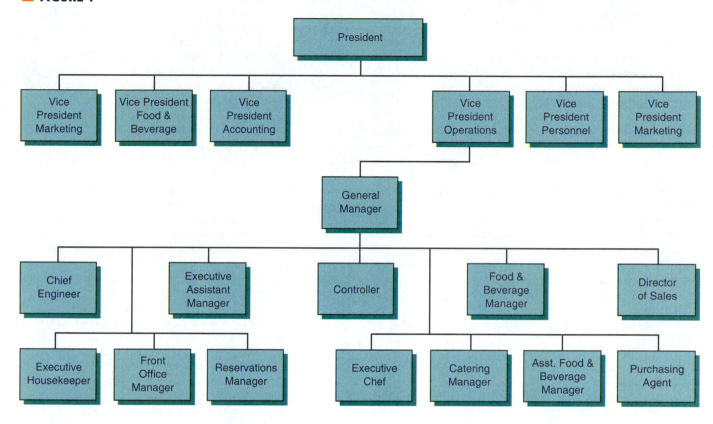

Benson: No, it doesn't. I've been working with Ryan Haase (accounts payable clerk) to determine the ingredient costs for all our menu items. Based on established menu prices in the restaurants and selling prices of last month's banquet menus, we should have been well below budget on our food costs.

Reynolds: Have you shared any of your concerns with John Anderson (general manager)?

Benson: Yes.

Reynolds: Well, don't keep me in suspense. What did he say?

Benson: Not much then, but he called me in a couple of days later and repeated most of the same things Mike had told me earlier. On top of that, he told me I was spending too much time counting pennies, and I shouldn't worry as long as we remained profitable and our percentage costs held steady.

Reynolds: Let me talk with John, and I'll get back to you as soon as possible.

Benson: I'd appreciate it if you'd keep my name out of this. Mike has been accusing me of being out to get him. If I'm wrong, I don't want to create any more hard feelings because Mike seems to be well liked by his staff.

Reynolds: No problem. I'll do a little checking on my own and try to bring the subject up for discussion at the right time.

As the executive assistant manager and member of the hotel's executive committee, Reynolds had access to all the information about the operation, but his primary responsibility was for operation of the rooms department. He and Mike Schwerzek had the same reporting relations to the general manager (see Figure 1), but in the general manager's absence, the executive assistant manager was officially in charge of all hotel operations. However, in practice, the executive assistant manager was expected to devote only limited time and attention to food and beverage operations.

Normally, food and beverage operations, as well as other operational issues in the hotel, were discussed during budget deliberations and at executive committee meetings. The executive committee was composed of the general manager, the executive assistant manager, food and beverage manager, director of sales, controller, and chief engineer. Under the direction of the general manager, this committee was responsible for the oversight and coordination of all hotel operations.

The opportunity to discuss food and beverage costs came up sooner than Reynolds had expected. John Anderson had asked him if he wanted to include any items on the agenda at the biweekly executive committee meeting. In addition to normal operating issues, Reynolds mentioned that he would be interested in discussing food and beverage costs because they were the only cost categories continually over budget. Reynolds was surprised when Anderson said that Nancy Benson must have been bending his ear. Reynolds admitted that she had but that he had also been doing some checking on his own to satisfy his curiosity.

Reynolds was surprised and troubled when Anderson cut the conversation short by saying that he had complete confidence in Mike Schwerzek and didn't want the subject brought up again. Reynolds definitely felt that he was between a rock and a hard place. Anderson had been the general manager when Reynolds entered the management training program and had become his mentor, but he also valued Nancy Benson's ability to spot potential trouble.

Although he could have walked away from the issue, Reynolds decided not to do so. Besides wanting to satisfy his own curiosity, he knew that a better understanding of food and beverage operations would be to his benefit when he finally became a general manager. He adjusted his schedule so that he could spend more time observing purchasing, receiving, food preparation, and service activities in the food and beverage department. Mike Schwerzek must have sensed Reynolds's increased presence because he openly complained at the next executive committee meeting that Reynolds was spending too much time in the food and beverage areas. Although Schwerzek continued to protest, John Anderson encouraged Reynolds to learn as much about the food and beverage areas as possible in order to prepare himself for his planned promotion to a general manager's position.

Two months passed before Reynolds brought up the subject of food and beverage costs again with Anderson. On a quiet Saturday morning, Reynolds stepped into Anderson's office, carrying a legal pad full of notes.

Reynolds: John, you and I have been with this company for a long time. I'm concerned about a potential problem and I need to share these concerns with you.

Anderson: Okay, have a seat and take your time.

Reynolds: It's about our food and beverage department. I think Nancy was right; there seems to be something that's just not quite right in those areas. I'm still not sure I can put my finger on it, but I've come up with some very interesting information. I think the problem may be bigger than just a cost issue. Let me tell you some of the things that I've picked up over the past two months.

First, I don't know whether you're aware of it, but Mike Schwerzek, Jeff Randall (executive chef), and Anna Ellingson (purchasing agent) all worked together before coming here. In fact, Jeff and Anna were hired based on Mike's recommendations.

Second, four months ago, Mike hired his brother, Larry Schwerzek, as a relief cook to work on weekends and to help out on extremely busy nights. The fact that they are related and working in the same department is a violation of company policy. When I mentioned the policy to Mike, he told me that the way he interpreted it, is that it doesn't apply to temporary help. Disregarding the questions of company policy, Larry has no previous culinary experience. In fact, right now, he is working as a maintenance helper for an apartment complex. Mike said that it's a good arrangement because he only works when needed, and he can depend on him to come in on short notice.

Third, eight months ago, we stopped purchasing from Southeastern Meats here in town and began purchasing all of our fresh fish, poultry, and meat and some frozen products from Carver Meats in Chattanooga. Mike and Jeff say we are getting the same quality product and service at a better price. I've reviewed the old invoices, and the quality (grade) specified and delivered on the invoice is the same, but the prices are a few pennies higher per pound or item. Although it's only a rumor around town, it's probably worth noting that some food and beverage people feel that Carver Meats sometimes substitutes lower grades of meats in its shipments, and there is some suspicion that it has given kickbacks to purchasing agents or chefs.

Fourth, Wendell Johnson (storeroom clerk) tells me that the night cooks are concerned because on several occasions Larry Schwerzek has used the chef's keys to get supplies from the storeroom and hasn't completed the required requisitions. They're afraid to say anything to Mike or Jeff because they know they are friends, but they're also afraid of being blamed if anything comes up missing.

Finally, last night, I was working late to assist with the end of the month inventories and to spot check the different departments. When I went to the kitchen, Anna Ellingson and Larry Schwerzek were taking inventory. When I asked Anna where the chef or the executive sous chef was, she told me they were both busy, so she had asked Larry to help her. This procedure seemed odd to me because it's company policy for either the chef or executive sous chef to supervise and participate in the inventory procedure. I decided to stick around and spend some time with the night audit crew. After the kitchen and all food and beverage outlets were shut down, I went back and reinventoried the meat cooler. The counts and weights I got and recorded on these inventory sheets were different and several pounds less than those reported on the inventory sheets.

Anderson: Mike told me you had been snooping around.

Reynolds: Hey, maybe if he thinks I'm "snooping," he has something to hide.

Anderson: It sounds like all of the things you've found are just judgment calls. Maybe Mike is right. He feels you two have a personality clash and you are envious of the strong support he gets from his staff.

Reynolds: Come off it, John! You know better than that. If you're not sure about my concerns, call in Victor Herche (vice-president of food and beverage) and let him or someone on his staff take a look into the situation.

Anderson: Cool down. Let me think about what you've said, and I'll get back to you.

Monday afternoon Anderson's secretary called Reynolds and asked him to come to Anderson's office. When he arrived, Anderson and Schwerzek were discussing food costs. Much to Reynolds's surprise, Anderson asked him to summarize the facts he had presented Saturday morning. Schwerzek comfortably defended his position on all the points raised. Even when pressed on the question of inventory procedures and company policy, he dodged the issue by saying that it had been a very busy period and that he was confident in Larry and Anna's abilities to do the job. As for the differences in meat counts and weights, he said that mistakes are possible when you're counting and weighing hundreds of items and working in several coolers and freezers. At the end of a fairly heated discussion, Schwerzek told Anderson to keep Reynolds out of his hair because his continual questioning and snooping were becoming disruptive. Anderson supported Schwerzek and told Reynolds to limit his future involvement in the food and beverage areas.

Feeling a bit let down and perhaps even betrayed after this meeting, Reynolds decided to vent his frustrations to Nancy Benson. He had visited with her many times during his investigation to ask her questions and get accounting information. However, this was the first time he'd had a detailed discussion with her about what he had observed. After recounting the events of the past few weeks, they agreed that there was a problem but that they weren't sure what to do next.

Questions

1. What problems are evident in the operating and/or control procedures in the Atlanta hotel? Are the controls adequate? Explain.

2. If you were Chad Reynolds, what courses of action could you take? Include in your response a discussion of how you would present controversial issues to your supervisor. What would you do if your supervisor wasn't responsive to your concerns?

3. Identify and discuss the roles of potential change agents. Could Chad Reynolds be considered one?

4. What are the potential causes of and possible approaches to dealing with the apparent conflict between the parties involved? Is Reynolds looking beyond his areas of the authority? Explain.

5. What sources of power are being used by the key players in this case? Are there other sources of power available to the participants?

6. Should Reynolds bypass the chain of command and contact the corporate office? What are the implications of doing so? Of not doing so?

7. Discuss the possible mentoring dynamics between Chad Reynolds and John Anderson. Is the deterioration of such a relationship common or uncommon? Why?

8. What role do you feel politics plays in this situation?

9. What ethical considerations should Reynolds consider in his decision of what to do next? What different perspectives should he consider?

10. Do you consider this a case of whistle-blowing? Why or why not? What effects would going forward likely have on Reynolds's career?

Source: This case was prepared by Roy A. Cook of Fort Lewis College, Durango, Colorado, and Jeryl L. Nelson of Wayne State College, Wayne, Nebraska. It was presented to and accepted by the refereed Society for Case Research. All rights reserved to the authors and the SCR. Copyright © 1994 by Roy A. Cook and Jeryl L. Nelson. Edited for *Organizational Behavior*, 8th edition, and used with permission.

What Do We Do with Howard?

Agrigreen, Inc., manufactures various agricultural fertilizers in several plants in the western United States and Canada. Tad Pierson, appointed three months ago as a project engineer at one of the Agrigreen plants, had been told last week by Burt Jacobs, the new manager of engineering to whom he reports, that he was to take on the added responsibility of supervising the plant surveying group. Having worked with members of this group in the past, Pierson was aware of some performance problems and conflicts that existed within the group. Contemplating what action, if any, he should take as their new supervisor, he reviewed the history of the surveying group with others in the company (see Figure 1) and then talked with each group member individually to arrive at the following picture of the situation.

Howard Lineberry, Lead Surveyor

After receiving his surveyor's certificate from the local civil technologies college, Howard Lineberry had gone to work for the State Highway Department as a chainman. The job hadn't paid very well, and he always felt that the lead surveyor didn't like him and often had him doing work that was better suited for a rodman, a position of lower status than chainman on a survey crew.

So, when a job for a lead surveyor had opened up at Agrigreen eighteen years ago, Lineberry had been glad to get it. He told Pierson how excited he had been to be hired into the newly created position. Previously, survey work at Agrigreen had been handled on a part-time basis by drafting personnel or project engineers, mainly Frank Silverton (see Figure 2). Because of significant growth during the preceding three years,

■ FIGURE 1

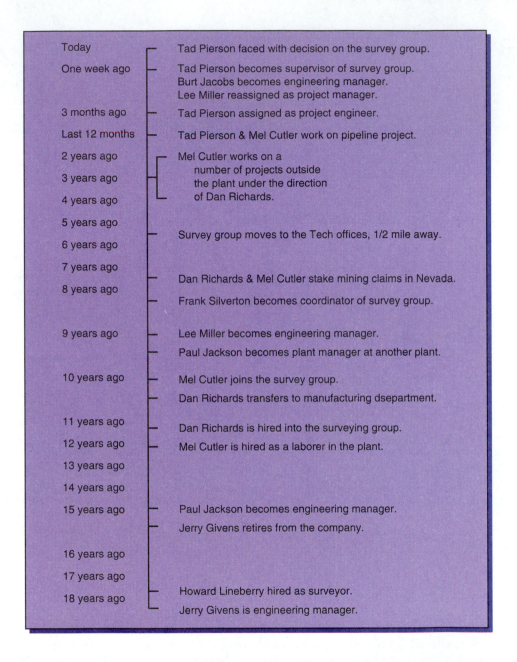

Today	Tad Pierson faced with decision on the survey group.
One week ago	Tad Pierson becomes supervisor of survey group. Burt Jacobs becomes engineering manager. Lee Miller reassigned as project manager.
3 months ago	Tad Pierson assigned as project engineer.
Last 12 months	Tad Pierson & Mel Cutler work on pipeline project.
2 years ago	Mel Cutler works on a
3 years ago	number of projects outside the plant under the direction
4 years ago	of Dan Richards.
5 years ago	
6 years ago	Survey group moves to the Tech offices, 1/2 mile away.
7 years ago	
8 years ago	Dan Richards & Mel Cutler stake mining claims in Nevada. Frank Silverton becomes coordinator of survey group.
9 years ago	Lee Miller becomes engineering manager. Paul Jackson becomes plant manager at another plant.
10 years ago	Mel Cutler joins the survey group. Dan Richards transfers to manufacturing dsepartment.
11 years ago	Dan Richards is hired into the surveying group.
12 years ago	Mel Cutler is hired as a laborer in the plant.
13 years ago	
14 years ago	
15 years ago	Paul Jackson becomes engineering manager. Jerry Givens retires from the company.
16 years ago	
17 years ago	
18 years ago	Howard Lineberry hired as surveyor. Jerry Givens is engineering manager.

survey work had begun to eat up nearly all of Silverton's working hours. As a project engineer, his salary was too high to justify using him for survey activities, so management had decided to hire someone with an education in surveying and some experience to support the work of Silverton and the five other project engineers.

Jerry Givens, manager of the engineering staff at the time, and since retired, was the man who had hired and first supervised Lineberry. Since being hired, he has worked for four different supervisors. He remembered Givens as a "cantankerous, hard-headed boss who had very specific things that he wanted done and definite ideas on how they should be accomplished." He often lost his temper and openly criticized Lineberry or

anyone else doing something he didn't like. Nevertheless, Lineberry felt that he got along well with Givens. He usually had Lineberry's daily work scheduled by the time Lineberry arrived in the morning and explained what needed to be done and how it should be done. Only occasionally would Givens have to stop by during the day to change the focus of activities.

After Givens retired, Lineberry reported to Paul Jackson, the new manager of engineering. Unlike Givens, Jackson expected Lineberry to plan his day based on the work that needed to be done and to go ahead and do it. About that time, Lineberry had been thinking that he could do a better job supporting the project engineers, who were increasingly busy on more and larger projects, if he worked with them more directly. The increased

■ FIGURE 2

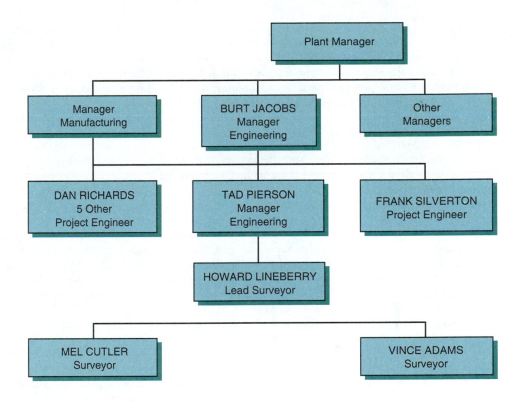

pace of work often resulted in last minute requests for Lineberry to provide information and field work. He felt that he had handled fairly well what had become frequent daily changes in his work schedule.

Then one day Jackson accused Lineberry, in front of a couple of the engineers, of being "disorganized and possibly lazy." Later, maybe as a result of thinking about what Paul had said, or maybe as a result of just bad luck, according to Lineberry, he made an error fixing the location of a building foundation. The error wasn't noticed until it was time to erect the new mill. What followed, Lineberry remembered, was "pure hell as the foundation was demolished and replaced at considerable cost in time and money." After that, people stopped talking when he walked up, and he often overheard "little biting comments" about him. Lineberry had "considered quitting, but good jobs were hard to get."

After the foundation incident, Jackson became increasingly critical and finally decided that Lineberry needed someone to assist him and double check his "error prone" work. At the same time, Agrigreen was planning to build a new wastewater holding pond, and the project would require extra surveying help. Jackson hired Dan Richards to assist Lineberry. Richards was a bright, hard-working young man who had the same training as Lineberry and who was also pursuing a degree in engineering. As the project proceeded, Richards had openly expressed his feelings that his leader, Howard Lineberry, was slow and stupid. Lineberry felt relieved a year and half later when Richards was transferred to the manufacturing department.

Mel Cutler, who had been employed in the plant for two years as a laborer, replaced Richards. He had previously worked for another employer as a draftsman and had also gained considerable experience in surveying. Lineberry immediately liked Cutler, something he had never felt for Dan Richards. Cutler was willing to work with Lineberry on how to do the jobs and often caught small errors before they became problems.

Ten years have passed since Cutler first joined Lineberry, who now felt a "slight pang" as he wished things were still the same between them. But, during the past five years, relations between them had become increasingly tense. Recently, the only verbal exchanges between them had been terse and directly concerned with the job. Much of the enjoyment of his job is gone, and Lineberry often dreaded coming to work.

A few months after Cutler had been hired, another supervisory change occurred. Lee Miller, a former project engineer, took the manager's job when Paul Jackson was promoted to plant manager at another Agrigreen plant. Miller had been very successful as an engineer but as a supervisor was somewhat indecisive.

Meanwhile, increasing workloads had resulted in the hiring of additional draftsmen, and office space was getting tight. Miller corrected the situation by remodeling some space in the basement of the Tech offices located about a half-mile from the plant, and Lineberry and Cutler moved there. Nobody bothered either of them much in the new location. Lineberry felt good about the change because he now had space for the survey equipment and he was away from the mainstream of the operation. He needed to see the engineers only when he felt like it and wasn't bothered as often by hearing their derogatory comments.

Four years ago, Miller had told Lineberry and the other surveyors that he would like them to coordinate their job assignments and schedules through Frank Silverton, indicating that Silverton had much more surveying experience than he did and would know better what the needs were. Lineberry remembered feeling uncomfortable about this arrangement because Silverton wasn't really his boss, and he still had to have Miller sign his time cards and approve his vacation.

During the past four years, Cutler had occasionally worked on small projects outside the plant, most frequently for Dan Richards, who always specified which individual he wanted when requesting help.

Recently, the company had constructed a fifty-mile pipeline to deliver raw material to the plant, and Cutler was chosen to work under Tad Pierson on that project. Pierson was a recent engineering graduate charged with overseeing the pipeline survey and construction, which had lasted from April through December the previous year. Lineberry still felt angry about Cutler's assignment to the project because he has had "more experience than Mel at surveying and could have used the overtime money." The only benefit to Lineberry resulting from Cutler's outside work was that Miller had hired Vince Adams to help Lineberry during the summer months. Lineberry and Adams thought much the same way about many things, and Lineberry had a genuine affection for this "just-out-of-high-school" young man.

Following completion of the pipeline project, Tad Pierson had been made a project engineer, and because of the lack of space in the plant offices, was given space in the Tech offices near Lineberry, Adams, and Cutler. Pierson was openly friendly with Cutler, but Lineberry felt that Pierson "acted coolly" toward him and Adams. They seemed to have nothing in common, and each time Lineberry had tried to talk to Pierson, Pierson seemed to cut the discussion short and make an excuse to leave.

A week ago, Lee Miller had stepped down as manager of engineering and resumed duties as one of the project engineers. Burt Jacobs, a big, loud, direct person (in Lineberry's opinion), who had been the manager of purchasing and stores (plant supplies) replaced him as manager. Jacobs was an engineer about half Miller's age and several years younger than Lineberry. Only this morning, Jacobs had called the engineering department together to say that change was needed because of the friction between engineering and the other departments in the plant. He also said that the surveyors were now to report to Pierson (which made Lineberry very uneasy) and that anyone needing surveying services must now schedule it through Pierson.

Mel Cutler, Surveyor's Helper

Mel Cutler arrived in town without a job and was a "happy man" when he got the call from Agrigreen. The company needed a plant laborer, and he needed a job. He remembered the job for the next two years as "the most exhausting and filthy job I have ever worked." Finally, ten years ago a surveyor's helper position had opened up, and with his background in surveying and drafting he was able to get the job.

Cutler was assigned to Howard Lineberry. For the first few years, they worked well together. Both men had young families, and they shared many of the same outside interests. Cutler had been willing to go along with the way Lineberry had always done things until about five years ago when he noticed that they "experienced continual problems due to the way Howard kept his notes." Cutler tried to show Lineberry the way he had been trained to keep notes, but "Howard would have nothing to do with it." The debate continued for several weeks.

Soon, Lineberry started keeping the work schedule to himself, and Cutler often had no idea what they were going to do next until Lineberry stopped the truck and started unloading equipment. In addition, Lineberry's frequent snack breaks were starting to bother Cutler. He began losing respect for Lineberry and thought that Lineberry was "growing less concerned about his job." No amount of criticism from Frank Silverton, their boss, seemed to have any effect on Lineberry or the number of errors he committed.

Moving the surveyors out of the plant had been wrong in Cutler's opinion. He said, "Howard started taking advantage of the situation almost immediately by coming in late and leaving early a couple of times each week." Lately, Lineberry had been taking naps after lunch, justifying it by saying that he often worked late and was just making up the time. For the past year or so, he had been far more likely to be late for work than to be on time. Whenever Silverton mentioned it, Lineberry always had an excuse. Silverton gave up trying to get him to work on time and settled for just getting some good work done.

Years ago, Dan Richards had first called to see if Cutler wanted to help him stake Agrigreen mining claims in Nevada, and Cutler had jumped at the chance. This turned out to be the first of many surveying expeditions that the two men made together. Looking back, Cutler could see how they had developed a "lot of respect and trust in each other's work." They often joked about Lineberry's laziness and what an idiot they thought he was.

Cutler had been extremely happy when he became part of the pipeline survey crew. He had met Tad Pierson, the pipeline field engineer, at a party that Richards had given and had immediately liked him. Shortly into the project, Pierson, on Richards's recommendation, put Cutler in charge of the pipeline survey crew and made him responsible for inspections for the eastern half of the pipeline.

Cutler felt good about the assignment and vowed that he would be "the best worker Tad had ever seen." The hours were long—he had averaged more than thirty-five hours overtime a week for fifteen weeks straight and had never once complained. Pierson was also working long days, and Cutler felt that they had developed an unspoken respect for each other as solid, hard workers. Pierson had backed him without question when Cutler had ordered the contractor to dig up a quarter mile of pipeline that had been buried rather hastily while he had been gone from the work site. Cutler had felt, and later proved, that the contractor buried the pipe to prevent proper inspection.

Cutler had talked with Pierson about Lineberry, indicating he didn't "look forward to working for him again when the pipeline is completed." Later, after Pierson had been reassigned to the plant, Cutler regularly stopped by to talk with him, often pointing out some of the things that Lineberry and Adams were doing; Cutler and Pierson laughed and shook their heads.

Cutler had been excited to hear at this morning's meeting that Tad Pierson was now in charge of the surveyors. He wondered how long it would take Pierson to fire Howard.

Tad Pierson, Project Engineer

In reviewing his own career with Agrigreen, Tad Pierson had the following thoughts.

I don't know; I guess I've known Dan Richards since I was about fourteen or so. We used to pal around in high school and have always been close. Dan told me he had wanted out of this area so badly because of Howard. He really hates the guy, and I guess I don't have much respect for him either. It's really ironic that now I'm Howard's boss.

Yeah, it was Dan that talked me into going back to school. When I was ready to give up as I'd done before, he told me, "You can always quit." He knew it'd make me mad enough to stay. I guess I owe him for that. That, and his pulling the strings that got me on here. When I called him yesterday, to let him know about the change, he almost fell off his chair laughing. Then he stopped and said that he wished he was me so he could fire Howard. He was serious; he really hates him.

I don't know what I'm going to do. I think the company would be money ahead to fire Howard. But, I went through the firing thing with a guy on the pipeline crew last summer. With all the letters and documentation and stuff you have to go through, it'd take two years to get rid of him. When I think of how long he's been here and his family and all, I get kind of squeamish. I guess I just don't know what to do. I'm going to think on it some.

When Burt asked me if I'd take the surveyors I told him I would, but not like Frank had. If I wanted to fire Howard, I wanted to be able to do it. He told me, "They'd be yours; just document it. I'm going to have my hands full trying to fix other messes without trying to handle that problem too." I almost get the feeling that both of us are in up to our ears.

With regard to Howard, about a month ago I went over to see Mel for a minute. There was Howard, with his head down on the drafting table, sound asleep. He didn't even hear me come or go. Vince wasn't any better, he was sitting there holding his hard hat and staring into it, dazed. I don't know if he knew I was there or not either. What a pair!

The pipeline was different. You knew it was just a summer thing, so we could put up with a lot of stuff. Mel's a good man. He's pretty sour on the company though. He doesn't think Howard should get paid more than he does and "still get away with the crap he does." He's already told me I should fire both Howard and Vince.

I just don't know what to do. I talked with some of the engineers. Half of them don't trust the work they get from Howard—they'd rather go out and do it themselves, and they do. I sometimes wonder what the heck we even have the surveyors for. I wonder what I should do?

Questions

1. What is the problem in this case?

2. What is your view of Howard Lineberry's performance? Discuss how motivational models can be applied to explain his behavior.

3. How would you describe the behaviors of Dan Richards and Mel Cutler? What was the nature of their relationships with Howard Lineberry?

4. What part do informal relationships play in the case? What do they indicate about the culture of the organization?

5. What problems, if any, were created with the placement of the surveying group within the structure of the organization?

6. What responsibility, if any, should management bear for the problems that developed?

7. What else can you discern about the culture of the organization? What factors in the culture help or hinder performance, or account for the behaviors observed? What should Tad Pierson do to resolve the situation involving Howard Lineberry?

Source: This case was prepared by William E. Stratton of Idaho State University, Pocatello, Idaho, and J. Dale Reavis. It was presented to and accepted by the refereed Society for Case Research. All rights reserved to the authors and the SCR. Copyright © 1995 by William E. Stratton and J. Dale Reavis. It was edited for *Organizational Behavior*, 8th edition, and used with permission.

Countrywide Quality: A Case of Managing Change

Countrywide Credit Industries, Inc., is a publicly held, diversified financial services company specializing in single-family home mortgage loans. Its net revenues for fiscal year 1996 (1997 projections shown in parenthesis) totaled more than $505 million ($937 million), with net earnings for fiscal year 1996 at more than $140 million ($171 million), or up 133 percent from fiscal year 1995 earnings. Countrywide Credit Industries comprises six subsidiary companies that operate independently. Countrywide Agency, Inc., is an affiliated insurance agent offering property, casualty, and mortgage life insurance to homeowners. Countrywide Securities Corporation markets mortgage-backed securities, typically to small investors and brokers. Countrywide Servicing Exchange is a servicing rights and loan portfolio broker. Countrywide Asset Management Corporation manages Countrywide Mortgage

Investment, an unaffiliated real estate investment trust. Countrywide Partnership, Inc., manages mobile home parks in Texas and Florida. The last of the subsidiaries is Countrywide Funding Corporation, which is involved in Countrywide's primary line of business, the origination of residential mortgage loans.

Countrywide Funding Corporation is the mortgage banking subsidiary and primary operating unit of Countrywide Credit Industries. The company's sole business is to originate and service residential mortgage loans. Owing to the state of the U.S. economy and low interest rates, Countrywide's recent growth is attributed to an increase in the demand for refinancing residential loans. As a result, the company had become the largest mortgage banker in the world.

The company was first established in 1969 by a partnership between two individuals: David Loeb, chairman, and Angelo Mozilo, vice-chairman. Both had the vision to create a company that would prosper by "delivering the American dream." Their continued success in the mortgage banking industry built a 3700 employee company that is still growing. Countrywide is known for its ability to employ hard-working individuals dedicated to help the business succeed by accomplishing its financial goals. Countrywide originated a record $32.4 billion in residential mortgage loans during fiscal year 1993. Residential mortgage loans are originated from a variety of sources nationwide, buffering the company against downturns in any specific region and market sector. The company's operations are divided into four lines of business:

1. The wholesale division acquires loans through relationships with mortgage brokers.

2. The retail division acquires loans through associations with real estate agencies and home buyers.

3. The consumer division acquires loans through direct connections with home buyers and owners via direct mail, telephone, and advertisements.

4. The correspondent division acquires loans through savings and loan associations, commercial banks, credit unions, and other mortgage bankers.

After acquiring loans by one of those methods, the company pools them into mortgage-backed securities and sells them on the secondary market to investors. These loans are guaranteed by government agencies such as Fannie Mae, Freddie Mac, and Ginnie Mae and by other investors for their completeness and validity "without recourse" (no credit risk to CFC). After selling these loans, Countrywide reserves the right to continue servicing these loans until maturity, charging the investor for this service. The servicing of these loans consists of the processing and administration of mortgage loan payments over the life of the loan. Thus loan servicing provides a steady revenue stream that is countercyclical to Countrywide's loan origination business. After the loans are sold on the secondary market, the cycle begins again.

To maintain its competitive edge, Countrywide does not employ commissioned loan sales agents, opting instead for cost-efficient advertising and promotional programs. Also,

located in Countrywide's retail branch offices are managers that are experienced underwriters with the authority to process, underwrite, and fund mortgage loans up to $1 million locally rather than at an offsite, centralized location. This effort, along with the advanced computer technology in Countrywide's branches allows a local office to underwrite and fund loans in less than thirty days, thereby keeping operating costs low. Efficiency and effectiveness have been the factors contributing to the company's productivity. The use of a quality assurance department was identified as a better way to accomplish these goals during a period of rapid growth.

Department Evolution

The quality assurance (QA) department was established approximately five years ago when Senior Managing Director and Chief Operating Officer (COO) Stan Kurland viewed a new concept while visiting First National Bank of Chicago (FNBC). What he learned from this visit was how to merge the philosophy of continuous improvement with total quality management (TQM) methods and performance measurements to achieve the strategic organizational objectives. He returned to company headquarters in Pasadena, California, to search for an individual to develop and maintain such a process at Countrywide. The quality assurance department was created and for approximately two years the department was involved in statistical analysis and the creation of company handbooks.

Kurland was not satisfied with the department's initial strategic direction. As a result, in an attempt to change it, he hired a new vice-president-director of quality assurance, Leland Louie. Louie set a different direction for the department, more aligned to the objectives that Stan Kurland had originally envisioned. One of the main objectives of the QA department was to implement performance measurements throughout the company, educate and sustain the idea of continuous improvement, and support the overall quality movement. These objectives were accomplished through a "hands-on" approach whereby the QA staff works directly with the line personnel in other departments.

Since its creation, the QA department has been involved in two major organizational changes. Originally the department was part of the operations division, headed by Scott Anderson, first vice-president of operations. In March 1992, the department was placed under Jeffrey Speakes, executive vice-president of strategic and financial planning. Louie was pleased with this organizational change because it increased the department's visibility to top management. He knew that in order for it to succeed the quality effort required a strong commitment from top management. Until this point, top management's support was not clearly evident within the company, especially to the departments that had been involved in QA activities. In December 1992, the quality assurance department was involved in yet another organizational change. This time the department was placed under the direction of Carlos Garcia, managing director and chief financial officer, with additional supervision by Andrew Hopping, senior vice-president of special projects. This change made Louie and the entire staff of the QA department somewhat uneasy. Instead of removing an additional layer of management as the preceding change had, another layer of management was added. Under Garcia's direction, Hopping was told to work closely with Dawn Duran, senior quality assurance consultant rather than directly with Louie. Hopping proceeded to collaborate closely with Duran regarding the strategic direction of the department—in effect, alienating not only Louie, but also most the people in the QA department. This situation continued for several months after the reorganization.

Management Evolution

Chairman David Loeb is approximately seventy years old and had maintained a low profile, behind the scenes position at Countrywide. Loeb had been involved with the back-office chores of fundraising and hedging interest rate exposure. He seldom appears at the Pasadena headquarters, instead opting to work from home. Recently, it had been rumored that Loeb would soon retire. Angelo Mozilo, in contrast, had maintained a high profile, running the day-to-day operations at headquarters. A strategic operations report by H. F. Ahmanson, described Mozilo to be a hands-on manager, totally consumed by the business, a perfectionist with a bottom-line attitude, and a risk taker. He is dictatorial about hours worked, resulting in most employees working long days and had been known to terminate employees the first time they make a mistake. However, Mozilo is the likely candidate to become chairman, which would leave his current position of president and chief executive officer vacant. Stan Kurland seemed to be the individual who would move into this position, but recent developments had changed the certainty of that happening.

In the production area the tremendous number of loan originations had given Gerald Baker, managing director of production and support divisions a strong position to campaign for the CEO spot. Such a major organizational change at Countrywide would affect the entire company. It had already made an impact on Louie and the QA department. Kurland had been a participant in promoting the changes occurring with the QA department, and recently had assigned a cost reduction (CORE) project to the QA team. In an effort to maintain the stability of his department, Louie had worked diligently with his team to ensure accurate results. Since the beginning of CORE, the QA team had identified various areas where costs could be reduced, and had presented its recommendations to Kurland and Garcia. However, few instances of actual implementation seemed to emerge from their studies.

Prior to assignment of this project, Hamid Nouri, a director in the management information services (MIS) department, had approached Mozilo regarding the quality effort and the importance of having strong support from top management. Mozilo reiterated his interest to ensure that the quality effort be pursued at Countrywide and expressed this view to Kurland and other managing directors. Currently, the QA department continues to undergo organizational changes, much to the chagrin of its employees and managers. There is a sense that the QA department has alienated many of the operating units they had "consulted" with under Louie's supervision. This feeling persists even though the QA involvement generally fostered some positive changes and increased productivity. Given all the turmoil, Louie wonders what his next move should be.

Questions

1. What was the main issue troubling the quality assurance department?

2. What could Leland Louie have done to prevent the situation from occurring, thus protecting his people and his own position?

3. Did particular events or the current financial situation assist in creating the changes that occurred in the QA department?

Source: This case was prepared by Ramon Haynes and Aimee Manansala, Engineering Management Program, California Polytechnic State University, San Luis Obispo, California. It was edited for *Organizational Behavior*, 8th edition, and used with permission.

Conflict Resolution at General Hospital

General Hospital was founded in 1968 as a nonprofit community hospital in the Northeast. In 1981, the facility was expanded from 175 beds to 275 beds, and the emergency room was upgraded. Also, in 1981, General Hospital signed an agreement with a nearby medical center for patient services that it wasn't equipped to provide.

During the 1980s, approximately 90 percent of General Hospital's beds were occupied. However, in 1994, the nearby medical center underwent renovations and obtained state-of-the-art equipment. As a result, the General Hospital's patient occupancy rate had dropped to 65 percent by the end of 1996.

It had to eliminate services in areas in which it couldn't compete. General Hospital also had a 35 percent increase in Medicare and Medicaid patients from 1993 to 1996. These government health insurance plans generated significantly less revenue than many private health insurance plans.

General Hospital CEO Mike Hammer realized that his hospital was in a nosedive and that a long-term, high-speed fix was in order. Without it, the hospital would soon begin to face survivability issues and possibly lose its accreditation. An experienced health-care executive, Hammer knew that he had to cut costs and increase revenues so that promising current services could be expanded and new services added in areas that General Hospital could successfully compete against the medical center. Hammer felt that under his leadership the current management team could get the job done with one exception: cost control.

In Mike Hammer's experience, physicians were a major factor in the inability of hospitals to regulate costs. He believed that physicians in the main didn't understand, nor were they interested in, the role of costs in determining the viability of hospitals. He felt that this lack of concern stemmed from the physicians' strong allegiance to their profession as opposed to the hospitals in which they had patient privileges.

In the past, Hammer had tried two approaches to controlling physician-driven costs, each of which had failed. Early in his tenure as General Hospital's CEO, he had tried to convince Director of Medicine Dr. Mark Williams to get the staff physicians to become cost sensitive in their decision making. Even when Hammer spotted a wasteful practice, physicians defended their actions as "the practice of good medicine." He rarely won any of these battles. Also, in 1993, he hired a consultant who studied the situation and recommended a formal comprehensive cost containment program. However, the hospital's board of trustees failed to support the program because the director of medicine vehemently opposed it. Even private meetings with Dr. Williams could not get him to change his mind or even to use the proposed program as a focus for constructive change. Dr. Williams felt that Hammer was asking for a cultural change that was impossible.

Forcing them to adhere to the plan would make it significantly more difficult to attract and keep talented physicians. Therefore the plan was not implemented.

The failure to achieve comprehensive cost control led Hammer to believe that physician-controlled costs had to be addressed on a step-by-step basis, one physician at a time. He theorized that, once a series of cost containment steps had been taken and reductions accrued, the culture would begin to change and more ambitious attempts at cost control would stand a better chance of success. Hammer had just hired a new hospital administrator, Marge Harding, who was effectively the hospital's chief operating officer (COO). He thought that perhaps the time had arrived to test his theory and see if cost control could begin to become a reality.

The Meeting

Hammer met with Harding and suggested a course of action.

Hammer: As I mentioned last week, we have to get aggressive in the cost area. Here's what I want you to do. Select something that the physicians are doing that can be done at less cost and implement the change. And remember, as COO you have the unilateral authority to place contracts and fire employees who are in an "at-will employment status." In fact, don't tell me what you're doing. That will allow us more time and help us play good cop-bad cop with the doctors.

Harding: I'll get right on it. I'm sure that I can get some good results.

Hammer: Good, Marge! That's all I have for now.

Harding was delighted that Hammer had given her a cost-reduction assignment. In her ten years in the health-care field, she had seen many financial abuses but until now never had the authority to do anything about them. She judged that her registered nurse experience, a three-year stint as assistant hospital administrator at another hospital, her baccalaureate degree in finance, and her masters degree in health-care administration would serve her well in a cost-cutting role. Also, her dad and one of her brothers were physicians, so she wasn't awed by medical doctors. In fact, she rather enjoyed challenging them, as she considered many of them to be one-dimensional. She felt that physicians knew the scientific elements of medicine well but lacked the sensitivity, knowledge, and skill needed to deliver patient care in a cost-effective manner. Harding also knew that health-care reform was a hot item and that, if she could improve the cost of operating General Hospital significantly, she would have a good chance of getting a CEO position, perhaps within the next five years, before she reached forty.

The Change

That night in the solitude of her condo while listening to a CD, Marge reviewed in her mind the orientation tour that she had gone through two weeks earlier at General Hospital. As she identified candidates for cost cutting, she listed the pros and cons of each. Next, she telephoned her friend, Joel Cohen, a 4.0 GPA MBA graduate of a prestigious business school. She got him to help her identify more clearly some cost-cutting alternatives, to formulate additional advantages and disadvantages, and to finalize her first choice: to computerize the interpretation of EKG readings.

All EKG readings at General Hospital were interpreted by Dr. James Boyer, an attending cardiologist. Dr. Boyer had been approved by both the board of trustees and the hospital medical staff to interpret EKGs. Furthermore, he was held in high esteem by his colleagues for accurate and timely reports. He had hardly ever missed a day of work in fifteen years and had always arranged for a suitable replacement when he went on vacation. Dr. Boyer was particularly valuable at dovetailing his services with the many other hospital activities involved in elective admissions.

Marge Harding knew that computerized EKG interpretations were the norm today. Furthermore, she determined that replacing Dr. Boyer with a computerized EKG interpretation service would save General Hospital at least $100,000 per year for the next three years and provide nearly instantaneous results.

She signed a one-year contract on behalf of General Hospital with Health Diagnostics. The equipment was installed and the hospital's EKG technicians were trained. Finally, the computerized EKG interpretation system was put online and Harding issued two directives, one to the EKG department to use the system and another to her assistant, John Will. She was taking a week's vacation and was instructing Will to provide liaison between the contractor and the hospital and to introduce the system and its benefits to the medical and nursing staffs. Finally, just prior to catching a plane to her vacation paradise, Harding sent a letter to Dr. Boyer notifying him that his services were no longer needed and that he was involuntarily separated from General Hospital unless he successfully competed for a vacant position within the next thirty days.

Early Problems

During the first week of computerized operations, many EKG problems emerged. Some EKG interpretations came back on time, others were a few hours late, and still others never arrived at General Hospital. At times, reports were returned inadvertently with a different patients' EKG analyses on them. Such mix-ups resulted in misfilings and at times confused physicians and even caused a few misdiagnoses. At other times, the patients were actually at other hospitals! The overwhelming problem was incorrect EKG interpretations in 25 percent of the reports.

The physicians were furious. They did not recognize the physicians who had certified the EKG reports. "What happened to Dr. Boyer?" became an echo. When they discovered that Dr. Boyer had been fired, they vehemently complained to Dr. Williams. Dr. Boyer's colleagues felt strongly that, as Dr. Boyer was part of the medical staff, a review of his termination was in order. Dr. Williams worried about the potential for legal liabilities resulting from inaccurate readings, as well as EKG reports signed by physicians not certified by General Hospital's certification committee. The nursing director, Nancy Ames, was unaware of the extent of the change and the ensuing problems.

The overall result was that the hospital's operation was quickly becoming seriously jeopardized. John Will was powerless to discontinue the computerized EKG service because he had no legitimate authority to do so.

The Following Monday

At 10:00 A.M. the following Monday, the medical staff convened to discuss the problem. Dr. Williams strongly urged Harding to come to the meeting, but she didn't attend. Instead she sent John Will with a message: "General Hospital needs to stay abreast of ongoing technological developments in science and medicine, especially when costs are reduced. The computerized EKG system stays." This incensed the medical staff. Dr. Williams sent Will back to Harding with a rebuttal message: "Either speak to us today and resolve this problem, or we will admit all new patients to other hospitals." Dr. Williams was totally frustrated. He had brought the matter up with Mike Hammer that morning but felt that he had been brushed off. Hammer said that he was very busy and that, hopefully the problem would get resolved by those directly involved.

Questions

1. Were the communications between the various parties effective? Why or why not?

2. How would you characterize Mike Hammer's leadership style relative to the attempted change?

3. How successful was Marge Harding in carrying out Hammer's directive to select and implement a cost-saving idea?

4. Should Harding meet with Dr. Williams? If so, what should be her position and how should the meeting be structured?

Source: This case was prepared by James W. Lawson and Charles Connant of St. Peter's College, Jersey City, New Jersey. It was presented to and accepted by the refereed Society for Case Research. All rights reserved to the authors and the SCR. Copyright © 1994 by James W. Lawson and Charles Connant. It was edited for *Organizational Behavior*, 8th edition, and used with permission.

AUTHOR INDEX

A

Abelson, M. A., 565
Adams, J. S., 159
Ader, R., 209
Adkins, C. L., 562
Adler, P. S., 480, 495, 516
Adler, S., 40
Affleck, G., 94
Agunis, H., 592
Ahearne, M., 309, 321
Aiken, M., 259
Ajzen, I., 52
Alban, B. T., 243
Albers, M. S., 235
Alderfer, C. P., 143
Alexander, K. L., 277
Aley, J., 579
Alger, A., 373
Allen, D. S., 209
Allen, J. S., 343
Allen, N. J., 565
Allen, R. E., 204, 602
Allen, R. W., 286
Alleven, M., 366
Allmendinger J., 525
Alvesson, M., 370
Amabile, T. M., 458
Amason, A.C ., 364
Amburgey, T. L., 507
Amsden, D. M., 15
Amsden, R. T., 15
Anderson, J. W., 408
Anderson, T., 381, 383
Andrews, S. B., 280
Anfuso, D., 113, 115, 150
Anmis, M., 402
Anonyus, C., 93
Arbose, J., 202
Arliss, L. P., 423
Armitage, M. A., 213
Armstrong, L., 485, 490
Arredondo, P., 7
Arthur, M. B., 349
Arzt, E. L., 535
Ashforth, B. E., 82, 212, 565
Ashkanasy, N. M., 338
Ashkenas, R., 9, 348, 523, 600
Atwater, L. E., 276, 344
Austin, J. T., 180
Austin, N., 555
Axley, S. R., 397
Azar, B., 90

B

Babladelis, G., 94
Bacharach, S. B., 274
Badaracco, J. R., Jr., 443
Baker, F., 13
Baker, S., 277, 485, 490
Balakrishnan, P. V., 156
Baldwin, M. W., 491
Bales, R. F., 245
Balkin, D. B., 189
Ball, G. A., 119
Band, W., 16
Bandura, A., 107, 121
Banks, W. P., 72
Barber, P., 76
Bargh, J. A., 173
Barksdale, K., 56
Barnard, C. I., 274
Barnes, F. C., 263
Barnes-Farrell, J. L., 485
Barnett, T., 630
Baron, R. A., 89, 92, 207, 216, 364
Baron, R. M., 50, 83, 199
Barone, M., 353
Barrett, F. J., 597
Barrick, M. R., 45
Barry, B., 156, 247
Bartlett, C. A., 603
Bartunek, J. M., 363
Barum, C. F., 401
Baskerville, D. M., 387
Bass, B. M., 306, 343
Bass, K., 630
Bastinautti, L. M., 259
Bateman, T. S., 247, 491
Baum, A. S., 199, 216
Bazerman, M. H., 19, 318, 442, 457
Beamer, L., 405
Beaubien, E.E., 258
Becker, F., 477
Becker, T. E., 56, 180
Becker, W. S., 144
Beckhard, R. 344, 370, 583
Beckmann, J., 52
Beemon, D. R., 287
Beer, M., 591, 593
Behar, R., 412, 417
Belasco, J. A., 305
Bell, C. H., 592, 593
Ben-Avi, I., 202
Bencivenga, D., 473
Benedict B. B., 243, 381

Bennett, N., 233
Bennis, W., 303, 340, 461
Berelson, B., 243
Berkowitz, M. W., 439, 440
Bernbeim, R. E., 341
Berner, J., 412
Bernstein, P. L., 454
Bertenthal, B., 72
Berton, L., 379
Besser, T. L., 114, 190, 249
Beswick, R. W., 412
Bettenhausen, K. L., 247
Beyer, J. M., 546, 553, 565, 596
Bhagat, R. S., 211
Bhawak, D. P. S., 286
Bibee, W., 625
Bickman, L., 620
Biddle, W., 370
Biederman, P. W., 461
Biggart, N. W., 272
Bikson, T. K., 236, 399, 412
Billings, R. S., 56, 180
Bing, S., 404
Birchard, B., 532
Bird, F. B., 405
Bitterman, D., 315
Black, J. S., 47, 383
Blake, R., 72, 79, 377, 386
Blanchard, K. H., 315, 319, 377, 405
Blass, T., 45
Bly, J. L. 621
Bobko, P., 131, 178, 177
Boccialetti, G., 606
Boehme, D. M., 154
Boes, R. F., 164
Boettger, R. D., 121, 152
Bohl, D. L., 138
Boisseau, C., 333, 344
Bommer, W. H., 309, 321, 344, 354
Bond, M. H., 83
Booth-Kewley, S., 214
Bornstein, R. F., 586
Borys, B., 480, 516
Bouchard, T. J., 42
Bourget, L., 272
Bowen, B. D., 624
Bowley, J. M., 412
Boyatzis, R. E., 147, 290
Bradford, D. L., 282
Bradford, S., 7
Bradley, S., 136
Brady, J., 531
Brass, D. J., 109, 178, 276

SUBJECT AND ORGANIZATIONAL INDEX

Brinker International, 301, 346
Britain, 73
Brooklyn Union, 353, 512
Bureaucracy, 516

C

Callaway Golf Corporation, 520
Calvert, 113
Campbell Soup, 300, 303, 308, 529
Career development, 203
Careers
    stress, 203
    women, 11
Carmike Cinemas, 506
Case study, 623
Categorical imperative principle, 441
Caterpillar, 578
Ceiba-Geigy, 534
Centralization, 516
Ceremonies, 553
Chain of command, 518
Chain Saw Manufacturers Association, 58
Change
    competencies, 21
    MCI, 22
    organizational culture, 554
    see organizational change
Change management, 592–605
Channels, 400
Chaparral Steel, 310
Charismatic leaders, 342
Charting behavior, 126
Chem-Bio Corporation, 183
Chevron Corporation, 218
Chilis, 625
China, 278, 556, 575
Chrysler Corporation, 594
Citicorp, 60
Classical conditioning
    defined, 105
    process, 105
    reflexive behaviors, 105
Closure, 80
Club culture, 545
Coacting group, 233
Coalitions, 237
Coca-Cola, 175, 545
Cohesiveness, 249
Coercive power, 273, 305
Cognitive conflict, 363
Cognitive dissonance, 367
Cognitive moral development, 57
Colgate Palmolive Company, 141, 272
Collaborating style, 376
Collateral organization, 602
Collectivism, 231
Commonwealth Electric Co., 559
Communicating, 23
Communication
    communicating, 23

cultural symbols, 547
    impression management, 84
    internet, 17
    intranet, 17
    network design, 531
    organizational change, 591
    perceptual errors, 84
    perceptual selection, 74
    performance appraisal, 185
    person perception, 82
    see interpersonal communication
    social information processing, 490
    voice quality, 83
Communication openness, 414
Compaq Computer, 311
Competencies
    achieving technical proficiency, 224
    communicating, 23
    communication, 303
    competency, 21
    conceptualization, 21
    conflict management, 23
    creativity, 21
    decision making, 22
    diversity, 7–14
    ethical standards, 25
    expert power, 274
    Ford Motor Co., 25
    independence, 350
    interdependence, 351
    job design, 484
    knowledge as power, 276
    leadership, 303
    leader style questionnaire, 331
    leading, 23
    learning, 24, 105
    listening, 23
    managing people and tasks, 22
    managing self, 24
    mobilizing innovation and change, 21
    oral communication, 23
    organizing, 504
    personal attributes, 25
    personal time management, 25
    planning, 22
    quality management, 15
    risk taking, 21
    self-mastery, 350
    self-understanding, 303
    skill, 21
    synergy, 351
    technical proficiency, 24
    vision, 303
    visioning, 22
    written communication, 23
Competency, 21
Competition, 576
Compliance conformity, 248
Compromising style, 377
Computer Language Research, 160
Concentration of effect, 438

Conceptualization, 21
Conference Board, 595
Confirmation bias, 455
Conflict
    accommodating style, 376
    affective conflict, 363
    aggressive behavior, 204
    Andersen Worldwide, 379
    approach-approach conflict, 366
    avoidance-avoidance conflict, 366
    avoiding style, 373
    balanced view, 365
    cognitive conflict, 363
    cognitive dissonance, 367
    collaborating style, 376
    compromising style, 377
    conflict management, 23
    culture, 450
    defined, 362
    diversity, 372
    dual-careers, 206
    exchange process, 284
    fight-or-flight response, 199
    Food & Drug Administration, 369
    forcing style, 374
    forms, 363
    goal conflict, 363
    handling styles, 373–378
    horizontal conflict, 371
    influence strategies, 283
    intergroup conflict, 371
    intergroup dialogue technique, 386
    interpersonal conflict, 368
    interrole conflict, 369
    intersender role conflict, 369
    intragroup conflict, 370
    intrapersonal conflict, 366
    intrasender role conflict, 369
    Lanteck, 371
    leadership, 325
    line-staff conflict, 372
    mediation, 384
    Motorola, 365
    negative view, 364
    negotiations, 378–384
    neurotic tendencies, 367
    Northeast Utilities, 375
    perceptual defense, 86
    person-role conflict, 369
    political behavior, 284
    positive view, 364
    principled organizational dissent, 558
    procedural conflict, 364
    quality, 365
    questionnaire, 387
    resistance to change, 584
    role ambiguity, 203, 370
    role conflict, 203, 368
    sexual harassment, 204
    Texaco, 568
    vertical conflict, 371

INTERNET ORGANIZATION INDEX